Fleshing Out Skull & Bones

Investigations into America's Most Powerful Secret Society

Kris Millegan - Editor

Fleshing Out Skull & Bones

Investigations into America's Most Powerful Secret Society

TrineDay
P.O. Box 577
Walterville, OR 97489

www.TrineDay.com • www.FleshingOutSkullAndBones.com • www.BoodleBoys.com

Support@TrineDay.com

Library of Congress Control Number: 2003095005

Millegan, Robert A (Kris) — Editor/Author

Fleshing Out Skull & Bones: Investigations into America's Most Powerful Secret Society

p.cm.

Includes bibliographical references

ISBN 0-9720207-2-1 (HardCover)

ISBN 0-9752906-0-6 (SoftCover)

1. Order of Skull & Bones—Political Activity. 2. Secret Societies—United States 3. Yale University—Students—Societies, etc. 4. Yale University—Alumni and alumnae—Societies, etc. I. Title

366 20 First Edition

10 9 8 7 6 5 4 3

Authors: Kris Millegan, Antony Sutton, Charlotte Thomson Iserbyt, Howard Altman, Toby Rogers, Steve Sewall, Ralph E Bunch, Daniel Hopsicker, Carl Oglesby, Webster Griffin Tarpley, Anton Chaitkin, Jedediah McClure.

Printed on acid-free paper in the United States of America.

Distribution to the Trade by:

Independent Publishers Group (IPG)
814 North Franklin Street
Chicago, Illinois 60610
312.337.0747.
www.ipgbook.com
frontdesk@ipgbook.com

Dedicated to My Father

At one time, he peddled Skull & Bones in his front job for the CIA.

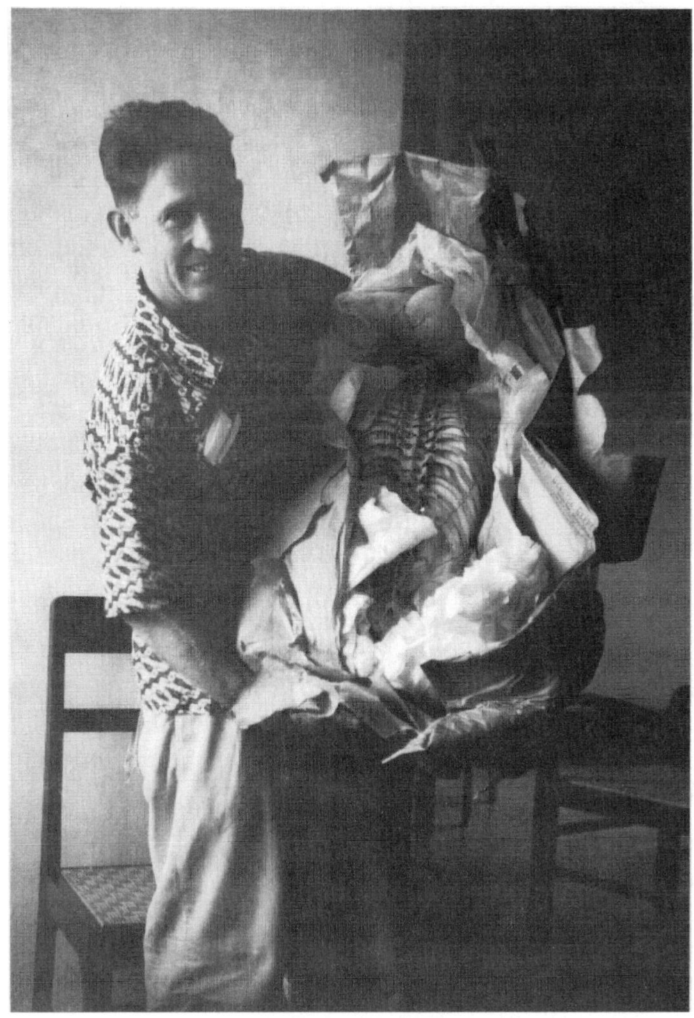

Lloyd Sidney Millegan
OSS/G2/CIA
August 18, 1918 — February 7, 1990
Picture taken in Indonesia - 1951

Table of Contents

Table of Contents (cont.)

ACKNOWLEDGEMENTS

I would like to thank all of those involved with this project, especially my family, who have allowed me the time for the task.

I would like to thank all the authors and other contributors, some who asked to be anonymous. The curators, archivists and the whole staff at Yale University, Manuscripts and Archives were most courteous and very helpful to this country boy. Thanks, to the folks at printing house McNaughton & Gunn for their excellent help and continual devotion to doing the job right.

With sadness that they didn't see this work but knowing that these two would be happy with this work. I would like to thank my Dad, for out of his concern for myself came the courage and will to speak about what he had seen, sparking with-in me a zest for historical research.

And to a very kind and gentle man, who could be cantankerous at times, Mr. Antony Sutton for sharing with me his thoughts, research and wondrous glee of discovery.

Thank-you, Ed B. and Kathy G., for all your support and help. And to all my friends that have put up with me.

High Times printed two of the articles in this book. I would like to thank the magazine and editor Steve Hager for allowing me delve into a subject that is generally censored from national discourse.

And thanks to all of the fellow sojourners on this bright blue ball spinning through space. For those who came before, for those who share this crazy beautiful space now — and then, there are those that will have to deal with what ever is left when we are gone …

Thank-you

Onwards to the Utmost of Futures

Kris Millegan

Preface

This book started as research into trying to understand some things my Dad told me. When I was first writing on the subject, I contacted several publishers and was politely told, by the *one* that answered, they "didn't want to *take on* Skull & Bones."

An article of mine was published online at www.parascope.com, which was well received. From that article and a friendship with Antony Sutton — came this book.

The Internet has become an astounding force whose cultural and political realities are still to be understood and it's power is forcing change that continues today — with an unknown ending. The Internet has allowed uncensored national discussion, engendered understandings and energized a potent plebeian power whose creativity is countering the secretive sophism that ruins our republic and economy through covert corrupt means. The question remains: will the dreamscape that enthralls vast numbers continue its hoodwink, and will our children wake up slaves in a mean, technologically *locked-down* fascist state, or will they continue to slumber in the propaganda and hidden corruption of the celebrity-laden delusion of the contrived virtual reality friendly fascism that the secret societies have created around us — or will the Internet and other factors bring about a revival of our civic heritage and liberty.

The most important thing that I would like folks to understand from this work is that the secrecy of these organizations is not good for our Republic. These secret societies are historically foreign-based and do not care about this country. Their ends justifies the means *zeitgeist* leads to massive corruption and the "institutionalized sociological" excess of "elite deviancy." Where a certain few believe that they are beyond the law and then through corrupted political and economic power — act above the law, through whatever means at their disposal. One question this book examines is whether there is any truth in the age-old lore of the *conspiracy theory* of history — are we are dealing with a multi-generational, necromantic, synarchistic phenomenon? Have secret societies created a national security state apparatus to beguile us hoi polloi of our economic, civic and spiritual integrity? Do these secret societies create and play both sides in controlled conflicts to produce outcomes to further their New World Order millenniumist designs?

Porch brethren are requirement for a secret society to work and many in these organizations, magickal and fraternal are unawares of any deeper motivations of the elite leadership of the group. It is when these secret organizations with members in high political office exert their influence towards goals unknown and/or unbecoming that we citizens should take notice — and action.

Mysticism and fellowship are not bad and evil things. They are just like any thing. It is what people do with them … their actions that do ill or good in this world.

Secrecy and our Republic do not mix.

Our children's future is what we leave them.

Om
K

From the 1918-19 Yale *Banner*

Everything You Ever Wanted to Ask, But Were Afraid to Know

Kris Millegan

Appeared online July 1996, at www.Parascope.com – now at www.Boodleboys.com

The story begins at Yale, where three threads of American social history — espionage, drug smuggling and secret societies — intertwine into one.

Elihu Yale was born near Boston, educated in London, and served with the British East India Company, eventually becoming governor of Fort Saint George, Madras, India in 1687. He amassed a great fortune from trade and returned to England in 1699. Yale became known as a philanthropist; upon receiving a request from the Collegiate School in Connecticut, he sent a donation and a gift of books. After subsequent bequests, Cotton Mather suggested the school be named Yale College in 1718.

Elihu Yale

A statue of Nathan Hale stands on Old Campus at Yale University. A copy of that statue stands in front of the CIA's headquarters in Langley, Virginia. Yet another stands in front of Phillips Academy in Andover, Massachusetts (where George H.W. Bush went to prep school and joined his first secret society at the age of 12).

Nathan Hale, along with three other Yale graduates, was a member of the "Culper Ring," one of America's first intelligence operations. Established by George Washington, it was successful throughout the Revolutionary War. Nathan was the only operative to be ferreted out by the British, and after speaking his famous regrets, he was hanged in 1776. Ever since the founding of the Republic, the relationship between Yale and the Intelligence Community has been unique.

Samuel Russell

In 1823, Samuel Russell established Russell and Company for the purpose of acquiring opium in Turkey and smuggling it to China. Russell and Company merged with the Perkins (Boston) syndicate in 1830 and became the primary American opium smuggler. Many of the great American and European fortunes were built on the "China"(opium) trade.

One of Russell and Company's Chief of Operations in Canton was Warren Delano, Jr., grandfather of Franklin D. Roosevelt. Other Russell partners included John Cleve Green (who financed Princeton), Abiel Low (who financed construction of Columbia), Joseph Coolidge and the Perkins, Sturgis and Forbes families. (Coolidge's son organized the United Fruit company, and his grandson, Archibald C. Coolidge, was a co-founder of the Council on Foreign Relations.)

William H. Russell

William Huntington Russell (S&B 1833), Samuel's cousin, studied in Germany from 1831-32. Germany was a hotbed of new ideas. The "scientific method" was being applied to all forms of human endeavor. Prussia, which blamed the defeat of its forces by Napoleon in 1806 on soldiers only thinking about themselves in the stress of battle, took the principles set forth by John Locke and Jean Rousseau and created a new educational system. Johan Wolfgang Fitche, in his "Address to the German People," declared that the children would be taken over by the State and told what to think and how to think it.

Georg Wilhelm Friedrich Hegel took over Fitche's chair at the University Of Berlin in 1817 and was a professor there until his death in 1831. Hegel was the culmination of the German idealistic philosophy school of Immanuel Kant.

To Hegel, our world is a world of reason. The state is Absolute Reason and the citizen can only become free by worship and obedience to the state. Hegel called the state the "march of God in the world" and the "final end." This final end, Hegel said, "has supreme right against the individual, whose supreme duty is to be a member of the state." Both fascism and communism have their philosophical roots in Hegelianism. Hegelian philosophy was very much in vogue during William Russell's time in Germany.

Georg Hegel

When Russell returned to Yale in 1832, he formed a senior society with Alphonso Taft (S&B 1833). According to information acquired from a break-in to the "tomb" (the Skull and Bones meeting hall) in 1876, "Bones is a chapter of a corps in a German University ... General Russell, its founder, was in Germany before his Senior Year and formed a warm friendship with a leading member of a German society. He brought back with him to college, authority to found a chapter here." So class valedictorian William H. Russell, along with 14 others, became the founding members of "The Order of Scull and Bones," later changed to "The Order of Skull and Bones."

The secretive Order of Skull and Bones exists only at Yale. Fifteen juniors are "tapped" each year by the seniors to be initiated into next year's group. Some say each initiate is given $15,000 and a grandfather clock. Far from being a campus fun-house, the group is geared more toward the success of its members in the post-collegiate world.

The family names on the Skull and Bones roster roll off the tongue like an elite party list — Lord, Whitney, Taft, Jay, Bundy, Harriman, Weyerhaeuser, Pinchot, Rockefeller, Goodyear, Sloane, Stimson, Phelps, Perkins, Pillsbury, Kellogg, Vanderbilt, Bush, Lovett and others.

William Russell went on to become a general and a state legislator in Connecticut. Alphonso Taft was appointed US Attorney General, Secretary of War (a post many "Bonesmen" have held), Ambassador to Austria, and Ambassador to Russia (another post held by many "Bonesmen"). His son, William Howard Taft (S&B 1878), is the only man to be both President of the United States and Chief Justice of the Supreme Court.

Alphonso Taft

William H. Taft

SECRETS OF THE "TOMB"

THE ORDER FLOURISHED from the very beginning in spite of occasional squalls of controversy. There was dissension from some professors, who objected to its secrecy and exclusiveness. And there was backlash from students, showing concern about the influence "Bones" was having over Yale finances and the favoritism shown to "Bonesmen."

In October, 1873, Volume 1, Number 1, of ***The Iconoclast*** was published in New Haven. It was only published once and was one of only a few openly published articles on the Order of Skull and Bones.

From ***The Iconoclast***:

> We speak through a new publication, because the college press is closed to those who dare to openly mention 'Bones'....
>
> Out of every class Skull and Bones takes its men. They have gone out into the world and have become, in many instances, leaders in society. They have obtained control of Yale. Its business is performed by them. Money paid to the college must pass into their hands, and be subject to their will. No doubt they are worthy men in themselves, but the many, whom they looked down upon while in college, cannot so far forget as to give money freely into their hands. Men in

Wall Street complain that the college comes straight to them for help, instead of asking each graduate for his share. The reason is found in a remark made by one of Yale's and America's first men: 'Few will give but Bones men and they care far more for their society than they do for the college ....'

Year by year the deadly evil is growing. The society was never as obnoxious to the college as it is today, and it is just this ill-feeling that shuts the pockets of non-members. Never before has it shown such arrogance and self-fancied superiority. It grasps the College Press and endeavors to rule it all. It does not deign to show its credentials, but clutches at power with the silence of conscious guilt.

To tell the good which Yale College has done would be well nigh impossible. To tell the good she might do would be yet more difficult. The question, then, is reduced to this – on the one hand lies a source of incalculable good – on the other a society guilty of serious and far-reaching crimes. It is Yale College against Skull and Bones!! We ask all men, as a question of right, which should be allowed to live?

At first, the society held its meetings in hired halls. Then in 1856, the "Tomb," a windowless, brown-stone meeting hall, was constructed, where to this day the "Bonesmen" hold their "strange, occultish" initiation rites and meet each Thursday and Sunday.

The Tomb - 1864

On September 29, 1876, a group calling itself *The Order of File and Claw* broke into the Skull and Bones' holy of holies. In the "tomb" they found lodge-room 324 "fitted up in black velvet, even the walls being covered with the material." Upstairs was lodge-room 322, "the *sanctum sanctorum* of the temple ... furnished in red velvet" with a pentagram on the wall. In the hall are "pictures of the founders of Bones at Yale, and of members of the Society in Germany, when the chapter was established here in 1832." The raiding party found another interesting scene in the parlor next to room 322.

FILE AND CLAW.

From *The Fall Of Skull And Bones*:

On the west wall, hung among other pictures, an old engraving representing an open burial vault, in which, on a stone slab, rest four human skulls, grouped about a fools cap and bells, an open book, several mathematical instruments, a beggar's scrip, and a royal crown. On the arched wall above the vault are the explanatory words, in Roman letters, 'We War Der Thor, Wer Weiser, Wer Bettler Oder, Kaiser?' and below the vault is engraved, in German characters, the sentence; 'Ob Arm, Ob Beich, im Tode gleich.'

The picture is accompanied by a card on which is written, 'From the German Chapter. Presented by D. C. Gilman of D. 50'.

Daniel Coit Gilman (1852), along with two other "Bonesmen," formed a troika which still influences American life today. Soon after their initiation in Skull and Bones, Daniel Gilman, Timothy Dwight (1849) and Andrew Dickinson White (1853) went to study philosophy in Europe at the University of Berlin. Gilman returned from Europe and incorporated Skull and Bones as the Russell Trust in 1856, with himself as Treasurer and William H. Russell as President. He spent the next 14 years in New Haven consolidating the order's power.

Gilman was appointed Librarian at Yale in 1858. Through shrewd political maneuvering, he acquired funding for Yale's science departments (Sheffield Scientific School) and was able to get the Morrill Land Bill introduced in Congress, passed and finally signed by President Lincoln, after being vetoed by President Buchanan.

Daniel C. Gilman

This bill, "donating public-lands for State College for agriculture and sciences," is now known as the Land Grant College Act. Yale was the first school in America to get the federal land scrip and quickly grabbed all of Connecticut's share at the time. Pleased by the acquisitions, Yale made Gilman a Professor of Physical Geography.

Daniel was the first President of the University of California. He also helped found, and was the first president of, John Hopkins.

Gilman was first president of the Carnegie Institution and involved in the founding of the Peabody, Slater and Russell Sage Foundations.

His buddy, Andrew D. White, was the first president of Cornell University (which received all of New York's share of the Land Grant College Act), U.S. Minister to Russia, U.S. Ambassador to Berlin and first president of the American Historical Association. White was also Chairman of the American delegation to the first Hague Conference in 1899, which established an international judiciary.

Andrew D. White

Timothy Dwight, a professor at Yale Divinity School, was installed as president of Yale in 1886. All presidents since have been either "Bonesmen" or directly tied to the Order and its interests.

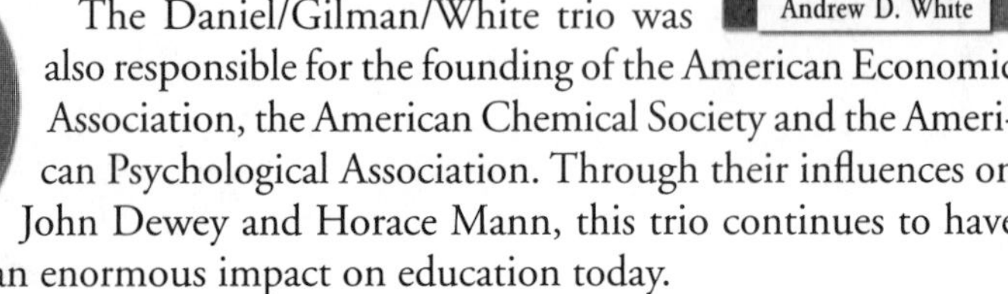

Timothy Dwight

The Daniel/Gilman/White trio was also responsible for the founding of the American Economic Association, the American Chemical Society and the American Psychological Association. Through their influences on John Dewey and Horace Mann, this trio continues to have an enormous impact on education today.

Networks of Power

In his book *America's Secret Establishment*, Antony Sutton outlined the Order of Skull and Bones' ability to establish vertical and horizontal "chains of influence" that ensured the continuity of their conspiratorial schemes.

The Whitney-Stimson-Bundy links represent the "vertical chain."

W. C. Whitney (S&B 1863), who married Flora Payne (of the Standard Oil/ Payne dynasty), was Secretary of the Navy. His attorney was a man named Elihu Root. Root hired Henry Stimson (S&B 1888), out of law school. Stimson took over from Root as Secretary of War in 1911, appointed by fellow Bonesman William Howard Taft. Stimson later became Coolidge's Governor-General of the Philippine Islands, Hoover's Secretary of State, and Secretary of War during the Roosevelt and Truman Administrations.

W.C. Whitney

Hollister Bundy (S&B '09) was Stimson's special assistant and point man in the Pentagon for the Manhattan Project. His two sons, also members of Skull and Bones, were William Bundy (S&B '39) and McGeorge Bundy (S&B '40) — both very active in governmental and foundation affairs.

The two brothers, from their positions in the CIA, the Department of Defense and the State Department, and as Special Assistants to Presidents Kennedy and Johnson, exercised significant impact on the flow of information and intelligence during the Vietnam "War."

McGeorge Bundy and LBJ

William Bundy went on to be editor of *Foreign Affairs*, the influential quarterly of the Council on Foreign Affairs (CFR). McGeorge became president of the Ford Foundation.

Another interesting group of "Bonesmen" is the Harriman/Bush crowd. Averell Harriman (S&B '13), "Elder Statesman" of the Democratic Party, and his brother Roland Harriman (S&B '17) were very active members. In fact, four of Roland's fellow "Bonesmen" from the class of 1917 were directors of Brown Brothers, Harriman, including Prescott Bush (S&B '17), George HW Bush's dad.

Prescott Bush

Averell Harriman

Since the turn of the century, two investment bank firms — Guaranty Trust and Brown Brothers, Harriman — were both dominated by members of Skull and Bones. These two firms were heavily involved in the financing of Communism and Hitler's regime.

Bonesman share an affinity for the Hegelian ideas of the historical dialectic, which dictates the use of controlled conflict (thesis versus anti-thesis) to create a pre-determined synthesis. This being a synthesis of their making and design, where the state is absolute and individuals are granted their freedoms based on their obedience to the state — a *New World Order.*

Funding and political maneuvering on the part of "Bonesmen" and their allies helped the Bolsheviks prevail in Russia. In defiance of federal laws, the cabal financed industries, established banks and developed oil and mineral deposits in the fledgling USSR.

Robert Lovett, Winston Churchill, Dean Acheson (Scroll & Key) and Averell Harriman

Later, Averell Harriman, as minister to Great Britain in charge of Lend-Lease for Britain and Russia, was responsible for shipping entire factories into Russia. According to some researchers, Harriman also oversaw the transfer of nuclear secrets, plutonium and US dollar printing plates to the USSR.

In 1932, the Union Banking Corporation of New York City was established with four directors from the 1917 S&B cell and two Nazi bankers associated with Fritz Thyssen, who had been financing Hitler since 1923.

From ***George Bush; The Unauthorized Biography***:

> President Franklin Roosevelt's Alien Property Custodian, Leo T. Crowley, signed Vesting Order Number 248 [11/17/42] seizing the property of Prescott Bush under the Trading with Enemy Act. The order, published in obscure government record books and kept out of the news,* explained nothing about the Nazis involved; only that the Union Banking Corporation was run for the *Thyssen family* of Germany and/or Hungary – nationals ... of a designated enemy country.

By deciding that Prescott Bush and the other directors of the Union Banking Corporation were legally *front men for the Nazis*, the government avoided the more important historical issue: In what way were Hitler's Nazis themselves hired, armed, and instructed by the New York and London clique of which Prescott Bush was an executive manager?

*New York Times, December 16, 1944, ran a five-paragraph page 25 article on actions of the New York State Banking Department. Only the last sentence refers to the Nazi bank, as follows: *The Union Banking Corporation, 39 Broadway, New York, has received authority to change its principal place of business to 120 Broadway.*

The Times omitted the fact that the Union Banking Corporation had been seized by the government for trading with the enemy, and the fact that 120 Broadway was the address of the government's Alien Property Custodian.

After the war, Prescott went on to become a US Senator from Connecticut and favorite golfing partner of President Eisenhower. Prescott claims some responsibility for getting Richard Nixon into politics and takes personal credit for bringing Dick on board as Ike's running mate in 1952.

Name Roster of the Secret Establishment

There were so many "Yalies" in the OSS (Office of Strategic Services) that Yale's drinking tune, the "Whiffenpoof Song," became an "unofficial" song of the OSS. Many in the OSS were "Bonesmen" or belonged to the other Yale senior societies.

Robert Lovett (S&B '18), Harriman's childhood friend, had been tapped into Skull & Bones by Prescott Bush's cell of '17 and was a director at Brown Brothers, Harriman.

Again, from ***George Bush: The Unauthorized Biography***:

On October 22, 1945, Secretary of War Robert Patterson created the Lovett Committee, chaired by Robert A. Lovett, to advise the government on the post-World War II organization of U.S. intelligence activities ... The new agency would 'consult' with the armed forces, but it must be the sole collecting agency in the field of foreign espionage and counterespionage. The new agency should have an independent budget, and its appropriations should be granted by Congress without public hearings. Lovett appeared before the Secretaries of State, War, and Navy on November 14, 1945 ... Lovett pressed for a virtual resumption of the wartime Office of Strategic Services (OSS) ... The CIA was established in 1947 according to the prescription of Robert Lovett, of Jupiter Island. [Florida]

Robert A. Lovett

Gaddis Smith, a history professor at Yale, said, "Yale has influenced the Central Intelligence Agency more than any other university, giving the CIA the atmosphere of a class reunion." And "Bonesman" have been foremost among the "spooks" building the CIA's "haunted house."

F. Trubee Davison (S&B '18) was Director of Personnel at the CIA in the early years. Some of the "Bonesmen" connected with the intelligence community have been:

- Sloane Coffin, Jr. (S&B '49)
- V. Van Dine (S&B '49)
- James Buckley (S&B '44)
- Bill Buckley (S&B '50)
- Hugh Cunningham (S&B '34)
- Hugh Wilson (S&B '09)
- Reuben Holden (S&B '40)
- Charles R. Walker (S&B '16)
- Yale's 'unofficial' Secretary of War, Robert D. French (S&B '10)
- Archibald MacLeish (S&B '15)
- Dino Pionzio (S&B '50), CIA Deputy Chief of Station during Allende overthrow
- William and McGeorge Bundy
- Richard A. Moore (S&B '36)
- Senator David Boren (S&B '63)
- Senator John Kerry (S&B '66)

...and, of course, George Herbert Walker Bush. Bush tapped Coffin, who tapped Buckley.

Some other prominent "Bonesmen" include:

- Henry Luce (S&B '20), Time-Life
- John Thomas Daniels (S&B '14), founder Archer Daniels Midland
- Gifford Pinchot (S&B 1889), President Theodore Roosevelt's chief forester
- Frederick E. Weyerhaeuser (S&B 1896)
- Harold Stanley (S&B '08), founder of Morgan Stanley, investment banker
- Alfred Cowles (S&B '13), Cowles Communications
- Henry P. Davison (S&B '20), senior partner Morgan Guaranty Trust
- Thomas Cochran (S&B '04) Morgan partner
- John Heinz (S&B '31) CEO Heinz Foods
- Pierre Jay (S&B 1892), first chairman of the Federal Reserve Bank of New York
- George Herbert Walker, Jr. (S&B '27), financier and co-founder of the NY Mets
- Fred Smith (S&B '66), founder, CEO and President of Federal Express
- Artemus Gates (S&B '18), President of New York Trust Company, Union Pacific, TIME, Boeing
- William Draper III (S&B '50), the Defense Department, UN, Import-Export Bank

- Dean Witter, Jr.(S&B '44), investment banker
- Senator Jonathan Bingham (S&B '36)
- Potter Stewart (S&B '36), Supreme Court Justice
- Senator John Chaffe (S&B '47)
- Harry Payne Whitney (S&B 1894), married Gertrude Vanderbilt, investment banker
- Russell W. Davenport (S&B '23), editor Fortune Magazine, created Fortune 500 list
- Evan G. Galbraith (S&B '50), Ambassador to France and Managing Director of Morgan Stanley
- Richard Gow (S&B '55), president Zapata Oil
- Amory Howe Bradford (S&B '34), husband of Carol Warburg Rothschild and general manager for the New York Times
- C. E. Lord (S&B '49), Comptroller of the Currency
- Winston Lord (S&B '59), Chairman of the Council on Foreign Relations, Ambassador to China and assistant Secretary of State in the Clinton administration

Barbara and George HW Bush in China

Ever since Nixon re-established America's political relationship with China, many of our ambassadors to that country have been Bonesmen, including George HW Bush, the first Chief U. S. Liaison Officer to the Peoples Republic of China.

China and the Opium Wars

Why all this interest in China? Well, among other things, China is one of the largest producers and users of opiates in the world.

For a period, in the 1800s, the Yankee Clippers in Connecticut and Massachusetts were the fastest ships on the ocean. Speed was crucial to the opium trade; whoever made the trip from Turkey/India to Macao/Hong Kong/Shanghai first got the most for their goods.

During the Opium Wars, the U.S. chose to stand on the sidelines and cheer for the English and French, knowing that treaty obligations would bring the U.S. a share in the spoils. Russell and Company was at times the only trading house operating in Canton and used the opportunity to developed strong commercial ties and handsome profits.

Charmer launched Oct. 1854 for Bush & Wildes, Boston

Powerful national interests were behind the drug trade. American traders were badly in need of trade goods that the Chinese would buy, since by this time our natural trade items, such as fur seals and ginseng were in depletion. If the Chinese had not bought opium from Americans, then United States imports of silk, porcelain and tea would have to paid in precious coin, which was in short supply. In 1843, when the Port of Shanghai was opened, Russell and Co. was one of its earliest traders.

In 1903, Yale Divinity School set up a program of schools and hospitals in China. Mao Zedong was among the staff. During the intrigues of China in the 1930s and '40s, American intelligence called upon the resources of "Yale in China," and George Bush's cousin and fellow "Bonesman" Reuben Holden.

Yale-in-China Hospital, 1931

After stints as UN Ambassador and Chairman of the Republican National Committee for the beleaguered Richard Nixon, George Bush was sent to look after the "China trade." The Bush family is still very much involved in the economic activities of "Red" China.

Many researchers contend that George Bush has been with the CIA since the early 1950s, and that one of his jobs was to consolidate and co-ordinate the worldwide narcotics industry, the largest industry on Earth. Some say that one of the reasons behind the Vietnam "Police Action" was a cover for the consolidation of the "Golden Triangle."

George HW Bush
UN Ambassador

THE WAR ON DRUGS: AN "INTELLECTUAL FRAUD"

BEFORE THE VIETNAM "WAR," the Golden Triangle was run by French intelligence operatives and Corsican mobsters. After the French bailed out and America moved in, the triangle was run by U.S. intelligence, with aid from Sicilian mobsters. This narcotics network is well documented in *The Politics of Heroin in S. E. Asia* by Alfred McCoy, *The Great Heroin Coup* by Henrik Kruger and *Double-Cross* by Sam and Chuck Giancana.

Vice-President George Bush, as Chairman of President Reagan's cabinet-level working group and as Director of the National Narcotics Interdiction System, was the highest US governmental official involved in the "war on drugs."

Frances Mullen, Jr., former head of the Drug Enforcement Agency (DEA), called Bush's efforts "an intellectual fraud" and "a liability rather than an asset." Soon after these statements, Mullen resigned and the resultant General Accounting Office (GAO) report was buried.

George HW Bush
CIA Director

In July, 1985, the suppressed GAO paper reported that there were "no benefits from the National Narcotics Border Interdiction System, directed by George Bush. In fact, the overall effect was to encourage supply ...."

Monika Jensen-Stevenson, a *60 Minutes* producer, quit her job after the CBS news program refused to air the story she had uncovered relating to the covert drug trade. Her book, *Kiss The Boys Goodbye*, among other things, details how the US intelligence community used the apparatus of the POW/MIA governmental agencies as a cover for the trafficking of opiates from the "Golden Triangle" area.

President Reagan appointed Reform Party founder and Texas billionaire Ross Perot to the President's Advisory Council on Foreign Intelligence. Reagan made Perot a special presidential investigator, looking into America's POW and MIAs from the Vietnam "War."

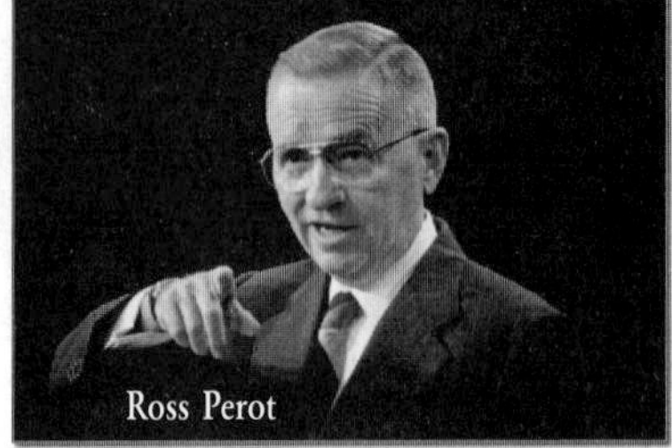
Ross Perot

Ross took the job to heart and spent considerable time and money in pursuit of the quest. He was given special clearance and access. He asked questions and interviewed everyone he could find.

From ***Kiss The Boys Goodbye***:

> Relations between Bush and Perot had gone downhill ever since the Vice-President had asked Ross Perot how his POW/MIA investigations were going.
>
> "Well, George, I go in looking for prisoners," said Perot, "but I spend all my time discovering the government has been moving drugs around the world and is involved in illegal arms deals.... I can't get at the prisoners because of the corruption among our own people."
>
> This ended Perot's official access to the highly classified files as a one-man presidential investigator. "I have been instructed to cease and desist," he had informed the families of missing men early in 1987.

The wholesale importation of cocaine into the U.S. during "Iran/Contra" is also well documented. George Bush is known "to be in the loop" with many of the players keeping in contact directly with his office.

Also, there has been much speculation as to the use of the off-shore rigs, pipelines and other assets of Zapata Offshore being used for narcotic trans-shipments.

Narcotics such as cocaine and heroin cannot be manufactured without the precursor chemicals. One of the largest makers of these precursor chemicals is the Eli Lilly Company of Indianapolis, Indiana. The Quayle family is a stockholder, and George Bush has been on the Board of Directors. Eli Lilly is also the company that first synthesized LSD for the CIA.

President George Bush & VP Dan Quayle are Delta Kappa Epsilon (DKE) fraternity brothers

George Bush, Skull & Bones and the JFK Assassination

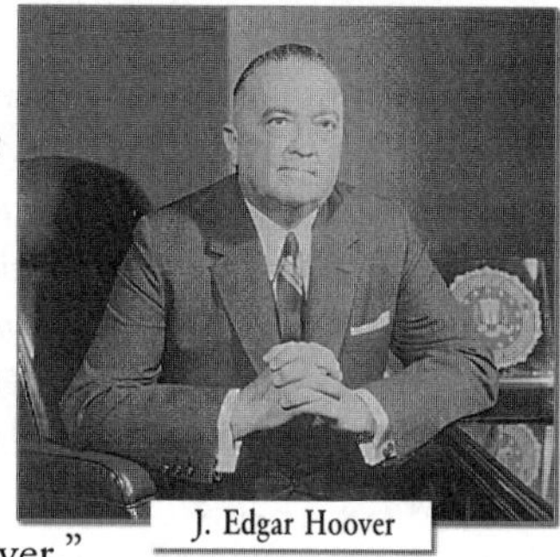
J. Edgar Hoover

Rodney Stich's book *Defrauding America* tells of a "deep-cover CIA officer" assigned to a counter-intelligence unit, code-named Pegasus. This unit "had tape-recordings of plans to assassinate Kennedy" from a tap on the phone of J. Edgar Hoover. The people on the tapes were "[Nelson] Rockefeller, Allen Dulles, [Lyndon] Johnson of Texas, George Bush and J. Edgar Hoover."

Could George Bush be involved in the JFK assassination?

In 1963, Bush was living in Houston, busily carrying out his duties as president of the Zapata Offshore oil company. He denied the existence of a note sent by the FBI's J. Edgar Hoover to "Mr. George Bush of the CIA." When news of the note surfaced, the CIA first said they never commented on employment questions, but later relented, said yes, a "George Bush" was mentioned in the note, but that it was "another" George Bush, not the man who took office in the White House in 1988.

Some intrepid reporters tracked down the "other" George Bush and discovered that he was just a lowly clerk who had shuffled papers for the CIA for about six months. He never received any interagency messages from anybody at the FBI, let alone J. Edgar.

It is also worth noting that a CIA code word for Bay of Pigs was Operation Zapata, and that two of the support vessels were named Barbara and Houston.

Many say that George Bush was high up on the CIA ladder at the time, running proprietorial vehicles and placed in a position of command, responsible for many of the Cubans recruited into "service" at the time. All through the Iran-Contra affair, Felix Rodriguez, the man who captured and had Che Guevara killed for the CIA, always seemed to call Bush's office first.

From *The Realist* (Summer, 1991):

> Bush was working with the now-famous CIA agent, Felix Rodriguez, recruiting right-wing Cuban exiles for the invasion of Cuba. It was Bush's CIA job to organize the Cuban community in Miami for the invasion.... A newly discovered FBI document reveals that George Bush was directly involved in the 1963 murder of President John Kennedy. The document places marksmen by the CIA. Bush at that time lived in Texas. Hopping from Houston to Miami weekly, Bush spent 1960 and '61 recruiting Cubans in Miami for the invasion ....
>
> George Bush claims he never worked for the CIA until he was appointed Director by former Warren Commission director and then President Jerry Ford in 1976. Logic suggests that is highly unlikely. Of course, Bush has a company duty to deny being in the CIA. The CIA is a secret organization. No one ever admits to being a member. The truth is that Bush has been a top CIA official since before the 1961 invasion of Cuba, working with Felix Rodriguez. Bush may

deny his actual role in the CIA in 1959, but there are records in the Bay of Pigs invasion of Cuba that expose Bush's role ... .

On the Watergate tapes, June 23, 1972, referred to in the media as the *smoking gun* conversation, Nixon and his Chief of Staff, H.R. Haldeman, were discussing how to stop the FBI investigation into the Watergate burglary. They were worried that the investigation would expose their connection to *the Bay of Pigs thing*. Haldeman, in his book *The Ends of Power*, reveals that Nixon always used code words when talking about the 1963 murder of JFK. Haldeman said Nixon would always refer to the assassination as *the Bay of Pigs*.

On that transcript we find Nixon discussing the role of George Bush's partner, Robert Mosbacher, as one of the Texas fundraisers for Nixon. On the tapes Nixon keeps referring to the *Cubans* and the *Texans*. The *Texans* were Bush, Mosbacher and Baker. This is another direct link between Bush and evidence linking Nixon and Bush to the Kennedy assassination.

President Nixon meets with Republican Party Chairman George Bush and others

MOTIVES FOR THE CONSPIRACY

SO, WHY WOULD an intelligence agency/secret society want to smuggle drugs and assassinate JFK?

Well, they make a lot of money and they garner intelligence assets through their participation. There is also the rationale that the world is a seamy and unseemly place, and if you're going to be the *big boy* on the block, you better know what's going on. And what better way of knowing than by running it yourself? There are also some who theorize that the covert drug trade fits with plans to destabilize American families and society. Through demoralizing and fracturing the body politic, they can impose their will using psychological warfare and the political alchemy of the Hegelian dialectic.

Moments before the murder

James Shelby Downard's article, *Sorcery, Sex, Assassination and the Science of Symbolism*, an underground classic, links American historical events with a wild, numerological, grand occult plan "to turn us into cybernetic mystery zombies." The assassination of JFK, this article contends, was the performance of a public occult ritual called *The Killing of the King*, designed as a mass-trauma, mind-control assault against our US national body-politic.

During Operation Sunrise, Operation Blowback, Operation Paperclip and others, thousands of Nazi scientists, researchers and administrators were brought to the United States after World War II. Many were *smuggled* into the country against direct, written orders from President Harry S. Truman.

Project Monarch was the resumption of a mind-control project called Marionette Programming, which started in Nazi Germany. The basic component of the Monarch Program is the sophisticated manipulation of the mind, using extreme trauma to induce Multiple Personality Disorder.

Mr. Downward feels that the perpetrators purposefully murdered JFK in such a way as to affect our national identity and cohesiveness — to fracture America's soul. Even the blatancy of their conspiracy was designed to show *their superiority* and *our futility*.

President Kennedy is hit

There have been studies that show a correlation between the JFK assassination and the rise in violence in society, distrust of government and other extensions of social ills.

The Illuminati: Subverting the Body Politic

WHY THIS ATTACK against our body politic?

In 1785, a courier died en route to Paris from Frankfort-on-the-Main. A tract written by Adam Weishaupt, founder of the Illuminati, *Original Shift in Days of Illuminations*, was recovered from the dead messenger, containing the secret society's long-range plan for "The New World Order through world revolution."

Adam Weishaupt

The Bavarian Government outlawed the society and in 1787 published the details of The Illuminati conspiracy in *The Original Writings of the Order and Sect of the Illuminati.*

In Adam Weishaupt's own words:

> By this plan, we shall direct all mankind in this manner. And, by the simplest means, we shall set all in motion and in flames. The occupations must be so allotted and contrived that we may, in secret, influence all political transactions.

There is disagreement among scholars as to whether or not the Illuminati survived its banishment. Nevertheless, the group had been quite successful in attracting members and had allied itself with the extensive Masonic networks.

The Illuminati was publicly founded May 1, 1776, at the University of Ingolstadt by Weishaupt, Professor of Canon Law. It was a very "learned" society; Weishaupt drew the earliest members of his new order from among his students.

On December 5, 1776, students at William and Mary College founded a secret society, Phi Beta Kappa. A second chapter was formed, at Yale, in 1780. The anti-Masonic movement in the United States during the 1820s held groups such as Phi Beta Kappa in a bad light. Because of pressure, the society went public.

This is noted by some researchers as the direct cause of the appearance of Yale's Order of Skull and Bones.

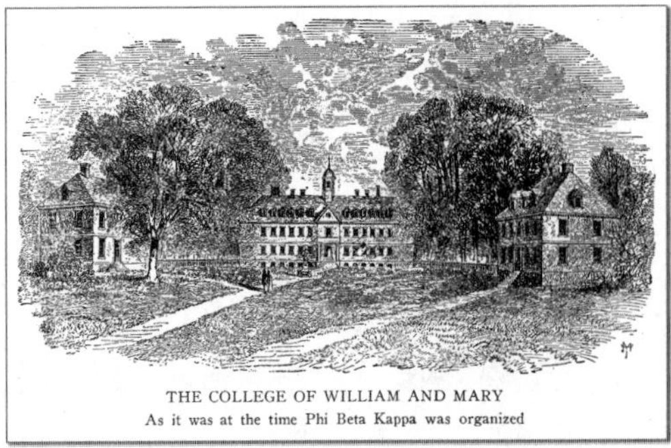

THE COLLEGE OF WILLIAM AND MARY
As it was at the time Phi Beta Kappa was organized

In *The Cyclopedia Of Fraternities*, a genealogical chart of general Greek-Letter college fraternities in the United States, shows Phi Beta Kappa as "the parent of all the fraternal systems in [American] higher education." There is only one "side" lineal descendant: the Yale chapter of 1780. The line then continues to Skull and Bones in 1832, and on through the other "only at Yale" senior societies, Scroll & Key and Wolf's Head.

Phi Beta Kappa is the "first three Greek letters, for 'Philosophia Biou Kubernetes' or 'Love of wisdom, the helmsman of life'." A skull homophone is scull, a quick, gliding boat and part of Skull & Bones first nomenclature.

John Robison, a professor of natural philosophy at Edinburgh University in Scotland and a member of a Freemason Lodge, said that he was asked to join the Illuminati. After study, he concluded the purposes of the Illuminati were not for him.

In 1798, he published a book called *Proofs Of A Conspiracy:*

> An association has been formed for the express purpose of rooting out all the religious establishments and overturning all the existing governments ... the leaders would rule the World with uncontrollable power, while all the rest would be employed as tools of the ambition of their unknown superiors.

Proofs Of A Conspiracy was sent to George Washington. Responding to the sender of the book with a letter, the president said he was aware the Illuminati were in America. He felt that the Illuminati had diabolical tenets and that their object was a separation of the People from their government.

In *Proofs Of A Conspiracy*, Robison described the ceremony of initiation of the "Regent degree" in Illuminism. In it "a skeleton is pointed out to him [the initiate], at the feet of which are laid a crown and a sword. He is asked *whether that is the skeleton of a king, nobleman or a beggar*. As he cannot decide, the president of the meeting says to him, *The character of being a man is the only one that is importance.*"

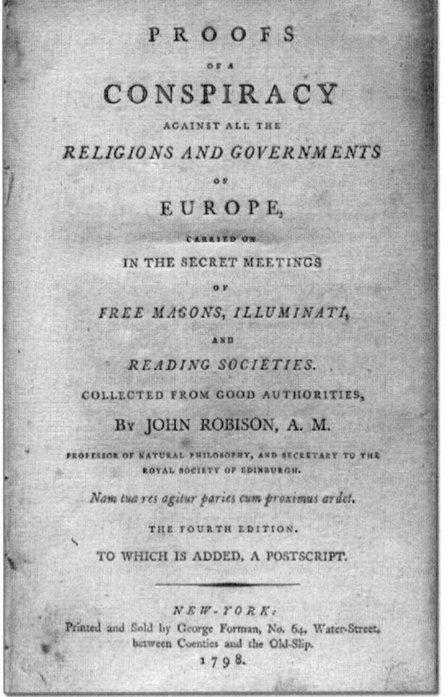

PROOFS
OF A
CONSPIRACY
AGAINST ALL THE
RELIGIONS AND GOVERNMENTS
OF
EUROPE,
CARRIED ON
IN THE SECRET MEETINGS
OF
FREE MASONS, ILLUMINATI,
AND
READING SOCIETIES.
COLLECTED FROM GOOD AUTHORITIES,
By JOHN ROBISON, A. M.
PROFESSOR OF NATURAL PHILOSOPHY, AND SECRETARY TO THE ROYAL SOCIETY OF EDINBURGH.
Nam tua res agitur paries cum proximus ardet.
THE FOURTH EDITION.
TO WHICH IS ADDED, A POSTSCRIPT.

NEW-YORK:
Printed and Sold by George Forman, No. 64, Water-Street, between Coenties and the Old-Slip.
1798.

BEGGARS ON FOOT: PRINCES AND QVEENS WHO RIDE,
IN SKVLL-AND-BONE LAND SAVNTER SIDE BY SIDE
EQVALITY

From a Bones membership book

This is, essentially, the same as the writing in the Skull & Bones' Temple:

"Wer war der Thor, wer Weiser, Bettler oder Kaiser? Ob Arm, ob Reich, im Tode gleich."

Which reads:

"Who was the fool, who the wise man, beggar or king? Whether poor or rich, all's the same in death."

SKULL & BONES = ILLUMINATI?

IS THE ORDER of the Skull & Bones part of the Illuminati?

When a person is initiated into Skull & Bones, they are given a new name, similar to the practice of the Illuminati. Many recorded Illuminati members can be shown to have contact and/or strong influences with many of the professors that taught "Bonesmen" in Berlin.

When a secret society conspires against the sovereignty of a king, they need to organize, raise funds, make their plans operational, and hopefully bring them to fruition.

Could we have in the United States a secret society that has used the "National Security State" as a cover for their nefarious plans?

From *George Bush: The Unauthorized Biography*:

Averell Harriman taking oath to serve as Director of the Mutual Security Agency

> That September [1951], Robert Lovett replaced Marshall as secretary of defense. Meanwhile, Harriman was named director of the Mutual Security Agency, making him the U.S. chief of the Anglo-American military alliance. By now, Brown Brothers, Harriman was everything but commander-in-chief.
>
> A central focus of the Harriman security regime in Washington (1950-53) was the organization of covert operations and *psychological warfare*. Harriman, together with his lawyers and business partners, Allen and John Foster Dulles, wanted the government's secret services to conduct extensive propaganda campaigns and mass-psychology experiments within the U.S.A., and paramilitary campaigns abroad ....
>
> The Harriman security regime created the Psychological Strategy Board (PSB) in 1951. The man appointed director of the PSB [was] Gordon Gray ... Gordon's brother, R.J. Reynolds chairman Bowman Gray Jr., was also a naval intelligence

officer, known around Washington as the *founder of operational intelligence*. Gordon Gray became a close friend and political ally of Prescott Bush; and Gray's son became for Prescott's son, George, his lawyer and the shield of his covert policy.

Gordon Gray

So you have the Whitney/Stimson/Bundy clan and the Harriman/Bush boys wielding a tremendous amount of influence on the political, economic and social affairs of America and the world. Then you have Prescott Bush's buddy Richard Nixon as an activist Vice-President. Then, a nation-chilling assassination, some time under LBJ with the Bundy boys keeping things in line, then Nixon as President with "Bonesmen" aides Ray Price ('51) and Richard A. Moore. Then DKE and Yale Law School graduate Gerald Ford. Some time out for a Trilateralist-patsy president, followed by Prescott's son as an activist Vice-President under Reagan. Then, Bonesman George HW Bush, who declares a *New World Order* while beating up on Saddam Hussein.

Presidents Ford, Nixon, Bush, Reagan and Carter

After 12 years of Republican administrations, Bush passes the reins to his drug smuggling buddy from Arkansas, Bill Clinton, who studied at Yale Law School. According to some researchers, Clinton was recruited as a CIA operative while a Rhodes Scholar at Oxford. Could this be the *ol' Hegelian historical dialectic two-step tango?*

WORLD HISTORY: PLAN OR ACCIDENT?

WILL WE GET ANOTHER FAILED Democratic administration? A scandal as disgraceful as Nixon's fall? When Robert P. Johnson (William Barr) told Clinton in a bunker in Arkansas that "you are our fair-haired boy, but you do have competition for the job you seek. We would never put all our eggs in one basket. You and your state have been our greatest asset … Mr. Casey wanted me to pass on to you, that unless you fuck up and do something stupid, you are number one on our short list for shot at the job you always wanted."

So, you have William Casey — CIA Director, George Bush's campaign manager and Sovereign Knight of Malta — speaking through the proxy of George Bush's last Attorney General to George's rival in the 1992 federal elections. Is it all just a show and sham for US hoi polloi?

Perhaps so, if there exists the type of control over the electoral process as told by Mae Brussell and the suppressed book, *VoteScam*, written by Jim and Ken Collier:

President William Clinton

Your vote and mine may now be a meaningless bit of energy directed by pre-programmed computers – which can be fixed to select certain pre-ordained candidates and leave no footprints or paper trail.

In short, computers are covertly stealing your vote.

For almost three decades the American vote has been subject to government-sponsored electronic theft.

William Casey

The vote has been stolen from you by a cartel of federal *national security* bureaucrats, who include higher-ups in the Central Intelligence Agency, political party leaders, Congressmen, co-opted journalists – and the owners and managers – of the major Establishment news media, who have decided in concert that how America's votes are counted, by whom they are counted and how the results are verified and delivered to the public is, as one of them put it, *[n]ot a proper area of inquiry.*

By means of an unofficial private corporation named News Election Service (NES), the Establishment press has actual physical control of the counting and dissemination of the vote, and it refuses to let the public know how it is done.

Is the American electorate subjected to cyclical propaganda, pre-selected candidates and winners, and psychological warfare to alienate Americans from the institutions established to serve them by the Constitution? Are the Democratic and Republican National Parties used for a Hegelian experiment in controlled conflict?

Pamela Churchill Harriman

Pamela Churchill Harriman, Averell's wife, is one of the Democratic Party's biggest fund-raisers. She once gave Bill a job as director of her PAM PAC when he was defeated for governor of Arkansas in 1980. Bill paid her back by appointing her as Ambassador to France.

Another Harriman/Bush friend, Eugene Stetson (S&B '34), was an assistant manager for Prescott Bush at Brown Brothers, Harriman's New York office. He organized the H. Smith Richardson Foundation. The foundation, in the late 1950s, participated in the MKULTRA, the CIA's domestic covert psychological warfare operation. The Richardson Foundation helped to finance the testing of psychotropic drugs, including LSD, at Bridgewater Hospital in Massachusetts, the center of some of the most brutal MK-ULTRA experiments.

During the Iran-Contra operations, the H. Smith Richardson Foundation was a "private donors steering committee," working with the National Security Council to co-ordinate the Office of Public Diplomacy. This was an effort to propagandize in favor of and run cover for the Iran-Contra operations, and to coordinate published attacks on opponents of the program.

The H. Smith Richardson Foundation also runs the Center for Creative Leadership in Virginia to "train leaders of the CIA," as well as another center near Greensboro, North Carolina, that trains CIA and Secret Service Agents. Almost everyone who achieves the military rank of general also gets this training.

This is just the tip of an iceberg. You also have eugenics and population control, suppressed history and technology, yearly retreats, profitable partnerships with brutal dictators, deals with "terrorists," the involvement of the Knights of Malta, war-mongering and profiteering, mind-control, secret societies for teens, ritual magic and more — all spinning the dark threads in the web of conspiracy that our spinning blue-green ball has become entangled.

A whole new crop of "Bonesmen" coming up, including George HW Bush's son George W Bush (S&B '68), Governor of Texas.

Bonesmen Bush

When Don Schollander (S&B '68), the Olympic gold-medalist and only known Skull and Bones member living in Portland, Oregon, was contacted by local Willamette Week reporter John Schrang regarding his involvement in the Order, he said, "It's really something I can't talk about."

Not wouldn't, but "couldn't."

In wake of Antony Sutton's first ground-breaking exposes of the Order, some of the Russell Trust papers at the Sterling Library at Yale have not been available.

Daniel Gilman, like most Bonesmen, makes no mention of Skull & Bones or the Russell Trust in his memoirs or biographies.

So, are we all just *fodder* for a secret society that is attempting to form a one world government with themselves at the helm? Or is the Order of Skull and Bones just a bunch of frat boys from Yale? Want to bet your future on it?

In the mid to late 90s there was very little mentioning George W Bush on the Internet. Consequently up until 1999, the above essay was always in the top 10 responses when searching Google for George W Bush. In 1998, the article was listed as the reference for Skull & Bones in Robert Anton Wilson's *Everything Is Under Control — Conspiracies, Cults and Cover-ups* — but most of all the story led to my personal introduction to author, historian and researcher, my friend, Antony Sutton.

THE SEPTEMBER 11TH ATTACK THE WAR ON TERROR AND THE ORDER OF SKULL & BONES

ANTONY SUTTON

JUNE 2002 – HIS LAST WRITTEN ARTICLE

THE WORLD TRADE CENTER TRAGEDY of September 11, 2001, murdered just under 3,000 Americans. The most costly attack ever on US soil. Today still uninvestigated, unsolved and virtually forgotten except for friends and relatives.

Why this suppression of WTC? Essentially because President Bush claims he cannot be bothered, he does not want his staff distracted, they are busy with the War on Terror.

Distracted? This matter could be disposed of in a 30-minute press conference.

The WTC episode was the initial, and so far the only, domestic physical act in this War on Terror. Now in denial Mr. Bush has apparently his own deep reasons for avoiding the topic. The country with less transitory interest has a right to know the reality of WTC. In one year this War on Terror has only this single disastrous WTC episode.

Mr. Bush has skillfully directed public attention to Afghanistan and Pakistan, but failed to show how Afghanistan and Pakistan tie to WTC.

Reality is where the public interest resides. For the public the WTC *is* the War on Terror, yet this is the core reality aspect where Bush ducks and weaves. Even further, he prevailed upon Senator Daschle to kill a Senate inquiry and pours cold water on any public inquiry.

Given this excellent opportunity for public exposure, Bush and the Administration have become shy and bashful. Our non-political question is ... what are they hiding?

According to *New York Times,* (June 6, 2002 page A-21), "... the Administration has a deep desire to avoid any investigation at all but this has become politically untenable."

While at the same time Mr. Bush is quoted, "I've seen no evidence today that said this country could have prevented the attacks." The latter statement does not accord with known facts.

As Kristen Breitweiser wrote in the *New York Times,* (May 17, 2002 page A 21), "Why was the President allowed to sit for 35 minutes with a group of second graders when the country was under attack?"

What is clearly obvious even to a *New York Times* reporter was not obvious to the echelons of officials surrounding the President ... of course the Miami photo shoot could have been deliberately planned as a deception move.

None of this is reflected in the public assessment and Bush retains a respectable 77% rating. This can plummet like a stone in a well.

Deaths Head of Mr. Bush

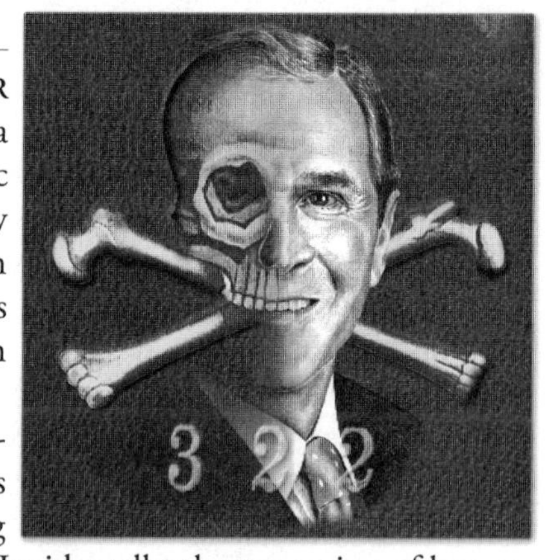

George W Bush and his father (as was *his* father) are members of a deeply submerged secret society, a satanic secret society, they would prefer you know nothing about. More suited to the 18th century than the 21st century it is known as Skull & Bones and is a real life anachronism in this modern world.

Bush is in the 1968 cell and a photograph of him and his 15 fellow cell-mates shows them grouped around a table bearing their symbol ... a skull and cross bones. (Incidentally, the possession of human remains is an offense against the laws in Connecticut, the home of S&B).

The Order of Skull and Bones is no mere innocent college fraternity, as Bush would have you believe. This is a post-graduate society geared to the outside world through the RTA (a tax exempt foundation, also known as the Russell Trust Association) and their retreat on Deer Island (See this author's *America's Secret Establishment* for further details)

One of the RTA's operating principles is the use of Hegelian creation of conflict to make "progress" or advance history, and is typical of two other omnipotent philosophies with Hegelian roots ... Nazism and Marxism.

As three members of the Bush family (grandfather Prescott, father George and George Junior) are members of RTA, we are interested in what this trio has done to further history using Hegelian methodology.

BACK TO WTC AND SEPTEMBER 11, 2001

Mr. Bush is *deeply* reluctant to tell us what he was doing between 8 AM and 9:15 AM on September 11, 2001. Yet this is a critical question for his fellow Americans. Because while Bush was meeting with Florida 2nd graders for 35 minutes — and according to the *New York Times* reporter this Florida meeting had *absolute* priority — almost 3,000 Americans were murdered.

The *New York Times* reporter found this strange, so do we. Mr. Bush has missed a key point here. His penchant for secrecy is not going to enable him to avoid the question. Why didn't he use this 35 minutes to partially rescue the US and send F-16s to shoot down the high-jacked planes? Then maybe only 300 lives, not nearly 3,000, would have been lost.

DOES BUSH HAVE A HEGELIAN HANGOVER?

The Reichstagg

The Bush family approach to the presidency is quite different from other presidents. The Bush family seemingly views the presidency as a personal fiefdom empowered with the divine right of kings, unassailable, not to be challenged, not to be doubted and potentially omnipotent.

This is an extraordinary error. The vast American public is just not on the same wavelength.

As an example of minefields down the road, take George Sr. and the Iran-Contra papers.

These are totally secret, not to be released and many believe will never be released. George Sr. was in charge of Iran-Contra.

How do we know this? Simply because 10 or so of the official participants (from DEA, CIA, NSA and on and on) had second thoughts, saw the illegalities, rebelled and placed their participation and what they knew on paper and the Internet.

So we have a personal and open account of the official suppressed record. We can well understand why Bush Sr. and his fellow operators want complete and permanent secrecy. Iran-Contra should place several dozen officials in jail.

An important part of Iran Contra was cocaine trafficking using a combination of official and private facilities with Bush Sr. in charge. For example, the deep sea drilling rigs, staffed by CIA and NSA persons of the Zapata Corporation (with Bones and Bush ties) were used as transit points for the cocaine. It may have been a joint operation with Israel because some cocaine packages were also labeled with the Star of David.

In brief, the private and public parts of this narcotics operation were merged and hidden, which is good enough reason for concealment of this episode from a long suffering public.

Then we have the deeply disturbing case of Prescott Bush, grandfather of George Bush, who with Averell Harriman helped finance Hitler through the Union Banking Corporation, which was later taken over by the Alien Property Custodian. Prescott seems to be a very active participant in The Order's efforts to create a Hegelian dialectic arms.

We know that this 1930's pro-Hitler maneuver even today creates alarm in Bush circles. We were interviewed for a documentary on this topic for Dutch National TV and great efforts were made to suppress the Dutch papers relating to this Bush-Harriman episode.

Prescott and Averell were members of the same secret society and supposedly opposite political parties — all while working together out of the same business office.

Our interest is purely research. We have two Bonesmen with private interests in a secret society, are they attempting to pursue Hegelian dialectic? We have every reason in the world to question Bush Junior's involvements in similar situations.

This is not a something Mr. Bush should avoid. If you lose control in these situations — as Mr. Bush well knows — you lose any influence you might have.

If we find three Bushes in a row involved in conflict creation situations … even the dumbest of American voters won't feel too happy.

This is where you find the limits of the American Historical Association, the major book publishers and establishment history. Any author in this field steers a path well clear of AHA and the major New York publishers. Why … because they have their marching orders. Also more interesting, we know how these blinker-equipped publishers became part of establishment mythology. And this is why the major publishers become smaller and smaller and ultimately will disappear.

Finale

No doubt the above news and similar yet to be published misdeeds will shock many — yet are really not cause for individual alarm.

The country has automatic ways of dealing with those who abuse, not always prompt or noticeable , but sooner or later Iran-Contra, the 2000 election episode and offshoots like Enron (Bush's biggest financier) will be called to account. That is the history of the United States. The country has an unusual ability to disgorge even its worst offenders and offenses.

Reichstagg Fire

Who remembers Teapot Dome, the Wall Street excesses of 1929, even the McCarthy era and segregation?

They have been dealt with.

Give this country enough time for information to spread and the system will right wrongs itself.

Even childish excesses like Skull & Bones will find their level and eventually be expunged.

The reaction will come from the bottom up.

What a Role Model For His Daughters!

Charlotte Thomson Iserbyt
July 2003

My grandfather, Samuel Clifton Thomson, The Order (Bones) 1891, was from Pottsville, Pa, an important coal mining center to this day. The Thomson family had been involved in coal mining from the early eighteen hundreds into the mid-twentieth century. The family was descended from Scottish Covenanters (Scottish Presbyterians who arrived in America in the mid seventeen hundreds. I have a beautiful sword presented to my great grandfather by officers in his Pennsylvania regiment at the conclusion of the Civil War.)

The original homestead exists in bad repair in Thompsontown, PA. My great grandfather changed the spelling of Thomson to Thompson adding a "p" since he wanted to show off his flourishing handwriting and a "p" really made the grade in this regard.

Grandpa graduated from Andover Boys Preparatory School, Yale University and from Columbia School of Mines with honors, in 1893. He received the School of Mines medal from the President of Columbia University, Nicholas Murray Butler.

Nicholas Murray Butler, on the Executive Committee of the Carnegie Endow-

Samuel C. Thomson at Noranda Mines, Quebec, 1922

ment for International Peace, delivered an address entitled "Higher Preparedness" on Nov. 27, 1915 to the Union League of Philadelphia in which he stated "The old world order changed when this war storm broke — the old world order died with the setting of the day's sun and a New World Order is being born while I speak." From *A World in Ferment, a Collection of Butler's Speeches,* Scribners 1917, page 106.

Butler's book *Across the Busy Years — Recollections and Reflections,* Scribners, 1935, pp 160-161 reveals much regarding Butler's role as Dean of the Faculty of Philosophy, Columbia University, in changing American education from its traditional academic orientation to a behaviorist (Wundtian/Pavlovian) orientation originating in Leipzig, Germany. This change was necessary for brainwashing (value change) and implementation of the present work force training required for a planned economy. It was Butler's access to Daniel Coit Gilman, an incorporator of Skull & Bones, and a key activist in the revolution of education which, resulted in bringing to Columbia University, Professor James McKeen Cattell. Butler's information ties in well with Tony Sutton's coverage of The Order's influence on American education. Sutton's book *America's Secret Establishment* is the only book on The Order which documents The Order's extraordinary influence in bringing about what this author refers to as "the deliberate dumbing down of America."

Butler's book also refers extensively to the activities of Charles D. Hilles, Sr. (not a member of The Order) whose role in the Republican Party included running for Governor of New York, Vice President of the United States, and who was Chairman of the Republican Party Platform Committee, 1916. Charles D. Hilles, Sr. was the father of Charles D. Hilles, Jr., one of my father's closest Bones' associates who stands behind the table in the Tomb (See photo of 1924 members of The Order. A few Bonesmen about whom I have written are seated as follows: my father, Clifton Thomson, is to the left of the table, Hilles behind table, Spofford standing left of the clock, and Blair standing, third from the left.)

What all of this has to do with Bones is not clear, but there surely must be connections. No doubt Grandpa's receiving the School of Mines medal was well-earned. However, it is also likely that Butler, an internationalist with connections all over the English-speaking world, selected Grandpa for the honor not only due to his engineering abilities, but also due to his connections through his membership in The Order.

Grandpa had good credentials for being tapped for The Order. He was a Unitarian and a Mason, from Pottsville, Pennsylvania. Had it not been for his being tapped for Bones, and his being awarded the mining medal, I rather doubt that he would have been invited to go to South Africa which took him to the pinnacles of the engineering profession and led him into a leadership role in the opening up of the gold mines. He had a close personal and working friendship with Sir Abe Bailey, who I believe was a South African Fabian socialist, and I understand he was an acquaintance of Cecil Rhodes. Upon returning to the United States, he explored in Quebec, Canada and founded Noranda Mines in the early twenties.

My memories of him are all wonderful. He was a most generous, unspoiled fellow who preferred to spend his evenings in the company of the less affluent on the West Side of NYC, eating hot dogs and drinking beer, rather than in his elegant suite at the Pierre Hotel on Fifth Avenue. I have a small silver trophy (cup), which I cherish, engraved "Grandpa to Charlotte for swimming, 1938" which he had made specially for me when I won a swimming race while on vacation with him at the Seigneury Club in Quebec. (I use it as a double shot measure in memory of grandpa who was an enthusiastic scotch drinker!)

Grandpa left for California in the late eighteen hundreds and worked at Grass Valley in a chlorination factory for a short while during the gold boom. He soon after was invited by the great John Hays Hammond to go to Africa, an invitation he declined, but later accepted from Thomas H. Leggatt. He arrived in the Rand in 1898 and spent twelve additional seasons (1902-1914) in charge of the mining operations of Norman and Company and Sir Abe Bailey. During that time Thomson's major concerns were the Witwatersrand Deep, the Treasury and Great Central mines. Many other properties came under his charge, as well, so that by the time he left Africa, he was widely known to the gold-mining fraternity. I have a solid gold cigarette box, the inside cover of which is engraved with the signatures of American mining engineers which they presented to him when he left the Rand in 1914.

During his stay in South Africa, Thomson saw service as a lieutenant in the British Army through the later phases of the Boer War. (He was in charge of protecting the mines from Boer sabotage.) It was Thomson's plan, on leaving the Rand in 1914, to engage in consulting practice in London, England, principally for Sir Abe Bailey and his associates. He evidently worked closely with Bailey while in South Africa. I had a wonderful black and white photo of my grandfather and Sir Abe Bailey, but somehow it has been lost.

World War I intervened while he was on holiday in the United States, however, thus reserving grandpa's future for Canadian mining, and to Noranda Mines. (He was one of the principals in the discovery and development of copper mines in Canada.) The Anglo-American connections are clear and of course, we are all aware of Carnegie's plan to bring America back to the mother's bosom, something we are looking at today. (George Bush and Tony Blair!)

My Dad, Clifton Samuel Thomson, a graduate of Hotchkiss Boys School, class of 1924 at Yale, Columbia Law School, 1926, and a Bonesman, was born in 1903 in Johannesburg, S.A., and lived there until 1914 when his family went to live in London for a while and then moved back to Englewood, N.J., U.S.A. Dad was also a member of Delta Kappa Epsilon while at Yale. This fraternity boasts many important members, including four Presidents of the United States: Hayes, Bush, Sr. Bush, Jr. Roosevelt, and Ford. I have always felt there was a very, very close connection between The Order and DKE. While in London he attended Cheam Boys School, the very elitist school outside of London, which caters to British royalty. He detested every minute of it (cold showers and lousy food) and his dislike of all things English, including the British cruelty exhibited in the Boer

War, remained with him until he died in 1984. Dad was, I believe, an unlikely candidate for Bones, being very down to earth, an individualist, honest to the core, and Christian. He served as Mayor of Sands Point, Long Island, N.Y., as a vestryman at St. Stephen's Episcopal Church at Port Washington, New York, and was elected councilman, Mendham Township Council, Mendham, New Jersey.

I knew three or four of his Bones classmates quite well: One, my sister's godfather, was I believe, instrumental in starting the Hemlock Society! This fellow who bounced me on his knees and told great stories ... was the last person I would ever have thought to be involved in bringing euthanasia to America. Dad also spent a couple of weeks at Bohemian Grove as a guest of his very close friend Edwin Blair, another Bones guy, who was nick-named "Mr. Yale" since he was such a good fund raiser. (Blair was also a partner with Chuck Spofford at Davis, Polk, Wardwell, Sunderland and Keindl ... see below.) Dad was not impressed by most of the activities at the Grove although he said a few presentations were noteworthy, food was excellent and accommodations top of the line. He had one big, and I mean "big" problem with pompous people, and there was no shortage of such types at Bohemian Grove functions. Henry Allen, another Bones friend of Dad's, was a director of the American Civil Liberties Union, set up by Amos Pinchot (The Order), and the daughter of his friend, Sherman Ewing, married a Rockefeller, but Ewing himself was not involved in any high level international or national policy planning.

Dad was at Hotchkiss School with E.O. Matthiessen (Bones 1923). An interesting aside follows: Matthiessen's daughter lived in the same town where I was on the local school board creating problems for the liberals ... in the seventies. She knew my father was her father's friend due to Hotchkiss and Bones, but that didn't make any difference to her ... she went after me with a vengeance, often, and in public (even at social occasions!) due to my opposition to the federally-funded non-academic and no right/no wrong programs being implemented in the seventies. She was a carbon copy of her father about whom Tony has written in his newsletters. Her Dad is quoted on the jacket of Tony's book as saying "As long as we have somebody from Bones who can bring pressure on the committee, I should think we'll be all right." — E.O. Matthiessen (S&B 1923) to Donald Ogden Steward (S&B 1916) about "Matty's" upcoming appearance before the House Committee on Un-American Activities.

In my opinion, the most important Bonesman in the Class of 1924, a close friend and roommate of my father's, was Charles Merville Spofford, who rose to great heights in international law and politics. Dad, once, close to the end of his life, related to me an account of Spofford's promotion to positions of international influence, much of which is covered in detail in *Yale '24-'24S* and which I am including since Spofford provides a most important case study in how a very few members of the Order become global shakers and movers.

An account of Spofford's meteoric rise to fame, taken from page 326 of *Yale '24-'24S*, published in 1955, follows:

> Chuck, who took his LL.B. at Harvard in 1928, was with Isham, Lincoln & Beal in Chicago until 1930 and has since been with Davis, Polk, Wardwell, Sunderland & Kiendl, in which he became a partner in 1940. He is a director of the Guaranty Trust Company of New York, the Distillers Company, Ltd., and the Gordon's Dry Gin Company, Ltd., and is on the boards of the Free Europe Committee, Union Theological Seminary, the Carnegie Corporation, the Juilliard Musical Foundation, the Juilliard School of Music, and the national council of the English-Speaking Union. He belongs to various bar associations and to the Council on Foreign Relations. He went on active duty as a lieutenant colonel in October, 1942, was assigned to the General Staff Corps, and had thirty-two months' service in the Eastern Theatre of Operations and Mediterranean Theatre of Operations, ranking as a brigadier general at his release in December, 1945; he was in the Reserve from 1947 to 1954. In addition to the U.S. Distinguished Service Medal and Purple Heart, he was awarded the Croix de Guerre with palm and was made a commander of the Legion of Honor, the Order of the British Empire, the Order of Ishan Iftikhar (Tunisia), and the Order of St. Maurice and St. Lazarus (Italian). Chuck was appointed U.S. deputy representative to the North Atlantic Council, with the rank of Ambassador, in June, 1950, the next month being elected chairman of the North Atlantic Council Deputies; for his work in this capacity (which continued until April 1952), he received the following decorations: officer, Legion of Honor; grand officer, Order of the Crown (Belgium); commander with star, Order of the Falcon (Iceland). He is the author of "The North Atlantic Treaty," in the *Journal of the Royal Empire Society*, "Toward Atlantic Security," in *International Affairs*, "North Atlantic Security," in the *Journal of the Royal United Services Institution*, and "NATO's Growing Pains" in *Foreign Affairs*.

I remember his coming into my office in Middle Eastern Affairs, U.S. Department of State, in 1956, at the peak of one of the continuing Mid-East crises, to participate as a board member of The Suez Canal Company.

After Chuck had divorced his wife of many years, he had a serious stroke, which confined him to a wheel chair. Surprisingly enough he remarried his former long-time secretary at Davis, Polk, a wonderful, down-to-earth woman with whom I had worked at one time. They lived in Easthampton, Long Island, in a house he bought from William Simon, former Secretary of the Treasury. I relate these seemingly unimportant bits of information to reveal how even those who rise to great heights in world affairs encounter the same difficult problems in marriage, severe illnesses, etc. that we plain *regulars* encounter, and that occasionally they survive through attachments to persons whose backgrounds are totally different (normal?). His second wife, who came from an entirely different background, took such wonderful care of Chuck until he passed on. She probably turned out to be the most important person in his life, outside of his children. There were other Bones friends of Dad's I knew fairly well but I don't have any interesting stories. I'd say only 3 or 4 out of the 15 were involved in important U.S. Government or international policy decisions.

Dad always supported the Bush family in its election efforts, while Mom, a true-blue conservative Catholic from Virginia, whose family served on the Confederate side during the Civil War, supported Reagan. The Order would solicit campaign contributions for Bush from its members. Dad attended the reunions on Deer Island, but not frequently.

Dad was a Senior Partner with Appleton, Rice, and Perrin, a small Wall Street law firm. Lee Perrin, Bones 1906, was a very fine gentleman who I suspect brought Dad on board at the firm. (Connections help!) Dad was also the attorney for a French company, the Matham Corporation, during World War II. I remember that he received all sorts of pins (medals) from Matham for his service to the company during the war. I believe Matham was involved in manufacturing arms.

Dad resigned his position with Matham due to its involvement with the Nazis. He was very principled, and I'm sure not at all on the Bones' wavelength of supporting both sides (i.e. Hitler and Stalin). Of interest and along the same lines was a comment he made to Alan Klotz, a Wall Street attorney, also a Bonesman from another year, regarding dropping the bomb on Hiroshima. Dad said he told Klotz, who reacted in shock, that, "we should have dropped it on Moscow instead." That doesn't jibe with Bones politics, does it? My mother always jokingly said, "One day Dad acts like a capitalist; the next day he acts like a communist." That's quite a comment, isn't it? I rather suspect that could be applied to most of those guys who received the same brainwashing at Yale. Isn't that known as *cognitive dissonance* in psychological circles?

On a personal level, that is, his attitude towards my work, he was "cool." Although he and I were very, very close as Dad and daughter and did many things together (tennis, swimming, long walks, talks, etc.), it always bothered him that I was critical of the public education system and U.S. foreign policy. (Although he would often make disparaging remarks about the "striped pants" guys running the world.) He once said he couldn't understand why I was opposed to world government and I responded "Dad, I can't believe what you are saying . . . whose Constitution will our country have?" (He was a conservative, constitutionally oriented, and had been mayor of our town!) He lent back in his chair, took a long puff on his cigar and slowly uttered the following in a deep voice: "Oh, Char, we'll take care of that when the time comes." He also once said when I complained about the national debt "not to worry, we owe it to ourselves!"

Although he considered me a very good writer, he said, "I don't agree with where you are coming from." He was brainwashed big time at Yale, especially considering how the brainwash *lasted* for such a long period of time (over the years) with someone who was so *fair*, *honest*, *unspoiled*, etc., and in constant pursuit of the *truth*. He was an avid reader ... I never saw him without a book in his lap. His favorite writer was Thoreau and he had read all the books in Will and Ariel Durant's *The History of Civilization* series.

My sister and I spent the last year of his life with him at his home in Gladstone, New Jersey. He was dying of cancer and my sister and I kept him at home; didn't allow him to be put in the hospital. Our mother was in a nursing home. Very sad they were separated like that at the end of their lives. He died in 1984 with his dog, Whiskers, a Welsh terrier, on the bed beside him!

1984 was the year Phyllis Schlafly's book, *Child Abuse in the Classroom*, which was really half mine since I had written most of the parts about the parents' testimony at U.S. Department of Education hearings. Phyllis and I worked on the book by phone, in order to have it available at the Republican Convention in Texas. Dad was able to hear our conversations about everything from death education to world government. His bedroom was on the ground floor next to the kitchen where I sort of lived with the phone. About a week before he died he looked at me and said, "If I had more time, I'd help you." That was so nice.

He had also told me several months before he died that he wished he had been a farmer rather than a Wall Street lawyer, and I really believe he meant that.

When not in town with his Wall Street friends, at the Downtown Association for lunch or in his office, all of which he surely enjoyed, he was painting landscapes, cooking, walking the dogs, creating a small pond, or turning the earth in his garden, a plain down to earth person and the greatest friend to many, many people. He never turned down a request for legal or other advice ... was available to everyone, free, no matter rich or poor. A more generous person never lived. He was a man of few words, had a laid back personality, and was incredibly witty with a very dry sense of humor.

What a role model for his daughters!

My parent's wedding was attended by all fifteen of his Bones friends who served as the ushers in 1926 and there is a photo of all fifteen Bones members in the Temple, all standing, with exception of my Dad and another Bones guy, who are sitting on either side of a table which holds the Skull and Bones. Yuk!

I also inherited the beautiful grandfather clock which I believe is given to Bones members when they marry. Dad always insisted that the women in the family never, ever allow the clock to stop. We were never told what would happen if we forgot and let it wind down. Sounded like some occult monkey business at work. Interestingly enough, since I inherited that clock it has broken down numerous times no matter how intent I am on not letting it wind down! I also have the little Skull and Bones pin each member is given upon initiation.

Charlotte Iserbyt is the consummate whistleblower! Iserbyt served as Senior Policy Advisor in the Office of Educational Research and Improvement (OERI), U.S. Department of Education, during the first Reagan Administration, where she first blew the whistle on a major technology initiative which would control curriculums in America's classrooms. Iserbyt is a former school board director in Camden, Maine and was co-founder and research analyst of Guardians of Education for Maine (GEM) from 1978 to 2000. She has also served in the American Red Cross on Guam and Japan during the Korean War, and in the United States Foreign Service in Belgium and in the Republic of South Africa. Iserbyt is a speaker and writer, best known for her 1985 booklet *Back to Basics Reform or OBE: Skinnerian International Curriculum* and her 1989 pamphlet *Soviets in the Classroom: America's Latest Education Fad* which covered the details of the U.S.-Soviet and Carnegie-Soviet Education Agreements which remain in effect to this day. She is a freelance writer and has had articles published in Human Events, *The Washington Times*, *The Bangor Daily News*, and included in the record of Congressional hearings.

www.DeliberateDumbingDown.com

GERONIMO'S BONES

HOWARD ALTMAN
JULY 2003

BACK IN THE LATE SUMMER OF 1989, when the *New Haven Advocate's* office was located on Chapel Street, it was not unusual for the odd and the insane to wander in off the streets.

Some came to sell purloined objects. Some came to babble. And some came because the office was open and there was no place else to go.

Most of the time, I was called upon to deal with the crazies, usually in the role of bouncer protecting the mostly female staff. On more than a few occasions, I had to physically remove such visitors.

Often, though, the crazies came looking for me.

Such was the case with the man in olive drab who had a story to tell.

"Hey Altman, someone's here to see you," said our receptionist.

Great. When she said it like that, it usually meant another paranoid crack head was coming to call.

I'd been visited by relatives of Jesus, descendents of UFO aliens and a man claiming to be great Caesar's ghost. The least I could do, I figured, was humor the man and send him, harmlessly, on his way.

I walked out of my office, to the front desk and greeted the man, a short, wiry guy with a craggily, weathered face and stringy hair. Instantly, I sensed there was something about him, something different than the other whackos who walked in off the street.

Extending his hand, he introduced himself.

"I am Geronimo's great-great grandson," he said.

"Yeah? And my name is Moses," I thought to myself.

Geronimo 1829-1909
May He Rest in Peace

By the look on the receptionist's face, I could tell that the man was making her nervous, so contrary to my usual rule, I invited him back to my office.

I sat down and invited him to do the same, but he refused, saying he was more comfortable standing.

As he stood, he began to tell me about his past, which, he claimed, included a stint in the US military, where he served with the special forces. He made it a point to tell me how he'd killed people, though it wasn't quite clear to me whether the killings took place as a member of the military or on his own.

Either way, I remember feeling just a might uneasy. He might have been hallucinating about being related to Geronimo, but the look in his eyes when he talked about killing people made me think that this guy was telling the truth about something.

After a few minutes more of small talk, I asked him a question.

"So what brings Geronimo's great-great grandson to New Haven?" I asked, a fairly legitimate question considering the circumstances.

And that's when he began to tell me an incredible story.

"I am here because my great-great grandfather Geronimo's bones are here," he said.

That was fantastic enough. But, the more he talked, the more fantastic the story became.

The bones, he said, were dug up by Prescott Bush, father of George Herbert Walker, the first President Bush. They were taken to the Skull and Bones, a secret society on the Yale campus that counts as members a number of Presidents and other high-ranking government and military officials.

The man, who said his name was Phillip Romero, said he wanted the bones returned to their rightful owner, the Apache. He asked if I would be interested in writing a story.

Well, of course I would be interested in writing a story about the President's father digging up Geronimo's bones and bringing them to a secret society in New Haven. There was just one little problem, I told Romero, the man who claimed to be a killer.

Being as tactful as possible, so as not to set him off unnecessarily, I explained that I needed more than his say-so to write a story implicating the father of the President in what amounts to a crime in the state of Connecticut, specifically, the illicit harboring of bones.

The great Apache chief's self-purported great-great grandson told me that such proof existed, in the form of a picture, which was in the hands of a man named Ned Anderson, a former tribal leader of the San Carlos Apache tribal council.

Anderson, said the man, had been tipped off about Geronimo's bones by a disgruntled Skull & Bonesman named "Pat," who told Anderson that Prescott Bush and others dug up the Apache chief's remains from their burial plot at Fort Sill, Oklahoma, and transported them to the Tomb — the Skull & Bones' formidable stone headquarters on High Street in New Haven — where they are to this day said to be used in society rituals.

(In addition to becoming a cult figure for his efforts to retrieve Geronimo's bones, Anderson, according to WaBun-Inini, of the White Earth Anishinabe Ojibwa Nation, would later be credited with helping to found Jesse Jackson's Rainbow Coalition and coining the phrase "Run, Jesse, Run," in conjunction with Jackson's nascent bid for the Presidency.)

His story finished, Romero thanked me for his time, turned around and walked out my office. I never heard from him again.

Anderson, on the other hand, I was in contact with frequently — though reaching him was no easy feat.

He lived on a reservation more than 20 miles from the nearest telephone and our conversations had to be scheduled far in advance so that he could hop a ride.

When we did speak, Anderson told a fascinating story, about how he discovered the whereabouts of Geronimo's bones after a very public battle with Geronimo's relatives, over where the great chief should be buried.

Anderson wanted the remains moved to his reservation in San Carlos, Arizona. Geronimo's family, represented by Wendell Chino, a family member and leader of the Mescalero Apache tribe, wanted the remains to remain where they were, or at least where everyone thought they were, in Fort Sill, where Geronimo died in captivity.

Anderson and Chino were never able to resolve their dispute — Chino calling Anderson's bid "a publicity stunt to attract tourists."

But that was not the end of the story.

The publicity, said Anderson, spurred a Bonesman named "Pat" to come forward and, perhaps out of guilt, tell Anderson that Geronimo was not buried in Fort Sill, but was instead on a shelf in the "Tomb."

The bones, said Anderson, were dug up in 1918 by Prescott Bush — father of the first President Bush and grandfather of the second — along with some cohorts.

In addition to telling Anderson about what happened to Geronimo's bones, "Pat" — whose real identity Anderson would never reveal despite my pleas, whimpers and other forms of persuasion — provided Anderson with a picture of what Anderson claimed are Geronimo's bones in New Haven.

Geronimo - 1890s

Anderson said he took that picture and tried to have his Senator at the time, Mo Udall, intervene. He also said he arranged a meeting with then President George H. W. Bush's brother Jonathan.

"Bush was taken aback when confronted with the evidence," Anderson told me. Just how far aback was hard to ascertain when I finally tracked down Bush. He was cordial, but did not want to talk about the meeting.

My research on the subject revealed that, with a lawyer willing to fight the battle, there might have been a case to investigate the corpse conundrum under Connecticut state law, which holds that it is unlawful to keep such remains.

But no one I talked to was willing to represent Anderson and everyone I talked to said no one would.

Armed with Anderson's evidence, I tried to pay a visit to the Tomb.

I slammed the great knocker, which bounced off the metal door with a tremendous thud. Eventually, someone answered and opened the door ever so slightly.

I introduced myself and told the man why I was there. He refused to talk or even let me in.

Taking a page out of the Obnoxious Salesman's Handbook, I stuck my foot in the heavy metal door in an effort to continue our conversation. The man slammed the door on my foot in an effort to end it.

Ultimately, his impatience (and pressure on my foot) outlasted my patience and I removed my foot, allowing him to close the door on me and any chance of my getting a comment from a Bonesman.

Although Anderson was unsuccessful in finding anyone to represent him and although I was unable to come to any definitive conclusion about Geronimo's bones, the story I wrote — *Bones of Contention: Skullduggery at Yale?* — made a bit of a splash. A local TV station covered it and interviewed me and I received a call from an Italian news magazine.

I left the *New Haven Advocate* in 1991 and the story about Geronimo's bones became a warm but distant memory until just a few years ago, when I began to read about the controversy in the CIA-Drugs Yahoo group and other places on the Internet, leading me to the conclusion that, no matter what happened, Geronimo's bones have legs.

PRESCOTT BUSH, $1,500,000 AND AUSCHWITZ

HOW THE BUSH FAMILY WEALTH IS LINKED TO THE JEWISH HOLOCAUST

TOBY ROGERS

APPEARED IN CLAMOR MAGAZINE, MAY/JUNE 2002

WHILE THE ENRON SCANDAL currently unfolds, another Bush family business scandal lurks beneath the shadows of history that may dwarf it.

On April 19, 2001, President George W. Bush spent some of Holocaust Remembrance Day in the Capital Rotunda with holocaust survivors, allied veterans, and their families. In a ceremony that included Jewish prayers and songs sung by holocaust victims in the camps, Benjamin Meed, a survivor of the Warsaw ghetto uprising, movingly described to the gathering what he experienced on April 19, 1943.

"I stood outside a Catholic church, which faced the ghetto," Mr. Meed said, "a young Jewish boy posing as a gentile. As I watched the ghetto being bombarded by the German artillery, I could see many of the Jews of my community jumping out of windows of burning buildings. I stood long and mute."

The survivor concluded his reminiscence saying, "We tremble to think what could happen if we allow a new generation to arise ignorant of the tragedy which is still shaping the future."

President Bush, appearing almost uncomfortable, read a statement that said that humanity was "bound by conscience to remember what happened" and that "the record has been kept and preserved." The record, Mr. Bush stated, was that one of the worst acts of genocide in human history "came not from crude and uneducated men, but from men who regarded themselves as cultured and well schooled, modern men, forward looking. Their crime showed the world that evil can slip in and blend in amid the most civilized surroundings. In the end only conscience can stop it."

But while President Bush publicly embraced the community of holocaust survivors in Washington last spring, he and his family have been keeping a secret from them for over 50 years about Prescott Bush, the President's grandfather. According to classified documents from Dutch intelligence and US government archives, President George W. Bush's grandfather, Prescott Bush made considerable profits off Auschwitz slave labor. In fact, President Bush himself is an heir to these profits from the holocaust which were placed in a blind trust in 1980 by his father, former President George Herbert Walker Bush.

Throughout the Bush family's decades of public life, the American press has gone out of its way to overlook one historical fact – that through Union Banking Corporation (UBC), Prescott Bush, and his father-in-law, George Herbert Walker, along with German industrialist Fritz Thyssen, financed Adolf Hitler before and during World War II. It was first reported in 1994 by John Loftus and Mark Aarons in *The Secret War Against the Jews: How Western Espionage Betrayed the Jewish People.*

The US government had known that many American companies were aiding Hitler, like Standard Oil, General Motors and Chase Bank, all of which were sanctioned after Pearl Harbor. But as The New York Times reporter Charles Higham later discovered, and published in his 1983 groundbreaking book, *Trading With The Enemy; The Nazi American Money Plot 1933-1949,* "the government smothered everything during and even after the war." Why?

According to Higham, the US government believed "a public scandal ... would have drastically affected public morale, caused widespread strikes and perhaps provoked mutinies in the armed services." Higham claims the government thought "their trial and imprisonment would have made it impossible for the corporate boards to help the American war effort."

However, Prescott Bush's banks were not just financing Hitler as previously reported. In fact, there was a distinct business link much deeper than Mr. Higham or Mr. Loftus knew at the time their books were published.

A classified Dutch intelligence file which was leaked by a courageous Dutch intelligence officer, along with newly surfaced information from U.S. government archives, "confirms absolutely," John Loftus says, the direct links between Bush, Thyssen and genocide profits from Auschwitz.

The business connections between Prescott Bush and Fritz Thyssen were more direct than what has been previously written. This new information reveals how Prescott Bush and UBC, which he managed directly, profited from the Holocaust. A case can be made that the inheritors of the Prescott Bush estate could be sued by survivors of the Holocaust and slave labor communities. To understand the complete picture of how Prescott Bush profited from the Holocaust, it is necessary to return to the year 1916, where it all began.

Post World War I: Thyssen Empire On The Ropes

By 1916, August Thyssen could see the writing on the wall. The "Great War" was spinning out of control, grinding away at Germany's resources and economy. The government was broke and his company, Thyssen & Co., with 50,000 German workers and annual production of 1,000,000 tons of steel and iron, was buckling under the war's pressure. As the main supplier of the German military, August Thyssen knew Germany would be defeated once the US entered the war.

At 74, "King" August Thyssen knew he was also running out of time. His first born "prince" Friedrich (Fritz) Thyssen, had been groomed at the finest technical business schools in Europe and was destined to inherit his father's estimated $100,000,000 fortune and an industrial empire located at Muehhlheim on the Ruhr.

In addition to Fritz, plans were also made for the second son Heinrich. At the outbreak of the war, Heinrich Thyssen discreetly changed his citizenship from German to Hungarian and married the Hungarian aristocrat Baroness Margrit Bornemisza de Kaszon. Soon Heinrich Thyssen switched his name to Baron Thyssen Bornemisza de Kaszon.

Near the end of World War I, August Thyssen opened the Bank voor Handel en Scheepvaart in Rotterdam. The neutral Holland was the perfect location outside of Germany to launder assets from the August Thyssen Bank in Berlin when the financial demands of the Allied forces surfaced. But the war ended much sooner than even Thyssen calculated and what developed caught the "Rockefeller of the Ruhr" off guard. On November 10, 1918, German socialists took over Berlin. The following morning at 5 a.m., what was left of Germany surrendered to the Allies, officially ending World War I. "At the time of the Armistice and the signing of the Treaty of Versailles, my Father and I were deeply saddened by the spectacle of Germany's abject humiliation," Thyssen recalled later in his autobiography, *I Paid Hitler.*

After the war, chaos descended on Germany as food ran short. Winter was looming over a starving nation when on Dec. 7, 1918, the socialist Spartacists League came knocking on the Thyssen Villa with armed militia. August and Fritz were arrested and dragged from jail to jail across Germany for four days. Along the way, they were lined up in staged executions designed to terrorize them.

It worked. When released, the two Thyssens were horrified at the new political climate in their beloved Germany. They could not accept that Germany was responsible for its own demise. All Germany's problems, the Thyssens felt, "have almost always been due to foreigners." It was the Jews, he and many others believed, who were secretly behind the socialist movement across the globe.

Meanwhile Fritz's younger brother Baron Thyssen Bornemisza de Kaszon moved to Rotterdam and became the principal owner of the Bank voor Handel en Scheepvaart. All the Thyssens needed now was an American branch.

1920s: The Business Ties That Bind

RAILROAD BARON E.H. HARRIMAN'S SON AVERELL wanted nothing to do with railroads, so his father gave him an investment firm, W.A. Harriman & Company in New York City. E.H. hired the most qualified person in the country to run the operation, George Herbert Walker. Averell hired his little brother Edward Roland "Bunny" Harriman as a vice president.

By 1920, George Herbert Walker had already built a fortune in Missouri. Walker, a charismatic former heavyweight boxing champion, was a human pit bull. He lived life to the fullest, owning mansions around the East Coast and one of the most extravagant apartments in Manhattan. His hobbies were golf, hunting, drinking scotch and beating his sons to a pulp. Elsie Walker, one of Walker's grandchildren described Walker as a "tough old bastard" whose children had no love "for their father." He was also a religious bigot who hated Catholics, although his parents raised him to be one. According to other sources, he also did not like Jews.

In 1922, Averell Harriman traveled to Germany to set up a W.A. Harriman & Co. branch in Berlin. The Berlin branch was also run by Walker. While in Germany, he met with the Thyssen family for the first time. Harriman agreed to help the Thyssens with their plan for an American bank.

The following year, a wounded Germany was growing sicker. The government had no solution and froze while Germany rotted from within. With widespread strikes and production at a near standstill, Fritz Thyssen later recalled, "We were at the worst time of the inflation. In Berlin the government was in distress. It was ruined financially. Authority was crumbling. In Saxony a communist government had been formed and the Red terror, organized by Max Hoelz, reigned through the countryside. The German Reich ... was now about to crumble."

In October, 1923, an emotionally desperate Fritz Thyssen went to visit one of his and Germany's great military heroes, General Erich Ludendorff. During the 1918 socialist rule in Berlin, Ludendorff organized a military resistance against the socialists and the industrialists were in great debt to him. When Thyssen met with Ludendorff, they discussed Germany's economic collapse. Thyssen was apocalyptic, fearing the worst was yet to come. Ludendorff disagreed. "There is but one hope," Ludendorff said, "Adolph Hitler and the National Socialist party." Ludendorff respected Hitler immensely. "He is the only man who has any political sense." Ludendorff encouraged Thyssen to join the Nazi movement. "Go listen to him one day" he said to Thyssen.

Thyssen followed General Ludendorff's advice and went to a number of meetings to hear Hitler speak. He became mesmerized by Hitler. "I realized his orator gifts and his ability to lead the masses. What impressed me most however was the order that reigned over his meetings, the almost military discipline of his followers."

Thyssen arranged to meet privately with Hitler and Ludendorff in Munich. Hitler told Thyssen the Nazi movement was in financial trouble, it was not growing fast enough and was nationally irrelevant. Hitler needed as much money as possible to fight off the Communists/Jewish conspiracy against Europe. Hitler envisioned a fascist German monarchy with a nonunion, antilock national work force.

Thyssen was overjoyed with the Nazi platform. He gave Hitler and Ludendorff 100,000 gold marks ($25,000) for the infant Nazi party. Others in the steel and coal industries soon followed Thyssen's lead, although none came close to matching him. Many business leaders in Germany supported Hitler's secret union-hating agenda. However, some donated because they feared they would be left out in the cold if he actually ever seized power.

Most industry leaders gave up on Hitler after his failed coup in 1923. While Hitler spent a brief time in jail, the Thyssens, through the Bank voor Handel en Scheepvaart, opened the Union Banking Corporation in 1924.

Union Banking Corporation

Early in 1924, Hendrick J. Kouwenhoven, the managing director of Bank voor Handel en Scheepvaart, traveled to New York to meet with Walker and the Harriman brothers. Together, they established The Union Banking Corporation. The UBC's headquarters was located at the same 39 Broadway address as Harriman & Co.

As the German economy recovered through the mid to late '20s, Walker and Harriman's firm sold over $50,000,000 worth of German bonds to American investors, who profited enormously from the economic boom in Germany. In 1926, August Thyssen died at the age of 84. Fritz was now in control of one of the largest industrial families in Europe. He quickly created the United Steel Works (USW), the biggest industrial conglomerate in German history. Thyssen hired Albert Volger, one of the Ruhr's most influential industrial directors, as director General of USW.

Thyssen also brought Fredich Flick, another German family juggernaut, on board. Flick owned coal and steel industries throughout Germany and Poland and desperately wanted to invest into the Thyssen empire. One of the primary motivations for the Thyssen/Flick massive steel and coal merger was suppressing the new labor and socialist movements.

That year in New York, George Walker decided to give his new son in law, Prescott Bush, a big break. Walker made Bush a vice president of Harriman & Co. Prescott's new office employed many of his classmates from his Yale class of 1917, including Roland Harriman and Knight Woolley. The three had been close friends at Yale and were all members of Skull and Bones, the mysterious on-campus secret society. Despite the upbeat fraternity atmosphere at Harriman & Co., it was also a place of hard work, and no one worked harder than Prescott Bush.

In fact, Walker hired Bush to help him supervise the new Thyssen/Flick United Steel Works. One section of the USW empire was the Consolidated Silesian Steel Corporation and the Upper Silesian Coal and Steel Company located in the Silesian section of Poland. Thyssen and Flick paid Bush and Walker generously, but it was worth every dime. Their new business arrangement pleased them all financially, and the collective talents of all four men and their rapid success astonished the business world.

In the meantime Hitler and the Nazi party were broke. Since the German economic recovery, members and donations had dried up, leaving the Nazi movement withering on the vine. In 1927, Hitler was desperate for cash; his party was slipping into debt. Hitler told his private secretary Rudolf Hess to shake down wealthy coal tycoon and Nazi sympathizer Emil Kirdorf. Kirdorf paid off Hitler's debt that year but the following year, he too had no money left to contribute.

In 1928, Hitler had his eyes on the enormous Barlow Palace located in Briennerstrasse, the most aristocratic section of Munich. Hitler wanted to convert the palace into the Nazi national headquarters and change its name to the Brown House but it was out of his price range. Hitler told Hess to contact Thyssen. After hearing the Hess appeal, Thyssen felt it was time to give Hitler a second chance. Through the Bank voor Handel en Scheepvaart, Thyssen said he "placed Hess in possession of the required funds" to purchase and redesign the Palace. Thyssen later said the amount was about 250,000 marks but leading Nazis later claimed that just the re-molding cost over 800,000 marks (equivalent to $2 million today).

Regardless of the cost, Hitler and Thyssen became close friends after the purchase of the Brown House. At the time, neither knew how influential that house was to become the following year when, in 1929, the great depression spread around the world. With the German economic recovery up in flames, Hitler knew there was going to be a line of industrialists out the door waiting to give him cash.

1930s: Hitler Rises – Thyssen/Bush Cash In

Thyssen would later try to claim that his weekends with Hitler and Hess at his Rhineland castles were not personal but strictly business and that he did not approve of most of Hitler's ideas, but the well-known journalist R.G Waldeck, who spent time with Thyssen at a spa in the Black Forest, remembered quite differently. Waldeck said when he and Thyssen would walk through the cool Black Forest in 1929-30, Thyssen would tell Waldeck that he believed in Hitler. He spoke of Hitler "with warmth" and said the Nazis were "new men" that would make Germany strong again. With the depression bleeding Europe, Thyssen's financial support made Hitler's rise to power almost inevitable.

The great Depression also rocked Harriman & Co. The following year, Harriman & Co. merged with the London firm Brown/Shipley. Brown/Shipley kept its name, but Harriman & Co. changed its name to Brown Brothers, Harriman. The new firm moved to 59 Wall St. while UBC stayed at 39 Broadway. Averell Harriman and Prescott Bush reestablished a holding company called The Harriman 15 Corporation. One of the companies Harriman had held stock in was the Consolidated Silesian Steel Company. Two thirds of the company was owned by Friedrich Flick. The rest was owned by Harriman.

In December 1931, Fritz Thyssen officially joined the Nazi party. When Thyssen joined the movement, the Nazi party was gaining critical mass around Germany. The charismatic speeches and persona of Hitler, the depression and the Thyssen's Bank voor Handel en Scheepvaart all contributed to Hitler's sudden rise in popularity with the German people.

In September 1932, Thyssen invited a group of elite German industrial tycoons to his castle to meet with Hitler. They spent hours questioning Hitler, who answered all their questions with the "utmost satisfaction," Thyssen remembered. The money poured in from the industrial circles mostly due to Hitler's "monarchistic attitude" towards labor and issues of class.

But by November, German voters grew weary of Hitler's antidemocratic tendencies and turned to the Communist party, which gained the most seats in the fall election. The Nazis lost a sweeping 35 seats in the Reichstag, but since the Nazis were already secretly negotiating a power sharing alliance with Hindenberg that would ultimately lead to Hitler declaring himself dictator, the outcry of German voters was politically insignificant.

By 1934, Hindenberg was dead and Hitler completely controlled Germany. In March, Hitler announced his plans for a vast new highway system. He wanted to connect the entire Reich with an unprecedented wide road design, especially around major ports. Hitler wanted to bring down unemployment but, more importantly, needed the new roads for speedy military maneuvers.

Hitler also wanted to seriously upgrade Germany's military machine. Hitler ordered a "rebirth of the German army" and contracted Thyssen and United Steel Works for the overhaul. Thyssen's steel empire was the cold steel heart of the new Nazi war machine that led the way to World War II, killing millions across Europe.

Thyssen's and Flick's profits soared into the hundreds of millions in 1934 and the Bank voor Handel en Scheepvaart and UBC in New York were overflowing with money. Prescott Bush became managing director of UBC and handled the day-to-day operations of the new German economic plan. Bush's shares in UBC peaked with Hitler's new German order. But while production rose, cronyism did as well.

On March 19, 1934, Prescott Bush handed Averell Harriman a copy of that day's *New York Times.* The Polish government was applying to take over Consolidated Silesian Steel Corporation and Upper Silesian Coal and Steel Company from "German and American interests" because of rampant "mismanagement, excessive borrowing, fictitious bookkeeping and gambling in securities." The Polish government required the owners of the company, which accounted for over 45% of Poland's steel production, to pay at least its full share of back taxes. Bush and Harriman would eventually hire attorney John Foster Dulles to help cover up any improprieties that might arise under investigative scrutiny.

Hitler's invasion of Poland in 1939 ended the debate about Consolidated Silesian Steel Corporation and Upper Silesian Coal and Steel Company. The Nazis knocked the Polish Government off Thyssen, Flick and Harriman's steel company and were planning to replace the paid workers. Originally Hitler promised Stalin they would share Poland and use Soviet prisoners as slaves in Polish factories. Hitler's promise never actually materialized and he eventually invaded Russia.

1940s: Business As Usual

Consolidated Silesian Steel Corporation was located near the Polish town of Oswiecim, one of Poland's richest mineral regions. That was where Hitler set up the Auschwitz concentration camp. When the plan to work Soviet prisoners fell through, the Nazis transferred Jews, communists, gypsies and other minority populations to the camp. The prisoners of Auschwitz who were able to work were shipped to 30 different companies. One of the companies was the vast Consolidated Silesian Steel Corporation.

"Nobody's made the connection before between Consolidated Silesian Steel Corporation, Auschwitz and Prescott Bush," John Loftus told Clamor.

"That was the reason why Auschwitz was built there. The coal deposits could be processed into either coal or additives for aviation gasoline."

Even though Thyssen and Flick's Consolidated Steel was in their possession, Hitler's invasions across Europe spooked them, bringing back memories of World War I. Thyssen and Flick sold Consolidated Steel to UBC. Under the complete control of Harriman and management of Bush, the company became Silesian American Corporation which became part of UBC and Harriman's portfolio of 15 corporations. Thyssen quickly moved to Switzerland and later France to hide from the terror about to be unleashed by the Nazi war machine he had helped build.

A portion of the slave labor force in Poland was "managed by Prescott Bush," according to a Dutch intelligence agent. In 1941, slave labor had become the lifeblood of the Nazi war machine. The resources of Poland's rich steel and coal field played an essential part in Hitler's invasion of Europe.

According to Higham, Hitler and the Fraternity of American businessmen "not only sought a continuing alliance of interests for the duration of World War II, but supported the idea of a negotiated peace with Germany that would bar any reorganization of Europe along liberal lines. It would leave as its residue a police state that would place the Fraternity in postwar possession of financial, industrial, and political autonomy."

Six days after Pearl Harbor and the US declaration of war at the end of 1941, President Franklin D. Roosevelt, Secretary of the Treasury Henry Morgenthau and US Attorney General Francis Biddle signed the Trading With the Enemy Act, which banned any business interests with US enemies of war. Prescott Bush continued with business as usual, aiding the Nazi invasion of Europe and supplying resources for weaponry that would eventually be turned on American solders in combat against Germany.

On October 20, 1942, the U.S. government had had enough of Prescott Bush and his Nazi business arrangements with Thyssen. Over the summer, The New York Tribune had exposed Bush and Thyssen, whom the Tribune dubbed "Hitler's Angel." When the US government saw UBC's books, they found out that Bush's bank and its shareholders "are held for the benefit of ... members of the Thyssen family, [and] is property of nationals ... of a designated enemy country." The list of seven UBC share holders was:

E. Roland Harriman .... 3,991 shares
Cornelius Lievense .... 4 shares
Harold D. Pennington............. 1 shares
Ray Morris................................ 1 shares

Prescott S. Bush........................ 1 shares
H. J. Kouwenhoven.................. 1 shares
Johann G. Groeninger............. 1 shares

The UBC books also revealed the myriad of money and holding companies funneled from the Thyssens and the government realized UBC was just the tip of the iceberg. On November 17, 1942, The US government also took over the Silesian American Corporation, but did not prosecute Bush for the reasons Higham noted earlier. The companies were allowed to operate within the Government Alien Property custodian office with a catch — no aiding the Nazis. In 1943, while still owning his stock, Prescott Bush resigned from UBC and even helped raise money for dozens of war-related causes as chairman of the National War Fund.

After the war, the Dutch government began investigating the whereabouts of some jewelry of the Dutch royal family that was stolen by the Nazis. They started looking into books of the Bank voor Handel en Scheepvaart. When they discovered the transaction papers of the Silesian American Corporation, they began asking the bank manager H.J. Kowenhoven a lot of questions. Kouwenhoven was shocked at the discovery and soon traveled to New York to inform Prescott Bush. According to Dutch intelligence, Kouwenhoven met with Prescott soon after Christmas, 1947. Two weeks later, Kouwenhoven apparently died of a heart attack.

1950s: Bush Sells UBC Stock

By 1948, Fritz Thyssen's life was in ruins. After being jailed by the Nazis, he was jailed by the Allies and interrogated extensively, but not completely, by US investigators. Thyssen and Flick were ordered to pay reparations and served time in prison for their atrocious crimes against humanity.

On February 8, 1951, Fritz Thyssen died bitterly in Argentina at the age of 78. Thyssen was angry at the way he was treated by Europe after the war and how history would remember him as Hitler's most important and prominent financier.

When Thyssen died, the Alien Property Custodian released the assets of the Union Banking Corporation to Brown Brothers Harriman. The remaining stockholders cashed in their stocks and quietly liquidated the rest of UBC's blood money.

Prescott Bush received $1.5 million for his share in UBC. That money enabled Bush to help his son, George Herbert Walker Bush, to set up his first royalty firm, Overby Development Company, that same year. It was also helpful when Prescott Bush left the business world to enter the public arena in 1952 with a successful senatorial campaign in Connecticut. On October 8th, 1972, Prescott Bush died of cancer and his will was enacted soon after.

In 1980, when George H.W. Bush was elected vice president, he placed his father's family inherence in a blind trust. The trust was managed by his old friend and quail hunting partner, William "Stamps" Farish III. Bush's choice of Farish to manage the family wealth is quite revealing in that it demonstrates that the former president might know exactly where some of his inheritance originated.

Farish's grandfather, William Farish Jr., on March 25th, 1942, pleaded "no contest" to conspiring with Nazi Germany while president of Standard Oil in New Jersey. He was described by Senator Harry Truman in public of approaching "treason" for profiting off the Nazi war machine. Standard Oil, invested millions in IG Farben, who opened a gasoline factory within Auschwitz in 1940. The billions "Stamps" inherited had more blood on it then Bush, so the paper trail of UBC stock would be safe during his 12 years in presidential politics.

It has been 60 years since one of the great money laundering scandals of the 20th century ended and only now are we beginning to see the true historical aspects of this important period of world history, a history that the remaining Holocaust survivors beg humanity to "never forget."

Loftus believes history will view Prescott Bush as harshly as Thyssen. "It is bad enough that the Bush family helped raise the money for Thyssen to give Hitler his start in the 1920s, but giving aid and comfort to the enemy in time of war is treason. The Bush bank helped the Thyssens make the Nazi steel that killed Allied solders. As bad as financing the Nazi war machine may seem, aiding and abetting the Holocaust was worse. Thyssen's coal mines used Jewish slaves as if they were disposable chemicals. There are six million skeletons in the Thyssen family closet, and a myriad of criminal and historical questions to be answered about the Bush family's complicity."

There is no question that the Bush family needs to donate at least $1.5 million to the proper holocaust reparation fund. Since Prescott Bush is dead, the only way to compensate is for the main inheritors of his estate to make amends with surviving slaves and the families of slaves who died in Bush and Thyssen's coal mines. If the Bush family refuses to contribute the money to compensate for Prescott Bush's involvement in the Holocaust, it is like denying the Holocaust itself and their role in one of the darkest moments in world history.

Toby Rogers is a contributing writer to *High Times, New York Times, The New York Post* and the *Village Voice.* In 1992, he won the Quill Award for Investigative reporting. In 2003, Toby Rogers was featured in *Horns and Halos,* a film about George W. Bush.

Special thanks to John Loftus, Emmy winning journalist, author and current president of the Florida Holocaust Museum.

This article and others on the same subject are posted at many sites on the Internet with no "official" or mainstream response. While we do not know if these articles are true or not, they should be explored with honest research and diligence. The only response I could find on this vexing question was/is at www.straightdope.com. Cecil Adams's defense of Prescott, is that everyone does it and that he "[will] buy the claim that Bush got his share of UBC back — it was an American bank, after all — but the idea that his German holdings increased in value despite being obliterated by Allied bombs is ridiculous." No refutation *just amused contempt* and *story.*

More on the use of these *stories* later.

REFLECTING ON THE YALE SUCCESSION

STEVE SEWALL

THIS OPINION PIECE APPEARED UNDER A DIFFERENT NAME IN THE *YALE HERALD* - FEBRUARY 21, 2003

IN 1949, *Yale Daily News* Editor William F. Buckley, Jr., DC '50, and my father, Yale English professor Richard B. Sewall, had a memorable exchange at Freshman Commons. They were there to help freshmen of the class of '53 make the most of their years at Yale. But they disagreed passionately about the purpose of education. Is it active (Buckley) or contemplative (Sewall)?

Buckley, the big man on campus, urged the freshmen to join, heel, compete and *succeed.* Yale, he said, is your chance to build the networks that will sustain you throughout life. Sewall, a teacher and scholar, urged the freshmen to read, write, discuss and *understand.* Yale, he said, is your chance to reflect on life itself. Years later, '53 alumnus Jim Thomson summed up the student response: "We all knew Sewall was right, but we wanted to *be like Buckley.*"

Since 1988, three Yale graduates have led the United States. This Yale succession is historic. Never before have three (or even two) successive U.S. presidents studied at the same university. During its tercentenary year, mother Yale codified this lineage by gathering its presidential progeny, separately, back to Yale. At graduation, President George W. Bush, DC '68, jokingly likened himself to the Prodigal Son.

Today, Yale uses its presidential lineage as a beacon to attract students, raise money and extend its global presence. But no one studies it. By falling silent on something historic happening in its own backyard, Yale's community of scholars risks losing its perspective on history. Equally at risk is America's political press, given its stunning silence on one university's four-term (and counting) lock on the White House.

So what's being overlooked? Under scrutiny, the Yale succession is a key to recent history and a gateway to leadership issues of concern to Yale as a "laboratory for future leaders," in President Richard Levin's phrase.

All three Yale presidents owe their White House tenures to the Big Money that has tightened its grip on local, state, and national government since the advent of televised attack ads in the 1960's. In addition, Big Money's grip on education and media has helped the Yale presidents advance America's post-Cold War bid for military and economic empire without ever consulting or informing voters. Finally, it was on the Yale presidents' watch that Big Money corrupted and inflated corporate and political America until the bubble burst, plunging the world into a recession that economists say could last for years.

No economy, national or global, can stand forever on a corrupt political base. Healthy societies, like healthy families, require trust. The seismic convergence of ethics and economics that toppled Japanese and American markets in 1991 and 2000, respectively, now rattles the entire world. Corruption and terror, widely seen as two unethical sides of the same coin of oil and empire, depress financial markets around the globe.

In America, the Dow Jones average reflects a general loss of faith in institutions fueled by Machiavellian venality in politics and by Enronitis in business. The restoration of integrity — a sea change in America's civic and commercial life — is the task of a generation. It entails creating a new "balance of public and private interests in the global economy," writes Jeffrey Garten of Yale's School of Management. If not apparent now, the need for change will become clear as investor mistrust causes market rally after market rally to fizzle.

Does the United States, in its commitment to freedom and democratic values, have the will to effect change? And does Yale, as a laboratory for future leaders, have the will to lead the way in imagining and implementing change? The unwillingness of Japan's elite universities to produce a generation of tough-minded reformers helps explain why that former economic superpower, now in its thirteenth year of recession, could be stagnate for years to come. Will America be next?

Significantly, the Ivy League aura that shields the Yale succession from scrutiny is fading. *In Secrets of the Tomb*, a recent history of Skull and Bones, Yale grad Alexandra Robbins, SY '98, shows how four generations of Bonesmen created the Bush dynasty that comprises two thirds of Yale's presidential troika. Looking ahead to 2004, Robbins describes a possible Bush/Kerry contest as "the first Bones versus Bones presidential race."

In this pairing, Yale comes off more as a club for oligarchs than as a laboratory for leaders. Three more Yale-trained presidential hopefuls bolster this impression: Vermont Governor Howard Dean, PC '71, and Senators Joe Lieberman, MC '64, LAW '67, and Hillary Clinton, LAW '67.

In 1949, Yale, in its wisdom, sent Bonesman Buckley and "barbarian" Sewall to Freshman Commons to encourage the class of '53 to pursue success and understanding. Today, Yale's silence on the Yale succession suggests that Yale, to its peril, may be pursuing success alone. The cure for non-reflection is thoughtful dialogue. The stakes are high. Let the dialogue begin.

***

Addendum: The Glass-top Table Conversation

Richard B. Sewall Professor, Dean and Master at Yale University
Picture taken early 1980s – courtesy the Sewall Family

As you know by now, my father, Richard B. Sewall, taught English at Yale for forty years. In the 1960's, he was the first Master of Ezra Stiles College. He retired in 1976. In June of last year, ten months before his death last April at age 95, he flew from Boston to Chicago to spend three months with me.

In his last years he suffered from dementia, a close cousin to full-blown Alzheimer's. He stopped writing letters and reading newspapers. Although he could take phone calls, he no longer made them. Most of the time, he seemed to be withdrawing from the world.

One evening in 1999, while he was still at his beloved country home in Bethany, outside of New Haven, I had phoned him and found him utterly disoriented. "Steve," he pleaded, "I don't know where I am. What are all these books doing on the walls?"

He was referring to the bookshelves of the cozy study with the little wood burning fireplace where for twenty years he had worked on his National Book Award-winning biography of Emily Dickenson. He was speaking from the house where he and my mother had enjoyed forty years of idyllic rural life, and where, since her death from pancreatic cancer in 1975, he had been bound and determined to end his days, like the New Englander he was, even at the cost of being apart from his three sons.

In his last years, he pursued a number of quests. One related to Yale. Sometimes after an afternoon nap he would appear in a jacket and tie. Glancing at his watch, he would say he had to be downtown at Yale in an hour to give a lecture. "What about, Dad?' I once asked. "I don't know," he said, with a hint of annoyance in his voice, "Whatever they want me to lecture about."

Another quest was to reunite with his family of birth. Just before we moved him to safety with my brother Rick's family near Boston, he would tell us he was waiting to be picked up and driven back to his childhood home in Rye, New York. His home in Bethany, with its splendid prospect of the New Haven reservoir and West Rock in the far distance, was now a mere way station in his search for a destination that always eluded him.

One of the joys of living with very old people is the knowledge that not all of their quests are imaginary. One of my father's real-life quests was visible in the luminous look of recognition he gave me when we met at O'Hare airport last June. He had reached a destination.

And here he was now, in high spirits, sitting opposite me at the sunlit, glass-top breakfast table at my home in Glenview, sipping from a bowl of chicken noodle soup and munching on a tuna fish sandwich. It was amazing to see him. He had made the flight by himself, without a hitch. And now he was bent over, utterly engrossed in the act of eating. Later that summer, I asked him what keeps him going. "Well," he said, "I get to eat three good meals a day. And I like being around you guys."

We hadn't seen each other in months. And I yearned to talk with him about the book I wanted to write. How would our conversation go? Where would it take us? I had no idea. Yet I knew it would be the latest installment in a running dialogue about Yale, education and, in effect, the modern world that began in 1965 while he was at Ezra Stiles, and where I lived while completing a Masters degree in teaching at Yale.

That was an eventful year for me. I studied Romantic poetry with Harold Bloom, sang with the Original Golden Stars, a New Haven gospel quartet, watched Vietnam War hearings conducted by Senator William Fulbright and his Senate Foreign Relations Committee on the color TV at the Yale Law School dining hall, I also met Allard K. Lowenstein, the Yale-trained lawyer, civil rights activist and future Congressman who then was building the student-based antiwar movement that in 1968 would unseat a sitting president, Lyndon Baines Johnson.

Al Lowenstein was the only visitor who was welcome to Stiles at any hour, day or night. He could wake my parents at midnight and within minutes be munching on a sandwich of his own, enthralling us with tales of political intrigue at the highest levels.

. . . .

The highlight of '65-'66 for me, however, was the English class I taught at Troup Junior High School in New Haven to 30 ninth grade boys diagnosed as slow learners. Most of these youngsters were nothing of the sort. They were students in a failed school system and residents of a failing city. By 1990, the City of New Haven, decimated by gangs and drugs, would have the highest per-capita murder rate of any city in America.

On my last day at Troup in 1966, school Principal Frank J. Carr asked me what I would change at Troup if could change just one thing. I said the school needed textbooks that were less than six years old. In response, he told me that while the New Haven Board of Education would spend $400,000 that summer on renovations for the Troup dining room, it would spend only $50,000 that year for textbooks for the entire system, grades 1 through 12.

In those days, fat cat general contractors ran the New Haven Board of Education. It was Big Money at the local level. I wonder who controls that Board today.

My year at Troup opened my eyes to the world. My students had problems, *but my students were not the problem.* To see if they could write, I assigned on the first day of class a one-page answer to the question, "What happened in English class today?" The paper Joe McVety (not his real name) handed me next day began, "At 9:27, Mr. Sewall walked into room 314 wearing his threadbare jacket." This kid could write. Another student, David Johns, was brighter than most people I met at Harvard, Yale and U. C. Berkeley.

It was not IQ problems but bad schooling and personal problems that held these students back. Take Dexter Matthews, a young man with a bladder problem but no written permission to leave class. Normally well behaved, Dexter would stand up and glare at me whenever I refused his urgent requests to go to the bathroom.

Well into the school year I asked students to write a story in which they tell me an enormous lie, wild and crazy, In his paper, Joe McVety championed Dexter's cause with a terrific yarn about how, after a global search, detective Dexter had finally tracked the evil Mr. Sewall down to the men's room of the Seaview Hotel in Paris, France, and, with a tremendous punch, knocked him clear through the skylight window.

The class howled with delight when I read Joe's paper aloud. But it still hadn't dawned on me that maybe Dexter did need to go to the john.

One day near the end of the school year, Dexter, in desperation, pulled a knife on me. Standing wide-eyed at his desk, he looked far more scared than I. The class froze. I told him scornfully to put away the knife, go take a leak, and be back in class in two minutes. He did. Finally I saw that Dexter wasn't trying to con me. But I can't say I taught him anything in English that year.

Then there was Anthony Tomasino, whose mom had a fresh-baked chocolate cake waiting for me when I visited her home to find out why her son was acting up in class. When I saw the front door had six locks on it, Mrs. Tomasino said that the sixth one was there because Anthony, a sleepwalker who still slept in his mom's bed, had learned to unlock the first five in his sleep.

At supper throughout the year, I regaled my parents with stories like these. But I learned less about teaching than I should have. My supervising teacher spent a total of 10 minutes with me during entire school year. Yale had never told me to expect any help from her, so I didn't. Still, after class most days, I wandered the school, taught as a substitute, or visited classes overseen by battle-scarred souls who had stopped teaching years ago, or never started. I got to know the school.

Although my father never visited my students at Troup, the late Paul Weiss did. Paul was a family friend, a Fellow at Stiles and a legend in the Yale philosophy department. He was also one of Yale's great teachers. What a day that was. Informed that a Yale professor was coming to class, my students expected John Wayne. But when Paul Weiss entered the room — the gnarliest, most eccentric looking guy you ever saw in your life — they thought they had got Mr. McGoo.

What they had was an incarnation of Socrates. Paul confronted them with Archimedes' paradox of the race between the hare and the tortoise. The discussion was pretty good. It came down to a contest between Paul and the super-sharp David Johns, who loved to argue, but who had a chip on his shoulder that kept him and Paul from coming to terms.

My most memorable moment at Troup, it turns out, was with my least memorable student. Nothing seemed to stand out about Kenny Brown. But here he was one day, in the passenger seat of my '65 green WV, getting a ride to the Dixwell Avenue bus after spending 45 minutes with me in after school detention. Kenny and I were on bad terms that day and neither of us felt like talking. Finally I broke the silence and asked him what he wanted to do when he got out of high school.

"I just want to get a job," he said in voice I had never heard before. It was low and guttural, like a man's. Dead serious. And yet despairing. What he yearned for in life, at age 15, was a job. What did I yearn for when I was 15? Stamps, girls and soccer. We talked. From then on, I respected Kenny Brown.

. . . .

At supper that night at the long rustic wooden dining table at Ezra Stiles, I told my parents that schools like Troup had broken the Jeffersonian promise of universal public education. My dad agreed. In the years to come, we came to feel that this promise — this fundamental right and indispensable cornerstone of democracy — survived at the national level mainly, and merely, in the "equal opportunity" and "no child left behind" platitudes of public figures who knew full well that American schools were sending millions of youngsters into the world utterly unprepared to survive in it.

Troup Junior High School brought out the Jonathan Kozoll in both of us. The gap between what Yale offered students and what the City of New Haven offered students was not only wrong, it was all but criminal. And we knew that this gap, if not corrected, would ultimately prove fatal to democracy itself.

Several years after granting me the M.A.T. degree in 1966, Yale summarily terminated its rickety M.A.T. program and replaced it with one that has made improvements in the New Haven schools, and, by example, in schools nationwide.

As the response of a torch-bearing university to the developing crisis in American education, however, my father and I felt this program was a drop in the bucket. The need, as we saw it, was for a Yale School of Education that would rival in size, quality and influence Yale's schools of law, management and medicine. Let this school train superb teachers and principals, much as Yale trains superb lawyers, businessmen and doctors.

Why is it, we asked ourselves, that great universities like Yale, in the quest to explore and to master every aspect of nature and every corner of the world, were so slow to see the obvious: the critical role of universal public education in sustaining a viable democracy?

To this paradox, we took bittersweet comfort in T. S. Eliot's celebrated account of the belatedness of all self-knowledge:

We shall not cease from exploration
And the end of all our exploring
Will be to arrive where we started
And know the place for the first time.

. . . .

At the glass-top table with my father last June, the knowledge that Eliot speaks of, and the day that my father and I had hoped for, seemed farther off than ever. The world had entered the era of Enronitis and the War on Terror.

My father had finished his meal. We had discussed family matters. I fell silent, wondering how I would resume the dialogue that had guided me over the past 35 years. His eyes, sunken and watery, were fixed on me. Age be damned, I told myself, we're gonna talk, full throttle, just like we always have.

At first I didn't let on that I wanted to write a book. I didn't have the nerve. Instead, I gave him the big picture, a sound-bite history of the 1990's, as if he had just gotten back from the planet Mars. I told him about the end of the cold war, the rise of the global economy, the boom in tech stocks, the bursting of the tech bubble, and the War on Terror triggered by 9/11.

He took it all in. For well over an hour, his eyes would neither wander or nor waiver.

I told him about the three Big Money "leadership issues" noted in the Yale Herald piece: campaign finance, America's post-Cold War drive toward global empire, and the endemic corruptions exposed by the bursting of the tech bubble. And I mentioned a fourth issue: the CIA's role in advancing the global drug trade that had corroded the American system of justice and decimated nearly every city in the nation, including New Haven and Chicago, the two cities I knew best.

I showed him my copy of the essential book on this topic, *The Politics of Heroin: CIA Complicity in the Global Drug Trade,* by Alfred W. McCoy, a Yale Ph.D. who teaches at the University of Wisconsin.

Then I brought it all home with a unifying insight. After several months of research, the idea of a Yale succession of U.S. presidents — Bush/Clinton/Bush and their possible Yale-trained successors — had suddenly dawned on me. Omens of Ivy League oligarchy!

To personalize this point, I placed on the glass-top table copy of the *American Heritage Dictionary* that he had handed me in 1975. "Read the entry for perquisite," he had said then, with undisguised pride. I asked him to look at it now. I read the entry to him, including the example of usage that follows the definition: "Politics was the perquisite of the upper classes. (Richard B. Sewall)"

He beamed and grasped my hand warmly. A former student of his, later a harmless drudge of a lexicographer at Random House, had recalled it from class, honored him with the attribution, and sent him the dictionary.

Pondering the "end of all our-exploring" belatedness of my discovery of the Yale succession, it struck me that Yale's string of White House occupants was itself hidden in plain view, celebrated and promoted by Yale, yet screened from critical analysis by 300 years of Ivy League venerability.

What was screened from analysis ran deeper still. Now I had to talk with my father about the covert Yale.

It will not surprise you to hear that two highly secretive, Yale-related institutions, CIA and Skull and Bones, are the wellsprings of this concept. The origins of Skull and Bones, however, just might. I told my father how William Huntington Russell, valedictorian of the Yale class of 1832, and recently returned from a transformative experience at a university-based secret society in Germany, had founded Skull and Bones with drug money provided by his uncle, Samuel Russell, an entrepreneur whose fleet of speedy Yankee Clippers had made him a fortune by transporting opium from Turkey, India and Burma to Canton and Shanghai in the so-called China Trade of the 19th century.

As his past students never cease telling me, Richard Sewall was among the most patient of men. For this reason, the rare moments of anger I saw in him as a child have stayed with me. One such, a recurrent one, had to do with Skull and Bones. At tea with Yale people in our living room, the mere mention of Bones would prompt him to declare it a "curse on the academic life of the university."

Having thrown down this gauntlet, he would fall silent, giving others the option of pursuing or dropping it. Sometimes someone would pursue it. That is how I first heard about the huge archive of old term papers, covering much of Yale's undergraduate course offering, that Bonesmen could touch up and resubmit as their own work. It was institutionalized plagiarism, he felt, and he was furious at Yale's inability to stop it.

In recent months, in overheated yet by no means unsubstantial online histories of Skull & Bones written by "outlaw historians" like Antony Sutton, Kris Millegan, Webster Tarpley and Anton Chaitkin, I had found weightier reasons to be concerned with Bones. Before sharing a few with my father, I wanted first to see if he could recall his old attacks on Bones. So I asked him.

"Sure I do," he replied, "but more than that, those guys were trying to run the whole damned university!"

This, to put it mildly, was news to me. Later I would read that Yale presidents have been Bonesmen or related to Bonesmen for 84 of the last 105 years up the time of his retirement in 1976 (See Appendix I)

How, I asked, was Bones trying to run the university? His response, while an answer to a different question, was passionate in its conviction.

"Skull and Bones will never succeed in running the university," he said. "Yale is too big and too diverse a place to be controlled by any one group." Suddenly, he was back in the 1950's, fighting some old battle that I had never heard about and never would. Sensing my interest, he cautioned me: "Watch out. You can never prove anything against those guys. They cover up everything they do."

For a moment, I had a queasy feeling of tilting at windmills. But anticipating that my father, even at age 95, would want documentation, I had at hand materials photocopied from the U. S. Government Documents Office at Northwestern University. These made reference to several Bonesmen, one of whom was the first of three generations of Bush family members who were Bonesmen.

I showed him four U.S. Treasury Department vesting orders issued in late 1941, after Pearl Harbor, and ordering the confiscation, under the terms of the Trading with the Enemy Act, of the assets of four corporations set up and run by Averell Harriman '13 and his chief lieutenant, Prescott Bush '17, grandfather of the current president, whom, as a child in 1950's, I remembered as a respected Republican senator from my home state of Connecticut. [See Appendix II, to be put online].

Identified by name on one of these orders were Prescott Bush, and another Bonesman, Roland Harriman '17, Averell's younger brother. Since the early 1920's, the four Harriman firms had raised millions from American investors not to build up Adolph Hitler's transportation or agriculture infrastructures, but to build up Hitler's military machine.

"Dad," I said, "If you spend a couple days on the Internet, you may get the feeling that the United States is run by a group of Ivy League arms merchants!" In the past, an incendiary assertion like this — and had I made one or two over the years — would have triggered a soothing, quietistic "yes, but" response. But not now.

I paused. We looked at each other. He seemed sad. "Dad, are you sure you want me to go on with all this?" I asked him, laughing as I spoke, "This ain't fun, and, believe me, it only gets worse!" He smiled affectionately and nodded yes. This was one of our moments. We were on a quest.

. . . .

I showed him *Houston Chronicle* accounts from the early 1990's describing long-standing business dealings between the Bush and bin Laden families. These, I said, began in the late 1970's when Sheik Mohammed bin Laden, the family patriarch and Osama's father, had, through a friend of the Bush family named James R. Bath, invested $50,000 in Arbusto, the oil exploration company founded by George W. Bush with his father's help.

I added that on September 11, 2001, Shafiq bin Laden, an estranged half-brother of Osama, had represented his family's investments at meeting of the Carlyle Group in Washington, D.C. Carlyle is a $16 billion private equity firm that buys up and turns around ailing firms, especially defense contractors. George H. W. Bush serves as a Senior Consultant there. And as Dan Briody establishes in his recent book on the firm, that Fred Malek put George W. Bush on the Caterair Board from 1990-94 while Caterair was owned by Carlyle.

It was important to understand, however, that questionable dealings of American industrialists and politicians were by no means limited to the Bush family or even to the Republicans. Averell Harriman, I told my father, was a career Democrat. I passed on the observation by one of the outlaw historians that Skull & Bones likes to have a voice on both sides of the political debate.

As it happens, Harriman's third wife, the glorious and glamorous Britisher, Pamela Harriman, had, after his death, presided over the neo-liberal refashioning of the Democratic Party in the 1980's to the point of advancing the young Bill Clinton to prominence as, of all things, the party's chief fundraiser.

No arms dealings here, but plenty of Big Money. Clinton was tied to a two-party system — and to a mass media and legal system as well — that had kept knowledge of American business dealings with Hitler and Stalin out of the political mainstream. Only Big Money, it seemed, could account for this act of suppression.

And Big Money had lots to hide. I told my father about two well-received recent books documenting the Nazi business dealings of Henry Ford and James Watson of IBM. In addition, General Motors, the du Ponts and the Rockefellers had all done business with Hitler. Finally, I mentioned Antony Sutton's controversial three-volume study of the buildup of Stalin's military machine, even during the Cold War years, by American businesses assisted by the U. S. Department of Commerce. Sutton was a Fellow at Stanford University's Hoover Institute. His book, as Harvard historian Richard Pipes indicated in endorsing Sutton's findings, would mark the end of Sutton's career as a mainstream academic.

Recently I had discussed these dubious dealings with my co-author Bob Back, a financial analyst with a CIA background who, as it happens, had worked during the 1970's at Brown Brothers, Harriman. "How in hell," I asked Bob in a moment of anger, "could American industrialists arm the two dictators who had turned the world into a living hell during much of the last half of the 20th century?"

In response, as I told my father, Bob, himself a Bush Republican who sees a need for uninhibited dialogue on these matters, had said, "Big money likes to play both sides of the game."

. . . .

To wrap things up, I read my father an excerpt from Joseph Trento's magisterial *Secret History of the CIA.* This extraordinary book is a history of American intelligence since World War II and, in many respects, of American foreign and domestic affairs as well. James Jesus Angleton '41, Yale's second most famous spy (the first being Nathan Hale), is a central figure in this book. Appointed by CIA founder Allen Dulles (a Princeton alum), Angleton was the founding Director of CIA Counterintelligence. His job was to protect the CIA from penetration by Soviet spies.

At Yale, Angleton had majored in English. My father recalled his name and said he had taught him. Angleton was a true aesthete. He created and edited a poetry magazine that he hand-delivered to subscribers at all hours of the night. On a visit to Harvard, he heard a lecture by the English critic William Empson and took it upon himself to bring Empson to lecture at Yale. Not bad for an undergraduate, we agreed.

In 1974, CIA Director William Colby dismissed Angleton for his failed attempt to expose a Soviet mole who, Angleton was convinced, had totally penetrated the CIA. Angleton's obsessive witch hunt had destroyed the careers of dozens of wrongly accused agents and demoralized the entire agency.

But time confirmed his worst fears. As Trento and David Wise before him have shown, CIA counterintelligence and FBI counterintelligence as well were indeed totally compromised by Soviet agent Igor Orlov, a "man with the soul of a sociopath" yet supremely disciplined and loyal to Stalin. Angleton missed nabbing Orlov by a hairsbreadth. Under scrutiny for years — CIA and FBI agents openly visited Gallery Orlov, the quaint art and picture-framing store that Igor and his wife Eleanore managed in Alexandria, Virginia — Orlov managed to pass two polygraph tests and got away clean.

Angleton, "written off as a crank and a madman by his critics," and dying of cancer, granted Trento an interview two years before his death in 1987. I read my father the following excerpt:

> *Within the confines of [Angleton's] remarkable life were most of America's secrets. "You know how I got to be in charge of counterintelligence? I agreed not to polygraph or require detailed background checks on Allen Dulles and 60 of his closest friends ... They were afraid that their own business dealings with Hitler's pals would come out. They were too arrogant to believe that the Russians would discover it all. ... You know, the CIA got tens of thousands of brave people killed. ... We played with lives as if we owned them. We gave false hope. We – I – so misjudged what happened."*
>
> *I asked the dying man how it all went so wrong.*
>
> *With no emotion in his voice, but with his hand trembling, Angleton replied: "Fundamentally, the founding fathers of U.S. intelligence were liars. The better you lied and the more you betrayed, the more likely you would be promoted. These people attracted and promoted each other. Outside of their duplicity, the only thing they had in common was a desire for absolute power. I did things that, in looking back on my life, I regret. But I was part of it and I loved being in it ... Allen Dulles, Richard Helms, Carmel Offie, and Frank Wisner were the grand masters. If you were in a room with them you were in a room full of people that you had to believe would deservedly end up in hell." Angleton slowly sipped his tea and then said, "I guess I will see them there soon."*

I read the last paragraph aloud twice. Then I paused. He was still with me. Shifting gears, I asked; "Who can tell for sure whether Dulles and his pals were liars? But Angleton sure doesn't sound like a madman."

I then tried to restore balance by suggesting that the world is a dangerous place, pure and simple. To read academics, journalists and public servants like George Kennan, Arnaud de Borchgrave, William Kristol, Robert Kagan, John Lewis Gaddis or Christopher Hitchens, I said, is to see that people like Allen Dulles and Averell Harriman, and the Yale succession presidents as well, have reason to believe they are addressing dangers that most Americans are too busy or afraid or uninformed to face up to.

The problem is, I told him, that the nation lacks a mechanism — public forums — for distinguishing between dangers real and unreal. Since the advent of network television, I said, civic discourse in America has degenerated to partisan strife. It's always been this way, the historians tell us, and this backward-looking argument has great force.

Yet America needs to look forward. It has the finest communications technologies ever devised. It should have a public communications system — a civic media — that brings out the best in citizens, not the worst. A problem-solving media, operating year round and prime time at local, state and national levels, that makes citizens and government responsive and accountable to each other.

With this, I had spoken my piece. The sunlight was gone from the dining area. Yet my father's watery eyes were still on me. He knew all about civic media, a concern of mine over the past 25 years. After a moment, sensing that I was waiting for him to speak, he lowered his eyes.

He had to be tired, I thought, and indeed, at that moment, he looked to be the oldest man I'd seen outside of a wheelchair or a hospital bed. A little puddle of drool flowing from his open mouth had formed on the glass top table beneath his chin. But the slight forward lean in his posture told me that his mind was working.

"So" he said, "What do you want to do with all this?"

"I want to write a book," I said. "An election year book. One that gives Yale, and the nation as well, a chance to reflect. And to act appropriately. But I need a good title. What do you think should I call it?"

Another moment passed. He leaned forward. "How about *Yale and the Modern World*?" he asked. It was simple. Yet Olympian in its detachment. I suddenly felt as if, it was I who was returning from Mars - and he who had been here all along.

. . . .

Our dialogue continued throughout that very hot summer. Wearing big old straw hats we took our twice daily walks, measured now not in miles covered, as in days gone by, but in houses passed. We dined alfresco at a Mexican restaurant on Waukegan Road overlooking a parking lot. A little fountain there sent water six feet into the air and brought out the best in children.

At twilight on June 20, my 62nd birthday, four generations of Sewalls – my father and I, my nephew Ethan ('00), and my four year old son, Joseph Richard Sewall – took to a big open field near our house and threw Frisbees.

During that summer I gave my father baths and backrubs. I played him "Open My Eyes That I May See", a favorite hymn. This, and songs by Paul Robeson — "Jacob's Ladder" and "Old Man River" — moved him to tears. And at several memorable gatherings, some of his former Yale students found that Richard Sewall himself could still perform, still make a telling point, even to point of moving others to tears.

. . . .

[to be continued] — www.yalesuccession.com

Appendix 1

President	Term	Years	Ties with Bones?
Richard Levin	1992-2003	11	No known ties
Benno Schmidt	1986-1992	6	No known ties
Bart Giamatti	1978-1986	8	Scroll & Key
Kingman Brewster	1963-1978	15	2 relatives in Skull & Bones
A. Whitney Griswold	1950-1978	18	2 relatives in Skull & Bones
Charles Seymour	1937-1950	16	Member, Skull & Bones
James R. Angell	1921-1937	16	No known ties. From Univ. of Chicago
Arthur T. Hadley	1899-1921	22	Member, Skull & Bones '76
Timothy Dwight	1886-1899	13	Skull & Bones '49
Noah Porter	1871-1886	16	(The last of Yale's clerical presidents)

Table based on Antony Sutton, *America's Secret Establishment*, pp. 68-69

Author's Note - Kris Millegan surprised me when he said he wanted to publish this long, rambling piece, originally written as background material for a class at Yale. The piece's concern with education and civic media does not relate directly to Kris' concern with Skull & Bones. And while the piece may tie some threads together for readers, it advances little that is new. Instead, it tries to introduce Yale people to aspects of Yale that are seldom discussed in print, yet which have national impact.

Kris wanted to publish the piece verbatim. This impressed me. An "outlaw historian," as I call him in the piece, was interested in the entirety of something written for academics. All my adult life I have tried to keep one foot in the learning camp of academics and the other in that of non-academics. So has my colleague Bob Back. That's how we learn, how we get closer to "the nuance," as Bob likes to call it.

I hope Kris' book takes us all a step closer to the day when, if we're able and lucky enough to reach it, outlaw and academic historians alike, and people on the left and right as well, will be astonished to discover how much there is to be learned when we learn from each other.

Steve Sewall, Harvard A.B. '64, Yale M.A.T '66, U. C. Berkeley Ph.D. '91, is a Chicago area educator and media activist. With Robert W. Back, Trinity College B.A. '58 and Yale GRD '60, he is writing, *Yale and the Modern World: Bush/Clinton/Bush, Big Money and the 2004 Presidential Election.*

The very word "secrecy" is repugnant in a free and open society; and we are as a people inherently and historically opposed to secret societies, to secret oaths and to secret proceedings. We decided long ago that the dangers of excessive and unwarranted concealment of pertinent facts far outweighed the dangers, which are cited to justify it.

President John F. Kennedy
Address to newspaper publishers, April 27, 1961.

SECRECY AND OUR CONSTITUTION: WHOM DO THEY SERVE?

RALPH E. BUNCH
EMERITUS PROFESSOR OF THE DEPARTMENT OF POLITICAL SCIENCE OF PORTLAND STATE UNIVERSITY

SECRECY IS AS AMERICAN AS APPLE PIE. Americans, often characterized as optimistic, naïve, and idealistic, might be momentarily put off by such an assertion, but a bit of thought and observation will confirm the ubiquity of secrecy in American public and private life.

The federal government's love affair with secrecy is well known and generally acknowledged in the fields of national security and police work. In the specialized fields of taxation, commerce, social programs, education, transportation, medicine, and perhaps all government activity, local, state, and national, secrecy exists officially and unofficially.

The law requires certain information — personnel records, personal information about citizens, plans for land purchases (lest speculators be advantaged and public costs increased), grand jury records, etc., be held tightly secret.

Government imposes secrecy on citizens as it does on its bureaucrats. The law requires some settlements in legal disputes be held confidential, and it prohibits some information about minors being made public. Libel and slander laws prohibit some known facts about persons being published or pronounced; thus, the law requires secrecy.

Corporate officers may not give out financial information to advantage some market players over other market players. Corporations, in keeping with the requirements of capitalist competition, have government- protected secrecy over their internal financial, marketing, and technological matters. Lawyer-client relations and doctor-patient relations are protected. In ordinary personal relations, everyone knows secrets, keeps some, and passes some on, at least occasionally.

Surely, most people keep financial and sexual matters secret.

The Constitution enshrines secrecy. Article I, Sec. 5, requires the Congress to publish its proceedings, that is, tell its secrets, except that by a majority vote in either house, it may keep some secrets. But by a twenty percent vote, a minority may cause any secret to be printed in the *Congressional Record.* Article VI requires that no religious test shall ever be required as a qualification to any office or public trust under the United States; that is, religious identity remains a secret for all in government, unless they should desire otherwise.

The government's desire for secrecy — a universal phenomena, according to German sociologist, Max Weber: "Every bureaucracy seeks to increase the superiority of the professionally informed by keeping their knowledge and intentions secret," has been in constant conflict with the First Amendment. President Nixon's request for an injunction against the *New York Times* for intending to publish the *Pentagon Papers* was struck down by the Supreme Court, even though, according to Nixon, national security and the Vietnam War effort were in danger from the publication. The Court, citing the First Amendment, has quite consistently held that government entities may not suppress speech or publishing, even in severe circumstances, unless there is a strong "clear and present danger that they will bring about the substantive evils that Congress has a right to prevent" (*Schenck v. United States,* 1919).

The Fourth Amendment is specifically aimed at protecting the rights of citizens to have and keep secrets from the government. "The right of the people to be secure in their persons, houses, papers, and effects, against unreasonable searches and seizures, shall not be violated ... " But the Court has had much difficulty in regulating the details; the requirements of effective police work run counter to an absolute requirement that a warrant be procured for a search. The police may need to search a person, on the person's apprehension, to protect the officer's safety and to prevent any relevant evidence being destroyed, for instance. What to do about phone taps of known criminals? Their acquaintances? How extensive may be a search for evidence of a person's car, home, or business at the moment of his arrest? If, in the search for evidence of a crime, evidence of another crime is found, but the warrant was issued for only the first crime, what evidence may be presented to a jury? How broad the rights to citizens' secrecy under the Fourth Amendment is the result of many Supreme Court cases, and changes often.

The Fifth Amendment's prohibition against a person charged with a criminal offense being forced to be a witness against his or her own self is based on the notion that there needs be a balance of respect between the citizen (or person) and the government; the government, at least in a democracy, must accord dignity and integrity to its subjects. Obviously, that would not be evident if the government were able to torture or intimidate a confession out of a person. Criminal law enforcement is more reliable and stronger when based on independently acquired evidence. Furthermore, as Justice Brandeis stated in *Olmstead v. United States (1928)*, in a dissenting opinion,

> Decency, security and liberty alike demand that government officials shall be subjected to the same rules of conduct that are commands to the citizens. In a government of laws, existence of the government will be imperiled if it fails to observe the law scrupulously. Our Government is the potent, the omnipresent teacher. For good or for ill, it teaches the whole people by its example.
>
> Crime is contagious. If the Government becomes a lawbreaker, it breeds contempt for law; it invites every man to become a law unto himself; it invites anarchy. To declare that in the administration of the criminal law the end justifies the means ... would bring terrible retribution. Against that pernicious doctrine this Court should resolutely set its face.

Thus, Miranda rights. But, on the other side, and in order to facilitate "good faith" conduct by officers, a citizen may not keep secret his identity when apprehended by an officer, according to the Supreme Court.

Amendment VI requires that the accused shall "have compulsory process for obtaining witnesses in his favor." In other words, a person may not keep secret exculpatory evidence, if ordered by a court to provide it in a criminal case. The fact that a witness is required to take an oath to tell the truth, sanctioned by the criminal offense of contempt of court, means that witnesses for one side in a trial may be forced, by cross-examination, to divulge evidence that favors the other side.

A detailed list of secret activities and secrecy impositions – by and on government and by and on citizens could fill this and several other books! So if secrecy is as American as apple pie, and as common as apple pie, it must have a function. It does; it functions as an integral aspect of all politics, or, at least, the politics practiced by less than perfect persons in less than perfect societies, i.e., *all* societies. (One might hypothesize a utopian situation in which all relationships were transparent and overt, thus needing no secrecy). But in the real world of human relations, politics requires — and would be impossible without secrecy. These assertions won't stand without explanation, nor would they be relevant to the subject of secrecy without an explanation based upon an uncommon definition of politics.

Politics, In Theory

PROFESSIONAL POLITICAL SCIENTISTS have had a bit of a problem with their central term. In the attempt to present themselves as scientists, they have, historically (if not hysterically) sought a definition of *politics* that would be acceptable and understandable to all. It would surely be a great achievement on the road to scientific acceptance if such a definition could be formulated. One must give the discipline credit for effort, if not for achievement; thousands of definitions exist. As it is, in recognition of the absence of a commonly accepted definition of *politics*, the discipline has agreed to disagree; every political scientist is free to create his own, on the convenient assumption that any agreed upon definition would inhibit free enquiry and cause a straitjacket mentality.

Recall President Bill Clinton's comment in his defense to the charge of inappropriate behavior in the Oval Office: "It all depends on what the meaning of *is* is." Ever the consummate politician, he was exactly right in noting that the definition is the crux of all matters. Likewise, for politics, which is *not* what you learned in PS 101 – constitutions, legislatures, elections, etc., all of which are but the idiosyncratic formal, organizational, and somewhat regularized, but ephemeral, expression of politics in the hundred plus nations of the world. While such knowledge is necessary and useful for partial understanding of formal governmental and political structures and machinations, one doesn't build a science on such ephemera; it would be like trying to develop a theory of botany by studying only the roses of the world, but only those roses found organized in formal gardens, or to develop a theory of biology by studying only aardvarks.

A scientifically adequate definition of *politics* would require that it be presented in terms of behavior known and practiced by all humans. As it is, most people know and care more about licorice than legislation, like elephants more than elections, and worry about constipation more than constitutions. The existing multitude of definitions of *politics* is the product of academicians and practitioners fascinated by those who hold the reins of public power. Their definitions might be useful and partially valid within the confines of that notable sphere of activity, but one should not confuse, say, a definition of water, adequate to discuss flood control, with a scientific definition of water at the level of its constituent elements of hydrogen and oxygen or, even at the lower level of its atomic structure. The social cost of defining politics in terms of governmental power was nicely noted by David Ignatius of the *Washington Post* who wrote, "When the big guys in Washington dream of transforming the world, it's the little guys who come home in body bags."

Politics, to be studied as a science, must first be defined as the universal form of human behavior that it is! Every human expresses politics throughout his or her life, just as all individuals expresses psychological, sociological, economic, and biological realities every day of their lives, and the psychologists, sociologists, economists, and biologist can speak to their cohorts sensibly because they have common understanding of their basic terms. Not so, political scientists.

But who can doubt that politics is a universal phenomenon not restricted to only those who govern, seek to govern, or seek to influence those who govern. There is a fundamental parallel between the behavior of Winston Churchill in defining the situation of England in 1940 as dire and seeking to convince Franklin Roosevelt to send guns and butter to England, and the behavior of a baby in the middle of the night. Thus, for example, the plaintive cry of the baby, at 3:00 AM, is a political act — defining its situation as hungry, wet, and/or lonesome. The baby's definition of the situation will be reinterpreted by the father, who will define it to his advantage; he will fake a few snores. His wife, acting politically in her own interests, using her elbow, will reject the father's definition and substitute one of her own: "You're faking, John! You know it's your turn! Get up and warm the bottle!" Now, that's politics at its universal human level.

By contrast, the definitions of the subject in the writings of major political science authorities are narrow and idiomatic. Twenty experts: twenty definitions. There is a British book, *What is Politics?*, in which each authority presents a different definition of the subject. One pundit will define politics as influence, another as power, another as self-interest, another as the art of the possible, and another as the skill of building consensus around a policy option. One expert, writing on the power of the presidency, determined that political power is the power to persuade. That's close, but he made the mistake of confusing means and results. Thus, all he had was a tautology, asking, then, what is the power to persuade? If, instead, he had concentrated on means, on behavior, he would have found that persuasive behavior (politics in a generic sense) is the effective skill of creating self –serving definitions of reality. Politics is the universal human behavior of defining reality so as to bring about acceptance of one's desired outcome.

Here are examples that prove the point: "Johnny, stop hitting your sister; be a good boy." "If you really loved me, you'd buy me that necklace." "Good friends don't let each other drink and drive." "Owning one's personal weapon is a sacred American right." "Dan Quayle is no Jack Kennedy!" "Osama bin Laden has insulted and degraded the Moslem faith." Accept any of these quotes, and you have accepted the speaker's definition of reality and his or her politics.

With this definition of politics, politics as a universal human goal-fulfilling behavior, consider the element of secrecy in the following example from Mark Twain's Huckleberry Finn. Huck finds himself in a real jam and has to come up quickly with an effective definition of the situation! He and the runaway slave, Jim, are on the raft, floating down the Mississippi, when a boat comes along side. In it are two fellows with guns, and they are looking for an escaped slave. Huck has hurried Jim under their tent to hide beneath some blankets. The conversation is pure Twain: The men ask if Huck has seen the slave, and he assures them that he has not, but if he had, he would surely turn him in. The men are somewhat convinced, but just to be sure, they say that they will come aboard and look around the raft.

Huck is feeling "scared as a rabbit," but he just up and says that, yes, you better come aboard, but don't get too close to my daddy in the tent, cause he has 'the sickness.' And nobody will let me land and take care of him. What do you say, 'Boy'? Your pappy has the plague? All ends well, with the men each putting a five-dollar gold piece on a shovel blade and, making sure not to get too close, poking the gold over to Huck, 'cause he's sure in a poor way!' Huck, the master politician, defining the situation to his advantage, by keeping the reality secret in order to manipulate his competitors into accepting his contrived redefinition of that reality.

Another example of how politics is an expression of different perspectives of reality is shown in four differing definitions of the little town of Denton, Texas, (where I taught in the late 60s). A huge billboard on Interstate 35 claimed that Denton was "just like Los Angeles, give or take six million people." Some of the local rednecks had crossed out "people" and painted in "Niggers!" Other citizens (I suspect some of my ACLU friends) had crossed out that obscenity and written in "Racist Trash!" But that had been crossed out by some of the local feminists, who had scrawled, "Male Chauvinist Pigs!" For obvious reasons, the authors of these insights chose to keep their identities secret.

Religion is essentially a subset of politics, the elaborate creation of a particular definition of life and eternity which is then offered to or imposed upon members and others. In requiring unquestioning acceptance, religions practice considerable secrecy. They exhibit much of the same behavior as governmental agencies that become convinced of their role as protector of the nation's security. Those agencies, such as the CIA and the FBI, approach totalitarian means of secrecy (on which, more later) to carry out what, to them, comes close to being considered a divine mission. Religions create absolute definitions of reality. There is no argument, in that context. (As a friend once said in response to one of my more arrogant pronouncements, "I see you have a very concrete view of this – all mixed up and permanently set"). Thus, some religions require members to police themselves – not read certain books, not allow evolutionary theory to contaminate their minds, not let authorities know of certain illegal practices such as polygamy, child abuse, narcotic use, etc., and violation of this secrecy is sanctioned by the ultimate punishments: banishment, and later, eternal hell.

Politics, In Practice

The material above, in summary, says secrecy is a necessary and integral aspect of American life. It is required and protected by the Constitution, practiced by all bureaucracies and all citizens, and is essential to politics in all its forms, formal and informal, public and private. What becomes apparent is that secrecy, like so many elements of life, is neither inherently 'good' nor 'bad.' Secrecy, like government, the law, the presidency, the military, the police, religion, politics, money, guns, or drugs, is a tool or device or resource that is to be judged according to the result of its use.

Some obviously bad uses of secrecy, in terms of public policy and social felicity, ironically, are quite well known, but, regardless, seem to be repeated over and over through our history. The exercise of governmental police power, defined as the authority to promote and safeguard the health, morals, safety, and welfare of the people, tends to enlarge the domain of government, local, state, and national, over the citizen.

Surely, the constant repetition of scandals wherein the local or state police have kept secret files on citizens, a practice prohibited by law, speaks to the weakness of dedication to the principle of a government of law by the very bureaucracies assigned to protect it. In Portland, Oregon, twenty years ago, the ACLU succeeded in forcing the police to eliminate such a file, but in 2002, police again were found to have kept illegal files on thousands of citizens. In that same year, the Denver, Colorado, police were ordered to purge their system of spying secretly on citizens.

In Denver, great-grandmother Helen Henry, 82, was noted in the secret files as having a "Free Leonard Peltier" bumper sticker on her Toyota sedan (*Sunday Oregonian*, 9/15/02, p. A21)! While such absurdities may cause a laugh, it is a serious matter; fear of one's name being placed in a secret file may cause that citizen to give up the constitutional right to protest peacefully. Hearing that a neighbor's name, or even an unknown citizen's name may be in a file has a chilling effect on the exercise of civil rights, the life blood of democratic government.

At the national level, the FBI under Director J. Edgar Hoover was found to have maintained extensive secret files on the rich, the famous, and the politically active. Hoover's long tenure was often attributed to the belief that he held embarrassing evidence on even the presidents and other top leaders, thus no president dared to fire him.

In response to the 9/11/01 terrorist attack on the nation, local police have been asked to work with the FBI-led Joint Terrorism Task Force. Many civil libertarians are troubled by the implicit conflict between the need to fight terrorist threats and the quite probable partial misuse of the police power. This fear is augmented by the creation of the Department of Homeland Security and the aggressive use of secrecy by Attorney General of the United States, John Ashcroft.

The AG's office has adopted a blanket policy to close hundreds of deportation hearings of noncitizens suspected of connection to terrorist activity. In August of 2002, a unanimous three-judge panel of the Sixth United States Court of Appeals declared that unlawful. Said Judge Damon J Keith, "Democracies die behind closed doors. When government begins closing doors, it selectively controls information rightfully belonging to the people. Selective information is misinformation."

It is upsetting to read constantly of the use of secrecy by national leaders. Both President Bush and Vice President Cheney have kept secret public information publicly demanded, in response to the recent corporate crime scandals, about their activities as CEOs of Harken Oil and Halliburton, respectively. President Bush wants the new Homeland Security Department to be exempt from the Freedom of Information Act and the Whistleblower Act. Dick Cheney has stonewalled the legitimate demand for the notes and list of attendees at his meetings to create a national energy policy; that "national energy policy development group" was a public body that met in secret. Even diehard Republican conservatives such as Senator Dan Burton of Indiana, who fear big and intrusive government, are aghast at a White House so hostile to open government.

The high cost of misused secrecy was made evident on September 11, 2001. It has become all too clear, in the public hearings in October, 2002, of the joint intelligence committee's investigating the attacks that the FBI, the CIA and the NSA had failed to protect the nation from calamity because of inefficiency tied to the overuse of secrecy. The agencies failed to communicate with each other, protecting bureaucratic turf rather than American soil. Though FBI Director Robert Mueller, the Director of the National Security Agency, Michael V. Hayden, and CIA Director George Tenet all spoke at length and provided many excuses, Senator Carl Levin of Michigan, a member of the Senate Select Committee on Intelligence, said, "At crucial points in the 21 months leading up to September 11th, this intelligence information was not shared or was not acted upon and, as a result, numerous opportunities to thwart the terrorist plots were squandered." (*The Oregonian*, October 18, 2002, p. A2)

As tragic as the incompetence leading up to 9/11 has been, an even more pervasive example of incompetent management of a governmental responsibility is reported by Senator Daniel Patrick Moynihan in his book, *Secrecy* (Yale University Press, 1998).

The extreme politics between the Right and the Left in America, in the period leading up to World War II and after, were based on allegations of secret conspiracies. The Right was sure that the Left was aligned with world communism, that Pearl Harbor was the result of a secret plan to bring the US into the war to save Stalin and Russia, and that the Communist International had spies in all the sensitive areas of government.

The Left, citing the Red Scare raids of the 1920s, pictured the Right as a group of fascists led by J. Edgar Hoover who wanted to destroy the legal protections of the Constitution, turn America over to Hitler, and was secretly involved in munitions and other manufacturing in Germany. Senator Joseph McCarthy astounded the Senate with the news that General George C. Marshall was a Communist traitor at the center of "a conspiracy so immense" as to dwarf any in history. McCarthy, it is now clear, would have been nothing without government secrecy. His ability to hypnotize the nation over the radio and the then-new television screen was based upon his claim that all his evidence came from secret documents held by the executive branch, which was dominated by communists.

Within this environment, says Moynihan, bazaar surreal events transpired. Hoover wrote an amazing letter to George E. Allen, Director of the Reconstruction Finance Corporation, intending that it would then be seen by President Truman (Hoover apparently could not bring himself to write directly to the President whom he personally detested). The letter outlined a huge conspiracy of top government officials working for a communist victory over America: Dean Acheson, Secretary of State; John J. McCloy, Former Assistant Secretary of War; Henry A. Wallace, Secretary of Commerce; Alger Hiss of the UN Organization; Dr. Edward U. Condon, Advisor to the Congressional Committee on Atomic Energy; popular journalists Raymond Gram Swing and Marquis Childs, and others. The message, six pages long, outlined Hoover's conclusions, from evidence by an 'informer,' that the secrets of the American atomic bomb were being funneled through these people directly to the Soviets! Moynihan characterizes it as a loony message not taken seriously. But what about its inclusion of the name, Alger Hiss!?

That was 1946. In 1949, after the very fortuitous breaking of the Soviet code by which the USSR was communicating with its agents in America, it was found that there was, in fact, an effective Soviet espionage effort in America. This information was in the hands of the forerunner agency of the current NSA, and its head, Admiral Stone, determined that President Truman should be informed immediately. However, General Carter W. Clarke, then chief of the army security agency, strongly disagreed; if the information were spread around, surely there would be a leak, and the Russians would know their code had been broken. At that point, General Omar Nelson Bradley, chairman of the Joint Chiefs of Staff, in spite of his admiration and loyalty to the President, agreed with General Clarke that the fact should be kept secret from the President and from Admiral Roscoe H. Hillenkoetter, the first director of the CIA! Secrecy triumphed!

President Truman was subjected to the very heated abuse of the McCarthy period and was required to defend his administration from some wild and baseless charges as well as other valid charges that were not supported by known evidence. Whittaker Chambers was right about Alger Hiss. But Truman was not allowed to know the fact that the Soviet code had been broken, the extent of the communist espionage ring's success, and the truth about Alger Hiss. The president of the United States was kept in the dark on a most important matter of national security because of the secrecy demands of underlings. The Venona files (the name applied to the deciphered Soviet spy messages) only became public knowledge decades later through the efforts of Moynihan and the Commission on Protecting and Reducing Government Secrecy, in 1996. If, as the Constitution requires, civilian leadership is centered in a civilian president who dominates the military service, and if Truman had been informed of the Venona files, how different would have been his handling of the communists-in-government issue that plagued his tenure as President, and how less would have been the trauma of national politics through the late forties and the fifties?

But the battle continues even into this century. Richard Perle, reviewing Moynihan's book in *Commentary* (www.findarticles.com/ct), barely concealing his conservative stiletto, writes:

> Curiously, Moynihan, a former vice chairman of the Senate Intelligence Committee, does not pause to wonder whether ***Washington*** might have had good reason to conceal its success in deciphering the Soviet codes. Although one would like to know what lies behind his thinking here, he never tells us. Nor do we learn anything more about his breathtaking revelation that even President Truman was kept in the dark about the decryptions. Can this be true? Or is there some metasecret of which Moynihan, too, remains ignorant? (My emphasis)

Apparently, "Washington," for Perle, means the CIA, the FBI, and the Military Joint Chiefs of Staff, rather than the democratic structures of the government — the Congress and the Office of the President. He is quick to conjure up a conspiracy theory, in loyalty to his preferred powers.

And surely, the seventies and eighties would have gone down differently if the CIA and the NSA had been less secret. The nation knows now that there was gross incompetence in those agencies in their efforts to evaluate the Soviet Union through the years of the Cold War. Soviet strengths were greatly exaggerated, and the weaknesses of the system were ignored. Only a few, Moynihan included, saw the errors in the analysis in the projections of Soviet power. Even Richard Perle accepts Moynihan's evaluation on this point.

There can be no doubt that the CIA seriously and consistently over-estimated the size, rate of growth, and potential of the Soviet economy. In 1958, the agency took the view that Soviet gross domestic product (GDP) was growing much faster than ours, and would come within 50 percent of ours by 1962. This was ludicrous, as was the CIA estimate in 1990 that the Soviet GDP stood at $2.5 trillion. . . . As Moynihan rightly observes, any casual visitor to Moscow would have seen more than enough of the appalling circumstances in which most Soviet citizens lived to cast doubt on the plausibility of the CIA's view.

The CIA soon after its creation at the end of World War II came to exhibit all the earmarks of a usual regulatory bureaucracy – and some quite unusual characteristics: in 1997, the first public statement of its budget was made, and it was $26.6 billion! But regardless of its more than fifty years of existence, its huge secret budget, its ability to exist out of the public eye, and amazing technological developments (communications, U-2s, satellites, and computers), "the overall quality of American intelligence may well have declined over time," says Moynihan (p. 78).

Surely, the most telling evidence of the CIA's incompetence was in its main task, evaluation of the 'enemy,' the USSR. It continually pictured the Soviet Union as a strong, modern, industrial behemoth single-mindedly pursuing the goal of world domination and equipped with a nuclear age armed force. The reality had not been spotted in the decades of U-2 and satellite photos or in the reams of secret documents. The USSR's incompetence in Afghanistan and the final collapse of the wall were surprises to those who should have known. Stanford Turner, the director of the CIA from 1977 to 1981, in 1991, claimed never to have heard from the intelligence or defense or state establishment even a hint that non-official sources in the Soviet Union were convinced that the system was broken and would disintegrate from its own internal weaknesses.

Daniel Patrick Moynihan's conclusion is that, at least in part, the reason is that collected information was kept secret, analyses were kept secret, and conclusions were kept secret; if these had been allowed to be known, discussed, criticized, and argued, errors, inconsistencies, and illogical aspects could have been eliminated. The price paid for the luxury of secrecy was staggering. What if, Moynihan asks, the US had been less secret, less bellicose, more conservative in its financing of military might, and had been prepared, when the inevitable collapse of the USSR came, to offer a parallel to the Marshall Plan that produced a renewed Europe and a friendly Germany and Italy?

One of the most outrageous uses of secrecy in government in a democracy is one of its most common. It happens at every level of government, local, state, and national. The policy making and enacting institutions of government, the legislative and executive branches, are overwhelmingly the sites of lobbying, a secret process in which the agents of private interests, in league with the majority of elected and appointed officials, work against the public interests.

The political aim of the lobbyists is to convince legislators and bureaucrats to accept a definition of reality favorable to the lobbyists, but to clothe that definition, which is kept secret, behind a definition of the reality that appears to be in the public interest. For example, lumber companies want to log state and national forest lands. They define their desire to see public money spent on roads throughout the forest as a desire to enhance the protection of the forest in case of forest fires, and to enhance the access to the public for hunting and camping activity.

Likewise, the pharmaceutical industry lobbies for extension of patent rights on profitable drugs "in order to ensure that they have enough money for their very important research in the war against devastating crippling diseases;" yet, most of their money goes for advertising, and most of their research money goes to invent drugs to fight the common cold, hemorrhoids, backache and zits. Why? As Willy Sutton said, "That's where the money is." Countless other examples may be found in the alphabet of economic activity in America from agriculture, banking, and commerce through X-rays, yacht ownership, and zinc mining.

Politicians, of course, enter into these conspiracies eagerly so as to collect campaign funds and to win a block of voters whose interests are enhanced. Additionally, coming to light all too often in scandals are the cases of officials accepting bribes or presents or paid trips, with family, to exotic spots to attend "important policy discussions" held quite often on golf courses. Many, even perhaps most, politicians develop great skill in presenting themselves as selfless agents working for the public weal, while secretly more concerned with job security and career goals in the struggle for power. That's politics!

THE POLITICS OF SECRET CONSPIRACIES

SECRECY, IN AN IMPERFECT WORLD, is an essential aspect of all politics. And, as noted above, the process of politics is the creation of self-serving definitions of reality. Secrecy, obviously, rests upon an assumption of mistrust in one's target of politics. Democrats mistrust Republicans, and vice versa. Nations mistrust each other. Husbands and wives mistrust each other, keeping their affairs secret, knowing their spouses just wouldn't understand. Likewise between parents and children. Thus, politicians define the reality of their ambitions in terms of service to the public good, nations talk peace but prepare for war, spouses define absence as the necessity of working late at the office, and children, intending to party, claim the need to get help on homework from a classmate.

James Madison, in *THE FEDERALIST PAPERS, "Number X,"* describes the essential elements in a republic to be freedom to form factions, the necessity that there be many factions, that they be spread over a large area, and that they be composed of a large number of individuals. Minority factions are controllable by the votes of a majority faction. But majority factions present the danger of deprival of rights of individuals and minorities. This danger, however, can be minimized by the difficulties of majorities to act in unison. First, they are, themselves, composed of minorities and, thus, find it hard to organize in concert to oppress a particular minority. And the fact that they are composed of many individuals spread over a large area also reduces their ability to act efficiently. Half of what anyone needs to know to understand American politics can be found in these insights presented by Madison in the five or six pages of *Number X*!

But the politics of conspiracies is not explained by the theory of democracy. Certainly, conspiracies are factions, and they are minority factions, but the defense Madison proposes, a majority vote, does not apply, because conspiracies see all non-members as opponents, and their secrecy aims to prevent opponents from even knowing of their existence, let alone offering themselves up for a vote by the citizens. This is true for the corporation clique that conspires to defraud the public or its own stockholders, for criminals planning a bank heist, for a political conspiracy planning a coup de etat, or a cabal of bureaucratic insiders intent upon using government power for personal and/or political purposes.

All secret societies are conspiratorial factions aimed at achieving goals that, by definition, are contrary to the public interest as determined by citizens in an open society. As Madison says, no faction can be allowed to be a judge in its own cause, because its interests would certainly bias its judgment and corrupt its integrity. And, as Karl Popper says, freedom is impossible unless it is guaranteed by the state; any secret society that weakens the rule of law, creates inequalities among citizens by illegal means, or frustrates the legitimate aims of democratic policy weakens a democratic republic and its objective of guaranteeing freedom to its citizens. Logically, then, secret societies are threats to democratic societies.

The question becomes one of determining how serious a threat to a democracy is a particular secret society. Certainly, Al-Queda is a very threatening conspiracy, as was the conspiracy led by Timothy McVeigh, and as is the mailer of the anthrax germs. One may create his or her own hierarchy of secret conspiracies threatening our society. The list is too long for this article, but would include some of these: all criminal activists, violent Right-to-Life factions, pedophilia traffickers, violent white-power advocates, anti-tax groups that practice fraud, illegal pornographers, a multitude of scam artists operating just within the law, the Elmer Gantrys of religious exploitation, gangs that use violence and intimidation, etc., etc.

Lastly, if I could be allowed a personal expression based on normative values rather than hard facts or academically sound theory, the conspiracies listed in the previous paragraph (other than the first three) are comparatively 'small potatoes' based on marginal personal greed or ego or fanaticism not reaching the level of serious threats to American democracy. They are the inevitable garbage created in a society that values liberty over totalitarian order. The real threats to the American democracy envisioned by Thomas Jefferson in his better moments, not contaminated by his aristocratic heritage and his personal needs, come from the misuse of political and economic power by an undemocratic wealthy elitist clique of materialist ideologues in secret cabals at the highest levels of American society.

RALPH E. BUNCH is an emeritus professor of the Department of Political Science of Portland State University. He was born in Portland, Oregon in 1927, served in the US Navy during WW II, graduated from Lewis and Clark College in 1951, received an M.S. (1961) and Ph.D. (1968) in political science from the University of Oregon. He has taught in public school in Oregon, Japan, and Canada, and during his twenty-five years as a professor, has taught in Oregon, Texas, Washington, and Russia. He served 16 years as Book Review Editor for *The International Journal of Comparative Sociology*, edited three books, and has authored numerous articles in professional journals. He is retired and lives with his wife, Eleonora, in King City, Oregon and in Moscow, Russia.

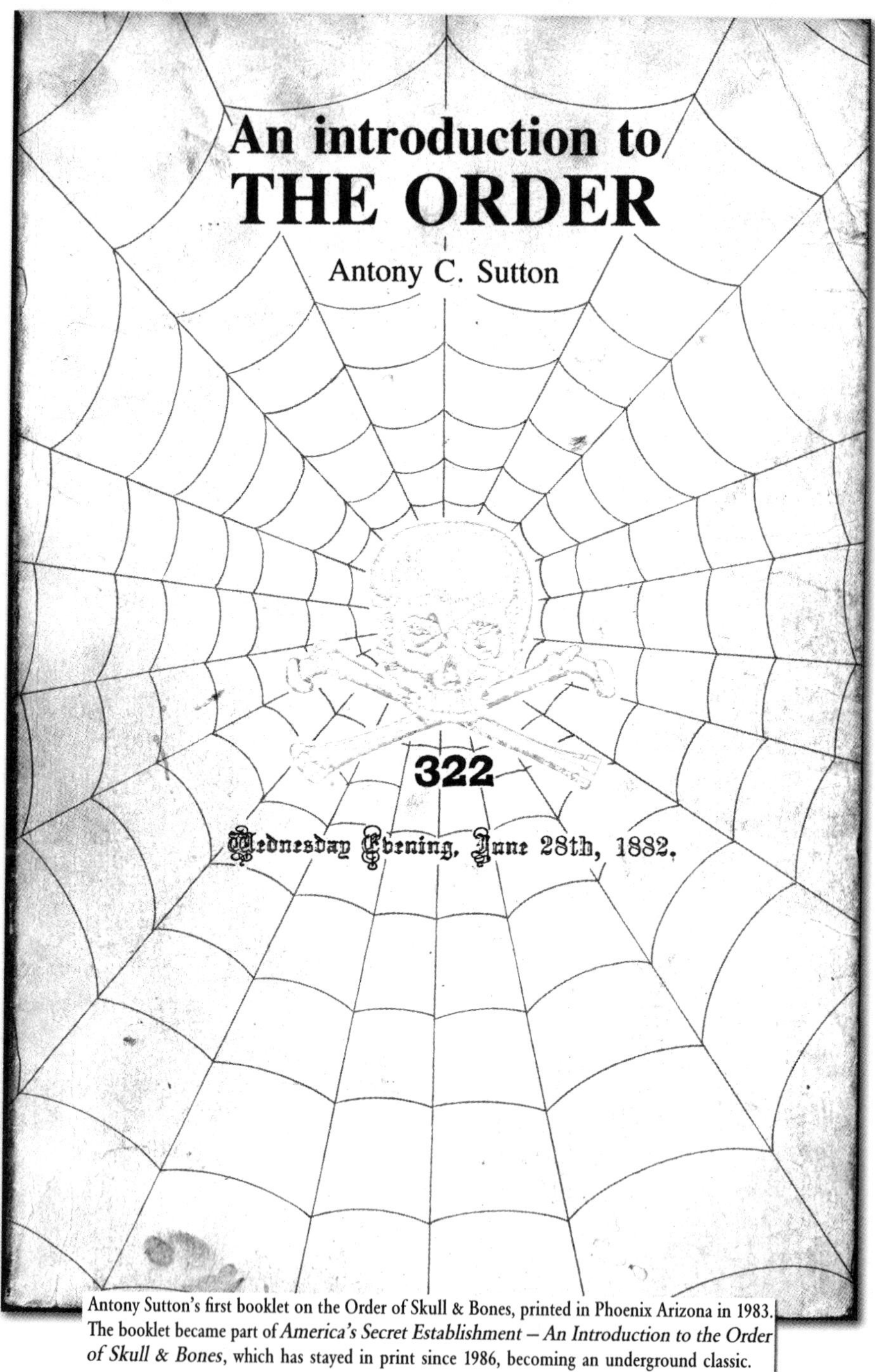

Antony Sutton's first booklet on the Order of Skull & Bones, printed in Phoenix Arizona in 1983. The booklet became part of *America's Secret Establishment – An Introduction to the Order of Skull & Bones*, which has stayed in print since 1986, becoming an underground classic.

W, S&B — AND THE TRUTH ... SHALL SET US FREE

A JULY 1, 1999 INTERVIEW WITH ANTONY C. SUTTON, RESEARCHER EMERITUS

Interviewers: Kris Millegan, Al Hidell, & David Guyatt

WELL, NOW, AIN'T LIFE GRAND here in these United States. Now, I don't know but I do believe I am being told, by our corporate media, that George W Bush is gonna be the next president and there ain't nothing us peons can do about it. W's already got the cash and all the *friends* a guy could want. Billy-boy has shown that personal peccadilloes don't matter. And, gee whiz, W's were just youthful indiscretions anyway.

Sutton and Millegan - July, 2000

The Mighty Wurlitzer is playing loud and strong; *Project Mockingbird* has come home to roost and it looks as though a foreign secret society will for the third time put their *juvenile* in the White House. The latest spin has W just being a president of his ol' college frat house, DKE, who *maybe* did some strange initiation rituals ... Yeah, right. Ya wanna buy a bridge?

George W Bush is a member of a 167-year-old secret society at Yale University, Skull & Bones. The Order of Skull & Bones has been shown to be founded as a chapter of a secret society based in Germany. Some say it is just a college club; other say much more and point to W's grandfather's filching of Geronimo's remains; of the financing of Nazis and Communism; of drug smuggling; of eugenics; of manipulation of our social and political arenas through the Hegelian method of thesis, antithesis — resulting towards the desired synthesis — a *New World Order,* and more ... .

But then this is not just a story about W, or Skull & Bones, but also the story of a courageous man, his dutiful journey and consequent battles with the 'powers-that-be.'

ANTONY C. SUTTON, FEB. 14, 1925 - JUNE 17, 2002, has been persecuted but never prosecuted for his research and subsequent publishing of his findings. His mainstream career was shattered by his devotion towards uncovering the truth. In 1968, his *Western Technology and Soviet Economic Development* was published by The Hoover Institute at Stanford University. Sutton showed how the Soviet state's technological and manufacturing base, which was then engaged in supplying the North Vietnamese the armaments and supplies to kill and wound American soldiers, was built by US firms and mostly paid for by the US taxpayers. From their largest steel and iron plant, to automobile manufacturing equipment, to precision ball-bearings and computers, the majority of the Soviet's large industrial enterprises had been built with the United States help or technical assistance.

Professor Richard Pipes, of Harvard, said in his book, *Survival Is Not Enough: Soviet Realities and America's Future* (Simon & Schuster; 1984):

> "In his three-volume detailed account of Soviet Purchases of Western Equipment and Technology ... [Antony] Sutton comes to conclusions that are uncomfortable for many businessmen and economists. For this reason his work tends to be either dismissed out of hand as ***extreme*** or, more often, simply ignored."

The reportage was too much and Sutton's career as a well-paid member of the academic establishment was under attack and he was told that he "would not survive."

His work led him to more questions than answers. "Why had the US built-up it's enemy? Why did the US build-up the Soviet Union, while we also transferred technology to Hitler's Germany? Why does Washington want to conceal these facts?"

Sutton, following his leads, proceeded to research and write his outstanding Wall Street financial expose series *Wall Street and FDR; Wall Street and the Rise of Hitler*; and *Wall Street and The Bolshevik Revolution.*

Then, someone sent Antony a membership list of Skull & Bones and … "a picture jumped out." And what a picture! A multigenerational foreign-based secret society with fingers in all kinds of pies and roots going back to *Illuminati* influences in 1830's Germany.

And what a list of members, accomplishments and … skullduggery!

Here, in a rare interview by email, are Antony Sutton's own reflections and answers to questions from myself and other researchers:

REMEMBER, ALL MY PAPERS on this are in deep storage 1000 miles away and cannot be accessed and I've not even thought about S&B for 15 years. I had no idea that any interest had been aroused out there. I know the book is a steady seller from the royalty reports; but that is all.

For the last 10 years I have been in complete seclusion working on future technology … I'm more engineer than historian. The only visitors I've had or meetings have been with three-letter agency people, who arrive on the doorstep unannounced and complain I am hard to find. Big Brother has the ability apparently to find anyone.

Nothing mysterious about this, I just dislike publicity and social interaction. You will see from the Dutch TV episode that my work still upsets the *powers-that-be* so these are merely reasonable precautions.

The Interview

KM - *Can you tell the story of how you learned about Skull & Bones, and how you felt?*

AS - I knew nothing of S&B until I received a letter in the early 80's asking if I would like to look at a genuine membership list. For no real reason I said yes. It was agreed to send the package by Federal Express and I could keep it for 24 hours, it had to be returned to the safe. It was a "black bag" job by a family member disgusted with their activities.

For the benefit of any S&B members who may read and doubt the statement; the membership list is in two volumes, black leather bound. Living members and deceased members in separate volumes. Very handsome books.

I spent all night in Kinko's, Santa Cruz, copied the entire volumes and returned within the 24 hour period.

I have never released any copies or identified the source. I figured each copy could be coded and enable S&B to trace the leak.

How did I feel? I felt then (as I do now} that these "prominent" men are really immature juveniles at heart. The horrible reality is that these little boys have been dominant in their influence in world affairs. No wonder we have wars and violence. Skull & Bones is the symbol of terrorist violence, pirates, the SS Deaths Head Division in WW Two, labels on poison bottles and so on.

I kept the stack of xeroxed sheets for quite a while before I looked at them–when I did look–a picture jumped out, THIS was a significant part of the so called establishment. No wonder the world has problems!

KM - *What is the percentage of active members?*

AS - I haven't checked for 15 years ... it used to be about one quarter. With the rise of the Bush dynasty it will increase somewhat, as they climb on the bandwagon. The Demos had their turn with Harriman in the 40's and 50's.

KM - *How many active members are there?*

AS - Usually about 600 alive at any one time ... recently more active.

***KM** - What is your take on the grandfather clock that each member allegedly receives?*

AS - They do get a clock. I've had that confirmed and you will see it in the photos in ASE (***America's Secret Establishment***). Might be symbolic, perhaps to state their organization goes on timelessly.

***KM** - Has Skull and Bones lost its clout?*

AS - Well look at the recent fund-raiser for George Bush ... Republicans are stuffing money into his pockets ... I suggest members recently got behind one of their own and decided to push George all out for president ... and Democrats can't do a thing because Democrat Bones are not going to allow the Party to use the ultimate weapon ... George's membership in a foreign secret society.

***KM** - What do you know of George W Bush?*

AS - He is a third generation Bonesman. My personal impression is that he doesn't have the drive of his father or the skills of his grandfather ... but I could be very wrong. He can beat anyone hands down – EXCEPT VENTURA.

If Bush handlers allow a face to face debate between Bush and Ventura. Ventura will win. Remember Ventura has admitted to his so-called "sins." Bush has a closet-full waiting to emerge. People are getting bored with cover ups and spin.

2000 may see the end of the Bones influence or – reality that these Bones people are powerful.

***KM** - Is the name of the German group known?*

AS - Almost certainly Illuminati.

***KM** - Some people say that there are other cells; what do you think?*

AS - There are many other secret societies. I've only looked at S&B. Unfortunately no historian will keep his job if he tries to explore conspiracy ... this is taboo for the American Historical Association. Sooner or later outsiders will take a look. I've long thought that S&B fits the legal definition of a conspiracy and needs to be officially investigated.

Yes there should be other cells. No secret society worth anything is going to keep its inner actions written down on paper. If the gigantic electronic monitoring apparatus is for national security purposes, then it should be monitoring these people 24 hours a day.

KM - *What are your thoughts on Wolf's Head? Scroll & Key? And the other Senior societies at Yale?*
AS - Wolfs Head, Scroll and Key seem to be pale imitations of S&B, but they have the same objective of deliberately building discrimination into a society. I listened to Jesse Ventura last night and he made the point that the Founding Fathers intended for CITIZENS to represent the people. I agree; a trucker, a farmer, a teacher represent the people not a bunch of professional pols or a secret society like S&B. All these societies place their own members ahead of the pack and give preference to their own members; this is discrimination par excellence.

KM - *Have you read Cathy O'Brien's book Tranceformation Of America? What do think of it?*
AS - The book does not contain one piece of hard physical evidence.. I think Cathy O'Brien BELIEVES SHE IS TELLING THE TRUTH ... but remember that Mark Phillips is a skilled neuro-linguistic-programmer.

Another point that really concerns me is this ... where did this story originate? It originated in Communist Chinese Intelligence and Mark Phillips had a contractual relationship with the ChiComs. This could be an attempt to destabilize the US.

No doubt these Washington pols are fully capable of these weird practices, just look at Bohemian Grove but that doesn't mean that the book is an accurate portrayal. If the book is credible, I would think the police would have raided Bohemian Grove long ago

My best guess is that the Chinese picked up whispers of Washington scandals and blew them out of proportion for their own purposes. This is a GUESS ... I don't know.

One thing that puzzled me, with all these sexual shenanigans how do Washington politicians find time to do anything else? According to the book this is a full time occupation for Senator Byrd and others.

KM - *What did your study of elites, economics, secrecy and technology do for your career?*
AS - Depends what you mean by *career*?

By conventional standards I am an abject failure. I've been thrown out of two major Universities (UCLA and Stanford), denied tenure at Cal State Los Angeles. Every time I write something, it appears to offend someone in the Establishment and they throw me to the wolves.

On the other hand I've written 26 books, published a couple of newsletters and so on ... even more important I've never compromised on the truth, and I don't quit.

In material terms ... hopeless failure. In terms of discovery ... I think I've been successful. Judge a man by his enemies. William Buckley called me a "jerk." Glenn Campbell, former Director of the Hoover Institution, Stanford called me "a problem."

***KM** - Do you believe that there has been suppression of technology? Has it been major or minor?*
AS - Yes there has been suppression but its going to be impossible to suppress the new emerging paradigm.

***KM** - The Federal Reserve, the House of Morgan, House of Rothschild and Skull and Bones are they related?*
AS - Best source for this is my book ***The Federal Reserve Conspiracy.***

***KM** - What are the good source materials for your research and writings about Skull and Bone's influencing John Dewey and Horace Mann?*
AS - Depends what you want to find. You could explore the 10 or so volume works of Dewey ... outrageous Hegelianism, the state is supreme, the individual merely a pawn to be trained. This is the basis of our 'educational system" ...or you could go and explore the members of S&B who brought the system to the US.

This trained "sausage mind" outlook has thoroughly permeated our universities ... that's why we have the peer review system ... we are all supposed to think alike and find the same answers. This political correctness garbage is another step to total thought control.

***AH** - Did any of Hitler's economic policies threaten the interests of the international bankers, and if so did that play a role in his downfall?*
AS - Hitler's economic policies were OK'd by the bankers right through the war ... ITT, Chase, Texaco and others were operating in Nazi-held France as late as 1945. In fact Chase in Paris was trying to get Nazi accounts as late as 1944. When we got to Germany in May, 1945, I remember seeing a (bombed-out) Woolworth store in Hamburg and thinking, "What's Woolworth doing in Nazi Germany?" While we were bombed and shelled it was "business as usual" for Big Business. Try the Alien Custodian Papers.

See my ***Best Enemy Money Can Buy*** for more.

Union Banking is very important. I made a documentary for Dutch National TV some years ago. It got all the way through the production process to the Dutch TV Guide ... at the last minute it was pulled and another film substituted. This documentary has proof of Bush financing Hitler – documents.

Maybe my Dutch friends will still get it viewed, but the apparatus reaches into Holland.

***KM** - What is the story that was going to be told on Dutch TV? And what is the story of it's censorship?*

AS - Couple of years back, a Dutch TV production company from Amsterdam – under contract to Dutch National TV–came to the US to make a documentary on S&B. They went to the Bones Temple and other places and interviewed people on the East Coast. On the West Coast, they interviewed myself and one other person.

I saw extracts from the original and it is a good professional job. They had documents linking the Bush family and other S&B members to financing Hitler through Union Banking of New York and its Dutch correspondent bank. More than I have in ***Wall Street And The Rise Of Hitler.***

The first version was later upgraded into a two part documentary and scheduled for showing this last March. It was pulled at the last minute and has never been shown.

AH *- Who has been financing Milosevic, and what role has the international banking community played in the Balkans?*

AS - I haven't looked at this one. Of course the notorious Black Hand society is located in the Balkans. See WW One.

DG *- What is the importance of your work on Skull and Bones?*

AS - The potential is extraordinary. IF we find that secret societies are indeed significant, the entire history of the last two centuries will have to be re-written.

At this point in 1999, the potential has not been explored by others and I've moved back to my original interest–technology. Apparently people see some merit in the work. It is never advertised. It is an underground word of mouth distribution but has sold steadily from 1986 to date. Every month I get a royalty check, so I know it is selling. But my original enthusiastic statement has not been fulfilled.

KM *- What do you see for the future?*

AS - Chaos, confusion and ultimately a battle between the individual and the State.

The individual is the stronger; and will win. The state is a fiction sanctified by Hegel and his followers to CONTROL the individual.

Sooner or later people will wake up. First we have to dump the trap of right and left, this is a Hegelian trap to divide and control. The battle is not between right and left; it is between us and them.

The message is getting through. ***ASE*** has sold for 15 years, small but steady. No advertising. Its an underground work. But the breadth of interest is amazing. From Black Africa, to Russia (12,000 copies), right, left ... it cuts across all ethnic, political, social lines..

The spirit of God is within us as individuals. Skull & Bones represents death. It has no life spirit and pretends that the State "is the march of God on earth."

The thinking of immature juveniles, deadly and destructive and has almost totally infected Washington.

What to do? Find yourself and then go to work ... tell your friends and put out the message.

The answer is within you.

NEW YORK EDITORS ...

IN TALKING TO A MAGAZINE in New York that is working on a feature story on George W. Bush and was thinking of doing a piece on S&B, I asked how about a sidebar on Antony Sutton? And got these responses:

"Someone is claiming he's a John Bircher. Liberty House is a right wing publishing company in Montana.

"Antony Sutton was at Stanford's conservative Hoover Institute.

"Among many other claims, Sutton's book accuses Skull and Bones of funding and encouraging 'the Maxist/Leftist '60s revolution'... and diverting attention by drawing students into disarmament and/or environmental groups and issues.

"Although there seems to be some real info in his book, it reads like a classic text of right-wing propaganda, filled with hyperbole and unsourced allegations."

Antony Sutton's response:

What's wrong with these editors?

I was thrown out of the Hoover Institution by the CIA types ... I am definitely persona non-grata. Director Glenn Campbell actually threatened me "you will not survive."

Some right winger!!

I've never been a member of the Birch Society or any society come to that.

I'd like to have that Editor say that to my face. They're sick!

Get his comments on the above ... and have him come up with some proof.

What's the legal definition of slander ... it has to be untrue and malicious. Do they have any money?

When it comes right down to it the NY people didn't even read my book ... else they would know that I see the right-left approach as a Hegelian trap ... as for lack of evidence I'll leave that to the readers. On second thought they probably never heard of Hegel.

When Lenin referred to 'useful idiots" he must have had these people in mind.

September 18, 1999 – More questions, More Answers

KM - *What has surprised you the most about America's Secret Establishment?*
AS - The most astonishing aspect of ASE is that the damn thing keeps selling with no advertising, no publicity, no help from me or the publisher. Astonishing and gratifying. It means that some readers see enough of value to pass the word. In terms of S&B discovery, nothing until very recently. I turned to other work (technology) and forgot about S&B. Recently I found extraordinary work by unknown people from the genealogical angle, This is definitely an advance.

All the royal families of Europe stem from the House of Saxe-Coburg-Gotha, that is where Weishaupt was installed. Its a 2 prong attack (1) via royal families and their descendents (2) via secret societies ... and the almighty State is the vehicle using dialectic methods.

KM - *Was there any reaction from Bones to your writings about the Order?*
AS - The material was removed from Yale Library promptly after the first edition was published in 1983, say within 4-6 months ... Members of S&B tried to make contact after about a year but both used phony names with their REAL ADDRESS, so I could find their real names. The content of their letters alerted me to check. Amateurs ... .

KM - *What was that material and did you make any copies?*
AS - From memory, it was about a magazine file thick, say 5 inches. Letters mostly, I selected a few for the book.

These materials still exist but so deeply hidden that it would cost several thousand dollars and much negotiation to regain. The holders don't know what they have and I don't know exactly where the material is. You can't say our spooky friends didn't teach us something ... .

KM - *What do you think S&B is planning now?*
AS - Plans ? I don't know. They look at the world through filters and "yes men." So while they have excellent information, they are dangerously off track in assessing the ordinary man. Their assumption is that they can buy, cajole or steal what they want and that everyone will go along. I see them as myopic juveniles ... .

KM - *Did ASE cause you any trouble?*

AS - From this book? Not at all ... The fireworks came much earlier in the early 1970's after publication of ***National Suicide*** (now ***Best Enemy Money Can Buy!***).

I am not looking for anything. Socially they are boring, so there is no basis for any discussion. One day they will hit a big bump in the road. Nothing to do with me.

KM - *Any last words?*
AS - Watch as events unfold. We are observers. They will destroy themselves. We can help a little but don't get any bright ideas about overturning the system. They have all the bombs but we have something stronger – the truth and freedom of spirit.

Be patient, spread the word among friends, do your little bit. The system will self destruct because it is founded on corruption and untruth.

Antony Sutton passed away on June 17, 2002. According to published accounts June 17th, 1933, was the date of the Order of Skull & Bone's *Century Celebration.* His death was sudden and unexpected. He was 77 and the local county coroner declared his passing, *natural causes.* Even after repeated contacts and pleas, no newspaper ran an obituary or story about his death and works. Tony died less than three weeks after the first hardbound copies of *America's Secret Establishment* were delivered from the printer. He was getting ready and was excited about appearing on radio shows to promote the book. The book was to be in West-Coast bookstores in September. Tony's death and a national book distribution opportunity changed the limited fall 2002 release to a national 2003 spring release. Meanwhile Little & Brown moved Alexandra Robbins' book (the first ever mainstream book on Bones) up to September, 2002 from January, 2003. Her book, *Secrets of the Tomb,* gets placed in the history section, whilst Tony's book gets placed in the *speculation* section with UFO's and such. Hmm, a book written by a member of the second oldest secret society at Yale, which declares Bones to be "the equivalent to the Wizard of Oz," that sometimes "Oz *needed* its Wizard" and disposes of the Nazi financing issue in one terse sentence is declared history, but a college professor's work on the same topic, that was the first book written about Bones and breaks many stories and research is just speculation. Such are the times we live in.

Antony had gone back to his engineering background and was producing a newsletter called *Future Technology Intelligence Review* (FTIR). Following is Tony's memoir about Stanford, some of his background and what happened to him because of his principles and courageous actions. After that are some of his thoughts on the September 11th attack and writings on the Order of Skull & Bones from FTIR and then some articles from *The Phoenix Newsletter,* Tony's newsletter from the 1980s and 90s, some from the time when he was first uncovering the story about Bones. The writing style is of a newsletter and that has been preserved, most of his underlined words and capitals have been turned to italics for presentation in book form

For more information about Antony Sutton visit
www.AntonySutton.com

Memoir Concerning Events At The Hoover Institution, Stanford University In The Period 1968 - 1974

[Relating to Suppression of Information by Washington, D.C.]

Antony Sutton
February 1996

BECAUSE THIS MEMOIR CONCERNS "PERCEPTIONS" of the Soviet Union and how this author avoided the conventional (and erroneous) artificial Soviet created propaganda perception, the memoir goes into formation of the author's own perceptions. These early paragraphs can be skipped.

The memoir also includes Appendix II, notes on a post-1974 event which repeated the perceptions problem in another context, and which the author tried to bring to official attention — again, unsuccessfully.

Early Background Of The Author

THE WRITER WAS EDUCATED at Bishopshalt Grammar School, Hillingdon Middlesex (outside London) from 1936 to 1941. This was the traditional English grammar school education with five years of two foreign languages, physics, biology, chemistry, music, history, geography, art, mathematics, English, wood and metal workshop with *no* elective courses and considerable homework. It was a thorough and no-nonsense basic education, very different from the U.S. high school.

My father was a coach builder for Thrupp & Mabberly, making Rolls Royce custom wood automobile bodies. My grandfather was former head coachman for the Duke of Beaumont. In the World War One period, he owned a fleet of a dozen London taxis. On my mother's side, the family stems from a line of substantial businessmen in the London furniture trade. My uncle formed the London Pattern company. In brief, I grew up in a family familiar with hand tools, jigs and fixtures, pattern making and automobile manufacture.

When I left Bishopshalt (in 1941 during World War II), I went to work for Richard Thomas Steel Company head office in London. This company had installed the first hot and cold strip steel mills in England. I worked in the mill scheduling department until called up to the Army in July 1943. Mill scheduling provides an excellent education in the capacity, operation and limits of steel mills and the end uses of various specifications.

In the Army, I was trained as a "driver-wireless operator" with extensive courses in radio communication (#19 and #22 sets), line laying, mine clearing, field maintenance, Morse code, codes and ciphers, all vehicles through personnel carriers. Just before D-Day, we were re-designated as the 42nd Armoured Division (a nominal deception unit with a handful of men and vehicles).

I landed in Normandy on D+10, and went through to Germany. For most of this time, numerous individual assignments gave me freedom for days at a time, and opportunity to learn something of European culture and industry. Seconded for six months to University of Gottingen for de-Nazification work. Demobilized 1947 with rank of sergeant.

In fall of 1947, I started at University of Southampton and obtained Honors Degree in Economics in 1951. The advantage of Southampton then (and now) is that students and faculty were flexible in study, ideas and work. Martin Fleischman and Stanley Pons did their early work on cold fusion at University of Southampton. In the 1940s, study was unregimented and free flowing. No grade point system.

A major plus was presence of an open Communist Party and recommended reading in Marx, Engels and Lenin. This proved to be an excellent foundation to understand the use of dialectical materialism and deception by the Soviets and their foreign Communists Party allies.

In 1951, I spent a few months as a clerk in a plant making gas meters and tinplate instruments; then returned to Richard Thomas & Co (now part of British Steel). I was appointed to a two years' management training course. This included visits to every major iron and steel plant in England with months spent on the floor of various plants including ore mining, blast furnaces, coke ovens, stripmills, tinplate and bypass mills, annealing and so on.

This two-year course gave me an understanding of the construction and operation of iron and steel plants and a reasonable grasp of metallurgy and metals testing.

By 1953, I had become disgusted with the laxity of nationalization. I left England and went to Canada via New York. I worked a year in Canadian steel firms, and then joined a mining exploration firm (Desmac Exploration, Ltd.) in charge of exploration logistics and information acquisition. By 1956, we had discovered major deposits of magnetite iron ore in Northern Quebec (Montgolfier Township) and had programs in several Canadian provinces. I acquired an introduction to geology and drilling techniques in order to evaluate potential mines. I left because it was too cold (i.e., -40° in winter!).

In 1957, I went to New York and was hired by Hoyland Steel as assistant to the manager of their Los Angeles branch, known as Great Western Steel, Inc. (the manager was an alcoholic, my job was to keep the firm on track, my eye on the manager, and quietly report back to New York). In this job, I visited every operating mine in the Western United States and Northern Mexico, and most of the significant plants, including the L.A. aircraft and electronics industries, i.e., Lockheed, Hughes, North American, and Douglas, as well as lumber mills, food processing and cement plants, quarries, and shipbuilding in California, to determine the potential for new alloys and specifications.

In November, 1957, 1 happened to be in the Motorola plant in Phoenix when the Russians sent up Sputnik. This had an enormous impact on the Motorola engineers, and I was struck by their naive acceptance, "The Russians are ahead of us." I knew from my steel experience that the gestation period for a strip mill was 6-8 years under western conditions, and the Russians could not have developed an indigenous strip process in the period 1917-1929 (the start of the first Five Year Plan). From my experience in post-war Germany, when the Soviets dismantled and shipped to Russia what was left of German industrial plants (really, a pile of junk), the "Russians are ahead" theory made no sense at all. Nowhere in my multi-country, multi-plant visits, had I encountered a Soviet process or innovation. My experience was the *opposite* to the prevailing perception of Soviet technological power.

My assessment was that the USSR in the 1950s and 1960s was a backward, technically dependent economy, without a support infrastructure.

In brief, by mid-1959, I had probably unique training with regard to on-the-floor exposure to industrial processes in five countries. I knew the equipment, who made it, its limits, and who used the equipment. Every technological process has its own "signature." For example, an iron blast furnace has precise shapes and measurements; it requires specific inputs of iron ore, coke, and limestone, of specific grades. You don't design a new blast furnace from scratch — you build on earlier designs with knowledge of limitations with each design change. These can be remarkably precise. Ask any engineer.

With this varied and detailed technological background, in 1959, 1 quit business and went to UCLA graduate school. My intent was to study the interface between economics and technology. Rather naively (I see today), I thought theoretical economics could teach me something about the efficiency factors behind engineering design. The immediate impact, however, was the rigid doctrinal structure of American graduate education. It turned out fine technicians, but was decidedly not happy with any original ideas or anything that challenged the textbooks.

Economics, I quickly found, treated technology as a constant given factor, not as a developing engineering dynamic. Once again, the assumption "The Russians are ahead" was the prevailing doctrine.

I spent considerable time in the UCLA Main Library and the Engineering Library where I located a wealth of material supporting my idea that everything Soviet had come from the West. I even found the original contract Averell Harriman signed with the Soviets to develop the Georgian manganese deposits. (He was taken! I had negotiated similar contracts in Canada, and could spot the loopholes.)

UCLA libraries also held several series of journals in Russian and English on 1930s construction by Western firms in Russia. These cited the foreign builders never mentioned in the UCLA textbooks on Soviet economic development. At first, I used these findings and ideas in seminars and papers, but soon found they were definitely not welcome, and the idea of challenging the textbooks bordered on treason. I found that prominent faculty such as Armen Alchian and Jack Hirschleifer, who also worked at Rand Corporation on Russian strategy, had naive ideas on Russian economic development and knew nothing — and I mean, *nothing*— about technology. Products were called, "widgets;" and technology was treated as a constant "given," rather than a dynamic engineering process. I did considerable research for Professor Dudley Pegrum and W.E. Baldwin in transportation and the African copper industry, and wrote an article on the Colombian iron industry, which was later published.

The textbooks and article literature on Soviet economic development had a truck-size omission: there was *nothing* on the development and *origins* of the technology used in the USSR. Every text and article had an extremely naive and erroneous description of Soviet development. There were no exceptions to this statement. Even Clark's ***The Economics of Soviet Steel***, an otherwise excellent book, had missed the Western origins. Another book was ***Economics of Technology***, published in the early 60s, and had no understanding of technology. It was a meaningless mass of mathematics with no relevance to technology in the slightest. Not one technological process was cited. I feel today as I did 30 years ago — the book is a fraud, but accepted in the academic community as an advance of knowledge.

Gradually, I developed a technique in my own research. Assume every Soviet design is indigenous; compare it to similar Western designs known from past experience; locate a transfer mechanism, i.e., installed by Western firms, taken from patent literature, copied within the Soviet Union in a "copying bureau." Then compare design specifications. Always assume the design is Soviet, unless the opposite can be proven.

The UCLA Ph.D. program was not completed. In one topic (macroeconomics), I was told to repeat one question of the Ph.D. finals, but to go ahead with the dissertation (which I did). The Department then gave me a new set of multiple questions. UCLA then denied the Ph.D. I later obtained two D.Sc. degrees elsewhere. Dr. Dudley Pegrum, Chairman of my Committee, then pushed me as Assistant Professor of Economics at (now) State University of California, Los Angeles.

The same kind of political pressure developed when I came up for tenure at Cal State in 1968. It was approved at the department level. Then tenure was rejected at the Administration level - even though my first book had been accepted at Hoover Institution and *no Cal State economics faculty member had a published book at that time.*

There is no question my views on Soviet weaknesses were the cause. In 1963, when I gave a lecture on Soviet development to the faculty, I made the blunt statement that Marxist central planning was not viable without outside help. The USSR stagnant, and this was a fatal flaw. When I stated that "Marxism is finished," one could feel the intense disapproval - almost, emotional distress - in the audience. By the early 1960s, it was clear that my perception of the Soviet Union as a technically backward and dependent economy was highly unwelcome to everyone else. The experiences at Motorola, UCLA and Cal State were consistent, in that I found no one agreed with my view of the Soviet Union as a backward, stagnant economy. Soviet propaganda was extraordinarily successful with its progressive image.

WESTERN TECHNOLOGY AND SOVIET ECONOMIC DEVELOPMENT

AS A UCLA GRADUATE STUDENT, I began in 1959 to explore the early technological history of the Soviet Union, and to learn technical Russian (enough to translate technical manuals). I said little about this work (except the one lecture cited above), which continued in my five years at Cal State Los Angeles. At Cal State, I engaged a tutor from the faculty to improve my Russian reading skills.

While at Cal State, I tried to obtain funding to speed up the work. All I could get was $400 for microfilm of State Department documents from Relm Foundation. In the early 1960s, I read scores of rolls of State documents, including reports from officers in Moscow, Leningrad, and Riga, Latvia. These included interviews with American businessmen returning from Russia, and detailed plans and specifications for plants installed by the West. (Magnitogorsk, Gorki, Uralmash, etc.). These businessmen were not always honest with State officers. They wanted to maintain Soviet good will. A few told State officials they were instructed to paint a rosy picture if they wanted contracts.

The State files supported my theory of technical dependence. However, I noted that State was reluctant to release certain documents on the purport lists. I made a special point to push for declassification, where I found State resistance. In practice, the resistance guided me to the real gold mines of information.

Through Blackwells (Booksellers) in Oxford, England, I bought hundreds of Soviet technical manuals and maintenance charts. It was fascinating to trace the technology in these manuals to systems I knew in the West. Even the Western language was adopted — for example, "Stilsona" for "Stilson wrench." The maintenance and training charts were invaluable in tracing origins. To this day, I don't understand why the Soviet Union allowed export of these items. For someone who knew the technology, it was like labeling the Western manufacturer. The Soviet copying bureaus were helpful. They duplicated EXACTLY the Western design. In consumer products, however, the Soviets often used military spec materials, yielding an overweight, clumsy product. Sometimes, the Soviets varied the way a part was made, i.e., by casting or stamping instead of forging.

In 1963, the State Department public view was "the Soviets have their own self developed technology" — i.e., *Directly contrary to their own files.*

By 1966, 1 had completed the first volume of *Western Technology and Soviet Economic Development (1917 to 1930).* It took about eight years, using my own funds (except $400), and with the facts consistently pointing away from academic and official statements and assumptions.

Soviet technology *was* western technology — period. Soviet attempts at innovation (i.e., the electric tractor) were pitiful.

The manuscript was sent unsolicited to Henry Regnery Company in Chicago. I was surprised to receive a reply letter from Henry Regnery himself, to the effect this was "an extremely important manuscript but not commercial." I wrote Hoover and received a letter back from Alan Belmont (Assistant Director). He had taken early retirement from the FBI, where he was Assistant Director for Domestic Intelligence. In response, I sent the manuscript to Hoover. Belmont suggested I spend the summer of 1966 at Hoover. I accepted. During this summer, I kept a low profile, avoided the social circuit (much to Director Glenn Campbell's disgust), and concentrated on work. Frankly, I didn't want a repeat of the UCLA and Cal State hostility. Only Al Belmont appeared to understand my hermit-like stance, and I will be eternally grateful for his understanding, and the "cover" he provided me, unasked.

I found that Belmont had insisted Roger Freeman, a long-time friend of Director Campbell, a man of many contacts and a former White House Aide, read the manuscript. Belmont then sent it to ex-Russian engineers for evaluation. The Russians were definite: "Sutton is right." Belmont told me this, and added the manuscript was also going to Sovietologists, but not to worry if they made adverse comments. (He once said something to the effect, "we do not accept them.") At some point, Roger Freeman told me that "they" (i.e., White House or CIA) didn't know about the "early period." I remember saying that my work should be repeated and double checked. It made our policy towards the Soviet Union naive and idiotic.

I agreed to return to Cal State for another year, and then go to Hoover as a Research Fellow to complete the two further volumes. Campbell has claimed that Hoover financed the first volume also. They did not. I submitted a complete Volume One, financed by myself. I returned to Hoover about mid-1968 and completed the two volumes by 1971. Volumes One and Two were brought into print fairly quickly. I had only one minor problem with the Editors. They wanted to remove everything on Soviet military use of our technology. I agreed to this.

I completed Volume Three by 1971 and anticipated it would be published promptly, like the first two volumes. In fact, it went quickly to page proof, which I corrected — then I heard nothing for a year. Normally, a book moves quickly from page proof to final book to recoup investment. My inquiries were met with a blank wall. All I could get from Al Belmont was, "It's coming."

We had a war in Vietnam, and I could daily see the product of U.S. and European technology killing our men in Vietnam, while we were still supplying technology for Soviet plants to manufacture weapons and supplies for North Vietnam. I considered this immoral and lunatic behavior. Further, I had personal experience of war in Normandy, in Belgium and the Rhine Crossing in March, 1945. Active war is not pleasant. Its cold, dirty, dangerous. My concern was with men on the ground in Vietnam rather than armchair academics and politicians who had probably never been on the dangerous end of a gun, but who were making technological decisions without knowing technology. In particular, I was horrified at State Department statements directly opposed to materials in their own files.

I decided to do an end-run around whomever was delaying the third volume, which had current application to policy, and was obviously being delayed. I agreed with Arlington House to quietly write another volume on the military use of our technological transfers and so-called, "peaceful trade." My planned, deliberate objective was to spring loose my Volume Three, by publishing the segments Hoover wanted "out" — i.e., the military end-use segments supplied by the West — and so, force their hand. I fully admit this was my intent. I would do the same again, only quicker, and with more publicity.

About this time, Henry Kissinger OK'd export of the Centalign B machines to the Soviet Union. These had only one end use — to machine ball-bearing races to extremely high accuracy for MIRV-ing Soviet missiles. The USSR could then pinpoint-target the United States. The Washington arguments were wrong. (However, DOD had people warning of the dangers.) The Soviets could not manufacture Centalign B machines, and no one else in the world had an equivalent machine.

Kissinger's action confirmed to me that something was badly wrong in Washington. His "detente" strategy was to give the Soviet long-term, needed technological advantage in exchange for short-term political promises which might or might not be kept. Kissinger called this policy "linkages." I called it "lunacy." We were handing over what Soviets *really* wanted (advanced technology) to receive empty words. It still baffles me how Kissinger can be regarded as an "expert." Anyone can hand over the keys to the safe and ask nothing in return.

Further, the McNamara "rules of engagement" had tied the hands of the military in Vietnam. In effect, we helped the Soviets build trucks, and then told our pilots not to shoot them up. When one looked at the entire picture, I could only arrive at one conclusion — treason.

I have never formed final conclusion on policy makers like Kissinger, Rusk and McNamara. It could be stupidity, ignorance, ego, or worse. Frankly, I don't know. When foreign diplomats and military people asked me, "do you think Kissinger is a Soviet agent?" I replied, "I don't know. He could be ignorant."

I told no one except Arlington House about National Suicide. It was written in three months, and rushed through production in another three months. It was published as, *National Suicide: Military Aid to the Soviet Union* (available today as, "*The Best Enemy Money Can Buy*"). My advance copy is marked, "Received August 27th, 1973." When it was received, Volume Three of Western Technology and Soviet Economic Development was still being held in page proofs, confirming my belief that the delay was deliberate to prevent the information becoming public. (This was 8 months after correction of page proofs.) From rumors, it appeared the pressure was coming from the White House.

Some days after receiving my advance copy of *National Suicide*, I received a call to go to the Director's office (Glenn Campbell). I found a group waiting, including Alan Belmont, Dick Staar (CIA), Stefan Possony, and perhaps a few others. Campbell immediately launched into an attack, stating that I had plagiarized the text of National Suicide, and that I had no right to produce such a book.

My reply was: (1) 1 cannot plagiarize my own work; (2) Hoover itself had asked for the military sections to be removed from Hoover volumes, thus releasing the material; (3) We had men being killed in Vietnam, and I had every right and duty to draw public attention to this if our policies were aiding the enemy; and (4) 1 remember saying, "tell me where I am wrong on a single fact." No one ever did.

I gave some examples, i.e., we were sending machine tools to the Gorki truck plant outside Moscow, and GAZ (Gorki) trucks were on the Ho Chi Minh Trail. The U.S. pilots even commented they looked like Ford trucks (Gorki was built by Ford Motor Company).

Soviet ships on the supply run to North Vietnam were larger, faster vessels, sold by the West under "peaceful trade." I had obtained a list of the vessels from sources that emerged from the woodwork after publication of my first book. From the Soviet Register of Shipping, I located the type, design and origin of every Soviet marine diesel engine. Most were Burmeister and Wain (Denmark), or Soviet copies.

In brief, my information was precise and accurate. Campbell asked me to have National Suicide withdrawn. I refused. End of meeting.

I called Arlington, and they assured me they would not buckle or withdraw the book.

Another meeting followed a few weeks later. Campbell said I had no agreement or contract with Hoover Institution, and I was no longer a Research Fellow. To stall for time, I said I did have a contract (actually, I did not), and I had no intention of changing my position.

I later heard that a few Senators and Congressmen had called Campbell to support me. A week later, Al Belmont came to my office and handed me a contract, signed by himself, with the words, "You are going to need this."

Hoover Institution then removed my name and that of my secretary from the Hoover personnel list. I became a non-person. In subsequent speeches, I found this Hoover Institution action to have significant impact on audiences. Apparently, it convinced people that I was probably right. Hoover also rapidly released Volume Three. They continued to pay me until I left voluntarily a year later. On the way out the door on the last day, Roger Freeman intercepted me and said, "We can work this out; let me talk with Campbell." I said thank you, but no thanks.

My sense was one of absolute disgust. I had, with my own funds and time, undertaken ten years of research of obvious value to the United States, and put up with the naive stupidity of academics at UCLA and Cal State to get the work into print. The response? — insult and harassment!

I concluded Campbell was a weak patsy, and that Washington didn't give a damn about our men in Vietnam. (This is still my assessment today.) The academic world by and large was more interested in preserving its little stock of knowledge. Academic freedom is a sham.

My thanks came from individual citizens. After speeches, scores would come up and say, "God bless you," or, "We are with you." One speech filled the Hollywood Palladium with standees at the back. At the end of the speech, I was called back three times to the podium. The more macabre would say, "it's a wonder you are still alive."

A few gestures were practical. A group of anonymous airline pilots gave me (through a friend) a gift of $10,000. A Congressman inserted my speeches into the Congressional record. I had a call from Antoine Pinay, former Prime Minister of France. Several VFW posts passed resolutions of commendation. And so on.

Not once did anyone challenge the data or the argument. The press ignored the books (with the exception of the *Manchester Union Leader* in New Hampshire and the *Telegraph* in London). However, on a later visit to London, The *Times* sent a message asking me to meet with the Editor (now Lord Rees-Mogg), who asked a key question: "Why do you think they are so upset?" Roughly, my answer was, "I really don't know. I guess I must be close to the truth."

I made a number of foreign trips, and met senior military or government people from Mexico, Argentina, South Africa, France, Belgium and other countries.

About 1969, Campbell urged me to submit my first volume to the University of London for a Ph.D. This I did. As I had scores of favorable academic reviews, the procedure should have been automatic. Peter Wiles was appointed examiner, and proceeded to raise every conceivable petty point possible. I made two trips to London, and did what I could to answer his points. In the end, I gave up, and figured it was another academic game.

In about 1970, I was contacted by a Colonel Samuel Clabaugh, who at one time had been U.S. military attache in London, a friend of Averell Harriman, and, formerly, with OSS and CIA. He was apparently in routine contact with Eleanor Dulles. Over perhaps a year or 18 months, we exchanged letters and meetings (I went to his apartment in Washington, D.C. for lunch). I was quite clear and definite: our policy is suicidal, developed by the naive or self serving. I remember repeatedly making the point; if I am wrong, someone will challenge me, but all we have is silence. *No one dares challenge me.* I know the technology, and I am right.

About 1971, Hoover Institution wanted me to give a paper at Ditchley Park in England to a group of businessmen, bankers and academics. This is where I met M. Pinay, former Prime Minister of France, who greeted me, "Tres bien; tres bien." At one point, the Chairman of Dunlop Holdings (who had built several plants in the Soviet Union) stood up and said, "Sutton's information is correct; we have built tire plants in the USSR for many years, and we will continue to build these plants even if it is my own suicide." Even today, I can't fully understand the motivation behind this statement. It's not rational, but that's what the man said. It raises the question of whether some form of brainwashing was used on foreign businessmen. I know there was pressure.

Over the years, my conclusions have firmed up roughly as follows:

1. The U.S. was suckered royally by Soviet propaganda (the "perception problem").

In most cases, the conduits were not agents (like Ames), but individual businessmen, academics, and politicians looking out for their own interests and proposing self-serving policies without challenge.

2. My argument was correct and remains correct today. The Soviet Union was incapable of self-sustaining development and relied on the West for most technical advance. The Russians are very capable people; it was the system that failed, the lack of a mechanism to transform ideas to technical reality in a rational, useful way.

3. My experience has been that the academic world is largely concerned with preserving the status quo and its own perks and prestige. Really new ideas are automatically dismissed. To me, this makes the entire fabric of degrees and honors suspect. These reflect merely an ability to absorb what is already known, not any contribution to future knowledge.

4. My greatest surprise is the sheer lack of moral action. No one asks, what is right?

What is moral? I find this entirely disgusting and shortsighted. The truth will always out, sooner or later. I prefer to be remembered as someone honestly concerned with others, rather than as a sham, self-serving political type. Glenn Campbell even sneered at my moral approach in one well-remembered conversation:

GC: "Tony, you have a problem."
TS: "What is that?"
GC: "You are a moralist."
TS: "So?"
GC: "You can't survive being a moralist. They will break your rice bowl."

On the other hand, no individual, and certainly no country survives without a set of principles. Pragmatism is shortsighted, a crutch for the weak, a cop-out for the greedy.

5. Certain names stand out as key in the Soviet perceptions program and successful operation at the highest levels in Washington:

Armand Hammer. Son of Julius Hammer (founder and financier for the Communist Party U.S.A.). Access to every President from Roosevelt onwards.

Protected at the highest levels in Washington.

Averell Harriman. Received $1 million gift from Soviets about 1928. (1 can provide the State Department file numbers if required.) State Department was told, "hands off" on Harriman. Key member of the Georgetown group that had major influence on policy and intelligence.

Henry Kissinger. I need only quote Anatoly Dobrynin (*In Confidence*, Random House, 1995). "... more than once when Kissinger knew I was going over to the State Department he would ask me to bear in mind that Rogers had not been told about this, that or some other aspect of the issue under discussion and I was not to tell Rogers about it."

Out of the hundreds of examples, I would select the export of Centalign B machines as the key to determine whose side Kissinger was on. I presume there was no mark program on our side (see Appendix), and in fact, it would be difficult because the product has precise measurable characteristics. *Kissinger, over numerous DOD protests, provided the USSR with MIRVing capability.*

Unless there was some deception program on our side which required Kissinger's action as a cover, then one is driven to the conclusion — unwelcome as it is —that Kissinger was a Soviet agent. Sutton was just one irritant in a larger game, but if the strings provided in the Sutton research were pulled, he had the capability of unraveling the entire Soviet perceptions program.

No one has stepped forward, in 1996 — or even in 2001 — to say, Sutton was right or wrong, because, even today, reputations are at stake. The United States owes me an official apology. When they should have encouraged me to work further to pull on the strings, I was squashed, threatened, harassed, and discarded — for whose benefit?

The Ames Case

The significance of Ames is not that a Soviet agent existed in CIA. This was discussed widely back in the 1970s and before. Even names were floating around. The significance is that Ames surfaces the perceptions program in a way that could not be done by any academic writer. The Soviets paid Ames well — very well, by Soviet standards — to maintain a facade. There were many ways Ames could be used; this was judged to be the most important. And it confirms what I had been saying since the late 1950s. When Lenin wrote about the "useful idiots," and the "deaf, mute blindmen," one wonders if he knew how successful his perceptions program was going to be. Lenin suckered the West royally. Ames is a pitiful pawn, but if you pull on the Ames string, you'll find the rest of the story — and more names.

Be prepared for some shocks.

Appendix 1: The Mark Program

In research on technical transfers, I was alert for specification changes in equipment which could affect quality, quantity and product obsolescence. In brief, it is possible by slightly changing specifications of manufacturing equipment, to affect quality and performance of the end product. For example, changing the dimensions and shape of a blast furnace has significant effect on cost, quality and quantity of output. By slight variations in equipment sold to the USSR, one could reduce the benefits. By changing the tensile strength of steel or design parameters, for example, one can influence the quality of the end product. On one or two occasions in State files, I caught reference to a "mark" program (i.e., to sell sub-standard equipment); and elsewhere, statements to the effect that Western businessmen sold outdated designs to the Soviets.

No mention is made in any of my books to this "mark" program. I did once mention it to Alan Belmont, i.e., that I knew of the possibility of such a program; that, if implemented, it was not effective; and I had not mentioned the possibility even in passing.

Possibly, Soviet political intervention into technology made such a program partly unnecessary. A great deal of equipment was ruined because Soviet political figures insisted on early and fast startups, insufficient maintenance and inadequate training. Russian engineers up to the 70s had about the same hands-on technical experience as a master mechanic in the United States. This has probably changed in some fields, i.e., computers and software.

Another factor is the absence of a secondary infrastructure in the Soviet Union. In the United States, thousands of machine shops, tool and die shops, and independent experts of all kinds give a wealth of backup experience where and when needed. This market-generated structure gives a richness of experience and flexibility to major corporations. The Soviet Union had nothing remotely similar; everything was handled "inhouse."

It is possible that CIA decided a "mark" program was unnecessary, i.e., it was *really* suckered by the Soviets, and truly believed the Soviet Union had a super-power industrial structure. Or, a mark program may have been inadequately designed. In any event, a mark program was not identified. However, it is difficult to believe that some key technologies (as the Centalign B) were not modified before shipment, if only as insurance. If we did not have such a program for key technologies, one has to ask, why not?

This raises another question. Why did policy debate always focus on the last sale or contract (i.e., the marginal unit) rather than the total of all sales in that technology. If debate was focused on the total industry, rather than single contract, then Soviet dependence is obvious.

In my exploration of the State files, I found that State Department officials filed reports with military information *without distribution.* The information was killed. To gauge the success of the Soviet perceptions program, one would have to thoroughly explore the hidden recesses of CIA to determine if a mark program was implemented at any point, in any way. If CIA considered such a program and rejected it, then the U.S. really *did* have a perceptions problem of extraordinary magnitude. For example, if Kissinger allowed the Centalign Bs to go forward without a mark program, then one has to have the most serious suspicions of Kissinger's motives.

I have no way of knowing the truth. However, one can deduce a problem from other technologies allowed to go forward, and where tracking subsequent operation proved that the Soviets had received the most advanced technology (i.e., advanced aluminum rolling equipment, marine diesels, and so on) *without modifications.* Example: the ships on the Haiphong run were the largest and fastest, and all had marine diesels imported from the West.

In brief, the U.S. should have had a mark program. I do not have enough data to say whether such a program existed or not. However, this would be a fruitful target for exploration of past files. If such a program was not implemented, why not? — and if it was, why did it fail?

APPENDIX TWO: LESSONS NOT LEARNED

THE HOOVER INSTITUTION SAGA starts up again in 1985 with a repeat of the perceptions disaster, and one that may have long-term consequences worse than the Soviet perceptions program. U.S. scientists are running what amounts to a scam to keep their gravy train flowing. This is losing lead time for the United States. A new technological paradigm is emerging and the science establishment is doing its best to deride and ignore the facts.

After leaving Hoover Institution, I continued to work on technological research. I found it relatively easy to earn a modest living as an author (in spite of Campbell's prediction that my rice bowl would be broken), and in the last 20 years, have authored another 20 or so books. I found regular bookstore distribution closed to my books. Campbell was right in this aspect. But apparently others were having *their* rice bowls broken, and a vast "alternative" book publishing industry is in great part due to the rise of new publishing houses scattered across the United States, handling the work of those who have been persecuted, or whose writing falls outside the narrow New York guidelines.

In any event, I generated enough spare time to work on technology. My exploration went back to ancient technology and science, through alchemy, Goethe, the Steiner movement, and Wilhelm Reich, as well as discarded discoveries of the last 200 years. I found hundreds of ideas and discoveries had been buried for political or financial reasons. In particular, I found that the ancients "knew something we don't today." I found that "underground" researchers were probing modern discoveries inconsistent with and wholly beyond our materialist view of the universe. The energy-matter equations, the basis of physics and the "laws" based on these equations were under assault - partly from researchers in Oriental traditions, and partly from workbench research picking up some of Faraday's observations back in 1831. Other developments were coming from the work of Wilhelm Reich and the anthroposophic tradition. Future 21st century technology will be a paradigm reflecting these discoveries, ignored in the materialist tradition.

Futurists see the future as extrapolation of the heat-pressure/centrifugal-expansion technologies of the industrial age, plus semiconductor technologies. What I see is an entirely new paradigm based on cold vacuum/centripetal vortex technologies, with semiconductors as enabling technology only. Quite different from, and far more powerful than our contemporary technology, and environmentally pure.

About 1985, 1 wrote to Glenn Campbell (who had been Reagan's Chairman of the Foreign Intelligence Advisory Board, and the logical recipient for any such ideas), and suggested the new paradigm should be investigated. Campbell probably thought I was looking for some kind of grant (I wasn't), and passed me on to Roger Freeman. I met with Roger Freeman at his house on the Stanford campus and briefly outlined my ideas. I told Freeman, "I am not looking for anything. I am concerned with the future of this country. The science establishment, like the Sovietological establishment, is protecting its turf for self-serving reasons."

Roger Freeman suggested I should see Edward Teller, whom he described as open minded. I found it difficult to get across the point that "open mindedness" is not enough when dealing with a scientific culture that has thoroughly permeated our society. What my analysis suggested was existence of a superior technology to our contemporary technological paradigm, and it would be most unlikely that Teller could grasp its elements, any more than Kissinger had grasped the elements of Soviet technological dependence.

I understand that Teller did agree to talk, but the meeting did not take place. Frankly, I wasn't going to waste my time. I had been insulted and abused trying to help the United States, and I wasn't going to risk any more abuse from "deaf mute blindmen" (Lenin). Time would show whether I was right or wrong. If the gatekeepers won't listen, *they* have the problem, not me.

Just three years after this Stanford meeting, Pons and Fleischman announced "cold fusion." This was instantly derided as *fraudulent* by the orthodox physics establishment, and Pons and Fleischman were driven out of the United States to France. Teller's reaction to cold fusion confirmed I was right in not pursuing the Freeman suggestion. Cold fusion is part of the new paradigm. In the last few months of 1995, the U.S. government has confirmed its viability. If Campbell had taken me seriously in 1985, it is quite possible that Pons and Fleischman would have had more favorable reception. In fact, the Japanese now finance their work in the south of France, and the U.S. now admits they are correct - but has lost a decade of lead time.

By extraordinary coincidence, Fleischman taught electrochemistry at University of Southampton (where I studied in 1948) and Pons was his graduate student also at Southampton. (Further, one of the leading researchers in the new paradigm is Harold Aspden, today, at Southampton.)

In January, 1990, 1 started Future Technology Intelligence Report to record my analysis, and as a device to pick up information. For six years, I have recorded monthly my ongoing work, a matter of record for history to read.

Once again the myopic vision of U.S. technical intelligence is highlighted. Ames is a disaster. Yet the gatekeepers of science and policy are creating another disaster, and will place the U.S. into irreversible technological decline by ignoring the new paradigm.

We have politicized decision making in technology, and U.S. politics is a poor guide to technological decision making. A moral approach would have saved the U.S. yet another embarrassment. If Campbell had taken steps to correct the injustice done to this writer in 1971 (and earlier), then the cold fusion reaction could have emerged in a different environment . I was already aware of over unity devices, and was looking at over unity N-machines when I approached Campbell in 1985. In fact, if Campbell had backed me in 1987, the U.S. would have arrived at a quicker and more accurate assessment of the emerging paradigm, and would have been ready for the hostile resistance that was forthcoming within the U.S. science establishment.

If anything, the treatment of my research is proof that in the long run, the moral approach is the only practical approach.

Just because Edward Teller designed the H-bomb doesn't ensure he will understand N-machines, cold fusion, or etheric weather control. These are outside the orthodox physicists' framework of understanding, outside the laws of physics, and require study of an entirely new framework of analysis, which is at this time incomplete. The only agreement in cold fusion, for example, is that "something" happens in the lattice structure. The "something" is under discussion and investigation. Much like electricity in the 1850s before Maxwell perfected the theoretical understanding. Etheric weather engineering is even more challenging. I have found that mathematicians (who appreciate golden proportions) are more understanding than meteorologists. In general, electrical engineers appear to grasp the new paradigm more readily. (Kincheloe, de Palma, Constable, Aspden, Tiller, Inomata, Tewari, etc.)

My greatest criticism and sorrow is that decisions on research directions are taken by those with the most to lose by change and who rationalize obstruction by clinging to obsolete ideas and citing obsolete, man-made "laws." That's no way to make progress — or for a country to survive.

Tony's Newsletters

ANTONY SUTTON produced several different newsletters during his lifetime as a way to stay in touch with his many readers and to continue his research on his many varied interests. The revenues were meager but did help to defray his research costs. From 1982 to 1997, he issued the *Phoenix Letter* and from 1990 until his passing, he published *Future Technology Intelligence Review (FTIR).* Here from October 2001 to April 2002 FTIRs is Tony sharing his thoughts on the September 11th attack and an article on Skull & Bones that he had written before the terror event. These are followed by articles from his *Phoenix Letter* about the Order of Skull & Bones. Some from when he first began writing about the Order.

FUTURE TECHNOLOGY INTELLIGENCE REPORT

A Monthly News Letter Devoted to Technical Prediction
Antony Sutton, DSc - October 2001: Vol 12, No. 10

The Future Is Here And Now – Bush Is Still Back In 1831

WHY 1831? Because German philosopher Georg Hegel died in 1831 and the Hegelian secret society (Yale) Skull & Bones, to which Bush has sworn eternal silence, was created in 1832.

Like Nazism, Communism, and Prussianism, groups, like S & B and Bohemian Grove are based on statist Hegelian idealism, the precise opposite of our ideal of Constitutional liberty and individual rights. The Owl of Minerva is the symbol of Bohemian Grove and the *Owl of Minerva* is also the title of the Hegelian Society Journal in the United States.

So what, you say? Because you will understand coming events in future technology and the roles of S & B and Bohemian Grove much better if you put to one side the artificial divisions of left and right, Republican and Democrat, and the hypocritical prattling of their members.

These elitist groups are Hegelian and believe the State is run for the benefit of the "Masters" (Hegel's term). We are mere "Slaves," the peons, who do their bidding. Understand this and you will understand the trials that await New Technology down the road a way. Okay, you say, but I always knew we were peons, and somebody unelected was running the show. The point is that no academic has yet pinned this control down to an operating philosophy working in defiance of the U.S. Constitution. Suspicion is not enough. Throwing names around is not enough. Big charts with lots of arrows is not enough. We have to pin down the how and why, the *operational procedures.* If we are right in our analysis, you will in coming years see another layer of the onion skin peeled back. *The Emperor really has no clothes.*

The Bush Administration is no different from the Clinton Administration when it comes to new and more efficient energy technology. Both Administrations publicly ignore new technology or define it as beefed up, old technology to favor those interests who pay vast sums to support the two major parties — and get a piece of the action.

We hesitate to recommend Hegel for your reading. We see Hegel as turgid nonsense, but very influential. If you want Hegel's statement on the relations between "Master" (them) and "Slave" (us), see pages 520 to 523 of *Phenomenology of Spirit.* This is the section on "Lordship and Bondage." (We term it, "Master and Slave"):

The self consciousness of the Lord is essentially related to the being of the mere things he uses and uses up, and these he enjoys through the bondsman's (slave) self consciousness. The bondsman prepares and arranges things for the enjoyment of the Lord.

In brief, the function of us — the slaves — is to work for the Master. See Bush/Cheney as the Lord and you and I as the slaves, then it all becomes clear. Our job is to go along. Theirs is to steal and grab and enjoy the product. The State is the vehicle they use to grab the product legally. The State is the Master, and we are supposed to be obedient slaves. Quite a racket, if you can keep it going. And this is the purpose of Bohemian Grove and Skull & Bones. Clever, isn't it? You are all running around thinking Republican and Democrat, while the real action is somewhere else.

So within this Hegelian frame, let's take a look at the Bush-Cheney energy plan.

The Bush-Cheney energy plan is wholly based on conventional fossil-atomic technology owned by the same interests that financed Bush and are prominent in the S & B and Bohemian Grove. If the steam and water wheel interests had kicked in for his re-election, no doubt they would have a place in the Bush-Cheney Plan. It's all about cash for re-election, put up enough cash, and you become one of the Masters.

Bush actions follow closely Hegel's plan for the "Masters." The Masters should not be interested (according to Hegel) in new discovery. Leave that for the slaves to develop. "Masters" prefer to milk the old, which generates profit and give them control. Hegel is therefore intimately related to Skull & Bones and Bohemian Grove. The reason that outside observers have not been able to get a handle on establishment power is because they have been trapped into a right-left dichotomy and kept there by carefully baited political promises, rarely kept except to financial contributors.

Collection of names and organizations is insufficient. One needs to know their operating philosophy to learn their goals and how they achieve their goals. This is not political meandering. Unless you understand the control features in today's world, you cannot make correct decisions on future technology.

The input for the Bush-Cheney energy plan came only from conventional energy interests. The Administration refuses to release the working papers. Why? Because these will demonstrate that only a few energy firms got access to Cheney with their proposals. These were clearly self-serving proposals. No one else was even considered. Certainly not renewable energy sources or free energy. Just as Hegel would have it. Those who gather at Bohemian Grove and Bones — the Masters — got the rewards. The citizen slaves who do the thinking and the development get nothing.

Same with Clinton. The Clinton Administration engineered a sabotage plan in 1996 to collapse the Congress on Free Energy scheduled to be held in Washington, D.C. Bush-Cheney just left them out of consideration.

This closed-shop procedure is, of course, the fascist tableau, and directly out of Hegel, who also provides the philosophic fuel for fascism and communism. So far, only a few commentators have made this observation, and wherever you took your "poli-sci" courses didn't tell you this.

Our name for the Bush-Clinton version is "smiling fascism," and it stems directly from the "right Hegelians" of the 19th century. Bush himself can trace to 1832 through Skull and Bones, and its formation in 1832 in Hegelian Germany and the U.S. Even Domhoff, who has written in detail about Bohemian Grove, missed the link to Hegel through Minerva the Owl.

Today, according to our sources, Morgan Stanley is preparing the IPO for Black Light Power (proven free energy). It will come to market in about two years. Wall Street (a lot of the Masters hang out in Wall Street) needs these two years to dump conventional energy assets. But don't be surprised if a wrench gets thrown into the works. We don't trust Washington, D.C. one bit when it comes to New Technology or what they will do with the technology as they try to seize control.

Similarly, California utilities are trying to dump their resource assets onto the State and the taxpayer before they become worthless. This is right on schedule as we predicted many years ago. First, fuel cells will have a run in about 2003 and 2004. Then free energy will start to emerge.

By 2005, everybody and his dog will be looking for free energy proposals. Another dot.com mania in the works. This will be the time to be very, very wary.

The most probable systems are already known today, but, suddenly, you will be offered participation in a score of systems whose free energy potential cannot be proven.

By 2005, the insiders will have dumped conventional energy assets long before the BLP IPO hits the market. Be careful. We know of only three, maybe four useful free energy technologies: BLP, MEG, Cold Fusion, and a Canadian project, already picked off by the U.S. Navy.

MEG is not in as strong a position as BLP because Colonel Bearden is U.S. Army (Retired), and subject to pressure. We like his technical approach, but Bearden himself well knows the pressures he faces.

Cold fusion is fully proven, but not yet repeatable. It was deliberately crippled, early on. The initial blow to destroy was cast by former President Bush (also S & B) in 1989. The Canadian project is based on nanotechnology and is way over unity (>1000%). This was demonstrated to the U.S. Navy — and then disappeared.

Note also that BLP has a director (Brewer) who was former Assistant Secretary of Energy in the Reagan Administration. BLP is described by the Internet service, <psst-heyu.com> as the "one that got away."

Maybe not quite a plausible theory is that if free energy is to emerge, the U.S. Government (run by the Masters) would much prefer a government monopoly or control by interests close to the Masters. In other words, make a profit out of something essentially free. How to seize it? There are many ways. At the moment, we say no more.

Free energy would of course be a useful lever to promote their New World Order. NWO could then come charging down the road as a White Knight to rescue the world from energy paralysis.

A SECOND TECHNOLOGICAL REVOLUTION

Almost simultaneously, the revolutionary potential in radionics is emerging. But out of England, not the U.S. The AMA believes it has this potential locked up. We don't think so. What may happen is this: the AMA will suddenly get religion and adopt radionics. Stranger things have happened.

Most important here is the theoretical justification for radionics formulated in the work of the late famed quantum physicist, David Bohm, one-time Professor of Physics at University of London.

Take a look at Chapter 7 of *The Undivided Universe*, by Bohm & Hiley, entitled "Non locality." Bohm says the opposition to "non locality" (this is what physicists call "action at a distance") has a historical explanation, and Einstein's "spooky action" comment is not based on science or logic, but on mere assumption.

While Maperton provides proof of concept for non locality and neatly gets around AMA/FDA dictates by computerization, David Bohm is the source for theoretical support.

But most people are like Einstein and think of all action as local. This assumption does not reflect observation, and in fact, is a continuation of Isaac Newton's comment that non locality is a "philosophical absurdity."

The establishment is headed, then, towards two roadblocks. Free energy is here, proven and scheduled for installation about 2004 - 2005. The earlier Bush administration shot down cold fusion with a stacked Blue Ribbon Committee, but Randall Mills was too persistent and thorough. The government will have to make a deal with Mills or go the seizure route.

Medical radionics is here, proven and available, free today.

Note the use of the word "free" in both cases. Not quite free, but close enough. If it is free, it cannot be controlled for private gain. Nobody can own it. What the U.S. can do is impose a tax to remove the free aspect or donate the technology to friends.

This, alone, guarantees more skullduggery in coming years. No way are the powers that be going to allow free energy without their control. This is fundamental. If Randall Mills is stubborn and won't make a deal, they use national security. And if you don't know how they use national security, then read our America's Secret Establishment. Randall Mills is not Tony Sutton. We would promptly put the BLP patents into the public domain, and make the lab information freely available. But Mills has sweated blood for 10- 15 years and deserves a payback; so do his loyal shareholders.

Does Washington know all this? Possibly most politicians and bureaucrats do not. But what about those who make the decisions?

We can go back 30 years, and cite CIA Director William Casey, who said CIA did not know the West built the Soviet Union until the 1970s. Yet the State Department files (State used to do the CIA's job) are crammed with information (Microcopy 316).

That's where we found the story in the 50s and 60s. (Casey was not courteous enough to cite this Editor as the source of his knowledge, but have you ever known a Government official to be courteous? — or truthful?)

Probably the strangest part of this story is that Secretary of State Dean Rusk and Assistant Secretary of State Main (in 1963) went on public record with statements like:

The Soviets have their own self-developed technology and are not dependent on U.S. technology. (Rusk)

These statements were nonsense, and directly opposed to the massive evidence in the State Department Decimal File. It took this writer three massive volumes to show the falsity. We then privately and quietly produced a fourth volume to show that the Soviets also depended on us for military technology as well. (National Suicide, 1974) — so privately that the book was on the street before the CIA picked up the news. When we refused to withdraw the volume, we were fired at a momentous meeting in August 1973.

The argument that we were killing our own men by shipping U.S. technology to the Soviets and Vietnam had no effect on the assembled CIA, FBI and academics. They had their orders. The Masters knew they were wrong, and wanted to avoid embarrassment and public exposure. A few, like Zbigniew Brzezinski and Richard Pipes, took our side, but were soon quieted. It took Casey and the CIA ten years to quietly repeat our work and find we were correct.

After this, we took nothing out of Washington at face value.

In brief, there is no sure thing about free energy. Wouldn't the government just love to gain control or make a deal and tax it? — and don't expect the truth.

Governments do a great job at making war, kicking their citizens around, especially those who make fundamental discoveries and maintain the status quo for their favored friends. They also do a great job at conning citizens.

Apart from this, politicians and bureaucrats have one aim: to keep on the government payroll, which they do very well! And if real ambitious, they want a freeway or building after their name. The welfare of citizens is very much secondary. Don't expect any change.

Look for legal theft; and as Hegel said, this must benefit the Masters. It is their right, and our duty is to go along, and if we behave, get some scraps. Huh!

Postscript

October's FTIR was written and in for typing before the World Trade Center attack.

Note:

a. We are intrigued that only the name Osama bin Laden (a CIA creation) is cited as a suspect. The media is totally absorbed with this one name. No other considered.

b. Bin Laden has been in terrorism for a decade and known to be a factor in all kinds of terrorist acts. Why wasn't he picked up before this? Journalists were able to locate and meet with him in Afghanistan, but not the U.S. government? We spend $30 billion a year on intelligence, and get hit by a massive surprise attack?

c. We suspect bin Laden was protected by certain powerful Western interests, specifically the Saudis and the oil companies fearful of disrupting oil markets.

d. Is it possible that the U.S. knew the latest WTC attack was coming, and let it occur? Like the 1992 WTC attack (F.B.I. knew), or Pearl Harbor, or the U.S.S. Maine in 1898. Why? For the reasons in the above text.

e. This writer is not alone in distrusting anything that comes out of Washington. Depressing, but realistic.

FUTURE TECHNOLOGY INTELLIGENCE REPORT

November 2001: Vol 12, No. 11

EDITORIAL COMMENTARY

1. The United States is a vast, wealthy, productive and intelligent country. The most successful society in all history. Above all, it has a working Constitution with the all-important separation of powers, a full-time restraint on the excesses of politics and government. Remember, the office of President is not the same as

the person who temporarily occupies the office. Without this separation, we could easily lapse into dictatorship.

2. The United States will recover from September 11, while mourning the loss of 3,000 citizens. It will do this with some loss of Constitutional rights. Proposals for ID cards, "roving wiretaps" and other devices from A/G Ashcroft are unnecessary — a hasty over-reaction to the situation. Quite rightly, these proposals are viewed suspiciously.

3. The U.S. took a hit. It will have to take some more hits. The response should be calm and reasoned, not hasty and emotional. But, above all, we need some explanations from Washington, D.C.

We need to know why this happened. The Presidential talk about *evil* and "America under attack" is ridiculous. *Why do these people hate America so much?* What have the government and the multi-nationals done to achieve this level of enmity? Why has Washington suppressed free energy development? We don't need Saudi Arabia or the other oil producers; we need open-mindedness in Washington.

Even further, we spend $30 billion a year on intelligence, yet no advance warning, and no action! This strains our credulity. The hijackers came into this country in mid summer, and were recorded on the CIA "terrorist watch list" as "terrorists." The ball stopped right there. *The White House was informed.* The people doing the watching did that *and no more.* They watched while terrorists were allowed to take *no-landing* flight training and do their planning in peace and quiet. It appears to us the operation was "allowed to go forward" — a scenario we have not seen discussed in the media. How can you spend $30 billion a year on intelligence, and ignore 19 *known* terrorists? We know the CIA informed the White House. *No one said, "stop them."*

This reminds us of a similar snafu in the 1960s. The CIA said it did not know that the U. S. had built the Soviet Union. Nothing has changed. Either we have the most unintelligent of intelligence agencies, throwing money at useless SIGNIT systems, or somebody has another agenda out there — and the power to order "don't do anything."

With hundreds of billions a year spent on defense, four planes are able to sneak in and bring down two landmark buildings and hit the Pentagon without triggering defenses. *This is incredible.* A complete collapse of defenses. We need a full and documented answer. How much was known and when? This put-off of "revealing our intelligence sources" is plain silly. We have no intelligence if we can't use it — period! To us, it looks very much like the Washington action pre-Pearl Harbor in 1941. Roosevelt had the Japanese code messages and allowed the attack to occur.

This is also a repeat of the collapse of U.S. intelligence in the technical "perceptions problem" with the Soviets. The U.S. never did figure out the technical weakness of the Soviet Union or chose *to* ignore the weaknesses. If you read, *Best*

Enemy Money Can Buy, you will see how the U.S. was assaulted by an army of disinformation. From Secretary of State Dean Rusk and his deputy Edwin Martin, who had an arsenal of absurdities presented as hard fact, to Armand Hammer, son of founder of the Communist party, U.S.A., and access to every president from Roosevelt onwards; to naive academics like Walt Rostow; to businessmen like Norris (Control Data).

In Iran Contra, the U.S. became a major cocaine supplier, and this was approved from the Bush White House. Nothing ambivalent about that — Colonel Olly North was flat-out lying, and the system will not release the papers, so as to provide a cover for Olly — and to hell with the public.

In the 1993 WTC attack, the FBI had a man inside the operation. It was allowed to go forward.

We refuse to believe that Osama bin Laden woke up one morning and decided to attack next Tuesday at 9:00 A.M. This is a man who lives in a cave, for heavens' sake!

What is his connection to the CIA? We are now set up for another whitewash, blue ribbon committee. There is a high probability that biological weapons will be used in jihad — cheap, portable, and sometimes effective. What is not discussed anywhere, probably not even in the Pentagon, is the use of radionics to counter pathogens.

The AMA-FDA complex has done an extraordinary job to eliminate knowledge and use of radionics in the U.S.A., an unbelievable disservice to humanity. And all for a few dollars' profit! Biological weapons by definition have a life energy, and radionics is the manipulation of life energy. This can be reversed, if you know how.

Radionics, discovered in 1924 by a San Francisco doctor, Albert Abrams, was ruthlessly suppressed by the American Medical Association in its effort to monopolize American medicine.

In fact, radionics may be the ideal defense for biological warfare. Radionics **can** protect up to 1/2 square mile, but thanks to AMA greed and myopia, the U.S. has no usable radionic defense. Any system using life energy can be influenced by radionics. But neither life energy nor radionics is officially recognized in the United States. If anything is to be done, it will be by individual citizens.

We don't believe that Al Queda cares what is officially recognized by the U.S. establishment. They have *one* question: does the United States have a defense?

The facts are extraordinary, but not surprising *to* those who follow government. There *is* a vaccine against anthrax — efficiency unknown. Only sufficient vaccine exists for the military. *None* is available for civilians. Antibiotics have very limited use.

Our personal view today *is "sauve qui peut" — it is up to* individual citizens *to* discover how they have been conned.

THIS IS YOUR GOVERNMENT AND WE ARE HERE TO HELP YOU

The Bush commentary — "bin Laden is an evil man..." and this is "a declaration of war," is a sophomore-level retort to a crisis. We need explanatory answers to a host of questions, and so far, we have very little.

QUESTION NO. 1: WHEN DID WASHINGTON KNOW OF THE WTC ATTACK – TIME AND DATE.

Did they know before 9:00 A.M. September 11?

Our information is, the White House knew on August 23, 2001, and had a list of the terrorists from CIA. We ask this because other Administrations have allowed attacks "to go forward" for political reasons. We can cite three or four such cases. The most well known is December, 1941, when Roosevelt had intercepts of the Japanese Pearl Harbor *attack* codes well beforehand, but allowed the attack to go forward to bring the U.S. into war. The code messages were forwarded to Hawaii by commercial routes, the slowest possible method. They arrived well after the attack.

In September, 2001, the entire New Utrecht High School in New York knew *a week beforehand* that the Twin Towers were to be attacked. (*Journal News,* October 11, 2001.) If a high school had advance warning, then someone in Washington *must* have had that same information.

QUESTION NO. 2: ISN'T CIA A WASTE OF MONEY?

We spend $30 billion a year on intelligence, and we are asked to believe no one in Washington had advance warning! Not impossible, but unlikely.

What *are* we doing? Well, we are *still* waiting for release of the Iran-Contra papers. Olly North was smuggling planeloads of cocaine into the U.S. under CIA auspices. This has been completely concealed by Congress. The Bush family supplied the oil rigs used as transit points for the cocaine. Very few know this today because Washington has clamped secrecy on the operation. In the early 1980s the U.S. Government was a major cocaine trafficker. Why? And why the continual denials in the face of operational documents?

QUESTION NO. 3: WHAT IS THE RELATIONSHIP BETWEEN BUSH, SR., AND THE BIN LADEN FAMILY?

www.judicialwatch.org

QUESTION NO. 4: JUST HOW MUCH DISTANCE IS THERE, REALLY, BETWEEN THE BIN LADEN FAMILY AND THE TERRORIST BIN LADEN?

Bush, Sr. meets with the bin Laden family on business, while a son is the terrorist bin Laden. It would not look good for Bush to be associated with a terrorist family; so did they invent a dispute to suggest distance? Funds were flowing for years from the family to bin Laden — this suggests cooperation. If there is no evidence to confirm cooperation, why not publish the FBI conclusions from the bank records?

QUESTION NO. 5: CAN WE SERIOUSLY BELIEVE BUSH, JR. WHEN HE CALLS SAUDI ARABIA AN "ALLY".

This is absurd. The Saudis are actively helping bin Laden — not the United States. Bush, Sr. has a business relationship with the bin Laden family. A constant stream of funds flows from Saudi businessmen to bin Laden. Saudi Intelligence is non-existent for the United States. We haven't caught up with bin Laden in great part because he is *protected* by Saudis.

Saudi Arabia is not an ally. It is virtually an enemy. Bush, Jr. is not facing the situation — why not?

QUESTION NO. 6: WE SPEND $30 BILLION A YEAR ON INTELLIGENCE AND COULD NOT FORESEE THIS WTC ATTACK?

There were, in fact, several reports from foreign allies — all ignored. Why?
Incompetence in Washington, D.C.

The November 2000 FTIR one year ago headlined a warning: we are on the verge of disaster. FTIR identified the Middle East, terrorism and the heavy overhang of gold supply. The significance is this: Washington has a thousand times more information than FTIR. It lacks a capability to analyze and then act on information. The prediction of a gold overhang is important, because it meant that in the event of a crisis, gold would not behave in its normal manner. This is exactly what happened in September, 2001. Gold responded only sluggishly to the WTC events.

The reluctance of Government to act is a recurring problem. Where oil and the Middle East are concerned, the word is "do nothing to upset the oil companies." As far back as 1985, we brought to the attention of the Foreign Intelligence Advisory Board the emerging free energy paradigm. Our argument: We don't need Saudi Arabia or any other oil producing country. Let's get out while we can.

This was back in 1985! — and is on record.

FUTURE TECHNOLOGY INTELLIGENCE REPORT

December 2001: Vol 12, No. 12

CIA RECRUITS OSAMA BIN LADEN TERRORIST

The following comes from London (BBC) and Australia and needs further investigation.

U.S. agents (FBI) in London were pulled off an investigation of bin Laden family and Saudi royals soon after Bush took office. (BBC has documents to show this.) In addition to Osama bin Laden, other members of the family were terrorists and under investigation by FBI.

SECRECY AND THE CIA

Intelligence agencies make a big deal out of secrecy. It makes them look important. Secrecy is sometimes needed to acquire information, and they paint a picture of clever CIA people acquiring secret documents.

In truth, this is nonsense. Almost all data can be acquired using *ingenuity* alone. For the four volumes of the *Western Technology* series, we acquired all the data needed without any skulking around, and that included the Russian technical manuals — hundreds of them — which came from inside the Soviet Union. What you do is ask for what you want, and have a reason ready.

The only problem I had was on some State {Department} documents. I had to jump up and down a little to get release. Then the reason for the trouble was obvious. State did not want public knowledge of the advanced systems the U.S. was shipping to the U.S.S.R.

This nonsense about the need for secrecy has two reasons:

1 . To conceal from the American public.

2. To make themselves look important, and keep the funds flowing from Congress.

About 5% of the material might be hard to obtain, but if you have Uncle Sam's checkbook, that is no problem.

Don't be confused by what I am saying: there have been, and maybe still are, some excellent CIA people. They will tell you that behind all the P.R. stuff, the real powers are (1) secret societies, and (2) drugs. But the bulk of CIA? — an expensive joke.

Congress is being fooled. And note this: the Chairman of the Intelligence Committee is Congressman Goss — a former CIA operative.

FUTURE TECHNOLOGY INTELLIGENCE REPORT

February 2002: Vol 13, No. 2

WORLD TRADE CENTER – 9/11

We have studied this event. Our suspicions were aroused at the time, and we now identify three areas where information and explanation are needed.

1. The precision, complexity, logistics and risk in this operation are way beyond the capability of any individual or group of individuals. Bin Laden, whatever his financial resources, does not have the technical resources of a state. There had to be a *state* entity involved, possibly in a covert partnership. Our short list of possible covert partners is:

United States, Great Britain, Saudi Arabia (very likely), Iraq, Iran, Israel

2. There is an interval of 75 minutes between the hijacking and alerting of the U.S. Air Force. Your choice is:

a. U.S. defenses were asleep, drinking coffee, or something else for 75 minutes.
b. *Or* - there was a deliberate delay, by official order — again, the state. At first, we thought it was *inefficiency*. Today, we are inclined to believe the WTC disaster was *allowed to go forward*.
3. The relations between the Bush family, bin Laden family, and the Saudi government. Of the 19 hijackers, 14 were Saudi.

F.B.I. Agent O'Neill has stated publicly he was blocked from investigation of the Saudi connection for *political* reasons. What *political* reasons are more important than investigation of the WTC destruction? This is supported by other information, confirming that Saudis are more deeply linked to Osama than has been stated, and Bush *stopped the investigation — why?*

Warning

In November, 2000 (that's one *year* before the WTC disaster) FTIR warned of "troublesome times ahead" and pointed to the Middle East and to financial arenas.

This warning holds. However, the turbulence may be in the financial and economic sectors, rather than airplanes crashing into buildings. WTC-9/11 was a wake-up call.

We are particularly concerned about reports of F.B.I. agents being pulled off investigations relating to Saudi Arabia. Further, we keep getting rumors of Washington, DC elements up to no good, who want expansion of war under the name of antiterrorism.

For the worst case, make sure you have a stock of gold and silver coins. If you have energy stocks, take a close look at the future for oil, gas and nuclear energy.

Battle In Washington

Keep your heads up, and let your Congressmen know what you think!

A group in the Pentagon wants more war with Iraq — *now*. Pentagon facilities are being used to leak reports and arguments supporting this policy. It appears to be behind the back of Secretary Rumsfeld and originates in the office of Deputy Secretary Wolfowitz, who has no military experience.

This group has gone back over past Iraqi actions and thinks it has a case for moving on Iraq. We see this as irresponsible with extraordinary consequences for the Near East. This is typical of the arrogant policies which upset U.S. allies.

The CIA has a better idea (for once): use covert action on Baghdad. Secretary of State Colin Powell, a former head of the Joint Chiefs, is against a military action policy.

The Future

The WTC debacle altered many things, not all yet apparent.

An attack right into the heart of New York City, and this Editor, four months later, is still uncertain of the identify of the attackers!

All this under the guidance of a President with more secrets than the public realizes — some pretty sleazy.

The U.S. has embarked on a ten-year world crusade — in effect, a global war. This, at a time of a rapidly declining economy and shocking revelations of corporate misdoings in Enron.

There is more to come, much more. And this takes us well beyond the original topic of future technology.

Our original task has broadened. The government is on the way to take over free energy technology; fuel cells are just the start. And what Kenneth Lay did with Enron, with off-the-budget entities, which carried the debt load, is no more than the U.S. government has done for decades, with its off-budget financing.

This changes our focus.

As you see, we have already broadened our scope to include the all-important geopolitical factors, and this will get us back to the core of *America's Secret Establishment.*

FUTURE TECHNOLOGY INTELLIGENCE REPORT

March 2002: Vol 13, No. 3

HIGH LEVEL GERMAN STATESMAN DISPUTES BUSH ON WTC AND 9/11

Former German Minister of Technology, Andreas von Buelow makes more sense than Bush and the White House on WTC and 9/11.

Von Buelow makes sense, but is almost totally ignored in the United States. He was the former Minister of Technology in Germany, an independent, sensible, down to earth thinker.

It is now nearly four months since 9/11, and according to general U.S. press articles, TV and radio reports, it is an unequivocal but unproven *fact* that the WTC event of 9/11 was the sole work of an *evil* madman — Osama bin Laden. Furthermore, we were promised an investigation, but all FBI investigative attempts have been blocked by the White House itself.

Then, conveniently, the Enron scandal emerged. Look at this: Enron has currently *twelve* Congressional investigations plus others on the board. The tragic event of WTC has none — *zero.*

Sure, Lay and his buddies ripped off millions, but someone was able to hijack four air planes, fly into New York landmark buildings, and kill a few thousand Americans. We spend billions of taxpayer dollars each year to stop this kind of thing — but our defenses spend 75 minutes drinking coffee!

Quite difficult to understand how a lone Arab who lives in a cave with four wives is able to bring about this stupendous act of cooperation, and our technical efficiency is not discussed or investigated! All we get in the U.S. is unsubstantiated lines about *evil* madmen!

But to the point, this gets no attention from Congress, only from a foreign statesman, while Lay and his fast-talking aides get twelve Congressional committees.

Our solution is simple: put Lay in jail, and put our effort into WTC - 9/11.

Something over 90% of Americans reportedly support Mr. Bush and accept his neurotic pleas *without question;* yet, overseas, some very important questions and investigations are in progress. At home, Enron commands all attention, while an extremely important interview of Andreas von Buelow appeared in the German daily, *Tagesspiegel* (January 13), with not one whisper in the U.S. And the topic is untouched, not only by the vast American Press, but also by Congressional investigators.

Here is one key point from von Buelow: "I can explain what's bothering me: I see that after the horrifying attacks of Sept. 11, all political public opinion is being forced into a direction that I consider wrong."

Some people in the U.S. feel the same way, but there is little coverage and few commentators even raise a hint that something is missing here.

Mr. von Buelow's views are important, not only by virtue of his former position, but also because his views match a few publicized in the United States. FTIR and the La Rouche people have expressed skepticism about the official monopoly view. We sense that many others have unexpressed skepticism, confusing the office of the President with the contemporary office holder.

In your mind, go back and look at how Mr. Bush came to occupy this office — courtesy of Enron — and consider how he can raise over 90% approval on the basis of a PR campaign with no evidence to support the claim.

The level at which Bush discusses Osama bin Laden is sophomoric. This discussion of an *evil,* seemingly uncatchable Osama is becoming ridiculous.

We need some solid answers to some solid questions, and we are not getting them. To remind you, 3000 citizens get wiped out, and the limit of our knowledge is — *evil madmen.*

Then we have absurd CIA statements from CIA Director George J. Tenet that this event was a *victory* for the United States! — *nonsense!* WTC was no victory. But all we get is amateurish, unproven accusations and claims of victory. The next thing we know, we shall have victory parades on the White House lawn!

The establishment press is little better. Read the *New York Times.* It is big on "the hole" and heroism (and indeed, there *were* some heroic actions) but not much else.

This is an intelligent nation. It needs more than this. The White House sees the U.S. as a beer-drinking, SUV-driving, chauvinistic Andy Griffth's Mayberry.

MORALITY

Something both vital and long overdue has happened in these United States — a deep-seated corruption is now emerging. We have to deal with it, not cover it up, else this country cannot survive.

The Enron case and Kenneth Lay are symptomatic. They reflect what some of us have long known. Basically, the problem stems from overwhelming greed in the political/economic system. Greed has brought Argentina to its knees, greed has brought Zimbabwe to the brink of starvation, and the results of greed over common good are all too obvious now in the United States and in the White House. Lay was the biggest subscriber to the Bush *election*, and also a major donor to Prince Charles in England — a mere $1.4 million for Charles. Lay was buying everyone who could be bought. The Russians adopted this *anything goes* philosophy at the Olympics — but too late in the day. They were caught!

We found this obeisance to corporate power in the Hoover Institution at Stanford University 30 years ago. We understand 3/4 of the Senate and perhaps 1/2 of the Congress have received donations from Kenneth Lay — all there, with their hands eagerly outstretched. So if an individual who has not bought his way into the game wants protection, it is not there.

Our personal case is the one *we know best*, and is very simple. Thirty years ago, we discovered something those in the industrial military establishment did not want you to know. We were told not to publish this by the Hoover Institution at Stanford. They even quietly went through the galleys of one of my books to pull out the material on military aid to the Russians. We refused to stay quiet, and wrote *National Suicide* and later *The Best Enemy Money Can Buy*. We published the whole dirty story.

We then found the Hoover Institution was maintained by private corporate donations, those who built the U.S.S.R. for profit — we found that our establishment actually built the Soviet Union while hypocritically claiming innocence. Just like Lay — "I know nothing."

Instead of thanks for our discovery, the establishment threatened and blustered to save its own skin and reputation. People like Dean Rusk, Robert McNamara and Henry Kissinger lied and made sure enormous pressure was brought out to stop the story. Congress stood by and did nothing.

They did not succeed, but thanks to the gullibility — and perhaps the greed of the Congressman in the street — there was enough pressure brought to silence Congress.

Many years ago, after I would present a speech, scores would come up and make statements, "We are with you." "God bless you." *But that was all.* We often wondered why — *why* people would stop at that point, and never go beyond empty words. We decided *fear* was the best explanation.

The fear system works. Almost everyone is accountable to someone just upstairs — his or her boss. As former Senator Mike Mansfield said, "To get along, you have to go along." But once you go along, you are committed. You have limited your own freedom of action.

What has happened is that many have limited their own freedom of action, and don't really want the greed-reward system to stop, because it has paid off for them. They have sacrificed their own freedom for security. Hence, Kenneth Lay & Co. today!

The many crooks baited the hooks and caught a raft of greedy fish. There have been many exceptions, but not enough. Sherron Watkins blew the whistle on Enron, but has to face hostility from co-workers and friends. How many whistle-blowers consider it necessary to hide, as if in fear?

We have no fear of the establishment. We can produce more than their complicity in build-up of the Soviet Union. Our delay is for others to wake up and demand these people crawl back into their holes.

Maybe the time is coming. Perhaps Enron and Kenneth Lay have brought enough of this terrible mess into focus. Hoover Institution Director Glenn Campbell mocked us as being a *moralist* and said "*you will not survive.*" We have survived so far.

If you want to know this story, read *Memoir* and *America's Secret Establishment.* Hopefully, you will be spurred to action — to destroy this monolithic corruption.

If you have silly ideas like rebellion — forget it. The solution is the mind and communication, that's all. Violence is self destructive. First enlighten yourself, and then your friends.

And remember one piece of advice. "They" are the ones who are afraid, not you. Do right, and fear no man.

MR. BUSH AND THE "AXIS OF EVIL"

Mr. Bush needs to check his history books when he talks about an "axis of evil." For many, including most Europeans, "axis of evil" refers to the unholy alliance of Nazi Germany and Fascist Italy. Mr. Bush has invented a new axis — Iraq, Iran and North Korea. No matter that Iran and Iraq are enemies. No matter that Saudi Arabia is more and more apparently the seat of power for our problems. *Fifteen of the nineteen hijackers were Saudi.* The Saudi finance Al Queda and Saudis are highly uncooperative.

Why doesn't Bush include Saudis? Politics again. Bush is buddy-buddy with Saudi Arabia for family and oil reasons, *and refuses to see any evil in that direction.*

Mr. Bush now has two major problems:

1. Get off the Osama kick, and tell us who was responsible for the World Trade Center bombing. "Condi" (Condoleezza. Rice, President George W. Bush's National Security Advisor) should remind him that assumption is not proof.
2. His "axis" is pure fabrication. There is no "axis" among these countries, except in his own imagination for his own purposes.

More and more, Bush sounds like one of his fraternity buddies in *Skull & Bones.*

Tenet and bin Laden

Now CIA Director George J. Tenet is claiming a *victory* for September 11th. That's about as far as you can stretch imagination! Some three thousand Americans died on September 11, 2001, at the World Trade Center — and we would like to know *why*. Tenet claims it was a *victory* for the CIA, and they had known about Osama bin Laden for five years. FTIR readers will ask a simple question: Why wasn't something done? Is it the CIA's job just to *look* at terrorism, say, "My, my!" and go back to sleep?

Tenet is implying that in five years, the agency could not find a way into the Osama group. To FTIR, that is a blunt admission of failure. *It is the job of intelligence agencies to find a way in.* That is what "operations" does.

To add to Tenet's advantages, the Bush family and many others have inside contacts with Saudi Arabia. No, Mr. Tenet — not victory, but downright failure. *Excuses won't do it.* At $30 billion a year, we need more.

THE VON BUELOW APPROACH

1. "There are 26 intelligence services in the U.S.A. with a budget of $30 billion (more than the total German defense budget) and they were not able to prevent the attacks."

(FTIR has pointed out the same statistic. We now find the CIA knew 10 days before the attacks, and did nothing. This $30 billion is in addition to a *secret budget* we understand to be at around $70 billion.)

2. "Then the U.S. immediately went to war ... but a Government which goes to war must first establish who the attacker, the enemy is. It has a duty to provide evidence, the U.S. has not been able to present any evidence that would hold up in court."

(FTIR makes a similar point. Bush has made an *assumption,* he has not presented *evidence.*

3. "The assumed chief terrorist is Mohammed Atta. This presumed terrorist then took some unusual risks ... and professionals do not take unusual risks. He catches a plane to reach Boston just a short time before the connecting flight. None of the stated terrorists was on the passenger list. None went through pre-flight procedures. None of the four pilots went to the agreed hijack code of 7700."

FUTURE TECHNOLOGY INTELLIGENCE REPORT

April 2002: Vol 13, No. 4

A BREAKTHROUGH. WHAT YOU MAY SUSPECT IS TRUE AND IS NOW IN PROGRESS BE WARNED

Sometimes surprises hit when least expected. This is certainly true in research.

In February 2002, we had a letter from an international, award-winning New York film maker, Roland Legiardi-Laura, currently making a film on John Taylor Gatto, the New York City and State Teacher of the Year. The film is entitled *The Fourth Purpose.*

In making the film, Roland had noted references to our book, *America's Secret Establishment.* These came from Gatto's fourth book, *Underground History of American Education.* (In case you need it, Roland's address is: The Odyssey Group, 269 East 8th Street, New York, NY 10009.)

Legiardi-Laura in particular had noted references in our book (a book he describes as "extraordinary") to Thomas Gallaudet, founder of Gallaudet College (for the deaf) in Washington, DC. A book by Gallaudet has apparently been expurgated. We have a photo of the title page, which proves the book did indeed exist, but Legiardi-Laura was unable to obtain a copy for the film.

Legiardi-Laura mailed me a copy of Gatto's book, and we found numerous references to a member of the *Illuminati,* a secret society, Johann Heinrich Pestalozzi (1746 - 1827), a close friend of Heinrich Hebart, the founder of so-called "enriched" education in the U.S. An odd combination. A Swiss *Illuminati* works closely and for some years lived with the American founder of the much-criticized domestic educational system in primary schools.

Legiardi-Laura achieved accidentally what so many have attempted. He found a way into the secret society octopus that threatens to extinguish our way of life.

This gives us an enormous research problem, and all we can do at the moment is present it to you. You are going to either solve it or let everything we have go to pieces. I cannot be any more clear than that.

What you cannot do is what happened 30 years ago when we discovered how the Soviet Union was built by the United States. People made all kind of supporting noises, but when it came down to *doing* something, they walked away and allowed a few to shoulder the burden. *Then the Soviet Union collapsed.* The Soviet chess piece was simply removed from the board, and today is replaced by "terrorism."

For a number of reasons, this "I see nothing" evasion tactic is not going to work this time around. This time, you either *do* something, or believe me, you will go under. I can't be any more blunt.

A NEW THEORY AND A HYPOTHESIS FOR INVESTIGATION

America's Secret Establishment is based on a genuine membership list of Skull and Bones, which is tied in with the older *Illuminati* secret society. When viewed side by side with Gatto's book, *Underground History of American Education,* a dramatic picture emerges.

Briefly, you have *already* been conditioned to accept secret society world control through the much-criticized educational system. Some of us have evaded this mechanism, because we did not receive our primary education in the United States. We *evaded the conditioning.* What *we* see clearly may not be available to *you.*

Remember, to achieve the *Illuminati-* Skull and Bones objective, they *must* conceal their intentions. The *Illuminati* were trapped in 1786, over 200 years ago, when the Elector of Bavaria intercepted their papers, found their objectives, and promptly broke up the *Illuminati* organization.

This is important. The *Illuminati* survived. Skull and Bones was founded in 1833, and has worked steadily since for its objectives. This is what Gatto has unknowingly discovered — a vital step in this plan for world domination. The President of the United States George W. Bush is a member of Skull and Bones.

WHAT PRIMARY EDUCATION DOES

As many parents have already found, the American primary education system has less to do with the development of the individual child, but rather prepares the child to be a cog in the State apparatus. This child conditioning can be looked at in two ways:

• First, the child is being raised as a tool of the State; barely able to read, and full of unnatural and non-educational ideas.

• But second, this conditioning can be viewed as a device to make a *New World Order* more acceptable. The kid grows up to be a pliant zombie.

This was not the Gatto objective. He started out by criticizing the *educational* objective. A teacher who was a real teacher, and objected to what is happening out there.

Because of the Pestalozzi aspect, we see this differently. We see a long-ranging conditioning objective to make the child accept these deeply secret objectives.

This is what the statistics portray. Just look at the literacy rate. Back 150 years ago, literacy was universal. Is it 100% in the U.S. today? Maybe 60% of the population can read! This is what we spend billions upon? — Something is *wrong*.

WHAT IS TO BE DONE?

First let's complete the Odyssey film on the educational system. This needs your help. This portrays a ridiculous affair. We spend billions — on what? — kids who can't read? The pilot film, *The Fourth Purpose,* produced by the Odyssey Group is available.

We took a look at a typical school schedule. Have you done this? One school has a period every day for — DRUMMING! Five days a week for drumming! No history, no Constitution, no literature, no science — but drumming!

Our conclusion was, shut this place down fast. This is not a school; it's an entertainment center.

This conditioning has been going on for well over 100 years. If it is not stopped, now, we shall have the entire population, except for immigrants, ready-made for the New World Order.

We have noticed that quite often the immigrant (there are 50 million of them) or the well-traveled American has evaded the conditioning. The vast group of younger Americans, those under 50 years of age, have been caught in the net.

Gatto and the Odyssey Group have caught this deeper purpose almost by accident.

Please think about this, and do what you can. You need to talk about this with your friends and relatives. You might see a note or review in a newsletter — that's about the sum of it. Nothing will appear in your newspaper, since newspapers do not report until a topic is widely notorious, and certainly not if the proverbial "telephone call" comes in from the publisher, i.e., "do not report." Some of you may remember 15 years ago, from time to time we received a report from a friend inside one of the major wire services: "News that is *not* reported on the wires."

We can only tell you what turns up in our research. As long as 40-50 years ago, we tried to tell people, for example, that the Soviet Union was *not* the almighty giant it appeared to the outside world. Our work was suppressed (see *Memoir).* Nobody would listen until we forced three books into the mainstream. Today, Mr. Gorbachev himself says the Soviet Union was a "propaganda hoax." For some reason, *people prefer the illusion to reality.*

Think about this, please: we have a President who is a member of Skull & Bones. We have described Skull & Bones in detail in *America's Secret Establishment.*

Our work is research. Whether you make use of the information is up to you.

THE WORLD TRADE CENTER DISASTER *(Continued)*

From the start, FTIR has been skeptical of the Bush explanation of the WTC disaster. Our skepticism is based on logic and common sense, up to now without evidence.

We now have evidence, which more or less confirms what at least some have already deduced.

As we stated last month, times have changed; you ignore today at your own peril.

Our doubts based on common sense were:

1. Mr. Bush claimed the culprit as an *evil bin Laden.* Not one piece of evidence was submitted. Bush jumped up and down, pointing a finger at bin Laden, and, according to reports, convinced over 90% of the *dumbed down* American public without a shred of proof.

2. Congress has over twelve investigations for the Enron case — and NONE for the WTC case. Just as we went to press, two committees were appointed — the House committee has a narrow focus. Chairman is Congressman Porter Goss, former CIA operations! Senate Chairman is Joseph Lieberman, with a wider scope. *Think about this.* Is the death of 3,000 Americans so insignificant that it can be brushed under the rug? Do the misdeeds of Kenneth Lay warrant twelve investigations, and the deaths of nearly 3,000 innocent Americans warrant *no* investigation?

Our conclusion: Congress doesn't *want* to investigate; maybe it fears some of the information below (and in following issues) is true, and will become public.

But Congress is supposed to represent the people!

3. After six months — no one can find Osama bin Laden, and Bush has stopped the FBI from investigation the Saudi angle.

4. And where is the press? This great big body of *investigative journalists* cannot even ask for proof of the Bush claim that Osama was to blame.

However: go to the Internet and you will find a different story. CNN and Rense.com (at: http://www.rense.com/general19/formergerman.htm); print the passenger lists for the four planes involved in the World Trade Center disaster. (More specifically, we routinely checked for Arab names — there are none (one possible). However, the FBI has given us Arab names for the hijackers without aliases. These names are not on any passenger manifest we have seen. What is the reason for this contradiction?

There is much more proof of an *alternative explanation.* The four American planes were hijacked by NORAD — i.e., U.S. Air Force, using remote control technology designed to rescue hijacked planes — not to fly them into buildings. *This is the story coming out of Britain and Germany.*

Is this why Britain — always a stout U.S. ally — refused to send 25,000 troops to Afghanistan? Is this why Germany refused to take over peace keeping in Kabul after Britain exits?

We will give you references next issue (June) where you can read the full version for yourself. Some of the references are not something we would rely on; they will need checking. You can read and decide for yourself.

When you pick yourself up off the floor, you will need to contact your Congressman, your local news editor, General Myers at NORAD, any honest newsletter editors you know, and others involved in this affair.

There are rumors this information will be expurgated. What you do after that is your business. From our perspective, we trust none of the above.

Approximately 10,000 people, probably a lot more, know this story, and we are skeptical of a variant — the Chinese version. Their interest is to destabilize the U.S.

Our starting point is:

1. You are not fully *dumbed down.*
2. Washington is unwilling to tell you the truth.
3. We pick up rumors that this same Washington is *frightened* that you will somehow learn the truth.
4. Many of you will download the story from Rense.com .

We start with the passenger lists from the four hijacked planes. Much more to come!

THE FUTURE: PLEASE READ

Sooner or later, we had to reach this point. Many, many are aware that the world has changed, but at FTIR, we see no signs that any are aware that knowing is not enough. You have to *do* something. Probably the United States of America has had it so good for so long, it is difficult to adjust.

We were burning many of our papers the other day, and the thought occurred — this is what Embassies do when war is imminent! The smoke from the chimney tells outsiders the end is approaching.

We first warned in November, 2000. September 11th, 2001, should have been another warning, and Washington over the past six months is confirmation. Our warnings have no effect. Congress is allowed to go six months without an investigation of September 11th. Allies are making their warning noises — they are not happy. When Britain refused to send 25,000 troops to Afghanistan, that should have been warning enough.

Rather than ignoring your Congressmen, you should be demanding answers from him about WTC — this is *your* representative, for heaven's sakes.

We can see the disintegration, but we do not see any part of the American people in protest. Everybody *seems* happy enough. Perhaps they do not see that "smiling fascism" can turn quickly to the real thing. Perhaps they do not recognize how the game is being played out in the military tribunals, the clamor for universal ID, and a lot worse. It is entirely possible that September 11th had nothing to do with Arabs, and a lot to do with NORAD.

Clearly worrisome is the fact that a former German Minister of Defense has picked up on this track, and clearly warns about it. Our other information confirms von Buelow. Von Buelow tells us that the U.S. is following the same track as 1930s Germany. *People would just not believe what was happening.*

Who was financing the German Nazi revolt of the 1930s? None other than Averell Harriman (Democrat) and Prescott Bush (Republican) through Union Banking, both Bonesmen, and Prescott Bush was the grandfather of today's George W. Bush — also a Yale Bonesman.

Same thing today. The counter-moves are not being made by citizens. Sure, a dozen or so commentators, especially on the Internet, are warning you. And FTIR was surprised to see a jump in renewals — so you are not all asleep.

But who is getting Congress on the ball? Who is writing to the Editor? Who is distributing literature?

If you have not read *America's Secret Establishment, I* urge you to do so. Published 20 years ago. And read *Electronically Hijacking the WTC Attack Aircraft*, at: www.geocities.com/mknemesis/homerun

Wake up and smell the coffee!

It looks as though *they* are willing to kill 3,000 Americans to advance their program. If that doesn't tell you something, nothing will. Take a look at the Internet, rense.com and Orlin Grabbe.

The next issue of FTIR will be June 2002; we are going to a bi-monthly schedule. Your subscriptions will be filled, except you have twice as long to read each issue.

This was Tony's last newsletter.

A REPORT ON THE ABUSE OF POWER

EDITOR: ANTONY C. SUTTON Vol. 2 No. 9 November, 1983

PUBLISHED BY RESEARCH PUBLICATIONS

Secret Skeletons From The Bush Closet

The bland self-effacing mask of Vice-President George Herbert Walker Bush conceals another man from another world.

The Bush family—and several allied families—are at the core of a secret society known as The Order. They are sworn to conceal its objectives. Even its very existence.

Three in the Bush family are members. Here is an extract from the membership "Catalogue" of this secret society listing the "Bush" entries.

BUSH, '48, George Herbert Walker—Grove Lane, Greenwich, Conn.
BUSH, '22, James Smith—[Finance]—Industrial Bank of St. St. Louis, 901 Washington Ave., St. Louis, Mo.; res., 5125 Lindell Blvd., Sgt., S.A.T.C., World War I; Lt. Col., U.S.A.A.F., World War II.
BUSH, '17, Prescott Sheldon—[Finance]—59 Wall St., New York City; res., Grove Lane, Greenwich, Conn. Member, Yale Corporation, 1944-; Capt., F.A., World War I (A.E.F.).

Prescott Sheldon Bush, father of Vice-President George Herbert Walker Bush, was initiated into The Order in 1917 along with Henry Neil Mallon, founder of Dresser Industries (an important supplier of strategic high technology to the Soviets).

After graduation from Yale both Prescott Bush and Henry Mallon were commissioned into the U.S. Army, Field Artillery.

As instant Captains, they were assigned (or perhaps rewarded) regiments as follows:

Captain Prescott Bush	322d Regiment Field Artillery
Captain Henry Mallon	323d Regiment Field Artillery

Readers of Introduction to THE ORDER will recall that "322" and "323" are room numbers in the "Bones" Temple on the Yale campus.

Editorial Offices
P.O. Box 39850
Phoenix, Arizona 85069

Subscriber to: INFOCEI — Confidential Wire Service, Paris
WONA — Wire Service, Berlin
Reuters — Wire Service

Subscription Offices
Research Publications
Box 39850, Phoenix, Arizona 85069
(602) 252-4477

THE PHOENIX LETTER

Vol 2 No 9 November 1983

SECRET SKELETONS FROM THE BUSH CLOSET

The bland self-effacing mask of Vice-President George Herbert Walker Bush conceals another man from another world.

The Bush family — and several allied families — are at the core of a *secret society* known as The Order. They are *sworn to conceal* its objectives. Even its very existence.

Three in the Bush family are members. Here is an extract from the membership "Catalogue" of this secret society listing the "Bush" entries.

BUSH, '48, George Herbert Walker-Grove Lane, Greenwich, Conn.

BUSH, '22, James Smith-(Finance-Industrial Bank of St. Louis, 901 Washington Ave., St. Louis, Mo.; res., 5125 Lindell Blvd., Sgt., S.A.T.C., World War 1; Lt. Col., U.S.A.A.F., World War 11.

BUSH, '17, Prescott Sheldon-(Finance-59 Wall St., New York City; res., Grove Lane, Greenwich, Conn. Member, Yale Corporation, 1944-; Capt., F.A., World War I (A.E.F.).

Prescott Sheldon Bush, father of Vice-President George Herbert Walker Bush, was initiated into The Order in 1917 along with Henry Neil Mallon, founder of Dresser Industries (an important supplier of strategic high technology to the Soviets).

After graduation from Yale both Prescott Bush and Henry Mallon were commissioned into the U.S. Army, Field Artillery.

As instant Captains, they were assigned (or perhaps rewarded) regiments as follows:

Captain Prescott Bush	322d Regiment Field Artillery
Captain Henry Mallon	323d Regiment Field Artillery

Readers of Introduction to THE ORDER will recall that "322" and "323" are room numbers in the "Bones" Temple on the Yale campus.

After World War One Prescott Bush joined W.A. Harriman (now Brown Brothers, Harriman) private bankers at 59 Wall Street, New York, to start a forty-year career with the firm. Brothers Averell Harriman ('13), Roland Noel Harriman ('17) and members of the Brown family are also members of The Order.

In 1921 Bush married Dorothy Walker, daughter of St. Louis banker George Herbert Walker, whose son Stoughton Walker was initiated in 1928. Walker also hired James Smith Bush (initiated 1922), brother of Prescott Bush into his bank, the Industrial Bank of St. Louis.

In brief, the Bush family is part of the *tightly woven inner core of The Order*, a secret society whose members are sworn to avoid discussion of objectives and membership — *or even its very existence.*

GEORGE HERBERT WALKER BUSH

George Bush was born June 12, 1924, in Milton, Massachusetts. His childhood was spent in Greenwich, Connecticut and Phillips Exeter Academy, Andover. During World War Two — and this is one of the few positive aspects of Bush's career — he spent three years in the Pacific with Naval Air Services, leaving as a Lieutenant Junior Grade.

Then, according to *Current Biography*:

> On his return to civilian life, Bush entered Yale University where he majored in economics, was elected to Phi Beta Kappa and joined Delta Kappa Epsilon fraternity.

Nowhere in this biography — nor in any other Bush biography — is initiation into the order cited. Membership is consistently *concealed* from the public record.

Moreover, suppression of this membership is consistent with the oath of initiation which forbids members to discuss membership or even be present when The Order is discussed by outsiders.

After Yale, Bush decided to go to work. According to *Current Biography:*

> After graduating from Yale ... Bush decided to strike out on his own rather than work for his father's banking firm (Brown Brothers, Harriman) and took a job as a salesman with Dresser Industries of Odessa, Texas, an oilfield supply company of which his father was a director.

One interesting point about Dresser Industries: it has always been a *supplier of top flight high technology to the Soviets* — some with more than obvious military applications. *Even* President Carter — who was actually tougher on holding the technological export line than President Reagan — allowed a Dresser-Soviet contract to go forward in 1977 *against the protests of the Department of Defense.*

AMBASSADOR BUSH AT UNITED NATIONS

In 1970 Bush ran for the U.S. Senate from Texas. *He lost.*

President Nixon then appointed Bush U.S. Ambassador to United Nations.

This appointment was widely criticized as a political pay-off-because Bush had absolutely *no experience whatsoever* in foreign affairs or diplomacy.

This deficiency led to *expulsion* of Taiwan from the U.N. General Assembly and a *seat for Communist China.*

Simultaneously Bush used his U.N. office to support "Mundialization," i.e., *the adoption by individual communities of world status.* Part of local taxes goes to support United Nations rather than the local community. It is a rejection of U.S. sovereignty.

The first U.S. city to join the New World Order was Richfield, Ohio (November 1970). Here's part of a letter sent by U.N. Ambassador Bush to Richfield, Ohio:

> Permit me to congratulate you and the other members of your community on your Proclamation of Mundialization. There cannot be anything more encouraging

> to us here than to hear from a community like yours that supports the United Nations and believes in it and in its importance to the establishment of world peace. Equally significant is your community's commitment to help increase understanding among the peoples of the world for without that understanding peace among peoples can never be achieved. What a profound contribution Richfield is making to man's greatest efforts to build a world in which all the pledges of the UN Charter will truly govern relations among nations!

Mr. Bush had sworn an oath of office to *support* the Constitution of the United States. He cannot support any measure that would *in any way dilute the sovereignty of the United States.* The "Mundialization" process and the Constitution of the U.S. are opposed to each other. They are mutually exclusive. You have to choose one or the other. *You can't support both simultaneously.*

After this Bush was moved along the fast track by Nixon and Ford:

- 1971-2 U.S. Ambassador to United Nations
- 1973-4 Chairman Republican National Committee
- 1974-5 Chief U.S. Liaison Office, Peking, Communist China
- 1976-7 Director, Central Intelligence Agency

In 1980 Bush ran for President. Financial backing came heavily from the so-called Eastern Establishment-not only did David Rockefeller send the maximum allowable contribution of $1,000, *but so did five other Rockefellers.*

Among members of The Order who backed Bush were:

- J. Richardson Dilworth ('38)
  (Administrator of the Rockefeller family) $1000
- John Cowles, Jr. (four Cowles in The Order) $1000
- George Weyerhaeuser $1000

As you know, Bush ended up on the Presidential ticket with Reagan — and made it into the White House.

Bush Meets Andropov

The October 1983 *Phoenix Letter* reported that individual Americans have met with Andropov *only twice.* And Andropov chose to meet members of The Order: Bush and Harriman. Not even U.S. Ambassador Hartman has seen Andropov alone.

What was Bush's assessment after the November 1982 meeting? This is Bush — a *former head of CIA* — on Andropov:

> My view on Andropov is that some people make this KGB thing sound horrendous. Maybe I speak defensively as a former head of CIA. But leave out the

naughty things they allegedly do: here's a man who has had access to a tremendous amount of intelligence over the years ... (and therefore) would be less apt to misread the intentions of the United States.

The Bush assessment was that Andropov *was misunderstood and really wanted to improve U.S.-Soviet relations.*

And what did *Phoenix Letter* print at that time (January 1983 The Russian Window)? As follows:

> Andropov is by far the most dangerous Soviet leader since the 1917 Bolshevik Revolution.
>
> *Andropov* has more education than Lenin, and probably equals Lenin's cunning. *Andropov* is as ruthless as Stalin, but this ruthlessness will be directed as much at the Free World as long suffering Russians. In the light of history Kruschev and Brezhnev will be seen as toothless tigers compared to the Andropov regime. In brief: KGB efficiency and terror will now be felt inside *and* outside Russia.

The "poor misunderstood" Andropov acted — in quick succession came these *terror strikes*:

- The attempted assassination of the Pope, traced back to Moscow,
- The massacre of KAL 007,
- The massacre of the South Korean cabinet in Bangkok,
- The Beirut Marine massacre,
- The Cuban-Soviet buildup on Grenada — aimed at revolution in Brazil.

Bush boasts he spent a year as head of CIA. He should buy a subscription to *The Phoenix Letter* — then his assessment of intentions will be 100% more accurate.

BUSH MEETS DICTATOR ROBERT MUGABE OF ZIMBABWE

After meeting with Andropov in November, 1982, Bush went on down to see Robert Mugabe in Zimbabwe and made a speech not exactly well covered by the U.S. media (it was not reported by *any* network or major newspaper). Reading extracts from the speech Bush made in Harare (capital of Zimbabwe) readers will understand why Bush may not have been anxious for domestic U.S. coverage of his views on Zimbabwe.

Back in May of this year we reported that Robert Mugabe was engaged in a quiet *slaughter* of his tribal enemies in Zimbabwe ... *while the U.S. was financing Zimbabwean housing projects at lower interest rates than could be obtained by American citizens.*

We described Mugabe as: " ... a smooth two-faced killer, who sneers when atrocities are mentioned and has conned the local U.S. representatives" (May 1983 p. 8).

While the slaughter was in progress Vice President Bush was in Zimbabwe-not to investigate the slaughter, *but to hail Mugabe.* Here are some of the fawning statements made by Bush at a State Dinner held in Harare, Zimbabwe on November 16, 1982:

> Your excellency ... thirty-one hours ago in Moscow, I discussed my mission to Africa with the President of Pakistan, Zia Al-Huk. When I mentioned Prime Minister Mugabe, President Zia made reference to something which informed men everywhere on earth agree .... I want to acknowledge that I stand in the presence of a genuine statesman, the Prime Minister of Zimbabwe, Robert Mugabe. His stature in the world is well established, highly respected, and it will be more formidable in the years to come ....

And more,

> Mr. Prime Minister ... you have faced awesome challenges ... I do want to say on behalf of the Reagan Administration that we support the policy of reconciliation to which you have committed yourself ... We have supported your country because its success is consistent with U.S. principles and U.S. interests ... shortly after President Reagan took office my government pledged nearly one quarter of a billion U.S. dollars in new aid. America has not only avowed its faith in Zimbabwe, but proven it.

Finally, Bush couldn't resist commenting on his response to Andropov's sucker bait:

> A moment ago I mentioned our journey to Moscow. No doubt you have all seen photographs of Secretary Brezhnev's funeral. The image that struck me most – one that I will never forget – was the magnificent, stately display of young Russian soldiers.

And there's more of the same preppie gee-whiz juvenile ramblings ... *this* is the Vice President of the United States — once they let him outside the U.S.

Now let's come up to date — to November 1, 1983, a few days before we go to press.

Over in Harare, statesman Robert Mugabe *has seized and imprisoned* Bishop Abel Muzorewa of the American-based United Methodist Church.

What is Bishop Muzorewa's sin?

Two days before Mugabe stormtroopers seized the bishop, Muzorewa made a comment that human oppression in Zimbabwe *was worse than under white minority rule* (Zimbabwe was formerly Rhodesia). This is how Bishop Muzorewa phrased his criticism of Mugabe:

> I continue to hope and pray that God can somehow help us to be delivered from the oppression of today imposed on us not by Ian Smith, not by Israel or

South Africa and not by people with white skins, but by our ruling party and government with black skins.

Bishop Muzorewa is today held in Harare Central Police Station. Muzorewa has not been formally charged with a crime. He cannot receive visitors or a lawyer.

And the man responsible is Vice President Bush's hero — *distinguished* statesman Mugabe — who is getting a one quarter billion dollar hand-out this year from the United States taxpayer.

CONCLUSIONS

1. Mr. Bush is a member of a "sordid" secret society (that's what one of its *own* members has called it). This membership has been *concealed* from the American public. It is obvious *deceptio*n.
2. Mr. Bush apparently has some difficulty in making *correct assessments of people and events.* Anyone who provides *rapturous* support for such psychopaths as Andropov and Mugabe has little understanding of traditional American values of freedom and human dignity.
3. These deficiencies have been *identified* by Andropov. Soviet psychological profiles of Bush are accurate. Bush apparently cannot restrain himself from reaction. Diplomatic precedence and goose-stepping military parades are two Bush baits which have succeeded.
4. Bush's actions confirm the conclusion of INTRODUCTION TO THE ORDER, i.e., that members of The Order have severe personality deficiencies.

RECOMMENDATION

1. That Vice-President Bush *resign* — today — before these facts become general public knowledge and rebound on the Reagan administration.

THE PHOENIX LETTER

Vol 2 No 12 February 1984

PATRIARCH "POPPY" BUSH OPTS FOR COVER UP

The *stupidity* of political sinners never ceases to amaze us.

Surely there must be one lesson from the Nixon White House — that cover-ups just don't work — that the public will accept a political sinner but not one who *conceals* his sinning.

P-T "Poppy" Bush (D. 146) is *scrambling* to hide a sordid segment of his life — his involvement with B---s, his membership in The Order.

(If you're wondering whether our typist is taking shortcuts with words, the answer is no — *they* know that P-T, D.146 and B---s stand for — it's a code *they* use in letters between members. Key: P-T is "Patriarch," D. 146 is a date of initiation and B --- s is "Bones").

Back to Patriarch "Poppy" Bush (alias Vice President George Herbert Walker Bush), in the November 1983 issue of *The Phoenix Letter* we printed an extract from the "Catalogue" of the-Russell Trust (a.k.a. Skull & Bones, a.k.a. The Order). This extract of the Bush family included Vice President Bush.

Within days we picked up the first of three events pointing to a cover-up:

(a) November 14, 1983, The Yale University Library *denied* researchers further access to Kingsley Trust and Russell Trust papers.

(b) December 13, 1983, Vice President Bush *denied* membership in a "sordid secret society."

(c) January 16, 1984, the White House *cancelled* the Republican regional platform hearings — a long-time GOP tradition.

Patriarch Bush Denies Membership In The Order

Mr. Bush is on the spot.

We have proof — absolutely irrefutable documentary proof-that Vice President Bush (as you know him) is a member of The Order.

On the other hand, members *take an oath* not to discuss membership. Even in letters between members, the entity "The Order" is coded in symbols.

Vice President Bush now *has a choice* — deny membership and so lie to the American people and betray his oath of office — *or* he can tell the truth, admit membership and betray The Order.

At this time Patriarch Bush has opted to deny membership.

In November 1983, a *Phoenix Letter* reader wrote the Vice President, requesting him to respond to the charges made in *The Phoenix Letter.* We will print two extracts from the reader's letter (it's too long to reproduce in full), then the Bush reply, then our comments (the complete Bush letter is reproduced on the next page).

(1) Reader To Bush:

> Are you now-or have you ever been – a member of and/or in any way affiliated with the alleged secret society cited by Mr. Sutton, also known as The Order?

Vice President Bush:

"The Vice-President is not now and never has been a member of any 'sordid secret society'" (see full context opposite).

Comment:

Mr. Bush attempts to *duck the question* by inserting a word, i.e., "sordid." The letter is signed by Shirley Green, Acting Press Secretary, so the letter can always be denied. *Obviously Vice President Bush is not in a position to make an outright denial.*

OFFICE OF THE VICE PRESIDENT

WASHINGTON

December 13, 1983

Dear Mr.

The Vice President asked me to thank you for your recent letter concerning the November issue of The Phoenix Letter.

The allegations contained in the Letter are so erroneous that they defy an item-by-item refutation. However, one of the areas that seems to be of concern to you has to do with something called "The Order." The Vice President is not now and has never been a member of any "sordid secret society." I am sure you know he has served his country as a Navy pilot in the Second World War and received the second highest medal awarded to our servicemen -- the Distinguished Flying Cross. He has also served at the United Nations as the U.S. representative in the People's Republic of China and was Director of Central Intelligence. He received the highest civilian awards given for service to country.

Vice President Bush's public career has been one of consistent loyalty and honor and has been conducted in full openness to the press for scrutiny of his performance.

The second area that appeared to cause you concern was an out-of-context and incomplete quotation following the Vice President's meeting with First Secretary Andropov. The Vice President simply stated that a Communist leader who had had access to full information about the United States and its people was less apt to misread the intentions of the United States and its peaceful desires than a Communist leader who was not familiar with the West and the values we hold dear. He at no time indicated that the change of leadership in the Soviet Union represented a change in their basic long-stated desires and goals vis-a-vis the rest of the world. Because of the Vice President's service at the CIA, he has a very realistic assessment of the Soviet system and is certainly not "misunderstanding" U.S.-Soviet relations.

The Vice President appreciated your bringing these concerns to his attention.

Sincerely,

Shirley Green

Shirley Green
Acting Press Secretary
to the Vice President

(2) Reader To Bush:

"Has Mr. Sutton accurately stated and/or quoted your position with regard to Soviet Premier Andropov and Dictator Mugabe of Zimbabwe? If not, then I request that you send me complete transcripts of what you actually stated."

Vice President Bush:

Bush ignores Mugabe. Neither did the Vice President fill the request for a full transcript. So *Phoenix Letter* sent a full transcript to the reader.

"Out of context and incomplete quotation" is the reason given for the Andropov part of the question, *but no transcript was sent to the reader.*

Comment:

None. Mr. Bush is obviously unable to support his allegations.

YALE UNIVERSITY LIBRARY JOINS THE COVER-UP

It is an *iron clad rule* among librarians throughout the civilized world that catalogue listed material should be freely available to all comers, without restricts, except where limitations on use are clearly stated and approved (rare books for example).

This is a basic tenet of professional librarianship — in thirty years around the academic world we have *never once* known this rule violated.

Even Soviet libraries by and large keep to this rule. This editor's three-volume study of Soviet technology relied heavily on Soviet material (the U. S. government classified its files on this topic) and even the paranoid Soviets were willing to ship abroad material listed in their Moscow catalogues.

Now let's come to that bastion of free inquiry in New Haven, Connecticut, known as Yale University.

Last August (1983) this Editor requested Yale University Library for a copy of items in their Yale catalogue under Call Numbers: Yeg2 K61c (Kingsley Trust) and Yeg2 R9c (Russell Trust).

Here is a copy of a relevant catalog card — as it (once) existed — at Yale University Library:

Kingsley Trust Association
Yeg2 C.S.P. 1842- C.C.J. [Catalogue]
K61C

Have: 1842-44,
1882, 1890, 1896,
1906. 1919, 1929, 1939,
1959, 1969

This is a temporary record for the serial being cataloged. Permanent cards will be filed soon.
recat
Subject Cataloguer: Analyzed
Serial Cataloguer: rtp() Not analyzed
Date: 2/3/78

Yale University Library

New Haven Connecticut 06520

Rutherford David Rogers
University Librarian

November 14, 1983

Mr. Anthony C. Sutton
P.O. Box 1791
Aptos, California 95003

Dear Mr. Sutton,

In reply to your letter of November 7 about the Kingsley Trust Association: Catalogue, please write:

Radley Daly, Treasurer
Box 1934 Yale Station
New Haven, CT 06520

I have reviewed our previous correspondence with you, and I suggest that you deal directly with the Kingsley Trust on this matter.

Cordially,

RD Rogers

Rutherford D. Rogers
University Librarian

RDR/jkw

The response denying access from the University Librarian is reproduced on the opposite page. The censor? Obviously Kingsley Trust. The Russell Trust request was ignored.

Who, or what, is Kingsley Trust? It is a.k.a. Scroll & Key-another Yale senior society. We suspect it is a part of, perhaps a chapter of The Order ... *members included Dean Acheson (NSC/68) and Cy Vance.*

Note this: the requested material was *open* to researchers as late as mid-1983 because previous requests were fulfilled promptly. Access was closed off sometime between July and November 1983, after remaining available for years, some for almost a century.

BUSH-BAKER GROUP CLOSE DOWN PLATFORM HEARINGS

Traditionally in election years the Republican Party holds *nationwide public* platform hearings.

This year, White House counselor Edwin Meese (in charge of writing the platform) and almost all Republican officials, legislators and Governors, wanted to continue the tradition.

The Bush-Baker forces said no. Said James Baker, "When you have the White House, why invite people to go out and criticize you."

Then Trent Lott (R-Miss.) arranged a compromise — *four* hearings only. *In January, even this compromise was scuttled by the Bush-Baker crowd.*

We understand individual Republicans are now organizing hearings on a local basis — in addition to the orchestrated show at Dallas.

We also know from internal correspondence among members of The Order (between their local cells or clubs) *that they are worried* — worried about the anti-elitist tide, worried that even Yale campus doesn't want them anymore.

Someone needs to come up with an idea — *how to get Vice President Bush on a public platform before nationwide TV cameras to answer a few questions.* For example:

"Are you or have ever been a member of a secret society?"

"Have you ever taken an oath to keep this membership secret?"

"Did you declare this secret membership to the FBI or the Senate when you were confirmed as Vice President?"

CONCLUSIONS:

1. George "Poppy" Bush is not only a member of a secret society, but *cannot deny this association.*

2. Bush has placed himself behind a *smoke screen,* i.e., he answers questions through a press secretary (who can be denied), keeps a *very* low profile, refuses to give the public a forum for questioning.

3. In brief, a *cover-up.*

RECOMMENDATIONS

1. *Mr. Bush should resign before he puts his other foot in it.*
2. *The Phoenix Letter* would appreciate any recent (since 1960) Yale yearbooks that publish Scroll & Key associations. We can return "borrowed" material within 24 hours by overnight Express mail.

WARNING

Do not assume ALL Yale graduates are suspect. *That would be grossly untrue and unfair.* We are talking about 15 men a year (the Yale 1945 entering class was 8,000). Not all those initiated became active. We are looking at 100 or so activists among 100,000 or so Yale graduates.

THE PHOENIX LETTER

Vol 2 No 12 February 1984

SECRECY OR PRIVACY?

Political conspiracy *demands* secrecy.

The Order (aka Skull & Bones or Russell Trust) will *not* comment on our charges.

The Order will *not* reply to letters. Members will *not* even admit membership (Vice President Bush, a public official, will not admit *or* deny).

Now Scroll & Key (aka Kingsley Trust) has presented us with a useful start point to attack the silence.

A few months ago on January 29, 1985, Radley H. Daly, Treasurer of Kingsley Trust, wrote that senior society secrecy was not secrecy but *privacy.* We reproduce this letter overleaf.

Daly *does not disclaim* concealment of information nor deny activities. Daly merely makes a bland claim for privacy. It is this claim of a *right to privacy* that we want to explore.

IS THE ORDER SECRET?

Let's go back 100 years: to the 1871 commentary on Yale senior societies by Lyman Bagg, FOUR YEARS AT YALE. The chapter on senior societies is reproduced in *America's Secret Establishment.* On pages 84-5 we find the following:

> ... the senior societies are such peculiarly Yale institutions, that it will be difficult for an outsider fully to appreciate their significance. Nothing like them exists in other colleges; and Harvard is the only college where, under similar conditions, they possibly could exist. In the first place, they are the only Yale

> societies whose transactions are really secret. Their members never even mention their names, nor refer to them in any way, in the presence of anyone not of their own number and, as they are all Seniors, there are no old members in the class above them to tell tales out of school.

Bagg's century-old observations are fully supported by *subsequent* ACTIONS.

A membership list for The Order — part of the Yale senior society system — is not freely available. If any reader wants to test this assertion, the address for The Order is:

> Russell Trust Association
> P. 0. Box 2138
> Yale Station
> New Haven, Conn 06520

Offer to pay Xeroxing costs and ask for:

> CATALOGUE, Volume One: Living Members
> CATALOGUE, Volume Two: Deceased Members
> Volume One is 193 pages in length and Volume Two is 141 pages.

If any reader succeeds in obtaining a copy, we would appreciate the news. We can then release for publication the copy we are now holding. We are presently reluctant to reproduce our copy in case it can be traced to a source.

Daly, of Scroll & Key, claims (opposite) that membership lists were at one time published in newspapers. This is partially true. *But* nothing more than bare names of those initiated were *ever* published. All procedures and objectives are carefully guarded and always have been.

In the past few decades secrecy has been extended *even to names* — as Daly admits. Daly states publication was "discontinued a few years back." In fact, it is almost a century since full lists were published to our knowledge, although we have not thoroughly researched this point.

The reason for non-publication presented by Daly is lack of newsworthiness. If it is *newsworthiness* alone, then why is it impossible to obtain a current list of members of Skull & Bones? Why is the catalogue treated as a state secret "For eye only."

We suggest the *true* reason for concealment is the precise opposite, i.e., that the list is indeed *highly* newsworthy. A quick scan of the 1983 list reveals an extraordinary correlation between The Order and the "powers that be" in the United States.

Furthermore, we have begun to print evidence of collusion among members for specific objectives. So we reject Radley Daly's argument out of hand.

KINGSLEY TRUST ASSOCIATION
YALE STATION NEW HAVEN
CONNECTICUT

January 29, 1985

Mr. Richard A. Landkamer

Dear Mr. Landkamer,

I am sorry to say that there are no more copies of the two volume set "A History of Scroll and Key." When this was published in 1978, only enough copies were printed to distribute to members of the society and to members of the academic administration at Yale. There is a set in the Sterling Memorial Library which you are welcome to refer to. The volume covering the first 100 years of the society was written by Professor Maynard H. Mack. A companion volume covering recent history was written by A. Bartlett Giamatti before he became president of Yale.

If you do visit the Sterling Memorial Library, you may wish to look at various documents going back a hundred years or more in which the names of the members of Yale's senior societies were routinely published at the time of election. You'll find these lists in the New York Herald Tribune, the New York Times, the New Haven newspapers, the Yale Daily News, and in class yearbooks. Not only the names, but often the pictures of the newly elected members were published openly, a practice that was discontinued a few years back, presumably for lack of newsworthiness.

In reading through the materials you have sent me, I have a sense that you and your colleagues have somehow lost the distinction between secrecy and privacy. I would have supposed you to be supportive of the concept of an individual's right to privacy.

Sincerely,

Radley H. Daly
Treasurer

RHD/ps

Privacy becomes unacceptable secrecy when the power and influence of fraternities is used to harm society or individuals outside the fraternity.

We can cite *The Brotherhood* in England (See *Phoenix Letter*, May 1984, Vol. 3, No. 3). The KGB infiltrated the Freemasons and used the Masonic fraternal preference structure to work their way to the top of British intelligence. The KGB ended up in control of MI-6, thanks to Masonic "Privacy." This, in spite of the fact that all British intelligence organizations *refuse* to recruit masons. (More recently this ban has been extended to Scotland Yard police.)

We have every right — and a civic duty-to demand that the Yale senior societies drop their protective shields and open up their records.

Even without the resources available to the FBI and Congress, we can print enough to demonstrate a prima facie case of illegal and possibly subversive actions.

FRATERNAL OBJECTIVES ARE THE KEY

Concealment of fraternal objectives is the key. Privacy is only guaranteed and acceptable in a free society if the privacy is used for legitimate ends.

Evidence is accumulating that Yale senior society power has been used for illegitimate ends. In the *Phoenix Letter* for December 1984, January and February 1985 we demonstrated — with only preliminary evidence — that the Yale senior society system has *generated the architects of defeat in U.S. foreign policy.* We demonstrated that members act jointly and consistently to the disadvantage of the United States.

Not only is *membership* concealed, but also *objectives* are concealed and members are *under oath* not to discuss membership or objectives.

We can deduce *objectives* from the actions of these blood brothers. Joint actions are the indicator and result of intentions. Joint actions are the proof of intentions.

Consider again, for example, the case of "The Brotherhood" in England as surfaced by Stephen Knight. The KGB infiltrated and manipulated British freemasonry to control British intelligence organizations. Yet British Freemasons claim a right to privacy. They are indeed entitled to privacy if their ends are *legitimate* and if they take precautions against misuse of privacy. But in England freemasonry was used for illegitimate ends. Privacy is used as a reason to hide perverted, illegal, socially harmful actions totally unacceptable in a free society.

In three issues of the Phoenix Letter we outlined joint use of power in the United States by members of Yale senior societies. These actions were to the disadvantage of the United States. We have so far outlined only 8 events. In fact, we have — even at this early stage — another 20 events ready to lay before you, including control of the Manhattan Project, target selection in World War Two, the Alger Hiss case, and a wide range of other situations.

Given the British case and these 28 events, we are entitled to view Mr. Daly's claim for privacy with extreme skepticism.

Not only can we demonstrate highly suspicious joint use of power, but also we have a situation where members are supposed to deny membership, membership lists are not published, and even Vice President Bush *in writing* will neither confirm nor deny membership. The "Temple" is not open to outsiders.

And we are supposed to accept this in the name of privacy?

THE POWER OF APPOINTMENT

The secret of The Order's acquisition of power is the *fraternal use of appointment.*

Any member who acquires a position of power uses this position to appoint blood brothers. This preferential pattern of appointment starts on the Yale campus itself and has been the target of past Yale criticism. Priority in appointment appears to be:

(1) Blood brothers in Skull & Bones (Russell Trust)

(2) Members of Scroll & Key (Kingsley Trust) and Wolfs Head (Phelps Trust)

(3) Other Yale graduates — except that it is not enough to be *just* a Yale graduate. Under certain circumstances other Ivy League graduates or outsiders with specific qualifications have priority over Yale graduates.

4) Other Ivy League Universities, especially Harvard, Princeton and Johns Hopkins

(5) Families of (1) and (2) above

(6) Outsiders with specific qualifications

For example: President William Howard Taft (Club D. 76) appointed Franklin MacVeagh (Club D. 60) as his Secretary of Treasury and Henry Lewis Stimson (Club D. 86) as his Secretary of War.

In brief: Taft's appointments were selected from category (1) above for two senior cabinet posts.

But Taft appointed Theodore Marburg, German born, (6) above, as U.S. Ambassador to Belgium. Why? In 1911 Marburg was the prime exponent of the League of Nations idea and used the Belgian post to push this concept. The League of Nations concept is an event we can trace to The Order and its associates.

HOW THEY PLAN TO PERPETUATE POWER

Of even greater significance is the way The Order has tried to institutionalize its power of appointment: *to remove power from the electorate.*

The selective appointment device has a weakness: sooner or later it may be identified and public protest will neutralize the power.

Hence, we find attempts to *lock in* the power of preferential appointment.

Consider these facts:

• Cord Meyer was founder of United World Federalists. Cord Meyer is on the Scroll & Key list.

• President Eisenhower's National Goals Commission had William P. Bundy (Club D. 137) as its director.

• The Hutchins-Luce Freedom of the Press Commission wanted to *restrict* the power of the press to inform. Henry Luce was Club D. 118 and Robert Hutchins was Phelps Trust.

These efforts came to a head with promotion of the "new Constitution." Here's how perpetuation of power *almost* came about in the 1960-1970 period:

Robert Maynard Hutchins (Phelps Trust) was Associate Director of the Ford Foundation, 1951-5. Ford Foundation established Fund for the Republic in 1954 and Hutchins became President. Fund for the Republic funded an outfit called Center for the Study of Democratic Institutions.

In the mid to late 1960s the Center got to work on the "new Constitution" and a member of The Order, McGeorge Bundy (Club D. 138), was President of the supporting Ford Foundation.

The Center's prime objective was to draft a "model Constitution for contemporary America."

Some of the provisions of this "new Constitution" follow: (taken from *The Center Magazine*, Volume III, No. 5, September/October 1970)

- Power of the Presidency is modified and shifted to the Senate
- Senators have *lifetime* tenure
- Senators *appointed*, not elected
- All enterprises regulated by a National Regulator
- The present Bill of Rights is either omitted or carefully circumscribed

The final version of this *dictatorial manifesto* was published in Rexford G. Tugwell, *The Emerging Constitution* (Harper & Rowe, 1974).

Current attempts to introduce the new "Constitution" through the back door include:

- Creation of 10 Federal Regions, equal to the ten "new States"
- A call to expand the Presidential term to nine years
- They plan for a Constitutional Convention in 1987. George Bush (D. 146) will be President of the Convention.

What You See Depends On Where You Stand

The vast majority of people look at events and activities as disconnected and independent. For most people the effort to establish a "new constitution" in 1970 has no connection with, for example, President Taft's cabinet appointments in 1911 or the Hutchins-Luce Commission on Freedom-of the Press, or the other 28 major events we have identified.

However, if one finds a *common thread* linking seemingly different events, people and activities, the viewpoint changes. This generates a search for other common links between the same people and events.

The common link or thread in 28 events (so far) is membership in Yale secret societies: Russell Trust, Kingsley Trust and Phelps Trust. Control or manipulation of these events and activities was in the hands of members of one or more of these trusts.

It is this common thread, a binding link, that secrecy keeps from public view. When you look at these events and activities from the viewpoint of secret fraternal organizations, the perspective changes.

Privacy then becomes unacceptable secrecy. Privacy becomes a device for manipulation of a free society. And if any reader doubts this can be done, please read Stephen Knight's *The Brotherhood* (Granada Press, 1984).

CONCLUSIONS

1. Radley Daly, Treasurer of Scroll & Key, claims a right to privacy for Yale senior societies.

2. We have introduced evidence that privacy has been used as a device to conceal joint activities to manipulate a free society.

3. Therefore the claim for privacy is rejected. Honest members of Yale senior societies — and they exist — should demand publication of all practices, traditions and "secrets."

THE LANDKAMER PROJECT

1. The network expands slowly but quite surely. A structure has evolved in which individuals work on specific projects in their own time at their own pace. Research results are coordinated with Landkamer, who makes them available to other interested parties.

2. Information is required on the following points:

(a) The Identity Church

(b) An alleged CIA operation entitled "Earl of Dysart"

(c) Names of Yale senior society members that have come up in connection with the Kennedy assassination, the Warren Commission and the Rockefeller Commission

NEWSNOTES

The Order And "Look Alikes"

Out of nowhere, in the last 12 months around the U.S., we find media stories about alleged criminal groups called The Order.

The media has given major space to these groups, but none to The Order as publicized in the *Phoenix Letter.*

Even more fascinating, we have received letters from prisoners in Federal Penitentiaries inquiring about The Order. So far, Federal prisons in California, Kansas, Texas and Alabama are represented in this unsolicited and unexpected prison mail.

There is no connection between The Order as publicized so far in the media and The Order described in the *Phoenix Letter.*

THE PHOENIX LETTER

Vol 7 No 3 May 1988

SECRET SOCIETIES

Vice President Bush is, as you know, a member of the super-secret Yale Skull & Bones. The following is from *Newsweek On Campus* (April 1988, page 17): "All references to Yale's 156-year-old Skull & Bones, which considers itself the ultimate secret society, are torn out of the card catalogs at the college library, and magazine articles about the group have been ripped from bound volumes. Those nosing around the Skull and Bones tomb may be followed or even threatened."

We can confirm the *Newsweek* reports of threats from our own sources. But what *Newsweek* doesn't know is that this makes investigators all the more curious and stubborn. Many seem to end up contacting us because we duplicated the Yale Library files many years ago. We are happy to make this suppressed information available to genuine researchers.

Personal note for Lee Atwood and Skull & Bones *thugs*, the files are duplicated, scattered and far distant from Arizona and California. Note for Yale Library: please reread the American Library Association regulations on suppressing materials. Thank you.

THE PHOENIX LETTER

Vol 8 No 12 December 1989

SKULL AND BONES SOCIETY

Sudden flurry of articles on Skull and Bones in establishment media ... picking up from where this editor left off in *Americas Secret Establishment.*

Louisville Courier-Journal (Magazine section Sunday, October 8, 1989) "The Bonesmen's Bond" with a subtitle "Presidents, Poets, Pundits and Pinkos have sworn allegiance to Skull and Bones, Yale's rich and powerful secret society, and the most exclusive college club of all. So what's all that Nazi stuff doing in the clubhouse?" Written by Steven M.L. Aronson.

Aronson charges that a room in the Bones Temple is "a little Nazi shrine inside, one room on the second floor has a bunch of swastikas, kind of an SS macho Nazi iconography."

Aronson forgets to mention that President Bush is (and his father was) in Skull and Bones.

The New Haven Advocate (New Haven is the home town of Yale and Skull and Bones).

The front page article in the October 19, 1989 issue is headed: "Bones of contention: skullduggery at Yale" by Howard Altman.

It's an extraordinary story — the Skull and Bones Temple at Yale is *illegally* holding the skull of Apache Chief Geronimo ... stolen from the grave by Senator Prescott Bush, father of President Bush, and other Bonesmen.

The Apaches want the skull back ... and under Connecticut law (Section 53-334 of Offenses Against Public Policy and Title 45-253 of the State Probate Law) the holding of human remains is *illegal.*

New Haven lawyers, according to Altman, are reluctant to sue or press for a civil or criminal complaint because of the power of Skull and Bones, to which *we* say "wait a minute, this isn't Russia" ... the local prosecutor *has a duty* to prosecute if the evidence is credible. *After all we live under the rule of law and that includes Presidents.* If Mr. Bush is accessory to a criminal offense, apparently compounded by satanism, he has to be brought to the bar of justice. In this case George Herbart Walker Bush is apparently not implicated directly except that he would have knowledge of illegal actions — which is indeed an offense.

[Other news sources please copy and give this charge some public exposure.]

The Altman article also cites a book, a history of Skull and Bones written in 1933 entitled *The Continuation of the History of Our Order for the Century Celebration.* Compiled by F.O. Matthieson. [Altman does not state that Matthieson was a prominent Marxist and a link between the old line Communists of the 1930's and the new progressives of the 1960's.]

If any reader can locate a copy of this book we will arrange for reprinting.

In any event:

(1) We now have clues that President Bush may be tied to *satanic practices.* This was a segment included in our *America's Secret Establishment*.

(2) We also have links between Skull and Bones and Naziism.

If you have read Trevor Ravenscroft *Sword of Destiny* ... *you will* immediately appreciate the significance. We suspect more information will surface in coming years.

Yale *Co-eds* before 1969
courtesy Manuscripts and Archives
Yale University Library

WHAT HATH WOMEN WROUGHT?

KRIS MILLEGAN
FEBRUARY 2001

KA-THUNK! THE SOUND BROUGHT MY ATTENTION to the very building that brought me to New Haven in the first place, "The Tomb," an expanded mausoleum, housing Yale's oldest senior secret society, The Order of Skull and Bones.

Out came a young, serious coed leaving the building into the cold afternoon snowscape. That started me wondering, what hath the ladies wrought? What had been the effect of allowing females into that venerable male bastion?

In 1991, the 15 outgoing members *tapped* 6 gals and 9 guys in early April as their replacements. Retribution came fast, the locks were changed on the heavy doors at High Street and board spokesman Reverend Sid Lovett (S&B 1950) declared, "There was no election. There is no society [next year]."

The "disagreement" caused more mainstream ink about the secret group's activities than ever before. There were stories in *Time, Newsweek* and *The Economist.* Even *People* magazine ran a 2-page spread about the Bones tiff in May '91, while Bonesman GHW Bush (S&B 48) sat in the Oval Office ... with no comment.

Walking around today at Yale, one can see and feel a strong feminine presence. Yale has been coed since 1969, the year after George W Bush (S&B 1968) graduated. By 1991 the undergrads were 45% female and a feeling on campus was that "gender differences between friends of different sexes is not a dominant issue." The Bones crowd was, as Yale was by 1991, a diverse group of races, creeds and sexual orientation. Also the *Tomb* had become a bone of contention with feminists and there had been a break-in by some determined ladies, who took pictures and spread *rumors.*

The board had offered an early compromise of separate his and hers secret societies but that was rejected by the then seniors, who went ahead, "tapped" the ladies and were locked-out of their High Street hideaway.

The "locked-outs" vowed to continue and they were soon offered the use of another senior society's (Manuscript) secret clubhouse. A then senior Bonesman contended, "It makes sense to be co-ed because the world is co-ed." One view on the other side, a Patriarch DC lawyer, felt "the admission of women would lead to 'date rape' in the 'medium-term future.'"

A vote-by-mail by Bones members produced a narrow vote in favor of the admittance of the co-eds. The *old guard* cried foul, filed charges that the *mail vote* was against *Bones by-laws* and scuttled the September '92 plans to initiate the ladies. Finally in November a second vote was taken, with members having to either appear in person or send a proxy by another Bonesman, at the *Tomb* and another slim decision was made to admit the gals. The 2000 senior group, outed by *Rumpus*, Yale's tabloid, included at least six women and maybe more. The *Rumpus* printed two different lists and some names could be either male or female. And it seems, judging from a list of Wolf Head's members for the year 2001, that Wolf's Head, the last all-male senior secret society at Yale, has also gone co-ed.

What has been the effect? Do the women tapped for Bones follow the "old guidelines" of captains of ball teams, a Yale Lit editor, maybe a radical (for excitement?), some old-blood money with a few minorities tossed in now and then? Is there a new sexual element? What about the sexual confession times? Is there a hot time on High Street now? Has the "nude mud wrestling" in the basement changed to "playtime in the dungeon?" Does the narrow vote show a political change at stodgy Bones? Will Bones be taken-over by radical-Amazons? What hath the women wrought?

"*My senior year, I joined Skull and Bones, a secret society, so secret I can't say anything more. It was a chance to make fourteen new friends.*"

From the autobiography of George W Bush, *A Charge to Keep.*

According to recent lists released by Yale's tabloid *Rumpus,* women are definitely here to stay at Bones. Women may actually revive some life and interest by students in the Order which was taking a beating from undergrads for its males-only stand. According to an article in the April 16, 1991, *Hartford Courant:* "My sense is that they get turned down these days more often than they get accepted," said Jacob Weisberg, a senior editor of the *New Republic,* who declined to become a Bonesman in 1985 when asked. "There have been years lately when their whole first string has turned them down."

Jacob even turned down a personal request from John Kerry to join Bones because "he felt he could not join a club that excludes women."

Skull & Bones

Kris Millegan
Appeared in *High Times*, January 2000

"These secret societies are behind it all," my father told me many years ago, During the early '50s he was a CIA branch chief, head of the East Asia intelligence analysis office. "The Vietnam War," he said soberly, "is about drugs." Many years later I finally had some understanding of what Dad was telling me. I wish I had asked more questions. Like, was he was talking about the Order of Skull and Bones?

It's a symbol used by pirates and poisons, but it's also a "fraternity" at Yale University. College kids having fun? Not quite.

Fifteen juniors are tapped on a Thursday in May each year. Around 2,500 have been members, mostly white males from wealthy Northeastern families: Bush, Ford, Goodyear, Harriman, Heinz, Jay, Kellogg, Phelps, Pillsbury, Pinchot, Rockefeller, Taft, Vanderbilt, Weyerhaeuser and Whitney are some of the names on its roster- Minorities were admitted in the 1950s, and the first women were admitted in 1991.

The Order of Skull and Bones is a secret society founded at Yale by **William Huntington Russell (S&B 1833)**. His cousin Samuel Russell's family enterprise, Russell & Company, was the largest American opium smuggler, working with the Scottish firm Jardine-Matheson, the world's largest opium smuggler.

Many New England and Southern families in the "China Trade" sent their sons to Yale, and many were "tapped" into Skull and Bones. From Yale, "Bonesmen" entered and were very influential in the worlds of commerce, communications, diplomacy, education, espionage, finance, law and politics.

There have been two Skull and Bones presidents, at least 10 Senators, two Chief Justices of the Supreme Court and many US Representatives and state governors.

Bonesmen have held myriad lesser appointed posts and positions, with a particular affinity for the Central Intelligence Agency. This year, a Bonesman — **George W. Bush (S&B 1968)** is the leading contender for the presidency.

The Bush Bonesmen

George W. Bush is the third generation of Bush Bonesmen to become prominent in national politics. His father, President George H.W. Bush, joined S&B, in 1948. His grandfather, **Prescott Bush (S&B, 1917)** was a senator from Connecticut, 1952-62, a partner in the Brown Brothers, Harriman investment-banking firm, and a director for CBS, Pan Am and Prudential. He was one of President Dwight Eisenhower's favorite golfing partners and a member of Washington's elite Alibi Club.

But there was more to Prescott than met the resume. He had served as a US Army Intelligence liaison officer during World War I. Prescott's boss, **W. Averell Harriman (S&B 1913)** worked closely with fellow "Bonesman" Secretary of Defense **Robert Lovett (S&B 1918)** to organize US intelligence activities in the early Cold War. They created a framework to run covert operations and psychological warfare.

In 1954, H.S. Richardson, the maker of Vick's cough drops and Vapo-Rub, wrote in a letter to Senator Bush; "l want to get your advice and counsel on a subject — namely what should be done with the income from a foundation, which my brothers and I are setting up."

Eugene Stetson (S&B 1934), an assistant manager at Brown Brothers, Harriman, organized the H. Smith Richardson Foundation. It participated in MK-ULTRA, a secret CIA domestic psychological-warfare operation, and helped to finance the testing of psychotropic drugs, including LSD, at Bridgewater Hospital in Massachusetts in the '50s.

In the '80s, the Richardson Foundation was a "private donors steering committee," working with the National Security Council to coordinate the Office of Public Diplomacy. This was an effort to provide money and cover for arming the Nicaraguan Contra rebels, and to coordinate published attacks on opponents of the program.

In 1962, Prescott founded the National Strategy Information Center, with his son, Prescott Bush, Jr. and future CIA director William Casey, an investment banker and veteran of the Office of Strategic Services (OSS), the CIA's predecessor. The center laundered funds for the dissemination of CIA-authored "news stories" to some 300 newspapers.

Gordon Gray, another of Prescott's golfing buddies, was Eisenhower's national security adviser and first director of the Psychological Strategy Board in the early '5Os. Along with Averell Harriman and others, he created the modern wall of "deniability" for US covert actions, such as the overthrow of leftist governments in Iran in 1953 and Guatemala in 1954. Gray's son C. Bowden Gray was President George Bush's White House counsel. As "protector of the president, come what may," he helped to keep Bush "out of the loop" as George became embroiled in the evolving Iran-Contra scandal. Iran-Contra, Watergate and other scandals have many of the same players — the Cubans from the "secret war" against Fidel Castro.

WHAT DID YOU DO IN THE SECRET WAR, DADDY?

HENRY NEIL MALLON (S&B 1917), Prescott's classmate at Yale and Dresser Industries chairman of the board, on April 10, 1953, wrote a letter to CIA Director Allen Dulles about a proposed meeting at the Carlton Hotel. At this meeting Mallon, Prescott Bush and Dulles discussed the use of drilling rigs in the Caribbean. Dresser Industries had "often provided cover employment to CIA operatives."

In reaction to the Cuban Revolution in 1959, Vice President Richard Nixon and the National Security Council formed a working group — the "5412 Committee." Members discussing "plausible deniability" and the option of assassinating Cuban leaders decided to use a third-party "cut-out" for the operation.The "cut-out," code-named Operation 40, was mobster Santos Trafficante, who had plenty of reasons to want Castro gone — and any actions could easily be laid at his doorstep. And with groundwork already laid with the World War II mob/docks deal and subsequent black-market activities in Italy, an informal financing arrangement between "intel," the mob, assassins and arms, and drug trafficking was made.

Zapata Off Shore, an offshore oil-drilling company headed by George Bush, provided a convenient cover. CIA veterans from 1960s covert actions against Castro maintain Zapata was used "as a front," and "Zapata's and their subsidiaries' offshore drilling platforms were used in operations." And according to former senior CIA Operations Directorate officials, Bush was a paymaster for "contracted services."

As liaison between the CIA and the Pentagon during the 1961 Bay of Pigs invasion of Cuba, Fletcher Prouty was put in charge of ordering supplies for the attack. "The CIA had code-named the invasion 'Zapata,'" recalls Prouty. "Two boats landed on the shores of Cuba. One was named Houston, the other Barbara. They were Navy ships that has been repainted with new names." At the time George Bush was living in Houston with his wife, Barbara.

In July, 1988, *The Nation* published a memo from FBI Director J. Edgar Hoover, stating that "Mr. George Bush of the Central Intelligence Agency" was providing information about State Department anxieties concerning the reaction of "some misguided anti-Castro" Cubans to President John F. Kennedy's assassination.

After Nixon resigned as President, his staff revealed that his code name for the assassination of John Kennedy was that "Bay of Pigs thing." One of the most important pieces of evidence in the assassination, Abraham Zapruder's film, was purchased by Time, Inc., and locked in a vault. Time, Inc. was founded by **Henry Luce (S&B, 1920).**

The Zapruder film got its first public screening after being subpoenaed by Judge Jim Garrison, who tried to prove CIA involvement in the killing. Ellen Ray, who now publishes Covert Action magazine, went to New Orleans to do a documentary on Garrison. After receiving many death threats, she canceled the project, but not before she met Prescott Bush at a private dinner arranged by a writer for the *New Yorker.* At the dinner, Prescott tried to pump her for information about Garrison's investigation.

Numerous government and ClA employees say that under Bush's successor, **Richard Gow (S&B 1955)**, the US and other governments used drill rigs owned by Zapata Off Shore and its subsidiary Rowan International for covert operations involving support and logistics for arms and drug trafficking operations.

"A great many of the drug smugglers in Miami today are Bay of Pigs veterans," a Florida drug prosecutor said in 1986. "That's why they are so tough. They are intelligence trained."

In 1998 former Green Beret William Tyree filed a $63 million federal lawsuit against Bush, the CIA and others. His court documents allege that US military personnel were used to assist arms and drug traffic. Tyree had started to become disenchanted with this "official" mission and his wife, Elaine, who was working for the Army Criminal Investigation Division, started to keep diaries. She was found beheaded with a hunting knife. Tyree was charged with the murder.

The charges were dropped by Massachusetts Judge James Killiam. "I didn't believe a word the prosecution's chief witness said," he said in a recent A&E special. The case had been re-filed by the Middlesex County DA's office. A young **John Kerry (S&B 1966)** was assistant DA at the time. In the late '80s Kerry chaired a special Senate committee on drugs, law enforcement and foreign policy, which made much noise about government-assisted drug-trafficking, but took no action. Much in the committee's files is still "classified."

One Army Intelligence and five Special Forces colonels associated with Tyree and these operations have since died, some under mysterious circumstances. Several have left amazing affidavits that detail massive hard drug trafficking by government personnel under the aegis of "national security." One of them, known as a "money man," had phone numbers for Bill Casey and a Gambino family crime boss in his address book.

The explosive lawsuit progresses slowly and nary a peep is heard from the media.

BUT IT'S NOT THE FIRST TIME

ON OCTOBER 20, 1942, 10 months after Pearl Harbor, US government ordered the seizure of "all the capital stock of the Union Banking Corporation, a New York corporation," by the Alien Property Custodian; the order stated "all of which shares are held for the benefit of members of the Thyssen family, [and] is property of nationals of a designated enemy country."

It seems that Averell Harriman and Prescott Bush — along with corporate lawyer John Foster Dulles and his brother Allen Dulles, spymaster for the CIA and the OSS — and others were involved in the buildup of Nazi Germany, supplying the Third Reich with capital and financial arrangements. This was kept quiet. Only a small notice appeared in the New York Times-years later — on Dec. 16, 1944: "The Union Banking Corporation, 39 Broadway, New York has received authority to change its principal place of business to 120 Broadway."

No mention was made of the fact that Union Banking Corporation had been seized for trading with the enemy, or that 120 Broadway was the address of the Alien Property Custodian.

Origins Of The Order

The Order of Skull and Bones was founded in 1832 by William Huntington Russell and Alphonso Taft. Many historians claim it appeared because Phi Beta Kappa, America's oldest Greek-letter college society, had abandoned secrecy.

Phi Beta Kappa was "founded with impressive ritual and high solemnity" on Thursday, December 5, 1776, at William and Mary College, in Williamsburg, Virginia. The chapter at William and Mary was disbanded in 1781, making the Yale branch, which was founded in November 1780, the oldest extant chapter.

Phi Beta Kappa became an "open honorary organization" in 1832. In protest, apparently, Russell, Yale valedictorian of 1833, influenced Taft and 13 others "to form what is now perhaps the most famous secret society in the United States."

From the very beginning there was resentment from fellow students. Faculty sent warning letters to early members' parents. But the chapter persisted and flourished, and by 1884 two other senior secret societies at Yale had been formed, Scroll and Key, and Wolf's Head. Also, Phi Beta Kappa was revived after disappearing in 1871.

On September 29, 1876, the Order of File and Claw broke into the "Tomb," the windowless Bones-owned and built meeting house. They wrote that they saw its walls "adorned with pictures of the founders of Bones at Yale, and of the members of the society in Germany, when the Chapter was established here in 1832."

In the cellar, they found a small room, with an "always-burning lamp" and "a dilapidated human skull." Upstairs, three rooms were found, a lodge room with its walls covered in black velvet, a table with skull and crossbones, and the "sanctum sanctorum," furnished in red velvet. The Order of File and Claw also reported an old engraving that, along with the decor, represented aspects of the Regent's degree in the outlawed Bavarian Illuminati.

The Links Of Power

For some understanding of the complex links between members of Skull and Bones, consider the first Bonesman to become president, **William Howard Taft (S&B 1878)**, who is the only man to have been both president and chief justice of the Supreme Court. His father, S&B cofounder Alphonso Taft, was appointed secretary of war by President Ulysses Grant, and was later Attorney General.

William Howard Taft was appointed by President William McKinley to be the first civil governor of the Philippines, displacing a disgruntled General Arthur MacArthur — General Douglas MacArthur's father — who had been the military governor. Theodore Roosevelt, who became president after the assassination of McKinley, appointed Taft secretary of war (1904-08). While secretary, he was the "master overseer and troubleshooter" for the Panama Canal, provisional governor of Cuba, and played a key role in foreign policy.

Taft was elected President in 1908. He was appointed chief justice of the Supreme Court by President Warren Harding in 1921, and served until just before his death in 1930.

President Taft made **Henry L. Stimson (S&B 1888)** his secretary of war (1911-13). Stimson was appointed to high government posts by seven presidents. He was governor general of the Philippines (1926-1928), secretary of state under President Herbert Hoover (1929-1933) and secretary of war under presidents Franklin Delano Roosevelt and Harry S. Truman (1940-1946). He was 'ultimately responsible" for the internment of Japanese-Americans in World War II, and oversaw the Manhattan Project, building the atomic bomb. He also took credit for swaying Truman into dropping the bomb.

Stimson groomed a generation of "Cold Warriors," in what was known as "Stimson's Kindergarten." Among these proteges were General George C. Marshall, John J. McCloy, Dean Acheson, and fellow Bonesmen Robert A. Lovett, **William Bundy (S&B 1939)** and his brother **McGeorge Bundy (S&B 1940)**.

"These men helped establish a distinguished network connecting Wall Street, Washington, worthy foundations and proper clubs," historian and Kennedy adviser Arthur Schlesinger, Jr., wrote. "The New York and legal community was the heart of the American Establishment. Its household deities were Henry L. Stimson and Elihu Root; its present leaders, Robert A. Lovett and John J. McCloy; its front organizations, the Rockefeller, Ford and Carnegie foundations and the Council on Foreign Relations."

Harriman and the Bundy brothers, in their positions in the State Department, Department of Defense, the CIA and as advisers to Presidents Kennedy and Johnson, exercised significant impact on the flow of information and intelligence during the Vietnam War. Harriman had busy careers in business and politics and led peace negotiations with North Vietnam in 1968. William Bundy went on to be editor of Foreign Affairs, the influential quarterly of the Council on Foreign Relations. McGeorge Bundy became president of the Ford Foundation.

The Fox And The Henhouse

George Bush was appointed by President Nixon to the White House Cabinet Committee on International Control in 1971. As vice president, he was the highest US official involved in the War on Drugs, as chairman of President Reagan's cabinet-level working group and as director of the National Narcotics Interdiction System.

Frances Mullen, Jr., former head of the Drug Enforcement Administration, called Bush's efforts "an intellectual fraud" and "a liability rather than an asset." Soon after these statements, Mullen resigned, and the resultant General Accounting Office report was buried.

In July 1985, the suppressed GAO paper reported that there were "no benefits from the National Narcotics Border Interdiction System, directed by George Bush. In fact, the overall effect was to encourage supply."

Bonesmen have helped create a prohibition where plants and their by-products are sold on the black market for precious-metal prices, using a corrupted "secret government" for trafficking and propaganda. A cabal that uses an unconstitutional Drug War for political, economic and social control.

Black Market Bones

Do the Origins of the Opium Trade Lead to the Most Dangerous Secret Society in America?

Kris Millegan
Appeared in *High Times*, October 2000

Motherships sail up and down the coast. Fast, small craft come out, load contraband and scoot back to shore day and night. Corrupt officials take bribes to look the other way. The smugglers live large, build yachts and send their kids to private schools. Banks and fronts are set up to launder money, move "product" and avoid scrutiny. Oodles and oodles of money are being made. The 1980s in Miami? Nope, we're talking about the mid-1800s, when some of America's oldest fortunes were made in the Chinese opium trade.

The *Sam Russell*

"The finest and fastest vessels of their size to be found in any sea, built by the best naval architects in England, Scotland and America. No cost is spared in their equipment, their crews large for rapid evolution, and their captains are the most skilled and dashing sailors to be found." So wrote missionary John Johnstone in the 1850s as he traveled by opium clipper to his station along the China coast.

You see, by the mid-1830s the trade in opium was the largest commodity market on the planet. And as Carl A. Trocki's excellent book *Opium, Empire and the Global Economy* (1999) points out:

> The trade in such drugs results in monopoly which not only centralizes the drug traffic, but also restructures the social and economic terrain in the process. Two major effects are the creation of mass markets and the generation of enormous ...

unprecedented, cash flows. [Which] results in the concentrated accumulation of vast pools of wealth. [Which] have been among the primary foundations of global capitalism and the modern nation-state itself. Indeed, it may be argued that the entire rise of the West, from 1500 to 1900, depended on a series of drug trades.

Drug trades destabilized existing societies not merely because they destroyed individual human beings but also, and perhaps more importantly [they] undercut the existing political economy of any state. They have created new forms of capital; and they have redistributed wealth in radically new ways.

It is possible to suggest that mass consumption, as it exists in modern society, began with drug addiction. And, beyond that, addiction began with a drug-as-commodity. Something was necessary to prime the pump, as it were, to initiate the cycles of production, consumption and accumulation that we identify with capitalism. Opium was the catalyst of the consumer market, the money economy.

Opium created pools of capital and fed the institutions that accumulated it: the banking and financial systems, the insurance systems and the transportation and information infrastructures.

One might say, *"Who controls opium controls? ...."*

Fast Ships, Drugs and Money

When we sold the Heathen nations rum and opium in rolls,
And the Missionaries went along to save their sinful souls.
The Old Clipper Days
— Julian S. Cutler

The Portuguese, Dutch, French, British and others began trading in opium soon after the first contact with China. Because the Chinese desired few trade goods, the Western nations soon became short of silver to purchase tea, silk, porcelain and other desired items. Fueled by both economic and imperialistic motives, the opium trade grew from around 200 chests (16 tons) a year to 4,200 chests (336 tons) by 1820, with the majority imported from India and in the hands of British traders. But the times were a'changing.

The upstart Americans introduced their famous clipper ships expressly for the "China trade," and in the 1830s the price of opium went down and shipments of opium to China went up. Shipments in 1830 were four times what they had been in 1820; by 1838, they'd more than doubled again. The opium clipper, with its ability to sail against the monsoons, sometimes made three round-trip journeys within one year, instead of taking up to two years to complete just one journey there and back. Profits were huge, and there was a large flow of silver being introduced from China into booming Western economies.

Canton Factories, circa 1825

In early 1837 there was a crash in the opium market, and the speculators' losses reverberated around the world in a financial panic, in which cash became scarce both in the US and Britain. Smuggler Robert B. Forbes lost his first opium fortune in the "Panic of 1837," and returned to China for more. He had built a house (now a museum) in Milton, Massachusetts (not far from where former President George Bush was born). Forbes had a special ship built: the "Lintin," a "storeship" named after an anchorage where he spent many years warehousing and selling contraband opium to Russell & Co. Chinese customers. Forbes would tell Chinese officials and others that he didn't deal in opium. But he was actually engaging in word games, and/or "transferring" the opium trade to front companies.

Russell & Co. was the largest American opium smuggler, and the third largest in the world, behind the British Dent firm and the largest smuggler of all, the Scottish merchants Jardine-Matheson. For many years Russell & Co and Jardine-Matheson worked together and were known as the "Combination." They virtually controlled the trade, manipulating market forces towards maximizing profits.

Thomas H. Perkins

Russell & Co. was started in 1824 by Samuel Russell of Middletown, Connecticut. In 1828 it "absorbed" the T.H. Perkins opium concern of Boston and became America's dominant force in China. Russell & Co. was very much a family affair, with uncles, cousins, brothers, fathers and sons dominating the firm and its allied banks and fronts.

The Russell family was steeped in Yale College history. The Rev. Nodiah Russell was a Yale founder. And in 1832, General William Huntington Russell, Samuel Russell's cousin, founded one of the US' most famous secret societies: the Order of Skull and Bones, along with Alphonso Taft. Taft's son, future President William Howard Taft (S&B 1878), would play many roles in the creation of international narcotics controls and the US Drug War.

Russell & Co. ships *Levant* and *Milo anchored off the Chinese island of Linton, an opium smuggling transhipment base.*

The Opium Wars

"I had not come to China for health or pleasure, and that I should remain at my post as long as I could sell a yard of cloth or buy a pound of tea."

—**R.B. Forbes** to Captain C. Elliot, British Superintendent of Trade, in refusing to leave Canton during the first Opium War.

Relations between the West and China had always been strained. The Chinese emperor would only receive Western ambassadors as if they were tribute-bearing vassals, and in the highly structured social caste of China, merchants were not worthy of respect, let alone discourse at an official level. For many years dealings with Westerners were delegated to a few "Hong" merchants, who paid for the privilege and had to vouchsafe the foreigners' commercial dealings. The term "pidgin" English came from the Hong merchant pronunciation of the word "business" in the trade dialect of English that was used to conduct affairs with the "white devils."

Chinese High Commissioner Lin Tse-hsu came to Canton in 1839 with an order to "investigate the port affairs." The first edict against opium had come in 1729; another against smoking came in 1796. The trade had grown to 40,000 chests by 1838. Smoking, a novel, more soporific and addictive manner of using opium, plus the encouragement of the trade by the British and others, had devastated all segments of Chinese society. Corruption, smuggling and smoking were rampant, creating apathy, and the trade was also draining China's treasury.

Commissioner Lin

Lin couldn't believe that opium was legal in Britain, and wrote a letter to Queen Victoria to implore her aid in stopping the trade. He disrupted the local merchants and published new edicts against the use and importation of the drug. Lin demanded that all chests of opium be forfeited as contraband, and all trading houses sign a bond, pledging to smuggle no more and becoming liable to Chinese law, which included the death penalty. Through threats, a servant walkout, giant gongs that were rung all night and other measures, he was able to collect over 20,000 chests of opium (about half of that year's Indian trade). Then, under orders from the emperor, he destroyed it all.

This sparked the first Opium War, made huge profits for those companies that had held on to chests, and left Russell & Company the only trading firm left open in Canton.

Warren Delano, Jr.

During that first Opium War, the chief of operations for Russell & Co. in Canton was Warren Delano, Jr., grandfather of Franklin Roosevelt. He was also the US vice-consul and once wrote home, "The High officers of the [Chinese] Government have not only connived at the trade, but the Governor and other officers of the province have bought the drug and have taken it from the stationed ships in their own Government boats." Wu Ping-chen, or Howqua II, the leading "hong" merchant, was considered by some to be one of the world's richest men, worth over $26 million in 1833.

Hoqua

SERIOUS BUSINESS

"If the trade is ever legalized, it will cease to be profitable from that time. The more difficulties that attend it, the better for you and us."
—Directors of Jardine-Matheson

THE PROFITS WERE HUGE and many fortunes were made. Warren Delano went home with one, lost it and went back to China to get more. Russell & Co. partners included John Cleve Green, a banker and railroad investor who made large donations to and was a trustee for Princeton; A. Abiel Low, a shipbuilder, merchant and railroad owner who backed Columbia University; and merchants Augustine Heard and Joseph Coolidge. Coolidge's son organized the United Fruit Company, and his grandson, Archibald C. Coolidge, was a cofounder of the Council on Foreign Relations. Partner John M. Forbes "dominated the management" of the Chicago, Burlington and Quincey

A. Heard

railroad, with Charles Perkins as president. Other partners and captains included Joseph Taylor Gilman, William Henry King, John Alsop Griswold, Captain Lovett and Captain J. Prescott. Captain Prescott called on F.T. Bush, Esq., his friend and agent in Hong Kong frequently. Russell & Co. families, relations and friends are well represented in the Order of Skull and Bones.

Shanghai - 1843

After the first Opium War, the port of Shanghai was opened up, with Russell & Co. as one of it first foreign merchants. In 1841, Russell brought the first steam ship to Chinese waters and continued to develop transportation routes as long as opium made them profitable. Russell partners were also involved in early railroad ventures in China, together with US railroad magnate E.H. Harriman, whose sons later became very active in Skull and Bones.

The second Opium War led to the legalization of opium in China in 1858, and the "country traders" began to lose their control of the business. They were just smugglers warehousing the "product" offshore and plying up and down the coast delivering opium to Chinese "compradors." Once opium was legalized, Chinese and Indian merchants started to take over the trade. Russell and others, with their limited role as smugglers, hadn't developed any structure to sell opium in inner China. The Chinese brokers could now just order opium just like any commodity, and the trade was transferred to firms with strong ties at the producing base, India, and the consuming giant, China.

Russell & Co. Shanghai, 1867

The old Western trading firms set up banks, transferred assets to other schemes and tried to capitalize on their "China trade" experience, but none of these ventures had quite the same level of profitability. Russell & Co. formed the Shanghai Steam Navigation Company, but in 1877 sold it to the China Merchant's Steam Navigation Company, and the American share of Chinese shipping dropped by 80%. Some sources say Russell failed in 1891, with British and German firms taken over their business. According to others, the company's successor in Shanghai was Shewan & Tomes.

In 1856, **Daniel C. Gilman (S&B 1852)**, a Russell & Co. partner relation, incorporated the Order of Skull & Bones as the Russell Trust Association, with General W.H. Russell as its president.

D.C. Gilman

THE MODERN WORLD: PROHIBITION, SMUGGLERS AND SPIES

The money from the drugs, produced the money for the guns, and that is how the operation worked, and Bush knew the whole god-damn thing.
—CIA operative Trenton Parker, in Rodney Stich's *Defrauding America*

IRONICALLY, THE SCIONS of these 19th-century opium fortunes would go on to play key roles in the Drug Wars of the 20th century: in both the enactment of drug prohibition and in the clandestine arrangements between smugglers and government spies.

In 1898, the Spanish-American War signaled the United States' debut as a global imperial power. American troops invaded Manila, and three years later, after a brutal guerrilla war, the Philippines became a colony of the US. President Theodore Roosevelt appointed Bonesman William Howard Taft to serve as the first civil governor of the islands. (Patriarch Bonesman Henry Stimson (S&B 1888) plus some Russell & Co. relations, later held that post.) Taft stayed on in the Philippines until 1904, even turning down a much-desired appointment to the US Supreme Court.

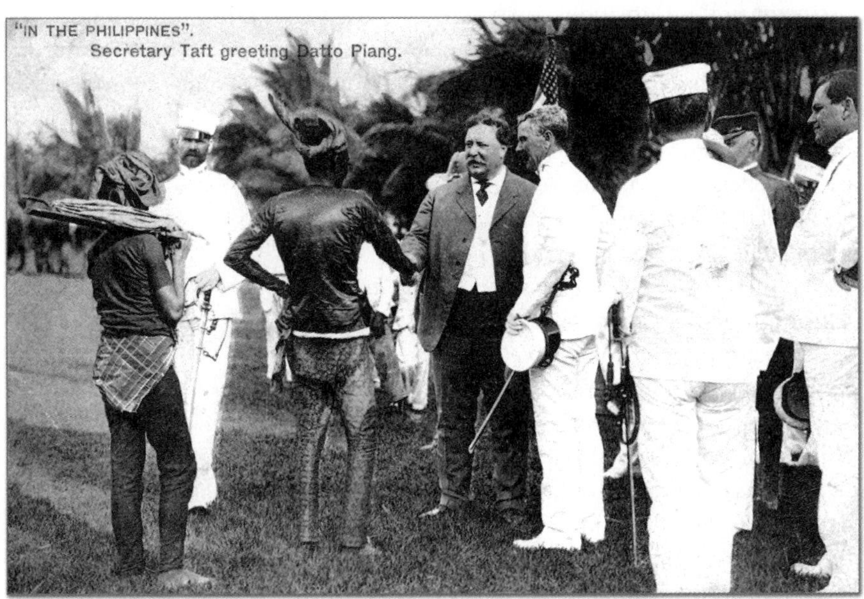
"IN THE PHILIPPINES".
Secretary Taft greeting Datto Piang.

Wrapper of legal opium packet, circa 1910

In 1903 the Philippines became the first modern nation in Asia to declare opium illegal. Soon there was a black market, and smuggling again began developing into a major force. Taft succeeded Roosevelt as President in 1909, and actively promoted federal legislation and international conventions to outlaw and "control" certain drugs. These international treaties helped to break down judicial reluctance, and brought claims of the extraconstitutional force of international treaty obligations into the enabling of US drug laws — thus creating a profitable prohibition.

And entangled in many of the recent nexuses of smugglers and spies is **George H.W. Bush (S&B 1948)**, one of scores of men from old-money families who wound up playing a prominent role in the covert-action realms of US foreign policy.

We have been told that the CIA agent George Bush who J. Edgar Hoover mentioned in a FBI memo concerning the John F. Kennedy assassination and Cubans was not THE George Bush. We have been told that Bush, then Vice President, was "out of the loop" for the Iran-Contra scandal of the 1980s, in which the US government either looked the other way or actively aided the Nicaraguan rebels' cocaine trafficking. Some of this we know to be lies.

Spooks, smugglers, and secrets seem to converge in a netherworld rapidly being exposed by researchers fueled by the Internet's capabilities of networking, discussion and informational exchange. Former federal prosecutors, journalists, authors, professors, researchers and others tracing the drug trade from many different directions all seem to end up with certain groups of high-level operatives being involved with this illicit trade in both drugs and arms. And many leads seem to point to George H.W. Bush and friends as the "elite deviants" involved in these schemes. "Many of the scandals that have occurred in the US since 1963 are fundamentally interrelated," sociologist David Simon wrote in Elite Deviance. "That is, the same people and institutions have been involved."

President George HW Bush

The mainstream media ignores it all, even the most recent startling revelations in Volume II of CIA Inspector General Frederick Hitz's report on "Allegations of Connections Between CIA and the Contras in Cocaine Trafficking to the United States." The Vol. II Hitz report depicts in no uncertain terms involvement in drug smuggling by US intelligence contract agents and their assets in Central America in the '80s, especially Lt. Col. Oliver North and other folks with strong contacts with George H.W. Bush.

Barry Seal

"And "Poppy" Bush also has kept alive the tradition of fast boats and smugglers. There was his friend Don Arnow, the "cigarette boat" builder/mob smuggler who was shot and died slumped over his steering wheel. As did another intelligence-connected drug-smuggler, Barry Seal, who, according to researcher Daniel Hopsicker, died in a hail of bullets with Bush's private phone number in his wallet."

With the current opiate epidemic closely mimicking the classic nation-destabilization/fortune-building imperialistic opium policy used against China in the 1800s, many drug-trade researchers question just what is going on where the higher echelons of the drug trade meet the secret branches of government.

Is the "official" prohibition one of collusion for political control, social engineering and the huge profits derived from illicit goods? Is all the heroin on the street there just because there exists a market full of desirous buyers? Or is a "secret government" using intelligence and military operatives in a massive drugging of our nation? Who runs it and where does the money go? Is it "government-sanctioned," under some twisted "national security" mantle?

Heroin is at an all-time high in purity, and at bargain-basement prices in a black market with younger and younger customers. It has gone from being less than 10% pure and scarce outside big-city ghettos to almost 70% pure and available nationwide, while the unaddictive marijuana has increased from $10 to $400 an ounce and has gotten somewhat harder to obtain.

Is this by chance?

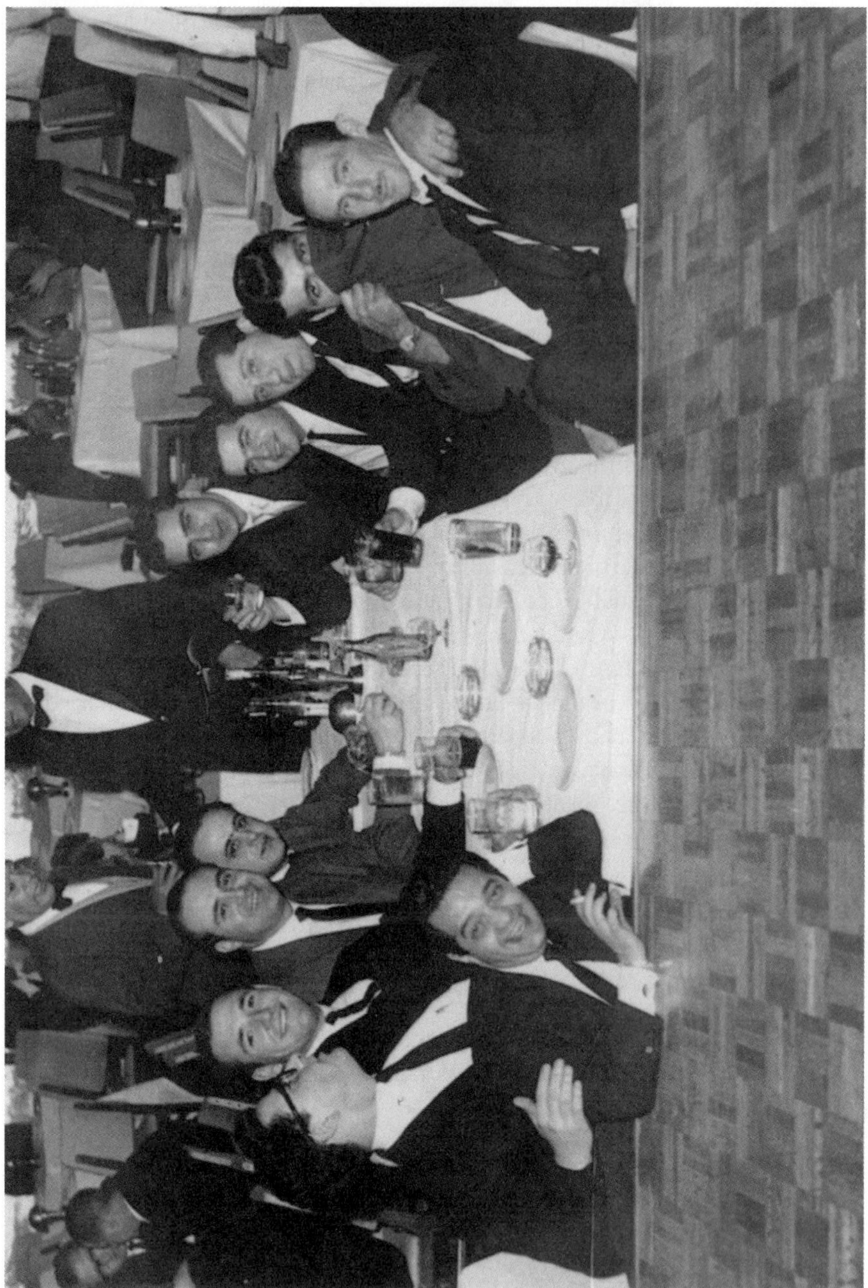

January 22, 1963, Mexico City – Only extant photo of CIA assassination squad Operation 40. Barry Seal, third from left. Felix Rodriguez, front left. William Houston Seymour, front right. To Seymour's left, hiding his face, is Frank Sturgis.

THE WAR OF '82

DANIEL HOPSICKER
FROM *BARRY AND 'THE BOYS' – THE CIA, THE MOB AND AMERICA'S SECRET HISTORY*

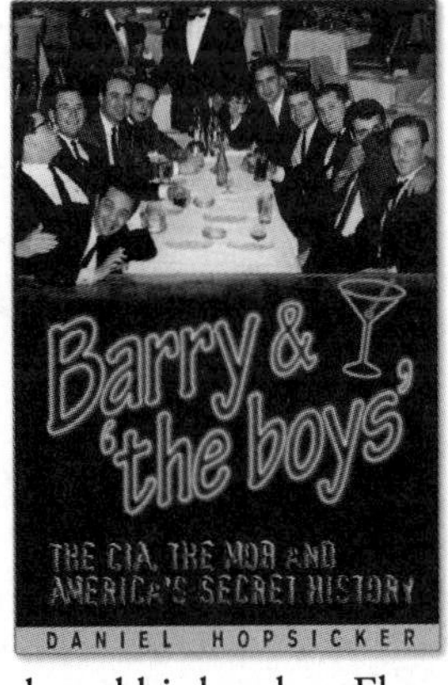

THE MOST TALKED-ABOUT EVENT in Barry Seal's much-talked about life concerns the persistent rumor, around since shortly after his assassination, that he had been murdered when he threatened to make use of a videotape of a Drug Enforcement Agency (DEA) cocaine sting which had netted George Bush's two sons, Jeb and George W.

Rumors are just that — rumors — still, when something has been whispered about for as long as this has, its very persistence becomes a story in itself. And this one has all the makings of a major box office thriller ....

Governor and Presidential contender George W. Bush and his brother, Florida's Governor Jeb Bush, allegedly caught on videotape in 1985 picking up kilos of cocaine at a Florida airport in a DEA sting set up by a vengeful Barry Seal.

Seal was said to have been angry over what he considered Vice President George Bush's shabby treatment of him. In the deal the two had cut, Seal felt, Bush was to take care of his (Seal's) legal difficulties; in exchange, Seal had gone to work for Bush and North at Mena, Arkansas.

Now he felt double-crossed by Bush, so the story goes; his reaction had been to use his DEA cover to set up a sting that ended up netting two very red-faced Bush boys.

Seal then stepped in and 'took care' of things. The Bushies were now supposedly in his debt. Plus he hung on to the videotape shot of the sting for insurance.

In retaliation, Seal was very publicly executed for his impudence less than a year later. When caught, members of the hit team all tell their lawyers that once they got to the US their actions had been directed by a military officer whom they all very quickly figured out to be National Security Council (NSC) staffer Lt. Colonel Oliver North.

Where are the tapes? What evidence was there for this story?

The evidence, if it existed, would have been in the three boxes of documents, audio and videotape that Seal had his employees move with him where-ever he went, and that were confiscated by the FBI Special Agent in Charge of the Baton Rouge office who showed up on the scene less than ten minutes after Seal's slaying.

Whatever Seal *was* carrying around with him when he died was so hot that, to get it, the FBI broke the law and violated both the rules of evidence and the US Constitution in their haste to recover Seal's files.

Was this why Barry Seal died?

Our investigation into persistent reports that there exists an incriminating videotape of Republican George W. Bush caught in an aborted (by Seal) DEA cocaine sting was unable to turn up anything to prove the allegation.

But what the search *did* uncover was almost equally shocking.

We discovered, first, that the plane from Seal's smuggling fleet suspected of being flown in the alleged incident had somehow, after Seal's death, ended up in the possession of the person who had supposedly been caught flying it in 1985, George W. Bush.

It was his favorite plane.

Small world? Or just coincidence?

We know what Bogie would have said ....

"Of all the planes in all the world, he had to fly in mine."

An even bigger shock awaited. The FAA ownership records of the turboprop King Air 200, which was part of Barry Seal's smuggling fleet of aircraft, and which was supposedly caught on tape in the sting, led directly to some of the major perpetrators of the financial frauds of the 1980's, Iran Contra, and the Savings and Loan Scandal.

Intrigue swirled around the successive owners of this particular Beech King Air 200 ... intrigue of a characteristically *spooky* kind.

The plane, in just the five years between Seal and the State of Texas Motor Pool, where it was Bush's favorite, had been involved with owners who found it necessary to make the papers on a regular and unflattering basis ....

The intrigue includes Greek shippers paying bribes to obtain loans from American companies which would never be repaid ....

An American executive snatching the charred remains of a payoff check from an ashtray in an Athens restaurant ....

Swiss police finding bank accounts used for kickbacks and bribes ... .

In trying to explain to ourselves how this plane went from being part of Barry Seal's smuggling fleet to becoming, according to Texas officials, a favorite airplane of Texan Governor George W. Bush, we had stumbled onto hard documentary evidence of Barry Seal's CIA involvement.

It was a major find. The FAA records confirm that Seal, with whom the CIA has (*natch*) consistently denied any relationship, piloted and controlled airplanes owned by the same Phoenix, Arizona, company, Greycas, which owned the majority interest in CIA proprietary airline, Southern Air Transport.

"Barry had a lot more to do with Southern Air Transport than has ever come out," we had been told by numerous sources.

Thanks to trying to track down an unsubstantiated rumor about those wastrel Bush boys, we had clear evidentiary *proof* that the biggest drug smuggler in American history flew CIA planes.

It had started with a lead into the history of the aircraft (a 1982 Beechcraft King Air 200 with FAA registration number N6308F - Serial Number BB-1014) found in records kept by Barry Seal's widow Debbie.

Through these files, and other "hard paper" records left by Seal after his assassination including leasing agreements, insurance policies and maintenance records we discovered a deliberately confusing paper trail of convoluted ownership exactly like those unmasked in the Iran Contra hearings and leading to the most interesting places.

Unraveling the King Air's tangled and colorful history first requires a look at the year the plane came into service ... 1982 was a momentous year. The plane was spanking-new. And President Reagan had just introduced "Project Democracy," which he called a "crusade for freedom."

It became, instead, a license to steal.

Here's how it started ... .

The detonations rumbled along the rocky course of the Rio Negro in Nicaragua throughout the night of March 14,1982.

Concrete bridges groaned under their own weight, and came crashing in avalanches of dust in a dark landscape seen through night-vision goggles. In certain quarters of Washington. D.C, it was time to uncork the champagne.

War was breaking out in Central America.

Two days later, Barry Seal took possession of the first of many planes supplied to him through CIA Director Bill Casey's "off-the-books" Enterprise, a King Air 200.

By March of 1982, more than 100 U.S. advisers were in Honduras. The chief of the Honduran Army, Barry's pal General Alvarez, said that his country would agree to U.S. intervention in Central America, if it were — *but of course!* — the only way to "preserve peace."

Some Generals will say anything to make a buck.

"Up to March 1982 you could still change your policy," recalled a member of the NSC later. "The issue was still the question of support for El Salvador's rebels. If that ended, so could pressure on Managua. But once the first forces of Nicaraguan exiles were trained and set in motion, any real negotiating became much harder. The blowing of the bridges was an announcement."

Democrats, fearing that Reagan was pushing the US into another Vietnam-style quagmire throughout early 1982 tried to cut off aid to the contras. And at precisely this time — at the height of CIA Director Bill Casey's frenetic efforts to ward off these Congressional efforts — Barry Seal acquired two brand new multi-million dollar Beech Craft King Air 200's.

The ownership of the planes was deliberately obscured through convoluted transactions involving Phoenix-based corporations which we were "fronts" for Phoenix-based General John Singlaub's "Enterprise."

In early 1982 Singlaub had organized an American chapter of the World Anti-Communist League (WACL), with a loan from Taiwan. Seal's King Air 200's came from sources close to these efforts.

Jack Singlaub has a long history of involvement in covert operations, beginning with the World War II Office of Strategic Services (OSS). He served as CIA desk officer for China in 1949 — yet another China hand — and deputy station chief in South Korea during the Korean War. During Vietnam he commanded the Special Operations Group Military Assistance Command, Vietnam—Studies and Observation Group, deeply involved in the CIA's Operation Phoenix assassination program.

Seal and Singlaub's covert efforts in 1982 were made necessary by the CIA's recent history. It had been forced, after the shocking scandals of the 1970's, to make drastic reductions in "official" CIA capabilities in the Carter years.

Until then, the CIA had controlled a huge network of planes, pilots and companies for use in paramilitary situations. But after the public revulsion at disclosures of out-of-control CIA covert operations, many of these assets, like the infamous Air America, were dissolved or sold off.

The Contra war put everything back into high gear; the Reagan Administration sought to expand covert paramilitary operations in Central America and elsewhere.

So the CIA and the Army jointly agreed to set up a special aviation operation called "*Seaspray*," New York Times reporter Seymour Hersh revealed in 1987. And the Agency rebuilt its capabilities illegally, relying on assets like Barry Seal.

This is old news to local and state police in areas, like Mena, affected by these extra-constitutional government operations. They more than most had seen the cynical manipulation of this operation to flood America with a river of drugs.

When law enforcement authorities debriefed convicted "drug smuggler" Seal in late 1985, one of the cops present brusquely began by stating, "We already know about *Seaspray*."

The spring of 1982 was an extraordinarily busy time. The boys were getting ready to go to war ....

- CIA agent Dewey Clarridge put a proposition to Contra leader Eden Pastora. "He would become the star of the second revolution as he had been the star of the first."
- John Hull, whom Congressional sources said worked for the CIA since at least the early 1970s, rented a contra safe house in San Jose, Coast Rica at CIA request.
- Retired Air Force General Richard Secord began managing an operation in which Israel shipped weapons captured in Lebanon to a CIA arms depot in San Antonio, Texas, for re-shipment to the contras.
- Felix Rodriguez drew on his Vietnam experience and wrote a proposal for the creation of an elite mobile strike force that would be "ideal for the pacification efforts in El Salvador and Guatemala."
- Medellin Cartel money man Ramon Milian Rodriguez began to launder, at Felix Rodriguez' request, $10 million from the cartel for the Contras. In secret testimony to a Senate committee he claimed he was solicited by 'old friend' Felix.
- Attorney General William French Smith signs a memorandum of understanding that gives the CIA carte blanche to ignore drug operatives working in the Contra movement. French's memo is widely considered the 'smoking gun' proving intent on the part of the CIA in the cocaine epidemic that coincided with the Contra war.
- And Barry Seal moves his base of operations from Louisiana to an obscure airport in the secluded mountains of western Arkansas to hook up with the CIA, which is anxious to use Seal's fleet of planes to ferry supplies to Contra camps in Honduras and Costa Rica.

Between March and December 1982, according to law enforcement records and Seal's own archives, Barry fitted nine of his aircraft with the latest electronic equipment, paying the $750,000 bill in cash...reminding us of an old Saturday Night Live gag about Chico Esquela, a clueless Latin ballpayer, changed only slightly:

"National security been berry berry good to me."

Early in 1982 a new cover unit of the Armed Forces was also set up. Known as the Intelligence Support Activity (ISA), it became a separate entity in the Army's secret world of special operations, with its own commander, Col. Jerry King. The secret operation ferried undercover Army operatives to Honduras where they trained Honduran troops for bloody hit-and-run operations into Nicaragua.

The Army went to outside businessmen and arms dealers to make off-the-books airplane purchases, with funds that had been "laundered" through secret Army finance offices at Fort Meade.

$325 million was appropriated for this Special Operations Division of the Army between 1981 and the autumn of 1983.

Through private front companies like the ones which supplied Barry Seal with his fleet of smuggling aircraft, Operations Seaspray and Yellow Fruit ferried weapons like rapid-fire cannons to CIA operatives busily mining Nicaragua's harbors.

All of this was in violation of Congressional legislation barring the Defense Department and the Agency from any action aimed at overthrowing the Sandinistas.

More importantly, they ignored the manifest wishes of the American people, who strongly rejected war with puny Nicaragua. According to a 1987 New York Times report by Seymour Hersh, had these operations become public, they would almost certainly have caused enormous damage to the Reagan Administration.

But that's why God made Special Forces...or so, at least, goes the rationale. Whatever the reason for the Central American war, Seal's drug enterprise grew to become a truly formidable 'funding engine.'

Vast fortunes were made, covertly, during the 1980's...and these are some of the people who made them, giving them a 'leg up' in achieving the coveted distinction of being 'global oligarchs.'

Seal's planes flew from Mena to airstrips in the mountains of Colombia and Venezuela. After making a refueling stop in Panama or Honduras, they would return to Mena. En route, the planes would drop parachute-equipped duffel bags loaded with cocaine over Seal-controlled farms in Louisiana... .

"His well-connected and officially-protected smuggling operation based at Mena accounted for billions in drugs and arms from 1982 until his murder four years later," said Dr. Roger Morris and Sally Denton in *Partners in Power.*

They reported that coded records of the Pentagon's Defense Intelligence Agency (DIA) showed Barry Seal on the payroll beginning in 1982.

The effects of the Barry Seal-directed efforts to take weapons one way and bring drugs the other soon began to become visible, in ruined lives in the U.S. and maimed bodies in Central America.

"My investigation established a conspiratorial period, chronologically, with a first overt act and a last overt act. The first overt act was April 12, 1982," stated Arkansas state criminal investigator Russell Welch.

Of course, Seal's operation was not alone. When private planes began to bomb the Nicaraguan capital, resulting in the crash of a Cessna 404 at the Managua airport, an account of how three Cessna's were secretly transferred from the New York Air National Guard to Central America for the raid on Managua leaked out.

Custody of a number of planes moved from the U.S. Air Force to a top-secret Joint Chiefs operation code-named "*Elephant Herd*," and then on to the CIA, through a Delaware company where they were first armed and then transferred to the Contras.

This company, Summit Aviation, was doing business with Barry Seal, proved by records in his widow's possession. According to congressional sources, Summit did "contract" work for the CIA, had former CIA personnel on the payroll, and had been linked through ownership records to the Cessna that crashed while bombing Managua.

And the downed Cessna's ownership records were equally as convoluted as were Barry Seal's King Air's. The 'fake paper' desk was doing a crackerjack job... .

The Cessna was purchased by Summit in October 1982 from Trager Aviation Center in Lima, Ohio. They covered their tracks on the same day, selling it to Investair Leasing Corp. of Mclean, Va. Investair, which had an unlisted telephone number, and also did contract work for the CIA, according to congressional sources.

The deal was "put together" by Patrick J. Foley, Summit's "military director," a Seal associate whose name and number are in Barry's files.

In addition to work for Investair, Summit maintained and modified planes for Armairco, another company involved in covert Government projects. Armairco, organized in 1982, also bought several multimillion-dollar Beechcraft King Airs like Seal's, purchased directly from Beech in a procedure used only for military projects, according to Beech officials and aviation experts.

They were all, in other words, mil-spec planes.

When asked whether Armairco's government work included activities in Central America, an Armairco official said, "That may well be."

The convoluted paper history of the airplane which once belonged to Barry Seal, and which was until recently the favorite plane of George W. Bush, begins when the title to the new aircraft was first recorded by Portland, Oregon, dealer Flightcraft, Inc, in early 1982.

Flightcraft's President, David Hinson, a former military and commercial airline pilot active in the Republican Party in Oregon, at the time was, according to *The Oregonian*, under consideration to head the FAA. The paper stated Hinson met with Transportation Secretary Elizabeth Dole to express interest in the job, even travelling to Washington to promote himself for the post.

Helping Bill Casey subvert the will of Congress and the American people presumably did nothing to hurt his chances ....

The King Air, N6308F, was spoken for even *before* it arrived at Flightcraft's facilities ... FAA records show a defunct Lake Arrowhead, California firm entered into leasing agreements with developer Eugene Glick in February of 1982, two months *before* the manufacturer's title was transferred to Flightcraft.

On paper the plane was 'owned' by a Greyhound Bus Lines subsidiary, Greycas, which in turn leased it to a mysterious Phoenix firm close to John Singlaub's Enterprise operations named Systems Marketing, Inc.

AP reporter Bryson Hull reported to us recently that some digging had revealed that Systems Marketing was a wholly-owned subsidiary of yet-another company, called... Military Electronics.

Can you say "Iran Contra?" (We knew that you could.)

Military Electronics, through its cutout, Systems Marketing, then leased the plane to Continental Desert Properties, a firm owned by Gene Glick ....

In the final step, Glick turned the plane over to Barry Seal. Insurance policies found in Seal's private papers confirm that he signed for an insurance policy on the aircraft.

What was the *purpose* of this convoluted ownership? What was it designed to conceal?

The answer lies in the very definition of "tradecraft," a term for what it is that spies and covert operators *do*: operate in the dark. The 'front' companies were in place to act as "cut-outs," layers of insulation, between the spy agency, in this case Bill Casey's CIA, and the covert operative, in this case, Barry Seal.

Gene Glick lived in the exclusive Hope Ranch, very near Ronald Reagan's Rancho Del Cielo Ranch in Santa Barbara, California. He leased not just this but several other Barry Seal's planes and helicopters as well, during the time Seal was most active in drug and weapons smuggling.

Other documents we uncovered revealed that Glick was also actively helping Seal purchase ocean-going vessels, for use in drug smuggling activities, and as stationary platforms for the CIA to use off the coast of Nicaragua.

FBI agent Del Hahn, who had dismissed Glick's importance to us, had instead fueled our suspicions.

"He's just a money launderer," said Hahn, Special Agent in Charge of an Inter-Agency Organized Crime Drug Task Force looking into Barry Seal's organization in the mid-'80s.

Not *quite*, Delbert .... He was a *cut-out.*

The circle was completed when we discovered that the Beech King Air, as well as several others used by Barry Seal, had been in reality owned all the time ... by the CIA, through the company revealed in 1998 bankruptcy proceedings to have owned Southern Air Transport (SAT). Southern Air was owned by an entity called Finova, which was disclosed when no one was looking when SAT went into bankruptcy in 1998.

Southern Air is a legendary CIA proprietary — second only to Air America — connected to Secord, Singlaub, Rodriguez, Casey and Vice President George Bush.

The company that supposedly 'owned' Barry Seal's King Air's is an Agency front, set up in Arizona and headquartered in Canada to escape American financial disclosure requirements.

Among its dubious achievements Southern Air owned the C123 used by Seal in the Nicaragua sting operation; the same aircraft that was later shot down over Nicaragua in 1986. When lone survivor Eugene Hasenfus was captured by Sandinistas, it had precipitated what became known as the Iran-Contra scandal.

Back then, no one knew — or admitted knowing — just who owned Southern Air Transport, although Government officials swore up and down that it *wasn't* the CIA.

On June 14, 1984, after passage of the second Boland Amendment and the consolidation of Contra operations under Oliver North, the plane was sold twice in one day, first to a Morgan B. Mitchell of Vale, Oregon, and then to Chevrolet Dealer Merrill Bean of Ogden Utah, who curiously gave the Dover, Delaware, address of the "Prentis Hall Corporation" on his FAA registration.

Students of the CIA have long been aware of the agency's affinity for hiding its assets in Delaware corporations. But many other companies do so for reasons of convenience. In an interview Bean stated that he had incorporated in Delaware as a legal necessity because of the needs of his investors.

"Delaware is a very convenient place for many kinds of corporations to incorporate and many large corporations and multi-nationals do so," Bean said. "Because other companies I was in partnership with were incorporated there I chose to do so also. It was much easier that way and it was a requirement of the partners who were investing."

A good answer. Unfortunately Delaware officials state that Bean's company, Prentis Hall, does not exist. And in the FAA records connected to Bean's ownership of the plane there are other gaps in the FAA records.

When major mechanical repairs are made on an aircraft, the mechanic is required to complete an FAA form; in December 1989, an FAA certified mechanic installed routine de-icing equipment on the plane, and, reviewing exact ownership documents, listed the owner as United Insurance of Ogden, Utah.

Nowhere in FAA title paperwork does United Insurance appear as an owner. And a spokesman for the Utah State Department of Insurance said there had never been a 'United Insurance' licensed to do business in the State.

So we took a closer look at Merrill Bean, and discovered that he, too, had been *involved in* — what else? — major financial fraud, in what The Salt Lake City Tribune called "the worst financial disaster in Utah since the Great Depression."

The disaster was the en massé failure of Utah thrifts—hybrid financial institutions that offered high interest rates and consumer loans—and the collapse of the insurance fund that was supposed to protect their deposits. And because Utah's thrifts were essentially uninsured, the failure of Bean's thrift left a trail of broken hearts and people.

One example will suffice:

"We had just moved to Utah from California two years ago," 58-year old Irene Culver told *The Salt Lake City Tribune* in 1986. "My husband Kent was an aircraft mechanic but he has Parkinson's disease. We put half our savings in there (Western Heritage) and bought a little fixer-upper with the other half. When the state closed everything, we were ruined."

"We were going to put a new roof on and install a gas furnace, because the electricity's expensive. Now we can't do it, so we've got half the house closed off."

Bean told us, "I was Director of that failed Thrift. I came aboard when it was almost going under. And I poured some money into it to try to save it and it didn't happen. I was hoping that my $75,000 that I put into it would help revive it."

How does a savvy businessman with aircraft and car dealerships believe that $75,000 will turn around a failing Savings & Loan?

The answer may be in "The Mafia, The CIA and George Bush," where Texas journalist Pete Brewton documented how much of the S&L scandal was connected to illegal covert operations of the CIA....

In many of those schemes a $75,000 or similar "buy-in" might have purchased a seat at a highly-lucrative but completely-criminal feeding frenzy.

The 'paper trail' of Barry Seal's King Air 200 revealed other connections to the unsavory perpetrators of the major financial frauds which — like the S&L scandal — marred the 1980's.

The plane's ostensible 'owner,' Greyhound Leasing, or Greycas, for short, was also at the center of a huge and seemingly-inexplicable financial fraud which, like the half-trillion dollar S&L scandal, no one ever seemed too concerned about unraveling.

The corporation was openly and eventually very publicly looted. Afterwards, company management pretended to be "baffled."

It went down like this: Greycas Inc. and another Greyhound unit, Greyhound Leasing, were bilked out of over $75 million by Sheldon Player, a Utah resident assumed to be in the machine and oilfield equipment sales business. He gained the money through fraudulently obtained loans from Greyhound.

Obligingly, Greycas then devised an elaborate cover-up scheme to prevent disclosure of details about the losses, which eventually topped one hundred million dollars.

It began with a $600,000 loan. Player would sell Greycas heavy machine tools, lease them back, and then pretend to sublease the expensive devices to end-users. In most cases the machines, collateral for the loans, were non-existent.

By 1984 Player had borrowed $8 million from Greyhound in the scheme. So he asked for $40 million in new loans to continue his transactions, and $23.5 million had been disbursed before the company got suspicious and confronted Player, telling him they wanted to inspect the machinery which they supposedly owned.

Player resisted, leading some company executives — not in on the joke — to question the "integrity of the transactions with Player."

But, remember, this was a company controlled by CIA-front Finova. So despite the company's doubts about Player's credibility and integrity, and in spite of Greycas' inability to obtain inspections of the equipment, the company lent Player *another $24 million* in new loans!

Anyone who has ever borrowed money for a car or home must admire the chutzpah of Sheldon Player, whom the business press took to calling an "admitted con artist" though he had no history of financial fraud that we could discover, which took place at the same time officers of a Swiss-based subsidiary of the company were also massively defrauding Greycas, of *another* $120 million, in a (supposedly) unrelated scandal.

"Many borrowers failed to make even the initial monthly payment," court documents stated, about this second scandal. The company's accountants wrote that "fraudulent and dishonest acts resulted directly in a loss of $119,684,598." Not so, said the company's hapless general counsel, responding weakly that the loss was a mere $72 million.

The double looting was an Iran-Contra 'bust-out' which left hapless shareholders holding the bag. The fraud included checks written as bribes on napkins in Swiss restaurants and then set afire, the reported possibility that one of the participants was blackmailing the company, and angry lawsuits filed by upset shareholders. But the *real* question, which puzzled business reporters were never able to answer, was: why were they were giving money away down at Greyhound during the 1980's?

The criminal trial of Sheldon Player is an illustration of our thesis that being connected means never having to say you're sorry. When Player was sentenced, he received just a five-year sentence. That's just one year for each $13 million he stole. This is clearly a deal which, if offered to regular Americans, would have them lined up around the Phoenix Federal Courthouse to sign up.

After receiving his 'draconian' sentence, Mr. Player was then given additional time to settle personal affairs before entering prison, which, for Mr. Player, consisted of the Lompoc Camp, a minimum-security facility known as one of the "country club" institutions in operation around the nation, according to Dick Murray of the U.S. Bureau of Prisons.

Even funnier is what happened to the President of hapless Greycas. Robert Bertrand, lucky fellow, never went to prison. Instead he resigned at Greyhound in 1986, and was appointed new president and chief executive officer of Finalco, an equipment finance and brokerage company based in Mclean, Virginia. That's the home of the CIA, folks. Probably just coincidence.

Completing the Barry Seal-to-George W. Bush plane chronology, Merrill Bean sold the plane in May of 1990 to Corporate Wings of Salt Lake City, which flipped it two days later to Gantt Aviation of Georgetown, Texas, which a month later sold it to the State of Texas Aircraft Pool, where it resides today.

Johnny Gantt, President of Gantt Aviation, said he probably knew that the State of Texas had a bid out when he acquired the plane. At the time the Governor of Texas was Bill Clements. His good friend, George W. Bush, was owner of the Texas Rangers.

It was Author Terry Reed who first announced that a videotape might surface during the 2000 presidential campaign "showing George W and Jeb arriving at Tamiami airport in 1985 to pick up two kilos of cocaine for a party." Statements in Reed's 1995 book *Compromised* recount how Seal bragged about how he had video of "the Bush boys" doing coke. Other witnesses have refused to go on the record. Are the rumors true? Did the Bush drug sting really happen? We must state honestly: we don't know.

What we do know is that by looking we connected the owners of this one plane to an incredible string of drug and money-related activities, activities carried out, in the normal course of things, by people who are properly called by a name many of them profess to hate:

"*Spooks.*"

from the book *Barry and 'the boys' — The CIA, the Mob and America's Secret History*
ISBN 09706591-0-5 (MadCow Press, PO Box 2687, Eugene, OR, 97402)

Daniel Hopsicker broke this story first in his book *Barry and the boys,* and in a article on the Internet (10/99) with Mike Ruppert at www.copvcia.com. Just after Hopsicker's book was in print, AP ran this *official* story:

From: *Corpus Christi Caller-Times* (9/10/2000)
TEXAS-OWNED PLANE ONCE OPERATED BY INFAMOUS DRUG RUNNER
Colombia cartel paid Adler 'Barry' Seal a reported $1 million for each flight
By C. Bryson Hull, Associated Press

HOUSTON — The state of Texas flies a plane that earned its wings at the hands of famed drug smuggler, government operative and eventual assassination victim Adler "Barry" Seal.

State officials have flown aboard N6308F, an 18-year-old twin turboprop that seats up to 10, on official business since Texas bought the plane in 1990. The Beech King Air is one of 53 in the state's fleet.

Gov. George W. Bush took office five years after the plane became Texas property and was unaware of its history. "We're glad to hear that the plane is on the straight and narrow and has landed on the right side of the law," Bush spokeswoman Linda Edwards said.

Airborne Smuggling

Seal leased the N6308F seven years before Texas brought it to ferry government officials, according to an Associated Press comparison of Federal Aviation Administration records with insurance and leasing documents.

In the early '80s, Seal was a top DEA informant by dint of his work as airborne smuggler for Colombia's Medellin cartel. He earned a reported $1 million a flight, hauling guns south and drugs north.

Seal, a former member of the Army's special forces and a one-time Trans World Airlines pilot, leased and operated the plane for at least a year, beginning on March 21, 1983, according to a leasing document.

B. Don Wineinger, who handled the insurance policies for Seal while working for a Kansas insurance firm, verified his signature on the documents and authenticated the lease.

Many Owners

The plane's owner at the time is unclear. Leasing records show the lessor as Continental Desert Properties Inc., a California real estate firm. But FAA title records show the owner to be Systems Marketing Inc., a now-defunct Arizona computer leasing business.

Continental Desert Properties owner Gene Glick has since died. The former owner of Systems Marketing was unavailable for comment.

N6308F passed through five other owners before it came to the state, but belonged for most of the time to a Utah Chevrolet dealer named Merrill Bean. Of the other owners, three were aircraft brokers and one was a leasing subsidiary of Greyhound Bus Lines called Greycas Inc. None, save Bean, owned the plane for more than 30 days.

Violent Death

The State of Texas Aircraft Pooling Board, which owns a fleet for use on official state business, purchased N6308F in May 1990 from Gantt Aviation, a Georgetown airplane broker.

Seal, 46, was machine-gunned to death in the parking lot of a Baton Rouge, La., halfway house on Feb. 19, 1986. Three Colombians were sentenced to life in prison for the killing, which occurred shortly before Seal was to testify in the Miami drug trial of Jorge Ochoa, a top Medellin cartel lieutenant. Medellin leader Pablo Escobar and Ochoa had offered $500,000 to have Seal killed and $1 million to have him brought back alive to Colombia, according to testimony at the trial.

Iran-Contra Connection

This is not the first time one of Seal's planes resurfaced in an unlikely place. In 1984, Seal flew his C-123K military transport plane, dubbed "The Fat Lady," to Nicaragua on an undercover Drug Enforcement Administration sting operation.

Using hidden cameras installed on the plane by the CIA, Seal snapped photos showing him taking bags of cocaine from Escobar and a corrupt Sandinista government official. President Reagan later used the photos during a nationally televised plea for support for the Contras.

But the plane that bore those public-relations fruits eventually gave Reagan fits. "The Fat Lady" was shot down over Nicaragua in October 1986 while carrying a load of weapons bound for the Contras. That crash and the Sandinistas' capture of the sole survivor, CIA operative Eugene Hasenfus, led to the unmasking of the Iran-Contra scandal.

THE SECRET TREATY OF FORT HUNT

This under-appreciated article is for background information and as a help in understanding our current world. There are no Bonesmen mentioned. Henry Stimson was Secretary of War at the time plus many other Bonesmen were in relevant positions.

CARL OGLESBY

APPEARED IN COVERT ACTION INFORMATION BULLETIN, FALL 1990

WILLIAM SHIRER CLOSED HIS 1960 MASTERPIECE, *The Rise and Fall of the Third Reich,* with the judgment that the Nazi regime "had passed into history,"[1] but we cannot be so confident today. On the contrary, the evidence as of 1990 is that World War II did not end as Shirer believed it did, that Nazism did not surrender unconditionally and disappear, that indeed it finessed a limited but crucial victory over the Allies, a victory no less significant for having been kept a secret from all but the few Americans who were directly involved.

THE ODESSA AND ITS MISSION

HITLER CONTINUED TO RANT OF VICTORY, but after Germany's massive defeat in the battle of Stalingrad in mid-January 1943, the realists of the German General Staff (OKW) were all agreed that their game was lost. Defeat at Stalingrad meant, at a minimum, that Germany could not win the war in the East that year. This in turn meant that the Nazis would have to keep the great preponderance of their military forces tied down on the eastern front and could not redeploy them to the West, where the Anglo-American invasion of Italy would occur that summer. Apparently inspired by the Soviet victory, President Franklin Delano Roosevelt and Prime Minister Winston Churchill announced at Casablanca, on January 24, 1943, their demand for Germany's unconditional surrender and the complete de-Nazification of Europe.[2]

Within the German general staff two competing groups formed around the question of what to do: one led by Heinrich Himmler, the other by Martin Bormann.[3]

Himmler was chief of the SS (Schutzstaffel, "protective echelon"), the black-shirted core of the Nazi party that emerged as Hitler's bodyguard in the late 1920s and grew into the most powerful of the Nazi political institutions. After the failure of the attempted military coup of July 20, 1944, which wounded but did not kill Hitler, the SS seized all power and imposed a furious blood purge of the armed services in which some seven thousand were arrested and nearly five thousand executed.[4] The SS was at that point the only organ of the Nazi state.

Himmler's plan for dealing with the grim situation facing Nazism found its premise in Hitler's belief that the alliance between "the ultra-capitalists" of the U.S. and "the ultra-Marxists" of the Soviet Union was politically unstable. "Even now they are at loggerheads," said Hitler. "If we can now deliver a few more blows, this artificially bolstered common front may suddenly collapse with a gigantic clap of thunder.[5] Himmler believed that this collapse would occur and that the U.S. would then consider the formation of a new anti-Soviet alliance with Nazi Germany. The Nazis would then negotiate "a separate peace" with the United States, separate from any peace with the USSR, with which Germany would remain at war, now joined against the Soviets by the United States.

But Martin Bormann, who was even more powerful than Himmler, did not accept the premise of the separate-peace idea. Bormann was an intimate of Hitler's, the deputy fuhrer and the head of the Nazi Party, thus superior to Himmler in rank. Bormann wielded additional power as Hitler's link to the industrial and financial cartels that ran the Nazi economy and was particularly close to Hermann Schmitz, chief executive of I.G. Farben, the giant chemical firm that was Nazi Germany's greatest industrial power.

With the support of Schmitz, Bormann rejected Himmler's separate-peace strategy on the ground that it was far too optimistic.[6] The Allied military advantage was too great, Bormann believed, for Roosevelt to be talked into a separate peace. Roosevelt, after all, had taken the lead in proclaiming the Allies' demand for Germany's unconditional surrender and total de-Nazification. Bormann reasoned, rather, that the Nazi's best hope of surviving military defeat lay within their own resources, chief of which was the cohesion of tens of thousands of SS men for whom the prospect of surrender could offer only the gallows.

Bormann and Schmitz developed a more aggressive, self-contained approach to the problem of the looming military defeat, the central concept of which was that large numbers of Nazis would have to leave Europe and, at least for a time, find places in the world in which to recover their strength. There were several possibilities in Latin America, most notably Argentina and Paraguay; South Africa, Egypt, and Indonesia were also attractive rear areas in which to retreat.[7]

After the German defeat in the battle of Normandy in June 1944, Bormann took the first external steps toward implementing concrete plans for the Nazis' great escape.

An enormous amount of Nazi treasure had to be moved out of Europe and made safe. This treasure was apparently divided into several caches, of which the one at the Reichsbank in Berlin included almost three tons of gold (much of it the so-called tooth-gold from the slaughter camps) as well as silver, platinum, tens of thousands of carats of precious stones, and perhaps a billion dollars in various currencies.8

There were industrial assets to be expatriated, including large tonnages of-specialty steel and certain industrial machinery as well as blueprints critical to the domination of certain areas of manufacturing

Key Nazi companies needed to be relicensed outside Germany in order to escape the reach of war-reparations claims.

And tens of thousands of Nazi war criminals, almost all of them members of the SS, needed help to escape Germany and safely regroup in foreign colonies capable of providing security and livelihoods.

For help with the first three of these tasks, Bormann convened a secret meeting of key German industrialists on August 10, 1944, at the Hotel Maison Rouge in Strasbourg.[9] One part of the minutes of this meeting states:

The [Nazi] Party is ready to supply large amounts of money to those industrialists who contribute to the post war organization abroad. In return, the Party demands all financial reserves which have already been transferred abroad or may later be transferred, so that after the defeat a strong new Reich can be built.[10]

The Nazi expert in this area was Hitler's one-time financial genius and Minister of the Economy, Dr. Hjalmar Horace Greeley Schacht, available to Bormann even though he was in prison on suspicion of involvement in the anti-Hitler coup of 1944. According to a U.S. Treasury Department report of 1945, at least 750 enterprises financed by the Nazi Party had been set up outside Germany by the end of the war. These firms were capable of generating an annual income of approximately $30 million, all of it available to Nazi causes.[11] It was Schacht's ability to finesse the legalities of licensing and ownership that brought this situation about.[12]

Organizing the physical removal of the Nazis' material assets and the escape of SS personnel were the tasks of the hulking Otto Skorzeny, simultaneously an officer of the SS, the Gestapo, and the Waffen SS as well as Hitler's "favorite commando."[13]

Skorzeny worked closely with Bormann and Schacht in transporting the Nazi assets to safety outside Europe and in creating a network of SS escape routes ("rat lines") that led from all over Germany to the Bavarian city of Memmingen, then to Rome, then by sea to a number of Nazi retreat colonies set up in the global south.

The international organization created to accommodate Bormann's plans is most often called "The Odessa," a German acronym for "Organization of Veterans of the SS." It has remained active as a shadowy presence since the war and may indeed constitute Nazism's most notable organizational achievement. But we must understand that none of Bormann's, Skorzeny's, and Schacht's well-laid plans would have stood the least chance of success had it not been for a final component of their organization, one not usually associated with the Odessa at all but very possibly the linchpin of the entire project.

Enter Gehlen

THIS FINAL ELEMENT OF THE ODESSA was the so-called Gehlen Organization (the Org), the Nazi intelligence system that sold itself to the U.S. at the end of the war. It was by far the most audacious, most critical, and most essential part of the entire Odessa undertaking. The literature on the Odessa and that on the Gehlen Organization, however, are two different things. No writer in the field of Nazi studies has yet explicitly associated the two, despite the fact that General Reinhard Gehlen was tied politically as well as personally with Skorzeny and Schacht. Moreover, Gehlen's fabled post-war organization was in large part staffed by SS Nazis who are positively identified with the Odessa, men such as the infamous Franz Alfred Six and Emil Augsburg of the Wannsee Institute. An even more compelling reason for associating Gehlen with the Odessa is that, without his organization as a screen, the various Odessa projects would have been directly exposed to American intelligence. If the Counter Intelligence Corps (CIC) and the Office of Strategic Services (OSS) had not been neutralized by the Gehlen ploy, the Odessa's great escape scheme would have been discovered and broken up.

At 43, Brigadier General Reinhard Gehlen was a stiff, unprepossessing man of five foot eight and a half inches and 128 pounds when he presented himself for surrender at the U.S. command center in Fischhausen. But there was nothing small about his ego. "I am head of the section Foreign Armies East in German Army Headquarters," he announced to the GI at the desk. "I have information to give of the highest importance to your government." The GI was not impressed, however, and Gehlen spent weeks stewing in a POW compound before an evident Soviet eagerness to find him finally aroused the Americans' attention.[14]

Gehlen became chief of the Third Reich's Foreign Armies East (FHO), on April 1, 1942. He was thus responsible for Germany's military intelligence operations throughout Eastern Europe and the Soviet Union. His FHO was connected in this role with a number of secret fascist organizations in the countries to Germany's east. These included Stepan Bandera's "B Faction" of the Organization of Ukrainian Nationalists (OUN/B),[15] Romania's Iron Guard,[16] the Ustachis of Yugoslavia,[17] the Vanagis of Latvia[18] and, after the summer of 1942, "Vlassov's Army,"[19] the band of defectors from Soviet Communism marching behind former Red hero General Andrey Vlassov. Later on in the war, Gehlen placed one of his top men in control of Foreign Armies West, which broadened his power; and then after Admiral Wilhelm Canaris was purged and his Abwehr intelligence service cannibalized by the SS, Gehlen became in effect Nazi Germany's over-all top intelligence chief.

The Great Escape

IN DECEMBER 1943, at the latest, Gehlen reached the same conclusion about the war that had come upon Bormann, Schacht, Skorzeny, and Himmler. Germany was losing and could do nothing about it. Several months later, Gehlen says, he began quietly discussing the impending defeat with a few close associates. As he writes in his memoir: "Early in October 1944 I told my more intimate colleagues that I considered the war was lost and we must begin thinking of the future. We had to think ahead and plan for the approaching catastrophe."[21]

Gehlen's strategic response to Gotterdammerung was a kind of fusion of Himmler's philosophy with Bormann's more pessimistic Odessa line: "My view," he writes, "was that there would be a place even for Germany in a Europe rearmed for defense against Communism. Therefore we must set our sights on the Western powers, and give ourselves two objectives: to help defend against Communist expansion and to recover and reunify Germany's lost territories."[22]

Just as Bormann, Skorzeny, and Schacht were beginning to execute their escape plans, so too was Gehlen. "Setting his sights on the Western powers," and in particular on the United States, Gehlen pursued the following strategic rationale: When the alliance between the United States and the USSR collapsed, as it was bound to do upon Germany's defeat, the United States would discover a piercing need for a top-quality intelligence service in Eastern Europe and inside the Soviet Union. It did not have such a service of its own, and the pressures of the erupting East-West conflict would not give it time to develop one from scratch. Let the United States therefore leave the assets assembled by Gehlen and the FHO intact. Let the United States not break up Gehlen's relationship with East European fascist groups. Let the United States pick up Gehlen's organization and put it to work for the West, the better to prevail in its coming struggle against a Soviet Union soon to become its ex-ally.

Gehlen brought his top staff people into the planning for this amazing proposal. Together, during the last months of the war, while Hitler was first raging at Gehlen for his "defeatist" intelligence reports, then promoting him to the rank of brigadier general, then at last firing him altogether (but promoting into the FHO directorship one of Gehlen's co-conspirators), Gehlen and his staff carefully prepared their huge files on East Europe and the Soviet Union and moved them south into the Bavarian Alps and buried them. At the same time, Gehlen began building the ranks of the FHO intelligence agents. The FHO in fact was the only organization in the whole of the Third Reich that was actually recruiting new members as the war was winding down.[23] SS men who knew they would be in trouble when the Allied forces arrived now came flocking to the FHO, knowing that it was the most secure place for them to be when the war finally ended.[24]

When Gehlen's plans were complete and his preparations all concluded, he divided his top staff into three separate groups and moved them (as Skorzeny was doing at the same time) into prearranged positions in Bavaria. Gehlen himself was in place before the German surrender on May 7, hiding comfortably in a well-stocked chalet in a mountain lea called Misery Meadow. Besides Gehlen, there were eight others in the Misery Meadow group, including two wounded men and three young women. For three weeks, maintaining radio contact with the two other groups, Gehlen and his colleagues stayed on the mountain, waiting for the American army to appear in the valley far below. "These days of living in the arms of nature were truly enchanting," he wrote. "We had grown accustomed to the peace, and our ears were attuned to nature's every sound."[25]

DESTRUCTION OF THE OSS

GEHLEN WAS STILL COMMUNING WITH NATURE when William Donovan, chief of the Office of Strategic Services (OSS), arrived in Nuremberg from Washington, dispatched by the new president to assist Supreme Court Justice Robert Jackson. Harry S. Truman had made Jackson the United States's chief prosecutor with the International Military Tribunal (IMT), established to try the Nazis' principal military leaders. Donovan's OSS was to function as an investigative arm of the IMT.

By the last half of the war if not before, President Roosevelt and Donovan were convinced that the U.S. needed a permanent intelligence service and that this service, like the OSS, should be civilian rather than military. They were convinced too that the OSS should be its foundation. On October 31, 1944, Roosevelt directed Donovan to prepare a memo on how such a service should be organized.[26]

Donovan consulted on this assignment with his colleague Allen Dulles, a force unto himself as wartime chief of OSS operations in Bern. Dulles advised Donovan to placate the military by proposing that the new agency be placed automatically under military command in time of war.[27] Donovan's proposal incorporated this idea,[28] but only in order to state all the more strongly the case for civilian control and for making the OSS the basis of the new organization. As he wrote in his memo to Roosevelt of November 18, 1944, "There are common-sense reasons why you may desire to lay the keel of the ship at once .... We now have [in the OSS] the trained and specialized personnel needed for such a task, and this talent should not be dispersed."[29]

Donovan proposed establishment of a civilian intelligence service responsible directly to the President and the Secretary of State, the chief mission of which would be to support the President in foreign policy. Except for the civilian Secretaries of War and the Navy, Donovan's plan did not even include a place for military representation on the advisory board, and he was careful to specify that the advisory board would merely advise and not control. The new service was to be all-powerful in its field, being responsible for "coordination of the functions of all intelligence agencies of the Government." The Donovan intelligence service, in other words, would directly and explicitly dominate the Army's G-2 and the Navy's ONI.[30]

Naturally, therefore, the Donovan plan drew an intense attack from the military. One G-2 officer called it "cumbersome and possibly dangerous."[31] Another referred to the OSS as "a bunch of faggots"[32] Nor was the FBI's J. Edgar Hoover silent. Hoover had fought creation of the OSS perhaps more bitterly than the military and had insisted throughout the war on maintaining an FBI intelligence network in Latin America despite the fact that this was supposed to be OSS turf.[33]

Certain elements within Army intelligence were not only opposed to Donovan's plan but were also beginning to formulate their own notions of what a post-war intelligence system should be like.

Roosevelt sent the Joint Chiefs of Staff ultra-secret copies of Donovan's proposal along with Roosevelt's own draft executive order to implement it. On January 1, 1945, the Chiefs formally reported to Roosevelt their extreme dissatisfaction with this scheme and leaked Donovan's memo to four right-wing newspapers, which leapt to the attack with blaring headlines accusing FDR and Donovan of conspiring to create "a super Gestapo." This attack put the Donovan plan on hold, and the death of FDR on April 12, 1945 destroyed it.[34]

In early May 1945, president for less than a month, Truman made the OSS the American component of the investigative arm of the IMT. It is one of the fascinating conjunctions of this story that Donovan should have left for Nuremberg just as Gehlen was coming down from his mountain. It is one of its riper ironies that Donovan would soon resign from Jackson's staff in a disagreement over trying German officers as war criminals, which Donovan objected to but Jackson and Truman supported.[35] Had Donovan lent his energies to the trial of Nazis within the German officer corps, he might have confronted the very adversaries who would shortly take his place in the American intelligence system, not only militarizing it, but Nazifying it as well.

GEHLEN MAKES HIS MOVE

GEHLEN HAD BEEN ON THE MOUNTAIN for exactly three weeks and the war had been over for almost two weeks when he decided on May 19 that it was time to make contact. He left the three women and the two wounded men at Misery Meadow and with his four aides began the descent to the valley town of Fischhausen on Lake Schliersee.

On the same day Soviet commissioners far to the north at Flensburg demanded that the United States hand over Gehlen as well as his files on the USSR. This was the first the U.S. command had heard of Gehlen.[36]

Gehlen and company took their time, staying three days with the parents of one of his aides and communicating by radio with those who had remained at Misery Meadow. On May 22, Gehlen at last decided the moment was right. He and his aides marched into the Army command center and represented themselves to the desk officer, a Captain John Schwarzwalder, to whom Gehlen spoke his prepared speech:

"I am head of the Section Foreign Armies East in German Army headquarters. I have information to give of the highest importance to your government." Schwarzwalder had Gehlen and his group jeeped to Miesbach where there was a OSS detachment. There Gehlen once again gave his speech, this time to a Captain Marian Porter: "I have information of the greatest importance for your supreme commander." Porter replied, "So have they all," and shunted him and his cohorts off to the prison camp at Salzburg.

Gehlen's disappointment at this reception was keen and his biographers all say he never forgot it, "lapsing," as one puts it, "into near despair" as he "presented the strange paradox of a spy-master thirsting for recognition by his captors."[37]

Recognition was inevitable, however, since the CIC was trying to find him. By mid June at the latest, his name was recognized by a G-2 officer, Colonel William H. Quinn, who had Gehlen brought to Augsburg for his first serious interrogation. Quinn was the first American to whom Gehlen presented his proposal and told of his staff dispersed at several camps in the mountains as well as the precious buried archives of the FHO. Unlike Captain Porter, Colonel Quinn was impressed. He promptly passed Gehlen up the command chain to General Edwin I. Sibert.

Sibert later recalled, "I had a most excellent impression of him at once." Gehlen immediately began educating him as to "the actual aims of the Soviet Union and its display of military might." As Sibert told a journalist years later, "With her present armed forces potential, he [Gehlen] continued, Russia could risk war with the West and the aim of such a war would be the occupation of West Germany."[38]

Acting without orders, Sibert listened to Gehlen for several days before informing Eisenhower's chief of staff, General Walter Bedell Smith.[39] Smith and Sibert then continued to develop their relationship with Gehlen secretly, choosing not to burden Eisenhower with knowledge of what they were doing "in order not to compromise him in his relations with the Soviets."[40] Eisenhower in fact had strictly forbidden U.S. fraternization with Germans.[41]

Gehlen was encouraged to resume contact with his FHO comrades who were still at large in Bavaria, releasing them from their vow of silence. Gehlen was sufficiently confident of his American relationships by this time that he dug up his buried files and, in special camps, put his FHO experts to work preparing detailed reports on the Red Army for his American captors. Well before the end of June he and his comrades were "discharged from prisoner of war status so that we could move around at will."[42] They were encouraged to form a unit termed a "general staff cell," first within G-2's Historical Research Section, then later in the Seventh Army's Intelligence Center in Wiesbaden, where they worked in private quarters and were treated as VIPs.[43]

Indeed, a partly declassified CIA document recapitulated this story in the early 1970s, noting at this time:

Gehlen met with Admiral Karl Doenitz, who had been appointed by Hitler as his successor during the last days of the Third Reich. Gehlen and the Admiral were now in a U.S. Army VIP prison camp in Wiesbaden; Gehlen sought and received approval from Doenitz too![44]

In other words, the German chain of command was still in effect, and it approved of what Gehlen was doing with the Americans.

Gehlen's biographers are under the impression that it took six weeks for someone in European G-2 to notice and recognize Gehlen in the POW cage, that Sibert did not tell Smith about finding him until the middle of August, and that it was much later still before Sibert and Smith conspired to circumvent Eisenhower and communicate their excitement about Gehlen to someone at the Pentagon presumably associated with the Joint Chiefs of Staff.[45] But documents released in the 1980s show that this part of Gehlen's story raced along much more quickly. Already on June 29, in fact, the Pentagon had informed Eisenhower's European command that the War Department wanted to see Gehlen in Washington.[46]

It was a fast time. By no later than August 22, one of Gehlen's top associates, Hermann Baun, was forming what would become the intelligence and counter-intelligence sections of Gehlen's new organization. Gehlen himself, with retinue, was departing for Washington in General Bedell Smith's DC-3 for high-level talks with American military and intelligence officials. And the whole concept of the deal he was about to offer his conquerors had been approved by a Nazi chain of command that was still functioning despite what the world thought and still does think was the Nazis' unconditional surrender.[47]

Gehlen arrived in Washington on August 24 with six of his top FHO aides and technical experts in tow.[48] World War II had been over about a week, the war in Europe about three and a half months.

THE SECRET TREATY OF FORT HUNT

As GEHLEN AND HIS SIX MEN were en route from Germany to Washington, Donovan's OSS troubles became critical. On August 23, Admiral William Leahy, chief of the JCS, the President's national security adviser and a man who despised Donovan, advised Truman to order his budget director Harold Smith to begin a study of the intelligence question. Stating "this country wanted no Gestapo under any guise or for any reason,"[49] Truman may not have known that the Gestapo's Odessa heirs were landing in the lap of the Pentagon even as he spoke. Smith in any case responded to Truman's directive by asking Donovan for his OSS demobilization plans.

Now, too late, Donovan tried to fight. The Gehlen party, "Group 6," was checking out its very comfortable accommodations at Fort Hunt at the very moment at which Donovan, writing from a borrowed Washington office, fired back a memo to Smith defending the OSS and its right to live:

Among these assets [of the OSS] was establishment for the first time in our nation's history of a foreign secret intelligence service which reported information as seen through American eyes. As an integral and inseparable part of this service, there is a group of specialists to analyze and evaluate the material for presentation to those who determine national policy.[50]

Much more significant than the question of the adequacy of U.S. intelligence on the Soviet Union, however, was the question of civilian versus military control of the intelligence mission. Germany and England had fought this battle in the 19th century, the military capturing the intelligence role in Germany and the civilians maintaining a position in England. Throughout the summer and fall of 1945, this same battle raged in the U.S. government.[51] The battle for intelligence control was indeed the background for the arrival of Gehlen and his six aides at

Fort Hunt, where Gehlen's party was housed and Gehlen himself provided with an NCO butler and several white-jacket orderlies.[52]

A momentous relationship was established at Fort Hunt, one that had the profoundest effects on the subsequent evolution of United States foreign policy during an exceptionally difficult passage of world history. The period of the Cold War as a whole, and more especially its early, formative years — from Gehlen's coming aboard the American intelligence service until he rejoined the West German republic in 1955 — was laden with the peril of nuclear war. On at least one occasion, in 1948,[53] Gehlen almost convinced the United States that the Soviet Union was about to launch a war against the West and that it would be in the U.S. interest to preempt it.

Clearly it is important to know who made and authorized the decisions that led to our national dependency on a network of underground Nazis. Yet because the relevant documents are still classified, this central part of the Gehlen story still cannot be reconstructed.

From the handful of published books about the Gehlen affair (none of which cite their sources on this point) we can list only seven Americans who were said to be involved with Gehlen at Fort Hunt:

- Admiral William D. Leahy, chief of staff and Truman's national security advisor.
- Allen Dulles, OSS station chief in Bern during the war.
- Sherman Kent, head of OSS Research and Analysis Branch and a Yale historian.
- General George V. Strong, head of Army G-2.
- Major General Alex H. Bolling of G-2.
- Brigadier General John T. Magruder, first head of the Army's Strategic Services Unit, a vulture of OSS.
- Loftus E. Becker, a lawyer assc. with G-2 and the Nuremberg war-crimes operation; the CIA's first deputy director.

We do not know if these people were involved as a committee, if they talked with Gehlen and his six aides a lot or a little, separately or all at once, or if they sent their own aides to work out the details. We do not know how a POW-interrogation was transformed into a bargaining process. Above all, we do not know what kind of communication the U.S. participants in the Fort Hunt-Gehlen talks had with the political authorities to whom they were responsible. Leahy is the only one who had obvious contact with President Truman. But there is nothing in the revealed record to indicate that he ever discussed Gehlen or the Fort Hunt deal with Truman, or took the least trouble to explain to Truman the implications of hiring a Nazi spy network. We have no idea, for that matter, how Leahy himself saw it.

What we do know is the outlines of the Gehlen deal itself, however it was hammered out and however it was or was not ratified by legal, political authority. That is because Gehlen himself laid out its terms in his autobiography, The Service. Gehlen says in this work (which has been attacked for its inaccuracies) that the discussion ended with "a 'gentlemen's agreement,'" that the terms of his relationship with the United States were "for a variety of reasons never set down in black and white." He continues, "Such was the element of trust that had been built up between the two sides during this year of intensive personal contact — that neither had the slightest hesitation in founding the entire operation on a verbal agreement and a handshake."[54] According to Gehlen, this agreement consisted of the following six basic points. His language is worth savoring. "I remember the terms of the agreement well," he wrote:

"1. A clandestine German intelligence organization was to be set up, using the existing potential to continue information gathering in the East just as we had been doing before. The basis for this was our common interest in a defense against communism."

"2. This German organization was to work not 'for' or 'under' the Americans, but 'jointly with the Americans.'

"3. The organization would operate exclusively under German leadership, which would receive its directives and assignments from the Americans until a new government was established in Germany."

"4. The organization was to be financed by the Americans with funds which were not to be part of the occupation costs, and in return the organization would supply all its intelligence reports to the Americans." (The Gehlen Organization's first annual budget is said to have been $3.4 million.[55])"

"5. As soon as a sovereign German government was established, that government should decide whether the organization should continue to function or not, but that until such time the care and control (later referred to as 'the trusteeship') of the organization would remain in American hands."

"6. Should the organization at any time find itself in a position where the American and German interests diverged, it was accepted that the organization would consider the interests of Germany first."[56]

Gehlen acknowledges that the last point especially might "raise some eyebrows" and make some think that the U.S. side "had gone overboard in making concessions to us." He assures his readers that actually "this point demonstrates better than any other Sibert's great vision: he recognized that for many years to come the interests of the United States and West Germany must run parallel."[57] Gehlen and his staff left Fort Hunt for Germany on July 1, 1946, having been in the United States for almost a year. They were temporarily based at Oberursel then settled into a permanent base in a walled-in, self-contained village at Pullach near Munich. Gehlen set up his headquarters in an estate originally built by Martin Bormann.[58] There a start-up group of 50 began to turn the "gentlemen's agreement" of Fort Hunt into reality. The first order of business being staff, Gehlen's recruiters were soon circulating among the "unemployed mass" of "former" Nazi SS men, the Odessa constituency, to find more evaluators, couriers and informers.[59] Gehlen had "solemnly promised in Washington not to employ SS and Gestapo men,"[60] although it will be noted that Gehlen includes no such provision in his list of terms. There is not the least question that he did recruit such men, supplying them with new names when necessary.

Two of the worst of them were Franz Six and Emil Augsburg. Six was a key Nazi intellectual, and both Six and Augsburg were associated with the Wannsee Institute, the Nazi think-tank in Berlin where SS leader Reinhard Heydrich, in January 1942, announced "The Final Solution to the Jewish Question." Both of them had commanded extermination squads roving in East Europe in pursuit of Jews and communists. And both had gone underground with the Odessa when the Third Reich crumbled. Augsburg hid in Italy, then returned in disguise when Gehlen called. Six was actually captured by Allied intelligence, tried at Nuremberg and imprisoned, only to be sprung to work with Augsburg running Gehlen's networks of East European Nazis.[61]

From the edge of total defeat, Gehlen now moved into his vintage years, more powerful, influential and independent than he had been even in the heyday of the Third Reich. Minimally supervised first by the War Department's Strategic Services Unit under Fort Hunt figure Major General John Magruder, and then by the SSU's follow-on organization, the Central Intelligence Group under Rear Admiral Sidney Souers,[62] the Org grew to dominate the entire West German intelligence service. Through his close ties to Chancellor Konrad Adenauer's chief minister, Hans Globke, Gehlen was able to place his men in positions of control in West Germany's military intelligence and the internal counterintelligence arm. When NATO was established he came to dominate it too. By one estimate "some 70 percent" of the total intelligence take flowing into NATO's military committee and Allied headquarters (SHAPE) on the Soviet Union, the countries of East Europe, the rest of Europe, and indeed the rest of the world was generated at Pullach.[63]

Not even the establishment of the CIA in 1947 and the official transfer of the Pullach operation into the West German government in 1955 (when it was retitled the Federal Intelligence Service, BND) lessened the reliance of American intelligence on Gehlen's product.[64] From the beginning days of the Cold War through the 1970s and beyond, the United States's, West Germany's, and NATO's most positive beliefs about the nature and intentions of the Soviet Union, the Warsaw Pact, and world communism would be supplied by an international network of utterly unreconstructed SS Nazis whose primary purposes were to cover the escape of the Odessa and make the world safe for Nazism.

The Cost of the Fort Hunt Treaty

Gehlen's story has many branchings beyond this point. These include several spy scandals that exposed his operation as dangerously vulnerable to Soviet penetration. They include the pitiful spectacle of U.S CIC agents pursuing Nazi fugitives on war-crimes charges only to see them summarily pardoned and hired by Gehlen. They include the dark saga of Klaus Barbie, the SS "Butcher of Lyon" who worked with the Gehlen Organization and boasted of 'being a member of the Odessa. They include assets of Operation Paperclip, in which right-wing forces in the U.S. military once again savaged the concept of de-Nazification in order to smuggle scores of SS rocket scientists into the United States. They include continuation of the civilian-vs.-military conflict over the institution of secret intelligence and the question of politically motivated covert action within the domestic interior. They include above all the story of the enormous victory of the Odessa in planting powerful Nazi colonies around the world — in such countries as South Africa, where the enactment of apartheid laws followed; or several countries in Latin America that then became breeding grounds for the Death Squads of the current day, and indeed even in the United States where it now appears that thousands of wanted Nazis were able to escape justice and grow old in peace.

In making the Gehlen deal, the United States did not acquire for itself an intelligence service. That is not what the Gehlen group was or was trying to be. The military intelligence historian Colonel William Corson put it most succinctly, "Gehlen' s organization was designed to protect the Odessa Nazis. It amounts to an exceptionally well-orchestrated diversion."[65] The only intelligence provided by the Gehlen net to the United States was intelligence selected specifically to worsen East-West tensions and increase the possibility of military conflict between the U.S. and the Soviet Union. It was exactly as the right-wing papers had warned in 1945 when they were aroused by Donovan's proposal for a permanent intelligence corps, warning their readers that a "super spy unit" could "determine American foreign policy by weeding out, withholding or coloring information gathered at his direction."[66] It was exactly as Truman had warned when he demobilized the OSS with the observation that the US, had no interest in "Gestapo-like measures." The fact that this lively concern for a police-state apparatus should have been focused on the relatively innocuous OSS while at the same time the red carpet was being rolled out for Gehlen's gang of SS men must surely count as one of the supreme wrenching ironies of the modern period.

Another dimension of the cost of the Gehlen deal is the stress it induced within American institutions, weakening them incalculably. The Gehlen Organization was the antithesis of the Allied cause, its sinister emergence on the scene of post-war Europe the very opposite of what the western democracies thought they had been fighting for.

Perhaps at least we can say that, despite Gehlen and despite the military, the United States did after all finally wind up with a civilian intelligence service. The National Security Act of 1947 did embody Donovan's central point in creating a CIA outside the military. But in fact the Gehlen Org substantially pre-empted the CIA's civilian character before it was ever born. The CIA was born to be rocked in Gehlen's cradle. It remained dependent on the Org even when the Org turned into the BND. Thus, whatever the CIA was from the standpoint of the law, it remained from the standpoint of practical intelligence collection a front for a house of Nazi spies.

The Org was not merely military, which is bad, not merely foreign, which is much worse, and not merely Nazi, which is intolerable; it was not even professionally committed to the security of the U.S. and Western Europe. It was committed exclusively to the security of the Odessa. All the Gehlen Org ever wanted the U.S. to be was anti-communist, the more militantly so the better. It never cared in the least for the security of the United States, its Constitution or its democratic tradition.

It is not the point of this essay that there would have been no Cold War if the Odessa had not wanted it and had not been able, through the naive collaboration of the American military Right, to place Gehlen and his network in a position that ought to have been occupied by a descendant of the OSS. But it was precisely because the world was so volatile and confusing as of the transition from World War II to peacetime that the U.S. needed to see it, as Donovan put it in his plaintive appeal to Truman in the summer of 1945, "through American eyes." No Nazi eyes, however bright, could see it for us without deceiving us and leading us to the betrayal of our own national character.

Second, there was no way to avoid the Cold War once we had taken the desperate step of opening our doors to Gehlen. From that moment on, from the summer of 1945 when the Army brought him into the United States and made a secret deal with him, the Cold War was locked in. A number of Cold War historians on the left (for example D.F. Fleming and Gabriel Kolko) have made cogent arguments that from the Soviet point of view the Cold War was thrust upon us by an irrational and belligerent Stalin. The story of the secret treaty of Fort Hunt exposes this "history" as a self-serving political illusion. On the contrary, the war in the Pacific was still raging and the United States was still trying to get the Soviet Union into the war against Japan when General Sibert was already deep into his relationship with Gehlen.

The key point that comes crashing through the practical and moral confusion about this matter, once one sees that Gehlen's Organization was an arm of the Odessa, is that, whether it was ethical or not, the U.S. did not pick up a Gift Horse in Gehlen at all; it picked up a Trojan Horse.

The unconditional surrender the Germans made to the Allied command at the little red schoolhouse in Reims was the surrender only of the German armed services. It was not the surrender of the hard SS core of the Nazi Party. The SS did not surrender, unconditionally or otherwise, and thus Nazism itself did not surrender. The SS chose rather, to seek other means of continuing the war while the right wing of the United States military establishment, through fears and secret passions and a naivete of its own, chose to facilitate that choice. The history that we have lived through since then stands witness to the consequences.

Carl Oglesby is the author of several books, notably *The Yankee and Cowboy War.* He has published a variety of articles on political themes. In 1965 he was the President of Students for a Democratic Society. He is the director of The Institute for Continuing de-Nazification. For information on the Institute write to: 294 Harvard Street, #3, Cambridge, MA 02139.

REFERENCES

1. William Shirer, *The Rise and Fall of the Third Reich* (New York: Simon & Schuster, 1960), p. 1140.
2. Ibid., p. 1033 fn. Enunciation of this policy surprised and upset some U.S. military leaders, who feared it would prolong the war. See, for example, William R. Corson (USMC ret.), *The Armies of Ignorance: The Rise of the American Intelligence Empire* (New York: Dial Press, 1977), pp. 8-10.
3. William Stevenson, *The Bormann Brotherhood: A New Investigation of the Escape and Survival of Nazi War Criminals* (New York: Harcourt Brace Jovanovich, 1973).
4. Op. cit., n. 1, p. 1072.
5. Ibi'd., pp. 1091 -92 \
6. This discussion of Bormann's strategy is based mainly on Glenn B. Infield, *Skorzeny: Hitler's Commando* (New York: St. Martin's Press, 1981); and op. cit., n. 3.
7. My summary of the Nazi survival plan is based on op. cit., n. 3; Infield, op. cit., n. 6; Ladislas Farago, *Aftermath: Martin Bormann and the Fourth Reich* (New York: Simon & Schuster, 1974); Charles Higham, *American Swastika* (New York: Doubleday, 1985); Brian Bunting, *The Rise of the South African Reich* (New York: Penguin, 1964); and Simon Wiesenthal, *The Murderers Among Us* (New York: McGraw-Hill, 1967). On "neo-Nazi" colonies in the Near and Middle East and South America, see Wiesenthal, pp. 78-95.
8. Infield, op. cit., n. 6, p. 192.
9. Ibid.- p. 179; and Wiesenthal, op. cit., n. 7, pp. 87-88.
10. Wiesenthal, op. cit., n. 7, p. 88. Also quoted in Infield, op. cit.,n.6,p. 183.
11. Infield, op. cit., n. 6, p. 183.
12. Schacht, who had lost favor with Hitler in 1938, was acquitted of war-crimes charges by the Nuremberg Tribunal. He was later convicted of being a "chief Nazi offender" by the German de-Nazification court at Baden-Wurttemberg, but his conviction was overturned and his eight-year sentence lifted on September 2, 1948. Infield, op cit., n. 6.
13. Infield, op cit., n. 6, p. 16.
14. Heinz Hohne and Hermann Zolling, *The General Was A Spy* (New York: Richard Barry, Coward McCann & Geoghegan, 1973), p. 54; and E.H. Cookridge, *Gehlen, Spy of the Century* (New York: Random House, 1971), p. 120.
15. Christopher Simpson, *Blowback* (New York: Weidenfeld and Nicolson, 1988), p. 160 ff. Simpson's is the best book on the Gehlen matter so far published. 16. Ibid., pp. 254-55.
17. Ibid., pp. 180, 193.
18. Ibid., pp. 10, 207-08.
19. Ibid ., pp. 18-22. Also see Hohne and Zolling, op. cit., n. 14, pp. 35-37; Cookridge, op. cit., n. 14, pp. 56-58.
20. Cookridge, op. cit., n. 14, p. 79.
21. Reinhard Gehlen, *The Service* (New York: World, 1972), p. 99.
22. Ibid, p. 107.
23. Cookridge, op. cit., n. 14, pp. 103, 106.
24. I do not know of an estimate of the size of the Foreign Armies East (FHO) as of the end of the war. Cookridge, op. cit., n. 14, p. 161, says that by 1948, when the Gehlen Organization was probably back up to war-time speed, its key agents "exceeded four thousand." Each agent typically ran a net of about six informants, Cookridge, op cit., n. 14, p. 167. Thus, the total Gehlen net might have numbered in the range of 20,000 individuals.
25. 0p. cit.,n.21, p. 115.
26. Corson, op. cit., n. 2, pp. 6, 20; Anthony Cave Brown, *The Last Hero, Wild Bill Donovan* (N.Y.: Vintage Books, 1982), p. 625; U.S. Senate, "Final Report of the Select Committee to Study Governmental Operations with Respect to Intelligence Activities," Book IV, Supplementary Staff Reports on Foreign and Military Intelligence (known as, *The Church Report*), p. 5.
27. Cookridge, op. cit., n. 14, p.l30.
28. Brown, op. cit., n. 26, p. 626.
29. Cookridge, op. cit., n. 14, p. 131.
30. William M. Leary, ed., *The Central Intelligence Agency: History and Documents* (Atlanta: University of Atlanta Press, 1984), pp. 123-25; Corson, op cit., n 2, pp. 214-17; Brown, op. cit., n. 26, p. 625.
31. Brown, op. cit., n. 26, p. 627.
32. Ibid., p. 170.

33. Thomas Powers, *The Man Who Kept the Secrets: Richard Helms and the CIA* (New York: Pocket Books,1981), p.31.
34. Ibid.
35. Brown, op. cit., n. 26, p. 744.
36. This account of Gehlen's surrender is based on Hohne and Zolling, op. cit., n. 14, pp. 52-56; Cookridge, op cit., n. 14, pp. l 18-21; op. cit., n. 3, pp. 89-90; op cit., n. 15, pp. 4143; and the BBC documentary, *Superspy: The Story of Reinhard Gehlen*, 1974. There are many trivial discrepancies in these four accounts but they are in perfect agreement as to the main thrust.
37. Cookridge, op. cit., n. 14, p. 120.
38. Holme and Zoll/≈ing, op. cit., n. 14, p. 58.
39. As to breaking orders, Gehlen is effusive in his praise of "Sibert's great vision.... I stand in admiration of Sibert as a general who took this bold step—in a situation fraught with political pitfalls—of taking over the intelligence experts of a former enemy for his own country.... The political risk to which Sibert was exposed was very great. Anti-German feeling was running high, and he had created our organizations without any authority from Washington and without the knowledge of the War Department." Op. cit., n. 21, p. 123.
40. Holme and Zolling, op. cit., n. 14, p. 58.
41. Ibid., pp. 58-59.
42. Op. cit., n. 21,p. 120.
43. Hohne and Zolling, op. cit., n. 14, p. 58.
44. Undated CIA fragment with head, "Recent Books," apparently published circa 1972, partly declassified and released in 1986 in response to a Freedom of Information (FOIA) suit.
45. Hohne and Zolling, op. cit., n. 14, pp. 56, 58-59.
46. U.S. Army document SHAEF D-95096, September 15, 1946, declassified FOIA release. The routing of this cable through SHAEF HQ raises a question as to whether Eisenhower was really kept in the dark about Gehlen.
47. As Gehlen was about to leave for the United States, he left a message for Baun with another of his top aides, Gerhard Wessel "I am to tell you from Gehlen that he has discussed with [Hitler's successor Admiral Karl] Doenitz and [Gehlen's superior and chief of staff General Franz] Halder the question of continuing his work with the Americans. Both were in agreement." Hohne and Zolling, op. cit., n. 14, p. 61.
48. There is variance in the literature concerning how many assistants Gehlen took with him to Washington. John Ranelagh, *TheAgency: The Rise and Decline of the CIA* (New York: Simon and Schuster, 1986), p. 92; Cookridge, op. cit., n. 14, p. 125; and op. cit., n. 15, p. 42, say it was three while Hohne and Zolling, op. cit., n. 14, p. 61, say four. A U.S. Army note of August 28, 1945 (a 1986 FOIA release) refers to "the 7 shipped by air last week," and that no doubt is the correct number. Another FOIA release, an unnumbered Military Intelligence Division document dated September 30, 1945, originated at Fort Hunt, labels the Gehlen party as "Group 6" and names seven members: Gehlen, Major Alberg Schoeller, Major Horst Hiemenz, Colonel Heinz Herre, Colonel Konrad Stephanus, and two others whose rank is not given, Franz Hinrichs and Herbert Feukner. The number is important for what it says about the nature of Gehlen's trip. Three might be thought of as co-defendants but six constitute a staff. Cookridge, op. cit., n. 14, p. 125, says Gehlen made the trip disguised in the uniform of a one-star American general, his aides disguised as U.S. captains. Hohne and Zolling, op. cit., n. 14, pp. 60-61, inflate the rank to two stars but then call the story spurious. Gehlen's memoir says nothing about it.
49. Corson, op. cit., n. 2, p. 239.
50. Ibid., p. 240.
51. Ranelagh, op. cit., n. 48, p. 102ff.
52. BBC documentary, Superspy, op. cit., n. 36. Corson, in an interview with the author, said the butler and the orderlies must have been CIC agents. Still, the detail rankles.
53. Cookridge, op. cit., n. 14, 203; op. cit., n. 15, p. 136.
54. Op. cit., n. 21, p. 121. Holme and Zolling, op. cit., n. 14, p. 64, say that the details of this "gentlemen's agreement" were put into writing by the CIA in 1949.
55. Hohne and Zolling, op. cit., n. 14, p. 65.
56. Op.cit.,n. 21,p. 122.
57. Ibid., pp. 122-23.
58. Hohne and Zolling, op. cit., n. 14, p.119; Cookridge, op. cit., n. 14, p. 155. BBC documentary, Superspy, op. cit., n. 36.

59. Hohne and Zolling, op. cit., n. 14, p. 67.
60. Cookridge, Op. Cil., n. 14, p. 144.
61. Op. cit., n. 15, pp. 17, 4647, 166, 225; Cookridge, Op. cit., n. 14, pp. 242-43.
62. Hohne and Zolling, op. cit., n. 14, p. 133.
63. Cookridge, op cit., n. 14, p. 218.
64. Ibid., p. 128.
65. Author's interview with Corson, May, 1986.
66. Cookridge, op. cit., n. 14, p. 131.

This is the Warren Commission. From the left: Rep. Gerald R. Ford, R-Mich.; Rep. Hale Boggs, D-La.; Sen. Richard B. Russell, D-Ga.; Chief Justice Earl Warren, the chairman; Sen. John Sherman Cooper, R-Ky.; John J. McCloy, New York banker; Allen W. Dulles, former Central Intelligence Agency director; and J. Lee Rankin of New York, general counsel.

SENATOR JOHN SHERMAN COOPER IS S&B 1923. GERALD FORD IS A *DEKE* AND ATTENDED YALE LAW SCHOOL

Mind Control, the Illuminati & the JFK Assassination

Kris Millegan

Appeared online November 1996, at www.Parascope.com – now at www.BoodleBoys.com

The nature of the universe is such that ends can never justify the means. On the contrary, the means always determine the end. – Aldous Huxley

Amidst anguish and outrage, a question has plagued the collective subconscious of America since 1963: ***Who killed President Kennedy?***

As one who was alive when it happened, I can testify to the effects of that act upon myself and to what I observed around me.

Tragedy is traumatic.

I was pulled out of junior high Spanish class and sent out on the street selling newspapers containing the grim news. Only twice in my lifetime were kids hawking papers on the street in our town; the day President John F Kennedy was assassinated and the day Jack Ruby shot Lee Harvey Oswald.

Kennedy's murder represents far more than the unlikely act of a "lone nut" or even a concealed political conspiracy. A four-tiered network of power interests was responsible for the *Killing of the King of Camelot*, with the all-seeing eye of the Illuminati at the top of the pyramid. Hanging from the Illuminati puppet strings are the Masons, Mafia and other *secret* societies, followed by the national security state apparatus/

Jack Ruby Shoots Lee Harvey Oswald

subculture. A rogue's gallery of various commercial, ideological, political and bureaucratic partners fill out the foundation of this conspiracy.

What is the Illuminati? In 1785, a courier died en route to Paris from Frankfort-on-the-Main. *Original Shift in Days of Illuminations,* a tract written by Adam "Spartacus" Weishaupt, founder of the Illuminati, was recovered from the dead messenger. It contained the secret society's long-range plan for *The New World Order through world revolution.*

The Bavarian Government promptly outlawed the society and in 1787 published the details of The Illuminati conspiracy in *The Original Writings of the Order and Sect of the Illuminati.*

The Illuminati was publicly founded May 1, 1776, at the University of Ingolstadt by Weishaupt, a Professor of Canon Law. It was a very "learned" society; Weishaupt drew the earliest members of his new order from among his students.

In Adam Weishaupt's own words:

Adam Weishaupt

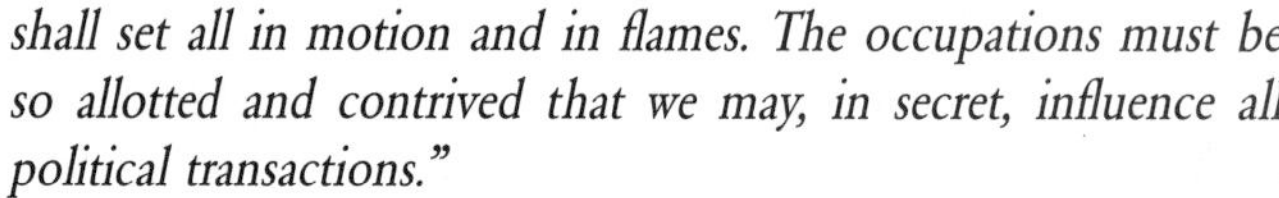

> *"By this plan, we shall direct all mankind in this manner. And, by the simplest means, we shall set all in motion and in flames. The occupations must be so allotted and contrived that we may, in secret, influence all political transactions."*

There is disagreement among scholars as to whether or not the Illuminati survived its banishment. Nevertheless, under Weishaupt's guidance, the group had been quite successful in attracting members and through various manipulations had allied itself with the extensive Masonic networks in Europe and the United States.

On December 5, 1776, students at William and Mary College founded a secret society, Phi Beta Kappa. A second chapter was formed at Yale in 1780. The anti-Masonic movement which erupted in the United States during the 1820s denounced the secrecy of groups such as Phi Beta Kappa. The society responded to this pressure by going public. Some researchers note this as the direct cause of the appearance of Yale's Order of Skull and Bones.

The alumni of Skull and Bones provide a direct link between secret societies and the state department/national security apparatus.

From *George Bush: The Unauthorized Biography:*

> ... Prescott Bush [Skull & Bones] was a U.S. senator from Connecticut, a confidential friend and golf partner with National Security Director Gordon Gray, and an important golf partner with Dwight Eisenhower as well. Prescott's old lawyer

from the Nazi days, John Foster Dulles, was Secretary of State, and his brother Allen Dulles, formerly of the Schroder bank, was head of the CIA.

... In the later years of the Eisenhower presidency, Gordon Gray rejoined the government. As an intimate friend and golfing partner of Prescott Bush, Gray complemented the Bush influence on Ike. The Bush-Gray family partnership in the ***secret government*** continues up through the George Bush presidency.

Gordon Gray had been appointed head of the new Psychological Strategy Board in 1951 under Averell Harriman's rule as assistant to President Truman for national security affairs. From 1958 to 1961 Gordon Gray held the identical post under President Eisenhower. Gray acted as Ike's intermediary, strategist and hand-holder, in the President's relations with the CIA and the U.S. and allied military forces.

Gordon Gray taking oath of office for Director of the Psycology Stategy Board

Eisenhower did not oppose the CIA's covert action projects; he only wanted to be protected from the consequences of their failure or exposure. Gray's primary task, in the guise of ***oversight*** on all U.S. covert action, was to protect and hide the growing mass of CIA and related secret government activities.

Dwight Eisenhower

It was not only covert ***projects*** which were developed by the Gray-Bush-Dulles combination; it was also new, hidden ***structures*** of the United States government.

From *The Immaculate Deception* by Russell Bowen:

According to Nixon's biography, his personal and political ties with the Bush family go back to 1946, when Nixon claims he read an ad placed in an L.A. newspaper by the Orange County Republican Party and a wealthy group of businessmen led by Prescott Bush, the father of George Bush.

Prescott Bush

They wanted a young candidate to run for Congress. Nixon applied and won the job, becoming a mouthpiece for the Bush group, progressing to the U.S. Senate and in 1952 the vice presidency.

In 1960, Vice President Nixon was scouring the world seeking the presidency. At his side was Prescott Bush. Congressman Gerald Ford was helping raise funds, as was George Bush.

It took Nixon eight more years to reach his goal. And the canny politician always remembered who helped him get there. So again it was payback time for George Bush. Nixon appointed him Chairman of the Republican National Committee, and later ambassador to China.

Bush & Nixon

By 1976, Ford, who succeeded Nixon after Watergate, paid his due bill. He picked out big job for his old crony, Bush: the CIA. But this time Bush would not be an underling. Now he would be head man.

MUDDY WATERS AND THE UNSEEN HAND

THE TRUTH ABOUT KENNEDY'S DEATH IS SUBMERGED IN CONSPIRATORIAL CHAOS

A century before the Roman Republic perished, two brothers, the Gracchi, emerged as popular leaders who were determined to check the corruption by wealth of the city's institutions. They were both killed. The murderers, who were never punished, came from the senatorial class which had felt threatened by the brothers' reforms.
— Peter Dale Scott, *Deep Politics*

One of the most effective tactics employed by the conspirators was to "muddy the waters" by bringing in as many "suspicious" individuals as possible into the assassination arena, even having different reasons for each person's presence — if there were a covert reason for being in Dallas on November 22, 1963, all the better. Scores of people were engaged in varied peripheral plots and sub-plots, many of which were related tangentially or not at all to the actual assassination. As a result, the pertinent facts drowned in a contrived whirlpool of suspicious, but not necessarily related, activity.

But who was *REALLY* involved?

Johnson & Nixon

Rodney Stich's book *Defrauding America* tells of a *deep-cover CIA officer* assigned to a counter-intelligence unit, code-named Pegasus. This unit *had tape-recordings of plans to assassinate Kennedy* from a tap on the phone of J. Edgar Hoover. The people on the tapes were *[Nelson] Rockefeller, Allen Dulles, [Lyndon] Johnson of Texas, George [HW] Bush and J. Edgar Hoover.*

Nelson Rockefeller in thought

According to Stich's source, *There were conversations between Rockefeller, [J. Edgar] Hoover, where Rockefeller asks, "Are we going to have any problems?" And he said, "No, we aren't going to have any problems. I checked with Dulles. If they do their job we'll do our job." There are a whole bunch of tapes, because Hoover didn't realize that his phone had been tapped.*

The inner core of the conspiracy is bound tightly together by oaths of secrecy and affiliations with various secret societies allied with various Nazi groups, mind control operations and business ventures. Much of the operational apparatus used in the conspiracy lay hidden in the shadow world of ultra-secret national security state entities such as Division Five of the FBI, the Defense Industrial Security Command and double/triple agents of various allegiances. *The Torbitt Document* and *The Man Who Knew Too Much* detail the workings of this actual operational framework. Agents from *psy* bureaus, future narcs, ultra-right-wingers, doubles and dead ringers, politicians, spies, cops all fall into the mix.

Hoover & Nixon

Another key aspect of the JFK assassination is mind control. Some researchers believe Lee Harvey Oswald was involved in the CIA's MKULTRA project and was subjected to extensive radio-hypnotic intracerebral control and electronic dissolution of memory while in Minsk, Russia. But the question of mind control extends far past the mechanics of the killing itself.

Oswald in handcuffs

SAVAGE NEW TIMES – MIND CONTROL AND THE ILLUMINATI

WAS KENNEDY'S MURDER ACTUALLY A RITUAL BLOOD SACRIFICE?

I think the subject which will be of most importance politically is Mass Psychology ... Its importance has been enormously increased by the growth of modern methods of propaganda. Although this science will be diligently studied, it will be rigidly confined to the governing class. The populace will not be allowed to know how its convictions are generated. — Bertrand Russell

The more one studies mind control, secret societies and the occult, the more one understands the subtlety and hidden symbolism of the Kennedy assassination.

James Shelby Downard's underground classic, *Sorcery, Sex, Assassination and the Science of Symbolism*, links American historical events with a grand occult plan to *turn us into cybernetic mystery zombies*. The assassination of JFK was a performance of the occult ritual called The Killing of the King, designed as a mass-trauma, mind-control assault against the national body-politic of the United States.

Mr. Downard's co-researcher and author, Michael A. Hoffman II, wrote in *Secret Societies and Psychological Warfare* that: "fabled alchemy had at least three goals to accomplish before the total decay of matter, the total breakdown we are witnessing all around us today, was fulfilled and these are:

> *The Creation and Destruction of Primordial Matter.*
> *The Killing of the Divine King.*
> *The Bringing of Prima Materia to Prima Terra."*

Hoffman writes: [The following excerpt is copyright © 1995 by Michael A. Hoffman II. All Rights Reserved. Used by permission.]

> Since ancient times these were the goals of the Gnostic-Rosicrucian-Masonic-Hermetic Academy, an elite as real and corporeal as President Bush's Skull and Bones society at Yale University; the Bohemian Grove in California; Dr. John Whiteside Parson's Ordo Templi Orientis (OTO) also in California; General Albert Pike's Scottish and Palladian Rites of Freemasonry and a host of lesser imitators. All of these cults have or had the highest possible offices, connections and old boy networks.

The Creation and Destruction of Primordial Matter was accomplished at the White Head ("Ancient of Days"), at White Sands, New Mexico, at the Trinity Site. The Trinity Site itself is located at the beginning of an ancient Western road known in old Mexico as the Jornada del Muerto (the Journey of the Dead Man).

Early in this century a Freemason named Peter Kern was ordered to build a highly symbolic "Gate of Death" at a key point on this ancient trail. It was known as the ***Gate with a Thousand Doors***.

At the front of this gate Kern was ceremonially murdered (decapitated) by a hooded executioner. Gary Trudeau satirized the Aztec-masonic Comazotz head-chopping cult of the American Southwest in a series of December, 1988, ***Doonesbury*** cartoons which depicted Skull and Bones initiates trying to dispose of a number of heads including that of Pancho Villa, a key political operative of the cryptocracy who was in fact also ritually decapitated.

Other occult rituals for the ***Creation and Destruction of Primordial Matter*** were played out in the general area of the 33rd degree of north parallel latitude in Truth or Consequences, New Mexico. The Trinity Site is also at this latitude.

There are 33 segments in the human spinal column which according to occult lore is the vehicle of the fiery ascent of the Kundalini serpent force which resides in the human body. 33 is the highest degree of Scottish Rite Freemasonry. Near the Trinity Site a derelict shack was symbolically dubbed "MacDonald House." The ***Creation and Destruction of Primordial Matter*** occurred exactly on the Trinity Site, the ***Place of Fire***, with the explosion of the first atomic bomb, culminating untold thousands of years of alchemical speculation and practice.

The ***Killing of the King*** rite was accomplished at another Trinity site located approximately ten miles south of the 33rd degree of north parallel latitude between the Trinity River and the Triple Underpass at Dealey Plaza in Dallas, Texas. Dealey Plaza was the site of the first masonic temple in Dallas. In this spot, which had been known during the 19th century cowboy era as "Bloody Elm Street," the world leader who had become known as the "King of Camelot," President John Fitzgerald Kennedy, was shot to death.

The Three Tramps – Dallas, Texas, November, 1963

A widely publicized image, which has become perhaps the key symbol of the enigma of the Kennedy hoodwink, emerged immediately in the wake of the assassination: a photograph of three "tramps" in official custody, who were unexplainably released and never identified, though speculation about who they really were has reached fever pitch among investigators.

This photograph is a ritual accompaniment of the Black Mass that was the ceremonial immolation of a king, the unmistakable calling card of masonic murder, the appearance of Jubela, Jubelo and Jubelum, the three "unworthy craftsmen" of Temple burlesque, "that will not be blamed for nothing." This ritual symbolism is necessary for the accomplishment of what James Shelby Downard and I described in the first edition of Apocalypse Culture, as the alchemical intention of the killing of the 'King of Camelot':

"... the ultimate purpose of that assassination was not political or economic but sorcerous: for the control of the dreaming mind and the marshaling of its forces is the omnipotent force in this entire scenario of lies, cruelty and degradation. Something died in the American people on Nov. 22, 1963 – call it idealism, innocence or the quest for moral excellence. It is the transformation of human beings which is the authentic reason and motive for the Kennedy murder ...."

JFK 11/14/63

The seemingly random and senseless slaughter of a President the week before Thanksgiving, by having his head blown apart in those now infamous Zapruder film frames, is the signpost of humanity's entry into what David Cronenberg in his Videodrome Rosicrucian cinematic manifesto termed, "Savage New Times."

The search for the three assassins has become a trip up and down Tim Finnegan's ladder, a ladder containing "one false step after another." It is a masonic riddle several magnitudes above the pedestrian, CIA-Mafia-Anti-Castro-Castro-KGB-Texas rightwing etc. etc. political "solutions" pushed by the various books and movies which sometimes only serve to confuse and demoralize us all the more.

THE ALCHEMY OF RITUAL MURDER

What ought to be unambiguous to any student of mass psychology, is the almost immediate decline of the American people in the wake of this shocking televised slaughter. There are many indicators of the transformation. Within a year Americans had largely switched from softer-toned, naturally colored cotton clothing to garish-colored artificial polyesters. Popular music became louder, faster and more cacophonous. Drugs appeared for the first time outside the Bohemian subculture ghettos in the mainstream. Extremes of every kind came into fashion. Revolutions in cognition and behavior were on the horizon, from the Beatles to Charles Manson, from Free Love to LSD.

The killers were not caught, the Warren Commission was a whitewash. There was a sense that the men who ordered the assassination were grinning somewhere over cocktails and out of this, a nearly-psychedelic wonder seized the American population, an awesome shiver before the realization that whoever could kill a president

LBJ taking oath of office, 11/22/63

of the United States in broad daylight and get away with it, could get away with anything.

A hidden government behind the visible government of these United States became painfully obvious in a kind of subliminal way and lent an undercurrent of the hallucinogenic to our reality. Welcome to Oz thanks to the men behind Os-wald and Ruby.

There was a transfer of power in the collective group mind of the American masses: from the public power of the elected front-man Chief Executive, to an unelected invisible college capable of terminating him with impunity.

For the first time in their history since the 1826 masonic assassination of writer William Morgan, Americans were forced to confront the vertiginous reality of a hidden power ruling their world. Sir James Frazer writing in ***The Golden Bough: A Study in Magic and Religion***, explains that when the "divine king" is murdered by one who is himself stronger or craftier, those powers of "divinity" which were the king's are "Sympathetically" and "Contagiously" transferred from the vanquished to the victor.

The entry of this awareness into the subconscious Group "Dreaming" Mind of the American masses instituted a new simulacrum. The shocking introduction of a diametrically different, new "reality" is a classic scenario of another phase of alchemical programming known to the cryptocracy as "Clamores."

Dave Marsh writing in ***Rolling Stone*** magazine (Feb. 24, 1977): "The Beatles have always had an intimate connection to the JFK assassination. He was shot the week before Thanksgiving 1963. By February 1964, the Beatles were number one in the national charts and the climactic appearance on Ed Sullivan's TV show occurred. Even Brian Epstein (the manager of the Beatles) believed the Kennedy assassination helped their rise – the Beatles appeared to bind our wounds with their messages of joy and handholding .... And the way was paved, replacing Camelot with Oz."

The Beatles and Ed Sullivan

Now the American people were forced to confront a scary alternative reality, the reality of a shadow government, over which they had neither control or knowledge. The shepherding process was thus accelerated with a vengeance. Avant-garde advertising, music, politics and news would hereafter depict (especially in the electronic media) – sometimes fleetingly, sometimes openly – a "shadow side" of reality, an underground amoral "funhouse" current associated with extreme sex, extreme violence and extreme speed.

The static images of the suit-and-tie talking heads of establishment religion, government, politics and business were subtly shown to be subordinate to the

Shadow State, which the American people were gradually getting a bigger glimpse of out of the corner of their collective eye. The interesting function of this phenomenon is that it simultaneously produces both terror and adulation and undercuts any offensive against it among its percipients, which does not possess the same jump-cut speed and funhouse ambiance.

There is a sense of existing in a palace of marvels manipulated by beautiful but Satanic princes possessed of so much knowledge, power and experience as to be vastly superior to the rest of humanity. They have been everywhere. They have done everything. They run the show which mesmerizes us. We are determined to watch it. We are transfixed and desperate to see their newest production, their latest thrilling revelation, even when the thrills are solely based upon the further confirmation of our dehumanization.

J.G. Ballard: "In this overlit realm ruled by images of the space race and the Vietnam War, the Kennedy assassination and the suicide of Marilyn Monroe, a unique alchemy of the imagination was taking place .... The demise of feeling and emotion, the death of affect, presided like a morbid sun over the playground of that ominous decade.

"The role assigned to us is that of zombies called upon by our shadow masters to perform bit parts and act as stock characters in their spectacular show. This mesmerizing process produces a demoralized, cynical, double-mind."

— *Secret Societies and Psychological Warfare*, pp. 91-95. (*Secret Societies and Psychological Warfare* is available for U.S. $17.95 plus $2.50 shipping (overseas remit $5.00 shipping), from: Independent History and Research, Box 849, Coeur d'Alene, Idaho 83816.)

John F. Kennedy

The perpetrators deliberately murdered JFK in such a way as to affect our national identity and cohesiveness — to fracture America's soul. Even the blatancy of their conspiracy was designed to show their *superiority* and our *futility*. *They* were doing to the nation what *they* had been doing to individuals for years.

Looking into the subject of mind-control, one finds that the scope is wide and methods used are sophisticated. Mind control traces its origins to religious institutional use by priesthoods. Techniques of mind control developed in our western culture were field-tested by the Jesuits, certain Vatican groups, and various mystery religions, secret societies and masonic organizations. Methods tested during the Inquisition were refined by Dr. Josef Mengele during the reign of the Third Reich.

Harry S. Truman

After World War II, hundreds of Nazi scientists, researchers and administrators were "smuggled" into the United States against direct written orders from President Harry S. Truman, through Operation Sunrise, Operation Blowback, Operation Paperclip and other covert operations.

Hitler at Nuremberg rally

Soon afterwards, a mind control project called Marionette Programming imported from Nazi Germany was revived under the new name, "Project Monarch." The basic component of the Monarch program is the sophisticated manipulation of the mind, using extreme trauma to induce Multiple Personality Disorder (MPD), now known as Disassociative Disorder.

In public testimony submitted to the President's Committee on Radiation, there are amazing allegations of severe torture and inhumane pogroms foisted upon Americans and other citizens, especially as children. These same children were used in radiation experiments. They detail the drug and traumatic methodology of sophisticated mind control. Survivors tell similar stories of brutal mind control experimentation as part of the CIA's MKULTRA program. Many mind control survivors speak of a "Dr. Greene." Some survivors and researchers have identified Dr. Greene as the infamous Dr. Mengele.

Dr, Josef Menegele

But mind control programs and assassinations are merely part of a much larger *enterprise* being carried out by an international network of power interests. In 1995, a researcher-lawyer anonymously posted on the Internet his ten-year investigation of this conspiracy on the Internet. Calling the JFK assassination part of a 50-year conspiracy, he detailed the structure of this international network, which he named "*the group.*" The inner workings and *New World Order* agenda of this group fit snugly with what other researchers have called the Illuminati.

THE NEW WORLD ORDER

Americans' trust of government has steadily declined since JFK's death.

After all, it was you and me. — The Rolling Stones, *Sympathy for the Devil"*

Soon after the American Revolution, John Robinson, a professor of natural philosophy at Edinburgh University in Scotland and member of a Freemason lodge, said that he was asked to join the Illuminati. After studying the group, he concluded that the purposes of the Illuminati were not compatible with his beliefs.

In 1798, he published a book called *Proofs Of A Conspiracy*, which states:

> An association has been formed for the express purpose of rooting out all the religious establishments and overturning all the existing governments .... The leaders would rule the World with uncontrollable power, while all the rest would be employed as tools of the ambition of their unknown superiors.

George Washington

Proofs of A Conspiracy was sent to George Washington. Responding to the sender of the book with a letter, President Washington said he was well aware of the Illuminati presence in America. He wrote that the Illuminati had *diabolical tenets* and that their object was *a separation of the People from their government.*

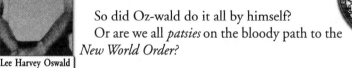

The decades following the JFK assassination have been marked by increasing cynicism and disillusionment among the American people towards a government which acts as an elite, aloof institution at the disposal of powerful forces both seen and unseen. Washington's statement of "a separation of the People from their government" has come to pass. As the glaciers of a contrived Cold War melt down, our "government" is steadily militarizing and expanding its police powers, turning away from foreign targets of aggression to focus on domestic "insurrection." Although the foundation of this conspiracy has been under construction for centuries, the poisoned fruits of these labors burst into bloom on that dark day in Dealey Plaza forty years ago.

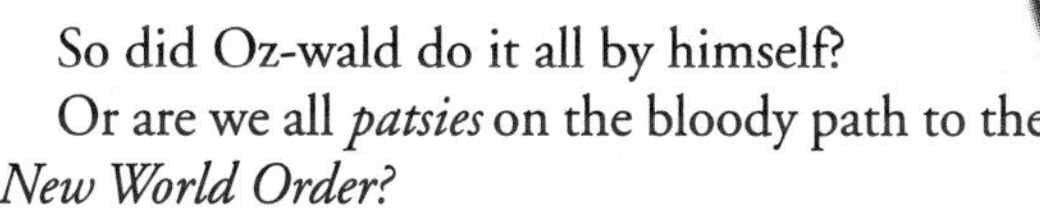

So did Oz-wald do it all by himself?
Or are we all *patsies* on the bloody path to the *New World Order?*

Lee Harvey Oswald

Supporting documentation and articles at:
www.boodleboys.com

Prescott Bush
BMOC
(Big Man on Campus)
Yale 1916-17
Glee Club
Football Cheerleaders
University Quartet
Varsity Baseball
Whiffenpoofs

PRESCOTT BUSH, THE UNION BANKING CORPORATION AND THE *STORY*

KRIS MILLEGAN
AUGUST 2003

"THERE'S THREE THINGS TO REMEMBER: claim everything, explain nothing, deny everything," recalled Prescott Bush as to how politics was explained to him by Clare Booth Luce, congresswoman and wife of fellow Bonesman and magazine magnate, Henry Luce. The remarks were recorded in a 1966 interview with Prescott for an oral history project about the Eisenhower Administration by Columbia University.

The Bush political family seems to have taken those words to heart, one example being the *story* of Prescott's involvement with the Union Banking Corporation and the financing of Hitler and fascism. Why there has been such a deliberate and hard cover-up of this affair is in no doubt due to its *sensitive* nature.

The who, what and where of this business is already covered in several of the other articles in this book. Here we will examine the *story* as it appears today.

The specific allegations about the Union Banking Corporation first surfaced in Antony Sutton's 1975 book, *Wall Street and the Rise of Hitler.* Sutton at that time did not know about the Order of Skull & Bones. After becoming aware of the Order in 1983 he expanded his writings on the subject in *How the Order Creates War and Revolution* in 1984, which was later published, with Antony's three other booklets on The Order of Skull & Bones, together as *America's Secret Establishment* in 1986. The charges were articulated again in 1988 in Sutton's *The Two Faces of George Bush.*

The mainstream press and establishment historians *ignored* Sutton's books and the accusations.

In 1992, Webster Tarpley and Anton Chaitkin authored *George Bush: The Unauthorized Biography* (some chapters are presented in this book), which took the investigations further. They found in U.S. government archives the vesting order seizing the Union Banking Corporation and documented other Harriman/Bush controlled interests that were doing business with the Nazis. Their book was published by Executive Intelligence Review, a Lyndon Laurouche organization, and again the reports were ignored.

John Loftus, a former attorney for the Office of Special Operations prosecuting Nazi war criminals in the US Justice Department also added information about the situation in his 1994 book, *The Secret War Against the Jews.*

A Dutch producer Daniël de Witt, from Dutch National Television interviewed Sutton, Chaitkin, Tarpley and others in 1996, for a documentary on Skull & Bones that included confirmation from Dutch officials concerning the Union Banking Corporation and its activities in financing Hitler through a Dutch bank, the Bank voor Handel en Scheepvart (Bank for Trade and Shipping). From the documentary: "Original documents of the Amsterdam based International Institute of Social History (Instituut voor Sociale Geschiedenis) clearly show the connection between the BHS, the August Thyssen Bank from Fritz Thyssen and Harriman's Union Banking Corporation."

The show — as produced — never aired.* The show was listed in printed schedules and there was a preview in a TV guide but the program was pulled just before being a televised in 1998. Finally in January 2001, a re-edited thirty minute segment of the original eighty minute film was aired plus ten minutes of new footage of interviews of the movie, *The Skulls,* writer and director.

With the advent and growth of the Internet and its ability to by-pass the mainstream media *editorial* bottleneck there was a growing awareness of the Nazi-Bush financial connections. Newspaper reporter Michael Kranish finally made the accusations *public* through a mainstream press article in the Boston *Globe* that became ***the story*** about the charges. A front-page article headlined *Triumphs, Troubles Shape Generations,* ran on April 23, 2001. The *story* was told in first three paragraphs.

The *story:*

Prescott Bush was surely aghast at a sensational article the New York *Herald Tribune* splashed on its front page in July 1942.

"Hitler's Angel Has 3 Million in US Bank," read the headline above a story reporting that Adolf Hitler's financier had stowed the fortune in Union Banking Corp., possibly to be held for "Nazi bigwigs." Bush knew all about the New York bank: He was one of its seven directors. If the Nazi tie became known, it would be a potential "embarrassment," Bush and his partners at Brown Brothers Harriman worried, explaining to government regulators that their position was merely an unpaid courtesy for a client. The situation grew more serious when the government seized Union's assets under the Trading with the Enemy Act, the sort of action that could have ruined Bush's political dreams.

As it turned out, his involvement wasn't pursued by the press or political opponents during his Senate campaigns a decade later. But the episode may well have been one of the catalysts for a dramatic change in his life. Just as the Union Banking story broke,

* see note, page 212

> Bush volunteered to be chairman of United Service Organizations, putting himself on the national stage for the first time. He traveled the country raising millions of dollars to help boost the morale of US troops during World War II, enhancing his stature in a way that helped him get elected US senator. A son and grandson would become presidents.

The next fifty plus paragraphs extolled Prescott's liberal virtues, proclaimed him to be "akin to the Kennedys" and mentions Prescott's membership in the Yale singing group the Whiffenpoofs, but failed to inform about his membership in the Order of Skull & Bones.

Alexandra Robbins, a member of Yale's second oldest senior secret society Scroll & Key, used the *story* in 2002 to deflect the charges in her faux exposé of the Order of Skull & Bones, *Secrets of the Tomb:*

> Nor was it Skull and Bones that specifically instructed members to aid Adolf Hitler, though Hitler's financier stowed $3 million in the Union Banking Corporation, a bank that counted among its seven directors Prescott Bush.

That's it. That is Ms. Robbins complete comment on the subject of the Union Banking Corporation, financing of Hitler and the Order of Skull & Bones. No mention about the American Ship and Commerce Company, Consolidated Silesian Steel Corporation, Hamburg-Amerika Lines, Harriman Fifteen Corporation, Harriman International Company, Holland-American Trading Company, Steamless Steel Corporation or the Silesian-American Corporation, companies of which Brown Brothers Harriman were involved and all of which were enmeshed with Hitler's rise to power. No mention that under the Trading with the Enemy Act many of these companies were seized and were placed at the US Office of Alien Property Custodian. No mention that the Union Banking Corporation was established in August 1924 with George Herbert Walker serving as president and working out of the offices of W. A. Harriman and Company. No mention that in 1932, four out of the eight bank directors were members of the Order of Skull & Bones. No mention that, in the fall of 1942 when Union Banking Corporation was taken over by the government, that a total of three out of seven directors were members of the Order and that a fourth director was an employee of Brown Brothers Harriman — effectively giving Brown Brothers Harriman voting control. No mention that while there were many other non-Bones personnel in partnership at Brown Brothers Harriman, none of them were directors of Union Banking, *only* Bones partners were on the Union Banking Corporation board. The only exception being not another partner but a Brown Brothers Harriman *employee.* No mention that two of the other directors have been identified as Nazis. There was no mention of published accounts such as "[a] 1934 congressional investigation alleged that Walker's Hamburg-Amerika Line subsidized a wide-range of pro-Nazi propaganda efforts both in Germany and the United States;" or that in June of 1936 "[i]nstead of divesting of the Nazi money, [Prescott] Bush hired a lawyer to hide his assets. The lawyer he hired … was Allen Dulles." Was it because Ms. Robbins didn't do her homework — or was she just *advancing* the *story*?

The *story* next gets extended and *massaged* in Mickey Herskowitz's craftily written just released 2003 biography of Prescott Bush, *Duty, Honor, Country:*

> In everyone's life there is a summer of '42; Prescott Bush spent his on Wall Street, where nostalgia and romance are not the hot commodities they were in the motion picture that made the phrase symbolic.
>
> A headline that landed on the front page of the New York *Herald Tribune* in July of that year read: "Hitler's Angel Has 3 Million in U.S. Bank." The reference was to the Union Banking Corporation. Prescott may have been upset or alarmed by the disclosure – he was one of its seven directors. A person of less established ethics would have been panicked.
>
> The story claimed that the bank held $3 million in deposits for a German businessman, described as a "financier" for Adolf Hitler. There was speculation that the account may have been intended for the later use of "Nazi bigwigs."
>
> Buried in the databases that dealt with the Bush family political tradition, the article was rediscovered and reported in the Boston *Globe*, in April 2001, by Michael Kranish. He concluded in the article that the connection had represented a potential "embarrassment" for Prescott. No one actually knew what purpose the fortune had been meant to serve, or who controlled it. Possibly, the money had been socked away as a hedge against Germany's defeat.
>
> Bush and his partners at Brown Brothers Harriman informed the government regulators that the account, opened in the late 1930s, was "an unpaid courtesy for a client. The situation," wrote Kranish, "grew more serious when the government seized Union's assets under the Trading with the Enemy Act, the sort of action that could have ruined Bush's political dreams." The phrase was an ominous one.
>
> The client was believed to be a friend of Charles Lindbergh, according to Roland Harriman. Prescott Bush acted quickly and openly on behalf of the firm, served well by a reputation that had never been compromised. He made available all records and all documents. Viewed six decades later in the era of serial corporate scandals and shattered careers, he received what can be viewed as the ultimate clean bill.
>
> A decade later when he ran for the Senate, his involvement in the bank went untouched by the press or his political opponents.
>
> Earlier that year he had accepted the chairmanship of the USO (United Service Organizations.) He traveled the country over the next two years raising millions for the National War Fund and, as the Boston Globe noted, "putting himself on the national stage for the first time ... (and) boosting the morale of U.S. troops." Out of adversity good things came.

Again the other companies are conveniently ignored and *new facts* appear out of thin air and a *theme* is laid down. Mr. Herskowitz doesn't cite any known sources for this new information. He cites the Kranish article but does not cite the *Herald-Tribune* or any other contemporaneous accounts; he says he had access to 46-hours of taped interviews and scrapbooks from the Bush family and mentions archives at the University of Connecticut. So we do not know where he gathered this particular new information. We do know that it is incorrect and misleading.

Let us examine the *story:*

First off the *Herald-Tribune* article *didn't appear* in July of 1942 it was actually printed in *July of 1941.* The article itself proved to be quite the challenge to find. I talked with several different researchers and none had been able to find it, although spending hours looking at microfilm. Since, there was never a complete date given, just July, 1942, researchers were having to look at the whole month of July and when it wasn't found there, began looking in June and August.

In a July 2003, call to Mr. Kranish at the *Globe* I was told that "several other people" had called him telling him that they were "unable to find it." That there wasn't a complete date reference on the *Herald-Tribune* article because the article — he had found it in an "archive of archives" — was cut out and there was not a full date just a month and year. He said he was sure it was July 1942. I asked Mike, if it was a special edition and if I could find out where this archive was? He said, "The *Herald-Tribune* doesn't exist anymore and it is hard to find, you are just going to have to take my *word* for it. The story definitely appeared." He then excused himself as being busy, that he had written the story over two years ago and he needed to go.

Well, we have found proof that the article did indeed appear — ***in July of 1941.*** First we found on Alex Jones' infowars.com website an article from the July 31, 1941, *Zanesville Signal* in Ohio. The Thyssen/Union Banking news story was in an INS (International News Service) wire report, which says that it was "disclosed today in a news story in the New York *Journal American.* We then found, at ancestry.com, an AP wire report in the *Sheboygan Press,* a Wisconsin newspaper of August 1, 1941 which stated: "The *Herald-Tribune* said Thursday [July, 31, 1941], that Fritz Thyssen, German industrialist credited with helping finance Adolf Hitler's rise to power, 'has $3,000,000 in American cash salted away in the bank vaults of downtown New York.'" Armed with the correct date, we were then able to find both the New York *Herald-Tribune* and New York *Journal American* stories. The articles are presented in full later in this chapter.

So, big deal, what difference does a year make? Well, let's see — in July of 1941 — when the article was *really* printed, there was no declared war, and the *story* allows the rehabilitation of Prescott's *honor* by allowing him to "enhance his stature" *before* the revealing newspaper article, instead of after. The truth of the matter, that Prescott was possibly running for cover in February 1942, by serving as the national chairman of USO, is not broached and the *scandal* is *covered-up.*

What "embarrassment" Prescott may have felt isn't known. The incident isn't discussed in his oral history interviews nor were there any contemporaneous news articles except for the one flurry in July/August 1941 and the articles that mention his name do so without any personal comments. Neither establishment historians nor the mainstream media have dealt with the episode in any depth. Sutton's works and others have been quietly ignored for years, it is only the power of the Internet that has brought forth the *story.*

In the *History Of The Class Of 1917 Yale College, Volume V — Twenty-Fifth Record* printed in 1942, Prescott proudly proclaims his directorship of the Union Banking Corporation, listing it third behind CBS and The Dresser Manufacturing Company and ahead of six other substantial companies. He had been on the bank's board since 1934, his father-in-law was a founder and had been the bank's president. It really wasn't a bank per sé, but acted has a holding company for Thyssen, the German Steel Trust and its related components in their dealings with American industrial and financial markets. It allowed the Thyssen interests to raise money, sell and buy goods in America and then use Union Banking Corporation as their reciprocal bank to transfer monies back and forth.

And the *theme* of poor ol' diligent, naïve Prescott and partners being flummoxed by Charles Lindbergh into such a position of "embarrassment" — is unfounded blame-shifting. The statements by Mr. Herskowitz of "[n]o one actually knew for what purpose the fortune had been meant to serve, or who controlled it" and "that the account [was] opened in late 1930's" are incorrect and disingenuous at best. The bank had working relations with the Thyssen interests since the 1920's and Prescott would have had access to information concerning business. Prescott had been a director of the bank since the early 1930s and he was "running the business" at Brown Brothers Harriman at the time of the scandal. In Prescott's own words, from the Columbia University oral history: "... the partners, like myself and Knight Wooley, who became — certainly after Lovett went to Washington in 1940 — from then on, we were really running the business, the day to day business, all the administrative decisions and the executive decisions. We were the ones that did it."

The Union Banking Corporation was capitalized at $400,000 (most of the stock held by Roland Harriman) and acted as a repository for Thyssen's funds earned in the United States. Tarpley and Chaitkin have written that government investigators reported "the Union Banking Corporation has since its inception [1924] handled funds chiefly supplied to it through the Dutch bank for Thyssen interests for American investment." Averell Harriman had been in Berlin in 1922 establishing a "Berlin Branch of W. A. Harriman & Co. under George Walker's presidency" at which time he "became acquainted with Fritz Thyssen."

In the 1941 articles it was reported that Union Baking Corporation's three million in funds had been frozen in May of 1940 and that the three million dollars, came from "organizations [that] did a thriving business rolling-up dollars." There were four and a half billion dollars in "foreign assets frozen by the US

Government since Adolf Hitler's armies began overrunning Europe" in US banks. Dutch, Belgian, Norwegian and French assets were frozen in 1940 — after the Nazis occupied those countries. German assets were frozen June 14, 1941.

> President Roosevelt ordered Axis funds in the United States frozen. In view of the unlimited national emergency declared by the President, ... The Executive Order is designed, among other things, to prevent the use of the financial facilities of the United States in ways harmful to national defense and other American interests, to prevent the liquidation in the United States of assets looted by duress or conquest, and to curb subversive activities in the United States. *Bulletin*, p. 718. See also Vol. 6, *Federal Register*, p. 2897 (http://www.ibiblio.org/pha/timeline/4106int.htm)

So had an intrepid reporter, tracking down leads about frozen assets uncovered the story? Or was it some sort of controlled leakage? Over a third of the article consists of the letters to and from the Superintendent of Banks of the State of New York which give some "patriotic" cover for the Brown Brothers Harriman partners. The article also sets out doctored facts, some in the bold subheads, such as "Enlisted Harriman in 1925, that is even contradicted in the newsstory. The theme of the *Herald-Tribune* article is a "chance" meeting, that it may be or not be that bad or duped Thyssen's fault, that no compensation was received and how *above-board* and approved the whole affair is from the government's view. The use of controlled scandal to deflect and cover-up deeper scandal has been used many times in US political life and it sometimes even gets a reporter off an editor's back. The story runs and is forgotten.

No matter what the reason, the reportage was quietly stifled. With Luce's *Time-Life* combine, Harriman's position at *Newsweek* and other Bones influenced media such as CBS, the New York *Times* and others, the *scandal* was effectively killed as an item of news.

There was *no* coverage of the *Herald-Tribune* article's information on the Thyssen/Union Banking Corporation connection in the national news weeklies, the New York *Times*, the *Wall Street Journal* or even the New York *Daily Worker*. The afternoon daily, Hearst-owned *Journal-American's* article was basically a condensed re-hash of the earlier *Herald Tribune* articles.

The next known mention of the Union Banking Corporation in the news was the cryptic one sentence in the December 16, 1944 New York *Times** financial pages saying that:

> The Union Banking Corporation, 39 Broadway, New York, has received authority to change its principal place of business to 120 Broadway.

The *real* story continued to be suppressed. No reportage that the corporation was taken over by the US Government under the Trading with the Enemy Act

* See page 264

in the fall of 1942, nor that the address to where Union Banking Corporation was moved was the Office of the Alien Property Custodian.

Maybe that power to suppress, to fabricate, *to deny everything and to explain nothing* was why Prescott was so blasé and felt no need to hide from his peers his directorship in a company that had already been reported by the New York press to be holding $3 million dollars in Nazi funds, prior to him putting the "bite" on classmates as the National Chairman in Charge of the 1942 Fund Drive for the USO.

The next mention of Thyssen in the news were reviews in newspapers, and in magazines, such as *Time, Newsweek* and *Nation,* for the book, *I Paid for Hitler,* by Fritz Thyssen. In Bonesman Henry Luce's *Time* magazine October 13, 1941 it was reported that a co-writer, Emery Reeves a journalist, who in April of 1940 met with Thyssen in Paris and persuaded Thyssen to go to Monte Carlo with Reeves, "a collaborator and a secretary." Where Thyssen would "dictate three solid hours every day, then revised and approved the copy."

In late May 1940. Reeves went "to Paris to check some names and dates." As the Germans were also on their way to Paris. Reeves left France for Britain on a British destroyer. "He never saw or heard from Thyssen again. After more than a year, it seemed obvious that Thyssen was a captive; for if he were free, he would have communicated with his family in South America. Alive or dead, he was Reeves decided, beyond the power of the book to hurt or help. So Reeves decided to publish."

The book has Thyssen pounding his head and muttering "'*Ein Dummkopf war ich!*' (What a dumbhead I was')" and reports about Thyssen's financial assistance to Hitler prior to the Beer Hall Putsch of 1923. The Thyssen role in financing Hitler is covered extensively in other chapters, so we will not recount that history here. A new revelation in the book was the novel conspiracy theory that Adolph Hitler was the illegitimate son of Baron Rothschild. *I Paid for Hitler* was published in New York, by Farrar & Rinehart. Chairman of the Board of Farrar & Rinehart was John Chipman Farrar a member of the 1918 cell of the Order of Skull & Bones. The class that had been tapped by Prescott's Bones cell. The 1918 Bones cell included US Congressman Malcolm Baldridge, CIA personnel Director F. Trubee Davison, mega-businessman Artemus Gates and the then, in 1941, Asst. Secretary of War and Brown Brothers Harriman partner Robert A Lovett. They had all been part of the famous Palm Beach, Florida, Yale WW I flying unit.

John C Farrar during WW II was a member of the Psychological Warfare Branch in the Office of War Information and was an editor for some of the OWI propaganda publications.

After the war, Thyssen "denied authorship" of *I Paid for Hitler.* Was there more to the book than met the eye? Was *I Paid for Hitler* created to confuse and possibly rehabilitate certain individuals and diffuse and confuse situations in the war-charged American atmosphere of the early 1940s? Similar to Bonesman

Luce's *Life* magazine reversing the Zapruder film frame of the JFK murder so as to accommodate the physics of the official *story* of that action.

You have got to be willing to do a lot of things furtively and secretly, to bring about a situation that will accomplish what you want to have accomplished. — Prescott Bush, speaking about the intelligence services in his oral history, done by Columbia University.

Prescott definitely understood this and it seems as though he and Brown Brothers Harriman were trying to keep the *scandal* in the dark — before some newshound broke the soon to be squashed news — because in the July 31, 1941, New York *Herald-Tribune* it says that seven months *before,* in January of 1941, Brown Brothers Harriman partner and Bonesman, Knight Wooley had written to the NY State Banking Board Superintendent that "[s]hould the United States enter the war, they [the Union Banking Corporation American directors] felt they might be under some embarrassment, ..."

Kept in the dark it was and Prescott won a special election in 1952, after the death of a sitting Senator, to serve as a US Senator from Connecticut. General Dwight Eisenhower, whom Prescott in November of 1951, had urged to run for the Republican party nomination for President of the US was also elected. Prescott golfed with President Eisenhower often, and spent a half-hour alone with him on Ike's last day as President.

Senator Bush served on the Banking Committee, many times as a contact person for World Bank and Federal Reserve officials, who sometimes looked for more casual places to do business than the Senate committee rooms. In his second term — protecting his state's interests — Prescott also served as a member of the Armed Service Committee. For years Connecticut had received more *per capita* of the defense dollar than any other state earning itself the sobriquet, the "Arsenal of Democracy." That the Military-Industrial Complex began in Connecticut in the 1800s is relevant ... but another tale.

Prescott was a member of two private clubs in Washington, the Alibi Club and the Alfalfa Club. Every presidential election season, the Alfalfa Club nominates one of its members in jest to run for President of the United States. In January 1959 Senator Bush was the nominee for Alfalfa Party. His acceptance speech was recorded and a transcript was included, by the Senator's request, in his oral history given to Columbia University. In this speech Prescott says:

> I recall here the immortal words of Granville Rice, when he wrote:
> *The rules of life apply the same*
> *To any sport you choose*
> *It matters not how you play the game,*
> *So long as you never lose.*

Prescott Bush retired from the Senate in 1962, returning to his work at Brown Brothers Harriman. He passed away in October of 1972. Antony Sutton didn't write his book about the Order of Skull & Bones and the Union Banking Corporation's involvement with financing Hitler until 1984. The *story* and Prescott's defense didn't appear till April 2001, just before his Bonesman grandson's selection to serve as the President of the United States.

Prescott never heard the *story*. Do we wonder … what he would have said?

*A NOTE FROM DANIËL DE WIT, DUTCH TELEVISION PRODUCER;

Amongst other things, what we had to cut was the information on the Bilderberg society and the CIA-drugs segment. What was left was as good as dead and was broadcast at the ultimate impossible hour of 5 PM on a Friday afternoon as every possible viewer is in traffic going home. There never was a rerun. The reason we had to, well, kill our 'child,' was because the new head of the documentary department at that time could not stand behind our findings. Even though they were based on facts and told by experts. There was also a cultural difference. The new head was just recently promoted to this documentary department from a news section that made very factual clips of maximum five minutes: 'There is a fire and two people died.' Whilst our documentary was about 'who lit the fire and why?' We had made a documentary — which is a view on reality based on facts — of one hour and twenty minutes and with a subject that is beyond the frame of mind of many people consuming the news that they are fed. This combination of events was the end of our documentary as such.

Making the program was quite an experience, not the least because of all the spooks we had to deal with for the CIA-drugs segment. When we first started in 1995 there was no Internet, just some old stencils of a hard to find book of a man known by only a few and the few who knew him, thought Antony Sutton was dead or lived on a high mountain. To communicate there was the fax and the telephone. In 1996 the Internet came (for us at least) but information on Skull & Bones was still hard to find. Try to explain that to anyone typing in "Skull and Bones" in Google today and getting swamped in information.

The subject of Bones and all these kinds of institutions and people was a real eye opener. As a matter of fact, it changed my life and made me see the world completely different. So much different that many times things are one hundred percent different than they seem. Not just ten of sixty percent, but really one hundred percent, turned upside down. On the one hand the subject of Skull & Bones became less 'dark,' because we found out the society is not some sort of spooky world government, on the other hand it became darker, because these Bones-like institutions and their members show a brute force and an enormous concentrated power that is overwhelming and could make anyone very cynical very easily. That also must be a reason people like to stay away from these realities.

Since corresponding and meeting with Antony Sutton he is my greatest example. He was just a player in the game that has to be played, but he played his role very well. He made a difference. I was then and still am 'in the research business', as Antony called it, digging deeper as ever, but it is extremely difficult to find resources to make new documentaries on the subjects I specialize in. Very frustrating, because the market is there. It's just not easy convincing the people who have the funds about this fact. In the meantime I began DaanSpeak.com, a web page that is an outlet for the information I collect and explain in my articles. It's a hobby, but a serious one. My main work is being a researcher for television programs. Through my website two program makers contacted me for their Dutch series that looks in a serious way at the phenomenon of conspiracies. The series will show that it is a very normal and obvious phenomenon. The program will air (although you never know) in Holland in January 2004.

Daniël de Wit
August 2003

THE WEATHER

Today: Thunder showers and warmer

Tomorrow: Fair and slightly cooler

Detailed Report on Page 16

NEW YORK

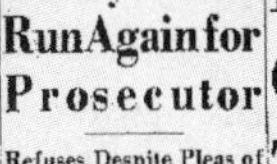

Herald Tribune

LATE CITY EDITION

VOL. CI No. 34,591 — Copyright, 1941, New York Tribune Inc. — THURSDAY, JULY 31, 1941 — LATE CITY LIFT — THREE CENTS — New York City and Vicinity

U.S. Protests to Japan on Bombs Near Gunboat and China Embassy

Welles Announces Strong Complaint: Capitol Hill Sentiment Is Indignant

Some Think Attack Not Just Error

Chungking Raiders Miss Tutuila by a Few Feet, Damage U. S. Property

By Wilfrid Fleisher

A CAUSE FOR PROTEST—The gunboat Tutuila at her anchorage in the Yangtze River at Chungking

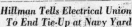

Dewey Won't Run Again for Prosecutor

Refuses Despite Pleas of Republicans and Other Anti-Tammany Groups

Asks Nomination Of One of His Aids

Does Not Want Office to 'Hinge' on One Man; Lockwood Is Favored

Roosevelt Asks Control Over Prices and Rents To Bar Inflation 'Disaster'

President Calls Situation 'Frighteningly Similar' to That in World War

Fight on Henderson Looms in Congress

Bills, Ready Today, Likely to Avoid Lid on Wages and Products of Farms

By Bert Andrews

Thyssen Has $3,000,000 Cash in New York Vaults

Union Banking Corp. May Hide Nest Egg for High Nazis He Once Backed

By M. Jay Racusin

In the tides of economic warfare now surging over the world, the New York Herald Tribune has discovered that Fritz Thyssen, the German industrialist, who was Adolf Hitler's original patron on a prodigal scale a decade ago, has $3,000,000 in American cash salted away in the bank vaults of downtown New York.

In the American colony of Thyssen enterprises perhaps the most interesting is the Union Banking Corporation, 39 Broadway, nominal guardian of the $3,000,000 cache, all in United States currency—a sort of nest egg for Herr Thyssen or perhaps for some of his high-placed Nazi friends when the present troublous days are over.

Among other Thyssen interests in New York are half a dozen corporations engaged in the shipping, export and import trades, centering chiefly about the coal and steel industries and operating under the wing of the Union Banking Corporation. These organizations did a thriving business in rolling up dollars for Herr Thyssen in years past, but have been brought virtually to a standstill during the last year by the war.

One of the most fascinating as-

(Continued on page 22, column 2)

Associated Press

Fritz Thyssen

Gotham Hosiery Closes a Mill in Silk Shortage

Philadelphia Plant Shut-down Is First Result of Cutting Japanese Supply

Nazis Await Fall of Leningrad; Fierce Battle Rages at Smolensk

Berlin Asserts Russia's Second City Is Threatened by Closing Pincers; Moscow Is Raided Again; Reds Report Hitler's Regiment Smashed

Hopkins Tells Stalin U.S. Will Fill Red Needs

Gets Note for Roosevelt and Says 'Anybody Who Fights Hitler Is on Right Side'

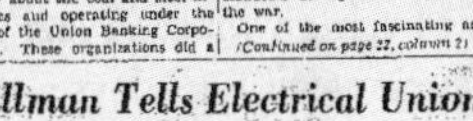

Hillman Tells Electrical Union To End Tie-Up at Navy Yard

Includes Other Defense Projects in City; Local Expected to Comply Today, but Will Continue Edison Strike; Mayor to See State Mediator

Senate Debate On Retention of Soldiers Opens

Elbert Thomas Warns of German Strength; House Committee Reports Bill

By Jack Beall

News on Inside Pages

Snub to Women in Home Defense Is Charged as Mrs. Kerr Quits

Club Federation President Notes LaGuardia Chose a Man to Fill O. C. D. Post

Tire Makers Raise Retail Prices 2.4% With Henderson Sanction

The front page of the New York *Herald-Tribune*, July, 31, 1941.

The Thyssen/Union Banking article was continued on page 22 in the financial news section, with three almost full columns plus another full column ancillary story on Thyssen. The articles are reproduced in full in the following pages.

Michael Kranish, the Boston Globe reporter, when we contacted in August 2003 to tell him that the articles were actually published in 1941 said, "Well, I wrote that so long ago, I can't remember now why – if it is '41 – why it says '42. It is a mystery to me. I do not know what the situation is. But it definitely was there, that is all I can say. The copy that I have, you know, someone put the date in it – maybe that was wrong. I certainly would have tried carefully to put the right date." Mike then wanted to know my purpose for looking in to this. I tell him I am a researcher and writer looking into Prescott Bush and Union Banking.

His then last words on the subject were, "I have looked very thoroughly and I did not find the evidence that the conspiracy theorist allege, so ... if the date is different I just don't know why that is."

New York *Herald-Tribune,* July 31, 1941

THYSSEN HAS $3,000.000 CASH IN NEW YORK VAULTS

Union Banking Corp. May Hide Nest Egg for High Nazis He Once Backed

By M. J Racusin

In the tides of economic warfare now surging over the world, the New York *Herald Tribune,* has discovered that Fritz Thyssen, the German industrialist who was Adolf Hitler's original patron on a prodigal scale a decade has $3,000,000 in American cash, salted away in the bank vaults of downtown New York.

In the American colony of Thyssen enterprises perhaps the most interesting is, the Union Banking Corporation, 39 Broadway, nominal guardian of the $3,000,000 cache, all in United States currency — a sort of nest egg for Herr Thyssen or perhaps for some of his high-placed Nazi friends when the present troublous days are over.

Among other Thyssen interests in New York are half a dozen corporations engaged in the shipping, export and import trades, centering chiefly about coal and steel industries and operating under the wing of the Union Banking Corporation. These organizations did a thriving business in rolling up dollars for Herr Thyssen in years past, but have been brought virtually to a standstill during the last year by the war.

One of the most fascinating aspects of this story is the mystery surrounding the Thyssen fortune. At the moment, of course, no can get at this Thyssen nest egg, because it is part of the $4,500,000,000 foreign assets frozen by the United States government since Adolf Hitler's armies began overrunning Europe.

Government circles assert that the assets of the Union Banking Corporation and its subsidiaries were frozen because capital and control came from Netherlands institution called the, Bank voor Handel en Scheepvaart (Bank for Trade, and Shipping) in Rotterdam one of the Thyssen string of banking houses on the Continent. It was subject to the freezing order, however, as a Dutch corporation and not as a German-owned property.

As the Custodian of all Dutch property outside the Netherlands, the Netherlands government in exile represents that it, too, would seem to have some rights in the, matter. Nevertheless all of Fritz Thyssen's properties were confiscated by the Nazi regime back in 1939, and thus it might appear that the assets here are legally a part of the German government's assets in the United States.

Rotterdam Bank Bombed

The Thyssen bank in Rotterdam which nominally owned the New York corporation was bombed out of existence by the invading Nazis in May, 1940. No one in New York professes to know what has happened to the officers of the Rotterdam institution. Not a word of instruction or advice has come from abroad.

Perhaps it wasn't Herr Thyssen's money at all, some persons suggest. Maybe he sent it here for safekeeping for some of the Nazi bigwigs — perhaps for Goering, for Goebbels, for Himmler, or even Hitler himself.

No matter how the story comes out, the United States government has the situation in hand. Every penny of known Thyssen assets is frozen, under the strictest control.

There are many Americans in responsible positions who do not think that the rift between Herr Thyssen and the Nazis was genuine at all, preferring to believe that Thyssen was in reality a sort of economic advance agent of the Hitler forces, a financial surveyor and softener-up posing as a refugee.

Reliable private information is that Thyssen has been wandering about Switzerland, France and other European countries before and after the Nazi armies arriving without much hindrance, from the Hitler government. Thyssen is now in Germany — not under confinement, free to move about but closely watched — perhaps a willing prisoner, perhaps a hostage for his wealth throughout the world.

Herr Thyssen's adventure in the American business world dates back to August, 1924, when without flourishes or ruffles the Union Banking Corporation was incorporated with a capital stock of $400,000, the money coming from the Bank voor Handel en Scheepvaart, of Rotterdam. It was licensed under the New York State banking laws as an investment corporation.

In addition to known lieutenants of the Thyssen interests in Europe, there appeared and continue to appear on the board of directors of this corporation the names of several partners of the private banking house of Brown Brothers Harriman & Co., 59 Wall Street.

Enlisted Harriman In 1925

This circumstance dates back to a chance meeting in Europe in 1925 between Fritz Thyssen and W. Averell Harriman, a partner of the Brown Brothers, Harriman firm and now minister plenipotentiary to England as expediter of lease-lend aid to the British. Herr Thyssen said to Mr. Harriman that he was opening a bank in the United States to take care of his financial and industrial interests here and, asked Mr. Harriman to serve on the board. Mr. Harriman agreed to have several other members of his firm, go on the directorate.

This took place, of course, at a time when the present world tangle could hardly have been foreseen and when such courtesies were part of the normal routine of international banking relations.

When a new world war began the Brown Brothers Harriman partners sensed possible embarrassment through association with a corporation stemming from German interests and considered withdrawal from the Union Banking Corporation's board. In a consultation with William R. White, State Superintendent of Banks, on the subject Mr. White requested them to remain on the board to assure efficient administration of the corporation's affairs by trustworthy and responsible persons during the emergency. They agreed to comply with Mr. White's request.

Brown Brothers Harriman & Co. have never had any financial interest in the Union Banking Corporation or any of its subsidiaries, and have never profited in any way from its activities. The association of some of its partners with the Thyssen corporation, it points, out, was entirely a matter of courtesy.

Relationship Explained

The circumstances of relationship were frankly set forth in a letter addressed by Knight Woolley, a partner of the, Brown Brothers Harriman firm, to Mr. White on Jan. 14 of this year. This letter follows:

"January 14, 1941.
"William R. White, Esq.,
"Superintendent of Banks, State Of New York,
80 Centre Street,
"New York, N, Y.

"'Dear Mr. White:

"As you are aware, my partners, E. R. Harriman, Ray Morris, Prescott S. Bush and our manager, H. D. Pennington, are directors of the Union Banking Corporation, a state institution under your supervision. This corporation is located, at 39 Broadway, and it is in effect a New York office, or agency, of the Bank voor Handel en Scheepvaart, in Rotterdam. Because of possible uncertainty as to whether the Bank voor Handel en Scheepvaart might be held to be a Dutch institution, or whether it is, in fact, a German institution under a Dutch name, my partners have been giving serious consideration to withdrawing from the board. Should the United States enter the war, they feel they might be under some embarrassment because of their connection with the bank, even though we have no financial interest in the Union Banking

Corporation, nor do we participate in its earnings. They act as directors merely as a matter of business courtesy.

"In order that you may understand clearly the reasons for our doubts, I should like to give you the background of our connection with the Union Banking Corporation. Our partner W.A. Harriman was in Europe in 1925, and at that time he became acquainted with Mr. Fritz Thyssen, the German industrialist. To the best of my knowledge, Mr. Thyssen formed the Bank voor Handel en Scheepvaart and presumably controlled that institution. At one of his meetings with Mr. Harriman, he told him he was forming a bank in New York to look after his interests in the United States and he asked Mr. Harriman to serve on the board. Mr. Harriman agreed that certain of his associates would serve in this capacity, and as a result various members of the Harriman organizations and now of Brown Brothers Harriman & Co., have been on the board ever since.

"The Union Banking Corporation does no commercial business, and its only depositor is the Bank voor Handel en Scheepvaart. Its activities are limited to occasional payments and a few purchases and sales of securities. All shares of the Union Banking Corporation are registered in the name of E. R. Harriman, who is chairman of the board, except the qualifying shares held by directors. As the company is Dutch-owned, its banking accounts were frozen under the Presidential Proclamation of May 10, 1940.

"The Union Banking Corporation maintains accounts with the Chase National Bank, the National City Bank, the Guaranty Trust Company, and ourselves. At present its account with us is the only one which is active, and the drawings are limited to the Payment of salaries and usual office expenses. To further control its operations, we have arranged that either Ray Morris or H. D. Pennington must sign checks jointly with the president of the company, Mr. C. Lievense, or with the, assistant treasurer, Mr. W Kauffmann, and that one of our gentleman from our organization must be present when access is desired to the company's safe deposit box at the Chase Bank.

"You have perhaps read in the newspapers recently that, Fritz Thyssen is no longer in Germany, and it has been reported that he has had differences with the Nazi regime. We have no knowledge as to whether he still retains an interest in the Bank voor Handel en Scheepvaart, nor are we able to obtain any information with respect to the stock ownership in the bank.

"In view, of these uncertainties, together with the censorship affecting communications to and from Rotterdam, I realize that the Union Banking Corporation might be placed in an embarrassing position if all the directors were to resign at this time. I feel sure however that you will understand the position of my Associates, and I would greatly appreciate, a frank expression from you as to the action which you feel that they should take should you believe that the interests of the Banking Department would be best served by their continuing as directors until the situation abroad has been somewhat clarified, I know that they will be glad to be guided by, your judgment and I shall greatly appreciate your reaction to this situation and your opinion as to what action, if any, should be taken by my associates.

Very truly yours,
"KNIGHT WOOLLEY."

Whites Reply

To this Mr. White replied:

"May 13, 1941.
"Mr. Knight Woolley,
"Brown Brothers Harriman & Co.,
"59 Wall Street,
"New York City.

Dear Mr. Woolley:

"Reference is made to your letter of January 14 and to conversations which you and certain of your partners have since had with me relative to the status of the Union Banking Corporation.

"During recent months this department has been obliged to give unusual attention to certain of the banking organizations in this country which have been affected by the freezing orders. This, however has not been true in the case of the Union Banking Corporation because of the confidence which the department has in the directors of this institution

"While the department would, not feel free to object if your partners, Mr. Harriman, Mr. Bush, and your firm's manager, Mr. Pennington, should desire to resign as directors of the corporation, nevertheless the department would be gratified if these gentlemen could find it possible to remain on the board during this period of uncertainty.

"I appreciate your thoughtfulness in bringing this matter to my attention and the willingness of yourself and your associates to consideration to the department's point of view in the matter.

"Sincerely yours,

"WILLIAM R. WHITE."

Personnel and Assets

The personnel and financial setup of the Union Banking Corporation is provided in the following report of the institution, issued on Jan 1, 1941:

UNION BANKING CORPORATION. NEW YORK, 39 BROADWAY, ORGANIZED 1924

Cornelis Lievense, President

Walter Kauffmann, Treasurer

Directors- Cornelis Lievense, E. Roland Harriman, R. D. Pennington, P. S. Bush, J. Kouwenhoven, Ray Morris, J. G. Groeninger

RESOURCES

Cash on hand and due from banks (domestic) $2,817,763.95

Bond and Stock investments 232,880.25

Other loans, notes and bills (including other acceptances) 53,000.00

Accrued Income 947.66

Total resources.................................$3,104,591.86

LIABILITIES

Deposits: Demand $115,880,14

Due to banks (domestic and foreign).......................................2,262,040,20

Other Liabilities 822.64

Capital stock 400,000

Surplus and undivided profits................302,339.70

Reserves...23,503,18

Total liabilities...................................3,104,591.86

Lievense a United States Citizen

The dominating personality in the administration of the Thyssen domain in the United States is the shy and little known Cornelis Lievense, a colorful little Hollander who arrived in this country by way of Montreal in May, 1926, two years after the Union Banking Corporation was set up Mr. Lievense is a naturalized American citizen having received his final citizen papers on Jan. 29, 1932, at Mineola, L.I.

Besides the Union Bank Corporation, Mr. Lievense is president of the Holland American Corporation, the Domestic Fuel Corporation, and the Seamless Steel Equipment Corporation.

All of these occupy offices with the Union Bank Corporation at 39 Broadway. Others in the group at that address are the Kemari Trading Corporation, the Riberena Fuel and Chartering Corporation, Kauffmann & Co. and Religious Publications Inc.

Mr. Lievense admitted that the assets of the Domestic Fuel Corporation, the Holland American Trading Corporation and the Seamless Steel Equipment Corporation had all been frozen along with those of the Union Banking Corporation by the Treasury Department. He said the business of the whole group, aside, from the bank, hardly approached $1,000,000 annually.

Blacklisted by Canada

He admitted also that the Domestic Fuel Corporation, which had been bringing cargoes of, coal from the Thyssen mining interests in Europe to Canada and other Western Hemisphere points, had been blacklisted by the Canadian Trade Commission in the fall of 1940.

Mr. Lievense would reveal little of the operations of the corporations beyond saying that they are now under the strict supervision of the Treasury Department and that there was "very little activity."

He insisted, however, that Religious Publications, Inc., although occupying offices with the Union Banking Corporation and the others, was not a Thyssen venture but was purely his personal affair.

"This is a philanthropic venture of mine," he explained with disarming sincerity, "undertaken to bring out the religious works of Dr. K Schilder, a Dutchman who has recently been released from a German concentration camp. This is in no sense a profit-making venture and must not be associated with these other business organizations."

Three of Dr. Schilder's books have been, brought out by the William B. Eerdmans Publishing Company, of Grand Rapids, Mich., and were translated from the Dutch by Henry Zylstra. They bear the titles, "Christ In His Suffering, "Christ on Trial" and "Christ Crucified."

On Other, Thyssen, Boards

Mr. Lievense speaks in soft, low tones and merely smiled broadly when questioned about his association with Herr Thyssen. His name appears as a director of the Thyssen Holland American Investment Corporation, at Rotterdam. He is a member of the board of the August Thyssen Bank, Aktiengesellschaft, at Berlin, and, he is also a director of the Handelscompagnie Ruilvkeer, a Thyssen bartering company at Amsterdam.

Two of Mr. Lievense's associates, on the board of the Union Banking Corporation,, J. G. Groeninger and N. J. Kouwenhoven, are among Herr Thyssen's chief managerial assistants in the conduct of many of his European Projects. Kouwenhoven is an old school friend of Mr. Lievense and is managing director of the Bank voor Handel en Scheepvaart. He is also managing director of the Holland American Investment Corporation and is on the board of the Thyssen-owned Vlaardingen Harborworks.

Groeninger is managing director of the Thyssen-owned Halcyon Line, with headquarters at Rotterdam. It was this corporation which refused to transfer its headquarters and assets outside Holland when the Netherlands government warned all industrialists to take their properties to Dutch colonies at the time of the Nazi Invasion. Just before the arrival of the German forces at Rotterdam, the British and Dutch navies seized eleven of the thirteen ships of the line and incorporated them in the British shipping pool. It is understood that three of these ships have since been destroyed. Only two ships of the line fell into the Nazis, hands.

Only One Has Visited U. S.

Both Groeninger and Kouwenhoven are directors of the local Holland American Trading Corporation. Groeninger is also on the board of the Bank voor Handel en Scheepvaart and is a director of the Vulcan Rhine Shipping Co., another unit in Thyssen's industrial kingdom. Kouwenhoven visited the United States about four or five years ago, Mr. Lievense said, but Groeninger appears never to have been here.

"I have told the government, Authorities everything I know and that is all I can say," Mr. Lievense said in a tolerant manner. "As, a matter of fact, I cannot say now who owns this money and this bank and these corporations. I cannot tell you if Mr. Thyssen owns it or not. You know, of course, that the building the Bank voor Handel en Scheepvaart has been bombed out of existence. Where is it now? Who owns it? Who knows?"

Pacing the floor of his office on the twenty-fifth floor of 39 Broadway, he said,

"All I know is that I am here and that the United States government is exercising strict supervision of all activities of the bank and these corporation. I cannot tell you whom I am working. You may be sure there is really little to do. All these corporations in their best years have done less than $1,000,000 annually."

Mr. Lievense added that his business had slowed down to such a degree that he had to let out two or three of his office force and had reduced his three-room office to two rooms.

Has Time to Play the Organ

"In fact" he said, " I have been, spending too much time indulging in my favorite pastime — playing the organ at my home. I also play the organ for the Whiteman Memorial Baptist Church at Oyster Bay, What else is there to do?"

Mr. Lievense and his wife, Maria Jacobs, have lived In a rambling two-story semi-Colonial home in Cedar Swamp Road, in the High Hills Farm section of Glen Head L. I., for the last eight or ten, years.

He passes much time visiting the tulip beds in the vicinity of his home. He is a member of the Netherlands Club, and was born In Maasslius, Holland, July 28, 1890.

Below is a sidebar article from *Herald Tribune* July 31, 1941, page 22.

Thyssen's Role In World Affairs Still a Mystery

Original Hitler Backer May Be Refugee or Nazi Agent if He's Alive and at Large

Fritz Thyssen, once ruler of the German steel trust and most important backer of Adolf Hitler In the early days of the Brown Shirt revolution in Germany, is the international mystery man of today. It is anybody's guess whether he is a genuine refugee from the Nazi terror or a Hitler agent wrapped in a fugitive's cloak. The world at large does not know where he is or even whether he is alive. And it has, apparently, no way of finding out.

On March 17 it was reported in Vichy. France, that he had been arrested on the Riviera in December, returned to Germany and lodged behind the barbed wire of Dachau concentration camp. Four days later German authorities announced that he was not in France or in Dachau but in South America. Earlier this month informed sources in Germany said he had been released from custody and was in a German sanatorium enjoying "limited freedom of movement."

Contradictory reports of Herr Thyssen's status are not new in the history of the man who, more than any other, financed Hitler's rise to power. Since 1934 vague rumors of breaks between Thyssen and Hitler have circulated from time to time. They came to a head on Nov. 11, 1939, when it was announced that he had left Germany for Switzerland "for an indefinite stay." The next day he arrived in Lucerne and for several months kept correspondents regarding his hints that he quit his country after protesting against the Nazi-Soviet pact and urging Hitler through Hermann Wilhelm Goering, not to go to war.

Property Confiscated

A week after his arrival in Switzerland it was announced in Berlin with fanfare that the Reich had confiscated his fortune and property estimated to be worth at least $88,000,000. It was done on the basis of a law aimed at persons inimical to the people and the state. On Feb. 12, 1940, a decree was published in the official German gazette stripping him and his wife of their citizenship. They were then living In luxury in a Locarno hotel.

From then until his disappearance from the Riviera his movements were of a nature to arouse suspicion, or at least puzzlement.

He was in Belgium in March, 1940, and within a few weeks Hitler's armies forced the surrender of that country. From Belgium he moved to France, where he remained unmolested long after the French bowed before Hitler's legions.

Thyssen's residence at the Hotel Crillon in Paris while the German armies gathered in front of the, Maginot Line puzzled the Parisians. It seemed strange to them that a man who was a declared enemy of France and the prime mover of Hitler's coup should be ensconced in the French capital at that particular time, able to get the ear not only of French industrialists but also of French politicians.

The same puzzlement arose after the French surrender when Thyssen supposedly an enemy of the Reich was allowed to sun himself for months on the sands of Cannes, although the German authorities could have had him for the asking.

Mentioned as Roehm Associate

All this maneuvering was an echo of in earlier incident in his career. In 1934 after Hitler had assumed the Chancellorship with the staunch help of Thyssen, Berlin began to buzz with rumors of a split among the Nazis. It was also said that Thyssen was seen frequently in the company of Captain Ernst Roehm, one of the leaders of the supposed plot against the Fuehrer.

In the blood bath of July 30, 1934, when Hitler purged his party by killing Roehm and others, there was no mention of Thyssen's having a part in the conspiracy. Yet, when he sailed in August for South America, it was reported that he was fleeing. Despite his intimacy with Roehm however, Thyssen apparently suffered none of Hitler's suspicion. After studying the steel business of South America, he returned in the spring to Germany and took up where he had left off.

In the various accounts of the string-pulling responsible for Hitler's rise in Germany, there in no suggestion that Thyssen shelled out his marks to the Nazi party for any reasons but selfish ones. He was firm believer In capitalism so far as capitalism was represented by the palatial Thyssen chateau, the roaring Thyssen steel furnaces in the Ruhr and Rhine valleys and the 120,000 workers who owed their daily bread to the Thyssen pay rolls. Hitler's main appeal to him was as a defender of Capitalism against tile Bolshevik bogey.

The Thyssen holdings were hard hit in the German inflation and the subsequent struggle of German industry against the restrictions imposed under the Versailles Treaty. Thyssen hated the French, distrusted the German Republic and dreaded socialism. He began to look around for an antidote to the three-headed monster of his imagination. In 1927 he found it in the person an Austrian former house painter.

Started Pushing In '30

Thyssen kept an eye on Hitler and, when the depression in 1930 rocked the Thyssen industrial empire, decided that it was time to push the Nazi leader. He introduced him to prominent industrialists, promised them that Hitler's National Socialism was only window dressing and helped to pry money for the cause from their pockets. In 1930 he and a business associate distributed 1,000,000 marks to the party and two years later, before the fateful presidential election leading to Hitler's Chancellorship, Thyssen donated 3,000,000 more.

His reward was to be made economic dictator of western Germany and a member of the Reich's Grand Economic Council and Prussian State Council. He also had a seat in the Reichstagg.

If the version that would picture him tossed over by Hitler is correct, he mistook his man when he patronizingly gathered the Fuehrer under his wing, His idea was to guide Hitler in the paths of safety for the Thyssen fortune. Like other German industrialists with same thought, however, it would appear that his supported puppet turned out to be a Frankenstein monster.

—

IN THE NEWS

BRITISH RAID FINNS, BOMB PORT, HIT SHIPS

Journal NEW YORK American
AN AMERICAN PAPER FOR THE AMERICAN PEOPLE
CITY EDITION
No. 19,579—DAILY   THURSDAY, JULY 31, 1941

Thyssen Fund Of $3,000,000 Found Here

JAPAN APOLOGIZES FOR GUNBOAT ATTACK

New Hopkins, Stalin Parley Due Today

MOSCOW, July 31 (AP).—Further conferences between Premier Josef Stalin and Harry L. Hopkins, personal representative of President Roosevelt, were expected today.

The Soviet army was reported battling the Nazi invaders to a standstill on the 40th day of the Russian-German war in vital sectors of the long battlefront.

Hopkins, who flew to Moscow from London Tuesday, was almost immediately granted an interview with the most important and most inaccessible man in Russia.

He said he came to see Stalin at Roosevelt's request and he expected another meeting today and perhaps several more before he leaves.

Bill O'Dwyer—His Life Story—by Austen Lake

Today's is the fifth installment in the absorbing life story of William (Bill) O'Dwyer, Democratic candidate for Mayor of New York, as written for the New York Journal-American by Austen Lake, noted newspaperman and author.

Earlier chapters described O'Dwyer's youth in Ireland, his education in Spain and his first struggles for a foothold in New York.

The "Frank Jones" was a floating farmhouse with decks like the flounces of an old lady's skirt, a seven-knot speed and the smell of a cabbage cellar.

Each evening, at twilight, it gave an hysterical hoot and began waggling its broad rump up the Hudson while its sister ship, the "Kaaterskilla," started churning down from Albany.

The next night the voyages were

Nazi Ace Who Fled U.S. Killed

Tokio Pledges U. S. Property Protection

TOKIO, July 31 (By Telephone to New York) (AP).—Foreign Minister Vice Admiral Teijiro Toyoda offered apologies and expressed regret today to United States Ambassador Joseph C. Grew for the bombing of the United States gunboat Tutuila at Chungking, China.

Grew and Toyoda talked at the Foreign Office for 20 minutes.

The chief aide of the Japanese Navy Ministry also visited the American naval attache, Commander Henri Smith-Hutton, to express his regrets.

The apologies and regret over the bombing, which occurred yesterday, were offered before the American envoy was able to make the representations he had been

Navy Acts To Support Russia

EXTRA

LONDON, July 31 (UP).—Britain made w[ar] against Finland for th[e] first time yesterday wh[en] naval aircraft attack[ed] Petsamo, Finnish Arc[tic] port, and Kirkenes, northern Norwegian p[ort], the Admiralty said today.

The British were acting in support of their Russian ally.

The attacking British planes hit the 1,460 ton German gunnery training ship Bremse, a fast vessel built in 1931, the Admiralty said.

In addition at least four supply ships at Kirkenes were hit and shipping and harbor works at Petsamo were damaged.

Indicating the great extent of the raid, the Admiralty said 16 British planes were lost.

Leningrad Capture Near, INS Reports

By PIERRE J. HUSS

The first and seventh edition's front-pages from the Hearst-owned afternoon daily, the *New York Journal American*, July 31, 1941. The day the Thyssen/Union Banking Corporation article was published. The first two editions name Prescott Bush on the front page with the rest of the article on page two. By the third edition the story went from 33 paragraphs to 12, with no mention of Harriman, Bush and friends on the front page. In the fourth, the Wall Street Closing edition, Thyssen's picture was much smaller. By the seventh edition, the Sports Final, the smaller story was moved to the fourth page and then — *forgotten.*

Journal NEW YORK American
AN AMERICAN PAPER FOR THE AMERICAN PEOPLE
7TH SPORT BASEBALL SPORTS FINAL
No. 19,579—DAILY   THURSDAY, JULY 31, 1941

BRITISH BOMBERS RAID FINN HARBOR

... Africa—an integral part of the British Empire on which the sun never squats?

Or are we better off through having become, because of our independence and our individuality and our true democracy, the greatest, the freest, the healthiest, the happiest, the richest, and the strongest nation in the world?

There is a poser for all proud, upstanding Americans—a difficult nut to crack apparently in this land where "every man is a king."

But we have got to crack it. So get out your nutcrackers.

IT IS TIME we decided definitely whether our fathers were the traitors and rebels that George the Third called them, or whether they were the exalted patriots we have always thought them.

Whether our nation is the pitiful failure that a band of royal refugees and some of our own snobs and sycophants declare it to be, or whether we are so splendid a success in civilized development, in spiritual attainment, in material progress, in liberty and enlightenment, in high standards of living and general popular welfare that we are the envy—and the jealousy—of all the peoples of the world.

And while we are struggling to solve these perplexing problems, let us find out whether we ourselves are a lot of kowtowing Tories or a nation of freedom-loving, independent American citizens—whether, indeed, we are mice or men.

MR. WEDGWOOD—a very honest Englishman, even if perhaps too free spoken—recently upbraided us Americans for our hesitation and delay in rejoining the British Empire.

He said the "Union Now" movement was "much farther advanced in England than in America."

Oil Stations Will Comply, Says Ickes

Firms in 17 States and D. of C. Pledge End of Night Sales

By KENNETH SCHEIBEL

WASHINGTON, July 31.—Oil Co-ordinator Ickes today announced that the major petroleum companies have agreed to close down 100,000 gasoline stations on the Atlantic seaboard at 7 p. m. nightly starting Sunday, to avert a threatened oil shortage in the area.

Twelve States, portions of five others and the District of Columbia come under the agreement, Ickes said.

The schedule calls for them to close at 7 p. m. nightly and not to reopen until 7 a. m. the following morning daily.

Ickes said the companies had agreed not to supply filling stations which fail to comply with the closing recommendation.

It was stressed that no individual stations had been approached. The shutdown is to be achieved through co-operation of companies supplying fuel.

LIST STATES AFFECTED.

The shutdown will ... in Maine, New Hampshire, ... ment, Massachusetts, Connecticut, Rhode Island, New Jersey, ... ware, Maryland, North Carolina, South Carolina, Georgia, peninsula of Florida, the District of Columbia.

Also in all marketing areas ... east of the Appalachian Mountains in New York, Pennsylvania, Virginia, and West Virginia, ... such additional marketing ... in said States or shipped into said areas from any point East."

Previously, the Oil Co-Ordinator had requested the public to reduce consumption 33 1-3 per cent on a voluntary basis. But he said today the public had not complied.

ICKES CITES SHORTAGE.

"The closing of retail ... serving the public generally ... necessary," Ickes asserted.

YANKEES GAME

14-INNING BOX SCORE (FIRST GAME)

DETROIT (A)

	AB	R	H	PO	A	E
Stainback, lf.	5	1	2	2	1	0
McCosky, cf.	4	2	2	5	0	0
Higgins, 3b.	4	0	1	2	2	0
York, 1b.	4	0	0	8	1	1
Campbell, rf.	4	0	1	3	0	0
Meyer, 2b.	4	0	0	4	2	0
Sullivan, c.	4	0	0	5	0	0
Croucher, ss.	4	0	0	1	3	0
Newsom, p.	3	0	0	0	1	0
McKain, p.	0	0	0	0	0	0
Gorsica, p.	0	0	0	0	0	0
Totals	36	3	6	30	10	1

NEW YORK (A)

	AB	R	H	PO	A	E
Sturm, 1b.	6	1	2	12	1	0
Rolfe, 3b.	4	0	0	1	2	0
Henrich, rf.	5	1	4	3	0	0
J.DiMaggio, cf	3	0	1	2	0	0
Keller, lf.	5	0	2	3	0	0
Dickey, c.	4	0	1	4	1	0
Gordon, 2b.	5	0	0	3	4	0
Rizzuto, ss.	5	1	1	1	2	0
Russo, p.	3	0	1	1	4	0

Bill O'Dwyer—His Life Story—by Austen Lake

Today's is the fifth installment in the absorbing life story of William (Bill) O'Dwyer, Democratic candidate for Mayor of New York, as written for the New York Journal-American by Austen Lake, noted newspaperman and author.

Earlier chapters described O'Dwyer's youth in Ireland, his education in Spain and his first struggles for a foothold in New York.

The "Frank Jones" was a floating farmhouse with decks like the flounces of an old lady's skirt, a seven-knot speed and the smell of a cabbage cellar.

Each evening, at twilight, it gave an hysterical hoot and began waggling its broad rump up the Hudson while its sister ship, the "Kaaterskilla," started churning down from Albany.

The next night the voyages were reversed—a 12-hour, go-as-you-please journey, popular with hop-

majesty of the Palisades and risking rheumatics.

It was the Summer of 1911 and Bill O'Dwyer was the "Frank Jones'" second fireman, a tough tyke who had grown lean as a hoe-handle in the blistering heat of the boiler room—125 pounds scant which won him the general title of "Slim."

The fire-room chief was a mid-

Welles Calls Jap Apology Insufficient

More Complete Reply from Tokio Awaited by U. S.

WASHINGTON, July 31 (AP).—Sumner Welles, Acting Secretary of State, said today Japanese apologies for the bombing of the U. S. gunboat Tutuila in China were insufficient to close the incident.

This government, he said, awaits a more complete reply from Japan to the American representations made here and in Tokio.

Welles said that immediately upon being informed of the incident at Chungking yesterday morning, a representative of the Japanese government called at the embassy in Tokio and ex-

New U.S. Defense Board

Wallace Heads 'Economic' Agency Aimed at Axis

WASHINGTON, July 31 (UP).—President Roosevelt today intensified this nation's economic warfare against the Berlin-Rome-Tokio Axis by creating an "economic Defense Board," headed by Vice-President Henry A. Wallace as chairman.

The President also acted to integrate more closely into the administration current efforts by this Government to solidify the Western Hemisphere.

He created the office of Co-ordinator of Inter-American affairs, selecting Nelson A. Rockefeller to head the new agency.

"PLANNING MINISTRY."

The new Economic Defense Board which will serve as a broad

16-Plane Loss Admitted by London

Ships in Norse Port Supplying Nazis in Russia Also Hit

LONDON, July 31 (UP).—Britain made war against Finland for the first time yesterday when naval aircraft attacked Petsamo, Finnish Arctic port, and Kirkenes, northern Norwegian port, the Admiralty said today.

The British were acting in support of their Russian ally.

The attacking British planes hit the 1,460-ton German gunnery training ship Bremse, a fast vessel built in 1931, the Admiralty said.

In addition, at least four supply ships at Kirkenes were hit and shipping and harbor works at Petsamo were damaged.

Thyssen Fund Of $3,000,000 Found Here

His Nazi nest egg in Uncle Sam's cold storage.

Existence of a $3,000,000 fund established here by Fritz Thyssen, German industrialist and original backer of Adolf Hitler at the beginning of the latter's rise to power, was disclosed today.

Whether the money is for Thyssen personally, or, perhaps, for some of his high-placed Nazi friends in the event of an "emergency" compelling them to leave Germany, no one knew.

However, it will do neither Thyssen nor any of his Nazi friends any good now, as it has been "frozen" along with the $4,500,000,000 Axis assets now held in this country.

INVESTMENT COMPANY.

The money exists in funds of the Union Banking Corporation, an investment company incorporated and licensed under new York State laws in August, 1924.

Money for its $400,000 capital stock came from Thyssen's Bank voor Handel en Scheepvaart in Rotterdam.

Among members of its board of directors are E. R. Harriman, Ray Morris and Prescott S. Bush, partner in the firm of Brown Brothers Harriman & Company, of which W. Averell harriman is now American minister plenipotentiary to England.

Also a director is H. D. Pennington, Brown Brothers Harriman & Co. manager.

On Jan. 14, 1941, Knight Woolley, another partner in the harriman company, wrote to State Banking Superintendent William R. White in behalf of Harriman, Morris, Bush and Pennington.

"Should the United States enter the war, they feel they might be under some embarrassment because of their connection with the bank, even thought we have no financial interest in the Union Banking Corporation, nor do we participate in its earnings," Woolley wrote.

SEEKS STEPS TO TAKE

He asked White for "a frank expression from you as to the action" the Harriman directors should take. Their own impulse, he indicated, was to resign en massé from Thyssen's bank.

White, however, replied on May 13:

"While the department would not feel free to object if your partners, Mr. Harriman, Mr. Morris and Mr. Bush, and your firm's manager, Mr. Pennington, should desire to resign as directors of the corporation, nevertheless the department would be gratified if these gentlemen could find it possible to remain on the board during this period of uncertainty."

He plainly indicated that he considered it best, if Thyssen or other Nazi money was tied up in the Union Banking Corporation, to keep the corporation under Harriman's Morris's, Bush's and Pennington's control, thus effectively checkmating whatever Thyssen's plan might be.

All of the shares of the Union Banking Corporation are registered in the name of E. R. Harriman, who is chairman of the board, except the qualifying shares held by other directors.

Mr. Woolley related the circumstances leading to the selection of the Harriman partners on the board of directors. He said:

'BUSINESS COURTESY.'

"Our partner, W. A. Harriman, was in Europe in 1925 and at that time he became acquainted with Fritz Thyssen.

"To the best of my knowledge, Thyssen formed the Bank voor Handel en Scheepvaart, and presumably controlled that institution.

"At one of his meetings with Mr. Harriman he told him he was forming a bank in New York to look after his interests in the United States, and he asked Mr. harriman to serve on the board.

"Mr. Harriman agreed that certain of his associates would serve in this capacity, and as a result various members of the Harriman organization, now Brown Brothers Harriman & Co., have been on the board ever since."

Mr. Woolley emphasized that these directors act "merely as a matter of business courtesy."

President of the Union Banking Corp. is Cornelis Lievense, Holland-born, who came to the United States by way of Montreal in May, 1926, two years after the bank was set up.

He is now a naturalized American citizen, having received his final papers in Mineola, L. I., Jan. 29, 1932.

He is president also of the Domestic Fuel Corp., Seamless Steel Equipment Corp., and Holland-American Trading Corp., all of which share the Union Banking Corp.'s offices at 39 Broadway.

ASSETS FROZEN

The assets of all three of these firms also have been "frozen" by the U. S. Government, Lievense admitted.

Last Fall, the Canadian Government blacklisted the Domestic Fuel Corp., which had been bringing coal from Thyssen's European mines to Canada.

Also housed in the same offices with the bank are the Kemari Trading Corp., Riberena Fuel Y Chartering Co. Religious Publications, Inc., and Kauffmann & Co.

Reached early today at his home on Cedar Swamp Road in the Glen Hills Farm section of Glen Head, L. I., Lievense said:

"I have nothing to say. I have no comment to make on anything, especially when I'm asleep."

Besides the Harriman officers on the board of the Union Banking Corp., there are J. G. Groeninger and N. J. Kouwenhoven.

Kouwenhoven is managing director of the Bank voor Handel en Scheepvaart, managing director of the Holland-American Investment Corp., and a member of the board of the Thyssen-owned Vlaardingsen Harborworks.

Groeninger is managing director of the Thyssen-owned Halcyon Line, which refused to obey the Netherlands government's order to all industries to remove their properties to the Dutch colonies, just before the Nazi invasion."

Thyssen himself, according to best obtainable advices, is now back in Germany. For a time he wandered about Switzerland, France and other European countries. His present status is said to be that of, perhaps, a willing prisoner, not in confinement but under surveillance, perhaps a hostage for his wealth throughout the world.

***

The next two and a-half pages are from the *History of the Yale Class of 1917, Twenty-Fifth Record* - 1942

Prescott Sheldon Bush

Business:	General Partner in the firm of Brown Brothers Harriman & Co. (private bankers), 59 Wall Street, New York City.
Residence:	Grove Lane, Greenwich, Conn.
Married:	Dorothy Walker, August, 1921, Kennebunkport, Me. Daughter of George Herbert Walker and Loulie Wear.
Children:	Prescott Sheldon, born August 10, 1922; George Herbert Walker, born June 12, 1924; Nancy Bush, born February 4, 1926; Jonathan James, born May 6, 1931; William Henry Trotter, born July 14, 1938.

Pres has been a General Partner of Brown Brothers, Harriman & Company since January 1, 1931. He is a director of the following corporations: Columbia Broadcasting System, The Dresser Manufacturing Co., The Union Banking Corporation, The Simmons Company, Massachusetts Investors Second Fund, The Rockbestos Products Corporations, The Vanadium Products Corporation of America, The United States Guarantee Company, Commercial Pacific Cable Company, and he is Chairman of the Board of the Pennsylvania Water & Power Company.

His son Prescott, Jr. is a member of the Class of 1944 at Yale, and his son George Herbert graduated this year from Andover Academy. Nancy is at Miss Porter's School at Farmington while Jonathan James attends the Greenwich Country Day School. William Henry Trotter Bush, age 3, better known as "Buck" is still too young to attend any school.

Pres is quite active in local town politics. He has been a member of the Representative Town Meeting of Greenwich since 1933 and has been Moderator of this body since 1935. He is a member of the Greenwich Defense Council. He is a member of the Republican party and has been active in local campaigns for the last eight years. Since 1938 he has been a director of the Greenwich Hospital Association. He is also a trustee of the Greenwich Boys Club. He belongs to the Yale Club of New York and has been a member of the Council since 1938. He belongs to the Lunch Club of New York, The Roundhill Club of Greenwich of which he was President from 1935 to 1938 and belongs to the Field Club of Greenwich.

period he also served successively as Secretary, Vice-President and President.

Pres writes: "It has been my good fortune to be closely associated in business for a good many years with Classmates of 1917. These are Bunny Harriman, Knight Woolley and Ellery James, who unfortunately died in 1932. In addition to these the firm of Brown Brothers Harriman & Co. has been rather heavily populated with Yale men, including — Averell Harriman, 1913; Bob Lovett, 1918; Thatcher M. Brown, 1897; Ray Morris, 1900, and a number of younger men who were graduated in the middle or late twenties, whose names are probably not familiar to the Class. The firm in which we have been associated has been established in business since 1818 and has the rather unique record of having maintained its place of business since that time in exactly the same location at 59 Wall Street, although the present building is the third one which has housed the business. In spite of the many changes in the political and economic life of the country over this long span of years the firm has been handed down from one group of partners to another in an unbroken line, and even today our senior partner is a direct descendant of the founder and his son is also now a member of the firm.

While the record of this firm is in no way spectacular, and while in comparison with our many huge banking institutions throughout the country the firm is relatively inconspicuous, it is nevertheless true that the firm today is larger and perhaps fully as vigorous as it has ever been. Thus, I feel that the association with this organization has been indeed a privilege and a satisfaction. I mention this because there is no doubt that my own participation in the business is traceable entirely to my acquaintance at Yale. I gratefully acknowledge the debt that I owe her for having made such a happy business life possible."

To the cognoscenti, and who of 1917 is not one of them, it is entirely unnecessary to announce that early this year Pres was appointed National Chairman in Charge of the 1942 Drive for funds for the United Service Organization (USO). At this writing, July, 1942, he is still in the midst of his campaign so it is impossible to state the measure of his success. Knowing Pres, however, we venture to predict that his total will eclipse that collected last year, and will give those that may follow him in this worthy project something to shoot at.

PRESCOTT SHELDON BUSH, care Simmons Hardware Company, St. Louis, Mo.

Enrolled for Plattsburg, 1916, but transferred to Battery A, Tobyhanna; Yale R. O. T. C.; first Officers' Training Camp, Fort Benjamin Harrison; commissioned Captain, Field Artillery, U. S. R., August 15, 1917; assigned as Instructor to second Officers' Training Camp at same post; attached to 322d Field Artillery, in command of Battery D, Camp Sherman, November 30, 1917; ordered to School of Fire, Fort Sill, about March 14, graduating May 24, 1918; went overseas June 14, assigned to Headquarters, 158th Field Artillery Brigade, as Intelligence Officer on General Fleming's staff; in August ordered to Verdun for special training in connection with the Intelligence Service, and assigned for period of three weeks to a staff of French officers; 158th Brigade, 32d Division, ordered to the front about September 15, serving continuously in the Meuse-Argonne Offensive until the Armistice; November 16, transferred to Headquarters, 7th Corps, serving as Operations and Intelligence Officer in march to the Rhine; transferred to the 132d Field Artillery, January, 1919; returned to the United States, March 25, and received discharge April 4, 1919.

From: History of the Class of 1917 Yale College, War Record – 1919

PRESCOTT SHELDON BUSH

Vice-president of W. A. Harriman & Company, Inc. (investment bankers), 39 Broadway, New York City.

***Residence,* Stanwich Road, Greenwich, Conn.**

BUSH accepted a position with the Simmons Hardware Company of St. Louis soon after his discharge from military service in 1919, and in January, 1921, he was made a member of the board of directors and assistant general manager of the company. About two years later he became general manager and treasurer of the Hupp Products Company of Columbus, Ohio, but resigned in November, 1923, to become president, in charge of sales, of the Stedman Products Company in South Braintree, Mass. He was made manager of the foreign division of the United States Rubber Company in New York City in February, 1925, but gave up that position in May, 1926, to become associated with W. A. Harriman & Company, Inc.

Bush is secretary of the United States Golf Association, and he belongs to the Yale and Lunch clubs in New York City and to the Round Hill and Field clubs in Greenwich. He is a member of St. Paul's Church, Greenwich.

He was married on August 6, 1921, at Kennebunkport, Maine, to Dorothy Walker. Mrs. Bush, who attended Miss Porter's School in Farmington, is the daughter of George Herbert and Lu-Jr., born at Kennebunkport in August, 1922; George Herbert Walker, born in Milton, Mass., in June, 1924; and Nancy, born in New York City in February, 1926.

From: History of the Class of 1917 Yale College, Decennial Record – 1928

REPRINT OF CHAPTER SEVEN OF ANTONY SUTTON'S

WALL STREET AND THE RISE OF HITLER

1976

Who Financed Adolf Hitler?

The funding of Hitler and the Nazi movement has yet to be explored in exhaustive depth. The only published examination of Hitler's personal finances is an article by Oron James Hale, "Adolph Hitler: Taxpayer,"[1] which records Adolph's brushes with the German tax authorities before he became *Reichskanzler.* In the 1920s Hitler presented himself to the German tax man as merely an impoverished writer living on bank loans, with an automobile bought on credit. Unfortunately, the original records used by Hale do not yield the source of Hitler's income, loans, or credit, and German law "did not require self-employed or professional persons to disclose in detail the sources of income or the nature of services rendered."[2] Obviously the funds for the automobiles, private secretary Rudolf Hess, another assistant, a chauffeur, and expenses incurred by political activity, came from somewhere. But, like Leon Trotsky's 1917 stay in New York, it is hard to reconcile Hitler's known expenditures with the precise source of his income.

Some Early Hitler Backers

We do know that prominent European and American industrialists were sponsoring all manner of totalitarian political groups at that time, including Communists and various Nazi groups. The U.S Kilgore Committee records that:

> *By 1919 Krupp was already giving financial aid to one of the reactionary political groups which sowed the seed of the present Nazi ideology. Hugo Stinnes was an early contributor to the Nazi Party (*National Socialistische Deutsche Arbeiter Partei*). By 1924 other prominent industrialists and financiers, among them Fritz Thyssen, Albert Voegler, Adolph [*sic*] Kirdorf, and Kurt von Schröder, were secretly giving substantial sums to the Nazis. In 1931 members of the coalowners' association which Kirdorf*

headed pledged themselves to pay 50 pfennigs for each ton of coal sold, the money to go to the organization which Hitler was building.[3]

Hitler's 1924 Munich trial yielded evidence that the Nazi Party received $20,000 from Nuremburg industrialists. The most interesting name from this period is that of Emil Kirdorf, who had earlier acted as conduit for financing German involvement in the Bolshevik Revolution.[4] Kirdorf's role in financing Hitler was, in his own words:

> *In 1923 I came into contact for the first time with the National-Socialist movement . . . . I first heard the Fuehrer in the Essen Exhibition Hall. His clear exposition completely convinced and overwhelmed me. In 1927 I first met the Fuehrer personally. I travelled to Munich and there had a conversation with the Fuehrer in the Bruckmann home. During four and a half hours Adolf Hitler explained to me his programme in detail. I then begged the Fuehrer to put together the lecture he had given me in the form of a pamphlet. I then distributed this pamphlet in my name in business and manufacturing circles.*
>
> *Since then I have placed myself completely at the disposition of his movement. Shortly after our Munich conversation, and as a result of the pamphlet which the Fuehrer composed and I distributed, a number of meetings took place between the Fuehrer and leading personalities in the field of industry. For the last time before the taking over of power, the leaders of industry met in my house together with Adolf Hitler, Rudolf Hess, Hermann Goering and other leading personalities of the party.*[5]

In 1925 the Hugo Stinnes family contributed funds to convert the Nazi weekly *Volkischer Beobachter* to a daily publication. Putzi Hanfstaengl, Franklin D. Roosevelt's friend and protegé, provided the remaining funds.[6] Table 7-1 summarizes presently known financial contributions and the business associations of contributors from the United States. Putzi is not listed in Table 7-1 as he was neither industrialist nor financier.

In the early 1930s financial assistance to Hitler began to flow more readily. There took place in Germany a series of meetings, irrefutably documented in several sources, between German industrialists, Hitler himself, and more often Hitler's representatives Hjalmar Schacht and

Rudolf Hess. The critical point is that the German industrialists financing Hitler were predominantly directors of cartels with American associations, ownership, participation, or some form of subsidiary connection. The Hitler backers were not, by and large, firms of purely German origin, or representative of German family business. Except for Thyssen and Kirdorf, in most cases they were the German multi-national firms — *i.e.*, I.G. Farben, A.E.G., DAPAG, *etc.* These multi-nationals had been built up by American loans in the 1920s, and in the early 1930s had American directors and heavy American financial participation.

One flow of foreign political funds not considered here is that reported from the European-based Royal Dutch Shell, Standard Oil's great competitor in the 20s and 30s, and the giant brainchild of Anglo-Dutch businessman Sir Henri Deterding. It has been widely asserted that Henri Deterding personally financed Hitler. This argument is made, for instance, by biographer Glyn Roberts in *The Most Powerful Man in the World.* Roberts notes that Deterding was impressed with Hitler as early as 1921:

> *. . . and the Dutch press reported that, through the agent Georg Bell, he [Deterding] had placed at Hitler's disposal, while the party was "still in long clothes," no less than four million guilders.*[7]

It was reported (by Roberts) that in 1931 Georg Bell, Deterding's agent, attended meetings of Ukrainian Patriots in Paris "as joint delegate of Hitler and Deterding."[8] Roberts also reports:

> *Deterding was accused, as Edgar Ansell Mowrer testifies in his* Germany Puts the Clock Back, *of putting up a large sum of money for the Nazis on the understanding that success would give him a more favored position in the German oil market. On other occasions, figures as high as £55,000,000 were mentioned.*[9]

Biographer Roberts really found Deterding's strong anti-Bolshevism distasteful, and rather than present hard evidence of funding he is inclined to assume rather than prove that Deterding was pro-Hitler. But pro-Hitlerism is not a necessary consequence of anti-Bolshevism; in any event Roberts offers no proof of finance, and hard evidence of Deterding's involvement was not found by this author.

Mowrer's book contains neither index nor footnotes as to the source of his information and Roberts has no specific evidence for his accusations. There is circumstantial evidence that Deterding was pro-Nazi. He later went to live in Hitler's Germany and increased his share of the German petroleum market. So there may have been some contributions, but these have not been proven.

Similarly, in France (on January 11, 1932), Paul Fauré, a member of the *Chambre des Députés*, accused the French industrial firm of Schneider-Creuzot of financing Hitler — and incidentally implicated Wall Street in other financing channels.[10]

The Schneider group is a famous firm of French armaments manufacturers. After recalling the Schneider influence in establishment of Fascism in Hungary and its extensive international armaments operations, Paul Fauré turns to Hitler, and quotes from the French paper *Le Journal*, "that Hitler had received 300,000 Swiss gold francs" from subscriptions opened in Holland under the case of a university professor named von Bissing. The Skoda plant at Pilsen, stated Paul Fauré, was controlled by the French Schneider family, and it was the Skoda directors von Duschnitz and von Arthaber who made the subscriptions to Hitler. Fauré concluded:

> *. . . I am disturbed to see the directors of Skoda, controlled by Schneider, subsidizing the electoral campaign of M. Hitler; I am disturbed to see your firms, your financiers, your industrial cartels unite themselves with the most nationalistic of Germans . . . .*

Again, no hard evidence was found for this alleged flow of Hitler funds.

Fritz Thyssen and W.A. Harriman Company of New York

Another elusive case of reported financing of Hitler is that of Fritz Thyssen, the German steel magnate who associated himself with the Nazi movement in the early 20s. When interrogated in 1945 under Project Dustbin,[11] Thyssen recalled that he was approached in 1923 by General Ludendorf at the time of French evacuation of the Ruhr. Shortly after this meeting Thyssen was introduced to Hitler and provided funds for the Nazis through General Ludendorf. In 1930-1931 Emil Kirdorf approached Thyssen and subsequently sent Rudolf Hess to negotiate further funding for the Nazi Party. This time Thyssen arranged a credit of 250,000 marks at the Bank Voor Handel en Scheepvaart N.V. at 18 Zuidblaak in Rotterdam, Holland, founded in 1918 with H. J. Kouwenhoven and D. C. Schutte as managing partners.[12] This bank was a subsidiary of the August Thyssen Bank of Germany (formerly von der Heydt's Bank A.G.). It was Thyssen's personal banking operation, and it was affiliated with the W. A. Harriman financial interests in New York. Thyssen reported to his Project Dustbin interrogators that:

> *I chose a Dutch bank because I did not want to be mixed up with German banks in my position, and because I thought it was better to do business with a Dutch bank, and I thought I would have the Nazis a little more in my hands.*[13]

Thyssen's book *I Paid Hitler*, published in 1941, was purported to be written by Fritz Thyssen himself, although Thyssen denies authorship. The book claims that funds for Hitler — about one million marks — came mainly from Thyssen himself. *I Paid Hitler* has other unsupported assertions, for example that Hitler was actually descended from an illegitimate child of the Rothschild family. Supposedly Hitler's grandmother, Frau Schickelgruber, had been a servant in the Rothschild household and while there became pregnant:

> *. . . an inquiry once ordered by the late Austrian chancellor, Engelbert Dollfuss, yielded some interesting results, owing to the fact that the dossiers of the police department of the Austro-Hungarian monarch were remarkably complete.*[14]

This assertion concerning Hitler's illegitimacy is refuted entirely in a more solidly based book by Eugene Davidson, which implicates the Frankenberger family, not the Rothschild family.

In any event, and more relevant from our viewpoint, the August Thyssen front bank in Holland — *i.e.*, the Bank voor Handel en Scheepvaart N.V. — controlled the Union Banking Corporation in New York. The Harrimans had a financial interest in, and E. Roland Harriman (Averell's brother) was a director of, this Union Banking Corporation. The Union Banking Corporation of New York City was a joint Thyssen-Harriman operation with the following directors in 1932:[15]

E. Roland HARRIMAN	Vice president of W. A. Harriman & Co., New York
H. J. KOUWENHOVEN	Nazi banker, managing partner of August Thyssen Bank and Bank voor Handel Scheepvaart N.V. (the transfer bank for Thyssen's funds)

TABLE 7-1: FINANCIAL LINKS BETWEEN U.S. INDUSTRIALISTS AND ADOLF HITLER

Date	American Bankers and Industrialists	U.S. Affiliated Firm		German Source		Intermediary for Funds/Agent
1923	Henry FORD	FORD MOTOR COMPANY		—		—
1931	E.R. HARRIMAN	UNION BANKING CORP		Fritz THYSSEN	250,000 RM	Bank voor Handel en Scheepvaart N.V. (Subsidiary of August Thyssen Bank)
1932-3		Flick (a director of AEG)		Friedrich FLICK	150,000 RM	Direct to NSDAP
February-March 1933		NONE		Emil KIRDORF	600,000 RM	"Nationale Treuhand" a/c at Delbrück Schickler Bank
February-March 1933	Edsel B. FORD C.E. MITCHELL Walter TEAGLE Paul M. WARBURG	AMERICAN I.G.		I.G. FARBEN	400,000 RM	"Nationale Treuhand"
February-March 1933		NONE		Reichsverband der Automobilindustrie	100,000 RM	"Nationale Treuhand"
February-March 1933	Gerard SWOPE Owen D. YOUNG C.H. MINOR E. Arthur BALDWIN	INTERNATIONAL GENERAL ELECTRIC	25 percent	A.E.G.	60,000 RM	"Nationale Treuhand" "Nationale Treuhand"

		NONE		DEMAG	50,000 RM	
February-March 1933	Owen D. YOUNG	INTERNATIONAL GENERAL ELECTRIC	16⅔ percent	OSRAM G.m.b.H.	40,000 RM	"Nationale Treuhand"
February-March 1933	Sosthenes BEHN	I.T.T.		Telefunken	35,000 RM	"Nationale Treuhand"
February-March 1933		NONE		Karl Herrman	300,000 RM	"Nationale Treuhand"
Febru ry-March 1933		NONE		A. Steinke (Director of BYBUAG)	200,000 RM	"Nationale Treuhand"
February-March 1933		NONE		Karl Lange Machine industry)	50,000 RM	"Nationale Treuhand"
February-March 1933		NONE		F. Springorum (Hoesch A.G.)	36,000 RM	"Nationale Treuhand"
February-March 1933	Edsel B. FORD	Ford Motor Co.		Carl BOSCH (I.G. Farben & Ford Motor A.G.)		
1932-1944	Walter TEAGLE J.A. MOFFETT W.S. FARISH	Standard Oil of N.J.	94 percent	Emil HELFFRICH (German-American Petroleum Co)		Heinrich Himmler S.S. via Keppler's Circle
1932-1944	Sosthenes BEHN	I.T.T.		Kurt von SCHRÖDER Mix & Genest Lorenz		Heinrich Himmler S.S. via Keppler's Circle

J. G. GROENINGEN	Vereinigte Stahlwerke (the steel cartel which also funded Hitler)
C. LIEVENSE	President, Union Banking Corp., New York City
E. S. JAMES	Partner Brown Brothers, later Brown Brothers, Harriman & Co.

Thyssen arranged a credit of 250,000 marks for Hitler, through this Dutch bank affiliated with the Harrimans. Thyssen's book, later repudiated, states that as much as one million marks came from Thyssen.

Thyssen's U.S. partners were, of course, prominent members of the Wall Street financial establishment. Edward Henry Harriman, the nineteenth-century railroad magnate, had two sons, W. Averell Harriman (born in 1891), and E. Roland Harriman (born in 1895). In 1917 W. Averell Harriman was a director of Guaranty Trust Company and he was involved in the Bolshevik Revolution.[16] According to his biographer, Averell started at the bottom of the career ladder as a clerk and section hand after leaving Yale in 1913, then "he moved steadily forward to positions of increasing responsibility in the fields of transportation and finance."[17] In addition to his directorship in Guaranty Trust, Harriman formed the Merchant Shipbuilding Corporation in 1917, which soon became the largest merchant fleet under American flag. This fleet was dis posed of in 1925 and Harriman entered the lucrative Russian market.[18]

In winding up these Russian deals in 1929, Averell Harriman received a windfall profit of $1 million from the usually hard-headed Soviets, who have a reputation of giving nothing away without some present or later *quid pro quo*. Concurrently with these successful moves in international finance, Averell Harriman has always been attracted by so-called "public" service. In 1913 Harriman's "public" service began with an appointment to the Palisades Park Commission. In 1933 Harriman was appointed chairman of the New York State Committee of Employment, and in 1934 became Administrative Officer of Roosevelt's NRA — the Mussolini-like brainchild of General Electric's Gerard Swope.[19] There followed a stream of "public" offices, first the Lend Lease program, then as Ambassador to the Soviet Union, later as Secretary of Commerce.

By contrast, E. Roland Harriman confined his activities to private business in international finance without venturing, as did brother Averell, into "public" service. In 1922 Roland and Averell formed W. A. Harriman & Company. Still later Roland became chairman of the board of Union Pacific Railroad and a director of *Newsweek* magazine, Mutual

Life Insurance Company of New York, a member of the board of governors of the American Red Cross, and a member of the American Museum of Natural History.

Nazi financier Hendrik Jozef Kouwenhoven, Roland Harriman's fellow-director at Union Banking Corporation in New York, was managing director of the Bank voor Handel en Scheepvaart N.V. (BHS) of Rotterdam. In 1940 the BHS held approximately $2.2 million assets in the Union Banking Corporation, which in turn did most of its business with BHS.[2] In the 1930s Kouwenhoven was also a director of the Vereinigte Stahlwerke A.G., the steel cartel founded with Wall Street funds in the mid-1920s. Like Baron Schröder, he was a prominent Hitler supporter.

Another director of the New York Union Banking Corporation was Johann Groeninger, a German subject with numerous industrial and financial affiliations involving Vereinigte Stahlwerke, the August Thyssen group, and a directorship of August Thyssen Hütte A.G.[21]

This affiliation and mutual business interest between Harriman and the Thyssen interests does not suggest that the Harrimans directly financed Hitler. On the other hand, it does show that the Harrimans were intimately connected with prominent Nazis Kouwenhoven and Groeninger and a Nazi front bank, the Bank voor Handel en Scheepvaart. There is every reason to believe that the Harrimans knew of Thyssen's support for the Nazis. In the case of the Harrimans, it is important to bear in mind their long-lasting and intimate relationship with the Soviet Union and the Harriman's position at the center of Roosevelt's New Deal and the Democratic Party. The evidence suggests that some members of the Wall Street elite are connected with, and certainly have influence with, *all* significant political groupings in the contemporary world socialist spectrum — Soviet socialism, Hitler's national socialism, and Roosevelt's New Deal socialism.

Financing Hitler in the March 1933 General Election

Putting the Georg Bell-Deterding and the Thyssen-Harriman cases to one side, we now examine the core of Hitler's backing. In May 1932 the so-called "Kaiserhof Meeting" took place between Schmitz of I.G. Farben, Max Ilgner of American I.G. Farben, Kiep of Hamburg-America Line, and Diem of the German Potash Trust. More than 500,000 marks was raised at this meeting and deposited to the credit of Rudolf Hess in the Deutsche Bank. It is noteworthy, in light of the "Warburg myth" described in Chapter Ten that Max Ilgner of the American I.G. Farben contributed 100,000 RM, or one-fifth of the total. The "Sidney Warburg" book claims Warburg involvement in the funding of Hitler, and Paul Warburg was a director of American I.G. Farben[22] while Max Warburg was a director of I.G. Farben.

There exists irrefutable documentary evidence of a further role of international bankers and industrialists in the financing of the Nazi Party and the *Volkspartie* for the March 1933 German election. A total of three million Reichmarks was subscribed by prominent firms and businessmen, suitably "washed" through an account at the Delbrück Schickler Bank, and then passed into the hands of Rudolf Hess for use by Hitler and the NSDAP. This transfer of funds was followed by the Reichstag fire, abrogation of constitutional rights, and consolidation of Nazi power. Access to the Reichstag by the arsonists was obtained through a tunnel from a house where Putzi Hanfstaengel was staying; the Reichstag fire itself was used by Hitler as a pretext to abolish constitutional rights. In brief, within a few weeks of the major funding of Hitler there was a linked sequence of major events: the financial contribution from prominent bankers and industrialists to the 1933 election, burning of the Reichstag, abrogation of constitutional rights, and subsequent seizure of power by the Nazi Party.

The fund-raising meeting was held February 20, 1933 in the home of Goering, who was then president of the Reichstag, with Hjalmar Horace Greeley Schacht acting as host. Among those present, according to I.G. Farben's von Schnitzler, were:

> *Krupp von Bohlen, who, in the beginning of 1933, was president of the Reichsverband der Deutschen Industrie Reich Association of German Industry; Dr. Albert Voegler, the leading man of the Vereinigte Stahlwerke; Von Loewenfeld; Dr. Stein, head of the Gewerkschaft Auguste-Victoria, a mine which belongs to the IG.*[23]

Hitler expounded his political views to the assembled businessmen in a lengthy two-and-one-half hour speech, using the threat of Communism and a Communist take-over to great effect:

> *It is not enough to say we do not want Communism in our economy. If we continue on our old political course, then we shall perish . . . . It is the noblest task of the leader to find ideals that are stronger than the factors that pull the people together. I*

> *recognized even while in the hospital that one had to search for new ideals conducive to reconstruction. I found them in nationalism, in the value of personality, and in the denial of reconciliation between nations ....*
>
> *Now we stand before the last election. Regardless of the outcome, there will be no retreat, even if the coming election does not bring about decision, one way or another. If the election does not decide, the decision must be brought about by other means. I have intervened in order to give the people once more the chance to decide their fate by themselves ....*
>
> *There are only two possibilities, either to crowd back the opponent on constitutional grounds, and for this purpose once more this election; or a struggle will be conducted with other weapons, which may demand greater sacrifices. I hope the German people thus recognize the greatness of the hour.*[24]

After Hitler had spoken, Krupp von Bohlen expressed the support of the assembled industrialists and bankers in the concrete form of a three-million-mark political fund. It turned out to be more than enough to acquire power, because 600,000 marks remained unexpended after the election.

Hjalmar Schacht organized this historic meeting. We have previously described Schacht's links with the United States: his father was cashier for the Berlin Branch of Equitable Assurance, and Hjalmar was intimately involved almost on a monthly basis with Wall Street.

The largest contributor to the fund was I.G. Farben, which committed itself for 30 percent (or 500,000 marks) of the total. Director A. Steinke, of BUBIAG (Braunkohlen-u. Brikett-Industrie A.G.), an I.G. Farben subsidiary, personally contributed another 200,000 marks. In brief, 45 percent of the funds for the 1933 election came from I.G. Farben. If we look at the directors of American I.G. Farben — the U.S. subsidiary of I.G. Farben — we get close to the roots of Wall Street involvement with Hitler. The board of American I.G. Farben at this time contained some of the most prestigious names among American industrialists: Edsel B. Ford of the Ford Motor Company, C.E. Mitchell of the Federal Reserve Bank of New York, and Walter Teagle, director of the Federal Reserve Bank of New York, the Standard Oil Company of New Jersey, and President Franklin D. Roosevelt's Georgia Warm Springs Foundation.

Paul M. Warburg, first director of the Federal Reserve Bank of New York and chairman of the Bank of Manhattan, was a Farben director and in Germany his brother Max Warburg was also a director of I.G. Farben. H. A. Metz of I.G. Farben was also a director of the Warburg's Bank of Manhattan. Finally, Carl Bosch of American I.G. Farben was also a director of Ford Motor Company A-G in Germany.

Three board members of American I.G. Farben were found guilty at the Nuremburg War Crimes Trials: Max Ilgner, F. Ter Meer, and Hermann Schmitz. As we have noted, the American board members — Edsel Ford, C. E. Mitchell, Walter Teagle, and Paul Warburg — were not placed on trial at Nuremburg, and so far as the records are concerned, it appears that they were not even questioned about their knowledge of the 1933 Hitler fund.

The 1933 Political Contributions

Who were the industrialists and bankers who placed election funds at the disposal of the Nazi Party in 1933? The list of contributors and the amount of their contribution is as follows:

FINANCIAL CONTRIBUTIONS TO HITLER: Feb. 23-Mar. 13, 1933:

(The Hjalmar Schacht account at Delbrück, Schickler Bank)

Political Contributions by Firms (with selected affiliated directors)	Amount Pledged	Percent of Firm Total
Verein fuer die Bergbaulichen Interessen (Kirdorf)	$600,000	45.8
I.G. Farbenindustrie (Edsel Ford, C.E. Mitchell, Walter Teagle, Paul Warburg)	400,000	30.5
Automobile Exhibition, Berlin (Reichsverbund der Automobilindustrie S.V.)	100,000	7.6
A.E.G., German General Electric (Gerard Swope, Owen Young, C.H. Minor, Arthur Baldwin)	60,000	4.6
Demag	50,000	3.8
Osram G.m.b.H. (Owen Young)	40,000	3.0

Telefunken Gesellschaft fuer drahtlose Telegraphie	35,000	2.7
Accumulatoren-Fabrik A.G. (Quandt of A.E.G.)	25,000	1.9
Total from industry	1,310,000	99.9

Plus Political Contributions by Individual Businessmen:

Karl Hermann	300,000
Director A. Steinke (BUBIAG-Braunkohlen—u. Brikett—Industrie A.G.)	200,000
Dir. Karl Lange (Geschaftsfuhrendes Vostandsmitglied des Vereins Deutsches Maschinenbau—Anstalten)	50,000
Dr. F. Springorum (Chairman: Eisen-und Stahlwerke Hoesch A.G.)	36,000

Source: See Appendix for translation of original document.

How can we prove that these political payments actually took place?

The payments to Hitler in this final step on the road to dictatorial Naziism were made through the private bank of Delbrück Schickler. The Delbrück Schickler Bank was a subsidiary of Metallgesellschaft A.G. ("Metall"), an industrial giant, the largest non-ferrous metal company in Germany, and the dominant influence in the world's nonferrous metal trading. The principal shareholders of "Metall" were I.G. Farben and the British Metal Corporation. We might note incidentally that the British directors on the "Metall" *Aufsichsrat* were Walter Gardner (Amalgamated Metal Corporation) and Captain Oliver Lyttelton (also on the board of Amalgamated Metal and paradoxically later in World War II to become the British Minister of Production).

There exists among the Nuremburg Trial papers the original transfer slips from the banking division of I.G. Farben and other firms listed on page 110 to the Delbrück Schickler Bank in Berlin, informing the bank of the transfer of funds from Dresdner Bank, and other banks, to their *Nationale Treuhand* (National Trusteeship) account. This account was disbursed by Rudolf Hess for Nazi Party expenses during the election. Translation of the I.G. Farben transfer slip, selected as a sample, is as follows:[25]

Translation of I.G. Farben letter of February 27, 1933, advising of transfer of 400,000 Reichsmarks to National Trusteeship account:

I.G. FARBENINDUSTRIE AKTIENGESELLSCHAFT

Bank Department

Firm: Delbrück Schickler & Co.,
BERLIN W.8
Mauerstrasse 63/65, Frankfurt (Main) 20
Our Ref: (Mention in Reply) 27 February 1933
B./Goe.

We are informing you herewith that we have authorized the Dresdner Bank in Frankfurt/M., to pay you tomorrow forenoon: RM 400,000 which you will use in favor of the account "NATIONALE TREUHAND" (National Trusteeship).

Respectfully,
I.G. Farbenindustrie Aktiengesellschaft
by Order:
(Signed) SELCK (Signed) BANGERT

By special delivery.[26]

At this juncture we should take note of the efforts that have been made to direct our attention away from American financiers (and German financiers connected with American-affiliated companies) who were involved with the funding of Hitler. Usually the blame for financing Hitler has been exclusively placed upon Fritz Thyssen or Emil Kirdorf. In the case of Thyssen this blame was widely circulated in a book allegedly authored by Thyssen in the middle of World War II but later repudiated by him.[27] Why Thyssen would want to admit such actions before the defeat of Naziism is unexplained.

Emil Kirdorf, who died in 1937, was always proud of his association with the rise of Naziism. The attempt to limit Hitler financing to Thyssen and Kirdorf extended into the Nuremburg trials in 1946, and was challenged only by the Soviet delegate. Even the Soviet delegate was unwilling to produce evidence of American associations; this is not surprising because the Soviet Union depends on the goodwill of these same financiers to transfer much needed advanced Western technology to the U.S.S.R.

At Nuremburg, statements were made and allowed to go unchallenged which were directly contrary to the known direct evidence presented above. For example, Buecher, Director General of German General Electric, was absolved from sympathy for Hitler:

> *Thyssen has confessed his error like a man and has courageously paid a heavy penalty for it. On the other side stand men like Reusch of the Gutehoffnungshuette, Karl Bosch, the late chairman of the I.G. Farben Aufsichtsrat, who would very likely have come to a sad end, had he not died in time. Their feelings were shared by the deputy chairman of the Aufsichtsrat of Kalle. The Siemens and AEG companies which, next to I.G. Farben, were the most powerful German concerns, and they were determined opponents of national socialism.*
>
> *I know that this unfriendly attitude on the part of the Siemens concern to the Nazis resulted in the firm receiving rather rough treatment. The Director General of the AEG (Allgemeine Elektrizitats Gesellschaft), Geheimrat Buecher, whom I knew from my stay in the colonies, was anything but a Nazi. I can assure General Taylor that it is certainly wrong to assert that the leading industrialists as such favored Hitler before his seizure of power.*[28]

Yet on page 56 of this book we reproduce a document originating with General Electric, transferring General Electric funds to the National Trusteeship account controlled by Rudolf Hess on behalf of Hitler and used in the 1933 elections.

Similarly, von Schnitzler, who was present at the February 1933 meeting on behalf of I.G. Farben, denied I.G. Farben's contributions to the 1933 Nationale Treuhand:

> *I never heard again of the whole matter [that of financing Hitler], but I believe that either the buro of Goering or Schacht or the Reichsverband der Deutschen Industrie had asked the office of Bosch or Schmitz for payment of IG's share in the elec tion fund. As I did not take the matter up again I not even at that time knew whether and which amount had been paid by the IG. According to the volume of the IG, I should estimate IG's share being something like 10 percent of the election fund, but as far as I know there is no evidence that I.G. Farben participated in the payments.*[29]

As we have seen, the evidence is incontrovertible regarding political cash contributions to Hitler at the crucial point of the takeover of power in Germany — and Hitler's earlier speech to the industrialists clearly revealed that a coercive takeover was the premeditated intent.

We know exactly who contributed, how much, and through what channels. It is notable that the largest contributors — I.G. Farben, German General Electric (and its affiliated company Osram), and Thyssen — were affiliated with Wall Street financiers. These Wall Street financiers were at the heart of the financial elite and they were prominent in contemporary American politics. Gerard Swope of General Electric was author of Roosevelt's New Deal, Teagle was one of NRA's top administrators, Paul Warburg and his associates at American I.G. Farben were Roosevelt advisors. It is perhaps not an extraordinary coincidence that Roosevelt's New Deal — called a "fascist measure" by Herbert Hoover — should have so closely resembled Hitler's program for Germany, and that both Hitler and Roosevelt took power in the same month of the same year — March 1933.

1, *The American Historical Review*, Volume LC, No. 4, July, 1955, p. 830.
2. Ibid, fn. (2).
3. *Elimination of German Resources*, p. 648. The Albert Voegler mentioned in the Kilgore Committee list of early Hitler supporters was the German representative on the Dawes Plan Commission, Owen Young of General Electric (see Chapter Three) was a U.S. representative for the Dawes Plan and formulated its successor, the Young Plan.
4. Antony C. Sutton, *Wall Street and the Bolshevik Revolution, op. cit.*
5. *Preussiche Zeitung*, January 3, 1937.
6. See p. 116.
7. Glyn Roberts, *The Most Powerful Man in the World*, (New York. Covici, Friede, 1938), p. 305.
8. Ibid., p. 813.
9. Ibid., p, 822.
10. See *Chambre des Députés — Debats*, February 11, 1932, pp. 496-500.
11, U.S. Group Control Council (Germany, Office of the Director Of intelligence. Field Information Agency, Technical). Intelligence Report No. EF/ME/I, 4 September 1945. "Examination of Dr. Fritz Thyssen," p. 13. Hereafter cited as Examination of Dr. Fritz Thyssen.
12. The Bank was known in Germany as *Bank für Handel und Schiff.*
13. Examination of Dr. Fritz Thyssen.
14. Fritz Thyssen, *I Paid Hitler*, (New York: Farrar & Rinehart, Inc., 1941), p. 159.
15. Taken from *Bankers Directory*, 1932 edition, p. 2557 and Poors, *Directory of Directors.* J.L Guinter and Knight Woolley were also directors.
16. See Antony C. Sutton, *Wall Street and the Bolshevik Revolution, op. cit.*
17. *National Cyclopaedia*, Volume G, page 16.
18. For a description of these ventures, based an State Department files, see Antony C. Sutton, *Western Technology and Soviet Economic Development*, Volume 1, op. cit.
19. See Antony C. Sutton, *Wall Street and FDR*, Chapter Nine, "Swope's Plan," *op. cit.*
20. See *Elimination of German Resources*, pp, 728-30.
21. For yet other connections between the Union Banking Corp. and German enterprises, see Ibid., pp 728-30.
22. See Chapter Ten. [Antony Sutton's *Wall Street and the Rise of Hitler*]
23. *NMT*, [Nuremburg Military Tribunals] Volume VII, p 555.
24. Josiah E. DuBois, Jr., *Generals in Grey Suits, op cit.*, p323
25. Original reproduced on page 64. [Antony Sutton's *Wall Street and the Rise of Hitler*]
26. *NMT*, Volume VII, p. 565. See p.64 for photograph of original document.
27. Fritz Thyssen, *I Paid Hitler*, (New York: Tronoto: Farrar & Rinehart, Inc., 1941)
28. *NMT*, Volume VI, pp. 1169-1170.
29. *NMT*, Volume VII, p565.

ANTITHESIS: FINANCING THE NAZIS

ANTONY C. SUTTON

FROM *AMERICA'S SECRET ESTABLISHMENT – AN INTRODUCTION TO THE ORDER OF SKULL AND BONES*, - 1986

The Marxist version of the Hegelian dialectic poses financial capitalism as thesis and Marxist revolution as antithesis. An obvious puzzle in this Marxian statement is the nature of the synthesis presumed to evolve out of the clash of these opposites, i.e., the clash of financial capitalism and revolutionary Marxism.

Lenin's statement that the State will wither away at the synthesis stage is nonsensical. In fact, as all contemporary Marxist states testify, the State in practice becomes all powerful. The immediate task of "the revolution" is to convey all power to the state, and modern Marxist states operate under a constant paranoia that power may indeed pass away from the hands of the State into the hands of the people.

We suggest that world forces may be seen differently, although still in terms of the Hegelian dialectic. If Marxism is posed as the thesis and national socialism as antithesis, then the most likely synthesis becomes a Hegelian New World Order, a synthesis evolving out of the clash of Marxism and national socialism. Moreover, in this statement those who finance and manage the clash of opposites can remain in control of the synthesis.

If we can show that The Order has artificially encouraged and developed **both** revolutionary Marxism **and** national socialism while retaining some control over the nature and degree of the conflict, then it follows The Order will be able to determine the evolution and nature of the New World Order.

RESTRICTED

U. S. GROUP CONTROL COUNCIL
(Germany)
Office of the Director of Intelligence
Field Information Agency, Technical

Mail Address: WS/ff
FIAT
c/o USFET Main
APO 757, U.S. Army

IN FIAT I 350.09-77

4 September 1945

INTELLIGENCE REPORT NO. EF/Me/1

1873

SUBJECT: Report No. 1, Parts I and II, on the Examination of Dr. FRITZ THYSSEN.

TO : FIAT Distribution.

1. The report consists of two parts:

a. Three statements prepared and signed by THYSSEN, in conjunction with his interrogations.

(1) THYSSEN's Relations with the Nazi Party.
(2) A second statement on the same subject.
(3) THYSSEN's Interview with GOERING, 29 January 1941.

b. Notes on various subjects, from stenographic transcripts of his interrogations.

(1) Real Estate and Personal Records
(2) Financial Resources
(3) Movements during the War
(4) Opinions at the Outbreak of Hostilities
(5) Examination by the Gestapo
(6) Personalities
(7) Financial Support of the Nazi Party
(8) Defence of his Support of the Nazi Party
(9) The Famous Meeting in DUESSELDORF, 1932
(10) The Book I Paid HITLER
(11) Opposition to the Nazi Party
(12) Resistance in the Ruhr, 1923
(13) The YOUNG Plan
(14) The HERMANN GOERING WERKE

2. The report is based on interrogations of THYSSEN by Mr. CLIFFORD HYNNING, U.S. Group Control Council (Germany), Finance Division, at DUSTBIN, on 13, 20, and 23 July 1945.

For the Director of Intelligence:

Walter K. Schwinn

WALTER K. SCHWINN
Chief, Economic and Financial Branch
FIAT (US)

PREPARED BY:

R. H. Super

R. H. SUPER
Economic & Financial Br.
FIAT (US)

RESTRICTED

RESTRICTED

I. WHERE DID THE NAZIS GET THEIR FUNDS FOR REVOLUTION?

In *Wall Street And The Rise of Hitler* we described several financial conduits between Wall Street and the Nazi Party. This was later supplemented by publication of a long suppressed book, *Hitler's Secret Backers.*[1] Still other books have emphasized the Fritz Thyssen financial connection to Hitler. After he split with Hitler, Thyssen himself wrote a book, *I Paid Hitler*. We are now in a position to merge the evidence in these books with other material and our documentation on The Order.

The records of the U.S. Control Council for Germany contain the post-war intelligence interviews with prominent Nazis. From these we have verification that the major conduit for funds to Hitler was Fritz Thyssen and his Bank fur Handel and Schiff, previously called von Heydt's Bank. This information coincides with evidence in *Wall Street And The Rise Of Hitler* and *Hitler's Secret Backers*, even to the names of the people and banks involved, i.e., Thyssen, Harriman, Guaranty Trust, von Heydt, Carter, and so on.

The document reproduced on page 167 slipped through U.S. censorship because the Office of Director of Intelligence did not know of the link between Fritz Thyssen and the Harriman interests in New York. Documents linking Wall Street to Hitler have for the most part been removed from U.S. Control Council records. In any event, we reproduce here the Intelligence report identifying Fritz Thyssen and his Bank fur Handel und Schiff (No. EF/Me/1 of September 4, 1945) and page 13 of the interrogation of Fritz Thyssen entitled "Financial Support of the Nazi Party."

II. WHO WAS THYSSEN?

Fritz Thyssen was the German steel magnate who associated himself with the Nazi movement in the early '20s. When interrogated in 1945 under Project Dustbin, Thyssen recalled that he was approached in 1923 by General Ludendorf at the time of French evacuation of the Ruhr. Shortly after this meeting Thyssen was introduced to Hitler and provided funds for the Nazis through General Ludendorf.

In 1930-31 Emil Kirdorf approached Thyssen and subsequently sent Rudolf Hess to negotiate further funding for the Nazi Party. This time Thyssen arranged a credit of 250,000 marks at the Bank Voor Handel en Scheepvaart N.V. (the Dutch name for the bank named by Thyssen in the attached document), at 18 Zuidblaak in Rotterdam, Holland.

Thyssen was former head of the Vereinigte Stahlwerke, The German

[1] *Wall Street And The Rise Of Hitler* and *Hitler's Secret Backers* are obtainable from Research Publications, P.O. Box 39850, Phoenix Arizona 85069. Some other aspects are covered in Charles Higham, *Trading With The Enemy* (Delacorte Press).

G. Financial Support of the Nazi Party.

My first connection with the Nazi party was through General LUDENDORF, following the evacuation of the Ruhr by the French troops. He told me about the Party and asked for my help. I agreed, but I did not want to give any money directly to the Party, so I gave it to LUDENDORF and he gave it to the Party. LUDENDORF introduced me to HITLER in 1923 before the Putsch. After the Putsch the two got separated, and I too got separated from the Nazis.

In 1930 or 1931, I think, EMIL KIRDORF asked me to obtain some foreign credits for the Nazi Party. I had known him for a long time, though not in connection with business. He was my neighbor. After the death of my father, he was the oldest industrialist in the Ruhr. KIRDORF sent HESS to me; HESS had gone first to KIRDORF and reported that he had purchased the Brown House in MUNICH and could not pay for it, and KIRDORF said he could not help him, but that he should apply to me. I told HESS that I could not do as he wished, but that in order to show my good will and because Mr. KIRDORF sent him I would arrange a credit for him with a Dutch bank in ROTTERDAM, the Bank für Handel und Schiff.

I arranged the credit by writing a letter in which I arranged that if the bank would give credit to HESS, he would pay it back in three years in equal rates. I was not officially guarantor of the loan, but because I had proposed it, I was really responsible. I chose a Dutch bank because I did not want to be mixed up with German banks in my position, and because I thought it was better to do business with a Dutch bank, and I thought I would have the Nazis a little more in my hands. HITLER pretended he never got any help. It was difficult to do nothing in those days when things were going, nobody knew where, and I always thought I would have some influence. It was for the same reason that I would not give up my position later as member of parliament, because I always thought perhaps I could prevent war.

The credit was about 250-300,000 marks--about the same sum I had given before. The loan has been repaid in part to the Dutch bank, but I think some money is still owing on it; it had not all been paid when I left Germany in 1939. I have had to make payments on it myself--perhaps 200,000-280,000 marks which the Nazi Party didn't pay; they did repay some.

The Nazis applied first to KIRDORF rather than direct to me because KIRDORF was a great friend of HITLER-- he was fascinated by him. But KIRDORF told me that he was not himself in a position to give such an amount, and so I made this arrangement. But I certainly would not have done it if KIRDORF had not sent this man HESS to me.

I do not know of anyone else among the industrialists who was supporting the Party financially in 1928; I was then its principal supporter. Later TENGELMANN, KIRDORF, VOEGLER, KNEPPER all contributed; that was some sort of tax imposed on the whole industry. The reason for it was that HITLER would fight the communists: it was clear that the power would fall either to the communists or to the Nazis. When the Reichstag was burned, everyone was sure it had been done by the communists. I later learned in Switzerland that it was all a lie.

My contributions to the Party since that day have not been important--part of what the industry gave. I did help them in the riding school in my place. In 1932 I made two small contributions to Gauleiter TERBOVEN. He came and asked for the winter help and assistance: the winter contribution was made every year. At that time I gave him a pretty nice sum, something like 20,000 marks. This became an annual contribution; I am not sure whether the sum was increased. You see, we had a winter contribution of our own. When the unemployment began, my family undertook a winter help of our own, and gave poor people food, clothing, and shelter.

I joined the Party when they offered me membership in the Reichstag, I think in the election of 1931 or 1932. Before that time I was a German Nationalist. It is correct to say that my only contributions from my personal resources to the Party were the small annual dues, the subscription to various publications of the Party, and the winter help to the amount of 20-30 thousand marks. In other words the total amount I paid to the Nazi Party and its affiliates in any one year may have been a little over 50,000 marks; certainly not so much as

- 13 -

R-E-S-T-R-I-C-T-E-D

steel trust, financed by Dillon, Read (New York), and played a decisive role in the rise of Hitler to power by contributing liberally to the Nazi Party and by influencing his fellow industrialists to join him in support of the Fuehrer. In reward for his efforts, Thyssen was showered with political and economic favors by the Third Reich and enjoyed almost unlimited power and prestige under the Nazi regime until his break with Hitler in 1939 over the decision to invade Poland and precipitate the Second World War.

This incident and Thyssen's subsequent publication, *I Paid Hitler*, has a parallel wtih the history of his father, August Thyssen. Through a similar confession in 1918 the elder Thyssen, despite his record as a staunch backer of pan-Germanism, succeeded in convincing the Allies that sole responsibility for German aggression should be placed on the Kaiser and German industrialists should not be blamed for the support they had given to the Hohenzollerns. Apparently influenced by August Thyssen and his associates, the Allies made no effort to reform German industry after World War I. The result was that Thyssen was allowed to retain a vast industrial empire and pass it on intact to his heirs and successors.

It was against this background that Fritz Thyssen took over control of the family holdings following the death of his father in 1926. The new German steel baron had already achieved fame throughout the Reich by his defiance of the French during their occupation of the Ruhr in 1923. Like Hitler, Thyssen regarded the Treaty of Versailles as "a pact of shame" which must be overthrown if the Fatherland were to rise again This is the story in *Hitler's Secret Backers*.

Thyssen set out along the same road as his father, aided by ample Wall Street loans to build German industry. August Thyssen had combined with Hugenburg, Kirdorf, and the elder Krupp to promote the All-Deutscher Verband (the Pan-German League), which supplied the rationale for the Kaiser's expansionist policies.

His son became an active member of the Stahlhelm and later, through Goring, joined the Nazis. Finally, after the crash of 1931 had brought German industry to the verge of bankruptcy, he openly embraced national socialism.

During the next 2 years Thyssen dedicated his fortune and his influence to bring Hitler to power. In 1932 he arranged the famous meeting in the Dusseldorf Industrialists' Club, at which Hitler addressed the leading businessmen of the Ruhr and the Rhineland. At the close of Hitler's speech Thyssen cried, "Heil Herr Hitler," while the others applauded enthusiastically. By the time of the German Presidential elections later that year, Thyssen obtained contributions to Hitler's campaign fund from the industrial combines. He alone is reported to have spent 3,000,000 marks on the Nazis in the year 1932.

III. THE UNION BANKING CONNECTION

This flow of funds went through Thyssen banks. The Bank fur Handel and Schiff cited as the conduit in the U.S. Intelligence report was a subsidiary of the August Thyssen Bank, and founded in 1918 with H.J. Kouwenhoven and D.C. Schutte as managing partners. In brief, it was Thyssen's personal banking operation, and **affiliated with the W.A. Harriman financial interests in New York.** Thyssen reported to his Project Dustbin interrogators that:

> "I chose a Dutch bank because I did not want to be mixed up with German banks in my position, and because I thought it was better to do business with a Dutch bank, and I thought I would have the Nazis a little more in my hands."

Hitler's Secret Backers identifies the conduit from the U.S. as "von Heydt," and von Heydt's Bank was the early name for Thyssen's Bank. Furthermore, the Thyssen front bank in Holland — i.e., the Bank voor Handel en Scheepvaart N.V. — controlled the Union Banking Corporation in New York.

The Harrimans had a financial interest in, and E. Roland Harriman (The Order 1917), Averell's brother, was a director of this Union Banking Corporation. The Union Banking Corporation of New York City was a joint Thyssen-Harriman operation with the following directors in 1932:

E. Roland Harriman (The Order 1917)	Vice President of W.A. Harriman & Co., New York
H.J. Kouwenhoven (Nazi)	Nazi banker, managing partner of August Thyssen Bank and Bank voor Handel Scheepvaart N.V. (the transfer bank for Thyssen's funds)
Knight Woolley (The Order 1917)	Director of Guaranty Trust, New York and Director Federal Reserve Bank of N.Y.
Cornelius Lievense	President, Union Banking Corp. and Director of Holland-American Investment Corp.
Ellery Sedgewick James (The Order 1917)	Partner, Brown Brothers, & Co., New York
Johann Groninger (Nazi)	Director of Bank voor Handel en Scheepvaart and Vereinigte Stahlwerke (Thyssen's steel operations)
J.L. Guinter	Director Union Banking Corp.
Prescott Sheldon Bush (The Order 1917)	Partner, Brown Brothers. Harriman. Father of President G.H.W. Bush.

The eight directors of Union Banking Corporation are an interesting bunch indeed. Look at the following:

- Four directors of Union Banking are members of The Order: all initiated at Yale in 1917 — members of the same Yale class. All four were members of the same cell (club) D 115.
- E. Harriman was the brother of W. Averell Harriman and a Vice-President of W.A. Harriman Company.
- Guaranty Trust was represented by Knight Woolley.
- Two of the Union directors, Kouwenhoven and Groninger, were Nazi directors of Bank voor Handel en Scheepvaart, formerly the von Heydt Bank. Von Heydt was the intermediary between Guaranty Trust and Hitler named in *Hitler's Secret Backer.*
- Ellery S. James and Prescott S. Bush were partners in Brown Brothers, later Brown Brothers, Harriman.

Out of eight directors of Thyssen's bank in New York, we can therefore identify six who are either Nazis or members of The Order.

This private bank was formerly named Von Heydt Bank and von Heydt is named by Sharp in *Hitler's Secret Backers* as the intermediary from Guaranty Trust in New York to Hitler between 1930 and 1933. Above all, remember that Shoup was writing in **1933** when this information was still only known to those on the inside. Out of tens of thousands of banks and bankers, Shoup, in 1933, names those that evidence surfacing decades later confirms as financing Hitler.

In brief, when we merge the information in PROJECT DUSTBIN with Shoup's *Hitler's Secret Backers,* we find **the major overseas conduit for Nazi financing traces back to THE ORDER and specifically cell D 115.**

IV. PROFIT FROM CONFLICT

Out of war and revolution come opportunities for profit.

Conflict can be used for profit by corporations under control and influence of The Order. In World War II, the Korean War and the Vietnamese War we can cite examples of American corporations that traded with "the enemy" for profit.

This "blood trade" is by no means sporadic or limited to a few firms; it is general and reflects higher policy decisions and philosophies. Corporations — even large corporations — are dominated by banks and trust companies, and in turn these banks and trust companies are dominated by The Order and its allies. (This will be the topic of a forthcoming volume).

Although the U.S. did not officially go to war with Germany until 1941, legally, and certainly morally, the U.S. was at war with Nazi Germany after the Destroyer deal with Great Britain in December 1940, i.e., the exchange of 50 old U.S. destroyers for strategic bases in British territory. Even before December 1940 the MS "Frederick S. Fales" owned by Standard Vacuum Company was sunk by a German submarine on September 21, 1940. Yet in 1941 Standard Oil of New Jersey (now EXXON) had six Standard Oil tankers under Panamanian registry, manned by Nazi officers to carry fuel oil from Standard Oil refineries to the Canary Islands, a refueling base of Nazi submarines.

A report on this dated July 15, 1941 from Intelligence at Fifth Corps in Columbus, Ohio is reproduced on page 172. The report is in error recording that no Standard Oil ships had been sunk by the Nazis; Major Burrows apparently did not know "Frederick S. Fales" in 1940.

Another example of profit from war is recorded in the document on page 173. This records the association of RCA and the Nazis in World War II. RCA was essentially a Morgan-Rockefeller firm and so linked to The Order.

Yet another example is that of Chase Bank. Chase was linked to The Order through the Rockefeller family (Percy Rockefeller, The Order 1900) and Vice-President Reeve Schley (Yale, Scroll & Key). Directors of Chase in The Order included Frederick Allen (The Order 1900), W.E.S. Griswold (The Order 1899) and Cornelius Vanderbilt, whose brother Gwynne Vanderbilt (The Order 1899) represented the family before his death. President of Chase was Winthrop Aldrich. This was the Harvard branch of the Aldrich family, another branch is Yale and The Order.

Chase Manhattan Bank is not only a firm that plays both sides of the political fence, but with Ford Motor Company, was selected by Treasury Secretary Morgenthau for post-war investigation of pro-Nazi activities:

> These two situations [i.e., Ford and Chase Bank] convince us that it is imperative to investigate immediately on the spot the activities of subsidiaries of at least some of the larger American firms which were operating in France during German occupation . . .

The extent of Chase collaboration with Nazis is staggering — and this was at a time when Nelson Rockefeller had an intelligence job in Washington aimed AGAINST Nazi operations in Latin America.

In December 1944 Treasury Department officials examined the records of the Chase Bank in Paris. On December 20, 1944 the senior U.S. examiner sent a memorandum to Treasury Secretary Morgenthau with the **preliminary** results of the Paris examination. Here's an extract from that report:

HEADQUARTERS FIFTH CORPS AREA
OFFICE OF THE CORPS AREA COMMANDER
FORT HAYES, COLUMBUS, OHIO

G-2 July 15, 1941

SUBJECT: Standard Oil Company of New Jersey Ships Under Panamanian Registry.

TO: A. C. of S., G-2,
War Department
Washington, D. C.

1. A report has been received from Cleveland, Ohio, in which it is stated that the source of this information is unquestionable, to the effect that the Standard Oil Company of New Jersey now ships under Panamanian registry, transporting oil (fuel) from Aruba, Dutch West Indies to Teneriffe, Canary Islands, and is apparently diverting about 20% of this fuel oil to the present German government.

2. About six of the ships operating on this route are reputed to be manned mainly by Nazi officers. Seamen have reported to the informant that they have seen submarines in the immediate vicinity of the Canary Islands and have learned that these submarines are refueling there. The informant also stated that the Standard Oil Company has not lost any ships to date by torpedoing as have other companies whose ships operate to other ports.

For the A. C. of S., G-2,

CHAS. A. [illegible],
Major, Military Intelligence,
Asst. A. C. of S., G-2

DEPARTMENT OF STATE

Memorandum of ~~Conversation~~ TELEPHONE

DATE: May 24, 1943.

SUBJECT: Communications.

PARTICIPANTS: Colonel Sarnoff, RCA

Mr. Long.

COPIES TO: PA, IH.

Messages fr B.A. by Axis powers to their Govts

I talked to Colonel Sarnoff on the telephone and explained to him that we had reason to believe that more messages than the agreed 700 code-groups a week were being sent from B. A. by the Axis powers to their Governments. I told him I could not disclose down there the source of our information. In an effort to obtain additional information our representatives down there had approached Hayes. Hayes had seemed to them noncooperative. There may have been very sound reasons why he refused to disclose the exact number of messages sent in code-groups by each of the Axis representatives to their Government. However, there didn't seem to be any reason why the managership should not request a report on all code-groups being sent over a period of time, day by day, and to include a report on all belligerents, and that if he would obtain that information through confidential channels we would be appreciative. I suggested it be not done by telegraph or telephone and suggested the mail, but offered to make the pouch available.

Colonel Sarnoff replied that he would talk to Mr. Winterbottom but he saw no reason why we should not do it and that he would communicate with us if they wanted to use the pouch.

After receipt of this information we will be in a better position to judge what our policy should be.

B. L.

A-L:BL:lag

a. Niederman, of Swiss nationality, manager of Chase, Paris, was unquestionably a collaborator;

b. The Chase Head Office in New York was informed of Niederman's collaborationist policy but took no steps to remove him. Indeed there is ample evidence to show that the Head Office in New York viewed Niederman's good relations with the Germans as an excellent means of preserving, unimpaired, the position of the Chase Bank in France.

c. The German authorities were anxious to keep the Chase open and indeed took exceptional measures to provide sources of revenue.

d. The German authorities desired "to be friends" with the important American banks because they expected that these banks would be useful after the war as an instrument of German policy in the United States.

e. The Chase, Paris showed itself most anxious to please the German authorities in every possible way. For example, the Chase zealously maintained the account of the German Embassy in Paris, "as every little thing helps" (to maintain the excellent relations between Chase and the German authorities).

f. The whole objective of the Chase policy and operation was to maintain the position of the bank at any cost.

In brief, Chase Bank was a Nazi collaborator, but the above preliminary report is as far as the investigation proceeded. The report was killed on orders from Washington, D.C.

On the other hand, Chase Bank, later Chase Manhattan Bank, has been a prime promoter of exporting U.S. technology to the Soviet Union. This goes all the way back to the early 1920s when Chase broke U.S. regulations in order to aid the Soviets. As early as 1922 Chase was trying to export military LIBERTY aircraft engines to the Soviet Union!

In conclusion, we have seen that the two arms of the dialectic described in Memoranda Three and Four clashed in World War II. Furthermore, the corporate segment of the elite profited from Lend Lease to the Soviets **and** by underground cooperation with Nazi interests. The political wing of The Order was at the same time preparing a new dialectic for the post World War II era.

S&B '41
S&B '21
S&B '17
S&B '18
S&B '17

Picture taken in 1959, while Averell Harriman was serving as Governor of New York and Prescott was serving in the US Senate.

Partners of Brown Brother Harriman & Co. are pictured against the background of a painting of the founders of the firm. The men responsible for operation of the bank were: seated *Moreau D. Brown, E. R. Harriman, Robert A. Lovett, Knight Woolley, Louis Curtis,* and, standing, *Elbridge T. Gerry, John B. Madden, L. Parks Shipley, Thomas McCance, Stephen Y. Hord, David G. Ackerman, F. H. Kingsbury, Jr.,* and *John C. West.*

William Averell Harriman - S&B '13
Founder - Brown Brothers Harriman
1913 Yale yearbook photo

Prescott S. Bush - S&B '17
w/Brown Brothers Harriman
1917 Yale yearbook photo

Brown Brothers Harriman
59 Wall Street, New York City

The House of Bush: Born in a Bank

Webster Griffin Tarpley and Anton Chaitkin

Chapter One of *George Bush – The Unauthorized Biography* - 1992. Used with permission.

Who is George Bush? How did he become the 41st U.S. President? He is said to be a man of the "old establishment," who "chose to seek his fortune as an independent oilman … ."[1]

In fact, Bush was never "independent." Every career step in his upward climb relied on his family's powerful associations. The Bush family joined the Eastern Establishment comparatively recently, and only as servitors. Their wealth and influence resulted from their loyalty to another, more powerful family, and their willingness to do anything to get ahead.

For what they did, Bush's forebears should have become very famous, or infamous. They remained obscure figures, managers from behind the scenes. But their actions — including his father's role as banker for Adolf Hitler — had tragic effects for the whole planet.

It was these services to his family's benefactors, which propelled George Bush to the top.

Prescott Goes to War

President George Herbert Walker Bush was born in 1924, the son of Prescott S. Bush and Dorothy Walker Bush. We will begin the George Bush story about a decade before his birth, on the eve of World War I. We will follow the career of his father, Prescott Bush, through his marriage with Dorothy Walker, on the path to fortune, elegance and power.

Prescott Bush entered Yale University in 1913. A native of Columbus, Ohio, Prescott had spent the last five years before college in St. George's Episcopal preparatory school in Newport, Rhode Island.

Prescott Bush's first college year, 1913, was also the freshman year at Yale for E. Roland ("Bunny") Harriman, whose older brother (Wm.) Averell Harriman had just graduated from Yale. This is the Averell Harriman who went on to fame as the U.S. ambassador to the Soviet Union during World War II, as a governor of New York State, and as a presidential advisor who was greatly responsible for starting the Vietnam War.

The Harrimans would become the sponsors of the Bushes, to lift them onto the stage of world history.

In the spring of 1916, Prescott Bush and "Bunny" Harriman were chosen for membership in an elite Yale senior-year secret society known as Skull and Bones. This unusually morbid, death-celebrating group helped Wall Street financiers find active young men of "good birth" to form a kind of imitation British aristocracy in America.

World War I was then raging in Europe. With the prospect that the U.S.A. would soon join the war, two Skull and Bones "Patriarchs," Averell Harriman (class of 1913) and Percy A. Rockefeller (class of 1900), paid special attention to Prescott's class of 1917. They wanted reliable cadres to help them play the Great Game, in the lucrative new imperial era that the war was opening up for London and New York moneycrats. Prescott Bush, by then a close friend of "Bunny" Harriman, and several other Bonesmen from their class of 1917 would later comprise the core partners in Brown Brothers Harriman, the world's largest private investment bank.

World War I did make an immense amount of money for the clan of stock speculators and British bankers who had just taken over U.S. industry. The Harrimans were stars of this new Anglo-American elite.

Averell's father, stock broker E.H. Harriman, had gained control of the Union Pacific Railroad in 1898 with credit arranged by William Rockefeller, Percy's father, and by Kuhn Loeb & Co.'s British-affiliated private bankers, Otto Kahn, Jacob Schiff and Felix Warburg.

William Rockefeller, treasurer of Standard Oil and brother of Standard founder John D. Rockefeller, owned National City Bank (later "Citibank") together with Texas-based James Stillman. In return for their backing, E.H. Harriman deposited in City Bank the vast receipts from his railroad lines. When he issued tens of millions of dollars of "watered" (fraudulent) railroad stock, Harriman sold most of the shares through the Kuhn Loeb company.

The First World War elevated Prescott Bush and his father, Samuel P. Bush, into the lower ranks of the Eastern Establishment.

As war loomed in 1914, National City Bank began reorganizing the U.S. arms industry. Percy A. Rockefeller took direct control of the Remington Arms company, appointing his own man, Samuel F. Pryor, as the new chief executive of Remington.

The U.S entered World War I in 1917. In the spring of 1918, Prescott's father, Samuel P. Bush, became chief of the Ordnance, Small Arms and Ammunition Section of the War Industries Board.[2] The senior Bush took national responsibility for government assistance to and relations with Remington and other weapons companies.

This was an unusual appointment, as Prescott's father seemed to have no background in munitions. Samuel Bush had been president of the Buckeye Steel Castings Co. in Columbus, Ohio, maker of railcar parts. His entire career had been in the railroad business — supplying equipment to the Wall Street-owned railroad systems.

The War Industries Board was run by Bernard Baruch, a Wall Street speculator with close personal and business ties to old E.H. Harriman. Baruch's brokerage firm had handled Harriman speculations of all kinds.[3]

In 1918, Samuel Bush became director of the Facilities Division of the War Industries Board. Prescott's father reported to the Board's Chairman, Bernard Baruch, and to Baruch's assistant, Wall Street private banker Clarence Dillon.

Robert S. Lovett, President of Union Pacific Railroad, chief counsel to E.H. Harriman and executor of his will, was in charge of national production and purchase "priorities" for Baruch's board.

With the war mobilization conducted under the supervision of the War Industries Board, U.S. consumers and taxpayers showered unprecedented fortunes on war producers and certain holders of raw materials and patents. Hearings in 1934 by the committee of U.S. Senator Gerald Nye attacked the "Merchants of Death" — war profiteers such as Remington Arms and the British Vickers company — whose salesmen had manipulated many nations into wars, and then supplied all sides with the weapons to fight them.

Percy Rockefeller and Samuel Pryor's Remington Arms supplied machine guns and Colt automatic pistols; millions of rifles to Czarist Russia; over half of the small-arms ammunition used by the Anglo-American allies in World War I; and 69 percent of the rifles used by the United States in that conflict.[4]

Samuel Bush's wartime relationship to these businessmen would continue after the war, and would especially aid his son Prescott's career of service to the Harrimans.

Most of the records and correspondence of Samuel Bush's arms- related section of the government have been burned, "to save space" in the National Archives. This matter of destroyed or misplaced records should be of concern to citizens of a constitutional republic. Unfortunately, it is a rather constant impediment with regard to researching George Bush's background: He is certainly the most "covert" American chief executive.

Now, arms production in wartime is by necessity carried on with great security precautions. The public need not know details of the private lives of the government or industry executives involved, and a broad interrelationship between government and private-sector personnel is normal and useful.

But during the period preceding World War I, and in the war years 1914-1917 when the U.S. was still neutral, interlocking Wall Street financiers subservient to British strategy lobbied heavily, and twisted U.S. government and domestic police functions. Led by the J.P. Morgan concern, Britain's overall purchasing agent in America, these financiers wanted a world war and they wanted the United States in it as Britain's ally. The U.S. and British arms companies, owned by these international financiers, poured out weapons abroad in deals not subject to the scrutiny of any electorate back home. The same gentlemen, as we shall see, later supplied weapons and money to Hitler's Nazis.

That this problem persists today, is in some respect due to the "control" over the documentation and the history of the arms traffickers.

World War I was a disaster for civilized humanity. It had terrible, unprecedented casualties, and shattering effects on the moral philosophy of Europeans and Americans.

But for a brief period, the war treated Prescott Bush rather well.

In June, 1918, just as his father took over responsibility for relations of the government with the private arms producers, Prescott went to Europe with the U.S. Army. His unit did not come near any fire until September. But on August 8, 1918, the following item appeared on the front page of Bush's home-town newspaper:

3 High Military Honors Conferred on Capt. Bush

For Notable Gallantry, When Leading Allied Commanders Were Endangered, Local Man is Awarded French, English and U.S. Crosses.

International Honors, perhaps unprecedented in the life of an American soldier, have been conferred upon Captain Prescott Sheldon Bush, son of Mr. and Mrs. S.P. Bush of Columbus.

Upon young Bush ... were conferred: Cross of the Legion of Honor, ... Victoria Cross, ... Distinguished Service Cross...

> Conferring of the three decorations upon one man at one time implies recognition of a deed of rare valor and probably of great military importance as well.
>
> From word which has reached Columbus during the last few days, it appears as if the achievement of Captain Bush well measures up to these requirements.
>
> The incident occurred on the western front about the time the Germans were launching their great offensive of July 15 ... The history of the remarkable victory scored later by the allies might have been written in another vein, but for the heroic and quick action of Captain Bush.
>
> The ... three allied leaders, Gen. [Ferdinand] Foch, Sir Douglas Haig and Gen. [John J.] Pershing ... were making an inspection of American positions. Gen. Pershing had sent for Captain Bush to guide them about one sector ... Suddenly Captain Bush noticed a shell coming directly for them. He shouted a warning, suddenly drew his bolo knife, stuck it up as he would a ball bat, and parried the blow, causing the shell to glance off to the right ...
>
> Within 24 hours young Bush was notified ... [that] the three allied commanders had recommended him for practically the highest honors within their gift... Captain Bush is 23 years old, a graduate of Yale in the class of 1917. He was one of Yale's best- known athletes ... was leader of the glee club ... and in his senior year was elected to the famous Skull and Bones Society ... [5]

The day after this astonishing story appeared, there was a large cartoon on the editorial page. It depicted Prescott Bush as a small boy, reading a story-book about military heroism, and saying: "Gee! I wonder if anything like that could ever truly happen to a boy." The caption below was a rehash of the batting- away- the-deadly-shell exploit, written in storybook style.[6]

Local excitement about the military "Babe Ruth" lasted just four weeks. Then this somber little box appeared on the front page:

> Editor State Journal:
>
> A cable received from my son, Prescott S. Bush, brings word that he has not been decorated, as published in the papers a month ago. He feels dreadfully troubled that a letter, written in a spirit of fun, should have been misinterpreted. He says he is no hero and asks me to make explanations. I will appreciate your kindness in publishing this letter...
>
> Flora Sheldon Bush.
> Columbus, Sept. 5.[7]

Prescott Bush later claimed that he spent "about 10 or 11 weeks" in the area of combat in France. "We were under fire there… It was quite exciting, and of course a wonderful experience." [8]

Prescott Bush was discharged in mid-1919, and returned for a short time to Columbus, Ohio. But his humiliation in his home town was so intense that he could no longer live there. The "war hero" story was henceforth not spoken of in his presence. Decades later, when he was an important, rich U.S. Senator, the story was whispered and puzzled over among the Congressmen.

Looking to be rescued from this ugly situation, Captain Bush went to the 1919 reunion of his Yale class in New Haven, Connecticut. Skull and Bones Patriarch Wallace Simmons, closely tied to the arms manufacturers, offered Prescott Bush a job in his St. Louis railroad equipment company. Bush took the offer and moved to St. Louis — and his destiny.

A THOROUGHBRED MARRIAGE

Prescott Bush went to St. Louis to repair his troubled life. Sometime that same year, Averell Harriman made a trip there on a project which would have great consequences for Prescott. The 28- year-old Harriman, until then something of a playboy, wanted to bring his inherited money and contacts into action in the arena of world affairs.

President Theodore Roosevelt had denounced Harriman's father for "cynicism and deep-seated corruption" and called him an "undesirable citizen."[9] For the still- smarting Averell to take his place among the makers and breakers of nations, he needed a financial and intelligence-gathering organization of his own. The man Harriman sought to create such an institution for him was Bert Walker, a Missouri stock broker and corporate wheeler-dealer.

George Herbert ("Bert") Walker, for whom President George H.W. Bush was named, did not immediately accept Harriman's proposal. Would Walker leave his little St. Louis empire, to try his influence in New York and Europe?

Bert was the son of a dry goods wholesaler who had thrived on imports from England.[10] The British connection had paid for Walker summer houses in Santa Barbara, California, and in Maine — "Walker's Point" at Kennebunkport. Bert Walker had been sent to England for his prep school and college education.

By 1919 Bert Walker had strong ties to the Guaranty Trust Company in New York and to the British-American banking house J.P. Morgan and Co. These Wall Street concerns represented all the important owners of American railroads: the Morgan partners and their associates or cousins in the intermarried Rockefeller, Whitney, Harriman and Vanderbilt families.

Bert Walker was known as the midwest's premier deal-arranger, awarding the investment capital of his international-banker contacts to the many railroads, utilities and other midwestern industries of which he and his St. Louis friends were executives or board members.

Walker's operations were always quiet, or mysterious, whether in local or global affairs. He had long been the "power behind the throne" in the St. Louis Democratic Party, along with his crony, former Missouri Governor David R. Francis. Walker and Francis together had sufficient influence to select the party's candidates.[11]

Back in 1904, Bert Walker, David Francis, Washington University President Robert Brookings and their banker/broker circle had organized a world's fair in St. Louis, the Louisiana Purchase Exposition. In line with the old Southern Confederacy family backgrounds of many of these sponsors, the fair featured a "Human Zoo"; live natives from backward jungle regions were exhibited in special cages under the supervision of anthropologist William J. McGee.

So Averell Harriman was a natural patron for Bert Walker. Bert shared Averell's passion for horse breeding and horse racing, and easily accommodated the Harriman family's related social philosophy. They believed that the horses and racing stables they owned showed the way toward a sharp upgrading of the human stock — just select and mate thoroughbreds, and spurn or eliminate inferior animals.

The First World War had brought the little St. Louis oligarchy into the Confederate-slave owner-oriented administration of President Woodrow Wilson and his advisors, Col. Edward House and Bernard Baruch.

Walker's friend Robert Brookings got into Bernard Baruch's War Industries Board as director of national Price Fixing (sic). David R. Francis became U.S. ambassador to Russia in 1916. As the Bolshevik Revolution broke out, we find Bert Walker busy appointing people to Francis's staff in Petrograd.[12]

Walker's earliest activities in relation to the Soviet state are of significant interest to historians, given the activist role he was to play there together with Harriman. But Walker's life is as covert as the rest of the Bush clan's, and the surviving public record is extremely thin.

The 1919 Versailles peace conference brought together British imperial strategists and their American friends to make postwar global arrangements. For his own intended international adventures, Harriman needed Bert Walker, the seasoned intriguer, who quietly represented many of the British-designated rulers of American politics and finance.

After two persuasion trips west by Harriman,[13] Walker at length agreed to move to New York. But he kept his father's summer house in Kennebunkport, Maine.

Bert Walker formally organized the W.A. Harriman & Co. private bank in November 1919. Walker became the bank's president and chief executive; Averell Harriman was chairman and controlling co-owner with his brother Roland ("Bunny"), Prescott Bush's close friend from Yale; and Percy Rockefeller was a director and a founding financial sponsor.

In the autumn of 1919, Prescott Bush made the acquaintance of Bert Walker's daughter Dorothy. They were engaged the following year, and were married in August, 1921.[14] Among the ushers and grooms at the elaborate wedding were Ellery S. James, Knight Woolley and four other fellow Skull and Bonesmen from the Yale Class of 1917.[15] The Bush-Walker extended family has gathered each summer at the "Walker country home" in Kennebunkport, from this marriage of President Bush's parents down to the present day.

When Prescott married Dorothy, he was only a minor executive of the Simmons Co., railroad equipment suppliers, while his wife's father was building one of the most gigantic businesses in the world. The following year the couple tried to move back to Columbus, Ohio; there Prescott worked for a short time in a rubber products company owned by his father. But they soon moved again to Milton, Mass., after outsiders bought the little family business and moved it near there.

Thus Prescott Bush was going nowhere fast, when his son George Herbert Walker Bush — the future U.S. President — was born in Milton, Mass., on June 12, 1924.

Perhaps it was as a birthday gift for George, that "Bunny" Harriman stepped in to rescue his father Prescott from oblivion, bringing him into the Harriman-controlled U.S. Rubber Co. in New York City. In 1925 the young family moved to the town where George was to grow up: Greenwich, Connecticut, a suburb both of New York and of New Haven/Yale.

Then on May 1, 1926, Prescott Bush joined W.A. Harriman & Co. as its vice president, under the bank's president, Bert Walker, his father-in-law and George's maternal grandfather — the head of the family.[16]

The Great Game

Prescott Bush would demonstrate strong loyalty to the firm he joined in 1926. And the bank, with the scope and power of many ordinary nations, could amply reward its agents. George Bush's Grandfather Walker had put the enterprise together, quietly, secretly, using all the international connections at his disposal. Let us briefly look back at the beginning of the Harriman firm — the Bush family enterprise — and follow its course into one of history's darkest projects.

The firm's first global lever was its successful arrangement to get into Germany by dominating that country's shipping. Averell Harriman announced in 1920 that he would re-start Germany's Hamburg-Amerika Line, after many months of scheming and arm-twisting. Hamburg-Amerika's commercial steamships had been confiscated by the United States at the end of the First World War. These ships had then become the property of the Harriman enterprise, by some arrangements with the U.S. authorities that were never made public.

The deal was breathtaking; it would create the world's largest private shipping line. Hamburg-Amerika Line regained its confiscated vessels, for a heavy price. The Harriman enterprise took "the right to participate in 50 percent of all business originated in Hamburg"; and for the next twenty years (1920-1940), the Harriman enterprise had "complete control of all activities of the Hamburg line in the United States."[17]

Harriman became co-owner of Hamburg-Amerika. The Harriman-Walker firm gained a tight hold on its management, with the not-so-subtle backing of the post-World War I occupation of Germany by the armies of England and America.

Just after Harriman's public statement, the St. Louis press celebrated Bert Walker's role in assembling the money to consummate the deal:

"Ex-St. Louisan Forms Giant Ship Merger"

"G. H. Walker is Moving Power Behind Harriman-Morton Shipping Combine … ."

The story celebrated a "merger of two big financial houses in New York, which will place practically unlimited capital at the disposal of the new American-German shipping combine … ."[18]

Bert Walker had arranged a "marriage" of J.P. Morgan credit and Harriman family inherited wealth.

W.A. Harriman & Co., of which Walker was president and founder, was merging with the Morton & Co. private bank — and Walker was "[p]rominent in the affairs of Morton & Co.," which was interlocked with the Morgan-controlled Guaranty Trust Co.

The Hamburg-Amerika takeover created an effective instrument for the manipulation and fatal subversion of Germany. One of the great "merchants of death," Samuel Pryor, was in it from the beginning. Pryor, then chairman of the executive committee of Remington Arms, helped arrange the deal and served with Walker on the board of Harriman's shipping front organization, the American Ship and Commerce Co.

Walker and Harriman took the next giant step in 1922, setting up their European headquarters office in Berlin. With the aid of the Hamburg-based Warburg bank, W.A. Harriman & Co. began spreading an investment net over German industry and raw materials.

From the Berlin base, Walker and Harriman then plunged into deals with the new dictatorship of the Soviet Union. They led a select group of Wall Street and British Empire speculators who re-started the Russian oil industry, which had been devastated by the Bolshevik Revolution. They contracted to mine Soviet manganese, an element essential to modern steelmaking. These concessions were arranged directly with Leon Trotsky, then with Feliks Dzerzhinsky, founder of the Soviet dictatorship's secret intelligence service (K.G.B), whose huge statue was finally pulled down by pro-democracy demonstrators in 1991.

These speculations created both channels of communication, and the style of accommodation, with the communist dictatorship, that have continued in the family down to President Bush.

With the bank launched, Bert Walker found New York the ideal place to satisfy his passion for sports, games and gambling. Walker was elected president of the U.S. Golf Association in 1920. He negotiated new international rules for the game with the Royal and Ancient Golf Club of St. Andrews, Scotland. After these talks he contributed the three-foot-high silver Walker Cup, for which British and American teams have since competed every two years.

Bert's son-in-law Prescott Bush was later secretary of the U.S. Golf Association during the grave political and economic crises of the early 1930s. Prescott became USGA President in 1935, while he was otherwise embroiled in the family firm's work with Nazi Germany.

When George was one year old, in 1925, Bert Walker and Averell Harriman headed a syndicate which rebuilt Madison Square Garden as the modern Palace of Sport. Walker was at the center of New York's gambling scene in its heyday, in that Prohibition era of colorful and bloody gangsters. The Garden bloomed with million-dollar prize fights; bookies and their clients pooled more millions, trying to match the pace of the speculation-crazed stock and bond men. This was the era of "organized" crime — the national gambling and bootleg syndicate structured on the New York corporate model.

By 1930, when George was a boy of six, Grandpa Walker was New York State Racing Commissioner. The vivid colors and sounds of the racing scene must have impressed little George as much as his grandfather. Bert Walker bred race horses at his own stable, the Log Cabin Stud. He was president of the Belmont Park race track. Bert also personally managed most aspects of Averell's racing interests-- down to picking the colors and fabrics for the Harriman racing gear.[19]

From 1926, George's father Prescott Bush showed a fierce loyalty to the Harrimans and a dogged determination to advance himself; he gradually came to run the day-to-day operations of W.A. Harriman & Co. After the firm's 1931 merger with the British-American banking house Brown Brothers, Prescott Bush became managing partner of the resulting company: Brown Brothers Harriman. This was ultimately the largest and politically the most important private banking house in America.

Financial collapse, world depression and social upheaval followed the fevered speculation of the 1920s. The 1929-31 crash of securities values wiped out the small fortune Prescott Bush had gained since 1926. But because of his devotion to the Harrimans, they "did a very generous thing," as Bush later put it. They staked him to what he had lost and put him back on his feet.

Prescott Bush described his own role, from 1931 through the 1940s, in a confidential interview:

> I emphasize ... that the Harrimans showed great courage and loyalty and confidence in us, because three or four of us were really running the business, the day to day business. Averell was all over the place in those days ... and Roland was involved in a lot of directorships, and he didn't get down into the "lift- up-and-bear-down" activity of the bank, you see– the day- to-day decisions ... we were really running the business, the day to day business, all the administrative decisions and the executive decisions. We were the ones that did it. We were the managing partners, let's say.[20]

But of the "three or four" partners in charge, Prescott was effectively at the head of the firm, because he had taken over management of the gigantic personal investment funds of Averell and E. Roland "Bunny" Harriman.

In those interwar years, Prescott Bush made the family fortune which George Bush inherited. He piled up the money from an international project which continued until a new world war, and the action of the U.S. government, intervened to stop him.

NOTES FOR CHAPTER I

1. *Washington Post*, Aug. 16, 1991, p. A1.
2. Gen. Hugh S. Johnson to Major J.H.K. Davis, June 6, 1918, file no. 334.8/168 or 334.8/451 in U.S. National Archives, Suitland, Maryland.
3. *Bernard M. Baruch, My Own Story* (New York: Henry Holt and Co., 1957), pp. 138-39. Baruch related that "our firm did a large business for Mr. Harriman... In 1906 Harriman had [us] place heavy bets on Charles Evans Hughes in his race for Governor of New York against William Randolph Hearst. After several hundred thousand dollars had been wagered, [our firm] stopped. Hearing of this, Harriman called ... up. 'Didn't I tell you to bet?' He demanded. 'Now go on.'|"
4. Alden Hatch, *Remington Arms: An American History*, 1956, copyright by the Remington Arms Co., pp. 224-25.
5. *The Ohio State Journal*, Columbus, Ohio, Thursday, Aug. 8, 1918.
6. *The Ohio State Journal*, Friday, Aug. 9, 1918.
7. *The Ohio State Journal*, Friday, Sept. 6, 1918.
8. Interview with Prescott Bush in the Oral History Research Project conducted by Columbia University in 1966, Eisenhower Administration Part II; pp. 5-6. The interview was supposed to be kept confidential and was never published, but Columbia later sold microfilms of the transcript to certain libraries, including Arizona State University.
9. Theodore Roosevelt to James S. Sherman, Oct. 6, 1906, made public by Roosevelt at a press conference April 2, 1907. Quoted in Henry F. Pringle, *Theodore Roosevelt* (New York: Harcourt, Brace and Company, 1931), p. 452. Roosevelt later confided to Harriman lawyer Robert S. Lovett that his views on Harriman were based on what J.P. Morgan had told him.
10. See *The Industries of St. Louis*, published 1885 by J.M. Elstner & Co., pp. 61-62 for Crow, Hagardine & Co., David Walker's first business; and p. 86 for Ely & Walker.
11. See Letter of G.H. Walker to D.R. Francis, March 20, 1905, in the Francis collection of the Missouri Historical Society, St. Louis, Missouri, on the organization of the Republicans and Democrats to run the election of the mayor, a Democrat acceptable to the socially prominent. The next day Walker became the treasurer and Francis the president of this "Committee of 1000." See also George H. Walker obituary, *St. Louis Globe-Democrat*, June 25, 1953.
12. Letter of Perry Francis to his father, Ambassador David R. Francis, Oct. 15, 1917, Francis collection of the Missouri Historical Society. "... Joe Miller left for San Francisco last Tuesday night, where he will receive orders to continue to Petrograd. I was told by Mildred Kotany [Walker's sister-in-law] that Bert Walker got him his appointment through Breck Long. I didn't know Joe was after it, or could have helped him myself. He will be good company for you when he gets there..."
13. Private interview with a Walker family member, cousin of President Bush.
14. Prescott Bush, Columbia University, op. cit., p. 7.
15. *St. Louis Globe Democrat*, Aug. 7, 1921. 16. This is the sequence of events, from Simmons to U.S. Rubber, which Prescott Bush gave in his Columbia University interview, op. cit.,) pp. 7-8.
17. Public statement of Averell Harriman, New York *Times*, Oct. 6, 1920, p. 1.
18. *St. Louis Globe-Democrat*, Oct. 12, 1920, p. 1.
19. Sports-as-business has continued in the family up through George Bush's adult life. Bert's son George Walker, Jr. — President Bush's uncle and financial angel in Texas — co-founded the New York Mets and was the baseball club's vice president and treasurer for 17 years until his death in 1977. The President's son, George Walker Bush, was co-owner of the Texas Rangers baseball club during his father's presidency.
20. Prescott Bush, Columbia University, op. cit., pp. 16-22.

"All the News That's Fit to Print"

The New York Times.

LATE CITY EDITION
Fair, windy, slightly warmer today. Mostly cloudy, colder tomorrow.

Copyright, 1944, by The New York Times Company.

VOL. XCIV. No. 31,738. NEW YORK, SATURDAY, DECEMBER 16, 1944. THREE CENTS NEW YORK CITY

U. S. FORCE LANDS UNOPPOSED ON MINDORO WITHIN 155 MILES OF PHILIPPINE CAPITAL; CHURCHILL BACKS RUSSIA ON POLISH ISSUE

CALL OF OLDER MEN INTO ARMED FORCES TO INCREASE FEB. 1

War Department Says Draft of Those Below 26 Will Not Keep the Ranks Full

FURLOUGHS AID OUTPUT

4,700 Soldiers to Go Into Key Plants and Get Army and Industrial Pay

Special to THE NEW YORK TIMES.

WASHINGTON, Dec. 15—As Selective Service headquarters announced today that a much larger proportion of older men would be inducted after Feb. 1, War Department officials disclosed that 4,700 soldiers had been furloughed to work in critical war industries until "civilian workers come forward to fill vacant jobs."

The order for the drafting of older men said that the estimates of the men to be available after Feb. 1 indicated that the armed forces could not be kept substantially filled "from men ages ... through 25 ..."

Finns' Debt Payment Held Up by Treasury

By The Associated Press.

WASHINGTON, Dec. 15—Finland offered today to pay her $235,445 war debt installment, but apparently it will not be accepted.

The Treasury Department, which would have to grant a license before Finland could use part of her frozen funds to pay the installment, said it had asked the State Department for guidance, but a Treasury spokesman said:

"We have received a letter from the State Department which appears on the surface to state a new policy, but the policy is not clear to us. We will have to study it before we can make any statement."

It was understood the State Department felt the Government should accept the payment, even though it had broken off diplomatic relations and officially considers Finland "enemy territory."

DEFERMENT IS SEEN FOR MEAT HOLIDAY

CURZON LINE BASIS

Prime Minister Advises Poles to Cede Area to Moscow Now

OFFERS LAND IN WEST

No U.S. Objection Made, He Says, Calling for Early Big 3 Parley

The text of Mr. Churchill's address is on Page 6.

By RAYMOND DANIELL
By Cable to THE NEW YORK TIMES.

LONDON, Dec. 15—Prime Minister Churchill, exposing in the House of Commons today "the grim, bare bones" of the Polish problem, ranged Britain at Russia's side in her demands for that part of Poland east of the Curzon Line, including Vilna and Lwow.

Britain, like Russia ...

M'ARTHUR STRIKES ANOTHER BLOW IN THE PHILIPPINES

...gh the islands along the course indicated by ...merican troops landed on the southwestern ... and drove a mile inland, meeting scant oppo- ... placed the landing near San José. Carrier ... more enemy aircraft in strikes at Luzon (2). The campaign north of Ormoc on Leyte (3) marked time. It was disclosed Filipino guerrillas had freed all Bohol (4) except the Tagbilaran area, had cleared most of the southern part of Cebu (5) and Negros (7), had seized four towns on Panay (6) and had liberated two provinces on northern Mindanao (8).

FOE IS SURPRIS...

Convoy Goes 600 Mi... Past Japanese Base for Big Advance

ENEMY FLIERS F...

Guerrillas in Offens... Throughout Philippin... With Our Help

By FRANK L. KLUCKHOH...
By Wireless to THE NEW YORK TIMES.

ADVANCED HEADQUARTE... on Leyte, Saturday, Dec. ... American troops were landed w... out the loss of a man on Mind... Island, just 155 miles south... Manila, at 7:30 yesterday morn...

[Domei, Japanese news age... cy, said Friday night in an ove... seas wireless dispatch that abo... one division of ground troo... had begun debarking in the ... cinity of San Jose in the sout... western part of Mindoro. "Ja... anese garrison units intercept... the enemy forces and fighting ... now in progress," said the d... patch, which was reported by t... Federal Communications Co... mission. A Tokyo broadcast ... corded by the Blue Network a... a sea and air battle was ragi... off the beachhead.]

In probably the most dar... move yet made in the Pacific, G... Douglas MacArthur by-pa...

FINANCIAL

BANKING DEPARTMENT REPORTS ON ACTIONS

Special to THE NEW YORK TIMES.

ALBANY, Dec. 15—The Continental Bank and Trust Company, 30 Broad Street, New York, has received permission to establish common trust funds under the titles "the first legal common trust fund of the Continental Bank and Trust Company of New York" and "the first discretionary common trust fund of the Continental Bank and Trust Company of New York," the State Banking Department announced today.

The Bankers Trust Company, 16 Wall Street, New York, has received approval of an increase of capital stock from $25,000,000 consisting of 2,500,000 shares valued at $10 each, to $30,000,000 consisting of 3,000,000 shares valued at $10 each.

It was announced that affairs of the Crescent Credit Union of Brooklyn, have been liquidated, and its corporate existence terminated.

By reason of a change in partnership, necessitating a new certificate of Brown Brothers Harriman & Co., 59 Wall Street, New York, to continue in business, the department's approval has been asked for in a verified certificate just filed. The members of the partnership were noted as Thatcher M. Brown, Moreau Delano Brown, Prescott S. Bush, Louis Curtis, W. Averell Harriman, E. Roland Harriman, Stephen Y. Hord, Thomas McCance, Ray Morris, Harold D. Pennington and Knight Woolley.

The Union Banking Corporation, 39 Broadway, New York, has received authority to change its principal place of business to 120 Broadway.

Railway to Change Route

WASHINGTON, Dec. 15 (AP)—

By reason of a change in partnership, necessitating a new certificate of Brown Brothers Harriman & Co., 59 Wall Street, New York, to continue in business, the department's approval has been asked for in a verified certificate just filed. The members of the partnership were noted as Thatcher M. Brown, Moreau Delano Brown, Prescott S. Bush, Louis Curtis, W. Averell Harriman, E. Roland Harriman, Stephen Y. Hord, Thomas McCance, Ray Morris, Harold D. Pennington and Knight Woolley.

The Union Banking Corporation, 39 Broadway, New York, has received authority to change its principal place of business to 120 Broadway.

Page 25 - *New York Times* - December 16, 1944
The public notice of the Union Banking Corporation being taken over by the US Government through the Under Trading with the Enemy Act. No mention that 120 Broadway is the address of the Office of Alien Property Custodian

THE HITLER PROJECT

WEBSTER GRIFFIN TARPLEY AND ANTON CHAITKIN
CHAPTER TWO OF *GEORGE BUSH – THE UNAUTHORIZED BIOGRAPHY* - 1992. USED WITH PERMISSION.

IN OCTOBER 1942, TEN MONTHS AFTER ENTERING WORLD WAR II, America was preparing its first assault against Nazi military forces. Prescott Bush was managing partner of Brown Brothers Harriman. His 18-year-old son George, the future U.S. President, had just begun training to become a naval pilot. On Oct. 20, 1942, the U.S. government ordered the seizure of Nazi German banking operations in New York City which were being conducted by Prescott Bush.

BUSH PROPERTY SEIZED – TRADING WITH THE ENEMY

Under the *Trading with the Enemy Act*, the government took over the **Union Banking Corporation**, in which Bush was a director. The U.S. Alien Property Custodian seized Union Banking Corp.'s stock shares, all of which were owned by Prescott Bush, E. Roland "Bunny" Harriman, three Nazi executives, and two other associates of Bush.[1]

The order seizing the bank "vests" (seizes) "all of the capital stock of Union Banking Corporation, a New York corporation," and names the holders of its shares as:

> "E. Roland Harriman – 3991 shares"
>
> [chairman and director of Union Banking Corp. (UBC); this is "Bunny" Harriman, described by Prescott Bush as a place holder who didn't get much into banking affairs; Prescott managed his personal investments]
>
> "Cornelis Lievense – 4 shares"
>
> [president and director of UBC; New York resident banking functionary for the Nazis]
>
> "Harold D. Pennington – 1 share"
>
> [treasurer and director of UBC; an office manager employed by Bush at Brown Brothers Harriman]

"Ray Morris – 1 share"
[director of UBC; partner of Bush and the Harrimans]

"Prescott S. Bush – 1 share"
[director of UBC, which was co-founded and sponsored by his father-in-law George Walker; senior managing partner for E. Roland Harriman and Averell Harriman]

"H.J. Kouwenhoven – 1 share"
[director of UBC; organized UBC as the emissary of Fritz Thyssen in negotiations with George Walker and Averell Harriman; managing director of UBC's Netherlands affiliate under Nazi occupation; industrial executive in Nazi Germany; director and chief foreign financial executive of the German Steel Trust]

"Johann G. Groeninger – 1 share"
[director of UBC and of its Netherlands affiliate; industrial executive in Nazi Germany]

"all of which shares are held for the benefit of ... members of the Thyssen family, [and] is property of nationals ... of a designated enemy country...."

By Oct. 26, 1942, U.S. troops were under way for North Africa. On Oct. 28, the government issued orders seizing two Nazi front organizations run by the Bush-Harriman bank: the **Holland-American Trading Corporation** and the **Seamless Steel Equipment Corporation.**[2]

U.S. forces landed under fire near Algiers on Nov. 8, 1942; heavy combat raged throughout November. Nazi interests in the **Silesian-American Corporation**, long managed by Prescott Bush and his father-in-law George Herbert Walker, were seized under the Trading with the Enemy Act on Nov. 17, 1942. In this action, the government announced that it was seizing only the Nazi interests, leaving the Nazis' U.S. partners to carry on the business.[3]

These and other actions taken by the U.S. government in wartime were, tragically, too little and too late. President Bush's family had already played a central role in financing and arming Adolf Hitler for his takeover of Germany; in financing and managing the buildup of Nazi war industries for the conquest of Europe and war against the U.S.A.; and in the development of Nazi genocide theories and racial propaganda, with their well-known results.

The facts presented here must be known, and their implications reflected upon, for a proper understanding of President George Herbert Walker Bush and of the danger to mankind that he represents. The President's family fortune was largely a result of the Hitler project. The powerful Anglo-American family associations, which later boosted him into the Central Intelligence Agency and up to the White House, were his father's partners in the Hitler project.

President Franklin Roosevelt's Alien Property Custodian, Leo T. Crowley, signed Vesting Order Number 248 seizing the property of Prescott Bush under the Trading with the Enemy Act. The order, published in obscure government record books and kept out of the news,[4] explained nothing about the Nazis involved; only that the Union Banking Corporation was run for the "Thyssen family" of "Germany and/or Hungary" — "nationals ... of a designated enemy country."

By deciding that Prescott Bush and the other directors of the Union Banking Corp. were legally *front men for the Nazis*, the government avoided the more important historical issue: In what way *were Hitler's Nazis themselves hired, armed and instructed by* the New York and London clique of which Prescott Bush was an executive manager? Let us examine the Harriman-Bush Hitler project from the 1920s until it was partially broken up, to seek an answer for that question.

ORIGIN AND EXTENT OF THE PROJECT

Fritz Thyssen and his business partners are universally recognized as the most important German financiers of Adolf Hitler's takeover of Germany. At the time of the order seizing the Thyssen family's Union Banking Corp., Mr. Fritz Thyssen had already published his famous book, *I Paid Hitler*,[5] admitting that he had financed Adolf Hitler and the Nazi movement since October 1923. Thyssen's role as the leading early backer of Hitler's grab for power in Germany had been noted by U.S. diplomats in Berlin in 1932.[6] The order seizing the Bush-Thyssen bank was curiously quiet and modest about the identity of the perpetrators who had been nailed.

But two weeks before the official order, government investigators had reported secretly that "W. Averell Harriman was in Europe sometime prior to 1924 and at that time became acquainted with Fritz Thyssen, the German industrialist." Harriman and Thyssen agreed to set up a bank for Thyssen in New York. "[C]ertain of [Harriman's] associates would serve as directors ...." Thyssen agent "H. J. Kouwenhoven ... came to the United States ... prior to 1924 for conferences with the Harriman Company in this connection ..."[7]

When exactly was "Harriman in Europe sometime prior to 1924[?]" In fact, he was in Berlin in 1922 to set up the Berlin branch of W.A. Harriman & Co. under George Walker's presidency.

The Union Banking Corporation was established formally in 1924, as a unit in the Manhattan offices of W.A. Harriman & Co., interlocking with the Thyssen-owned *Bank voor Handel en Scheepvaart* (BHS) in the Netherlands. The investigators concluded that "the Union Banking Corporation has since its inception handled funds chiefly supplied to it through the Dutch bank by the Thyssen interests for American investment."

Thus by personal agreement between Averell Harriman and Fritz Thyssen in 1922, W.A. Harriman & Co. (alias Union Banking Corporation) would be transferring funds back and forth between New York and the "Thyssen interests " in Germany. By putting up about $400,000, the Harriman organization would be joint owner and manager of Thyssen's banking operations outside of Germany.

How important was the Nazi enterprise for which President Bush's father was the New York banker?

A 1942 U.S. government investigative report said that Bush's Nazi-front bank was an interlocking concern with the Vereinigte Stahlwerke (United Steel Works Corporation or **German Steel Trust**) led by Fritz Thyssen and his two brothers. After the war, Congressional investigators probed the Thyssen interests, Union Banking Corp. and related Nazi units. The investigation showed that the *Vereinigte Stahlwerke* had produced the following approximate proportions of total German national output:

50.8% of Nazi Germany's pig iron
41.4% of Nazi Germany's universal plate
36.0% of Nazi Germany's heavy plate
38.5% of Nazi Germany's galvanized sheet

45.5% of Nazi Germany's pipes and tubes
22.1% of Nazi Germany's wire
35.0% of Nazi Germany's explosives.[8]

Prescott Bush became vice president of W.A. Harriman & Co. in 1926. That same year, a friend of Harriman and Bush set up a giant new organization for their client Fritz Thyssen, prime sponsor of politician Adolf Hitler. The new **German Steel Trust**, Germany's largest industrial corporation, was organized in 1926 by Wall Street banker Clarence Dillon. Dillon was the old comrade of Prescott Bush's father Sam Bush from the "Merchants of Death" bureau in World War I.

In return for putting up $70 million to create his organization, majority owner Thyssen gave the Dillon Read company two or more representatives on the board of the new Steel Trust.[9]

Thus there is a division of labor: Thyssen's own confidential accounts, for political and related purposes, were run through the Walker-Bush organization; the German Steel Trust did its corporate banking through Dillon Read.

The Walker-Bush firm's banking activities were not just politically neutral money-making ventures which happened to coincide with the aims of German Nazis. All of the firm's European business in those days was organized around anti-democratic political forces.

In 1927, criticism of their support for totalitarianism drew this retort from Bert Walker, written from Kennebunkport to Averell Harriman: "It seems to me that the suggestion in connection with Lord Bearsted's views that we withdraw from Russia smacks somewhat of the impertinent .... I think that we have drawn our line and should hew to it."[10]

Averell Harriman met with Italy's fascist dictator, Benito Mussolini. A representative of the firm subsequently telegraphed good news back to his chief executive Bert Walker: " ... During these last days ... Mussolini ... has examined and approved our c[o]ntract 15 June."[11]

The great financial collapse of 1929-31 shook America, Germany and Britain, weakening all governments. It also made the hard-pressed Prescott Bush even more willing to do whatever was necessary to retain his new place in the world. It was in this crisis that certain Anglo-Americans determined on the installation of a Hitler regime in Germany.

W.A. Harriman & Co., well-positioned for this enterprise and rich in assets from their German and Russian business, merged with the British-American investment house, Brown Brothers, on January 1, 1931. Bert Walker retired to his own G.H. Walker & Co. This left the Harriman brothers, Prescott Bush and Thatcher M. Brown as the senior partners of the new Brown Brothers Harriman firm. (The London, England branch of the Brown family firm continued operating under its historic name — Brown, Shipley.)

Robert A. Lovett also came over as a partner from Brown Brothers. His father, E.H. Harriman's lawyer and railroad chief, had been on the War Industries Board with Prescott's father. Though he remained a partner in Brown Brothers Harriman, the junior Lovett soon replaced his father as chief executive of Union Pacific Railroad.

Brown Brothers had a racial tradition that fitted it well for the Hitler project! American patriots had cursed its name back in U.S. Civil War days. Brown Brothers, with offices in the U.S.A. and in England, had carried on their ships fully 75 percent of the slave cotton from the American South over to British mill owners. Now in 1931, the virtual dictator of world finance, Bank of England Governor Montagu Collet Norman, was a former Brown Brothers partner, whose grandfather had been boss of Brown Brothers during the U.S. Civil War. Montagu Norman was known as the most avid of Hitler's supporters within British ruling circles, and Norman's intimacy with this firm was essential to his management of the Hitler project.

In 1931, while Prescott Bush ran the New York office of Brown Brothers Harriman, Prescott's partner was Montagu Norman's intimate friend Thatcher Brown. The Bank of England chief always stayed at the home of Prescott's partner on his hush-hush trips to New York. Prescott Bush concentrated on the firm's German activities, and Thatcher Brown saw to their business in old England, under the guidance of his mentor Montagu Norman.[12]

HITLER'S LADDER TO POWER

Adolf Hitler became Chancellor of Germany January 30, 1933, and absolute dictator in March 1933, after two years of expensive and violent lobbying and electioneering. Two affiliates of the Bush-Harriman organization played great parts in this criminal undertaking: Thyssen's German Steel Trust and the Hamburg-Amerika Line and several of its executives.[13]

Let us look more closely at the Bush family's German partners.

Fritz Thyssen told Allied interrogators after the war about some of his financial support for the Nazi Party: "In 1930 or 1931 ... I told [Hitler's deputy Rudolph] Hess ... I would arrange a credit for him with a Dutch bank in Rotterdam, the Bank für Handel und Schiff [i.e. Bank voor Handel en Scheepvaart (BHS), the Harriman-Bush affiliate]. I arranged the credit ... he would pay it back in three years .... I chose a Dutch bank because I did not want to be mixed up with German banks in my position, and because I thought it was better to do business with a Dutch bank, and I thought I would have the Nazis a little more in my hands ....

"The credit was about 250-300,000 [gold] marks — about the sum I had given before. The loan has been repaid in part to the Dutch bank, but I think some money is still owing on it ...."[14]

The overall total of Thyssen's political donations and loans to the Nazis was well over a million dollars, including funds he raised from others — in a period of terrible money shortage in Germany.

Friedrich Flick was the major co-owner of the German Steel Trust with Fritz Thyssen, Thyssen's long-time collaborator and occasional competitor. In preparation for the war crimes tribunal at Nuremberg, the U.S. government said that Flick was "one of leading financiers and industrialists who from 1932 contributed large sums to the Nazi Party ... member of 'Circle of Friends' of Himmler who contributed large sums to the SS."[15]

Flick, like Thyssen, financed the Nazis to maintain their private armies called *Schutzstaffel* (S.S. or Black Shirts) and *Sturmabteilung* (S.A., storm troops or Brown Shirts).

The Flick-Harriman partnership was directly supervised by Prescott Bush, President Bush's father, and by George Walker, President Bush's grandfather.

The Harriman-Walker Union Banking Corp. arrangements for the German Steel Trust had made them bankers for Flick and his vast operations in Germany by no later than 1926.

The Harriman Fifteen Corporation (George Walker, president, Prescott Bush and Averell Harriman, sole directors) held a substantial stake in the Silesian Holding Co. at the time of the merger with Brown Brothers, Jan. 1, 1931. This holding correlated to Averell Harriman's chairmanship of the **Consolidated Silesian Steel Corporation**, the American group owning one-third of a complex of steel-making, coal-mining and zinc-mining activities in Germany and Poland, in which Friedrich Flick owned two-thirds.[16]

The Nuremberg prosecutor characterized Flick as follows:

"Proprietor and head of a large group of industrial enterprises (coal and iron mines, steel producing and fabricating plants) ... '*Wehrwirtschaftsfuhrer*', 1938 [title awarded to prominent industrialists for merit in armaments drive —'Military Economy Leader'] ... [17]

For this buildup of the Hitler war machine with coal, steel and arms production, using slave laborers, the Nazi Flick was condemned to seven years in prison at the Nuremberg trials; he served three years. With friends in New York and London, however, Flick lived into the 1970s and died a billionaire.

On March 19, 1934, Prescott Bush — then director of the German Steel Trust's Union Banking Corporation — initiated an alert to the absent Averell Harriman about a problem which had developed in the Flick partnership.[18] Bush sent Harriman a clipping from the *New York Times* of that day, which reported that the Polish government was fighting back against American and German stockholders who controlled "Poland's largest industrial unit, the Upper Silesian Coal and Steel Company ..."

The *Times* article continued: "The company has long been accused of mismanagement, excessive borrowing, fictitious bookkeeping and gambling in securities. Warrants were issued in December for several directors accused of tax evasions. They were German citizens and they fled. They were replaced by Poles. Herr Flick, regarding this as an attempt to make the company's board entirely Polish, retaliated by restricting credits until the new Polish directors were unable to pay the workmen regularly."

The *Times* noted that the company's mines and mills "employ 25,000 men and account for 45 percent of Poland's total steel output and 12 percent of her coal production. Two-thirds of the company's stock is owned by Friedrich Flick, a leading German steel industrialist, and the remainder is owned by interests in the United States."

In view of the fact that a great deal of Polish output was being exported to Hitler Germany under depression conditions, the Polish government thought that Prescott Bush, Harriman and their Nazi partners should at least pay full taxes on their Polish holdings. The U.S. and Nazi owners responded with a lockout. The letter to Harriman in Washington reported a cable from their European representative: "Have undertaken new steps London Berlin ... please establish friendly relations with Polish Ambassador [in Washington]."

A 1935 Harriman Fifteen Corporation memo from George Walker announced an agreement had been made "in Berlin" to sell an 8,000 block of their shares in Consolidated Silesian Steel.[19] But the dispute with Poland did not deter the Bush family from continuing its partnership with Flick.

Nazi tanks and bombs "settled" this dispute in September, 1939 with the invasion of Poland, beginning World War II. The Nazi army had been equipped by Flick, Harriman, Walker and Bush, with materials essentially stolen from Poland.

There were probably few people at the time who could appreciate the irony that when the Soviets also attacked and invaded Poland from the East, their vehicles were fueled by oil pumped from Baku wells revived by the Harriman/Walker/Bush enterprise.

Three years later, nearly a year after the Japanese attack on Pearl Harbor, the U.S. government ordered the seizure of the Nazis' share in the Silesian-American Corporation under the Trading with the Enemy Act. Enemy nationals were said to own 49 percent of the common stock and 41.67 percent of the preferred stock of the company.

The order characterized the company as a "business enterprise within the United States, owned by [a front company in] Zurich, Switzerland, and held for the benefit of Bergwerksgesellschaft George von Giesche's Erben, a German corporation ...."[20]

Bert Walker was still the senior director of the company, which he had founded back in 1926 simultaneously with the creation of the German Steel Trust. Ray Morris, Prescott's partner from Union Banking Corp. and Brown Brothers Harriman, was also a director.

The investigative report prior to the government crackdown explained the "NATURE OF BUSINESS: The subject corporation is an American holding company for German and Polish subsidiaries, which own large and valuable coal and zinc mines in Silesia, Poland and Germany. Since September 1939, these properties have been in the possession of and have been operated by the German government and have undoubtedly been of considerable assistance to that country in its war effort."[21]

The report noted that the American stockholders hoped to regain control of the European properties after the war.

CONTROL OF NAZI COMMERCE

Bert Walker had arranged the credits Harriman needed to take control of the Hamburg-Amerika Line back in 1920. Walker had organized the **American Ship and Commerce Corp.** as a unit of the W.A. Harriman & Co., with contractual power over Hamburg-Amerika's affairs.

As the Hitler project went into high gear, Harriman-Bush shares in American Ship and Commerce Corp. were held by the Harriman Fifteen Corp., run by Prescott Bush and Bert Walker.[22]

It was a convenient stroll for the well-tanned, athletic, handsome Prescott Bush. From the Brown Brothers Harriman skyscraper at 59 Wall Street — where he was senior managing partner, confidential investments manager and adviser to Averell and his brother "Bunny" — he walked across to the Harriman Fifteen Corporation at One Wall Street, otherwise known as G.H. Walker & Co. — and around the corner to his subsidiary offices at 39 Broadway, former home of the old W.A. Harriman & Co., and still the offices for American Ship and Commerce Corp., and of the Union Banking Corporation.

In many ways, Bush's Hamburg-Amerika Line was the pivot for the entire Hitler project.

Averell Harriman and Bert Walker had gained control over the steamship company in 1920 in negotiations with its post-World War I chief executive, **Wilhelm Cuno**, and with the line's bankers, M.M. Warburg. Cuno was thereafter completely dependent on the Anglo-Americans, and became a member of the Anglo-German Friendship Society. In the 1930-32 drive for a Hitler dictatorship, Wilhelm Cuno contributed important sums to the Nazi Party.[23]

Albert Voegler was chief executive of the Thyssen-Flick German Steel Trust for which Bush's Union Banking Corp. was the New York office. He was a director of the Bush-affiliate BHS Bank in Rotterdam, and a director of the Harriman-Bush Hamburg-Amerika Line. Voegler joined Thyssen and Flick in their heavy 1930-33 Nazi contributions, and helped organize the final Nazi leap into national power.[24]

The **Schroeder** family of bankers was a linchpin for the Nazi activities of Harriman and Prescott Bush, closely tied to their lawyers Allen and John Foster Dulles.

Baron Kurt von Schroeder was co-director of the massive Thyssen-Hütte foundry along with Johann Groeninger, Prescott Bush's New York bank partner. Kurt von Schroeder was treasurer of the support organization for the Nazi Party's private armies, to which Friedrich Flick contributed. Kurt von Schroeder and Montagu Norman's protégé Hjalmar Schacht together made the final arrangements for Hitler to enter the government.[25]

Baron Rudolph von Schroeder was vice president and director of the Hamburg-Amerika Line. Long an intimate contact of Averell Harriman's in Germany, Baron Rudolph sent his grandson Baron Johann Rudolph for a tour of Prescott Bush's Brown Brothers Harriman offices in New York City in December 1932 — on the eve of their Hitler — triumph.[26]

Certain actions taken directly by the Harriman-Bush shipping line in 1932 must be ranked among the gravest acts of treason in this century.

The U.S. embassy in Berlin reported back to Washington that the "costly election campaigns" and "the cost of maintaining a private army of 300,000 to 400,000 men" had raised questions as to the Nazis' financial backers. The constitutional government of the German republic moved to defend national freedom by ordering the Nazi Party private armies disbanded. The U.S. embassy reported that the **Hamburg-Amerika Line was purchasing and distributing propaganda attacks against the German government, for attempting this last-minute crackdown on Hitler's forces.**[27]

Thousands of German opponents of Hitlerism were shot or intimidated by privately armed Nazi Brown Shirts. In this connection we note that the original "Merchant of Death," Samuel Pryor, was a founding director of both the Union Banking Corp. and the American Ship and Commerce Corp. Since Mr. Pryor was executive committee chairman of Remington Arms and a central figure in the world's private arms traffic, his use to the Hitler project was enhanced as the Bush family's partner in Nazi Party banking and trans-Atlantic shipping.

The U.S. Senate arms-traffic investigators probed Remington after it was joined in a cartel agreement on explosives to the Nazi firm I.G. Farben. Looking at the period leading up to Hitler's seizure of power, the Senators found that "German political associations, like the Nazi and others, are nearly all armed with American ... guns... . Arms of all kinds coming from America are transshipped in the Scheldt to river barges before the vessels arrive in Antwerp. They then can be carried through Holland without police inspection or interference. The Hitlerists and Communists are presumed to get arms in this manner. The principal arms coming from America are Thompson submachine guns and revolvers. The number is great."[28]

The beginning of the Hitler regime brought some bizarre changes to the Hamburg-Amerika Line — and more betrayals.

Prescott Bush's American Ship and Commerce Corp. notified Max Warburg of Hamburg, Germany, on March 7, 1933, that Warburg was to be the corporation's official, designated representative on the board of Hamburg-Amerika.[29]

Max Warburg replied on March 27, 1933, assuring his American sponsors that the Hitler government was good for Germany: "For the last few years business was considerably better than we had anticipated, but a reaction is making itself felt for some months. We are actually suffering also under the very active propaganda against Germany, caused by some unpleasant circumstances. These occurrences were the natural consequence of the very excited election campaign, but were extraordinarily exaggerated in the foreign press. The Government is firmly resolved to maintain public peace and order in Germany, and I feel perfectly convinced in this respect that there is no cause for any alarm whatsoever."[30]

This seal of approval for Hitler, coming from a famous Jew, was just what Harriman and Bush required, for they anticipated rather serious "alarm" inside the U.S.A. against their Nazi operations.

On March 29, 1933, two days after Max's letter to Harriman, Max's son, Erich Warburg, sent a cable to his cousin Frederick M. Warburg, a director of the Harriman railroad system. He asked Frederick to "use all your influence" to stop all anti-Nazi activity in America, including "atrocity news and unfriendly propaganda in foreign press, mass meetings, etc." Frederick cabled back to Erich: "No responsible groups here [are] urging [a] boycott [of] German goods[,] merely excited individuals." Two days after that, On March 31, 1933, the **American-Jewish Committee**, controlled by the Warburgs, and the **B'nai B'rith**, heavily influenced by the Sulzbergers (New York Times), issued a formal, official joint statement of the two organizations, counseling "that no American boycott against Germany be encouraged," and advising "that no further mass meetings be held or similar forms of agitation be employed."[31]

The American Jewish Committee and the B'nai B'rith (mother of the "Anti-Defamation League") continued with this hardline, no-attack-on-Hitler stance all through the 1930s, blunting the fight mounted by many Jews and other anti-fascists.

Thus the decisive interchange reproduced above, taking place entirely within the orbit of the Harriman/Bush firm, may explain something of the relationship of George Bush to American Jewish and Zionist leaders. Some of them, in close cooperation with his family, played an ugly part in the drama of Naziism. Is this why "professional Nazi-hunters" have never discovered how the Bush family made its money?

The executive board of the **Hamburg Amerika Line** (Hapag) met jointly with the North German Lloyd Company board in Hamburg on Sept. 5, 1933. Under official Nazi supervision, the two firms were merged. Prescott Bush's American Ship and Commerce Corp. installed Christian J. Beck, a long-time Harriman executive, as manager of freight and operations in North America for the new joint Nazi shipping lines (**Hapag-Lloyd**) on Nov. 4, 1933.

According to testimony of officials of the companies before Congress in 1934, a supervisor from the **Nazi Labor Front** rode with every ship of the Harriman-Bush line; employees of the New York offices were directly organized into the Nazi Labor Front organization; Hamburg-Amerika provided free passage to individuals going abroad for Nazi propaganda purposes; and the line subsidized pro-Nazi newspapers in the U.S.A., as it had done in Germany against the constitutional German government.[32]

In mid-1936, Prescott Bush's American Ship and Commerce Corp. cabled M.M. Warburg, asking Warburg to represent the company's heavy share interest at the forthcoming Hamburg-Amerika stockholders meeting. The Warburg office replied with the information that "we represented you" at the stockholders meeting and "exercised on your behalf your voting power for Rm [gold marks] 3,509,600 Hapag stock deposited with us."

The Warburgs transmitted a letter received from Emil Helfferich, German chief executive of both Hapag-Lloyd and of the Standard Oil subsidiary in Nazi Germany: "It is the intention to continue the relations with Mr. Harriman on the same basis as heretofore .... In a colorful gesture, Hapag's Nazi chairman Helfferich sent the line's president across the Atlantic on a Zeppelin to confer with their New York string-pullers.

After the meeting with the Zeppelin passenger, the Harriman-Bush office replied: "I am glad to learn that Mr. Hellferich [sic] has stated that relations between the Hamburg American Line and ourselves will be continued on the same basis as heretofore."[33]

Two months before moving against Prescott Bush's Union Banking Corporation, the U. S. government ordered the seizure of all property of the Hamburg-Amerika Line and North German Lloyd, under the Trading with the Enemy Act. The investigators noted in the pre-seizure report that Christian J. Beck was still acting as an attorney representing the Nazi firm.[34]

In May 1933, just after the Hitler regime was consolidated, an agreement was reached in Berlin for the coordination of all Nazi commerce with the U.S.A. The **Harriman International Co.**, led by Averell Harriman's first cousin Oliver, was to head a syndicate of 150 firms and individuals, to conduct *all exports from Hitler Germany to the United States.*[35]

This pact had been negotiated in Berlin between Hitler's economics minister, Hjalmar Schacht, and John Foster Dulles, international attorney for dozens of Nazi enterprises, with the counsel of Max Warburg and Kurt von Schroeder.

John Foster Dulles would later be U.S. Secretary of State, and the great power in the Republican Party of the 1950s. Foster's friendship and that of his brother Allen (head of the Central Intelligence Agency), greatly aided Prescott Bush to become the Republican U.S. Senator from Connecticut. And it was to be of inestimable value to George Bush, in his ascent to the heights of "covert action government," that both of these Dulles brothers were the lawyers for the Bush family's far-flung enterprise.

Throughout the 1930s, John Foster Dulles arranged debt restructuring for German firms under a series of decrees issued by Adolf Hitler. In these deals, Dulles struck a balance between the interest owed to selected, larger investors, and the needs of the growing Nazi war-making apparatus for producing tanks, poison gas, etc.

Dulles wrote to Prescott Bush in 1937 concerning one such arrangement. The German-Atlantic Cable Company, owning Nazi Germany's only telegraph channel to the United States, had made debt and management agreements with the Walker-Harriman bank during the 1920s. A new decree would now void those agreements, which had originally been reached with non-Nazi corporate officials. Dulles asked Bush, who managed these affairs for Averell Harriman, to get Averell's signature on a letter to Nazi officials, agreeing to the changes. Dulles wrote:

> Sept. 22, 1937
> Mr. Prescott S. Bush
> 59 Wall Street, New York, N.Y.
> Dear Press,
>
> I have looked over the letter of the German-American [sic] Cable Company to Averell Harriman .... It would appear that the only rights in the matter are those which inure in the bankers and that no legal embarrassment would result, so far as the bondholders are concerned, by your acquiescence in the modification of the bankers' agreement.
>
> Sincerely yours,
>
> John Foster Dulles

Dulles enclosed a proposed draft reply, Bush got Harriman's signature, and the changes went through.[36]

In conjunction with these arrangements, the German Atlantic Cable Company attempted to stop payment on its debts to smaller American bondholders. The money was to be used instead for arming the Nazi state, under a decree of the Hitler government.

Despite the busy efforts of Bush and Dulles, a New York court decided that this particular Hitler "law" was invalid in the United States; small bondholders, not parties to deals between the bankers and the Nazis, were entitled to get paid.[37]

In this and a few other of the attempted swindles, the intended victims came out with their money. But the Nazi financial and political reorganization went ahead to its tragic climax.

For his part in the Hitler revolution, Prescott Bush was paid a fortune.

This is the legacy he left to his son, President George Bush.

AN IMPORTANT HISTORICAL NOTE: HOW THE HARRIMANS HIRED HITLER

IT WAS NOT INEVITABLE that millions would be slaughtered under fascism and in World War II. At certain moments of crisis, crucial pro-Nazi decisions were made outside of Germany. These decisions for pro-Nazi actions were more aggressive than the mere "appeasement" which Anglo-American historians later preferred to discuss.

Private armies of 300,000 to 400,000 terrorists aided the Nazis' rise to power. W.A. Harriman's Hamburg-Amerika Line intervened against Germany's 1932 attempt to break them up.

The 1929-31 economic collapse bankrupted the Wall-Street-backed German Steel Trust. When the German government took over the Trust's stock shares, interests associated with Konrad Adenauer and the anti-Nazi Catholic Center Party attempted to acquire the shares. But the Anglo-Americans — Montagu Norman, and the Harriman-Bush bank — made sure that their Nazi puppet Fritz Thyssen regained control over the shares and the Trust. Thyssen's bankrolling of Hitler could then continue unhindered.

Unpayable debts crushed Germany in the 1920s, reparations required by the Versailles agreements. Germany was looted by the London-New York banking system, and Hitler's propaganda exploited this German debt burden.

But immediately *after* Germany came under Hitler's dictatorship, the Anglo-American financiers granted debt relief, which freed funds to be used for arming the Nazi state.

The North German Lloyd steamship line, which was merged with Hamburg-Amerika Line, was one of the companies which stopped debt payments under a Hitler decree arranged by John Foster Dulles and Hjalmar Schacht.

Kuhn Loeb and Co.'s Felix Warburg carried out the Hitler finance plan in New York. Kuhn Loeb asked North German Lloyd bondholders to accept new lower interest steamship bonds, issued by Kuhn Loeb, in place of the better pre-Hitler bonds.

New York attorney Jacob Chaitkin, father of coauthor Anton Chaitkin, took the cases of many different bondholders who rejected the swindle by Harriman, Bush, Warburg, and Hitler. Representing a women who was owed $30 on an old steamship bond — and opposing John Foster Dulles in New York municipal court — Chaitkin threatened a writ from the sheriff, tying up the 30,000 ton transatlantic liner *Europa* until the client received her $30. (*New York Times*, January 10, 1934, p. 31 col. 3).

The American Jewish Congress hired Jacob Chaitkin as the legal director of the boycott against Nazi Germany. The American Federation of Labor cooperated with Jewish and other groups in the anti-import boycott. On the other side, virtually all the Nazi trade with the United States was under the supervision of the Harriman interests and functionaries such as Prescott Bush, father of President George Bush.

Meanwhile, the Warburgs demanded that American Jews not "agitate" against the Hitler government, or join the organized boycott. The Warburgs' decision was carried out by the American Jewish Committee and the B'nai B'rith, who opposed the boycott as the Nazi military state grew increasingly powerful.

The historical cover-up on these events is so tight that virtually the only exposé of the Warburgs came in journalist John L. Spivak's "Wall Street's Fascist Conspiracy," in the pro-communist *New Masses* periodical (Jan. 29 and Feb. 5, 1934). Spivak pointed out that the Warburgs controlled the American Jewish Committee, which opposed the anti-Nazi boycott, while their Kuhn Loeb and Co. had underwritten Nazi shipping; and he exposed the financing of pro-fascist political activities by the Warburgs and their partners and allies, many of whom were bigwigs in the American Jewish Committee and B'nai B'rith.

Given where the Spivak piece appeared, it is not surprising that Spivak called Warburg an ally of the Morgan Bank, but made no mention of Averell Harriman. Mr. Harriman, after all, was a permanent hero of the Soviet Union.

John L. Spivak later underwent a curious transformation, himself joining the cover-up. In 1967, he wrote an autobiography (*A Man in His Time*, New York: Horizon Press), which praises the American Jewish Committee. The pro-fascism of the Warburgs does not appear in the book. The former "rebel " Spivak also praises the action arm of the B'nai B'rith, the Anti-Defamation League. Pathetically, he comments favorably that the League has spy files on the American populace which it shares with government agencies.

Thus is history erased; and those decisions, which direct history into one course or another, are lost to the knowledge of the current generation.

NOTES

1. Office of Alien Property Custodian, Vesting Order No. 248. The order was signed by Leo T. Crowley, Alien Property Custodian, executed October 20, 1942; F.R. Doc. 42-11568; Filed, November 6, 1942, 11:31 A.M.; 7 Fed. Reg. 9097 (Nov. 7, 1942). See also the *New York City Directory of Directors* (available at the Library of Congress). The volumes for the 1930s and 1940s list Prescott Bush as a director of Union Banking Corporation for the years 1934 through 1943.
2. Alien Property Custodian Vesting Order No. 259: Seamless Steel Equipment Corporation; Vesting Order No. 261: Holland-American Trading Corp.
3. Alien Property Custodian Vesting Order No. 370: Silesian-American Corp.
4. The *New York Times* on December 16, 1944, ran a five-paragraph page 25 article on actions of the New York State Banking Department. Only the last sentence refers to the Nazi bank, as follows: `` The Union Banking Corporation, 39 Broadway, New York, has received authority to change its principal place of business to 120 Broadway."
   The *Times* omitted the fact that the Union Banking Corporation had been seized by the government for trading with the enemy, and even the fact that 120 Broadway was the address of the government's Alien Property Custodian.
5. Fritz Thyssen, *I Paid Hitler*, 1941, reprinted in (Port Washington, N.Y.: Kennikat Press, 1972), p. 133. Thyssen says his contributions began with 100,000 marks given in October 1923, for Hitler's attempted "putsch" against the constitutional government.
6 Confidential memorandum from U.S. embassy, Berlin, to the U.S. Secretary of State, April 20, 1932, on microfilm in *Confidential Reports of U.S. State Dept.*, 1930s, *Germany*, at major U.S. libraries.
7. Oct. 5, 1942, Memorandum to the Executive Committee of the Office of Alien Property Custodian, stamped CONFIDENTIAL, from the Division of Investigation and Research, Homer Jones, Chief. Now declassified in United States National Archives, Suitland, Maryland annex. See Record Group 131, Alien Property Custodian, investigative reports, in file box relating to Vesting Order No. 248.
8. *Elimination of German Resources for War:* Hearings Before a Subcommittee of the Committee on Military Affairs, United States Senate, Seventy-Ninth Congress; Part 5, Testimony of [the United States] Treasury Department, July 2, 1945. P. 507: Table of Vereinigte Stahlwerke output, figures are percent of German total as of 1938; Thyssen organization including Union Banking Corporation pp. 727-31.
9. Robert Sobel, *The Life and Times of Dillon Read* (New York: Dutton-Penguin, 1991), pp. 92-111. The

Dillon Read firm cooperated in the development of Sobel's book.

10. George Walker to Averell Harriman, Aug. 11, 1927, in the W. Averell Harriman papers at the Library of Congress (designated hereafter WAH papers).
11. "Iaccarino"to G. H. Walker, RCA Radiogram Sept. 12, 1927. The specific nature of their business with Mussolini is not explained in correspondence available for public access.
12. Andrew Boyle, *Montagu Norman* (London: Cassell, 1967).
    Sir Henry Clay, *Lord Norman* (London, MacMillan & Co., 1957), pp. 18, 57, 70-71.
    John A. Kouwenhouven, *Partners in Banking ... Brown Brothers Harriman* (Garden City: Doubleday & Co., 1969).
13. Coordination of much of the Hitler project took place at a single New York address. The Union Banking Corporation had been set up by George Walker at 39 Broadway. Management of the Hamburg-Amerika Line, carried out through Harriman's American Ship and Commerce Corp., was also set up by George Walker at 39 Broadway.
14. Interrogation of Fritz Thyssen, EF/Me/1 of Sept. 4, 1945 in U.S. Control Council records, photostat on page 167 in Anthony Sutton, *An Introduction to The Order* (Billings, Mt.: Liberty House Press, 1986).
15. *Nazi Conspiracy and Aggression—Supplement B,* by the Office of United States Chief of Counsel for Prosecution of Axis Criminality, United States Government Printing Office, (Washington: 1948), pp. 1597, 1686.
16. "Consolidated Silesian Steel Corporation - [minutes of the] Meeting of Board of Directors," Oct. 31, 1930 (Harriman papers, Library of Congress), shows Averell Harriman as Chairman of the Board.
    Prescott Bush to W.A. Harriman, Memorandum Dec. 19, 1930 on their Harriman Fifteen Corp.
    Annual Report of United Konigs and Laura Steel and Iron Works for the year 1930 (Harriman papers, Library of Congress) lists "Dr. Friedrich Flick ... Berlin" and "William Averell Harriman ... New York " on the Board of Directors.
    "Harriman Fifteen Corporation Securities Position February 28, 1931," Harriman papers, Library of Congress. This report shows Harriman Fifteen Corporation holding 32,576 shares in Silesian Holding Co. V.T.C. worth (in scarce depression dollars) $1,628,800, just over half the value of the Harriman Fifteen Corporation's total holdings.
    The New York City Directory of Directors volumes for the 1930s (available at the Library of Congress) show Prescott Sheldon Bush and W. Averell Harriman as the directors of Harriman Fifteen Corp.
    "Appointments," (three typed pages) marked "Noted May 18 1931 W.A.H.," (among the papers from Prescott Bush's New York Office of Brown Brothers Harriman, Harriman papers, Library of Congress), lists a meeting between Averell Harriman and Friedrich Flick in Berlin at 4:00 P.M., Wednesday April 22, 1931. This was followed immediately by a meeting with Wilhelm Cuno, chief executive of the Hamburg-Amerika Line.
    The "Report To the Stockholders of the Harriman Fifteen Corporation," Oct. 19, 1933 (in the Harriman papers, Library of Congress) names G.H. Walker as president of the corporation. It shows the Harriman Fifteen Corporation's address as 1 Wall Street — the location of G.H. Walker and Co.
17. *Nazi Conspiracy and Aggression--Supplement B, op. cit.*, p. 1686.
18. Jim Flaherty (a BBH manager, Prescott Bush's employee), March 19, 1934 to W.A. Harriman.
    "Dear Averell:
    In Roland's absence Pres[cott] thought it advisable for me to let you know that we received the following cable from [our European representative] Rossi dated March 17th [relating to conflict with the Polish government] ...."
19. Harriman Fifteen Corporation notice to stockholders Jan. 7, 1935, under the name of George Walker, President.
20. Order No. 370: Silesian-American Corp. Executed Nov. 17, 1942. Signed by Leo T. Crowley, Alien Property Custodian. F.R. Doc. 42-14183; Filed Dec. 31, 1942, 11:28 A.M.; 8 Fed. Reg. 33 (Jan. 1, 1943).
    The order confiscated the Nazis' holdings of 98,000 shares of common and 50,000 shares of preferred stock in Silesian-American.
    The Nazi parent company in Breslau, Germany wrote directly to Averell Harriman at 59 Wall St. on Aug. 5, 1940, with "an invitation to take part in the regular meeting of the members of the Bergwerksgesellsc[h]aft Georg von Giesche's Erben ...." WAH papers.

21. Sept. 25, 1942, Memorandum To the Executive Committee of the Office of Alien Property Custodian, stamped CONFIDENTIAL, from the Division of Investigation and Research, Homer Jones, Chief. Now declassified in United States National Archives, Suitland, Maryland annex. See Record Group 131, Alien Property Custodian, investigative reports, in file box relating to Vesting Order No. 370.
22. George Walker was a director of American Ship and Commerce from its organization through 1928. Consult *New York City Directory of Directors.*
    "Harriman Fifteen Corporation Securities Position February 28, 1931," *op. cit.* The report lists 46,861 shares in the American Ship & Commerce Corp.
    See "Message from Mr. Bullfin," Aug. 30, 1934 (Harriman Fifteen section, Harriman papers, Library of Congress) for the joint supervision of Bush and Walker, respectively director and president of the corporation.
23. Cuno was later exposed by Walter Funk, Third Reich Press Chief and Under Secretary of Propaganda, in Funk's postwar jail cell at Nuremberg; but Cuno had died just as Hitler was taking power. William L. Shirer, *The Rise and Fall of the Third Reich* (New York: Simon and Schuster, 1960), p. 144. *Nazi Conspiracy and Aggression — Supplement B, op. cit.*, p. 1688.
24. See "Elimination of German Resources for War," *op. cit.*, pp. 881-82 on Voegler.
    See Annual Report of the (Hamburg-Amerikanische-Packetfahrt-Aktien-Gesellschaft (Hapag or Hamburg-Amerika Line), March 1931, for the board of directors. A copy is in the New York Public Library Annex at 11th Avenue, Manhattan.
25. *Nazi Conspiracy and Aggression--Supplement B, op. cit.*, pp. 1178, 1453-54, 1597, 1599.
    See "Elimination of German Resources for War," *op. cit.*, pp. 870-72 on Schroeder; p. 730 on Groeninger.
26. Annual Report of Hamburg-Amerika, *op. cit.*
    Baron Rudolph Schroeder, Sr. to Averell Harriman, Nov. 14, 1932. K[night] W[ooley] handwritten note and draft reply letter, Dec. 9, 1932.
    In his letter, Baron Rudolph refers to the family's American affiliate, J. Henry Schroder [name anglicized], of which Allen Dulles was a director, and his brother John Foster Dulles was the principal attorney.
    Baron Bruno Schroder of the British branch was adviser to Bank of England Governor Montagu Norman, and Baron Bruno's partner Frank Cyril Tiarks was Norman's co-director of the Bank of England throughout Norman's career. Kurt von Schroeder was Hjalmar Schacht's delegate to the Bank for International Settlements in Geneva, where many of the financial arrangements for the Nazi regime were made by Montagu Norman, Schacht and the Schroeders for several years of the Hitler regime right up to the outbreak of World War II.
27. Confidential memorandum from U.S. embassy, Berlin, *op. cit.*
28. U.S. Senate "Nye Committee " hearings, Sept. 14, 1934, pp. 1197-98, extracts from letters of Col. William N. Taylor, dated June 27, 1932 and Jan. 9, 1933.
29. American Ship and Commerce Corporation to Dr. Max Warburg, March 7, 1933.
    Max Warburg had brokered the sale of Hamburg-Amerika to Harriman and Walker in 1920. Max's brothers controlled the Kuhn Loeb investment banking house in New York, the firm which had staked old E.H. Harriman to his 1890s buyout of the giant Union Pacific Railroad.
    Max Warburg had long worked with Lord Milner and others of the racialist British Round Table concerning joint projects in Africa and Eastern Europe. He was an advisor to Hjalmar Schacht for several decades and was a top executive of Hitler's Reichsbank. The reader may consult David Farrer, *The Warburgs: The Story of A Family* (New York: Stein and Day, 1975).
30. Max Warburg, at M.M. Warburg and Co., Hamburg, to Averill [sic] Harriman, c/o Messrs. Brown Brothers Harriman & Co., 59 Wall Street, New York, N.Y., March 27, 1933.
31. This correspondence, and the joint statement of the Jewish organizations, are reproduced in Moshe R. Gottlieb, *American Anti-Nazi Resistance, 1933-41: An Historical Analysis* (New York: Ktav Publishing House, 1982).
32. *Investigation of Nazi Propaganda Activities and Investigation of Certain Other Propaganda Activities:* Public Hearings before A Subcommittee of the Special Committee on Un-American Activities, United States House of Representatives, Seventy Third Congress, New York City, July 9-12, 1934—Hearings No. 73-NY-7 (Washington: U.S. Govt. Printing Office, 1934). See testimony of Capt. Frederick C. Mensing, John Schroeder, Paul von Lilienfeld-Toal, and summaries by Committee members.
    See *New York Times*, July 16, 1933, p. 12, for organizing of Nazi Labor Front at North German Lloyd, leading to Hamburg-Amerika after merger.

33. American Ship and Commerce Corporation telegram to Rudolph Brinckmann at M.M. Warburg, June 12, 1936.
    Rudolph Brinckmann to Averell Harriman at 59 Wall St., June 20, 1936, with enclosed note transmitting Helfferich's letter.
    Reply to Dr. Rudolph Brinckmann c/o M.M. Warburg and Co, July 6, 1936, in the Harriman papers at the Library of Congress. The file copy of this letter carries no signature, but is presumably from Averell Harriman.
34. Office of Alien Property Custodian, Vesting Order No. 126. Signed by Leo T. Crowley, Alien Property Custodian, executed August 28, 1942. F.R. Doc. 42-8774; Filed September 4, 1942, 10:55 A.M.; 7 F.R. 7061 (No. 176, Sept. 5, 1942.) July 18, 1942, Memorandum To the Executive Committee of the Office of Alien Property Custodian, stamped CONFIDENTIAL, from the Division of Investigation and Research, Homer Jones, Chief. Now declassified in United States National Archives, Suitland, Maryland annex. See Record Group 131, Alien Property Custodian, investigative reports, in file box relating to Vesting Order No. 126.
35. *New York Times*, May 20, 1933. Leading up to this agreement is a telegram which somehow escaped the shredder and may be seen in the Harriman papers in the Library of Congress. It is addressed to Nazi official Hjalmar Schacht at the Mayflower Hotel, Washington, dated May 11, 1933: "Much disappointed to have missed seeing you Tuesday afternoon .... I hope to see you either in Washington or New York before you sail.
    with my regards W.A. Harriman"
36. Dulles to Bush letter and draft reply in WAH papers.
37. *New York Times*, January 19, 1958

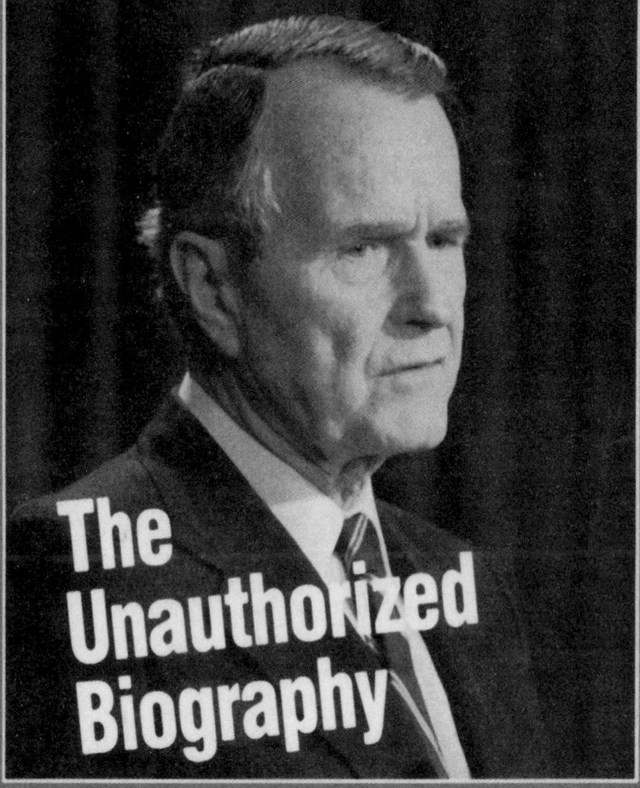

FIVE CHAPTERS here are from the very well researched, and very much ignored by the mainstream Media, *George Bush: The Unauthorized Biography* by Webster Griffin Tarpley and Anton Chaitkin. The 659-page book is hard to find and sell for $175 to $250 a copy.
The complete text is available online courtesy the authors at www.tarpley.net/bushb.htm

Race Hygiene: Three Bush Family Alliances

Webster Griffin Tarpley and Anton Chaitkin

Chapter Three of *George Bush – The Unauthorized Biography* - 1992. Used with permission.

"The [government] must put the most modern medical means in the service of this knowledge... Those who are physically and mentally unhealthy and unworthy must not perpetuate their suffering in the body of their children... The prevention of the faculty and opportunity to procreate on the part of the physically degenerate and mentally sick, over a period of only 600 years, would ... free humanity from an immeasurable misfortune."

"The per capita income gap between the developed and the developing countries is increasing, in large part the result of higher birth rates in the poorer countries... Famine in India, unwanted babies in the United States, poverty that seemed to form an unbreakable chain for millions of people — how should we tackle these problems?... It is quite clear that one of the major challenges of the 1970s ... will be to curb the world's fertility."

These two quotations are alike in their mock show of concern for human suffering, and in their cynical remedy for it: Big Brother must prevent the "unworthy" or "unwanted" people from living.

Let us now further inquire into the family background of our President, so as to help illustrate how the second quoted author, **George Bush**[1], came to share the outlook of the first, **Adolf Hitler**[2].

We shall examine here the alliance of the Bush family with three other families: **Farish**, **Draper** and **Gray**.

The private associations among these families have led to the President's relationship to his closest, most confidential advisers. These alliances were forged in the earlier Hitler project and its immediate aftermath. Understanding them will help us to explain George Bush's obsession with the supposed overpopulation of the world's non-Anglo-Saxons, and the dangerous means he has adopted to deal with this "problem."

Bush and Farish

When George Bush was elected Vice President in 1980, Texas mystery man William ("Will") Stamps Farish III took over management of all of George Bush's personal wealth in a "blind trust." Known as one of the richest men in Texas, Will Farish keeps his business affairs under the most intense secrecy. Only the source of his immense wealth is known, not its employment.[3]

Will Farish has long been Bush's closest friend and confidante. He is also the unique private host to Britain's Queen Elizabeth II: Farish owns and boards the studs which mate with the Queen's mares. That is her public rationale when she comes to America and stays in Farish's house. It is a vital link in the mind of our Anglophile President.

President Bush can count on Will Farish not to betray the violent secrets surrounding the Bush family money. For Farish's own family fortune was made in the same Hitler project, in a nightmarish partnership with George Bush's father.

On March 25, 1942, U.S. Assistant Attorney General Thurman Arnold announced that William Stamps Farish (grandfather of the President's money manager) had pled "no contest" to charges of criminal conspiracy with the Nazis. Farish was the principal manager of a worldwide cartel between Standard Oil Co. of New Jersey and the I.G. Farben concern. The merged enterprise had opened the Auschwitz slave labor camp on June 14, 1940, to produce artificial rubber and gasoline from coal. The Hitler government supplied political opponents and Jews as the slaves, who were worked to near death and then murdered.

Arnold disclosed that Standard Oil of N.J. (later known as Exxon), of which Farish was president and chief executive, had agreed to stop hiding from the United States patents for artificial rubber which the company had provided to the Nazis. [4]

A Senate investigating committee under Senator (later U.S. President) Harry Truman of Missouri had called Arnold to testify at hearings on U.S. corporations' collaboration with the Nazis. The Senators expressed outrage at the cynical way Farish was continuing an alliance with the Hitler regime that had begun back in 1933, when Farish became chief of Jersey Standard. Didn't he know there was a war on?

The Justice Department laid before the committee a letter, written to Standard president Farish by his vice president, shortly after the beginning of World War II (Sept. 1, 1939) in Europe. The letter concerned a renewal of their earlier agreements with the Nazis:

> Report on European Trip
> Oct. 12, 1939
> Mr. W.S. Farish
> 30 Rockefeller Plaza
>
> Dear Mr. Farish: ... I stayed in France until Sept. 17th... In England I met by appointment the Royal Dutch [Shell Oil Co.] gentlemen from Holland, and ... a general agreement was reached on the necessary changes in our relations with the I.G. [Farben], in view of the state of war... [T]he Royal Dutch Shell group is essentially British... I also had several meetings with ... the [British] Air Ministry...
>
> I required help to obtain the necessary permission to go to Holland... After discussions with the [American] Ambassador [Joseph Kennedy] ... the situation was cleared completely... The gentlemen in the Air Ministry ... very kindly offered to assist me [later] in reentering England...

> Pursuant to these arrangements, I was able to keep my appointments in Holland [having flown there on a British Royal Air Force bomber], where I had three days of discussion with the representatives of I.G. They delivered to me assignments of some 2,000 foreign patents and *we did our best to work out complete plans for a modus vivendi which could operate through the term of the war, whether or not the U.S. came in...* [emphasis added]
>
> Very truly yours, F[rank] A. Howard[5]

Here are some cold realities behind the tragedy of World War II, which help explain the Bush-Farish family alliance — and their peculiar closeness to the Queen of England:

- Shell Oil is principally owned by the British royal family. Shell's chairman, Sir Henri Deterding, helped sponsor Hitler's rise to power,[6] by arrangement with the royal family's Bank of England Governor, Montagu Norman. Their ally Standard Oil would take part in the Hitler project right up to the bloody, gruesome end.
- When grandfather Farish signed the Justice Department's consent decree in March 1942, the government had already started picking its way through the tangled web of world-monopoly oil and chemical agreements between Standard Oil and the Nazis. Many patents and other Nazi-owned aspects of the partnership had been seized by the U.S. Alien Property Custodian.

Uncle Sam would not seize Prescott Bush's Union Banking Corporation for another seven months.

The Bush-Farish axis had begun back in 1929. In that year the Harriman bank bought Dresser Industries, supplier of oil-pipeline couplers to Standard and other companies. Prescott Bush became a director and financial czar of Dresser, installing his Yale classmate Neil Mahlon as chairman.[7] George Bush would later name one of his sons after the Dresser executive.

William S. Farish was the main organizer of the Humble Oil Co. of Texas, which Farish merged into the Standard Oil Company of New Jersey. Farish built up the Humble-Standard empire of pipelines and refineries in Texas.[8]

The stock market crashed just after the Bush family got into the oil business. The world financial crisis led to the merger of the Walker-Harriman bank with Brown Brothers in 1931. Former Brown partner Montagu Norman and his protégé Hjalmar Schacht paid frantic visits to New York that year and the next, preparing the new Hitler regime for Germany.

The most important American political event in those preparations for Hitler was the infamous "Third International Congress on Eugenics," held at New York's American Museum of Natural History August 21-23, 1932, supervised by the International Federation of Eugenics Societies.[9] This meeting took up the stubborn persistence of African-Americans and other allegedly "inferior" and "socially inadequate" groups in reproducing, expanding their numbers, and amalgamating with others. It was recommended that these "dangers" to the "better" ethnic groups and to the "well-born," could be dealt with by sterilization or "cutting off the bad stock" of the "unfit."

Italy's fascist government sent an official representative. Averell Harriman's sister Mary, director of "Entertainment" for the Congress, lived down in Virginia fox-hunting country; her state supplied the speaker on "racial purity," W.A. Plecker, Virginia commissioner of vital statistics. Plecker reportedly held the delegates spellbound with his account of the struggle to stop race-mixing and inter-racial sex in Virginia.

The Congress proceedings were dedicated to Averell Harriman's mother; she had paid for the founding of the race-science movement in America back in 1910, building the

Eugenics Record Office as a branch of the Galton National Laboratory in London. She and other Harrimans were usually escorted to the horse races by old George Herbert Walker — they shared with the Bushes and the Farishes a fascination with "breeding thoroughbreds" among horses and humans.[10]

Averell Harriman personally arranged with the Walker/Bush Hamburg-Amerika Line to transport Nazi ideologues from Germany to New York for this meeting.[11] The most famous among those transported was Dr. Ernst Rüdin, psychiatrist at the Kaiser Wilhelm Institute for Genealogy and Demography in Berlin, where the Rockefeller family paid for Dr. Rüdin to occupy an entire floor with his eugenics "research." Dr. Rüdin had addressed the International Federation's 1928 Munich meeting, speaking on "Mental Aberration and Race Hygiene," while others (Germans and Americans) spoke on race-mixing and sterilization of the unfit. Rüdin had also led the German delegation to the 1930 Mental Hygiene Congress in Washington, D.C.

At the Harrimans' 1932 New York Eugenics Congress, Ernst Rüdin was unanimously elected president of the International Federation of Eugenics Societies. This was recognition of Rüdin as founder of the German Society for Race Hygiene, with his co-founder, Eugenics Federation vice president Alfred Plötz.

As depression-maddened financiers schemed in Berlin and New York, Rüdin was now official leader of the world eugenics movement. Components of his movement included groups with overlapping leadership, dedicated to:

- sterilization of mental patients ("mental hygiene societies");
- execution of the insane, criminals and the terminally ill ("euthanasia societies"); and
- eugenical race-purification by prevention of births to parents from "inferior" blood stocks ("birth control societies").

Before the Auschwitz death camp became a household word, these British-American-European groups called openly for the elimination of the "unfit" by means including force and violence.[12]

Ten months later, in June 1933, Hitler's interior minister Wilhelm Frick spoke to a eugenics meeting in the new Third Reich. Frick called the Germans a "degenerate" race, denouncing one-fifth of Germany's parents for producing "feeble-minded" and "defective" children. The following month, on a commission by Frick, Dr. Ernst Rüdin wrote the "Law for the Prevention of Hereditary Diseases in Posterity," the sterilization law modeled on previous U.S. statutes in Virginia and other states.

Special courts were soon established for the sterilization of German mental patients, the blind, the deaf and alcoholics. A quarter million people in these categories were sterilized. Rüdin, Plötz and their colleagues trained a whole generation of physicians and psychiatrists — as sterilizers and as killers.

When the war started, the eugenicists, doctors and psychiatrists staffed the new "T4" agency, which planned and supervised the mass killings: first at "euthanasia centers," where the same categories which had first been subject to sterilization were now to be murdered, their brains sent in lots of 200 to experimental psychiatrists; then at slave camps such as Auschwitz; and finally, for Jews and other race victims, at straight extermination camps in Poland, such as Treblinka and Belsen.[13]

In 1933, as what Hitler called his "New Order" appeared, John D. Rockefeller, Jr. appointed William S. Farish the chairman of Standard Oil Co. of New Jersey (in 1937 he was made president and chief executive). Farish moved his offices to Rockefeller Center, New York, where he spent a good deal of time with Hermann Schmitz, chairman of

I.G. Farben; his company paid a publicity man, Ivy Lee, to write pro-I.G. Farben and pro-Nazi propaganda and get it into the U.S. press.

Now that he was outside of Texas, Farish found himself in the shipping business — like the Bush family. He hired Nazi German crews for Standard Oil tankers. And he hired **Emil Helfferich**, chairman of the Walker/Bush/Harriman Hamburg-Amerika Line, as chairman also of the Standard Oil Company subsidiary in Germany. Karl Lindemann, board member of Hamburg-Amerika, also became a top Farish-Standard executive in Germany.[14]

This interlock between their Nazi German operations put Farish together with Prescott Bush in a small, select group of men operating from abroad through Hitler's "revolution," and calculating that they would never be punished.

In 1939, Farish's daughter Martha married Averell Harriman's nephew, Edward Harriman Gerry, and Farish in-laws became Prescott Bush's partners at 59 Broadway.[15]

Both Emil Helfferich and Karl Lindemann were authorized to write checks to Heinrich Himmler, chief of the Nazi S.S., on a special Standard Oil account. This account was managed by the German-British-American banker, Kurt von Schroeder. According to U.S. intelligence documents reviewed by author Antony Sutton, Emil Helfferich continued his payments to the S.S. into 1944, when the S.S. was supervising the mass murder at the Standard-I.G. Farben Auschwitz and other death camps. Helfferich told Allied interrogators after the war that these were not his personal contributions — they were corporate Standard Oil funds.[16]

After pleading "no contest" to charges of criminal conspiracy with the Nazis, William Stamps Farish was fined $5,000. (Similar fines were levied against Standard Oil — $5,000 each for the parent company and for several subsidiaries.) This of course did not interfere with the millions of dollars that Farish had acquired in conjunction with Hitler's New Order, as a large stockholder, chairman and president of Standard Oil. All the government sought was the use of patents which his company had given to the Nazis — the Auschwitz patents — but had withheld from the U.S. military and industry.

But a war was on, and if young men were to be asked to die fighting Hitler ... something more was needed. Farish was hauled before the Senate committee investigating the national defense program. The committee chairman, Senator Harry Truman, told newsmen before Farish testified: "I think this approaches treason."[17]

Farish began breaking apart at these hearings. He shouted his "indignation" at the Senators, and claimed he was not "disloyal."

After the March-April hearings ended, more dirt came gushing out of the Justice Department and the Congress on Farish and Standard Oil. Farish had deceived the U.S. Navy to prevent the Navy from acquiring certain patents, while supplying them to the Nazi war machine; meanwhile, he was supplying gasoline and tetraethyl lead to Germany's submarines and air force. Communications between Standard and I.G. Farben from the outbreak of World War II were released to the Senate, showing that Farish's organization had arranged to deceive the U.S. government into passing over Nazi-owned assets: They would nominally buy I.G.'s share in certain patents because "in the event of war between ourselves and Germany ... it would certainly be very undesirable to have this 20 percent Standard-I.G. pass to an alien property custodian of the U.S. who might sell it to an unfriendly interest."[18]

John D. Rockefeller, Jr. (father of David, Nelson and John D. Rockefeller III), controlling owner of Standard Oil, told the Roosevelt administration that he knew nothing of the day-to-day affairs of his company, that all these matters were handled by Farish and other executives.[19]

In August, Farish was brought back for more testimony. He was now frequently accused of lying. Farish was crushed under the intense, public grilling; he became morose, ashen. While Prescott Bush escaped publicity when the government seized his Nazi banking organization in October, Farish had been nailed. He collapsed and died of a heart attack on Nov. 29, 1942.

The Farish family was devastated by the exposure. Son William Stamps Farish, Jr., a lieutenant in the Army Air Force, was humiliated by the public knowledge that his father was fueling the enemy's aircraft; he died in a training accident in Texas six months later.[20]

With this double death, the fortune comprising much of Standard Oil's profits from Texas and Nazi Germany was now to be settled upon the little four-year-old grandson, William ("Will") Stamps Farish III. Will Farish grew up a recluse, the most secretive multi-millionaire in Texas, with investments of "that money" in a multitude of foreign countries, and a host of exotic contacts overlapping the intelligence and financial worlds — particularly in Britain.

The Bush-Farish axis started George Bush's career. After his 1948 graduation from Yale (and Skull and Bones), George Bush flew down to Texas on a corporate airplane and was employed by his father's Dresser Industries. In a couple of years he got help from his uncle, George Walker, Jr., and Farish's British banker friends, to set him up in the oil property speculation business. Soon thereafter, George Bush founded the Zapata Oil Company, which put oil drilling rigs into certain locations of great strategic interest to the Anglo-American intelligence community.

Will Farish at 25 years old was a personal aide to Zapata chairman George Bush in Bush's unsuccessful 1964 campaign for Senate. Will Farish used "that Auschwitz money" to back George Bush financially, investing in Zapata. When Bush was elected to Congress in 1966, Farish joined the Zapata board.[21]

When George Bush became U.S. Vice President in 1980, the Farish and Bush family fortunes were again completely, secretly commingled. As we shall see, the old projects were now being revived on a breathtaking scale.

Bush and Draper

Twenty years before he was U.S. President, George Bush brought two "race-science" professors in front of the Republican Task Force on Earth Resources and Population. As chairman of the Task Force, then-Congressman Bush invited Professors William Shockley and Arthur Jensen to explain to the committee how allegedly runaway birth-rates for African-Americans were "down-breeding" the American population.

Afterwards Bush personally summed up for the Congress the testimony his black-inferiority advocates had given to the Task Force.[22] George Bush held his hearings on the threat posed by black babies on August 5, 1969, while much of the world was in a better frame of mind — celebrating mankind's progress from the first moon landing 16 days earlier. Bush's obsessive thinking on this subject was guided by his family's friend, Gen. William H. Draper, Jr., the founder and chairman of the Population Crisis Committee, and vice chairman of the Planned Parenthood Federation. Draper had long been steering U.S. public discussion about the so-called "population bomb" in the non-white areas of the world.

If Congressman Bush had explained to his colleagues *how his family had come to know General Draper*, they would perhaps have felt some alarm, or even panic, and paid more healthy attention to Bush's presentation. Unfortunately, the Draper-Bush population doctrine is now official U.S. foreign policy.

William H. Draper, Jr. had joined the Bush team in 1927, when he was hired by Dillon Read & Co., New York investment bankers. Draper was put into a new job slot at the firm: handling the Thyssen account.

We recall that in 1924, Fritz Thyssen set up his Union Banking Corporation in George Herbert Walker's bank at 39 Broadway, Manhattan. Dillon Read & Co.'s boss, Clarence Dillon, had begun working with Fritz Thyssen sometime after Averell Harriman first met with Thyssen — at about the time Thyssen began financing Adolf Hitler's political career.

In January 1926, Dillon Read created the **German Credit and Investment Corporation** in Newark, New Jersey and Berlin, Germany, as Thyssen's short-term banker. That same year Dillon Read created the *Vereinigte Stahlwerke* (German Steel Trust), incorporating the Thyssen family interests under the direction of New York and London finance.[23]

William H. Draper, Jr. was made director, vice president and assistant treasurer of the German Credit and Investment Corp. His business was short-term loans and financial management tricks for Thyssen and the German Steel Trust. Draper's clients sponsored Hitler's terroristic takeover; his clients led the buildup of the Nazi war industry; his clients made war against the United States. The Nazis were Draper's direct partners in Berlin and New Jersey: Alexander Kreuter, residing in Berlin, was president; Frederic Brandi, whose father was a top coal executive in the German Steel Trust, moved to the U.S. in 1926 and served as Draper's co-director in Newark.

Draper's role was crucial for Dillon Read & Co., for whom Draper was a partner and eventually vice president. The German Credit and Investment Corp. (GCI) was a "front" for Dillon Read: It had the same New Jersey address as U.S. & International Securities Corp. (USIS), and the same man served as treasurer of both firms.[24]

Clarence Dillon and his son C. Douglas Dillon were directors of USIS, which was spotlighted when Clarence Dillon was hauled before the Senate Banking Committee's famous "Pecora" hearings in 1933. USIS was shown to be one of the great speculative pyramid schemes which had swindled stockholders of hundreds of millions of dollars. These investment policies had rotted the U.S. economy to the core, and led to the Great Depression of the 1930s.

But William H. Draper, Jr.'s GCI "front" was not *apparently* affiliated with the USIS "front" or with Dillon, and the GCI escaped the Congressmen's limited scrutiny. This oversight was to prove most unfortunate, particularly to the 50 million people who subsequently died in World War II.

Dillon Read hired public relations man Ivy Lee to prepare their executives for their testimony and to confuse and further baffle the Congressmen.[25] Lee apparently took enough time out from his duties as image-maker for William S. Farish and the Nazi I.G. Farben Co.; he managed the congressional thinking so that the Congressmen did not disturb the Draper operation in Germany — and did not meddle with Thyssen, or interfere with Hitler's U.S. moneymen.

Thus in 1932, William H. Draper, Jr. was free to finance the International Eugenics Congress as a "Supporting Member."[26] Was he using his own income as a Thyssen trust banker? Or did the funds come from Dillon Read corporate accounts, perhaps to be written off income tax as "expenses for German project: race purification"? Draper helped select Ernst Rüdin as chief of the world eugenics movement, who used his office to promote what he called Adolf Hitler's "holy, national and international racial hygienic mission."[27]

W.S. Farish, as we have seen, was publicly exposed in 1942, humiliated and destroyed. Just before Farish died, Prescott Bush's Nazi banking office was quietly seized and shut down. But Prescott's close friend and partner in the Thyssen-Hitler business, William H. Draper, Jr., *neither died nor moved out of German affairs.* Draper listed himself as a director of the German Credit and Investment Corp. through 1942, and the firm was not liquidated until November 1943.[28] But a war was on; Draper, a colonel from previous military service, went off to the Pacific theater and became a general.

General Draper apparently had a hobby: magic — illusions, sleight of hand, etc. — and he was a member of the Society of American Magicians. This is not irrelevant to his subsequent career.

The Nazi regime surrendered in May 1945. In July 1945, General Draper was called to Europe by the American military government authorities in Germany. Draper was appointed head of the Economics Division of the U.S. Control Commission. He was assigned to take apart the Nazi corporate cartels. There is an astonishing but perfectly logical rationale to this — Draper knew a lot about the subject! General Draper, who had spent about 15 years financing and managing the dirtiest of the Nazi enterprises, was now authorized to decide *who was exposed, who lost and who kept his business, and in practical effect, who was prosecuted for war crimes.*[29]

(Draper was not unique within the postwar occupation government. Consider the case of John J. McCloy, U.S. Military Governor and High Commissioner of Germany, 1949-1952. Under instructions from his Wall Street law firm, McCloy had lived for a year in Italy, serving as an advisor to the fascist government of Benito Mussolini. An intimate collaborator of the Harriman/Bush bank, McCloy had sat in Adolf Hitler's box at the 1936 Olympic games in Berlin, at the invitation of Nazi chieftains Rudolf Hess and Hermann Göring.)[30]

William H. Draper, Jr., as a "conservative," was paired with the "liberal" U.S. Treasury Secretary Henry Morgenthau in a vicious game. Morgenthau demanded that Germany be utterly destroyed as a nation, that its industry be dismantled and it be reduced to a purely rural country. As the economic boss in 1945 and 1946, Draper "protected" Germany from the Morgenthau Plan ... but at a price.

Draper and his colleagues demanded that Germany and the world accept the *collective guilt of the German people* as *the* explanation for the rise of Hitler's New Order, and the Nazi war crimes. This, of course, was rather convenient for General Draper himself, as it was for the Bush family. It is still convenient decades later, allowing Prescott's son, President Bush, to lecture Germany on the danger of Hitlerism. Germans are too slow, it seems, to accept his New World Order.

After several years of government service (often working directly for Averell Harriman in the North Atlantic Alliance), General Draper was appointed in 1958 chairman of a committee which was to advise President Dwight Eisenhower on the proper course for U.S. military aid to other countries. At that time, Prescott Bush was a U.S. Senator from Connecticut, a confidential friend and golf partner with National Security Director Gordon Gray, and an important golf partner with Dwight Eisenhower as well. Prescott's old lawyer from the Nazi days, John Foster Dulles, was Secretary of State, and his brother Allen Dulles, formerly of the Schroder bank, was head of the CIA.

This friendly environment emboldened General Draper to pull off a stunt with his military aid advisory committee. He changed the subject under study. The following year the Draper committee recommended that the U.S. government react to the supposed threat of the "population explosion" by formulating plans to depopulate the poorer countries. The growth of the world's non-white population, he proposed, should be regarded as dangerous to the national security of the United States![31]

President Eisenhower rejected the recommendation. But in the next decade, General Draper founded the "Population Crisis Committee" and the "Draper Fund," joining with the Rockefeller and Du Pont families to promote eugenics as "population control." The administration of President Lyndon Johnson, advised by General Draper on the subject, began financing birth control in the tropical countries through the U.S. Agency for International Development (USAID).

General Draper was George Bush's guru on the population question.[32] But there was also Draper's money — from that uniquely horrible source — and Draper's connections on Wall Street and abroad. Draper's son and heir, William H. Draper III, was co-chairman for finance (chief of fundraising) of the Bush-for-President national campaign organization in 1980. With George Bush in the White House, the younger Draper heads up the depopulation activities of the United Nations throughout the world.

General Draper was vice president of Dillon Read until 1953. During the 1950s and 1960s, the chief executive there was Frederic Brandi, the German who was Draper's co-director for the Nazi investments and his personal contact man with the Nazi German Steel Trust. Nicholas Brady was Brandi's partner from 1954, and replaced him as the firm's chief executive in 1971. Nicholas Brady, who knows where all the bodies are buried, was chairman of his friend George Bush's 1980 election campaign in New Jersey, and has been United States Treasury Secretary throughout Bush's presidency.[33]

BUSH AND GRAY

THE U.S. AGENCY FOR INTERNATIONAL DEVELOPMENT says that surgical sterilization is the Bush administration's "first choice" method of population reduction in the Third World.[34]

The United Nations Population Fund claims that 37 percent of contraception users in Ibero-America and the Caribbean have already been surgically sterilized. In a 1991 report, William H. Draper III's agency asserts that 254 million couples will be surgically sterilized over the course of the 1990s; and that if present trends continue, 80 percent of the women in Puerto Rico and Panama will be surgically sterilized.[35]

The U.S. government pays directly for these sterilizations.

Mexico is first among targeted nations, on a list which was drawn up in July 1991, at a USAID strategy session. India and Brazil are second and third priorities, respectively.

On contract with the Bush administration, U.S. personnel are working from bases in Mexico to perform surgery on millions of Mexican men and women. The acknowledged strategy in this program is to sterilize those young adults who have not already completed their families.

George Bush has a rather deep-seated personal feeling about this project, in particular as it pits him against Pope John Paul II in Catholic countries such as Mexico. (See Chapter 4 below, on the origin of a Bush family grudge in this regard.)

The spending for birth control in the non-white countries is one of the few items that is headed upwards in the Bush administration budget. As its 1992 budget was being set, USAID said its Population Account would receive $300 million, a 20 percent increase over the previous year. Within this project, a significant sum is spent on political and psychological manipulations of target nations, and rather blatant subversion of their religions and governments.[36]

These activities might be expected to cause serious objections from the victimized nationalities, or from U.S. taxpayers, especially if the program is somehow given widespread publicity.

Quite aside from moral considerations, *legal* questions would naturally arise, which could be summed up: **How does George Bush think he can get away with this?**

In this matter the President has expert advice. Mr. (Clayland) Boyden Gray has been counsel to George Bush since the 1980 election. As chief legal officer in the White House, Boyden Gray can walk the President through the dangers and complexities of waging such unusual warfare against Third World populations. Gray knows how these things are done.

When Boyden Gray was four and five years old, his father organized the pilot project for the present worldwide sterilization program, from the Gray family household in North Carolina.

It started in 1946. The eugenics movement was looking for a way to begin again in America.

Nazi death camps such as Auschwitz had just then seared the conscience of the world. The Sterilization League of America, which had changed its name during the war to "Birthright, Inc.," wanted to start up again. First they had to overcome public nervousness about crackpots proposing to eliminate "inferior" and "defective" people. The League tried to surface in Iowa, but had to back off because of negative publicity: A little boy had recently been sterilized there and had died from the operation.

They decided on North Carolina, where the Gray family could play the perfect host. Through British imperial contacts, Boyden Gray's grandfather, Bowman Gray, had become principal owner of the R.J. Reynolds Tobacco Co. Boyden's father, Gordon Gray, had recently founded the Bowman Gray (memorial) Medical School in Winston-Salem, using his inherited cigarette stock shares. The medical school was already a eugenics center.

As the experiment began, Gordon Gray's great aunt, Alice Shelton Gray, who had raised him from childhood, was living in his household. Aunt Alice had founded the "Human Betterment League," the North Carolina branch of the national eugenical sterilization movement.

Aunt Alice was the official supervisor of the 1946-47 experiment. Working under Miss Gray was Dr. Claude Nash Herndon, whom Gordon Gray had made assistant professor of "medical genetics" at Bowman Gray Medical School.

Dr. Clarence Gamble, heir to the Proctor and Gamble soap fortune, was the sterilizers' national field operations chief.

The experiment worked as follows. *All children enrolled in the school district of Winston-Salem, N.C. were given a special "intelligence test." Those children who scored below a certain arbitrary low mark were then cut open and surgically sterilized.*

We quote now from the official story of the project:[37]

> In Winston-Salem and in [nearby] Orange County, North Carolina, the [Sterilization League's] field committee had participated in testing projects to identify school age children who should be considered for sterilization. The project in Orange County was conducted by the University of North Carolina and was financed by a `Mr. Hanes,' a friend of Clarence Gamble and supporter of the field work project in North Carolina. The Winston-Salem project was also financed by Hanes." ["Hanes" was underwear mogul James Gordon Hanes, a trustee of Bowman Gray Medical School and treasurer of Alice Gray's group]...
>
> The medical school had a long history of interest in eugenics and had compiled extensive histories of families carrying inheritable disease. In 1946, Dr. C. Nash Herndon ... made a statement to the press on the use of sterilization to prevent the spread of inheritable diseases...

> The first step after giving the mental tests to grade school children was to interpret and make public the results. In Orange County the results indicated that three percent of the school age children were either insane or feebleminded... [Then] the field committee hired a social worker to review each case ... and to present any cases in which sterilization was indicated to the State Eugenics Board, which under North Carolina law had the authority to order sterilization...

Race science experimenter Dr. Claude Nash Herndon provided more details in an interview in 1990:[38]

> Alice Gray was the general supervisor of the project. She and Hanes sent out letters promoting the program to the commissioners of all 100 counties in North Carolina... What did I do? Nothing besides riding herd on the whole thing! The social workers operated out of my office. I was at the time also director of outpatient services at North Carolina Baptist Hospital. We would see the [targeted] parents and children there... I.Q. tests were run on all the children in the Winston-Salem public school system. Only the ones who scored really low [were targeted for sterilization], the real bottom of the barrel, like below 70.
>
> Did we do sterilizations on young children? Yes. This was a relatively minor operation... It was usually not until the child was eight or ten years old. For the boys, you just make an incision and tie the tube... We more often performed the operation on girls than with boys. Of course, you have to cut open the abdomen, but again, it is relatively minor.

Dr. Herndon remarked coolly that "we had a very good relationship with the press" for the project. This is not surprising, since Gordon Gray owned the *Winston-Salem Journal*, the *Twin City Sentinel* and radio station WSJS.

In 1950 and 1951, John Foster Dulles, then chairman of the Rockefeller Foundation, led John D. Rockefeller III on a series of world tours, focusing on the need to stop the expansion of the non-white populations. In November 1952, Dulles and Rockefeller set up the Population Council, with tens of millions of dollars from the Rockefeller family.

At that point, the American Eugenics Society, still cautious from the recent bad publicity vis-a-vis Hitler, left its old headquarters at Yale University. The Society moved its headquarters into the office of the Population Council, and the two groups melded together. The long-time secretary of the American Eugenics Society, Frederick Osborne, became the first president of the Population Council. The Gray family's child-sterilizer, Dr. Claude Nash Herndon, became president of the American Eugenics Society in 1953, as its work expanded under Rockefeller patronage.

Meanwhile, the International Planned Parenthood Federation was founded in London, in the offices of the British Eugenics Society.

The undead enemy from World War II, renamed "Population Control," had now been revived.

George Bush was U.S. ambassador to the United Nations in 1972, when with prodding from Bush and his friends, the U.S. Agency for International Development first made an official contract with the old Sterilization League of America. The League had changed its name twice again, and was now called the "Association for Voluntary Surgical Contraception." The U.S. government began paying the old fascist group to sterilize non-whites in foreign countries.

The Gray family experiment had succeeded.

In 1988, the U.S. Agency for International Development signed its latest contract with the old Sterilization League (a.k.a. Association for Voluntary Surgical Contraception), committing the U.S. government to spend $80 million over five years.

Having gotten away with sterilizing several hundred North Carolina school children, "not usually less than eight to ten years old," the identical group is now authorized by President Bush to do it to 58 countries in Asia, Africa and Ibero-America. The group modestly claims it has directly sterilized "only" two million people, with 87 percent of the bill paid by U.S. taxpayers.

Meanwhile, Dr. Clarence Gamble, Boyden Gray's favorite soap manufacturer, formed his own "Pathfinder Fund" as a split-off from the Sterilization League. Gamble's Pathfinder Fund, with additional millions from USAID, concentrates on penetration of local social groups in the non-white countries, to break down psychological resistance to the surgical sterilization teams.

NOTES:

1. Phyllis Tilson Piotrow, *World Population Crisis: The United States Response* (New York: Praeger Publishers, 1973), "Forward" by George H.W. Bush, pp. vii-viii.
2. Adolf Hitler, *Mein Kampf*(Boston, Houghton Mifflin Company, 1971), p. 404.
3. "The Ten Richest People in Houston," in *Houston Post Magazine*, March 11, 1984. "$150 million to $250 million from ... inheritance, plus subsequent investments ... chief heir to a family fortune in oil stock... As to his financial interests, he is ... coy. He once described one of his businesses as a company that `invests in and oversees a lot of smaller companies ... in a lot of foreign countries."'
4. The announcements were made in testimony before a Special Committee of the U.S. Senate Investigating the National Defense Program. The hearings on Standard Oil were held March 5, 24, 26, 27, 31, and April 1, 2, 3 and 7, 1942. Available on microfiche, law section, Library of Congress. See also *New York Times*, March 26 and March 27, 1942, and *Washington Evening Star*, March 26 and March 27, 1942.
5. *Ibid.*, Exhibit No. 368, printed on pp. 4584-87 of the hearing record. See also Charles Higham, *Trading With The Enemy* (New York: Delacorte Press, 1983), p. 36.
6. Confidential memorandum from U.S. embassy, Berlin, *op. cit.*, chapter 2. Sir Henri Deterding was among the most notorious pro-Nazis of the early war period.
7. See sections on Prescott Bush in Darwin Payne, *Initiative in Energy: Dresser Industries, Inc.* (New York: Distributed by Simon and Schuster, 1979) (published by the Dresser Company).
8. William Stamps Farish obituary, *New York Times*, Nov. 30, 1942.
9. *A Decade of Progress in Eugenics: Scientific Papers of the Third International Congress of Eugenics held at American Museum of Natural History New York, Aug. 21-23, 1932.* (Baltimore: Williams & Wilkins Company, Sept., 1934).
   The term "eugenics" is taken from the Greek to signify "good birth" or "well-born," as in aristocrat. Its basic assumption is that those who are not "well-born" should not exist.
10. See among other such letters, George Herbert Walker, 39 Broadway, N.Y., to W. A. Harriman, London, Feb. 21, 1925, in WAH papers.
11. ***Averell Harriman to Dr. Charles B. Davenport,*** President, The International Congress of Eugenics, Cold Spring Harbor, L.I., N.Y.
    January 21, 1932
    Dear Dr. Davenport:
    I will be only too glad to put you in touch with the Hamburg-American Line ... they may be able to co-operate in making suggestions which will keep the expenses to a minimum. I have referred your letter to Mr. Emil Lederer [of the Hamburg-Amerika executive board in New York] with the request that he communicate with you.
    Davenport to Mr. W.A. Harriman,
    59 Wall Street, New York, N.Y.
    January 23, 1932

Dear Mr. Harriman:

Thank you very much for your kind letter of January 21st and the action you took which has resulted at once in a letter from Mr. Emil Lederer. This letter will serve as a starting point for correspondence, which I hope will enable more of our German colleagues to come to America on the occasion of the congresses of eugenics and genetics, than otherwise.

Congressional hearings in 1934 established that Hamburg-Amerika routinely provided free transatlantic passage for those carrying out Nazi propaganda chores. See *Investigation of Nazi Propaganda Activities and Investigation of Certain Other Propaganda Activities* ,*op. cit.* , chapter 2.

12. Alexis Carrel, *Man the Unknown* (New York: Halcyon House, published by arrangement with Harper & Brothers, 1935), pp. 318-19.
The battle cry of the New Order was sounded in 1935 with the publication of *Man the Unknown* , by Dr. Alexis Carrel of the Rockefeller Institute in New York. This Nobel Prize-winner said "enormous sums are now required to maintain prisons and insane asylums... Why do we preserve these useless and harmful beings? This fact must be squarely faced. Why should society not dispose of the criminals and the insane in a more economical manner? ... The community must be protected against troublesome and dangerous elements... Perhaps prisons should be abolished... The conditioning of the petty criminal with the whip, or some more scientific procedure, followed by a short stay in hospital, would probably suffice to insure order. [Criminals including those] who have ... misled the public on important matters, should be humanely and economically disposed of in small euthanasic institutions supplied with proper gases. A similar treatment could be advantageously applied to the insane, guilty of criminal acts."
Carrel claimed to have transplanted the head of a dog to another dog and kept it alive for quite some time.
13. Bernhard Schreiber, *The Men Behind Hitler: A German Warning to the World*, France: La Hay-Mureaux, ca. 1975), English language edition supplied by H & P. Tadeusz, 369 Edgewere Road, London W2. A copy of this book is now held by Union College Library, Syracuse, N.Y.
14. Higham, *op. cit.* , p. 35.
15. Engagement announced Feb. 10, 1939, *New York Times* , p. 20. See also *Directory of Directors* for New York City, 1930s and 1940s.
16. Higham, *op. cit.* , pp. 20, 22 and other references to Schroeder and Lindemann.
Anthony Sutton, *Wall Street and the Rise of Hitler* (Seal Beach: '76 Press, 1976). Sutton is also a good source on the Harrimans.
17. *Washington Evening Star* , March 27, 1942, p. 1.
18. Higham, *op. cit.* p. 50.
19. *Ibid.* , p. 48.
20. *Washington Post* , April 29, 1990, p. F4. Higham, *op. cit.* , pp. 52-53.
21. Zapata annual reports, 1950s-60s, Library of Congress microforms.
22. See Congressional Record for Bush speech in the House of Representatives, Sept. 4, 1969. Bush inserted in the record the testimony given before his Task Force on Aug. 5, 1969.
23. Sobel, *op. cit.* , pp. 92-111. See also Boyle, *op. cit.* , chapter 1, concerning the Morgan-led Dawes Committee of Germany's foreign creditors.
Like Harriman, Dillon used the Schroeder and Warburg banks to strike his German bargains. All Dillon Read & Co. affairs in Germany were supervised by J.P. Morgan & Co. partner Thomas Lamont, and were authorized by Bank of England Governor Montagu Norman.
24. See *Poor's Register of Directors and Executives* , (New York: Poor's Publishing Company, late 1920s, '30s and '40s). See also *Standard Corporation Records* (New York: Standard & Poor), 1935 edition pp. 2571-25, and 1938 edition pp. 7436-38, for description and history of the German Credit and Investment Corporation. For Frederic Brandi, See also Sobel, *op. cit.* , pp. 213-14.
25. Sobel, *op. cit.* , pp. 180, 186. Ivy Lee had been hired to improve the Rockefeller family image, particularly difficult after their 1914 massacre of striking miners and pregnant women in Ludlow, Colorado. Lee got old John D. Rockefeller to pass out dimes to poor people lined up at his porch.
26. Third International Eugenics Congress papers *op. cit.* , footnote 7, p. 512, "Supporting Members."
27. Schreiber, *op. cit.* , p. 160. The Third Int. Eugenics Congress papers, p. 526, lists the officers of the International Federation as of publication date in September, 1934. Rüdin is listed as president — a year after he has written the sterilization law for Hitler.
28. *Directory of Directors for New York City* , 1942. Interview with Nancy Bowles, librarian of Dillon Read & Co.
29. Higham, *op. cit.* , p. 129, 212-15, 219-23.

30. Walter Isaacson and Evan Thomas, *The Wise Men: Six Friends and the World They Made — Acheson, Bohlen, Harriman, Kennan, Lovett, McCloy* (New York: Simon and Schuster, 1986), pp. 122, 305.
31. Piotrow, *op. cit.* , pp. 36-42.
32. *Ibid.* , p. viii. "As chairman of the special Republican Task Force on Population and Earth Resources, I was impressed by the arguments of William H. Draper, Jr… Gen. Draper continues to lead through his tireless work for the U.N. Population Fund."
33. Sobel, *op. cit.* , pp. 298, 354.
34. Interview July 16, 1991, with Joanne Grossi, an official with the USAID's Population Office.
35. Dr. Nafis Sadik, "The State of World Population," 1991, New York, United Nations Population Fund.
36. See *User's Guide to the Office of Population* , 1991, Office of Population, Bureau for Science and Technology, United States Agency for International Development. Available from S&T/POP, Room 811 SA-18, USAID, Washington D.C. 20523-1819.
37. "History of the Association for Voluntary Sterilization [formerly Sterilization League of America], 1935-64," thesis submitted to the faculty of the graduate school of the University of Minnesota by William Ray Van Essendelft, March, 1978, available on microfilm, Library of Congress. This is the official history, written with full cooperation of the Sterilization League.
38. Interview with Dr. C. Nash Herndon, June 20, 1990.

THE CENTER OF POWER IS IN WASHINGTON

WEBSTER GRIFFIN TARPLEY AND ANTON CHAITKIN
CHAPTER FOUR OF *GEORGE BUSH – THE UNAUTHORIZED BIOGRAPHY* - 1992. USED WITH PERMISSION.

Brown Brothers Harriman & Co.
59 Wall Street, New York
Cable Address "Shipley-New York"
Business Established 1818
Private Bankers
September 5, 1944

The Honorable W.A. Harriman
American Ambassador to the U.S.S.R.
American Embassy,
Moscow, Russia

Dear Averell:

Thinking that possibly Bullitt's article in the recent issue of "LIFE" may not have come to your attention, I have clipped it and am sending it to you, feeling that it will interest you.

At present writing all well here.

With warm regards, I am,

Sincerely yours,

Pres – –

"AT PRESENT WRITING ALL IS WELL HERE." Thus the ambassador to Russia was reassured by the managing partner of his firm, Prescott Bush. Only 22-1/2 months before, the U.S. government had seized and shut down the Union Banking Corp., which had been operated on behalf of Nazi Germany by Bush and the Harrimans (see Chapter 2). But that was behind them now and they were safe. There would be no publicity on the Harriman-Bush sponsorship of Hitlerism.

Prescott's son George, the future U.S. President, was also safe. Three days before this note to Moscow was written, George Bush had parachuted from a Navy bomber airplane over the Pacific Ocean, killing his two crew members when the unpiloted plane crashed.

Five months later, in February 1945, Prescott's boss, Averell Harriman, escorted President Franklin Roosevelt to the fateful summit meeting with Soviet leader Joseph Stalin at Yalta. In April Roosevelt died. The agreement reached at Yalta, calling for free elections in Poland once the war ended, was never enforced.

Over the next eight years (1945 through 1952), Prescott Bush was Harriman's anchor in the New York financial world. The increasingly powerful Mr. Harriman and his allies gave Eastern Europe over to Soviet dictatorship. A Cold War was then undertaken, to "counterbalance" the Soviets.

This British-inspired strategy paid several nightmarish dividends. Eastern Europe was to remain enslaved. Germany was "permanently" divided. Anglo-American power was jointly exercised over the non-Soviet "Free World." The confidential functions of the British and American governments were merged. The Harriman clique took possession of the U.S. national security apparatus, and in doing so, they opened the gate and let the Bush family in.

Following his services to Germany's Nazi Party, Averell Harriman spent several years mediating between the British, American and Soviet governments in the war to stop the Nazis. He was ambassador to Moscow from 1943 to 1946.

President Harry Truman, whom Harriman and his friends held in amused contempt, appointed Harriman U.S. ambassador to Britain in 1946.

Harriman was at lunch with former British Prime Minister Winston Churchill one day in 1946, when Truman telephoned. Harriman asked Churchill if he should accept Truman's offer to come back to the U.S. as Secretary of Commerce. According to Harriman's account, Churchill told him: "Absolutely. The center of power is in Washington."[1]

Jupiter Island

The reorganization of the American government after World War II — the creation of the U.S. Central Intelligence Agency along British lines, for example — had devastating consequences. We are concerned here with only certain aspects of that overall transformation, those matters of policy and family which gave shape to the life and mind of George Bush, and gave him access to power.

It was in these postwar years that George Bush attended Yale University, and was inducted into the Skull and Bones society. The Bush family's home at that time was in Greenwich, Connecticut. But it was just then that George's parents, Prescott and Dorothy Walker Bush, were wintering in a peculiar spot in Florida, a place that is excluded from mention in literature originating from Bush circles.

Certain national news accounts early in 1991 featured the observations on President Bush's childhood by his elderly mother Dorothy. She was said to be a resident of Hobe Sound, Florida. More precisely, the President's mother lived in a hyper-security arrangement created a half-century earlier by Averell Harriman, adjacent to Hobe Sound. Its correct name is Jupiter Island.

During his political career, George Bush has claimed many different "home" states, including Texas, Maine, Massachusetts and Connecticut. It has not been expedient for him to claim Florida, though that state has a vital link to his role in the world, as we shall see. And George Bush's home base in Florida, throughout his adult life, has been Jupiter Island.

The unique, bizarre setup on Jupiter Island began in 1931, following the merger of W.A. Harriman & Co. with the British-American firm Brown Brothers.

The reader will recall Mr. Samuel Pryor, the "Merchant of Death." A partner with the Harrimans, Prescott Bush, George Walker and Nazi boss Fritz Thyssen in banking and shipping enterprises, Sam Pryor remained executive committee chairman of Remington Arms. In this period, the Nazi private armies (S.A. and S.S.) were supplied with American arms — most likely by Pryor and his company — as they moved to overthrow the German republic. Such gun-running as an instrument of national policy would later become notorious in the "Iran-Contra" affair.

Samuel Pryor's daughter Permelia married Yale graduate Joseph V. Reed on the last day of 1927. Reed immediately went to work for Prescott Bush and George Walker as an apprentice at W.A. Harriman & Co.

During World War II, Joseph V. Reed had served in the "special services" section of the U.S. Army Signal Corps. A specialist in security, codes and espionage, Reed later wrote a book entitled *Fun with Cryptograms.*[2]

Now, Sam Pryor had had property around Hobe Sound, Florida, for some time. In 1931, Joseph and Permelia Pryor Reed bought the entirety of Jupiter Island.

This is a typically beautiful Atlantic coast "barrier island," a half-mile wide and nine miles long. The middle of Jupiter Island lies just off Hobe Sound. The south bridge connects the island with the town of Jupiter, to the north of Palm Beach. It is about 90 minutes by auto from Miami — today, a few minutes by helicopter.

Early in 1991, a newspaper reporter asked a friend of the Bush family about security arrangements on Jupiter Island. He responded, "If you called up the White House, would they tell you how many security people they had? It's not that Jupiter Island is the White House, although he [George Bush] does come down frequently."

But for several decades before Bush was President, Jupiter Island had an ordinance requiring the registration and fingerprinting of all housekeepers, gardeners and other non-residents working on the island. The Jupiter Island police department says that there are sensors in the two main roads that can track every automobile on the island. If a car stops in the street, the police will be there within one or two minutes. Surveillance is a duty of all employees of the town of Jupiter Island. News reporters are to be prevented from visiting the island.[3]

To create this astonishing private club, Joseph and Permelia Pryor Reed sold land only to those who would fit in. Permelia Reed was still the grande dame of the island when George Bush was inaugurated President in 1989. In recognition of the fact that the Reeds know where *all* the bodies are buried, President Bush appointed Permelia's son, Joseph V. Reed, Jr., chief of protocol for the U.S. State Department, in charge of private arrangements with foreign dignitaries.

Averell Harriman made Jupiter Island a staging ground for his 1940s takeover of the U.S. national security apparatus. It was in that connection that the island became possibly the most secretive private place in America.

Let us briefly survey the neighborhood, back then in 1946-48, to see some of the uses various of the residents had for the Harriman clique.

RESIDENTS ON JUPITER ISLAND

Jupiter Islander **ROBERT A. LOVETT**, [4] Prescott Bush's partner at Brown Brothers Harriman, had been Assistant Secretary of War for Air from 1941 to 1945. Lovett was the leading American advocate of the policy of terror-bombing of civilians. He organized the Strategic Bombing Survey, carried out for the American and British governments by the staff of the Prudential Insurance Company, guided by London's Tavistock Psychiatric Clinic.

In the postwar period, Prescott Bush was associated with Prudential Insurance, one of Lovett's intelligence channels to the British secret services. Prescott was listed by Prudential as a director of the company for about two years in the early 1950s.

Their Strategic Bombing Survey failed to demonstrate any real military advantage accruing from such outrages as the fire-bombing of Dresden, Germany. But the Harrimanites nevertheless persisted in the advocacy of terror from the air. They glorified this as "psychological warfare," a part of the utopian military doctrine opposed to the views of military traditionalists such as Gen. Douglas MacArthur.

Robert Lovett later advised President Lyndon Johnson to terror-bomb Vietnam. President George Bush revived the doctrine with the bombing of civilian areas in Panama, and the destruction of Baghdad.

On Oct. 22, 1945, Secretary of War Robert Patterson created the Lovett Committee, chaired by Robert A. Lovett, to advise the government on the post-World War II organization of U.S. intelligence activities. The existence of this committee was unknown to the public until an official CIA history was released from secrecy in 1989. But the CIA's author (who was President Bush's prep school history teacher; see chapter 5) gives no real details of the Lovett Committee's functioning, claiming: "The record of the testimony of the Lovett Committee, unfortunately, was not in the archives of the agency when this account was written."[5]

The CIA's self-history does inform us of the advice that Lovett provided to the Truman cabinet, as the official War Department intelligence proposal.

Lovett decided that there should be a separate Central Intelligence Agency. The new agency would "consult" with the armed forces, but it must be the sole collecting agency in the field of foreign espionage and counterespionage. The new agency should have an independent budget, and its appropriations should be granted by Congress without public hearings.

Lovett appeared before the Secretaries of State, War and Navy on November 14, 1945. He spoke highly of the FBI's work because it had "the best personality file in the world." Lovett said the FBI was expert at producing false documents, an art "which we developed so successfully during the war and at which we became outstandingly adept." Lovett pressed for a virtual resumption of the wartime Office of Strategic Services (OSS) in a new CIA.

U.S. military traditionalists centered around Gen. Douglas MacArthur opposed Lovett's proposal.

The continuation of the OSS had been attacked at the end of the war on the grounds that the OSS was entirely under British control, and that it would constitute an American Gestapo.[6]

But the CIA was established in 1947 according to the prescription of Robert Lovett, of Jupiter Island.

CHARLES PAYSON and his wife, **JOAN WHITNEY PAYSON**, were extended family members of Harriman's and business associates of the Bush family.

Joan's aunt, Gertrude Vanderbilt Whitney, was a relative of the Harrimans. Gertrude's son, Cornelius Vanderbilt ("Sonny") Whitney, long-time chairman of Pan American Airways (Prescott was a Pan Am director), became Assistant Secretary of the U.S. Air Force in 1947. Sonny's wife Marie had divorced him and married Averell Harriman in 1930.

Joan and Sonny's uncle, Air Marshall Sir Thomas Elmhirst, was director of intelligence for the British Air Force from 1945 to 1947.

Joan's brother, John Hay ("Jock") Whitney, was to be ambassador to Great Britain from 1955 to 1961 — when it would be vital for Prescott and George Bush to have such a friend. Joan's father, grandfather and uncle were members of the Skull and Bones secret society.

Charles Payson organized a uranium refinery in 1948. Later he was chairman of Vitro Corp., makers of parts for submarine-launched ballistic missiles, equipment for frequency surveillance and torpedo guidance, and other subsurface weaponry.

Naval warfare has long been a preoccupation of the British Empire. British penetration of the U.S. Naval Intelligence service has been particularly heavy since the tenure of Joan's Anglophile grandfather, William C. Whitney, as Secretary of the Navy for President Grover Cleveland. This traditional covert British orientation in the U.S. Navy, Naval Intelligence and the Navy's included service, the Marine Corps, forms a backdrop to the career of George Bush — and to the whole neighborhood on Jupiter Island. Naval Intelligence maintained direct relations with gangster boss Meyer Lansky for Anglo-American political operations in Cuba during World War II, well before the establishment of the CIA. Lansky officially moved to Florida in 1953.[7]

GEORGE HERBERT WALKER, JR. (Skull and Bones 1927), was extremely close to his nephew George Bush, helping to sponsor his entry into the oil business in the 1950s. "Uncle Herbie" was also a partner of Joan Whitney Payson when they co-founded the New York Mets baseball team in 1960. His son, G.H. Walker III, was a Yale classmate of Nicholas Brady and Moreau D. Brown (Thatcher Brown's grandson), forming what was called the "Yale Mafia" on Wall Street.

WALTER S. CARPENTER, JR. had been chairman of the finance committee of the Du Pont Corporation (1930-40). In 1933, Carpenter oversaw Du Pont's purchase of Remington Arms from Sam Pryor and the Rockefellers, and led Du Pont into partnership with the Nazi I.G. Farben Company for the manufacture of explosives. Carpenter became Du Pont's president in 1940. His cartel with the Nazis was broken up by the U.S. government. Nevertheless, Carpenter remained Du Pont's president as the company's technicians participated massively in the Manhattan Project to produce the first atomic bomb. He was chairman of Du Pont from 1948 to 1962, retaining high-level access to U.S. strategic activities.

Walter Carpenter and Prescott Bush were fellow activists in the Mental Hygiene Society. Originating at Yale University in 1908, the movement had been organized into the World Federation of Mental Health by Montagu Norman, himself a frequent mental patient, former Brown Brothers partner and Bank of England Governor. Norman had appointed as the federation's chairman, Brigadier John Rawlings Rees, director of the Tavistock Psychiatric Clinic, chief psychiatrist and psychological warfare expert for the British intelligence services. Prescott was a director of the society in Connecticut; Carpenter was a director in Delaware.

PAUL MELLON was the leading heir to the Mellon fortune, and a long-time neighbor of Averell Harriman's in Middleburg, Virginia, as well as Jupiter Island, Florida. Paul's father, Andrew Mellon, U.S. Treasury Secretary 1921-32, had approved the transactions of Harriman, Pryor and Bush with the Warburgs and the Nazis. Paul Mellon's son-in-law, **DAVID K.E. BRUCE**, worked in Prescott Bush's W.A. Harriman & Co. during the late 1920s; was head of the London branch of U.S. intelligence during World War II; and was Averell Harriman's Assistant Secretary of Commerce in 1947-48. Mellon family money and participation would be instrumental in many domestic U.S. projects of the new Central Intelligence Agency.

CARLL TUCKER manufactured electronic guidance equipment for the Navy. With the Mellons, Tucker was an owner of South American oil properties. Mrs. Tucker was the great aunt of Nicholas Brady, later George Bush's Iran-Contra partner and U.S. Treasury Secretary. Their son Carll Tucker, Jr. (Skull and Bones 1947), was among the 15 Bonesmen who selected George Bush for induction in the class of 1948.

C. DOUGLAS DILLON was the boss of William H. Draper, Jr. in the Draper-Prescott Bush-Fritz Thyssen Nazi banking scheme of the 1930s and 40s. His father, Clarence Dillon, created the *Vereinigte Stahlwerke* (Thyssen's German Steel Trust) in 1926. C. Douglas Dillon made Nicholas Brady the chairman of the Dillon Read firm in 1971 and himself continued as chairman of the executive committee. C. Douglas Dillon would be a vital ally of his neighbor Prescott Bush during the Eisenhower administration.

Publisher **NELSON DOUBLEDAY** headed his family's publishing firm, founded under the auspices of J.P. Morgan and other British Empire representatives. When George Bush's "Uncle Herbie" died, Doubleday took over as majority owner and chief executive of the New York Mets baseball team.

GEORGE W. MERCK, chairman of Merck & Co., drug and chemical manufacturers, was director of the War Research Service: Merck was the official chief of all U.S. research into biological warfare from 1942 until at least the end of World War II. After 1944, Merck's organization was placed under the U.S. Chemical Warfare Service. His family firm in Germany and the U.S. was famous for its manufacture of morphine.

A.L. COLE was useful to the Jupiter Islanders as an executive of *Readers Digest* . In 1965, just after performing a rather dirty favor for George Bush (see Chapter 9), Cole became chairman of the executive committee of the *Digest* , the world's largest-circulation periodical.

From the late 1940s, Jupiter Island has served as a center for the direction of covert action by the U.S. government and, indeed, for the covert management of the government. Jupiter Island will reappear later on, in our account of George Bush in the Iran-Contra affair.

TARGET: WASHINGTON

GEORGE W. BUSH GRADUATED FROM YALE IN 1948. He soon entered the family's Dresser oil supply concern in Texas. We shall now briefly describe the forces that descended on Washington, D.C. during those years when Bush, with the assistance of family and powerful friends, was becoming "established in business on his own."

From 1948 to 1950, Prescott Bush's boss Averell Harriman was U.S. "ambassador-at-large" to Europe. He was a non-military "theater commander," the administrator of the multi-billion-dollar Marshall Plan, participating in all military/strategic decision-making by the Anglo-American alliance.

The U.S. Secretary of Defense, James Forrestal, had become a problem to the Harrimanites. Forrestal had long been an executive at Dillon Read on Wall Street. But in recent years he had gone astray. As Secretary of the Navy in 1944, Forrestal proposed the racial integration of the Navy. As Defense Secretary he pressed for integration in the armed forces and this eventually became the U.S. policy.

Forrestal opposed the utopians' strategy of appeasement coupled with brinkmanship. He was simply opposed to communism. On March 28, 1949, Forrestal was forced out of office and flown on an Air Force plane to Florida. He was taken to "Hobe Sound" (Jupiter Island), where Robert Lovett and an army psychiatrist dealt with him.[8]

He was flown back to Washington, locked in Walter Reed Army Hospital and given insulin shock treatments for alleged "mental exhaustion." He was denied all visitors except his estranged wife and children — his son had been Averell Harriman's aide in Moscow. On May 22, James Forrestal's body was found, his bathrobe cord tied tightly around his neck, after he had plunged from a sixteenth-story hospital window. The chief psychiatrist called the death a suicide even before any investigation was started. The results of the Army's inquest were kept secret. Forrestal's diaries were published, 80 percent deleted, after a year of direct government censorship and rewriting.

North Korean troops invaded South Korea in June 1950, after U.S. Secretary of State Dean Acheson (Harriman's very close friend) publicly specified that Korea would not be defended. With a new war on, Harriman came back to serve as President Truman's adviser, to "oversee national security affairs."

Harriman replaced Clark Clifford, who had been special counsel to Truman. Clifford, however, remained close to Harriman and his partners as they gained more and more power. Clifford later wrote about his cordial relations with Prescott Bush:

> Prescott Bush ... had become one of my frequent golfing partners in the fifties, and I had both liked and respected him... Bush had a splendid singing voice, and particularly loved quartet singing. In the fifties, he organized a quartet that included my daughter Joyce... They would sing in Washington, and, on occasion, he invited the group to Hobe Sound in Florida to perform. His son [George], though, had never struck me as a strong or forceful person. In 1988, he presented himself successfully to the voters as an outsider – no small trick for a man whose roots wound through Connecticut, Yale, Texas oil, the CIA, a patrician background, wealth, and the Vice-Presidency.[9]

With James Forrestal out of the way, Averell Harriman and Dean Acheson drove to Leesburg, Virginia, on July 1, 1950, to hire the British-backed U.S. Gen. George C. Marshall as Secretary of Defense. At the same time, Prescott's partner, Robert Lovett, himself became Assistant Secretary of Defense.

Lovett, Marshall, Harriman and Acheson went to work to unhorse Gen. Douglas MacArthur, commander of U.S. forces in Asia. MacArthur kept Wall Street's intelligence agencies away from his command, and favored real independence for the non-white nations. Lovett called for MacArthur's firing on March 23, 1951, citing MacArthur's insistence on defeating the Communist Chinese invaders in Korea. MacArthur's famous message, that there was "no substitute for victory," was read in Congress on April 5; MacArthur was fired on April 10, 1951.

That September, Robert Lovett replaced Marshall as Secretary of Defense. Meanwhile, Harriman was named director of the Mutual Security Agency, making him the U.S. chief of the Anglo-American military alliance. By now, Brown Brothers Harriman was everything but Commander-in-Chief.

These were, of course exciting times for the Bush family, whose wagon was hitched to the financial gods of Olympus — to Jupiter, that is.

> Brown Brothers Harriman & Co.
> 59 Wall Street, New York 5, N.Y.
> Business Established 1818
> Cable Address "Shipley-New York"

Private Bankers
April 2, 1951

The Honorable W.A. Harriman,
The White House, Washington, D.C.

Dear Averell:
I was sorry to miss you in Washington but appreciate your cordial note. I shall hope for better luck another time. I hope you had a good rest at Hobe Sound.
With affectionate regard, I am,
Sincerely yours,
Pres [signed]
Prescott S. Bush.

A central focus of the Harriman security regime in Washington (1950-53) was the organization of covert operations, and "psychological warfare." Harriman, together with his lawyers and business partners, Allen Dulles and John Foster Dulles, wanted the government's secret services to conduct extensive propaganda campaigns and mass-psychology experiments within the U.S.A., and paramilitary campaigns abroad. This would supposedly ensure a stable world-wide environment favorable to Anglo-American financial and political interests.

The Harriman security regime created the Psychological Strategy Board (PSB) in 1951. The man appointed director of the PSB, Gordon Gray, is familiar to the reader as the sponsor of the child sterilization experiments, carried out by the Harrimanite eugenics movement in North Carolina following World War II (see Chapter 3).

Gordon Gray was an avid Anglophile, whose father had gotten controlling ownership of the R.J. Reynolds Tobacco Company through alliance with the British Imperial Tobacco cartel's U.S. representatives, the Duke family of North Carolina. Gordon's brother, R.J. Reynolds chairman Bowman Gray, Jr., was also a Naval Intelligence officer, known around Washington as the "founder of operational intelligence." Gordon Gray became a close friend and political ally of Prescott Bush; and Gray's son became for Prescott's son, George, his lawyer and the shield of his covert policy.

But President Harry Truman, as malleable as he was, constituted an obstacle to the covert warriors. An insular Missouri politician vaguely favorable to the U.S. Constitution, he remained skeptical about secret service activities that reminded him of the Nazi Gestapo.

So, "covert operations" could not fully take off without a change of the Washington regime. And it was with the Republican Party that Prescott Bush was to get his turn.

Prescott had made his first attempt to enter national politics in 1950, as his partners took control of the levers of governmental power. Remaining in charge of Brown Brothers Harriman, he ran against Connecticut's William Benton for a seat in the U.S. Senate. (The race was for a two-year unexpired term, left empty by the death of the previous Senator.)

In those days, Wisconsin's drunken Senator Joseph R. McCarthy was making a circus-like crusade against communist influence in Washington. McCarthy attacked liberals and leftists, State Department personnel, politicians and Hollywood figures. He generally left unscathed the Wall Street and London strategists who donated Eastern Europe and China to communist dictatorship — like George Bush, their geopolitics was beyond left and right.

Prescott Bush had no public ties to the notorious Joe McCarthy, and appeared to be neutral about his crusade. But the Wisconsin Senator had his uses. Joe McCarthy came into Connecticut three times that year to campaign for Bush and against the Democrats. Bush himself made charges of "Korea, Communism and Corruption" into a slick campaign phrase against Benton, which then turned up as a national Republican slogan.

The response was disappointing. Only small crowds turned out to hear Joe McCarthy, and Benton was not hurt. McCarthy's pro-Bush rally in New Haven, in a hall that seated 6,000, drew only 376 people. Benton joked on the radio that "200 of them were my spies."

Prescott Bush resigned from the Yale Board of Fellows for his campaign, and the board published a statement to the effect that the "Yale vote" should support Bush — despite the fact that William Benton was a Yale man, and in many ways identical in outlook to Bush. Yale's Whiffenpoof singers appeared regularly for Prescott's campaign. None of this was particularly effective, however, with the voting population.[10]

Then Prescott Bush ran into a completely unexpected problem. At that time, the old Harriman eugenics movement was centered at Yale University. Prescott Bush was a Yale trustee, and his former Brown Brothers Harriman partner, Lawrence Tighe, was Yale's treasurer. In that connection, a slight glimmer of the truth about the Bush-Harriman firm's Nazi activities now made its way into the campaign.

Not only was the American Eugenics Society itself headquartered at Yale, but all parts of this undead fascist movement had a busy home at Yale. The coercive psychiatry and sterilization advocates had made the Yale/New Haven Hospital and Yale Medical School their laboratories for hands-on practice in brain surgery and psychological experimentation. And the Birth Control League was there, which had long trumpeted the need for eugenical births — fewer births for parents with "inferior" bloodlines. Prescott's partner Tighe was a Connecticut director of the league, and the Connecticut league's medical advisor was eugenics advocate Dr. Winternitz of Yale Medical School.

Now in 1950, people who knew something about Prescott Bush knew that he had very unsavory roots in the eugenics movement. There were then, just after the anti-Hitler war, few open advocates of sterilization of "unfit" or "unnecessary" people. (That would be revived later, with the help of General Draper and his friend George Bush.) But the Birth Control League was public — just about then it was changing its name to the euphemistic "Planned Parenthood."

Then, very late in the 1950 senatorial campaign, Prescott Bush was publicly exposed for being an activist in that section of the old fascist eugenics movement. Prescott Bush lost the election by about 1,000 out of 862,000 votes. He and his family blamed the defeat on the exposé. The defeat was burned into the family's memory, leaving a bitterness and perhaps a desire for revenge.

In his foreword to a population control propaganda book, George Bush wrote about that 1950 election: "My own first awareness of birth control as a public policy issue came with a jolt in 1950 when my father was running for United States Senate in Connecticut. Drew Pearson, on the Sunday before Election day, 'revealed' that my father was involved with Planned Parenthood... Many political observers felt a sufficient number of voters were swayed by his alleged contacts with the birth controllers to cost him the election..."[11]

Prescott Bush was defeated, while the other Republican candidates fared well in Connecticut. When he tried again, Prescott Bush would not leave the outcome to the blind whims of the public.

Prescott Bush moved into action again in 1952 as a national leader of the push to give the Republican presidential nomination to Gen. Dwight D. ("Ike") Eisenhower. Among the other team members were Bush's Hitler-era lawyer John Foster Dulles, and Jupiter Islander C. Douglas Dillon.

Dillon and his father were the pivots as the Harriman-Dulles combination readied Ike for the presidency. As a friend put it: "When the Dillons ... invited [Eisenhower] to dinner it was to introduce him to Wall Street bankers and lawyers."[12]

Ike's higher-level backers believed, correctly, that Ike would not interfere with even the dirtiest of their covert action programs. The bland, pleasant Prescott Bush was in from the beginning: a friend to Ike, and an original backer of his presidency.

On July 28, 1952, as the election approached, Connecticut's senior U.S. Senator, James O'Brien McMahon, died at the age of 48.*

This was *extremely* convenient for Prescott. He got the Republican nomination for U.S. Senator at a special delegated meeting, with backing by the Yale-dominated state party leadership. Now he would run in a special election for the suddenly vacant Senate seat. He could expect to be swept into office, since he would be on the same electoral ticket as the popular war hero, General Ike. By a technicality, he would instantly become Connecticut's senior Senator, with extra power in Congress. And the next regularly scheduled senatorial race would be in 1956 (when McMahon's term would have ended), so Prescott could run again in that presidential election year — once again on Ike's coattails!

With this arrangement, things worked out very smoothly. In Eisenhower's 1952 election victory, Ike won Connecticut by a margin of 129,507 votes out of 1,092,471. Prescott Bush came in last among the statewide Republicans, but managed to win by 30,373 out of 1,088,799 votes case, his margin nearly 100,000 behind Eisenhower. He took the traditionally Republican towns.

In Eisenhower's 1956 reelection, Ike won Connecticut by 303,036 out of 1,114,954 votes, the largest presidential margin in Connecticut's history. Prescott Bush managed to win again, by 129,544 votes out of 1,085,206 — his margin this time 290,082 smaller than Eisenhower's.[13]

In January 1963, when this electoral strategy had been played out and his second term expired, Prescott Bush retired from government and returned to Brown Brothers Harriman.

The 1952 Eisenhower victory made John Foster Dulles Secretary of State, and his brother Allen Dulles head of the CIA. The reigning Dulles brothers were the "Republican" replacements for their client and business partner, "Democrat" Averell Harriman. Occasional public posturings aside, their strategic commitments were identical to his.

Undoubtedly the most important work accomplished by Prescott Bush in the new regime was on the golf links, where he was Ike's favorite partner.

Toward the "National Security State"

Prescott Bush was a most elusive, secretive Senator. By diligent research, his views on some issues may be traced: He was opposed to the development of public power projects like the Tennessee Valley Authority; he opposed the constitutional amendment introduced by Ohio Senator John W. Bricker, which would have required congressional approval of international agreements by the executive branch.

But Prescott Bush was essentially a covert operative in Washington.

* McMahon had been Assistant U.S. Attorney General, in charge of the Criminal Division, from 1935 to 1939. Was there a chance he might someday speak out about the unpunished Nazi-era crimes of the wealthy and powerful?

On June 10, 1954, Bush received a letter from Connecticut resident H. Smith Richardson, owner of Vick Chemical Company (cough drops, Vapo-Rub):

"... At some time before Fall, Senator, I want to get your advice and counsel on a [new] subject — namely what should be done with the income from a foundation which my brother and I set up, and which will begin its operation in 1956..."[14]

This letter presages the establishment of the **H. Smith Richardson Foundation,** a Bush family-dictated private slush fund which was to be utilized by the Central Intelligence Agency, and by Vice President Bush, for the conduct of his Iran-Contra adventures.

The Bush family knew Richardson and his wife through their mutual friendship with Sears Roebuck's chairman, Gen. Robert E. Wood. General Wood had been president of the America First organization, which had lobbied against war with Hitler Germany. H. Smith Richardson had contributed the start-up money for America First and had spoken out against the U.S. "joining the Communists" by fighting Hitler. Richardson's wife was a proud relative of Nancy Langehorne from Virginia, who married Lord Astor and backed the Nazis from their Cliveden Estate.

General Wood's daughter Mary had married the son of Standard Oil president William Stamps Farish. The Bushes had stuck with the Farishes through their disastrous exposure during World War II (see Chapter 3). Young George Bush and his bride Barbara were especially close to Mary Farish, and to her son W.S. Farish III, who would be the great confidante of George's presidency.[15]

The H. Smith Richardson Foundation was organized by Eugene Stetson, Jr., Richardson's son-in-law. Stetson (Skull and Bones, 1934) had worked for Prescott Bush as assistant manager of the New York branch of Brown Brothers Harriman.

In the late 1950s, the H. Smith Richardson Foundation took part in the "psychological warfare" of the CIA. This was not a foreign, but a domestic, covert operation, carried out mainly against unwitting U.S. citizens. CIA Director Allen Dulles and his British allies organized "MK-Ultra," the testing of psychotropic drugs including LSD on a very large scale, allegedly to evaluate "chemical warfare" possibilities. In this period, the Richardson Foundation helped finance experiments at Bridgewater Hospital in Massachusetts, the center of some of the most brutal MK-Ultra tortures. These outrages have been graphically portrayed in the movie, *Titticut Follies.*

During 1990, an investigator for this book toured H. Smith Richardson's **Center for Creative Leadership** just north of Greensboro, North Carolina. The tour guide said that in these rooms, agents of the Central Intelligence Agency and the Secret Service are trained. He demonstrated the two-way mirrors through which the government employees are watched, while they are put through mind-bending psychodramas. The guide explained that "virtually everyone who becomes a general" in the U.S. armed forces also goes through this "training" at the Richardson Center.

Another office of the Center for Creative Leadership is in Langley, Virginia, at the headquarters of the Central Intelligence Agency. Here also, Richardson's Center trains leaders of the CIA.

Prescott Bush worked throughout the Eisenhower years as a confidential ally of the Dulles brothers. In July 1956, Egypt's President Gamel Abdul Nasser announced he would accept the U.S. offer of a loan for the construction of the Aswan Dam project. John Foster Dulles then prepared a statement telling the Egyptian ambassador that the U.S.A. had decided to retract its offer. Dulles gave the explosive statement in advance to Prescott Bush for his approval. Dulles also gave the statement to President Eisenhower, and to the British government.[16]

Nasser reacted to the Dulles brush-off by nationalizing the Suez Canal to pay for the dam. Israel, then Britain and France, invaded Egypt to try to overthrow Nasser, leader of the anti-imperial Arab nationalists. However, Eisenhower refused (for once) to play the Dulles-British game, and the invaders had to leave Egypt when Britain was threatened with U.S. economic sanctions.

During 1956, Senator Prescott Bush's value to the Harriman-Dulles political group increased when he was put on the Senate Armed Services Committee. Bush toured U.S. and allied military bases throughout the world, and had increased access to the national security decision-making process.

In the later years of the Eisenhower presidency, Gordon Gray rejoined the government. As an intimate friend and golfing partner of Prescott Bush, Gray complemented the Bush influence on Ike. The Bush-Gray family partnership in the "secret government" continues up through the George Bush presidency.

Gordon Gray had been appointed head of the new Psychological Strategy Board in 1951 under Averell Harriman's rule as assistant to President Truman for national security affairs. From 1958 to 1961, Gordon Gray was national security chief under President Eisenhower. Gray acted as Ike's intermediary, strategist and hand-holder, in the President's relations with the CIA and the U.S. and allied military forces.

Eisenhower did not oppose the CIA's covert action projects; he only wanted to be protected from the consequences of their failure or exposure. Gray's primary task, in the guise of "oversight" on all U.S. covert action, was to protect and hide the growing mass of CIA and related secret government activities.

It was not only covert *projects* which were developed by the Gray-Bush-Dulles combination; it was also new, hidden *structures* of the United States government.

Senator Henry Jackson challenged these arrangements in 1959 and 1960. Jackson created a Subcommittee on National Policy Machinery of the Senate Committee on Governmental Operations, which investigated Gordon Gray's reign at the National Security Council. On January 26, 1960, Gordon Gray warned President Eisenhower that a document revealing the existence of a secret part of the U.S. government had somehow gotten into the bibliography being used by Senator Jackson. The unit was Gray's "5412 Group" within the administration, officially but secretly in charge of approving covert action. Under Gray's guidance, Ike "'was clear and firm in his response' that Jackson's staff *not* be informed of the existence of this unit [emphasis in the original]."[17]

Several figures of the Eisenhower administration must be considered the fathers of this permanent covert action monolith, men who continued shepherding the monster after its birth in the Eisenhower era:

GORDON GRAY, the shadowy assistant to the President for national security affairs, Prescott Bush's closest executive branch crony and golf partner along with Eisenhower. By 1959-60, Gray had Ike's total confidence and served as the Harrimanites' monitor on all U.S. military and non-military projects.

British intelligence agent Kim Philby defected to the Russians in 1963. Philby had gained virtually total access to U.S. intelligence activities beginning in 1949, as the British secret services' liaison to the Harriman-dominated CIA. After Philby's defection, it seemed obvious that the aristocratic British intelligence service was in fact a menace to the western cause. In the 1960s, a small team of U.S. counterintelligence specialists went to England to investigate the situation. They reported back that the British secret service could be thoroughly trusted. The leader of this "expert" team, Gordon Gray, was the head of the counterespionage section of the President's Foreign Intelligence Advisory Board for Presidents John Kennedy through Gerald Ford.

ROBERT LOVETT, Bush's Jupiter Island neighbor and Brown Brothers Harriman partner, from 1956 on a member of the President's Foreign Intelligence Advisory Board. Lovett later claimed to have criticized — from the "inside" — the plan to invade Cuba at the Bay of Pigs. Lovett was asked to choose the cabinet for John Kennedy in 1961.

CIA DIRECTOR ALLEN DULLES, Bush's former international attorney. Kennedy fired Dulles after the Bay of Pigs invasion, but Dulles served on the Warren Commission, which whitewashed President Kennedy's murder.

C. DOUGLAS DILLON, neighbor of Bush on Jupiter Island, became Undersecretary of State in 1958 after the death of John Foster Dulles. Dillon had been John Foster Dulles's ambassador to France (1953-57), coordinating the original U.S. covert backing for the French imperial effort in Vietnam, with catastrophic results for the world. Dillon was Treasury Secretary for both John Kennedy and Lyndon Johnson.

AMBASSADOR TO BRITAIN JOCK WHITNEY, extended family member of the Harrimans and neighbor of Prescott Bush on Jupiter Island. Whitney set up a press service in London called Forum World Features, which published propaganda furnished directly by the CIA and the British intelligence services. Beginning in 1961, Whitney was chairman of the British Empire's "English Speaking Union."

SENATOR PRESCOTT BUSH, friend and counselor of President Eisenhower.

Bush's term continued on in the Senate after the Eisenhower years, throughout most of the aborted Kennedy presidency.

In 1962, the National Strategy Information Center was founded by Prescott Bush and his son Prescott, Jr., William Casey (the future CIA chief) and Leo Cherne. The center came to be directed by Frank Barnett, former program officer of the Bush family's H. Smith Richardson Foundation. The center conduited funds to the London-Based Forum World Features, for the circulation of CIA-authored "news stories" to some 300 newspapers internationally.[18]

"Democrat" Averell Harriman rotated back into official government in the Kennedy administration. As Assistant Secretary and Undersecretary of State, Harriman helped push the United States into the Vietnam War. Harriman had no post in the Eisenhower administration. Yet he was perhaps more than anyone the leader and the glue for the incredible evil that was hatched by the CIA in the final Eisenhower years: a half-public, half-private Harrimanite army, never since demobilized, and increasingly associated with the name of Bush.

Following the rise of Castro, the U.S. Central Intelligence Agency contracted with the organization of Mafia boss Meyer Lansky to organize and train assassination squads for use against the Cuban government. Among those employed were John Rosselli, Santos Trafficante and Sam Giancana. Uncontested public documentation of these facts has been published by congressional bodies and by leading Establishment academics.[19]

But the disturbing implications and later consequences of this engagement are a crucial matter for further study by the citizens of every nation. This much is established:

On Aug. 18, 1960, President Eisenhower approved a $13 million official budget for a secret CIA-run guerrilla war against Castro. It is known that Vice President Richard M. Nixon took a hand in the promotion of this initiative. The U.S. military was kept out of the covert action plans until very late in the game.

The first of eight admitted assassination attempts against Castro took place in 1960.

The program was, of course, a failure, if not a circus. The invasion of Cuba by the CIA's anti-Castro exiles was put off until after John Kennedy took over the presidency. The invasion at the Bay of Pigs was a fiasco, and Castro's forces easily prevailed. But the program continued.

In 1960, Felix Rodriguez, Luis Posada Carriles, Rafael "Chi Chi" Quintero, Frank Sturgis (or "Frank Fiorini") and other Florida-based Cuban exiles were trained as killers and drug-traffickers in the Cuban initiative; their supervisor was E. Howard Hunt. Their overall CIA boss was Miami station chief Theodore G. Shackley, seconded by Thomas Clines. In later chapters we will follow the subsequent careers of these characters — increasingly identified with George Bush — through the Watergate coup, and the Iran-Contra scandal.

NOTES

1. Walter Isaacson and Evan Thomas, *The Wise Men: Six Friends and the World They Made — Acheson, Bohlen, Harriman, Kennan, Lovett, McCloy* (New York: Simon and Schuster, 1986), p. 377.
2. Reed was better known in high society as a minor diplomat, the founder of the Triton Press and the president of the American Shakespeare Theater.
3. *Palm Beach Post*, Jan. 13, 1991.
4. For Lovett's residency there see Isaacson and Thomas, *op. cit.*, p. 417. Some Jupiter Island residencies were verified by their inclusion in the 1947 membership list of the Hobe Sound Yacht Club, in the Harriman papers, Library of Congress; others were established from interviews with long-time Jupiter Islanders.
5. Arthur Burr Darling, *The Central Intelligence Agency: An Instrument of Government, to 1950* (College Station: Pennsylvania State University, 1990), p. 59.
6. The *Chicago Tribune*, Feb. 9, 1945, for example, warned of "Creation of an all-powerful intelligence service to spy on the postwar world and to pry into the lives of citizens at home." Cf. Anthony Cave Brown, *Wild Bill Donovan: The Last Hero* (New York: Times Books, 1982), p. 625, on warnings to FDR about the British control of U.S. intelligence.
7. Dennis Eisenberg, Uri Dan, Eli Landau, *Meyer Lansky: Mogul of the Mob* (New York: Paddington Press, 1979) pp. 227-28.
8. See John Ranelagh, *The Agency: The Rise and Decline of the CIA* (New York: Simon and Schuster, 1987), pp. 131-32.
9. Clark Clifford, *Counsel to the President* (New York: Random House, 1991).
10. Sidney Hyman, *The Lives of William Benton* (Chicago: The University of Chicago Press, 1969), pp. 438-41.
11. Phyllis Tilson Piotrow, *World Population Crisis: The United States Response* (New York: Praeger Publishers, 1973), "Foreward," by George H.W. Bush, p. vii.
12. Herbert S. Parmet, *Eisenhower and the American Crusades* (New York: The Macmillan Company, 1972), p. 14.
13. *New York Times*, Sept. 6, 1952, Nov. 5, 1952, Nov. 7, 1956.
14. Richardson to Prescott Bush, H. Smith Richardson Papers, University of North Carolina, Chapel Hill.
15. Wayne S. Cole, *America First: The Battle Against Intervention, 1940-1941* (Madison: the University of Wisconsin Press, 1953); interviews with Richardson family employees; H. Smith Richardson Foundation annual reports; Richardson to Prescott Bush, March 26, 1954, Richardson Papers. *Washington Post*, April 29, 1990.
16. Parmet, *op. cit.*, p. 481.
17. John Prados, *Keepers of the Keys: A History of the National Security Council from Truman to Bush* (New York: William Morrow, 1991) pp. 92-95.
18. Robert Callaghan in *Covert Action*, No. 33, Winter 1990. Prescott, Jr. was a board member of the National Strategy Information Center as of 1991. Both Prescott Sr. and Jr. were deeply involved along with Casey in the circles of Pan American Airlines, Pan Am's owners the Grace family, and the CIA's Latin American affairs. The center, based in Washington, D.C., declines public inquiries about its

founding.

See also *EIR Special Report:* "American Leviathan: Administrative Fascism under the Bush Regime" (Wiesbaden, Germany: Executive Intelligence Review Nachrichtenagentur, April 1990), p. 192.

19. For example, see Trumbull Higgins, *The Perfect Failure: Kennedy, Eisenhower, and the CIA at the Bay of Pigs* (New York: W.W. Norton and Co., 1987), pp. 55-56, 89-90.
Unverified information on the squads is provided in the affidavit of Daniel P. Sheehan, attorney for the Christic Institute, reproduced in *EIR Special Report:* , "Project Democracy: The `Parallel Government' behind the Iran-Contra Affair" (Washington, D.C.: Executive Intelligence Review, 1987), pp. 249-50.
Some of the hired assassins have published their memoirs. See, for example, Felix Rodriguez and John Weisman, *Secret Warrior* (New York: Simon and Schuster, 1989); and E. Howard Hunt, *Undercover: Memoirs of an American Secret Agent* (New York: G.P. Putnam's Sons, 1974).

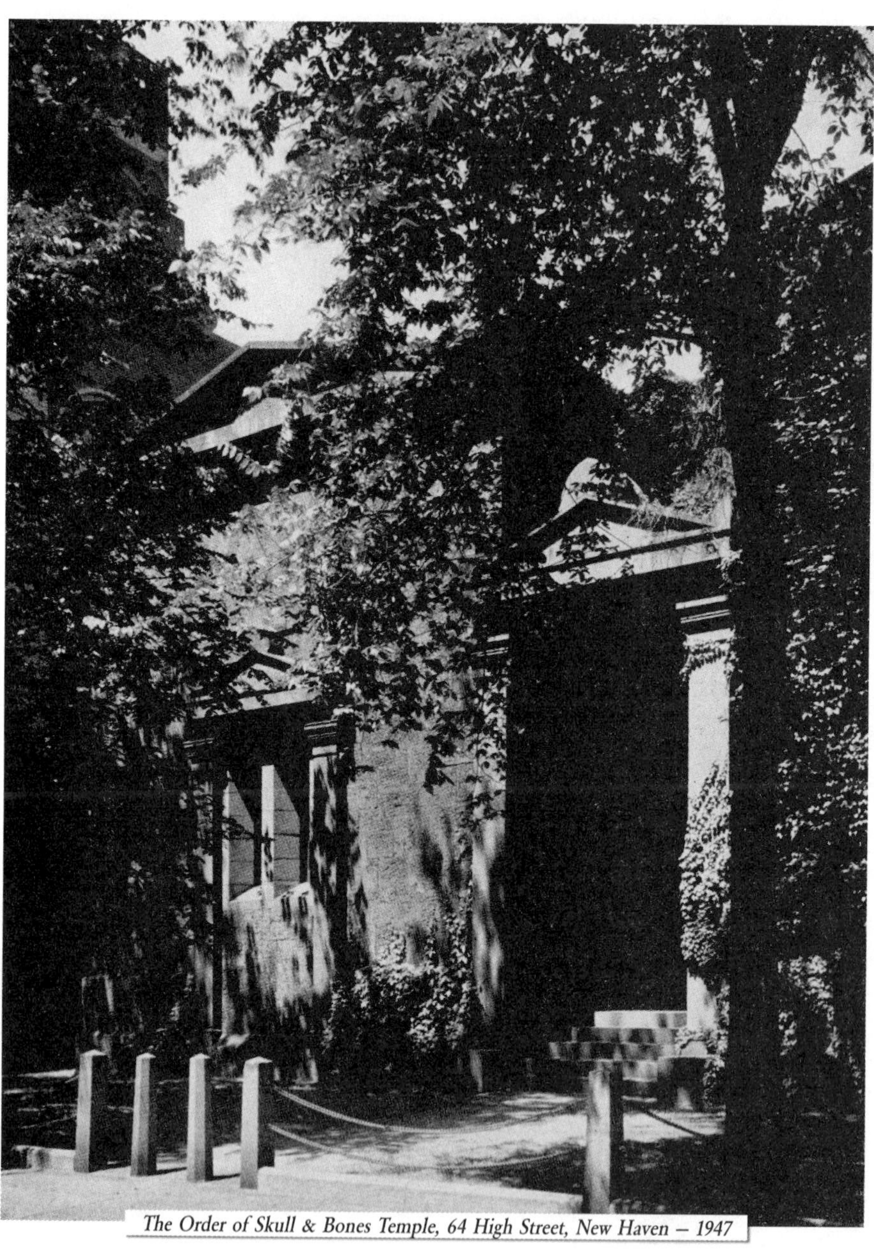

The Order of Skull & Bones Temple, 64 High Street, New Haven – 1947

Wise statesmen ... established these great self-evident truths, that when in the distant future some man, some faction, some interest, should set up the doctrine that none but rich men, or none but white men, were entitled to life, liberty and the pursuit of happiness, their posterity should look up again at the Declaration of Independence and take courage to renew the battle which their fathers began ...[1]

— Abraham Lincoln

Skull and Bones: The Racist Nightmare at Yale

Webster Griffin Tarpley and Anton Chaitkin

Chapter Seven of *George Bush – The Unauthorized Biography* - 1992. Used with permission.

The U.S. Navy delivered George Bush back home for good on Christmas Eve, 1944; the war in the Pacific raged on over the next half year, with Allied forces taking Southeast Asia, the Netherlands East Indies (Indonesia), and islands such as Iwo Jima and Okinawa.

Honeymoon

Barbara Pierce quit Smith College in her sophomore year to marry George. Prescott and Mother Bush gave a splendid prenuptial dinner at the Greenwich Field Club. The wedding took place January 6, 1945, in the Rye, New York Presbyterian Church, as the U.S. Third Fleet bombarded the main Philippine island of Luzon in preparation for invasion. Afterwards there was a glamorous reception for 300 at Appawamis Country Club. The newlyweds honeymooned at The Cloisters, a five-star hotel on Sea Island, Georgia, with swimming, tennis and golf.

George's next assignment was to train pilots at Norfolk, Virginia Naval Air Station. "George's duty ... was light. As for other young marrieds, whose husbands were between warzone tours, this was kind of an extended (and paid) honeymoon."[2]

Japan surrendered in August. That fall, George and Barbara Bush moved to New Haven where Bush entered Yale University. He and Barbara moved into an apartment at 37 Hillhouse Avenue, across the street from Yale President Charles Seymour.

College life was good to George, what he saw of it. A college career usually occupies four years. But we know that George Bush is a rapidly moving man. Thus he was pleased with the special arrangement made for veterans, by which Yale allowed him to get his degree after attending classes for only two and a half years.

Bush and his friends remember it all fondly, as representatives of the Fashionable Set: "[M]embers of [Bush's] class have since sighed with nostalgia for those days of the late 1940s ... Trolley cars still rumbled along the New Haven streets. On autumn afternoons they would be crowded with students going out to football games at the Yale Bowl, *scattering pennies along the way and shouting 'scramble' to the street kids diving for them*" [emphasis added].[3]

In 1947, Barbara gave birth to George W. Bush, the President's namesake.

By the time of his 1948 graduation, he had been elected to Phi Beta Kappa, an honor traditionally associated with academic achievement. A great deal is known about George Bush's career at Yale, except the part about books and studies. Unfortunately for those who would wish to consider his intellectual accomplishment, everything about that has been sealed shut and is top secret. The Yale administration says they have turned over to the FBI custody of all of Bush's academic records, allegedly because the FBI needs such access to check the resumés of important office holders.

From all available testimony, his mental life before college was anything but outstanding. His campaign literature claims that, as a veteran, Bush was "serious" at Yale. But we cannot check exactly how he achieved election to Phi Beta Kappa, in his abbreviated college experience. Without top secret clearance, we cannot consult his test results, read his essays, or learn much about his performance in class. We know that his father was a trustee of the university, in charge of "developmental" fundraising. And his family friends were in control of the U.S. secret services.

A great deal is known, however, about George Bush's *status* at Yale.

His fellow student John H. Chafee, later a U.S. Senator from Rhode Island and Secretary of the Navy, declared: "We didn't see much of him because he was married, but I guess my first impression was that he was — and I don't mean this in a derogatory fashion — in the inner set, the movers and shakers, the establishment. I don't mean he put on airs or anything, but … just everybody knew him."

Chafee, like Bush, and Dan Quayle, was in the important national fraternity, Delta Kappa Epsilon (DKE or the "Dekes"). But Chafee says, "I never remember seeing him there. He wasn't one to hang around with the fellows."[4]

THE TOMB

GEORGE BUSH, IN FACT, PASSED his most important days and nights at Yale in the strange companionship of the senior-year Skull and Bones Society.[5]

Out of those few who were chosen for Bones membership, George was the last one to be notified of his selection — this honor is traditionally reserved for the highest of the high and mighty.

His father, Prescott Bush, several other relatives and partners, and Roland and Averell Harriman, who sponsored the Bush family, were also members of this secret society.

The undoubted political and financial power associated with Skull and Bones has given rise to many popular questions about the nature and origin of the group. Its members have fed the mystery with false leads and silly speculations.

The order was incorporated in 1856 under the name "Russell Trust Association." By special act of the state legislature in 1943, its trustees are exempted from the normal requirement of filing corporate reports with the Connecticut Secretary of State.

As of 1978, all business of the Russell Trust was handled by its lone trustee, Brown Brothers Harriman partner John B. Madden, Jr. Madden started with Brown Brothers Harriman in 1946, under senior partner Prescott Bush, George Bush's father.

Each year, Skull and Bones members select ("tap") 15 third-year Yale students to replace them in the senior group the following year. Graduating members are given a sizeable cash bonus to help them get started in life. Older graduate members, the so-called "Patriarchs," give special backing in business, politics, espionage and legal careers to graduate Bonesmen who exhibit talent or usefulness.

The home of Skull and Bones on the Yale campus is a stone building resembling a mausoleum, and known as "the Tomb." Initiations take place on Deer Island in the St. Lawrence River (an island owned by the Russell Trust Association), with regular reunions on Deer Island and at Yale. Initiation rites reportedly include strenuous and traumatic activities of the new member, while immersed naked in mud, and in a coffin. More important is the "sexual autobiography": The initiate tells the Order all the sex secrets of his young life. Weakened mental defenses against manipulation, and the blackmail potential of such information, have obvious permanent uses in enforcing loyalty among members.

The loyalty is intense. One of Bush's former teachers, whose own father was a Skull and Bones member, told our interviewer that his father used to stab his little Skull and Bones pin into his skin to keep it in place when he took a bath.

Members continue throughout their lives to unburden themselves on their psychosexual thoughts to their Bones Brothers, even if they are no longer sitting in a coffin. This has been the case with President George Bush, for whom these ties are reported to have a deep personal meaning. Beyond the psychological manipulation associated with freemasonic mummery, there are very solid political reasons for Bush's strong identification with this cult.

Observers of Skull and Bones, apologists and critics alike, have accepted various deceptive notions about the order. There are two outstanding, among these falsehoods:

1) that it is essentially an *American* group, an assembly of wealthy, elite "patriots"; it is in fact, an agency for British Empire penetration and subversion of the American republic; and

2) that it is somehow *the* unique center of conspiratorial control over the United States. This misconception is certainly understandable, given the rather astonishing number of powerful, historically important and grotesquely anti-human individuals, who have come out of Skull and Bones. But there are in fact congruent organizations at other Ivy League colleges, which reflect, as does Skull and Bones, the over-arching oligarchical power of several heavily intermarried financier families.

The mistaken, speculative notions may be corrected by examining the history of Skull and Bones, viewed within the reality of the American Eastern Establishment.

Skull and Bones — the Russell Trust Association — was first established among the class graduating from Yale in 1833. Its founder was William Huntington Russell of Middletown, Connecticut. The Russell family was the master of incalculable wealth derived from the largest U.S. criminal organization of the nineteenth century: Russell and Company, the great opium syndicate.

There was at that time a deep suspicion of, and national revulsion against, freemasonry and secret organizations in the United States, fostered in particular by the anti-masonic writings of former U.S. President John Quincy Adams. Adams stressed that those who take oaths to politically powerful international secret societies cannot be depended on for loyalty to a democratic republic.

But the Russells were protected as part of the multiply-intermarried grouping of families then ruling Connecticut (see accompanying chart). The blood-proud members of the Russell, Pierpont, Edwards, Burr, Griswold, Day, Alsop and Hubbard families were prominent in the pro-British party within the state. Many of their sons would be among the members chosen for the Skull and Bones Society over the years.

The background to Skull and Bones is a story of Opium and Empire, and a bitter struggle for political control over the new U.S. republic.

Samuel Russell, second cousin to Bones founder William H., established Russell and Company in 1823. Its business was to acquire opium from Turkey and smuggle it into China, where it was strictly prohibited, under the armed protection of the British Empire.

The prior, predominant American gang in this field had been the syndicate created by Thomas Handasyd Perkins of Newburyport, Massachusetts, an aggregation of the self-styled "blue bloods" or Brahmins of Boston's north shore. Forced out of the lucrative African slave trade by U.S. law and Caribbean slave revolts, leaders of the Cabot, Lowell, Higginson, Forbes, Cushing and Sturgis families had married Perkins siblings and children. The Perkins opium syndicate made the fortune and established the power of these families. By the 1830s, the Russells had bought out the Perkins syndicate and made Connecticut the primary center of the U.S. opium racket. Massachusetts families (Coolidge, Sturgis, Forbes and Delano) joined Connecticut (Alsop) and New York (Low) smuggler-millionaires under the Russell auspices.

John Quincy Adams and other patriots had fought these men for a quarter century by the time the Russell Trust Association was set up with its open pirate emblem — Skull and Bones.

With British ties of family, shipping and merchant banking, the old New England Tories had continued their hostility to American independence after the Revolutionary War of 1775-83. These pretended conservative patriots proclaimed Thomas Jefferson's 1801 presidential inauguration "radical usurpation."

The Massachusetts Tories ("Essex Junto") joined with Vice President Aaron Burr, Jr. (a member of the Connecticut Edwards and Pierpont families) and Burr's cousin and law partner Theodore Dwight, in political moves designed to break up the United States and return it to British allegiance.

The U.S. nationalist leader, former Treasury Secretary Alexander Hamilton, exposed the plan in 1804. Burr shot him to death in a duel, then led a famous abortive conspiracy to form a new empire in the Southwest, with territory to be torn from the U.S.A. and Spanish Mexico. For the "blue bloods," the romantic figure of Aaron Burr was ever afterwards the symbol of British feudal revenge against the American republic.

The Connecticut Tory families hosted the infamous Hartford Convention in 1815, toward the end of the second war between the U.S. and Britain (the War of 1812). Their secessionist propaganda was rendered impotent by America's defensive military victory. This faction then retired from the open political arena, pursuing instead entirely private and covert alliances with the British Empire. The incestuously intermarried Massachusetts and Connecticut families associated themselves with the British East India Company in the criminal opium traffic into China. These families made increased profits as partners and surrogates for the British during the bloody 1839-42 Opium War, the race war of British forces against Chinese defenders.

Samuel and William Huntington Russell were quiet, wary builders of their faction's power. An intimate colleague of opium gangster Samuel Russell wrote this about him:

> While he lived, no friend of his would venture to mention his name in print. While in China, he lived for about twenty-five years almost as a hermit, hardly known outside of his factory [the Canton warehouse compound] except by the chosen few who enjoyed his intimacy, and by his good friend, Hoqua [Chinese security director for the British

> East India Company], but studying commerce in its broadest sense, as well as its minutest details. Returning home with well-earned wealth he lived hospitably in the midst of his family, and a small circle of intimates. Scorning words and pretensions from the bottom of his heart, he was the truest and staunchest of friends; hating notoriety, he could always be absolutely counted on for every good work which did not involve publicity.

The Russells' Skull and Bones Society was the most important of their domestic projects "which did not involve publicity."

A police-blotter type review of Russell's organization will show why the secret order, though powerful, was not the unique organ of "conspiracy" for the U.S. Eastern Establishment. The following gentlemen were among Russells' partners:

- Augustine Heard (1785-1868): ship captain and pioneer U.S. opium smuggler.
- John Cleve Green (1800-75): married to Sarah Griswold; gave a fortune in opium profits to Princeton University, financing three Princeton buildings and four professorships; trustee of the Princeton Theological Seminary for 25 years.
- Abiel Abbott Low (1811-93): his opium fortune financed the construction of the Columbia University New York City campus; father of Columbia's president Seth Low.
- John Murray Forbes (1813-98): his opium millions financed the career of author Ralph Waldo Emerson, who married Forbes's daughter, and bankrolled the establishment of the Bell Telephone Company, whose first president was Forbes's son.
- Joseph Coolidge: his Augustine Heard agency got $10 million yearly as surrogates for the Scottish dope-runners Jardine Matheson during the fighting in China; his son organized the United Fruit Company; his grandson, Archibald Cary Coolidge, was the founding executive officer of the Anglo-Americans' Council on Foreign Relations.
- Warren Delano, Jr.: chief of Russell and Co. in Canton; grandfather of U.S. President Franklin Delano Roosevelt.

*• Russell Sturgis: his grandson by the same name was chairman of the Baring Bank in England, financiers of the Far East opium trade.

Such persons as John C. Green and A.A. Low, whose names adorn various buildings at Princeton and Columbia Universities, made little attempt to hide the criminal origin of their influential money. Similarly with the Cabots, the Higginsons and the Welds for Harvard. The secret groups at other colleges are analogous and closely related to Yale's Skull and Bones.

Princeton has its "eating clubs," especially Ivy Club and Cottage Club, whose oligarchical tradition runs from Jonathan Edwards and Aaron Burr through the Dulles brothers. At Harvard there is the ultra-blue-blooded Porcelian (known also as the Porc or Pig club); Theodore Roosevelt bragged to the German Kaiser of his membership there; Franklin Roosevelt was a member of the slightly "lower" Fly Club.

A few of the early initiates in Skull and Bones went on to careers in obvious defiance of the order's oligarchical character; two such were the scientists **Benjamin Silliman, Jr.** (Skull and Bones 1837), and **William Chauvenet** (Skull and Bones 1840). This reflects the continued importance of republican factions at Yale, Harvard and other colleges during the middle three decades of the nineteenth century. Silliman and Chauvenet became enemies of everything Skull and Bones stood for, while the Yale secret group rapidly conformed to the Russells' expectations.

* Certain of the prominent Boston opium families, such as Cabot and Weld, did not affiliate directly with Russell, Connecticut and Yale, but were identified instead with Harvard.

Yale was the northern college favored by southern slave-owning would-be aristocrats. Among Yale's southern students were John C. Calhoun, later the famous South Carolina defender of slavery against nationalism, and Judah P. Benjamin, later Secretary of State for the slaveowners' Confederacy.

Young South Carolinian Joseph Heatly Dulles, whose family bought their slaves with the money from contract-security work for the British conquerors in India, was in a previous secret Yale group, the "Society of Brothers in Unity." At Yale Dulles worked with the Northern secessionists and attached himself to Daniel Lord; their two families clove together in the fashion of a gang. The Lords became powerful Anglo-American Wall Street lawyers, and J.H. Dulles's grandson was the father of Allen Dulles and John Foster Dulles.

In 1832-33 Skull and Bones was launched under the Russell pirate flag.

Among the early initiates of the order were **Henry Rootes Jackson** (S&B 1839), a leader of the 1861 Georgia Secession Convention and post-Civil War president of the Georgia Historical Society (thus the false accounts of the "good old slavery days" and the "bad northern invaders"); **John Perkins, Jr.** (S&B 1840), chairman of the 1861 Louisiana Secession Convention, who fled abroad for 13 years after the Civil War; and **William Taylor Sullivan Barry** (S&B 1841), a national leader of the secessionist wing of the Democratic Party during the 1850s, and chairman of the 1861 Mississippi Secession Convention.

Alphonso Taft was a Bonesman alongside **William H. Russell** in the Class of 1833. As U.S. Attorney General in 1876-77, Alphonso Taft helped organize the backroom settlement of the deadlocked 1876 presidential election. The bargain gave Rutherford B. Hayes the presidency (1877-81) and withdrew the U.S. troops from the South, where they had been enforcing blacks' rights.

Alphonso's son, **William Howard Taft** (S&B 1878), was U.S. President from 1909 to 1913. President Taft's son, **Robert Alphonso Taft** (S&B 1910), was a leading U.S. Senator after World War II; his family's Anglo-Saxon racial/ancestral preoccupation was the disease which crippled Robert Taft's leadership of American nationalist "conservatives."

Other pre-Civil War Bonesmen were:

• **William M. Evarts** (S&B 1837): Wall Street attorney for British and southern slaveowner projects, collaborator of Taft in the 1876 bargain, U.S. Secretary of State 1877-81;

• **Morris R. Waite** (S&B 1837): Chief Justice of the U.S. Supreme Court 1874-88, whose rulings destroyed many rights of African-Americans gained in the Civil War; he helped his cohorts Taft and Evarts arrange the 1876 presidential settlement scheme to pull the rights-enforcing U.S. troops out of the South;

• **Daniel Coit Gilman** (S&B 1852): co-incorporator of the Russell Trust; founding president of Johns Hopkins University as a great center for the racialist eugenics movement;

• **Andrew D. White** (S&B 1853): founding president of Cornell University; psychic researcher; and diplomatic cohort of the Venetian, Russian and British oligarchies;

• **Chauncey M. Depew** (S&B 1856): general counsel for the Vanderbilt railroads, he helped the Harriman family to enter into high society.

By about the mid-1880s, the Skull and Bones membership roster began to change from its earlier, often "scholarly," coloration; the change reflected the degradation of American political and economic life by imperialist, neo-pagan and racialist ideology.

Irving Fisher (S&B 1888) became the racialist high priest of the economics faculty (Yale professor 1896-1946), and a famous merchant of British Empire propaganda for free trade and reduction of the non-white population. Fisher was founding president of the American Eugenics Society under the financial largesse of Averell Harriman's mother.

Gifford Pinchot (S&B 1889) invented the aristocrats' "conservation" movement. He was President Theodore Roosevelt's chief forester, substituting federal land-control in place of Abraham Lincoln's free-land-to-families farm creation program. Pinchot's British Empire activitism included the Psychical Research Society and his vice-presidency of the first International Eugenics Congress in 1912.

Helping Pinchot initiate this century's racialist environmentalism were his cohorts **George W. Woodruff** (S&B 1889), Teddy Roosevelt's Assistant Attorney General and Acting Interior Secretary; and **Henry Solon Graves** (S&B 1892), chief U.S. forester 1910-20. **Frederick E. Weyerhaeuser** (S&B 1896), owner of vast tracts of American forest, was a follower of Pinchot's movement, while the Weyerhauser family were active collaborators of British-South African super-racist Cecil Rhodes. This family's friendship with President George Bush is a vital factor in the present environmentalist movement.

With **Henry L. Stimson** (S&B 1888) we come to the Eastern Liberal Establishment which has ruled America during the twentieth century. Stimson was President Taft's Secretary of War (1911-13), and President Herbert Hoover's Secretary of State (1929-33). As Secretary of War (1940-45), this time under President Harry Truman, Stimson pressed Truman to drop the atomic bomb on the Japanese. This decision involved much more than merely "pragmatic" military considerations. These Anglophiles, up through George Bush, have opposed the American republic's tradition of alliance with national aspirations in Asia; and they worried that the invention of nuclear energy would too powerfully unsettle the world's toleration for poverty and misery. Both the U.S. and the Atom had better be dreaded, they thought.

The present century owes much of its record of horrors to the influential Anglophile American families which came to dominate and employ the Skull and Bones Society as a political recruiting agency, particularly the Harrimans, Whitneys, Vanderbilts, Rockefellers and their lawyers, the Lords and Tafts and Bundys.

The politically aggressive Guaranty Trust Company, run almost entirely by Skull and Bones initiates, was a financial vehicle of these families in the early 1900s. Guaranty Trust's support for the Bolshevik and Nazi revolutions overlapped the more intense endeavors in these fields by the Harrimans, George Walker and Prescott Bush a few blocks away, and in Berlin.

Skull and Bones was dominated from 1913 onward by the circles of Averell Harriman. They displaced remaining traditionalists such as Douglas MacArthur from power in the United States.

For George Bush, the Skull and Bones Society is more than simply the British, as opposed to the American, strategic tradition. It is merged in the family and personal network within which his whole life has been, in a sense, handed to him prepackaged.

BRITAIN'S YALE FLYING UNIT

DURING PRESCOTT BUSH'S STUDENT DAYS, the Harriman set at Yale decided that World War I was sufficiently amusing that they ought to get into it as recreation. They formed a special Yale Unit of the Naval Reserve Flying Corps, at the instigation of F. Trubee Davison. Since the United States was not at war, and the Yale students were going to serve Britain, the Yale Unit was privately and lavishly financed by F. Trubee's father, Henry Davison, the senior managing partner at J.P. Morgan and Co. At that time, the

Morgan bank was the official financial agency for the British government in the United States. The Yale Unit's leader was amateur pilot Robert A. Lovett. They were based first on Long Island, New York, then in Palm Beach, Florida.

The Yale Unit has been described by Lovett's family and friends in a collective biography of the Harriman set:

> Training for the Yale Flying Unit was not exactly boot camp. Davison's father ... helped finance them royally, and newspapers of the day dubbed them "the millionaires' unit." They cut rakish figures, and knew it; though some dismissed them as dilettantes, the hearts of young Long Island belles fluttered at the sight ....
>
> [In] Palm Beach ... they ostentatiously pursued a relaxed style. "They were rolled about in wheel chairs by African slaves amid tropical gardens and coconut palms," wrote the unit's historian ... "For light exercise, they learned to glance at their new wristwatches with an air of easy nonchalance"... [Lovett] was made chief of the unit's private club, the Wags, whose members started their sentences, "Being a Wag and therefore a superman"...
>
> Despite the snide comments of those who dismissed them as frivolous rich boys, Lovett's unit proved to be daring and imaginative warriors when they were dispatched for active duty in 1917 with Britain's Royal Naval Air Service.[6]

Lovett was transferred to the U.S. Navy after the U.S. joined Britain in World War I.

The Yale Flying Unit was the glory of Skull and Bones. **Roland Harriman**, **Prescott Bush** and their 1917 Bonesmates selected for 1918 membership in the secret order these Yale Flying Unit leaders: **Robert Lovett**, **F. Trubee Davison**, **Artemus Lamb Gates**, and **John Martin Vorys**. Unit flyers **David Sinton Ingalls** and F. Trubee's brother, **Harry P. Davison** (who became Morgan vice chairman), were tapped for the 1920 Skull and Bones.

Lovett did not actually have a senior year at Yale: "He was tapped for Skull and Bones not on the Old Campus but at a naval station in West Palm Beach; his initiation, instead of being conducted in the 'tomb' on High Street, occurred at the headquarters of the Navy's Northern Bombing Group between Dunkirk and Calais."[7]

Some years later, **Averell Harriman** gathered Lovett, Prescott Bush and other pets into the utopian oligarchs' community a few miles to the north of Palm Beach, called Jupiter Island (see Chapter 4 [George Bush: The Unauthorized Biography]).

British Empire loyalists flew right from the Yale Unit into U.S. strategy-making positions:

• F. Trubee Davison was Assistant U.S. Secretary of War for Air from 1926 to 1933. David S. Ingalls (on the board of Jupiter Island's Pan American Airways) was meanwhile Assistant Secretary of the Navy for Aviation (1929-32). Following the American Museum of Natural History's Hitlerite 1932 eugenics congress, Davison resigned his government Air post to become the Museum's president. Then, under the Harriman-Lovett national security regime of the early 1950s, F. Trubee Davison became Director of Personnel for the new Central Intelligence Agency.

• Robert Lovett was Assistant Secretary of War for Air from 1941-45.

• Lovett's 1918 Bonesmate Artemus Gates (chosen by Prescott and his fellows) became Assistant Secretary of the Navy for Air in 1941. Gates retained this post throughout the Second World War until 1945. Having a man like Gates up there, who owed his position to Averell, Bob, Prescott and their set, was quite reassuring to young naval aviator George Bush; especially so, when Bush would have to worry about the record being correct concerning his controversial fatal crash.

Other Important Bonesmen

• **Richard M. Bissell,** Jr. was a very important man to the denizens of Jupiter Island. He graduated from Yale in 1932, the year after the Harrimanites bought the island. Though not in Skull and Bones, Bissell was the younger brother of **William Truesdale Bissell**, a Bonesman from the class of 1925. Their father, Connecticut insurance executive Richard M. Bissell, Sr., had put the U.S. insurance industry's inside knowledge of all fire-insured industrial plants at the disposal of government planners during World War I.

The senior Bissell, a powerful Yale alumnus, was also the director of the Neuro-Psychiatric Institute of the Hartford Retreat for the Insane; there, in 1904, Yale graduate Clifford Beers underwent mind-destroying treatment which led this mental patient to found the Mental Hygiene Society, a major Yale-based Skull and Bones project. This would evolve into the CIA's cultural engineering effort of the 1950s, the drugs and brainwashing adventure known as "MK-Ultra."

Richard M. Bissell, Jr. studied at the London School of Economics in 1932 and 1933, and taught at Yale from 1935 to 1941. He then joined Harriman's entourage in the U.S. government. Bissell was an economist for the Combined Shipping Adjustment Board in 1942-43, while Averell Harriman was the U.S. leader of that board in London.

In 1947 and 1948, Bissell was executive secretary of the "Harriman Commission," otherwise known as the President's Commission on Foreign Aid. When Harriman was the administrator of the Marshall Plan, Bissell was assistant administrator.

Harriman was director of Mutual Security (1951-53), while Bissell was consultant to the director of Mutual Security 1952.

Bissell then joined F. Trubee Davison at the Central Intelligence Agency. When Allen Dulles became CIA Director, Bissell was one of his three aides.

Why could this be of interest to our Floridians? We saw in Chapter 4 [George Bush — The Unauthorized Biography], that the great anti-Castro covert initiative of 1959-61 was supervised by an awesome array of Harriman agents. We need now add to that assessment only the fact that the detailed management of the invasion of Cuba, and of the assassination planning, and the training of the squads for these jobs, was given into the hands of Richard M. Bissell, Jr.

This 1961 invasion failed. Fidel Castro survived the widely-discussed assassination plots against him. But the initiative succeeded in what was probably its core purpose: to organize a force of multi-use professional assassins.

The Florida-trained killers stayed in business under the leadership of Ted Shackley. They were all around the assassination of President Kennedy in 1963. They kept going with the Operation Phoenix mass murder of Vietnamese civilians, with Middle East drug and terrorist programs, and with George Bush's Contra wars in Central America.

• **Harvey Hollister Bundy** (S&B 1909) was Henry L. Stimson's Assistant Secretary of State (1931-33); then he was Stimson's Special Assistant Secretary of War, alongside Assistant Secretary Robert Lovett of Skull and Bones and Brown Brothers Harriman.

Harvey's son **William P. Bundy** (S&B 1939) was a CIA officer from 1951 to 1961; as a 1960s defense official, he pushed the Harriman-Dulles scheme for a Vietnam war. Harvey's other son, **McGeorge Bundy** (S&B 1940), co-authored Stimson's memoirs in 1948. As President John Kennedy's Director of National Security, McGeorge Bundy organized the whitewash of the Kennedy assassination, and immediately switched the U.S. policy away from the Kennedy pullout and back toward war in Vietnam.

• There was also **Henry Luce**, a Bonesman of 1920 with David S. Ingalls and Harry Pomeroy. Luce published Time magazine, where his ironically-named "American Century" blustering was straight British Empire doctrine: Bury the republics, hail the Anglo-Saxon conquerors.

• **William Sloane Coffin**, tapped for 1949 Skull and Bones by George Bush and his Bone companions, was from a long line of Skull and Bones Coffins. William Sloane Coffin was famous in the Vietnam War protest days as a leader of the left protest against the war. Was the fact that he was an agent of the Central Intelligence Agency embarrassing to William Sloane?

This was no contradiction. His uncle, the **Reverend Henry Sloane Coffin** (S&B 1897), had also been a "peace" agitator, and an oligarchical agent. Uncle Henry was for 20 years president of the Union Theological Seminary, whose board chairman was Prescott Bush's partner Thatcher Brown. In 1937, Henry Coffin and John Foster Dulles led the U.S. delegation to England to found the World Council of Churches, as a "peace movement" guided by the pro-Hitler faction in England.

The Coffins have been mainstays of the liberal death lobby, for euthanasia and eugenics. The Coffins outlasted Hitler, arriving into the CIA in the 1950s.

• **Amory Howe Bradford** (S&B 1934) married Carol Warburg Rothschild in 1941. Carol's mother, Carola, was the acknowledged head of the Warburg family in America after World War II. This family had assisted the Harrimans' rise into the world in the nineteenth and early twentieth centuries; in concert with the Sulzbergers at the New York Times, they had used their American Jewish Committee and B'nai B'rith to protect the Harriman-Bush deals with Hitler. This made it nice for Averell Harriman, just like family, when Amory Howe Bradford worked on the Planning Group of Harriman's NATO secretariat in London, 1951-52. Bradford was meanwhile assistant to the publisher of the New York Times, and went on to become general manager of the Times.

Other modern Bonesmen have been closely tied to George Bush's career.

• **George Herbert Walker, Jr.** (S&B 1927) was the President's uncle and financial angel. In the 1970s he sold G.H. Walker & Co. to White, Weld & Co. and became a director of White, Weld; company heir William Weld, the current Massachusetts governor, is an active Bush Republican.

• Publisher **William F. Buckley** (S&B 1950) had a family oil business in Mexico. There Buckley was a close ally to CIA covert operations manager E. Howard Hunt, whose lethal antics were performed under the eyes of Miami Station and Jupiter Island.

• **David Lyle Boren** (S&B 1963) was assistant to the director of the Office of Civil and Defense Mobilization, and a propaganda analyst for the U.S. Information Agency, before graduating from Yale. Thus while he was imbibing the British view at Oxford University (1963-65), Boren was already an Anglo-American intelligence operative, listed in the "speakers bureau" of the American embassy in London. David Boren was elected to the U.S. Senate in 1979 and became chairman of the Senate Intelligence Committee.

Though a Democrat (who spoke knowingly of the "parallel government" operating in Iran-Contra), Boren's Intelligence Committee rulings have been (not unexpectedly) more and more favorable to his "Patriarch" in the White House.

BUSH'S OWN BONES

AMONG THE TRADITIONAL ARTIFACTS collected and maintained within the High Street Tomb are human remains of various derivations. The following concerns one such set of Skull and Bones.

Geronimo, an Apache faction leader and warrior, led a party of warriors on a raid in 1876, after Apaches were moved to the San Carlos Reservation in Arizona territory. He led other raids against U.S. and Mexican forces well into the 1880s; he was captured and escaped many times.

Geronimo was finally interned at Fort Sill, Oklahoma. He became a farmer and joined a Christian congregation. He died at the age of 79 years in 1909, and was buried at Fort Sill. Three-quarters of a century later, his tribesmen raised the question of getting their famous warrior reinterred back in Arizona.

Ned Anderson was Tribal Chairman of the San Carlos Apache Tribe from 1978 to 1986. This is the story he tells[8]:

Around the fall of 1983, the leader of an Apache group in another section of Arizona said he was interested in having the remains of Geronimo returned to his tribe's custody. Taking up this idea, Anderson said that the remains properly belonged to his group as much as to the other Apaches. After much discussion, several Apache groups met at a kind of summit meeting held at Fort Sill, Oklahoma. The army authorities were not favorable to the meeting, and it only occurred through the intervention of the office of the Governor of Oklahoma.

As a result of this meeting, Ned Anderson was written up in the newspapers as an articulate Apache activist. Soon afterwards, in late 1983 or early 1984, a Skull and Bones member contacted Anderson and leaked evidence that Geronimo's remains had long ago been pilfered — by Prescott Bush, George's father. The informant said that in May of 1918, Prescott Bush and five other officers at Fort Sill desecrated the grave of Geronimo. They took turns watching while they robbed the grave, taking items including a skull, some other bones, a horse bit and straps. These prizes were taken back to the Tomb, the home of the Skull and Bones Society at Yale in New Haven, Connecticut. They were put into a display case, which members and visitors could easily view upon entry to the building.

The informant provided Anderson with photographs of the stolen remains, and a copy of a Skull and Bones log book in which the 1918 grave robbery had been recorded. The informant said that Skull and Bones members used the pilfered remains in performing some of their Thursday and Sunday night rituals, with Geronimo's skull sitting out on a table in front of them.

Outraged, Anderson traveled to New Haven. He did some investigation on the Yale campus and held numerous discussions, to learn what the Apaches would be up against when they took action, and what type of action would be most fruitful.

Through an attorney, Ned Anderson asked the FBI to move into the case. The attorney conveyed to him the Bureau's response: If he would turn over every scrap of evidence to the FBI, and completely remove himself from the case, they would get involved. He rejected this bargain, since it did not seem likely to lead toward recovery of Geronimo's remains.

Due to his persistence, he was able to arrange a September 1986 Manhattan meeting with Jonathan Bush, George Bush's brother. Jonathan Bush vaguely assured Anderson that he would get what he had come after, and set a followup meeting for the next day. But Bush stalled — Anderson believes this was to gain time to hide and secure the stolen remains against any possible rescue action.

The Skull and Bones attorney representing the Bush family and managing the case was Endicott Peabody Davison. His father was the F. Trubee Davison mentioned above, who had been president of New York's American Museum of Natural History, and personnel director for the Central Intelligence Agency. The general attitude of this Museum crowd has long been that "Natives" should be stuffed and mounted for display to the Fashionable Set.

Finally, after about 11 days, another meeting occurred. A display case was produced, which did in fact match the one in the photograph the informant had given to Ned Anderson. But the skull he was shown was that of a ten-year-old child, and Anderson refused to receive it or to sign a legal document promising to shut up about the matter.

Anderson took his complaint to Arizona Congressmen Morris Udahl and John McCain III, but with no results. George Bush refused Congressman McCain's request that he meet with Anderson.

Anderson wrote to Udahl, enclosing a photograph of the wall case and skull at the "Tomb," showing a black and white photograph of the living Geronimo, which members of the Order had boastfully posted next to their display of his skull. Anderson quoted from a Skull and Bones Society internal history, entitled *Continuation of the History of Our Order for the Century Celebration, 17 June 1933, by The Little Devil of D'121.*

> From the war days [W.W. I] also sprang the mad expedition from the School of Fire at Fort Sill, Oklahoma, that brought to the T[omb] its most spectacular "crook," the skull of Geronimo the terrible, the Indian Chief who had taken forty-nine white scalps. An expedition in late May, 1918, by members of four Clubs [i.e. four graduating-class years of the Society], Xit D.114, Barebones, Caliban and Dingbat, D.115, S'Mike D.116, and Hellbender D.117, planned with great caution since in the words of one of them: "Six army captains robbing a grave wouldn't look good in the papers." The stirring climax was recorded by Hellbender in the Black Book of D.117: "... The ring of pick on stone and thud of earth on earth alone disturbs the peace of the prairie. An axe pried open the iron door of the tomb, and Pat[riarch] Bush entered and started to dig. We dug in turn, each on relief taking a turn on the road as guards ... Finally Pat[riarch] Ellery James turned up a bridle, soon a saddle horn and rotten leathers followed, then wood and then, at the exact bottom of the small round hole, Pat[riarch] James dug deep and pried out the trophy itself ... We quickly closed the grave, shut the door and sped home to Pat[riarch] Mallon's room, where we cleaned the Bones. Pat[riarch] Mallon sat on the floor liberally applying carbolic acid. The Skull was fairly clean, having only some flesh inside and a little hair. I showered and hit the hay ... a happy man ... ."[9]

The other grave robber whose name is given, Ellery James, we encountered in Chapter 1 [*George Bush : The Unauthorized Biography*] — he was to be an usher at Prescott's wedding three years later. And the fellow who applied acid to the stolen skull, burning off the flesh and hair, was Neil Mallon. Years later, Prescott Bush and his partners chose Mallon as chairman of Dresser Industries; Mallon hired Prescott's son, George Bush, for George's first job; and George Bush named his son, Neil Mallon Bush, after the flesh-picker.

In 1988, the Washington Post ran an article, originating from the Establishment-line Arizona Republic, entitled "Skull for Scandal: Did Bush's Father Rob Geronimo's Grave?" The article included a small quote from the 1933 Skull and Bones History of Our Order: "An axe pried open the iron door of the tomb, and ... Bush entered and started to dig ..." and so forth, but neglected to include other names beside Bush.

According to the Washington Post, the document which Bush attorney Endicott Davison tried to get the Apache leader to sign, stipulated that Ned Anderson agreed it would be "inappropriate for you, me [Jonathan Bush] or anyone in association with us to make or permit any publication in connection with this transaction." Anderson called the document ``very insulting to Indians." Davison claimed later that the Order's own history book is a hoax, but during the negotiations with Anderson, Bush's attorney demanded Anderson give up his copy of the book.[10]

Bush crony Fitzhugh Green gives the view of the President's backers on this affair, and conveys the arrogant racial attitude typical of Skull and Bones:

> Prescott Bush had a colorful side. In 1988 the press revealed the complaint of an Apache leader about Bush. This was Ned Anderson of San Carlos, Oklahoma [sic], who charged that as a young army officer Bush stole the skull of Indian Chief [sic] Geronimo and had it hung on the wall of Yale's Skull and Bones Club. After exposure of 'true facts' by Anderson, and consideration by some representatives in Congress, the issue faded from public sight. Whether or not this alleged skullduggery actually occurred, *the mere idea casts the senior Bush in an adventurous light*'[11] [emphasis added].

George Bush's crowning as a Bonesman was intensely, personally important to him. These men were tapped for the Class of 1948:

Thomas William Ludlow Ashley
Lucius Horatio Biglow, Jr.
George Herbert Walker Bush
John Erwin Caulkins
William Judkins Clark
William James Connelly, Jr.
George Cook III
David Charles Grimes
Richard Elwood Jenkins
Richard Gerstle Mack
Thomas Wilder Moseley
George Harold Pfau, Jr.
Samuel Sloane Walker, Jr.
Howard Sayre Weaver
Valleau Wilkie, Jr.

Survivors of this 1948 Bones group were interviewed for a 1988 Washington Post campaign profile of George Bush. The members described their continuing intimacy with and financial support for Bush up through his 1980s vice-presidency. Their original sexual togetherness at Yale is stressed:

> The relationships that were formed in the "Tomb" ... where the Society's meetings took place each Thursday and Sunday night during the academic year, have had a strong place in Bush's life, according to all 11 of his fellow Bonesmen who are still alive.
>
> Several described in detail the ritual in the organization that builds the bonds. Before giving his life history, each member had to spend a Sunday night reviewing his sex life in a talk known in the Tomb as CB, or "connubial bliss"...
>
> "The first time you review your sex life ... We went all the way around among the 15," said Lucius H. Biglow Jr., a retired Seattle attorney. "That way you get everybody committed to a certain extent ... It was a gradual way of building confidence."
>
> The sexual histories helped break down the normal defenses of the members, according to several of the members from his class. William J. Connelly, Jr. ... said, "In Skull and Bones we all stand together, 15 brothers under the skin. [It is] the greatest allegiance in the world."[12]

Here is our future U.S. President with the other wealthy, amoral young men, excited about their future unlimited power over the ignorant common people, sharing their sex secrets in a mausoleum surrounded by human remains. The excited young men are entirely directed by the "Patriarchs," the cynical alumni financiers who are the legal owners of the Order.

THE YALE TORIES WHO MADE SKULL AND BONES

THIS CHART DEPICTS FAMILY RELATIONSHIPS which were vital to the persons appearing on the chart. At less exalted levels of society, one is supposed to be praised or blamed only according to one's own actions. But in these Yale circles, "family' — genealogy — is an overwhelming consideration when evaluating individuals. Thus what we present here is more than simply a system of associations. It is a tradition which has operated powerfully on the emotions and judgment of the leaders of Yale University; they have merged their own identities into this tradition.

Lines are directed downwards from parents to their children. A double hyphen (- -) signifies the marriage of the persons on either side.

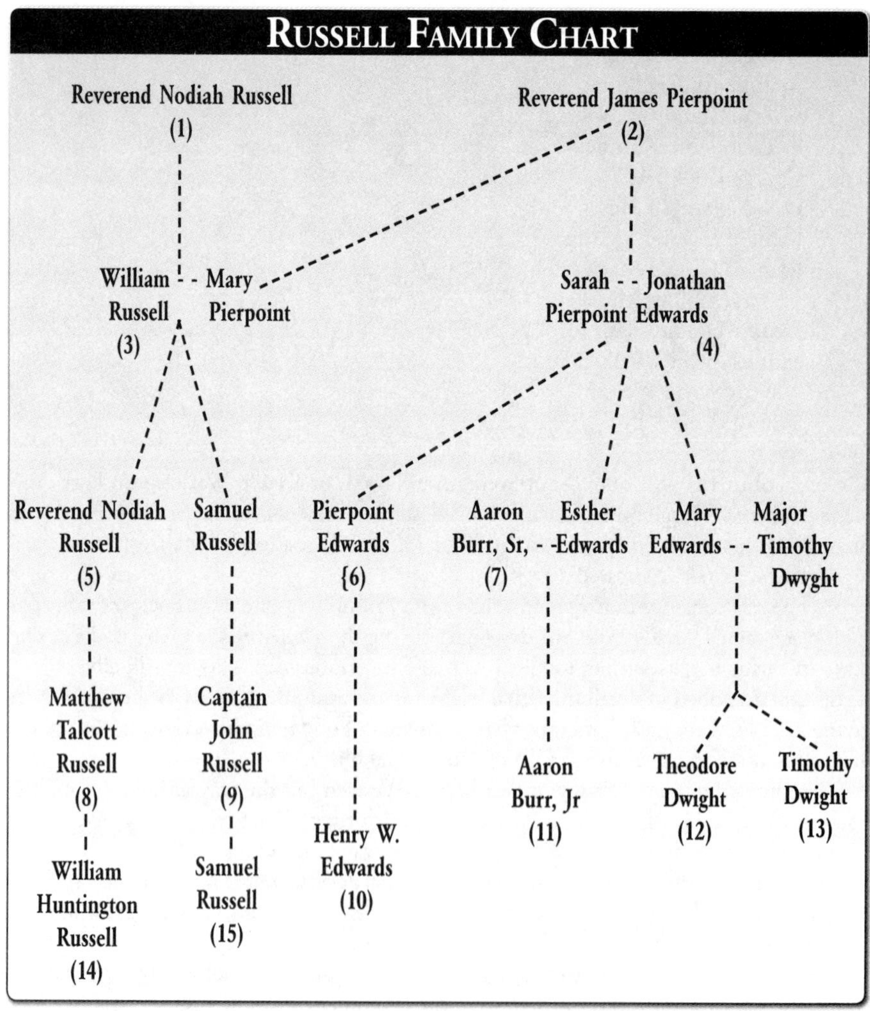

Guide To The Yale Family Chart

1) Rev. Nodiah Russell: One of 10 or 12 men who founded Yale University in 1701. Yale Trustee 1701-13. Pastor, First Congregational Church, Middletown, CT, ca. 1691-1716.
2) Rev. James Pierpont: Most celebrated of the Yale founders. Yale Trustee, 1701-14.
3) William Russell: Yale Trustee 1745-61. Pastor, First Congregational Church, Middletown, CT, 1716-61.
4) Jonathan Edwards: Graduated Yale 1720. Ultra-Calvinist theologian, president of Princeton University (called then "College of New Jersey").
5) Rev. Nodiah Russell: Graduated Yale 1750.
6) Pierpont Edwards (1750-1826): Made Master of Connecticut Masons by the British Army occupying New York in 1783; he administered the estate of the traitor Benedict Arnold.
7) Aaron Burr, Sr.: Graduated Yale 1735. President of Princeton University ("College of New Jersey").
8) Matthew Talcott Russell: Graduated Yale 1769. Deacon of First Congregational Church, Middletown, CT for 30 years. Lawyer for the Middletown Russell family. Died ca. 1817.
9) Captain John Russell. Died 1801 or 1802.
10) Henry W. Edwards: Governor of Connecticut 1833, 1835-38. Protector of Samuel Russell's opium-financed enterprises, patron of William Huntington Russell's new secret society, Skull and Bones.
11) Aaron Burr, Jr.: U.S. Vice President 1801-08. Killed Alexander Hamilton in a duel in 1804. Secession conspirator. Acquitted of treason in 1807, but wanted for murder, he fled to England. Returned to U.S.A. in 1812. Wall Street lawyer, 1812-36. Hero of imperial Anglo-Americans.
12) Theodore Dwight (1764-1846): Law partner of his cousin Aaron Burr, Jr. Secretary of the secessionist Hartford Convention, 1815. He united the Connecticut pro-British party with Massachusetts "Essex Junto."
13) Timothy Dwight: Secessionist. President of Yale, 1795-1817.
14) William Huntington Russell (1809-85): Graduated Yale 1833. Founder of Skull and Bones Society (or Russell Trust Association), which came to dominate Yale. Founded prep school for boys, 1836. His secret organization spread in the 1870s to Phillips Academy, the Andover, Massachusetts prep school.
15) Samuel Russell: Born in 1789 in the main ancestral house of the Russell family of Middletown. This house had been owned by the co-founder of Yale, Nodiah Russell (1), and by William Russell (3) and his wife Mary, sister-in-law to Jonathan Edwards.

He became head of the Middletown Russells. He established Russell and Co. in 1823, which by the 1830s superseded Perkins syndicate as largest American opium smuggling organization. His partners included leading Boston families.

He founded the Russell Manufacturing Company, Middletown, in 1837; he was president of Middlesex County Bank. During the formative years of Skull and Bones, the fabulously wealthy Samuel Russell was undisputed king of Middletown.

Note to Reader:

For the sake of clarity, we have omitted from this chart the ancestral line from Rev. James Pierpont (2) to his great grandson Rev. John Pierpont. Rev. John Pierpont wrote poetry for the pro-British secessionists; he denounced President Thomas Jefferson for saying that Pierpont's New England relatives were "under the influence of the whore of England." Rev. John was an employee of Aaron Burr's family during Burr's western conspiracy. Rev. John's daughter Juliet married Connecticut-born British banker Junius Morgan and gave birth to U.S. financial kingpin John Pierpont Morgan, named for his grandfather Rev. John.

NOTES:

1. Speech at Lewistown, Illinois, August 17, 1858; quoted in James Mellon (editor), *The Face of Lincoln* (New York: Viking Press, 1979), p. 35.
2. Fitzhugh Green, *George Bush: An Intimate Portrait* (New York: Hippocrene Books, 1989), p. 41.
3. Nicholas King, *George Bush: A Biography* (New York: Dodd, Mead & Company, 1980), p. 38.
4. Green, op. cit., p. 47.
5. Ibid., p. 48.
6. Among the sources used for this section are:
   Skull and Bones membership list, 1833-1950, printed 1949 by the Russell Trust Association, New Haven, Connecticut, available through the Yale University Library, New Haven.
   Biographies of the Russells and related families, in the Yale University Library, New Haven, and in the Russell Library, Middletown, Connecticut.
   Ron Chernow, *The House of Morgan: An American Banking Dynasty and the Rise of Modern Finance* (New York: Atlantic Monthly Press, 1990).
   Anthony C. Sutton, *How the Order Creates War and Revolution*, (Phoenix: Research Publications, Inc., 1984).
   Anthony C. Sutton, *America's Secret Establishment: An Introduction to the Order of Skull and Bones*, (Billings, Mt.: Liberty House Press, 1986).
   Anton Chaitkin, *Treason in America: From Aaron Burr to Averell Harriman*, second edition (New York: New Benjamin Franklin House, 1985).
   Anton Chaitkin, "Station Identification: Morgan, Hitler, NBC," New Solidarity, Oct. 8, 1984.
   Interviews with Bones members and their families.
7. Walter Isaacson and Evan Thomas, *The Wise Men: Six Friends and the World They Made — Acheson, Bohlen, Harriman, Kennan, Lovett, McCloy* (New York: Simon and Schuster, 1986), pp. 90-91.
8. Ibid., p. 93.
9. Interview with Ned Anderson, Nov. 6, 1991.
10. Quoted in Ned Anderson to Anton Chaitkin, Dec. 2, 1991, in possession of the authors.
11. Article by Paul Brinkley-Rogers of the Arizona Republic, in the Washington Post, Oct. 1, 1988.
12. Green, op. cit., p. 50.
13. Bob Woodward and Walter Pincus, "Bush Opened Up To Secret Yale Society," Washington Post, Aug. 7, 1988.

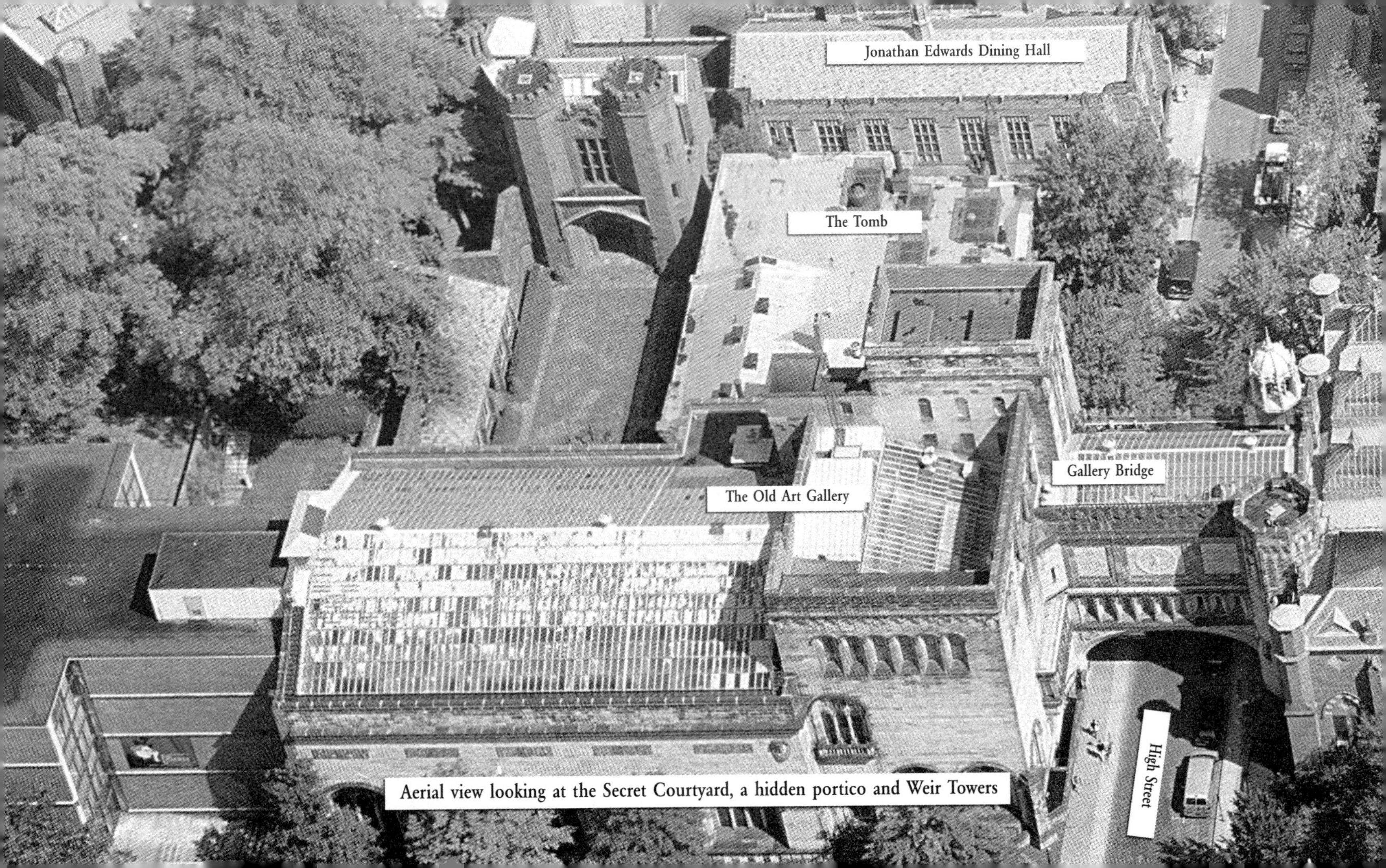

Aerial view looking at the Secret Courtyard, a hidden portico and Weir Towers

FEDERAL REGISTER, *Saturday, November 7, 1942*

[Vesting Order Number 248]

ALL OF THE CAPITAL STOCK OF UNION BANKING CORPORATION AND CERTAIN INDEBTEDNESS OWING BY IT

Under the authority of the Trading with the enemy Act, as amended, and Executive Order No. 9095, as amended,[1] and pursuant to law, the undersigned, after investigation, finding:

(a) That the property described as follows:

All of the capital stock of Union Banking Corporation, a New York corporation, New York, New York, which is a business enterprise within the United States, consisting of 4,000 shares of $100 par value common capital stock, the names of the registered owners of which, and the number of shares owned by them respectively, are as follows:

Names	Number of shares
E. Roland Harriman	3,991
Cornelius Lievense	4
Harold D. Pennington	1
Ray Morris	1
Prescott S. Bush	1
H. J. Kouwenhoven	1
Johann G. Groeninger	1
Total	4,000

[1] 7 F.R. 5205.

all of which shares are held for the benefit of Bank voor Handel en Scheepvaart, N. V., Rotterdam, The Netherlands, which bank is owned or controlled by members of the Thyssen family, nationals of Germany and/or Hungary,

is property of nationals, and represents ownership of said business enterprise which is a national, of a designated enemy country or countries (Germany and/or Hungary);

(b) That the property described as follows:

All right, title, interest and claim of any name or nature whatsoever of the aforesaid Bank voor Handel en Scheepvaart, and August Thyssen-Bank, Berlin, Germany, and each of them, in and to all indebtedness, contingent or otherwise and whether or not matured, owing to them, or each of them, by said Union Banking Corporation, including but not limited to all security rights in and to any and all collateral for any or all of such indebtedness and the right to sue for and collect such indebtedness.

is an interest in the aforesaid business enterprise held by nationals of an enemy country or countries, and also is property within the United States owned or controlled by nationals of a designated enemy country or countries (Germany and/or Hungary);

and determining that to the extent that any or all of such nationals are persons not within a designated enemy country, the national interest of the United States requires that such persons be treated as nationals of the aforesaid designated enemy country or countries (Germany and/or Hungary), and having made all determinations and taken all action, after appropriate consultation and certification, required by said executive order or Act or otherwise, and deeming it necessary in the national interest, hereby vests such property in the Alien Property Custodian, to be held, used, administered, liquidated, sold or otherwise dealt with in the interest of and for the benefit of the United States.

Such property and any or all of the proceeds thereof shall be held in a special account pending further determination of the Alien Property Custodian. This shall not be deemed to limit the powers of the Alien Property Custodian to return such property or the proceeds thereof, or to indicate that compensation will not be paid in lieu thereof, if and when it should be determined that such return should be made or such compensation should be paid.

Any person, except a national of a designated enemy country, asserting any claim arising as a result of this order may file with the Alien Property Custodian a notice of his claim, together with a request for a hearing thereon, on Form APC-1, within one year from the date hereof, or within such further time as may be allowed by the Alien Property Custodian. Nothing herein contained shall be deemed to constitute an admission of the existence, validity or right to allowance of any such claim.

The terms "national", "designated enemy country" and "business enterprise within the United States" as used herein shall have the meanings prescribed in section 10 of said executive order.

Executed at Washington, D. C., on October 20, 1942.

[SEAL] LEO T. CROWLEY,
Alien Property Custodian.

[F. R. Doc. 42-11568; Filed, November 6, 1942; 11:31 a. m.]

THE ORDER OF SKULL & BONES AND ILLEGAL FINANCE:

A STUDY OF THE ANALYTICAL FRAMEWORK OF CONSPIRACY THEORY

JEDEDIAH MCCLURE
2003

THIS WORK PRESENTS AND EXAMINES the analytical framework of conspiracy theorists in relation to the Order of Skull and Bones in an attempt to illuminate the clash between scholars of conspiracy theory and social science. This work specifically examines in detail the illegal financing activities of members of the Order of Skull and Bones to designated enemy regimes during two specific periods of war in the first half of the twentieth century.

1 — INTRODUCTION

THE ACADEMIC QUARREL with the traditional mode of conspiracy theory is, in short, that conspiracy theory takes for granted certain conditions of generality and fixity which are not always, or always completely, satisfied; that rigid adherence to long- range assumptions narrowly limits the range of what can be properly defined; and entails that conspiracy theory, being unique, indeterminate, and subject to change, is indefinable. Conspiracy theory maintains a lack of simplicity in its theoretical explanation of historical events often incorporating complex explanations when other, more simplistic explanatory models may exist. Furthermore, conspiracy theory is an unfalsifiable explanation of events.

As a result, conspiracy theory has come to represent a political other to 'proper' democratic politics through the use of potentially illegitimate assumptions that seem to question that the Unites States is a benign, pluralistic democracy, and that seem to reject the popular notion that history moves through the triumph of progress and leadership, as well as through the vagaries of coincidence and mistake.

In regards to conspiratorial assumptions of illegal financing and the Order of Skull and Bones, specialists in the field of political science, who are confronted by ragged evidence, are likely to insist that a similar lack of uniformity and/or causation characterized financial decisions in the first half of the century, and that no conspiratorial collusion existed. To generalize about legality and motives of early international financing is undoubtedly hazardous, and one should be on guard against projecting bias and contemporary theories too far back into the past. Yet one must also be on guard against ignoring important evidence and its implications on society at that period of time.

The actual number of firms involved and level of international financing to both Germany and the Soviet Union during this time period is inevitably open to dispute. Even apart from the problem of trying to estimate the number of firms and amount of finance that went uncataloged by Senate investigations, contemporary evidence must be handled with caution, for it often yields false clues to the number of firms involved and the motives of the financiers. Furthermore, drawing correlations between firms that were involved in illegal financing requires listing managers, presidents, vice-presidents and directors who might have been involved in the decision making process. Such information is difficult to come by, and almost impossible to determine who was directly making individual decisions. As a result, certain assumptions have to be made and adhered to without the benefit of supporting evidence. This is one of many reasons that social scientists discredit conspiracy theory and the issues of illegal finance during times of war are largely ignored.

Nevertheless, although it has to be considered in conjunction with many other issues, the correlations between The Order of Skull and Bones and illegal finance certainly does deserve a closer study. One must be careful not to skew these historical events with speculation and assumption. But it is equally important not to go too far in the other direction and underestimate and/or ignore these correlations. In order to avoid this problem, a falsifiable test will be created in order to minimize problems associated with traditional conspiracy theory and to provide a framework through which the conspiracy theory evidence can be reexamined.

This work will begin with a historical look into the background of conspiracy theory and its prevalence in American culture. Section 2 will outline the framework of conspiracy theory in an attempt to illustrate the analytical approach used by conspiracy theorists in interpreting contemporary events. An abbreviated history of the Order of Skull and Bones and how this organization is interpreted through the framework of conspiracy theory will also be presented in this section. Section 3 will outline the benefits and problems of a conspiracy theory approach to history, focusing on terminology, the formulation of arguments and the assumptions necessary for a conspiracy theory. Section 4 will develop a cross-sectional, falsifiable test in order to determine if a relationship between membership in the Order of Skull and Bones and participation in illegal financing exists. The results of the cross-sectional test will be applied to a larger set of evidence used by conspiracy theorists in order to minimize the degree of bias associated with conspiratorial interpretations in section 5. This work will then conclude with an examination of the results of the cross-sectional test in light of the conspiracy theorists' evidence.

2 – A History of Conspiracy Theory

With the recent election of President, and Skull and Bones member, George W. Bush, as well as increased political support for presidential hopeful Senator John Kerry, also a Skull and Bones member, the subject of the Order of Skull and Bones has become very popular with certain media outlets, as well as very marketable. Hollywood recently produced a movie based loosely on the Order of Skull and Bones, an investigative documentary was produced for television and three books covering the subject of Skull and Bones are scheduled to be released between 2002 and 2003.

Such a rapid growth in the recent attention directed at Skull and Bones begs the question of why; why has this organization received so much attention of late, and why is much of the attention focused on allegations of conspiracy? Skull and Bones has been in existence since 1832; however, until the election of our former President and Skull and Bones member George H. W. Bush, only about half a dozen articles were written about this organization. So why are we seeing such recent explosive popularity and interest regarding this subject?

I propose two possibilities that tend to feed into each other compounding the underlying focus of recent attention. The first is the secrecy of this organization. Skull and Bones, whose actual name is "The Order 322" or "The Order of Skull and Bones," is the most prestigious and influential of nine secret, senior societies at Yale University. Their meetings are held secretly, their initiations are held secretly, and until recently their membership was kept secret. The secrecy of this society is so prevailing that a member of The Order is allegedly required to leave the room when the subject of The Order is being discussed. As a result of this adamant secrecy, outsiders are left no option but to speculate about the purpose and intent of Skull and Bones.

Second, the secret society of Skull and Bones is very small. Membership is limited to the initiation of only 15 seniors each year. This fact was known at Yale since The Order's founding; however, it was kept from public attention until 1984 when an anonymous member of Skull and Bones provided an author with inside information, thus allowing the author to obtain the previously secret membership list. This membership list provided the groundwork from which all speculation about the organization's goals and intentions derive. The small size of Skull and Bones is not at all indicative of the power and influence that they have had on American society in the past 150 years.

As one investigative reporter so aptly claimed, " For two centuries, the initiation rite of Skull and Bones has shaped the character of the men who have shaped the American character,"[1] including three Presidents. This secret society is dominated by old-line wealth and power. In Skull and Bones we find family names such as Bush, Russell, Taft, Whitney, Lord, Phelps, Wadsworth, Allen, Bundy and Adams. Other Skull and Bones families that attained influence during the nineteenth century include Harriman, Rockefeller, Payne and Davison. A brief list of some of the members of Skull and Bones during the past century better illustrates the level of wealth, power and influence this small group wields.

George W. Bush ('68): President
George H.W. Bush ('48): CIA, Vice Pres. (1980-88), Pres. (88-92), Zapata Oil
Prescott Bush ('17): Union Banking Corporation, Brown Brothers, Harriman
William H. Taft (1878): President, Chief justice of Supreme Court
Alphonso Taft (1833): Secretary of war, Attorney General
Henry Stimson (1888): served 7 Presidents
Robert Lovett ('18): Advisor Kennedy administration
Harvey Bundy ('09): Advisor at war Department
McGeorge Bundy ('40): National Security Advisor, Kennedy
William Bundy ('39): Senior post CIA
Potter Stewart ('37): Supreme Court Justice
Winston Lord ('59): CIA, President of the Council on Foreign Relations.
Harold Stanley ('08): Founder of Morgan Stanley
Henry Davison ('20): Founder of Guaranty Trust
Averell Harriman ('13): Brown Brothers Harriman, Presidential advisor to 6 Pres.,
Thomas Daniels ('14): Founder of Archer-Daniels-Midland
Russell Wheeler Davenport ('23): Creator of Fortune 500 list
Alfred Cowles ('13): Founder of Cowles communications
Henry Luce ('20): Founder of Time-Life
Artemus Gates ('18): President of NY Trust Company, Union Pacific, Time, Boeing
Dean Witter, Jr. ('44)
Pierre Jay (1892): First Chairman of the New York Federal Reserve
Knight Woolley ('17): director of Federal Reserve Bank

As this short list indicates, these members were very influential leaders in American society. Because of the existence of a membership list, researchers are able to trace the activities of the members of Skull and Bones in an attempt to determine the goal of that secret society. However, instead of providing answers, such research only succeeded in generating new questions, assumptions and speculations. Such speculation resulted in numerous conspiracy theories ranging from organized crime and drug trafficking to the direct manipulation of education and brain washing of America; to the Nazi eugenics movement and ultimately the active creation and manipulation of war through illegal finance.

It is the latter subject that this thesis will explore. The claim of active creation and manipulation of war through illegal finance was chosen because there exists very strong and verifiable evidence documenting the illegal financing of enemy regimes by members of Skull and Bones prior to and during times of war.

This evidence and the subsequent claims are significant because of the positions of influence that members of Skull and Bones occupy in our government. If the members of this secret society who hold political positions in the government are involved in illegal activities, how will their actions affect the United States as a whole, as well as the creation of government policies that those members are able to influence? Second, how does public knowledge of illegal activities by political officials affect the democratic process? The focus of this thesis then is an attempt to answer the question: Does a causal relationship exist between membership in Skull and Bones and participation in illegal finance?

But first, it would be of value to provide a brief history of the emergence and growth of conspiracy theory in general. How and where did conspiracy theory start? How has conspiracy theory grown, and among whom is it most prevalent? An exploration of the emergence of conspiracy theory will then be followed by a brief history of the "Order of Skull and Bones."

Theoretical Understanding of Conspiracy Theory

Conspiracy theory in the United States has received a great deal of popular attention in the past several decades. In the wake of the cold war, with events such as the Vietnam War and the Watergate scandal still etched in the minds of millions of Americans, a strong sentiment of distrust aimed at the government arose. Groups, such as the John Birch Society, were formed for the purpose of combating the 'government conspiracy,' while numerous citizens harbor varying degrees of distrust toward politics and/or feelings of insignificance in the American political system.

As Professor Mark T. Reinhardt states, "On the one hand, conspiracy theory is often characterized as illegitimate, pathological, and a threat to political stability; on the other hand, it seems an entertaining narrative form, a populist expression of a democratic culture, that circulates deep skepticism about the truth of the current political order through contemporary culture."[2] Author Mark Fenster, in his book Conspiracy Theories: Secrecy and Power in American Culture, makes a powerful argument for regarding conspiracism (the belief in conspiracy theory) as an integral product of the political system, reflecting inadequacies the establishment itself is blind to and expressing strong desires for the realization of frustrated ideals. Fenster notes that conspiracy theory serves a useful purpose as a balm to the politically alienated segments of society, and he optimistically interprets the popular pursuit of uncovering the hidden mechanics of power as evidence of a latent populism waiting to be harnessed.[3]

Nevertheless, conspiracy thinking is not confined to the marginal and politically alienated segments of society as Fenster might imply. Rather conspiracy thinking is becoming a popular way of viewing the world around us. Political figures such as Joseph McCarthy and Barry Goldwater both made names for themselves through the claims and pursuance of conspiracy within the government. Numerous movies and television shows incorporate the themes of government conspiracy, abuse of power and political cover-up while New York Times best selling authors such as Dean Koontz consistently focus attention on secret government agencies and plots.

In 1996, the Gallup Organization and the Post-Modernity Project of the University of Virginia conducted a survey concerning American political beliefs entitled, *The State of Disunion: 1996 Survey of American Political Culture.* This study involved face-to-face interviews with a national sampling of over 2,000 adults. Among the many findings reported in the survey were the following:

> *Three out of four Americans (77 percent) agree with the statement that "the government is pretty much run by a few big interests looking out for themselves." (Twenty-nine percent completely agree.) Similarly, 63 percent of all Americans say that America's governing elite is "only concerned about its own agenda." This same percentage agrees that "our country is run by a close network of special interests, public officials, and the media." (Twenty-five percent completely agree.)*[4]

The survey also revealed, "one quarter of the population repeatedly express the conviction that the government is run by a conspiracy, and one in ten Americans strongly subscribes to this view."[5]

Conspiracy theory provides a framework, which for many, helps explain much of what would otherwise seem illogical or implausible in our contemporary society. Conspiracy theory does not question the foundations of our societal structure but rather conspiracy theory provides the ability for people to maintain their ideological convictions while scapegoating blame onto the ruling elite. Conspiracy theory centers on the surpluses of political and economic power, understanding them as integral to the maintenance of power, while attempting to discern who has the surpluses of power, how they obtained those surpluses and what they are doing with them.

Popular Understanding of Conspiracy Theory

CONSPIRACY THEORIES were arguably a large influence on American thinking before the Revolutionary War. It was popularized just after World War I and the Bolshevik Revolution, asserting Communism as the manifested form of the global conspiracy, and has steadily gained influence and attention since then through its insistence on the rejection of both socialism and global governing organizations such as the United Nations. Conspiracy theory is not limited to certain segments of society nor is it exclusive to American culture.

The predominance of conspiracy thinking is found in numerous writings, speeches and records including U.S. congressional records and investigations, and many powerful and influential people have promoted it. For example, the California Senate Investigating Committee on Education states in their 1953 report on education that,

> *So called modern Communism is apparently the same hypocritical and deadly world conspiracy to destroy civilization that was founded by the secret order of the Illuminati in Bavaria May 1, 1776.*[6]

Conspiracy thinking is not exclusive to American Culture. In a speech before the British Parliament in 1920, Winston Churchill stated,

> *From the days of Sparticus-Weishaupt to those of Karl Marx, ... this world-wide conspiracy for the overthrow of civilization ... has been steadily growing. It has been the mainspring of every subversive movement during the Nineteenth century, and now at last this band of extraordinary personalities from the underworld of the great cities of Europe and America has gripped the Russian people...*[7]

Both of these passages refer to a worldwide conspiracy originating with the "secret order of the Illuminati of Bavaria." The Illuminati of Bavaria, for a vast majority of conspiracy theorists is the corner stone to understanding the worldwide conspiracy that allegedly exists today. Conspiracy theorist John F. McManus states,

> *"Let us openly assert, that there is operating in the world today, and especially within our own nation, a conspiracy that is either a direct descendant of the Illuminati of 1776 or something closely patterned after it."8*

So who or what is the Illuminati of Bavaria and why is so much attention focused on this group?

HISTORICAL UNDERSTANDING OF CONSPIRACY THEORY

ADAM WEISHAUPT formed the "Order of the Illuminati" in Bavaria on May 1, 1776. The philosophy of Weishaupt's Illuminism "propose[d] as the end of Illuminism the abolition of property, social authority, and of nationality,"[9] and was based primarily on revolution and secrecy as a means to bring about social change. Weishaupt's goal was the complete and revolutionary restructuring of society, and to this end Weishaupt "felt the need of a powerful secret organization to support him in the conflict with his adversaries and in the execution of his rationalistic schemes along ecclesiastical and political lines."[10]

By 1778, only two years after its creation, Weishaupt was able to secure more then 1000 members for the Illuminati in Bavaria alone, and there were lodges in 12 other countries including France and the United States.[11] In 1784, a messenger was struck by lightning while carrying letters from Weishaupt to other members of the Illuminati. The police authorities confiscated these letters, which resulted in the raid of the homes of several leading members of the Illuminati. Weishaupt's Order of the Illuminati was declared as subversive to the German government and the leaders of the Illuminati were banished from Germany.

After the French Revolution numerous books outlining alleged connections between the French Jacobins and Weishaupt's Illuminati were produced. These books focused on the many shared members between the Illuminati and the Jacobins, showing that the leaders of the French Revolution were also high ranking members of the Illuminati, according the Illuminati's records which were confiscated by the Bavarian government.

Concern over the influence of the Illuminati during the French Revolution spread all over the world, including America. In a letter to Rev. G.W. Snyder dated October 24, 1798, Former President George Washington States,

> *Reverend sir: It was not my intention to doubt that the doctrine of the Illuminati had not spread in the United States. On the contrary, no one is more satisfied of this fact then I am.*[12]

Many organizations that were allegedly involved with the conspiratorial Illuminati, because of their many shared members, became suspect. These various groups included Eclectic Freemasonry, the German Union and the League of the Just. The connection between the League of the Just and the Illuminati is of significance to conspiracy theorists because it was the League of the Just who "commissioned [Karl] Marx and [Frederick] Engels to draw up a definitive statement of its aims and program."[13] According to J. Edgar Hoover, the League of the Just was a secret society that later became publicly known as the Communist League.

Conspiracy theorists emphasize the alleged link between the Illuminati of Bavaria and Communism. A comparison of the Communist Manifesto and of the writing of Adam Weishaupt, as confiscated by the Bavarian government and later published by John Robison in 1798, show that the two philosophies are essentially identical in both goals and in methodology. Other superficial evidence presented by conspiracy theorists include the Communist National holiday celebrated on May 1, the same day that the Illuminati was officially formed; the stated goal of Communism as expressed by former Communist leaders such as Lenin, Stalin, Khrushchev and Gorbachev as being World Communism or Novus Ordo Seclorum (New World Order), is both the same goal and same terminology expressed by Adam Weishaupt; both the Illuminati and Communism were regarded by numerous political figures throughout the world as a well organized international conspiracy in pursuit of a ruinous end.

Following a three year investigation of the 1886 riot in Chicago that resulted in the death of 7 police officers and the injury of 63 more, Police Captain Michael Schaack stated,

> *In London there are all the factors for the most dangerous mob the world can produce. In France, the commune is stronger than ever it was and the Red terror may appear with every turn of the whirligig of politics. In Spain and Italy, the Socialists are busy while in Germany and Russia a crisis is at hand. Let none mistake either the purpose or the duration of these fanatics, nor their growing strength. This is a methodical, not a haphazard conspiracy. The ferment in Russia is controlled by the same heads and the same hands as the activity in Chicago. There is a cold-blooded, calculating purpose behind this revolt manipulating every part of it the world over to a common and ruinous end.*[14]

A majority of conspiracy theorists base their method of analysis of contemporary events on the assumption that Communism is still alive and active and that it is a manifestation of Weishaupt's secret order of the Illuminati because members of the Illuminati created the Communist League and commissioned Marx and Engels to write the Communist Manifesto. As a result of the publication of the Illuminati's records detailing their subversive agenda, conspiracy theorists assume a long-range plan of world domination by any group that might be aligned with the original Illuminati. This basis for analysis is critical to understanding the conspiracy theorists' claims against the Order of Skull and Bones, because, as will be discussed shortly, the Order of Skull and Bones is considered to be a single lodge of the original Illuminati.

But why would wealthy capitalists support or finance communist or fascist regimes? There are three possible answers to this question. The first, and most obvious, is profit. It is possible that businesses seek profits regardless of ideology. In this case, expanding business to a larger market that includes communist or fascist regimes would increase revenues and profits for the firm. Second, capitalistic industrialists might favor a degree of social control and development by the government. Industrialists Henry Ford and Frederick Winslow Taylor, along with their revolutionary ideas on the efficiency of the individual in the work place such as specialization, departmentalization, mass production and employee satisfaction, also favored a stronger welfare state to provide the necessary atmosphere for maximum production. The third possibility, as expressed by conspiracy theorist Antony Sutton, claims that the eventual power structure between a communist state, a fascist state and a monopoly is essentially the same: control of production and elimination of industrial competition. Both communism and fascism control the means of production and the degree of competition while a monopoly attempts to do the same. Sutton maintains that these American capitalists might aid these regimes in an attempt to gain favor with the regime and gain industrial dominance.

SKULL AND BONES

WILLIAM HUNTINGTON RUSSELL AND ALPHONSO TAFT established the Order of Skull and Bones, officially called the "Order 322," at Yale University in 1833. It was later incorporated as the Russell Trust in 1856. It is one of nine secret societies at Yale, and one of three senior societies that are exclusive to Yale University. Fifteen juniors are "tapped" each year by the seniors to be initiated into next year's group. Each initiate is allegedly given $15,000 and a grandfather clock, although no one has yet been able to discover the significance of the clock.

The original founder of Skull and Bones, William Russell, studied in Germany from 1831-1832. While in Germany, it is believed that Russell joined a secret society at the German University and was then given permission to start a section of that same secret society at Yale. According to information acquired from a break-in to the "tomb" (the Skull and Bones temple and meeting hall located on Yale's campus) in 1876, "Bones is a section of a corps in a German University ... General Russell, its founder, was in Germany before his Senior Year and formed a warm friendship with a leading member of a German society. He brought back with him to college, authority to found a section here."[15]

This same break-in team, who mockingly referred to themselves as "the Order of File and Claw," claimed that within the Skull and Bones Tomb was a room numbered 322, an elaborately decorated ceremonial room furnished in red velvet with a pentagram on the wall. In the parlor next to room 322 the break-in group found:

> *On the west wall, hung among other pictures, an old engraving representing an open burial vault, in which, on a stone slab, rest four human skulls, grouped about a fools cap and bells, an open book, several mathematical instruments, a beggar's scrip, and a royal crown. On the arched wall above the vault are the explanatory words, in Roman letters, "We War Der Thor, Wer Weiser, Wer Bettler Oder, Kaiser? And below the vault is engraved, in German characters, the sentence: 'Ob Arm, Ob Beich, im Tode gleich.*[16]

The picture is accompanied by a card on which is written, 'From the German section, Presented by D.C. Gilman of D. 50'. D.C. Gilman refers to Daniel Coit Gilman, initiated into the Order of Skull and Bones 1850. The two German phrases translate into "Who was the fool, who the wise man, beggar or king? Whether poor or rich, in death we are the same. This quote, and the initiation rituals that each new member must experience are extremely similar to the initiation ceremony of the Illuminati. An expose on the initiation rites of Skull and Bones by reporter Ron Rosenbaum, *The Last Secrets of Skull and Bones*, highlights the various initiation activities along with a comparison of the same Illuminati ceremonies as recorded by former Illuminati member John Robison. Many conspiracy theorists conclude that the Order of Skull and Bones is either a section of the original Illuminati or an extension thereof.

Conspiracy theorists, in light of potential Illuminati affiliation, emphasize three aspects of society in which members of Skull and Bones were profoundly influential: namely government, education and illegal finance. It is this latter subject that will be explored to some degree in this work.

Given the historical framework of the Illuminati/Communist long-range goal of world domination used by conspiracy theorists, and the possible connection between the Order of Skull and Bones and the Order of the Illuminati, it is easy to understand the concerns of conspiracy theorists in regard to illegal financing of enemy regimes by members of Skull and Bones. As conspiracy theorist Antony Sutton states,

> *Revolution is always recorded as a spontaneous event by the politically or economically deprived against an autocratic state. Never in Western textbooks will you find the evidence that revolutions need finance and the source of the finance in many cases traces back to Wall Street.*[17]

More importantly, concludes Sutton, is that members of Skull and Bones provide a large part of Wall Street's financing to revolutionary movements.

3 – An Evaluation of the Analytical Framework of Conspiracy Theory

CONSPIRACY THEORY MAINTAINS that, in a given state, power "is exercised from behind the scenes by a small secretive group of private citizens who want to change the government system or put the country under the control of a world government."[1] These conspiratorial groups are always made up of a group of powerful and/or influential businessmen or politicians who are intent on running the world. In essence, these small, secretive groups form a shadow government that is not elected but controls political decision-making not only for their own benefit but also at the detriment of the rest of society.

"In the past, the conspirators were usually said to be secret Communist sympathizers who were intent on bringing the United States under a common world government in conjunction with the Soviet Union, but the collapse of the Soviet Union in 1991 changed the focus to the United Nations as the likely controlling force in the 'New World Order."[2] However, with deterioration of Soviet economies, the maintenance of Communist party leaders in positions of power and publicly popular soviet appeals for a return to Communism, many conspiracy theorists are reverting back to claims of the "Communist Threat."

Smaller groups of conspiratorial thinkers, on the other hand, focus on a secret group of individuals whom, it is claimed, are located in the government itself. This secretive group is held responsible for the creation of government organizations such as the CIA, think tanks like the Council on Foreign Relations and the Trilateral Commission as well as the creation of war through both illegal finance in the corporate world and government policy-making in the political realm. One secret organization that receives a great deal of attention by conspiracists is the Order of Skull and Bones.

The allegations made against Skull and Bones by Antony Sutton and other conspiracy theorists undoubtedly fall into the realm of power politics. It would be highly enlightening to examine the claims made against Skull and Bones using other methods of analysis; however, because other methods of analysis have not yet been used to examine Skull and Bones activities, and because all Skull and Bones activities are generally presented through use of the conspiracy theory framework, we will focus our attention on a critical analysis of conspiracy theory.*

TENETS OF CONSPIRACY THEORY

THERE ARE BOTH POSITIVE AND NEGATIVE aspects to using a conspiracy theory framework. As with many theories on power politics, the focus is on a specific framework, with a tendency to disregard or downplay the importance of other factors. An understanding of the strengths and weaknesses of conspiracy theory will aid in the overall assessment of the conspiracy theory's evaluation of the claims against Skull and Bones.

The advantages of conspiracy theory are threefold: 1) conspiracy theory aids in the discovery of important facts and assessing personal guilt; 2) it allows society to admit horrors and express indignation without rejecting the basic norms of society; 3) it acts as a scapegoat for societal frustrations. These three advantages occur simultaneously within conspiracy theory and are inseparable. A conspiracy theory could not occur without assessing personal guilt for a societal atrocity. The blame for that atrocity is then placed solely on the individual and, by extension, any network or group he may be affiliated with, thereby disregarding any fundamental flaws in the fabric of society that may contribute to the problem.

Conspiracy theories can act as a forum through which members of society are able to admit horrors and express indignation about the outcomes and problems of society. However the discoveries of conspiracy theory are often dismissed because they are presented in a conspiracy theory framework that does not acknowledge errors in the basic norms of society, but rather shifts blame to clandestine networks working behind the scenes. The result of illegal financing then is not the result of a capitalist system which allows for profit maximization at the expense of others, but rather illegal financing occurs because a select, secretive group chose for it to happen in order to advance their global agenda. In this way, the blame is shifted from the political structure of society to a small group who are then held responsible for all the ills of society.

A conspiracy theory is a version of historical events that redirects an audience's anger toward a scapegoat group. The theory seeks to lay blame for a legitimate issue on a perceived common enemy. As with any societal issue, there are legitimate concerns that need to be addressed. Conspiracy theories, however, fail to address legitimate concerns because realistic solutions are lost in the process of laying blame for the common problem on a select group. By only laying blame for the problem, the issue becomes, in effect, a renewable source of fuel for the audience.

Author Mark Fenster makes a powerful argument for regarding conspiracism as an integral product of the political system, reflecting the inadequacies of the establishment and expressing strong desires for the realization of frustrated ideals.

Fenster notes that conspiracy theory should be perceived "as an active, indeed endless, process that continually seeks, but never fully arrives at, a final interpretation. It displaces the citizen's desire for political significance onto a signifying regime in which interpretation replaces political engagement.[3] Mark T. Reinhardt interprets Fenster's claims when stating, "conspiracy theory serves a useful purpose as a balm to the politically alienated segments of society, and he optimistically interprets the popular pursuit of uncovering the hidden mechanics of power as evidence of a latent populism waiting to be harnessed."[4]

The political significance of conspiracy theory is its ability to represent disenfranchised segments of society through expressions of distrust toward the government and the establishment of blame for society's ills. The interpretation of conspiracy theory must begin with the observation that conspiracy theory is an attempt to apprehend the past and the present by placing potentially disparate events within a unifying interpretive frame. However, the process through which conspiracy theory results is very problematic. The problems of conspiracy theory can be arranged into 4 categories: 1) terminology, 2) information, 3) formulation of the argument and 4) formulation of conclusions. Each of these categories will be addressed separately so that the significance of each can be fully understood.

PROBLEMS OF CONSPIRACY THEORY – TERMINOLOGY

THE FIRST AND MOST BASIC PROBLEM of conspiracy theory lies in the terminology and ambiguous meanings associated with the term "conspiracy theory." A definite distinction exists between a *conspiracy* and a *conspiracy theory.* The former describes an actual instance of covert collusion, while the latter describes something that exists only in the imagination of an observer.

A conspiracy involves two or more *conspirators* jointly and secretly aiming to achieve a prohibited goal. Conspiracies do occur. The European powers did conspire to divide up the Middle East during World War I (the Sykes-Picot agreement); the Israelis did bomb American targets in Egypt in 1954 to put the blame on Gamal Abdel Nasser (the Lavon Affair); and the U.S. government did send arms to Iran in the mid-1980s (the Iran/contra scandal).

Conspiracies subdivide into *petty conspiracies,* which work within the existing order, and *grand conspiracies,* which aspire to world domination. The former are limited affairs that involve a handful of individuals plotting to make money or to seize power. They aim at transferring money from one pocket to another or replacing one set of rulers with another. With some exceptions, petty conspiracies receive little attention in the media and are generally not referred to as a conspiracy. Rather, grand conspiracies are what conspiracy theorists refer to when they use the term conspiracy. Larger and more vague, grand conspiracies go beyond plots for personal gain or for power or money; they seek to destroy religion, subvert society, change the political order, and undermine truth itself. Grand conspiracies involve not duplicitous politicians or evil merchants but covert international movements. They capture the imagination and inflame political passion; they are big enough to cause all the world's ills. It is important to distinguish between a petty conspiracy and a grand conspiracy during our evaluation of Skull and Bones activities.

A *conspiracy theory,* on the other hand, is the unproven version of a conspiracy. Anyone might speculate about the odd conspiracy theory, but the *conspiracy theorist* makes this a habitual practice. He discerns malignant forces at work wherever something displeases him; plots serve as his first method for explaining the world around him. He suspects a plot or cover-up even when other, less malign explanations better fit the facts. This preoccupation with conspiracy theories is variously called *conspiracism* or the *conspiracy mentality.* Just as conspiracies divide into two sorts, the petty and the grand, so do conspiracy theories. Petty theories deal with limited aims; grand conspiracy theories involve fears of world domination.

Grand conspiracy theories may also have local manifestations, but they invariably fit into a larger scheme that maintains the ultimate goal of world hegemony. Such theories have a finite history as previously illustrated. They began during the Enlightenment in northwestern Europe, became a major factor with the French Revolution, and peaked in importance in the three decades after 1918. Grand conspiracy theories have a well-established structure and form. The story begins with a small group attempting to benefit itself by clandestinely making plans to take over the government or expand its influence abroad. Its means can be many - propaganda, destroying a political system, controlling multinational corporations - but the immediate goal is usually economic.

Information

Good research is based on the ability to uncover accurate information. Hypotheses are formulated with information and historical events are analyzed using information recovered through research. However, there are three important problems with research information that play a major role in conspiracy theories. First, conspiracy theories, by their very definition, are not provable. Incomplete and/or insufficient evidence is the primary component of conspiracies, effectively moving the conspirator's claims into the world of the uncertain and unknown. Conspiracy theories focus on relationships and events that are rarely covered in the media and are generally given very little attention. As a result, it is difficult to find records and information that would support a conspiracy theorist's hypotheses. The question of legitimacy also comes into play disputing both the validity of records and/or information as well as disputing the context in which the records occurred verses the context in which it is used by conspiracy theorists.

Incomplete information is often used by conspiracy theorists to paint a limited picture of events in society from which certain assumptions must be drawn and which prescribes specific conclusions. Because causation is never known to conspiracy theorists, they focus on inconclusive correlations drawn from incomplete information. Certain assumptions must then be applied, generally of a secretive, collective, long-range nature, which then require conspiratorial conclusions. The use of conspiratorial assumptions in order to produce conspiratorial conclusions will become more evident as we analyze Skull and Bones involvement in both the Bolshevik Revolution and the rise of Hitler.

Second, the excessive amount of information used by conspiracy theorists in and of itself becomes problematic. Conspiracy theorists commonly rely on large amounts of information to prove their point. The assumption that since there is so much information available on the subject it must be true is based on a common fallacy of logic; resulting in the conclusion that the sheer enormity of printed text unquestionably makes the accusation fact, despite generally large amounts of irrelevant information and correlations that are unnecessarily included.

Third, the majority of conspiracy theory information and research is either unfalsifiable or unverifiable, or both. The strength and weakness of conspiracy lies at the fact that a conspiracy theory is unfalsifiable. The conspiracy theory generates a large amount of information that draws correlations and which, under certain interpretation, may point toward a specific conspiratorial explanation. However, the theory as a whole cannot be proven as a legitimate conspiracy, nor can it be proven as false, again drawing strength on correlations. Furthermore, conspiracy theories are based on "privileged information" provided by an insider who claims to shed light on a given conspiracy. By the very nature of the claims of an insider, there is no verifiability. Generally, an insider is alone when he attempts to illuminate a conspiracy, and supporting testimony is rare.

Such is the case with author Antony Sutton. He was the first non-member of Skull and Bones to allegedly obtain a membership list of Skull and Bones. According to Sutton, an insider disenchanted with the goals of Skull and Bones gave him a membership list. Much of the completed research on Skull and Bones is based on the membership list that Sutton was given. However, later research discovered that the membership list of Skull and Bones was annually printed in the annual reports of RTA (Russell Trust Association) under whom Skull and Bones is formally incorporated.* If the connection between Skull and Bones and RTA was not discovered, then Sutton's list of Skull and Bones members might never have been verified. As it stands, many of Sutton's claims, based on insider information, remain unverified.

As a result, information used in conspiracy theory is almost always incomplete and inconclusive, unnecessarily excessive and unfalsifiable or unverifiable.

Formulation of the Argument

As opposed to a systematic approach to analysis, the approach and formulation of arguments for conspiracy theories are all too often circular, ad hoc, and biased. A circular argument is one of the most common fallacies for conspiracy theorists. This fallacy occurs when one tries to prove point A by using point B, which in turn is proved by the first point. An example of such an argument would be the claim that Skull and Bones is involved in a grand conspiracy. As evidence for this, theorists focus on the illegal financing activities of members.

*Editor's note: I do not know what annual reports these are. Annual state corporation filings list only the directors and officers.

Conspiracy theorists argue that illegal financing of enemy regimes is a way to advance a global, conspiratorial agenda. Conspiracy theorists then claim that Skull and Bones involvement in illegal financing proves that Skull and Bones is involved in a Grand conspiracy. Did this circular endorsement prove anything about the nature of Skull and Bones?

An ad hoc explanation of events occurs when the fundamental criteria for a conspiracy changes from one event to the next, after the fact. Conspiracy theorists examine situation 1 and determine that factors A, B and C are the fundamental factors required for a conspiracy. An examination of situation 2 yields factors A, D and E, and not A, B and C as in situation 1. Conspiracy theorists then alter the fundamental criteria that are required for a conspiracy theory to exist in order to include situation 2. This alteration of fundamental criteria occurs after the occurrence and examination of each new situation.

Many social scientists would argue that the trademark of conspiracy theory is its lack of objectivity. It is difficult, if not impossible to find conspiracy theory literature that is not biased. Such literature is filled with the demonization of the alleged conspiracy group, and it too often appears that the alleged conspirators become the scapegoats of societal problems. Focus is spent on reiterating negative affiliations of individuals and negative representations of those affiliate groups. A great deal of emphasis is based on those groups that either use secrecy or which wield a great deal of power. Furthermore, all conspiracy research is presented in the conspiratorial framework, often focusing on one or two elements that fit the prescribed framework while dismissing or all together ignoring information or events that do not fit the framework.

Formulation of Conclusions

There are two common errors that occur in the formulation of conclusions of conspiracy theories. The first is a faulty conclusion that is drawn from faulty information. The second is a faulty conclusion that is based on good evidence. These errors are not exclusive to conspiracy, but rather they are problems of any scholarly discipline.

A faulty conclusion drawn from faulty information is common with conspiracy theory for many reasons. Legitimate information on a true conspiracy will be nearly impossible to obtain. There is a lack of complex data; as a result, conspiracy researchers are forced to draw conclusions from very limited information. They are given to misinterpretation of information, which results in the furtherance of faulty conclusions as conspiracy researchers rely heavily on secondary sources to obtain their information. Many conspiracy researchers focus on work already completed by others and generally fail to check their primary sources in order to prevent misinterpretation and/or the misquoting of primary sources. This problem is furthered by the Internet, where large amounts of information is passed along, but very rarely provides primary documentation of claims, which lends itself toward misunderstanding and misquoting from other secondary sources.

A simple key word search of Skull and Bones on the Internet will yield 100's of websites with information pertaining to Skull and Bones. A careful study of these web pages show that they all reiterate the same basic information, but as the information is passed from one secondary source to the next, it loses its informational accuracy. Names are misused and dates are confused. Each new site attempts to add its own information and conclusions to be passed to the next person for further evaluation and change. In the end we are left with 100's of web sites each dedicated to Skull and Bones, each with its own conclusions and assumptions based on information that may have lost its original accuracy.

Faulty conclusions based on good evidence can result from a fundamental element of any scholarly work: the assumptions of each argument. Incorrect assumptions can misdirect and bias any research, resulting in a logical fallacy. For example, the claim that Skull and Bones is involved in the illegal financing of enemy regimes is based on the assumption that illegal financing is a focus of Skull and Bones, and that its members, as a whole, are engaged in this practice. Evidence indicates between 25 to 30 members of Skull and Bones were involved with firms who provided illegal financing, over a 30-year period. Noting that during any given year there are about 700 members of Skull and Bones living, 25-30 members does not seem to be an accurate representation of Skull and Bones as a whole. Further research indicates that the majority of members, during this time period, pursued fields in education or business, and were not involved in illegal activities. The above assumption that Skull and Bones is involved in illegal financing because a very small percentage of members are involved in such activities leads to a logical fallacy.

Another basic assumption of conspiracy theorists derives from the terminology and definition of a conspiracy. As we stated earlier, the definition of a conspiracy is when two or more conspirators jointly and secretly aim to achieve a prohibited goal. However, the definition used by conspiracy theorists is slightly different. As stated by John F. McManus, a conspiracy is "an endeavor engaged in secretly by two or more persons for the accomplishment of an evil goal."[5] From the very outset conspiracy theorists have attached specific values of good and evil to certain behaviors. No longer is a conspiracy an attempt to achieve a prohibited goal, or an act against the law, but a conspiracy becomes ambiguous as it begins to include anything and anyone who might aid in the accomplishment of an "evil" goal, as defined by the conspiracy theorists. The ambiguity of the conspiracy theorists' definition becomes far-reaching and too inclusive as it begins to include any liberal or non-conservative program or behavior.

Often the assumptions of conspiracy theory are not explicitly stated but implicitly assigned through the use of complex questions. A complex question is formed when your proposition affirms more than one thing, but your question allows for an answer to only one. An example of this line of questioning would be "how was Skull and Bones involved in illegal financing?" In order to answer the question, we must assume and acknowledge that Skull and Bones was involved in illegal financing without having proved that Skull and Bones was actually involved. In this manner, conspiracy theorists focus not on whether or not a group is involved in a conspiracy, but rather the focus is on how they are involved in a conspiracy, already assuming that a conspiracy is occurring without proper examination and proof.

Conclusion

This section discussed the many potential flaws that surface when dealing with conspiracy theory: namely the lack of uniformity in definition, the inadequacy of information and the formulation of both argument and conclusion. In order to fully understand the connection between Skull and Bones and illegal financing, I will attempt to reduce these problems by eliminating both the assumptions of conspiracy and the conspiratorial framework in an effort to create a falsifiable test. This test will be used to then assess any possible correlations that may exist between Skull and Bones and illegal financing.

4 – Method of Analysis

Experimental Test vs. Non-experimental Test

In order to accurately study and assess correlations between membership in Skull and Bones and participation in illegal financing, a reliable scientific test design must be created. Although scientific methods are not always necessary to answer research questions, they can be very effective in minimizing the biases that affect subjective opinion. Many scientific designs rely on experimentation. Experimental designs allow researchers the ability to control one or more variables thereby eliminating potentially confounding factors. Such designs are powerful because they can be effective in determining causal relationships between variables.

However, because we are unable to control the variables that we are studying (membership in Skull and Bones and participation in illegal financing), we are forced to rely on a non-experimental test design. Non-experimental test designs do not allow for control or manipulation of variables, but rather strict observations are used, from which conclusions can be drawn. Non-experimental test designs do not yield results that are as strong as those of experimental test designs, and they generally do not establish a causal relationship between the variables. However, non-experimental tests are generally effective at determining correlations among variables, and continuation of the test design over a period of time dramatically strengthens its conclusions.

There are two problems associated with non-experimental test designs. First the quality of information that is observed and used for the test could be incomplete, inaccurate or biased, which could result in unreliable and/or inconclusive conclusions. Furthermore, the information that is used in the test could be selectively chosen and biased, again resulting in unreliable and/or inconclusive conclusions. Second, a lack of direct manipulation or control in the non-experimental design can cause problems in the interpretation of results because the investigator might not be able to properly handle extraneous factors. As a result, variables may become compounded and factors that are not of concern in the study may complicate or taint the conclusions.

Why a Non-Experimental Test Design Was Chosen

For the purpose of testing the relationship between membership in Skull and Bones and participation in illegal financing, a non-experimental cross-sectional test design will be used. This test design is simplistic in that it "requires nothing more than the collection of two or more measures on a set of subjects or social entities at one point in time and requires no treatments or manipulations."[1] The cross-sectional design can be effective in determining whether or not two or more variables are related. Because we will be unable to determine causation through a non-experimental test, the establishment of correlations will be the goal of our test.

A cross-sectional test design is useful in this study because it provides a scientific framework through which the specified events can be studied. A scientific hypothesis maintains validity when the hypothesis can be tested and can, potentially, be falsified. On the other hand, as previously noted, conspiracy theory relies on ad hoc explanations, explanations that do not provide a testable hypothesis because their basic assumptions change with each new event in order to maintain specific conclusions. The conspiracy theory does not provide a process for systematic evaluation of more then one situation. As a result, its conclusions are not generally considered scientifically valid. The cross-sectional test will provide both testable hypotheses and a framework for systematic evaluation of the hypotheses through the studied events.

A cross-sectional test design has both limitations and advantages. It does not allow us to control specific variables; as a result we are forced to examine historical events. Not only are we limited in how we conduct the study, but we are also limited in the information available for testing. Information pertaining to this subject is scarce and often biased in its traditional presentation by conspiracy theorists. Second, the conclusions of a cross-sectional test do not show causation and depending on the rigidity of the hypothesis that is used, could lend itself to misinterpretation. Third, a cross-sectional test over one period in time produces weak conclusions. Continuation of the same test is required with a large test sample over a long period of time in order to add strength to any conclusion produced.

However, the advantages of a cross-sectional test far outweigh the limitations. Given a random sample, the testing of several hypotheses will not show causation but can indicate correlations between the variables. The test is also able to show a much broader picture of the behavior of segments of society or society as a whole, thereby reducing the occurrence of sample bias. The test also provides a means of systematically testing various hypotheses in order to sustain or disprove a given hypothesis.

The Test Framework

The purpose of the cross-sectional test is to determine a relationship between membership in Skull and Bones and participation in illegal financing. The data for this test will be drawn from historical records as well as research and claims made by several conspiracy theorists. The test will have two variables each specifically measured. These variables will be tested against five separate hypotheses in order to 1) maintain an unbiased examination of events and evidence as well as 2) examine the results of a hypothesis that will be acceptable to both social scientists and conspiracy theorists. This test will examine illegal financing to the Bolshevik Revolution and the rise of Hitler by United States based financial firms.

Variables

Two variables will be used on our cross-sectional test design: 1) membership in Skull and Bones and 2) participation in illegal financing by a firm.

Measurements

Membership in Skull and Bones will be determined through the membership records of Skull and Bones. Membership in Skull and Bones is only important to this study if the individual was a member of Skull and Bones during the time period being examined (1917-1945).

A firm will be defined as a financial institution whose primary activity is providing financing to industrial corporations or other entities. This definition intentionally excludes industrial and production companies. A company such as Ford or GE, who participated in illegal financing will not be included in this study because the primary activities of both Ford and GE are production and not financing. On the other hand, a company such as Guaranty Trust Company, whose primary objective is to provide financing to production companies, would fit the requirements.

Participation in illegal financing will be determined when a firm participates in providing funds to a state or group against the established laws of the country where the financing took place.

A firm is determined to be associated with Skull and Bones in one or more of the following ways: if it was directly created by members of Skull and Bones; if its president, chief executive officer, or chairman of the board is a member of Skull and Bones; or if 25 percent or more of its managing directors are members of Skull and Bones. Conversely, a firm is determined to not be associated with Skull and Bones if fewer then 25 percent of its managing directors are members of Skull and Bones, if it was not created by a member of Skull and Bones or if neither its president, CEO or Chairman are not members of Skull and Bones. I am requiring 25 percent of a firm's directorship to be members of Skull and Bones before that firm is classified as being associated with Skull and Bones in order to eliminate the effects of confounding variables.

The variables to be studied are binary. In other words, a firm either participates in illegal financing or it does not; Skull and Bones is either present, according to the above definition, or it is not. I am not allowing for variations of illegal financing, nor am I examining intentions behind illegal financing at this time.

Likewise, there occur variations of Skull and Bones affiliations with various firms. However, a firm will only be classified as affiliated with Skull and Bones if it fits the specific requirements above. The elimination of variance in variables will aid in the interpretive process.

The use of a binary state of variables is intended to avoid pitfalls such as the following example: a corporate financier is a director of company A and company B. He is not a member of Skull and Bones, but company A is heavily dominated by Skull and Bones members. Both companies A and B are involved in illegal financing. The link between company A and company B through the mentioned financier would lead some to conclude that company B is also under the influence of Skull and Bones through the common financier. However, such a link does not indicate Skull and Bones influence over company B, and inclusion of company B as a Skull and Bones dominated firm could skew the results of the data.

POSSIBILITY OF ERROR

AS WITH ALL FORMS OF MEASUREMENT, there is always some degree of error. Establishing membership in Skull and Bones through reference to a private membership list is subject to error because, despite strong research supporting the validity of the membership list, Skull and Bones is secretive about its membership and no member of Skull and Bones has either confirmed or denied the accuracy of the membership list. In the case of participation in illegal financing, we cannot know which directors initiated and/or were involved in illegal financing. We are forced to assume that all managing directors, by the very nature of their position, were aware of the illegal financing, and with at least 25 percent of the directorship consisting of members we can conclude that members of Skull and Bones had some degree of influence and/or leverage in the decisions made.

EVENTS TO BE EXAMINED

FOR ANALYSIS I CHOSE TO EXAMINE the financing activities of firms during the Bolshevik Revolution (1917-1926) and the rise of Hitler (1923-1942). I chose these two historical events because during both time periods the United States government had established very specific laws forbidding financial support to the belligerent regimes by United States residents. Second, these two events occurred in a relatively close time frame and the structure and laws pertaining to international finance were relatively similar. Third, these two events are the primary focus of conspiracy theorists when claiming that Skull and Bones is involved in a conspiracy.

The further examination of an additional historical period of conflict such as the Vietnam War or the Gulf War would add strength to the conclusions that will result from our test, however very little research has been completed by conspiracy theorists or scholars in regards to potentially illegal financial transactions of US firms after World War II. Furthermore, the occurrence of changes in international law after World War II resulted in a change in both the definitions of international finance and the methods through which international finance occurred. As a result, it would be very difficult to find another situation of finance that maintained similar circumstances, laws and public opinion.

HYPOTHESES

AS PREVIOUSLY STATED, the core of the validity of scientific test designs is a hypothesis that can be tested and potentially disproved. For our cross-sectional test we will propose four separate hypotheses that were derived from the conspiracy theorists' allegations in order to determine the existence of relationships as well as provide a testing method that may be accepted by both social scientists and conspiracy theorists. Four hypotheses will be presented, starting with a very strict hypothesis and then loosening the restrictions with each consecutive hypothesis.

The term "strict hypothesis" refers to a hypothesis that has strong and clear assumptions resulting in a strong prediction of results. A hypothesis that is "loose" is one that is weak and unclear and results in weak predictions. A hypothesis that is very restrictive or strict will be more favorable to a social scientist's analytical framework and will be rejected by conspiracy theorists because of its strict assumptions, while a hypothesis that is too loose could result in the failure to explain the events in question. The hypothesis that will be most beneficial will most likely be one that falls somewhere between the very strict hypothesis and the very loose hypothesis; being strict enough to point toward important correlations without potentially ignoring other possibly significant connections.

As previously stated, the cross-sectional test has two variables: membership in Skull and Bones, and participation in illegal financing. As shown by Figure 1, the presence of members of Skull and Bones is demonstrated by boxes A and B, while the absence of members of Skull and Bones is demonstrated by boxes C and D. Participation in illegal financing is represented by boxes A and C and the absence of participation in illegal financing is represented by boxes B and D. Each of the four falsifiable hypotheses will be presented in detail separately. Each hypothesis will include requirements for falsification, the predictions of the hypothesis and the significance of each possible outcome of the hypothesis. After all four hypotheses are presented, the falsifiable test for event 1 (Bolshevik Revolution) and event 2 (rise of Hitler) will be presented, followed by the results of the test in relation to each hypothesis.

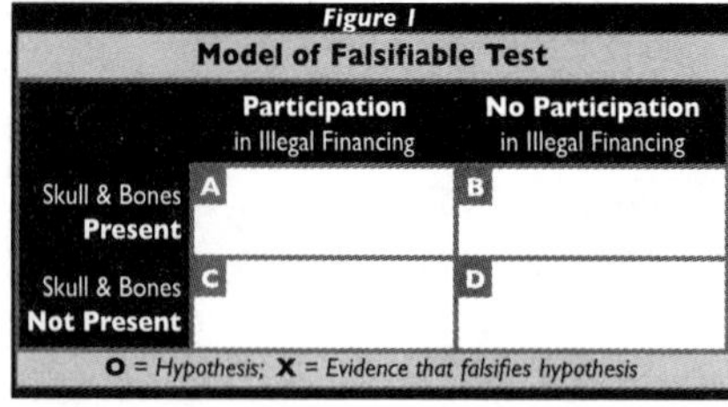

THE FIRST HYPOTHESIS, the most restrictive, is the hypothesis that Skull and Bones related firms will provide illegal finance to enemy regimes while non-Skull and Bones related firms will not provide illegal financing. In this hypothesis, we will predict that all of the test data will fall into either box A or box D, will all

Skull and Bones related firms participating in illegal finance and all non-Skull and Bones related firms not participating in illegal finance.

The occurrence of data in boxes B and/or C will disprove this hypothesis. Data in box B indicates that some Skull and Bones related firms did not participate in illegal financing, while data in box C indicates that some non-Skull and Bones related firms did participate in illegal financing.

If we were to find our data in box B, regardless of where other data falls, our hypothesis that Skull and Bones is directly related with illegal financing would be falsified, because it would indicated that members of Skull and Bones were in a position to provide illegal financing but did not.

If our data were to fall exclusively in boxes C and D then again the hypothesis would be disproved, however because we are examining the relationship between membership in Skull and Bones and participation in illegal financing, we can conclude that at least some of the data will fall into box A.

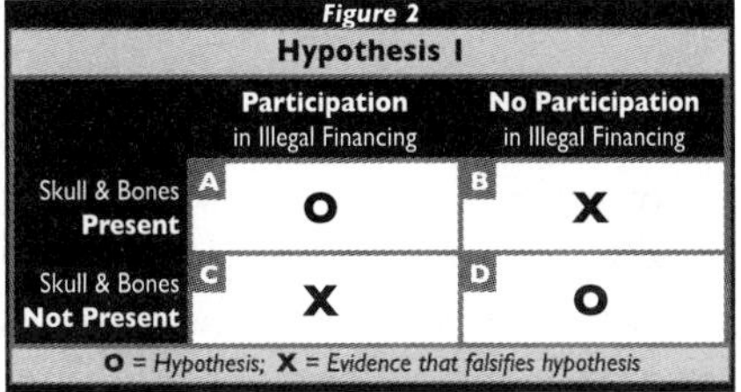

Figure 2

Hypothesis I

	Participation in Illegal Financing	No Participation in Illegal Financing
Skull & Bones **Present**	A O	B X
Skull & Bones **Not Present**	C X	D O

O = *Hypothesis;* X = *Evidence that falsifies hypothesis*

If the data were to fall into boxes A and C, the results would also disprove the hypothesis. Although, a collection of the data falling into boxes A and C does not necessary disprove that a relationship might exist between members of Skull and Bones and involvement in illegal financing, it does demonstrate that other firms in similar positions are engaging in illegal financing; and may indicate that there are other factors responsible for the illegal activity which does not include membership in Skull and Bones.

Hypothesis 1 will be rejected by conspiracy theorists because conspiracy theorists will consider the assumptions of the hypothesis to be inaccurate. The hypothesis limits participation in illegal finance exclusively to Skull and Bones related firms while also making participation in illegal financing mandatory of Skull and Bones members. However, a falsification of this hypothesis is useful to this study and the establishment of relationships in that a falsification of hypothesis 1 would indicate that illegal finance is not an exclusive behavior of Skull and Bones. A falsification of hypothesis 1 also indicates that other factors may exist that may influence a firm's decision regarding participation in illegal financing.

THE SECOND HYPOTHESIS states that the presence of Skull and Bones may or may not result in the participation in illegal financing but non-Skull and Bones related firms will not participate in illegal financing. In hypothesis 2 we predict that the presence of Skull and Bones may or may not result in participation in illegal financing. Therefore, if hypothesis 2 is correct, our data will fall in boxes A, B, and D, with Skull and Bones related firms either participating or not participating in illegal financing while non-Skull and Bones related firms would not be participating in illegal financing.

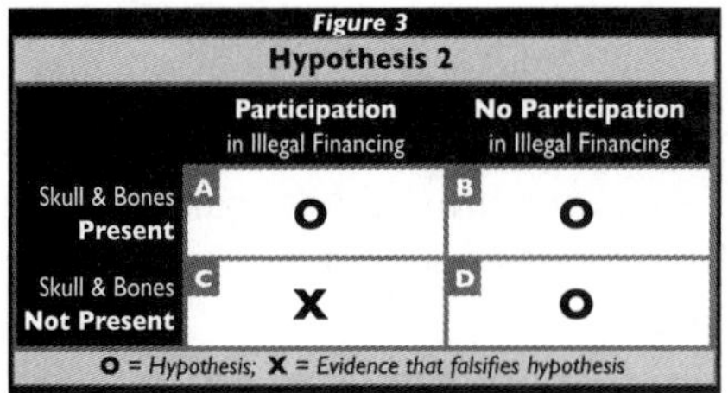

This hypothesis indicates that if a relationship exists between Skull and Bones and participation in illegal financing, then it would be a weak relationship and participation in illegal financing would not be a primary behavior of Skull and Bones. In other words, Skull and Bones may not be the primary motivation for participation in illegal financing. Hypothesis 2 will be falsified if any of the data falls into box 3, indicating that non-Skull and Bones related firms are also participating in illegal financing. Again, a falsification of hypothesis 2 indicates that illegal financing is not an exclusive behavior of Skull and Bones and indicates that there are other factors influencing the decision to participate in illegal financing.

Figure 4

Hypothesis 3

	Participation in Illegal Financing	No Participation in Illegal Financing
Skull & Bones **Present**	A O	B X
Skull & Bones **Not Present**	C O	D O

O = *Hypothesis;* X = *Evidence that falsifies hypothesis*

THE THIRD HYPOTHESIS is that the presence of Skull and Bones will always result in illegal financing while the non-presence of Skull and Bones may or may not result in illegal financing. In hypothesis 3 we predict that all of our data will fall into boxes A, C and D, with Skull and Bones related firms participating in illegal financing and non-Skull and Bones related firms participating in both illegal financing and non-illegal financing.

This hypothesis would indicate that a relationship did exist between Skull and Bones and participation in illegal financing but it would also indicate that other factors exist which are driving participation in illegal financing. Therefore, a relationship between Skull and Bones and participation in illegal financing would exist, but would be weak. This hypothesis would be falsified if any Skull and Bones related firms did not participate in illegal financing, indicating that no relationship between Skull and Bones and participation in illegal financing exists.

THE FOURTH HYPOTHESIS is that all firms will participate in illegal financing. In this hypothesis we predict that all of our data will fall into boxes A and C.

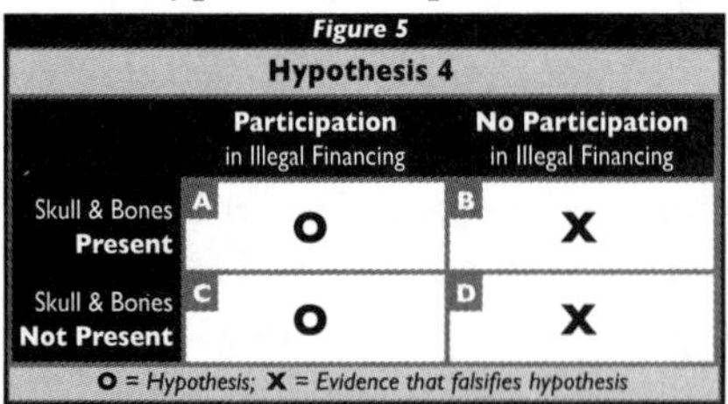

All firms will participate in illegal financing and there will be no firms that will not participate in illegal financing. This hypothesis would indicate that Skull and Bones is not a contributing factor to participation in illegal financing, but that there are other motivating factors that are enticing other segments of society to participate in illegal financing. If data falls into boxes B or C, then this hypothesis is falsified. A falsification of hypothesis 4 indicates participation in illegal financing is not a behavior of all financial firms and there must exist some separating factor that influences some firms to participate in illegal financing while not influencing other firms.

THE TEST

TWO MODELS ARE BEING EXAMINED. Model 1 demonstrates financial activities of several firms during the Bolshevik revolution, while Model 2 demonstrates financial activities of several firms during the rise of Hitler. Each model will be examined separately followed by a comparison of the conclusions of each model.

An error in our methodological framework is that much of the evidence used for observation was drawn from government records and from conspiracy work already completed, which also draws from government records. Consequently, the available evidence provides a very narrow sample, which presents two fundamental problems. First, the sample itself is too small and lends itself toward a large deviation in results. In the observation of the Bolshevik Revolution, seven firms are a small portion of the American financial community. With a sample of only seven firms, only a few of the firms would be required to both participate in illegal financing and to be involved with Skull and Bones in order for a relationship to appear to exist between the two. As it stands in our test, 28 percent of the firms involved in the Bolshevik revolution were also involved in Skull and Bones. A larger sample could very well decrease that percentage and show a different relationship.

Furthermore, the sample is not representative of the society as a whole. For example, the inclusion of illegal financial assistance to Germany by American industrialists would show more then 300 American firms involved in trade with Germany that aided in the development of the German war machine. Thus, illegal financing of Germany was not an exclusive behavior committed by a very small few. However, it is difficult to determine what percentage of industrialists were involved in illegal financing verses those industrialists who were not without counting all industrial companies at the time, which would negate the purpose of using a sample.

The second problem is that of sample bias. The original research question of this work is based on the knowledge that some Skull and Bones dominated firms were providing illegal financing to enemy regimes. Further research indicates that there were other companies that were also involved in illegal financing but were not involved with Skull and Bones. However, the inclusion of these firms in our sample negates random sampling and steers our conclusions in a particular direction. Furthermore, a lack of sufficient research in regards to those firms who did not participate in illegal financing, and more importantly, those firms who did not participate in illegal financing and who were associated with Skull and Bones definitely lends itself toward a biased conclusion.

RELATIONSHIP BETWEEN A FIRM'S PARTICIPATION IN ILLEGAL FINANCING AND MEMBERSHIP IN SKULL & BONES

RESULTS - MODEL 1. In the cross-sectional analysis of a firm's participation in illegal financing and membership in Skull and Bones during the Bolshevik Revolution we find that just over 28 percent of our sample data (or two of the seven firms studied) fell into box A, showing that roughly 28 percent of our sample were firms that participated in illegal financing and were affiliated with Skull and Bones. We also find that roughly 56 percent of our sample (four of the seven firms studied) participated in illegal financing but were not affiliated with Skull and Bones. We also find that roughly 14 percent of our sample (one of the seven firms studied) did not participated in illegal financing and was not affiliated with Skull and Bones. An interesting point is that there was no data for box B, representing Skull and Bones affiliated firms that did not participate in illegal financing. This result is due in part to a lack of investigation into the careers of all Skull and Bones members during this time period. Rather then investigate the careers of each member during this time period, I examined the board of directors of various firms to determine if there was influence by Skull and Bones, according to the previously stated definition of what Skull and Bones influence requires. It is possible that Skull and Bones members entered various financial firms and did not participate in illegal financing, but our evidence does not indicate whether this is or is not the case.

Figure 6 — Bolshevik Revolution

Falsifiable Test #1

	Participation in Illegal Financing	**No Participation** in Illegal Financing
Skull & Bones **Present**	A 1) W.A. Harriman & Co. 2) Guaranty Trust Company	B ?
Skull & Bones **Not Present**	C 1) National City Bank 2) Chase National Bank[1] 3) Kuhn, Loeb & Company 4) Mechanics & Metals National Bank	D 1) J.P. Morgan & Co.[2]

1: Chase National Bank had Percy Rockefeller, a member of Skull and Bones, on the board of directors, but membership in Skull and Bones did not make up 20 percent of the directorship.
2: the J.P. Morgan firm was involved heavily with illegal financing during World War I and gained control of Guaranty Trust Company in 1912. However, there is no existing evidence to indicate that the firm of J.P. Morgan was involved in illegal financing during the Bolshevik revolution, nor is there evidence to indicate an influence of J.P. Morgan on the affairs of Guaranty Trust Company during the Bolshevik revolution.

Given the results of the data, model 1 disproves hypothesis 1, hypothesis 2 and hypothesis 4. Non-Skull and Bones related firms did participate in illegal financing while some non-Skull and Bones related firms did not participate in illegal financing. These results indicate that participation in illegal financing is not an exclusive behavior of Skull and Bones. It also indicates that there exist other factors, which motivate participation in illegal financing. However the data does not necessarily reject hypothesis 3; that the presence of Skull and Bones will always result in illegal financing while the non-presence of Skull and Bones may or may not result in illegal financing. The sample evidence indicates that there does exist a relationship between Skull and Bones and participation in illegal financing. However, it appears that membership in Skull and Bones is not a driving motivation; rather there exist other motivating factors that encourage firms to participate in illegal financing. The data also shows that whatever external factor is motivating firms to participate in illegal financing, it is not affecting all firms equally. No evidence exists to determine if there were Skull and Bones related firms that did not participate in illegal financing, as a result our conclusions are weakened.

The objective in using a cross-sectional test was two-fold: First, although it is not effective in determining causation, the cross-sectional test is able to point toward significant correlations. Second, those correlations can then be used to provide a framework, or new perspective, through which the evidence can be re-examined and bias can be reduced. On the other hand, the cross-sectional test was unable to provide us with a direct answer as to what relationship exists between membership in Skull and Bones and illegal financing. As a result, we will need to turn to the evidence and arguments of conspiracy theorists for further insight. The results of the cross-sectional test will aid this evaluation of evidence by forcing us to focus on specific correlations and minimize any bias or assumptions that have traditionally accompanied such evidence.

RESULTS - MODEL 2. In the cross-sectional analysis of a firm's participation in illegal financing and membership in Skull and Bones during the rise of Hitler, we find that 50 percent of our sample (five of the ten firms studied) were firms that participated in illegal financing and were affiliated with Skull and Bones. We find that 40 percent of our sample (four of the ten firms studied) participated in illegal financing but were not affiliated with Skull and Bones. We also find that 10 percent of our sample (one of the ten firms studied) did not participated in illegal financing and was not affiliated with Skull and Bones. Again there was no data for box B, representing Skull and Bones affiliated firms that did not participate in illegal financing.

Given the results of the data, model 2 also disproves hypothesis 1, hypothesis 2 and hypothesis 4. Once again, non-Skull and Bones related firms did participate in illegal financing. Some non-Skull and Bones related firms did participate in illegal financing while other

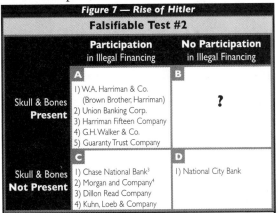

Figure 7 — Rise of Hitler

Falsifiable Test #2

	Participation in Illegal Financing	**No Participation** in Illegal Financing
Skull & Bones **Present**	A 1) W.A. Harriman & Co. (Brown Brother, Harriman) 2) Union Banking Corp. 3) Harriman Fifteen Company 4) G.H. Walker & Co. 5) Guaranty Trust Company	B ?
Skull & Bones **Not Present**	C 1) Chase National Bank[3] 2) Morgan and Company[4] 3) Dillon Read Company 4) Kuhn, Loeb & Company	D 1) National City Bank

3-4: There may be some dispute as to whether or not Chase National Bank and Morgan and Company should be included in this box. Both companies did indeed provide illegal financial assistance to the German army. However, the Paris offices of both these companies agreed to provide financial assistance to the German army only after Paris was invaded by Germany. An argument can be made that these two companies acted purely out of economic necessity in order to prevent asset confiscation by the invading forces, whereas the companies in box A deliberately provided illegal financial assistance to the German army long before war began. Disregarding the issue of intent, these companies match the definition for participation in illegal financing.

non-Skull and Bones related firms did not participate in illegal financing. This model also indicates that participation in illegal financing is not an exclusive behavior of Skull and Bones, and indicates that other motivating factors may exist. The data of model 2 also does not necessarily reject hypothesis 3; that the presence of Skull and Bones will always result in illegal financing while the non-presence of Skull and Bones may or may not result in illegal financing. The sample evidence indicates that there does exist a relationship between Skull and Bones and participation in illegal financing; however, membership in Skull and Bones is not a driving motivation. There appear to exist other motivating factors that are encouraging non-Skull and Bones related firms to participate in illegal financing. The data also shows that whatever external factors are motivating firms to participate in illegal financing, they are not affecting all firms equally.

The conclusions of models 1 and 2 appear almost identical. Both models disproved hypotheses 1, 2 and 4 while accepting hypothesis 3. Both models appear to confirm that a relationship does exist between being a member of Skull and Bones and participating in illegal financing; however, that relationship is weak. Both models indicate that Skull and Bones is not a motivating factor for participating in illegal financing but rather other factors exist which motivate firms to participate in illegal financing. In light of the results of this test, namely: 1) a relationship does exists between being a member of Skull and Bones and participation in illegal financing, 2) the relationship is weak and Skull and Bones is not a motivating factor, and 3) other factors exist in society that are driving participation in illegal finance; an examination of the evidence of illegal financing by Skull and Bones members, as presented by conspiracy theorists, is necessary.

The results of our cross sectional test will provide us with a new perspective and framework through which we can reevaluate the evidence proposed by conspiracy theorists. The goal of the cross-sectional test was threefold: first, it was intended to help eliminate interpretive bias; second, to show possible relationships between the variables, and three to provide a larger view of the behavior of society. The results of the cross-sectional test will aid in the re-evaluation of the evidence as it will bring into perspective the behavior of the financial community during this time period as well as aid in recognizing and eliminating biased representation of information.

5 — Bolshevik Revolution and the Rise of Hitler
An evaluation of evidence

THE CROSS-SECTIONAL TEST completed in section four highlighted some very important correlations regarding Skull and Bones and illegal financing. Nevertheless, it did not provide strong answers to our question regarding the nature of the relationship between Skull and Bones and illegal financing. A further evaluation of the evidence presented by conspiracy theorists is now needed in conjunction with the results of the cross-sectional test in order to gain additional insight.

Because conspiracy theorists focus on the existence of a grand conspiracy aimed at taking over the world, events such as the Bolshevik revolution and the rise of Hitler will be examined in order to see how members of Skull and Bones are allegedly advancing the grand conspiracy. The conspiracy theorists argument, as formulated by Skull and Bones researcher Antony Sutton, emphasizes the illegal financial activities of Skull and Bones members through three Skull and Bones dominated firms between the years 1917 to 1943. These firms include W. A. Harriman and Co. (later became Brown Brothers, Harriman), Guaranty Trust Company, and the Union Banking Corporation. Additional emphasis is then placed on the corporate subsidiaries and affiliated corporations of these three firms.

Sutton states that both the W. A. Harriman and Co. and Guaranty Trust Company were the "operational vehicles" through which Skull and Bones was able to concentrate its illegal financing efforts, focusing on both the large percentage of Skull and Bones members who make up the board of directors of each of these companies as well as the many directors shared between these two companies. By extension of the W.A. Harriman & Co., the Union Banking Corporation is also included for the same reasons mentioned above as well as its unique financial agenda for which it was created.

Furthermore, according to Sutton, the goal of Skull and Bones, through its illegal financial efforts, is to advance a financial domination of the world through support of fascism and communism. As explained in section two, conspiracy theorists believe that Skull and Bones supports both fascist and communist regimes because both style of regime maintains a government controlled economy, which would benefit Skull and Bones firms through the elimination of competition. Yet, the financing of these regimes would only be a means to an end. Sutton argues that financial support of the extreme left (communism) and the extreme right (fascism) would cause a popular rejection of both extremes in favor of a different form of government that could both prevent and control extremist regimes. Eventually a New World Order would be adopted with the members of Skull and Bones in control.

Sutton argues that this plan will be accomplished through the use of the Hegelian Dialectic process, or managed conflict. This process involves the creation of a conflict, and the control of both sides of the conflict in order to steer the conflicts resolution toward a desired goal. In the case of Skull and Bones, according to Sutton, through the financing of both Communism (thesis) and Germany's National Socialism (Antithesis), a conflict would arise which, if controlled correctly, would result in an increased policy and public approval for the implementation of a world government. The assumption being that a world government would control the world's finances and would in turn be controlled by members of Skull and Bones.

An illustration of the Managed Conflict process involving Skull and Bones and the illegal financing of the Bolshevik Revolution and the rise of Hitler, as proposed by Sutton, breaks down into five basic parts, as illustrated in Figure 8.

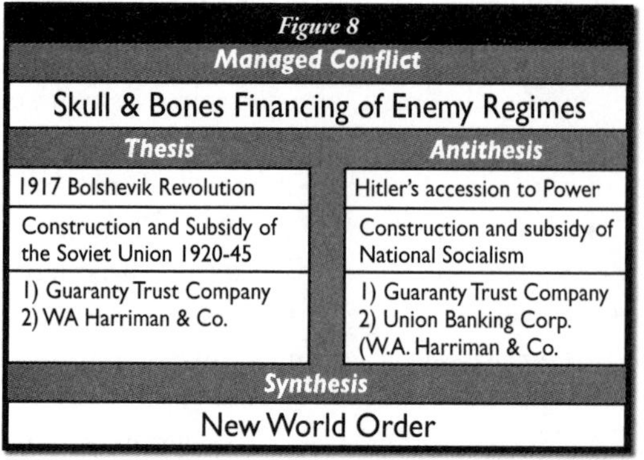

Figure 8
Managed Conflict
Skull & Bones Financing of Enemy Regimes
Thesis
Antithesis
1917 Bolshevik Revolution
Hitler's accession to Power
Construction and Subsidy of the Soviet Union 1920-45
Construction and subsidy of National Socialism
1) Guaranty Trust Company
2) WA Harriman & Co.
1) Guaranty Trust Company
2) Union Banking Corp. (W.A. Harriman & Co.
Synthesis
New World Order

The top box indicates what the subject of the diagram is focusing on: Skull and Bones involvement in the illegal financing of enemy regimes. The diagram then splits into two columns to show the Controlled thesis on the left and the antithesis on the right. The first set of boxes indicates the two sides of the conflict that are being managed along with a general period of time. The subsequent row of boxes indicates how the thesis and antithesis are being created and managed followed by the third set of boxes showing the method by which Skull and Bones is attempting to accomplish the creation and management of the thesis and antithesis. The final box then shows the controlled goal as a result of the management of conflict.

As was discussed in section 3, the conspiracy framework of analysis is far too limiting and problematic. Sutton maintains that the illegal financing of enemy regimes by members of Skull and Bones "can only be explained in the terms of the Hegelian dialectic" [1], process. This framework assumes that Skull and Bones is involved in a conspiracy of a grand nature without proving that to be the case. Second, because it assumes a conspiracy is at work, it eliminates other possibilities that might explain the situation. Using the results of the cross-sectional test performed in section 4 as a framework, a new analysis of the claims against Skull and Bones must be conducted.

The evidence that will be examined in the following pages is in no way an exhaustive study of illegal financing activities during the Bolshevik Revolution or the rise of Hitler. Instead, we will focus our attention on the evidence that is presented by conspiracy theorists against Skull and Bones in an attempt to better explain the events in question as well as to draw further insights as to the correct nature of the relationship between Skull and Bones and illegal financing by using the results of the cross-sectional test.

To begin this analysis of evidence, we will start with an examination of the Guaranty Trust Company and Brown Brothers, Harriman (formerly W.A. Harriman & Co.) in order to explain why conspiracy theorists focus so heavily on the activities of these two companies, and why these companies were labeled as affiliated with Skull and Bones in the cross-sectional test. The activities of these companies and their subsidiaries will then be presented for evaluation starting with the illegal financing during the Bolshevik Revolution and then followed by the activities of these firms during the rise of Hitler, in order to show that the aid of these companies was critical to the development and/or maintenance of Soviet communism and German fascism.

In addition to following these three companies, we will also follow the activities of specific members of Skull and Bones through their involvement with the above-mentioned firms. This work will examine the activities of Averell Harriman ('13), Prescott Bush ('17), Roland Harriman ('17), Ray Morris ('01) and George H. Walker, highlighting their illegal activities through these firms and their subsidiaries.

For simplicity, and in order to accurately present the correlations stressed by conspiracy theorists, members of Skull and Bones will be indicated by including the year of their initiation into the Order of Skull and Bones next to their name.

GUARANTY TRUST COMPANY

GUARANTY TRUST COMPANY WAS FOUNDED IN 1864 in New York. It grew rapidly by the absorbing other banks and trust companies including the Morton Trust Company, the Standard Trust Company, and the National Bank of Commerce. Guaranty Trust Company became a subsidiary of the J.P. Morgan firm in 1912 when the Harriman family sold 8,000 shares of 20,000 total outstanding shares to J.P. Morgan, and has been known as Morgan-Guaranty Company since 1954.

The original capital for Guaranty Trust came from the Whitney, Rockefeller, Harriman and Vanderbilt family, all of which are represented in The Order of Skull and Bones, and on the Board of Guaranty Trust throughout the time period being discussed. Directors of Guaranty Trust Company during this time frame, who were also members of Skull and Bones, include:

Membership in The Order Of Skull and Bones and Guaranty Trust Company:
* *indicates directorship in both W.A. Harriman & Co. and Guaranty Trust Company.*

Harold Stanley ('08)
W. Murray Crane ('04)
Harry P. Whitney (1894)
W. Averell Harriman ('13) *
Knight Woolley ('17) *
Frank P. Shepard ('17) (VP from 1920-1934)
Joseph R. Swan ('02)
Thomas Cochrane (1894)
Percy Rockefeller ('00)
George H. Chittenden ('39)
William Redmond Cross ('41)
Henry P. Davison, Jr. ('20)
Thomas Rodd ('35)
Clement D. Gile ('39)

This concentration of members of Skull and Bones, according to Sutton, represents a tight collusion that could be very influential in the decision-making process of the firm. This firm was classified as affiliated with Skull and Bones because this firm: 1) was created by Skull and Bones members, 2) the Vice-President of the Firm was a member of Skull and Bones during the time period discussed, and 3) more then 25 percent of the firms directors were members of Skull and Bones.

Guaranty Trust Company was involved in illegal financing both before and after the Bolshevik Revolution; was the backer of Ludwig Martens and his soviet bureau; was the first Soviet representative in the United States; the first Soviet fiscal agent in the United States; and received the first shipments of Soviet gold to the United States.[2]

W.A. HARRIMAN & CO.

W.A. HARRIMAN & CO. WAS ESTABLISHED IN 1920 by Averell Harriman('13) with George Herbert Walker (father-in-law of Prescott Bush ('17)) as President and Roland Harriman ('17) as Vice-President. W.A. Harriman & Co. merged with the British-American investment house, Brown Brothers, on January 1, 1931. George Herbert Walker retired to his own G. H. Walker & Co, leaving the Harriman brothers, Prescott Bush and Thatcher M. Brown of the Brown Brothers firm as the Senior-partners. From its inception, the W.A. Harriman & Co. (Brown Brothers, Harriman) housed members of The Order.

Like the Guaranty Trust Company, members of The Order of Skull and Bones also established the original W.A. HARRIMAN & CO. Furthermore, this firm was also dominated and substantially owned by members of the Order of Skull and Bones. It is in this context that some investigators attempt to unravel episodes of illegal financing to both the Bolshevik Revolution and Hitler's rise to power.

Membership in The Order of Skull and Bones and of Brown Brothers, Harriman (Formerly W.A. Harriman & Co.):

** indicates directorship in both W.A. Harriman & Co. and Guaranty Trust Company.*
^ indicates directorship in both W.A. Harriman & Co. and the Union Banking Corporation.

W. Averell Harriman ('13) *
E. Roland Harriman ('17) ^ (VP from 1920-1926)
Ellery S. James ('17)
Ray Morris ('01)^
Prescott Sheldon Bush ('17)^ (VP 1926 -)
Knight Woolley ('17) *
Mortimer Seabury ('09)
Robert A. Lovett ('18)
Eugene WM. Stetson, Jr. ('34)

Walter H. Brown ('45)
Stephen Y. Hord ('21)
John Beckwith Madden ('41)
Grange K. Costikyan ('29)
Partners *not* in The Order:
Matthew C. Brush
Thatcher M. Brown

Here too we find a large concentration of members of Skull and Bones within W.A. Harriman & Co. although the board of directors of W.A. Harriman & Co. has grown since the World War II, during the period of time in question only four partners existed, three of whom where members of Skull and Bones. This firm was also included in my classification as affiliated with Skull and Bones because 1) it was created by members of Skull and Bones, 2) both the President and Vice-President were members of Skull and Bones, and 3) more then 25 percent of the directors were members of Skull and Bones.

BOLSHEVIK REVOLUTION

CONSPIRACY THEORISTS GENERALLY FOCUS THEIR ATTENTION on the illegal financing activities of W.A. Harriman & Co. and Guaranty Trust Company which benefited the Soviet regime during and following the Bolshevik Revolution. Special emphasis is placed on those industrial companies that were controlled by these two firms, namely the International Barnsdall Corporation, the Georgian Manganese Company, which provided the technology and equipment needed for industrial production in the Soviet Union, and the USSR's first national bank, Ruskombank, which provided a means by which the Soviet regime could establish credit with the United States. Conspiracy theorists also draw attention to the anti-communist activities conducted by these companies domestically as evidence of the Hegelian managed conflict process.

INTERNATIONAL BARNSDALL CORPORATION

THE BOLSHEVIKS TOOK CONTROL OF THE CAUCASUS and the Baku oil fields in 1920-21. As a result of mismanagement and political chaos, the oil field drilling in the Baku almost ceased between 1921-1923. The Chairman of Azneft (The Soviet oil production trust), put forward a program for recovery of the oil fields, however the program required equipment and technology that was not available in Russia. In an article published in Pravda, September 21, 1922, Serbrovsky states,

> But just here American capital is going to support us. The American firm International Barnsdall Corporation has submitted a plan ... Lack of equipment prevents us from increasing the production of the oil industry of Baku by ourselves. The American firm ... will provide the equipment, start drilling in the oil fields and organize the technical production of oil with deep pumps. [3]

International Barnsdall Corporation, together with Lucey Manufacturing Company and other major foreign oil well equipment firms fulfilled Azneft 's plan. The first International Barnsdall Corporation concession was signed in October 1921 and was followed by two more in September 1922,[4] despite the fact that Federal Authorities prohibited trading in Russian credits in the United States[5].

Guaranty Trust Company, W.A. Harriman & Co. and Lee, Higginson Company owned the Barnsdall Corporation. The Barnsdall Corporation owned 75 percent of the International Barnsdall Corporation, with the other 25 percent owned by H. Mason Day. A member of Skull and Bones represented the Lee, Higginson Company on the Board of Directors of International Barnsdall Corporation. The Chairman was Matthew C. Brush, one of the very few directors of W.A. Harriman & Co. who was not a member of The Order of Skull and Bones. It is argued that Skull and Bones had a significant hold and influence on the affairs of the International Barnsdall Corporation through its strong representation in three of the four companies owning the International Barnsdall Corporation. Nevertheless, evidence tends to ignore the other major firms involved in this transaction. Conspiracy theorists argue that members of Skull and Bones, through the W.A. Harriman & Co. and Guaranty Trust Company, were able to use the International Barnsdall Corporation in order to aid in the development of communism (the Hegelian thesis.) We shall see similar behavior with the Georgian Manganese Company.

Georgian Manganese Company

W. Averell Harriman, with Matthew C. Brush as Chairman, formed the Georgian Manganese Company in 1923. On July 12th, 1925, a concession agreement was made between the W. A. Harriman & Co. of New York and the USSR to provide loans and foreign exchange for the purpose of exploitation of the Chiaturi manganese deposits and extensive introduction of modern mining and transportation methods.[6] Under this agreement $4 million was spent on mechanizing the mines and converting them from hand to mechanical operation, including the production of a railroad system, an aerial tramway for the transfer of manganese ore and loading elevators.

On August 10, 1920, the U.S. State Department adopted the policy of unrecognition to be the official U.S. policy toward the Soviet Union.[7] This policy prevented the extension of credit to the Soviet Union and permitted only preapproved trading. This policy was in effect until President Roosevelt took office in 1933. The activities of both the International Barnsdall Corporation and the Georgian Manganese Company in the years of 1921-22 and 1925 respectively, were not approved by the U.S. government and were in direct violation of the State Department's prohibition.

Both the International Barnsdall Corporation and the Georgian Manganese Company were both heavily involved in illegal activity in support of Soviet development while receiving a large percentage of their financing through W.A. Harriman & Co. A member of Skull and Bones, Averell Harriman('13) founded the Georgian

Manganese Company, while W.A. Harriman & Co. and Guaranty Trust Company owned more then two-thirds of the Barnsdall Corporation, which in turn owned 75 percent of the International Barnsdall Corporation. Despite having partial ownership, it is difficult to tell what role the members of Skull and Bones in the W.A. Harriman & Co. and Guaranty Trust Company firms played in the decision making process of either the International Barnsdall Corporation or the Georgian Manganese Company. I did not include these two companies in the cross-sectional test because the primary function of these companies is not to provide financing to other corporations or entities, but rather their primary function is industrial.

GUARANTY TRUST COMPANY AND RUSKOMBANK

IT IS ARGUED THAT MEMBERS OF SKULL AND BONES were not only providing technology and equipment to the Soviet Union, but they were involved in the creation of a bank that would allow Credit to the Soviet Union. In 1920 the Anglo-Russian Chamber of Commerce was created to promote trade with Russia. The Chairman of its Executive Committee was Skull and Bones member Samuel R. Bertron('85), a Vice President of Guaranty Trust Company. In a letter from the Anglo-Russian Chamber of Commerce to the State Department, dated July 1, 1921, requests, "What date trading in Russian credits was prohibited in the United States by Federal Authorities?"[8]

Despite knowledge of Guaranty Trust Company's Vice-President Samuel Bertron('85) that trading and banking with the Soviet Union was deemed illegal by the State Department, Guaranty Trust Company initiated trade with the Soviet Union against State Department regulations. Guaranty Trust Company, in association with several German, Swedish and British bankers, formed a joint banking agreement with the Soviets in the fall of 1922. Ruskombank (Foreign Commercial Bank or the Bank of Foreign Commerce) became the first Soviet commercial bank, and was headed by Olof Aschberg.[9] A Vice-President of Guaranty Trust Company was installed as the first VP of Ruskombank in charge of its foreign operations.[10] Guaranty Trust Company came to represent Ruskombank the in the US.

The objectives of Ruskombank "were to raise short-term loans in foreign countries, to introduce foreign capital into the Soviet Union, and generally to facilitate Russian overseas trade."[11] At the opening of the bank, Olof Aschberg commented, "The new bank will look after the purchasing of machinery and raw material from England and the United States and will give guarantees for the completion of contracts."[12]

Conspiracy theorists point toward the illegal financing that was provided by U.S. firms as evidence of a conspiracy, as well as the joint directorship of these firms by Skull and Bones members such as Averell Harriman as proof of collusion. There is a link between membership in Skull and Bones and directorship in both W.A. Harriman & Co. and Guaranty Trust Company. There also exists a link between these firms and their subsidiaries: the Georgian Manganese Company and the International Barnsdall Corporation. The most dominant link that appears to exist is the presence of Averell Harriman in the directorship of W.A. Harriman & Co. and Guaranty Trust Company, as well as both subsidiaries.

A broader view of society shows that during this time period the Soviet government had enacted their New Economic Program (NEP). The NEP promised a reform of Communist policies and cooperation with capitalist business and resulted in a massive infusion of financial and technological aid from numerous countries. Although the U.S. State Department refused to acknowledge the new Soviet government and deemed trade with the USSR illegal, numerous American companies, both industrial and financial, provided aid to the USSR during the NEP.

As the results of the cross-sectional test indicated, a broader view of society does show similar illegal involvement by non-Skull and Bones related firms. Conspiracy theorists who emphasize Skull and Bones involvement in illegal financing rarely evaluate the illegal financing of other firms and their subsidiaries. A few of these non-Skull and Bones related firms that were involved in illegal financing include National City Bank who was involved in illegal financing before WWI as well as after the Bolshevik Revolution, the Chase National Bank who was involved in illegal financing during WWI, Kuhn, Loeb and Company who was involved in illegal financing before and during WWI as well as post Bolshevik Revolution, and the Mechanics and Metals National Bank who was also involved in illegal financing before and during WWI. Important production companies and industrialist who received financing from the above-mentioned firms, and who also aided in the industrial development of the Soviet Union include the Daniel Williard of Baltimore & Ohio Railroad, Westinghouse Air Brake Company, General Electric, Henry Ford and the Vacuum Oil Company.

RISE OF HITLER

IN ORDER FOR THE HEGELIAN MANAGED CONFLICT process to work, an antithesis is required. Hitler's fascist NAZI party became the antithesis, according to Sutton, and as a result became the benefactor of heavy financing and aid from members of Skull and Bones. Brown Brothers Harriman (formerly W.A. Harriman & Co.) headed by Averell Harriman ('13), the Sullivan and Cromwell Law Firm headed by John Foster Dulles, and the Union Banking Corporation (UBC) headed by Roland Harriman ('17) and Prescott Bush ('17), came to represent the entire business interests of the NAZI cartels in the U.S. before and during World War II.[13] On October 1942, the U.S. government charged Prescott Bush ('17) with running NAZI front groups in the United States. Under the Trading with the Enemy Act, all the shares of the Union Banking Corporation were seized, including those held by Prescott Bush ('17), W. Averell Harriman ('13) and Roland Harriman ('17) as being, in effect, held for enemy nationals. The Union Banking Corporation was an affiliate of Brown Brothers, Harriman (formerly W.A. Harriman & Co.), where Prescott Bush, Averell Harriman and Roland Harriman were partners.

Once the government obtained access to The UBC's records, an intricate web of Nazi front corporations began to unravel. Within days two of Union Banking Company's subsidiaries (the Holland American Trading Corporation and the Seamless Steel Equipment Corporation) were also seized. The government later went after the Harriman Fifteen Holding Company (which was shared by Prescott Bush, his father-in-law George Herbert Walker and the Harriman brothers), the Hamburg-Amerika Line, and the Silesian-American Corporation. The U.S. government found that huge sections of the UBC Empire was operated on behalf of Nazi Germany and had greatly assisted the German war effort.

By determining that Prescott Bush ('17), Roland Harriman ('17), George Herbert Walker and other directors of Union Banking Corp. were legally front men for the Nazis, a host of business networks for the build-up of Germany emerged. In light of the results of the cross-sectional analysis we will re-analyze the Union Banking Corporation's role in financing Germany during the rise of Hitler, to determine whether or not illegal support for a violent regime was intentional as well as what role members of Skull & Bones played in these activities.

Again, the evidence presented here is not a comprehensive examination of the available evidence nor is it a comprehensive presentation of the argument against Skull and Bones, however it is more then sufficient to show the connections and relationships between firms in an attempt to show the intent of each firm.

Union Banking Corporation

Conspiracy theorists claim that Averell Harriman('13) began plans to take advantage of the economic crisis in Germany during the post-World War I period, starting in the early 1920's. Government investigators reported that "W. Averell Harriman was in Europe sometime prior to 1924 and at that time became acquainted with Fritz Thyssen, the German industrialist." During this time Harriman and Thyssen agreed to set up a bank for Thyssen in New York. "Certain of Harriman's associates would serve as directors..." while Thyssen's agent "H.J. Kouwenhoven ... came to the United States ... prior to 1924 for conferences with the Harriman Company in this connection."[14]

The Union Banking Corporation was formally established in 1924 as a unit of the Manhattan offices of W.A. Harriman & Co., interlocking with the Thyssen-owned bank voor Handel en Scheepvaart (BHS) in the Netherlands. Thus by personal agreement between Averell Harriman and Fritz Thyssen in 1922, W.A. Harriman and Co., through the Union Banking Corporation, would be transferring funds back and forth between New York and the Thyssen interests in Germany by way of BHS in the Netherlands. By fronting $400,000 during the upstart, W.A. Harriman and company became joint owner and manager of Thyssen's banking operations in the U.S., the UBC.[15] Government investigators concluded "the Union Banking Corporation has since its inception handled funds chiefly supplied to it through the Dutch bank by the Thyssen interests for American investment."[16]

An article in the Herald Tribune on July 31, 1941 declared that while the majority of Thyssen's interest within the United States had been frozen, the Union Banking Corp was currently holding $3 million for Thyssen.[17] This article launched an investigation by the U.S. government's Justice Department, and on October 20, 1942 the U.S. government, under the trading with the Enemy Act, seized the assets of the Union Banking Corporation including stock shares, all of which were owned by E. Roland Harriman, Prescott Bush, three Nazi executives and two associates of Bush.[18]

The list of Directors and their affiliations at the time of seizure are important in order to understand the aid that the UBC provided to the Nazi movement in Germany. These directors and their affiliations are:

E. Roland Harriman - 3991 shares
[Chairman and director of Union Banking Corp. (UBC); Partner in Brown Brothers Harriman; Member of Skull & Bones ('17).]

Cornelis Lievense - 4 shares
[President and Director of UBC; New York resident banking functionary for the Nazi party.]

Harold D. Pennington - 1 share
[Treasurer and Director of UBC; an office manager employed by Bush at Brown Brothers, Harriman.]

Ray Morris - 1 share
[Director of UBC; Partner of Prescott Bush and both Averell and Roland Harriman; member of Skull & Bones ('01).]

Prescott S. Bush - 1 share
[Director of UBC, which was co-founded and sponsored by his father-in-law George Herbert Walker; senior managing partner for E. Roland Harriman and Averell Harriman; Partner Brown Brothers, Harriman; member of Skull & Bones ('17).]

H.J. Kouwenhoven - 1 share
[Director of UBC; organized UBC as the emissary of Fritz Thyssen in negotiations with George Herbert Walker and Averell Harriman; managing director of UBC's Netherlands affiliate under Nazi occupation; industrial executive in Nazi Germany; director and chief foreign financial executive of the German Steel Trust.]

Johann G. Groeninger - 1 share
Director of UBC and of its Netherlands affiliate (BHS); German industrial executive.]

At the time of the US Government's seizure, of the six Directors, three were members of Skull and Bones while three other Directors were members of Germany's Nazi party.

Investigators soon discovered that illegal financing of Germany by the UBC was just the tip of the iceberg. On October 28, 1942, the US government seized two Nazi front organizations run by the UBC: the Holland-American Trading Corporation and the Seamless Steel Equipment Corporation.[19] Then on November 17, 1942, Nazi interest in the Silesian-American Corporation (long managed by Averell Harriman, Prescott Bush and father-in-law George Herbert Walker) was seized under the Trading with the Enemy Act.[20] These three front organizations, along with two UBC affiliates, the German Steel Trust and the Hamburg-Amerika Line, played a great part in the arming of Germany before and during World War II. The U.S. based UBC became the pivotal component of US aid to Germany prior to and during the war.

GERMAN STEEL TRUST

THE 1942 US GOVERNMENT INVESTIGATIVE REPORT states that the UBC was an interlocking concern with the *Vereinigte Stahlwerke* (United Steel Works Corporation or German Steel Trust.)[21] The UBC began making financial arrangements for the German Steel Trust and its co-owner, Friedrich Flick, before 1926.[22] Flick was the major co-owner of the German Steel Trust with Fritz Thyssen. At the wartime tribunal at Nuremberg, the US government said that Flick was "one of the leading financiers and industrialist who from 1932 contributed large sums to the Nazi party [and] to the SS."[23]

After the war, a Congressional investigation examined the Thyssen interests in relation with the UBC (The UBC was also the New York office for the German Steel Trust) and other Nazi entities, and determined that the Vereinigte Stahlwerke (German Steel Trust) had produced the following approximate proportions of total German national output as of 1938:

50.8% of Germany's pig iron
41.4% of Germany's universal plat
36.0% of Germany's heavy plate
38.5% of Germany's galvanized sheet
45.5% of Germany's pipes and tubes
22.1% of Germany's wire
35.0% of Germany's explosives[24]

The major co-owners of the Germany Steel Trust were Fritz Thyssen and Friedrich Flick. Both of these men were long-time supporters of the Nazi movement in Germany and were held on trial after the war for their financial and industrial support to Germany during the War.

Fritz Thyssen told Allied interrogators after the war that he provided financing to the Nazi party in several different ways. Arrangements were made with Hitler's deputy Rudolph Hess to received credit with the Dutch bank in Rotterdam, the Bank Handel und Schiff (i.e. Bank voor Handel en Scheepvaart (BHS), the UBC affiliate bank).[25] Thyssen also donated large sums of money for the maintenance of Hitler's private armies: the Schutzstaffel (S.S. or Black Shirts) and the

Sturmabteilung (S.A., Brown Shirts).[26] Flick also, since 1932, donated large sums to the Nazi party and was a member of the infamous "Circle of Friends" who contributed large sums to the maintenance of the S.S.[27] For the role he played in the buildup of Hitler's army, Flick was condemned to seven years in prison at the Nuremberg trials.

The 1929-31 economic collapse bankrupted the German Steel Trust and the German government took over the Trust's stock shares. Konrad Adenauer and interest associated with the anti-Nazi Catholic Center Party attempted to acquire the shares. However, the UBC, with the help of British financier Montagu Norman, made the financial arrangements that guaranteed Fritz Thyssen would regain control over the shares and the Trust.[28]

Silesian-America Corporation

The Silesian-America Corporation was founded in 1926 by Herbert Walker at the same time as the German Steel Trust, and was held as a unit of the *Harriman Fifteen Corporation.* The Harriman Fifteen Corporation consisted entirely of George Walker as president, and Prescott Bush ('17) and Averell Harriman ('13) as the sole directors of the corporation. At the time of the merger of W.A. Harriman & Co. and Brown Brothers in 1931, The Harriman Fifteen Corporation held a substantial stake in the Silesian Holding Co., which resulted in Averell Harriman's Chairmanship of the Consolidated Silesian Steel Corporation, with the Harriman Fifteen Corporation owning one-third of a complex of steel-making, coal-mining and zinc-mining activities in Germany and Poland, while Friedrich Flick owned the majority of the other two-thirds.[29] A director of the Silesian-America Corporation was Ray Morris ('01), a partner of Prescott Bush ('17) and the Harrimans at both The UBC and Brown Brothers, Harriman.

An investigative report of the Silesian-American Corporation determined the "NATURE OF BUSINESS: The subject corporation is an American holding company for German and Polish subsidiaries, which own large and valuable coal and zinc mines in Silesia, Poland and Germany. Since September 1929 these properties have been in the possession of and have been operated by the German government and have undoubtedly been of considerable assistance to that country in its war effort."[30]

Hamburg-Amerika Line

In 1920 Herbert Walker, as president of the W.A. Harriman and Co., arranged the necessary credits to take control of the Hamburg-Amerika Line. Walker then organized the American Ship and Commerce Corp. as a unit of the W.A. Harriman and Co., with contractual power over Hamburg-Amerika's affairs.[31] The Bush-Harriman shares in American Ship and Commerce Corp. were held by the Harriman Fifteen Corp., which was run by Prescott Bush ('17) and Herbert Walker.[32]

Directors of the Hamburg-Amerika Line included Baron Rudolph von Schroeder and Albert Voegler: Voegler was the chief executive of the German Steel

Trust associated with the UBC and a director of the BHS Bank in Rotterdam which was also the Dutch bank affiliated with the UBC. Voegler donated heavily to the Nazi party between 1930-1933 and helped to organize the Nazi leap into national power.[33]

The Hamburg-Amerika Line was not only involved in the buildup of Hitler's army, but was an active agent in the promotion and arming of Hitler's Nazi party. Before Hitler's accession to power, his private army of an estimated 300,000 men raised concern with Germany's established government, which moved to defend national freedom by ordering the Nazi party's private armies to be disbanded. The U.S. Embassy reported that the Hamburg-Amerika Line was purchasing and distributing propaganda attacks against the German government for attempting to disband Hitler's forces.[34]

Furthermore, the Hamburg-Amerika Line and its affiliates were being used to ship American weapons to Germany. A key figure in these activities was Samuel Pryor. Pryor was a founding director of both the UBC and the American Ship and Commerce Corp. with Herbert Walker and Averell Harriman. Pryor was also the executive committee chairman of Remington Arms.[35] A US Senate investigation on arms trafficking began after Remington contracted to supply the German firm I.G. Farben with explosives. The Senators found that,

> German political associations, like the Nazi and others, are nearly all armed with American ... guns ... Arms of all kinds coming from America are transshipped in the Scheldt to river barges before the vessels arrive in Antwerp. They then can be carried through Holland without police inspection or interference. The Hitlerists (sic) and Communists are presumed to get arms in this manner. The principal arms coming from America are Thompson submachine guns and revolvers. The number is great.[36]

On September 5, 1933, under official Nazi supervision, the Hamburg Amerika Line (Hapag) and the North German Lloyd Company merged. On November 4, 1933, Prescott Bush, through the American Ship and Commerce Corp, personally chose Christian J. Beck to be the manager of freight and operations in North America for the new joint Nazi shipping lines (Hapag-Lloyd).[37]

According to testimony of officials of the companies before Congress in 1934, a supervisor from the Nazi Labor Front rode with every ship of the Hapag-Lloyd line; employees of the New York offices were directly organized into the Nazi Labor Front organization; Hamburg-Amerika provided free passage to individuals going abroad for Nazi propaganda purposes; and the line subsidized pro-Nazi newspapers in the USA, as it had done in Germany against the constitutional government.[38]

Two months before the seizure of the UBC, the US government ordered the seizure of all property of the Hamburg-Amerika Line and the North German Lloyd Company under the Trading with the Enemy Act. The investigators noted in the pre-seizure report that Christian J. Beck was still acting as an attorney representing the Nazi firm.[39]

As is argued by Sutton and other conspiracy theorists, the Guaranty Trust Company and the W.A. Harriman & Co. were both involved in illegal financial activities, which resulted in the economic and industrial build-up of the Soviet Union and Hitler's army. However, the conspiracy theorists conclude that because a large percentage of these firms are made up of Skull and Bones members, Skull and Bones must then be involved in a conspiracy. An examination of other companies who received financing from these firms might show that the majority of companies aided by either the Guaranty Trust Company and the W.A. Harriman & Co. were not involved in the build-up of Hitler's Nazi party. However, this information is not available.

Second, it is difficult to determine how much of the decision making was done by members of Skull and Bones verses non-member partners and directors. As was indicated in the presented evidence, many of the managers and presidents of subsidiary companies were not members of Skull and Bones, and it was these latter companies that were providing the material build-up of Germany and the Soviet Union.

Furthermore, it might be erroneous to argue that because members of Skull and Bones were involved in illegal financing that it is a behavior of the Skull and Bones group. Conspiracy theorists, despite showing individual guilt, have largely failed to provide proof that causation exists between being a member of Skull and Bones and participating in illegal financing.

Throughout all the evidence, we not only find W.A. Harriman & Co. and Guaranty Trust Company with all its subsidiaries, but more importantly we find five individuals at the head of all these affairs. The presence of Skull and Bones members Averell Harriman ('13), Prescott Bush ('17), Roland Harriman ('17), Ray Morris ('01) and non-member George H. Walker. Many of these members were involved in the creation of the majority of the above-mentioned firms.

This evidence demonstrates the personal blame for illegal financing on the five above-mentioned individuals, at the very least. It also demonstrates important family correlations such as Averell and brother Roland Harriman or Prescott Bush and father-in-law George H. Walker. Furthermore, although George H. Walker was not a member of Skull and Bones, his progeny were initiated, along with the progeny of the other four financiers. The evidence also indicates that illegal financing is not an exclusive behavior of members of Skull and Bones, but rather many firms were engaged in such practices.

6 — Conclusion

The falsifiable test conducted in section four yielded three important results. First, a relationship between being a member of Skull and Bones and participation in illegal financing did appear to exist. Despite the behavior of non-Skull and Bones related firms, our evidence indicated that all members of Skull and Bones who were in a position that allowed them to provide illegal financing did so. Second, the existence of many non-Skull and Bones related firms who were also providing illegal financing indicates that the relationship between being a member of Skull and Bones and participation in illegal financing may be spurious, and membership in Skull and Bones does not appear to be a motivating factor in the participation of illegal financing. Third, the participation of non-Skull and Bones related firms in illegal financing indicates that other factors exist in society that are acting as the motivating force behind illegal finance.

RESULTS OF THE EXAMINATION OF EVIDENCE

AN EXAMINATION OF THE EVIDENCE USED BY CONSPIRACY THEORISTS against Skull and Bones during both the Bolshevik Revolution and the rise of Hitler was enlightening for three reasons: it assessed personal blame, it presented a broader view of society, and it highlighted important family connections that were not discernible in the falsifiable test.

The presentation of evidence in both cases showed clearly a number of companies that acted illegally during this time period. In some instances the evidence was able to indicate individual guilt and intent, although evidence for the latter is generally incomplete and circumstantial. The assessment of personal guilt is important in criminal investigations. However, the assumption that a grand conspiracy is taking place or that Skull and Bones is involved in such a conspiracy remains unproven.

Using the evidence illustrated in section five, we were able to present the charges made against Skull and Bones members while at the same time glimpse a broader view of society during that time period. Although conspiracy theorists tend to focus only on those firms controlled or associated with Skull and Bones members, a closer examination of society shows that several hundred firms and industrial companies illegally aided in the build-up of the Soviet Union during and after the Bolshevik Revolution as well as Hitler's accession to power. No evidence exists showing correlations between being a member of Skull and Bones and these other companies who were also providing illegal financing. The evidence also indicates that many of America's largest corporations, such as General Electric, Ford, Standard Oil and the Vacuum Oil Company participated in illegal financing during this time period.

Participation in illegal financing by such a large group of the corporate elite indicates that other factors in society might exist that motivates firms to participate in illegal activity. The most obvious factor is the profit maximization of financial gains. These corporations were able to take advantage of post war Germany and Russia in an attempt to increase profits through the sale of products these countries desperately needed. As indicated in section five, several companies formed a lobbying group in an attempt to persuade congress to recognize the USSR and aid in the new government's development. Certainly any financial aid to the USSR by the US government would have ended up in the pockets of the American businesses that were providing the USSR with technology and equipment. Other companies such as Standard Oil and W.A. Harriman & Co. were granted ownership, by the foreign country, over portions of the industry they were financially aiding.

Another factor that might motivate firms to participate in illegal activity could be the desire for power. However, power seems to be directly connected to financial gains. Increased profits would allow a company to gain a larger share of the industry and thus create even larger profits. The company could gain stronger influence in government through increased lobbying and the creation of foundations and think tanks. The company could also gain stronger influence among the public through propaganda and advertising, publications by the company's foundations and think tanks, and through goal-specific grants and donations. By extension, an individual would gain these same powers through the company. Or more accurately, the company would act as the vehicle through which the individual is able to gain and exercise power.

Status is another factor that might motivate a firm to participate in illegal finance, although again, status is also directly related with financial gains as well as power.

Conspiracy theorists assert that these factors are legitimate factors for explaining why so many companies were involved in illegal financing. However, conspiracy theorists go one step further to argue that there exists a few individuals who are encouraging and even organizing the activities of others in order to accomplish their conspiratorial goals. Examples would include the financing of dozens of industrial companies who were intent on illegally conducting business with the USSR or Germany by W.A. Harriman & Co. and Guaranty Trust Company. Or conspiracy theorists point toward the exclusive representation of American firms in their dealings with pre-World War II Germany by the Sullivan and Cromwell Law Firm headed by John Foster Dulles.

These claims would suggest that the majority of business is intent on profit maximization, and businesses would engage in illegal activity if there was a possibility of not suffering consequences. But conspiracy theorists also suggest that there exist a few individuals who are trying to carry out a hidden agenda. These clandestine individuals position themselves in situations where they are able to steer the actions of others. In such a way, these clandestine few could position themselves in the financial world and then aggressively aid those companies that are willing to act in a way that benefits the financier's agenda. In the same way, these conspiratorial financiers would be able to prevent companies from acting in a way that harms the agenda of the financiers through the denial of business finance.

However, proving that a select few individuals are steering the actions of others is nearly impossible as it involves proving intent. Second, such agenda-based manipulation of the corporate world could still be explained through profit maximization, which would not necessarily require secrecy or a conspiracy of a grand nature.

The third benefit of the examination of evidence is that it highlights important family correlations that were not discernible in the falsifiable test. Evidence shows two strong family links that were heavily involved in illegal finance in both case studies. The Harriman family, which includes W.A. Harriman('13) and brother Roland Harriman ('17), were responsible for the creation of the W.A. Harriman & Co. and the Union Banking Corporation. These firms, of which both the Harrimans were directors, were the focal points of illegal financing to the Bolshevik Revolution and the rise of Hitler. W.A. Harriman was also a director of Guaranty Trust Company.

The second family correlation is that of Prescott Bush ('17), which includes his father-in-law George Herbert Walker. George Herbert Walker was one of the original directors of W.A. Harriman & Co.; he helped set up the Union Banking Corporation and later established G.H. Walker & Co. and the Harriman Fifteen Company. His son-in-law, Prescott Bush ('17) was a director of both the Union Banking Corporation and W.A. Harriman & Co. Although George Herbert Walker was not a member of Skull and Bones, both his son and grandson were initiated into the Order of Skull and Bones. Prescott was the first in his family to be initiated, but his son, George H.W. Bush, and grandson, George W. Bush, were initiated as well as numerous relatives. There are no other prominent family connections between the members of Skull and Bones that participated in illegal financing.

Possible Explanations

THE EVIDENCE OF ILLEGAL FINANCING could lead to numerous conclusions and explanations. The methodological framework used in section four was intended to reduce those possibilities. However, even with both the falsifiable test and a reevaluation of the evidence we are left with several possible conclusions.

As previously explained, power, prestige and wealth could be the ultimate motivating factor for illegal financing, whether by members of Skull and Bones or by non-Skull and Bones related firms; however, this does not exclude occasional non-profit, agenda-based motivators. The results of the falsifiable test indicate that a weak relationship exists between being a member of skull and Bones and participation in illegal financing, however a relationship still appears to exist. A much stronger correlation exists between being involved in a powerful firm and participation in illegal financing. As a result, we could conclude that Skull and Bones membership appears to have nothing to do with illegal financing as a whole.

However, our evidence indicates that a relationship does exist between being a member of Skull and Bones and participation in illegal financing. It is difficult to determine what that relationship is, or if our test is accurate. Because of the small size of the test sample the results could be skewed, incorrectly indicating that a relationship may exist when in reality it might not. Nevertheless, for the purpose of evaluation we are going to assume that the test sample is an accurate representation of each case study. With that assumption, our results indicate that a relationship between the two variables exists, but now we need to explore the possible forms the relationship between Skull and Bones and illegal finance might take.

Conspiracy theorists claim that the relationship is direct and conspiratorial, stating that the appearance of several members of Skull and Bones indicates group collusion. Often in the arguments presented by conspiracy theorists, no distinction is made between the organization of Skull and Bones and its members. Rather, each is generically referred to as Skull and Bones. In this way, an implicit assumption and accusation is made against the Skull and Bones organization whenever one of its members is accused of a crime. Firms are not referred to as being dominated by *members* of Skull and Bones but rather the firm is referred to as being Skull and Bones dominated. Illegal financing is not referred to as illegal financing by members of Skull and Bones, but rather it is illegal financing by Skull and Bones. The potentially erroneous assumption is that a direct relationship exists between the behavior of Skull and Bones members and the Skull and Bones organization itself, despite the fact that no evidence exists to prove that illegal financing is the agenda of the Skull and Bones organization.

Another simple cross-sectional test might help to bring into perspective the conspiracy theorists assumptions about the proposed Skull and Bones agenda. If illegal financing was the agenda of Skull and Bones, then a significant percent of the group's members should be involved in this activity. Never the less, not enough significant evidence exists which would allow us to calculate the percentage of Skull and Bones members that were involved in illegal financing during this time period.

Explanation of Relationship

So what then is the nature of the relationship between Skull and Bones and illegal financing? The research indicates four possible explanations for the relationship that appears to exist: 1) positive networking, 2) agenda based networking, 3) status and 4) collective guilt of Skull and Bones.

It could simply be a coincidence that there are so many members of Skull and Bones working together at firms where illegal financing is taking place; however, that seems highly unlikely. A better explanation would be to examine the networking capabilities among alumni members of Skull and Bones. Networking with alumni, and especially among fraternity pledge classes is quite common in most American universities. There is no evidence to suggest that networking was any less useful between the years of 1917 and 1943. It is reasonable to conclude that members of Skull and Bones who were interested in international finance were able to network with alumni Skull and Bones members to gain access to particular jobs, especially when members such as Averell Harriman and Prescott Bush were so well connected in the financial world.

Given the high concentration of members of Skull and Bones found in certain firms such as W.A. Harriman & Co., or Guaranty Trust Company, it is reasonable to conclude that some form of networking was taking place. At this point however, the question shifts from whether or not members of Skull and Bones networked with each other, to what role networking played in illegal financing. On the one hand, positive networking could have occurred in which case members of Skull and Bones networked with each other to gain particular positions of employment. Nothing conspiratorial would exist in this relationship, and the existence of numerous members of Skull and Bones located within a single firm where illegal finance occurs is simply coincidental. On the other hand, could agenda-based networking have occurred? More specifically, if deviant members of Skull and Bones wanted to engage in illegal financing, did they network within the membership of Skull and Bones to find other members who would also be willing to engage in illegal financing? This variation seems plausible, and given that members of the Order of Skull and Bones are already bound by oaths of secrecy, it does not seem to be a far stretch to accept a claim that deviant members are able to network within the Order of Skull and Bones for deviant purposes.

Regardless, there is no information as to whether or not the many Skull and Bones members who were employed by the firms that participated in illegal finance were actively participating in the decision making process to provide illegal finance. We must assume that by the very nature of their positions as directors of the company, that they were aware of such activity, but that is an assumption that remains unproven. It could be that these members of Skull and Bones networked to gain jobs with various firms but were not involved in illegal activity. If this is true, then the number of Skull and Bones members who were actively participating in illegal finance would be much smaller then originally indicated.

A third possible explanation is that the Order of Skull and Bones merely represents status. Skull and Bones is the most prestigious of the nine secret societies at Yale University. It is made up of very wealthy prestigious family names. As previously stated, Prescott Bush was the first in his family to be initiated into the Order, but both his son and grandson were initiated; the same is true of Averell Harriman. George H. Walker was not a member, but was associated in all his business ventures with prominent members. Both his son and grandson were initiated into the Order of Skull and Bones. It is plausible to conclude that there exists no relationship between being a member of Skull and Bones and participation in illegal financing, but rather the bonds that were established between individuals such as the Harrimans, Prescott Bush and George H. Walker resulted in the initiation of the progeny of these men into the prestigious Order of Skull and Bones.

However, a very slight twist on this third conclusion might state that the Skull and Bones organization is not, in and of itself, goal oriented, but rather Skull and Bones becomes the reflection of the agenda of its members during any given time period. If members of prominent families within Skull and Bones collectively work to accomplish a given goal, how does that effect the Skull and Bones organization as a whole as well as the potential agenda of the organization? Furthermore, if the progeny of individuals who were involved in illegal financing are initiated into Skull and Bones as a status symbol, does that not represent an implicit acceptance (or even reward) for illegal financing?

The fourth possible relationship is that Skull and Bones is collectively guilty of illegal financing. Our falsifiable test indicated that the relationship between membership in Skull and Bones and illegal financing may be spurious, but it does not negate possible guilt of the Skull and Bones organization. Conspiracy theorists have long argued that a conspiracy only requires a few collaborative individuals in key positions to successfully accomplish a goal. Recent events involving Enron and Arthur Anderson certainly showed how only a few well-placed individuals were able to commit illegal financial activities and hide such activities from other officers in the firm. It is possible that a secret agenda of Skull and Bones is illegal financing, and only certain members are chosen to accomplish that specific agenda while other members or kept out of the loop, or more ominously, other members are pursuing other Skull and Bones promoted activities.

The cross-sectional test was unable to indicate if causation between membership in Skull and Bones and participation in illegal finance exists. The research and evidence was useful in assessing the personal guilt of members of Skull and Bones, yet it too failed to prove causation. As a result, it is still unclear as to whether or not membership in Skull and Bones is the reason that the guilty members participated in illegal financing.

PROBLEMS WITH TEST RESULTS

THE PURPOSE OF USING A SCIENTIFIC TEST DESIGN is to eliminate error and problems associated with bias; however, those problems can still occur. The primary problem associated with the test conducted in section four is that of sample size and bias. As previously stated, the sample for our test was very small, which leads to a larger margin of error. A sample of 10 companies, with four of those companies affiliated with Skull and Bones, indicates that 40 percent of the sample was associated with Skull and Bones. If the sample were to be increased to 20 firms, holding the number of Skull and Bones related firms constant, then the percentage of firms that would be associated with Skull and Bones would be reduced by 50 percent, indicating that only 20 percent of the firms were affiliated with Skull and Bones.

The purpose of a sample is to try to show an accurate representation of society as a whole. That task is difficult to do with so small a sample. Second, increasing our sample size by 100 percent while holding constant the number of firms that are affiliated with Skull and Bones shows a dramatic decrease in comparison with the rest of the sample.

Biased sampling further complicates this problem. This study was initiated by the knowledge that some firms that were affiliated with Skull and Bones were also participating in illegal finance. By intentionally including those firms in our sample we begin to bias our results, especially considering that the sample is so small. Second, a majority of the research for this work focused on those firms that did participate in illegal finance, generally lacking sufficient research of those firms that were not participating in illegal finance. As a result there is further biasing of the test sample. An unbiased test sample would most likely show that a great deal of firms did not participate in illegal financing.

In addition, no evidence was presented that fit the requirements of box B in our testing sample: Membership in Skull and Bones and non-participation in illegal financing. Again, further research into those firms that did not participate in illegal financing might show Skull and Bones members in the directorship of those firms, indicating that members of Skull and Bones members were in a position to participate in illegal finance but did not. However, no research was completed in that area and as a result the conclusions from the cross-sectional test are further weakened.

Social Science vs. Conspiracy theory: Problems with the acceptability of a cross sectional test

The hypotheses of this particular cross-sectional test find themselves caught in much the same dilemma as any other conspiracy verses social science work; it is not accepted or supported by both social scientists and conspiracy theorists alike. This particular work will fall into the favor of social scientists while conspiracy theorists might argue that by comparing large sections of society we are dismissing the potentially critical links that need to be explored between Skull and Bones and any conspiracy that may stem from it. While social scientists can argue that illegal financing may have been a behavior practiced by several firms of influential power without the benefit of Skull and Bones membership, conspiracy theorists would counter that the activities of other firms does not downplay the importance of the activities of firms dominated by Skull and Bones.

The difference in the interpretations of these events stem from the very different methodologies used in the analytical frameworks of conspiracy theorists and social scientists. These differences include the testing of assumptions, differing definitions and induction.

Social scientists rely on controlled assumptions in order to test their hypotheses. As stated previously in this section, scientists run tests by controlling certain variables while manipulating others to determine relationships. These relationships are then tested in order to find a universality that holds true. As one theory is proven false, a new theory is designed from the new evidence and is then tested, and this process is repeated until the theory utterly fails or until it cannot be proven false. On the other hand, conspiracy theorists tend to create theories of a grand conspiracy using the evidence of one or two situations. Then as new situations arise, new characteristics of the conspiracy theory emerge to adapt to the new situation. As a result, a tightly constructed universal framework for the classification of a conspiracy is not possible because each situation requires different defining characteristics in order to classify it as a conspiracy.

In many ways, social scientists examine the micro events of particular situations in order to develop a theory that will apply to the macro level. The events of the Bolshevik revolution are examined to develop the defining characteristics of a conspiracy and are then used and tested on other similar historical events. On the other hand, conspiracy theorists focus on the macro level in order to interpret the micro events that take place. Because conspiracy theorists focus on the existence of a grand conspiracy aimed at taking over the world on the macro level, events such as the Bolshevik revolution and the rise of Hitler are then examined in order to see how the grand conspiracy is being advanced through these events. The framework of conspiracy theory and a long-range goal of world socialism and domination are used to interpret historical events, rather then using an accumulation of historical events to determine whether or not a conspiracy is taking place.

There also exists the confusion of terminology with conspiracy and conspiracy theory. As previously stated, two forms of a conspiracy can exist. A grand conspiracy aspires to world domination while a petty conspiracy works within the existing order. A petty conspiracy is limited to affairs that involve a handful of individuals plotting to make money or to seize power. A petty conspiracy aims at transferring money from one pocket to another or replacing one set of rulers with another. With a few possible exceptions, grand conspiracies are extremely difficult to prove, while petty conspiracies are very rarely referred to as a conspiracy. When conspiracy theorists say that a conspiracy exists, they are referring to a grand conspiracy, and therein lies the problem. As the evidence in section five indicates, very likely a conspiracy was indeed taking place. Numerous companies were involved in the illegal financing of enemy regimes against specific instructions issued by the U.S. State Department. This conspiracy was of a petty nature as the seemingly obvious goal of this conspiracy was financial gain. If conspiracy theorists would emphasize that their evidence points toward a petty conspiracy, it might be more acceptable to social scientists. Never the less, conspiracy theorists use the evidence of a petty conspiracy to point toward the possible existence of a grand conspiracy, which also requires the affiliation of a secret and subversive organization such as the Order of Skull and Bones.

In testing, a social scientist will often examine the evidence of many different events in order to draw correlations and create hypotheses. These hypotheses are tested against other events to determine if they will hold up or be rejected. On the other hand, conspiracy theorists tend to create a theory, and then only use the favorable evidence of other events to prove it. As we saw in the presentation of evidence, focus is on the Skull and Bones related firms in order to prove that Skull and Bones is involved in a grand conspiracy. No attention is given to those companies who are involved in illegal activity and are not affiliated with Skull and Bones, nor is there an investigation into the activity's of Skull and Bones related firms that might not have participated in illegal finance.

The selective presentation of only favorable evidence also leads to problems of induction. Because only Skull and Bones members who are involved in illegal activity are presented, the reader is left to the conclusion that all Skull and Bones members are involved in illegal activity. If a book were written celebrating the great amount of influence Skull and Bones members had on the American educational system, only listing those members who contributed significantly to education as well as the great percentage of members who become professors, the reader would plausibly induce from the evidence that Skull and Bones membership is focused on higher education and teaching. Again, biased representation of evidence leads both the conspiracy theorists and the reader to fallible conclusions.

Never the less, the evidence presented by conspiracy theorists is valuable as it helps to assess individual guilt. Furthermore, the scientific cross-sectional test did not produce strong conclusions, and therefore did not necessarily negate the conspiracy theory. Rather, it helped to see through the shortcomings of the conspiracy theory evidence as well as provide insight into important correlations that can be further evaluated in conjunction with the evidence. The results of the cross-sectional test provided a framework that, when combined with the evidence and commentary, helps to better explain a larger view of the situation. In order to gain additional explanations and insights into the relationship of illegal finance and membership in Skull and Bones, it would be useful to use the results of the cross-sectional test in conjunction with other theories of power politics.

REQUIREMENTS FOR A CONSPIRACY THEORY

THIS STUDY DID NOT PROVE OR DISPROVE the existence of a conspiracy in relation to Skull and Bones and illegal financing, but it did provide interesting insights into possible explanations. In order to prove that a conspiracy exists, very specific requirements must be met. First, the conspiracy must be jointly planned and acted upon. There must be direct collusion between the members of the conspiracy. There is the possibility that not all members of the conspiracy will be actively involved, but a large percentage of the members of the conspiracy should be actively involved. Second, the conspiracy must be secret. By the very definition of a conspiracy, secrecy is required for individuals to achieve a prohibited goal. If the goals of the group are public knowledge and the group is still trying to accomplish them, then it cannot be classified as a conspiracy. Third, the goals of the conspiracy must be prohibited by law. Conspiracy theorists make a distinction here by stating that the goals of the conspiracy must be evil, but evil is too ambiguous a term for proper evaluation.

If a group of students jointly and secretly decided to earn a grade of "A" on their final exams, then this would not fit the requirements of a conspiracy. If these same students jointly and secretly plotted to steal the answer key to the exams, then it would fit the requirements of conspiracy. Likewise, if all of the members of an extremist group such as the Ku Klux Klan began rallies and demonstrations in an attempt to segregate the community, this would not be classified as a conspiracy. Although there is group collusion and they are attempting to achieve a prohibited goal, there is no secrecy in their actions. On the other hand, the assassination of civil rights leaders during the 1960's and 70's would fit the requirements or a conspiracy provided that more then one person was involved in the planning of the assassination.

In regards to the Order of Skull and Bones and participation in illegal financing, the group as a whole meets the requirement of secrecy, but there is no evidence that the Order of Skull and Bones is secretly planning specific and illegal actions. Conspiracy theorists would need to prove that the Order of Skull and Bones is in some way promoting illegal financing. Second, group collusion in regards to participation in illegal financing is uncertain. Collusion between certain members exists, but it is unknown as to whether or not that collusion is representative of the Skull and Bones organization. Third, conspiracy theorists would need to prove that the stated goals of the Order of Skull and Bones are conspiratorial or are attempting to achieve a prohibited goal. No such stated goal of Skull and Bones has been proven to exists (although if a conspiracy does exist then no such goal will be found.)

Conspiracy theorists attempt to prove these three requirements by first demonstrating a possible link between the Order of the Illuminati and the Order of Skull and Bones. Existing records do indicate that the Order of the Illuminati was involved in a conspiracy of a grand nature. Conspiracy theorists use these claims against the Illuminati along side strong similarities between both the Illuminati and Skull and Bones in an attempt to show that these two organizations are really one and the same. Conspiracy theorist conclude that if the Order of Skull and Bones was originally a section of the Order of the Illuminati then the revealed goals of the Order of the Illuminati must be the same for Order of Skull and Bones.

Conspiracy theorists do not focus on group cohesion in micro activities such as illegal finance, but rather on a cumulative cohesion to the ultimate goals of the conspiracy. In which case, it is argued that only a few members need to be involved in illegal finance while other members can be involved in government, in education, in media, etc. This way, the goals of the conspiracy can be furthered through many different means all working together. This point is also consistent with the plans of the Order of the Illuminati.

Finally, the general and extreme policy of secrecy by members of Skull and Bones is referred to as a fulfillment of the final requirement of secrecy. If they exist, the goals of Skull and Bones are not known by anyone outside of the Order. It is assumed by conspiracy theorists that goals do exist and that they are conspiratorial in nature. The secrecy of the group only adds fuel to the fire of suspicion.

In reality, a conspiracy theory version of history assumes a top-down, macro framework of a long-range global conspiracy, which is then used to interpret all historical events. Such a framework is required in order to arrive at the conclusion of a grand conspiracy. As already stated, conspiracy theorists showed the individual guilt of members of Skull and Bones, but assessing the collective guilt of Skull and Bones is a difficult task. The burden of proof lies with the conspiracy theorists. This work has provided valuable insights into the nature of the relationship between membership in Skull and Bones and participation in illegal finance, yet that relationship remains unclear.

Appendix

Confiscation of Union Banking Corporation

Federal Register, Saturday, November 7, 1942

[Vesting Order Number 248]

All of the capital stock of Union Banking Corporation and certain indebtedness owing by it.

Under the authority of the Trading with the Enemy Act, as amended, and Executive Order No. 9095, as amended, and pursuant to law, the undersigned, after investigation, finding:

(a) That the property described as follows:

All of the capital stock of Union Banking Corporation, a New York corporation, New York, New York, which is a business enterprise within the United States, consisting of 4,000 shares of $100 par value common capital stock, the names of the registered owners of which, and the number of shares owned by them respectively, are as follows:

Names	Number of Shares
E. Roland Harriman	3,991
Cornelius Lievense	4
Harold D. Pennington	1
Ray Morris	1
Prescott S. Bush	1
H. J. Kouwenhoven	1
Johann G. Groeninger	1
Total	4000

all of which shares are held for the benefit of Bank voor Handel en Scheepvaart, N.V., Rotterdam, The Netherlands, which bank is owned or controlled by members of the Thyssen family, nationals of Germany and/or Hungary, is property of nationals, and represents ownership of said business enterprise which is a national, of a designated enemy country or countries (Germany and/or Hungary);

(b) That the property described as follows:

All right, title, interest and claim of any name or nature whatsoever of the aforesaid Bank voor Handel en Scheepvaart, and August Thyssen-Bank, Berlin, Germany, and each of them, in and to all indebtedness, contingent or otherwise and whether or not matured owing to them, or each of them by said Union Banking Corporation, including but not limited to all security rights in and to any and all collateral for any or all of such indebtedness and the right to sue for and collect such indebtedness.

is an interest in the aforesaid business enterprise held by nationals of an enemy country or countries, and also is property within the United States owned or controlled by nationals of a designated enemy country or countries (Germany and/or Hungary);

and determining that to the extent that any or all of such nationals are persons not within a designated enemy country, the national interest of the United States requires that such persons be treated as nationals of the aforesaid designated enemy country or countries (Germany and/or Hungary), and having made all determinations and taken all action, after appropriate consultation and certification, required by said executive order or Act or otherwise, and deeming it necessary in the national interest, hereby vests such property in the Alien Property Custodian, to be held, used, administered, liquidated, sold or otherwise dealt with in the interested of and for the benefit of the United States.

Such property and any or all of the proceeds thereof shall be held in a special account pending further determination of the Alien Property Custodian. This shall not be deemed to limit the powers of the Alien Property Custodian to return such property or the proceeds thereof, or to indicate that compensation will not be paid in lieu thereof, if and when it should be determined that such a return should be made or such compensation should be paid.

Any person, except a national of a designated enemy country, asserting any claim arising as a result of this order may file with the Alien Property Custodian a notice of his claim, together with a request for a hearing thereon, on Form APC-1, within one year from the date hereof, or within such further time as may be allowed by the Alien Property Custodian. Nothing herein contained shall be deemed to constitute an admission of the existence, validity or right to allowance of any such claim.

The terms "national," "designated enemy country" and "Business enterprise with the United States" as used herein shall have the meanings prescribed in section 10 of said executive order.

Executed at Washington, D. C. on October 20, 1942.

Leo T. Crowley
Alien Property Custodian,

[F.R. Doc. 42-11568; Filed, November 6, 1942; 11:31 a.m.]

ENDNOTES

SECTION 2

1 Ron Rosenbaum, *The New York Observer,* August 23, 2001
2 Mark Fenster. *Conspiracy Theories: secrecy and power in American Culture.* P.69
3 Ibid p 18
4 Gallup Organization and the Post-Modernity Project of the University of Virginia. *The State of Disunion: 1996 Survey of American Political Culture.*
5 Ibid
6 1953 California Senate Investigating Committee on Education: As presented in *An Overview of Our World: An Analysis of the Great Conspiracy and Its Effect on Contemporary History.* By John F. McManus. Appleton, WI: The John Birch Society, 1991, videotape.
7 In a speech before the British Parliament in 1920, Winston Churchill ... video
8 John F. McManus. *An Overview of Our World: An Analysis of the Great Conspiracy and Its Effect on Contemporary History.*
9 Webster, Nesta. *Secret Societies and Subversive Movements.* p. 207
10 Gruber, Hermann. *Illuminati, The Catholic Encyclopedia.* p. 661
11 Ibid, p. 662
12 In a letter to Rev. G.W. Snyder dated October 24, 1798, Former President George Washington; as presented in *An Overview of Our World: An Analysis of the Great Conspiracy and Its Effect on Contemporary History.* By John F. McManus. Appleton, WI: The John Birch Society, 1991, videotape.
13 J. Edgar Hoover, *A Study of Communism.* N.Y. p.25
14 Schaack, Michael. *Anarchy and Anarchist: A History of the Red Terror and the Social Revolution in America and Europe.*
15 Lawrence, John. *A Brief History of Skull and Bones Society at Yale University.*
16 Rosenbaum, Ron. *The Last Secrets of Skull and Bones.*
17 Sutton, Antony C. *America's Secret Establishment: An Introduction to the order of Skull and Bones.* p. 122

SECTION 3

1 Domhoff, G. William. *Who Rules America?,* p. 14
2 Ibid, p. 14
3 Fenster, Mark. *Conspiracy theories: Secrecy and Power in American Culture,* p. 72.
4 Reinhardt, Mark T. *Publishers Weekly.*
5 John F. McManus. *An Overview of Our World: An Analysis of the Great Conspiracy and Its Effect on Contemporary History.*

SECTION 4

1 Spector, Paul E. *Research Design,* p 32.

SECTION 5

1 Sutton, Antony C. *America's Secret Establishment: An Introduction to the order of Skull and Bones.* p. 115.
2 Sutton, Antony C. *Wall Street and the Bolshevik Revolution.* p. 163
3 *Pravda,* September 21,1922; Presented in *America's Secret Establishment: An Introduction to the Order of Skull and Bones.* p. 150.
4 Sutton, Antony C. *America's Secret Establishment: An Introduction to the Order of Skull and Bones.* p. 150
5 Ibid p. 158.
6 *U.S. State Decimal File* 316-138-12/331.
7 State Department Policy as Stated in *Revolutionary Cyclone,* http://history.sandiego.edu/gen/20th/1910s/cyclone.html
8 Letter from the American-Russian Chamber of Commerce to the U.S. State Department, Russian Division, Washington, D.C., July 1st, 1921. Photostat presented in *America's Secret Establish-*

ment: An Introduction to the Order of Skull and Bones. p. 158

9 Sutton, Antony C. Wall Street and the Bolshevik Revolution. p. 60

10 US state department decimal file 861.516/140. Published in Sutton, Antony C. *America's Secret Establishment: An Introduction to the Order of Skull and Bones.* p. 157.

11 Sutton, Antony C. *Wall Street and the Bolshevik Revolution.* p. 66.

12 *U.S. State Department Decimal File,* 861.516/140, Stockholm, October 23, 1922.

13 Webster G. Tarpley & Anton Chaitkin. *George Bush: The Unauthorized Biography,* p. 14.

14 Oct. 5, 1942, Memorandum to the executive Committee of the Office of Alien Property Custodian, stamped CONFIDENTIAL, from the division of Investigation and Research, Homer Jones, Chief. Now declassified in United States National Archives, Suitland, Maryland annex. See Record Group 131, Alien Property Custodian, investigative reports, in file box relating to Vesting Order no. 248.

15 Webster G. Tarpley & Anton Chaitkin, *George Bush: The Unauthorized Biography,* section 2, page 3.

16 Oct. 5, 1942, Memorandum to the executive Committee of the Office of Alien Property Custodian, stamped CONFIDENTIAL, from the division of Investigation and Research, Homer Jones, Chief. Now declassified in United States National Archives, Suitland, Maryland annex. See Record Group 131, Alien Property Custodian, investigative reports, in file box relating to Vesting Order no. 248.

17 *Herald Tribute,* Associated Press, July 31, 1941.

18 Office of Alien Property Custodian, Vesting Order No. 248. The order was signed by Leo T. Crowley, Alien Property Custodian, executed October 20, 1942; F.R. Doc. 42-11568; Filed, November 6, 1942. 11:31 AM; 7 Fed. Reg. 9097 (Nov. 7, 1942). See also the *New York City Directory of Directors* (available at the Library of Congress). The volumes for the 1930s and the 1940s list Prescott Bush as a director of Union Banking Corporation for the years 1934 through 1943.

19 Alien Property Custodian Vesting Order No. 259: Seamless Steel Equipment Corporation; Vesting Order No. 261: Holland-America Trading Corp.

20 Alien Property Custodian Vesting Order No. 259: Seamless Steel Equipment Corporation; Vesting Order No. 261: Holland-America Trading Corp.

21 Webster G. Tarpley & Anton Chaitkin. *George Bush: The Unauthorized Biography,* p. 3

22 Webster G. Tarpley & Anton Chaitkin. *George Bush: The Unauthorized Biography,* p. 6

23 *Nazi Conspiracy and Aggression Supplement B,* by the Office of United States Chief of Counsel for Prosecution of Nazis Criminality, United States Government Printing Office, (Washington: 1948), pp. 1597, 1686.

24 *Elimination of German Resources for War: Hearings before a Subcommittee of the Committee on Military Affairs, United States Senate, Seventy-Ninth Congress; Part 5, Testimony of [the United States] Treasury Department, July 2, 1945.* P. 507: Table of Vereinigte Stahlwerke output figures are percent of German total as of 1938; Thyssen organization including Union Banking Corporation pp. 727-731.

25 Interrogation of Fritz Thyssen, EF/Me?1 of Sept. 4, 1945 in U.S. Control Counsel records, Photostat on page 167 in Anthony Sutton, *An introduction to the Order* (Billings, Mt.: Liberty House Press, 1986).

26 Ibid

27 *Nazi Conspiracy and Aggression Supplement B,* by the Office of United States Chief of Counsel for Prosecution of Nazis Criminality, United States Government Printing Office, (Washington: 1948), pp. 1597, 1686

28 Webster G. Tarpley & Anton Chaitkin. *George Bush: The Unauthorized Biography,* p.13.

29 *Consolidated Silesian Steel Corporation [minutes of the] meeting of Board of Directors,* Oct. 31, 1930 (Harriman papers, Library of Congress), shows Averell Harriman as Chairman of the Board. Prescott Bush to W.A. Harriman, Memorandum Dec. 19, 1930 on their Harriman Fifteen Corp. Annual Report of United Konigs and Laura Steel and Iron Works for the year 1930 (Harriman papers, Library of Congress) lists "Dr. Friedrich Flick … Berlin " and " William Averell Harriman … New York" on the Board of Directors.

"Harriman Fifteen Corporation Securities Position February 28, 1931," Harriman papers, Library of Congress. This report shows Harriman Fifteen Corporation holding 32,576 shares in Silesian Holding Co. V.T.C. worth $1,628,800, just over half the value of the Harriman Fifteen Corporation's total holdings.

The *New York City Directory of Directors* volumes for the 1930s (available at the Library of Congress) show Prescott Sheldon Bush and W. Averell Harriman as the directors of Harriman Fifteen Corp.

"Appointments," marked "Noted may 18, 1931 W.A.H., " (among the papers from Prescott Bush's New York Office of Brown Brothers Harriman, Harriman papers, Library of Congress), lists a meeting between Averell Harriman and Friedrich Flick in Berlin at 4:00 P.M., Wednesday April 22, 1931. This was followed immediately by a meeting with Wilhelm Cuno, chief executive of the Hamburg-Amerika Line.

The "Report To the Stockholders of the Harriman Fifteen Corporation," Oct. 19, 1933 (in the Harriman papers, Library of Congress) names G.H. Walker as president of the corporation. It shows the Harriman Fifteen Corporation's address as 1 Wall Street the location of G.H. Walker and Co.

30 Sept. 25, 1942, Memorandum To the Executive Committee of the Office of Alien Property Custodian, stamped Confidential, from the Division of Investigation and Research, Homer Jones, Chief. Now declassified in United States National Archives, Suitland, Maryland annex. See Record Group 131, Alien Property Custodian, investigative reports, in file box relating to Vesting Order NO. 370.

31 Webster G. Tarpley & Anton Chaitkin. *George Bush: The Unauthorized Biography*, p. 8.

32 George Walker was a director of American Ship and Commerce from its organization through 1928. Consult *New York City Directory of Directors.*

33 See *Elimination of German Resources for War, op. cit.*, pp. 881-882 on Voegler.

34 Confidential memorandum from U.S. embassy, Berlin, op.cit.

35 Webster G. Tarpley & Anton Chaitkin. *George Bush: The Unauthorized Biography*, p. 9.

36 U.S. Senate "Nye Committee" hearings, Sept. 14, 1934, pp. 1197-98, extracts from letters of Col. William N. Taylor, dated June 27, 1932 and Jan. 9, 1933.

37 Webster G. Tarpley & Anton Chaitkin. *George Bush: The Unauthorized Biography*, p. 11.

38 Investigation of Nazi Propaganda Activities and Investigation of Certain Other Propaganda Activities: Public hearings before A Subcommittee of the Special Committee on Un-American Activities, United States House of Representatives, Seventy Third Congress, New York City, July 9-12, 1934 Hearings No. 73 NY-7 (Washington: U.S. Govt. Printing Office, 1934). See testimony of Capt. Frederick C. Mensing, John Schroeder, Paul von Lilienfeld-Toal, and summaries by Committee members.

See New York *Times*, July 16, 1933, p. 12, for organizing of Nazi Labor Front at North German Lloyd, leading to Hamburg-Amerika after merger.

39 Office of Alien Property Custodian, Vesting Order No. 126. Signed by Leo T. Crowley, Alien Property Custodian, executed August 28th, 1942. F.R. Doc. 42-8774; Filed September 4, 1942, 10:55 A.M.; 7F.R. 7061 (No. 176, Sept. 5, 1942.) July 18, 1942, Memorandum To the Executive Committee of the Office of Alien Property Custodian, stamped CONFIDENTIAL, from the Division of Investigation and Research, Homer Jones, Chief. Now declassified in United States National Archives, Suitland, Maryland annex. See Record Group 131, Alien Property Custodian, investigative reports, in file box relating to Vesting Order No. 126.

APPENDIX A

22 Office of Alien Property Custodian, Vesting Order No. 248. The order was signed by Leo t. Crowley, Alien Property Custodian, executed October 20, 1942; F.R. Doc. 42-11568; Filed, November 6, 1942. 11:31 AM; 7 Fed. Reg. 9097 (Nov. 7, 1942). See also the New York City Directory of Directors (available at the Library of Congress). The volumes for the 1930s and the 1940s list Prescott Bush as a director of Union Banking Corporation for the years 1934 through 1943.

Jedediah McClure was born in Indiana in 1978, and graduated with a B.A. in international political economics from DePauw University. He is currently the President of Freedom-Medical, Phoenix, Arizona.

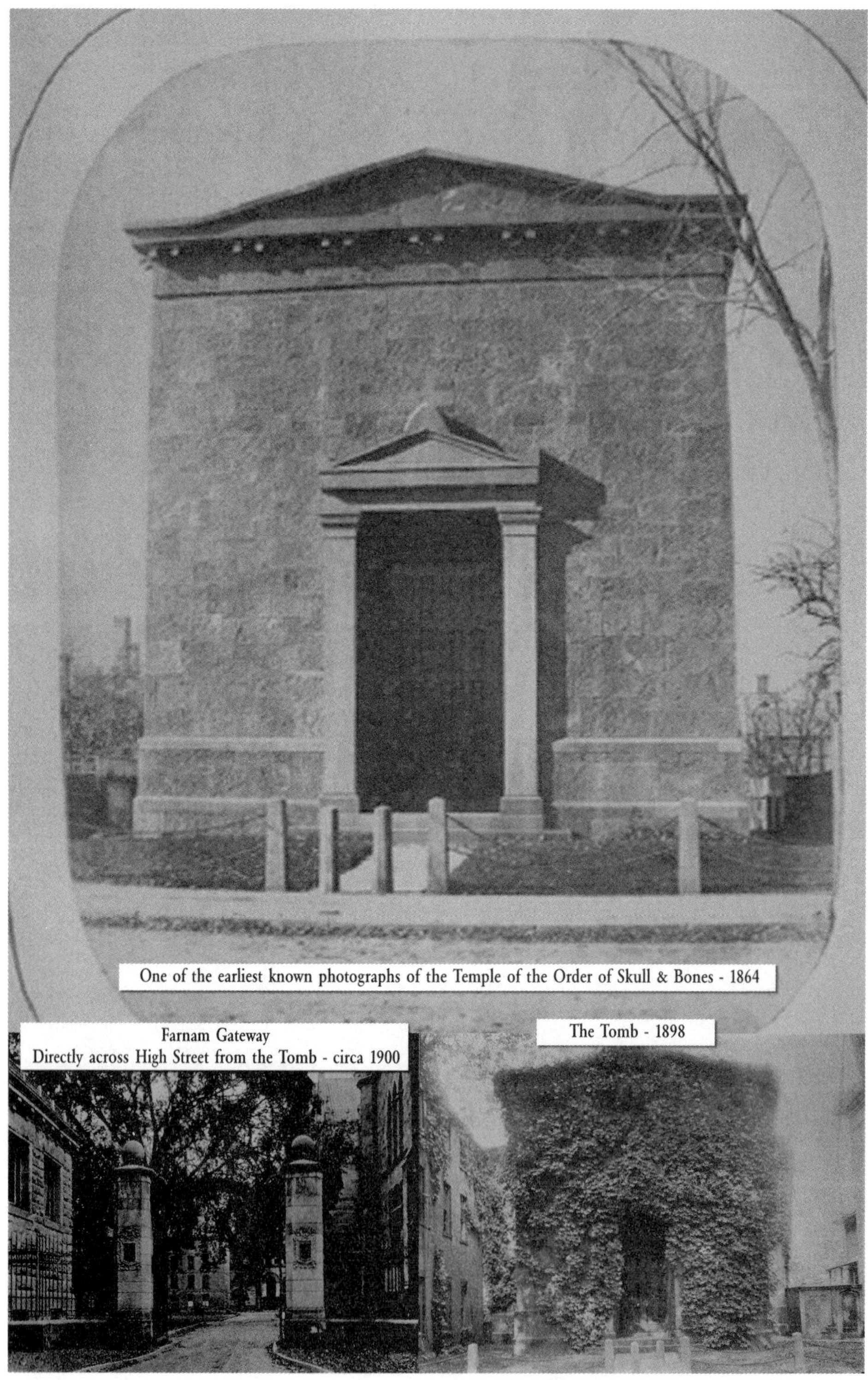

One of the earliest known photographs of the Temple of the Order of Skull & Bones - 1864

Farnam Gateway
Directly across High Street from the Tomb - circa 1900

The Tomb - 1898

The Tomb

Kris Millegan
August 2003

There it sits at 64 High Street, looming large and innocent, a squat funny looking building with slits for windows and big black doors that clang loudly when they shut. The building known as the Temple to members is most often referred to by its very appropriate nickname — the Tomb. You cannot walk completely around the building, and hidden behind the building and its high stonewalls is a secret courtyard.

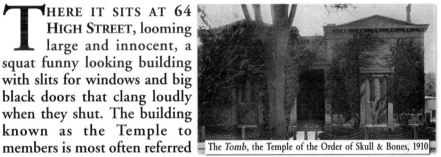

The *Tomb*, the Temple of the Order of Skull & Bones, 1910

The Art Gallery Bridge

One may actually view the Tomb from a Starbucks on Chapel Street by looking underneath, through the Art Gallery Bridge. Interestingly, there are no tables and chairs in that corner of the cafe, so you may not sit and stare, you may only peek while perusing coffee paraphernalia.

The intersection of High and Chapel Streets is one of the gateways to the Yale campus, a transition point between "Town & Gown." When the Temple was built in 1856, across the street from the Yale campus, it was pretty much by itself. Then in 1864 through a bequest from Augustus Russell Street the Yale Art School and Gallery or Street Hall was built "specifically at Mr. Street's direction" on the northeast corner of Chapel & High with one entrance for New Haven citizens and one for the college.

Street Hall's entrance to the town of New Haven on Chapel Street

Later in the 1920's the Gallery of Fine Arts, now known as the Old Art Gallery, was built on the northwest corner of High and Chapel Streets and an elaborate gallery bridge walkway was built over High Street connecting the two art buildings. With Weir Hall on one side and later with the modernistic Yale Art Gallery built in 1953, the Tomb was flanked on three sides by Yale art galleries and schools. In the 1920's there was thought of moving the museum and galleries next to the new Peabody museum on Whitney Avenue, but that was nixed by Street's original bequest restrictions.

There have always been strong relationships in New England between the art community and secret societies. The Age of Enlightenment, Calvinism, Spiritual Awakenings, The Revolutionary War, Millennialism and other influences had brewed an interesting social stew with the secret societies, primarily Freemasonry and Phi Beta Kappa playing very visible roles. The year Skull & Bones was formed, America's first college campus art gallery *and the first Tomb-like building at Yale,* the Trumbull Gallery, was opened on October 25, 1832. John Trumbull, famous early American historical painter, had fallen on hard times and his nephew and Yale's first science faculty member, Professor Silliman, established the gallery and arranged for him to receive an annuity in exchange for the donation of his paintings to Yale. An early design for the gallery was likened to a *traditional Greek Temple.* Trumbull designed the building that was finally built. The gallery contained two large windowless rooms and had an eastern entrance flanked by Doric columns and Doric pilasters.

Trumbull Gallery in 1864

Professor Silliman was the founder and editor of the *American Journal of Science and Arts.* He was a founding member of the National Academy of Sciences and a member of Phi Beta Kappa, which in 1832, in reaction to the Ant-Masonic movement ceased being a secret society and became an *open and honorary* organization. A reported reaction to the Phi Beta Kappa secrecy change was that Yale students William Huntington Russell and Alphonso Taft asked 13 of their classmates to form with them the *Order of Scull & Bones.* Phi Beta Kappa did continue also, with Russell, Taft and three other Bonesmen as members.

The school of chemistry, which Professor Silliman founded at Yale in 1847, later developed into the Sheffield Scientific School (SSS) through which Bones was able to *take-over* Yale. Professor Silliman retired in 1853 to be succeeded by his son, Professor Benjamin Silliman, Jr., a member of a very active group of Bonesmen, the class of 1837. Junior, among other things, discovered in 1855 the process known as *cracking,* the distillation of paraffin, gasoline and other products from oil. As Professor Silliman, Jr. noted in his report:

Professor Benjamin Silliman, Jr (S&B 1837)

> *Gentlemen, it appears to me that your Company may have in their possession a raw material from which, by a simple and not expensive process, they may manufacture very valuable products.*

His findings spurred the first *oil rush* and brought America's first oil company, The Pennsylvania Rock Oil Company of New York *into the hands of New Haven investors,* and made fortunes for Townsend and Bissell families, who soon had sons in the Order of Skull & Bones. The thread of the petroleum business continues through the history of Yale, the Tomb and the members of the Order of Skull & Bones.

A drawing of the Tomb from 1860

The Tomb as first built was a nearly windowless two-story mausoleum/ Masonic hall style building. It was constructed from brownstone and is generally considered to be the work of local architect Henry Austin, although officially the architect is unknown. There have been no public events held within it, so information about the interior comes from reportage of various *break-ins* and some people with commercial access. The Order of File & Claw issued a pamphlet in 1876 on a break-in on September 29th of that year. That report is reproduced in full, starting on page 469.

The most recent reportage about a break-in or "sort of a quick canter through the premises" by some Yale co-eds in the summer of 1979, who were "invited in by a dissident member ..." was in an article by Stephen ML Aronson in *Fame* magazine, Volume 2, Number 2, August 1989:

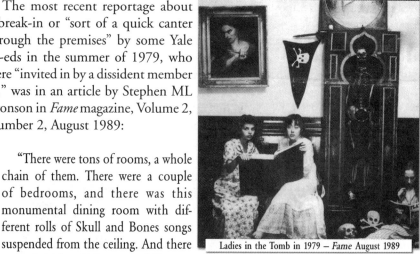

Ladies in the Tomb in 1979 – *Fame* August 1989

> "There were tons of rooms, a whole chain of them. There were a couple of bedrooms, and there was this monumental dining room with different rolls of Skull and Bones songs suspended from the ceiling. And there was a President Taft memorabilia room filled with flyers, posters, buttons – the whole room was like a Miss Haversham's shrine. And a big living room with a beautiful rug. And then this big, huge, expensive-looking ivory carving in the hallway. The whole thing was on a very medieval scale. But it was all kind of a shambles. It looked like a boy's dorm room, like it hadn't been cleaned up in six months. There were a lot of old bones around – believe me, it could use a women's touch.
>
> "The most shocking thing – and I say this because I do think it's sort of important – I mean, President Bush does belong to Skull and Bones, everyone knows that – there is, like a little Nazi shrine inside. One room on the second floor has a bunch of swastikas, kind of an SS macho Nazi iconography. Somebody should ask President Bush about the swastikas in there. I mean, I don't think he'll say they're *not* there. I think he'll say, 'Oh, it wasn't a big deal, it was just a little room.' Which I don't think is true and which I wouldn't find terribly reassuring anyway. But I don't think he'd deny it altogether, because it's true. I mean, I think the Nazi stuff was no more serious than all the bones that were around, but I still find it a little disconcerting."

The Tomb – Scribner's Magazine, April 1876

Alexandra Robbins in her book, *Secrets of the Tomb* adds to the public's knowledge of the interior, although she dismisses the idea that the Tomb may be reached by Yale's infamous steam tunnels — even when the subject is brought up by New Haven's finest. There are most definitely extensive tunnel and underground building complexes at Yale. Exploring the steam tunnels is still "among the offenses that are subject to disciplinary action." The *Yale Bulletin*

& Calendar September 1-8, 1997 Volume 26, Number 2 reports about a $90 million "comprehensive reconstruction" and "modernization" of the power plants and the "interconnecting network of underground pipes and tunnels provide steam for heating, chilled water for air conditioning, electricity and telecommunication systems throughout central campus." From the relative positions of the power plants and Yale buildings, it is very probable that there is underground access to the Bones clubhouse, as claimed by the New Haven police officers in Ms. Robbins' book.

Just a little over a block away is the Cross Campus Library, a huge multi-storied underground complex in the central campus core. Next-door just beyond the Tomb's secret courtyard wall underneath Weir Court is a large underground auditorium.

According to Ms. Robbins there is an underground tunnel going underneath the secret courtyard garden then turning north going only as far as Weir Towers. With the Order's government intelligence background, I am sure that there could be constructed an entrance into Yale's hundred-plus year old underground system with a blind alley so that those without the need to know would think that there was only passage to the basement of Weir Towers.

Bones Hall, Century Magazine – September1888

The wall between the Old Art Gallery and the Tomb as viewed looking west from High Street

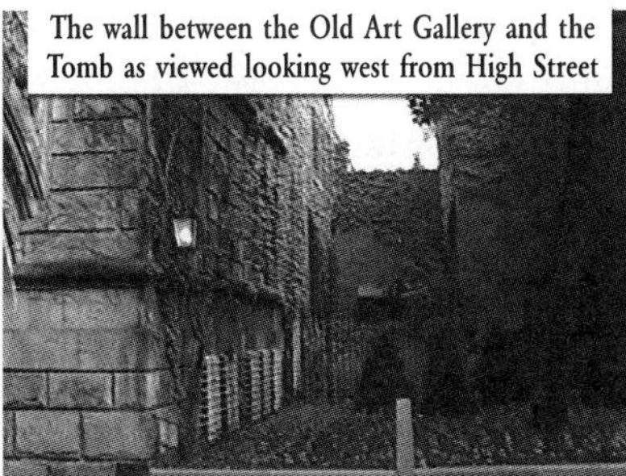

The Tomb was first enlarged in 1883 with the addition of a large dining hall attached at a tee on the rear of the building. The dining hall is two stories with large windows. The additional building doesn't directly abut the Old Art Gallery building, built later in 1926-27 on the south, but there is a high stonewall between the two buildings that blocks vision and movement.

When the dining room addition was added, George Douglas Miller, a member from 1870, *owned* the surrounding property and "[h]e raised a great mound of earth and surrounded the property for secrecy."

The Order writes very little about Mr. Miller. In their catalogues all that is said is that he was an industrialist. George Douglas Miller also gave to the Order one of his private islands, Deer Island, inherited from his father Samuel.

George Douglas Miller, 1847-1932
Benafactor of Bones?

For some time George lived on the property surrounding the Tomb. His son Samuel was born in 1881 and died in 1883 on the "premises." According to the *Biographical Record of the Class of Seventy, Yale University, 1870-1904*, Miller had "prepared" for Yale at Skull & Bones co-founder, William H. Russell's Collegiate Institute in New Haven. Miller had been in the employ of a New York publishing house, the secretary of the New England Car Spring Company and then he worked with the New York and Straitsville Coal and Iron Company, "a position which came to him through William Walter Phelps (S&B 1860), who had a controlling interest in the company. He was afterwards secretary of the New Haven Electric Light Company"

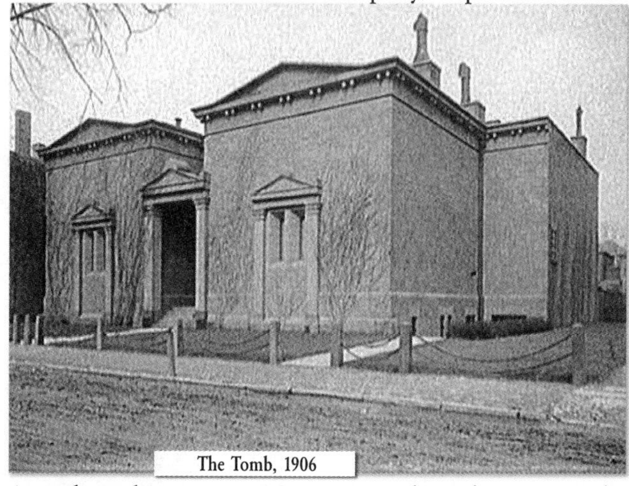
The Tomb, 1906

W W Phelps is a member of the Order who was involved extensively in the Order's influence on Yale.

George didn't reminisce about his time in New Haven, his relatives I spoke with knew nothing about his time there and written records are sketchy and sometimes contradictory. As far as I can ascertain, is that George purchased the property all around the Tomb, almost the complete block in the 1870s and early 1880s. There were various buildings both commercial and residential. He then proceeded to raze many of the buildings and built a flat-topped berm around the sides of the Tomb and wanted to build a college such as the Magadelan College at Oxford University. Evarts Tracy (S&B 1890), a member of the NYC architect firm, Tracy & Swartwout began building this college in 1910.

The exterior of the Tomb that we see today was constructed in 1903. The building was reproduced, the original door was turned into a pair of slit windows and the doorway was put in the middle of the two. The north building is the most recent.

Alumni Hall being torn down, 1911

In 1911, Alumni Hall was demolished and it's two large Gothic stone towers were brought down the street and re-erected at the northwest corner of the new addition to the Tomb.

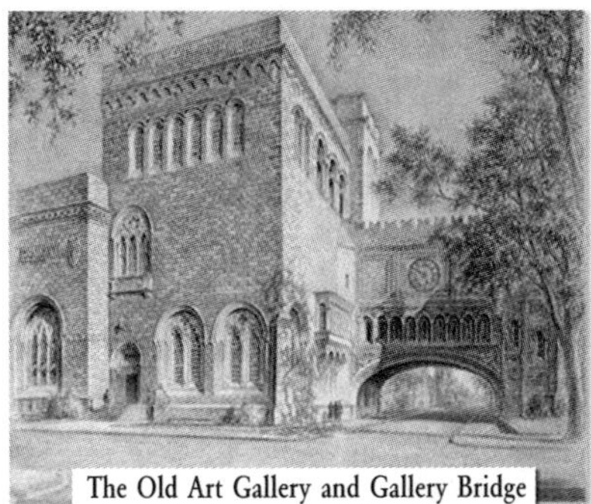
The Old Art Gallery and Gallery Bridge

The old Trumbull Gallery was torn down in 1903, after having had windows put in 1868 and then serving as the central administration building until demolished.

John Trumbull and his wife were buried beneath their gallery in 1843. They were moved to Street Hall for a while to be finally laid to rest across High Street in the basement of the Old Art Gallery, right next to the Tomb. Notably above the bridge between the two art school buildings is a "dimensionally correct (30 feet by 60 feet)" windowless replica of a gallery at the Trumbull Gallery.

The cloister quadrangle that Miller began was abandoned and in 1912 was purchased by Yale. The building was finally completed in 1924 and was named Weir Hall. It was the home to the School of Architecture for many years. The building was finished using funds from Yale graduate Edward S. Harkness, the son of Stephen Harkness, a Cleveland harness-maker, who was an early investor with John D. Rockefeller and wound up as the second largest shareholder in Standard Oil.

Looking down the small pathway to Weir Hall and Towers. The northeast corner of the Tomb Library is on the left and the dining hall of Jonathan Edwards College is on the right

Harkness donated funds again, some sources say in 1924 others say is 1926, but nonetheless, Harkness bought the rest of the Miller property to the south of the Tomb and Yale commissioned Tracy & Swartwout to design the Old Art Gallery. The original design filled up the whole block from High to York Streets and there were designed perpendicular arms connecting to Weir Hall that would have completely enclosed the Tomb. This design was not built with just about half being built. This was just enough to seal off the south side of the Tomb and secret courtyard.

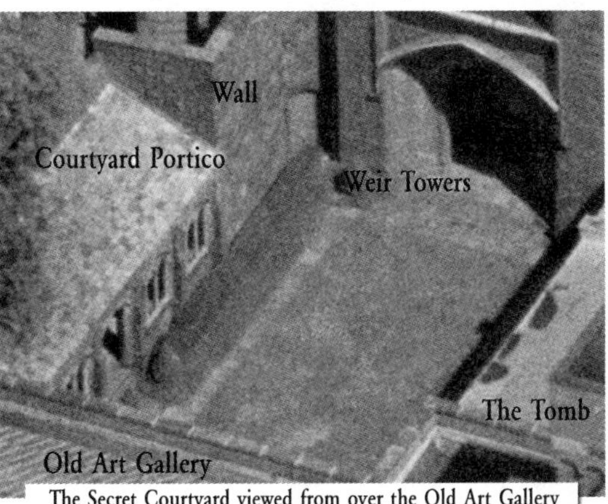

The Secret Courtyard viewed from over the Old Art Gallery

There appears to be a vestibule at or a door into Weir Towers from the secret courtyard. Inside the courtyard there is a portico and according to reports there are some memorial benches and a statue of a knight.

The secret courtyard gate

A gate entrance to the courtyard is on the northwest corner and a high wall encompasses the courtyard completely on the west side connecting again to the Old Art Gallery.

At certain times of the day you may pass through the locked doors of the antechamber of Weir Hall Towers and into Weir Court. Weir Court, abutting on the west side the Tomb's secret courtyard 20-foot tall ivy-covered wall, was built on part of the same plateau that Miller had built up. The space is a small and usually private park amid the bustle of the urban campus and probably very similar to the Bones' secret courtyard on the other side of the wall.

Southern view from Weir Court toward Kahn's Yale Art Gallery

Until 1947, the Department of Architecture was housed in Weir Hall with a view of the secret courtyard, a view they kept when they moved to the top floors of the Louis Kahn designed modernistic completion of the Art Gallery over to York Street. The Tomb was now completely sealed behind the protective façade of the art schools. In 1963 the architecture school moved across York Street but they "still return to Miller's courtyard every spring for the hopeful rituals of commencement."

Looking from Weir Court to the northeast, Weir Hall on left, Weir Towers in middle – note, boarded-up windows. The secret courtyard wall goes from right to center

Underneath the Weir Court in 1974-76 there was built, as already mentioned, a large auditorium. This was done without disturbing the large old elm trees. The park-like setting above-ground was restored as it was before the underground structure was built and is natural looking. Personally after visiting the court several times, I didn't realize that there was an underground structure at the site until reading about it later. It was not evident in casual use and perusal of the area.

After the architecture school moved, Weir Hall became part of Jonathan Edwards College, most of the Weir Hall building becoming the college library. The Towers at this time appeared to have become more part of Bones than Yale, with access curtailed to public and Yalies alike. What the policy is and who owns the Towers are not completely clear.

The Tomb property today is the only private property within the blocks from High to York Streets and Chapel and Grove Streets, the rest belonging to Yale University. From 1911 to 1928 Yale acquired 36 different parcels on the two blocks from Elm to Grove Streets through a series of interesting transactions using "trusts and trusted friends in order to acquire property for itself while vesting legal title in another's name." This was done to keep the University's name off the public records thus not allowing the property owners "to exact a holdout premium." Yale's "false front" acting as the Trustee holding the property was "almost exclusively the Union & New Haven Trust Company," A company with at least three Bones members in the firm, one serving as president for 20 years and Chairman of the Board for 10. Some of these transactions were just simple actions with the trust company holding the property for a few months.

Sterling Law School, Yale University

The University's purchase of the three lots, which gave Yale the entire frontage of High Street from Wall to Grove Streets — where today, stands the Sterling Law School — was a bit more complex.

The University acquired the property in a convoluted four-year scheme with Edward Harkness again supplying oil money for the purchase. The parcel was placed in the name of Bonesman Samuel H Fisher (S&B 1889), a New Haven lawyer, a Yale general counsel, a Fellow of the Yale Corporation and Director of New York Trust among many others. Part of the property deal was the site of the Hopkins Grammar School, a prestigious school of long tradition, which many Bonesmen including founder William Huntington Russell attended.

Hopkin's Grammar School

The chairman of the Hopkins School, Bonesman Simeon E. Baldwin (1861), facilitated the deal. Baldwin was part of a very powerful Bones Machine in Connecticut and Yale at the time. He served as Governor of Yale 1911-15, after serving from 1907-10 as the Chief Justice of the Connecticut Supreme Court, having been on the court since 1893 — all the time holding a Yale Professorship of Law.

The Hopkins' property was "held" by Yale University Press, a separate "entity legally distinct from the university," that was very much under the influence of Bones and friends at Yale. Yale even engineered a little detour in Grove Street to undercut a Mr. Edward Bishop who had brokered for Yale some of the harder to secure residential and commercial properties, when he tried to exact a *holdout premium.* The land acquisition operation was handled by the office of the Treasurer of Yale, which was held by the Order of Skull & Bones for many years.

Treasurers of Yale 1862-1978			
Name	Bones Year	Treasurer Years	Notes
Henry Coit Kingsley	1834	1862-87	Daniel Coit Gilman's uncle
Timothy Dwight	1849	acting - 1887-89	President of Yale 1886-99
William Farnam	1866	1889-99	Yale Corp member, Trustee of SSS 1894-23
Morris Tyler		1900-03	Graduated Yale, 1870, w/George Douglas Miller, Phi Beta Kappa
Thomas Lee McClung	1892	1904-09	Treasurer of US, 1909-12, Bones cellmate of Pierre Jay, first president of NY Federal Reserve Bank
Arthur T. Hadley	1876	acting - 1909-10	President of Yale 1899-1921
George Parmly Day		1910-42	9 members of Day family in Skull &Bones
Lawrence G. Tithe	1916	1942-54	Director and Partner at Brown Brothers Harriman, Dir of many of New Haven's banks and utilities
Charles Stafford Gage	1925	1954- 66	For many years w/Bones-family firm Mathiesson Chemical, Director, Union & New Haven Trust Company among others
John E. Ecklund	1938	1966-78	Partner in the Bones-dominated New Haven law firm of Dana & Wiggin

As seen a member of the Order was Treasurer of Yale from 1862 to 1978 except two gentlemen who served for 36 years of that 116 year stretch. The one serving longest, 32 years, hailed from a Bones family.

THE ORDER TAKES CONTROL, FIRST YALE, THEN ...

The manipulation for control had been going on at Yale for many years, **From *America's Secret Establishment* by Antony Sutton:**

> Daniel Coit Gilman is the key activist in the revolution of education by The Order. The Gilman family came to the United States from Norfolk, England in 1638. On his mother's side, the Coit family came from Wales to Salem, Massachusetts before 1638.
>
> Gilman was born in Norwich, Connecticut July 8, 1831, from a family laced with members of The Order and links to Yale College (as it was known at that time). Uncle Henry Coit Kingsley (The Order '34) was Treasurer of Yale from 1862 to 1886. James I. Kingsley was Gilman's uncle and a Professor at Yale. William M. Kingsley, a cousin, was editor of the influential journal *New Englander*.

On the Coit side of the family, Joshua Coit was a member of The Order in 1853 as well as William Coit in 1887.

Gilman's brother-in-law, the Reverend Joseph Parrish Thompson ('38) was in The Order.

Gilman returned from Europe in late 1855 and spent the next 14 years in New Haven, Connecticut – almost entirely in and around Yale, consolidating the power of The Order.

His first task in 1856 was to incorporate Skull & Bones as a legal entity under the name of The Russell Trust. Gilman became Treasurer and William H. Russell, the cofounder, was President. It is notable that there is no mention of The Order, Skull & Bones, The Russell Trust, or any secret society activity in Gilman's biography, nor in open records. The Order, so far as its members are concerned, is designed to be secret, and apart from one or two inconsequential slips, meaningless unless one has the whole picture. The Order has been remarkably adept at keeping its secret. In other words, The Order fulfills our first requirement for a conspiracy - i.e., IT IS SECRET.

The information on The Order that we are using surfaced by accident. In a way similar to the surfacing of the Illuminati papers in 1783 when a messenger carrying Illuminati papers was killed and the Bavarian police found the documents. All that exists publicly for The Order is the charter of the Russell Trust, and that tells you nothing

On the public record then, Gilman became assistant Librarian at Yale in the fall of 1856 and "in October he was chosen to fill a vacancy on the New Haven Board of Education." In 1858 he was appointed Librarian at Yale. Then he moved to bigger tasks.

The Sheffield Scientific School

The Sheffield Scientific School, the science departments at Yale, exemplifies the way in which The Order came to control Yale and then the United States.

In the early 1850s, Yale science was insignificant, just two or three very small departments. In 1861 these were concentrated into the Sheffield Scientific School with private funds from Joseph E. Sheffield. Gilman went to work to raise more funds for expansion.

Gilman's brother had married the daughter of Chemistry Professor Benjamin Silliman (The Order, 1837). This brought Gilman into contact with Professor Dana, also a member of the Silliman family, and this group decided that Gilman should write a report on reorganization of Sheffield. This was done and entitled *Proposed Plan for the Complete Reorganization of the School of Science Connected with Yale College*.

While this plan was worked out, friends and members of The Order made moves in Washington, D.C., and the Connecticut State Legislature to get state funding for the Sheffield Scientific School. The Morrill Land Bill was introduced into Congress in 1857, passed in 1859, but vetoed by President Buchanan. It was later signed by President Lincoln. This bill, now known as the Land Grant College Act, donated public lands for State colleges of agriculture and sciences ... and of course Gilman's report on just such a college was ready. The legal procedure was for the Federal government to issue land scrip in proportion to a state's representation, but state legislatures first had to pass legislation accepting the scrip. Not only was Daniel Gilman first on the scene to get Federal land scrip, he was first among **all** the states and grabbed all of Connecticut's share for Sheffield Scientific School! Gilman had, of course, tailored his report to fit the amount forthcoming for Connecticut. No other institution in Connecticut received even a whisper until 1893, when Storrs Agricultural College received a land grant.

Of course it helped that a member of The Order, Augustus Brandegee ('49), was speaker of the Connecticut State Legislature in 1861 when the state bill was moving through, accepting Connecticut's share for Sheffield. Other members of The Order, like Stephen W. Kellogg ('46) and William Russell ('33), were either in the State Legislature or had influence from past service.

The Order repeated the same grab for public funds in New York State. All of New York's share of the Land Grant College Act went to Cornell University. Andrew Dickson White, a member of our trio, was the key activist in New York and later became first President of Cornell. Daniel Gilman was rewarded by Yale and became Professor of Physical Geography at Sheffield in 1863.

In brief, The Order was able to corner the total state shares for Connecticut and New York, cutting out other scholastic institutions. This is the first example of scores we shall present in this series – how The Order uses public funds for its own objectives.

And this, of course, is the great advantage of Hegel for an elite. The State is absolute. But the State is also a fiction. So if The Order can manipulate the State, it in effect becomes the absolute. A neat game. And like the Hegelian dialectic process we cited in the first volume, The Order has worked it like a charm.

Back to Sheffield Scientific School. The Order now had funds for Sheffield and proceeded to consolidate its control. In February 1871 the School was incorporated and the following became trustees:

Charles J. Sheffield
Prof. G.J. Brush (Gilman's close friend)
Daniel Coit Gilman (The Order, '52)
W.T. Trowbridge
John S. Beach (The Order, '39)
William W. Phelps (The Order, '60)

Out of six trustees, three were in The Order. In addition, George St. John Sheffield, son of the benefactor, was initiated in 1863, and the first Dean of Sheffield was J.A. Porter, also the first member of Scroll & Key (the supposedly competitive senior society at Yale).

How The Order Came To Control Yale University

From Sheffield Scientific School The Order broadened its horizons.

The Order's control over all Yale was evident by the 1870s, even under the administration of Noah Porter (1871-1881), who was not a member. In the decades after the 1870s, The Order tightened its grip *The Iconoclast* (October 13, 1873) summarizes the facts we have presented on control of Yale by The Order, without being fully aware of the details:

> *They have obtained control of Yale. Its business is performed by them. Money paid to the college must pass into their hands, and be subject to their will. No doubt they are worthy men in themselves, but the many whom they looked down upon while in college, cannot so far forget as to give money freely into their hands. Men in Wall Street complain that the college comes straight to them for help, instead of asking each graduate for his share. The reason is found in a remark made by one of Yale's and America's first men: "Few will give but Bones men, and they care far more for their society than they do for the college." The Woolsey Fund has but a struggling existence, for kindred reasons.*
>
> *Here, then, appears the true reason for Yale's poverty. She is controlled by a few men who shut themselves off from others, and assume to be their superiors ...*

The anonymous writer of *Iconoclast* blames The Order for the poverty of Yale. But worse was to come. Then-President Noah Porter the last of the clerical Presidents of Yale (1871-1886), and the last without either membership or family connections to The Order.

After 1886 the Yale Presidency became almost a fiefdom for The Order.

From 1886 to 1899, member Timothy Dwight ('49) was President, followed by another member of The Order, Arthur Twining Hadley (1899 to 1921). Then came James R. Angell (1921-37), not a member of The Order, who came to Yale from the University of Chicago where he worked with Dewey, built the School of Education, and was past President of the American Psychological Association.

From 1937 to 1950 Charles Seymour, a member of The Order, was President followed by Alfred Whitney Griswold from 1950 to 1963 Griswold was not a member, but both the Griswold and Whitney families have members in The Order. For example, Dwight Torrey Griswold ('08) and William Edward Schenk Griswold ('99) were in The Order. In 1963 Kingman Brewster took over as President. The Brewster family has had several members in The Order, in law and the ministry rather than education.

We can best conclude this memorandum with a quotation from the anonymous Yale observer:

> *Whatever want the college suffers, whatever is lacking in her educational course, whatever disgrace lies in her poor buildings, whatever embarrassments have beset her needy students, so far as money could have availed, the weight of blame lies upon the ill-starred society. The pecuniary question is one of the future as well as of the present and past. Year by year the deadly evil is growing. The society was never as obnoxious to the college as it is today, and it is just this ill-feeling that shuts the pockets of nonmembers. Never before has it shown such arrogance and self- fancied superiority. It grasps the College Press and endeavors to rule in all. It does not deign to show its credentials, but clutches at power with the silence of conscious guilt.*
> (pages 65-69)

WHERE DID THE MONEY COME FROM? WHERE DID IT GO?

Where did George Douglas Miller's money come from and how did it happen that he owned the land around the Tomb? My surmise is that Mr. Miller was acting as a *beard* for the Skull & Bones Trust. The main *front man* for the Order's activities in New Haven since the mid 1850s, Mr. Gilman, had moved on in the early 1870s to serve as the first President of the University of California in 1872.

Daniel Coit Gilman

The *Boodle Boys*, as Skull & Bones members were being called at the time, needed a new *front man* and prevailed upon the obliging Mr. Miller. George spent his first year after graduation, 1871, working in the college library system — similar to Mr. Gilman's return to Yale. He then went off into the world but he didn't really get all that far and soon came back to New Haven. Once back in town, George soon began to buy up the property around the Tomb and served as a secretary for a local utility.

He held many of his positions from his association with Bonesman W.W. Phelps, who was the son-in-law and estate trustee of John Sheffield the benefactor of Sheffield Scientific School (SSS). Phelps was a congressman, US Minister to Austria and Germany and a very successful business man. He was on the Board of Directors of the National City Bank, The Second National Bank of NY, the United States Trust Company, nine railroad firms and others. Mr. Phelps was an incorporator and trustee for many years of Sheffield Scientific School, which was phased out in the 1950s and became officially part of Yale but with the Trust still exercising control over the land.

Back in 1911 when Miller's money *ran out*, the Order had assumed the Presidency of Yale for over 20 years and in the Treasurer's office for over 40 years. They kept this influence into the 1970s through personnel in powerful positions and the distribution of oil monies. And — the great Gothic Yale University was built.

Why spend theirs, when it could all so easily be done with other people's money?

And Bones wouldn't get the rap for being too haughty and powerful.

The secret society holdings are now little private islands surround by the burgeoning Yale University.

Why George Miller left New Haven is unrecorded, he spent his life after New Haven as an international traveler and dabbled some in real estate in Albany, New York. He didn't pass on a large estate. The only thing that a grandchild remembers are trips to Deer Island and something called *Miller's Folly* — some strange building that their grandfather had owned.

Miller's Folly was a famous spite building in Albany, New York, where George, described as "an eccentric man of means," lived in a fashionable part of town.

The Hampton Hotel a fashionable destination place in Downtown Albany at State and Broadway and "was noted in the 1920's for its roof gardens, which offered a romantic view of the city and the river.

"George built a building on a very small piece of property that wasn't large enough to be occupied but tall enough to block the hotel's vistas. George expected the hotel owners to pay him money to reclaim their scenery. Instead, the Hampton built higher, so did George!

"The Hampton closed its roof and turned it into guest rooms. George's building, never finished, with no stairs to its upper stories, became a home for pigeons, unused for a generation, a monument to perversity … ."

Sources other than noted in text:
The Campus Guide - Yale University, Pinnell, Patrick
New Haven - A Guide to Architecture and Urban Design, Brown, Elizabeth Mills
Journal of the New Haven Historical Society - Fall 1998
O' Albany, Kennedy, William

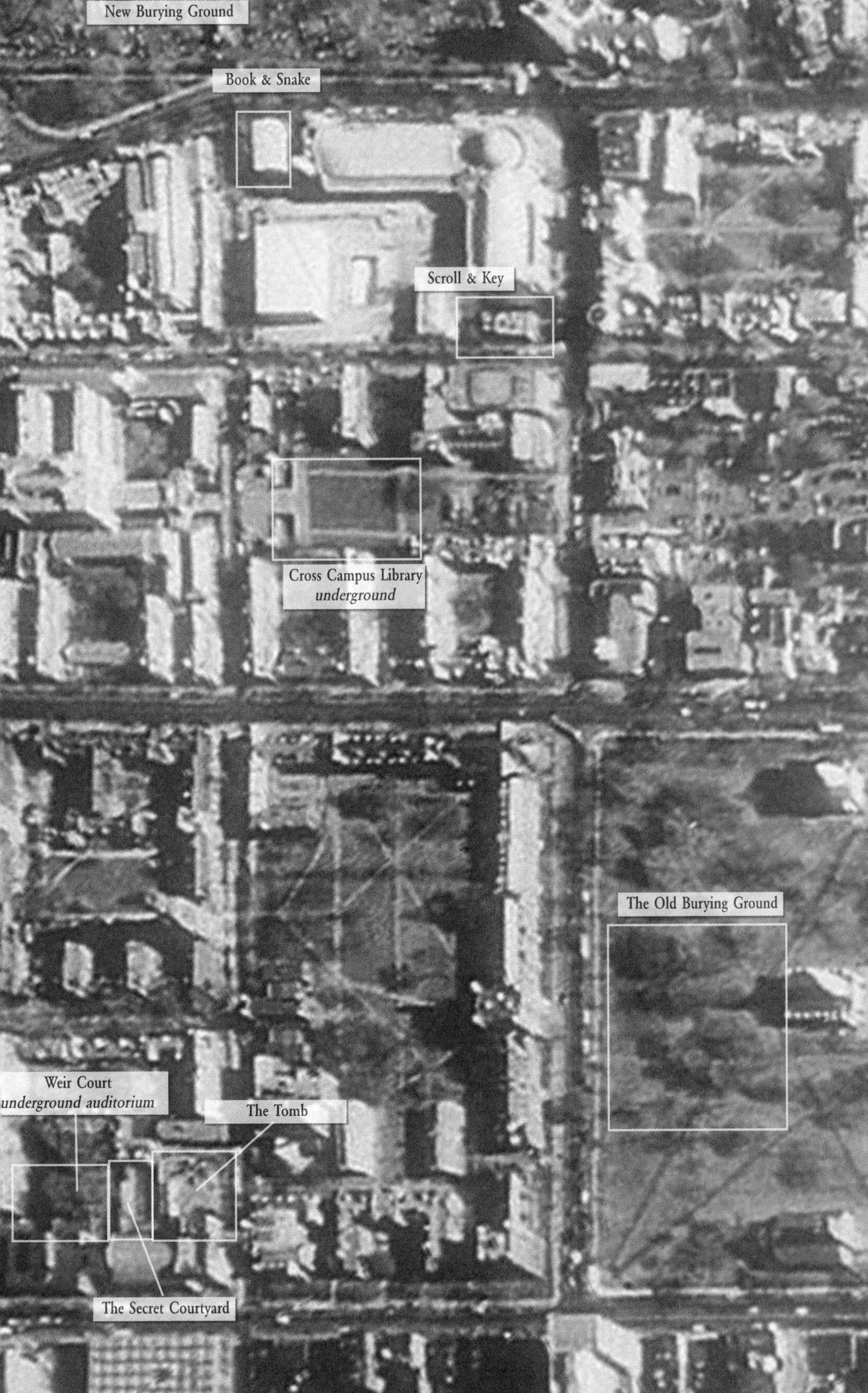
New Burying Ground
Book & Snake
Scroll & Key
Cross Campus Library
underground
The Old Burying Ground
Weir Court
underground auditorium
The Tomb
The Secret Courtyard

St. John Crypt
Power Plant
Egyptian Gate
Book & Snake
Sterling Law School
Scroll & Key
Cross Campus Library - *underground*
The Green
Wolf's Head
The Secret Courtyard
The *Tomb*
Weir Court - *undergound* auditorium

God and Man and Magic at Yale

Kris Millegan
August 2003

Walking around Yale, I found myself in amazement at the architecture and was thinking, "When did the Goths invade?" If a person hasn't been to the Yale campus one truly has no idea at the many awe-inspiring buildings — many resembling Gothic cathedrals. A cathedral is a sanctified church containing the cathedra, the bishop's seat of power from which is ruled the diocese.

The Saint Denis Basilica near Paris is considered by many to be the first example of Gothic architecture. It was begun in 1136 and finished near the end of the thirteenth century. It was built on the site where, according to legend, Saint Denis, the patron saint of France and legendary first bishop of Paris, stopped preaching, lay down his head and died. Quite literally, or so the tale goes (according to *Golden Legends,* compiled in the 13th century and destined to be a bestseller in the 15th century, second only to the Bible) that, around the year 250 AD, St. Denis went to convert the Gauls and was beheaded by the Romans for his ministrations. The decapitated St. Denis began to preach a sermon and, carrying his head in his hands, he then walked to the cathedral site and expired.

It eventually became known as the "royal necropolis of France" because of all the bluebloods buried there. From the Merovigans to Carolingians to Carpetians to Valois to Bourbons, they are all there, all mixed together it seems. This is because, during the revolutionary fervor of the late 1700s in France, the tombs were opened and the remains were all dumped into two mass graves. When the Bourbons were briefly restored they weren't able to tell who's who and, so, buried them all together in a big vault with brass plaques on the outside telling us who all is inside. It's sort of like a big bone pile. Funny, there are lots of bones in this story.

Chartres Cathederal

These massive stone buildings, cathedrals, especially ones such as Chartres, are known for their mathematical and alchemical aspects. The rise of the cathedrals — some of the most significant buildings of the medieval period — are linked by many historians and researchers with the rise of the Knights Templar and, later, the Freemasons. The builder of St. Denis, Abbot Suger, used the Templars for a capital transfer transaction with King Louis VII of France in 1148, while he was on the Second Crusade.

Gutenberg

In the 1430s Johannes Gutenberg took four years building his press and then, in another fifteen years (1455), printed his famous Bibles. This helped to usher in the Renaissance and the downfall of the Papacy and its fiefdoms. On Halloween in 1517, a well-read Martin Luther nailed his ninety-five theses to the church door, marking the beginning of the Protestant Reformation. Later, in the early 1530s, when snubbed for a divorce, Henry VIII started his own church, the Church of England. By the 1550s people were going to jail in London for practicing their faith differently from proscribed ecclesiastical tradition.

FAITH OF OUR FATHERS

Pilgrims giving thanks in the New World

As time and Gutenberg's press spread the Word, the Reformation increased the ferment for social, religious and political change. Around the 1560s in England there emerged a group who were, because of their endeavors to *purify* the Church of England in theological and liturgical matters, derisively called Puritans. They called themselves *Saints* and *people of God.* Other of the faithful wished to separate completely from the mother-church and start a new church. They were called Pilgrims and settled in New England in Massachusetts, landing at Plymouth Rock on December 21, 1620.

Not quite twenty years later a very devout group of Puritans settled in Connecticut on land purchased from the Quinnipiac Indians in 1638. The land was not theirs by legal right and they had no deed. The new colony, named New Haven, based part of its claim on the discovery by John Cabot, who had landed somewhere on the North American shore on the feast-day of St. John the Baptist, June 24, 1497. The New Haven Colony was the wealthiest group to settle in the new world so far. The leaders and their congregation wished to build a new Zion on biblical principles and prepare for Christ's return and final judgment.

Saint John the Baptist

The story of New Haven begins in the parish of Saint Stephen's, Coleman Street, London. Saul/Paul stoned St. Stephen to death outside Damascus. St. Stephen was one of the original seven deacons and the first Christian

St. Stephenns, Coleman Street, London

martyr. Saint Stephen's feast day is December 26th.

Saint Stephen

Saint Stephen's was "one of London's most influential" pulpits at the time. In October of 1624, 27 year-old, John Davenport was elected vicar. After fending off accusations of being a Puritan, he was allowed his position and became quite celebrated.

Later in 1633, when Charles I appointed William Laud to the office of Archbishop of Canterbury with complete authority to deal with dissenters within the Church of England, Davenport left England for exile in the Netherlands. While there, Davenport read the impassioned accounts from his friend John Cotton about New England and soon proceeded back to England to gather his flock to save them from the coming *punishment* from God soon to be visited upon England in retribution for its *manifold and persistent wickedness.* He was hoping to congregate the faithful and seek shelter in New England where the *saints could prepare for Christ's return and the final judgment.*

John Davenport

Puritans were true believers and proponents of the strict doctrines of John Calvin, a French-born, theologian whose influence can be still felt today. Calvinism beliefs codified at the Synod of Dordt in 1618/19 are based on total dependence on God and predestination. These are:

- that all humans are, inherently wicked and offend God;
- that there is an elect that God chose to be saved regardless of their actions and how deserving;
- that Jesus died just for those special elect, not for everyone;
- that once God has chosen an elect they are saved by irresistible grace no matter what;
- that these elect or Saints cannot fall from grace once saved.

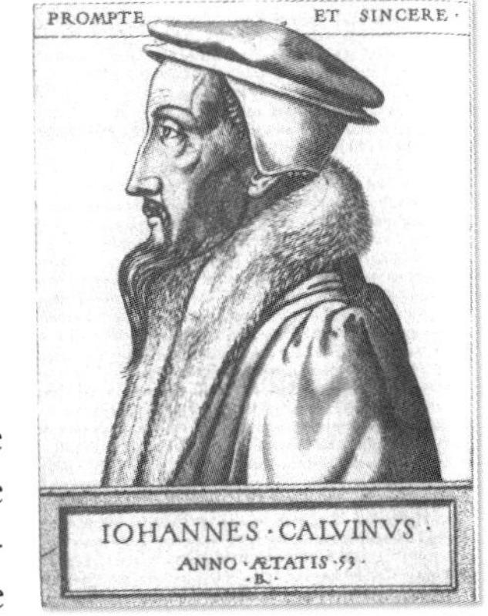

The most pious, the Hyper-Calvinists (which the New Haven Colony were) hold to the tenet of the doctrine of *reprobation,* the belief that God purposefully foreordains damnation. In other words, there are those who are *predestined to Hell.* Some being the *Elect* doing "God's work" through "sanctified" devilish activities. Regular *Hell's Angels* ....

NEW HAVEN

Wisdom hath builded her house, she hath hewn out her seven pillars.

Davenport's main ally was his childhood playmate Theophilius Eaton, a commercial agent handling James I affairs in Denmark and the London agent for Christian IV of Denmark. Eaton was deputy-governor of the Eastland Company, an original subscriber to the Massachusetts Bay Company and a fervent Puritan

This group didn't starve their first winter, and Eaton was Governor of the colony until his death in 1658. Mr. Eaton had married Anne Lloyd, widow of Thomas Yale and grandmother of Elihu Yale, benefactor and namesake of Yale University.

New Haven was a theocracy with only male church members — *The Elect* — allowed to vote and hold office. Although they were a small fraction of the total population, they ruled over the majority. No matter their actual piety, to the *people of God,* the rest of the populace was considered hopelessly damned. A person only became one of the *Saints* through pre-ordained mystical unavoidable grace that was made manifest through a somewhat mystical "born-again" experience. Mosaic Law was the rule of the colony with Mr. Eaton as "Judge" and Rev. Davenport their preacher/prophet. They were the two main players of the New Haven plantation's original "seven pillars." This all eventually fell apart when the contested title to the land and other forces led to absorption of the Colony by Connecticut in 1664.

Governor Elihu Yale and his cousin David. Elihu's father was one of the original settlers of New Haven.

The town of the New Haven Colony was laid out in 1638 into nine squares using magnetic north. The first street "was laid out half a mile in length and upon it as a base, a square was described." Plot allocations were completed by 1641 with the center square being public. The four streets State, Church, College and York run east/west, with George, Chapel, Elm and Grove as cross streets. New streets bisecting the originals in 1784 were named Orange, Wall, Crown, Temple and High.

In 1640 in the middle of the public square there was built a wooden meetinghouse. Over the years there have been many different congregations on the green: the "Prime Ancient Church," the "First Society," the White Haven Society," the "New Lights," the "Old Lights" and others. Over the years there has been much theological discord about just who was saved and who wasn't, and through the many revivals the congregations split, reformed and reunited several times.

Behind the center church is the "Old Burying Ground," directly opposite Yale College. By 1800, in this relatively small area, there were packed more than 5,000 skeletons and, as time

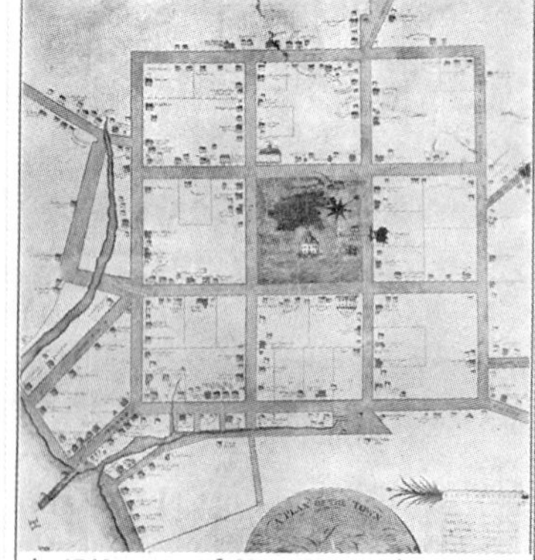
A 1748 map of New Haven by General Wadsworth. Yale College is one building on the corner of College and Chapel.

passed, the overcrowding became a problem. A new center church was built "on top over some of the graves" in the early 1810s when it "was not an uncommon sight to see animals digging up the bones."

Saint John the Evangilist

The "official" founding date of the Masonic Grand Lodge of England, June 24, 1717, is the feast day of their primary patron saint, St. John the Baptist. The oldest lodge in Connecticut is New Haven's Hiram Lodge. It was given its charter November 12, 1750 and held it's first meeting on Thursday, December 27, 1750, the feast day of the other patron saint of Masonry, mystic and apocalyptic writer, St. John the Evangelist. The Masons still meet on Thursday nights, the same night another *secret society* also gathers together in a Temple on High Street surrounded by the Yale campus and New Haven, The Order of Skull & Bones.

When New Haven grew from a town to a city in 1784, the first new street was High Street, going only *within* the original town square area from George to Grove.

In the middle of town at the corner of High and Chapel Streets, turning-up High and going under the Art Gallery bridge, on the west side of the street, is the Tomb, built in 1856 and expanded several times. Behind it is the Secret Courtyard and towers of Weir Hall. Down High Street is the world famous Sterling Library. At the next corner down High St. is the Yale Law School, alma mater of Bill & Hillary Clinton, Gerald Ford, Joe Lieberman and Clarence Thomas, among others. Across the street, on the other corner, is a three story white-marble mausoleum-looking building. This is the "meeting-hall" of the secret society, Book & Snake. Reporter Bob Woodward and former Treasury Secretary Nicklaus Brady are members.

THE NEW BURYING GROUND

Directly at the end of High Street is the oldest family-plot cemetery in the country, built in 1797 as a *garden for the dead.* This "New Burying Ground" was built "in the country" at the end of High Street at Grove Street by a syndicate of 32 prominent families. The old graves were relocated there from the old churchyard on The Green in 1821. Many famous persons are buried there, including Eli Whitney, Roger Sherman, Charles Goodyear and many of Yale's presidents. Surrounded by Yale University, it encompasses 16 acres in downtown modern New Haven, and has hundreds of obelisks and monuments.

The entrance is via a huge Egyptian Revival-style gate built by Henry Austin in 1845 out of the same type of brownstone as the "Tomb." It displays the inscription *"The Dead Shall Be Raised"* beneath the outstretched winged-sun disk.

The Legend of the Egyptian Winged-Sun-Disk

Horus, was one the main Egyptian gods, son and heir to Ra. There was a Horus the elder and a Horus the younger. He was generally depicted as a falcon headed being, but Horus had at least seven different forms. Asked by his sister, Isis, to avenge the death of her brother/husband, Osiris, Horus asked the god Thoth, the master magician, for help. With Thoth's aid, Horus became "a great sun-disk, with resplendent wings outstretched on either side." After many battles, Horus defeats Set and Osiris is resurrected.

"Horus then commanded Thoth that the Winged-Sun-Disk, with Uraei [snakes], should be brought into every sanctuary wherein he dwelt, and into every sanctuary of all the gods of the lands of the South and the North, and in Amentet, in order that they might drive away evil from therein ..."

THE QUICK AND THE DEAD?

Ezra Stiles, president of Yale College, was the first to suggest that freed slaves be sent back to Africa. Funds for such a colony began to be collected in 1776 and the American Colonization Society was founded in 1817. This was not some altruistic crusade but was "formed solely for the sending to Africa of free Negroes, who were considered extremely dangerous."

Ezra Stiles's son was a founder of Phi Beta Kappa at Yale.

Ezra Stiles is buried at the New Haven Burying Ground, so is Jehudi Ashmun, who some consider the "founder" of Liberia (1822). Some praise him, others say he was dictatorial and "convinced that African-Americans were not capable of running their own political affairs." He rescheduled an election after *his* candidates lost and fixed the next one. This set the stage for years of factional strife.

Jehudi Ashmun

Jehudi left Africa ill with fever and died just a few days after landing, in Boston on August 25, 1828. His funeral was held two day later in New Haven and he was interned in a sarcophagus that today lies just inside the massive Egyptian gate.

Jehudi wasn't a Yalie, (his Whitney family connection may be what brought him to rest in New Haven) but the main road curving around the outside of the cemetery was renamed in the 1840s Ashmun Street, near the time when the Egyptian gate was built.

The Ashmun tomb just inside the gate. The New Burying Ground is commonly known now as the Grove Street Cemetery

Ashmun is the Egyptian name for Hermopolis, the home of the sacred eight, the site of the world's creation out of chaos, the cosmic egg. Hermopolis, believed to be city

"where the sun first rose on earth," was also the center of the god of wisdom and learning, the ibis-headed moon-god Thoth. The Greeks called him Hermes Trismegistus, the god of time and "conductor of the dead," the inventor of alchemy and magic, and a traditional source for Western ritual magic

THE CRYPT OF SAINT JOHN

In the middle of the *"garden for the dead"* is a most interesting mausoleum dating from the 1870s: the crypt of *St. John.* It seems to be built of the same brownstone as both the Skull & Bone's "Tomb" and the massive Egyptian entrance gate. Note that the winged-sun disk with snakes is prominently displayed. On each side are flanking white marble sepulchers, and the plot is completely enclosed by an iron fence and stone pillars. The stone pillars are similar to those along the cemetery fence. This *bone house* is in Yale's section of the cemetery with many Bonesmen nearby.

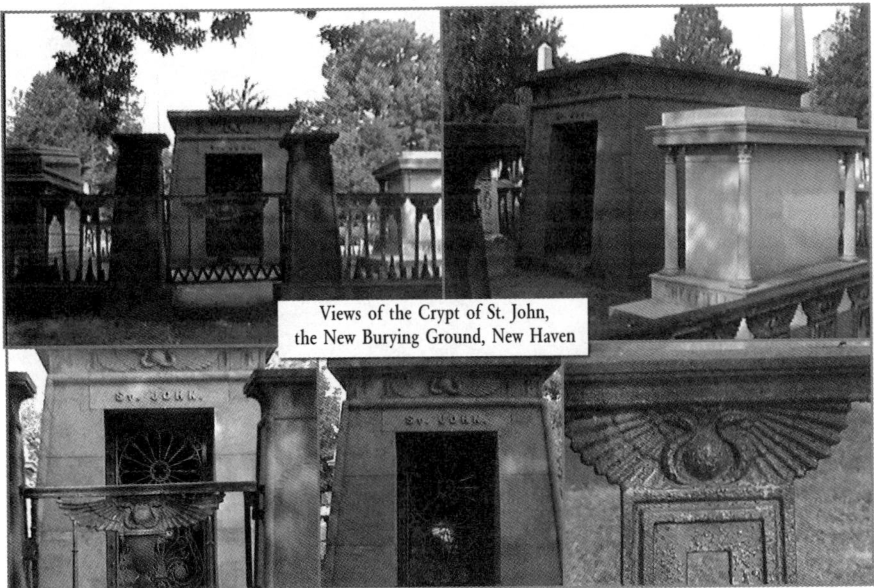

Views of the Crypt of St. John, the New Burying Ground, New Haven

No other headstones or crypts in the cemetery use the winged-disk motif. Buried inside are Samuel St. John and wife and on either side in non-identical white sarcophagi are Sheffields.

Sheffield Scientific School circa 1905

Joseph Sheffield's many bequests to Yale earned for him the honor of having the science department, the Sheffield Scientific School (SSS), named after him. It was through the 'SSS' that Skull & Bones came to *control* Yale. Daniel Gilman, an incorporator of the Russell Trust Association, officially incorporated SSS in 1871, with two other Bonesmen including William W. Phelps financier, congressman, ambassador and son-in-law of Mr. Sheffield. Soon Yale, as written in 1873, became "controlled by a few men who shut themselves off from others, and assume to be their superiors ..."

BOOK & SNAKE

The secret society, Book & Snake, began at 'SSS' in 1865. The founding club's picture shows them gathered around a similar skull, one without a jawbone, as does Bones in its annual photos. Across from the cemetery's gate in 1901,

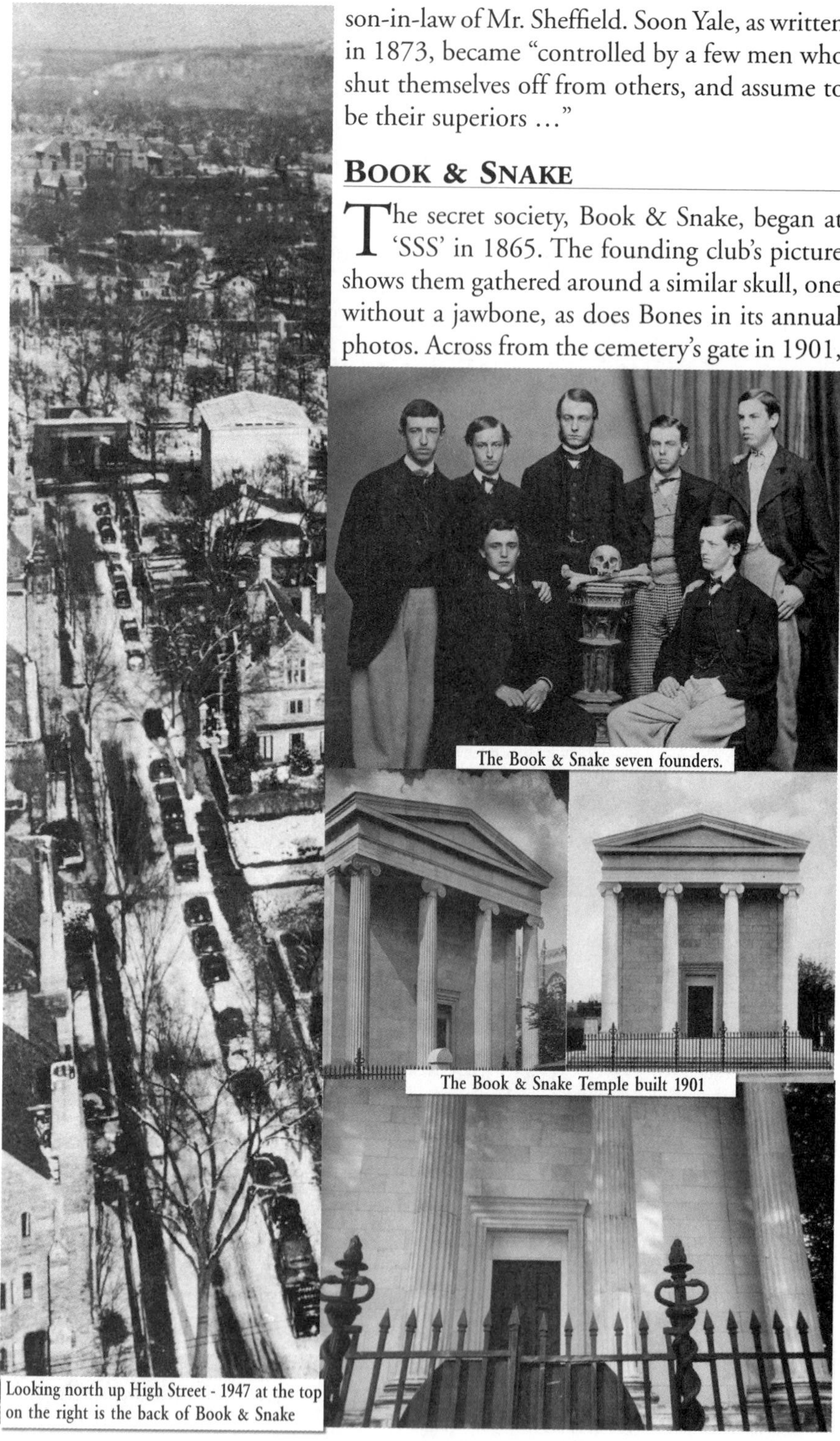

The Book & Snake seven founders.

The Book & Snake Temple built 1901

Looking north up High Street - 1947 at the top on the right is the back of Book & Snake

Book & Snake built their huge Greek Ionic white windowless mausoleum clubhouse surrounded by iron fencing using iron Thoth's staff as posts. When you put together the winged circle and the entwined snakes you have the caduceus or staff of Mercury.

The Cloister, S.S.S.

The Book & Snake Pin

A connection between Book & Snake and Skull & Bones appears to exist. There is the very simple reversal of the initials of the groups, S&B and B&S. For many years Book & Snake had a living-quarters house further down Grove Street known as the Cloister Club, which associated itself with the symbol of the jawless skull chained to a cross.

The Book & Snake Temple viewed from the New Burial Ground early 1900s

From the Yale Banner

The Cloister Club circa 1888

Magic is as Magic Does

According to the *US News & World Report*, May 13, 1991 When asked by a reporter "if he had news about the rebellion in Iraq?" George HW Bush answered only with the code-word *seven.* According to the magazine's source *seven* refers to the fact that, because Skull & Bones has fifteen members, a majority eight vote means yes and seven votes represents a *no, lose* or *fail.* "The source also reports that when the president was invited to a meeting in the Tomb, … he declined because he could not enter its inner sanctum without his Secret Service officers, none of whom are members. Bush was then fined — and he subsequently paid — $3.22 for missing a meeting."

"322" is the Order's particular, peculiar number, and is on the door and inlaid on the floor of their *sanctum sanctorum* in the upstairs of the original hall. What "322" means has been debated for years. Some say that it relates to the year 1832 when the Yale society was founded and the second '2' meant it was a second chapter of a German secret society. Some say it represents the date of the death of Demosthenes, claiming it was upon his philosophy that Bones was founded. Others point to the occultic and numerological aspects of the number. Again there are several differing explanations. One being that 322 represents "the symbolic dimensions for an isosceles triangle with three as the base and the twos becoming equal sides. "In an isosceles triangle with the point of the apex representing a Logos, and the two equal sides flowing from it representing the masculine and feminine rays, the horizontal base-line stands for the physical foundation from which the manifested objective world starts into existence."

The most visible and recognized symbol of the group is the skull and crossbones. A symbol of death, that is found on bottles of poison, pirates flags and the Nazi totenkopf, "death's head" the insignia of the Nazi Schutzstaffel or, as commonly known, the SS. It has been used in Prussia for elite troops as far back as 1740.

Some historians date the origin of the skull and crossbones to the late Middle Ages, during that period doctors were using the symbol as a sign of quarantine. It was drawn on doors of patients with strange and/or deadly maladies. After the Inquisition began in the 13th century, and the persecution of heretics by ecclesiastical tribunals drove non-Catholic thought underground, the heretics began using skull and crossbones *to ward off persecutors.* There was a slight difference in the heretic's skull and crossbones. It had no lower jaw, which signified secrecy and silence. Many don't even notice the missing mandible. The symbol soon began showing up on ship's masts, at first used to keep people away. Later it was used by privateers and pirates.

An understanding of Masonry, the Knights Templars and the preservation of the old mystery schools is emerging, and evidence is accumulating about the Knights Templars devotions to St. John, Mary Magdalene and their use of the Skull and Crossbones in their symbology, both by the original Knights Templars, who were disbanded in 1307, and by the current Masonic commanderies. I have a Xeroxed page from a very old Masonic book that uses the same exact skull and bones woodcut that Bones uses as a symbol of Knights Templars.

From a private paper on Skull & Bones:

> the skull represented the Temple of wisdom, which was later Christianized for concealment and referred to as the *upper room*. It is the room at the top of the 33 vertebra of the spine which represented the path to the upper room; the equivalent of the journey through life or the road to enlightenment.
>
> ... The crossed bones represents the two pillars, which stand at the threshold to the pathway to the Temple of Wisdom. One bone represents Knowledge the other represents Understanding. This Temple of Wisdom is believed by the occultists to be the structure within which the human consciousness resides. When the neophyte becomes *the dweller at the Threshold*, he symbolically stands at the intersection of the crossed bones. If he chooses to pass through the threshold, he no longer resides only in the outer, material world; but he has become a dweller in a land of new consciousness to grow in self-awareness through Knowledge and Understanding. The neophyte symbolically dies or falls asleep to the outer world as the consciousness turns from outward concerns to inner concerns, knowing when he arrives at the Temple of Wisdom he will awaken or become resurrected to a new world order.

A new world order! Illuminatist Adam Weishaupt called for cosmopolitanism. Hitler and Goebbels proclaimed the Third Reich a New World Order. George HW Bush, an Order of Skull & Bones member, used the term several times during his US presidential term. On September 11, 1990 in an address to a Joint Session of the US Congress, exactly eleven years before Flight Eleven crashed into the twin towers, President George HW Bush said:

> We stand today at a unique and extraordinary moment. The crisis in the Persian Gulf, as grave as it is, also offers a rare opportunity to move toward an historic period of cooperation. Out of these troubled times, our fifth objective – a new world order – can emerge: a new era – freer from the threat of terror, stronger in the pursuit of justice, and more secure in the quest for peace. An era in which the nations of the world, East and West, North and South, can prosper and live in harmony. A hundred generations have searched for this elusive path to peace, while a thousand wars raged across the span of human endeavor. Today that new world is struggling to be born, a world quite different from the one we've known.

WHAT IS IT WITH THIS PREOCCUPATION WITH NEW WORLD ORDERS AND NEW ERAS?

Some of the most interesting research to come out about the Knights Templars and Freemasons are the researches by Christopher Knight & Robert Lomas in their books the *Hiram's Key* and *The Second Messiah*. The books of Michael Baigent, Richard Lee and Henry Lincoln were some of the first to explore these topics. Also there are the books by Lynn Picknett and Clive Prince, *The Templar Revelation* and *The Stargate Conspiracy*. And one last one I would like to mention by name, *The Warriors and the Bankers* by Alan Butler and Stephen Dafoe. Many others are also relevant to understanding this history of secret societies, some specifically about the chapel at Rosslyn, Scotland and the chapel of Sauniere at Renne-le-Chateau, France. First century studies, the study of intelligence services and methods, financial studies and banking histories are helpful in understanding the reach and rolodexes of these small but powerful secret organizations.

The basic story is that in 70 AD, when Titus was sacking Jerusalem various familial groups responsible for differing duties, generally connected with Temple obligations, gathered their items of diligence such as sacred oils, treasures, and hid them in caves in the Temple Mount and other areas of the country. These families comprised of members of the various priesthoods and royal lines then dispersed, many towards Europe, producing the "bluebloods." According to Knight and Lomas, a familial secret society existed named *Rex Deus* that was revealed by a father to his chosen son, upon this son reaching the age of 21. This group emerged above-ground with the Crusades, supposedly in accordance with prophecies in Daniel and Isaiah.

From *The Second Messiah:*

> The picture that was emerging was of a group of European noble families, descended from Jewish Lines of David and Aaron, who escaped from Jerusalem shortly before, or possibly even after, the fall of the Temple. They had passed down the knowledge of the artifacts concealed beneath the Temple to a chosen son (not necessarily the eldest) of each family. Some of the families involved were the Counts of Champagne, Lords of Gisors, Lords of Payens, Counts of Fontaine, Counts of Anjou, de Bouillon, St Clairs of Roslin, Brienne, Joinville, Chaumont, St Clair de Gisor, St Clair de Neg and the Hapsburgs.

From this group developed the Knights Templar, who went to Jerusalem, were housed on the Temple Mount, later returning to Europe to become what many call the first international bankers, They were soldiers, sailors and large landholders and were a very strong political force. The Templars were arrested by Phillip the Fair, King of France on Friday, October 13, 1307 and driven underground or into exile.

The Templars, according to several sources, had knowledge and had explored the North American continent before Columbus. The Rosslyn Chapel in Scotland, built between 1440 and 1490, has stone reliefs of plants found only in the Americas. John Cabot, whom many of the major Bones players claim as a relation, sailed from Bristol, England (a port very beholden to the Templars) and Cabot named his American settlement, St, John.

The history of Freemasonry is long and tedious. Nevertheless, we know that Freemasonry emerged officially in 1717 in England and soon enjoyed royal protection. During the preceding and proceeding centuries much activity took place in various secret societies both fraternal and magickal orders. One very interesting ideology that developed out of these circles is *synarchy.*

An excerpt from Picknett and Prince's *The Stargate Conspiracy:*

... a specific politico-esoteric system, a movement known as Synarchy. This is 'government by secret societies,' or by a group of initiates who operate from behind the scenes. It is an analogue of 'theocracy,' or rule by a priesthood. ...

The founder of Synarchy, a Frenchman named Joseph Alexandre Saint-Yves d'Alveydre (1824-1909), explained that the term was the opposite of anarchy. Whereas anarchy is based on the principle that the state should have no control over individuals, Synarchy proposes that it should have complete control. He proposed that Synarchists achieve power by taking over the three key institutions of social control: political, religious and economic. With its own members in positions of power, the Synarchists would, in effect, secretly govern entire states. And why stop there? One of the aims of Synarchy, from its very inception, was – from the words of a Synarchist document – the creation of a 'federal European Union.' Is it any coincidence that we are now moving rapidly towards such a European state? Significantly, those words were written as far back as 1946. ...

As might be expected from a movement dedicated to governing by secret societies, Synarchy had close ties with some of the most powerful of such organizations, including the Martinist Order, of which Saint-Yves d'Alveydre was Grand Master. As the French writer Gerard Galtier states: "The synarchic ideal influenced all the Martinists and occultists of the beginning of the century."[25] Not unexpectedly, Synarchists were also members of French Masonic Lodges, ...

Synarchy is by definition a shadowy group lurking behind many uprisings and revolutions, and whose jealous gaze is automatically fixed on any stable regime or established government unless it already conforms to their ideals. ...

There is another aspect to Synarchy. The concept of nine legendary leaders plays a large part in its philosophy. ... the Knights Templar, founded by nine French knights shortly after the First Crusade. The Templars were believed by Saint-Yves d'Alveydre to have represented the supreme expression of Synarchy in the medieval world, because they had almost total political, religious and financial control during the two centuries of their existence yet remained at heart a secret, heretical order whose real agenda was known only to its membership.

In nineteenth-century France several secret societies all claimed to be the true descendants of the medieval Knights Templar. Saint-Yves drew upon their ideals and practices for his movement, especially those of certain types of occult Freemasonry known as the Strict Templar Observance and its successor, the Rectified Scottish Rite, thus bestowing on the primarily political movement a strong undercurrent of mysticism And magical rites. This proved to be a two-way traffic, for the Synarchist ideal was adopted by several occultists and their organizations, such as Papus Gerard Encausse, (1865-1916), an enormously influential figure who was the French Grand Master of both the Ordo Templi Orientis (OTO) and the Masonic Order of Memphis-Misraim, whose rituals, significantly, were based on the rites and ceremonies of the ancient Egyptian priesthood. Papus considered Saint-Yves to be his 'intellectual Master.' As Gerard Galtier wrote: "Without doubt, the Martinist directors such as Papus ... had the ambition to secretly influence the course of political events, notably by the diffusion of synarchic ideals."

Papus put the Synarchist ideals into practice by working to bring together the various secret societies of his day, merging orders where possible and creating 'confederations' where representatives of the organizations could meet. The bodies he created fragmented during the First World War, but others, notably Theodore Reuss and H. Spencer Lewis, created similar groups afterwards.

Undoubtedly, Saint-Yves was hugely influential on the development of Western occultism. Theo Paijmans, an authority on nineteenth-century European esotericism, pointed out to us that Saint-Yves introduced the seminal idea of Agartha, the mysterious underground realm from which highly evolved Adepts psychically direct the development of the human race. This was to become a common feature of Western occultism – as in the works of Madame H.P. Blavatsky – and was the basis for a belief in Hidden Masters, or Secret Chiefs, which we will discuss shortly. Saint-Yves claimed that he had travelled astrally to Agartha, and that he was in telepathic contact with its inhabitants. He also claimed that he had derived his Synarchist ideology from them.

... The twentieth-century legacy ... involves one of the most flamboyant and controversial figures of our times – the ritual magician Aleister Crowley.

Conjurations of the 'Beast'

In March 1904 the – even by then – notorious occultist Aleister Crowley (1875-1947) and his new wife Rose paid a visit to Cairo where they carried out a 'magickal' operation (a 'working') in their rented apartment. The result was unexpected. The untrained Rose, totally ignorant of magickal workings (and, if Crowley's somewhat disloyal description is anything to go by, of much else too), went into trance, repeating, 'They are waiting for you.' During the next few days, she revealed that 'they' were primarily the god Horus, who had chosen Crowley for a special task, telling him the ritual to facilitate contact. At first Crowley was irritated by Rose's words – after all, he was the great magus, not her – but then he gave her a series of questions to test the authenticity of the communicator. When he asked her which planet was traditionally associated with Horus, she answered, correctly, Mars.

A few days later, in the Cairo Museum, Rose – who had never visited it before – confidently led her husband through the halls to stand before one particular exhibit, a rather unremarkable Twenty-Sixth-Dynasty painted wooden stele showing an Egyptian priest standing before Horus in his form of Ra-Hoor-Khuit (a variation of Ra-Horakhti, who is closely associated with the Sphinx). This has been known ever since in the occult world as the Stele of Revealing. Crowley was impressed by the synchronicity of the exhibit's number – 666, the number of the Great Beast of Revelation, which also happened to be Crowley's own proud alter ego, thanks to an overliteral interpretation of the Bible by his religious-maniac mother. (When we saw the stele in April 1998, we were amused to note that, although it is now exhibit 9422, the original 1904 label, bearing the number 666 in a beautiful but faded copperplate hand, has been laid beside it in the display case. Could there be Crowleyite sympathizers; on the staff of the Cairo Museum?)

This led Crowley, somewhat reluctantly, to take his wife's words seriously. He duly carried out the magickal ritual – now known simply as the Cairo Working – which turned out to be a pivotal moment not only in his own bizarre career, but also in the whole history of modern occultism. As a result of this working, he came into contact with an entity called Aiwass (sometimes, for magickal reasons, spelt Aiwaz) who over the course of three days –8-10 April 1904 – 'dictated' to Crowley what has become his 'gospel,' *The Book of Law*. pp 264-269

The works of Aleister Crowley still carry a profound effect upon Western occultic traditions and practice. *The Book of Law* redeveloped a theme written in 1532, by Francois Rabelais in *Gargantua and Pantragruel*, wherein a story speaks of the "Abbey of Thelma," and the only rule is "do what thou wilt." Crowley reworked it into his famous codex "Do what thou wilt shall be the whole of the Law."

DO CALVINISM AND RITUAL MAGIC MIX?

Yale and Harvard, both schools were founded and run for many years by Calvinist clerics soon became hot beds of secret societies and magical ritual.

From *Washington Allston — Secret Societies and the Alchemy of Anglo-American Painting:*

> Allston was a member of the Phi Beta Kappa Society, which not only organized the leading members of the New England intelligentsia, but closely associated them with the broader, middle class social base of Freemasonry. A secret fraternity of students and alumni, Phi Beta Kappa derived its rituals and symbols from the Masonic brotherhood. Like Masonry, the "master image" of Phi Beta Kappa was the animating sun, symbol of alchemical wisdom originated from Ancient Egypt.
>
> ... They [Masons] celebrated the arts for transmitting an ancient body of original truths, deriving not only from the Jews and the masons who built Solomon's Temple, but also from Pythagoras and the Greeks, and from the ancient Egyptian mythology of Isis, Osiris, and Hermes Trismegistus.
>
> ...
>
> The society [PBK] created a magical aura to honor wisdom *through initiation ceremonies that led blindfolded candidates toward sudden illumination and arcane emblems expressing esoteric truths*. [emphasis added]

The whole art community that surrounded the birth of Bones and later surrounded the Tomb were largely members of Phi Beta Kappa (PBK). Many being both Bones and PBK. Such as founders Russell and Taft, plus the ever-handy Daniel Coit Gilman.

Charles Tracy, an 1832 Yale graduate writes in his *Yale College, Sketches from Memory:*

> In those days free-masonry and anti-masonry fought their battles: and a grave question of consience [sic] arose about the promise of secrecy exacted on initiation to the Phi Beta Kappa Society. Harvard was for dissolving the secrecy, and it sent Edward Everett to the private meeting at Yale to advocate the cause. He used a tender tone stood half drooping as he spoke, and touchingly set forth that the students at Harvard had such conscientious scruples as to keep them from taking the vow of secrecy, and the society's life was endangered. There was stout opposition, but the motion prevailed, and the missionary returned to gladden the tender consiences[sic] of the Harvard boys. The secret was of course out. The whole world did not stare at the discovery; and a few years had passed the society took back its secrecy and revived its grip.

Most secret societies have structure akin to an onion or pyramid with a large base or outer layer that makes-up the majority of the members. These members, called porch brethren in Masonic circles are there for window-dressing and generally have very little idea of the true function of the organization. Then there are the administrators and then at the core a "secret society within a secret society" with many times certain key personnel overlapping into several secret societal organizations.

The Yale secret society Wolf's Head's logo is the head of a wolf over an upside down ankh. "In the Egyptian mysteries a candidate would assumed the mantle of Osiris and wore a wolf skin. Wolf in French is *louve* and the word *louvteau* means "the son of a Mason." The ankh is an old Egyptian symbol generally associated with life and eternity. The mystical and ritual magickal significance of the Wolf's Head logo is there for all to see.

There are those who say this is just folderol, just "fads and fancy" of students. To others it adds to the evidence that the secret societies at Yale are much more than a *supplemental educational program* of Yale University or even just a crazy college "club." Demonstrative links to the mystery schools and ritualistic initiatory paraphernalia abound. Do some Bonesmen experience an initiatory death and rebirth through Yale's underground? Is the crypt of Saint John part of that ritual?

Do we find in New Haven a multi-generational *cult* that uses conspiratorial tactics and ritualistic magic in its drama for control?

A bigger picture emerges when you look in depth at the historical, architectural and genealogical threads, and at the physical geomantic forces at play in New Haven.

You could make a case that what exists at Yale is a multi-generational cult that believes in the power of death to bring about change, a group of *Zeitgeist* initiates believing that the ends justify the means, and using massive deaths to feed their necromancy.

Just a bit farther up the geographical draw from the cemetery is the Winchester Repeating Arms plant, where many of the rifles for deadly warfare have been manufactured, producing many piles of bones — many through conflicts with Bones members playing major political roles.

Ron Rosenbaum reported in the *New York Observer*, April 23, 2001, this chant used in the Order's initiation rites:

> The Hangman Equals Death!
> The Devil Equals Death!
> Death Equals Death.

In Alexandra Robbins' *apologia* for the Order, *Secrets of the Tomb*, Bonesmen claim that they just played a joke on Rosenbaum and the ritual was a show. Scroll & Key member Ms. Robbins, after saying that she thought "the ceremony described in Rosenbaum's article sounded much to vulgar for Skull and Bones, then quotes a Bonesman "laughing heartily" and saying, "We wanted to fuck with that prick."

As Governor of Texas, George W Bush "hung" all prisoners sentenced to death that he had an opportunity to kill, *except one*, Henry Lee Lucas — a confessed serial killer for a shadowy cult. Bonesman and US political power player Henry L Stimson takes credit for talking President Truman into dropping *the bombs* on Hiroshima and Nagasaki. These are just two of the Order's death-dealing activities.

The primary families of the Order are all inter-related and related to European royalty. In a private letter* from one Bonesman to another, a member does treat another of its members as royalty. When one takes into consideration that George W Bush has more royal relations that any other US President, along with royalty's heavy involvement in Masonry and other western ritual magical circles, one wonders about the mindset created from the influences of the Hyper-Calvinist beliefs of Hell predestination, and infallible salvation mixed with potent duality of Western Ritual Magic tradition. Is our republic being undermined by a fervent multi-generational death-magic cult that is trying to bring about an apocalyptic New World Order through synarchical means — with themselves playing the leading roles — no matter the cost to the rest of us? Do *they* know?

The Order of Skull & Bones is a secret society and they aren't saying.

To the tables down at Mory's
To the place where Louie dwells
To the dear old Temple bar we love so well
Sing the Whiffenpoofs assembled
With their glasses raised on high
And the magic of their singing casts its spell

Yes, the magic of their singing
If the songs we love so well
"Shall I Wasting" and "Mavourneen" and the rest
We will serenade our Louie while life and voice shall last
Then we'll pass and be forgotten with the rest

We are poor little lambs who have lost our way
Baa, baa, baa
We are little black sheep who have gone astray
Baa, baa, baa

Gentleman songsters off on a spree
Doomed from here to eternity
Lord have mercy on such as we
Baa, baa, baa

* See pages 430-431

Skull and Bones

FOUNDED 1832

Archibald John Allen
Charles Booth Alling, Jr.
Edward Williamson Andrews, Jr.
*Gillam Dorr Blake
William Michael Bouliaratis
David Bennet Bronson
Walter Henderson Brown
Louis Connick, Jr.
John Carey
John Lester Hubbard Chaffee
Edwin Lyon Dale, Jr.
Endicott Peabody Davison
Francis Bolton Elwell, Jr.
John George Gilpin Finley
John Warren Finney
William Skinner Goedecke
Archer Harman, Jr.
George Burgwin Holmes
Gordon Buckland Hurlbut
Donald Loyal Leavenworth
Russell Vincent Lynch
Benjamin Thomas McElroy
Guy Ennis McGaughey
Thomas Ridgway Mallon
James Ivan Moore
William Singer Moorhead, Jr.
Frank O'Brien, Jr.
Philip O'Brien, Jr.
Charles Edgar Palmer
Richard Rollins Read
Howard Copland Robinson, Jr.
Irving Seaman, Jr.
Josiah Augustus Spaulding
William Sayer Sumner
Carll Tucker, Jr.
Charles Pratt Twichell
Elliot Evans Vose
George Upson Warren

* Deceased.

The 1947 Yale *Banner* listing for the Order. WW II interrupted the Order's initiations. These 38 members were then spread out through several year's cells.

PICTURES FROM THE CRYPT

Seated left - Sextus Shearer seated right - William Henry Fuller

L-R, Robert L Chamberlain, Simeon Eren Baldwin, Hubert S Brown, Frances E Kernochan, William E Park, Ralph O Williams, Franklin B Dexter, John Mitchell, Edward R Sill, Alexander P Root, Stanford Newell, Tracey Peck, Jr., Anthony Higgns

COURTESY ARCHIVES & MANUSCRIPTS –YALE UNIVERSITY LIBRARY

Seated left - Anson Phelps Tinker seated right - LeBaron Bradford Colt
L–R, Thomas Chalmers Sloane, Henry Park Wright, James Kingsley Thacher, Coburn Dewees Berry, Samuel Tweedy, James Coffin, Chauncey Bunce Brewster, William Allison McKinney, Charles Henry Farnam, Edward Jefferson Tytus,

COURTESY ARCHIVES & MANUSCRIPTS –YALE UNIVERSITY LIBRARY

Seated left - John Norton Pomeroy seated right - William Kent
L–R, John Bennetto, Robert Nelson Corwin, William Hutchinson Cowles, Willard Robinson Douglas, William Larned Thacher, Clinton Larue Hare, Georger Griswold Haven, Alexander Brown Coxe, John Rogers, William Burrage Kendall, Jr., Walter Bradley Sheppard, Samuel Knight, Oliver Gould Jennings

COURTESY ARCHIVES & MANUSCRIPTS –YALE UNIVERSITY LIBRARY

The Order of Skull & Bones 1892

Seated left - Ernest Ryle seated right - Knight Dexter Cheney, Jr.,
L–R, Benjamin Lewis Crosby, Jr., Clive Day, William Lloyd Kitchel, Henry Solon Graves, Pierre Jay, Howell Cheney, Hugh Aiken Bayne, Stanford Newel Morison, Frank Julian Price, Edward Boltwood, Lee McClurg, James Wernham, Dunsford Ingersoll. James William Husted

COURTESY ARCHIVES & MANUSCRIPTS –YALE UNIVERSITY LIBRARY

Book & Snake 1865

Samuel R Throckmorton, third from right second row, Joseph Thomspon Whittlesy, seated left

COURTESY ARCHIVES & MANUSCRIPTS –YALE UNIVERSITY LIBRARY

Founders of "Book & Snake – [illegible]"
1865

[illegible] in 1863

Hooded Students and Crowd - Tap Day - 1930s
COURTESY ARCHIVES & MANUSCRIPTS –YALE UNIVERSITY LIBRARY

John Ecklund tapped for Bones, 1938
COURTESY ARCHIVES & MANUSCRIPTS
YALE UNIVERSITY LIBRARY

Skull & Bones, Do you accept? TapDay - 1960s
COURTESY ARCHIVES & MANUSCRIPTS
YALE UNIVERSITY LIBRARY

Tap Days - 1940s
COURTESY ARCHIVES & MANUSCRIPTS –YALE UNIVERSITY LIBRARY

Hooded Students, 1930s
COURTESY ARCHIVES & MANUSCRIPTS –YALE UNIVERSITY LIBRARY

Under the Oak Tree – Tap Day
COURTESY ARCHIVES & MANUSCRIPTS –YALE UNIVERSITY LIBRARY

Tap Day - 1950

Tap Day - 1900

The form of Tap Day has changed many times but the function has remained the same — the choosing of next year's members in the secret societies. For many years the junior class would assembly in a large group outdoors and then there would be a series of taps from the various societies. Later the *tapping* moved indoors. Today at Yale, Tap Day has turned into Tap Night — a huge costumed extravagandic bacchanal.

Tap Day - 1930s
COURTESY ARCHIVES & MANUSCRIPTS
YALE UNIVERSITY LIBRARY

Tap Day - 1893
COURTESY ARCHIVES & MANUSCRIPTS –YALE UNIVERSITY LIBRARY

Tap Day - 1890

Wednesday Evening, June 17th, 1925.

☞ VIII. S. B. T

Pars magna bonitatis est velle fieri bonum.
Seneca, Ep. 34, 3

Charles Graydon Poore, S. E. C

YALE COLLEGE,
June 4, 1925.

Notice sent to all members inviting them to meet the newly tapped initiates - 1925

P. 2124.	D. 124.
Daniel Allen,	Cheshire, Conn.
James Davis Bronson, Jr.,	Stillwater, Minn.
Henry Cornick Coke,	Dallas, Texas
Henry Stetson Crosby,	Minneapolis, Minn.
Benjamin Crawford Cutler,	Andover, Mass.
John Alfred Davenport,	Philadelphia, Pa.
Alfred Ludlow Ferguson, Jr.,	Greenwich, Conn.
John McArthur Hoysradt,	Bronxville, N. Y.
Howard Thayer Kingsbury, Jr.,	New York City
Oswald Bates Lord,	Tarrytown, N. Y.
Anthony Lee Michel,	Oak Park, Ill.
Charles Graydon Poore,	Saint Paul, Minn.
Reginald Dean Root,	Le Roy, N. Y.
Frank Ford Russell,	Hempstead, Long Island, N. Y.
Charles Hastings Willard,	Minneapolis, Minn.

This listing of new members was sent with the meeting announcement and may be pasted in the formal membership book – 1926

In Memory

of

Henry Brodhead, D. 57
✠ January 26, 1925 ✠

Roger Sherman White, D. 57
✠ July 9, 1924 ✠

Joseph Leonard Daniels, D. 58
✠ October 22, 1924 ✠

George St. John Sheffield, D. 61
✠ December 14, 1924 ✠

LeBaron Bradford Colt, D. 66
✠ August 18, 1924 ✠

Thomas Hooker, D. 67
✠ October 28, 1924 ✠

Henry Warren Raymond, D. 67
✠ February 18, 1925 ✠

Charles Clerc Deming, D. 70
✠ July 23, 1924 ✠

Samuel Oscar Prentice, D. 71
✠ November 2, 1924 ✠

Almet Francis Jenks, D. 73
✠ September 18, 1924 ✠

Oliver David Thompson, D. 77
✠ June 10, 1925 ✠

Walter Chauncey Camp, D. 78
✠ March 14, 1925 ✠

Arthur Sherwood Osborne, D. 80
✠ November 4, 1924 ✠

Frank Bosworth Brandegee, D. 83
✠ October 14, 1924 ✠

Samuel Johnson Walker, D. 86
✠ August 19, 1924 ✠

Horace Sheldon Stokes, D. 87
✠ December 19, 1924 ✠

Edward Boltwood, D. 90
✠ September 6, 1924 ✠

James William Husted, D. 90
✠ January 2, 1925 ✠

Ralph Delahaye Paine, D. 92
✠ April 29, 1925 ✠

Alexander Ray Clark, D. 93
✠ March 19, 1925 ✠

Grenville Parker, D. 96
✠ July 18, 1924 ✠

Stuart Brown Camp, D. 98
✠ September 25, 1924 ✠

Albert De Silver, D. 108
✠ December 7, 1924 ✠

[July 1, 1924—June 30, 1925]

Death Notices were sent at the same time, again formatted so as to be added to members membership book. The membership books had blank pages to attach the notices

1925

ARDREY, Rushton Leigh—East St., Rye, N. Y. Business.
ASHBURN, Frank Davis—West Point, N. Y. Law.
BENCH, Edward Cajetan—Linden Ave., Englewood, N. J. Business.
BISSELL, William Truesdale—Farmington, Conn. Student.
BLAIR, James Grant—4607 Ross Ave., Dallas, Tex. Student.
GAGE, Charles Stafford—317 81st St., Brooklyn, N. Y. Business.
IVES, Gerard Merrick—145 East 35th St., New York City. Business.
JONES, Walter Clyde, Jr.—1637 Judson Ave., Evanston, Ill. Law.
LOVEJOY, Winslow Meston—Armory St., New Haven, Conn. Law.
LUFKIN, Elgood Moulton—Kirby Lane, Rye, N. Y. Business.
LUMAN, Richard John—Pinedale, Wyo. Business.
NORTON, William Bunnell—Mt. Hermon, Mass. Teaching.
SCOTT, Henry Clarkson—Allerton House, 39th St., New York City. Business.
STEVENS, Marvin Allen—1407 Yale Station, New Haven, Conn. Medicine.
STEVENSON, Donald Day—86 Mercer St., Princeton, N. J. Medicine.

[Insert—P. 100-B of 1923 Catalogue.]

This listing is also sent of the graduating members. This may be added to the *Catalouge*, which also includes some biographical information. These catalouges are now issued in two volumes – Living and Deceased members.

322

New Haven, Conn., Nov. 5, 1925

The annual meeting of the Russell Trust Association will be held at the usual place in this city, at eight o'clock, on Friday Evening, Nov. 13, 1925, to hear the Treasurer's Report, to elect two directors to serve in the place of Messrs. H. De F. Baldwin and M. A. Seabury, whose terms expire at that time, and to transact such other business as may properly come before the meeting.

S. B. T. at 7.15 o'clock.

GUSTAV GRUENER, Secretary.

The building will be open to the graduates Saturday evening, November 14.

Announcement of annual meeting - 1925

BEGGARS ON FOOT: PRINCES AND QVEENS WHO RIDE,
IN SKVLL-AND-BONE LAND SAVNTER SIDE BY SIDE.
MAX BACHMANN FEC
MCMV
·EQVALITY·

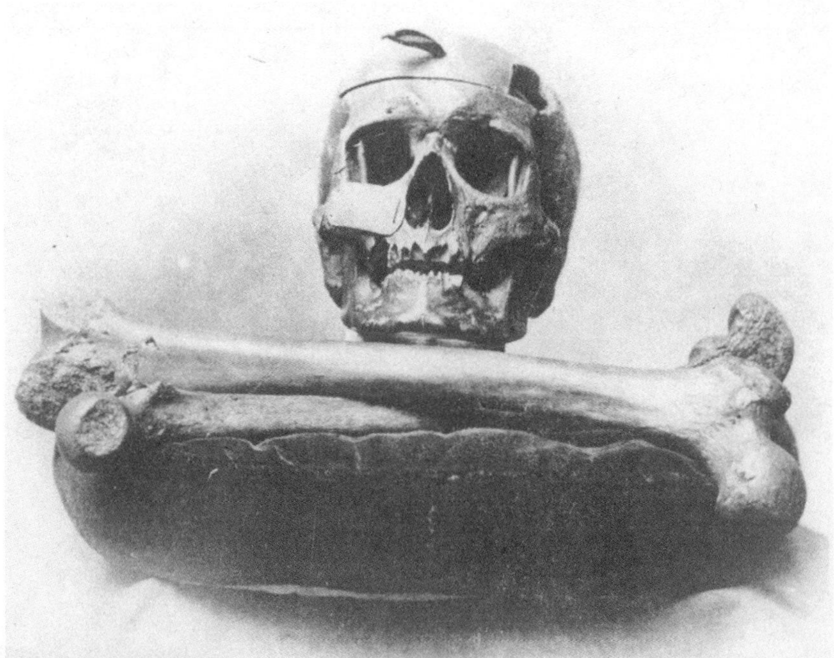

These pictures come from various membership books made available to us. The number 322 is on the back cover of the older formal membership book.
The page at the bottom right with the strange word has been called by some the Order's secret word.

OTIKUNBCDITF.

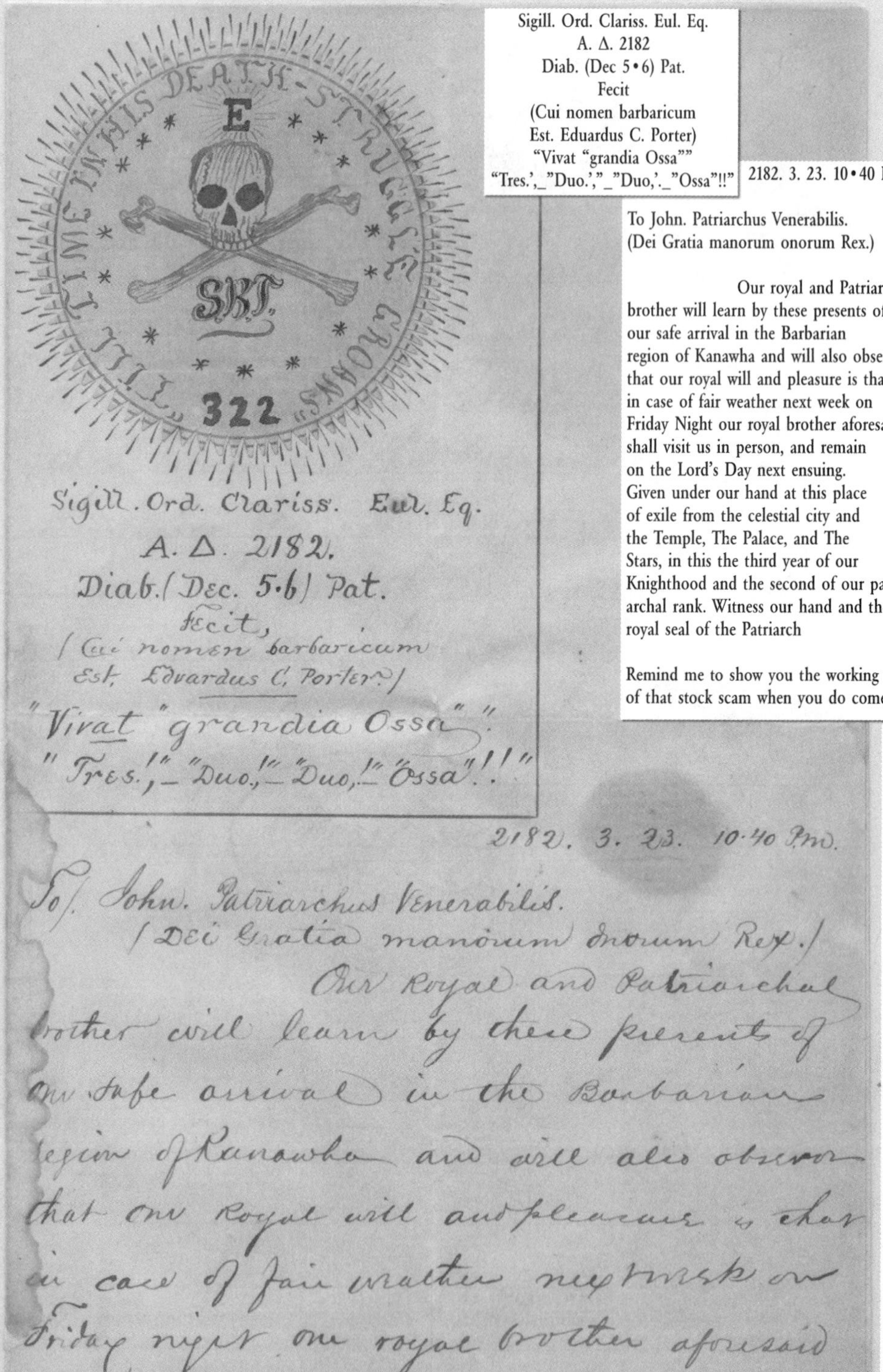

Sigill. Ord. Clariss. Eul. Eq.
A. Δ. 2182
Diab. (Dec 5•6) Pat.
Fecit
(Cui nomen barbaricum
Est. Eduardus C. Porter)
"Vivat "grandia Ossa""
"Tres.',_"Duo.',"_"Duo,'._"Ossa"!!"

2182. 3. 23. 10•40 P.M.

To John. Patriarchus Venerabilis.
(Dei Gratia manorum onorum Rex.)

Our royal and Patriarchal brother will learn by these presents of our safe arrival in the Barbarian region of Kanawha and will also observe that our royal will and pleasure is that in case of fair weather next week on Friday Night our royal brother aforesaid shall visit us in person, and remain on the Lord's Day next ensuing. Given under our hand at this place of exile from the celestial city and the Temple, The Palace, and The Stars, in this the third year of our Knighthood and the second of our patriarchal rank. Witness our hand and the royal seal of the Patriarch

Remind me to show you the working of that stock scam when you do come

COURTESY ARCHIVES & MANUSCRIPTS
YALE UNIVERSITY LIBRARY

shall visit us in person, and remain
on the Lord's Day next ensuing.
Given under our hand at this place
of exile from the celestial city and
the Temple, the Palace, and the
stars. in this the third year of our
Knighthood and the second of our patriarchal rank. Witness our hand and the
royal seal of the Patriarch

Edwardus R

Remind me to show you the working
of that stock seen when you do come

This letter was found in the archives of Yale University Library in a box that no one had asked to see for years. The letter was deteriorating and came as a surprise to the curators that it was in their collection.
Edward C. Porter was a member in 1858 and was an Episcopal Minister. As to what it all means, I do not know. It does give some very interesting insights into how some members feel and act about Bones. Kanawha is in West Virginia.

COURTESY ARCHIVES & MANUSCRIPTS
YALE UNIVERSITY LIBRARY

Chauncey DePew
Arthur Hadley
Fredrick Jones
Donald Mitchell
George Peabody Wetmore
Alfred Vanderbilt
Edward Trudeau, Jr.
Walter Camp
Anthony Higgins
Thomas Thacher
Henry L. Stimson
William Bissell
Timoth Woodru
Orris Ferry
William Sumner
Ward Cheney
Arthur Darling
Joseph Ord

The entire Yale Class of 1878 from which 15 were members of the Order.

St. John Crypt
Power Plant
Wolf's Head
Weir Court - *undergound* auditorium

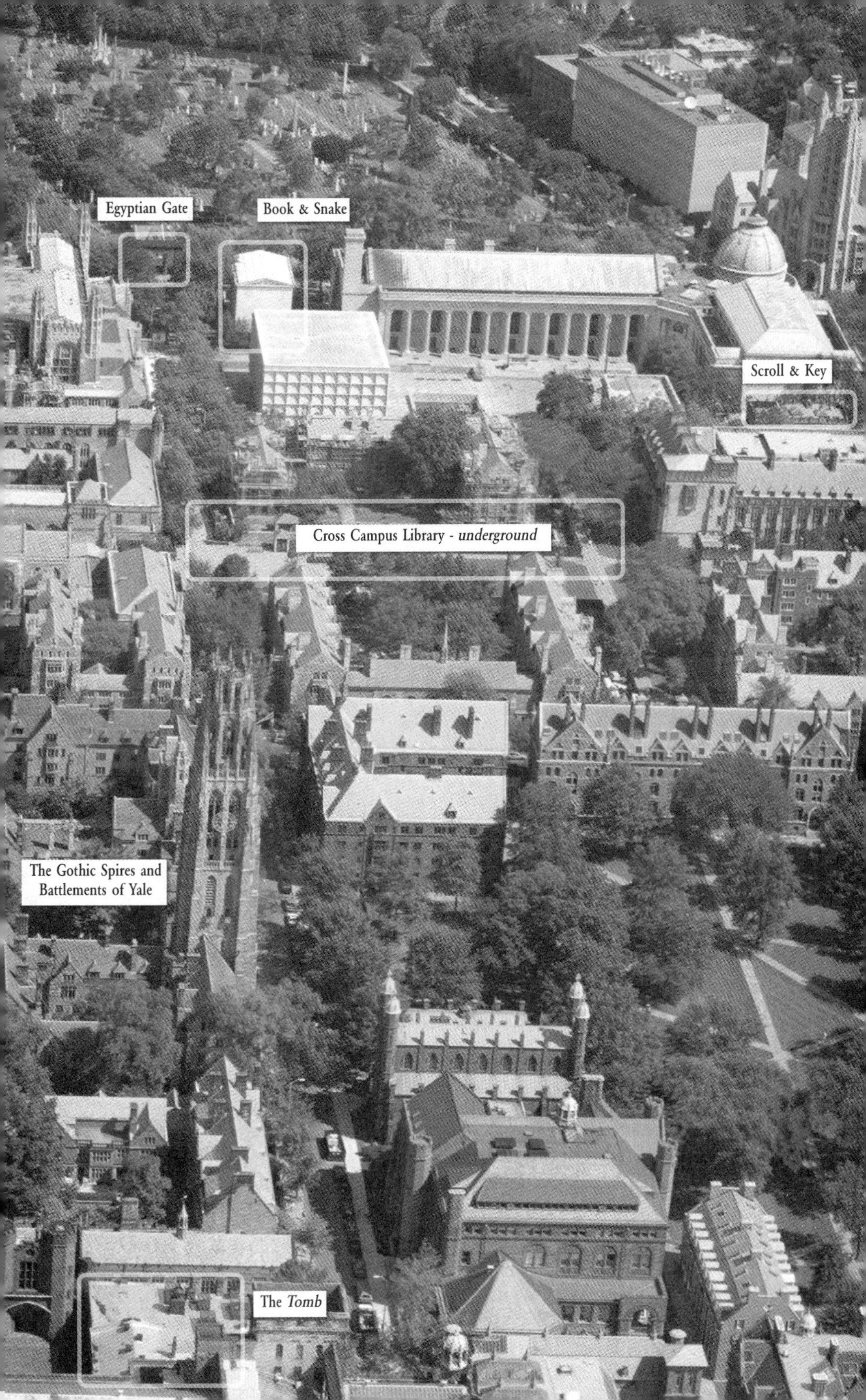

Egyptian Gate
Book & Snake
Scroll & Key
Cross Campus Library - *underground*
The Gothic Spires and Battlements of Yale
The *Tomb*

SKULL & BONES "TOMB"
FLY-BY — SEPT. 3 1998
1
Weir Towers
Jonathan Edwards Dining Hall
Weir Court
The *Tomb*
The Old Art Gallery
Gallery Bridge
3

2
4
The New Art Gallery

Deer Island

Based on a 1994 USGS Aerial Photo

0 — 100m   0 — 100yd

The Farmhouse

The Stone House

The Ledges

The Outlook & Boathouse

Satellite Photo Of NE United States Showing Location Of Deer Island

The Deer Island Club

1908

Friends of Deer Island:

This customary report and appeal to our scattered members was issued soon after our annual meeting, as the disabilities of age forced me to ask for help.

It is rather a "Bon Voyage" to old friends (for Deer Island has been my summer home for 71½ years) than behest to our new management.

The inclosed circular was not mailed before, partly because the writer was minded to first gather in the stray sheep who failed to pay annual dues; but, chiefly, because he feared that earlier issue might seem to some to harm the University Endowment movement. So we waited until now to voice any solicitude for the future of our child – the D. I. Club.

Deer Island, my friends, has meant so much to the best part of me! I do entreat you to safeguard it in every way.

It's raison d'etre is now unquestioned. Keep it out of Mrs. Grundy's clutches. You can't improve it much. But you must satisfy the butcher, the baker, the lordly plumber, and the omnivorous tax-collector.

May 1927 –G. D. M.

THE DEER ISLAND CLUB OFFICIAL BOOKLET REPRINTED HERE AND THE ABOVE COVER LETTER WERE ACQUIRED FROM THE CARY FAMILY OF VIRGINIA, DESCENDENTS OF GEORGE DOUGLAS MILLER.

The Deer Island Club

THE OUTLOOK AND BOATHOUSE

...1908...

DIRECTORS

GUSTAV GRUENER
WILLIAM BEEBE
G. D. MILLER
WILLIAM M. BARNUM
FRANK J. PRICE

OFFICERS

President
GUSTAV GRUENER

Secretary
FRANK J. PRICE

Treasurer
WILLIAM BEEBE

THE OUTLOOK LANDING

The Deer Island Club Corporation

ARTICLES OF ASSOCIATION

Be it know that we, the subscribers, do hereby associate ourselves as a body politic and corporate, pursuant to the statute laws of the State of Connecticut regulating the formation and organization of corporations without capital stock, and the following are our articles of association :

ARTICLE I. The name of said corporation shall be "THE DEER ISLAND CLUB CORPORATION."

ARTICLE II. The purposes for which said corporation is formed are the following, to wit:—to promote the social intercourse of its members, and to provide for them facilities for recreation and social enjoyment; and to this end, to purchase, hold and convey any property, real or personal, which may be necessary or convenient therefor; to maintain a Club House for the use and benefit of its members; and to adopt suitable by-laws and generally to exercise all the usual powers of corporations not prohibited by said statutes.

Article III. The members of said corporation shall be the subscribers, and such persons as may from time to time be elected or constituted members under the by-laws adopted by said corporation. Dated at New Haven, Conn., this 18th day of February, A. D. 1907.

William Beebe
Henry W. Farnam
Gustav Gruener
J. C. Schwab
Heathcote M. Woolsey

New Haven, February 18, 1907.

State of Connecticut }
County of New Haven } *ss.*

Then and there personally appeared William Beebe, Henry W. Farnam, Gustav Gruener, John C. Schwab and Heathcote M. Woolsey, signers of the foregoing instrument, and acknowledged the same to be their free act and deed, before me.

[Notarial Seal] SAMUEL H. FISHER,
Notary Public

Approved Feb. 20, 1907.
THEODORE BODEWEIN,
Secretary.

Corporation Fee, $10.00
Paid February 20, 1907.
L. MOSES
for Treasurer.

Per A. R. Parsons.

The foregoing is a true copy of the original articles of association of THE DEER ISLAND CLUB ASSOCIATION and of the endorsements thereon.

Attest,

HEATHCOTE M. WOOLSEY
Temporary Clerk

BY-LAWS

OF

The Deer Island Club Corporation

ARTICLE I.

SECTION 1. *Annual Meeting.* The corporation shall hold its first annual meeting on the evening of February 21, 1907, in New Haven, and thereafter shall hold its annual meeting in New Haven, in the month of February of each year, at such time and place as the Directors shall appoint. Due notice of the time and place of holding such meeting, and of the business to be transacted thereat shall be given by the secretary to the members of the corporation.

SEC. 2. Special meetings of the corporation shall be called by the president at the written request of ten members of the corporation, and one week's notice of such meeting and of the object of the call shall be given by the secretary.

SEC. 3. Fifteen members shall constitute a quorum. Any member may constitute an agent to vote in the meetings of this corporation by writing signed by him for that purpose.

ARTICLE II.

SECTION 1. All the property and affairs of the corporation shall be under the control and management of a board of directors, consisting of five members elected at each annual meeting by ballot by the members of the corporation from their own number. The directors shall hold office for one year and until their successors are elected, and shall be eligible for re-election.

SEC. 2. The directors shall have power:—

(*a*) To appoint a president, secretary and treasurer and to define the duties of such officers.

(*b*) To appoint such committees and sub-committees as they may from time to time deem necessary, with power to perform the duties assigned to them.

(*c*) To make rules for the use of the corporation's premises by members, and for their conduct of the same.

(*d*) To call special meetings of the corporation.

(*e*) To solicit subscriptions for purposes which they deem in keeping with the general objects of the corporation.

(*f*) To fill any vacancies in the offices or committees of the corporation, or in their own number, provided, however, that any person thus chosen to be a member of the board of directors shall hold office only until the next annual meeting of the corporation and until his successor is elected.

(*g*) To buy, lease or otherwise control property for the corporation.

(*h*) To collect dues from the members.

(*i*) And generally to do whatever is usual or convenient for the maintenance and welfare of the corporation.

ARTICLE III.

SEC. 1. Any person who shall be a member of the Russell Trust Association, a corporation organized under the laws of the State of Connecticut, and located in the Town of New Haven, County of New Haven, and State of Connecticut, shall be eligible to membership in this corporation.

SEC. 2. Any such person upon signifying his intention in writing to the secretary, and upon the payment of the annual dues, shall become a member of this corporation.

ARTICLE IV.

The annual dues of members shall be ten dollars a year, payable on the first day of January in each year.

ARTICLE V.

These by-laws may be amended at any meeting of the members of this corporation by a two-thirds vote of the members present.

OUTDOOR FIREPLACE—OUTLOOK

Copy of Circular Sent Out July 1, 1907.

Covering directions of general interest for each season.

The following memorandum is prepared especially for the benefit of the subscribers to the DEER ISLAND CLUB, but the Directors wish it to be generally known that the privileges of the Island are extended to all men entitled thereto whether subscribers or not.

Those who expect to go there immediately after Commencement, especially if accompanied by their wives or other members of their families, should notify Mr. Miller of the time of their arrival and the number of their party.

The Bungalow at the head of the Island has been offered by Mr. Miller for this season for the entertainment of ladies. Its equipment is excellent throughout and its situation is the best on the Island.

The rate fixed for this season is $2.00 per day for members and all ladies, and $2.50 per day for all other visitors. The extra charge when amounting to $10.00 includes membership.

Visitors are requested to observe strictly the rule which is in force at all clubs against feeing servants. All servants at Deer Island receive good wages.

The night express leaving New York at 9 P. M. reaches Clayton without change at 7 A. M., Alexandria Bay, 9.30 A. M. The Empire State (8 A. M.) and the Second Empire (1 P. M.) from New York connect at Utica to reach Clayton at 4 P. M. and 9 P. M. respectively. Alexandria Bay 6.30 P. M. and 10.20 P M.

Fifteen-day excursion tickets from New York to Alexandria Bay and return are $12.75. Fare by mileage books is $14.70, and extra mileage will be redeemed at the island.

Passengers from the West change for Alexandria Bay at Syracuse, or they can come by boat direct to Alexandria Bay from Toronto or intermediate ports without change. The club launch will meet visitors at Alexandria Bay.

The trip to Alexandria Bay can be combined with excursions down the St. Lawrence to Quebec and the Saguenay, or to Montreal and New York, or up through the Lakes.

THE DEER ISLAND CLUB submits the following informal report of its third season.

No less than sixty-eight entitled to its privileges have visited the island during the past summer, most of whom have remained for two weeks or longer, while several have brought their wives and children to the "Ledges." The expectations of the club are being realized, especially by those who come in groups and renew their old time friendships under the ideal conditions there presented.

Attention is again called to the fact that all those eligible to membership, whether members of THE DEER ISLAND CLUB or not, are welcome on the island.

It is suggested that all who can include a trip to Deer Island in their next summer's tour should make plans therefor at an early date, in order that the various groups who intend to do so may assemble at a time arranged in advance. This will enable the management to make adequate provision for all visitors, and will make possible, in many instances, the meeting of friends there who might otherwise miss seeing one another.

INFORMATION

For the benefit of those who have not been to Deer Island the following details may be of interest.

BESIDE THE OUTLOOK

FIREPLACE AND LIBRARY—OUTLOOK

Deer Island lies in the St. Lawrence River two miles north of Alexandria Bay. The river at that point is about three miles wide and the American ship channel sweeps the eastern side of the island. Being thus near the center of the river, the island commands a superb view for many miles both up and down the river and is exposed to the prevailing breezes which blow north and south along the course of the stream. The island is irregular in form, with a shore line two miles in length, following the bays and indentations. It is covered to the water's edge by a natural forest which has been preserved and is traversed in all directions by wooded paths, of which more than fifteen miles have been laid out.

THE "OUTLOOK"

This is the main club house, located on the eastern side of the island, with a rocky bay on one side and the broad St. Lawrence in front. The house rises from a granite ledge on the river bank, and a wide gallery opening out of the lounging room projects over the clear green waters, which are there more than 100 feet deep. In the "Outlook" are fifteen bed rooms, each with hot and cold water; and five bath rooms. Each room is furnished in a unique way. All have a fine outlook on the river and seven of them open on balconies on the water side of the house. In the northern part is the dining room, comfortably and picturesquely furnished, commanding light and air and beautiful river views through the broad windows at its either extremity. The lounging room opens out of this, and with its large windows and water gallery seems poised over the brink of the river. In the south wing is the main hall filled with a collection of curious and beautiful mementos and relics gathered from many lands, while beside the great fire place a short stairway leads to the library, a semi-circular room back of the chimney—a room that must be seen to be appreciated and understood.

THE "STONE HOUSE"

This is located 100 yards from the "Outlook," close to the shore and in a heavily wooded dell. It is a large building of native stone with a Flemish roof. In the lower part is a great hall (not yet finished.) Its walls are to be hung with a collection of ancient armor which is now in the keeping of the Albany Historical Society. At the rear of the hall is a gallery, and on the floor above it is a suite of six bed rooms with several baths, while on the floor above that is a similar suite of five bed rooms, surrounded by a gallery, which comes well above the tree tops and looks out on a magnificent view.

THE STONE HOUSE

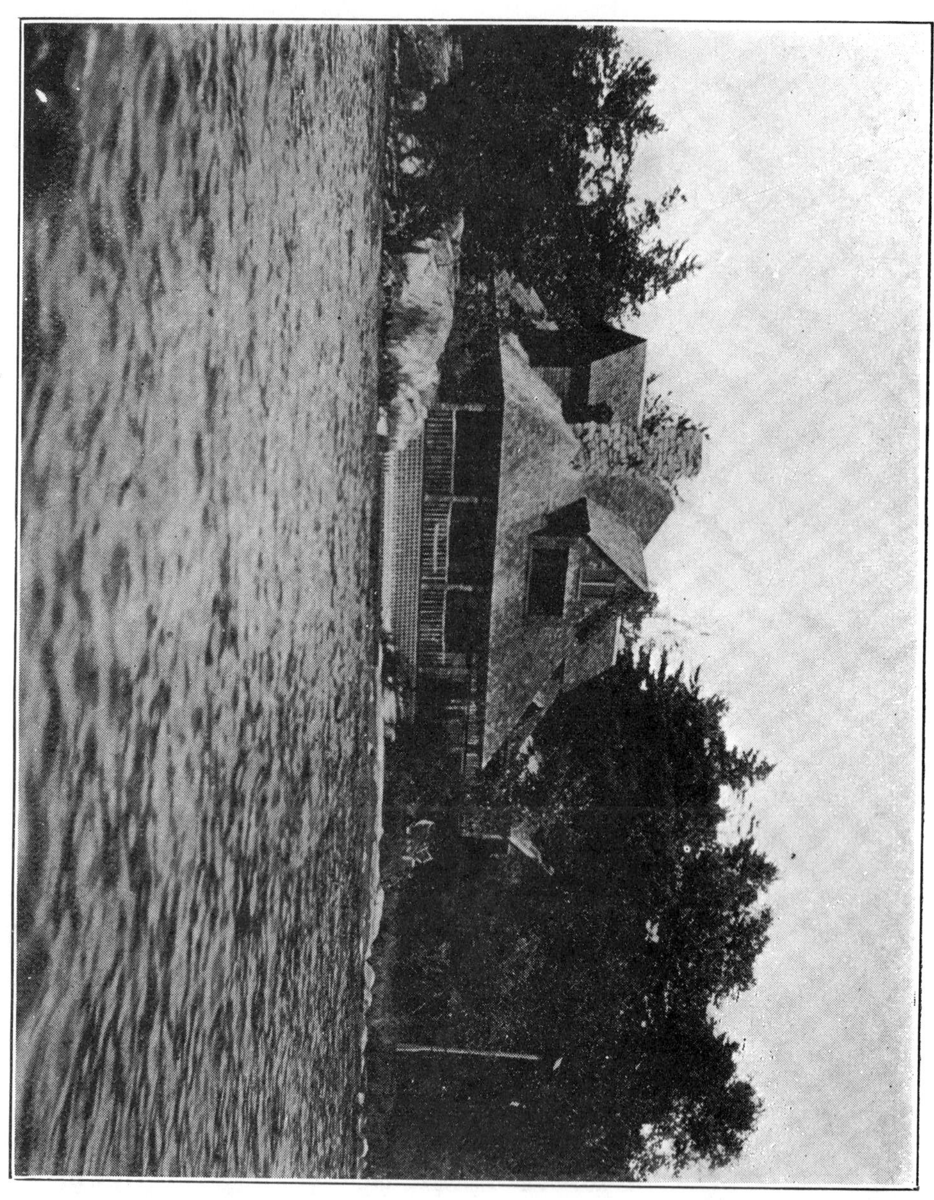

THE LEDGES

THE "LEDGES"

This is for the accommodation of men bringing their wives and families or friends. It is located on the southern extremity of the island, less than half a mile from the "Outlook," and comprises a group of semi-detached houses at the water's edge. Here are nine bed rooms with a large social room, surrounded on all four sides by a wide veranda, which is also the dining room, one of the four sides being always sheltered and available for that purpose.

Both the "Outlook" and the "Ledges" are provided with commodious boat houses. The club now owns several boats and canoes, and during the past season added a motor launch. During the coming season it is expected that other boats will be purchased and installed as may be needed.

At the "Outlook" a competent housekeeper is in charge whenever guests are present At the "Ledges" Prof. and Mrs. Beebe have kindly acted as house committee, while in the event of their absence, suitable provision will be made for members and guests.

CLUB MEMBERS

E. Alexander........... '73
F. W. Allen............ '00
M. H. Arnot............ '56

W. I. Badger........... '82
H. A. Bayne............ '92
S. E. Baldwin.......... '61
O. T. Bannard.......... '76
W. M. Barnum......... '77
W. Beebe .... '73
S. B. Bertron......... .. '85
E. M. Bentley.......... '80
W. McC. Blair.......... '07
L. W. Bowers........... '79
G. C. Brooke........... '97
F. H. Brooke........... '99
J. W. Brooks........... '75
H. S. Brooks........... '85
L. F. Burpee........... '79
S. C. Bushnell.......... '74
F. S. Butterworth...... '95

E. Coffin .... '66
W. Camp .... '80
W. H. Cowles.......... '87

H. M. Denslow......... '73
M. Dexter .... '67
H. F. Dimock........... '63
T. P. Dixon............ '07
P. L. Dodge........... '07
T. E. Donnelly.......... '89
W. E. Dwight.......... '93

F. MacVeagh .... '62
J. G. Magee............ '06
T. S. Maffitt............ '99
H. Mansfield .... '71
L. McClung .... '92
G. D. Miller............ '70
W. S. Moorehead....... '06

J. B. Neal.............. '96

J. P. Ord............... '73
F. O'Brien .... '06

H. M. Painter.......... '84
W. Parker .... '80
W. Parkin .... '74
J. R. Parrott........... '83
J. H. Perry............. '70
W. A. Peters........... '80
A. R. E. Pinchot........ '97
Gifford Pinchot .... '89
H. B. Platt............. '82
L. A. Platt............. '79
F. J. Price............. '92
S. O. Prentice.......... '73

D. Sage .... '97
H. M. Sage............. '90
W. D. Simmons........ '90
E. C. Smith............ '75

S. J. Elder............. '73
W. P. Eno.............. '82

C. H. Farnam........... '68
H. W. Farnam.......... '74
S. Fish, Jr............. '05
I. Fisher .... '88
G. T. Ford............. '65
E. B. Frost............. '83

E. E. Garrison......... '97
E. F. Green............. '80
G. Greuner.......... .. '84

L. S. Haslam........... '90
G. G. Haven, Jr........ '87
E. N. Hidden........... '85
C. B. Hobbs............ '85

H. A. James............ '74
N. James .... '90
W. B. James............ '79
P. H. Jennings......... '04
D. A. Jones............. '75

W. Kent .... '87
C. H. Kelsey............ '78
J. F. Kernochan........ '63
A. B. Kerr.............. '97
A. R. Kimball.......... '77
H. L. S. Knox.......... '07

A. E. Lamb............. '67

E. R. Stearns........... '70
A. P. Stokes............ '96
C. M. Stone............ '78

F. B. Tarbell........... '73
J. P. Taylor............ '62
J. S. Thatcher.......... '77
S. D. Thatcher.......... '83
T. Thatcher .... '71
W. L. Thatcher......... '87
C. H. Thomas.......... '73
S. Thorne .... '96
S. B. Thorne........... '96
J. C. Thornton......... '08
J. B. Townsend......... '91
J. M. Townsend......... '74
J. M. Townsend, Jr..... '08
G. C. Tuttle............ '07

J. W. Wadsworth, Jr.... '98
F. C. Walcott........... '91
W. H. Welch........... '70
F. E. Weyerhaeuser..... '96
F. S. Witherbee........ '74
W. C. Witherbee........ '80
A. D. White............ '53
J. L. Whitney.......... '56
T. L. Woodruff......... '79
T. S. Woolsey.......... '72

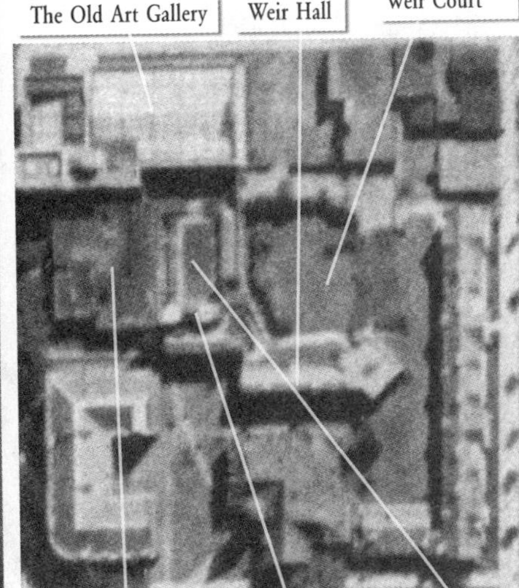

George Douglas Miller 1847 - 1932

Benefactor of Bones? George at one time owned the whole block surrounding the Order's Temple in New Haven. He was a member of Bones in 1870 and owned the property from the late 1870s until the 1920s. George moved the Gothic towers of Alumni Hall next to the Tomb and started the building that became Weir Hall. He gave to the Order its private retreat on the US/Canadian border, Deer Island.

The Ledges

The Stone House, 1908 Deer Island Handbook

Stone House 1998

The Stone House is now jus
a ruin.

Photos of the Deer Island ruin
were taken in the year 2000
and appear here courtesy of
www.newruins.com

Stone House Chimney, 2000

Stone House ruins viewed through the bushes from the water, 2000

The Ledges from 1908 Deer Island Handbook

The Ledges in 2000

The stone chimmney and some rock foundations are all that is left of the Outlook. It is reported that this building burned down in 1949. The Outlook housed a collection of valuable antiques and books which were all lost in the fire.

Remains of the granite chimney from The Outlook on the channel side of Deer Island.

HARPER'S WEEKLY.
A JOURNAL OF CIVILIZATION.

VOL. XVIII.—No. 893.] NEW YORK, SATURDAY, FEBRUARY 7, 1874. [WITH A SUPPLEMENT. PRICE TEN CENTS.

THE EMANCIPATOR OF LABOR AND THE HONEST WORKING-PEOPLE.—[SEE NEXT PAGE.]

SECRET SOCIETIES AT YALE.

FROM *HARPER'S WEEKLY*, FEBRUARY 7, 1874

SECRET SOCIETIES AT YALE COLLEGE.—[FROM A DRAWING BY MISS ALICE DONLEVY.]

THE SECRET SOCIETY SYSTEM of Yale College is a peculiar characteristic of that institution, and is so prominent a feature there that it is quite as much talked about as the college curriculum itself. Whether this be an advantage or the reverse is a question which may of course be argued either way. The society system at Yale is different from that which prevails at any other institution of learning in this feature, that there are no societies — except in the scientific school — which run through the entire course, but the societies change with each succeeding year. After Freshman year the members of the next year's society are elected by the class above, and is the number is necessarily limited, a society election is one of the coveted boners. Every college in the land has its secret societies — even Harvard cannot deprive them of in existence within its halls. But at all the other colleges and universities except Yale the Freshmen are elected soon after entering, and remain active members of the organization during the entire four years.

Beginning, then, with the societies of Freshmen year, we find three such societies now in existence at Yale. As with the organizations in the two succeeding classes, these societies are known and designated by letters of the Greek alphabet, the letters selected being the initial letters of the secret motto of the society. They are known as Delta Kappa (ΔK), founded in 1845; Kappa Sigma Epsilon, or "Sigma Fps" (KΣE), founded in 1840; and Gamma Nu (ΓN), a sort of half-and-half secret society, founded in 1855, A fourth society, Sigma Delta (ΣΔ), founded in 1849, expired in 1860. A Freshman on entering college has an opportunity to join either one of these three societies, and if he has friends in an upper class, is pretty sure to join whichever **one** they may recommend. The rivalry between the societies is solely one of numbers, and many interesting and humorous stories of the influences used to induce a would-be Freshman to join one or the other of the two first-named might be repeated *ad libitum*, Zealous Sophomores have paid hotel bills, driven in hired carriages all around the city, carried carpet-bags, and furnished With an unlimited supply of cigars, wine, and suppers, Freshmen whom they wished to secure for their organization, only to fie mortified in the end by the discovery that the Freshman was already pledged to the rival organization, or was a smooth-faced graduate of many years' standing. The society meetings in this year are held on Saturday nights, breaking up at midnight, and the exercises, are of a literary character, sometimes varied by a dramatic entertainment. Despite the popular belief to the contrary, not a drop of wine is allowed within any society hall in college, and this rule, we have been informed on good authority, is seldom if ever violated. "Sigma Eps" has one chapter or branch at Dartmouth College; Delta Kappa has one at Amherst as well as one at Dartmouth; Gamma Nu has no chapters, and is a weak society at the best. All told, the first named society has had about 1600 members, the second about 1900, and the third 400. An allusion to these societies would not be complete without a reference to their initiations, which are known of and cited throughout the country as illustrations of pandemonium broken loose. Until 1869 they were very rough in character, and often resulted in serious injury to some of their victims; but since then a professor has been present during the sports, to interfere in case they are carried too far. Tossing in a blanket, rolling in a wheel, stowing away in a coffin, sitting, suddenly in a tub of ice, or put under a guillotine, where the knife is arrested within a few inches of the victim's nose, and members yelling, blowing horns, burning phosphorus, and masked as skeletons and demons-these are what a candidate has to pass through before being invested with the dignity of membership.

The Sophomore societies are now mere stepping-stones to a Junior organization, and are almost entirely of a social character. They are at present two in number — Delta Beta Chi (ΔBX), and Phi Theta Psi (ΦΘΨ) — and have each from thirty to thirty-five members. In a class of ordinary size this leaves about half the members out in the cold. The first Sophomore society I was established in 1838, and was known as Kappa Sigma Theta, and flourished until 1858. Alpha Sigma Phi was established in 1846; and was-broken up in 1864 by the faculty, and from its ashes sprang the two organizations already mentioned. All the college societies have rooms of their own, guarded by ponderous iron doors, and furnished, so report says, elaborately and elegantly. They are in Sophomore year more like jolly, free-and-easy clubs than any thing else, having of course their grips and pass-words, but beyond an occasional dramatic entertainment the literary feature of the Freshmen societies has disappeared.

In Junior year there are three -societies, two of which own handsome buildings of their own, illustrations of which accompany this article. Alpha Delta Phi, founded in 1832 at Hamilton College, is the weak member of the triad, its chapter at, Yale, which was established in 1836, ranking the lowest in the college estimation. It has twenty-two chapters in the different colleges throughout the Union, and numbered 3650 members all told when its last catalogue was issued. Among its prominent members may be cited D. G. MITCHELL ('Ilk Marvel"), W. L. KINGSLEY (editor of the *New Englander),* General DICK TAYLOR, President D. C. GILMAN (of the California University), G. W. SMALLET, Governor DENNISON (of Ohio), and Senator PUGH, HORACE MAYNARD, Dr. STORRS, J. R. LOWELL, Rev. E. E. HALE, MANTON MARBLE, and others, while the late Chief Justice CHASE, Rev. H. W. BEECHER, and CASSIUS M. CLAY are among its honorary members. This society has no hall of its own at Yale.

The society of Psi Upsilon is one of the best-known of college societies; it was founded at Union College in 1833, and established a chapter at Yale in 1838 ; has now fifteen chapters, and a roll of membership with about 3500 names. Among its members are Senator FERRY, DWIGHT Foster, ANDREW D. WHITE, CHAUNCEY M. Depew, F. W. SEWARD, GALUSHA A. GROW, Amos F. AKERMAN and a host of other equally well-known names. It owns a beautiful hall on High Street, with a front of twenty-six feet and a depth of sixty-six feet. The material is red pressed brick, inlaid with ornamental work in black, and it has a Mansard-roof. Inside is a fine theatre or exhibition-hall and several other rooms. The cost of the property was about $15,000.

The other Junior society is that of Delta Kappa Epsilon, founded at Yale in 1.844. It has now no less than thirty-eight chapters and nearly 5000 members. Among them are CHARLTON F. LEWIS, Major-General SWAYNE, Professor NORTHROP, J. H. DRUMMOND, General F. A. WALKER, J. Q. ADAMS, Jun.; find among its honorary members General BURNSIDE, SCHUYLER COLFAX, BAYARD TAYLOR, and others. Its hall is on York Street, and was built in 1861 of red brick, and has a front of twenty-four feet six inches, with a depth of forty-five feet, and the property is valued now at about $10,000.

Last, though by no means least, come the Senior societies, two in number, whose mysteries are "deep, dark, unfathomable," and an election to either of which is one of the coveted college honors. Skull and Bones, and Scroll and Key are the euphonious names by which these two organizations are known to the college world. Of the two the first-named is also first in position and in honor. Not much is known about its origin, except that it is supposed to have been founded in 1933. It takes each year fifteen new members, who are claimed to be the most prominent in their respective class either as scholars, literary men, or social companions. Its hall is on High Street near Chapel and is a grim-looking, windowless, tomb-like structure, built of brown sandstone, and with a front of thirty-five and a depth of forty-four feet. It stands in a lot forty by seventy, and the value of the property is estimated at $30,000.

Scroll and Key was founded in 1841, and it also takes fifteen new members every year. Its hall is undoubtedly the handsomest college society structure in the United States, and it stands on the corner of College and Wall streets. It has a front of thirty-six feet, with a depth of fifty-five feet, in a lot forty-eight by ninety-two, and the light yellow Cleveland stone is the chief material of which it is composed. This is set off by thin layers of dark blue marble, while four pillars of Aberdeen granite with marble cappings sustain the three projecting arches in front. The value of the entire property can not be less than $50,000.

Among the prominent members of the Skull and Bones Society are found the names of W. M.. EVARTS, Colonel H. C. DEMING, General W. H. RUSSELL, Professor THACHER, Professor SILLIMAN, Professor HOPPIN, Rev. Dr. THOMPSON, Senator FERRY, D. G. MITCHELL, H. B. HARRISON, ANDREW D. WHITE, C. M. DEPEW, E. R. SILL, General CROXTON, and others. Among the notable members of Scroll and Key are General RUNYON, S. F. MORSE, General SWAYNE, Professor EATON, and W. R. BACON.

So far we have sketched the history of the societies of the academic department. Two more remain, Phi Beta Kappa, which is represented in every college, and has for its members the leading scholars in every class, and Chi Delta Theta, a revived society, which formerly comprised the leading literary men, and now is confined to the five editors of the *Yale Literary Magazine.* The Sheffield. Scientific School has also several secret societies, but the school itself is too young for them to have any history.

In leaving the subject of secret societies of Yale, much of course remains unsaid as not being pertinent to the limits of a newspaper article. College politics are kept alive in all their intricacies by the societies, which represent in that respect the parties of the outside world. Friendships are formed in them which last through life, and the old graduate finds an old familiar spot in his society hall when he returns to his alma mater and meets none but strange faces and new buildings about him. 'The secret societies form the college life, and their existence is apparently assured. They

"Mask their business from the common eye;"

but even if their doings were open to public inspection, but little would be revealed not already known or surmised. And as to their existence, they believe in

"Giving it an understanding, but no tongue."

* *

FILE AND CLAW.

Badge.

THE FALL OF SKULL AND BONES

COMPILED FROM THE MINUTES OF THE 7TH REGULAR MEETING OF THE

ORDER OF THE FILE AND CLAW

9,29,76

De oesibus—quid dicam? Ilium fuit!

— Published by the Order, 1876 —

BABYLON IS FALLEN.

ANY one who was noticing the Bones men of '77, on the morning of Sunday, October 1st, 1876, was probably struck by the crest-fallen air which characterized all of them. At any rate there were those who observed that during the church services their eyes suspiciously scanned the faces of one neutral after another, and invariably dropped if their glance was returned. The reason for this is a simple one. As long as Skull and Bones Society shall exist, the night of September 29th will be to its members the anniversary of the occasion when their Temple was invaded by neutrals, some of their rarest memorabilia confiscated, and their most sacred secrets unveiled to the vulgar eyes of the uninitiated.

We have thought that a description of how this was done might be of interest to the college world. The back-cellar windows of the Eulogian Temple were fortified as follows :

First, to one seeking entrance from the outside, was a row of one-inch iron bars; behind them a strong iron netting fastened to a wooden frame; behind this another row of iron bars, one and one quarter inches thick; and still behind this a heavy wooden shutter. Formidable as these defenses appear, the ORDER OF THE FILE AND CLAW, having procured a supply of files, skeleton keys, etc., determined to attempt to effect an entrance. For reasons that need not be rehearsed here, the work proceeded slowly, and it was only after many hours of patient and cautious labor that one of the outside bars was cut in two. Next, by means of a powerful claw, the long nails that fastened the iron netting to the wooden frame were drawn out. Then the bar was re-fastened in its place by means of a little putty, and we retired to await a favorable night for finishing the job. Eight o'clock Friday evening, September 29th, was the hour selected.

First, one of our number proceeded to remove the iron bar and the netting, and then, for the sake of more room, he, with considerable difficulty, got out the strong wooded frame to which the latter had been fastened. Pushing head and shoulders into the opening thus made, there still remained a strong row of one and one quarter inch iron bars. Fortunately there was no need to file through these. It was found that they were fastened above in a thick joist, but below ran into a brick " damp-wall " that was built up inside, and two inches from, the stone foundation-wall of the building. By the aid of a claw and a hatchet, it was the work of but a few moments to dig away about twenty inches of this wall, and thus loosen an iron plate through which the lower ends of the bars ran. Upon pushing this plate inward, the bars all fell out with their own weight; the flimsy wooden shutter was then easily wrenched from its position, and at just half past ten o'clock an entrance into the cellar was obtained. Passing in through the window, we broke open the wooden door at the top of the cellar stairs, opened the two iron shutters which close the back windows of the main hall, and proceeded to examine the Temple at our leisure. For the benefit of future explorers, and as a directory for new-fledged Bones men for all time, we will now give a brief description of

THE INTERIOR OF SKULL AND BONES HALL.

Besides the cellar, the Temple is divided into two stories. Fig. 1 is a rough plan of the cellar :

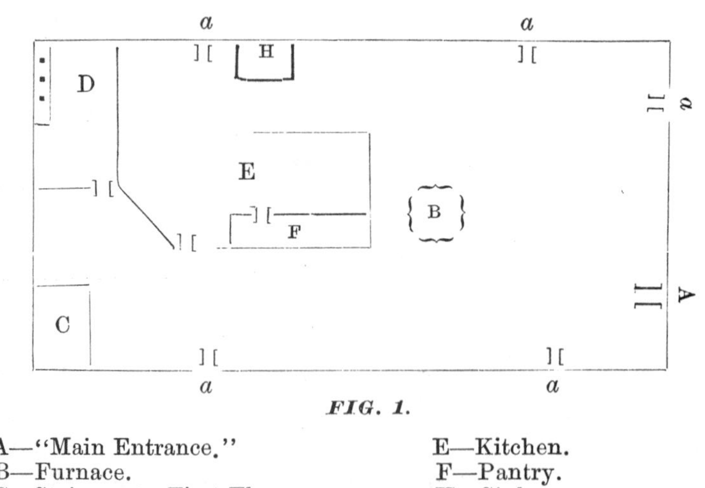

FIG. 1.

A—"Main Entrance."
B—Furnace.
C—Stairway to First Floor.
D—Jo.
E—Kitchen.
F—Pantry.
H—Sink.
a—Other Windows.

A light is always kept burning in the Jo (D), which is ornamented with a dilapidated human skull and a framed set of "Directions to Freshmen," signed THOMAS CLAP, and dated *Yale College*, 1752. Here is also a tombstone marked SPERRY, seemingly taken from the same grave as the skull. On the west wall of the kitchen (E), which contains the ordinary conveniences, hangs a picture of Napoleon Bonaparte. In the Pantry (F) are large quantities of dishes, each piece of crockery ornamented with a picture of a skull and crossbones, and each spoon and fork marked S. B. T.

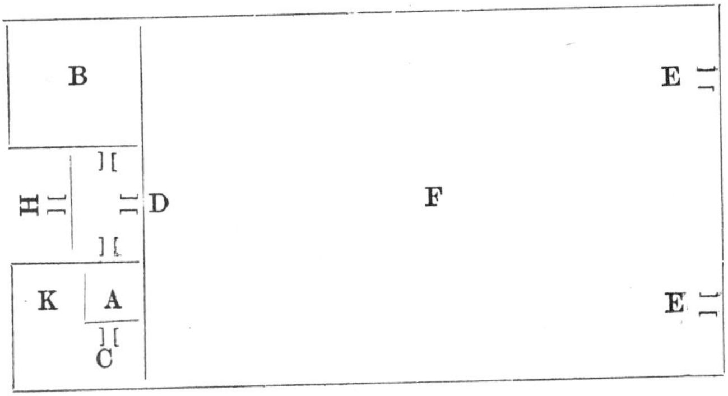

FIG. 2.

On ascending the stairs from the cellar, you find yourself, after bursting open the door C, Fig. 2, in an entry (A), from which a winding staircase (K) leads to the next floor. The door C, which is of wood, we found locked, but broke open without difficulty. H is the outside iron door, covered on the inside with a pair of light frame doors. B is a small toilet room. The door D, which is without a lock, opens into the main hall (F), called by the initiated "324." The floor is of colored tiles; the walls are rather gaudily frescoed, mainly in red and black, somewhat like those of D K hall. A few settees, resembling those in Linonia Hall, and a table, make up the furniture of the room. The wood work is painted white, and, like the walls, is in many places scratched and dirty. E E are two narrow windows, guarded by strong iron shutters. The latter are concealed from view by some light wooden blinds stained to look like walnut. The only objects of interest in the room were a glass case in the southeast corner containing a large number of gilded base-balls, each inscribed with the date, score, etc., of a university game, and a well-thumbed text-book, either a Physics or a Human Intellect, on the fly-leaf of which was inscribed the autograph of Bones' irrepressible annoyer, Arjayjay of '76.

Thus far we had found little to compensate us for our trouble, but on ascending to the next floor, and passing, on our right. a little store-room and draw-bridge which extend over the front entrance from High street, our pains was rewarded.

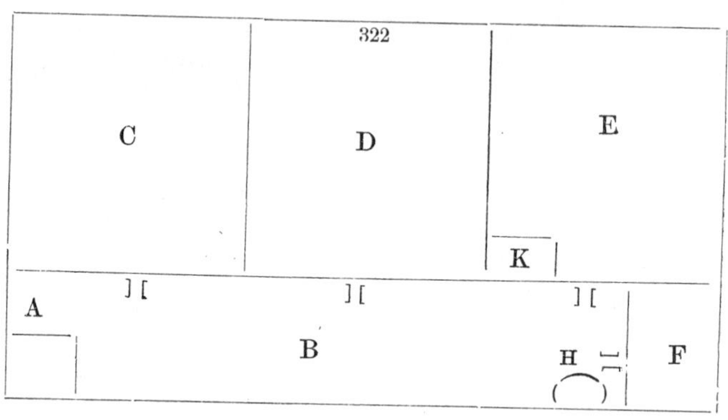

FIG. 3.

A—Staircase.
B—Hall.
C—Parlor 323.
D—Parlor 322.
E—Storeroom.
F—Storeroom.
H—Safe.
K—Closet.

Entering the room C, Fig. 3, immediately on the left is seen a book-case, which contains the Skull and Bones library, including a complete set of the Yale Lit., handsomely bound college catalogues and books published by Bones men. Here, too, was the Constitution of the Phi Beta Kappa and a catalogue of SCROLL AND KEY Society, containing a list of members down to 1868. It was bound in black, and had on the front cover the letters C. S. P. and on the back C. C. J. in Old English text. For the year LI only eleven names are given, and for XLII only twelve. It contains several typographical errors, as for instance, D. Cady Eaton's first name is printed Samuel. Opposite the names of the first two Keys men for LXII, some one has written, in a bold hand, the mystic symbol "*Ass.*" And at the top of the page which gives the men of LII, is written, "Croud packed by Boies," and Boies is the name of a Keys man of that year. From the catalogue we learn that the President and Secretary of Scroll and Key are known " inside " as CHILO and EUMENES, and that, as in Bones, each member has a nickname given him. Some of these are handed down from class to class, and of these

Glaucus, Prisaticus and Arbaces appear to be the favorites.

Hanging on the wall towards High street was a handsomely-framed cushion of dark velvet, on which were fastened the pins of all the societies which have existed in college, including Spade and Grave, Bull and Stones, and the like. On the south side of the room is a fire-place, and above this a mantel and mirror. Upon the mantel were a Skull and Bones of silver, the skull about two inches in diameter, and engraved "322 from the S. E. C. of 1858;" another of bronze, a little larger than the silver one, and various other insignia relating to Skull and Bones, On the west wall hung, among other pictures, an old engraving representing an open burial vault, in which, on a stone slab, rest four human skulls, grouped about a fool's-cap and bells, an open book, several mathematical instruments, a beggar's scrip, and a royal crown. On the arched wall above the vault are the explanatory words, in Roman letters, "WER WAR DER THOR, WER WEISER, WER BETTLER ODER KAISER?" and below the vault is engraved, in German characters, the sentence :

"Ob Arm, ob Reich, im Tode gleich."

The picture is accompanied by a card, on which is written, "From the German Chapter. Presented by Patriarch D. C. Gilman of D. 50." The room is handsomely furnished; tobacco and pipes were abundant, and packs of well-worn cards served to indicate how the society manages to kill five or six hours every Thursday evening. The pipe-bowls, which are representations of skulls, and bear the stamp of M. Gambier, Paris, have the Eulogian name of the owner and his decade written upon them with red ink ; for instance, the one belonging to the present "Member from Bath" was marked "TRIM, D. 75."

Room D, the Bones name of which is "322," is the *sanctum sanctorum* of the Temple. Its distinguishing feature is a life-size *fac simile* of the Bones pin, handsomely inlaid in the black marble hearth. Just below the mantel, and also inlaid in marble, is the motto :

Rari Quippe Boni,

in old English text. This room is even more richly furnished than "323," but contains no book-case, and no pictures of special significance.

On the walls of the long hall B are hung a couple of score of photographs, about 12x20 inches, each representing fifteen Bonesmen grouped around a table, on which rest a human skull and crossbones. As the finish of these pictures is poor and of an antiquated style, it is probable that they are taken each year with the apparatus belonging to the society. H is an old-fashioned plain-lock safe, size about 20x26 inches, and 15 inches deep, set in the wall. It is probably used as a place of deposit for money and valuables, but on the night of the 29th contained only a bunch of keys and a small gold-mounted flask half filled with brandy.

K is a small closet in which are kept unbound sheets of the Bones Society catalogue and a set of handsome memorabil books, one for each year. Some of the old memorabil is quite curious, and the collections relating to recent years are very complete.

The Bones catalogue is essentially as described in Four Years at Yale.

The doors to E and F, which are used as general storerooms, are protected by plates of sheet-tin, but the locks were not "what we may call" proof against skeleton keys. The memora bilia in these rooms was noteworthy for amount rather than quality. However, in the midst of a good deal of rubbish we found four or five boating flags, and a number of old Greek, Latin and German works in MS. None of these were society records, but works of well-known authors; into the genuine antiquity of the MSS. we have not as yet been able to examine.

In conclusion, we will say that a thorough examination of every part of the Temple leads us to the conclusion that "the most powerful of college societies" is nothing more than a pleasant convivial club. The kitchen contains the materials for serving refreshments for the inner man; there are neither billiard tables nor any kind of musical instrument in the building; there is a total absence of all the "machinery" which we had been led to expect; the bell heard on initiation nights is not "the old college bell;" Skull and Bones has no secrets beyond a few that may be handed down annually by word of mouth, and no written constitution beyond a few directions similar to the suggestions appended to the Delta Kappa by-laws.

Before leaving the hall, it was asked whether we should inform other members of the college of what we had done, and throw open the hall to the public. We think no one will deny that we had it in our power at one stroke not only to take away forever all the prestige which her supposed secresy has given this society, but to make her the laughing-stock of all college, and render her future existence extremely doubtful. But while we had no consideration for the mysterious popiecock of Skull and Bones Society, we nevertheless remembered that some of the Bones men of '77 are our warm personal friends, and therefore we preferred a less radical course. To Bones as a pleasant convivial club, we have no objections. Let her live on as long as men enjoy good suppers and quiet whist. But her mystery and her secresy are at an end, and we hope her absurd pretensions and her popiecock are dead also.

The burglary was not discovered until the following evening, at about eight o'clock. All day Saturday the great Skull and Bones lay at the mercy of any one who might notice the back window.

How thoroughly the society was frightened can be seen by the way they have sealed up the window through which we entered, as well as more recently all of the other five basement openings. We have no idea that Skull and Bones will deny that their hall has been entered, for we are not without proofs that our tale is true. We have above spoken of different manuscripts, trinkets and memorabilia as existing in the Temple. In several cases we should have written "*existed,*" for the place that knew them shall know them no more forever. In short, while robbery was not our errand, on the principle that the second thief is the best owner we helped ourselves to a few pieces of memorabil, which can be put on exhibition, and a few documents which can be printed, should any authoritative denial be made to any essential point in this statement. Nor will Bones' usual policy of silence avail to throw discredit upon our story. Part of our memorabil has been seen by Senior neutrals, and the remainder will be put where it will do the most good, as soon as the protection of a sheepskin has been placed between us and the Faculty and the law.

YALE COLLEGE, 1877.

SCROLL AND KEY FOUNDED 1842

Raymond Jacob Albright
Delavan Munson Baldwin jr.
John Robert Halsey Blum
Prosser Gifford
Roger Lee Hadlich
Henry Brandebury Hager
Larry Lee Jenney
Robert Charles Johnson

Scroll & Key Membership Listing, Yale *Banner*, 1951

William Redington Lynch
John Thomas Mackelfresh
Briton Martin jr.
Edward Andrew Mearns jr.
Larom Beckley Munson
Raymond MacFarlane Reid jr.
James Stillman Rockefeller jr.

The Temple of the Order of Scroll & Key, 1898

THE TOMB GRAFFITI TRIAL OF 1878

FROM *THE YALE NEWS*

VOL. II – NO. 47. JUNE 17, 1878. NEW HAVEN, CT

LAST THURSDAY NIGHT

LAST THURSDAY NIGHT the hall on the corner of College and Wall streets, occupied by the Scroll and Key Society, was painted by some unknown person in such a manner as to deface and seriously mar the fine effect of the marble front. All college disapproved the act, and many were glad when it was known that two detectives were engaged in working up the matter. Many, however, considered that the more dignified stand taken by the Skull and Bones Society which had suffered a similar, though from the nature of the building material, less injury would have been the proper treatment.

Friday afternoon several suspicious looking men went through South college in a vague sort of a way, inquiring for bed-room sets, etc., and during annual, one room at least was searched.

Early in the evening Edmund R. Terry, a Senior, from Brooklyn, was pointed out to a constable by a classmate named Jewett. Several men were at the fence at the time, and so the demand for a warrant was met by the answer: "You can't come any Sandy Hollow game over me," allusion being made, according to Chief Allen, to a resident in Sandy Hollow, a low part of New Haven, who demanded to see a warrant and, on its being produced, relieved the constable of it. He was finally persuaded to exhibit his warrant to Terry at a distance from the, party. Terry was taken to the Station House, and bailed out by a classmate, Mr. Briggs. Herbert W. Bowen, also a Senior and Brooklynite, was arrested a little later, and bailed by Mr. A. A Dershimer, '78.

The warrants were examined, and the charge found to be, "defacing the building of the Kingsley Trust Association.

The names of E. S. Charlier, and J. W. Eaton, '79; M. Wilcox, '78; and Tutor E. S. Dana appeared as prosecuting witnesses.

By nine o'clock Friday morning, the Court room was crowded with students, among whom were the following Keys men: Tutor Dana, John A. Porter and M. Wilcox, '78, and TenEyck and Donaldson, '79, and several graduates, among them Frank Ingersoll and John W. Alling of this city. No Bones men were visible.

The disposal of three drunks, and a family jar occupied the Court until. 10, and during this time some of the audience got tired and departed. Finally the case of E. R. Terry was called, and the charge of defacing Keys hall read. Terry plead not guilty, and E. S. Dana took the stand. Tutor Dana testified that he was a member of the Kingsley Trust Association, and one of the trustees of the building. He saw the building after the defacement of Thursday night. Mr. Doolittle, attorney for the defence, objected to the word defacement. It was changed, and the witness proceeded to testify that "the hall had been ornamented — we will say decorated, adorned, — " by laying on in black paint, in front and at the side, of certain ,figures.

"What were those figures?"

"A 5, a 2, and a 2."

E. S. Charlier testified that he was a member of the Junior class resident at 82 Wall street. First saw Terry on Thursday night at 10:30 near Farnam College. He came up and peered into my face. We went over to Key's Hall. There Terry came up and looked into my face. I saw a man at work in front of the hall. Quite a number of men, presumably students were on the N. E. corner. They crossed the street one by one, and, without addressing the painter inspected his work.

Mr. C. testified to a conversation with Bowen, in which Bowen warned him, not to interfere. He did not see the painter's face. Failed to recognize him. Could not describe him. Does not know whether he was a collegian or not.

When the work was done, he followed the painter, endeavoring to ascertain who he was. Bowen went with him. They went down Wall to High, but failed to overtake the painter, although neither party ran. Three or four men were with the painter, who had a pot or vessel of paint with him.

The inscription on the steps was

522

SCULL & BONE.

On the side were two or three 522's.

Does not know to what purpose the building is applied.

The Keys society has no peculiar number to his knowledge. One society in college employs the number 322. Mr. C. was asked if he belonged to any college society. "I belong to Linonia."

"Are you a secret member of Keys?

"I am a member of no secret organization in Yale College."

James W. Eaton was called and testified that he met Terry near the south entry of Farnam, between 10:30 and 11:30 Thursday evening. Had a conversation with him. Terry told him of the decoration of the hall, and stating that he had taken no part in the procedure. Had produced a small tube of pigment done up in foil, with the remark that it would make "first-class memorabil."

This closed the case against Terry.

The defense did not introduce any evidence. Pickett, for the prosecution, claimed that Terry had aided and abetted in a conspiracy to deface the hall.

Doolittle, for the defense, called the act a harmless college prank. All injury to the hall could have been removed in a few hours with a little common sense and some potter's clay. The numbers were evidently placed there merely to cause laughter. If Terry had no right to be present, how came Charlier there? Charlier was equally guilty. Eaton's evidence was for the defense, for he had testified that Terry had stated at the time that he had no part in the proceedings.

The Court very justly pronounced the work as low and mean and beneath the dignity of any one who pretended to be a gentleman, but said that there being no conclusive proof, he would have to nolle the case.

Bowen's case came next and seeing no hope of convicting him by Mr. Pickett's tactics, Alling came to the rescue.

E. S. Charlier testified that he had seen Bowen on the corner of Wall and College streets, Thursday evening. He had but a slight acquaintance with Bowen, having been casually introduced a week before. Nevertheless, he went up to Bowen, notwithstanding the fact that Bowen was an upperclass-man.

Bowen had remarked "Good evening." Charlier replied, "I think this is nice, don't you?" Bowen said in effect that it was none of his business. Charlier said, "I call this low business for a gentleman, a gentleman of Yale." All the rest of the party crossed the street separately. Bowen and Charlier crossed together. They followed the, painter together until Bowen advised Charlier to give tip the pursuit, saying, "What are you meddling here for? You will get into trouble."

Mr. Alling: "Is Bowen a member of Scroll and Key?"

Charlier: "No. He has the reputation of being 'sat on' in his own class."

Mr. Doolittle: "Have you the reputation of making bets and not paying them in your own class?"

Pickett objected and the question was not pressed.

Pickett began asking about Senior societies, but Ailing and Marion Wilcox spoke to him and he desisted.

Doolittle wanted to know if Charlier was a candidate for membership in Keys. Pickett objected. Charlier's impression was that Bowen was superintending the matter. He, supposed Bowen was engaged in mischief and "volunteered, the information that he thought it was a low business for a gentleman." Doolittle considered such remark to a mere bystander an insult.

Charlier considered himself "as much a gentleman as you are, and" [with a splendid stage gesture] "I appeal to you, your honor."

His honor told him to go on with his evidence. After some evidence of' trifling importance, Eaton was called, and testified that he had seen Bowen enter the South entry of Farnam rapidly, Thursday evening, in a dark suit of presumably old clothes. He wore a slouch hat, and had his coat collar turned up about his neck.

E. R. Terry was called and testified. Saw Bowen last Thursday night across from Keys hall. Could not say whether he had seen Bowen on College, West of Wall, that evening or not. Did not know who painted the hall. Had not asked. Did not see or recognize the man, as his back was turned. Thought he was disguised. Did not know. Did not know whether the painter was a college main or not. Had not entered into any conspiracy with Bowen to deface the hall. Did not, wish to testify for fear of criminating himself. He refused to "give away" the parties who were present, and then made a slip and mentioned the name of a well known Senior. He had purchased some black paint from Cutler for ten cents. Had painted signs with it. Asked if he had lent any paint to some one named Moore or Moores, or something similar. He had. Had he been in this man's room. Was in considerable doubt. Finally said he believed he had. He was in the habit of going there.

He had seen some paint there. It was less than four pounds. Had no conversation relative to Keys hall on the evening and in the room mentioned. Had however a prior knowledge of the decoration. Had gone over to the hall on purpose to see it. Did not know who invited him — went in response to a mere campus rumor.

Did not belong to same society as Bowen; B. was a Psi U. man, T. a member of D. K. E. Was not a member of 522. If he had been he would have objected to the name of the society being painted in such a place. Terry's paint can was not out of his room that night. Refused to say who was across the street from Keys hall.

Tutor Dana was called. He saw B. pass him with a rush and enter his, room, Thursday night. Came out in response to a call. "He and a crowd started off on a brisk walk, attended by a peculiar motion of the heel and toe, characteristic of the Keys society; an old but, somewhat childish custom, I should like to be permitted to observe. I heard Bowen start up a song of a popular character, sometimes sung by the society of Scroll and Key, and hence these gentlemen — ." He was stopped by Mr. Doolittle.

Alling spoke for the prosecution, and Doolittle for the defense.

Doolittle gave Ailing some "taffy" about his membership in Keys. Called him the real conspirator, compared him to Catiline. So sensitive, you know. Argued that there was no proof of Bowen's participation or conspiracy. Called it a college jest. The society considered its hall not disfigured and disgraced by the paint, but by the emblem of a rival Society.

Judge Peck spoke a few minutes treating the perpetrators of the outrage with the contempt they so well deserve, but acquitted Mr. Bowen with the remark that he considered the case as beneath the dignity and unworthy the attention of the Court, and the remark that though he considered Terry's testimony as sufficient proof of the existence of a conspiracy, there was no proof of Bowen's participation. The case was therefore nolled.

***

Some other notes from same issue:

The man who arrested Terry told I him that if he would turn State's evidence he would be released.

Within a quarter of an hour after court adjourned Saturday, one of the prosecuting witnesses was discharging debts of honor, the result of the spring regatta.

A lawyer was heard Saturday afternoon to say, "This is the first time in the history of the college that one Yale man has testified in Court against another."

The college generally will support the sentiment expressed by some one, Saturday, after the trial. There is just one man in college meaner than the man who painted Keys Hall. He is the man who went into Court and testified against a fellow student.

***

FROM AN UNNAMED LOCAL NEW HAVEN NEWSPAPER ACCOUNT
(CUT OUT - CIRCA JUNE, 1878.)

COLLEGIATE VANDALISM

TRIED FOR DEFACING A BUILDING.

HOW THE HALL OF SCROLL AND KEY WAS DEFACED.

JUDGE PECK THINKS THE MATTER ONE TO BE SETTLED OUT OF COURT.

THE CITY COURT ROOM was crowded with students this morning, who had gathered to witness the trial of Edmund R. Terry and Herbert W. Bowen, arrested on a charge of having aided, abetted and conspired to deface the hall occupied by the Scroll and Key Society on the corner of College and Wall streets, on the night of the 13th inst. The accused were defended by Tilton E. Doolittle, and Mr. Pickett was assisted in the prosecution by John W. Alling, of the class of '62, and a former member of Scroll and Keys.

The first party tried was Mr. Terry. Edward S. Dana, a tutor at Yale, testified that he saw the building after its defacement on the night of the 13th, and also on the same day. He saw the figures "522" on the wall between the staircases leading into the building, painted on the white wall in black figures. He also testified that the building belonged to the Kingsley Trust association, of which he was one of the trustees. Mr. E. S. Charlier, a Junior, who "gave the business away," next told his story. He was going by Farnam hall on the night when the ornamentation of the hall took place, and there saw Mr. Terry, who looked at him full in the face two or three times, he returning the look, so as to be able to fully recognize Terry. He then went along up to Wall street where he has rooms, and found some one engaged in artistic work at Keys hall, and fonr[sic] students, two of whom he recognized as Terry and Bowen, looking at the work, the latter apparently superintending it. He addressed Bowen with whom he had a[n] jgh[sic] acquaintance and returned the salutation. Then Charlier said "Don't you think this is nice business," and Bowen responded "It's none of your business." Mr. Charlier said "I call it low business for a gentleman of Yale to be engaged in." He was then informed that it would be a very healthy thing for him to do to avoid meddling and go about his own business. At this point the painter whose back was kept studiously turned toward him went away, being escorted by one of the party, the other three remaining behind and intimating to him that he must not interfere and that if he did there would be trouble. He followed the painter for some distance and finally thinking discretion the better part of valor, left the party and went home. Mr. James W. Eaton another junior testified to having seen the ornamentation, as it had pleased Mr. Doolittle to call the defacement. He had also seen Mr. Terry at Farnam college that evening, and they had some conversation in relation to the matter of the decoration, Mr. Terry telling him what was done, and taking a small can of pigment from his market remarked, "This will make a first-class memorabil.' He described the disfiguring of the walls of Keys Hall, which bore in black paint the legend "522 Scull and Bone 522[.]" This closed the case against Terry who did not testify at that time, and after short arguments in which Mr. Doolittle claims that nothing was proven and Mr. Pickett that there was a clean case against Terry of his having cognizance of, and aiding in or abetting the disgraceful work. The court pronounced the work as low, mean, and beneath the dignity of any one who pretended to be a gentleman, but said he should have to order the case nolled, as there was no conclusive proor[sic] against him.

Then came the case against Bowen, and Mr. Alling, seeing there was no hope of convicting him in the way in which Mr. Pickett had been conducting the first, came to the rescue, in order to convict, if possible, the one who was supposed to be the principal in the affair. Tutor Dana testified to having seen a party of four or five students on the Campus, among whom was Bowen, who, when they saw him, started off in the childish walk assumed by the members of the Scroll and Key society, and began to sing a song which is sung by the members of that society almost exclusively. Where they went to he did not know. Mr. Charlier repeated his testimony given in the case against Terry, identifying Bowen fully as the man to whom he said that the "ornamentation" in progress was low business, altogether too low for a gentleman at Yale to be implicated it. He also reaffirmed his statement that Brown said "You'll get into trouble if you meddle." He testified further that he saw Bowen go over or and instruct the painter who was engaged in the disgraceful job, and that Bowen stood within a few feet of him while the painting was in progress. When the party left the building he saw the one that did the painting, whom he did not recognize, and another of the students, each carrying a paint pot.

There was considerable talk about secret societies, witness answering that he belonged to no society in Yale, and he was asked if Mr. Bowen did not belong to one the secret societies. His reply was, "No, sir, Mr. Bowen has the reputation of being one of the men in his class who was …

{unreadable}

… statement was greeted with hisses by the students in the room. One of them sitting near the reporters table said, "He'll get h—l for that when he gets to college."

Mr. Doolittle turned to the witness when the excitement had subsided and asked, "Haven't you the reputation among the students of being one of those men who refuse to pay bets they have made, when you lose?" This question was greeted with laughter and applause by the students, but court -ordered the witness not to answer the question, and ordered the crowd to keep quiet. The cross-examination elicited no new facts, and Mr. James W. Eaton was called, and testified to having seen Bowen go into Farnham college soon after 11 o'clock, with an old suits of clothes on, his collar turned up, and a slouch hat pulled down over his eyes. He recognized him by his height.

There was considerable excitement when Edmund R. Terry was called, and as he took the stand he appeared to be a most unwilling witness, and appearances in the case were not deceitful this time. He testified to having seen Bowen on the evening on which the outrage was committed, and also to having seen him during the daytime of the same day, but denied that he had entered into any conspiracy with him to deface the building, giving his testimony hesitatingly and guardedly. He testified that he had purchased some black paint, which he had used in painting a sign of furniture for sale. He said he had loaned the paint to one Moore, living in the same building, but on the floor below him, the paint to be used for the same purpose he had used it, and acknowledged having been in Moore's room during the evening, but denied that any conversation relative to the painting of Keys' hall had been had there. He refused to tell who was there beside him, or what the conversation was, on the ground that it might tend to criminate him. He acknowledged having visited Keys hall to see the "decoration," and said that Mr. Charlier's statement was substantially correct, as to his visit. He refused to tell who were in the party besides himself and Bowen, the court sustaining him in his refusal, he claiming that his sense of honor would not allow him to "give away" the parties who were present. He said the party who did the work was disguised, but that he could not tell what the disguise consisted of, as the party kept his back constantly turned toward the street. He acknowledged that both he and Bowen were witnesses of a portion of the defacing, but denied that they knew of it before it was done.

Short arguments by Mr. Doolittle and Mr. Alling followed, the former claiming that no conspiracy was proven and that the boys happened to be there as spectators as did Mr. Charlier, and that if there had been a conspiracy, Mr. Bowen would have tried to keep out of the way himself. Mr. Alling held that there was a clear case against the men who, with others of the "Mythical 522" failing to gain elections to either of the secret societies had taken this method of revenge.

The court (Judge Pack) nolled the case, saying that there was no doubt but that the accused knew of the outrage, but that it was a college prank. If a Grand street boy had done the work, he said, I should fine him $25 and costs, and perhaps send him to jail. This is a student's frolic, done in a spirit of fun, and should be settled at the college, and not brought to this court. He therefore, greatly to the surprise of the majority present, ordered a nolle entered in the case.

Wolf's Head

FOUNDED 1883

HENRY HORNBLOWER ATKINS
DONALD ADELBERT BOYNTON
EDMOND TAYLOR CHEWNING, JR.
WILLIAM WELCH COLLIN, III
WINTHROP PALMER ELDREDGE
ROBERT ANDERS EMILE
JAMES HINCHMAN GOODENOUGH
BENJAMIN AVERY HAMMER
WILLIAM FRANCIS HOWE, JR.
JULIAN STEVENS KAISER
JOHN STUART LOVEJOY
JOHN CURTIS MCILWAINE
EDWARD GOWLING OAKLEY
JOHN HIGGINS REMER
FREDERIC LINCOLN ROCKEFELLER
WILLIAM SUTCLIFFE SAGAR, JR.
THOMAS FRANCIS SCANNELL, JR.
MICHAEL SCOTT
WILLIAM HAMMEL SHANNON
ROBERT KASTOR ZELLE

WOLF'S HEAD MEMBERS – 1947
FROM THE YALE *BANNER*

THE FOUNDING OF WOLF'S HEAD

JOHN WILLIAM ANDREWS
THE FOUNDING OF WOLF'S HEAD – 1934

THE GREAT GOD POPPYCOCK

CROTONIA was certainly one of the first of the Yale societies. Little is known of it but it serves us here, for just as Wolf's Head was the product of a wave of protest against the things for which Skull and Bones and Scroll and Key stood in 1883, so the first society to enjoy a long and distinguished life at Yale was started, in part, as a protest against the ways of Crotonia.

THE WOLF'S HEAD SOCIETY'S ORIGINAL HOUSE CIRCA 1900

Linonia, organized in 1753, was apparently a "crusading" movement designed to bring more democracy to the College. One reads this between the lines of the brief story of Linonia's origin (the italics in the following quotation are the writer's): "Of the class which graduated that year [1754], numbering 17 in all," says the author of *Four Years at Yale,* "one only belonged to the society [Linonia]. He was the seventeenth on the list-the names at that time being arranged *according to the 'gentility' of the families they represented, instead* of *alphabetically."* Crotonia lived on for a few years only, while Linonia came into blossoming days and survived, finally only as a shell of former glory, for over a hundred years.

Linonia, however, was at first closed to freshmen, who "in those days of servitude" were never "admitted to any Society whatever"; and in 1768 Brothers in Unity was founded, definitely a crusading movement. We are told that it was organized "by 21 individuals in the four classes of [17]68, '69, '70, and '71 — seven being upper-class men who seceded from Linonia, and the remaining 14 being Freshmen, who were of course neutrals." The hero of this movement was a freshman "who stood up for the dignity of his class; and having found two Seniors, three juniors and two Sophomores, who were willing that Freshmen ... be admitted to a literary Society, he, with thirteen of his classmates fought for and established their own respectability." Brothers in Unity forced the pace on Linonia, just as Wolf's Head did later on Skull and Bones and Scroll and Key. Linonia opened its doors to the freshmen and thereafter for many years the two societies competed on a basis of equality.

Both Linonia and Brothers in Unity were secret societies; but their secrecy never reached the dignity of "poppycock " — the generic term adopted later by the Yale undergraduate to denote all the elements in the secret society system to which he objected. The chief competition between these societies was in the matter of numbers, each attempting to get "the largest number of the incoming class." Such rivalry in secrecy as existed was a rivalry between two groups of "ins," stimulated to a friendly game of hide-and-seek, it being thought "a great — as it was an infrequent — triumph for a man to find out the name of the president or other officers in a rival society." Both societies, too, had much to engross their attention besides the preservation of mystery. They served an important function in a College still inadequately organized. The accumulation of books was begun by them at a very early period; and by 1870, the number of books in each of the two libraries had reached approximately thirteen thousand. The societies also had reading rooms, which were in general use. In addition, the meetings in their halls, while in part devoted to the popular "pea-nut bums," initiations, elections and the like, included also formal and informal debates, the delivery of orations and the reading of essays and poems, all so much the vogue in those times; and in their hey-day — after 1825 — the societies occasionally put on "exhibitions": "a dramatic poem, a tragedy, and a comedy, all written for the occasion," being delivered or acted, each society trying to outdo the other.

They were general societies in the truest sense of the word, and lived for many years without creating a need for reform.

A third important society was founded in 1779 — the Yale Chapter of Phi Beta Kappa. It was not, apparently, a crusading movement, for it did not compete with the existing societies. It was a national society, giving the "bulk" of its elections to the juniors during the third term, as the senior societies do to this day. Admission to the Society was considered "one of the greatest honors in college"; and in spite of stray cases of personal prejudice and personal favoritism, scholastic achievement was the sole criterion for membership, "the society confining its elections pretty closely to the list recommended it by the faculty, in response to its own application therefor."

Phi Beta Kappa also had important educational activities, supplementing, like those of the general societies, only more seriously, the aIl-too-rigid curriculum of the day. "The exercises consisted of an oration and a debate. ... The day after Commencement, it was customary to hold an 'exhibition,' when two orations were delivered by tutors or other graduates, and a debate was engaged in by four undergraduates." As these exhibitions gradually grew in interest and importance, it was decided to make them public, "and in the 42 years, 1793-1834, there were only 12 Commencements when the Society failed to display itself." Like Linonia and Brothers in Unity, Phi Beta Kappa was an institution with an important private and public life in the College.

It was, however, a secret society; more secret — though in exactly what manner we are not told — than the general societies and hence more open to the temptations of generating "poppycock." Certainly its secrecy was the secrecy of a small group of "ins" against a much larger group of "outs"; and as was to happen so often and so notoriously later on in the case of Skull and Bones and Scroll and Key, "poppycock" was accompanied by its corollary-attacks of a physical nature by the "outs."

In the history of Phi Beta Kappa there is record of at least two breakings-in by the "neutrals" of the College, acting, we are told "under the united influence of envy, resentment and curiosity." In 1786 three seniors broke open the door of the secretary's study and "feloniously took, stole, and carried away the secretary's trunk, with all its contents." They were discovered, the papers returned and the thieves appeared before a general meeting of the society with a "voluntary" written confession, swearing never to divulge whatever secrets they had discovered. A year and a half later the trunk was once more raided and its contents stolen, the perpetrators, this time, never being discovered.

But about 1825 a much more serious event took place. "A clamor against Masonry and secret societies generally... swept over the country." It seems to have swept through the American colleges as well and to have resulted in the removal of its secret character from Phi Beta Kappa. "With its mystery departed its activity also; and for forty years past" — the statement is from *Four Years at Yale,* published in 1871 — "it has been simply a 'society institution' possessed of but little more life than it claims to-day, though membership in it was thought an honor worth striving for until quite a recent period." By 1884, when the Founders of Wolf's Head were getting ready to graduate, Phi Beta Kappa was dead. The College press of the time contains reports of the efforts made by the Yale faculty to revive it. It was dead, however, past all saving except as a symbolic institution.

In 1832 with the founding of Skull and Bones begins the era of the senior societies of the type which existed in 1883. Skull and Bones was organized "by fifteen members of the class which graduated the following year" and was, in all probability, an "outs" movement, it being recorded that "some injustice in the conferring of Phi Beta Kappa elections seems to have led to its establishment." It was not a crusading movement unless — and this may well be possible — the need of the human animal for secrecy and mystery is a real need which must be satisfied. The elimination of these elements from Phi Beta Kappa-the only important grouping in senior year at this time except Chi Delta Theta, which was distinctly literary — may have left a gaping void. Certainly, like all new institutions, Skull and Bones was not taken seriously at first, being "for some time regarded throughout college as a sort of burlesque convivial club." Certainly too, there is no evidence of any very serious purpose behind its founding. In fact all of the evidence points to its being a group of congenial individuals enjoying, behind their closed doors, a rather riotous good time.

The same elements seem to have motivated the founding of Scroll and Key in 1841. It was definitely an "Outs" movement, "its founders not being lucky enough to secure elections to Bones." But unlike Skull and Bones which had created an organization quite different from Phi Beta Kappa and not in competition with it, Scroll and Key, at least in the eyes of the College, set out from the beginning to rival the older society on its own ground. "Its ceremonies, customs and hours of meeting were all patterned after those of Bones, as well as its manner of giving out elections." That it was considered a "sour grape" society is indicated by the burlesque in *The Yale Banger* of 1845, in which the Keys scroll bears the legend, "Declaration of Independence and Rejection of the Skull & Bone," and has for its Great Seal "a view of the historical fox reaching after the equally celebrated grapes." This, the author of *Four Years at Yale* remarks, "probably represents, with substantial accuracy, the motive which originated Keys."

Even more than Skull and Bones the new society had hard sledding at first, failing on at least four occasions prior to 1851 to make up its full quota of fifteen, the number in 1850 falling as low as seven; but like Skull and Bones it seems to have had no important purpose of existence other than pleasant social intercourse.

Being thus limited, these two societies were in a more precarious position than the older societies which had had definite activities, intellectual and otherwise, within and without their halls. Their very secrecy was a temptation and a handicap. It would seem that at first — during the days of their youth, ten, twenty years after their respective foundings — they were merely negatively mysterious. Their members, it seems, said nothing about their activities inside their buildings and concealed the arrangement of rooms and furniture. They used their moments of public appearance to strut a bit before they retired for another year into their " impenetrable mystery." They wore their badges merely as symbols of membership and took themselves more or less lightly as human beings in a human world.

But with no relation to the world except the self-imposed duty of perpetuating the species, and no formalized basis for choice other than a social one, these societies fell, after a while, into the temptation of using what they had most of — their mysteries and ritual — to startle the College into taking them seriously. From a negative manifestation of mystery they gradually turned to a positive manifestation; and to the ever increasing ranks of the non-society men — the College was growing slowly, but steadily — it appeared each year that the members of these societies were becoming more self-conscious in their position as the "elect" of the College; were interfering more, as societies, in College affairs; and, in general, were thrusting themselves too much upon the attention of the College world.

By 1873 the word "poppycock" was in current use and the "god" who had started life so modestly had become great. But already in 1870 he was strutting and had been strutting for some years. The elements which had gradually come to constitute his most objectionable features will be familiar to all, for many of the hydra-heads have not been severed even to this day, and some which were once severed have grown back again.

It is to be supposed, since there is no evidence to the contrary, that from the beginning the members of both Skull and Bones and Scroll and Key wore their badges on their neckties. But by 1870 the light-hearted wearing of a symbol of membership had become a solemn ritual surrounded by ritual. "This badge is constantly worn by active members," says the author of *Four Years at Yale* (from which volume many of the preceeding[sic] quotations have been taken), "by day upon the shirt bosom or necktie, by night upon the night dress. A gymnast or boating man will be sure to have his senior badge attached to what little clothing he may be encumbered with while in practice; and a swimmer, divested of all garments whatever, will often hold it in his mouth or hand, or attach it to his body in some way, while in the water." And as for anyone touching the pin or speaking of it or of the society, the words of the *Horoscope,* written much later, vividly describe the result: "[the society men] rise up abruptly, put their ears behind their beads and sneak off."

A similar ritual was built up around the society buildings: the mystery that might rightly have attached to the four walls of the meeting place being extended to unwarranted distances. The impressive Skull and Bones tomb was erected in 1856, and Scroll and Key inhabited, until the completion of their fine hall on College Street in 1870 rooms "in the fourth story of the Leffingwell Building, corner of Church and Court Streets, across from the Tontine Hotel." We are not told directly that the entire Leffingwell Building was held sacred; but we know that by 1870 the senior society men had progressed to the length of at times refusing "to speak while passing in front of their hall" and even "in some cases [of refusing] to notice a neutral classmate whom they may chance to meet after eight o'clock of a Thursday evening."

Such items of ritual, inasmuch as they related specifically to society paraphernalia, might not have been deemed offensive by the "neutrals" of the College and might have been without harmful results had they been restricted at this point. But once embarked upon, the habit of flaunting their special position in the face of the College grew upon the society men of successive classes like the growing hold of the drug habit.

In 1867 an all-time "high" for the period up to 1870 had been reached. In that year the College, which was apparently not too much concerned over bad manners on the part of senior society men where their pins and buildings were concerned, was distinctly shocked. We know one of the causes. "Two Bones men," we read, "brought from their meeting a sick classmate and put him to bed in his room, without paying any attention to his neutral chum who was there present, though he was also a classmate with whom they were on friendly terms." But there must have been other incidents which have not come down to us, for the young author of Four *Years at Yale,* an undergraduate at this time, speaks of "exaggerated secrecy" as "a modern outgrowth," and refers to 1867 as the year of its "highest pitch." He indicates clearly that the College did not take it lying down and that as a result of the furore the senior society men thereafter "conducted themselves much more sensibly."

But this temporary recession of the tide was to be followed by new "highest pitches." It is easy to imagine the process, for ritual is a coral growth: new ceremonies are added, but few are ever cut away. With the intense rivalry that existed between Skull and Bones and Scroll and Key the inventive genius of the immature youngesters[sic] of the successive delegations must have been continuously at work. They took what they found after their election and then, consciously and unconsciously, set about devising new ways and means of impressing the underclassmen. They invented new taboos to emphasize a superiority they may or may not have felt at first. Later, by a boomerang effect, the taboos became hourly proof of an existing superiority, till it came to be believed. Ultimately, they and all those with whom they came in contact were unhappily aware of a chasm between the "elect" and the "non-elect."

The proof of the process is partly illustrated by a story appearing in an 1890 Buffalo, New York, newspaper. The story contains no hint as to the date of the incident, though it is evidently ancient history. It may be apocryphal. It is illuminating, nevertheless. As in the 18 67 incident a member of Skull and Bones was lying sick in his room at the hour of the regular Thursday evening meeting. His "neutral" roommate was in attendance. Members of Skull and Bones made their appearance; but this time their care and attention was not limited to a putting to bed and a departure. The technique had become enlarged. In one-hour shifts the members of the delegation came to sit by the sick man's bed. They ignored the roommate completely and their relation with their brother member was that of the deaf and dumb.

This particular story ended happily. After the second visitation the roommate bolted the door and stoutly informed the next arrival that no deaf-mutes need apply.

The God's Enemies

It was not to be expected that the College "neutrals," already at a disadvantage through their position as "outs" and sometimes smarting under a sense of injustice, should have remained inhibited in the expression of their feelings or that they should always have been as restrained as the roommate of the deaf-mute invasion.

Each "highest pitch" on the part of the society men was met by a corresponding "highest pitch" counter-activity on the part of the enemy, this activity taking on forms ranging from cat-calls and physical violence to diatribes in anonymous pamphlets and bitter complainings in such College publications as might by chance become available.

THE CURRENT WOLF'S HEAD SOCIETY COMPOUND AT YALE. THE PROPERTY IS COMPLETELY SURROUNDED BY A HIGH STONE WALL. THE BACK BUILDING APPEARS VERY CHAPEL-LIKE.

An entirely unofficial institution, first known as "Bowl and Stones" and later as "Bull and Stones," was the rallying ground for the attacks. *Four Years at Yale* gives us the picture for the years 1865-1869. "It is in senior year alone," says its author, "that the neutrals largely outnumber the society men, that they have nothing to hope for in the way of class elections, and that they are not overawed by the presence of the upper-class men. These circumstances combine to foster in some of them a sort of reckless hostility toward these societies. ... It was in the class of '66 that this hostility first definitely displayed itself, in the institution of a sort of mock 'society' called 'Bowl and Stones" the name being a take-off on that of Bones, and the duties of its members being simply to range about the colleges at a late hour on Thursday night, or early on Friday morning when the senior societies disbanded, singing songs in ridicule of the latter, blocking up the entries, and making a general uproar. The refrain of one song, to the tune of 'Bonnie Blue Flag,' was 'Hurrah! Hurrah! for jolly Bowl and Stones'; of another to the tune of 'Babylon,' 'Haughty Bones is fallen, and we gwine down to occupy the skull.' ... In the class of '67 they were at their worst, and wantonly smashed bottles of ink upon the front of Bones hall and tore the chains from its fence."

By the early 1870's "Bowl and Stones" had become "Bull and Stones," a well established institution occupying a definite and permanent place in the minds of the undergraduate "neutrals" and the object of constant comment by them. The *Naughty-Gal All-Man-Ax,* for example, devoted much time and space in its issue for 1875 to the origin-entirely imaginary, of course — of this Yale institution. "Of all the college societies now in existence," it says, "Bull and Stones is the oldest. Before even Hasty Pudding or Phi Beta Kappa were thought of, this fraternity could number its years by the score. Bull and Stones was founded Commencement Day, 1776, by the Rev. Elisha Williams, Rector of Yale College, Ezra Stiles, Jeremiah Day (both Presidents of the University), the Governor of the State, and other prominent men … . Its hall is — no one knows where. However, there is a rumor current that the elected from '76 are to build a fine new hall on Hillhouse Avenue."

In one class the "neutrals" went so far "as to procure a small gilt representation of 'a bull' standing upon 'stones,' which was worn … even in public … during the first term of their senior year."

And in very close proportion to the widening of the taboos by the society men, the activities of the "Bull and Stones" men grew more and more violent and spread deeper and deeper among the "neutrals" of all classes.

The *Yale News* had not been founded in those days, and even if it had been it is to be doubted in view of its subsequent history whether it would have encouraged or even permitted editorials or communications on such a hush subject as the senior societies. The *Yale Courant* had re-acquired independent existence as an undergraduate organ in 1870; but a search in the un-indexed volumes prior to 1874-75 fails to disclose any editorial, communication or news article, or even a list of members elected, where the senior societies are concerned. And after the 1864 attack upon Skull and Bones in *The Yale Literary Magazine* (via the *leader "Co*llegial Ingenuity") had resulted in the violent war between the "neutral" editors and the Skull and Bones editors on the Board, and in the formation the same year of the unhappy "Diggers" society, "Spade and Grave," the pages of this aristocrat of the College papers were closed forever to "Bull and Stones" material.

The discontented of the College who were not satisfied with "direct action" but needed the printed word for the release of their emotions, were driven, therefore, to publications of their own creating. Even more than the "physical" violences which they often chronicled, the ideas expressed in these publications were effective in crystalizing[sic] and perpetuating from one class to another the antagonism to the societies and their methods.

The one and only issue of the *Iconoclast,* which must have startled the College when it was put on sale on October 13, 1873, was frankly directed against Skull and Bones. "Our object," said the editors, "is to ventilate a few facts concerning 'Skull and Bones,' to dissipate the awe and reverence which has of late years enshrouded this order of Poppy Cock. … Our reason for doing this, is … because we believe that Skull and Bones, directly and indirectly, is the bane of Yale College. …We speak through a new publication, because the college press is closed to those who dare to openly mention 'Bones.'"

The eight pages were full of a variety of charges. Bones, said the editors, takes upon itself to put the final stamp of approval on those whom the Class and the College have seen fit to honor: it is an insult to both Class and College. …Yale is a poor college; it cannot afford to build adequate buildings, to pay its officers properly, or even to have its magazines bound. Why? It is said that all the rich men go to Harvard. This is not so I The reason is that Bones men have "obtained control of Yale" ; "money paid to the College must pass into their hands"; no doubt "they are worthy men in themselves, but the many whom they looked down upon while in college, cannot so far forget as to give money freely into their hands." ... Again, Bones men are shown special favor by the faculty: "Is it not strange, to say the least, that on *Friday* the *Bones* men are invariably called up on the *review* by our *Bones* professor? . . ."Bones was responsible for the low state of College baseball ... Bones was responsible (by implication) for the demise of the general societies, Linonia and Brothers in Unity. ... Bones was responsible for everything that ever went wrong in the College-if one were to believe the editors of the *Iconoclast!*

And there were interminable verses:

We are not 'soreheads.' God forbid that we should cherish strong
Desires to be identified with principles that long
Have been a blight upon the life and politics of Yale, —
Before whose unjust aims the glow of 'Boss Tweed's brass would pale.
We represent the neutral men, whose voices must be heard,
And never can be silenced by a haughty look or word
Of those whose influence here at Yale could be but void and null
Did they not wear upon their breasts two crossed bones and a skull.

****

"What right, forsooth, have *fifteen* men to lord it over all?
What right to say the college world shall on their faces fall
When they approach? Have they, indeed, to 'sickly greatness grown'
And must each one with servile speech them his 'superiors own?
And after much more the "poetic" venture ends:
And if they will not hear our claims, or grant the justice due,
But still persist in tarnishing the glory of the blue,
Ruling this little college world with proud, imperious tones,
Be then the watchword of our ranks — DOWN, DOWN WITH SKULL AND BONES !"

The leading article in the *Iconoclast* contained also this statement: "When Skull and Bones was founded, the evil which we are about to unfold did not exist. It is an evil which has grown up-which is growing today." It closed with a cry which was to grow persistently louder as time went on: *"It is Yale College against Skull and Bones!!* We ask all men, as a question of right, which should be allowed to live?" All italics, capitalization and punctuation in quotations from the *Iconoclast* appear in the original.

In the same college year, 1873-74, a new departure cropped up in the war between the "ins and the "outs."

The main attack was directed this time at Scroll and Key as a result of activities which were to acquire for this society an "unsavory reputation in regard to memorabil' thieving." But there was also a subsidiary attack on Skull and Bones; and for the first time apparently, the attacks were carried on not by seniors and juniors as previously, but by members of the *sophomore* class.

The vehicle was another private publication, a pamphlet printed in the guise of an issue of the *Yale Literary Magazine* and identical with it in general appearance, except that the dignified and bewigged head of Saint Elihu Yale, and his feet, legs and knee breeches, were replaced by the corresponding members of a lowly bull, the cloven hoofs resting upon a floor of cannon-ball-like stones.

The title gave the tone of the whole: *Seventh Book of Genesis, otherwise known as the Gospel according to Scrohleankee.* It is recorded by the *Naughty-Gal All-Man-Ax,* for 1875, that it was written "by a sophomore in revenge for having some of his *memorabilia* appropriated by one of the college societies." It is dated February 1874.

The author set forth, first, the alleged state of mind of the men who founded Scroll and Key in 1841. "Wherefore do they of Pscullenbohnes," the founders were made to say, "for a space of nine years set themselves up for us to bow down before and worship? Behold, they are no better than we. Go to now, let us congregate together to make unto ourselves a graven image and a great mysterie. Let it be called Scrohleankee. And let us afterward take unto ourselves from Phortietoo such of them as are to be saved like unto ourselves. Also let Phortietoo dososummore unto Phortiethrie and so on until perchance by doing sosummore we may rival our enemy, even Pscullenbohnes." "And," said the chronicle, they did sosummore."

The pamphlet then sketched, in an irreverent manner, the progress of "Keeze" down to the year 1872, "when one Noah, surnamed Pohrturr, was King" and the freshman "Klasuv Psevventie Psyx journed that way" and, having become sophomores, beheld "the foolishness and thomfoollerrie of the mysterie of the great Poppiekock," and how "very many of the lesser tribes not yet within reach of the Gospel of Dososummore ... cast to the dogs their natural rights and groveled upon their bellies in the dust, that, peradventure, they might be accepted." It told how "a Nootrahl, bold and skillful, did fasten a banner by night from the top of the chief synagogue of the land ... and on it was written in symbolical characters, Death to Pschullenbohnes"; how a certain sophomore, "named Arayjay," brought down the flag and "loaned it ... to a Nootrahl to keep till Xmas for an altar cloth when offering burnt offerings to Bullensthone his god"; how Scrohleankee" stole the flag from the "neutral's room; how in revenge the "Nootrahls congregated 'round about the new tabernacle [the recently completed Scroll and Key tomb], reviling Keeze and singing their hymns of sacrifice"; and how "Scrohleankee [did] wax exceeding wroth, and would have gone forth and slain all, but they could not."

The story then passed to Arayjay who "vexed over the loss of his flag ... cast about him what he might do." It told how "he spake thus within himself: ... 'I will wear their pihn; yea, verily, the golden image which they worship.' ... And he did so ... and ... the Keeze men were black with rage ... Howbeit, they did not touch him for fear of his Klasmaytes." Finally it was told how certain men of the class of "Psevventie Psyx," "about the fourth watch... gathered up their loins, and taking their pots came unto Keeze Hall ... and behold, they wrote upon the door, in large characters, PSEVVENTIE PSYX. Then did they hastily depart ... and when the Keeze men saw what was done, their fury surpassed the rage of a mad cow in her wildest cavortings ... and they held Arayjay in suspicion and would have crucified him, but they could not."

The tale ended with a parable of a ram with two horns, attacked by a he-goat with one horn, who smote the ram and broke both horns; and the parable was thus interpreted: "The ram with the two horns is Scrohleankee. The horns ...are the Gospel of Dusosummore, and the doctrine of the Great Poppiekock ... . The he-goat ... is Psevventie Psyx ... and the rest of the prophecy showeth the hostility of Psevventie Psyx to Scrohleankee with its Dusosummore and its Poppiekock, and the manner in which Psevventie Psyx will destroy Scrohleankee and exterminate it utterly."

A few months before the Seventh *Book of* Genesis, another pamphlet had appeared, The Yale Literary Chronicle. The covers of the two are identical, except in color, and they are probably by the same author, for the Chronicle couches its main story in the peculiar language which was brought to such perfection in the Seventh Genesis. It celebrated, among other things, the "many jokes and tricks ... the Bullenstohnes men [did] play upon the Chosen-phew" and especially how "they did fall upon the chariot [carrying "to the Bohns men their provender"] ... and ... did seize the food ... and that night the Pscullenbohns men went hungry to bed " — a tale reminiscent of the incident related in *Four Years at Yale*: "The Stones men seized upon and confiscated for their own use the ice-cream and other good things which the confectioner was engaged in taking into Bones hall."

The year of the Iconoclast and the Scroll and Key war was memorable, however, for another event. In May of 1874, the Yale Courant, for the first discovered time, opened its editorial and news columns to discussion and news of the senior societies.

"It would be an unpardonable oversight," said the issue of May 23d," to pass without notice ... an event which occupies so much of the attention and interest of the college world as the announcement of elections to Senior societies." And the elections were not only announced and Tap Day described in detail, but the Courant embarked on a long editorial discussion of the evils of the system, particularly its creation of the politician type among the undergraduates, and closed with the bold words: "May the time soon come when Yale shall be delivered of them [the politicians] and of the system which has produced them."

Such outspokenness may have accounted in part for the quietness of the next college year. When Tap Day was approaching in May, 1875, and the Courant was once more launching its editorials, it was able to say: "The Senior society men of '75 have, as a general thing, conducted themselves in a non-offensive manner;

a great deal of that ostentatious 'poppicock' which caused so much trouble with '74 has not been put on; in fact, the way in which they have acted throughout the year has led us to the belief that a wise choice [in the coming elections] is to be made." But a warning was issued. "However," said the Courant, "whether the following year is to be a quiet one or a season of Iconoclasts, bogus pins, bum thieving, etc., rests entirely with the Society men of the Senior class, and it is to be hoped that they are fully alive to the fact."

When Tap Day was over the Courant was not satisfied and said so. The elections, on the whole, were properly given, it thought, but one man was left out of Skull and Bones "for no other earthly reason than a petty personal dislike." "That is the sentiment," said the Courant, "of the majority of men in the College"; and there was no lack of frankness in the Courant's opinion of such an act. In addition there were three surprises in the elections to Scroll and Key, and while not finding fault with the men taken in, the Courant was troubled about the men omitted. "There has been some talk," it remarked, "about setting Spade and Grave on its legs again and we think that it would be a desirable thing if it could possibly be done ... a third society is really needed in Senior year. Of course it would be difficult to start such a society, but it would surely be a success in the end, provided however, that it was a respectable organization, and not got together to 'grind' the other two."

Most illuminating of all was the Courant's news-story of Tap Day itself. "It has been handed down by tradition that Senior election night is a legitimate time for the non-society men of the Senior and junior classes to range around Bones' Hall, and make as much disturbance and trouble as possible, and then to howl, in the college yard for the rest of the evening, the praises of Bull and Stones, interfering with the society men as they give out elections, rushing them round the campus, locking them up in the entries and building bonfires .... But this year matters have been different .... Instead of congregating around Bones' Hall and making the welkin ring there, the crowd thronged the yard between Farnam and Durfee, eagerly comparing notes as the elections were given out, passing a few remarks upon the general make-up of some well-dressed Keys man, and rushing round to congratulate the fortunate or to sympathize with others. As the Bones' men went around they greeted salutations from the crowd with good natured grins, once or twice answering back in a joking way; a thing never before done and which materially assisted in repressing any tendency to rowdyism."

The Courant closed its year with another editorial: "The organizations in question propose to take in only the 'cream' of the class, and when the best part of that ingredient is left out, what else can be expected than adverse criticism?" It also printed at Commencement time a communication from a graduate of '69. "Well, really," asks E. P. W., the graduate, "has the writer [of the Courant's first editorial after Tap Day] come to regard an election to a society as one of the prizes?... The Alumni do not so regard it. ..."And at the same time the *Courant,* not to be found in support of such a system, answered: "The writer has mistaken us entirely. We never said that it was an honor to receive a Senior election. What we did say, was that it is *considered* an honor....'" (Italics theirs.)

But such frankness could not last. In the College year 1875-76, the *Courant* was once more feeding the College on a milk and water diet. There is an editorial on the society system, but the high point of criticism was that the evils were known and felt in every class. The news-story was a conventional, a fine time was had by all, and the results of the elections were "anticipated and satisfactory to the crowd and to the class." In 1877 and 1878 reference had dwindled to a mere list of names. In 1879 even the lists had disappeared, reappearing in 1880 and 1881 and vanishing again in 1882. *Courant* men, strictly "neutrals" before 1880, began in that year to receive elections: one member of the board to Skull and Bones in each of the years 1880 and 1882, and one member to Scroll and Key in 1881.

One suspects a Machiavellian technique for the muzzling of the College press. At all events, with the first return to milk and water in 1876 whether by coincidence or something more, the "Bull and Stones" violences returned.

In 1870 the author of *Four Years at Yale* had written with a measure of pride and a larger measure of foreboding: "Not yet do they [the "Bull and Stones" men] ever attempt to break into the halls of the [senior societies]." But among the memorabilia of the year 1876-77, we find a small brown pamphlet bearing the title: "The *Fall of Skull and Bones, compiled from the minutes of the 76th regular meeting of the Order of the File and Claw.*" It is dated 1876, and tells the story of an alleged breaking into the Skull and Bones tomb, "File and Claw" being obviously another manifestation of the chameleon, "Bull and Stones."

"Anyone who was noticing the Bones men of 77," the pamphlet begins, "on the morning of Sunday, October 1st, 1876, was probably struck by the crest-fallen air which characterized all of them. ... The reason for this is a simple one. As long as Skull and Bones Society shall exist, the night of September 29th will be to its members the anniversary of the occasion when their Temple was invaded by neutrals, some of their rarest memorabilia confiscated, and their most sacred secrets unveiled to the vulgar eyes of the uninitiated."

It may have been on this occasion that the theft reported in *The New Haven Register* for March 7, 1887, occurred, for dates meant as little to newspapers then as now. "The original by-laws of the Russell Trust association,'" says the *Register*, "... were stolen from the temple on High Street by a sorehead student in 1872 or '73, who had failed to get into the society itself, but did succeed in getting into the building through the roof and then making away with the by-laws."

The pamphlet says nothing about by-laws. It deals first with the details of the fortifications of the Eulogian Temple."

"The back-cellar windows," it says, "were fortified as follows: First ... was a row of one-inch iron bars; behind them a strong iron netting fastened to a wooden frame; behind this another row of iron bars, one and one quarter inches thick; and still behind this a heavy wooden shutter."

It then proceeds to the tale of the breaking-the outside bars cut "only after many hours of patient and cautious labor"; the long nails in the iron netting drawn "by means of a powerful claw"; the brick "damp-wall" dug away with a claw and hatchet; and the building entered "at just half-past ten o'clock" on the night of Friday, September 29th.

The Skull and Bones tomb is described floor by floor and room by room, the invaders having discovered, in essence, nothing which they might not have known or guessed before; but "for the benefit of future explorers, and as a directory for new-fledged Bones men for all time," they give the description and include detailed floor plans. The narrative is in all ways uninteresting. It is only important in that it is the first recorded breaking into a senior society building and that the note upon which it ends — a sincere, if slightly bombastic note-fits so accurately with all else that is known of the thoughts and activities of "neutrals."

"Before leaving the hall," the author says, "it was asked whether we should inform other members of the college of what we had done, and throw open the hall to the public. We think no one will deny that we had it in our power at one stroke not only to take away forever all the prestige which her supposed secrecy has given this society, but to make her the laughing-stock of all college, and render her future existence extremely doubtful. But while we had no consideration for the mysterious poppiecock of Skull and Bones Society, we nevertheless remembered that some of the Bones men of '77 are our warm personal friends, and therefore we preferred a less radical course. To Bones as a pleasant convivial club, we have no objections. Let her live on as long as men enjoy good suppers and quiet whist. But her mystery and her secrecy are at an end, and we hope her absurd pretensions and her poppiecock are dead also."

The Changing College and the God Challenged

THROUGH all these years one can detect a distinct change taking place in the College, fostered by the faculty, but responded to readily by the undergraduates. Yale College was growing up, "hallowed institutions" were being abolished right and left and among them, in 1875, the two sophomore societies, Beta Xi and Theta Psi.

Their abolition had been mooted for a long time, the faculty merely waiting for the proper moment and excuse. It came on Monday, May 24, 1875, a few days before that so-peaceful Tap Day of the year after the Scroll and Key "memorabil'" war, though just what happened is not clear. The Courant said of the recently tapped senior society members: "The newly elected were requested to remain in their rooms all night, probably to prevent any possible repetition of Monday night's scene"; and added, "It was no use, no one stayed in; but everyone kept sober." The Courant also, in announcing that the freshmen had been notified by their division officers not to be initiated into sophomore societies until further notice, said: "Last Monday's spree ... was the last straw that broke the camel's back."

The burial of the societies was as tumultuous as their lives. Both halls were raided by undergraduates and the appurtenances-" hymn books, the archives, the old Sigma Phi curtain, the ballot box, posters and pictures " — carried off as "memorabil'." Most bemourned was the Theta Psi raven "imported from

England and … valued at fifty dollars." The thefts were charged to the senior societies — to Scroll and Key, "that society having an unsavory reputation in regard to memorabil' thieving"; to Skull and Bones, "as a prominent Bones man was seen going up there Wednesday evening" and two Bones men were caught "at the doors of Theta Psi Thursday morning, and immediately ran away upon the approach of the Sophomores."

But significant of the changing times, no one mourned the demise of the organizations. "Talk of the Faculty disbanding them has been rife at frequent periods," wrote the Courant," it is probably done for a good reason. … The majority of thinking men in college will not be sorry for this action of the Faculty." The horseplay and general disorder they bred was becoming, intellectually at least, unfashionable.

Five years later when the Founders of Wolf's Head from the class of '84 had barely settled themselves in New Haven as freshmen "on probation," the freshmen societies, Delta Kappa and Sigma Epps, met a similar fate.

Like the sophomore societies these freshmen organizations had been notorious for years as riot breeders and wasters of time. The author of *Four Years at Yale* gives us the picture in a description that still applied in 1880: "When 'the candidate for admission to the freshman class in Yale College' draws near to New Haven," he says, "he is usually accosted with the utmost politeness by a jaunty young gentleman, resplendent with mystic insignia. …" The "jaunty young gentleman" then attempted to pledge the sub-freshman to his society, which might be Sigma Epps, Delta Kappa or Gamma Nu. On arriving at New Haven the sub-freshman was surrounded by society runners. "At a sign from the first," the account continues, it one takes his valise, another his umbrella, a third his bundle. … And before the sub-Fresh has time to protest, he is rolling along in a hack, and his new found friends are enquiring the number of his boarding house. … Sometimes the transfer to the hack is not so easily accomplished, for the runners of another society may scent the prey, rush for it, and bear it off in triumph. There are plenty of representatives from all three societies hanging about the railroad station. … They jump upon the platforms of the moving cars, they fight the brakemen, they incommode the travelers, they defy the policemen, — but they will offer the advantages of 'the best freshman society' to every individual 'candidate.'"

This picture is supplemented by the *Yale Courant,* already, in 1872, forecasting the abolition of these societies: "If they [the freshmen society runners] do their duty as we used to do it, they must visit the depot *twenty-three times a day, besides attending to the morning and night boat."* (Italics ours.)

Quite apart from all this local disorder, the vast campaign machinery that had been built up was an impossible drain on student time and money. "I was pledged while at Williston," writes Francis Bartlett Kellogg, Founder, Of '83, of his freshman society experience; and this was merely typical of the general policy of sending emissaries broadcast to the prep. schools just before Commencement to pledge members — often futily and foolishly, for we have a record that, in 1880, representatives of Gamma NO were sent to the Hartford High School and there pledged all the members of the graduating class although none of them came to Yale or, it seems, had any prospect of coming.

In addition, as had been the case with the sophomore societies, the freshman initiations, pea-nut bums, and purposeless meetings and politics were seats of continuous disorder.

The excuse to disband them appeared at the freshman initiations of 18 So. These ceremonies were held in the middle of the Garfield-Hancock presidential campaign, and presidential campaigns of that day were as immature as the horseplay of the undergraduates. Yale was largely Republican. The Democratic candidates were apparently associated in Republican minds with the rebels of the Civil War. Organization for the campaign was not casual, as witness the notice in the *Yale News:* "Order No. 2. The University Garfield and Arthur Regiment will meet for company drill at 9:30 A.M. Saturday." And by a stroke of fate the hall of the Jeffersonian Club, boosters of General Hancock, was just across the street from the initiation hall of Sigma Epps; and between the two halls was hung a "flag of the union with Hancock's name across its sacred folds."

The inevitable happened. "The initiation," writes Frank Kellogg, "turned out to be an historical event. It rang down the curtain for the freshmen societies. Incidentally, being tossed in a blanket is rather exhilarating. The grand climax, however, came with the discovery of a rope tied to a bar across one of the front windows. Investigation disclosed that the rope extended across Chapel Street and that from it, in mid-street, hung a large American flag with the words 'Hancock and English' emblazoned upon it. These were the Democratic candidates for President and Vice President. Political stupidity had anchored that rope within reach of student hands which were promptly in action. The flag was quickly hauled in and as quickly torn into a thousand pieces, henceforth to function as memorabilia of a momentous occasion."

This act, coming when the New Haven political blood was hot, assumed major political proportions.

A despicable outrage, cried the *New Haven Register,* Democratic. Give us the sacred pieces, shouted the Jeffersonian Club. It was an unpardonable act, said the *Yale News* calmly, but stop making political capital out of what was simply the act of a few rowdy Sophs at a freshman initiation. Not rowdy Sophs — upperclassmen, protested "Justice" in a communication to the *News.* And committees from the College waited on the Jeffersonian Club with apologies and offers of cash payment. The *Register* then acquired-feloniously according to the *News* the Sigma Epps constitution, publishing it in full. Dastardly, thieving act, howled the *News,* and a secret society tool The Jeffersonian Club, having turned down the cash offer and still crying for the "sacred pieces," waited surreptitiously upon President Porter and demanded-of all things-money, which commodity "peace-loving" President Porter dug out of his own pocket to quell the uproar-one hundred and two dollars and some cents. The entire College was furious at this traitorous act of the "rebs" Then the campaign ended; and with the approval "of all thinking men" the freshman societies were abolished forever.

That is, Delta Kappa and Sigma Epps were abolished. Gamma Nu, the third freshman society, and as far as can be learned, quite as much involved as the other two in the evils of campaigning, was permitted to survive. But Gamma Nu was a "reform" society. Its founders had suffered "the fate of all reformers ... despised, derided and abused." Gamma Nu men, by and large, were "harder workers, and in proportion to their numbers ... [secured] a far larger share of the substantial college awards." Even in 1870 Gamma Nu "was sometimes favored ... [by the faculty] as against the others." But most important of all, Gamma Nu was an *open* society-not exactly an open club, the ideal of the College "neutrals '!---but still not a typical "Yale secret society." Its survival was a symptom of the times.

Two other "immemorial traditions" were sacrificed in this period to the eradication of immaturity: the Thanksgiving jubilee, a more than usually riotous affair frequently censored by the faculty, and the custom of the senior societies of giving their elections in the rooms of the candidates.

The Tap Day tradition had already undergone one major change. Much earlier it had been the rule for all fifteen undergraduates of each senior society to march in a body to the room of each candidate where the elections were offered, the leader of the group, in the case of Skull and Bones, "displaying a human skull and bone," and in the case of Scroll and Key, in addition to "the large gilt scroll-and-key" being borne by the leader, with each member carrying "a key some two feet in length." This marching of an army, however, called forth the best efforts of the "neutrals" in mass formation. Free-for-alls in the rooms and entries resulted until, after a period, a major break with tradition was made and the senior society men were sent out one by one, each individual tendering an election to an individual candidate.

As we have seen this change had achieved nothing substantial and the "neutral " activities — the catcalls, bonfires and kidnappings — grew burdensome. Daylight and supervision-probably by the faculty — were required. The rites were, therefore, transferred to the Campus, to the corner under the elms next to the Chapel, and the Tap Day known to most living Yale men and objectionable to so many of them, came into existence.

Under the impact of all these abolitions the "Bull and Stones" violences dwindled. We know that the breaking into Skull and Bones —" this unprecedented vandalism " — was followed "in 1878, by another set of marauders defacing with paint both Senior buildings," that "the offenders were tried in the City Court" and that they "escaped free of fine or imprisonment, through technicalities." We know, too, that in the same year, probably as a part of this same anti-society wave, a supplement to the *Yale Year Book* was devoted in part to a cut of the Keys scroll, with key-crossing, sealed with the "Great Seal " — the fox and grapes view — and bearing the legend, obviously an imitation of the *Banger* burlesque already referred to: "Declaration of Imbecility and Rejection of Skull and Bones." The accompanying letter-press reads: "The club occupying the so-called striped zebra Billiard Hall ... after acting in the most unaccountable, ungentlemanly and underhand way during the past year, decided not to permit their cut to be used by anything except their own masterpieces of publications as the Yale Index. ... The following cut has been agreed upon by the dub as a proper heading for all college papers except the enterprising (1) *valuable* (!) yea, PRICELESS (!!) Index." (Italics, etc., in the original.)

But after 1878 there seems to have been a cessation of physical violences and less of the old childish forms of attack.

"What were the 'Bull and Stones' activities in your time?" was the question put in the recent questionnaire to the living members of the first three delegations to Wolf's Head who, together, cover the college generation, 1879-1885. "None," is the substance of the statements of the nine men who answered: Frank Bartlett Kellogg and Frank Cunningham; Founders, of '83; Franklin Davis Bowen, Henry Raup Wagner and Harry Augustus Worcester, Founders, of '84; and Albert Heman Ely, Lafayette Blanchard Gleason, William Procter Morrison and William T. G. Weymouth, of '85; either by direct statement, or indirectly by failing to answer the question. Weymouth says, "I hardly remember the name," and Gleason adds, "Not until the meeting of the Senior class in 1884."

This does not mean, however, that the "poppycock" of the society men had diminished in intensity or scope or that the College had grown reconciled to it.

We read in the New Haven press of those days of an operation in Bridgeport, Connecticut, upon a Skull and Bones man in a very serious condition after having swallowed his society pin: humorous, if it were not so sad; and Frank Kellogg writes:

"I recall a prank of Sophomore year. The D'Oyly Carte Musical Comedy Company gave 'The Pirates of Penzance' in New Haven. The pirate king wore a Napoleon hat with a skull and cross bones emblazoned on it. I enlisted the co-operation of Ted Buell and Charlie Foote in my plot and we visited the 'king' at his hotel. We told him that it would make a local hit if he would put '322' below the death's head. Then we went to the evening performance and sat in the front row of the balcony. When the 'king' appeared he had the mystic number on the hat all right.

"I don't suppose the singer noticed that several students in the audience got up and left the hall. Much less did he know that they were 'Bones' men. However, we did, and got quite a kick out of it, but more especially out of the universal grin on the faces of all the other Yale men in the audience."

But whether these activities and all they typify were confined to Skull and Bones men, or were affected by Scroll and Key men as well, and whether by all fifteen men in each society or by a few only, there is no direct evidence to show. Scroll and Key as a rule seemed to confine its unpleasantness to "memorabil'" raids and such, leaving to Skull and Bones the development of "haughty manners." In all probability, it was the old story of "high pitches" and "low pitches," for we know that the society men of '82, like their predecessors of a few classes after the "highest pitch" of 1867, conducted themselves " more sensibly." That there was an immediate reaction is proven by the tidal wave of antagonism that threatened to overwhelm the societies in 1883 and 1884.

The forerunner of this wave was a " daily anti-senior society newspaper … vigorously conducted so as to thwart the society men in every way." No copy of this publication has been discovered; but the fact that it was issued *daily* proves that its attack was, like that of the *Iconoclast,* general and not specific, and that the antagonism behind it unlike the quickly released antagonisms of the *Iconoclast,* the *Seventh Book of Genesis* and the *Fall of Skull and Bones,* was something functioning twenty-four hours a day.

The wave itself, however, was characterized by a rebellion in the ranks of the senior societies themselves, as is evidenced by an " elaborate pamphlet from a man who had belonged to the societies from each year, from first to last," and who, in spite of these affiliations, " sought to prove that the whole system was pernicious and should be abolished." This was alarming enough, but worse followed. The crusade against the societies, until then confined to the Campus activities of the "Bull and Stones" men and the presentation of views in special publications of limited circulation, spread violently outward and "was transferred to the columns of prominent metropolitan journals." The alumni bodies were infected: " alumnus and undergraduate emulated each other in striving to point out the enormities committed by the societies," and before the astonished eyes of the world-at-large, and aided and abetted by editors forever welcoming dissension at Yale to increase their circulation, "the good name of the University ... [was) dragged through the mire by her own sons."

The situation affected all Yale men, but from the point of view of the harassed societies the immediate danger lay in the fact that the attacks upon them had lost their informal and indirect characteristics. A few isolated expressions of adverse opinion could be ignored by the Yale authorities as unrepresentative. "Bull and Stones" physical violences could be cried down as immature horseplay of undergraduates and counter-attacked as clean-cut violations of law. But when "the faculty and corporation were directly appealed to" by the enemies of the system, then the situation was obviously out of hand. It was entirely possible that, legally and drastically approached, the faculty and corporation would be driven into legal and drastic action.

We have this general picture on the unimpeachable authority of John Addison Porter, prominent Yale and Scroll and Key man, in his article in the *New Englander* for May, 1884, "The Society System of Yale College." It is to be gathered directly from what he says and indirectly from what he implies. The vital nature of the question is to be read in his choice of vehicle: a publication traditionally devoted to Yale matters of the highest importance. The quality of the danger appears in his statement that whereas "the societies have never yet : been forced to ... offer explanations to their assailants, and it is extremely improbable that they will ever condescend to do so," nevertheless the occasion has now arisen "for plain words between man and man ... the time for delay, for allowing things to 'adjust' themselves, would appear to have passed."

"Whether the Yale Societies are guilty or not of the charges made against them," says Mr. Porter," is not the first question. ... The very fact that almost every year the students are more or less divided on this score, that twice within the past ten years the faculty have thought necessary to exercise their rarely used prerogative of suppressing time-honored customs the Freshmen and the Sophomore Societies augurs that germs of further dissension may exist fatal to that harmony which is indispensible(sic) to the greatest usefulness of the University."

He then proceeds to a series of charges and answers to the charges, that may well be taken as typical of the attacks and defences of the "societies war and of their extraordinary futility. The "neutrals were in the grip of psychological factors created, in part, by the presence and growth of "poppycock," while the societies were unable to recognize the impossibility of a reconciliation of views without a major change of policy.

Charge: "The Senior Societies … have muzzled the college press … ."

Answer: "On all the college press proper *(i.e.,* excepting the *Yale Literary Magazine)* the nonSenior-society men always greatly outnumber the elect"; but "to preserve a constant equilibrium [in the College] would be simply an impossibility … if general society discussions were allowed to overload the columns of college news-papers."

Charge: "The evil worms itself into our religious life … *i.e.,* by estranging from their classmates the 'deacons' who are society men."

Answer: "Coming merely as an anonymous and unauthenticated assertion, in the *N. Y. Nation,* it may be dismissed … .

Charge: The societies are over-expensive.

Answer: No men, however bitter, have boasted that they were left out of the societies simply on this score."

Charge: "College work deteriorates about the time the society elections are announced."

Answer: It is "the hottest portion of the Spring. … The discerning faculty … invariably shorten the advance work and institute review lessons … . What connection there is between the societies … and deterioration in scholarship, is not patent on the surface."

Charge: "Politics … are to some extent increased by the presence of the societies."

Answer: "The author of *Four Years at Yale,* a non-Senior Society man, and not over partial to them, states in his book, 'The part played by them in politics is simply a negative one.'"

Charge. "Favoritism rules the elections … relationships and personal friendships are acknowledged before merit."

Answer: "Year after year the nearest relatives, sons, brothers, nephews, the most cordial friends and room-mates are left out … simply because they fall below the required standard for membership."

Charge: "Men admit just *before* they join the societies … that they tend to keep the non-society men from coming back to Commencements and other reunions after graduation."

Answer: "Yale non-society men come back to New Haven more regularly and in larger numbers than the alumni of non-society colleges."

Admission and defence. "The societies ... are tempted occasionally to abuse their privileges ... . Their 'etiquette' ... which prevents them from discussing society matters with outsiders, thus being directly opposed to wirepulling, is ... commendable. When it is perverted into rudeness to strangers, or swaggering with under-classmen, it is puerile and snobbish."

Charge in conclusion: "Society influence pervades the faculty and corporation, influencing the bestowal of prizes, appointments to tutorships, etc."

Admission in conclusion: "If such cases can be authenticated they are danger signals of the downfall of the one society, or both."

Defence desperate: "It is doubtful if the faculty and corporation themselves could abolish them without legal proof that they had abused the privileges which had been guaranteed them.

The immediate cause for the publication of this article was the direct, open and organized attempt, on February 1, 1884, to kill or cure the diseased society "pyramid" by the amputation of its senior society top-knot. Said *The New Haven Register,* in 1887, "In 1884 ... opposition to 'poppycock' ... was at its height"; and *The New York Tribune,* in 1896, "From time to time the opposition to the senior society system takes organized form, but perhaps the most vigorous attack ... was made by the class of 1884"

The wave was breaking.

The senior class had met, according to custom, for the election of its class day committees: Promenade, Class Supper, Class Day, Class Cup, Ivy, and the election of a Class Secretary. Well beforehand, however, it had become known that after the transaction of this business, a resolution against the senior societies would be introduced. "[The movement] was fostered and conducted," writes Lafayette Gleason, "by William McMurtrie Speer, afterwards prominent in newspaper and legal circles in New York"; and Speer had done a thorough job. "The supporters of this motion entered the meeting confident of their ability to put it through," the *Yale News* says, and this is confirmed by the statement of the Horoscope of a year later: "There were a sufficient number who had promised to vote for it to make it a success."

The society men were genuinely alarmed. One more "abolition" in a season of "abolitions" was entirely within the bounds of possibility. They themselves conducted a counter-canvass of the class insofar as their policy of never condescending to face an opponent man to man would permit them; but this policy had them at a distinct disadvantage. The mathematics of the meeting disclose two illuminating possibilities. There were 151 men in the senior class. 117 of these voted "yea" or "nay" on the anti-society motion. 117 Plus 30 equals 147. Allowing for a few natural absences, the conclusion is inevitable either that not a single member of Skull and Bones or Scroll and Key was present at the meeting or that, being present, they were too proud to vote. In either event, they were forced to rely on such allies as could be induced to support them.

The Class Day officers were duly elected, among them a number of the men to be found among the Founders of Wolf's Head: Charles Walker, William Bristow and Charles Phelps, to the Promenade Committee of nine; William Holliday, Harry Worcester, Harry Wagner, and James Dawson, to the Class Supper Committee of five; Edwin Merritt, Henry Cromwell and Sidney Hopkins to the Class Cup Committee of three.

"The way was now clear," says the *Yale News*, for Mr. Speer to introduce the following resolution, which the meeting had declined to receive before, prefering[sic] to postpone its discussion until all other business had been transacted:

"WHEREAS, The present senior society system creates a social aristocracy, exercises an undue influence in college politics, fosters a truckling and cowering disposition among the lower classes, creates dissensions and enmities in every class, alienates the affections of the graduates from the college, stifles the full expression of college sentiment by its control of the college press.

"*Resolved,* That we believe this system detrimental to the best interest of Yale College and injurious to, ourselves. That we request the college press to publish this resolution of the senior class. That the chairman and two others, to be appointed by him, be a committee of three to lay this resolution before the president, faculty and members of the corporation."

Debate then followed, but true to the general policy of suppressing society news and views as far as possible, not a word appears in the College press, or elsewhere, of the sentiments expressed. We know only the outline of the parliamentary procedure: that after the resolution had been read, "Mr. Merritt " — no other than Edwin Albert Merritt, of '84, a Founder of Wolf's Head —" demanded that the mover should make known to the meeting his reasons for supporting it. Mr. Speer, thereupon, did so, when Mr. Merritt spoke at some length in reply. The debate was continued by Mr. Kinlay, for the resolution, and Mr. Judson, against."

Then after some skirmishing — a majority vote to lay on the table having been ruled insufficient by the chair, with a two-thirds vote impossible to secure — the motion was put to a vote. The chair ruled "that the voter, on his name being called, could answer from his seat, could whisper his vote in the ear of the chairman, or could deposit a ballot in the hat at the desk"; and amid great excitement, 117 men of the senior class, one by one, recorded their vote in these varying fashions. The process was slow, with the outcome unrevealed and in doubt. At length all the votes were in and counted.

There were 67 "nays" and 50 "yeas."

"It is a disgrace to the Yale manhood so often spoken of," writes the *Horoscope* bitterly in 1885, "that the last graduating class was unable to pass resolutions condemning the methods of the two eyesores." This from the "neutral" side. On the "society" side haste was made to follow up the advantage gained and within a few hours almost, John Addison Porter had been spurred into the preparation and proposed publication of a "defense" of the system and was abroad on the Campus collecting his material before worse should happen.

The outcome seems to have been a complete surprise both to the two older societies and to the College. It was due, however, to the introduction of a new element. In June of 1883, eight months before, entirely unknown to the College or the world-at-large, a third senior society had been successfully founded — the society which was to be called later Wolf's Head " and "The Phelps Association."

"I remember the meeting ... very well," writes Harry Wagner. "On this occasion the two older societies requested our assistance. I think that most of our members voted with them." Lafayette Gleason says: "Speer counted upon the votes of Wolf's Head members, as we were supposed to be organized in opposition to the two societies, but for obvious reasons, such as the Hall being under construction, etc., he did not get those votes."

Wolf's Head Society buildings from the front and inside the wall. Notice bricked-up windows.
From Yale *Banner* 1947

The shift of fifteen votes would, of course, have reversed the "yeas" and "nays" and brought victory to the proponents of the resolution, so that the Founding may be said to be directly responsible for the outcome. But while some of the fifteen Founders must have voted as they did from loyalty to a system of which they were now a part or from a feeling that the system was too entrenched to be affected by a mere vote, nevertheless, from an historical perspective the reason for the defeat appears to lie much deeper.

The Founders of the new Society had been, of course, of the great body of the College "outs." For this very reason they had not been bound by tradition and were able with dear eyes to discern the defects in the existing system, and to attempt its cure through the introduction of new and progressive elements rather than through the over-drastic process of the axe. Not by accident had they gathered into the platform of their institution the spirit of the ideas expressed over long years by the "neutrals" of the College-the spirit of the *Courant's* description of that one peaceful Tap Day after the bitter Scroll and Key memorabilia war: "As the Bones men went around they greeted salutations from the crowd with good-natured grins, once or twice answering back in a joking way; *a thing never before done ...*";

the spirit of the *Courant's "third* society" proposal: "a respectable organization … not *got together to 'grind 'the other two* "; the spirit of the constructive elements of the *Iconoclast,* the *Seventh Book of Genesis* and the *Fall of Skull and Bones.*

In addition, like the founders of Linonia and Brothers in Unity, they had embarked upon their venture with something of a crusading fervor — " to bring more democracy to the College." As a first witness of this, unlike the members of Skull and Bones and Scroll and Key who were skulking in their tents — haughtily absent or more haughtily present but not voting — the fifteen members of the new society were full participants in the meeting with their non-society classmates.

It would not have been possible in the course of a bitter and long debate to have kept the basic principles of the founding of the new Society wholly hidden. Wolf's Head, at this time, was still without a name; its building was no more than a foundation covered with snow; but its existence was known by this time and its membership, in part at least, identified and something of the ideas behind its founding must have percolated into the College. When, therefore, Edwin Merritt spoke "at some length" in defense of the society system — or more probably in defense of a society system in which a sense of humor would play a large part and "poppycock" none at all — it is impossible not to believe that he was listened to by his classmates with deep interest as the possible prophet of a new order, or that 'votes — whether of some of the Founders or of the "neutrals" — previously "promised" to Speer were changed under the persuasiveness of the new idea.

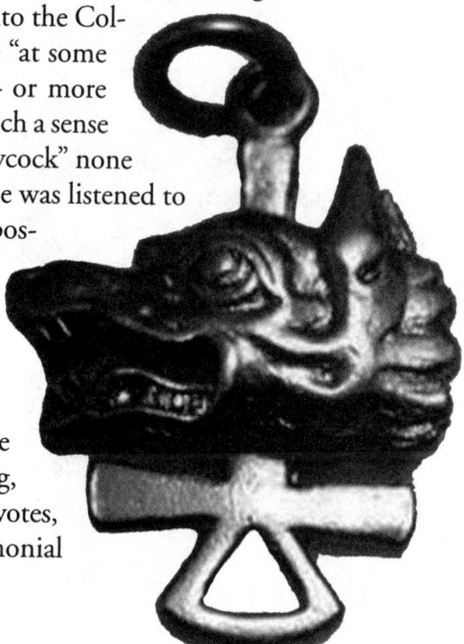

More than this, the very presence of the members of the new society at the meeting, taking part in the debate and registering their votes, must have been a happy and effective testimonial of the possibility of a new order.

Pages 17-67 of *The Founding of Wolf's Head,* by John Williams Andrews. The Phelps Association, 1934.

UNDERGRADUATE DAYS

HENRY SELDEN JOHNSTON
APPEARED IN THE *DECENNIAL RECORD OF THE CLASS OF 1896, YALE COLLEGE* – 1906

IN LOOKING ABOUT FOR A FURTHER OBSERVANCE of the general history of the Class it seems proper to count among those changes it saw transpire and those new experiences common to all, an institution not very closely connected with the University, not created at the instance of the faculty or student body, but bringing an amusement and diversion that was quite generally indulged in — namely, Poli's Theatre. Prior to the coming of the vaudeville performances the succeeding classes of Freshmen and others had made periodic descents in bands upon some dreadful melodrama or cheap comic opera at Proctor's Theatre, where was to be found more trouble than amusement; but times are now so changed in these affairs that not only is Poli's a regular resort for students, but it is even said to be a place where New Haven's superior society and Yale's Faculty are not above attending.

The mummer's art that so flourished in the universities situated in the larger cities had not racked the simple souls of Yale before our day. They had been content to read of lutes trimmed to the beating foot and to imitate in cheers the classic chorus of the frogs. The secret societies, however, had long found amusement in giving on their own hallowed stages plays that were not seriously prepared or skillfully performed, and in our middle years the junior Fraternities sought the clamor and the glare of the theatre by the public production of musical comedies, in one of which our classmates appeared as brigands, nymphs, and gallowglasses. It is amazing, now that the enthusiasm of seeing our college favorites in new roles has waned, to think of the bad acting, singing and dancing that an audience, fetched from afar and exhilarated by the conscious presence of its "nice people," would tolerate. After two performances the Faculty, not outraged at the quality — for that could be forgiven — but fearful of offending puritanism by a toleration of Dionysian revelry, forbade a further trial of the art.

No commentary, however abbreviated, on the life at Yale would be adequate without some allusion to the system of secret societies existing there. The establishment of societies is fixed, although they are continually undergoing a series of changes and developments, thereby indicating some disorder of the social state. When we entered college there were two Sophomore societies that kept the entire Class in a state of unrest throughout Freshman year; their only outward indications being exhibited by machinations in Freshman politics and by their marching in a body, as of course, into the two larger junior societies, Psi Upsilon and Delta Kappa Epsilon. In our junior year a third Sophomore society was started by the members of Ninety-Six, but shortly after our day all these Sophomore societies, having met with a widespread condemnation, were abolished by the Faculty.

At the close of our course Alpha Delta Phi, which had been a general four-year society, was made a junior fraternity, resulting in a shifting in the system to overcome the criticism then prevailing. The Senior secret societies have continued without change, except that there is to be recorded the recent birth of a non-secret Senior group styled the Elihu Club.

The subject of societies is so abundantly, though furtively, discussed in undergraduate days that any consideration of the various views would perhaps be unwelcome here, and the social problem involved is referred to only to cut the ten-year notch in our opinions, and to pause, as we reflect once more upon that powerful undercurrent of Yale life, for the observing of the modifications that a decade of experience and of contact with a different community have made in us.

A comment on the American people has been frequently made that they are inordinately given to forming a multiplicity of secret orders and associations. Certainly in the colleges this propensity has developed to a high degree, and Yale has indulged in it in due proportion. Secret societies abound, especially in preparatory schools, where they are subjected to no very intelligent control. Boys are entranced by the appeal of mysticism newly awakened in a dawning life, and captivated in their unbalanced days by an apparent superiority established by themselves and accepted by the uninitiated. They bring to Yale all the ardor and all the undesirable attitudes that school societies can create, and, with the latter, supply to the social life an element that is in constant conflict with more wholesome influence.

A Yale graduate will be most likely to form an opinion uncolored by loyalty to his fraternity, or without bias as to the society system, if he calmly considers the characteristics of some outside fraternal order of whatever species of Independent Reindeers it may happen to be. The very fact that he himself is not a member—as not many college men join in after years such associations—is an expression of his opinion of their allurements; he knows that their secrets amount to nothing, that their symbolism is the emptiest kind of trumpery. He recognizes the valuable features which abound, — the insurance securities, the commercial opportunities, and the social benefits, — but utterly scouts the serious claims of hidden power in their secrecy. He turns again at this extended day to view the societies of Alma Mater, to discover, doubtless with some shock of surprise, how like in part they are to those fraternal orders viewed with his indulgent eye. True, there is a marked divergence, but on the point of secrecy he finds college men no less ridiculous, except they are not so old and fat.

To turn over the pages of the Yale Banner, or any college year book, is to find emblematic engravings of secret orders with smouldering sarcophagi, exhaling the odor of mystery, skulls, masks, spades, keys to the secret of knowledge, books of sibylline prophecy, and a host of gewgaws that symbolize the ages of credulity and ignorance. The sacred iron doors at Yale no more close on the world than do the wicker wings of a summer barroom; the societies have no secrets, except for the pitiful agreement not to tell the meaning of A.B.C. or the significance of chained hearts and clasped hands.

It cannot be denied that a spirit of mysticism, finding its only expression in tokens of tragedy and darkness, appeals strongly to all men and especially to the spirited and immature temperament of youths. If Yale men take a delight in the allurements and romances of the occult, they are to be allowed that liberty, even at the seat of a university, where it is the business of the Faculty to enlighten the blind, and the practice of a student body to seriously administer the social law. In general the liberty is harmless, but the spectacle is to be tolerated only where it does not interfere or conflict with the wellbeing of the college community. Whether it does so at Yale is the question now raised for our maturer judgments.

It has been stated that but few graduates join fraternal orders. A further reason for this is found in the fact that those orders cannot bestow the favors or inflict the pains that lie in the laps of the college fraternities. In the world at large we have courts of law to govern the conduct of men, and the requirements of the entire community over conduct extend not much beyond the reach of the penal statutes. For the vast admixture of society there are many standards imposed on as many classes, among which the fraternal organizations by their paucity in membership are entirely lost, so that a breach of any particular requirement of a fraternal order not corresponding with a general rule of conduct of the entire community will bring no penalty except from the order. One is permitted to observe a march of decorated Templars without much concern for his own welfare, but at Yale the underclass man lurks to watch a midnight parade as fearful of detection as a Peeping Tom.

The college community is quite differently constituted from the general, and the system of ethics which prevails richly transcends that penumbra closely clinging to the portals of the jail. Undergraduates come largely from a single stratum of society and respond with almost equal sensitiveness to the praise or blame of their fellow-men. Their numbers are few, all are eligible to the same clubs, and most regard an election as a thing greatly to be desired. The secret societies dominate the entire activity of college life, they establish by their elections a system of rewards that are accepted by the community as the highest gifts that man can have for man, and of punishments whose sting no one is too independent to ignore or too degraded to feel. They establish a morale, their imposition of social regulations is accepted by all, and the violation of their rules brings not only the disapproval of the initiated and a failure of election, but shapes the judgment of expectant underclassmen on the propriety of conduct. Whether this situation is deplorable or beneficent is for the moment immaterial; the fact to be noted is that it exists.

The government by a tribunal of public opinion, so constituted, exercises a control, powerful, sustained, and complete, over the behavior of men from the moment they arrive in New Haven as Freshmen; it is powerful only because its standards are high, sustained because it affects a class superior in culture, and complete because it manages men in their most dependent days. This system, unique in its class progression and wholesome in its achievement, is highly valuable. Yet in spite of its wide and efficient control of conduct, and because of its great authority, it has established a certain attitude and exercises some requirements that neither appeal to reason nor freely meet the approval of sober-minded graduates. It is out of the feature of secrecy that there arises a strong doubt.

It has been maintained here that the secret societies have no substantial secrets, and that their claims of the supernatural or of hidden experience are as unreal as they are pretentious, yet the power and the prestige they have gained, coupled with the show of secrecy, give birth to a feeling of superiority and exclusiveness that quite intoxicates. If men want to feel superior and exclusive, of course they may be allowed the opportunity so to indulge their intellects, but when they are the same men whom circumstance has elevated to a position of authority, the maintenance of their attitude may, and in undergraduate days ought to be fairly questioned. That the entire system is conducted with a fostered exclusion is beyond doubt; the countless prohibitions that are imposed on non-members is proof enough. The quality of exclusion is displayed not in an aloofness from non-members, such conduct could be nicely tolerated, but in a pointed commingling, a subtle insistence on a difference, and a constant appreciation of a barrier, perhaps as wilfully raised by the non-member, but certainly the fabric of the other. It may be urged that men need not accept these prohibitions, but the college world does submit to them—the worst being a restriction upon free discussion. The decrees of exclusiveness are administered conjointly with the wholesome rules of conduct, and most men while willingly submitting to the latter feel hotly the effrontery offered in the former, for effrontery and chivalry can be maintained together in any community and they so thrive in Yale's societies. As the secrecy is false, the exclusiveness is manufactured, and as it is manufactured it is offensive. A proper answer is not given if it be said that no man need feel the exclusion unless he chooses to take it as such, for when a condition is ostentatiously created, as this is, and a prohibition against open recognition is decreed, then exclusiveness is deliberately maintained. Objection arises not out of pique at the assumption of the chosen few but out of the injury submitted to, perhaps weakly, by the uninitiated. In a hundred ways Yale men have been hurt, have received wounds that have smarted even in later years, wounds that could have been avoided only by refraining from entering Yale, and it is difficult to believe that among those who have removed the spectacles of loyalty there are not many who have come to think that the whole system of societies, in so far as they are 'secret, is prejudicial to the best possible undergraduate life.

The societies at Yale are essentially clubs for the development of friendships, all have the interest of Yale at heart, and election to their number is an honor not lightly considered and a trust not wilfully violated. Their power is great, their influence inspiring. Without secrecy and the offense growing out of it, these clubs would still maintain their high position and authority, and they would remove from life at Yale a feature that long has been an object of criticism and regret.

While the society system has a strong influence on college social life it is still only an undercurrent above which is a stronger, wider stream, rich with experience and opportunity from earliest Freshman days. At a casual glance it seems amazing to think how quickly the members of the Class in Freshman year came to know each other. An universal intimacy sprang up that finds, as we continually observe, no correspondence in the outside world. Mere boys, shy and diffident, from all corners of the country, made up the membership; they were not thrown together by the force of college regulations, but were marshalled in divisions of thirty or so, and yet in no time they were on terms of Nym and Pistol from A to Z. This of course was due to the men coming in groups from the preparatory schools, like Andover and St. Paul's, and lesser institutions, where they lived in closest relation. Each group stood practically as a unit, so that to know one meant immediately to know all. Those who came singly from remotest towns and isolated high schools soon became attached to and a part of one of the larger groups, with the consequence that from the very start of the course the men gained acquaintances widespread that later were to develop into friendships, fraternities, clubs, and carousals.

Henry Selden Johnson (Yale 1896)

How it looks to us now

A Tabulation of the answers to Hawkes' circular letter of December, 1905

Herbert E Hawkes

QUESTION *VIII*

What relative importance would you now place on study and on activities outside the curriculum (e. g., athletics, societies) ?

A few more than half the men answering this question (151) are clear that study is of first importance, very many regarding the outside activities merely as a relish. The sentiment of the entire body of answers is contained in the reply: "1. Study, 2. Social associations with classmates and others, 3. Athletics, 4. Societies." Other suggestive replies of men who look on study as of primary importance are: "To any one of ordinary intelligence, there seems to be time for both. An honest day's work *every day* on the studies and all the rest of the time devoted to outside activities or to recreation would seem to be desirable." "Study first. Many activities which at college seemed of first importance lose much of that importance in the retrospect."

A number of men (about 40) seem to place general association with their classmates (including athletic and social activities) in the first place, though the common intellectual interests seems to be the substratum that makes this association valuable, or in fact possible.

"Study is the basis of college life, and indispensable, but the greatest good from the stay at Yale comes in my experience from the constant intercourse with men. Athletics and societies are first-rate mediums through which the pressure of many may cause the individual to modify his peculiarities and faults. Four years at New Haven seeing no one but instructors, and devoting the whole time to study would be less valuable than four years under the present system, with study left out and some regular physical labor substituted as the reason for our presence,—No, on reading this I convert myself to the contrary. The improvement would not come without the mental activity of study. It is absolutely essential."

The chief complaint against athletics is that comparatively few are encouraged to take part in them. A very common sentiment is expressed by the man who says: "I think athletics should be more generally indulged in and less attention paid to University teams."

Although the question does not suggest a criticism of the society system, about 20 men add such criticism. Their replies are mostly to the effect either that societies are very much over-emphasized or that they should be abolished. Six of them, however, feel that the societies do more good than harm. Of these six men five were in Senior societies. The only Senior society man to criticize the society system stated the following: "I do not think a man should make a Senior society unless he has a junior appointment." Of the critics a very few were members of junior societies. Sentiments expressed are as follows: "The fetish of Senior societies seems to me wholly bad. Its evil influence penetrates even the lower grades of preparatory schools." "Societies (all of them) root and branch should be abolished." "Societies seem to me of less importance each year." These from Junior society men who did not make a Senior society. Non-society men who mention them at all criticize severely.

Our epigrammatic member says: "The four things which did me more good than all the curriculum were learning:

1. In Freshman year, that a man is a fool to sport.
2. In Sophomore year, that a 'pull' is a great help.
3. In Junior year, that general acquaintance with current affairs is very desirable.
4. In Senior year, that the best man doesn't always win."

YALE UNIVERSITY

EDWIN E. SLOSSON
AN EXCERPT FROM: *THE INDEPENDENT - A WEEKLY MAGAZINE* VOL. LXVI THURSDAY, FEBRUARY 4, 1909, NEW YORK

A stranger who tries to see Yale will be disappointed because so much of it and the best of it is invisible. I felt on the campus as I do in the dynamo room of a great power house. I knew that I was in the presence of forces obviously powerful but imperceptible to my senses. There is not enough tangible machinery about Yale to account for the work it is doing. The Yale undergraduates seem to train, control and discipline themselves, leaving little for the official authorities to do in this way. In fact President Hadley has explicitly recognized this in saying that "if the chairman of the Yale News Board is a man of the right type — and he almost always is — he is the most efficient disciplinary officer of the university.

However strained the relations between the officers of the university and the student body might become the *News* would never attack the President so bitterly as did the Harvard *Crimson* President Eliot or the Stanford *Sequoia* President Jordan last year. The *Record* never prints malicious jokes on the professors, as do so many "college comics." The Yale men who have patiently endeavored to explain to me the influences which mold the undergraduate into the Yale type have laid great stress on the common dormitory life and the effect of the senior societies. There are three secret societies, Skull and Bones, Scroll and Keys, and Wolf's Head, and it is the ambition of every normal College man to get into one of them. Toward this all his efforts are directed from his freshman year, and Tap Day marks for him the success or failure of his college career. As one graduate said to me: "I would willingly have sacrificed a year of my life if it had been necessary in order to make Bones."

Since the ideals of the senior societies set the standard for the college it is important to know what are regarded as the qualifications for selection. In so far as I have been able to ascertain them from talking with Yale alumni these qualifications may be formulated as two, one passive and one active: First, conformity; second, achievement. The first requirement of eligibility is that the student "be a gentleman" according to the prevailing definition of that word; that he be clubbable; that he conform to Yale customs and violate none of its traditions. The second distinguishes the few men of prominence from the crowd of those who are merely negatively eligible thru conformity with establisht ideals of manners and conduct. A man must have done something, particularly something that has brought glory upon the college; he must be a leader among his mates in college activities, such as athletics, journalism, college politics, or religious work.

These criteria are on the whole good ones, at least very similar to those that measure a man's success in the outside world, but some questions would arise as to their interpretation. Youth is naturally intolerant and exclusive, even, or perhaps especially, college youth, and probably too rigid a conformity is insisted upon and too narrow a definition given to the word "gentleman." Then, too, the activities in which prominence is rewarded are rather apart from the purposes for which the university exists, and devotion to some of these activities may easily become so absorbing as to give rise to a general sentiment that high grades are indicative of a narrow mind.

The societies should in my opinion add scholarship to their list of undergraduate activities in which a student may legitimately attain distinction, and should take cognizance of the fact that a man who presents an original thesis, who discovers a new species of plant or writes a genuine poem, may be said in a sense to have brought glory upon his university as well as a man who has won a game.

That scholarship has very little weight in the question of eligibility to the senior societies was shown by Mr. Maurice F. Parmelee in the Yale *Courant* of December, 1906, from which I obtain the following figures:

TABLES OF GRADUATES FROM ACADEMIC DEPARTMENT, 1882-1905			
		Honor men	**%**
Wolf's Head	**308**	**19**	**6.1**
Scroll & Keys	**349**	**37**	**10.6**
Skull & Bones	**358**	**83**	**23.1**
Society Men	**1,015**	**139**	**13.6**
Non-Society Men	**3,984**	**967**	**24.2**
Total	**4,999**	**1,106**	**22.6**

The "Honor Men" are those that have received the highest marks in their classes and are, according to tradition, placed upon the commencement program for Philosophical Orations, High Orations and Orations, altho these are not now given. These men also become members of the Phi Beta Kappa, a national non-secret honorary society. The figures show that only one of the three secret senior societies contains a higher percentage of honor men than the College as a whole, and even that society had a less percentage than the student body outside. That is, if a blindfolded man had entered the crowd assembled around the oak tree near Battell Chapel on the third Thursday in May and tapped forty-five men at random, the chances are that he would have obtained men of higher standing than those actually chosen, after the long and anxious deliberations of the secret conclaves. Or, in other words, after the forty-five happy men had gone to their rooms there was better picking in the crowd than there was before, so far as scholarship goes.

But the faculty estimate of a man's ability based on grades alone is as narrow as the student estimate based on activities which often interfere with the making of high grades. To get some light on this point, I asked seven Yale graduates in classes from 1872 to 1896, to mark in the directory of graduates the names of their classmates who had in some way distinguished themselves since graduation. No instructions were given as to the degree of prominence or the proportion of the class to be indicated, but they checked on an average 24 per cent. of the names on their class rolls. On comparing these with the lists of living graduates in these classes who are members of the three senior societies and of Phi Beta Kappa (the latter being Honor Men), the following results were obtained:

38 per cent. of the Phi Beta Kappa men became prominent.
37 Per cent. of the Society men became prominent.
19 per cent. of the men not in Phi Beta Kappa became prominent.
18 per cent. of the men not in the societies became prominent.

Of course the question of which men in these classes had shown special ability depended upon the personal judgment of the men marking the lists and their knowledge of their classmates and the examination was not extensive enough to give accurate figures.* [* But two men marking the same class gave practically the same figures.] No allowance can be made for the fact that the honors conferred upon an undergraduate give him thereafter a certain prominence in the eyes of his classmates and may directly contribute to his success in life. Still we should probably be justified in concluding that the senior societies and the Phi Beta Kappa, tho their standards of judgment are different, are equally successful in picking out the men of superior ability and that a student belonging to either of these groups has twice the chance of future prominence as one belonging to neither. There are several interpretations that might be given to these figures. One is that the importance attached to non-scholastic activities in Yale draws a large proportion of the ablest students away from their university duties.

Most conspicuous of the activities is, of course, athletics, which at Yale as in all the other American colleges, absorbs too much of the student's time, energy, ,and enthusiasm. By athletics I do not mean physical exercise or even sport, for these two desirable elements of student life have been so overshadowed by other features of the intercollegiate contest system as to be negligible in the consideration of the question. Whenever the number of spectators exceeds the number of players the limit of true sport has been past, and when the spectators outnumber the players a hundred to one, the game becomes merely an exhibition. If there were some way by which the strength and agility, or rather the health and symmetrical development of the entire student body of one university could be matched against those of another, some good might come of it, but under present conditions success in intercollegiate contests does not prove that the winning university is superior to its rival in these important qualities nor does it do much to promote them. Young men got excited enough over their games naturally without outside pressure, and when they know that in every city of the United States crowds are assembled to watch and bet on their feats the pressure is too great. Overstrain, physical and moral, necessarily results, as in the boat race of last June, when, with a President rooting on one side and a future President on the other, a Yale student collapsed and has since died and two Harvard men broke the rules of the university and were expelled.

I find that I am expected to say something about democracy in this article on Yale. I will therefore take this opportunity of explaining that I have not been able to find out much about democracy in American universities because it means different things or takes different forms in the different institutions I have visited. In Yale, for example, the students resent the introduction of valets and automobiles as a menace to democracy. In Princeton the authorities regard the use of Greek letters in the name of a club as too dangerous to be tolerated. In Wisconsin it is thought democracy will be lost if the tickets to the junior Prom are raised from \$3 to \$5. In Michigan any system of marking grades except "passed" and "not passed" is considered undemocratic and it was only this year that that aristocratic institution, the Phi Beta Kappa, was allowed to be establisht. In Harvard the word "democracy" seems to mean "promiscuity" or else some spiritual condition altogether unaffected by external circumstances. When I started out on my quizzing tour I had at the head of the list of questions which I proposed to ask, in one form or another, "Does the spirit of democracy prevail in this university.

But I soon dropped that question as unnecessary and fruitless, because it was answered everywhere before I asked it, and always in the same way. There were two things about which faculty, students and alumni of each university visited agreed, that is on the purity of their democracy and the beauty of their campus. In admitting deficiencies in other respects they were usually frank enough and on some points even effusive, but on these two they would acknowledge no superiors. Therefore as the net result of a hundred conversations bearing on this subject I have left in my memory a hazy composite something like this: "There are other universities that are richer or older than ours; some that have at present more students. Our president is not all that he should be. The trustees do not always do the right thing. The faculty might be improved by process of elimination and substitution. But nowhere will you find a prettier campus or a more democratic body of students." On the former point I was able to use my own eyes, and shall take the liberty of expressing my personal opinions, but on the latter I was obliged to rely on hearsay evidence. Having just given this evidence I shall dismiss the subject with the remark that in view of alarmist reports about the growth of luxury, narrowness and class distinction, it is distinctly encouraging to find that the democratic spirit is still regarded as a desirable thing to have in a university, even tho there may be a disposition to assume that it is already attained.

I have observed a curious difference between Eastern and Western colleges in regard to the influence of the alumni. In the West the alumni are always urging forward their Alma Mater into untried paths. Sometimes a State Alumni Association will take things into its own hands and, overruling president, trustees and faculty, will, by control of the legislature, force the university to take steps which it believes are necessary to bring it closer into touch with modern life. In the East on the contrary the alumni seem to be, as a whole, a conservative, even a reactionary influence, opposing almost any change, wise or unwise. I have asked many persons the reason of this and tho they generally have agreed that it is so, they have not given any explanation which, in my opinion, satisfactorily accounts for it. The most plausible of the explanations suggested to me is that the Eastern alumni are older on the average. But are not the freshly graduated about as reluctant to have their Alma Mater changed as the older men? Whatever the cause it raises the question whether the present movement to give the alumni a larger representation on the governing boards of State universities may not ultimately result in impeding rather than accelerating these institutions.

Eastern alumni are generous in the matter of financial support and certain individuals initiate important changes thru specific gifts, but as a body they are inclined to regard their Alma Mater as a relic of happy schooldays and as such to keep it intact and unaltered, so that when they return they may find it as they remembered it. In 1888 several thousand of the Yale alumni signed a petition to the corporation remonstrating against the removal of an old fence that was in the way of one of the new buildings, and what is worse, they celebrated twenty years later the anniversary of "the fight that failed." It is the alumni, I believe, who are responsible for the preservation of Old South Middle, which makes Yale look like a full-grown rooster with a bit of the shell from which it was hatched stuck on its back. In important matters it is the same. If it were proposed to cut down the college course to three years or to raise the Sheffield course to four; to make the Sheffield boys go to chapel or to release the college boys from going; to abolish the senior societies or to have more of them, probably the majority of the alumni would oppose the change regardless of its advantages or disadvantages. I presume that Secretary Stokes, altho I have never heard him say so, is more often called upon in local alumni associations to explain why some things have been changed than why more have not been changed.

The finest thing about Yale is the student body. I do not think this is true of all the universities in this country. In some laboratories and libraries I have visited the students appeared out of place, unworthy of their beautiful buildings. In some classrooms 1 have pitied the instructors because they were expending so much good teaching on such poor material. But I did not pity the instructors in Yale. If they could not do something worth while with the earnest, energetic, wide-awake, well-ordered young men in the scats before them, they could not anywhere. The Yale students as a rule are not blase, cynical and prematurely aged, nor on the other hand are they awkward, unruly and obstreperous. They are not so studious and diligent as the average run of students in the State and city universities, but they come from more cultured homes and with more thoro preparation. After seeing the Yale boys in mass, I have come to think that the university gets more credit than it deserves for the achievements of its graduates. This educational machinery that we talk so much about is, after all, of minor importance. The product of the mill depends mostly on what kind of grain is poured into the hopper.

I liked the way a man would stroll across the campus in the evening, bareheaded and hand-pocketed, and call "Oh Billy Rogers!" to a four-story building, then hold a confidential conversation with the student who stuck his head out of one of the upper windows. I like the way they played diabolo and tops. I liked the way they heeled for the *News.* I liked the way they sang. Altogether they are a likable lot of fellows.

Social System in the College

Clarence W. Mendel

from *Fifty Years of Yale News: Yale Daily News*, January 28, 1928, New Haven Connecticut

The oldest secret society at Yale is Phi Beta Kappa. It may seem curious at present to think of the learned society as a secret fraternity but such it was from its first year at Yale in 1780 down to 1825 and it is more truly in many ways the predecessor of the modem fraternity than are the ungainly open societies that preceded it at Yale. Chi Delta Theta was also a secret fraternity for many years and the societies that succeeded these two always maintained at least a political interest in things intellectual.

The whole question of societies and fraternities and their place on the campus does not seem today to be the leading question that it was fifty years ago. At that time, or approximately then, appeared the greatest book on Yale life that has ever been written in the way of a compilation of facts. "Four Years at Yale" devotes the first 186 pages to societies and only in what follows deals with student life in general. Probably the best way to understand the changes is to visualize the situation in the early 70's.

At the top of the system were the two Senior societies, Bones and Keys, then as now taking fifteen members each, elected at the end of junior year. These societies were local and entirely secret. Bones, which was originally Skull and Bone, was founded by fifteen men of the Class of 1833 as a result, it is said, of some injustice in the Phi Beta Kappa elections so that in another way Phi Beta Kappa may be considered the unintentional sponsor for the system. There was never any pledging or discussion of elections which were given out on a Thursday evening in the individual rooms. A sharp distinction from all other societies except Keys which was modeled exactly upon Bones lay in the fact that graduates attended initiations and commencement dinners in large numbers. Keys and an unsuccessful society called Spade and Grave were the only other Senior societies at the time. Spade and Grave started as the result of a quarrel between three Bones editors of the Yale Lit and two non-society editors, but was soon buried.

In Junior year there were three fraternities, Alpha Delta Phi, Psi U and DKE, all established between 1836 and 1844. In the 70's the last two had what were considered extravagant houses, one on High street and the other on York of which the more elaborate was valued at nearly $15,000. These junior societies were chapters of national fraternities and took about thirty men each. Their chief function seems to have been to engineer the election of the Wooden Spoon Committee and the Yale Lit editors. There were nine men on the former and five of the latter. Coalitions between various pairs of societies always determined who should be the Spoon man and the editor in chief of the Lit. Beyond this political function the only object of the fraternities seems to have been self-perpetuation. So far as we can judge there was absolutely no fraternity feeling. Only the Junior Class members were interested or attended meetings. There was no Senior delegation at all.

In Sophomore year we find the societies which really created some intense interest. Kappa Sigma Theta and Alpha Sigma Phi had died out. But the result of a ruction between Psi U and DKE in 1864 had produced two societies known as Phi Theta Psi and Delta Beta Xi, vouched for by no lesser notables than Professor Thacher and Cyrus Northrop. The motto of the former was the familiar but tantalizing *amici usque ad aras.* Freshmen were pledged for these societies early in the year, about thirty to each. There was a notification night preceded by marching on the campus with dark lanterns and songs outside the rooms of the chosen. The Freshmen furnished the banquets. Initiations were secret and inside the houses, followed by a play and dinner. The meetings were on Friday and the graduates had nothing to do with the fraternities except by invitation. In these Sophomore societies are to be found most of the traditions which have continued in the modern fraternities and they rather than the junior fraternities were the hunting grounds of the Senior society campaigners. Probably this was one of the reasons why they and one or two others founded later were short lived. They were the step in the pyramid around which centered the most severe general criticism, especially that which came from the faculty who in those days wielded rather a big stick.

At the bottom of the social pyramid were the Freshman societies Kappa Sigma Epsilon, Delta Kappa, and Gamma Nu. The last was an open society, the other two semi-secret. At first in the 40's the membership of a Freshman society had been twenty but in the 70's the whole class was divided between the three societies after a vigorous campaign for the best men which extended back into pre-college days. One blackball rejected a man but every Freshman must belong to one of the three societies! How this worked out is something of a puzzle today. These Freshman societies tried to extend themselves to other colleges as the fraternities had done, but without much success. At some period certain schools regularly supplied particular societies. There was some open hazing of candidates, and each initiate was in charge of one Sophomore to see that life did not become dull for him at any moment.

Such in abstract was the society situation fifty years ago. The two great debating societies so-called, Linonia and Brothers in Unity, established in the middle of the eighteenth century, were purely voluntary and included all four years. They had rooms in Alumni Hall, held debates and listened to orations, poems, and essays. Their chief treasures were their libraries, which were kept in the wings of the old library. They had over 13,000 books each in 1870. There was a reading room supported by the societies and run by the College in the central part of South Middle with space for the College Book Store. On the racks of the reading room were to be found one hundred and twenty periodicals, including Punch. A tax of $8.00 per annum was assessed on the members, and the reading room was presided over by an "indigent student." This reading room superseded a newspaper rack in the bowling alleys of the old gymnasium.

The evolution from this situation of the 70's to the present day social system is fairly obvious. The general societies, Linonia and Brothers, have become in part a library collection, in part mere names in Harkness Quadrangle. The most iron clad democracy could not maintain "societies" that took in every one of the increasingly numerous boys that came to Yale. Phi Beta Kappa, the source of the whole trouble, is now a respected badge of scholarship. At the bottom of the pyramid the great unwieldy Freshman societies died in the 80's. There seems to have been some merciful assistance given them from without to hasten their last moments, and the assistance was even more effective in the case of the Sophomore societies, which died a little later. There soon sprang into existence, however, a new group of Sophomore societies taking in fifteen men apiece and quite obviously out of tune with the pyramid principle. Hé Boulé, Eta Phi, and Kappa Psi formed a group of forty-five men who quite regularly stuck together and furnished the material for the three Senior societies (Wolf's Head had been founded meanwhile). Quite obviously they injured the system in two ways. In the first place they selected and established a chosen group early in the college course, shattering the existing ideals of democracy. In the second place they produced something of a continuity of experience which the old class system of societies had, in the interests of class spirit, prevented. They were abolished by faculty action in 1902, and the present system really dates from that time. With no Sophomore or Freshman societies the Junior fraternities slipped down to the beginning of Sophomore year, and in place of a pyramid there came into being a large group of fraternities with continuous existence through three years, the group of smaller senior societies in the final year continuing as before.

From this survey of the situation fifty years ago and now it is clear that most of our older customs and methods are more or less intact although they now belong to different organizations and different kinds of organization. The fixed element amongst the many changes has been the Senior society and even there the Elihu Club has introduced some relaxation of the old austerity. In spite of external resemblances in custom and tradition the fraternities have largely reversed the theory of the early years that only the members of a given class should be interested in a given society. The delegation system inside of the fraternities is, however, a direct outcome of this old theory, a trait persisting within a system which has practically discarded the theory as a whole.

One distinct change is to be found in the present day principle that in general less than half of a class should be comprised within the fraternities. In the 70' s everybody belonged to a Freshman society and a good deal more than half the class to a Junior society. The modern principle is different.

Fraternities have increased in numbers in the College but only in proportion with the growth of the College. From decade to decade the Sophomore societies were always a little out of gear with the rest of the system. A curious incongruity in the system of the 70's, namely the appearance of fraternities as the junior group in the society system, probably accounts for the traditional difficulty which the Yale chapters have always had with their national organizations.

The fraternal urge was originally connected with scholarly interests. Witness Phi Beta Kappa and Chi Delta Theta. Witness the great debating societies — open and general to be sure, but always cultivating club rivalry. Throughout the history of societies at Yale, and even in the last fifty years, the various organizations have never entirely thrown overboard the principle of intellectual stimulation as an excuse for existence in association with the principles of good fellowship and service to Yale. The relative importance of the various principles is a most variable quantity. In the seventies we are told "the sight of a Phi Beta key would raise a cry of derision." Today it may be that we have gone too far in the direction of shuffling off onto Phi Beta Kappa, The Elizabethan Club, The Pundits and so on, all the responsibility of carrying our intellectual burden. But still the debates of the old freshman societies, the essays and orations and poems of the others have left their mark on our present society procedure. The descriptions of the absurdities of rushing week in the seventies and in the present decade are interchangeable. The solemnities and the excesses and the constantly renewed agreements — these are all recurring motifs throughout the fifty years.

And what of the resulting situation? Senior Societies still loom overwhelmingly large on the Yale College horizon. In the past they have been the conservation of the best traditions of Yale. Today they do not maintain the standards as they have been reputed to in the earlier days. They must meet the fact that last year more than half their men were taken from the graduates of three preparatory schools and that only two high school men were chosen. They must face the charge that the senior society men are no longer, through the fraternities, establishing standards which in themselves justify their existence.

The Junior Fraternities are confronted today with a considerable body of honest conviction that they are worthless or even harmful at Yale. The foolish, small-town quality of open initiating is to say the least in bad taste. The marked tendency to encourage (some would say compel) drinking on the part of the initiate is intolerable. The open house system now inaugurated has a tendency to increase the drift toward snobbish aloofness.

All true — much of it too true. But the answer is what it always has been and must be. The human animal will make for itself groups within its social confines. The value of the smaller group is to accentuate and perpetuate the best in the larger group. To justify themselves the societies must do this, otherwise they must give way to something better. They can be a blessing to Yale and Yale will not tolerate their being a curse.

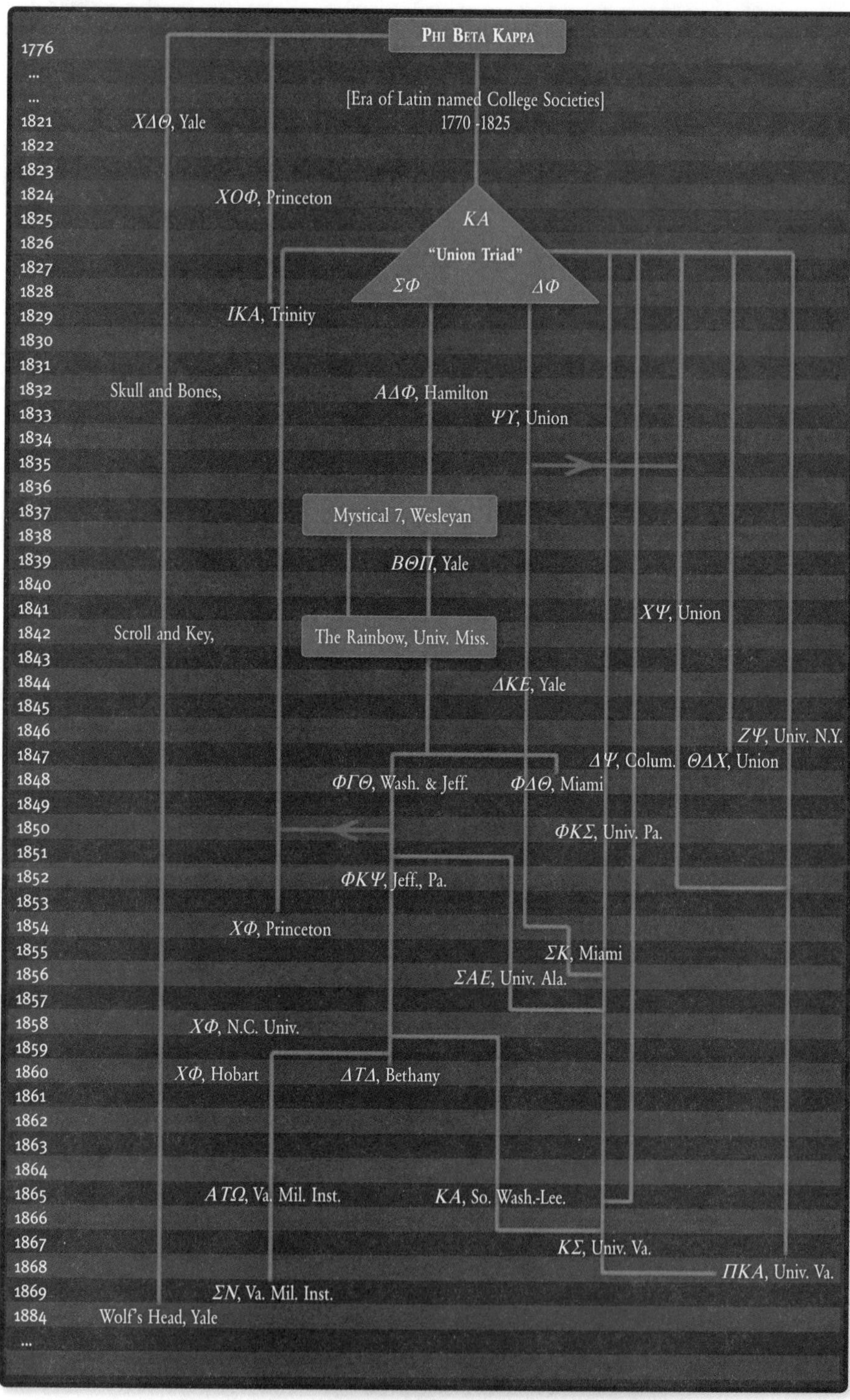

GENEALOGICAL CHART OF GENERAL, GREEK-LETTER, COLLEGE FRATERNITIES IN THE UNITED STATES

The Cyclopædia of Fraternities

Albert C Stevens
1907

Greek-letter Or College Fraternities

College Fraternities — Secret, literary, and social organizations of students at American colleges and universities; sometimes called Greek-letter societies, because the names of nearly all of them are made up of two or three Greek letters, which are presumed to refer to mystical words or to mottoes known only to members. It is as if the Odd Fellows called themselves the "F. L. T. " Fraternity, referring to their well-known watchwords, "Friendship, Love, and Truth." College fraternities may be classified as general, local, professional, and women's. There are twenty-six fraternities in the first group, which have chapters or branches in from four to sixty-four of the higher institutions of learning in the United States. Membership is confined in almost all instances to students studying the classics or those in the literary and scientific departments; membership originally was, and in a few instances to-day is, restricted to upper-class men. This has resulted in the formation of similar societies among students in professional schools, of which four have achieved prominence and a considerable membership. With the increase of institutions for the higher education of women, there have appeared nearly a dozen Greek and Roman letter secret societies for women undergraduates, half a dozen of which made themselves known beyond the walls of the colleges where they have an active existence. There are many college secret societies classed as local, that is, existing only at colleges where founded, some with Greek-letter and some with other titles, among the better known of which are the three senior class societies at Yale. If to the foregoing there be added those which have lived, shone, and left a record, American college life will be found to have given birth to almost one hundred secret societies of this particular and unique type.

The form of government prior to 1870 was weak, consisting of general supervision by a Grand, usually the parent Chapter, or by one chapter after another in turn, which made laws and regulations as it pleased, communicated the fact to the other chapters and left it to their option to obey them. But within the last quarter of a century conventions made up of delegates from chapters, with administrative bodies or councils, composed of alumni members, have had a general supervision over and management of affairs, and in leading, instances have taken the place of an imperial form of government. Annual conventions are held with undergraduate chapters, in turn, when undergraduate delegates act in the capacity of legislators, leaving the duties of all executive to the council of alumni. These reunions generally end with a banquet and formal public exercises at which distinguished members deliver addresses of welcome, poems, and orations in the presence of delegates and other undergraduate members, their relatives and friends. These exercises are rendered the more attractive because of the long list of alumni prominent in the various walks of life, who may be called on to discourse eloquently touching the fraternity and what it means to those who enjoy its privileges, or on literary and economic topics.

Membership in college fraternities includes active, alumni, and honorary; but the latter, with a few exceptions, is no longer permitted to increase, initiations being confined to undergraduates. At some of the larger cities, graduate members have established alumni chapters or clubs. The older fraternities, for they do not rank necessarily according to membership, have published accounts of their origin and growth; a number have issued elaborate and ornate catalogues, with lists of names of members arranged alphabetically by States and by colleges, with memoranda as to rank in the society or at college and biographical sketches of members distinguished in public life; not a few issue magazines and other periodicals, some of which are circulated privately. Nearly all have published music and song books of their own, in some instances have adopted distinctive colors, and in others, flowers, as having a special significance. But most important, perhaps, are college fraternity badges, almost always made of gold, sometimes enamelled, and generally set with precious stones. These are worn conspicuously by undergraduate members and by many long after leaving college. In a number of instances the badge consists of a monogram formed of the Greek letters composing the name of the fraternity; in others, of a representation of one or more emblems and in many instances of shields or rhombs, ornamented with enamelled, jewelled, or engraved letters and emblems.

The Greek-letter fraternity is unique among secret societies, in that it is the only organization of the kind founded on an aristocracy of social advantage and educational opportunity. Students have to be invited to join them, and the undergraduate who should prove so unfamiliar with college customs as to ask to join one would probably never be permitted to do so. So "secret" are the Greek-letter fraternities, or most of them, that, although wearing jewelled badges, members generally refuse to mention the organization in the presence of profanes. Instances have been known where a member of one college fraternity resigned and joined another, or was expelled and elected by a rival society, but they are like hens' teeth. Though this does happen, the member is said to be "lifted." A student whose acquaintance has been cultivated, has been "rushed;" when he has been asked to join, he has been "bid;" and when he has agreed to do so, he is "pledged;" when he has been initiated and appears wearing the society's badge, he is" swung, out." In "rushing" a man it is customary to invite him to the fraternity house, where he meets the members, who watch his conduct and his conversation. If he makes a good impression, he is invited again, taken to football games, to the theatre, and invited to social affairs, and if all are satisfied the new man is a desirable acquisition he is invited to join. After initiation the watch over a new member is kept up. He is guarded against falling behind in class work and is taught during all his first year that neither he nor his opinions are of importance. By the time he is a sophomore he has learned to make allowance for every one's point of view.

Among about six hundred and fifty chapters of American college fraternities nearly seventy possess houses or temples valued at over $1,000,000, costing from $1,200 to $100,000. Some of them are elaborate and fanciful in design, others severely classic and still others sombre piles of brick and stone. In many instances members lodge in fraternity houses, in others out of them. The tabular exhibit on page 330 respecting some of the better known general Greek-letter fraternities is condensed from data for 1890 and 1891, furnished by William Raimond Baird in Johnson's Encyclopedia.

The system of Greek-letter fraternities, nearly if not all of which are chartered corporations, is fitly characterized by John Addison Porter, private secretary to President McKinley, in a "Century Magazine" article, September, 1888, as "the most prominent characteristic of American undergraduate social life." A reference to brief sketches of them will reveal the names of a few of the 125,000 members who during, the greater part of the present century have done much to add lustre to the professional, political, and business life of the Republic. The novitiate of the college fraternity soon learns to think of these men not only as brethren, but as models. President Seelye of Amherst College, in an address on June 28, 1887, said:

> It is not accidental that the foremost men in college, as a rule, belong to some of these societies. That each society should seek for membership the best scholars, the best writers and speakers, the best men of a class, shows well where its strength is thought to lie. A student entering one of these societies finds a healthy stimulus in the repute which his fraternity shall share from his successful work. The rivalry of individuals loses much of its narrowness, and almost all of its envy, when the prize which the individual seeks is valued chiefly for its benefit to the fellowship to which he belongs. Doubtless members of these societies often remain narrow-minded and laggard in the race, after all the influence of their society has been expended upon them, but the influence is a broadening and

> a quickening one notwithstanding. Under its power the self-conceit of a young man is more likely to give way to self-control than otherwise.

Mr. Porter adds this

> These "little societies" have supplied forty governers [sic] to most of the largest States of the Union, and had, in the last administration, the President of the United States and the majority of his Cabinet. On the Supreme Bench of the United States the fraternities are now (1888) represented by five of the associate justices. A summary, published in 1885, showed Alpha Delta Phi, Psi Upsilon, and Delta Kappa Epsilon, to have furnished of United States senators, 39, 25, and 36, respectively; while in the last Congress thirteen representatives and two senators were members of the last-named fraternity alone; and in the membership of these three fraternities are included twenty-four bishops of the Protestant Episcopal Church.

In view of the foregoing, it is with amusement rather than concern that one recalls the active opposition to college secret societies between 1845 and 1885 by the faculties of a few distinguished colleges and officers of a number of other institutions of learning. This was due in part to the antipathy for all secret societies engendered in the minds of some who were close to but partly ignorant of the facts underlying the anti-Masonic agitation of from 1827 to 1840; partly to the warfare waged against secret associations of all kinds by one or two religious denominations, and to some extent, to ignorance of all that pertains to these societies, or because antagonists had been refused by or expelled from membership in such organizations, or for special reasons applying to particular instances. All of this opposition, except that at Princeton, has practically disappeared, the other colleges prohibiting Greek-letter fraternities not having either the standing as institutions of learning or the personnel among their students which would suggest the propriety of establishing chapters of these societies.

The earliest warfare of this character was at Harvard College in 1831, when John Quincy Adams and others, notably Joseph Story and Edward Everett, induced the parent Greek-letter society, Phi Beta Kappa, to make public its so-called secrets and become an open, honorary organization. It is worth recalling that in 1831 Mr. Adams was elected an anti-Masonic and Whig candidate for Congress and that he had been defeated for reelection to the Presidency three years before by Andrew Jackson, a Freemason, at a time when public feeling ran high against the Masonic Fraternity, owing to its supposed responsibility for the mysterious disappearance of one Morgan who, it was said, proposed to reveal its secrets. Mr. Adams was led to"' hate Freemasonry," not from any personal knowledge he had of it, but because of the attitude of politicians toward the institution who exercised a great influence over him. One result was a series of letters abusive of Freemasonry which he published in the papers between 1831 and 1833, and another evidently, was his rescuing the chapter of Phi Beta Kappa at Harvard, his alma mater from the depths of iniquity to which he evidently thought its secrecy was leading it. Associate Justice Story was professor of law at Harvard at the time, and Edward Everett, then member of Congress, was the candidate (such is the irony of fate) for the Vice-Presidency of the Constitutional Union party in 1860. The latter organization, it will be recalled, was the residuary legatee of the so-called Know Nothing party, a proscriptive, political secret society, which antagonized aliens and Roman Catholics from behind closed doors and at the ballot-box during the early fifties. [1850s] (See Know Nothing Party.) There were few chapters of college secret societies in 1831, not more than a dozen scattered throughout New England, New York, and New Jersey, and communication between them either by mail or in, person was infrequent. There was no other effect of the effort by Adams, Story, and Everett until in 1834, when a "non-secret" Greek-letter society, Delta Upsilon,* [*There is an anti-secret society called Delta Upsilon which exists at a number of colleges and grew out of a confederation of societies having their origin in opposition to the secret societies. It makes more or less point, of the alleged immorality of the secrecy of the fraternities and its chapters work with or against the fraternities as may seem to them expedient.—*Baird's American College Fraternities*, New York,] was formed at Williams College. It exists to this day, with chapters in twenty-six colleges, and has many of the outward peculiarities of the secret Greek-letter fraternities. It reveals very little more of what it does than the latter, and calls itself private instead of secret. Eleven years later, 1845, the faculty of the University of Michigan demanded the disbandment of chapters of Alpha Delta Phi, Chi Psi, and Beta Theta Pi under penalty of expulsion of members and required new students to sign a pledge not to join such societies. The fight between the faculty and the few members of the then far western branches of those fraternities lasted five or six years. The members of Beta Theta Pi tried to 'evade the rule and killed the chapter in the attempt, Alpha Delta Phi and Chi Psi fought the faculty tooth and nail, in the press throughout the State, by means of an informed and healthy public sentiment, and with the aid of Freemasons and Odd Fellows, until the rule was rescinded. Two professors were expelled from the faculty by the Board of Regents and one was allowed to resign. A new president of the university was appointed shortly after and there was no further trouble. This anti-fraternity war, almost one of extermination, was another outcome of anti-secret society sentiment created by the anti-Masonic agitation a few years before. Opposition to the Greek-letter fraternities continued to show itself at some colleges through faculty regulations prohibiting their organization, notably at the Universities of Alabama, North Carolina, and Illinois; at Oberlin and others by requiring students to sign a pledge at matriculation, not to join such societies, which was the course pursued at Princeton in 1857, at Purdue, Dennison, and elsewhere. The refusal of the University of California in 1879 to permit a chapter of one of these societies to exist roused the press of that State, and the order was speedily rescinded. At Purdue University, Indianapolis, the faculty opposed Greek-letter ' fraternities, on the ground that they exercised an undue influence to enlarge the classical course of studies at the expense of the scientific. A test case was made of the faculty's refusing to admit to college a member of the Sigma Chi Fraternity who was otherwise eligible. The case was taken to the Supreme Court and the college authorities were beaten,* [*Baird's American College Fraternities] "the fraternities" being placed by this decision "in a position entirely similar to that of other secret societies," putting the burden of proof upon the faculty passing anti-fraternity laws, "to show that attendance -upon the meetings of a fraternity interfere with the relation of the members of the college." The president of Purdue resigned soon after and was succeeded, strange to relate, by a member of the Sigma Chi fraternity. Within the past fifteen years anti-fraternity laws have been repealed or ignored by Harvard as well as Vanderbilt, and by the Universities of North Carolina, Georgia, Iowa, Missouri, and Alabama. The secrecy of these societies is confined to so little besides privacy of meetings that it hardly calls for comment. While largely social, their aims are high and ideals lofty. Advantages secured and friendships gained through them are often among the most valuable acquisitions of the college student.

Origin and Extension. — American Greek-letter college secret societies began with the formation of Phi Beta Kappa at the College of William and Mary, Williamsburg, Va., December 5, 1776. Secret or semi-secret, as well as open, literary college societies, usually with Latin names, already existed, where debates and annual elections of officers were often the first training of the young student in public speaking and in politics. William and Mary was a successful and prosperous college one hundred and twenty-one years ago, and there it was that five young men formed a new and, as they believed, more effective students' organization. There was already a society there with a Latin name, and as one of the five students was a good Greek scholar, it has been thought that may have suggested the propriety of a Greek-letter name. In any event, they chose a Greek motto of three words, the initials of which are Phi Beta Kappa; decided to keep the society's proceedings secret; declared themselves a fraternity; established a few local branches, of which nothing has been heard since, and chapters at Yale and Harvard, which preserved the society and founded what has grown into a veritable world of Greek-letter fraternities. (See Phi Beta Kappa; also accompanying genealogical charts showing the order and place of establishment of earlier chapters of Phi Beta Kappa, and some of the other older Greek-letter fraternities, whether imitators of or merely inspired by a spirit of rivalry to those which preceded them.) The parent chapter of Phi Beta Kappa became dormant at the approach of Lord Cornwallis in 1781. The Yale Chapter was established in 1780, and that at Harvard a year later. These were originally the Zeta and Epsilon Chapters, Beta, Gamma and Delta having been assigned to now extinct, local, non-collegiate Virginia chapters. They subsequently became the Alphas, respectively of Connecticut and Massachusetts. From this, doubtless, arose the custom in many of the Greek-letter fraternities of designating chapters by Greek letters, the oldest in a State as Alpha, and so on. Six years later, in 1787, the Yale and Harvard Chapters took Phi Beta Kappa to Dartmouth, at Hanover, N. H., and in 1817 thirty years after, it was established at Union College at Schenectady, N. Y. It was during this thirty years' interval that the older college literary societies flourished, many of which had Latin names, some of which are still active, but most of which have given way to the Greek-letter fraternities, except at Princeton, where Whig and Clio continue features -of student life; and at Lafayette, where Washington and Jefferson claim a large share of attention. Four years after Phi Beta Kappa was taken to Union College, a second Greek-letter fraternity was founded at Yale, manifestly suggested by Phi Beta Kappa, which had been there forty-one years. It was called Chi Delta Theta, and differed from its progenitor in that it never established branches or chapters at other colleges, but remained a local, and, more recently an honorary society, membership in it being practically an honor conferred upon the editorial staff of the Yale "Literary Magazine." Two years later, in 1823 according to tradition, a Kappa Alpha club was formed at Union College, there being at that time no intention of making it a secret society. Whether the thought of rivalling the then comparatively widespread Greek-letter fraternity Phi Beta Kappa was the inspiration is not known, but the probabilities indicate that the second Greek-letter fraternity at Union was modelled after the first. Their names are suggestively alike and a comparison of the watchkey badges of both would seem to settle the question. In 1825 Kappa Alpha club blossomed out as a regular Greek-letter fraternity, and two years later, stimulated by a spirit of emulation, Sigma Phi was founded and within a few months Delta Phi was organized, the third at Union College, which institution has proved a veritable mother of fraternities. These three societies, the "Union Triad," are, more than any others, except Phi Beta Kappa, responsible for the widespread interest shown during the past sixty years in this department of secret, social, and literary life at American colleges. Sigma Phi was the first to follow the example of Phi Beta Kappa by establishing chapters, its original branch being at Hamilton College, Clinton, N. Y., where it was established in 1831. Kappa Alpha was quick to follow the example, but the Hamilton students who were approached by the "Kaps" declined to become members of that society, and in 1832 founded one of their own, calling it Alpha Delta Phi. It was in 1832 also that the Yale society commonly called Skull and Bones appeared. It has continued a purely local organization, on the lines of other college fraternities, without a Greek-letter title, but with more mystery and prestige than usually surrounds a society which does not venture beyond the place of origin. It is due to Skull and Bones that what is known as the Yale secret society system differs from that at almost all other colleges. At the latter, members of a fraternity would as soon think of committing treason as join a second college society; but at Yale the sophomore joins one of the junior Greek-letter fraternities, if asked, and then lives in the unuttered hope of being invited to join one of the local senior-year fraternities.

Whether successful or not, his interest in his junior society (one of the three most renowned which have chapters at the older institutions of learning) is not, as a rule, of that deep and lasting nature which characterizes members of the same society at other colleges. In 1829, three years before Skull and Bones was founded, I. K. A. (not Greek), appeared at Washington, now Trinity College, Hartford, Conn., and, like the former, has remained a local senior society ever since. In 1833 Union College gave birth to another fraternity, Psi Upsilon, which, within a few years, followed Alpha Delta Phi, which led in placing chapters in the then foremost colleges and universities. Alpha Delta Phi shocked some of the conservative spirits of 1835 by placing chapters at the University of New York and in what was then regarded as the far West, at Miami University, Oxford, Ohio. In 1836 it appeared at Columbia in New York City and at Amherst in 1837 at Yale, Harvard, and Brown, and in 1838 at the Cincinnati Law School; so that within six years it possessed nine chapters as contrasted with only four chapters of Phi Beta Kappa, four of Sigma Phi, one of Delta Phi, all older societies, and as compared with two chapters of Psi Upsilon. A brief account of the local, senior-class society, The Mystic Seven founded at Wesleyan University (since absorbed by Beta Theta Pi), may be found in the sketch of the Heptasophs, or Seven Wise Men. The advent of Alpha Delta Phi at Miami resulted in the formation of Beta Theta Pi. In 1837 Psi Upsilon went to the University of New York, to Yale, and in 1840 to Brown, in which year Alpha Delta Phi was established at Hobart. In 1841 Union arose to the occasion again and gave birth to another, its fifth fraternity, Chi Psi, and in 1842, stimulated by the success of Skull and Bones at Yale, Scroll and Key made its appearance there, to choose fifteen juniors annually and divide the honors, as far as possible, with the older senior society. In 1844 a schism from the Yale Chapter of Psi Upsilon resulted in the formation of a third "junior-year fraternity" Delta Kappa Epsilon, the only living society originating at Yale which has established chapters at other colleges and has conformed to the college society system existing out of New Haven. Alpha Delta Phi, Psi Upsilon, and Delta Kappa Epsilon, for fifty years, have been closely associated in the minds of the members of the college world, and are fairly classed as the three great college fraternities. They are great rivals and number many distinguished names in professional, political, commercial, and industrial life on the lists of their alumni. A large proportion of their chapters own their own houses or temples. At most of the older Eastern and Middle State colleges and universities chapters of two of these fraternities are to be found, and at many such institutions the three meet as rivals. In the latter instance, as pointed out by Baird,* [**American College Fraternities*; New York, James P. Downs, 1890.] the colleges are historic, which is due to the fact that forty years ago such colleges were the centres of the literary activity of the country.

New chapters of Alpha Delta Phi, Psi Upsilon, Delta Kappa Epsilon, and Beta Theta Pi were established with comparative frequency between 1844 and 1861, the societies ranking during that period about in the order named. During those years thirteen new college fraternities appeared to dispute supremacy, so far as possible, with those which were practically their inspiration, Zeta Psi at the University of New York in 1846; Theta Delta Chi at Union in 1847; Delta Psi at Columbia in the same year; Phi Delta Theta at Miami, and Phi Gamma Delta at Washington and Jefferson in 1848; Phi Kappa Sigma at the University of Pennsylvania in 1850; Phi Kappa Psi at Jefferson in 1852; Sigma Chi at Miami in 1855; Sigma Alpha Epsilon at the University of Alabama in 1856; Chi Phi (southern) at the University of North Carolina in 1858; another Chi Phi, this at Hobart College in 1860, and Delta Tau Delta at Bethany College in the same year. The original Southern college fraternity, "The Rainbow," founded at the University of Mississippi in 1841, believed to have been an offshoot from the Mystical Seven of Wesleyan, did not live long. (See Order of the Heptasophs.) The Princeton and Hobart orders of Chi Phi united in 1867, and the Southern order of Chi Phi joined them in 1874, when the amalgamated orders took the name of the Chi Phi fraternity. After the Civil War there was not much opportunity for new college fraternities to compete with those already in the field, except in the South, where chapters of Northern fraternities had disappeared. As shown in an accompanying genealogical chart of these organizations, five Greek-letter fraternities were established at Southern educational institutions between 1864 and 1870: Alpha Tau Omega at Virginia Military Institute, and Kappa Alpha (southern) at Washington-Lee University, Virginia, in 1865; Kappa Sigma at the University of Virginia in 1867; Pi Kappa Alpha at the same place in 1868, and Sigma Nu at the Virginia Military Institute in 1869, all of which have sent out branches and prospered. Aside from the founding in 1884 of a third local senior society, Wolf's Head, at Yale, the past twenty-seven years have developed few, if any, college fraternities of national repute except professional and women's societies. The quarter of a century in this department of college life has witnessed a rapid growth on the part of some fraternities which, just after the war, were not ranked among the first half dozen, and by others, the development of abnormal conservatism, with a tendency to let well enough alone, and in some instances to live on prestige. An accompanying chart makes it plain that after Kappa Alpha, Sigma Phi, and Delta Phi at Union bad given rise to Alpha Delta Phi and to Psi Upsilon, the former to Beta Theta Pi and the latter to Delta Kappa Epsilon, that the line of propagation, as it were, was divided. One course was the outcome of the activity of Alpha Delta Phi and Beta Theta Pi, resulting in Phi Gamma Delta, Phi Delta Theta, Phi Kappa Psi, Sigma Alpha Epsilon Delta Tau Delta, Alpha Tau Omega Kappa Alpha (southern) and Sigma Nu, the other, the result of Psi Upsilon and Delta Kappa Epsilon stimulus, including Sigma Chi, Kappa Sigma, Pi Kappa Alpha, and Phi Kappa Sigma. Among remaining prominent societies Chi Psi and Theta Delta Chi had their origin at Union, and Delta Psi and Zeta Psi in New York city, where Alpha Delta Phi, Psi Upsilon and Delta Phi had each preceded them. The foregoing suggests a classification of college fraternities into general, honorary, professional, women's and local.

The older societies in the first group may be subdivided according to seniority and place of origin as follows:

GENERAL FRATERNITIES.

Union Triad.—Kappa Alpha, Sigma Phi, Delta Phi.
Historic Triad.—Alpha Delta Phi, Psi Upsilon, Delta Kappa Epsilon.
Pennsylvania Triad.—Phi Gamma Delta, Phi Kappa Sigma, Phi Kappa Psi.
Double Triad (East).—Mystical Seven, Chi Psi, Zeta Psi, Theta, Delta Chi, Delta Psi, Chi Phi (Princeton, 1854).
Miami Triad (West)—Beta Theta Pi, Phi Delta, Theta Sigma Chi
Triple Triad (South)—W. W. W., or The] Rainbow (dead), Sigma Alpha Epsilon, Chi Phi (University of North Carolina), Delta Tau Delta, Alpha Tau Omega, Kappa Alpha, Kappa Sigma, Pi Kappa Alpha, Sigma Nu.

The characteristics of the three earlier fraternities at Union College are broadly marked. Twenty years ago and for a long time preceding, the membership of the few chapters of Kappa Alpha (very few had or have been established) was limited and exclusive, while the policy of the fraternity was distinctly one of non-extension. Its immediate imitator, Sigma Phi, was not long in securing a like classification. It, too, had a restricted number of chapters, and a tendency to regard the grandfather as having much to do with the man. Delta Phi was less exclusive, but did not establish many new chapters and has held to its earlier standard with less success than the other two. Baird says of the three great fraternities, Alpha Delta Phi, Psi Upsilon, and Delta Kappa Epsilon, that "they are rivals of each other more frequently than of other societies, and have the common characteristics of chapters of large size, literary work in their meetings, and wealth in their outward appointments." He thinks the first excels in literary spirit, the second in the cultivation of the social side of life, and that the third "occupies a middle ground." At Yale they are junior societies, and at that place, more often than otherwise, are stepping _tones to the senior societies. They are found as rivals at Hamilton, Columbia, Yale, Amherst, Brown, Bowdoin, Dartmouth, Michigan Rochester, Wesleyan, Kenyon, Cornell, Trinity, and Minnesota; the first and third at Western Reserve, Williams, and College of the City of New York; the second and third at Chicago and Syracuse, and the first two at Union. Psi Upsilon also has chapters at New York University, University of Pennsylvania, and Lehigh; Alpha Delta Phi at Harvard, Johns Hopkins and Toronto; and Delta Kappa Epsilon at Colby, Lafayette, Colgate, Rutgers, Middlebury, Rensselaer Polytechnic Institute, De Pauw, Central, Miami, California, Vanderbilt, Virginia, North Carolina, Alabama, and Mississippi. Alpha Delta Phi and Psi Upsilon continue to pay that attention to the social standing and literary excellence among their members which has ever characterized almost all of the chapters of each, but are more conservative as to extension than formerly. Delta Kappa Epsilon is noticeable for good fellowship and numerous chapters, some of which as noted, are at minor colleges.

Beta Theta Pi, the first western fraternity, is now one of the largest and best governed. It places less weight on the propriety or desirability of what has been called conservatism with respect to increase of chapters and maintains as high literary excellence among members as older and formerly more distinguished fraternities. Chi Psi, while not so restricted as to number of chapters as Sigma Phi or Kappa Alpha, continues one of the smaller societies; its reputation is as much for good fellowship as for social or literary excellence. Zeta Psi was formerly one of the smaller fraternities, but adopted a policy of extension and has grown rapidly. It is very secret, was founded by Freemasons, and in recent years has made a remarkable advance in standing and membership. The socially exclusive members of Delta Psi, like those of Sigma Phi and Kappa Alpha, do not add to their few chapters. There is considerable wealth centred in this organization. Among western societies which have shown enterprise and have become prominent of late years are Phi Kappa Psi, Phi Delta Theta, and Phi Gamma Delta. Some of the relatively smaller or younger societies, such as Theta Delta Chi, the (amalgamated) Chi Phi, Sigma Chi, and Delta Tau Delta, are particularly strong at a number of colleges. The fraternities in the Pennsylvania and Miami groups, as a whole, have paid more attention to extension than to the exclusiveness which has marked societies forming the Union, Historic, and Double Triads. Most of the Chapters of the Southern group are confined to colleges in the South. Since 1880, Beta Theta Pi, Phi Delta Theta, Delta Tau Delta, Phi Kappa Psi, Sigma Chi, and Phi Gamma Delta, which, prior thereto, were found almost exclusively in western and southern colleges, began to invade colleges and universities of the North and East, where to-day, in some instances, they dispute supremacy with older fraternities.

HONORARY FRATERNITIES.

Phi Beta Kappa; Chi Delta Theta, local Yale, and Sigma Xi, local, Cornell, 1886.

PROFESSIONAL FRATERNITIES.

Theta Xi, English and scientific, Rensselaer Polytechnic Institute, 1864: four chapters in 1890; membership estimated. 450.

Phi Delta Phi, law, University of Michigan 1869; sixteen chapters in 1890; membership in 1897 estimated,. 2,000.

Q. T. V., (not Greek-letter), agricultural and scientific , Massachusetts Agricultural College, 1809; four chapters, in 1890; membership estimated, 650.

Phi Sigma Kappa, scientific and medical, Massachusetts Agricultural College' 1873; three chapters in 1890; membership estimated, 210.

Nu Sigma Nu, medical, University of Michigan, 1882; three chapters in 1890; membership in 1897 estimated, 200.

Alpha Chi Omega, music (women students), De Pauw University, 1885; two chapters in 1890; membership estimated, 200.

Phi Alpha Sigma, medical, Bellevue Hospital, 1887; two chapters and an estimated membership of 150.

College Sisterhoods.

Pi Beta Phi, founded at Monmouth College, Illinois, by eleven young women; originally called the I. C. Sorosis, now known by the Greek letters which, placed on the feather of a golden arrow constitute the society's badge; colors are wine red and pale blue and its flower is the carnation; there were nineteen chapters reported in 1890 in Illinois, Iowa, Indiana, Kansas, Michigan, Nebraska, Colorado, District of Columbia, Ohio, and Minnesota. Total membership is probably not over 1,600.

Kappa Kappa Gamma, organized at Monmouth, Ill., 1870 by four young women, in preference to accepting membership in a proposed sisterhood. It spread to colleges through the central western and northwestern States, and by 1890 had twenty-two active chapters, with a form of government similar to that of many Greek-letter fraternities. It's colors are dark and light blue and the badge is a jewelled key with the letters Kappa Kappa Gamma and Alpha Omega Omicron enamelled in black thereon. Present membership: about 2,200

Kappa Alpha Theta, organized at De Pauw University, Indiana, in 1870, by a daughter of a member of Beta Theta Pi and three other women students, assisted by the father of the founder. Its government was vested in the parent chapter until 1883, when it was placed in the hands of a Grand Chapter composed of one member from each chapter. Its flower is the pansy, its colors are black and gold and its badge is a kite shaped shield with a black- field and white chevron bearing the Greek letters forming its name. Its twenty active chapters in 1890 were scattered through the central western and northwestern States, with a few in California, Pennsylvania, New York, and Vermont. Present membership is approximately 1,900.

Delta Gamma, founded at the University of Mississippi, in 1872, by three women, the outgrowth of a social organization at a neighboring educational institution. The twelve active chapters in 1890 were distributed through southern, central, northwestern, a few far western, and in eastern States. March 15 is observed as a day of reunion, when the alumni, so far as possible, visit active chapters or communicate with them by mail. A Grand (governing) and a Deputy Grand Chapter is chosen every four years. There are alumni chapters at Cleveland, Milwaukee, Chicago, and other cities. Its colors are pink, blue, and bronze, and the pearl rose is the society flower. The badge is a gold anchor, with a shield above the flukes bearing the letters forming the name of the organization.

Alpha Phi, founded at Syracuse University in 1872, by ten women students. Nine years later it established the second or Beta, Chapter, that at Northwestern University, but has continued a conservative policy in this respect, having formed only five chapters by 1890, the others being at Boston University, De Pauw, and Cornell. There are several alumni chapters. The first society chapter house among

Greek-letter sisterhoods was erected by the Alpha (Syracuse) Chapter of Alpha Phi. Lilies of the valley and forget-me-nots are the flowers of the sisterhood. Its colors are silver gray and red, and its badge is a monogram formed of the letters composing its name. Frances Willard, late President of the W. C. T. U., was one of its alumni.

Gamma Phi Beta, founded at Syracuse University, 1874, by four women students, aided by Bishop E. 0. Haven, then Chancelor [sic] of the University. Its four other chapters in 1890 were located at Ann Arbor, University of Wisconsin Boston University, and Northwestern University. The society flower is the carnation. Its colors are fawn and seal brown, and the badge is a monogram of the three Greek letters within a crescent.

Sigma Kappa was organized at Colby University, Waterville, Me., 1874. Estimated membership 130.

Alpha Beta Tau was founded in 1881, at Oxford Female Institute, Oxford, Miss., with a branch at the University of Mississippi. Its total membership is about 290.

P. E. 0. (Not Greek-letter,) Little is known of this society, which exists West and South, both at and without college cities and towns. There appears to be an especial element of secrecy attached to it. Its membership, has been estimated at about 2,000.

Delta Delta Delta was organized in 1888 at Boston University by four young women. In 1890 it had five chapters. It is governed by convention, and during recess by the officers and parent chapter. It displays the pansy, gold, silver, and blue colors, and a badge consisting of a crescent with three deltas upon it and three stars between the horns. Its membership is about 300.

Beta Sigma Omicron was founded at the University of Missouri in 1889.

LOCAL FRATERNITIES.

1. K. A. (not Greek), Trinity, 1829. Founded by six students of the classes of '29, '30, and '32. Its color is royal purple. The badge is a St. Andrew's cross, bearing the initials of its title on three of the arms, and 1776 on the fourth. Rev. Thomas Gallaudet, St. Ann's, New York, and Rev. George Mallory, editor of the "Churchman "New York, are among its best known alumni.

Skull and Bones was founded at Yale College, as a senior society, by fifteen members of the class of 1832. A writer in the New York "Tribune," in 1896, states that:

> The father of "Bones," first of the senior societies, is believed to have been General William H. Russell, '37, who died a few years ago, after having been for many years at the head of a famous military academy in the city of New Haven. It is a part of college tradition that "Bones" is a branch of a university corps in Germany, in which country General Russell spent some time before his graduation. One of the classmates who joined with him in establishing the society at Yale was the late Alphonso Taft of Cincinnati, President Hayes's Attorney-General. The

> society flourished from the start. For a long time it held its meetings in hired rooms; but in 1856 the windowless, vine-covered brown stone hall in High Street, near Chapel Street, opposite the campus, was erected. A few years ago the society found more space necessary and built a large wing to the hall. The building is about 30 feet high, 33 feet wide, and 44 feet deep. The property is held by the Russell Trust Association, a name assumed in honor of General Russell. On the last Thursday in May the entire college assembles before Durfee Hall, among whom the juniors are conspicuous, for they all know that lightning is to strike forty-five of them. Soon a "Bones" man appears who, however good natured, wears a solemn look as he passes in and out among the crowd. Suddenly he taps or slaps a junior on the shoulder,* and says sternly, "Go to your room." Amid wild cheering the lucky man obeys mutely followed by the one who tapped him, who says, "Will you accept an election to the society known as 'Skull and Bones?'" and goes away in silence, while the junior returns to receive the congratulations of friends. About the same time a Keys man, and a "Wolf's Head" man in his wake, go through the same evolutions. Between "tapping time" and initiation a week elapses. During this time the slapper and the slapped preserve a sacred mutual silence, except when the new man is notified of the time and place of the awful ordeal, to be consummated in the recesses of the society house.

This peculiar ceremony of nominating or choosing new members of the Yale senior societies, original there with Skull and Bones and imitated by "Keys" and by Wolf's Head, is, doubtless, derived from the accolade, or conferring of knighthood, in ancient times an embrace; but more recently a blow on the shoulder with the flat of a sword. But still more singular is the custom of the Yale juniors in assembling on the campus between four and six o'clock, on the particular Thursday in May, accompanied by half the college, and hundreds of other spectators, entirely without announcement from or arrangement by any one. The writer first referred to points out, in addition to the fact that Yale's senior societies meet Thursday nights in closely guarded society houses, that a "Bones" man, while in college, is never without his badge, a skull and bones, with the figures "322" in place of the lower jaw; that if in swimming without bathing costume, he carries it in his mouth; that one of the newly chosen "Bones" men wears two (overlapped) badges for six months, and that the "sanctum sanctorum" in the "Bones" house is referred to by the figures "322." There is a tradition, however, that the "322," the sum of which is the perfect number and suggests a "mystical seven," means "founded in '32, 2nd chapter (the first being "the German corps"); also, that the members trace their society "to a Greek patriot organization, dating back to Demosthenes, 322 B.C. The 'Bones' records of 1881, it, is alleged, are headed 'Anno-Demotheni 2203.' " An election to "Bones" is generally the secret ambition of almost all Yale men, even over the bones of the Greek-letter societies, although Scroll and Key, and Wolf's Head, of late, have made such

*Secret Societies at Yale. Rupert Hughes, McClure's Magazine, June, 1894.

[Editor's Note: The article was in *Munsey's Magazine*, not *McClures Magazine* and is reprinted in this book.]

strides as to frequently dispute the first place which the older senior society has had in the minds of available material. "Bones" generally elects honor men and athletic stars. Scroll and Key takes men of the same rank, but more frequently from among the social element, while Wolf's Head has taken men which might have been welcome additions to either

Bones" or "Keys." The following are the names of some of the better known Yale graduates who are "Bones" men: President Dwight, Ellis H. Roberts, William W. Crapo, Daniel C. Gilman, Andrew D. White, Chauncey M. Depew, Moses Coit Tyler, Eugene Schuyler, William Walter Phelps, Anthony Higgins, Daniel H. Chamberlain, Franklin McVeagh, William Collins Whitney, William Graham Sumner, George Peabody Wetmore, Wilson Shannon Bissell, John C. Eno, Theodore S. Woolsey, Walker Blaine, Arthur T. Hadley, Robert J. Cook, Judge William II. Taft, Walter Camp, Sheffield Phelps, and Alonzo A. Stagg. The three historic junior societies at Yale are Alpha Delta Phi, Psi Upsilon, and Delta Kappa Epsilon, although Zeta Psi has figured there of late years as a sophomore and junior society. Skull and Bones, Scroll and Key, and Wolf's Head, as a matter of practice, each elect fifteen members annually, generally from among members of the first three societies named, seldom from members of that last named, and still less frequently elect a junior who is not a member of any, of the Greek-letter fraternities.

Lambda Iota was founded at the University of Vermont by thirteen students, where it has since maintained a prosperous existence. Its badge consists of an owl on the top of a column or pillar between the letters forming the society's name. It numbers three governors of Vermont among its alumni. Its membership is more than 400.

Scroll and Key was founded at Yale in 1841, by members of the class of '42, as a rival senior society to Skull and Bones, most of the peculiarities of which it copied. (See Skull and Bones.) It celebrated its fiftieth anniversary with a three days' jubilee in May, 1892, in its society house at New Haven, one of the handsomest structures of the kind in the country. It is incorporated as the Kingsley Trust Association. It is related that on the nights when the society meets all the active "Keys" men in New Haven are required to be in the society house from half-past six until half-past twelve, and that none of them is allowed to leave the building during that period, "unless accompanied by another man." In preserving a deep mystery about its affairs, in not mentioning the society in the presence of an outsider, and in retaining constant possession of badges by undergraduate members, "Keys" parallels its prototype. While members of the latter wear their badges on their vests, "Keys" men frequently wear theirs on their necktie. The "Keys" badge consists of a gold key across a scroll, with the letters "C. S. P." above, and "C. C. I." below. It selects annually fifteen members of the junior class by the same process described as originating with Skull and Bones. Its membership, on the whole, is characterized as conspicuous for social standing and wealth rather than for college or athletic honors, though many Yale athletes and honor men have joined it. Among its prominent graduates are Theodore Runyon, John Addison Porter, George Shiras, General Wager Swayne, the Rev. Joseph IT. Twitchell, Dr. James W. McLane, George A. Adee, Edward S. Dana, Isaac Bromley, Bartlett Arkell, and James R. Sheffield.

Wolf's Head was founded at Yale by a number of members of the class of '84, as a rival senior society to Skull and Bones and to Scroll and Key. (See those societies.) It copies most, if not all, of the peculiarities of the two older senior societies. For a few years it was not rated as highly as either "Bones" or "Keys," and was able to take only the so-called better men in the Junior Class overlooked by "Bones" and "Keys;" but with the increase in the size of classes, and the fact that each of the senior societies takes only fifteen men each year, with increased age and its handsome ivy-clad society house. Wolf's Head continues to gain upon its older rivals. It is incorporated as the Phelps Trust Association. Its badge consists of a wolf's head transfixed on an inverted Egyptian tau, the symbolism suggested by which is significant, yet probably different from that taught within the pale of the society.

Phi Nu Theta was organized at Wesleyan University, 1837, shortly after the appearance there of the Mystical Seven which is now dead, and in some respects one of the most remarkable college societies in the country. Phi Nu Theta sought to bring together a few members of each class for mutual helpfulness and within the past sixty years has initiated about 460 members. It has a handsome house, and ranks well among Middletown college fraternities. Its badge is a scroll watch-key with the letters forming its name engraved thereon. Among its alumni are Rev. Dr. Winchell, formerly of Syracuse University, the late Bishop Haven and Professor W. O. Atwater.

Kappa Kappa Kappa. Founded at Dartmouth, Hanover, N. H., in 1842, by six students, assisted by Professor C. B. Haddock, the year following the appearance of Scroll and Key at Yale. It numbers about 850 members. The badge is a Corinthian column and capital of gold with the letters K. K. K. at the base. It has generally ranked with other fraternities at Dartmouth.

Delta Psi. Organized at the University of Vermont in 1850. For a few years it was an anti-secret society. It has no connection with the fraternity by the same name which was founded at Columbia in 1847. It numbers about 350 members.

Alpha Sigma Pi. Organized at Norwich University, Vermont, in 1857, by seven students. The military character of the society was the natural outcome of the college where it appeared. Its colors are blue and white, and the badge is a gold shield displaying a flag and musket crossed over a drum and the Greek letters forming the name of the organization. Present membership, about 290. General Granville M. Dodge is, perhaps, its most widely known alumnus.

Phi Zeta Mu was organized in the scientific school, Dartmouth, in 1857, by five students, members of '58 and '59. It has a monogram badge, a fine society building, and about 400 members.

Alpha Sigma Phi was founded at Yale in 1846 as a sophomore society. It established chapters at Harvard in 1850, Amherst in 1857, Marietta College, Ohio, in 1860, and at Ohio Wesleyan University in 1865. The parent chapter died from internal disagreements, the first two branches were suppressed by college faculties, and the fourth was withdrawn by the society itself, which flourishes, therefore, solely at Marietta College. It has about 300 names in its catalogue, and there are several organizations of its alumni. The society has a fine house. Its badge consists of a shield bearing an open book on which are hieroglyphics, across it a quill and letters forming the name of the society.

Berzelius was established at Sheffield, Yale College, in 1863. Its membership is about 370. The badge "is a combination of potash bulbs in gold," over which is the letter "B." It ranks high among Yale scientific students.

Sigma Delta Chi was founded at Sheffield Scientific School, Yale, in 1867. It is sometimes referred to as Book and Snake, because its badge consists of an open book displaying the letters Sigma Delta Chi, surrounded by a serpent. It is prosperous and has about 300 members.

The foregoing makes it plain that the secret society system at Yale is something radically different from that at other colleges. The difference may be made clear by stating that at almost all colleges the freshman who receives a bid from and joins a Greek-letter fraternity unites with an interstate or national society which represents the social, literary, and human side of college life and binds him closely to itself not only while an undergraduate, but for life.

At Yale when there used to be freshmen as well as sophomore,' junior, and senior societies, the same general cliques or group of "fellows" were taken into the same freshman, sophomore, junior, and senior societies in a mass, a sort of four degrees system, each society representing a different "degree." The freshmen societies were merely Yale affairs, with no ligaments reaching to other colleges, and the like is true to-day of Yale's sophomore societies. Its three junior fraternities are, indeed, parts of as many national college societies, with a prestige not second even to Yale's senior societies, but one must leave the shadows of Yale to appreciate the fact. The Yale senior societies, owing to this exceptional and unfortunate system so far as the Yale sophomore and junior societies are concerned, are goals, and the sophomore and junior societies are merely stepping-stones. Twenty-five years ago the rival freshmen societies were "D. K." (Delta Kappa) and "Sigma Epps" (Kappa Sigma Epsilon). The sophomore members endeavored to select freshmen most likely to make a mark while in college, and great efforts were made by the rival societies to outwit each other and get "the best men." When the initiation ceremonies were held, a month later, the sophomores felt that they were rewarded for their trouble. A correspondent of the New York "Sun" has described substantially what took place at the initiation of freshmen during the palmy days of "D. K." and "Sigma Epps," as follows:

The candidate received a black-bordered notification of his election, with instructions to repair the following evening to some remote street corner. There he was met by two sophomore members who straightway blindfolded him and grasped him firmly on either side. Then ensued a Walhalla dance through bypath and wood and dell. Now the candidate was run at full speed against a tree, now he trembled astride a picket fence, now the bandage was slipped so as to give one glance of an open grave or the dizzy verge of East Rock. Then, after many miles and countless turns he was hurried, all panting, struggling, and stumbling, through a busy street, made evident by jostlings and derisive calls. He was forced step by step to mount backward a seemingly interminable flight of stairs, and to wait in a close and heated room until there was a sudden upward jerk, the bandage was removed, and be found himself on the roof of a high building with others of his classmates, equally confused and exhausted. When at length the candidate's name was called in sombre tones he advanced all uncertain to the scuttle. There he was bound and blindfolded. Strong arms grasped him from above and from below. He descended rapidly with many a bump. He was dragged into the main hall, flung into a great canvas blanket with rope handles, and then, with all the force of a score of excited young devotees, tossed and slapped again and again against the lofty ceiling. He was rolled in a cask and nailed in a coffin, and stretched on a guillotine with one blade—all to an accompaniment of sulphurous smoke and lurid flashes and piercing yells of "'My poor fresh."

But these ceremonies were not always without unfortunate results, and at times were marked, by a degree of hilariousness not explained entirely on the ground of good nature and a desire to look on the humorous side of life. The displeasure of the faculty was an outcome, and in 1880 the societies were abolished. The only remaining Yale freshman fraternity, Gamma Nu, founded in 1859 as a non-secret, literary society, died from internal weakness in 1889, since which time Yale Greek-letter or other secret freshmen societies have been extinct. Twenty-five years ago Yale's sophomore fraternities were Phi Theta Psi and Delta Beta Xi, founded on the ruins, as it were, of Kappa Sigma Phi and Alpha Sigma Theta. The first, called "Theta Psi," was practically a stepping-stone to Psi Upsilon, and Delta Beta" was all ante-room leading to the sanctum sanctorum of Delta Kappa Epsilon. They took about thirty men each and held weekly meetings, features of which were mild-mannered literary exercises and sometimes punch that was anything but mild. So serious were the results of one occasion of that kind, in 1878, that the faculty unceremoniously "twisted the neck" of the "phoenix of Theta Psi" and closed "the book of Delta Beta forever." The two existing sophomore societies are Hé Boulé and Eta Phi, the first formed in 1875 and the latter in 1879, among the most powerful organizations at Yale, it being seldom that a member of each fails of an election to the junior societies. They are almost if not quite as secret in their workings as the senior societies, and constitute a formidable factor in college politics. The names of the seventeen members of each, together with their places of meeting, are confidently believed by members to be unknown to the outside world; and while, as a matter of fact, such is seldom or never the case, the fiction is encouraged. The owl and initials of He Boule and the mask of Eta Phi are worn near the left armholes of the waistcoat. Alpha Delta Phi, Psi Upsilon, and Delta Kappa Epsilon of national fame, with chapters at many other colleges, each takes thirty-five sophomores at the end of the year. Zeta Psi, a two-year society at Yale, also takes its quota. As explained in the sketch of Skull and Bones, these elections have an important bearing on the chances of those selected for securing membership in one of the three senior societies. About twenty-five years ago Alpha Delta Phi refused to continue to be made a means to an end, merely a way to a senior society, and withdrew its Yale Chapter. For nearly a score of years thereafter Psi Upsilon and Delta Kappa Epsilon monopolized desirable junior recruits on their way to "Bones" and "Keys," and after 1881 to Wolf's Head. Six or seven years ago Alpha Delta Phi revived its Yale Chapter, the oldest secret society at Yale except Skull and Bones, as a four-year fraternity, and tried to make it a Yale organization on a par with even the senior year fraternities. It met with only moderate success, owing to the overpowering, weight of Yale sentiment in favor of class societies, and within a few years accepted the situation, became a junior society again, so far as that chapter is concerned, built one of the handsomest and most expensive fraternity houses at New Haven, and revived its ancient standing as a worthy rival of the Yale variety of Psi Upsilon and Delta Kappa Epsilon.

This junior society rivalry, however, is more on the surface than otherwise, the three fraternities being practically private social clubs which meet separately, of course, to cooperate in the production of plays and burlesques and in even more distinctively social entertainments. The "Alpha Delt," "Psi U," and "Deke" halls, or houses, at New Haven are among the most elaborate and costly structures of the kind in the country. In the week prior to the "tapping" ceremonial of the senior societies, in May (see Skull and Bones), the junior societies appear on the campus attired in gowns and hoods, singing each its own peculiar songs, after which they retire to their several buildings and proceed to initiate the thirty-five newly pledged members who are to act as heirs and assigns of these fraternities for the ensuing college year.

The inspiration, development, rituals, and function of the general college fraternities, those which do not live in vain, which hold the remembrance and affection of members well on into their declining years, which often divide the regard felt for alma mater, call for an analysis which the mere chronicler may well be excused for not attempting. A recent writer stated that many men who have belonged to a Greek Letter society during their undergraduate days lose interest in the matter before they are five years away from their alma mater. This is almost inevitable because of new interests and because a large number of graduates are not associated in their homes with men who belong to their fraternity. "One can hardly refrain from believing the author of the sentiment is a Yale man. The "Bones" or "Keys" graduate of Yale might naturally find the height of his ambition in an election to a senior society. Neither his sophomore nor junior year fraternities cuts much of a figure beyond the fact that he used them in an effort to get to "Bones," "Keys," or Wolf's Head. But the alumnus of Cornell, Columbia, Amherst, the

University of Michigan, and many other colleges, who is an Alpha Delt," a "Psi U, " a "Deke," a Beta," a "Zete," a "Kap," a "Sig," or a member of any of a score of others with a national reputation, remains more often than otherwise a faithful son of such society so long as he lives, and treasures its records, its traditions and its influences to' the latest days of his life. The Greek-letter fraternities antedate all other existing secret societies in America, except the fraternity of Freemasons. They vary more than might be supposed, for members are always convinced of the superiority of their own fraternities over all rivals and confident of the greater loyalty of their own alumni. Some have elaborate rituals and others ceremonials which would be regarded by good judges as commonplace. The world at large, unfortunately, has had abundant evidence during the past twenty-five years of the sensational if not solemn character of the initiation ceremonies of some, as the results were such as to endanger the lives of initiates.

Heckethorn [*Secret Societies of All Ages.*] and some others attribute the founding, in 1776, of Phi Beta Kappa, the mother of American college Greek-letter fraternities, to the Illuminati, of Weishaupt, in Bavaria, but this is undoubtedly mere conjecture. The Illuminati itself was founded in 1776, and it is hardly likely that a few boys at the College of William and Mary in Virginia, in those days of extremely infrequent letter-writing and trans-Atlantic voyages, were inspired in their formation of a Greek-letter secret society by the illustrious foreigner whose name is linked to an order which for a short time was grafted upon Freemasonry and then disappeared forever. There is no reason for believing that American college Greek Letter societies had any inspiration beyond what appeared on the surface, until after 1828, the year following the disappearance of Morgan, who was accused of being about to betray Masonic secrets. In that and several succeeding years politicians made use of this "good enough Morgan until after election," and so fanned the anti-Masonic flame that thousands of well-meaning people discovered prejudices against the fraternity which they never till then suspected themselves of possessing. Reference has been made to the effect on John Quincy Adams, Edward Everett, and others, and the history of that time will reveal some, notably Thurlow Weed, who were less sincere in their antagonism to Freemasonry, even though no less bitter. This presented an opportunity to cranks and charlatans which was not to be despised, and the country was speedily flooded with supposititious Masonic ceremonies and alleged accounts of revelations of Masonic secrets. The public mind was directed to that subject as it never had been before, and probably never will be again. Secret societies of the middle ages, the mysteries of Isis and Osiris and of Eleusis, and the revolutionary secret societies of this and of other countries, all came in for a critical examination and premeditated condemnation and got both. The only importance attaching to this reference is to recall what seems not to have been pointed out before, that it was during the period from 1828 to 1845, covering the anti-Masonic agitation, that the older among the best known national Greek-letter college fraternities were born. At that time the English Order of Foresters was just being introduced here; the

English Order of Odd Fellows had not been domesticated more than a decade and had only a few members; the English Order of Druids was a newcomer; the American Improved Order of Red Men as at present organized, was only then taking shape, and the Ancient Order of Hibernians had just arrived at New York City from Ireland. Curiosity and prejudice had been mingled in an effort to find out something with which to condemn the type of the secret society, Freemasonry, and the effort resulted, among other things, in a study of secret societies

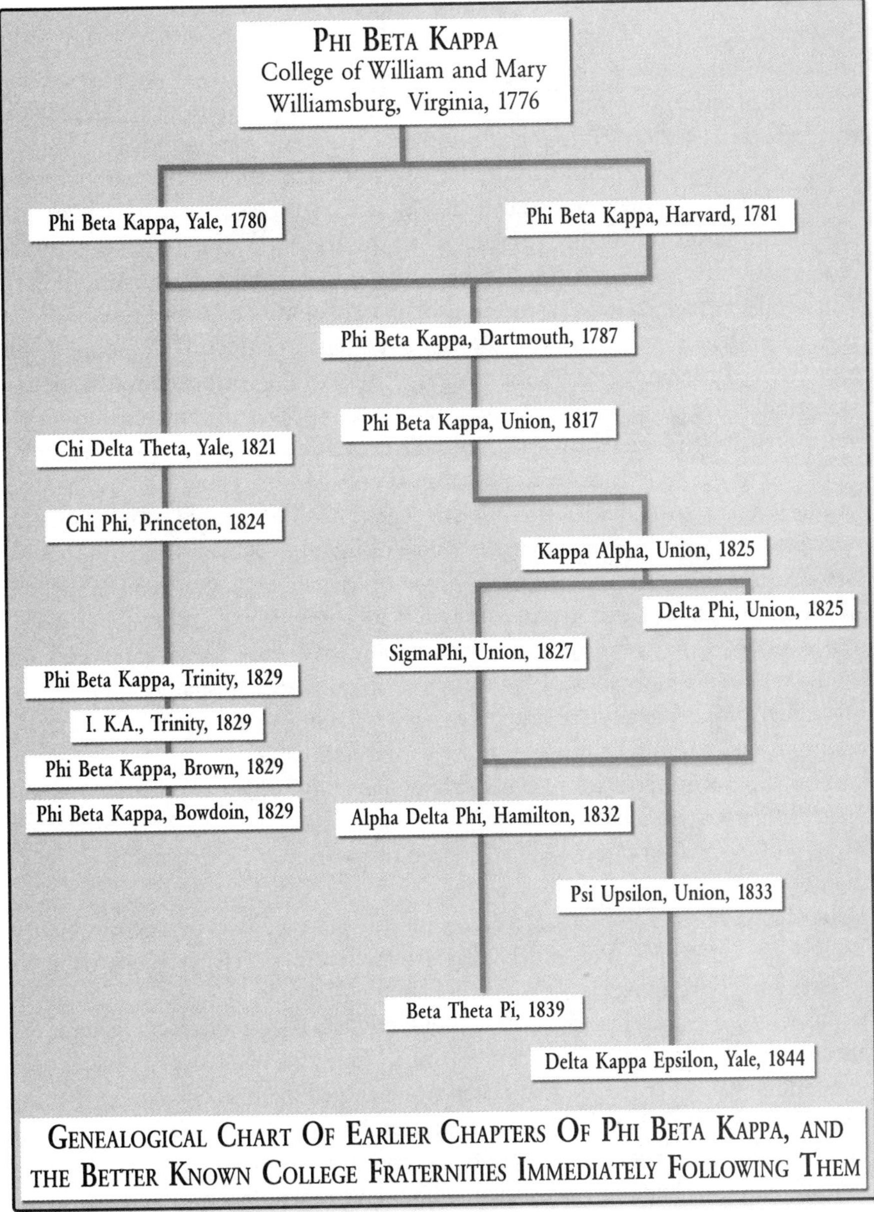

GENEALOGICAL CHART OF EARLIER CHAPTERS OF PHI BETA KAPPA, AND THE BETTER KNOWN COLLEGE FRATERNITIES IMMEDIATELY FOLLOWING THEM

in general. If one can read of groups of college students at New York and New England centres of intelligence organizing Greek Letter secret societies on the outward lines established by Phi Beta Kappa, Kappa Alpha, Sigma Phi, and Delta Phi without appreciating that they must have utilized some of the raw material which was floating in the air, he must be deficient in imagination. The societies which saw the light in 1825 and 1827, Kappa Alpha, Sigma Phi, and Delta Phi, probably did not have elaborate rituals at that time. There are those who know they had them later. Then came Alpha Delta Phi and Skull and Bones in 1832, Psi Upsilon, in 1833, 'Mystical Seven in 1837, Beta Theta Pi in 1839, Chi Psi and Scroll and Key in 1841, and Delta Kappa Epsilon in 1844. In these one finds the practical inspiration for all that came after in the family of Greek-letter societies. That college fraternities multiplied fast and grew rapidly during this period is more than significant. As a matter of fact, some of the better known college fraternities give unmistakable evidence, to those of their members in a position to judge, of having rummaged in the bureau drawers of Freemasonry, Odd Fellowship, Forestry, the Templars, Knights of Malta, and other "orders" for ritualistic finery. Zeta Psi was founded by Freemasons. Delta Psi, Columbia, 1847, was dressed up by some one who had access to rituals of the bastard Masonic rites of Misraim and Memphis. Psi Upsilon hung its harp low on the tree of symbolic Masonry while its offspring, Delta Kappa Epsilon, read up on the Vehmgerichte and ancient Grecian mysteries before selecting a few ceremonials which would better fit nineteenth-century college life. Theta Delta Chi went far afield and returned with the Forestic legend, while the earlier "Alpha Delts" were evidently inspired by what they knew of Royal Arch Masonry and the Red Cross degree as conferred in commanderies of Masonic Knights Templars. There would appear to be little room to-day for additions to the Greek-letter world. There are too many of these fraternities already, and while there is no tendency on the part of stronger societies to unite, weaker ones occasionally find their way into older or stronger fraternities. The latter, having the prestige of age and a distinguished alumni, are naturally well-nigh invincible.

The general fraternities publish catalogues containing, as estimated, about 111,000 names, honorary about 6,500, professional 4,400, and the ladies, perhaps, 9,000; in all about 131,000, a large proportion of which are of deceased members.

Delta Kappa Epsilon. — Organized on June 22, 1844, at Yale College, by William W. Atwater, Edward G. Bartlett, Frederick P. Bellinger, Jr., Henry Case, George F. Chester, John B. Conyngham, Thomas L. Franklin, W. Walter Horton, William Boyd Jacobs, Edward V. Kinsley, Chester N. Righter, Elisha Bacon Shapleigh, Thomas D. Sherwood, Alfred Everett Stetson and Orson W. Stow, who had just completed their sophomore year. They had contemplated being elected members of Psi Upsilon in a body, but some of them failing to secure an election to that junior society, the fifteen stood together and formed a new junior society with the foregoing title, to compete with Alpha Delta Phi and Psi Upsilon, which, until then, had monopolized junior year Greek-letter society interests at Yale. Delta Kappa Epsilon, or "D. K. E." as it is usually called, beat all records at extension, by placing chapters at thirty-two colleges and universities between the year it was founded and the outbreak of the war in 1861, going as far as Miami and the University of Michigan in the West and to colleges in Virginia, Kentucky, Tennessee, Mississippi and Louisiana at the South. The southern chapters were rendered dormant by the war, and since 1866 the fraternity has been much more particular in creating branches, has made more of an effort to revive inactive chapters than to place new ones. Its original plan did not contemplate a general fraternity, but early opportunities for new chapters presenting themselves, a plan for the propagation of "D. K. E." was organized and was carried out with a thoroughness which, owing in part to the war, reacted upon the general standing of the society. From 1870 to date the society has built upon far better foundation and with more care and skill, and ranks as the largest general college fraternity, with more than 12,000 members, nearly 10 per cent of the total membership of the world of Greek-letter societies. The impression has always prevailed that the parent chapter of "D. K. E." exercises a dominant influence over the entire organization, but this has been denied. Certain it is that, at times, the tie between the Yale "Deke" and his fraters from other colleges is not as strong as that between members of different chapters of almost any other college fraternity. But this may be due to the peculiar society system at Yale rather than to a peculiarity in the government or personnel of Delta Kappa Epsilon. Its Harvard chapter ran against the anti-fraternity laws there in 1858 and practically ceased to exist as a chapter of Delta Kappa Epsilon until 1863. It had not initiated members, for several years, but held meetings in Boston, where it became known as the "Dicky Club." The chapter was revived as a sophomore society in 1863, and exists to-day, occasionally challenging attention when some accident reveals to the public its ridiculous and at times reprehensible method of initiating candidates. Dicky Club is no longer "D. K. E." Quite a number of chapters of "D. K. E." have houses of their own; the "D. K. E." club in New York stands as high as similar institutions there, and there are associations of "D. K. E." alumni at a score of cities which hold annual reunions and cultivate the fraternal relations begun during college life. The fraternity is governed by an advisory council which is incorporated. The badge resembles that of Psi Upsilon, except that in the centre of the black field the golden letters Delta Kappa Epsilon appear upon a white scroll. Much is made of armorial bearings, each chapter having a distinct blazon. The fraternity emblem is a lion rampant, in black, on a gold background. On its list of names of distinguished members are those of United States Senators M. C. Butler and Calvin S. Brice ; Perry Belmont, W. A Washburn, John D. Long, A. Miner Griswold, A. P. Burbank, Theodore Roosevelt, John Bach McMaster, George Ticknor Curtis, Julian Hawthorne, Robert Grant, Theodore Winthrop, William L. Alden, ex-Governor McCreary of Kentucky; Wayne McVeagh, Charles S. Fairchild, General Francis A. Walker, Whitelaw Reid, Robert T. Lincoln, Stewart L. Woodford, Marl, H. Dunnell, and Henry Cabot Lodge.

This is the heraldry for Delta Kappa Epsilon. ΔΚΕ is known in its own literature as an international secret society. It was begun at Yale in 1844 as a junior society. Both President George W and George HW are members of the founding Phi Chapter at Yale University. Notice the use of the Winged Sun-Disk, the eye of Horus in a upside down triangle

SIGMA DELTA CHI CLOISTERS AND CHAPEL, S. S. S., YALE.

OF college fraternities in the United States one significant fact may pass unquestioned—they have retained the affection and kept the support of a large number of those who knew them best. On their rosters are found not only the names of undergraduates, but also those of men who long since left youth and folly far behind. Indeed, one now and then runs across a name that adds a certain dignity to the catalogue and becomes an inspiration for ambitious youth. Of these many find no small satisfaction in identifying themselves from time to time with the life of the various clubs and societies of which they were members when boys at college; they take a mild, half-melancholy pleasure in reminiscent talk, and delight to meet and wander with half-regretful sadness in halls where youth wears the crown.

The charm of life in the society hall is much easier for one to imagine than for another to relate. A stereotyped phrase, "mere boyishness," fails to explain it; a compendium of dry facts and arguments would be farther still from picturing the life that often masquerades under the thin veil of a half-pretended secrecy. More "sweetness and light" seems always to have been the goal towards which the fraternities strove, and the story of their development is a plain tale of natural and steady growth from small beginnings.

Towards the end of the first quarter of the present century the social life of our colleges had become barren—not more barren, perhaps, than it had been for many years, but relatively so in view of the fact that life was becoming richer and the spirit of the times more liberal. Boys from families in which puritanical methods were obsolete naturally hated the puritanism of college discipline; they chafed at the petty decorum of the stuffy class-rooms, and fretted at the deadness of the iron-bound curriculum. Almost the only means of relaxation countenanced by the faculties were open debating societies, which met on the college grounds, and to the meetings of which both professor and student might go. In view of the fact that students, from the days of Horace down, were wont to hold their preceptors as their natural enemies, the presence of professors did not increase the popularity of these societies. Indeed, they languished. Here was the opportunity of the typical college fraternity.

KAPPA ALPHA LODGE, CORNELL.

WHIG HALL, PRINCETON.

Of these societies the first to assume the characteristics that are now recognized as their essential, albeit it soon lost them, had been Phi Beta Kappa. It was founded at Williamsburg, Virginia, December 5, 1776, in the very room where Patrick Henry had voiced the revolutionary spirit of Virginia. The story is a simple one: John Heath, Thomas Smith, Richard Booker, Armistead Smith, and John Jones,

* For friendly assistance in the preparation of this article the writer cordially acknowledges his obligation to Mr. John De Witt Warner, of New York.

HASTY PUDDING CLUB-HOUSE, HARVARD.

students at William and Mary College, then the most wealthy, flourishing, and aristocratic institution of learning in America, believing that there was room for a more effective student organization than the one of a Latin name that then existed there, and recalling that one of their number was the best Greek scholar in college, resolved to found a new society, the proceedings of which were to be secret, to be known by the name of the three Greek letters that formed the initials of its motto — Phi Beta Kappa. The minutes are discouraging to those who would like to consider Phi Beta Kappa as a band of youthful enthusiasts planning a union of the virtuous college youth of this country, who were afterward to reform the world; and even more so to those who have declared infidel philosophy to be its cult. Youths of fine feelings and good digestion, they enjoyed together many a symposium like that on the occasion of Mr. Bowdoin's departure for Europe, when, "after many toasts suitable to the occasion, the evening was spent by the members in a manner which indicated the highest esteem for their departing friend, mixed with sorrow for his intended absence and joy for his future prospects in life." They called themselves a "fraternity." More thoroughly to enjoy the society of congenial associates, to promote refined good-fellowship, was the motive of these hearty young students who founded the first of the true Greek-letter fraternities, with (to quote from its ritual) "friendship as its basis, and

"KEYS" HALL, YALE.

benevolence and literature as its pillars"— one which thrived in their day as its successors on the same basis flourish in ours. So far from being inspirers, or a product, of American national spirit, or of a union of the wise and virtuous to which they invited all known American colleges, the only reference in their record to the Revolution is the single mention of the "confusion of the times" in the record of the final meeting; and the only recognition of the existence of other colleges is the record of the granting of charters for "meetings" at Harvard and Yale, which institutions were never mentioned again.

Meanwhile Cornwallis was coming nearer, and after having chartered additional chap-

"BONES" HALL, YALE.

ters,— Beta, Gamma, Delta, Epsilon, Zeta (Harvard), Eta (Yale), and Theta,— the Alpha, or mother chapter, passed out of existence.

From Epsilon and Zeta have descended the latter-day chapters of Phi Beta Kappa. Of the fate of Beta, Gamma, Delta, Eta, and Theta nothing is known. After a lapse of seventy years, William Short, of the mother chapter, at the age of ninety, traveled from Philadelphia to Williamsburg and revived the Alpha, which, however, soon succumbed to the vicissitudes of its college. It is not known what was its first follower. But of those whose activity have been continuous to date, Kappa Alpha, founded in 1825 at Union College, adopting with its Greek name a badge planned similarly to that of Phi Beta Kappa (except that it was suspended from one corner, instead of from the center of one of its equal sides), and inspired by similar ends, began

BERZELIUS HALL, S. S. S., YALE.

the career that has made it the mother of living Greek-letter societies. For Phi Beta Kappa has long since become an honorary, as distinguished from an active, institution, though the reunions of its chapters, especially of the old Zeta, now the "Alpha of Massachusetts," founded at Cambridge in 1779, are still noteworthy events.

Even before Phi Beta Kappa came into existence, Oliver Ellsworth, afterward Chief-Justice of the Supreme Court of the United States, had founded Clio Hall at Princeton, and a few years later, in 1769, Whig Hall arose at the same college with James Madison, afterward twice President of the United States, for its founder; and from that day to this these friendly rivals have never ceased to exert a healthful influence on the intellectual life of Princeton. These were the prototypes, and are the most vigorous survivals, of what, for nearly a century, were the most flourishing and numerous of student societies — the twin literary societies, or "halls," generally secret, and always intense in mutual rivalry, which have been institutions at every leading college in the land.

Another and a third, though less homogeneous, class of student societies may be best described by noting separately its only important examples — at Harvard and Yale. The Hasty Pudding Club of Harvard also took its rise in those interesting and formative years just subsequent to the close of the Revolutionary war, and was founded, as its constitution says, "to cherish the feelings of friendship and patriotism." For the display of the latter virtue the club for many years was wont to celebrate Washington's Birthday with oration and poem, with toasts and punch. Alas, for these degenerate days! Conventional theatricals have taken the place of poem and oration, though, for aught I know, the toasts and punch may yet survive. "Two members in alphabetical order"— so ran the old by-laws — "shall provide a pot of hasty pudding for every meeting," and it is said that this practice is still religiously kept. That the banquet was not lightly considered by the old Harvard clubs may be seen in the tendency to exalt in the name of the club the peculiar feature of the club's fare, the Porcellian taking its name from the roasted pig — classical token of hospitality — that one of its bright young members provided for the entertainment of his fellows on a time when the feast fell to his providing. But the Porcellian has not wholly given itself up to the things that go with banqueting, for no other college society has so fine a library as it possesses. Indeed, its seven thousand well-selected and finely bound volumes might be coveted by many less fortunate small colleges. The A. D. Club is a younger rival of the "Pork," and, in the comfort of its house, the brilliancy of its dinners, and its good-fellowship, is by no means inferior. The development of this species of undergraduate activity has taken a widely different and rather unique form at Yale. The Yale senior societies are the most secret and clannish of college societies. No outsiders ever enter their buildings, and their goings and comings are so locked in mystery that one can only guess what their aims and purposes are. A passion for relic worship and a taste for politics are generally ascribed to both, though the class of men taken by Scroll and Key differs widely from that chosen by Skull

DELTA KAPPA EPSILON HALL, YALE.

ALPHA DELTA PHI (EELL'S MEMORIAL) HALL, HAMILTON.

and Bones — the men of the former being selected, it is supposed, for their social position and qualities of good-fellowship, while those of the latter are usually good scholars or prominent athletes.

Thus we have the three classes of student societies — the old literary societies, still flourishing in the older colleges of the South, but languishing elsewhere, except at Princeton, where Clio and Whig are still the great institutions of the student body, and at Lafayette, where the Washington and Jefferson are scarcely less prosperous; the peculiar local institutions of Yale and Harvard, *sui generis* and not to be propagated; and the Greek-letter system of chaptered fraternities, the chartered corporations of which are to-day the most prominent characteristic of American undergraduate social life.

The interval of thirty-five years from the founding of Kappa Alpha to the outbreak of the civil war was the golden age of these fraternities. They sprang up and multiplied with a persistency that should forever make firm the doctrine of the strengthening power of persecution. They were not confined to any one grade of college or to any particular part of the country. They flourished everywhere, and increased in number through almost every imaginable combination of the letters of the Greek alphabet. Many, of course, have vanished from the face of the earth. Of those that still remain, Delta Kappa Epsilon, founded at Yale in 1844, is the largest, and has now above 9000 members, representing 32 active chapters situated in 19 different States; Psi Upsilon, originated at Union in 1833, enrolls some 6600 members, distributed among 19 chapters in 10 States; and Alpha Delta Phi, founded at Hamilton in 1832, has a membership nearly as large. Delta Kappa Epsilon appears to have made good its claim to be recognized as a national institution; and while certain smaller fraternities are favorites in particular parts of the country, all barriers are rapidly disappearing before these three favorite societies in their march towards representation at all the important colleges of the country.

ALPHA TAU OMEGA HALL, SEWANEE.

Though fraternities are organized less frequently now than formerly, because of the

DELTA KAPPA EPSILON HALL, ANN ARBOR.

increased difficulty of competing with those that have been long established, still, as the colleges themselves grow, the chapters of the most flourishing fraternities grow with them; so that the increase of the system, as a whole, is both very regular and very considerable. Up to 1883, the date at which the latest general manual of the fraternities appeared, there were enrolled among the 32 general college fraternities of this country, forming an aggregate of 505 active chapters, no less than 67,941 members, representing every possible profession and branch of business, every shade of religious and political opinion, and every State and Territory of the United States. But these figures by no means tell the whole story of

ALPHA PHI (LADIES') LODGE, SYRACUSE.

the growth and spread of the "little" college fraternities. Many colleges and advanced technical schools in every section of the country, besides welcoming the general fraternities to their privileges, have ambitiously started and preserved local fraternities that are limited or have no branches at other institutions, but nevertheless often enjoy a large share of local patronage. These societies, of which there are 16 now in existence, had a membership of 4077. But this is not all. The female students, not to be outdone, about a dozen years ago began to organize sisterhoods, from which males were ignominiously debarred from membership, and had meantime succeeded in building up 7 prosperous societies, with 16 chapters and 2038 members, situated mostly in co-educational institutions. When to this grand total of 74,056 names are added the large membership of the Princeton halls, the Harvard clubs, and the Yale senior societies, already described, together with the very numerous class organizations in various colleges, it may be seen how firm a hold the spirit of coöperation has taken upon the collegians of the country. The fraternities have grown far away from the persecutions of their early days, when the hands of all men and faculties were raised against them. Because they met in secret, and held themselves free from the intrusion of the faculty for one night in the week, and adorned their poor little badges with Greek letters, all evil and rebellious conduct was charged against them. Though their purposes were sensible enough, and good rather than evil has come from them, a nameless stigma of bad parentage still rests upon the whole system, to live down which, by an overplus of actual and visible good attainment, has not been possible till within recent years. But prejudice has an unequal contest with conviction. Through persecution, and poverty of opportunity, and lack of means the new society men fought their way towards solid ground, finding in their struggles and in their ambitions for the success and honors of their fraternities an incentive and charm college life had till then never yielded.

Whatever may have been the shortcomings of the American college boy of a quarter of a century ago, want of energy was not one of them. To take off his coat and go to work with his hands seemed to him the most natural thing when he needed a society lodge. In this way was built, in 1855, the famous "log-cabin" of Delta Kappa Epsilon at Kenyon College, Gambier, Ohio. The site selected was a deep ravine, far away from any human dwelling. Neighboring farmers were hired to fell the trees and to raise the frame of this ark of a house, forty-five feet in length by ten in height. The entire chapter (including its youngest member, now an orator of national reputation several times elected to Congress) rested not until they had plastered the outside crevices with mud. Inside the room was nicely ceiled, and furnished with good tables and chairs, a carpet, and several pictures. The walls and roof of the building were ingeniously deadened with saw-dust and charcoal, so that not the remotest whispers could reach the ears of curious eavesdroppers, if any such should have the temerity to penetrate to the recesses of this sylvan retreat. "A cooking-stove, with skillet, griddles, and pots complete, was the pride of the premises," writes an old member, "where each hungry boy could roast his own potatoes, or cook his meat on a forked stick, in true bandit style."

DELTA KAPPA EPSILON LOG-CABIN, KENYON.

The building of this lodge gave a great impetus to the owning of society homesteads. Before this the various chapters had been accustomed to rendezvous stealthily in college garrets, at village hotels, or anywhere that circumstances and pursuing faculties made most convenient. But when the assurance was once gained that the fraternities might own their premises and make them permanent abiding-places, the whole system became straightway established on a lasting foundation. In 1861, at Yale, the parent chapter of

ALPHA DELTA PHI LODGE, ANN ARBOR.

the same fraternity, Delta Kappa Epsilon, built for itself a two-story hall in the form of a well-proportioned Greek temple, and this proved to be the beginning of a long epoch of more and more elaborate house-building, the culmination of which has scarcely been reached at the present day.

From the temple-shaped hall with its facilities for the routine work of the chapter, its dramatic and social festivities, the most enterprising fraternities progressed gradually towards ample homesteads, thoroughly equipped for dealing with every phase of student life, including the furnishing of comfortable board and lodging, which, in some features, excelled the average dormitories. The work began in earnest about fifteen years ago, but the past two or three years have excelled all the others combined, both in an intelligent understanding of what was needed to make the houses thoroughly habitable and creditable in appearance, and in the amount of superior work planned in detail or actually accomplished. A critical comparison of the specimens in existence reveals the fact that pretty nearly every kind of known architecture has been tried. At Princeton one may see in the twin temples of Whig and Clio copies of the Ionic architecture; at Cambridge, should he visit the A. D. Club, he could scarcely fail to notice that this hospitable mansion is the veritable traditional New England homestead, with its air of little pretense and much comfort. At Yale, "Bones Hall" is venerable and picturesque when covered by the foliage of its ivy; the magnificent building of "Keys" is of Moorish pattern; the new "Wolf's Head" society, at the same college, honors our ancestors in the "Old Home" by choosing a corbel-stepped gable, "fretting the sky," to which the English and the Dutch of several centuries ago were noticeably partial; the stone Delta Psi lodges at New Haven and Hartford are veritable castles for strength and ruggedness of outline; no gentleman would need a more tasteful or finely located villa than one of the fraternity houses which he would find at Ithaca; while by Delta Kappa Epsilon at Amherst has been introduced, and by Sigma Delta Chi at Yale has been elaborated, what seems probable to become the reigning type — that of "cloisters," in which are lodged the members, joined by gallery or covered way to the "chapel," where are celebrated the rites of the chapter.

CHI PSI LODGE, AMHERST.

DELTA PSI HALL, S. S. S., YALE.

If the fraternities as a whole have had a weakness, it has been for what they were pleased to believe was the "Queen Anne style" — a "spread" of red bricks, irregular, very irregular, tile roofs, and an unknown quantity of bowed windows, with the usual accessories of modern stained-glass "Venetian" blinds, and unlimited opportunity for portières. These experiments, as embodied by some amateur architect, most likely a well-meaning but untrained member of the chapter, have not always been successful; but lately the bizarre mode has given way to better taste, and in all probability the next efforts of the fraternities at house-building will be characterized by solidity rather than show, by harmony rather than conspicuousness. Several of the college faculties have, with the consent of their boards of trustees, presented enterprising societies with valuable building-sites on their grounds; and where their invitations have been accepted, they have no cause to regret their generosity.

SIGMA PHI LODGE, WILLIAMS.

In interior decoration the houses of the American college fraternities differ no less radically than in external appearance. At a Western lodge the members are often content with, and indeed think themselves fortunate if

DELTA PSI LODGE, TRINITY.

they have at their command, the bare necessities of life, while not a few of the wealthy chapter-houses of the East are furnished with all the luxury and refined taste of the highest modern art as applied to club life. For instance, the lodge-room of the Delta Psi fraternity in New York City is magnificently furnished in Egyptian designs especially imported from Thebes for this purpose, at a cost of several thousands of dollars; and in the buildings of the Alpha Delta Phi at Wesleyan, the Psi Upsilon at Cornell, the Chi Psi at Amherst, and the Sigma Phi at Williams may be found wood-work, furniture, and objects of art which would be in no wise out of place in the most attractive of modern city homes. Several of the foremost chapters, such as the Sigma Phi, the Alpha Delta Phi, and the Kappa Alpha of Williams College, have been presented with valuable memorials by the friends or relatives of deceased members, which are introduced so as to form conspicuous features of the buildings. Thus the last of the three societies just named contains a strikingly beautiful emblematic window, designed by Tiffany & Co. of New York. The Samuel Eell's Memorial Hall, at Hamilton College, is itself a tribute to the brilliant young founder of the Alpha Delta Phi fraternity, who died after a short career of great promise at the Cincinnati bar as a law partner of the late Chief-Justice Chase. Other representative lodges have been built or beautified by the generosity of individuals.

With the aid of rich sons and generous parents and friends, the loading down of college lodge-rooms might easily be carried to an unfortunate extreme, especially if a false spirit of rivalry should gain a foothold in our college world. But at present there seems little danger of this. An honorable ambition prevails among the leaders of the best fraternities to make their homes complete and attractive in every particular, but beyond this they do not seek to go. The energies of those who

DELTA PSI HALL, NEW YORK CITY.

DELTA KAPPA EPSILON LODGE AND HALL, AMHERST.

have charge should be directed especially to adorning the chapter-houses with what illustrates and improves student life in general, and with what is of particular importance to the members of the college or university at which the chapter-house is located.

Of the value of the real and personal property belonging to the ten American college fraternities that are represented by at least one chapter-house each, and the leaders by

ALPHA DELTA PHI LODGE, WILLIAMS (MEMORIAL PORCH).

five or more, it may safely be said that the sum is fast approaching a million of dollars; while numerous other fraternities and chapters have well-invested and rapidly accumulating building-funds.

The fraternity literature is another interesting subject. The hideous reptiles and winged monsters, the burning altars and dungeon bars, and other such fantastic symbolism with which the magazines and newspapers of some of the fraternities are decorated, prove to cover interesting and oftentimes useful tables of contents, including reminiscences of college life and literary articles by prominent graduates, news-letters from the chapters at the different colleges, personal gossip concerning alumni, official notices from the officers of the fraternity, editorial comments, and notes from exchanges. Two or three of these society periodicals have attained a large circulation. The fraternities have not confined their energies to current papers, however, but have compiled elaborate record books of their members, in the form of catalogues, which, besides containing the names and occupations of members, give succinct sketches of the chapters and the colleges at which they are situate, interesting tables of residence and relationship, and brief biographical sketches of the most distinguished graduates. But decidedly the freshest and most characteristic literature possessed by the fraternities are their song-books, where, in varied and not always correct verse, the youthful laureates have sung the praises of their clans, comrades, festal nights, the charms of good-fellowship, and many other such tempting themes for the imagination and the heart.

Till about a dozen years ago few or none of the fraternities had a strong executive government, but were managed by the oldest chapter, or by several chapters in turn, and by the hasty edicts of the general conventions of the order. But this system proving inadequate, the leaders conceived and boldly acted on the idea of taking the general executive administration of the college fraternities out of the hands of the undergraduate members, at the same time appealing to the graduate members to assume an active share in their welfare. So far their success has been noteworthy. The graduate councils, which now form the executive department of most of the leading fraternities, are ably managed, and graduate associations of the larger fraternities have been formed in most of the important cities. They hold reunions, banquets, and business meetings, and in most essentials serve as graduate chapters of their orders, cementing old college ties and forming new ones between members of different colleges; and several of the fraternities, such as the Delta Psi, the Delta Phi, the Delta Kappa Epsilon, the Alpha Delta Phi, the Psi Upsilon, the Zeta Psi, and the Delta Upsilon, have lately taken the advanced step of establishing in the large cities regular club-houses, which are well equipped, and well patronized by men of all ages; while at Chautauqua, the "Wooglin" club-house, with its ample accommodations and grounds, is the summer headquarters of the Beta Theta Pi, by a graduate corporation of which it is owned.

The legislative functions of the fraternities still rest with the annual conventions, which are usually held with the different undergraduate chapters in turn, when, besides the transaction of routine business, the several hundred students present from all parts of the country are occupied with social courtesies extended to them by local residents, and with literary efforts in the form of orations and poems, often delivered by members of the fraternity who have attained eminence in public life.

FIELD MEMORIAL WINDOW, KAPPA ALPHA LODGE, WILLIAMS.

KAPPA ALPHA LODGE, WILLIAMS.

In view of the facts already presented in the course of this narrative, a defense of the fraternities, a summing-up of all the reasons on which their existence and continuance might be justified, seems altogether superfluous. This one significant feature of the case may however be offered to the dubious without comment, as pointing its own moral—that so far, whenever the majesty of the law has been invoked by still obstinate faculties or trustees to drive the fraternities from their institutions, the law has upheld the continuance of the societies and the free rights of the students to join them, provided that in doing so they do not violate any of the proper functions of the college. It was so in 1879, when the faculty of the University of California tried to disband a society which had been allowed to erect a house on college land, and was met by the hostile criticisms of the entire press of that State; it was so in 1882, when the president of Purdue University, Indiana, striving to compel students entering his university not to join any of the societies, was prevented by a decision of the superior court of that State, and in the end resigned his office. The one notable exception to this rule is the case of the College of New Jersey. Here the faculty succeeded in expelling all the fraternities; but it was before the era of their house-building. All of those chapters

PHI KAPPA PSI (MEMORIAL) LODGE, GETTYSBURG.

which have built houses are now incorporated institutions, paying taxes on their real and personal property, and entitled to the full privileges and protection of local and State laws.

They therefore appear to rest on a more solid basis than mere sufferance; and however ardently certain individuals may wish to see them abolished, it is extremely doubtful if even an organized crusade against them, headed by all the college presidents in the United States and the majority of the faculties under them, could succeed in doing more than to drive the reputable societies into a temporary seclusion, from which, in a few years, they would emerge stronger than ever. Such at least has been the case at many representative institutions.

But the above supposition is relegated to the realms of the impossible when one discovers that a large portion of the educators referred to are themselves members of the fraternities, and in many cases actively associated with their progress. This list includes such men as President Eliot of Harvard, Dwight of Yale, Walker of the Boston Institute of Technology, Seelye of Amherst, White of Cornell, Dwight of the Columbia Law School, Gilman of Johns Hopkins University, Johnston of Tulane, and Northrop of the University of Minnesota. There is not a faculty of any size in the United States that does not contain society members, and few professorial chairs at the largest colleges are not filled by representatives of the leading fraternities. These "little societies" have supplied forty governors to most of the largest States of the Union; and had in the last administration the President of the United States and the majority of his Cabinet. On the Supreme Bench of the United States the fraternities are now represented by five of the associate justices. A summary, published in 1885, showed Alpha Delta Phi, Psi Upsilon, and Delta Kappa Epsilon to have furnished of United States senators and representatives 39, 25, and 36 respectively; while in the last Congress 13 representatives and 2 senators were members of the last-named fraternity alone; and in the membership of these 3 fraternities are included 24 bishops of the Protestant Episcopal Church. In the class-room they are represented by Whitney and Marsh; in the pulpit, by R. S. Storrs and Phillips Brooks; in the paths of literature, by James Russell Lowell, George William Curtis, Donald G. Mitchell, Charles Dudley Warner, Edward Everett Hale, and E. C. Stedman; in recent public life, by Presidents Arthur and Garfield, by Wayne MacVeagh, Charles S. Fairchild, Robert T. Lincoln, John D. Long, William M. Evarts, Joseph R. Hawley, and William Walter Phelps. These gentlemen were not elected into the fraternities after graduation, but were active supporters of these organizations during their undergraduate days. Whatever, then, may be the shortcomings of college secret societies, it is to their credit that their exponents are men noted for ability and prominence in every useful sphere of life, as well as for mere culture and congeniality, while from end to end of the catalogued chapter-lists run in thick procession the starred names of the most brilliant and lamented of the young officers who fell in the battles of our civil war — in the blue and gray ranks alike. Judging the system by its deeds only, it is difficult to escape the conclusion that the best societies have in reality been groups of picked men among the fortunate few, comparatively speaking, who are able to incur the expense of a college education.

In almost every college where the secret societies have flourished attempts have been made, some of them quite successful, to carry on local anti-secret societies; and there has existed for many years an anti-secret fraternity, with chapters placed in different colleges, which has been patterned very closely after the societies calling themselves secret, both as to means and ends. But in one case only, that of Delta Upsilon, have the anti-secret orders

DELTA PSI LODGE, WILLIAMS.

PSI UPSILON LODGE, HAMILTON.

been able to keep pace with their secret rivals, in either the quality of their membership, their activity in college affairs, or their increase in material resources. Even here this has been the result of assimilation to the secret fraternities, till now, so far as Delta Upsilon can effect it, the distinction between itself and the secret fraternities is simply that the latter exposes somewhat more private business than do they, and, as to the rest, terms "privacy" what they call "secrecy."

Mr. Warner has said:

> Notwithstanding their formation is only in obedience to an ancient and universal love in human nature, they are attacked because they are secret. I suppose that some of them are guardians of the occult mysteries of Egypt and India, that they know what once was only known to augurs, flamens, and vestal virgins, and perhaps to the priests of Osiris; others keep some secret knowledge of the formation of the alphabet, or preserve the secret of nature preserved in the Rule of Three, and know why it was not the Rule of Four; while others, in midnight conclave, study the ratio of the cylinder to the inscribed sphere. It matters not. I have never yet met any one who knew these secrets, whatever they are, who thought there was any moral dynamite in them; never one who had shared them who did not acknowledge their wholesome influence in his college life. I mean, of course, the reputable societies; I am acquainted with no other.

The constitutions of many college fraternities are now open to the inspection of faculties; the most vigorous publish detailed accounts of their conventions and social gatherings; nearly all of the homesteads are on occasions opened for the reception of visitors; their rites, ceremonies, and even the appearance of their *sancta sanctorum*, are quite accurately apprehended by rival societies—in short, the old shibboleth of secrecy is a myth rather than a reality.

The shrewdest college presidents have long since discovered that to control undergraduate action with a firm though gentle hand they have only frankly to bespeak the aid and win the confidence and assistance of the fraternities represented at their institutions. It is thus that we come to see and to realize the importance of such unique departures from the traditional, ever-antagonistic relations between the faculties and the students of large colleges as those lately put into operation at Amherst, Bowdoin, and other colleges; where all matters relating to the privileges and penalties of the students are adjusted to a code of laws which is administered, and from time to time amended, by a council of undergraduates, representing the fraternities, acting in concert with one or more members of the faculty. This simple and amicable relationship between those desiring to obtain knowledge and those desiring to impart it has already been attended with very gratifying results.

Illustrated by such cases as that of Amherst and Bowdoin, and reënforced by the healthy tone of the fraternity press, which has not failed to wage war on what is reprehensible or deficient in our college life, and has labored to inculcate in their members the obligations which they owe to their college and to the members of rival societies as well as of their own, the words of General Stewart L. Woodford, in speaking of the early days of the societies, seem amply justified, and to promise even larger and still more excellent fruit in the near future:

> To no one cause more than to the fraternity movement has been due the altered conditions of college culture. . . . In matters of study and discipline each student is now largely guided by his personal predilections, by the advice of those whom he sees fit to consult, by the moral force of his chosen associates. These associations are now determined in many colleges by the Greek-letter societies or fraternities.

PHI NU THETA LODGE, WESLEYAN.

DELTA UPSILON LODGE, MADISON.

That they can use without abusing their privileges was very well expressed by President White, at the dedication of the new Psi Upsilon house at Cornell:

Both theory and experience show us that when a body of young men in a university like this are given a piece of property, a house, its surroundings, its reputation, which for the time being is their own, for which they are responsible, in which they take pride, they will treat it carefully, lovingly, because the honor of the society they love is bound up in it.

He added the following profound observations as the result of his long experience, both here and abroad:

One of the most unpleasant things in college life hitherto has been the fact that the students have considered themselves as practically something more than boys, and therefore not under tutors and governors; but something less than men, and therefore not amenable to the ordinary laws of society. Neither the dormitory nor the students' boarding-house is calculated to better this condition of things, for neither has any influence in developing the sense of manly responsibility in a student. But houses such as I am happy to say this society and its sister societies are to erect on these grounds seem to solve the problem in a far better way. They give excellent accommodations at reasonable prices; they can be arranged in such a manner and governed by such rules as to promote seclusion for study during working-hours; they afford opportunities for the alumni and older students to exercise a good influence upon the younger; they give those provisions for the maintenance of health which can hardly be expected in student barracks, or in the ordinary student boarding-house, and in the long run can be made more economical. But what I prize most of all in a house like this is its educating value; for such a house tends to take those who live in it out of the category of boys and to place them in the category of men. To use an old English phrase, it gives them "a stake in the country."

President Seelye of Amherst College, in an address on June 28, 1887, states, referring to the Greek-letter fraternities:

The aim of these societies is, I say, improvement in literary culture and in manly character, and this aim is reasonably justified by the results. It is not accidental that the foremost men in college, as a rule, belong to some of these societies. That each society should seek for its membership the best scholars, the best writers and speakers, the best men of a class, shows well where its strength is thought to lie. A student entering one of these societies finds a healthy stimulus in the repute which his fraternity shall share from his successful work. The rivalry of individuals loses much of its narrowness, and almost all of its envy, when the prize which the individual seeks is valued chiefly for its benefit to the fellowship to which he belongs. Doubtless members of these societies often remain narrow-minded and laggard in the race, after all the influence of their society has been expended upon them, but the influence is a broadening and a quickening one notwithstanding. Under its power the self-conceit of a young man is more likely to give way to self-control than otherwise. . . .

To represent all the fraternities as standing on anything like the same high plane as to membership, progress in the past, and prospects for the future would be misleading. My thoughts have naturally turned to the standing, the equipment, the aspirations, or perhaps only the pretty dreams of those fraternities which deserve to be ranked as the leaders in the race — that some day all the colleges of the United States will be veritable and acknowledged student democracies; that the fraternity buildings, though smaller than the college halls, will equal the latter in durability and completeness of appointment; that all the large cities will have graduate clubs, where the college fraternity man can renew the old associations that he cherished when a student.

The leading fraternities are fond of affirming the difference in their standard qualifications for membership. Some venerate high scholarship; others pride themselves on the aristocracy of birth or wealth; still others recognize the claims of a heartier and more democratic spirit. This may be true; and yet in all of them there is enough good-fellowship to attract the cultured and enough culture to improve the sociable. They illustrate a law of nature and a law of man, in the tendency of atoms with affinities to form into groups. Having outgrown weaknesses and prejudices, they may be expected to enjoy a career of prosperity.

PSI UPSILON LODGE, TRINITY.

John Addison Porter.

[Editor's Note - Mr. Porter was a member of Scroll & Key and a booster of the Yale's senior secret societies]

SECRET SOCIETIES AT YALE.

One of the most remarkable features of college life at New Haven—The undergraduates' secret organizations, their fine club houses, their prestige and influence—"Skull and Bones," "Scroll and Key," "Wolf's Head," and others.

By Rupert Hughes.

LIFE at Yale is almost devoid of society in the ordinary acceptance of the word. The stern, conservative Puritanism of the New Englanders who make New Haven their home, is inclined to frown on the levity and recklessness of college men, and seldom encourages their attentions to the local Priscillas; while the Yale man is too much wrapped up in the joys of campus life to miss the luxury. The only social life enjoyed by the average undergraduate is that of an occasional spasm like "Prom." week, when the long starved appetite overfeeds on imported delicacies; for a Yale man never thinks of taking a New Haven girl to a college event if he can, by hook or by crook, manage to bring to town a fair maiden, duly chaperoned, from his own city.

But society life, as the Yale man interprets it, is quite the most important factor of college existence, and should be spelled with a capital "S." It is in the mysterious halls of the secret societies that the student finds his dearest pleasures, and from them it is that the powers that direct the college democracy issue.

The first noticeable feature of the Yale societies is that they are only class societies, and not fraternal organizations to be enjoyed for the three or four years of college life. The one important exception to this, Alpha Delta Phi, only emphasizes the strong class spirit at Yale by the many difficulties against which it has had to contend. And yet, though this fact is undeniable, the society life is, in a sense, similar to that where the fraternity membership extends through the whole course. The same men, in general, clique together and pass almost *en masse* through the different class societies, as through successive strata, or through different degrees and orders.

For example, a member of Kappa Omicron Alpha (one of the secret societies at the Phillips Andover Academy, and probably the most powerful preparatory school society in the country) is almost certain of an election to one of the two Sophomore societies at Yale. This is an excellent introduction to the Junior societies, and they are but stepping stones to that peak of Yale advancement, a home in one of the Senior societies.

The evolution, or retrogression, of the Yale chapters of various national four year fraternities, like Delta Kappa Epsilon and Psi Upsilon, into mere class societies, presents interesting features

The Yale Campus.

not to be dwelt upon here, further than to note how permanently the class principle is now imbedded in the college tradition and spirit. So firmly imbedded, indeed, is it, that many outside fraternities do not dare attempt an entrance into Yale; and there is a strong sentiment even in Alpha Delta Phi that looks towards turning it also into a class society.

The history of secret societies at Yale contains the obituaries of some fifteen victims to the rule of the survival of the fittest. Among these were several Freshman societies that withered and died under the disapproval of the faculty, which found too much reason for suspicion of any dark organizations among the immature and unassimilated new comers. The last of these to die was the local society, Gamma Nu, which for some time kept up a struggling existence unknown to the faculty, but finally fell apart from internal weakness in 1889. This ended Freshman club life, and it is only natural, to the Yale mind, that the men who are forbidden canes, high hats, and a seat on what is left of the famous fence, should also be denied anything so dignified as a society.

The policy of the faculty, though it does not forbid secret societies *in toto*, like the Princeton faculty, is, or at

Wolf's Head Society House.

mysteries. The fac that almost any under graduate can tell yo both the names of th members and the loca tion of their societ rooms, does no weaken the bond of th members, however, s long as they suppos their secrets inviolate

The badges of thes organizations are wor on the waistcoat, unde the coat, and near th left armpit. That o Hé Boulé is an ow with the initials unde it, and that of Eta Ph is a mask.

In choosing th

least has been, more or less adverse to Sophomore organizations also. In spite of this, two Sophomore societies maintain a flourishing existence. They were founded respectively in 1875 and 1879, and are called Hé Boulé and Eta Phi.

In some respects these are the most powerful cliques in college, since the high place of society membership in the Yale mind cannot be overestimated, and since initiation into one of these two clubs practically insures admission to those of the Junior and Senior years. The power of Hé Boulé and Eta Phi is mightily strengthened, too, both in the firmness of fraternal ties and in the underground workings of college politics, by their almost absolute secrecy. Even the names of the seventeen members of each, and the places of meeting, are supposed to be dark

Delta Psi Society House.

members a certain number of popular men are given "hold offs;" that is, intimations that they are likely to receive "bids." But inasmuch as only about forty per cent of these men are actually taken in, and inasmuch as some men receive a "hold off" from each of

The number never varies, the outgoing class electing twenty five of the number, and the quota being filled up by the new men themselves.

It is noteworthy that the sharp distinctions and fierce rivalries that once separated these two societies have grad-

Delta Kappa Epsilon Society House.

the societies, many unlucky wights, in deliberating which horn of the dilemma to take, get hold of neither; or in the more picturesque Yalese, "Stacks of fellows, in trying not to chump themselves on either, horse themselves on both."

So far as the writer knows, no member of Hé Boulé or Eta Phi has ever failed of admission to one of the two great Junior societies, Delta Kappa Epsilon and Psi Upsilon. Both of these are chapters of great national three year fraternities. The former, commonly called "Deke" at Yale, is a chapter of the fraternity to which the Harvard "Dicky," of rather unenviable fame, originally belonged. Each takes in thirty five new members every year.

ually disappeared, until now they are hardly more than friendly social clubs, the members of which meet and collaborate in the authorship and production of plays, like the burlesque opera, "Robin Hood, Jr.," which was given with immense success last year, and was marked with quite a professional finish of cleverness.

The initiations are now nothing more than picturesque, since the lamentable death of Wilkins Rustin, '94, in the spring of 1892. He was blindfolded and instructed to run at his highest speed along an unfrequented street. In his enthusiasm he outstripped the two men in whose charge he was. Misunderstanding a cry of warning from them, he suddenly swerved from his

Psi Upsilon Society House.

direct course and ran into the sharp pole of a wagon, receiving injuries that proved fatal. The keen anxiety and deep grief of his initiators acquitted them of anything more serious than blind folly, but the faculty very wisely forbade all initiation further than the taking of the oath. Indeed, in deference to the storm of indignation throughout the country, they almost decided to wipe out the societies altogether; but, fortunately for the delight of Yale life, this radical step was not taken.

On the night of initiation, which is always the last Friday in May, the two societies march about the campus in hoods and gowns, singing their rival songs as they march. They then retire to their halls, where the formal initiation takes place, and a local burlesque is given as a welcome to the new comers. In order to make a whole night of it, the two societies indulge in a hilarious game of base ball, between daylight and sunrise, those who are not on the nines usually falling asleep in a shed near by.

Badge of Delta Kappa Epsilon.

Perhaps the strongest bond of fellowship in the two Junior societies, besides the conviviality they foster, is the large number of very creditable plays written and performed in their halls, the works of Boltwood, Perkins, and Paine deserving especial mention. The connection of these societies with their national organizations grows weaker and weaker every year, and many advocate its complete dissolution. Perhaps their principal value in the eyes of the students is their service in securing admission to the societies of the Seniors, who retain a limited voice and vote in the Junior clubs. The expenses are not high, being seldom more than seventy five dollars for the year.

Badge of Hé Boulé.

The Psi Upsilon badge shows two clasped hands and a monogram; that of "Deke" is a scroll bearing the word "Yale," and the initials of the society's name.

This is as good a place as any to refer to two societies which are, in a sense, rivals of the two last named, though they are hardly formidable opponents.

Zeta Psi, commonly known as "Zate," is a two year society which usually takes in fifteen or twenty of the men that fail of admission to Delta Kappa Epsilon and Psi Upsilon. Though Zeta Psi is not held in very high favor at Yale, it has a handsome chapter house, and a number of very good men on its list of members. Its pin is a monogram.

A more important body is Alpha Delta Phi, a chapter of the great national fraternity of that name. It is a three year society, and leads a somewhat precarious existence, harrowed as it is by its inevitable conflict, first against the power and activity of the Sophomore societies, and later against the *dolce far niente* of the Juniors. Unlike a member of Zeta Psi, the "Alpha Delt" stands a fair chance of election to the poorest of the three Senior societies and "a shadow of a show" for the two better ones. But the spirit of the college is against a three year society, and it is hard to get an ambitious student to lose the possibility of a place in the more popular clubs even for a sure membership in Alpha Delta Phi.

Should the latter be turned into a Junior society, as many desire, it would soon be a dangerous rival to Delta Kappa Epsilon and Psi Upsilon. It has a great history, but suffers for lack of a chapter house. Money is now being collected for this purpose, however, and the society has already bought a lot on Hillhouse, the most elegant avenue in New Haven.

Skull and Bones Society House.

Alpha Delta Phi was founded in 1836, but was extinct for many years, and was only reorganized in 1888, the year that saw the birth of Zeta Psi. Psi Upsilon has had a continuous existence since 1838, and Delta Kappa Epsilon since 1844. The badge of Alpha Delta

Phi is a star and crescent, and the membership is about forty.

We have now climbed to that sublime height of the Yale career known as Senior society life. Whatever hardships the student may have endured, whatever disappointments may have embittered his lot, if he can only find a haven in one of the Senior societies, his cup of joy is full. Omitting mention of Phi Beta Kappa, the association of men that have taken honors for scholarship, and Chi Delta Theta, composed of the editors of the *Yale Literary Magazine* (founded respectively in 1780 and 1821), the social societies are three in number: Skull and Bones, founded in 1832, Scroll and Key 1842, and a newcomer, Wolf's Head, born only eleven years ago.

These societies are all endowed and incorporated, "Bones" being incorporated as the Russell Trust Association, "Keys" as the Kingsley Trust Association, and Wolf's Head as the Phelps Trust Association. They all have graduate organizations, and are quite an expensive luxury.

Scroll and Key Society House.

As "Bones" is the oldest and richest (having one fund of forty thousand dollars), so it is the greatest, and he is not a Yale man that would prefer any scholarship honors or prizes to membership in old "Bonesy." Every year it takes in the fifteen "biggest" men in the incoming Senior class. By this I do not mean that it is a fat men's club, but that it takes the fifteen men who stand head and shoulders above their class for distinction—literary, scholastic, athletic, social, or otherwise. An impression prevails, however, that here, as with the other societies, in many cases heredity has much to do with the selection, and that the son or younger brother of a former member is often preferred to more capable candidates. But this is stoutly contradicted by Bones men.

The Bones badge consists of a gold skull and cross bones over the number "322," and it is worn on the lower left side of the waistcoat.

Badge of Psi Epsilon.

"Keys," whose pin is worn on the neck scarf, and is a gold key on a scroll with the letters "C. S. P." and "C. C. I.," is not far behind Bones in prominence. It takes annually the fifteen most convivial and socially prominent men left by Bones. Wolf's Head is much less highly rated, and instances are not wholly unknown wherein students unnoticed by either Bones or Keys have yet refused to join Wolf's Head. Its pin is a golden wolf's head transfixed on a loop, and it has a magnificent chapter house.

The day of election into these societies is perhaps the quaintest feature of Yale life. It is called "tapping time," or "slap day," and falls on the third Thursday in May, at five in the afternoon. Then all the anxious Juniors congregate in front of what is now used as "the fence," and pray that they may be chosen. Soon a solemn Senior issues from one of the society halls and threads the crowd till he finds the man he has been delegated to notify. He deals him a vigorous slap on the back, and says sternly, "Go to your room."

Amid wild cheering, the lucky man obeys mutely, followed by his slapper, who says to him, "Will you accept an election to the society *known as* Skull and Bones?" and goes back in silence to the hall whence he came, while the happy Junior returns to receive the envious congratulations of his friends. About the same time a Keys man, with a Wolf's Head man in his wake, goes through the same evolutions.

Between "tapping time" and initiation a week elapses. During this the slapper and the slapped preserve a sacred mutual silence, except on one occasion, when the new man is notified of the time and place of the awful ordeal, which is consummated in the dark recesses of the mysterious chapter house.

Besides these Academic societies there are many others at Yale. Among those not yet mentioned are Phi Gamma Delta, a very small university chapter of the national fraternity; the University Club,

Berzelius Society House.

which is like any city club; the two Law School societies, Corbey Court and Book and Gavel, and the societies of the Sheffield Scientific School. These last are quite as important as the minor Academic societies, and deserve more detailed mention than space permits, notably "Book and Snake," or Sigma Delta Chi, whose club house, "The Cloister," is the handsomest in New Haven; "Berzelius," named after the great chemist; the "Tea Company," or Delta Psi; and Chi Phi, besides which there are three smaller societies, Theta Psi, Theta Delta Chi, and Delta Phi.

The Cloister.

There are many interesting customs in vogue among these secret brotherhoods, such as their habit of returning home from meetings in absolute oblivion of each other and everybody else, walking at opposite sides of the pavement and crossing each other's paths on entering their houses. In the training seasons, too, the athletes are always escorted home from meetings at ten o'clock. The Academic Sophomores meet on Friday nights; the Juniors, on Tuesdays; the Sheffield men, on Thursdays; and the Seniors, on Thursdays and Saturdays.

Most inexplicable to an outsider is the fact that a Yale man is unwilling to breathe a word about his college society, and seemingly feels insulted at any mention of it. Even the most bewitching young woman is warned not to make any remark about his badge (which, by the way, is supposed never to leave his person, even during a bath, when it is carried in his mouth) for the student will feel compelled to receive your question in absolute silence.

The ethics of the subject cannot be discussed here, but it is noteworthy that the chief arguments against these organizations come from men who have failed of admission to them, and that Yale's greatest alumni have been members of the secret societies.

Badges of Berzelius, Book and Snake, and Delta Psi.

SCRIBNER'S MONTHLY.

VOL. XI. APRIL, 1876. No. 6.

YALE COLLEGE.

PLANTING THE IVY, YALE COLLEGE.

NEW HAVEN, the seat of Yale College, lies in a small alluvial plain on the edge of Long Island Sound. The city is built at the head of a narrow bay four miles long, and its suburbs stretch back across the plain to the foot of a range of trap dikes. The boldest members of this range are the two sheer and naked precipices known as East and West Rock. These are some 370 feet high, and the most striking objects in sight, as one sails up the winding channel of the bay, or enters the city by rail across the trestle-work over the "flat marshes, that look like monster billiard-tables with hay-stacks lying about for balls."

The following somewhat rose-colored picture of the city, is painted by Willis from his recollections of it as an undergraduate in 1827:

"If you were to set a poet to make a town, with *carte blanche* as to trees, gardens and green blinds, he would probably turn out very much such a place as New Haven. The first thought of the inventor of New Haven was to lay out the streets in parallelograms; the second was to plant them from suburb to water-side, with the magnificent elms of the country. The result is that, at the end of fifty years, the town is buried in leaves. If it were not for the spires of the churches, a bird flying over on his autumn voyage to the Floridas would never mention having seen it in his travels. The houses are something between an Italian palace and an English cottage,—built of wood, but, in the dim light of those overshadowing trees, as fair to the eye as marble, with their

THE DIVINITY SCHOOL.

triennial coats of paint; and each stands in the midst of its own encircling grass-plot, half buried in vines and flowers, and facing outward from a cluster of gardens divided by slender palings, and filling up with fruit-trees and summer-houses the square on whose limit it stands. Then, like the vari-colored parallelograms upon a chess-board, green openings are left throughout the town, fringed with triple and interweaving elm rows, the long weeping branches sweeping downward to the grass, and, with their inclosing shadows, keeping moist and cool the road they overhang."

In spite of its growth from a small university town to a city of over 50,000 inhabitants, New Haven keeps its rural look. This is owing partly to its architecture, and partly to its tree-planting traditions, inherited from the times of James Hillhouse, who set out the great elms that now shadow the older streets. The immediate suburbs of New Haven are far from imposing,—acres of flat ground covered with rows of small wooden houses, of a dreary sameness of pattern, with here and there a waste lot intersected by foot-paths, and nibbled by bleating goats that tug restlessly at their tethers. Yet even in these unsightly outskirts, and wherever the hand of the real estate speculator has been at work laying out new "boulevards," there are planted ranks of young elms, the germ of future Temple streets. Hence, from the top of East or West Rock, the straggling town, with its wooden houses and shade trees, looks like an overgrown village. From the upper stories of Divinity Hall in June the tree-tops of the City Green and the College Campus strike on the eye as a sea of billowy verdure, the church steeples and the belfries, clock towers and gables of the University, seeming not so much to emerge therefrom as to be themselves the craft of some fantastic navy sailing on the leaves. The round

DURFEE HALL.

observatory of the Athenæum serves for the cheese-box turret of a Monitor, and the steep roof-ridge of Durfee, with chimneys for smoke-pipes, does duty as a hog-backed Merrimac.

The scenery about New Haven is uncommonly rich and varied, tempting constantly to holiday walks and sails, and lending a romantic charm to the memories of undergraduate life. There is an intimate blending of sea-side and inland. Brackish creeks empty and fill their sluices with tide water, at the bases of cliffs miles from the sea. Following a path through woods, you come out suddenly on the borders of a salt marsh, where gulls are flying about. Lying under the trees of an orchard seemingly in the heart of the continent, you lift your eyes and see across the clover-tops the sparkle of the sun on the waters of the Sound, and the sail of a vessel bound for New York. You could put out your hand and touch it, lying under the apple-trees.

New Haven was settled in 1638 by a company of immigrants from London, who bought the land from Momauguin, sachem of the Quinnipiacs, "for 12 coats of English cloth, 12 alchymy spoons, 12 hatchets, 12 hoes, 2 dozen knives, 12 porringers and 4 cases of French knives and scissors." Like other New England towns, it has its romance of colonial history. In 1661 Whalley and Goffe, two of the regicide judges of Charles the First, came to New Haven. Tradition connects their names with a sort of den, formed by two bowlders on the back of West Rock, where they lay hidden while the King's officers were making search for them in the town. The Judges' Cave is the first shrine to which the Freshman makes pilgrimage, and on one of the bowlders some lover of liberty, whose enthusiasm outran his orthography, has cut the inscription: "*Oposition* to tyrants is obedience to God."*

Long before the close of the 17th century, the project of a college in the Colony of Connecticut had been mooted. The distance of Harvard College in those days of unrapid transit (mostly on horseback) was felt as a serious evil. But not until the year 1700 did the movement take definite shape. In that year ten of the foremost ministers in the colony, nominated by general consent, assembled at New Haven, and formed themselves into a society for founding and carrying on a collegiate school. Later in the year tradition reports that they again came together at Branford, each bringing a number of books—in all some forty folios—which he laid on the table with the words: "I give these books for founding a college in this colony." So that the library is to be regarded as the corner-stone of the university. In 1701, the society was incorporated by Act of the Colonial Assembly, in consequence of a petition numerously signed, setting forth that "from a sincere regard to, and zeal for, upholding the Protestant religion by a succession of learned and orthodox men, they [the petitioners] had proposed that a collegiate school should be erected in this colony, wherein youth should be instructed in all parts of learning, to qualify them for public employments in church and civil state."

STATUE OF RECTOR PIERSON.

Abraham Pierson, of Killingworth [Kenelworth], was chosen Rector of the school, and held office till his death in 1707. In the summer of 1874 a bronze statue of Yale's first president was erected on the college grounds in front of the Art Gallery, and unveiled at Commencement with appropriate ceremonies. The statue was designed by Launt Thompson, and presented to the col-

* For a fuller account of the topography and antiquities of New Haven, see President Dwight's "Statistical Account of New Haven;" and Prof. Dana's "Walks about New Haven," in the "College Courant" for 1868-9.

lege by Mr. Charles Morgan, of New York. It is not properly a likeness but an ideal—assisted, however, by reference to portraits of members of the Pierson family. The straight figure and aquiline features of the fine old Puritan scholar have something typical and even prophetic, carrying the mind back to the times when, *Teucro duce et auspice Teucro*, the students were "weekly caused *memoriter* to recite the Assembly's Catechism in Latin and Ames's Theological Theses." A memorial of Rector Pierson is also preserved in the library—a square oaken chair of the true antique solidity.

The school was located provisionally at Saybrook. The first student on its rolls was Jacob Hemingway, who took his Bachelor's degree in 1704. He entered college in March, 1702, and continued in his sole person to represent the whole body of undergraduates until September of the same year, when the number was swelled to eight, who were distributed into classes according to their scholarship. At the same time the Faculty received an addition by the appointment of Mr. Daniel Hooker as tutor. The first Commencement was held at Saybrook in 1702, and some honorary degrees conferred; but there was no proper graduating class until the following year, when the Triennial Catalogue makes the following record:

1703.

*Johannes Hart, A. M. Tutor. *1731.

This first graduate of Yale had already spent three years at Harvard before he removed to Saybrook and became the Senior sophister of the sister university. These modest beginnings recall the affectionate banter of a Harvard poet about the infant years of his own Alma Mater:

> " And who was on the catalogue when college was begun?
> Two nephews of the President and *the* Professor's son: * * * *
> Lord! How the Seniors kicked about the Freshman class of one!"

YALE ART BUILDING.

It should be borne in mind that in 1700 Connecticut had a poor and thinly scattered agricultural population of little more than 15,000.

During its first seventeen years the new college led a wandering life. Rector Pierson lived at Killingworth, and taught his classes there. The Rector who succeeded him resided at Milford with the Seniors, the lower classes being instructed by the tutors at Saybrook. In 1716, many of the students, being dissatisfied with Saybrook, seceded to Wethersfield and put themselves under the teaching of Mr. Elisha Williams, who thus became a kind of tutor extraordinary. The few who remained at Saybrook shortly after fled from the small-pox to East Guilford. There was much local jealousy touching the permanent settling of the college; New Haven, Hartford, Saybrook, Wethersfield and Middletown, all making bids for it.

The up-river interest was in the minority in the Corporation, and memorialized the Assembly. But most of the Trustees declaring for New Haven, the college was removed thither in 1717—not, however, without violent opposition. The Governor and Council had to assemble at Saybrook to help the sheriff. The bridges between Saybrook and New Haven were broken down, and the library was a week on the road. The carts in which the latter was carried were attacked, and two hundred and sixty volumes lost or destroyed in the scuffle.

The Commencements at Saybrook had been mostly private. A public Commencement was held at New Haven in 1718. A few recalcitrant members of the graduating class still lingered at Wethersfield, where a rival Commencement took place. But the up-river faction was finally conciliated, and Mr. Elisha Williams was appointed tutor, and afterward, in 1725, Rector. Meanwhile a house for the reception of the college had been built at New Haven, and was dedicated on Commencement Day. It stood in the south-eastern corner of the yard, near "the fence," whose top rail, crowded with singers in the summer evenings, now forms the favorite lounging-place of the undergraduates (see page 768). This building was of wood, three stories high, with steep roof and dor-

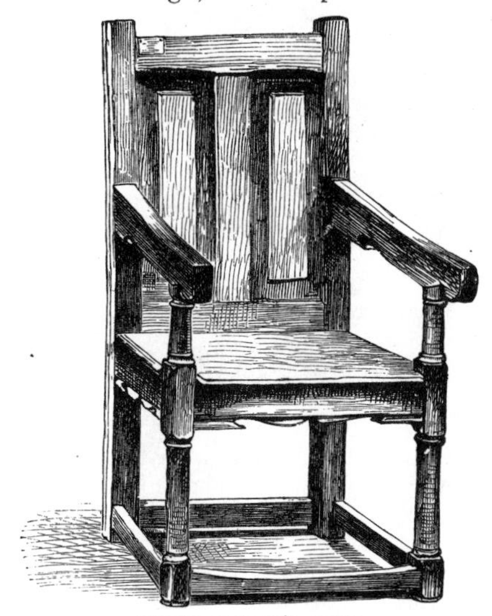

RECTOR PIERSON'S CHAIR.

mer windows, and had, besides chambers for the scholars, a hall, library and kitchen. A part of it was standing as late as 1782. About the time of the removal of the college to New Haven, there were received from Gov. Elihu Yale, of London, a large box of books, the portrait (by Sir Godfrey Kneller) and the arms of King George, and £200 sterling worth of English goods. The portrait is preserved in the Art Gallery, but the coat-of-arms was destroyed at the time of the Revolution. In acknowledgment of this gift the Trustees "solemnly named" the new building Yale College; "upon which," proceeds the contemporary account, "the Hon. Col. Taylor represented Governor Yale in a speech expressing his great satisfaction; which ended, we passed to the church and there the Commencement was carried on. * * * * After which were graduated ten young men, whereupon the Hon. Gov. Saltonstall in a Latin speech congratulated the Trustees in their success and in the comfortable appearance with relation to the school. All which ended, the gentlemen returned to the college hall, where they were entertained with a splendid dinner, and the ladies at the same time were also entertained in the Library. After which they sung the four first verses of the 65th Psalm, and so the day ended."

Elihu Yale, whose name was thus almost accidentally bound up forever with the fortunes of a university whose future greatness he surely could not have foretokened, was born in New Haven in 1648. He was educated in England, and made a fortune in the East Indies, where he was made Governor of Fort St. George, now Madras. "He was a gentleman," says President Clap, "who greatly abounded in good humor and generosity as well as in wealth." A grandson of Gov. Yale presented the college, in 1789, with an original full-length portrait of its distinguished sponsor. From this is taken the picture which figures on the cover of the "Yale Literary Magazine," but the elegiac couplet just beneath it,

"*Dum mens grata manet nomen laudesque Yalenses*
Cantabunt suboles unanimique patres."

comes from a MS. inscription, under an engraving of Gov. Yale sent to the college at an earlier period. The college is also in possession of a silver snuff-box once belonging to its benefactor, having a tortoise-shell lid with medallion, coat-of-arms, and the motto *Præmium virtutis gloria*. The following lines, from Yale's epitaph in the church-yard at Wrexham in Wales, are curious, and have been often quoted:

"Born in America, in Europe bred,
In Afric travelled and in Asia wed,
Where long he lived and thrived; at London dead.
Much Good, some Ill he did; so hope's all's even,
And that his Soul through Mercy's gone to Heaven."

The college had now a local habitation and a name, and was fairly launched upon its course. By the close of the century, the number of students had risen to 130. Instruction continued in the hands of the President and tutors, who varied from one to five. A Professorship of Divinity was founded in 1755; one of Mathematics, Natural Philosophy, and Astronomy, in 1770. An instructor in Hebrew was appointed in 1798. But these chairs were slenderly endowed, and often empty. Sometimes the President performed the duties of a Professor, as well as his own.

PORTRAIT OF GOVERNOR YALE.

A house for the Rector had been built in 1722. A second President's house was built in 1799, and was standing in 1860. In laying the foundations of Farnam Hall, in 1869, a bottle of mulberry wine was dug up from the ruins of the President's cellar, "which, if any have tasted, they have far exceeded the palates of antiquity." In 1752 South Middle College was built, and paid for partly by the proceeds of a lottery, and partly by a grant from the Assembly of the money that came from the sale of a French prize captured by a Connecticut frigate. In acknowledgment of this gift, the building was originally named Connecticut Hall. It was modeled upon "red Massachusetts" at Cambridge, and was described in the dedication ceremonies as *ædes hæc nitida et splendida Aula Connecticutensis.* It is the oldest college building now remaining. Its lower story is partly occupied by the reading-room. In 1763 was completed the Athenæum, now used for Freshman recitation-rooms, but at first for a chapel, and the upper floor for a library; for the steeple has been substituted a wooden turret, used as an astronomical observatory. In 1793–4 South College was built, the third member of "the logues. Down to 1767, the names of undergraduates were arranged, not alphabetically, but in order of rank. The first name in the class of 1725 is Gurdon Saltonstall, the

PRESIDENT NOAH PORTER.

Governor's son. Then follow names of sons of clergymen, lawyers, artisans, and tradesmen. "Every student," runs one of the old laws, "shall be called by his sir name, except he be the son of a nobleman, or a knight's eldest son." As between the college classes, a strict subordination was enforced, and a somewhat laborious etiquette prevailed between Faculty and students. The Freshmen were almost in the condition of fags in the English public schools. The following statutes from a book of "Freshman Laws" seem incredible, but were gravely meant, and put in practice:

"The Freshmen, as well as other undergraduates, are to be uncovered, and are forbidden to wear their hats (unless in stormy weather) in the front door-yard of the President's or Professor's house, or within ten rods of the person of the President, eight rods of the Professor, and five rods of a tutor."

"A Freshman shall not play with any members of an upper class without being asked."

"In case of personal insult, a Junior may call up a Freshman and reprehend him. A Sophomore, in like case, must obtain leave from a Senior, and then he may discipline a Freshman."

"Freshmen shall not run in college-yard, or up or down stairs, or call to anyone through a college window."

The Academic costume of cap and gown was worn at Yale in the last century. A curious wood-cut, "View of Yale College," in the library, printed at New Haven in 1786, represents South Middle College and the Athenæum, with figures of President Stiles, tutors, and scholars, walking in the yard. Some are in cap and gown, others in frock coat, cocked hat, and peruke. Each has a little spot of green to stand on, like the wooden lozenges which support the feet of the *dramatis personæ* in a Noah's Ark. The figure of President Stiles is fearfully and wonderfully made.

The scholars were not allowed to use English in addressing each other, but must talk in Latin. Discipline was maintained chiefly by a system of graded fines. Freshmen and "commencing Sophomores" were sometimes cuffed or boxed on the ear by the President in a solemn and formal manner in chapel; but there seems to have been no

THE COLLEGE FENCE.

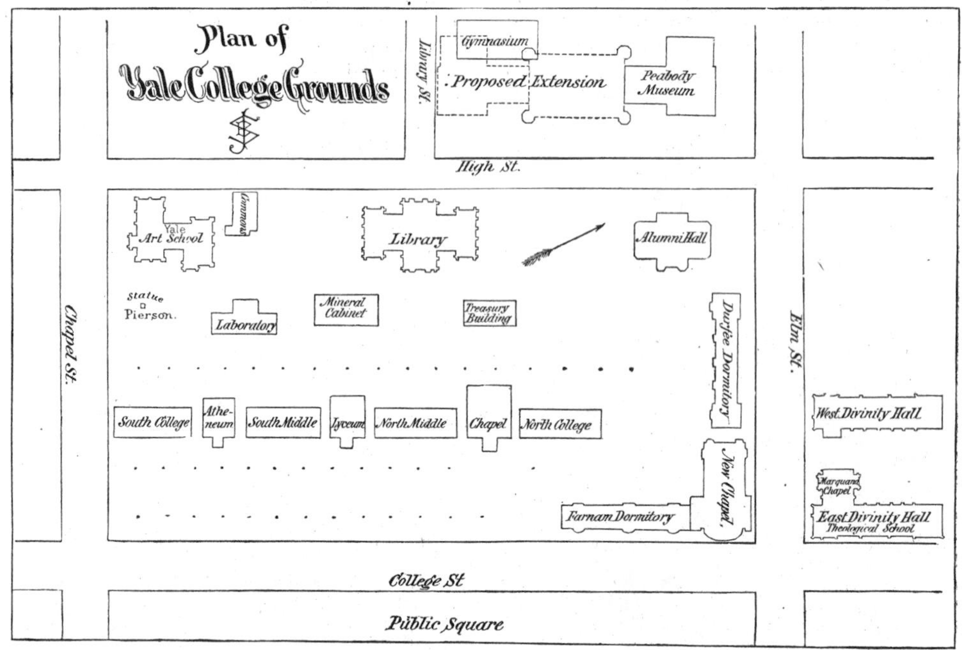

instance at Yale of that bodily flogging sometimes administered at Harvard—notably in the case of Thomas Sargent, of painful memory, who was "whipped before the scholars" in 1674. We cannot pause to describe those shadowy functionaries, the Beadle and the Scholar of the House, or do more than allude in passing to the College Butler, a licensed monopolist, who held his buttery in the ground floor front corner room in the south entry of South Middle, wherefrom he dispensed to such as had money or credit "cider, metheglin, strong beer, together with loaf sugar ('saccharum rigidum'), pipes, tobacco, etc,"—being, indeed, a sort of ancient and official "Hoad." He it was who furnished the candles which glimmered in the chapel at early prayers in the dark winter mornings. He had charge of the college bell, and a disorderly student was sometimes, with a certain grim humor on the part of the authorities, appointed to the office of "Butler's waiter," and compelled to ring the bell for a week or two.

FRANKLIN'S CLOCK IN THE LIBRARY.

In 1729 arrived in Rhode Island, Dean, afterward Bishop, George Berkeley, with a train of English gentlemen. He came to the province in furtherance of his romantic project of founding a college in Bermuda to christianize the Indians, and be the center of civilization in the New World. The imaginative spirit in which Berkeley undertook this enterprise appears from his fine "Verses on the Prospect of Planting Arts and Learning in America." The closing stanza is familiar, the first line having passed into proverb:

"Westward the course of empire takes its way;
The four first acts already past,
A fifth shall close the drama with the day;
Time's noblest offspring is the last."

In Rhode Island Berkeley sojourned three years, waiting for the £20,000 promised him by the British Ministry toward his Bermuda College. This, of course, never came. Sir Robert Walpole's statesmanship was anything but visionary, and he found more practical uses for the money at home. In the interior of the island Berkeley built himself a mansion, still standing, which he named Whitehall, in a pleasant valley, neighbor to a hill that commands the land and the ocean with its outlying islands. Here he lived in scholarly retirement, writing his "Minute Philosopher," and the dialogues of "Alciphron."

In 1719 Timothy Cutler had been chosen Rector of Yale College. He is described and the Trustees excused Mr. Cutler from any further service as Rector, and accepted Mr. Brown's resignation of his tutorship. It is honorable to both sides that the new converts never put themselves in hostility to the college. Mr. (afterward Dr.) Johnson in particular continued zealous in its interests. He had accompanied Cutler to England, and received ordination and degrees.* In 1754 he was chosen first President of King's (now Columbia) College. His son was edu-

"THE OLD BRICK ROW."

by President Stiles as "a great Hebrician and Orientalist," "a noble Latin Orator," and a man of "a high, lofty, and despotic mien." "He made a grand figure as the head of a college. But his head being at length turned with the splendor of Prelacy, and carried away with the fond enterprise of Episcopizing all New England, he, in 1722, turned Churchman, left his Rectorate of Yale College, and was re-ordained by the Bishop of Norwich, and was honored with the Doctorate in Divinity from Oxford and Cambridge. Returning, he settled in Boston, but failed of that influence and eminence which he figured to himself in prospect."

Rector Cutler drew after him a number of ministers, including Mr. Samuel Johnson, a former tutor, and Mr. Daniel Brown, then acting tutor in the college. This apostacy created alarm throughout New England, cated at Yale, and became, like his father, President of King's College.

On Berkeley's arrival at Newport, Johnson visited him there, and a friendship was begun which had important results for Yale. The two friends kept up a correspondence, partly on philosophical matters, and Johnson embraced Berkeley's idealism, as did also, though independently, a thinker in some respects greater than Berkeley—Jonathan Edwards, once a pupil of Johnson at Yale. Johnson embodied the Berkeleian system in his "Elementa Philosophica," printed at Philadelphia in 1752 by Benjamin Franklin. Through Johnson, Berkeley became interested in "the college at Newhaven," and in 1732, on his return to England, conveyed to the Trustees his farm of

* He is said to have visited Pope, and brought home cuttings from the Twickenham willow, which he planted at Stratford, Conn.

ninety-six acres at Whitehall, the rent to be appropriated to three scholarships, awarded for excellence in Greek and Latin, determined by a competitive examination in the presence of the President and the "Senior Episcopal Missionary of the Colony or Province of Connecticut." In 1733 he sent the college nearly 1,000 volumes, valued at £500,—the best collection of books that had ever been brought at one time to America. The collection included the chief works of classical literature and philosophy, the Greek and Latin Fathers, church history, Anglican divinity, modern philosophy, mathematics, natural history and medicine, English poetry, and modern French literature. Berkeley kept up a correspondence with the college till his death in 1753. His name has been kept alive at Yale, not only by the Berkeley scholarships,—"the Dean's bounty" they were formerly called,—but by many other mementos; among others by his portrait now in the Art Gallery, painted by Smibert, an English artist who came with him to America as Professor of Fine Arts in the future University of Bermuda. Smibert staid in America after Berkeley's departure, and died at Boston. Copley was one of his pupils. The painting shows Berkeley standing by a table, with his hand resting on a volume of Plato, and surrounded by his family. North Middle College, finished in 1803, was at first called Berkeley Hall, but "swell names" have never flourished at Yale. In 1869 a Berkeley Association was started by the Episcopal students in college.

FARNAM HALL.

During the long administration of President Clap, from 1739 to 1766, there arose in the colony serious dissatisfaction with the college management. In 1740 the great revival preacher, Whitefield, visited New England, and, raised by his eloquence, a kind of religious inflammation. All sorts of Enthusiasts and Separatists started up to trouble the decorous orthodoxy that had hitherto reigned unbroken in Connecticut. Authority everywhere took ground against the movement, and the heads of the college criticised Whitefield and his followers in a printed document. David Brainerd, then a Junior in college, and afterward a famous missionary among the Indians, a man of fervent and even fanatical piety, said of a

GOING TO PRAYERS IN THE OLDEN TIME.

certain tutor Whittelsey, that "he had no more of the grace of God than that chair." For this offense, and for attending against the rules a Separatist meeting in New Haven, he was expelled from college. This and other harsh measures gave great offense

"HANNIBAL."

to many in the colony. Anonymous pamphlets were directed against the government of the college; its orthodoxy was questioned, and complaints were made of its system of discipline and instruction; the students were encouraged in insubordination by civilians in New Haven. Finally, in 1763, a memorial was presented to the Assembly, praying the appointment of a Commission of Visitation to inquire into and rectify the abuses in the college. In answer, President Clap presented an address, showing conclusively that no visitorial powers resided in the Legislature, but in the real founders of the college, the ten ministers who made the first donation of books, and their successors, the Trustees under the charter of 1701, *and the President and Fellows of Yale College in New Haven* under the amended charter of 1745. Of the legal ability shown in this argument Chancellor Kent spoke in the highest terms. The Assembly took no action on the memorial. This controversy was of great value to the college, as it established thus early in its history the independence of the corporation from State interference. Nevertheless the college continued for a time widely unpopular, and a fresh grievance was added when, in 1765, two of the tutors who had become infected with Sandemanian principles were forced by the President to resign. President Clap was a man of ability and firmness of will, who devoted himself with untiring fidelity to the interests of the college. The study of mathematics and natural philosophy especially received impetus from his teaching; but he seems to have been rigid and intolerant.

During the Revolution the college was all but broken up. Owing to the high price of provisions at New Haven, the Freshmen were removed to Farmington, and the Juniors and Sophomores to Glastonbury, the Seniors alone staying at New Haven under Tutor Dwight. No public Commencement was held between 1777 and 1781. It was voted that the college bell might be transported to Glastonbury if the inhabitants would pay the cost of its conveyance. In July, 1779, New Haven was occupied by the British. The invading force landed on the shore of the Sound west of the town, and advanced

COMING FROM PRAYERS.

along the Milford turnpike. Beyond West River they were met by the militia, including a number of undergraduates. These irregular troops were soon dispersed after a skirmish. Among other citizens, ex-President Daggett had shouldered his fowling-piece and gone forth to battle. He was taken prisoner, put at the head of the British column, and prodded with bayonets into town. Being a portly man, "subject to continual dissolution and thaw," and the day being intensely hot, Dr. Daggett sustained injuries from his forced march at the point of the bayonet, which are believed to have hastened his death. In this skirmish Major Campbell, reputed the handsomest man in the British army, was shot by a farmer from behind a stone wall. He was buried in the fields near by, and the spot is still marked by a small stone, and sometimes visited by the curious. It is said that the first body of troops reviewed by Washington after his appointment as Commander-in-Chief, was a company of Yale students that he put through the maneuvers on the New Haven green while on his way to take command at Cambridge. By reason of the depreciation and fluctuation of the currency during the Revolution and just after, the salaries of the college officers were paid in terms of beef, pork, wheat, and Indian corn, a medium not so elastic as Continental paper, but seemingly preferred by these ancient bullionists.

One of the most interesting of the early Presidents of the college was Dr. Ezra Stiles, who served from 1777 to 1795. He was the best scholar of his time in New England, and, it is said, would have been elected President of Harvard, but for his being a graduate of another college. He had an eager and credulous curiosity, which led him into a wide range of rather unrelated pursuits. Thus we find him experimenting with an electrical apparatus sent to the college by Dr. Franklin; corresponding with Winthrop about the comet of 1759; writing letters of inquiry to the head of the Jesuits' College in Mexico respecting the discoveries of the Catholic Missions in the North-west; to a Greek bishop in Syria asking for an account of the Gentiles beyond the Caspian, "with reference to the remains of the ten tribes;" to Sir William Jones suggesting a search for copies of the Pentateuch among the Black Jews in India. As an antiquarian and Orientalist he was specially famous. He wrote an entertaining but uncritical treatise on King Charles's Judges in America. He pursued his Oriental studies with the help of the learned Rabbi Haigim Isaac Carigal, who had charge of the synagogue at Newport. He was active in the controversy between the colonies and the mother country, and later in projects for the abolition of the slave trade. He pursued a more liberal policy than President Clap, and it was during his administration that the Hon. James Hillhouse, Treasurer of the College,

INTERIOR OF STUDENT'S ROOM.

originated the conciliatory measure by which, in return for a grant from the State, the Governor, Lieutenant-Governor, and six senior Senators were made *ex-officio* members of the Corporation. South College, built in 1794, was named Union Hall, to commemorate this union of Church and State in the college government.

The successors of Dr. Stiles in the Presidency have been Timothy Dwight (1795–1817); Jeremiah Day (1817–1846); Theodore Dwight Woolsey (1846–1871); and Noah Porter, the present head of the College.

At the time of the Revolution there flourished at New Haven a school of Yale poets and patriots, who aided the cause of Independence with sword and pen—Trumbull, Dwight, Humphreys, and Barlow. They wrote immense epics in rhyme; essays in the style of "The Spectator;" satires and epistles after the manner of Pope; epigrams against Tom Paine, Ethan Allen and Thomas Jefferson; and burlesques in imitation of Hudibras. This galaxy of literati, together with three Hartford wits, contributors to "The American Mercury," formed a mutual admiration society and were spoken of as "The Seven Pleiades of Connecticut." Their poems are little read nowadays, but are historically interesting as the beginnings of our national literature, and abundantly filled with the spirit of '76. The two first named, John Trumbull and Timothy Dwight, were chosen tutors in the college in 1771. Their influence served to broaden the course of study by the introduction of the humanities,—Trumbull's first satire, "The Progress of Dullness," being directed in part against the dry and unpractical character of the old logical curriculum. Trumbull's best poem was "M'Fingal," a satirical account of the war, which was very popular in its day. Thirty pirated impressions were hawked about by newsmongers and chapmen, and the classical Marquis de Chastellux wrote from Paris complimenting Trumbull in good critical form for having observed all the rules of burlesque poetry obtaining since the age of Homer. Could Dr. Johnson have said more?

Two or three couplets of "M'Fingal" still circulate as proverbs generally credited to Butler, *e. g.:*

> "No man e'er felt the halter draw
> With good opinion of the law:"

and,

> "But optics sharp it needs, I ween,
> To see what is not to be seen."

Trumbull afterward studied law in John Adams's office at Boston, and finally became Judge of the Superior Court of Connecticut.

Timothy Dwight is less known to posterity as a writer than as the vigorous scholar who, as President of Yale College, impressed his strong personality upon every one of a generation of students. Yet his contributions to literature were by no means valueless. Prominent among these were his "Theology," and his entertaining "Travels in New England and New York," of which latter Southey spoke with respect, though he made game of his poems. Of these, "The Conquest of Canaän," finished at the age of twenty-three, is the longest and most pretentious. This is a scriptural epic in rhymed heroics, which was favorably criticised by Cowper in "The Analytical Review." Trumbull, "in allusion to the number of thunder-storms described in the portion of the poem handed him to read, requested that, when he sent in the remainder, a lightning-rod might be included." Of this epic, with its thunder-storms and Niagaras, its Irads and Selimas, and the rest, one would wish to speak warily as of the *manes* of the illustrious dead. Peace be with them! Dwight's best poem is, perhaps, his "Greenfield Hill," a rural idyl in the reflective and descriptive vein of Goldsmith. His once famous song, "Columbia," was written during his chaplaincy in the Revolutionary army, and gave voice to the new feeling of American nationality. The psalm included in most collections beginning, "I love Thy kingdom, Lord," was written by Dwight.

The third star in this constellation was Colonel David Humphreys, who was graduated in 1771. He fought in the Revolution, first as staff officer to General Putnam, and afterward as one of Washington's aids, and was presented with a sword by Congress for gallantry at Yorktown. He continued a life-long friend of Washington, and a frequent inmate at Mount Vernon. He was appointed Minister to Spain and introduced into America the breed of Merino sheep. From his woolen factory was furnished the coat in which President Madison took his oath of office. Colonel Humphreys' muse was always patriotic, and, withal, somewhat stately and monotonous. He sung "The Happiness of America," "The Future Glory of the United States," "Love of Country," "The Death of General Washington," and "The Industry of the United States of America." He exchanged poetic epistles with Barlow, "whom Nature formed her

ANNUAL EXAMINATION IN ALUMNI HALL.

loftiest poet," and with Dwight, "that bard sublime, the father of our epic song." His poem, entitled "Address to the Armies of the United States of America," was translated into French by the Marquis de Chastellux. Humphreys was the patron saint and one of the founders of the Brothers in Unity Society, and, as such, his name has come down in college song almost to the present generation of undergraduates. Another Revolutionary hero, Nathan Hale, the martyr spy, was the founder of the rival society, Linonia.

Joel Barlow made his début as a poet on his Commencement Day, in 1778, by the delivery of a poem on the "Prospect of Peace." Like Dwight, he served as chaplain in the Revolutionary army. When the war was over, this knot of New Haven poets turned their pens into the service of the Federalist party. Barlow settled at Hartford and wrote for the "Mercury," in connection with Trumbull, Humphreys and Dr. Lemuel Hopkins, a series of papers called "The Anarchiad," in favor of a strong Constitution. But later, he strayed to Paris and went after false gods, becoming a convert to French democracy and taking part in the struggles of the Revolution. He attacked Burke in a pamphlet printed at London, and wrote, among other rather wild things, a famous song in praise of the guillotine to the tune of "God Save the King." He made a fortune abroad by speculation, and, returning to America, after an absence of seventeen years, built a residence near Washington, which he called *Kalorama*. He was sent as Minister to France by Mr. Monroe, and caught his death by exposure while traveling through Poland to get an interview with Napoleon, then engaged on his Russian campaign. Barlow's best poem is "Hasty Pudding," an excellent mock heroic after the manner of Philip's "Cider." The couplet,

> "E'en in thy native regions, how I blush
> To hear the Pennsylvanians call thee *mush*,"

is familiar, as, indeed, are other passages. But Barlow's chief title to fame in his own time was "The Columbiad," a sort of Fourth of July epic in ten books, splendid with the boom of cannon and the blaze of rockets, with geographical surveys of the continent from "hills of vision," accompanied with remarks by guardian angels and geniuses of America, and ending in a grand holocaust of ancient errors and superstitions. This was published at Philadelphia in 1807, with prints by the best English engravers, and was the costliest book that had ever been issued from an American press. Many of the pieces of this early school of Connecticut poets were published in a volume of "American Poems," at Litchfield, in 1793.

With the opening of the present century, and the accession of President Dwight in 1795, the college entered upon a career of development so rapid and manifold that, from a school attended by scarcely more than one hundred and thirty pupils, and conducted by half a dozen teachers, it has become a university of six separate faculties, numbering some ninety officers of instruction and nearly eleven hundred students, and occupying about thirty buildings, This development has been double: First, an unfolding of the college in itself; Secondly, a throwing off by the parent stem of vigorous shoots in the shape of special departments and technical schools.

The increase in the number of college buildings may first be mentioned, as the outward and visible sign of this progress. The plan of the first builders was as simple as their architecture—mere accretion in a right line. Hence "the old brick row," comprising, besides the structures already mentioned, the Lyceum, begun in 1800; North College, in 1821; the Old Chapel, in 1824, and Old Divinity, in 1835. The buildings of this row are all standing, except the last, which was pulled down in 1870, to make room for Durfee Hall. The Lyceum is occupied by recitation-rooms. All these buildings are excessively plain, resembling nothing so much as a line of red brick factories. The four dormitories are almost precisely alike. Each is four stories high and has two entries; each entry gives access to sixteen rooms, four on a floor. Though plain in appearance, they furnish comfortable lodgings. Two of them are heated by steam. All have water on the ground floor, and gas in the entries and in some of the rooms.

SOCIETY HALLS.
1. Skull and Bones.
2. Psi Upsilon. 3. Scroll and Keys.
4. Delta Kappa Epsilon.

These buildings are old without being venerable; yet sometimes, in the long summer vacation, when the yard is deserted, their bricky fronts, with the shadows of the elms playing quietly over them, take on a mellow tone of age that appeals to one with a certain pathos for recognition. The rooms in the older colleges have a faint aroma of association. In many, lists of former inmates are kept pasted on the closet doors. The floors are uneven, the low ceilings are crossed by beams, and there are old-fashioned fire-places in the chimney, now chiefly bricked or boarded up. Altogether, it is not strange that so much sentimental opposition was developed among the alumni when, a few years since, it was proposed to move the college from its present site.

PRESENTATION DAY.

Behind the main row stand three other buildings irregularly placed—the Laboratory, the Cabinet, and the Trumbull Gallery. The first is a low brick edifice put up in 1782 for a commons hall and kitchen, but used since 1819 for a chemical lecture-room, laboratory, optical chamber, working-rooms, etc. The cabinet is a large building covered with dark stucco, constructed in 1819. The upper story is used as a cabinet of minerals; the lower was occupied by a dining-hall until the abolition of the commons in 1843, but now by recitation-rooms and the "philosophical chamber." The Trumbull Gallery is a mausoleum-like affair erected in 1832, to hold the paintings presented by Colonel John Trumbull, the historical painter of the Revolution. Some of these pieces are widely known by copies, as, "The Signing of the Declaration of Independence" and "The Death of Montgomery." In 1868 the paintings were removed to the new art school, and the upper floor of Trumbull Gallery is now taken up by the rooms of the President and Treasurer of the college. On the lower floor are working-rooms for entomology, popularly known as the "Bug Lab."

The most modern buildings are ranged along the outer edge of the college square, an area of some nine acres, facing inward. They are designed in time to form a continuous quadrangle completely inclosing this square. It is unfortunate that, when this arrangement was decided upon no general plans were drawn for such a quadrangle. As it is, the new colleges, though in some cases individually creditable, are of so many materials and shapes, that it will be impossible to harmonize them architecturally in a close quadrangle. The first of these is the Library, a graceful Gothic building of rough-dressed Portland sandstone, begun in 1842. Here the books of the college at last found permanent shelter after lodging successively in the upper stories of the Athenæum, the Lyceum, and the Chapel. Including the consolidated libraries of the Linonia and Brothers Societies in the north wing, the college owns one hundred and eleven thousand volumes, exclusive of pamphlets.

Alumni Hall, completed in 1853, is a squat, castellated structure of red sandstone,* built in that order of architecture known to readers of "Cecil Dreeme" and the Bohemian frequenters of "Chrysalis" as *mock-Gothic.* The lower story is a large hall used for the annual examinations and for Commencement meetings of the Alumni. It is hung around with portraits of college benefactors and distinguished graduates. There are two medieval-looking towers (with wooden battlements), whose corkscrew staircases conduct to the two handsome rooms on the upper floor, once the rival debating halls of Linonia and Brothers, but now used as lecture-rooms.

By far the most elaborate building on the square is the Art School, completed in 1866 at a cost of $200,000 and upward. It is built of smooth-dressed New Jersey sandstone, in the shape of an irregular H, and has one entrance, through a tower, from the college side, and another from Chapel street through a fine porch with columns of polished granite. The floors are of oak and black walnut, and the inside finish of the halls and the handsome staircases of chestnut. The second story contains two large sky-light galleries, in one of which is hung the Jarves collection of paintings illustrative of the history of Italian art; in the other the Trumbull collection and other paintings belonging to the college, conspicuous among which is Allston's "Jeremiah." The school also owns a well-chosen gallery of casts, collections of photographs, etc. The lower floor is devoted to studios and lecture-rooms.

The only portion of the "quad" at present closely built, is the north-eastern corner, formed by Farnam, Durfee, and the new chapel. Farnam Hall was finished in 1870. It is built of brick and North River blue-stone, is four stories high, and furnishes accommodation for 89 students. The rooms are grouped on three staircases. Durfee Hall, completed in 1871, is perhaps the most thoroughly satisfactory to the eye of all the college buildings. It is of rough-dressed New Jersey sandstone, four stories high, and accommodates 80 lodgers. The rooms are grouped on five staircases. Both of these houses are heated by steam and lighted by gas throughout, and have water on each floor. Filling the space between Farnam and Durfee is the new chapel, not yet finished, a cruciform building with a rounded apse at the eastern, and two towers at the western end of the nave. Like Durfee, it is of New Jersey sandstone with trimmings of the light-colored Ohio sandstone. Two scutcheons on the Elm street side present the coats of arms of the college and the State, with their respective legends: *Lux et Veritas* and *Qui transtulit sustinet.* The chapel will seat 1,150 persons.

During the year 1868-9 the question was agitated whether it might not be well to move the college into the suburbs, on account of the rise in the value of land from the rapid growth of the city. The proposed new site was a lot of fifty acres near the Observatory grounds, on the ridge between East and West Rocks, half a mile north of the Old Hillhouse Place. The plan was given up because of the impossibility of raising money enough to equip the college properly in a fresh location.

President Dwight inaugurated the policy of appointing to permanent professorships young men who had given promise as tutors. Among those first appointed were Jeremiah Day, who succeeded Dr. Dwight in the Presidency; Benjamin Silliman and James L. Kingsley. A Professorship of Jurisprudence, the nucleus of a Law School, was founded in 1801; of Chemistry, Mineralogy, and Geol-

THE LIBRARY.

* Much, in fact, like the cock's comb in Chaucer:
" —— redder than the fine coral,
Embattailed, as it were, a castle wal."

ogy in 1802; of Ancient Languages (Hebrew, Greek and Latin) in 1805; of Rhetoric in 1817. These chairs were afterward divided, and others were added. At present the teaching force of the college proper (or *Academical Department*) consists of the President, who is also the Professor of Moral Philosophy and Metaphysics; eleven Professors in the following subjects: Natural Philosophy and Astronomy; Geology and Mineralogy; Latin; Mathematics; Greek; Rhetoric and English Literature; History; Chemistry and Molecular Physics; Modern Languages; German; and Political and Social Science; three Assistant Professors in Mathematics, Latin and English Literature; and ten tutors.

The first of the professional schools in operation was the Medical School, organized in 1810 with assistance from the State Medical Society, which retains the right of choosing members of the Examining Board. The Faculty consists of seven Professors and a Demonstrator in Anatomy. Since 1859 the School has occupied a three-story brick building on York street, about two blocks from the college, containing a lecture-room, anatomical museum, dissecting-rooms, offices, etc. The catalogue of 1875 shows an attendance of forty-two students.

In 1822 was organized the Divinity School, developing in time into one of the most prosperous branches of the University. Instruction is in the hands of six permanent Professors and several special lecturers. A popular feature was added to the course of study in 1871, by the endowment of the Lyman Beecher Lectureship on Preaching, which has been held in successive years by several eminent divines. Four volumes of "Yale Lectures on Preaching" have already issued from the press. The Divinity School is quartered in two fine buildings opposite the new Chapel and Durfee. These are known as East and West Divinity Halls, and were built respectively in 1870 and 1874. They are alike in appearance—each five stories high, and furnish jointly rooms for 150 students. The lower floors are devoted to class-rooms, libraries, etc. Connected with East Divinity is the small but elegant Marquand Chapel. The number of students at the Seminary averages 100.

The Law School was started in 1824 and celebrated its semi-centennial in 1874; on which occasion Chief-Justice Waite presided. The Hon. Edwards Pierrepont delivered an oration and ex-President Woolsey an historical address. The School has been

NEW CHAPEL.

located since 1873 in fine apartments, occupying the entire third floor of the new County Court House. Its efficiency has increased greatly within the last decade, and the number of its students has been nearly trebled. On the last catalogue it stood 76. The Law School has four regular Professors and seven or eight lecturers.

The most powerful department of the University, after the Academical, is the Sheffield Scientific School. Although this has had many benefactors, and although its success has been due in great part to the exceptional energy and ability of its Professors, yet it may be regarded as mainly the work of one man, Mr. Joseph E. Sheffield, of New Haven. The School was started in 1847, but led a struggling existence till 1860, when Mr. Sheffield bought the old Medical College at the head of College street and presented it to the School, after having refitted it, added two wings, and furnished it with apparatus. The building has received later additions; among others, two towers for astronomical purposes. It is known as Sheffield Hall. In 1873 the same generous patron built and equipped a second building, North Sheffield Hall, immediately north of the former. Both are occupied by laboratories, collections, drawing rooms, observatories, libraries, lecture and recitation rooms and private rooms for instructors. The large lecture-room in North Sheffield seats 400. The *known* gifts of Mr. Sheffield to the School exceed $350,000. But he has given much privately in addition.

The Faculty of the Sheffield School consists of sixteen Professors, and thirteen instructors and assistants. The number of undergraduates is 224. Although the sphere of the school is primarily the Natural Sciences, it is by no means a mere professional or technical institute. It secures a liberal basis for special study by enforcing, in Freshman year, a uniform course in mathematics, physics, chemistry, botany, physical geography, drawing, German, English and political economy. Some knowledge of Latin is required for admission. There is a "select course," embracing linguistics, political economy, and history (under such instructors as Professor William D. Whitney and General Francis A. Walker), English language and literature, German, French, and English composition.

SHEFFIELD HALL.

The Scientific School has, indeed, attained the dimensions of a second and independent college. It is not unlikely that, by an enlargement of its courses in language and history (adding perhaps the classical tongues), the Academic Department in the meanwhile gradually opening elective courses, and increasing its facilities for the teaching of natural science, the two may eventually come to cover nearly the same ground.

Here may be mentioned the Peabody Museum of Natural History, endowed by Mr. George Peabody of London. This is a handsome four-story building, just erected on the corner of Elm and High streets, opposite Alumni Hall. It contains lecture-rooms, offices, and cabinets for collections in zoölogy, geology, mineralogy, paleontology, and American archæology. The valuable collections of fossils made by the annual Yale expedition in the West, under the leadership of Professor Marsh, will be arranged in the Peabody Museum. The building already erected is merely one wing of a larger structure which will stretch from Elm to Library street.

The Yale School of the Fine Arts is, like the Sheffield School, mainly the creation of a single donor, Mr. Augustus R. Street of New Haven, whose gifts to the college have amounted to $280,000, besides other sums of unknown amount not yet realized. The Faculty of the Art School consists of a Professor of Painting and Design, a Professor of the History of Art, a Professor of Drawing, and an Instructor in Perspective. It has some thirty students, and is open to both sexes.

These various departments, though subject to the general government of the University,—the original *President and Fellows of Yale College*,—are practically independent in their internal discipline and instruction. The President of the college is *ex officio* President of each of the schools; but these have also a Dean, Chairman, or Director, who acts as executive officer of his department. All degrees, of course, are conferred by the University.

One of the most encouraging symptoms in the recent development of the University is the establishment of a school for the advanced instruction of graduate students. At present, however, this department has no separate organization, instruction being given by members of the undergraduate Faculties in the intervals of their other work. The annual report by the Executive Committee of the Society of the Alumni, published June 1st, 1875, says: "There have been this year 29 [graduate] students distributed in the following classes: In History, 13; in Political Science, 12; in Sanskrit and General Philology, 9; in English Literature, 7; in Greek, 7; in Hebrew, 6; in Mental Science, 4; in Mathematics, 3; in Latin, 2; in Gothic, 2." This is exclusive of graduate students in Natural Sciences. The number of graduate students now in attendance is 63. The recent establishment of several Fellowships will do much toward stimulating graduate study; but what is most needed is provision for a number of University Professors who should devote themselves exclusively to this department.

It would be impossible, within the limits of this paper, to mention the many gifts, in the shape of endowment funds, building funds, scholarships, books, money, specimens, apparatus, etc., which have contributed to the rapid advance thus briefly sketched in all departments of the University. It is worthy of note, however, that Yale owes nearly all that she has to private liberality. The gifts of the commonwealth of Connecticut to the college do not, all told, exceed $100,000, if we except $135,000, the product of the sale of public lands granted to the Scientific School as the State Agricultural Institute. The productive property of the University, according to the last Treasury Exhibit, is about $1,500,000. If to this be added the value of the land, and the amount that has been spent in buildings, books, apparatus, etc., the University may be roughly estimated as worth five millions of dollars—a small sum, if we consider what has been accomplished with it. Indeed, the history of the college is a story of unceasing struggle with poverty—almost with bankruptcy; of self-denying effort by its officers, and of a system of small and patient economies on the part of its financial managers.

In addition to the buildings belonging to the separate departments ought perhaps to be mentioned the College Gymnasium, and the building opposite it on Library street, occupied by graduate students; the elegant new boat-house of the Yale Navy on Mill River, and the halls of the Skull and Bones, Scroll and Keys, Psi Upsilon, and Delta Kappa Epsilon Societies.

About the years 1869–71 appeared what was called "the Young Yale movement," a rather vaguely expressed, though clearly shown, dissatisfaction among the younger graduates with the conservatism of the college government. It was urged especially that there was too large a clerical element in the corporation, and that the Alumni ought to be represented. There was much controversy in and out of print, Dr. Leonard Bacon taking a prominent part on the Old Yale, and Mr. William Walter Phelps on the Young Yale, side. Finally, in accordance with a suggestion of President Woolsey, made as long ago as 1866, the State agreed to relinquish a share of its claim in the government of the college, and the six Senior Senators were replaced by an equal number of gentlemen, chosen, one each year, by the Alumni at their annual Commencement meetings.

In speaking of the influence which the college has had on the intellectual development of the country, a comparison naturally suggests itself between Yale and the sister University at Cambridge. Founded under similar auspices, and for similar purposes, the two have diverged widely in spirit. Cambridge, with the neighboring city of Boston, is widely known, not only as the seat of Harvard College, but as the center of most that is best in American letters. New Haven can claim no such distinction. There has always been in the training given at Yale a certain severity. Discipline, rather than culture; power, rather than grace;

PEABODY MUSEUM.

"light," rather than "sweetness," have been, if not the aim, at least the result of her teachings. Her scholars have been noted for solid and exact learning. Perhaps Dwight and Woolsey on one hand, and Everett and Felton on the other, may be taken as the types of Yale and Harvard Presidents. This difference is owing to many causes. Harvard has had at her back a wealthy and cultivated city. Boston is the chief point on this continent where the electric sparks have been taken off from the current of European thought. Yale, on the contrary, has been situated in a small provincial city, with little "atmosphere" beyond what the college itself might impart to the town. Again, the Unitarian and Transcendental movements in Massachusetts during the first half of this century, whatever may have been their effect on the Church, undoubtedly stimulated literary activity.

The course of study at the two colleges has been much the same. The influences of place have differed *toto cœlo*. The imagination and the feelings may be chastened, but they cannot be aroused to original expression by any scheme of study. For this there are needed fresh and joyous impressions from without; a free and even audacious reception and interchange of new thought. These impulses the Massachusetts come-outers of the last generation had and profited by.

Before the recent changes in its system,

YALE BOAT-HOUSE.

Harvard was not very a large and by no means popular college, drawing most of its students from Eastern Massachusetts. Its Alumni settled largely in Boston and neighboring towns, and there thus grew up about the college a cultivated body of its sons, and in time a school of brilliant writers. Of

DR. LEONARD BACON.

Yale the reverse has been true. She has not kept her boys at home. They came from all over the country, largely from New York and the West, and, before the war, from the South; and after graduation they cut loose from Alma Mater's apron-strings, and were scattered more widely than before. This, which has been her weakness, has also been her strength. She has a national character, and her investments are everywhere.

Yale is by no means deficient in distinguished names in poetry, fiction, criticism, and belles-lettres generally, numbering among her graduates of the present century Pierpont, Hillhouse, Cooper,* Percival, Willis, Bushnell, Judd (the author of "Margaret,") Bristed, Mitchell, Winthrop, and Stedman, with others perhaps less famous. But the centrifugal force of New Haven is shown in the fact that of this list only three have resided there since their graduation, and these at different times. There has never been a Yale school of writers since the

* Non-graduate, class of 1806.

Revolutionary "Pleiades" already mentioned.

But in the literature of knowledge, in the professions, in business, politics, and practical life, Yale's record is a proud one. In scholarship she is represented by such names as Webster, Worcester, Woolsey, Hadley, and Whitney; in science and invention by Silliman, Morse, Whitney, Dana, and Chauvenet; in divinity by Edwards, Hopkins, Emmons, Dwight, and Taylor; in the State and at the bar by Grimke, Mason, Kent, Calhoun, and Evarts. The class of 1837, *e. g.*, contributed to the number of prominent men now in public life the names of the Hon. William M. Evarts, Chief-Justice Waite, Attorney-General Pierrepont, and Governor Samuel J. Tilden.

Yale is, in a sense, the daughter of Harvard. Her founders and early Presidents and tutors were of necessity Harvard men. But the younger college has since been far more active in founding and officering new colleges—a work, be it said, which has proved to be of doubtful expediency. Yale may be called, like Virginia, "Mother of Presidents." She has furnished Presidents to Princeton, Columbia, Dartmouth, Williams, Amherst, Trinity, Middlebury, Cornell, and the Universities of Vermont, California, Pennsylvania, and many others. Presidents Barnard of Columbia, White of Cornell, Gilman of the Hopkins University, and Chancellor Stillè of the University of Pennsylvania, are all graduates of Yale.

This paper has been devoted mainly to tracing the growth of the university as an educational institution. The social life of the undergraduates falls outside our compass. Much might be written of the old college commons, of the Bully Club, of Town and Gown fights, of Linonia and Brothers and the Secret Societies; of the ceremonies of Presentation Day; of college journalism and college boating, and of many other customs, traditions, and institutions, but they would easily fill a chapter by themselves. Probably at no other American college has so distinctive a social life been developed as at Yale, nor one so rich in humorous and picturesque traits. This life has never been adequately described. In conclusion, it

PROFESSOR WEIR'S STUDIO.

may be permissible to quote what has elsewhere been written as expressing the hopes and aspirations of "Young Yale."

"We care not that the dawn should throw
Its flush upon our portico;
But rather that our natal star,
Bright Hesper in the twilight far,
Should beckon toward the distant West
Which he—our Berkeley—loved the best;
Whereto, his prophet line did say,
'The course of empire takes its way.'
And in the groves of that young land
A mighty school his wisdom planned,
To teach new knowledge to new men—
Strange sciences undreamed of then.
She comes—had come, unknown, before—
Though not on 'vext Bermoothes' shore;
Yet will she not her prophet fail—
The Old—the New—the same dear Yale."

The article below is from *Life* magazine April 3, 1913. This is not the same *Life* magazine begun in 1936 by Bonesman Henry Luce. This was one of the last articles about The Order of Skull and Bones in the popular press until *Esquire* magazine in September 1977

WE read in the papers that the Yale worm has turned and that the whole Sophomore class, except two members, have signed in a book not to be joined to Bones, Keys or Wolf's Head Senior Societies, as now constituted. The said organizations, it seems, must abolish secrecy and get in a new line of consecration, if they are to enjoy the patronage of the present Yale Sophomore class.

This is great news.

Who would be free themselves must strike the blow. It is much more suitable for the Yale Sophomores to take this action than for the faculty to do it, because a Sophomore can better afford to be foolish than a faculty can. If the little Senior clubs at Yale can be broken of some of their silly habits, and shorn of their importance as arbiters of destinies and standardizers of character, there is no reason why they should not renew their health and live joyful and comparatively innocuous ever after. For the last forty years they have been getting more and more out of date and more and more in the way of what Dr. Wilson calls "The New Freedom." Surely they must know it, and must be glad of a chance to rid themselves of buncombe and an uncomfortable prestige, and shake down into something that will fit into a modern institution.

It is not the fault of their members that they have come to be a nuisance. That is something that has just happened to them, in the march of events, just as it has happened to the trusts and the tariff and the House of Lords. And the revolt of the Sophomores is just a piece of the contemporary unheaval. Everybody who cares for Yale is to be congratulated on it, especially Bones, Keys and Wolf's Head. Now these amusing organizations will be able to modernize themselves, let daylight into their club houses, exhibit the enlightened selfishness which is all that is possible to any club that lives by exclusion and permit themselves some of the exercises of hospitality, from which hitherto they have been debarred.

It is obvious that something happen between their sophomore and senior years, because the societies lived on with their secrets intact – and still act secretly today.

The Order of Skull & Bones
1888

Seated left - George Metcalf Gill seated right - Fredrick Palmer Solley
L–R, Henry Lewis Stimson, David Whipple Morison, James Howard McMillan, Samuel Johnson Walker, Morrison R. Waite, Richard Melancthon Hurd, Amos Alonzo Stagg, Frederic Augustus Stevenson, Harlan Ward Cooley, Irving Fisher, Samuel Sidney Roby, Orland Sidney Isbell, William Henry Seward COURTESY ARCHIVES & MANUSCRIPTS –YALE UNIVERSITY LIBRARY

The Order of Skull & Bones
1900

Seated left - Hulbert Taft seated right - Frederick Baldwin Adams
L–R, John Morgan Hopkins, Ashley Leavitt, Frank Dexter Cheney, Stuart Brown Camp, James Cowan Greenway, Malcom Douglas, Corlis Esmonde Sullivan, John Walter Cross, Percy Avery Rockefeller, William Sloane Coffin, Brace Whitman Paddock, Frederick Winthrop Allen, George Armstrong Lyon COURTESY ARCHIVES & MANUSCRIPTS –YALE UNIVERSITY LIBRARY

THE SKELETON CREW

KRIS MILLEGAN
JULY 2003

THIS LIST IS COMPILED from material from the Order of Skull and Bones membership books at Sterling Library, Yale University and other public records. The latest books available are the 1971 ***Living Members*** and the 1973 ***Deceased Members*** books. The last year the members were published in the ***Yale Banner*** is 1969. ***The Rumpus,*** a Yale tabloid, has printed some of the members of recent years. There is no known verifiable public source for the members from 1972 on and no available private source for 1986 on. Please inform the publisher of any errors or omissions. Skull & Bones is an increasingly *secret* secret society and our materials are not, therefore, current. The Period and Decade numbers are peculiar to the Order of Skull & Bones.

1833		**PERIOD 2, DECADE 31**
NAME	OCCUPATION	NOTES
Bates, Samuel Henshaw	Farming	Priv, Union Army, Civil War
Beach, John Campell	Law	
Bishop, Noah	Ministry	Presbyterian Minister
Crump, John	Med Student	
Davis, Benjamin Franklin	Medicine	Served Seminole War
Hart, Rufus Erastus	Law	Mbr 1845-47, OH State Senate
Lewis, Asahel Hooker	Literary	Mbr 1847-48, OH State Legislature
Marshall, Samuel Davies	Law, Literary	Mbr, IL State Legislature; Major, Mexican War
Mather, Frederick Ellsworth	Law	Mbr 1845, NY State Legislature
Miller, Phineas Timothy	Medicine	
—— —— ——		
Robertson, Robert	Literary	
Russell, William Huntington	Education	Mbr 1846-47, CT State Legislature, Founder Collegiate and Commercial Institute (New Haven); Maj-Gen 1862-70, CT Ntnl Guard, Co-Founder of Bones
Taft, Alphonso	Law	US Minister Austria 1882-84, Russia 1884-85; Sec 1876, War US; Attny Gen 1876-77, US; Mbr 1872-82, Yale Corp; Co-Founder of Bones
Wood, George Ingersoll	Ministry	Congregational Minister

1834		PERIOD 2, DECADE 32
NAME	OCCUPATION	NOTES
Beaumont, George Anson O.	Law	
Burr, William Shedden	Industrial	Iron Industry
Coffing, Churchill	Law	
Emerson, Alfred	Ministry	Congregational Minister; Prof Mathematics and Astronomy 1853-56, Western Reserve College
Foster, Eleazar Kingsbury	Law	Spkr 65, Mbr 1844-45, CT State Legislature; Judge of Probate 1845-46, 1848-49 (New Haven, CT)
Gordon, Alexander Blucher	Law	
Hall, Daniel Emerson	Law	
Houston, John Wallace	Law	Assoc Justice 1855-93, DE Superior Court; Mbr 1845-51, Congress; Sec of State 1841-44, DE
Kendall, John Newton	Medicine	
Kingsley, Henry Coit	Law, Finance	Treas 1862-87, Yale U
Lea, James Neilsen	Law	Assoc Justice, LA Supreme Court 1855-63; Mbr 1846, LA State Legislature
Southmayd, Samuel Gray	Industrial	
Spencer, George Gilman	Business	Wholesale grocer
Tweedy, John Hubbard	Transportation	Mbr 1853, WS State Legislature; Mbr 1847-48 US Congress;
Washington, William Henry	Law	Mbr 1841-43 US Congress; Mbr, NC State Legislature

1835		PERIOD 2, DECADE 33
NAME	OCCUPATION	NOTES
Anderson, Edwin Alexander	Medicine	Pres NC Med Society; Surgeon, Confederate Army, Civil War
Davis, John	Law	
Howard, Oran Reed	Ministry	Episcopal Minister
Johnston, Frank	Literary	
McLellan, William	Law	Bank Pres
Mills, Ethelbert Smith	Law	Pres, Brooklyn Trust; drowned
Rafferty, John Chandler	Law	Mbr, PA State Senate
Seeley, John Edward	Law	Mbr 1870-71, US Congress; Judge
Seymour, John Forman	Business	
Sheffey, Hugh White	Law	Judge 1865-69, Superior Court; Spkr 1861-65, Mbr 1846, VA State Legislature
Strong, Caleb	Ministry	Presbyterian Minister
Stubbs, Alfred	Ministry	Episcopal Minister
Sturges, Thomas Benedict	Ministry	Congregational Minister
Thacher, Thomas Anthony	Education	Prof 1842-86, Latin Yale College; Mbr 1856-77, CT State Bd Educ
Walsh, Hugh	Medicine	

1836		PERIOD 2, DECADE 34
NAME	OCCUPATION	NOTES
Darling, Thomas	Finance	Banker; USN, Civil War
Deming, Henry Champion	Law	Mbr 1863-67, US Congress
Dent, Henry Hatch	Law	
Dunwody, James Bulloch	Ministry	Presbyterian Minister
Harris, Henry Reeder	Farming	
Hurd, John Codman	Literary	
Martin, John Griffith	Law	
Marvin, George Lockwood	Law	
Pierson, William Seward	Law	Brig Gen, Union Army, Civil War
Preston, Henry Kirk	Law	
Rowland, William Sherman	Law	
Sherman, Frederick Roger	Law	
Swift, John Morton	Farming	
Tyler, George Palmer	Ministry	Presbyterian Minister
Wray, James McAlpin	Law	

1837		PERIOD 2, DECADE 35
NAME	OCCUPATION	NOTES
Carter, Edwin Osgood	Law	Judge 1863, (MA); 1862 US Asst Assessor; Civil Engineer, 1845 (Chile), 46-49 (Peru)
Coit, William	Law	

Day, Thomas Mills	Literary	State printer, CT; Aide to Governor, CT; Newspaper Publisher, Editor, 1855-66, Hartford *Courant*; Lt Col, Militia, CT
Evarts, William Maxwell	Law	Mbr 1885-91, US Senate; Secretary of State 1877-81, US; Attny Gen 1868-69, US; Deputy US District Attorney 1849, Southern NY; Mbr 1872-91, Yale Corp; Counsel for Andrew Johnson's Impeachment trial
Hatch, Walter Tilden	Finance	Banker & Broker, WT Hatch & Sons (NYC)
Hyatt, Robert Underwood	Law	Lawyer, Dane School (Cambridge, MA)
Law, William Fabian	Law	Farmer, Lawyer, Dane Law School (Cambridge, MA); US District Attny (GA)
Lyman, Chester Smith	Education	Prof Emeritus 1889-90, Prof 1884-89, Astronomy, 1871-84, Physics, 1859-71, Industrial mechanics, Yale U
Owen, Allen Ferdinand	Law	Mbr 1848-52, US Congress; Mbr 1843-47, GA State Legislature; US Consul Havana; Dane Law School (Cambridge, MA)
Robeson, Abel Bellows	Medicine	
Scarborough, William Smith	Law	Mbr 1846, CT State Senate
Silliman, Benjamin Jr.	Education	Prof 1846-49 54-85, Chemistry Yale U; Prof 1849-1854, Medical Chemistry, Toxicology U Louisville; Mbr, Common Council (New Haven); Dir, New Haven Gas Works; Original member National Academy of Sciences
Waite, Morris Remmick	Law	Chief Justice, 1874-88, U.S. Supreme Court; Mbr 1849, OH State Legislature; Mbr 1882-88, Yale Corp
Williams, Henry	Law	US Dist Attny 1849-54 (GA); Dane Law School (Cambridge, MA); Lt, Confederate Army, Civil War
Yerkes, Stephen	Education	Pres, Prof 1857-66, 67-96, Biblical and Oriental Lit, Danville Theological Seminary (KY); Acting Prof 1866-67, Greek, Centre College (Danville); Prof 1852-57, Ancient Languages, Transylvania U

1838 — PERIOD 2, DECADE 36

NAME	OCCUPATION	NOTES
Bartlett, John Knowlton	Medicine	Pres, WS Med Society
Cooper, William Frierson	Law	Judge1861-62, 77-86, TN Supreme Court
Dodd, Albert	Law	Drowned
Fleming, William Stuart	Law	Chancellor 1870-86, 8th Div of TN
Jones, Seaborn Augustus	Farming	Planter
Key, Thomas Marshall	Law	Mbr 1858-61, KY State Senate; Col Union Army Civil War
Law, William Lyon		
Lynde, Charles James	Law	
Ribeiro, Carlos Fernando	Farming	Planter
Rich, Charles	Business	
Spaulding, Ebenezer	Law	
Talcott, Thomas Grosvenor	Law	
Thompson, Joseph Parrish	Ministry	Congregational Minister
Varnum, Joseph Bradley	Law	Mbr 1849, 50, 57 (Spkr 51), NY State Legislature
Williams, Thomas Scott	Law	Drowned

1839 — PERIOD 2, DECADE 37

NAME	OCCUPATION	NOTES
Beach, John Sheldon	Law	RTA Incorporator
Biddle, Thomas Bradish	Law	
Chandler, William Henry	Farming	Mbr 1867-71, CT State Senate; Mbr 1847, CT State Legislature
Eldridge, Charles St. John	Student	
Faulkner, Endress	Finance	
Hubbard, Richard Dudley	Law	Gov 1877-79, CT; Mbr 1867-69, US Congress; Mbr CT 1842-43 55,58, State Legislature; Mbr 1877-79, Yale Corp
Jackson, Henry Rootes	Law	Pres 1894-98, American National Bank of Brunswick; US Minister Mexico 1885-88, Austria 1854-58; US Dist Attny 1843-49, (GA); Judge for Eastern Circuit GA Superior Court; 1861, Georgia Secession Convention; Pres, Georgia Historical Society; Brig Gen, Confederate Army, Civil War; Col, Mexican War
Norris, William Herbert	Ministry	Episcopal Minister
Putnam, James Osborne	Law	Chancellor U Buffalo; US Minister 1880-82, Belgium; US Consul 1861-66, Havre, France; Mbr 1854-55, NY State Senate,
Stille, Charles Janeway	Literary	Provost 1868-82, Prof 1866-68, Belles-Letteres U PA; Mbr, US Sanitary Comm, Civil War
Trotter, Silas Flournoy	Business	Lawyer & Planter
Washington, George	Industrial	

Watson, John Marsh	Law	
Williams, William Perkins	Student	
Wolcott, Elizer	Industrial	

1840 — **PERIOD 2, DECADE 38**

NAME	OCCUPATION	NOTES
Beirne, Christopher James	Law	Mbr, WV State Legislature
Benedict, Theodore Hudson	Government	Mbr 1850, NY State Legislature
Burnham, Curtis Field	Law	Mbr 1899, 1903, KY State Senate; Asst Treasurer 1875-76, US; Mbr 1851, 59-63, KY State Legislature
Chauvenet, William	Education	Chancellor, Washington U, (St Louis)
Fisk, Stuart Wilkins	Law	Col, Inf Confederate Army Civil War
Hoppin, James Mason	Education	Prof Emeritus 1899-1906, Prof History of Art 1879-99, Prof of Homiletics 1861-79, Yale U
Hoyt, Joseph Gibson	Education	Chancellor, Prof 1858-62, Greek, Washington U
Hudson, Ward Woodridge	Law	
Jesup, James Riley	Law	
March, Daniel	Ministry	Congregational Minister
McCall, Henry	Farming	
Perkins, John	Law	Mbr 1853-57, US Congress; Sec Navy, Confederate States, Civil War; Chairman of the 1861 Louisiana Secession Convention.
Perkins, William	Law	Drowned, 1854
Richards, George	Ministry	Mbr 1868-70, Yale Corp; Congregational Minister
Tiffany, William Henry	Business	Mining

1841 — **PERIOD 2, DECADE 39**

NAME	OCCUPATION	NOTES
Barry, William Taylor Sullivan	Law	Chairman 1861, Mississippi Secession Convention; Mbr1861, Confederate Provisional Congress; Mbr US Congress 53-55; Mbr 1849-53, MS State Legislature; Served Confederate Army, Civil War
DeSa, Pompeo Ascenco	Farming	Planter
Emerson, Joseph	Education	Prof, Greek 55-88, Ancient Languages 1848-55, Beloit College
Eustis, William Tappan	Ministry	Congregational Minister
Field, David Irvine	Farming	Planter
Gillette, Augustus Canfield	Law & Literary	
Helfenstein, Charles Philip	Industrial	Coal Business
Leaf, Edmund	Ministry	Episcopal Minister
Learned, William Law	Law	Justice 1870-92 (presiding justice 1875-92), NY Supreme Court; Pres, Albany Law School
Mitchell, Donald Grant	Literary	US Consul 1854, Venice
Raymond, Henry Hunter	Law	Maj, Confederate Army, Civil War
Sturges, Hezekiah	Law	Judge, NY Supreme Court
Willis, Richard Storrs	Music, Literary	
Woolfolk, William Grey	Farming	Planter; Confederate Army, Civil War
Yarnall, Thomas Coffin	Ministry	Episcopal Rector

1842 — **PERIOD 2, DECADE 40**

NAME	OCCUPATION	NOTES
Benton, Joseph Augustine	Education	Pres, Prof 1869-92, Pacific Theological Seminary
Brown, Joseph Venen	Business	
Buttles, Albert Barnes	Law	
Edwards, Newton	Law	
Gready, William Postell	Ministry	Presbyterian Minister
Halsey, Jacob	Law	
Henen, William Davison	Law	Major Confederate Army Civil War
Huggins, William Sidney	Ministry	Presbyterian Minister
Lewis, Henry	Student	
MacWhorter, Alexander	Ministry	Episcopal Minister; Prof 1859-60, Metaphysics, English Lit, Troy U
Mathews, Albert	Literary	
Miller, Francis William	Law	
Perkins, Nathaniel Shaw	Business	

Peters, John Andrew	Law	Chief Justice 1883-00, Assoc Justice 1873-83, ME Supreme Court; Mbr 1866-73, US Congress; Attny Gen 1864-66, (ME); Mbr 1864, ME State legislature; Mbr 1862-63, ME State Senate
Pratt, Julius Howard	Business	Mngr, Arlington Cemetery

1843 — PERIOD 2, DECADE 41

NAME	OCCUPATION	NOTES
Baratte, Julius Adolphus	Law	Collector of Customs
Chambers, William Lyon	Business	Pres, Chambersburgh National Bank
Eames, Benjamin Tucker	Law	Mbr 1881-79, Congress; Mbr 1854-56, 59, 63, 84, RI State Senator; Mbr, 1868, Spkr 69, RI State legislature
Gachet, Charles Nicholas	Law	Served Confederate Army, Civil War
Grammar, Christopher	Law	
Granger, Gideon	Law	
Hart, Roswell	Finance	Mbr 1864-66, US Congress
Havens, Daniel William	Ministry	Presbyterian Minister
Lambert, Alfred	Medicine	
Lane, William Griswold	Law	Judge
Lent, John Abram	Business, Law	Judge
Moody, Thomas Hudson	Business	
Robb, John Hunte	Law	
Robinson, Lucius Franklin	Law	w/Robinson & Robinson
Stevens, Henry	Literary	Bibliophile, Fellow, London Society of Antiquaries

1844 — PERIOD 2, DECADE 42

NAME	OCCUPATION	NOTES
Bell, Richard Dobbs Spaight	Business	
Breed, Edward Andrews	Business	
Elliot, William Horace	Law	
Felder, John Henry	Farming	Mbr 1852-61, SC State Legislature; 1st Lt, Inf Confederate Army, Civil War
Ferry, Orris Sanford	Law	Mbr 1866-75, US Senate; Mbr 1859-61, US Congress; Mbr 1855-56, CT State Legislature; Brig Gen Union Army Civil War
Fewsmith, William	Education	US Civil Service Commissioner; Examiner, US Civil Commission
Fisk, Samuel Augustus	Medicine	
Foote, Thaddeus	Law	Col, Cavalry Union Army Civil War
Lanier, Alexander Chalmers	X	
Lovell, Joseph	Law	Brig Gen, Confederate Army, Civil War
Robb, James Madison	Law	
Walker, Joseph Burbeen	Farming, Business	Mbr 1893, NH State Senate; 1866-67, NH State Legislature; Pres 1889-93, Mbr 1885 NH State Forestry Comm; Mbr, NH Bd Agriculture; Trustee, NH College of Agriculture and Mechanic Arts
Washburn, William Barrett	Industrial, Finance	Mbr 1874-75, US Senate; Gov 1872-74, MA; Mbr 1862-72 US Congress; Mbr 1853-54 MA State Legislature; Mbr 1850, MA State Senate; Mbr 1872-81, Yale Corp
Wetherell, John Walcott	Law	Col, Union Army Civil War
Wilson, Archelaus	Law	Inventor

1845 — PERIOD 2, DECADE 43

NAME	OCCUPATION	NOTES
Brickell, James Noaille	Law	1st Lt, Ord Confederate Army, Civil War
Conner, Lemuel Parker	Law	Maj, Confederate Army, Civil War
Conner, William Gustine	Farming	Planter; Maj, Confederate Army, Civil War
Cushman, Isaac LaFayette	Education	
Esty, Constantine Canaris	Law	Mbr 71-79, MA Bd of Education; Mbr 1872-73 US Congress; Mbr 1866, MA State Legislature; Mbr 1857-58, MA State Senate
Gould, James Gardner	Law	
Harding, John Wheeler	Ministry	Congregational Minister
Hill, George Canning	Literary Work	
Hyde, Alvan Pinney	Law	Hyde, Gross & Hyde (Hartford); Mbr 1854, 58, 63, CT State Legislature
Kennedy, Thomas	Ministry	
Metcalfe, Orrick	Medicine	Prof 1845-47, Languages Jefferson College; Surgeon, Confederate Army, Civil War
Nickerson, Sereno Dwight	Finance	Sec, Grand Lodge of Freemasons MA
Rankin, Robert	Law	

Taylor, Richard	Farming	Planter; Mbr 1856-60, LA State Senate; Service Mexican War; Lt Gen, Confederate Army Civil War
Wales, Leonard Eugene	Law	Judge 1884-97, US Dist Court (DE); Union Army, Civil War

1846 — **PERIOD 2, DECADE 44**

NAME	OCCUPATION	NOTES
Backus, Joseph Willes	Ministry	Congregational Minister; Mbr 1875-99 Yale Corp
Brisbrin, John Ball	Law	Mbr 1858, 1864, MN State Legislature
Eakin, William Spencer	Business	Merchant
Harrison, Henry Baldwin	Law	Gov 1885-87, CT; Mbr 1865, 1873, Spkr 1883, CT State Legislature; Mbr 1854-56, CT State Senate; Mbr 1872-85, Yale Corp; RTA Incorporator
Hawley, David	Law	
Kellogg, Stephen Wright	Law	Mbr 1869-73, US Congress; Judge 1864, New Haven City Court; Judge 1854-61, Probate, Waterbury Dist; Mbr 1856, CT State Legislature; Mbr 1853, CT State Senate
Linton, Stephen Duncan	Farming	Cotton Planter
Mulford, David Humphrey	Business	Iron Business
Nelson, Rensselaer Russell	Law	Assoc Justice 1857-58, Supreme Court (Territory MN); Judge 1858-96, US District Court (MN)
Nevins, William Russell	Law	
Phinney, Elihu	Industrial	drowned
Savage, Josiah	Law	
Steele, Henry Thornton	Law	
Stiles, Joseph	X	Civil Engineer
Trask, Charles Hooper	Business	Rhodes Scholar (Oxford)

1847 — **PERIOD 2, DECADE 45**

NAME	OCCUPATION	NOTES
Allison, Samuel Perkins	Law	General; Lawyer
Baldwin, Roger Sherman	Law	
Bayne, Thomas Levingston	Law	Lt Col Artillery, Confederate Army, Civil War
Coon, John	Industrial	Mngr, Rocky Mt Oil Co. Pueblo CO; Paymaster, Union Army, Civil War
Fitch, James	Law	
Haight, Ducald Cameron	Law	Drowned
Hayden, William Hallock	Industrial	Mfg Saddlery Hardware
McLallen, Philemon Fred	Law	
Mills, Alfred	Law	
Moore, William Eves	Ministry	Presbyterian Minister; 2d Lt Union Army, Civil War
Munn, John	Law	
Olmstead, John Hull	Literary	
Sanford, Charles Frederick	Law	Judge
Smith, John Donnell	Science	Capt, Confederate Army Civil War
Wilson, John	Law	

1848 — **PERIOD 2, DECADE 46**

NAME	OCCUPATION	NOTES
Abbe, Frederick Randolph	Ministry	Congregational Minister
Aitchison, William	Minisitry	Missionary (Peking, China)
Blake, Henry Taylor	Law	Incorporator RTA
Colton, Henry Martin	Education	Congregational Minister
Condit, Charles	Law	
Emerson, Samuel	Education	
Foster, Dwight	Law	Assoc Judge 66-69, MA Supreme Court; Attny Gen 1861-64, MA
Hitchcock, Henry	Law	Dean 1867-79; Prof of law 1867-84, St Louis Law School, Washington U; Adj-Gen, Union Army, Civil War
Kinne, William	Education	
Mesick, Richard Smith	Law	Mbr, CA State Senate; Dist Judge; Judge Supreme Court NV
Pinckard, Thomas Cicero	Education	
Strickler, Samuel Alexander	Finance	
White, George	Law	
Willcox, Giles Buckingham	X	
Young, Benham Daniel	Education	

1849		PERIOD 2, DECADE 47
NAME	OCCUPATION	NOTES
Brandegee, Augustus	Law	Mbr 1863-67, US Congress; Mbr 1854-57, Spkr 61, CT State Legislature; Lawyer, Brandegee, Noyes & Brandegee
Came, Charles Green	Literary Work	Editor *Boston Journal*; Mbr 1852-55, Maine State Legislature
Campbell, James	Transportation	RR business
Clarke, William Barker	Ministry	Chittenden Prof 1863-66, Divinity Yale U; Pastor (Durham, CT)
Dwight, Timothy	Education	Pres Emeritus 1899-1916, Pres 1886-99, Acting Treas 1886-88, Prof of Sacred literature, 1858-86; Yale U; Changed Yale College to Yale U; Editor 1866-74, *New Englander*; Editor, Translator 1874-84, American Comm Revision of New Testament
Finch, Francis Miles	Law	Dean 1896-1903, Prof, History and evolution of Law 1895-1903, Cornell Law School; Assoc Judge 1880-1896, NY Court of Appeals
Fisk, Franklin Woodbury	Education	Pres 87-1900, Prof, Sacred Rhetoric 1857-1900, Chicago Theological Seminary; Prof, Rhetoric and English Literature 1854-59, Beloit College
Hough, Edward Clement	Finance	
Hurlbut, Joseph	Theological Student	
Kirby, Jacob Brown	Farming, Industrial	
Metcalfe, Henry Laurens	Business	Confederate Army, Civil War
Miles, James Browning	Ministry	Congregational Minister; Sec, Am Peace Society
Morris, Edward Dafydd	Ministry	Presbyterian Minister; Prof 1868-98, ecclesiastical history, Lane Theological Seminary
Richardson, Walker	Farming	Planter; Confederate Army, Civil War
Rockwell, John	Finance	

1850		PERIOD 2, DECADE 48
NAME	OCCUPATION	NOTES
Bentley, Edward Warren	Ministry	Dutch Reform Minister
Bliss, Robert	Finance	
Bliss, William Root	Insurance	w/Equitable Life Assurance Co
Camp, Clinton	Theological Student	
Chase, Henry	Law	Mbr 1865, VT State Legislature; Inspector of Immigration
Colton, Willis Strong	Ministry	Congregational Minister
Condit, Albert Pierson	Law	Mbr 1886, 67, NJ State Legislature, Spkr 1871
Converse, George Sherman	Ministry	Episcopal Minister
Dechert, Henry Martyn	Law	Lawyer, Pres, Commonwealth Title Ins & Trust Co. (Philadelphia); Pres, State Asylum for Chronic Insane of PA; 1st Lt, Inf, Union Army
Foote, Joseph Forward	Law	
Ludden, William	Music	Music Author, Publisher and Musical Merchandise Dealer
Manross, Newton Spaulding	Science	Prof 1861-62, Chemistry Amherst College; Capt, Union Army Civil war
Roberts, Ellis Henry	Finance	Treas 1899-1903, Asst Treas 1889-1893, US; Mbr 1871-75, US Congress; Mbr 1867, NY State Legislature
Storrs, Cordial	Law	
Woodford, Oswald Langdon	Ministry, Farming	Mbr 1865, CT State Legislature; Congregational Minister

1851		PERIOD 2, DECADE 49
NAME	OCCUPATION	NOTES
Alexander, William Felix	Finance	Cotton Broker, Insurance agent; served Confederate Army during Civil War
Beman, Henry DeWitt	Law	Served Confederate Army, Civil War
Brinsmade, Horatio Walsh	Medical Student	
Crampton, Rufus Cowles	Education	Pres 1877-81, Prof 1854-88, Mathematics & Astronomy, Illinois College; Lt Col, Union Army, Civil War
Dana, William Buck	Industrial	Publisher, WB Dana & Co
Evans, Evan Wilhelm	Education	Prof, Mathematics 1868-72, Cornell U; Prof, Natural Philosophy and Astronomy 1857-64, Marietta College
Haldeman, Richard Jacobs	Literary	Mbr 1869-73, US Congress
Hebard, Albert	Student	
Little, Robbins	Library Work	Supt 1878-96, The Astor Library (NYC); Examiner of Claims 1873-78, War Dept; Instr 1865-69, International Law, US Naval Academy
Manice, William DeForest	Law	
Slade, John Milton	Business	dry goods

Vose, James Gardiner	Ministry	Congregational Minister; Prof 1856-64, Rhetoric, Amherst College; Trustee 1886-08 Andover Theology Seminary
Wells, Henry Dorrance	Business	
White, Henry Dyer	Law	1st Treas, Incorporator, RTA
Whitney, Emerson Cogswell	Education	

1852 — **PERIOD 2, DECADE 50**

NAME	OCCUPATION	NOTES
Bigelow, Albert	Ministry	Presbyterian Minister
Blakeslee, Henry Clay	Engineering	
Bliss, Charles Miller	Literary	2nd Lt, Inf, Union Army, Civil War
Cooper, Jacob	Education	Prof of Logics and Metaphysics 1893-04, Prof of Greek 66-93, Rutgers Col , Prof of Greek 1855-62, 63-66 Center College; Chaplin, Union Army Civil War
Crapo, William Wallace	Law	Pres 13, Bedford Institution for Savings, MA; Pres 13, Wamsutta Mills; Pres 1893 Mechanics' National Bank; Mbr 1875-83, US Congress; Mbr 1857, MA State Legislature
Gilman, Daniel Coit	Education	Co-incorporator of the Russell Trust; Pres 02-05, Carnegie Institution of Washington; First Pres 1875-1901, John Hopkins U; First Pres 1872-75, U of CA; Prof, Geology 1863-72, Sheffield Scientific School; Librarian 1858-65, Yale College; Sec 1865-66, CT State Bd Education
Helmer, Charles Downs	Ministry	Congregational Minister
Houghton, Edward	Farming	
Johnston, William Preston	Education	1st Pres 1883-1899, Tulane; Pres 1880-1883, LSA; Prof 1867-77, English Lit, History & Political Economy Washington & Lee U; Col, Confederate Army Civil War
Marmaduke, Vincent	Literary	Mbr 1882-84, State Legislature; Col, Confederate Army, Civil War
McCormick, Henry	Industrial	Farmer, Banker, Iron Business; Co, Union Army Civil War
Ross, William Baldwin	Law	Union Army, Civil War
Safford, George Blagden	Ministry	
Sill, George Griswold	Law	US Dist Attny CT 1888-1892; Mbr 1882-83, CT State Legislature; Lt Gov 1873-77, CT; Mbr Yale Corp 1873-77
Stanley, William	Law	

1853 — **PERIOD 2, DECADE 51**

NAME	OCCUPATION	NOTES
Aiken, William Pope	Minisitry	Congregational Minister
Babcock, Henry Harper	Industrial	
Baldwin, George William	Law	Asst, Adjunct Gen of Volunteers Spanish-American War
Capron, Samuel Mills	Education	Principal, Hartford High School
Coit, Joshua	Ministry	Congregational Minister
Davies, Thomas Frederick	Ministry	1889-1905 Episcopal Bishop of MI; Prof Hebrew 1862, Berkeley Divinity School
Gleason, William Henry	Ministry	Mbr 1864-65, NY State Legislature; Dutch Reform Minister
Grout, Alfred	Law	
Heard, Albert Farley	Government	
Jack, Thomas McKinney	Law	Mbr 1859-61, TX Legislature; 1856-58, City Judge; Lt Col, Calvary Confederate Army Civil War
Johnson, George Asbury	Law	Attny Gen 1886-90, CA; Mbr 1882-1886, CA State Senate; Judge 1872-1874, 17th Judicial Circuit Court
Kent, Albert Emmett	Business	Banker, AE Kent & Sons (San Rafael, CA)
White, Andrew Dickinson	Education	Founding Pres 1866-85, Prof 1866-85, Hist, Cornell U; US Minister 1892-94 Russia; US Minister 1879-81,1897-1902 Germany; Prof 1857-66, Hist and English Lit, U MI; Trustee, Carnegie Institute and Carnegie Endowment for Peace; psychic researcher
Whiton, James Morris	Ministry, Literary	Editorial Staff 13, *The Outlook* (NYC); Prof 1893-94 Ethics & Economist, Meadville Theological School; Congregational Minister;
Willard, Andrew Jackson	Medicine	

1854 — **PERIOD 2, DECADE 52**

NAME	OCCUPATION	NOTES
Blackman, Samuel Curtis	Law	
Cutler, Carroll	Education	Pres 1871-86, Prof of Metaphysics and Rhetoric 1860-89, Western Reserve College; Prof of Theology Biddle U
Denny, Thomas	Finance	Thomas Denny & Co
Fenn, William Henry	Ministry	Congregational Minister

Hooker, John Worthington	Medicine	Prof of Hygiene 1860-63, Amehurst College
Lambert, Edward W.	Medicine	
Lombard, James Kittredge	Ministry	Episcopal Minister
Lord, George DeForest	Law	
Morris, Luzon Burritt	Law	Gov CT 1892-94; Mbr 1855, 56, 70, 76, 80, 81, CT State Legislature; Mbr 1874, CT State Senate
Potwin. Lemuel Stoughton	Education	Prof 06-07 Emeritus, 1892-1906 English, 1871-92 Latin, Western Reserve U
Purnell, Charles Thomas	Law	
Slade, Francis Henry	Business	dry goods
Twombly, Alexander S.	Ministry	Congregational Minister
White, Charles Atwood	Law	
Whitney, Edward Payton	Med Student	disappeared

1855 — PERIOD 2, DECADE 53

NAME	OCCUPATION	NOTES
Alexander, William DeWitt	Government	Surveyor General 1871-1900 (Hawaii); VP Bd Educ HI; Pres 1864-71, Prof of Greek 1858-64, Oahu College, Commisioner HI Government to DC; Member HI Privy Council; Historian of HI
Barnes, William H. Lienow	Law	
Bumstead, Nathaniel Willis	Industrial	Mining; Pres JF Bumstead Co, (Boston); Capt, Inf, Union Army, Civil War
Child, Linus Mason	Law	Mbr 1868-69, MA State Legislature
Cobb, Henry Nitchie	Ministry	Sec of Bd of Foreign Missions of the Reformed Church in America
Granger, John Albert	Farming	
Johnson, Charles Frederick	Education	Prof Emeritus 06-31, Prof English 1884-1906, Trinity College; Asst Prof 1865-70, Mathematics, US Naval Academy
Kittredge, George Alvah	Business	Dir, Bombay Tramway Co; Am Vice-Consul (Bombay)
Lampson, George	Law	
Mulford, Elisha	Ministry, Literary	Episcopal Minister
Spring, Andrew Jackson	Education	Sgt Major Confederate Army Civil War
Tyler, Charles Mellen	Education	Trustee, 1886-1892, 1907-18, Prof Emeritus 03-18, Sage Prof 1891-03, History and Philosophy of Religion, Cornell U; Mbr 1862, MA State Legislature; Chaplin Capt, Union Army Civil War
Wheeler, William	Law	Capt, Union Army, Civil War
Woodward, Stanley	Law	Judge, Supreme Court, 11th Judicial Dist, PA; Capt, Union Army, Civil War
Yardley, Henry Albert	Education	Prof 1867-82, Homiletics and Christian Evidences, Berkeley Div School

1856 — PERIOD 2, DECADE 54

NAME	OCCUPATION	NOTES
Arnot, Matthias Hollenback	Finance	Banker, Elmira NY
Barker, George Payson	Law	
Brown, John Mason	Law	Cav, Union Army, Civil War
Campbell, William H. Wilson	Literary	Journalist
Condit, Stephen	Law	
Depew, Chauncy Mitchell	Law	Mbr 1899-1911, US Senate; Regent 1874-1904, U of the State of NY; Appointed US Minister 1866, Japan, (resigned); Sec of State, 1863-65 US; Mbr 1861-63, NY State Legislature; Chmn Bd, Dir, NY Central Lines, NYC; Mbr 1888-1906, Yale Corp; Col, Judge Advocate, Civil War
Dickinson, Arthur	Business	Commissary Dept, Confederate Army, Civil War
Eakin, Emmet Alexander	Farming	
Fischer, Louis Christopher	Finance	Sec, Treas, Mercantile Trust and Deposit Co (Baltimore)
Magruder, Benjamin Drake	Law	Justice 1891-1900, Chief Justice 1885-1906, IL Supreme Court
Nettleton, Edward Payson	Law	Asst 1869-73, US Dist Attny (Boston); Col Union Army Civil War
Packard, Lewis Richard	Education	Hillhouse Prof 1867-84, Asst Prof 1863-67 Greek Yale U
Paine, Levi Leonard	Ministry	Dean of Faculty, Prof 1870-1902, Church History, Bangor Theological Seminary
Robinson, George Chester	Ministry	Methodist Minister
Whitney, James Lyman	Library Work	Librarian, Boston Public Library

1857 — PERIOD 2, DECADE 55

NAME	OCCUPATION	NOTES
Blackman, Charles Seymour	Business	
Blake, Eli Whitney Jr	Education	Prof 70-95, Physics Brown U; Prof 1868-1870, Physics, Cornell

Buckland, Joseph Payson	Education	Judge
Butler, Francis Eugene	Ministry	Presbyterian Chaplain, Inf, Union Army, Civil War
Croxton, John Thomas	Law	US Minister 1873-74, Bolivia; Brig Gen, Inf Union Army Civil War
Day, John Calvin	Law	
Edwards, Alfred Lewis	Law	
Green, James Payne	Education	Planter; Prof Greek, Mathematics 1857-59, Jefferson College; Lt Cavalry, Confederate Army, Civil War
Holmes, John Milton	Ministry	Congregational Minister
Jackson, Joseph Cooke	Law	US Commissioner Naval Credits; Asst US Dist Attny 1870, (Southern Dist NY); Brig Gen, Union Army Civil War
Northup, Cyrus	Education	Pres Emeritus 11-22, Pres 1884-1911 U MN; Prof 1863-84, English Rhetoric & Literature, Yale U
Pratt, George	Law	Mbr 1860, 64, 65 & 69, CT State Legislature
Seymour, Storrs Ozias	Ministry	Mbr 1880-84, CT State Bd Education; Trustee Berkeley Divinity School; Episcopal Minister
Tyler, Moses Coit	Education	Prof 1881-00, Am History Cornell U; Prof English Lang, Lit 1873-81, Prof 1867-73 Rhetoric and English Lit, U MI
Wells, Nathan Dana	Law	

1858 — Period 2, Decade 56

Name	Occupation	Notes
Blake, Edward Foster	Law Student	Maj, Inf, Union Army, Civil War
Eichelberger, Martin Smyser	Law	Pres, York Wire Cloth Co (York, PA)
Grant, Edward Dromgoole	Real Estate	Real Estate Broker
Haskell, Robert Chandler	Industrial	Mfg Floor Oil Cloth
Heermance, Edgar Laing	Ministry	Presbyterian Minister
Hollister, Arthur Nelson	Education	
Kimball, John Edwin	Education	Supt Schools (Newton, MA)
Lee, Samuel Henry	Ministry, Education	Pres Emeritus 08-18, Pres 1893-1908, Prof History, Political Economy 1890-1908, Am International College (Springfield, MA); Prof Political Economy 1872-76, Oberlin College
MacLellan, George Boardman	Education	Asst Engineer, Confederate Army Civil War
Perkins, Thomas Albert	Finance	Cotton Broker; Sgt Union Army, Civil War
Porter, Edward Clarke	Ministry	Episcopal Minister
Scott, Eben Greenough	Law	1st Lt, Union Army Civil War
Stevens, Frederic William	Law, Finance	
Van Name, Addison	Library Work	Librarian Emeritus 05-22, Librarian 1865-05, Yale U
Woodward, William Herrick	Industrial	

1859 — Period 2, Decade 57

Name	Occupation	Notes
Bristol, Louis Henry	Law	Lawyer, Bristol, Stoddard & Bristol
Brodhead, Henry	Law	
Carpenter, Robert John	Industrial	Paper Mfg
Clay, Green	Farming	Mbr 1902, MO State Legislature; 1891 Mbr MO State Senate; Sec 1861-62, US Legation Russia, 62-68 to Italy; Mbr MS State Legislature; Pres MS Levee Bd; Col Union Army, Civil War
Dunham, George Elliott	Student	Drowned
Hall, William Kittredge	Ministry	Presbyterian Chaplain, Union Army, Civil War
Hannahs, Diodate Cushman	Law Student	Capt, Calvary Union Army Civil War
Harrison, Burton Norvel	Law	Asst Prof 1859-60, Physics, U of MS; Private Secretary, Jefferson Davis, Civil War
Robertson, Charles Franklin	Ministry	Episcopal Bishop (MO)
Schuyler, Eugene	Government	Service in US Diplomatic Service as Sec, Consul and Minister 1867-90, to Russia, Turkey, England, Italy, Greece, Roumania, Serbia and Egypt
Smith, Eugene	Law	
Stiles, William Augustus	Literary	Editor & Treas, *Garden and Forest* (NYC)
Taylor, Alfred Judd	Law	
White, Roger Sherman	Law	
Wilcox, Asher Henry	Ministry	Congregational Minister

1860 — PERIOD 2, DECADE 58

NAME	OCCUPATION	NOTES
Beckley, John Werley	Business	Merchant
Boies, Charles Alred		Theological Student
Boltwood, Edward	Insurance	Pres, Berkshire Life Insurance Co
Daniels, Joseph Leonard	Education	Prof of Greek 1865-1906, acting Pres 1903-04, Dean of faculty 1892-93, Olivet College; Congregational Minister
Davis, Lowndes Henry	Law	Mbr 1879-1885, Congress; Mbr 1876, MO State Legislature; Attny 1865-69, 10th Judicial Dist of MO; Circuit Attny (Cape Girardeau, MO);
Davis, Robert Stewart	Industrial	Proprietor, The Call; Mngr, Atlantic City RR
Fowler, William	Law	Capt, Inf Union Army, Civil War
Furbish, Edward Brown	Ministry	Congregational Minister; Chaplain, Union Army Civil War
Hebard, Daniel	Education	Deaf Mute instr; Asst Adj-Gen Union Army Civil War
Johnston, William Curtis	Ministry	Presbyterian; Chaplain, Inf Union Army Civil Wars
Jones, Luther Maynard	Law	Brown, Shipley & Co (London, England); Union Army, Civil war
Owen, Charles Hunter	Literary	Mbr 1882, CT State Legislature; Capt Heavy Artillery, Union Army Civil War
Phelps, William Walter	Law, Government	Mbr 1873-74, 83-89, US Congress; US Minister 1881-82 Austria, 1889-93 Germany; Judge 1893-94 NJ Court Errors & Appeals 1893-94; Mbr 1872-92 Yale Corp
Seeley, John Frank	Law	
Smith, William Thayer	Medicine	Dean 1896-1909, Prof Surgery 1907-09, Prof 85-1907 Assoc Prof 1883-85, Physiology, Dartmouth Med School

1861 — PERIOD 2, DECADE 59

NAME	OCCUPATION	NOTES
Baldwin, Simeon Eren	Law	Prof Emeritus 1919-1927, Prof of Law 1872-1919, Yale; Governor 1907-10, CT; Assoc Justice 1893-1907, Chief Justice 1907-1910, CT Supreme Court of Errors; Mbr 1911-14, Yale Corp
Brown, Hubert Sanford	Business	Lt Col, Union Army, Civil War
Chamberlain, Robert Linton	Law	Priv Inf, Union Army, Civil War
Dexter, Franklin Bowditch	Education	Asst Librarian 1869-1912, Sec 1869-99, Larned Prof of American History 1877-88, Yale U
Fuller, William Henry	Industrial	Mfr, Wall Paper
Higgins, Anthony	Law	Mbr 1889-95, US Senate; US Dist Attny 1869-76, (DE)
Kernochan, Francis Edward	Industrial	Proprietor, Bell Air Mill
Mitchell, John Hanson	Law	
Newel, Stanford	Law	US Minister 1897-1905, Netherlands
Park, William Edwards	Ministry	Congregational Minister
Peck, Tracy	Education	Prof Emeritus 08-21, Prof 1880-1908, Latin, Yale U; Prof 1871-1889, Latin, Cornell U,
Root, Alexander Porter	Finance	Pres, First National Bank, Houston; Maj, Cavalry Confederate Army, Civil War
Shearer, Sextus		Theological Student
Sill, Edward Rowland	Literary	Prof 1874-82, English U CA
Williams, Ralph Omsted	Literary	Union Army, Civil War

1862 — PERIOD 2, DECADE 60

NAME	OCCUPATION	NOTES
Adams, Frederick	Law	Judge 03-19, Circuit Court Essex County NJ; 1897-1903, Circuit Court of Errors and Appeals of NJ
Chamberlain, Daniel Henry	Law	Governor 74-76, SC; Atty Gen 1868-72, SC; 1st Lt, Union Army, Civil War
Coe, Edward Benton	Ministry	Dutch Reform Minister; Street Professor of Modern Languages 1864-79, Yale U
Day, Melville Cox	Law	
Eaton, Sherburne Blake	Law	Eaton, Lewis & Rowe (NYC); Eaton & Lewis (NYC); Capt, Union Army, Civil War
Johnston, Henry Phelps	Education	Prof Emeritus 16-23, Prof 1863-1916, History, College of the City of NY; 2nd Lt, Union Army, Civil War
Kitchel, Cornelius Ladd	Ministry, Education	Sec Emeritus 09-29, Sec 04-09, Bureau of Appointments, Yale U; Priv, Union Army, Civil War
Lampson, William	Finance	Pres, Bank of LeRoy (Leroy NY)
MacVeagh, Franklin	Business	Sec 09-13, Treasury US; Trustee 01-13 (U Chicago); Chmn 14, First International Congress of Social Insurance; Wholesale Grocers, Franklin MacVeagh & Co (Chicago)
Ripley, George Coit	Law	1st Lt, Inf Union Army, Civil War
Seely, William Wallace	Education	Dean Faculty 1881-1900, Prof 1866-1900, Opthalmology, Otology Med Col OH, now U Cincinnati
Stebbins, Henry Hamlin	Ministry	Presbyterian Minister

Taylor, John Phelps	Ministry	Trustee, Abbot Academy; Prof 1883-99, Biblical Theology Andover Theological Seminary
Ward, John Abbott	Student	
Weeks, Robert Kelley	Literary.	

1863 — **PERIOD 2, DECADE 61**

NAME	OCCUPATION	NOTES
Allen, Walter	Literary Work	Editor *NY World*; Acting Asst Paymaster, USN, Civil War
Arms, Charles Jesup	Law	Mbr 1894-95, RI State Senate; Cpt Union Army, Civil War
Bingham, Egert Byron	Ministry	Congregational Minister
Bull, Cornelius Wade	Medicine	Acting Asst Paymaster, USN, Civil War
Butler, John Haskell	Government	Mbr 1880-81, MA State Legislature; USN, Civil War
Chamberlain, Leander T.	Ministry	Judge Advocate, USN, Civil War
Dimock, Henry Farnam	Business	Treas, Metropolitan Steamship Co; Mbr 1899-1911, Yale Corp
Fowler, Horace Webster	Law	Capt, Artillery Union Army, Civil War
Kernochan, Joseph Frederick	Law	
Perry, David Brainard	Education	Pres 1881-1912, Prof 1873-81, Greek, Latin, Doane College; Congregational Minister
Sheffield, George St. John	Finance	
Southworth, George Champlin Shepard	Education	Prof 1889-1900, English Language and Literature, Case School Applied Science; Prof 1881-88, Belles-lettres, Kenyon College; Prof Sacred Theology Bexley Theological Seminary 1885-88; Mbr 1871, MA Legislature
Sumner, William Graham	Education	Prof Emeritus 1909-10, Pelatiah Perit Prof 1885-1909, Prof 1872-85, Political and Social Science, Yale U
Wesson, Charles Holland	Law	
Whitney, William Collins	Law	Sec 1885-89, Navy, US; and many business ventures

1864 — **PERIOD 2, DECADE 62**

NAME	OCCUPATION	NOTES
Boltwood, Thomas Kast	Law	
Borden, Matthew Chaloner Durfee	Industrial	Owner, The American Printing Co, (Fall River, MA)
Boyden, Henry Paine	Literary	
Clark, Albert Barnes	Farming	Insurance, Fruit Raising; Asst Paymaster USN, Civil War
Hewitt, Thomas Browning	Law	
MacLean, Charles Fraser	Law	Police Commissioner; Justice 1895-1909, NY Supreme Court
Merriam, George Spring	Literary	
Miller, Allanson Douglas	Ministry	Episcopal Minister
Owen, Henry Elijah	Medicine	
Palmer, William Henry	Medicine	
Pratt, William Hall Brace	Medicine	
Pugsley, Isaac Platt	law	Judge 1883-1903, Court of Common Pleas; Asst Paymaster, US Navy, Civil War
Sterling, John Williams	Law	Shearman & Sterling (NYC)
White, Oliver Sherman	Law	
Woodruff, Francis Eben	Government	Commissioner 1865-97, Custom Service of China

1865 — **PERIOD 2, DECADE 63**

NAME	OCCUPATION	NOTES
Bent, Joseph Appleton	Law	
Brooks, John Edward	Business	Brooks Bros clothier
Brown, Henry Armitt	Law	
Bulkey, Tuzar	Law Student	
Bushnell, William Benedict	Industrial	
Caskey, Taliaferro Franklin	Ministry	Rector Emeritus, St John's (American) Church Dresden, Germany
Charnley, Charles Meigs	X	Pres, American Cooperage Co, (Chicago, IL)
Ewell, John Lewis	Education	Prof, Church History and Hebrew Exegesis 1891-1910, Howard U; Prof, Latin 1866-67, Washington U; Congregational Minister
Ford, George Tod	Law	
Merrill, Payson	Law	Merrill & Rogers (NYC); Mbr 05-22, Yale Corp; Founder, Chmn 00-02, Yale Alumni U Fund Assn; Union Army, Civil War
Riggs, Benjamin Clapp	Medicine	
Smith, Charles Edgar	Law	Priv Union Army Civil War

Stimson, Henry Albert	Ministry	Lecturer, Oberlin Theological Seminary, Andover, Chicago, Yale; Acting Prof, of Homiletics Hartford Theology Seminary; Trustee Carleton College, Drury, Mt Holyoke, Hartford Theology Seminary; Dir, Chicago Theology Seminary, Congregational Minister
Stone, William	Art	
Warren, Henry Waterman	Industrial	Mbr 1882, 85, MA State Legislature; Mbr 1870-75, MS State Legislature

1866 — PERIOD 2, DECADE 64

NAME	OCCUPATION	NOTES
Adams, Charles Hemmenway	Literary work	Editor Hartford *Courant*
Brand, James	Ministry	Congregational Minister; Sgt, Union Army, Civil War
Coffin, Edmund	Law	
Cole, Hamilton	Law	
Farnam, William Whitman	Education	Treas 1889-99, Yale U; Trustee 1894-1923, Sheffield Scientific School; Mbr 1885-89, Yale Corp
Foote, Harry Ward	Law student	
Hall, John Manning	Law	Pres 1893-03, NY, NH & H RR Co; Pres 1899, CT State Senate; Judge 1889-93, CT Superior Court; Mbr 1870-72, 1878, Spkr 1882, CT State Legislature
Hincks, Edward Young	Education	Prof emeritus 22-27, Prof Biblical Theology 08-22, Harvard U; 00-08, w/*The Christian*; Prof Biblical Theology 1883-00, Andover Theological Seminary
Holt, George Chandler	Law	Holt & Butler (NYC); US Dist Judge 03-14, Southern Dist of NY
Judson, Frederick Newton	Law	Mbr 10-11, National Securities Comm; Mbr 12, Bd Arbitration Eastern RRs & Engineers; Pres 07, Am Assoc Political Science; 1893, Judson & Taussig (St Louis, MO)
Lampman, Lewis	Ministry, Education	Presbyterian
Sloane, Henry Thompson	Business	Treas, W & J Sloane, carpet business (NYC)
Southgate, Charles McClellan	Ministry	Trustee 1894-1912, Hartford Theological Seminary; Congregational Minister
Wade, Levi Clifford	Transportation	Mbr 1876-75 (Spkr 79) MA State Legislature; Pres Mexican Central R'y
White, George Edward	Industrial	Treas, The Yale & Towne Mfg Co

1867 — PERIOD 2, DECADE 65

NAME	OCCUPATION	NOTES
Bissell, Arthur Douglas	Finance	Pres, The People's Bank of Buffalo
Dexter, Morton	Literary Work	Congregational Minister and Editor, *The Congregationalist*
DuBois, John Jay	Law	
Dunning, Albert Elijah	Ministry	Editor, *The Congregationalist*
Harding, Wilder Bennett	Farming	Principal, Washington Academy (Salem, NY)
Hartshorn, Joseph William	Ministry	Congregational Minister
Hedge, Thomas	Law	Lawyer, Hedge & Blythe (Burlington, IA); Mbr 1899-07, US Congress; 2nd Lt, Union Army Civil War
Lamb, Albert Eugene	Law	Johnson & Lamb, Brooklyn
Libbey, Frank	Business	Lumber business, 13, wFrank Libbey & Co (NY/DC); 1893 w/Libbey, Bittlinger & Miller (DC)
Merriam, James Fiske	Finance	investment banker
Seymour, Horatio	Engineering	Managing Dir, MI Land & Iron Co; State Engineer & Surveyor 1877-81, of NY
Spencer, James Magoffin	Education	Prof 1867-73, Mathematics, Gallaudet College (DC), Writer 13 (Munich, Germany)
Taft, Peter Rawson	Law	
Wetmore, George Peabody	Law	Mbr 1895-13, US Senate; Gov 1885-57, RI
Woodward, Richard William	Science	

1868 — PERIOD 2, DECADE 66

NAME	OCCUPATION	NOTES
Berry, Coburn Dewees	Law	
Brewster, Chauncey Bunce	Ministry	Episcopal Bishop 1899-1928, (CT)
Coffin, James	Finance	Sugar Merchant, Mining & Banking
Colt, LeBaron Bradford	Law	Mbr 1913-24, US Senate; US Circuit Judge 1884-1913; US Dist Judge 1881-84, RI
Dixon, William Palmer	Law	1893, Peckham & Dixon, (NYC); 1913, Dixon & Holmes NYC; Trustee, Mutual Life Ins Co; Dir, Am Exchange Ntl Bank, Fidelity & Casualty Co, Lawyers Title & Trust Co, Mortgage Bond Co, City of NY Ins Co
Farnam, Charles Henry	Archaeologist	
Lewis, John	Law	w/Am RR & Corp, IL; Union Army, Civil War
McKinney, William Allison	Law	Union Army, Civil War

Sloane, Thomas Chalmers	Business	Mbr 1889-1890, Yale Corp
Thacher, James Kingsley	Medicine	Prof 1887-91, Clinical Medicine, 1879-91, Physiology, Yale Med School
Tinker, Anson Phelps	Ministry	Congregational minister
Tweedy, Samuel	Law	Tweedy, Scott & Whittlesey (Danbury, CT)
Tytus, Edward Jefferson	Business	wholesale paper dealer
Wood, William Curtis	Education	
Wright, Henry Park	Education	Prof Emeritus 09-18, Dunham Prof 1876-09, Latin , Asst Prof 1871-76, Latin Yale U; Dean 1884-1909 Yale College; Trustee, CT College for Women; Sgt, Inf Spanish-American War

1869 — PERIOD 2, DECADE 67

NAME	OCCUPATION	NOTES
Bannard, Henry Clay	Industrial	
Beers, Henry Augustin	Education	Prof Emeritus 16-26, Prof 1880-1916, Asst Prof 1874-80, English Lit, Yale U
Bissell, Wilson Shannon	Law	Postmaster 1893-95, US; Vice-Chancellor 1895-1902, Chancellor 02-03, U Buffalo
Brown, Alexander Lardner	Business	Druggist
Eno, John Chester	Finance	
Foster, John P. Codington	Medicine	
Freeman, Henry Varnum	Law	Presiding Justice 1898-1915, Appellate Court (IL); Judge 1893-1898, Superior Court; Dir, Chicago Public Library; Lawyer, Freeman & Walker (Chicago); Capt, Inf Union Army Civil War
Heaton, Edward	Law	Lt, Artillery Union Army, Civil War
Hooker, Thomas	Finance	Pres, First Ntl Bank (New Haven)
Isham, John Beach	Medicine	
Lear, Henry	Law	Pres, Doylestown National Bank; Pres, Doylestown Electric Co (PA)
Perrin, Bernadotte	Education	Prof Emeritus 09-20, Prof 1893-1909, Greek, Yale U; Prof 1881-93, Greek, Western Reserve College; Pres Am Philosophy Assn
Raymond, Henry Warren	Literary	Editor & Publisher, *Germantown Telegraph*; lecturer on US Navy
Richardson, Rufus Byam	Education	Prof 1882-1893, Dartmouth; Prof 1880-82, IN U, Dir 1893-1903, Am School Classical Studies at Athens; Corp, Inf Union Army, Civil War
Shirley, Arthur	Ministry, Education	Congregational Minister

1870 — PERIOD 2, DECADE 68

NAME	OCCUPATION	NOTES
Andrews, John Wallingford Jr.	Law	US district attorney 1879-80, MT
Gulliver, William Curtis	Law	
Johnston, Ross	Business	Whsl Shoe Business
Learned, Dwight Whitney	Education	Prof 1876-1928, Church History, Bible Theology, Greek, Doshisha College, Japan; Prof 1873-75, Greek, Mathematics, Thayer College; Mbr Comm for revision of Japanese version of New Testament
Mason, Henry Burrall	Law	Mason Brothers
McClure, James Gore King	Education	Pres Emeritus 28-32, Pres 05-28, McCormick Theological Seminary; Pres 1897-1901, Lake Forest U
McCutchen, Sam St. John	Law	
Miller, George Douglas	Industrial	Owner of Deer Island, Builder of Weir Hall; Sec, Thompson Paper & Pulp Co; Sec, New Haven Electric Light, New Haven Heat Supply Company; w/ NY *& Straitsville Coal & Iron Co; Sec, New England Car Spring co; Dir of Deer Island Corp
Perry, John Hoyt	Law	Pres, Savings Bank of Southport, CT; Pres 10-21, Bd Commissioners CT State Police; Mbr 13-15, CT State Senate; Mbr CT 1877, 78, 81-, Spkr 1889, State Legislature
Selden, Edward Griffin	Ministry	Minister Reformed Church; Congregational Minister
Shattuck, John Waldon	Business	dry goods
Stearns, Edwin Russell	Industrial	Treas, The Stearns & Foster Co, Cotton Mfg (Cincinnati)
Strong, Charles Hall	Ministry	Episcopal Minister
Tilney, Thomas Joseph	Industrial	
Welch, William Henry	Medicine	Prof Emeritus 31-34, Prof Hist Medicine 26-31, Dir 16-26, School Hygiene and Public Health, Dean 1893-98, Medical Faculty, Baxley Prof 1884-16, Anatomy, John Hopkins U; Pres 1898-1922, MD State Bd Health; Pres Bd of Dir 10-34, Rockefeller Institute of Med Research; Trustee 06-34, Carnegie Inst; Prof Pathological Anatomy 1879-84, Bellevue Hosp Medical College; Assoc fellow, Trumbull College Yale U; Col, Med Corps WWI

1871 — PERIOD 2, DECADE 69

NAME	OCCUPATION	NOTES
Clark, Charles Hopkins	Literary Work	Editor Hartford *Courant*; Dir, Collins Co, CT Mutual Life Ins Co, Phoenix Ins Co, Wadsworth Athenaeum Mbr 10-25, Yale Corp
Collin, Frederick	Law	Assoc Judge 1910-21, NY Court of Appeals; Mayor 1894-98, Elmira, NY
Elliot, Henry Rutherford	Literary	Sec, Textile Publishing Co
Hine, Charles Daniel	Education	Sec 1883-1920, CT State Bd Educ; Mbr, State Council of Defense WWI
Kinney, Herbert Evelyn	Law	
Lea, Robert Brinkley	Law	
Mansfield, Howard	Law	Treas 02-29, Met Museum Art; Chmn Advisory Bd, Compulsory Service, WWI
Mason, Alfred Bishop	Business	Managing Dir, Sprague, Duncan & Hutchinson, Ltd (NYC), electrical engineers
Mead, Frederick	Business	Merchant, Frederick Mead & Co (NYC)
Perry, Wilbert Warren	Law	Mbr CT 1883, State Legislature; Asst 1877-81, State's Attny (CT)
Sperry, Watson Robertson	Literary	Editorial Writer, Hartford *Courant*; US Minister 1892-94, Persia
Strong, George Arthur	Law	Martin & Strong (NYC)
Sweet, Edwin Forrest	Law	Asst Sec 13-21, Dept Commerce US; Mbr 11-13, US Congress; Mayor 04-06 (Grand Rapids MI); Mbr, War Industries Bd WWI
Thacher, Thomas	Law	
Townsend, William Kneeland	Law	Prof 1881-07, Yale Law School; Judge 02-07, US Circuit Court of Appeals 2d Circuit; Judge 1892-02, US Dist Court (CT)

1872 — PERIOD 2, DECADE 70

NAME	OCCUPATION	NOTES
Coe, Robert Elmer	Student	
Cushing, William Lee	Education	Founder, Princpal, Westminster School, (NY)
Deming, Charles Clerc	Law	Journalist
Deming, Clarence	Literary	Collector 1869-72, Internal Revenue; Mbr 1863-67, US Congress; Mbr 1849, 50, 59, 60, CT State Legislature; Col, Union Army, Civil War
Deming, Henry Champion	Finance	Sec, Mercantile Trust
Dennis, Frederic Shepard	Medicine	Prof Emeritus 10-34, Prof of Clinical surgery 1898-1910, Cornell U Medical School; Prof of Surgery 1883-93, Bellevue Hosp Medical College
Hincks, John Howard	Ministry, Education	Prof History, Social Science, Dean of Faculty, VP, U GA (Atlanta)
Hoppin, Benjamin	Literary Work	w/Robert Peary 1896
Merriam, Alexander Ross	Ministry	Prof Emeritus 1918-1927, Prof 1893-1918, practical theology, Christian sociology, Hartford Theological Seminary
Moore, George Foot	Education	Prof Emeritus 28-31, Frothingham Prof History Religion 04-28, Prof 02-04, Theology Harvard U; Pres 1899-1901, Prof 1883-1902, Hebrew Andover Theological Seminary
Owen, Edward Thomas	Education	Prof Emeritus, Prof 1879-1915, French U WI
Payson, Henry Silas	Farming	
Ramsdell, Charles Benjamin	Ministry	Acting Pres, Winsdor College; Pastor, North Presbyterian Church(DC); Union Army Civil War
Spaldin, George Atherton	Medicine	
Woolsey, Theodore Salisbury	Education	Prof Emeritus 11-29, Prof 1878-1911, International Law, Yale U

1873 — PERIOD 2, DECADE 71

NAME	OCCUPATION	NOTES
Alexander, Eben	Education	US Minister 1893-97, Greece; 1877-86, 1897-1910 Prof of Greek UNC; 1877-86 Prof of Ancient Languauges U of TN
Allen, Arthur Huntington	Ministry	Presbyterian Minister
Beebe, William	Education	Prof, 1898-1917, Asst Prof 1882-87, Math, Astronomy 1887-98, Yale U; Treas, Dir, Deer Island Club Corp
Daniels, Rensselaer Wilkinson	Finance	Grain Merchant; w/Title Guarantee and Trust Co, LA, CA
Denslow, Herbert McKenzie	Ministry	Prof Emeritus 1927-1944, Prof of Pastoral Theology 1902-27, General Theological Seminary; Instructor 1873-74, Gen Russell's Collegiate and Commercial Institute, (New Haven CT)
Elder, Samuel James	Law	Elder, Whitman & Barnum (Boston); Elder, Wait & Whitman (Boston); Mbr 1885, MA State Legislature
Flagg, Wilbur Wells	Business	w/Rock Mountain Bell Telephone Co
Grubb, Charles Ross	Finance	1913, c/o Morgan, Harjes & Co, Paris; Investment Officer, International Finance Corp, (DC); Lt Cmndr 42-46, USNR
Johnes, Edward Rudolph	Law	Johnes & Willcox (NYC)
Judson, Issac Nichols	Education	Teacher, Central High School (St Louis, MO)

Lathe, Herbert William	Ministry	Congregational Minister
Ord, Joseph Pacificus	Finance	Comptroller, GE Co
Prentice, Samuel Oscar	Law	Chief Justice 13-20, Judge 01-20, CT Supreme Court; Prof 01-16, Pleading, Yale Law School
Tarbell, Frank Bigelow	Education	Prof 1894-18, Classical Archaeology, Assoc Prof 1893-94, Greek, U Chicago; Dir 18898-89, 1892-93 Am School Classical Studies, Athens; Asst Prof 1882-87, Greek, Yale U
Thomas, Charles Henry	Business	

1874 — PERIOD 2, DECADE 72

NAME	OCCUPATION	NOTES
Aldis, Owen Franklin	Law	Real Estate, Aldis, Aldis & Northcote
Barnes, Pearce	Law	
Bushnell, Samuel Clarke	Ministry	Congregational Minister
Farnam, Henry Walcott	Education	Pres 27-33, Hopkins Grammar School; Prof Emeritus 18-33, Prof of economics 12-18, Prof of Political Economy 1880-1912, Yale U; Mbr, CT State Council of Defense, WWI; Editor, Yale Review; Pres, Am Economic Assn
Grover, Thomas Williams	Education	
James, Henry Ammon	Law	
Munroe, George Edmund	Medicine	
Parkin, William	Law	MacFarland & Parker (NYC)
Robbins, Edwards Denmore	Law	Prof 1899-1903, Gen Medical & Jurisprudence Yale U; Mbr 1882-83, CT State Legislature; Mbr 1884-1919, CT State Bd Education; Trustee CT College for Women; General Counsel, NY, NH & H RR Co
Stapler, Henry Beidleman Bascom	Law	Asst Dist Attny 1891-93, (NYC); w/Stapler, Smith & Tomlinson
Townsend, James Mulford	Law	Pres 12-13, Trustee 04-13, NY Law School
Walden, Russell	Law	
Wickes, Thomas Parmelee	Law	Hatch & Wickes (NYC)
Witherbee, Frank Spencer	Industrial	Iron and mining business, Witherbee, Sherman & Co (NY)
Wood, John Seymour	Law	

1875 — PERIOD 2, DECADE 73

NAME	OCCUPATION	NOTES
Avery, Charles Hammond	Law	
Brooks, James Wilton	Law/Literay	Mbr 1882-1884, NY State Legislature; Pres Univ Magazine Co
Chester, Carl Thurston	Law	Prof, Buffalo Law School
Clarke, Thomas Slidell	Law	
Day, Robert Webster	Real Estate	Proprietor, Hyde Park Hotel (Chicago); Sec, Ellicott Square Co (Buffalo)
Gulliver, Henry Strong	Education	Principal, Waterbury HS
Hotchkiss, William Henry	Business	Dry Goods, Mbr JN Adams & Co (Buffalo, NY)
Jenks, Almet Francis	Law	Judge 1896-1921, presiding Judge 11-21, Supreme Court (NY); Judge Advocate Gen 1891-95, NY
Jones, Dwight Arven	Law	Pres, St Joseph Lead Co; Pres, Doe Run Lead Co (MI) Pres 13, River and Bonne Terre RR 1913 NYC
Jones, Frank Hatch	Finance	Sec 13, Continental and Commercial Trust and Savings Bank (Chicago); 1st Asst Postmaster Gen 1893-97, US
Patton, John Jr	Law	Mbr 1894-95, US Senate
Seymour, John Sammis	Law	US Commissioner Patents 1893-1897; Mbr 1891-92, CT State Senate
Smith, Edward Curtis	Transportation	Pres, Central VT RR; Gov 1898-1900, VT; Mbr 1890, VT State Legislature
Southworth, Edward Wells	Law	
Tillinghast, Charles	Medicine	

1876 — PERIOD 2, DECADE 74

NAME	OCCUPATION	NOTES
Allen, John DeWitt Hamilton	Business	Wholesale Commission and Grocery Business, CA
Andrews, John Wolcott	Industrial	Manufacturing
Bannard, Otto Tremont	Law/Finance	Pres, The NY Trust Co (NYC); Commissioner of Educ (NYC); Mbr 10-28 Yale Corp
Blaine, Walker	Law	Examiner of Claims 1889-90, State Department; 82-85 Asst attorney for the US before Court of Commissioners of Alabama Claims; 3rd Asst 1881-82, Sec of State;
Bottum, Elisha Slocum	Law	Asst States Attny (Cook Co, IL)
Cook, Robert Johnston	Industrial	Editor, Publisher *Philadelphia Press*

Dawes, Chester Mitchell	Law	Asst US Attny 1884-86, (northern district of IL); Gen Counsel for CB&Q RR
Fowler, Charles Newell	Law	Pres, Equitable Mortgage Co (NYC); Mbr 1895-1911, Congress
Hadley, Arthur Twining	Education	Pres Emeritus 21-30, Pres 1899-1921, Acting Treas 09-10, Dean Grad School 1892-1895, Prof Pol Econ 1891-99, Prof Pol & Society Science 1886-91, Tutor 1879-83; Yale U; One of original editors, 1892 *Yale Review*; Writer, Asst Editor 1883-86, *Railroad Gazette*; Commissioner 1885-87, Labor Statistics, CT; Father-in-law, Luzon B Morris, CT Gov 1882; Pres, American Economic Association 1899; Chmn 1910, Railroad Securities Commission; Bd Dir 13, NY, New Haven & Hartford; Dir, Atchinson, Topeka & Santa Fe RR
Howe, Elmer Parker	Law	
Hyde, William Waldo	Law	Hyde, Gross & Hyde; Mayor 1892-94, Hartford
Marvin, Joseph Howard	Law	
Russell, Philip Gray	Law	Prindle & Russell (DC)
Smith, Rufus Biggs	Law	Judge Superior Court, Cincinnati; Prof 1896-1900, Law, Chmn Bd Trustees Cincinnati Law School
Worcester, Edwin Dean	Law	13 w/Worcester, Williams & Saxe; 1893 w/Saunders, Webb & Worcester (NYC)

1877 — PERIOD 2, DECADE 75

NAME	OCCUPATION	NOTES
Barnum, William Milo	Finance	Banking 04-08, Harvey Fisk & Sons; Lawyer, Simpson, Thatcher & Barnum 04; Dir American Locomotive; Pres, Chmn Bd, Pacific Coast Co, Steamers SF, Seattle, AK; Dir Yale Alumni Fund; Dir, Deer Island Club Corp
Bigelow, Walter Irving	Finance	Broker, AM Bigelow & Co; Dir, Whitney-Adams Co, Gorton-Pew Fisheries Co
Brooks, Walter	Business	Brooks Bros clothier, lived abroad many years, Brussels, BE; author A Child and a Boy Bretanos NY
Chapin, Charles Frederick	Literary	Editor, Waterbury American, (CT)
Collin, William Welch	Business	Lumber Merchant, Crosby-Collin (Pittsburgh), Iron ore, Founder Collinwood TN
Cooke, Eldridge Clinton	Finance	Pres Minneapolis Trust Company, Chmn Bd Dir First Minneapolis Trust Company; Dir First Ntl Bank of MN
Eaton, Samuel Lewis	Medicine	Medical Examiner, Prudential Ins Co; Trustee, Staff Newton Hosp (MA); Newton Highlands Nervine (private sanatorium)
Gould, Anthony	Literary	
Hoysradt, Albert	Law	Mbr 1886-87, NY State Senate
Kimball, Arthur Reed	Literary	Editorial Writer, Assoc Editor, *Waterbury American*; Pres, Morris Plan Bank (Waterbury); Pres, Second Mortgage Co; Pres, CT Chamber of Commerce; Dirs, Colonial Trust Co, Dime Savings Bank, Chase Companies, Waterbury Clock Company; Mbr, Yale Corp
Percy, Frederick Bosworth	Medicine	Prof Emeritus 15-28, Prof Clinical Medicine 08-15, Assoc Prof 1891-89, Prof 1898-1909, Materia Medica Boston U Med School; Physician 1893-1914, MA Homeopathic Hosp; Physician 05-18, Westboro Hosp for the Insane
Sears, Joshua Montgomery	Farming	Capitalist & Farmer
Thacher, John Seymour	Medicine	Prof 03-22, Clinical Medicine, Columbia U; Bellevue Hosp (NY)
Tuttle, George Montgomery	Medicine	Prof 1885-03, Gynecology, College of Physicians and Surgeons, Columbia U
Winston, Frederick Seymour	Law	Winston & Meagher (Chicago)

1878 — PERIOD 2, DECADE 76

NAME	OCCUPATION	NOTES
Campbell, Treat	Law	
Carter, Charles Francis	Ministry	Congregational Minister; Mbr State Council of Defense, WWI
Curtis, George Louis	Ministry	Presbyterian Minister
Edwards, George Benjamin	Finance	Pres, National Deposit Bank, (Russellville, KS)
Foster, Roger	Law	Lecturer, Yale Law School on Federal Jurisprudence
James, William Knowles	Law	1893, w/Reed, James & Randolph (St Joseph, MO); Circuit Judge; Mbr, MO State Legislature
Jenks, Tudor Storrs	Literary	
Kelsey, Clarence	Finance	Pres, Title Guarantee & Trust Co (NYC); Mbr 10-25, Yale Corp
Knott, George Tapscott	Farming	Fruit Growing; Collector, IRS
Pollock, George Edward	Industrial	
Seely, Edward Howard Jr.	Literary	Editor, *The New Peterson Magazine*, Philadelphia
Spencer, Charles Langford	Welfare	Clerk 1892-1921, US Dist Court MN; US Commissioner 1895-1921
Stone, Charles Martin	Industrial	Crandal, Stone & Co, Mfg, Real Estate (Binghamton, NY)

Taft, William Howard	Law	Chief Justice US 21-30; Kent Prof 13-21, Law Yale College and Prof of Constitutional Law Yale Law School; Pres US 08-12; Sec War 1904-08; Gov 01-04, Philippine Islands; Prof Law, Dean 1896-00, Cincinnati Law School; Judge 1890-92, US Circuit Court; Solicitor-Gen 1890-92 of US; Mbr Yale Corp 1906-13, 22-25; Trustee Carnegie Institution
Whitney, Edward Baldwin	Law	Justice 09-11, NY Supreme Court; Asst Attny Gen 1893-97, US

1879 — PERIOD 2, DECADE 77

NAME	OCCUPATION	NOTES
Bowers, Lloyd Wheaton	Law	Solicitor-General, 09-10 US
Burpee, Lucien Francis	Law	Judge 21-24, CT Supreme Court of Errors; Judge 09-21, CT Superior; Lt Col, Judge Advocate US Vols Spanish-American War
Foster, George Ferris	Business	Sec, FA Stokes Co
Green, Henry Sherwood	Library Work	Mgr 1913, Acme Press (Morgantown, WV); Prof Greek 01-12, Assoc Prof Greek 00-01, Yale U; Prof Greek 1896-00, Bethaney College
Hitchcock, Henry	Law	
Hyde, Frank Eldridge	Law	US Consul 1893-97, Lyons France; Mbr 1887-89, CT State Legislature
James, Walter Belknap	Medicine	Prof 19-18, Clinical Medicine, Bard Prof of Medicine 04-09, Prof of Medicine 02–4, College of Physicians & Surgeons; Am Red Cross WWI (Fgn Service)
Livingston, Herman	Industrial	Iron Ore Mining
Perrin, John Orlando	Finance	Federal Reserve Agent, Federal Reserve Bank (Chicago); Chmn Bd, VP, Perrin National Bank (Lafayette, IN)
Platt, Lewis Alfred	Industrial	Sec, Pres, The Platt Bros & Co, Mfg (Waterbury, CT); Mbr 10-12, CT State Senate
Rodman, Robert Simpson	Farming	viticulture, olives
Swinburne, Louis Judson	Literary	
Thompson, Oliver David	Law	
Tighe, Ambrose	Law	Special Asst 17-19, Attny Gen MN; Mbr 03, 07, MN State Legislature
Woodruff, Timothy Lester	Business	Lt Gov 1897-1903, NY; Pres, The Maltine Mfg Co (Brooklyn)

1880 — PERIOD 2, DECADE 78

NAME	OCCUPATION	NOTES
Allen, William Palmer	Literary Work	Lawyer
Amundson, John Arnold	Law	
Bentley, Edward Manross	Engineering	Patent Lawyer, Bentley & Blodgett, Boston; Sheffield, Bentley & Betts NYC
Camp, Walter	Industrial	Pres, Treas, Gen Mgr & Asst Treas, New Haven Clock Co; Head advisory football coach 1888-1912, Yale; Chmn U Athletic Assn; Chmn Intercollegiate Football Rules Comm; Chmn Athletic Div, Navy Comm on Training Camp activities and Dir of Athletics, Naval Training Camps WWI
Green, Edmund Frank	Insurance	Pres, Pacific Coast Casualty Co (SF, CA)
Jennings, Walter	Industrial	Pres 13, Ntl Fuel Gas Co, (NYC); 1893 w/Standard Oil Co; Dirs, Standard Oil NJ, Manhattan Bank, NY Trust Co
Nichols, Alfred Bull	Education	Prof 03-11, German, Simmons College
Ordway, Henry Choate	Finance	Butts & Ordway (Boston)
Parker, Wilbur	Business	Oil & Gas; Mbr 1892-93, OH State Senate; Mbr 1890-1891, OH State Legislature;
Partridge, Sidney Catlin	Ministry	in charge, Divinity School, Wuchang China; Protestant Episcopal Bishop of 11-30, West MO; 00-11, Kyoto, Japan
Peters, William Allison	Law	Strudwick & Peters (Seattle)
Scudder, Doremus	Ministry	Congregational Minister; Minister Central Union (Honolulu); Maj, Am Red Cross WWI (Fgn Service).
Spencer, Edward Curran	Medicine	
Taft, Henry Waters	Law	13 w/Strong & Cadwalader NYC; 1893 w/Page & Taft (NYC); Spec Asst to 05-07, Attny Gen of US; Mbr 25-26, Comm on Reorganization of NY State Government; Trustee, College of the City of NY
Witherbee, Walter Crafts	Mining	Treas, Witherbee, Sherman and Co; Pres, Ntl Bank; VP, Port Henry Iron Ore Co; Secret Service work for DOJ, WWI

1881 — PERIOD 2, DECADE 79

NAME	OCCUPATION	NOTES
Aiken, Edwin Edgerton	Minisitry	Missionary (Peking, China)
Barney, Danford Newton	Business	Mbr 1905, CT State Senate
Bartlett, Philip Golden	Law	Lawyer, Simpson, Thatcher & Barnum
Burrel, Joseph Dunn	Ministry	Presbyterian Minister; Chaplain Capt, American Red Cross, WWI (Fgn Service)
Coleman, John Caldwell	Law	

Evarts, Sherman	Law	
Fuller, Philo Carroll	Industrial	Treas, Fuller & Rice Lumber & Mfg Co; Dir, First Ntl Bank (Grand Rapids)
Ives, Henry	Business	Broker 1913, Zurich Insurance Co; Pres, Treas 1893, The Edgewood Co (CT)
Leighton, James	Law Student	
Osborne, Thomas Burr	Science	
Thompson, Norman Frederick	Finance	Asst Sec, Teas, Equitable Mortgage Co 1893; Pres Manufacturers Ntl Bank, Treas City Rockford IL 1913
Van deGraaff, Adrian Sebastian	Law	Hargrave & Van de Graaf (Tuscaloosa, AL); Mbr 18-22, AL State Legislature; Judge 15-22, 6th AL Dist; Prof 1891-97, Statutory and Common Law, U AL Law School
Vernon, Frederick R.	Industrial	
Walden, Howard Talbott	Law	
White, Henry Charles	Law	13 w/White, Dagget & Hooker; 1893 w/White & Dagget (New Haven)

1882 — PERIOD 2, DECADE 80

NAME	OCCUPATION	NOTES
Badger, Walter Irving	Law	
Brewster, Benjamin	Ministry	Episcopal Bishop 16-40, (ME); Missionary Bishop13, (Western CO)
Campbell, James Alexander	Law	
Eno, William Phelps	Transportation	Real Estate; Author of world's first street traffic regulations (NYC, London and Paris) and other traffic control systems, including road traffic control codes of allied troops in WWI and II; Dir, Home Defense League of DC WWI
French, Asa Palmer	Law	US District Attny 1906-14 (MA); US District Attny 1902-06, (SE MA),
Johnson, Barclay	Law	
Knapp, Howard Hoyt	Law	Seymour & Knapp, (Bridgeport, CT); City Attny
Lyman, Chester Wolcott	Industrial	Intrnl Paper Co; Chmn, Red Cross and War Work Comm, WWI
McBride, Wilber	Law	
Osborne, Arthur Sherwood	Law	Chemist, CT Agricultural Experiment Station
Platt, Henry Barstow	Insurance, Transportation	Gen Supt, US Express Co (NYC); Dir Bureau Personnel, Overseas Service, Atlantic Div, Am Red Cross WWI; VP Fidelity and Deposit Co
Pollock, William	Transportation	
Wells, John Lewis	Law	
Whitney, Joseph Ernest	Education	
Worcester, Franklin Eldred	Transportation	RR business

1883 — PERIOD 2, DECADE 81

NAME	OCCUPATION	NOTES
Burpee, Charles Winslow	Literary Work	Asst Editor, *Bridgeport Standard*, (CT); Phoenix Mutual Life Insurance Co, Hartford); Col, CT State Guard, WWI; 1st CT Inf, Spanish-American War
Deming, Lawrence Clerc	Transportation	Asst Sec, Atchinson, Topeka & Santa FE RR
Folsom, Henry Titus	Business	Merchant
Foote, Charles Seward	Law	Mbr 1900-01, NJ State Assembly; lawyer w/Parrish & Pendleton, (NYC)
Frost, Elihu Brintnal	Law	
Hillard, Lord Butler	Law, Business	Pres, WY Valley Lumber Co (Wilkes-Barre PA); Pres, Bd of Prison Comm
Hull, Louis Kossuth	Law	US Dist Attny 1885-87, ND; Col, Spanish-American War
Kellogg, Fred William	Education	
McLaughlin, Edward Tompkins	Education	Asst Prof 1890-93, English, Prof 1893, Rhetoric and Belles lettres, Yale U
Moore, Eliakim Hastings	Education	Prof Mathematics 1892-1931, Assoc Prof 1891-1892, U Chicago; Asst Prof 1889-91, Mathematics Northwestern U
Palmer, Harry Herbert	Literary	
Parrott, Joseph Robinson	Law, Transportation	VP, Gen Counsel Jack, St Aug. & I R R'y Co; Pres, FL East Coast R'y Co; Pres, FL East Coast Hotel Systems; Pres, P & O SS Co (Jacksonville)
Taft, Horace Dutton	Education	Founded the Taft School, 1890 , Headmaster 1890-1936, Headmaster Emeritus 36-43, Trustee 26-43, Pres of the Bd 26-36
Thacher, Sherman Day	Education	Founded Thacher School 1899; Teacher Casa Peidra Ranch School, (Ojai Valley, CA)
Woodward, John Butler	Law	Judge 13-25, Court of Common Pleas, 11th Judicial Dist PA; Wheaton, Darling & Woodward (Wilkes-Barre, PA)

1884 — PERIOD 2, DECADE 82

NAME	OCCUPATION	NOTES
Blodgett, George Reddington	Law	Lawyer, Bentley & Blodgett (Boston)
Booth, Samuel Albert	Law	Lawyer, Ripley, Brennan & Booth, (Minneapolis)
Booth, Wilbur Franklin	Law	Judge 25-44, 8th US Circuit; US Dist Judge 14-25, (MN); MN State Dist Judge 1909-14 (MN); Asst Counsel, St Louis RR Co

Evarts, Maxwell	Law	Asst US Attny 1890-92, (Southern NY)
Foster, Reginald	Law	
Gruener, Gustav	Education	Prof German 13, Yale U; Iron Mines; Pres, Dir, Deer Island Corp
Jenks, Paul Emmott	Government	Pres, Continental Filter Co; Asst Deputy City Treas, (Brooklyn); US Vice-Counsel 16-23, Yokohama, Japan
Jones, Frederick Scheetz	Education	Dean Emeritus 26-44, Dean 09-26, Yale U; Assoc Fellow 33-44, Berkeley College, Yale U; Chmn 18-39, CT State Bd Education; Chmn Bd 21-42, The Hotchkiss School; Dean 01-09, College of Engineering, Prof 1899-1909, Physics, U MN
Lambert, Alexander	Medicine	Prof 1898-1931, Clinical Medicine Cornell U Med College; Col, Med Corps WWI AEF
Lawrance, Thomas Garner	Student	
McMillan, William Charles	Industrial	Dir, MI Peninsular Car Co; Pres, Detroit Gas Co
Painter, Henry McMahon	Medicine	Prof 06-20, Obstetrics, College of Physicians and Surgeons, Columbia U
Tompkins, Ray	Finance	wholesale grocer, CM & R Thompkins
Twombly, Henry Bancroft	Law	Putney & Bishop (NYC); Putney, Twombly, Hall & Skidmore (NYC); Dirs, Gen Counsel, Intrnl Salt Co, Lobsitz Mills, Berkshire Industrial Farms
Wilder, Amos Parker	Literary	Editorial Writer 1893, *Commercial Advertiser* (NYC); Editor, *WS State Journal*; US Counsel Gen 06-09 Hong Kong, 09-14 Shanghai

1885 — Period 2, Decade 83

Name	Occupation	Notes
Arnot, John Hulett	Finance	Banker (Elmira NY)
Baldwin, Henry DeForest	Law	Pres 08-25, Queens Co Water Co; Chmn 22-23, NY City Charter Comm; 1900 w/Lord, Day & Lord; Asst Corp Counsel 1895-98, NYC; CFR
Bertron, Samuel Reading	Finance	Banker, Bertron, Griscom & Co, NYC; Advisor 17-21, Excess Profits Tax Bd; Mbr 18, US Mission to Russia; VP Equitable Mortgage Co; established French War Relief Bureau, WWI
Brandegee, Frank Bosworth	Law	Mbr 05-24, US Senate; Mbr 02-05, Congress; Mbr 1888, Spkr 1899, CT State Legislature; Lawyer, Brandegee, Noyes & Brandegee
Bridgeman, John Cloyse	Industrial	Gen Mgr, Hazard Mfg Co (Wilkes-Barre, PA)
Brooks, Henry Stanford	Business	Spec Agent ATT; General Commercial Supt, ATT Co, (NYC); Chmn 1916-18, Yale Alumni Fund
Flanders, Henry Richmond	Insurance	
Hidden, Edward	Finance	VP 13, Commonwealth Trust Co (St Louis); Chmn, US Comm on relations w/Hati
Hobbs, Charles Buxton	Law	Ptnr 13, Gifford, Hobbs & Beard (NYC); 1893, Hobbs & Gifford (NYC)
Mallon, Guy Ward	Law	Mallon, Coffey & Mallon, Cincinnati; Trustee 1896-1933, VP 32-33 Berea College; Mbr 1890-91, OH State Legislature; Mbr 06-08, Cincinnati City Council; Trustee 03-19, OH State U
McHenry, John	Finance	Asst Sec, Treas, Mercantile Trust and Deposit Co (Baltimore); Sec, Treas MD & PA R'y Co
Richards, Eugene Lamb	Law	NY Deputy Attny Gen 1896-70; Janeway, Thacher & Richards. NYC
Robinson, Lucius Franklin	Law	Pres 1890-91, Hartford Common Council; Pres 33, CT Constitutional Convention; Chmn 17-38, CT State Park and Forest Comm; w/Robinson & Robinson; w/ Robinson, Robinson & Cole
Terry, Wyllys	Insurance	Insurance broker; Benedict & Terry; Sec & Treas, Van Brunt St & Erie Basin RR Co.
Worcester, Wilfred James	Finance	Sec 13, US Trust Co of NY; 1893 w/Kerr & Worcester (NYC)

1886 — Period 2, Decade 84

Name	Occupation	Notes
Anthony, Benjamin Harris	Industrial	Publisher, *Evening Standard* (New Bedford, MA); Trustee, Dir, Savings Bank; VP, Assoc Press
Bremmer, Samuel Kimball	Medicine	
Cowles, Alfred	Law	
Crapo, Stanford Tappan	Industrial	Pres, BF Berry Coal Co; Pres, Treas 1913, Huron, and Wyandotte Portland Cement Co (Detroit); w/ Flint & Pere Marquette RR, 1893
Day, Thomas Mills	Law	
Knapp, Wallace Percy	Law	Larned, Warren & Knapp (NYC)
Lewis, Charlton Miner	Education	w/Sullivan and Cromwell
Peters, Frank George	Law	
Phelps, Edward Johnson	Finance	Pres of Bd Dir, Yale U; Sec & Treas, Northern Trust Safe Deposit Company (Chicago); Mbr 10-16, Yale Alumni Bd;
Phelps, Sheffield	Literary	Editorial Writer, *New York Mail and Express*

Pierson, Charles Wheeler	Law	w/Alexander & Green (NYC)
Schwab, John Christopher.	Education	Librarian of Yale U 05-16, Prof 1898-1905 Asst Prof 1893-98, Political Economy Yale U; Trustee Mt Holyoke College
Shipman, Arthur Leffingwell	Law	04–08, CT Corp Counsel of Hartford; Mbr 1892, Hartford Common Council; 13 w/Gross, Hyde & Shipman; 1893 w/Henney & Shipman
Stewart, Philip Battel	Finance	
Winston, Dudley	Finance	mortgage banker, Winston & Co (Chicago, IL)

1887 — PERIOD 2, DECADE 85

NAME	OCCUPATION	NOTES
Bennetto, John	Law	
Corwin, Robert Nelson	Education	Prof 1899-1944, Asst Prof 1897-99, German, Chmn Bd of Admissions 19-33, Assoc Fellow 33-44, Pierson College, Yale U; Pres 29-30, NE Assoc of College and Secondary Schools
Cowles, William Hutchinson	Journalism	Publisher, *Spokane Review*
Coxe, Alexander Brown	Farming	Coal Mining
Douglass, Willard Robinson	Law	
Hare, Clinton Larue	Business	
Haven, George Griswold	Finance	Banker 13, Strong, Sturgis & Co (NYC); Sec, Treas 1893, St Paul & Duluth RR and of NY & Northern R'y
Jennings, Oliver Gould	Law	Editorial Staff, *St Nicholas*; Dir, Am Trading Co and others
Kendall, William Burrage Jr.	Business	Carpet Business, WB Kendall & Sons (NYC)
Kent, William	Business	Banker, AE Kent & Sons (Chicago); Mbr 11-27, US Congress; Mbr 17-21 US Tariff Comm
Knight, Samuel	Law	w/Myrick & Deering, (CA); asst US Attny 1893-98, US Attny 27-31, (Northern Dist CA); Maj, Judge Advocate General's Dept WWI AEF
Pomeroy. John Norton	Education	Prof 11-24, Asst Prof 10-11, Law, U IL
Rogers, John	Medicine	Prof Emeritus 26-39, Prof Clinical Surgery 10-26, Cornell U Medical College
Sheppard, Walter Bradley	Literary	
Thacher, William Larned	Education	Emeritus 31-, Teacher, Assoc, Hdmstr 1895-31, Thacher School (Ojai, CA); Sec 1889-94, Students Movement Assoc (NYC)

1888 — PERIOD 2, DECADE 86

NAME	OCCUPATION	NOTES
Cooley, Harlan Ward	Insurance	
Fisher, Irving	Education	Prof Emeritus 35-47, Prof of Political Economy1898-1935, Asst Prof, Political Economy 95-98, Asst Prof, Mathematics 1893-95, Yale U; Founding President of the American Eugenics Society
Gill, George Metcalf	Industrial	Sec, Treas, The Gill Engraving Co (NYC)
Hurd, Richard Melancthon	Finance	Mbr 15-18. Prison Comm NY State; Pres 1913, Lawyers Mortgage Co, (NYC); Mbr 1893, US Mortgage Co of NYC
Isbell, Orland Sidney	Law	1913, w/Lawyer Mortgage Co NYC; 1893 w/Jerome & Hood (Denver, CO)
McMillan, James Howard	Law	Transportation; Maj, Spanish-American War
Morison, David Whipple	Transportation	13 w/Coffee Business (NYC); 1893 w/Great Northern R'y Co
Roby, Samuel Sidney Brese	Business	
Seward, William Henry	Law, Finance	Banking, WH Seward & Co (Auburn, NY)
Solley, Fred Palmer	Medicine	
Stagg, Amos Alonzo	Education	Prof Emeritus 33, Prof, Dir 00-33, Assoc Prof 1892-1900 , Dir Dept Physical Culture and Athletics, U Chicago 1892-1900; Prof Emeritus 47, Football Coach 33-46, College of the Pacific; Adv Football Coach, Susquehanna U 47-52; Adv Coach Stockton College 53; Olympic Committees
Stevenson, Frederic Augustus	Communication	Gen Supt of Plant, ATT (NYC)
Stimson, Henry Lewis	Law	Sec War 40-45; Chmn Am Delg 30, London Naval Conferences; Mbr 32, Am Delg to Disarmament Conferences; Sec State 29-33; Gov Gen 27-29, Philippines; Spec Rep of Pres 27, Nicaragua; Sec War 11-13; Attny 06-09, Southern Dist NY; 1901 w/Winthrop & Stimson; 1897 w/Root, Howard, Winthrop & Stimson; 1893, w/Root & Clarke (NYC); Lt Col AEF WWI
Waite, Morison Remick	Law	Gen Solicitor 18-46, B&O Western Lines; Gen Attny 17-19, for OH, IN of B&O RR Co; Gen Solicitor 09-17, C, H&D R'wy Co, 11-14, B&O SW R'wy Co; 09-16, w/ Waite & Schipdel 16- Waite, Schindel & Bayless; Law, Cincinnati 1890; Bankruptcy Referee 1898-1906; Trustees Kenyon College, Cincinnati Public Library
Walker, Samuel Johnson	Medicine	Prof Pediatrics 08-19, Asst Prof 00-08, Neurology, Chicago Polyclinic Post Graduate School; Clinical Prof 08-19, Rush Medical College; Major, American Red Cross, WWI (fgn Service)

1889 — PERIOD 2, DECADE 87

NAME	OCCUPATION	NOTES
Buchanan, Thomas Walter	Literary Work	Editor
Corbin, William Herbert	Business	Pres 39-45, Hartford Pub Library; Tax Commissioner 1907-20, CT; Sec & Treas 1913, The Wm H Wiley & Son Co, (Hartford); Hdmstr 1893, Pingry School (Elizabeth, NJ); Mbr 10-30, Yale Alumni Bd
Donnelley, Thomas Elliott	Industrial	RR Donnelley & Sons Co; Dir, Pulp & Paper Div, War Industries Bd, WWI; Chmn 1922, Citizens' Comm (Chicago); Mbr 25-32, Council Yale-in-China
Fisher, Samuel Herbert	Law	Bristol, Stoddard, Beach & Fisher (New Haven); Pollok & Mason; Dir, NY Trust Co, Nazarerth Cement Co (NY) and others; 41-42 Admin of Defense, (CT); Chmn 36-40, CT Highway Safety Comm; Chmn 33-35, CT Tercentenary Comm; Fellow 20-35, Yale Corp
Gill, Charles Otis	Ministry	Sec, Treas The Gill Engraving Co, (NYC); InterChurch World Movement Work in New England; Fed Council of Churches of Christ in Am, (OH)
Griggs, John Cornelius	Education	Prof English, Dept Head 1920-27, Assoc Prof English 19-29, Canton Christian College; Assoc Prof Music 1897-19, Vassar College
McQuaid, William Adolph	Law	1st Deputy 11-14, Attny Gen NY; Asst Dist Attny NYC
Pinchot, Gifford	Government	Gov 23-27, 31-35, PA; Public Emeritus 36-46, Prof 03-36, Forestry Yale U; Commissioner 20-23, Forestry, PA; US Forester & Chief of Division 1889-1910, US; Mbr, US Food Admin, WWI; VP 12, First International Eugenics Congress
Reed, Harry Lathrop	Education	Pres Emeritus 37-; Pres, Prof, asst Prof, Dir 03-37, Auburn Theological Seminary; Pastor First Presbyterian Albany, OR 1897-1903; Trustee 14-49, Wells College 14-49; Congregational Minister 1897
Robinson, Henry Seymour	Insurance	
Smith, Herbert Augustine	Forestry	Instr 1892-98, English Yale U; 01-37 w/US Forest Service
Stokes, Horace Sheldon	Medicine	
Walker, Horace Fletcher	Education	
Wells, Herbert Wetmore	Ministry	Episcopal Minister; Instr, Army Educ Corps WWI (Fgn Service)
Woodruff, George Washington	Law	Public Service Commissioner 31-33, PA; Attny Gen 23-27, PA; Fed Judge 09-10 (HI); Acting Sec 07, Interior US; Asst Attny Gen 07-09, US

1890 — PERIOD 2, DECADE 88

NAME	OCCUPATION	NOTES
Bayard, Thomas Francis	Law	Mbr 22-29, US Senate; Solicitor 17-19, Wilmington City; Govt. Appeal Agent Wilmington, WWI
Corwith, John White	X	
Crosby, John	Law & Industrial	Pres, Washburn Crosby, Minneapolis; Trustee, Dunwoody Industrial Inst; Mbr, Federal Adv Council (DC); Mbr 1894-1948, Minneapolis City Council
Day, Arthur Pomeroy	Finance	Chmn Bd, Hartford Trust Co; Treas 1893, LE Rhodes Co; Sec, VP, CT Trust & Safe Deposit Co, (Hartford); Dir, CT Gen Life Ins Co, EG Whittlesey & Co, Russell Mfg Co, Spencer Turbine Co, Am Hardware Co, Arrow, Hart & Hegeman Electric Co, Aetna Ins Co, World Fire & Marine Ins Co, Century Indemnity Co, Spencer Aircraft Motors Inc; Trustee Mechanic Savings Bank; Mbr, Hartford Redevelopment Comm, CT River Bridge and Hwy Comm
Farnham, John Dorrance	Law	
Harrison, Fairfax	Transportation	Chmn 17, Railroad War Bd
Haslam, Lewis Scofield	Law	Counsel, Asst Treas 13, Simmons Hardware Co, (St Louis MO); Attny 1893, Lord, Day & Lord (NYC); Mbr 33-35, Alumni Bd
James, Norman	Industrial	13 w/N W James & Co, Lumber Merchants, (Baltimore); Sec 1893, Central R'y Co, Baltimore; Dirs, Citizen's National Bank, Safe Deposit and Trust Co, Savings Bank of Baltimore
Kellogg, Charles Poole	Welfare	Sec 1895-1928, CT Dept of Public Welfare
Kneeland, Yale	Business	Grain Merchant, Kneeland & Co (NYC)
Morse, Sidney Nelson	Education	
Sage, Henry Manning	Real Estate	wholesale lumber HW Sage & Co, Albany; Pres, Sage Land & Improvement Co Albany; Chmn 22-32, Hudson River Regulating Bd; Mbr 11-21. NY State Senate; Mbr 1898-99, NY State Legislature; Trustee 00-04, Cornell U
Simmons, Wallace Delafield	Industrial	Asst Treas, Pres, Simmons Hardware Co (St Louis); War Industries Bd, WWI
Stewart, Percy Hamilton	Law	Mbr 31-32 US Congress; Mbr 23-29, NJ State Highway Comm; Mbr 19-21, NJ State Bd Education; Mayor Plainfield, NJ 12-13; Civilian Aide to the Adj Gen WWI
Tracy, Evarts	Architecture	Tracy & Swartwout; Lt Col, Eng Corps, WWI AEF

1891 — PERIOD 2, DECADE 89

NAME	OCCUPATION	NOTES
Calhoun, Governeur	Business	Attny 1913 (St Louis); Supt Office 1877, Western Div LS&MS RR

Cox, John Joughin	Law Student	
Doane, John Wesley Jr.	Finance	Broker, Diltons, Ltd (Montreal); Wholesale drug business (NYC); 1893, w/Pullman's Palace Car Co (Chicago)
Estill, Joe Garner	Education	Mbr 32-34,34-36, CT State Legislature; Master Mathematics, Hotchkiss School
Graves, William Phillips	Medicine	Prof, Emeritus 32-33, Prof, Gynecology 11-32, Harvard Med School
Isham, Edward Swift	Industrial	dry goods
Kenerson, Vertner	Medicine	Surgeon, Spanish-American War
McClintlock, Norman	Education	Faculty 32-36, Rutgers; Prof 25-30, Dept Zoology, U PA; w/Westinghouse Electric & Mfg Co
Morison, Samuel Benjamin	Business	13, w/Coffee Business (NYC)
Poole, William Frederick	Law	
Simms, William Erskine	Farming	
Thomson, Samuel Clifton	Engineering	Trade Advisor 17-18, Export Div, War Trade Bd
Townsend, John Barnes	Finance	Mgr, The Press (Philadelphia)
Tweedy, Henry Hallam	Education	Prof 09-37, Practical Theology, Yale Div School
Walcott, Frederic Collin	Government	Mbr 25-29, CT State Senate; Mbr 29-35, US Senate; Welfare Commissioner 35-39, (CT); Mfg cotton cloth; Banker, Mfgr 07-15, Officer & Dir many Corps until 1922; Mbr 21-29, State Bd of Fisheries & Game and State Water Comm; Mbr Exec Comm 15-17, Carnegie Inst of Washington; Belgian, Polish Relief Work; US Food Admin 17-19, WWI

1892 — PERIOD 2, DECADE 90

NAME	OCCUPATION	NOTES
Bayne, Hugh Aiken	Law	Counsel 20-26, Reparation Comm (Paris); Counsel 19, Liquidation Com of War Dept; Attny 05-14, Strong & Cadwalader; Lt Col, Judge Advocate Generals' Depts, WWI AEF
Boltwood, Edward	Literay work	
Cheney, Howell	Industrial	Silk Manufacturer 1893-35; Dir, Sec 25-35, Cheney Bros; Trustee 1900-05, Manchester Savings Bank; Mbr 07, CT Comm on Consolidation of State Comm; Mbr 09-19, CT State Bd of Education; Chmn 13-38, CT Unemployment Comm; Chmn Comm on State Prison Systems, Mbr 13-38, Yale Corp; Chmn War Savings Comm CT
Cheney, Knight Dexter Jr.	Industrial	Silk Manufacturer
Crosby, Benjamin Lewis Jr.	Law Student	
Day, Clive	Education	Prof 22-38, Political Economy, Prof 07-22, Asst Prof 02-07, Economic History, Yale U; Instr 1895-98, History U CA; Mbr 31-33, CT Unemployment Comm; Chmn 18, Balkan Div, US Peace Comm, Paris
Graves, Henry Solon	Education	Prof Emeritus 39, Dean 22-39, Prof, Dir 00-10, Yale Forestry School, Provost 23-27, Yale U; Asst Chief 1898-1900, Div of Forestry, Chief Forester 10-20, USDA; Lt Col, Eng Corps WWI AEF
Husted, James William	Law	Mbr 15-23, Congress; Mbr Congressional Investigation Comm in France, WWI; Mbr 1895-97, NY State Legislature
Ingersoll, James Wernham Dunsford	Education	Asst Prof 1897-1921, Latin, Yale U
Jay, Pierre	Finance	Hon Chmn 45, Chmn Bd 30-45, Fiduciary Trust Co of NY; Ntl Treas 41, Russian War Relief; Am Mbr 26-30, Transfer Comm, Deputy Agent of Reparations (Berlin); Chmn Bd, Federal Reserve Agent 14-26, Federal Reserve Bank of New York; VP 09-14, Manhattan Co, NY; Bank Commissioner 06-09, (MA); VP 03-06, Old Colony Trust Co, Boston; 1899-1903 w/Post & Flagg,(NY); 1893 w/The Beni Gum Co, La Paz, Bolivia; Gov, Yale Publishing Assn.
Kitchel, William Lloyd	Law	
McClung, Thomas Lee	Finance	Treasurer of 09-12, US; Treas 04-09, Yale U; Furniture Business (TN)
Morison, Stanford Newel	Farming	Raising Coffee
Price, Frank Julian	Law	Asst Corp Counsel 11-18 (NYC); Mbr 00-01, NY State Legislature; ; Dir, Sec Deer Island Club
Ryle, Ernest	X	Iron Business, Scranton; Canteen worker, WWI (French Army)

1893 — PERIOD 2, DECADE 91

NAME	OCCUPATION	NOTES
Begg, William Reynolds	Law	
Cooke, James Barclay	Industrial	Sec & Treas, Passaic Structural Steel Co, NJ
Dwight, Winthrop Edwards	Law	Assoc Fellow 35-44, T. Dwight College, Yale U
Gallaudet, Edson Fessenden	Engineering	Pres, Gallaudet Engineering Co; Instructor Physics 1897-00, Head Crew Coach 00, Yale U

Hay, Logan	Law	Mbr 07-14, IL State Senate
Ives, Sherwood Bissell	Medicine	
Jones, Alfred Henry	Law	
Lambert, Adrian VanSinderen	Medicine	NY Hosp, Lincoln Hosp, Roosevelt Hosp, Bellevue Hosp, College Physicians and Surgeons, Columbia U
Martin, George Greene	Communication	
Parker, William White W.	Law, Finance	
Parsons, Francis	Finance, Law	Mbr 25-37, Yale Corp; Trustee 36-37, Peabody Museum Ntnl History; Capt, Am Red Cross, WWI (fgn service)
Robinson, John Trumbull	Law	US Attny 08-12, Dist of CT
Roby, Joseph	Medicine	
Rogers, Derby	Law	Supply Sgt, CT State Guard
Wallis, Alexander Hamilton	X	Cprl 17, CT Home Guard

1894 — PERIOD 2, DECADE 92

NAME	OCCUPATION	NOTES
Case, George Bowen	Law	Mbr, Red Cross War Council, WWI
Cochran, Thomas	Finance	VP Astor Trust Co NYC; Mem JP Morgan and Co; Pres Liberty Ntl Bank, NY; Dir various Corps; Trustee numerous Companies and RRs
Davies, Thomas Frederick	Ministry	Episcopal Bishop 11-36, (Western MA); Representative YMCA War Work Council, WWI (fgn service)
Hall, John Loomer	Law	Choate, Hall & Stewart (Boston); Dir, NY, NH & H RR, Merchants Ntl Bank of Boston, Westinghouse Electric & Mfg Co, The CT R'wy Co, MA Fire & Marine Ins Co, Am Sugar Refining Co, United Shoe Co; VP, Boston Herald-Traveler Corp; Pres, Trustee, Boston Public Library; Naval Intelligence WWI
Hare, Meredith	Law	
Holter, Edwin Olaf	Law	State Commissioner 13, Prisons (NY); Pres Prison Assn NY; Trustee, Am Scandinavian Foundation; 2nd Lt, Signal Corps US Vol Spanish American War
Howland, John	Medicine	Prof 12-26, John Hopkins; 10-12, Pediatrics Washington U; Maj, Med Corps WWI
James, Robert Campbell	Finance	
McMillan, Philip Hamilton	Law, Business	Pres, Detroit and Cleveland Navigation Co; Sec, Treas, *Detroit Free Press*; Trustee Estate of James McMillian
Paine, Ralph Delahaye	Literary	Mbr 18-20, NH State Legislature; Mbr 18, Fed Fuel Comm; War correspondent Cuba, Spanish-American War, China-Bover Rebellion; Bureau of Public Information & Navy Department, WWI (fgn service)
Stewart, Walter Eugene Jr.	Law	2d Lt, Inf Spanish-American War
Stillman, Leland Stanford	Law, Finance	Asst Sec, Astor Trust Co; Priv, Cav Spanish-American War
Walcott, William Stuart	Farming	
Whitney, Harry Payne	Finance	Married Gertrude Vanderbilt, investment banker.
Word, Charles Francis	Law	Mbr 03-04, MT State Legislature; Sec to 1897-1901, Gov MT

1895 — PERIOD 2, DECADE 93

NAME	OCCUPATION	NOTES
Beard, Anson McCook	Business	
Buckner, Mortimer Norton	Finance	Pres, VP, NY Trust Co, (NYC); Mbr Bd 28-40, Yale Corp; Assoc Fellow 34-42, Calhoun Coll; Mbr 22-28, Yale Alumni Bd
Butterworth, Frank Seiler	Finance	Mbr 07-09, CT State Senate; 2nd Lt Chemical Warfare Service, WWI, AEF
Cable, Benjamin Stickney	Law	General Attny, C, RI & P Ry; Asst Sec of Commerce and Labor 09-13, US
Carter, Walter Frederick	Law	
Clark, Alexander Ray	Finance	Stockbroker w/Jewett Brothers NYC
Cooke, Walter Evans	Industrial	w/Passaic Structural Steel Co
Davis, Benjamin	Law	Asst US Attny 1913, (Chicago)
Denison, Lindsay	Literary	Journalist, *The Evening World*, (NYC); Capt, QMC WWI AEF
Harrison, Francis Burton	Government	Governor General Philippines 13-21, later Advisor to Pres. Philippines; Mbr 03-05 07-13 US Congress; Capt, Adj Gen
Hinkey, Frank Augustus	Finance	Zinc Smelting
McKee, Lanier	Law	Author, *The Land of Nome*
Phelps, Zira Bennett	Insurance	VP, Comptroller, Dir Security Mutual Life Insurance Co (NY); Dir, Bayless Pulp and Paper Co; Dare Lumber Co
Shepley, Arthur Behn	Law	Prof 10-13, Equity, Washington U, Law School; Service Spanish-American War
Sloane, William	Business	Pres, W & J Sloane, Inc (NYC); Trustee, Robert College (Istanbul); Chmn, Ntl War Work Council, YMCA, WWI

1896		PERIOD 2, DECADE 94
NAME	OCCUPATION	NOTES
Beard, William Mossgrove	Business	VP, Union Carbide (NY); Ptnr, Beard & Paret (NYC); Mbr 12, NJ State Legislature
Brown, Alexander	Government	Brown Brothers & Company; Asst Paymaster, USN, Spanish-American War
Cheney, Ward	Literary	1st Lt, Inf, US Army, Spanish-American War
Cross, William Redmond	Finance	Keeper of Maps 31-39, Yale U Library; Broker, Redmond & Co (NY); Mbr, Sec 1898-1905, Morton Bliss & Co, Morton Trust Co, Treas, Cuba Co, (NY); Mbr 1897-98, Manhattan Trust Compnay (NY); Pres 37-40, NY Zoologocal Society
DeSibour, Jules Henri	Architecture	Architect for French Embassy and other public buildings
Griggs, Maitland Fuller	Law	Attny, (NY); Chmn 26-41, Originator, Founder, Associates in Fine Arts, Chmn Comm on Accessions 28-40, Yale Art Gallery, Yale U; Lt Col, Ord Dept WWI
McKee, McKee Dunn	Insurance	Pres, Two Kings Mining Co, (Mexico); Buck Run Coal Co, (PA); Compressed Gas Capsule Co (NY); Bertron & Storrs, (NY); 2nd Lt, Spanish-American War
Neale, James Brown	Mining	VP, Dir 05-, Sonman Shaft Coal; Worker, Pennsylvania Coal Co; Treas, Dir 03-, Darkwater Coal Co; Pres, 1899-, Buck Run Coal Co (Minersville, PA)
Smith, Winthrop Davenport	Business, Finance	Merchant, Ptnr, Keller & Smith; Fred Macey Co, Ltd (NY); Baltimore, Chesapeake & Atlantic RR; Hartley & Graham (NY)
Stokes, Anson Phelps	Ministry, Education	Extensive World Traveler; Founder, Trustee, Am U Union in Europe; Trustee, Rockefeller Foundation, Gen Education Bd, International Educ Bd; Dir, Educ Dept YMCA; AEF WWI; Sec1899-21, Yale U; Canon 24-30, Washington Cathedral; Chmn Bd Trustees, Yale-in-China; Pres Emeritus, Stokes Foundation; Trustee Brookings Inst; Author
Thorne, Samuel	Law	Delafield, Howr, Thorne & Rogers; Dirs, Leonia-Englewood Estates, Mandings Development Corp, Missionary Aexposition Co, Silver Bay Assn; Attny, w/Joline, Larkin & Rathbone; Deputy Asst Dist Attny 01-05 (NYC); Attny 00-01 w/Stimson & Williams; Dirs, Pemeta Oil Co, Church Properties Fire Insurance Co, Church Life Ins Corp; Dirs, Pres, Church Pub Assn Inc, Church Army in the USA; Trustee, Yale-in-China; Pvt, Home Guard WWI
Thorne, Samuel Brinckeroff	Business	Chmn Bd 22-24, Dir 14-22, Treas, 01-03, Temple Coal, Co; Pres, 09-30 Thorne, Neale & Co NYC; Treas 01-30 Buck Run Coal Co; Pres 03-07, Darkwater Coal; Trustees, East River Savings Bank, Title Guarantee & Trust Co (NY), Museum Natural History (NY); Captain, hero Yale football; service on Comm sent abroad by Fed Fuel Admin, WWI
Treadway, Ralph Bishop	Law	Attny 00-13, Land Dept Chicago & Northwestern RR Co (Chicago); Attny 1899-00, Jackson, Busby & Lyman; Russia Merchant, W Ropes & Co; Pres 1893, Petroffshy Oil Works Co
Trudeau, Edward Livingston Jr	Medicine	
Weyerhaeuser, Frederick Edward	Industrial	Pres 28-45, Treas 06-28, Weyerhaeuser Timber Company; Founder 03, Weyerhaeuser Sales Company; Pres 00, Southern Lumber Company (AR); Various Dir; Comm of Fine Arts, Yale; Gov, Yale Publishing Assoc

1897		PERIOD 2, DECADE 95
NAME	OCCUPATION	NOTES
Bailey, Philip Horton	Business	2nd Lt, Regular Army Spanish-American War
Brooke, George Clymer	Finance	George S Fox & Sons (Philadelphia)
Coffin, Henry Sloane	Ministry	Mbr 44-46, NY City Comm on Racial and Religious Tolerance; Mbr 43-44, NY State Comm on Birth Control legislation, Moderator Gen Assembly of the Presbyterian Church; Mbr 21-45, Yale Corp; YMCA Chaplin WWI Fgn service
Fincke, Clarence Mann	Finance	Chmn Bd, Dir 48, Home Life Ins Co, Manhattan Fire & Marine Ins Co, Seaboard Surety Co; 32, w/Greenwich Savings Bank, (NYC); 20-31,w/Bank of Am; Asst Sec 17-20, Franklin Trust Co
Garrison, Elisha Ely	Engineering	Mngr, WS State Journal (Madison); US Volunteer Calvary (Rough Riders) Spanish American War, Lt Col FA WWI AEF
Gerard, Sumner	Law	Pres, Aeon Realty Corp, GBW Construction Co, Aeonitt Realty Corp; Sgt US Vol Cavalry (Rough Riders) Spanish American War, Maj FA WWI
Gillette, Curtenius	Medicine	Post-Grad U Bavaria; Bellevue Hosp; Manhattan State Hosp; Lt Col, Med Corps WWI AEF
Kerr, Albert Boardman	Law	Chief Counsel 18, US Housing Corp; Ptnr 1913, Zabrinskie, Murray, Sage & Kerr (NYC)
Kitchel, Cornelius Porter	Law	
Pinchot, Amos Richards Eno	Law	Priv Calvary, Spanish-American War; Founder 17, ACLU, Inc; Organizer 17, Am Comm War Finance

Sage, Dean	Law	Chmn Bd of Trustees 29-43, Atlanta U; Mayor Mendham NJ 17-22; Deputy Asst 02, Dist Attny NY County; Civilian Army Transport Service WWI
Smyth, Nathan Ayer	Law	Asst Dir 17-18, Gen US Employment Service; Asst Gen Counsel 21 Gen Counsel 22-25, US Shipping BD Emergency Fleet Corp; Asst Dist Attny 02-10, (NYC)
Sumner, Graham	Law	13 w/Simpson, Thacher & Bartlett (NYC)
Wheelwright, Joseph Storer	Medicine	Major, Med Corps WWI AEF
Williams, Norman Alton	Industrial	Mfg

1898 — PERIOD 2, DECADE 96

NAME	OCCUPATION	NOTES
Cheney, Clifford Dudley	Industrial	Silk Manufacturer; Capt, Cav, Mexican Border; Lt Col, Ord Dept, WWI AEF
Fearey, Morton Lazell	Law	Chmn Selective Service Bd, WWI
Gallaudet, Herbert Draper	Literary	Congregational Minister; Capt FA WWI AEF
Hale, Eugene Jr.	Finance	Broker 1913, (NYC); Priv, Med Corps WWI
Hinsdale, Frank Gilbert	Industrial	Asst to Treas, Wilkes-Barre Lace Mfg Co (PA)
Kernochan, Frederic	Law	Chief Justice 16-37, Assoc Justice 13-16, NY Court of Spec Sessions; Asst Dist Attny 03-05, NYC; Light Artillery Spanish American War
Lord, Franklin Atkins	Law	Sec US Shipping Bd 23-32; Deputy Police Commissioner NYC
Montgomery, Grenville Dodge	Finance	Cadet, USN Spanish-American War; Officer Candidate, FA WWI
Parker, Grenville	Finance	Emanuel, Parker & Co (NYC); Officer Candidate FA WWI
Rogers, David Francis	Finance	Bonds, Rogers & Gould NYC
Simmons, Frank Hunter	Industrial	1913 w/Iron Business (NYC); Treas, John Simmons Co; Dir, Vulcan Rail & Construction Co, Essex Foundry
Wadsworth, James Wolcott Jr.	Government	Chmn 50, Ntl Security Training Comm 50; Mbr 32-50, US Congress; Mbr 15-27 US Senate 15-27; Livestock, Farming 1899-; Mgr 11-15, Ranch Palodoro (TX); Dir Genesee Valley Ntl Bank & Trust Co (Geneseo, NY); Spkr 06-10, NY State Legislature; Pvt, Spanish American War
Whitney, Payne	Finance	Pres, Interlake Pulp and Paper Co; VP, Whitney Realty Co; 13 w/Great Northern Paper Co (NY); Dir, Knickerbocker Trust Co
Wickes, Forsyth	Law	13 w/Crocker & Wickes; Sr Ptnr, Wickes, Riddell, Bloomer, Jacobi & McGuire (NYC); Founder, Bd Chmn, The French Lycee (NY); Maj, AEF WWI
Wright, Henry Burt	Education	Prof 14-23, Christian Methods, Asst Prof 11-14, History, Asst Prof 07-11, Roman History and Latin Lit, Yale U; acting Sec 1899-1900, Yale U; Yale College in China

1899 — PERIOD 2, DECADE 97

NAME	OCCUPATION	NOTES
Adams, Mason Tyler	Industrial	Missionary
Ames, Sullivan Dobb	Law Student	
Bowles, Henry Thornton	Engineer	
Brooke, Frederick Hiester	Architecture	Capt Air Service, WWI
Brown, Jamot	Business	Real Estate
Callahan, Hugh Andrew	Insurance	Mbr 30-33, AZ House of Reps; City Clerk, City Magistrate 22-27, Phoenix; Chief Clerk 17-18, AZ House of Rep; Sec Bd Dirs, 17-18, AZ State Institutions; Deputy Factory Inspector 1913, IL: Lumber Dealer Chicago
Day, Dwight Huntington	Finance	Treas, Foreign Mission Bd, Presbyterian, NYC; YMCA Sec WWI
Griswold, William Edward Schenck	Business	Dir, W&J Sloane, Commercial Solvents Corp, CT Light & Power Co, Greenwich Savings Bank, Northern Pacific Rwy Co; Sec 09-11, Railroad Securities Comm
Maffitt, Thomas Skinner	Industrial	VP, MO Iron Co (St Louis); Capt, Military Intelligence Div WWI
Magee, James McDevitt	Law	Beatty, Magee & Martin (Pittsburgh); Mbr 23-27, US Congress; Capt, Air Service WWI
Preston, Ord	Finance	Chmn Bd 45-46, Pres 32-45, Dir 12, Union Trust Co; Mbr NY Stock Exchange, Mbr 05-12, E Welles & Co; Pres 23-30, Dir 10, Washington (DC) Gas & Light Co; 02-05, w/Neale & Thorne coal operators, PA; Clerk 00-02, WH Goadby & Co, Brokers, (NYC); Major, Air Service, WWI
Sweet, Carroll Fuller	Industrial	Grand Rapids Lumber Co
Vanderbilt, Alfred Gwynne	Finance	
Welles, Charles Hopkins Jr.	Law	13, w/Wells & Torrey; Ptnr 1893, Welles & Mackie (Scranton, PA);
Whitehouse, William Fitzhugh	Finance	Mbr 24, 26, RI State Senate; Maj, WWI AEF

1900 — PERIOD 2, DECADE 98

NAME	OCCUPATION	NOTES
Adams, Frederick Baldwin	Transportation	Banking, NYC; Pres West Indies Sugar Corp; Chmn Atlantic Coast Line RR, Louisville & Nashville RR, Clinchfield RR; Dir of many subsudary and affiliated RR corps; also officer or dir of many other corps

Allen, Frederick Winthrop	Finance	Private Banker, Lee, Higginson & Co (NY); Trustee 28-33, Barnard College; 31-33 Trustee John Hopkins; 23-27 Yale Alumni Brd; Mbr Raw materials Cmtte; Dir 17, War Savings for Greater NY; VP 1913, Mechanics & Metals, Nat Bank (NY)
Camp, Stuart Brown	Industrial	
Cheney, Frank Dexter	Industrial	Silk Manufacturer; CT State Council of Defense
Coffin, William Sloane	Business	Pres 31-33, Metropolitan Museum of Art; YMCA Work; WWI Foreign Service
Cross, John Walter	Architecture	1907-42, Cross & Cross (NYC), Ross & Son, (NYC); Chief Architect 18, US Housing Corp; Mbr, Ntl Comm of Fine Arts; NY Art Comm
Douglas, Malcolm	Medicine	Maj, Med Corps, AEF WWI
Greenway, James Cowan	Medicine	Assoc Attending Physician 08-16, NY Hosp; Dir 16-36, Yale U Health Dept; Major 17-18, Medical Corps
Hopkins, John Morgan	Education	
Leavitt, Ashley Day	Ministry	Congregational Minister, (Hartford, CT, Concord, NH, Brookline MA); National Council Preacher; Chmn 26-38, 44-46, Prudential Comm ABCFM
Lyon, George Armstrong	Finance	Investment Banker, NW Halsey & Co (Boston); Capt, Inf WWI AEF
Paddock, Brace Whitman	Medicine	
Rockefeller, Percy Avery	Finance	Founder, VP Owenoke Corp; Dirs, Air Reduction Co, Am International Corp, Atlantic Fruit Co, Anaconda Copper Mining Co, Bethlehem Steel Corp, Bowman Biltmore Hotels Co, Cuba Co, Chile Copper Co, Consolidated Gas Co, Greenwich Trust Co, WA Harriman& Co, Mesabi iron Co, National City Bank of NY, National City Company, New York Edison Co, North Am Reassurance Co, National Surety Company, Provident Loan Society, Remington Arms Co, United Electric Light & Power Co, Western Union Telegraph Co; Trustee John Sterling, Yale-1863
Sullivan, Corlis Esmonde	Finance	VP, Glens Run Coal Co (Cleveland); Mbr 21-24, Advisory Council Fed Reserve Bd
Taft, Hulbert	Journalism	Pres 30, Editor 07, Assoc Editor 02-07, Reporter 01-02, *Cincinnati Times-Star*; Mbr, Cincinnati Home Guard WWI

1901 — PERIOD 2, DECADE 99

NAME	OCCUPATION	NOTES
Allen, Arthur Dwight	Art	
Carlisle, James Mandeville	Law/Finance	Maj, Adj Gen Dept WWI
Cheney, Philip	Industrial	Silk Manufacturer; Capt, Inf, WWI AEF
Cheney, Thomas Langdon	Industrial	Silk Manufacturer
Christian, Henry Hall	X	
Coy, Sherman Lockwood	Industrial	Cloquet Lumber Co, (MN); The Northern Lumber Co, (MN)
Edwards, Richard Henry	Ministry	Dir, Ntl Council on Religious Education in Higher Education; Ntl War Council YMCA WWI; Mbr 41-46, Fed Council of Churches
Eels, John Shepard	Ranching	Real Estate Broker (Marin County CA)
Hixon, Robert	Business	Lumber; Maj, Am Red Cross, WWI (fgn service)
Hoysradt, J Warren	Finance	1913, w/Guaranty Trust Co (NYC)
Keppelman, John Arthur	Law	Federal Food Administrator (Berks City, PA)
Morris, Ray	Finance	Mbr 49, Brown Bros Harriman; Pres Investment Bankers Assn of America 25-26; Mbr 10-20, White, Weld & Co (NYC); Editor RR Gazette 1903-10; Dir, Exec Comm, Gen Security Assurance Corp, Am Woolen Co; Dir, Finance Comm, Symington-Gould Corp; Dirs, Holly Sugar Co, Sinclair Oil & Refining Corp, McCall Corp, Sidney Blumenthal & Co, The Best Foods, Inc, Grand Union Co, Punta Alegre Sugar Corp, SKF Industries, Inc
Richardson, Allan Harvey	Insurance	Pres, The McCall Co; Treas 12-15, Puerto Rico
Welch, George Arnold	Law	
Wright, Alfred Parks	Student	

1902 — PERIOD 2, DECADE 100

NAME	OCCUPATION	NOTES
Carpenter, George Boone	Farming, Writer	
Cressler, Alfred Miller	Finance	Treas, Kerr Murray Mfg Co, (Wayne, IN)
Cushing, Charles C. Strong	Literary	YMCA Secretary, WWI (fgn Service)
Day, William Edwards	Finance/Industry	w/Thomas C Day Co, (Indianapolis)
Ferguson, Alfred Ludlow	Business	Treas, Windsor Print Works (MA)
Guernsey, Raymond Gano	Law	Officer Candidate, FA WWI
Potter, Roderick	Business	Treas, Ellicot Square Co, Buffalo
Rumsey, Bronson Case	Education, Farming	Mbr 32-40, WY St Senate; Capt, Am Field Service WWII

Sincerbeaux, Frank Huestis	Law	44- w/Sincerbeaux & Shrewsbury; Assoc 44, Bowers & Sands; 26-44 w/ Middlebrook & Sincerbeaux; 06-26 w/Middlebrook & Borland; Trustee, The Greenwich Savings Bank; Dirs, Eugene A Hoffman Estate, Inc, Forest Hills Garden, Inc, Eva Gebhard Gourgaud Foundation
Stebbins, Edwin Allen	Finance	Pres, Rochester Savings Bank; Dirs, Savings Banks Trust Co, Sibley, Lindsay & Curr Co; Dir, Rochester C of C and Bureau Municipal Research; Fruit Grower & Wholesale Merchant (Rochester, NY)
Stone, Harold	Finance	US Public Service Res, US Employment Service, Dept Labor, WWI
Swan, Joseph Rockwell	Finance	Pres, Dir Am Hard Wall Plaster Co; 38-44 w/Smith Barney & Co; Ptnr 34-37, EB Smith & Co; Pres 28-34, Dir, VP 19-28, Guaranty Co of NY; Ptnr 10-19, Kean Taylor & Co (NYC); Treas, Union Trust Co, Albany 07-10; Chmn Bd 46-, Pres 38-46 NY Botanical Gardens; Maj, Am Red Cross WWI
Taylor, Alan McLean	Welfare	Rector, Episcopal Church (Boston)
Trowbridge, Mason	Law	Asst Prof 15-16, Yale Law School; Asst 04-05, English Dept Yale U; Deputy Asst 06, 09 Dist Attny NYC
White, Percy Gardiner	Welfare	

1903 — PERIOD 2, DECADE 101

NAME	OCCUPATION	NOTES
Chadwick, George Brewster	Education	Mgr, The Patterson Mfg Co, Ltd East (Toronto): Capt Chemical Warfare Service, WWI
Clark, Harold Terry	Law	Mbr 13-38, Squire, Sanders & Dempsy; Dir, Cleveland Electric Illuminating Co, Kelley Island Line & Transport Co, Cleveland Quarries Co, Fisher Bros Co, Rayen Co; Pres, Dir, Lakeside Marblehead RR Co; Sec, Dir, Cleveland City Forge; Trustee, Society for Savings, Cleveland; Asst to Chmn 18, US War Industries Bd, Bernard Baruch; Mbr 18, American Peace Commision, Paris;
Corning, Erastus	Medicine	Chief Surgeon 1919-, AM Expeditionary Force, Archangel, Russia; Lt Col Med Corps WWI AEF
Dreisbach, John Martin	Business	VP, Macan Jr Co, (Easton PA)
Hamlin, Chauncey Jerome	Investment Banker, Law	Ptnr 41- , Hamlin & Lunt; Ptnr 40-41, Langdon B Wood & Co; Spec Ptnr 37-, Wood, Trubeee & Co; O'Brien & Hamlin, later Obrian, Hamlin, Donovon & Goodyear; 05-07 Rogers, Locke & Milburn (Buffalo); Dir 1931, Buffalo, Rochester & Pittsburgh R'wy; Trustee, Am Museum Natural Hist; Capt, FA AEF WWI
Hewitt, Brower	Industrial	RR Business 1913; Treas, Marine Historical Assn of Mystic Seaport
Holt, Henry Chandle	Finance	Chmn, Treas, International Grenfell Assn; Pres, Central Hanover Safe Deposit Co; Clerk, Asst Sec, VP 06-46, Central Trust Co (NYC)
Lamb, Albert Richard	Medicine	Presbyterian Hosp (NYC); Maj, Med Corps WWI
Moore, Frank Wood	Ministry	Prof Emeritus 30-47, Asst Prof Homiletics 17-30, Auburn Theological Seminary
Sutphin, Stuart Bruen	Business	Dir, Ntl Bank; Capt QMC
Thompson, Donald	Law	
Wallace, Henry Mitchell	Industrial	VP, American Brass Co
Waring, Antonio Johnston	Medicine	Capt, Med Corps WWI
White, John Richards	Education	
Wilhelmi, Frederick William	Industrial	Supt 13, Cloquet Tie & Post Co (Cloquet MN); Intelligence Branch, US Army WWI

1904 — PERIOD 2, DECADE 102

NAME	OCCUPATION	NOTES
Adams, Charles Edward	Industrial	Banker (NYC); Chief Iron and Steel Div, War Production Board WWII
Adams, George Webster	Finance	
Cheney, Russell	Art	Mbr, CT Academy of Arts and Sciences
Crane, Winthrop Murray	Industrial	Pres, Gen Mgr 23-, Crane & Co, Inc; Dir, Otis Elevator Co, Inc, Guaranty Trust Co (NY), Am Banknote Co, Air Reduction Co, Agricultural Ntl Bank (Pittsfield), Berkshire Life Insurance Co, Eaton Paper Co ; Yale Alumni Bd; Lt Col, Ord Dept WWI
Cross, Walter Snell	Ministry	Pres 50-51, The Mother Church, First Church of Christian Scientist, (Boston MA); Lt, Chaplin Army WWI
Dodge, Francis Talmage	Business	Pres 04-52, Dodge & Olcott, Co
Jennings, Percy Hall	Industrial	Asst Treas, Am Trading Co NYC; Maj Air Service AEF WWI
Kittle, John Caspar	Art	Sec, Kittle Construction Co (CA); Capt, QMC WWI AEF
Metcalf, Harold Grant	Industrial	w/mill 04, asst Treas 05-21, VP 21-28, Pres 28-41, Vice Chmn 41-48, Chmn Bd 48-52, Colombian Rope Co (Auburn NY)

Name	Occupation	Notes
Miller, James Ely	Finance	Capt, Air Service AEF WWI
Pierce, Frederick Erastus	Education	Assoc Prof 26-35, Asst Prof 10-26, English Yale U
Reed, Lansing Parmalee	Law	Trustee 29-37, Union Theological Seminary; Chmn Yale 30-32, U Fund Assoc
Soper, Willard Burr	Medicine	Assoc Clinical Prof 27-31, Medicine Yale U; Maj, Med corps WWI
Thacher, Thomas Day	Law	Judge 43-48, NY Court Appeals; Corp Counsel 43, City of NY; Solicter Gen 30-33, US; Judge 25-30, US Dist Court Southern Dist NY; 19-24, 33-43 w/Simpson, Thacher & Bartlett; Asst US Attny Southern Dist NY 07-08; Chmn NYC Charter Comm; Maj, Am Red Cross, WWI (Fgn Service)
Wiggin, Frederick Holme	Law	34- w/Wiggin & Dana (New Haven); Ptnr 16-34, Bristol & WhiteLaw; 07-13 w/Bristol, Stoddard, Beach & Fisher; Dir, First Ntl Bank & Trust Co (New Haven); Capt, FARE WWI

1905 — PERIOD 2, DECADE 103

NAME	OCCUPATION	NOTES
Bradford, Arthur Howe	Ministry	Minister 18-52, Central Congregational (Providence RI); 13-18 Rutland Congregrational; Asst Minister 09-12, South Congregrational Church (Springfield MA); preacher Yale, Phillips Exeter Acad; Mbr 25-52 Yale Corporation
Ellsworth, John Stoughton	Farming	Asst Treas, The Arlington Co (NYC)
Fish, Stuyvesant	Finance	Broker; Lt. FA WWI
Hogan, James Joseph	Law	
Hollister, Buell	Finance	Broker, Sr Ptnr, Pyne, Kendall & Hollister (NYC); Pres, Dir, Independent Gold Mining Co; Chmn Bd, Cornell Dubilier Electric Corp; Bd, YMCA NYC; Am Red Cross WWI
Hughes, Berrien	Law	Capt, FA WWI
Lathrop, John Hiram	Law	Mbr 44-49, Appellate Judicial Comm of MO
Richardson, Gardner	Government	First Sec 38-47, Dept of State; Commercial Attache 26-38, Dept of Commerce; 12-14 w/White, Weld & Co (NYC); Asst Pub 05-12, Independent Mag; 12-14; Am Ambulance Field Service 14-15; Comm for Relief, Belgium 15-17; Chief Amer Relief Admin, Hungary 19-20, Austria 20-23; Dir for Austria of Commonwealth Fund 23-25; Commercial Attache 26-29 Athens, 29-30 Vienna & Belgrade, 30-33, 34-38 Vienna, 38-39, Bucharest, 39-41, Istanbul, 41, First Sec Berlin, 41 Berne; Exec Asst to Dir 48, Gen International Refugee Org; Capt Inf 17-18, Assigned to Intelligence Sec GHQ US Army; AEF WWI
Rogers, Edmund Pendleton	Finance	Banker & Broker; Officer Candidate, FA WWI
Sargent, Murray	Industrial	Pres, Bd Chmn 1907, Sargent & Co, New Haven; Dir 27-34, 1st National Bank (New Haven); Trustee, Blue Cross Plan; Pres, Knickerbocker Hosp; War industries Board
Sloane, John	Business	Chmn Bd, Dir, W J Sloane; Pres, Dir William John Corp; Dirs, Duttons, Inc, Gorham Inc, Centennial Ins Co, Alexander Smith & Sons Carpet Co; Trustees, Am Surety Co of NY, Atlantic Mutual Indemnity Co, Mutual Ins Co of NY, US Trust Co of NY; Dirs, Company of Master Craftsmen; 18 w/WWI Mil Intelligence Div, Combat Sec, General Staff (DC); Intelligence Officer, NY State Guard, retired as Col
Tilney, Robert Fingland II	Engineering	
Turner, Harold McLeod	Business	Lt, NY Ntl Guard WWI
Van Reypen, William K. Jr.	Law Student	
Whitehouse, Edwin Sheldon	Government	US Minister 33-34, Columbia; US Minister 30-33, Guatemala

1906 — PERIOD 2, DECADE 104

NAME	OCCUPATION	NOTES
Bruce, Donald	Forestry	Forest Service Missoula MT; Ptnr, Mason, Bruce & Girad; Capt, Eng Corp AEF, WWI
Dousman, Louis deVierville	Insurance	Mbr, Billings City Park Bd, MT State Park Bd
Ely, Grosvenor	Finance	Treas, Ashland Cotton Co (CT); Dir, Thames Ntl Bank, Chelsea Savings Bank; Capt, CT State Guard, Chief of Section, War Industry BD, WWI; VChmn, CT State War Finance Comm, WWII; Mbr, CT State Banking Advisory Council
Flinn, Alexander Rex	Business	Mbr 43-50, Bd of Educ (Pittsburgh); AEF WWI
Hoyt, Lydig	Law	Sec to US 07, Ambassador to Great Britain; Deputy Police Commissioner (NYC); 1st Lt, FA AEF WWI; Capt, Am Field Service WWII
Magee, John Gillespie	Ministry	Fellow Jonathan Edwards College 46-53; Chmn, International Red Cross, Nanking, China WWII

McClure, James Gore King Jr.,	Farming	Pres 20-, Farmer's Federation, Inc; Pres, Farmers Loan Corp; Pres, Appalachian Mutual, Inc; Pres 37-41, Am Forestry Assn; Mbr 25-33, NC Bd of Conversation & Development; Mbr, Ntl Comm for Public Schools; Pub Dir 37-40, Home Loan Corp; VChmn, Farmer's Cooperative Council, Inc
McGee, Donald Ashbrook	Finance	Mbr 16, Troop D Ntnl Guard NJ, Mexico Border Service; Dist Dir, War Dept Comm Training Camp Activities, WWI
Moorhead, William Singer	Law	Attny w/Moorhead & Knox, Pittsburgh; Chmn 22-24, US Tax Simplification Bd; Lecturer 09-18, U Pittsburgh School Law; Trustees, Carnegie Library, Carnegie Inst, Carnegie Inst Technology
O'Brien, Frank	Education	
Perrin, Lee James	Law	Officer Candidate, FA WWI
Rockwell, Foster Haven	Finance	Chmn 08-11, AZ Horticulture Comm; Maj, Am Red Cross WWI (fgn service)
Smith, Bruce Donald	Finance	Consultant to Gen Mgr 48, Atomic Energy Comm; 34-41 w/Red Cross; 13 w/Northern Trust Co Chicago; Capt Chemical Warfare Service WWI AEF
Turner, Spencer	Business	Exec Dir, Cotton Goods Section, War Industries Bd, WWI
Wilson, Hugh Robert	Government	Assoc Fellow 41-46, T Dwight College, Yale U; 41-45 w/OSS; US Diplomatic Service 1912-41; Sec - Lisbon, Guatemala, Buenos Aires, Berlin, Berne, Washington 11-21; Counselor - Tokyo, Mexico and Washington 24-27; Minister Berne, Switz 27-37; Asst Sec State 37-38; Ambassador Germany 38; Spec Asst to Sec State 39-41; Sec Gen 27, Three Power Naval Arms Limitation Conference (Geneva); Advisor 30, Naval Conference London; Mbr 32-37, Am Delegation to 54 Nation Disarmament Parley (Geneva); US Representative 31, Advisory Comm on Manchuria;

1907 — PERIOD 2, DECADE 105

NAME	OCCUPATION	NOTES
Barnes, William Deluce	Ministry/Public Works	Congregational Minister; Mbr 49-51 CT State Legislature; Chmn, State Comm of Crime & Delinquency; Pres CT Probation and Parole Assoc; Exec Sec CT Prison Assoc
Blair, William McCormick	Finance	Ptnr, William Blair Co; Dir, Continental Casualty Company, Continental Assurance Co, Peoples Gas Light and Coke Co; Life Trustee & Pres 58-66, Art Inst of Chicago; Trustee Field Museum; Life Trustee, U of Chicago; Trustee, 38-58, Groton Schl; Exec Com, Alumni Bd Yale U; Pvt, 18 Army
Camp, Arthur Goodwin	Insurance	
Daniels, Forest Leonard	X	
Danielson, Richard Ely	Literary	Pres, Editor 40, *The Atlantic Monthly*; Pres 27-37, Sportsman Pub Co ; Editor 24-28, *Boston Independent;* Bond Business 13, w/Central Trust Co (IL, Chicago); Capt Inf WWI AEF; Intelligence, Lt Col GSC WWII
Dixon, Theodore Polhemus	Finance	Capt, Intelligence WWI
Dodge, Philip Lyndon	Finance	Ptnr, Laird, Bissell & Meeds; Yale Alumni Fund
Glaenzer, Georges Brette	Industrial	
Knox, Hugh Smith	Education	Yeoman, USN WWI
Little, Mitchell Stuart	Industrial	Founder, Pres 12-, MS Little Mfg Co; Pres The Smyth Mfg Co, Sigourney Tool Co; Chmn EC Fuller Co; Sec 10-12, Whitlock Coil Pipe; Dirs, Terry Steam Turbine Co, Aetna Life Ins Co, Aetna Casualty & Surety Co, Automobile Ins Co, Hartford Gas Co, The Collins Co, Whitlock Mfg Co, Arrow-Hart & Hegeman Electric Co, Standard Screw Co, Hartford Ntl Bank & Trust Co; Trustee, Society for Savings; Mbr, Alumni Bd
Morse, Samuel Finley Brown	Business	Chmn Bd, Del Monte Properties Co; Pres 19-68, Peeble Beach; Mgr 15-62 Pacific Improvement Co; Pres 08-10 SFB Morse Development Co; Mgr 10-15, Crocker Huffman Land & Water Co
Truesdale, Calvin	Business	Bonds; Lt, FA Res Corps WWI
Tuttle, George Coolidge	Law, Mfg	
Wells, Harold Sherman	Industrial	13, w/Public Utility, Pacific Power & Light (Portland OR); Capt, Am Red Cross, WWI (Fgn Service)
Woolsey, Heathcote Muirson	Architecture	Goodwin, Bullard & Woolsey; Officer's Training School, WWI

1908 — PERIOD 2, DECADE 106

NAME	OCCUPATION	NOTES
Biglow, Lucius Horatio	Law	Mbr 49, CT Legislature; Capt 17-19, Inf AUS
Dahl, George	Education	Holmes Prof Hebrew 1910-49, Yale Divinty School; Congregational Minister; YMCA, Education Division WWI
Davis, Walter Goodwin	Law & Finance	Mbr 1921, ME House of Rep; Pres ME Historical Society; Pres Maine Gen Hosp Corp; Capt WWI AEF Military Intelligence
Dines, Tyson Manzey	Law	Durham Coal & Iron Co, (Chattanooga)

Foster, Joseph Taylor	Finance	Dines, Dines & Holme (Denver)
Griswold, Dwight Torrey	X	Mining
Perrin, Lester William	Finance	Ptnr, Lazard Feres et Cie (NYC); Mayor 40-44, (Bernardsville, NJ); Capt 17-19, Inf
Seymour, Charles	Education	Pres Emeritus 50-63, Pres 37-50, Provost 28-37, Master Berkeley College 33-37, Prof 18-37, Instr 11-17. History, Yale U; Trustee Carnegie Found, Archaeological Institute; Curator Edward M House Collection, Yale U; 18-19, American Comm to Negotiate Peace; US Delegate 19, Czechoslovak and Rumanian Comm (Paris); Chmn 43-45, Post War Planning Comm; Dept State WWI; Dir, 2d Ntl Bank (New Haven); Close friend of Col Edward M House
Shepard, Roger Bulkley	Finance	Chmn, Bd Dirs 40-, Federal Reserve Bank (Minneapolis, St Paul MN); Pres 23-, Sec & Treas 14-23, Asst Treas 10-14, Finch, Van Slyck & McConville (St Paul); Clerk 08-10, Harris Trust & Savings Bank (Chicago); Dir, Merchants Bank (merged w/First Ntnl Bank; Ensign 17-18, USN
Stanley, Harold	Finance	Founder, Pres 35-41, Morgan, Stanley & Co, Inc (NY); Ptnr 28-35, JP Morgan & Co; VP 16-28, Guaranty Trust; 10-15, w/JG White & Co (NYC); w/Ntnl Commercial Bank, Albany, NY
Thornton, James Carlton	Finance	Treas, Watkins Coal Co (NYC); Capt, FA WWI AEF
Townsend, George Henry	Industrial	Pres, Motometer Co (NY); Industrial War Service, WW I & II
Townsend, James Mulford Jr	Business	Sec & Treas, Watkins Coal Co; Lt, Inf WWI
Watkins, Charles Law	Education	Organizer, Dir 29-45, Phillips Gallery Art School; adjunct Prof 43-45, Social Art, American U; lecturer, Consultant 37-45, Fine Arts, Hood College 37-45; 13 w/Watkins Coal Co (NYC); Aspirant, French Army WWI
Williams, James Willard	Education	Gov 45, Drummer Acad; Master 30-44, Gunnery Sch; Hdmstr 25-30, Tamalpais Sch; Instr 22-25, Biology Phillips Andover; Teacher 16-22, Biology, College of Yale in China, Changsha, China; Teacher 10-13, English, Choate School

1909 — PERIOD 2, DECADE 107

NAME	OCCUPATION	NOTES
Bundy, Harvey Hollister	Law	Ptnr Choate, Hall & Stewart, (Boston); Chmn of Trustees, Carnegie Endowment for Intrnl Peace; Chmn 46-52, Boston Chptr, Am Red Cross; Asst Sec State, 31-33; Special Asst 41-45, Sec of War, US; Asst Counsel 17-19, US Food Admin; Yale Alumni Bd; Pres World Peace Foundation; Sec 14-15, Justice OW Holmes
Burch, Robert Boyd	Law	Judge 39-67, Superior CT (San Diego County); Judge 49, Juvenile Court; Major Inf, WWI AEF
Campbell, Charles Soutter	Industrial	Asst Headmaster Kingsley School, NJ; Chmn Advisory Bd, Yale Christian Assn
Clark, Avery Artison	Industrial	Sugar Mfg
Dominick, Gayer Gardner	Finance	Limited Ptnr, Dominick & Dominick, (NYC); Governor 3 terms, Stock Exchange; Pres 48-53, Roosevelt Hosp; Trustee 55, Iolani School, Honolulu, HI; Lt, WWI Navy-Submarine, Lighter-than-Air
Howard, James Merriam	Ministry	Dir 30-35, Union Theological Seminary; Pastorates 14-20 Bronx, 20-25, South Street Presbyterian, 25-36 Bedford Park; occasional preacher 21-46, Sec Dwight Hall 09-10 Yale U; Capt Chaplain FA WWI
Howe, Henry Almy	Finance	Exporter; Maj FA WWI AEF
Jefferson, Edward Francis	Education	Hotchkiss School; YMCA Sec, WWI (Fgn Service)
Klots, Allen Trafford	Law	Chmn 57- , Mayor's Comm on the Courts (NYC); Mayor 42-48, (Laurel Hollow NY); Spec Asst 31-32, Sec of State; Lt, FA WWI
Lippitt, Henry	Industrial	
Perrin, John Bates	Finance	
Rand, Stuart Craig	Law	Mbr 43-46, MA State legislature; Mbr Yale Alumni Bd; Capt, Air Service WWI
Sanderson, Benjamin Blethen	Law	Chmn 40-44, Portland Chapter, Red Cross; Corporator Maine Medical Ctr
Seabury, Mortimer Ashmfad	Finance	Investment Counselor; Yale Alumni Bd; AUS Ordnance, WWI
Stokes, Harold Phelps	Journalism	Sec 24-25, Commerce, US; Editorial Staff *NY Times* 26-37; DC Corres 19-23; Corres Paris Peace Conference 19, Albany Corres 13-17, Reporter 11-13, *NY Evening Post*; traveled Europe 04-05, Far East 09-10; 1st Lt FA WW1

1910 — PERIOD 2, DECADE 108

NAME	OCCUPATION	NOTES
Bayne-Jones, Stanhope	Medicine	Consultant in Medical Research to Surgeon Gen; Chmn 57-58, Med Edu US Dept HEW; Pres 47-53, Joint Adm Bd, NY Hsp/Cornell U Med Ctr; Prof Bacteriology 32-47, Dean 35-40, Yale Med School, Master 32-38, Trumbull Coll, Yale U; Prof of Bacteriology/Immunology 24-32, Univ ofRochester; Assoc Prof 19-24, Bacteriologyy, John Hopkins; Mbr 57-58 Yale Corp;17-19 WWI; Brig Gen 42-46, Military Cross (British) WWII

Coy, Edward Harris	Insurance	Dir, Munsey Trust Co, (DC); Treas, Girl Scouts of Am; Durham Coal & Iron Co, (Chattanooga)
DeSilver, Albert	Law	
Franchot, Charles Pascal	Law	Pres, Gen Counsel Buffalo Electric Furnace Corp; Chmn Bd Dir, Gen Counsel Sonotone Corp; Pres, Dir Burden Iron Co; Dir, Gen Counsel, Neville Island Glass Co; VP, Gen Counsel 26-27, Rand Kardex Bureau Inc; Dir, Gen Counsel 27-45, Remington Rand Inc; Mbr 46, Franchot, Corwin & Dressner (NY, DC); 44-48, Franchot & Dressner; 37-42, Franchot & Schachtel; 22-37, Franchot & Warren; 20-26, Kenefick, Cooke, Mitchell & Bass; Consular agent for France 16-26, Buffalo; Special Legal Adviser to Dir 46-50, Naval Petroleum Reserves; Maj Calvary WWI AEF; Capt USNR JAG WWII
French, Robert Dudley	Education	Chmn English Dept 45-47, Prof 30-54, Assoc Prof 26-29, Asst Prof, English 1919-26, Master Jonathan Edwards College 1930, Yale U; Known as Yale's Secretary of War.
Harrison, George Leslie	Law , Insurance	Pres Dir 41-, NY Life Ins Co; Pres 36-40, Gov 28-36, Deputy Gov 20-28, Fed Res Bank NY; Asst Gen Counsel 14-18, General Counsel 19-20, Federal Reserve Bd, DC; ; Dir First Ntl Bank NY; Trustee Columbia U; Mbr NY State Banking Bd, Mbr 48, Ntl Council of the Comm for the Marshall Plan; Special Consultant to Sec of War 43-46; Legal Sec 13-14, OW Holmes; Vice Chmn, NY Red Cross; Mbr Exec Comm, Pilgrims of the US; Capt Am Red Cross WWI (Fgn Service)
Heron, John	Law	Capt, Inf WWI AEF
King, Lyndon Marrs	Business	Pres, Chmn Bd Northrup, King Co (Minneapolis)
Knight, Augustus	Finance	Bond Broker; Alderman 27-31 (Evanston)
Logan, Walter Seth	Law	VP, Gen Counsel 28-53, Fed Reserve Bank NY; 22-28, w/Reynolds, Richards, McCutcheon & Logan; General Counsel 20-22, Fed Reserve Bd; 1st Lt 18-19, Chemical Warfare Service
Lohmann, Carl Albert	Education	Mbr 54-56, NH, CT Bd Park Comm; Sec 27-53, Yale U; Sec 25-27, Alumni Advisory Bd; Curator 26-30, 46-53, Prints Yale Art Gallery; Assoc Fellow, Jonathan Edwards; Mbr Alumni Bd
Murphy, Frederick James	Insurance	Coach Football, Basketball Northwestern U (Evanston IL); Dirs Archer Daniels Midland, Cherry-Burrel Corp; Container Corp Am; Mbr 58-66, U Council; Mbr 66-, Yale Corp; Capt 42-44, 50-53, USMC
Philbin, Stephen H II	X	
Taft, Robert Alphonso	Law	Mbr 38-53, US Senate; Mbr 31-32, OH Senate, 21-26 OH House of Rep; 23- w/Taft, Stettinius & Hollister; 13-17 w/Maxwell & Ramsey; Dirs, Central Trust Co, Covington & Cincinnati Bridge Co; Asst Counsel 17-18, US Food Admin; Counsel 18-19, Am Relief Admin; Mbr 36-53, Yale Corp
Wodell, Ruthven Adriance	Law	Chief Yeoman, USNRF WWI

1911 — PERIOD 2, DECADE 109

NAME	OCCUPATION	NOTES
Badger, Paul Bradford	Industrial	Socony Oil; Bond Salesman, Merrill, Oldham & Co, MA
Corey, Alan Lyle	Finance	1913, Guarantee Trust Co (NYC); Ensign USNRF WWI
Daly, Frederick Joseph	Education	Phillips Academy; 1st Lt. Motor Transport Corps WWI AEF; Major AUS WWII
Davis, Clinton Wildes	Industrial	w/Portland Packing Co (Portland ME); Maj FA WWI
Day, Sherwood Sunderland	Ministry	Presbyterian minister; YMCA Sec in India, (Calcutta)
Dempsey, John Bourne	Law	Mbr 23-27, OH House of Representatives; Mbr 48-55, Yale U Council; Chmn 40-43, Alumni Bd; Capt FA WWI
Gammell, Arthur Amory	Law	Mbr 24-55, Milbank, Tweed, Hadley & McCloy; Dir 33-45, Albany & Susquehanna RR; Mbr 42-45, Selective Service Bd #50 NYC; Major 17-19, FA AEF
Hyde, Frederick Walton	Industrial	CCI Co, Lumbering Dept (Marquette, MI)
Lombardi, Cornelius Ennis	Law	Chmn Bd Comm, Redevelopment Authority (KC, MO); Mbr, Yale Alumni Bd; 1st Lt, FA AEF WWI
McDonnell, John Vincent	Industrial	Columbia Oil Co (NYC); Sgt, Inf WWI

Randolph, Francis Fitz	Finance	Sr Ptnr 40-, J&W Seligman & Co 23-; Chmn Exec Comm, Tricontinental Investment Co (NYC); 14-17 w/Cravath & Henderson; Asst Counsel 15-16, B&O RR; Chmn Bd, Exec Comm 40-52, Globe & Rutgers Fire Ins Co and American Home Fire Ins Co; Pres 46-60, M-K-T RR Co; Mbr Exec Comms, Tri-Continental Corp, National Investors Corp, Bond St Investing Co, Union Service Corp, Union Securities Corp, Gen Shareholdings Inc, Whitehall Fund, Inc; Mbr Exec Comms, Dirs General Properties Corp, Am Reisurance Co, Park Properties Corp; Chmn Bd, Exec Comm, Globe & Rutgers Fire Ins Co, Am Home Fire Assurance Co; Chmn Exec Comm, Ins Co State of PA; Chmn Exec Comm, Dir 40-61, Newport News Shipbuilding & Drydock Co; Trustee, Mbr Exec Comm, Bowery Savings Bank; Trustee Chmn Find Comm, Vassar 46-65, College; Trustee 52-58, College Retirement Equities Fund; Treas 46-48, Metro Opera Guild; Chief 19, Paris Bureau Armenia Rumania amer Relief Admin; Mbr 19-20, War Loan Staff, US Treasury, Peace Conference Paris; Mbr Jekyll Island Club; Treas, RTA; Capt 16-19, US Army Calvary & FA
Rowland, John Tilghman	Literary	Author; Editor Outing Pub Co; Lt 17-21, Naval Air Service; Cmndr 42-45, USNR
Soule, Leslie	Industrial	Treas, Masoneilan Div, Worthington Corp; Lt 17-18, USN
Van Sinderen, Henry Brinsmade	Business	Bd Chmn, Pres 45-, VP 19-45, C Tennant Sons & Co (NYC); 11-17 w/Am Trading Co (Yokohama, Japan); Dir 17-18, Bureau of Exports War Trade Bd (DC); Capt AUS WWI
Wheeler, Lawrence Raymond	Industrial	Senior Editor 35-38, US Forest Service

1912 — PERIOD 2, DECADE 110

NAME	OCCUPATION	NOTES
Boyd, Francis T	Business	VP, Natl Research Bureau; 1st Asst Sec 28-35, NY Stock Exchange; Capt 17-19, 2nd Mobile Ordinance Repair Unit, 2nd Div AEF, WWI
Gardner, Robert Abbe	Finance	Mbr 19, Mitchell-Hutchins & Co; 15-19, w/Peabody Coal; 12-15 w/Consumers Co (Chicago); Dir, Chicago & Great Western R'wy; Trustee, Phillips Andover Academy; Mbr Alumni Bd, 1st Lt, FA WWI AEF; Col, GSC WWII
Hartley, Cavour	Business	Real Estate; 2nd Lt, FA AEF WWI; Lt, USNR WWII
Howe, Arthur	Education	Pres 31-40, Hamptom Inst; Asst Prof 27-30, Citizenship Dartmouth; Asst Hdmstr, Chaplin 18-27 Taft School, Watertown CT; 16-18, Loomis School, Winsdor CT; Mbr Ntl Council, Boy Scouts of Am; Dir, CT US Boys, WWI
Hyde, Donald Robertson	Industrial	Treas, John G Patton Co; Chmn 50-54, Greenwich Recreation Comm; Col Artillery, Ordnance WWI, WWII
McClure, Archibald	Ministry	
Merritt, Henry Newton	Law	Deputy Attny Gen 31-35, PA
Mullins, Frederic Parsons	Finance	Ptnr, AE Masten & Co (Pittsburgh); Pres, School Bd; 1st Lt AEF WWI
Murphy, Gerald Clery	Business	United Shoe Machinery Co (NYC)
Paul, Charles Henry	Law	Lawyer; Judge 25-27, WA State Superior Court (King County); 1st Lt 17-19, 364th Inf 91st Div
Smith, James Gregory	Industrial	Pres, Equities, Inc; Welden National Bank
Street, Henry Abbott	Business	Capt, Ord Dept WWI AEF
Strout, Edwin Augustus Jr.	Finance	Capt, FA WWI AEF; Lt Col, GSC AUS WWII
Tener, Alexander Campbell	Law	Judge 43-45, Orphans Court (Allegheny City PA); Renegotiation Bd Pittsburgh
Twombly, Edward Bancroft	Law	Sr Ptnr, Putney, Twombly, Hall & Skidmore (NYC); Mbr Common Council, 22-25, Pres 26-28, Mayor 29-31 (Summitt NJ); Dir, Mbr Finance Comm, Preferred Accident Ins Co. NY and Protective Indemnity Co; Dirs, Gen Counsel Mica Insulator Co, Eugene Munsell & Co, Distributors Group Inc, Johnson Magazines; Counsel, Group Securities; Trustee, Temple U; Chmn Defense Council WWII; Lt Col 16, Calvary Inf, Mexican Border War; Capt 18-19, WWI; Lt Col 21

1913 — PERIOD 2, DECADE 111

NAME	OCCUPATION	NOTES
Allen, Calvin Durand	Insurance	CT Mutal Life Ins Co; Capt 17-18, AUS
Allen, Clarence Emir Jr.	Law	1st Lt, Inf, WWI
Baker, Richard Wheeler	Law	2nd Lt, Air Services WWI
Colgate, Henry Auchincloss	Finance	Ptnr, Wood, Struthers Co; Dir, Colgate-Palmolive-Peet Co, International Paper Co, Grand Union Stores, Morristown Trust Co; Mbr Bd Trustees, Colgate U; Trustee, Boys Club NY; Trustee, Ntl Society for Prevention of Blindness; 2nd Lt Air Service WWI

Cortelyou, George Bruce	Business	Sr. Consultant James Talcott, Inc; Asst Treas 55-retired, NY Life Ins Co; Pres 30-32, Distributors Group; Asst Treas Central Trust Co of IL; Capt 17-19, 17th Engineers WWI
Cowles, Alfred	Finance	Pres 33- , Cowles Comm for Res in Economics; Pres 25-38, Cowles & Co, (CO Springs); Dir 39-68, (Chicago) Tribune Co, WGN Inc, Ontario Paper Co Ltd, Illinois Atlantic Corp, Marlhill Mines Ltd, News Syndicate Inc, Chicago Tribune-New York News Syndicate Inc, Quebec & Ontario Transportation Co, Quebec North Shore Paper Co, WI Radio Inc; Dir, Chmn Rialto Trust; Dir 55-63, Continental IL Ntl Bank & Trust Co, (Chicago); Dir 52-65, VSI Corp; Dir 48-65, Passavant Memorial Hosp; Trustee 25-53, CO College
Harman, Archer	Education	Dir of Guidance, Wellesly High School (MA); Capt, FA WWI
Harriman, William Averell	Government	Ltd Ptnr 46- , Ptnr 31-46, Brown Bros Harriman & Co; Chmn Bd 32-46, VP 15-17, Union Pacific RR; Chmn Bd 17-25, Merchant Shipbldg Corp; WA Harriman & Co, Inc 20-31; Chmn Exec Comm 31-42, Dir 15-46, IL Central RR; US Rep 68-69, Vietnam Peace Talks (Paris); Ambassador at large 65-69; Asst Sec of State 61-65, Far Eastern Affairs; Ambassador at large 61; Gov 55-59, NY; Dir Mutual Security Agency 51-53; Spec Asst to Pres 50-52; American Rep at NATO 51-52; US rep in Europe under Econ Coop Act 48-50; Sec of Commerce 46-48; US Ambassador 46, Great Britain; 41-46, Lend-Lease Russia/Great Britain; US Ambassador 43-46, Russia; Rep 42, London of Combined Shipping Bd; Spec Rep of Pres 41, Great Britain; US Ambassador 41, USSR; NRA 34
Lovett, August Sidney	Ministry, Finance	Dir Memorial Gifts, Yale Alumni Fund; Exec Sec Yale-in-China 59-64; Chaplain 32-58, Yale U; Master 53-58, Pierson College Yale U; Woolsey Prof Biblical Lit; Minister, Mt Vernon Church, Boston 19-32; Pres RTA
McAndrew, Alexander	X	
Philbin, Jesse Holladay	Law, Business	Asst Gen Counsel & Sec 27, Fed Reserve Bank (NY); 2d Lt & Aide to Gen Hatch AEF WWI; State Dept WWII
Sawyer, Homer Eugene Jr	Industrial	Capt, AEF WWI
Schwab, Laurence vonPost	Business	2d Lt, Air Service, WWI
Shelden, Allan	Finance	Lt USNRF WWI
Waters, William Otis	Finance	2nd Lt, WWI AEF

1914 — PERIOD 2, DECADE 112

NAME	OCCUPATION	NOTES
Avery, Benjamin F.	Industrial	Pres 27-29, Canadain Soc of Forest Engineers; 2nd Lt, Inf, AUS
Cornish, Percy Gillette Jr	Medicine	Prv 17-18, Medical Corps
Daniels, Thomas Leonard	Industrial	Founder, Dir, Emeritus 14-17, 29- , Archer-Daniels-Midland Co; US Diplomatic Service 22-29, (Brussels, Rio, Rome); War Board Production & War Food Admin 42-43; Dir, Northwestern Ntl Bank & Trust Co (MN); Trustee, Carlton College (St Paul); Major 17-19, US Army
Gile, Clement Moses	Finance	Lt, USNR WWI
Hobson, Henry Wise	Ministry	Retired 1959, Bishop, Protestant Episcopal Church, Diocese of Southern Ohio; Chmn Exec Comm Forward Movement Publications Episcopal Church 34-; Exec Council 37-46, 49-55 Episcopal Church; Bishop 30-59, Rector 21-30, All Saints Church Worcester MA; Asst Minister 20-21, St John's Waterbury CT; Trustee Phillips Acad, Andover 37-66; Pres 47-66; Trustee 30-59, Kenyon College; Major, Inf Army WWI
Jenks, Almet Francis	Literary	Magazine Writer, *Saturday Evening Post, Harper's*; 1st Lt Cav AEF WWI; Maj USMCR WWII
Jones, George Gill	Communications	Lt, USNR WWI
Ketcham, Henry Holman	Industry	Chmn, Henry H Ketchum Lumber Co (Seattle); Dir, Seattle Trust & Savings Bank; Belgium Consul for WA; 68, Ntl Footbal Hall of Fame; Major 17-19, FA
King, Stoddard	Literary	Capt, Inf WA Ntnl Guard WWI
Lippincott, William Jackson	Finance	
Osborn, Richard	Finance	Broker, Towne, Brayton & Osborn (MA); Service Sanitaire, 5th French Army, 1st Lt, Coast Artillery Res Corps.
Patterson, George W.	Advertising	Artillery, French Army WWI
Rogers, Herman Livingston	Engineering	Maj, FA WWI AEF; Chief French Section WWII
Shepard, Lorrin Andrews	Medicine	Asst Sec to Reuben Holden 59-62, in charge of Foreign visitors Yale U; Dir 57-58, Intrnl House; Medical Dir and Surgeon 27-57, Am Hosp Istanbul; Med Dir Mission Hosp, Gaziantep 19-25; Daughter Constance Jolly
Warren, William Candee Jr.	Law	Attny w/Magavern, Lowe & Beilewech (Buffalo); Trustee, Sec Counsel, Buffalo Gen Hosp; Trustee, Treas, Fresh Air Mission; Trustee, Treas, Pres Bd, Presbyterian of Western NY; Mbr, Yale Alumni Bd; Capt, FA AEF WWI; ordnance Dept WWII

1915 — PERIOD 2, DECADE 113

NAME	OCCUPATION	NOTES
Burtt, Edwin Arthur	Education	Sage Prof 32-60, Philosophy, Cornell; Philosophy Staff 21-23, Columbia; 23-32, U of Chicago
Carter, Lyon	Finance	1st Lt, CAC WWI
Cornell, Thomas Hilary	Business	1st Lt FA WWI AEF
Davenport, Stephen Rintoul	Industrial	VP, Yardley of London, Inc; Capt 17-19, CAC AEF WWI
Denegre, Thomas Bayne	Finance	W/First Ntl Bank of Biloxi; 1st Lt FA WWI AEF
MacDonald, Ranald Hugh Jr	Finance	Consultant, Gen Ptnr, Dominick & Dominick; Pres 48-58, Ntl Shares Corp; Trustee Exec Comm 37-61, Franklin Savings Bank (NY); Trustee, Finance Comm 44-61, Pratt Inst; Gov 42-46, Invest Bankers Assn, 42-46 Assn Stock Exch Firms, 44-50, NY Stock Exchange; 2nd Lt 17-19, USAF
MacLeish, Archibald	Literary, Education	Boylston Prof Harvard 49-62; Asst Sec 44-45, State; Librarian 39-44, of Congress; Dir 41-42, US Office of Facts and Figures; OSS; Asst Dir 42-43, OWI (Office of War Information); Yale U Council 66-71; Poetry 32, 52 Drama 69, Pulitzer Prize; Capt 17-18, AEF
Middlebrook, Louis Shelton	Industrial	1st Lt, FA AEF WWI
Paris, Irving	Finance	Lt, Naval Aviation, WWI
Pumpelly, Harold Armstrong	Mining	Lt, Naval Service WWI
Reilly, John Sylvester	Industrial	Pres, Gordon & Dilworth, Inc & Diplomat Products, Inc; Capt 17-19, Ordnance
Shedden, William Martindale	Medicine	Instr, Anatomy, Harvard Sch; Instr Surgery, Tufts U Med Sch; Chief Surgeon, Veterans Admin Hosp (Lake City FL); Cmdr 42-45, USN MC 42-45
Slocum, Edwin Lyon	Finance	Acct Exec, Francis I Dupont (NYC); Capt 17–18, Inf
Stackpole, Edward James	Publishing	Salesman 15-17, Gen Mgr 21-36, Pres, Treas, Dir 36- *Telegraph Press* (Harrisburg PA); Pres, Treas, Dir WHP radio 31-; Sec-Treas, Dir 36, Am Aviation Assoc Inc; Dirs Harrisburg Trust Co, Penn-Harris Hotel Co, Harrisburg Hotel Co; Dir, Pres, Soldiers Orphans School (Scotland PA); Capt Inf WWI, Brig Gen of the line WWII
Swift, Walker Ely	Medicine	

1916 — PERIOD 2, DECADE 114

NAME	OCCUPATION	NOTES
Darling, Arthur Burr	Education	Engaged in research and writing on British-American Relations; Fullbright Sr Fellow 55-56, Italy; Historian 51-54, US Govt; Chmn 33-51, History Dept, Phillips Academy (Andover); Instr/Assoc Prof 22-33, Yale; Current History Assoc 24-31, NY Times; Ensign 17-19, USNRF
Gaillard, Samuel Gourdin Jr.	Industrial	1st Lieut, Ord Dept WWI AEF
Hadley, Morris	Law	Ptnr, Milbank, Tweed, Hadley & McCoy (NYC); Mbr 31-41, Yale Corp; Trustee, Chmn Bd 39-41, Vassar College; Trustee 38, Pres 43-58, NY Pub Library; Trustee 47-67, Chmn 55-66, Carnegie Corp of NY; Deputy Dir 41-42, OWI; Maj 16-19, FA Army AEF
Johnstone, Henry Webb	Industrial	Sr VP, Dir, Merck & Co, Inc; Dir 58-64, Kent & Queen Anne's Hosp, Chestertown MD; 1st Lt 17-19, Army
Knapp, Farwell	Law	Pres 38-42, Dean, Instructor Law 28-38, Hartford College of Law; Asst Tax Commissioner 25-37, CT; Sgt, FA WWI AEF
Oler, Wesley Mardon	Business	Dir 42-65, PR Overseas Operations Div, General Motors Corp; Ptnr 29-42, Pershing & Co; VP 17-29, American Ice Co; 1st Lt 17-18, USAF, Flying Instr, Army Test Pilot
Porter, Gilbert Edwin III	Finance	1st Lt, FA WWI
Putnam, Howard Phelps	Literary	
Roberts, Charles Holmes Jr.	Finance	Rep 39-41, MA General Court; Lt, Naval Air Service WWI (fgn service)
Shepard, Donald Carrington	Industrial	1st Lt FA WWI
Stewart, Donald Ogden	Literary	Author, Playwright, Screen Writer; Academy Award 1941 Best Screenplay, Philadelphia Story, Kitty Foyle, The Barretts of Wimpole, Life with Father; Chief Quartermaster 18-19, USNRF
Tener, Kinley John	Law	Capt, FA WWI AEF

Tighe, Laurence Gotzian	Finance	Treas 42-53, Assoc Treas 38-42, Yale U; Dir 34-38, Ptnr 30-34, 24-34, w/Brown Bros, Brown Bros Harriman; 21-24 w/Stacy & Braun (Boston); Sales 21, SW Straus & Co, Boston; Asst Treas 19-20, FH Swift & Co, Inc (Boston); 19 w/Kalman, Matteson & Wood (St Paul, MN); Clerk 16-17, Equitable Trust Co (NYC); dir PA Water & power Co, CT Light & power Co, Ntl Sugar Refining Co, Industrial Enterprises Inc, NY, First Ntl Bank & Trust Co, New Haven; Corporator New Haven Savings Bank; Treas Bd Trustees Shefield Scientific Schl; Treas Yale Alumni Fund, Yale athletic Assn, Yale Library Assoc; Trustee Yale-in-China; Capt FA WWI
von Holt, Herman Vademar	Business	Estate Mngmt (Honolulu); Treas 23-48, St Andrew's Cathedral Parrish; Mbr 32-38, Honolulu Parks Bd; Dir, Chmn Invest Comm 32-69, Episcopal Church HI; 2nd Lt, 17-19 US Tanks Corps AEF
Walker, Charles Rumford	Librarian	Curator 62-, Yale Technology and Society Collection, Sterling Memorial Library, Yale U; Asst Sec 42-45, Yale U; Dir 45-62, Technology Project, Sr Research Fellow 55-62 Yale U; 1st Lt 18-19,

1917 — PERIOD 2, DECADE 115

NAME	OCCUPATION	NOTES
Bellinger, Alfred Rammond	Education	Prof Emeritus of Latin 59-78, Faculty 23-59 Yale U; Acting Dean 53-54, Fellow 33- Saybrook Coll; Pres, Sec 68, RTA; 1st Lt 17-19, Air Service WWI
Bush, Prescott Sheldon	Finance	Mbr 52-63, US Senate R-CT; Ptnr 1930-72 Brown Brothers Harriman & Co, NY; VP 26-30 WA Harriman & Co; Dir Pan Am Airways, CBS, Dresser Industries, Inc, Simminos Co, Vanadium Corp of Am; Chmn Bd PA Water & Power Co, US Guarantee Co; Chmn 42 Natl Campgn USO; Pres 1935, USGA; Trustee Yale U, Mbr 48-58 Yale Corp
Cooper, Henry Sage Fenimore	Medicine	Physician, Park Ave NYC; Attending Surgeon 37-60, Presbyterian Hosp, NYC; 2nd Surgical Service 26-36, Bellevue Hosp; Capt 17-19, FA
Cunningham, Oliver Bulg	Student	Capt, FA WWI AEF
Duryee, Samuel Sloan	Law	Lawyer, of Counsel, Parker, Duryee, Zunino, Malone & Carter (NYC); Chief 40-41, Tax Amortization Section, Office under Sec War; Chmn 41-42, Tax Amortization Bd; Pres 48-58, Hosp for Special Surgery; Dir, Am Subsidiaries of Zurich Ins Co; Pres, Trustee 48-65, Groton School; Capt 17-19, FA AEF
Harriman, Edward Roland *Bunny* Noel	Finance	Pres 34-57, Chmn 57- Ptnr Brown Bros Harriman; Chmn Bd Dir, UP RR; Dirs, Delaware & Hudson Co, Merchants Sterling Corp, Am Bank Note Co, Anaconda Copper Mining Co, *Newsweek*, Mutual Life Ins Co of NY, Provident Fire Insurance Co; Mbr Finance Advisory Comm, Royal Exchange Assurance; Trustee, Boys Club NY; Pres 50-53, Chmn 63-, American Red Cross; Lt 17-19, US Army
Isham, Henry Porter	Business	Isham, Lincoln & Beale, Chicago; Pres Clearing Industrial Dist Inc; Dirs, Marshall Field & Co, Clearing Machine Corp, First Ntl Bank of Chicago, Am Shipbuilding Co; Chmn Bd, Clearing Industrial Dist Inc, (Chicago); Sec, Pres 33-47, Passavant Memorial Hosp; Trustee Field Museum; Capt FA AEF WWI; Chief Purchaser 43-46, Termination and Renegotiation Policy, Chicago Ordnance Dist AUS
James, Ellery Sedgewick	Finance	Capt FA AEF WWI
LeGore, Harry William	Industrial	Mbr 34-38, MD State Senate; Mbr 30-34, MD House of Delegates; w/Legore Lime Co, Capt, USMC AEF WWI
Mallon, Henry Neil	Industrial	Chmn Bd, Pres, Dir 29-, Dresser Industries (Cleveland), Pres 31-, Dresser Mfg Ltd (Toronto); Chmn Bd, Dir Bryant Heater Co (Cleveland); Factory Mgr, Gen Mgr, Dir 20-29, US Can Co (Cincinnati); 19-20 w/Continental Can Co (Chicago); Dirs Bovaud & Seyfang Mfg Co (Bradford Pa), Clark Bros Inc (Olean NY), Day & Night Mfg Co (Monrovia CA), Intrnl Derrick & Equipment Co (Columbus OH), Kobe, Inc (Huntington Park CA), Pacific Pumps, Inc (CA), Roots-Connesville Blower Corp (Connersville IN), Security Engineering Co (Whitter CA), Stacey Bros, Gus Construction Co (Cincinnati), Pharis Tire & Rubber Co (Newark, OH), Petrolite Corp (St Louis), Magazines of Industry (NYC), Hydrocarbon Research Inc (NY), Carthage Hydrocol Corp (NY); Maj 17-19, FA
Olsen, Albert William	Finance	VP, NY Trust Co; 1st Lt 18, FA US Army
Overton, John Williams	Student	1st Lt, Marine Corps, WWI AEF
Shepard, Frank Parsons Jr.	Finance	VP Banker's Trust Co (NYC); 1st Lt 18-19, FA
Simpson, Kenneth Farrand	Law	Mbr 40-41 US Congress; US Attny 25-27, Southern Dist NY; Spec Asst 26, Attny Gen US; Mbr 37-40, Rep Ntl Comm; Capt, FA WWI AEF
Woolley, Knight	Finance	Ptnr 31-, Brown Brothers Harriman & Co, NYC; Ptnr 27-31, Harriman Bros; 20-27 w/Am National Exchange Bank; 19-20 w/Guaranty Trust Co; Dirs Southern RR System, Merchants Sterling Corp, Orama Corp, Tiger Corp, Air Reduction Co, Inc, Am Hawaiian SS Co, Caledonia Am Ins Co, Ntl Sugar Refining Co, Hewitt-Robins, Inc; Trustee, Treas, Boy's Club NY; Major 17-19, FA US Army

1918 — PERIOD 2, DECADE 116

NAME	OCCUPATION	NOTES
Ames, Allen Wallace	Finance	Marine Midland Trust; LT USN Air Service, WWI; Capt, USNAS WWII
Baldridge, Howard Malcolm	Law	Mbr US Congress; Capt FA WWI; Col AF WWII
Clay, Cassius Marcellus	Law, Farming	Mbr 53-55, KY Senate, 57 Pres pro tem; Mbr 33-41, KY State Legislature; 1941-45 Gen Solicitor B&O RR; re-organization Mgr 41-42, MP RR Co; Asst Gen Counsel 33-41, Reconstruction Finance Corp, (in charge of RR section) DC; Assoc 27-32, Beekman, Bogue; 21-27, Simpson, Thacher & Bartlett; 1st Lt FA WWI
Davison, Frederick Trubee	Museum	Director of Personnel at the CIA 51; Pres 33-53, American Museum of Natural History; Assistant U.S. secretary 26-33 War for Air; Trustee, Mutual Life Ins Co; Mbr 21-26, NY State Legislature; Mbr 31-53, Yale Corporation; Lt jg, Naval Air Service WWI; Brig Gen, USAF WWII
Deans, Robert Barr	Finance	Ptnr, CS Halsey & Co, Dillon & Read; Acct Exec, Travel Consultants, Inc (DC); Mbr 48-61, CIA; Col 17-19, 42-46, USAF; OBE, Crown of Italy, Order of St George, Bronze Star
Farrar, John Chipman	Literary	Chmn Bd Farrar, Straus & Giroux Inc NYC; Editor, Chmn Bd 46, Farrar & Strauss; 29-44 Editor, VP Chmn Bd Farrar & Rinehart; Editor 21-27, The Bookman; Dir 27, Doubleday Doran & Co; Editor 25, George H Doran; 1919-21 Reporter, *NY Sunday World*; Lecturer 46, Publishing course, Columbia U; Mbr 40-43, Writers Bd for World Government; Mbr 46-50, Federal Grand Jury Assoc; 1st Lt 17-19, USAF; Mbr 43-44 Psychological Warfare Branch OWI; Editor, *USA* and *Die Amerikanische Rundschau* 44-45, Overseas Publications of OWI,
Garfield, Newell	Industrial	VP Zephyr Textiles (Ormestown, Canada); Dir, Riggs & Lombard, Ames Textiles (Lowell, MA); Major 17-18, FA
Gates, Artemus Lamb	Finance	Chmn Bd, Dir, Lawyers Title Corp of NY; President of New York Trust Company 29-41; Dir, Union Pacific, TIME, Boeing Company, Am Superpower Corp, North British & Mercantile Ins Cos; Trustee, Mutual Life Insurance; Assistant 41-45, Navy Secretary for Air; Under Sec 45, Navy; Lt Cmndr 17-19, Naval Air Service
Gould, James	Finance	Capt, FA WWI AEF
Lovett, Robert Abercrombie	Finance	Ptnr 1928-40, 46-, Brown Brothers Harriman & Co (NY); Sec 51-53, Defense; Deputy Sec 50-51, Defense ; Under Sec 47-49, State; Assistant Secretary 41-45, War for Air, War; Chmn Exec Comm 53-66, Union Pacific RR; Clerk 1926, Ntl Bank of Commerce (NY); Trustee 49-61, Rockefeller Found; Trustee 37-65, Carnegie Found for Adc Teaching; Trustee 48-, Carnegie Inst of Washington, DC; Trustee 31-40, Met Museum Art; Dirs, Los Angeles & Salt Lake City RR Co, OR Short Line RR Co, OR-WA RR & Navigation Co, Royal-Liverpool Group Ins Cos, St Joseph & Grand Island R'wy Co; Mbr, CFR; Harriman's childhood friend; Lt Cmndr 17-18, USN Air Service
Snell, Raymond Franklin	Finance	Financial Management (NYC); 2d Lt 17-19, FA
Stewart, Charles Jacob	Finance	Chmn Bd, Manufacturers Hanover Trust Co; Dir, Greenwich Savings Bank; 2d Lt 18-19, FA
Taft, Charles Phelps	Law	Headley, Taft & Headley 46-; 24-37 w/Taft, Stettinius & Hollister; 23 w/Taft & Taft; Prosecuting Attny 27-28; Mayor 55-57, City Councilman 38-42, 48-51, 55 (Cincinnati); Dir 43-45, Wartime Econ Affairs, Dept. of State; Pres 47-48, Federal Council of Churches 47-48; Central Comm 37-54, World Council of Churches; Trustee, Twentieth Century Fund;
Vorys, John Martin	Law	Mbr 39-59, US Congress; 26-38 w/Vorys, Sater, Seymour & Pease; Sec 21-22, Am Delegation Conference on Limitation of Armaments (DC); Dir 25-65, YMCA; Rep 23-25, OH General Assembly; Mbr 25-27, OH State Senate; Dir 29-31, of Aeronautics (OH); Teacher 19-20, College of Yale China; USN pilot WWI, CAP pilot 42
Woolley, John Eliot	Publishing	2d Lt, FA WWI; Lt Col USAAF WWII

1919 — PERIOD 2, DECADE 117

NAME	OCCUPATION	NOTES
Allen, Parker Breese	Industrial	Chmn Bd, Meriden Gravure Co; 2nd Lt17-19, FA, Lt Col 42-45 AF; OBE
Baldwin, Sherman	Law	Trustee 34-54, Brearley Schl; Trustee 51-61, 62-65, Vassar College; 30-48 Trustee Pomfret School; Mbr Bd, Exec Comm 47- , NY Botanical Garden; Trustee 63-67, Metro Museum of Art, Trustee, Sec, Exec Comm 45-69, American Academy of Rome; Mbr 35-50 Yale Alumni Bd
Campbell, Alan Barnette	Industrial	2nd Lt FA WWI
Carter, Frederic Dewhurst	Finance	Mbr Alumni Bd; 1st Lt, FA WWI
Depew, Ganson Goodyear	Law	Asst Dist Attny 22-24, (Western NY); Lt, Naval Air Service

Gaillard, Edward McCrady	Finance	Pres 43-63, Chmn 63-68, Union & New Haven Trust Co; Mbr 56, Yale Development Board; Dir 48, United Illuminating Co; Dir 56-60, Wallace Silversmith Co; Pres 37-40, CT Bankers Assn; 1st Lt, FA WWI 17-19; Dir RTA
Hadley, Hamilton	Law, Writer	Ptnr 29-40, Winthrop, Stimson, Putnam & Roberts; Dir (now emeritus) 33, Research Corp; Trustee 36, US Trust Co, (NYC); Dir, VP 29-40, Am Superpower Corp; VP, Niagara Hudson Power Corp, Commonwealth and Southern Corp; Capt 17-19, AEF Air Service
Haffner, Charles Christian Jr.	Industrial	Treas 35-40, VP 45-, Chmn Finance Comm, formerly Chmn, CEO RR Donnelley & Sons Co (Chicago); Exec VP 33-34, City Ntl Bank & Trust Co; Exec VP 31-33, Central Republic Bank & Trust Co; Cashier-VP 27-28, Central Trust Co (Chicago); Major General 40-46, Division Cmndr 103rd
Mallon, John Howard	Industry	Sr VP, Louisville Cement Co; Dir 59-64, 70-77, Louisville Water Co; 1st Lt 17-19, 151st FA
McCormick, Alexander Agnew Jr.	Student	Lt Naval Air Service, WWI (Fgn Service)
McKee, Elmore McNeill	Ministry	64-67 w/Albuquerque Public schools; Conslt-lecturer 63-64, Peace Corps training Ctr Latin America U NM; Field Reporter & Originator 50-51, The People Act Project 20th Century Fund; Dir 52-55, same project, Ford Foundation; Head of Mission 46-47, Am Friends Service Co (US Zone Germany); 36-46, St George's NYC; Rector 30-36, Trinity Church (Buffalo); Chaplain 26-30, Yale U; Rector 22-26, St Pauls (New Haven); Asst 21-22, St John's (Church Waterbury); Trustee 26-30, Taft School; Exec Comm 40-43, Comm on Just and Durable Peace Fed Council Churches; Author; 1st Lt 17-19, Sanitary Corps
Mead, Winter	Business	Mbr, Bd Assessors (Morristown, NJ); 2nd Lt, FA WWI; Chmn Civil Defense (Morristown) WWII
Otis, James Sanford	Finance	Lt, Naval Aviation
Smith, Traver	Farming	Rancher; Lt USN 17-18, Aviation
Walker, George Nesmith	Industrial	w/Moboil Oil Corp; Capt 17-18, FA AEF

1920		**Period 2, Decade 118**
Name	**Occupation**	**Notes**
Adams, Lewis G.	Architecture	Ptnr, Adams & Woodbridge; Cmdr 17-19, 41-45, USNR
Davison, Harry Pomeroy	Finance	Sr VP, JP Morgan & Co. (NYC); Lt, Naval Air Service WWI; Cmndr, USN WWII
Hadden, Briton	Literary	Co-Founder 1923, *Time* Magazine; 2nd Lt, FA WWI
Heffelfinger, Frank Peavey	Business	Hon Chmn Bd, Exec Comm, Peavey Co (MN); VP, Gen Mgr 29-39, Monarch Elevator Co; VP 25-29, Globe Elevator Co; Sec 21-25 Northern Elevator Co; British Am Elevator Co 20, Port Arthur Elevator Co 1920; Dir, Great Northern R'wy Co; Mbr, Republican Ntl Finance Co; Trustee Hazelden Found; Dirs Trout Unlimited, North Star Res & Dev Inst, Ntl Football Found, Ntl Tax Equality Assn; 2nd Lt US Army WWI; Reg Dir, War Production Bd WWII
Hincks, John Morris	Insurance, Finance	Chmn 44, Middlesex Mutual Assurance Co (Middletown, CT); 30-42, w/Calvin Bullock; 22-30, w/Hincks Bros
Hobson, Francis Thayer	Literary	Chmn Bd 31-, Pres William Morrow & Co Publishers (NYC); Ptnr, Thayer Hobson & Co; Dir, MS Mill Co Inc, Jefferson House Inc
Ingalls, David Sinton	Law	Pres, Publisher 54-58, Cincinnati Publishing Co; VP & Mngr 40-42, Charge of Overseas Operations 45-49 Pan American World Airways; Dir 33-35, Health & Welfare (Cleveland); Asst Sec 29-32, Navy for Aeronautics; Mbr 26-29, Ohio House of Rep; 23-29 w/Squire, Sanders & Dempsey (Cleveland); US Naval Aviation 17-19, 42-45; Capt; Rear Admiral USNR WWI, WWII
Luce, Henry Robinson	Literary	Founder of/and editor-in-Chief *Time* '23, *Life* '36, *Fortune* '30, *Sports Illustrated, Architectural Forum, House & Home*, NYC; Dir Aid Refugee Chinese Intellectuals, American Korean Found, Korea Society, Union Theological Seminary, Univ of Andes Found; trustee Am heritage Found, China Inst of Am, Met Museum Art, Yale-in-China Assn; Sponsor, Intrnl Friendship League, Save the Children Fund, World Brotherhood; Mbr 47-56, Yale U Council.; 2nd Lt FA WW
McHenry, James	Finance	Ptnr, Alex, Brown & Sons, Baltimore; 2nd Lt FA WWI; Capt USMCR WWII
Patterson, Morehead	Industrial	VP, Dir, International Cigar Machinery Co; Dir, Durham-Enders Razor Co; Deputy US Rep 54, UN Disarmament Comm (London); US Rep 54-55, International Atomic Agency Negotiations; Asst Counsel, Asst VP, VP, Pres, Dir, Chmn 26-27-, American Machine & Foundry Co (NYC); 2d Lt, FA WWI
Safford, Theodore Lee	Ministry	2d Lt, FA WWI
Sargent, Joseph Weir	Insurance	2d Lt 17-18, FA
Schermerhorn, Alfred Cosler	Finance	2d Lt, FA WWI; Lt Col, USAAF WWII

Van Slyck, DeForest	Government	Pres, Hon Chmn Bd, Intrnl Student House (DC); 46-60 w/CIA (DC); Ptnr 37-46, Fahnestock & Co (NYC); Assoc 29-37 Lazard Freres (NYC); Instr and Asst Prof 20-29, Yale; Mbr 57-67, Yale Dev Comm; WWI Quartermaster 18, USNR; Col 42-45, USAAF WWII
Winter, Daniel Robbins	Business	Asst Gen Mgr, Direct Marketing, Gulf Oil (Pittsburgh, PA); Vol Ambulance Field Service 17, WWI; 2d Lt 18-79, FA

1921 — PERIOD 2, DECADE 119

NAME	OCCUPATION	NOTES
Acosta, John Sidney	Insurance	2nd Lt FA WWI
Bradley, Charles Harvey	Business	Pres 24-55, WJ Holliday & Co; Pres, Monarch Steel Co; Pres, Chmn Bd, PR Mallory & Co, Inc; Pvt 17-18, USMC
Brewster, Walter Rice	Law	Mbr Milbank, Tweed, Hadley & McCloy; Assoc Fellow 70-, Trumbull College, Yale U; Dir 60-62, Rogers Peet Co; Assoc Govt Appeal Agnt 41-42, US Selective Service; 2nd Lt, 18-23, FA Officers Reserve Corp WWI; Lt Cmdr, 42-45, USNR WWII
Bundy, Frederick McGeorge	Finance	Chmn Bd Cape Ann Bank & Trust; Asst Treas, Chmn Bd 23-68, Groton's of Gloucester, (MA); Mbr 53-54, Ntl Fisheries Inst; Mbr 56-59, Yale Alumni Bd; 2nd Lt, US Army
Cowles, William Sheffield	Finance	Ptnr 30-69, Wood, Walker & Co; Mbr 49-55, CT State Legislature, Spkr of House 54-55; Mayor 56-60, Farmington; Lt 18-20, USMC; Capt 41-46, USN Admiral Halsey's staff
Heminway, Bartow Lewis	Industrial	Pres, Heminway Corp (CT); Dir, Exec Comm, Colonial Bank & Trust Co (CT); Trustees, Taft School, St Margaret's School for Girls; 2nd Lt, FA WWI
Hord, Stephen Young	Finance	Gen Ptnr 45- , 32-45, w/Brown Bros Harriman & Co; 27-32, w/Lee Higginson & Co Chicago; 21-27 w/Chicago; Northern Trust Co Chicago; Dir 68- , Chmn Investment Comm Pension Fund 70- , Abex Corp; Dir, Mbr Finance Comm 47-69, Am Auto Ins Co; Dir 57-69, Assoc Indemnity Corp; Dir Mbr Exec Comm 62- , IL Central Industries, Inc; Dir 45- , IL Central RR; Dir 52-57, Rotary Elec Steel Co Detroit; Dir 57-61, Calvert Drilling Inc ; Dir 64-69, Ntl Surety Corp (NY); Dir 57-68, Symington Wayne Corp; Dir 47-70, Midwest Stock Exchange; Dirs, Chicago Tunnel Co, Tunnel Transport Co, Clearing Machine Corp, Yazoo & MS Valley RR; Mbr 54- ,Chicago Panel of Arbitrators NYSE; Charter Trustee 63-68, Phillips Academy Andover; CFR; Pvt 18-22, USMC AEF 5th reg
Jenckes, Marcien	Law	Ptnr Choate, Hall & Stewart, Boston; 2nd Lt 18-19, FA Army
Litt, Willard David	Finance	2nd Lt FA WWI, Lt USNR WWII
Lunt, Storer Boardman	Literary	Chmn, WW Norton Co, Inc (NYC); Mbr, Gov Bd 55-65, Yale U Press; Pres 62-65, Am Book Publisher's Council; Pres 65-69, National Publisher's Ass; 2nd Lt 17-18, FA
Neville, James Eugene	Law	Asst US Attny, Coolidge Admin
Parsons, Langdon	Medicine	Gynecologist, Surgeon; Dir 63-71, Alumni Relations, Harvard Med School; Prof Emeritus 66-, Clinical Prof 63-66, Gyn Harvard Med School; Prof 49-62, Obs & Gyn, Boston U School Med; Lt Col 42-46, MC, US Army
Shevlin, Edward Leonard	Business	2d Lt, FA WWI
Stewart, John	Finance	Investment Counsel; VP Cooke & Bieler; Pres 55, Baxter & Stewart, Inc; VP 65, Cooke & Beller, Inc; Chmn Bd 50-54, Henry B Warner & Co; Salesman 54-55, Harrison & Co; Mgr Stock Dept 37-40, Merrill, Lynch, Fenner & Smith, Phils; Pres 40-49, Donner Corp; Dirs, Teleflex, Inc, Bryn Mawyr Hosp, Chesapeake Utilities Corp; Wellington Tech Industries, Inc, Cooke & Bieler, Inc; Chmn Bd, Church Farm School (PA); Lt 18, FA US Army 18
Winter, Edwin Wheeler II	Finance	2d Lt, FA WWI

1922 — PERIOD 2, DECADE 120

NAME	OCCUPATION	NOTES
Aldrich, Malcolm Pratt	Finance	Chmn of Bd The Commonwealth Fund; Dir, Trustee 31-59, NY Trust; 33-40, 58-72 Southern Pacific; 40-55 NY Central RR; 53-58 Natl Distillers & Chmcl Corp; 56-72 Equitable Life; 62-66 Phelps Dodge; 64-70 American Elec Pwr; 38-68 Am Mus. Of Nat Hist; 51-70 Met Mus of Art; Spec Asst to Asst Sec of Navy for Air, 42-45 Capt USN; Mayor 31-39, North Hills NY; Assoc Fellow 32- Davenport Coll; Pres, 57-58, Mbr 53-58, Unvrsty Council; Yale Alumni Fund
Bush, James Smith	Finance	Pres Inter Mundi; Curator 50-56, U Of MO; managing Dir 59-63, Export-Import Bank of WA; Lt Col 42-45, USA
Cheney, Ward	Industrial	Pres, Dir Cheney Bros, Textile Mfrs; Dir, Pioneer Parachute Co; Chmn, Comm for Dept of Fine Arts at Yale; Pvt, OTC, WWI; Cmdr, USN, WWII
Crosby, Albert Hastings	Finance	Priv, SACT WWI
Frost, Albert Carl, Jr.	Finance	Rep, Bache & Corp

Hilles, Frederick Whiley	Education	Bodman Prof English Emeritus Chmn 47-56, 62-64, Mbr 26-65 English Dept, Dir of Humanities 56-59 Yale U; VP 58-, Yale U press; App Seaman, USN WWI; Lt Col, AUS WWII; Hon OBE; Pres RTA
Larner, Robert Johnson	Finance	Gunnery Sgt, USMCAR WWI
Lord, William Galey	Industrial	Pres, Galey & Lord, Exec VP, Burlington Industries; Dir 49-69, V Chmn Brooklyn Museum; Mbr 62-67, Yale U Council
Page, Robert Guthrie	Business	Chmn Exec Com, formerly Pres, Bd Chmn Phelps Dodge Corp (NYC); Spec Asst to Under Sec of Navy 40; Reg Adminis 35, SEC; Sec 26-27, Justice Louis D Brandeis
Root, Wells	Writing	Instructor, Theatre Arts, UCLA, CA; Author, 32 Feature Screenplays, 75 TV Shows, books, Maj 42-45, AAF
Solley, Robert Folger	Medicine	Physician, Asst Pathologist, Asst, Assoc, Attending then Consulting Physician 29-70, St Lukes Hosp (NYC); Consulting Physician Nantucket Cottage Hosp; Asst Physician 35-46, Presbyterian Hosp and Neurological Inst (NYC); Cmdr 42-46, MC USNR
Strong, Henry Barnard	Government	Rep, Gen Assembly CT; Exec Sec 43-47, Govs Baldwin, McConaughy; Navy WWI
Thomas, John Allen Miner	Literary	
Townsend, Frederic dePeyster Jr	Law	
Woodward, Stanley	Government	US Foreign Service 25-53, except 34-37, when Commissioner Fairmount Park, Phila, PA; Ambassador 50-53, Canada; Chief of Protocol 45-50, US Dept State; Yale-in-China; Sgt 18, FA US Army

1923 — PERIOD 2, DECADE 121

NAME	OCCUPATION	NOTES
Becket, George Campbell	Law	Attny, Ptnr, Shipman & Goodwin (CT); Justice of the Peace 40-71, 78-83, Trial Justice 42-60 (Salisbury, CT); Dir, Torrington Savings Bank
Bulkey, Jonathan Ogden	Business	Pulp & Paper Dist, (NYC); Corporal SSU, WWII
Cooper, John Sherman	Government	of Counsel, Covington & Burling, DC; Mbr 47-49, 53-55, 57-73, US Senate KY; County Judge 30-38, (Pulaski County KY); elected 45, Circuit Judge; Mbr, 49-51 Gardner, Morrison & Rogers (DC); US Delegate 49, UN General Assembly Session; Ambassador 55-56, India & Nepal; Advisor 50, Sec of State Acheson; Mbr 63-65 Warren Comm named by Pres Johnson to investigate assassination of President Kennedy; 60-65 Yale U Council, Pvt to Capt 42-46, US Army, Military Police
Davenport, Russell Wheeler	Literary	Pub Officer 47, CBS; Chief Editorial Writer 42-44, *Life*; Editor, Writer, Chmn Bd 1930-41, Fortune Magazine (created the Fortune 500 companies list); Reporter 24-25, *Spokane Review*, (WA); Editorial Staff 23-24, *Time*; Pvt Ambulance Services, WWI AEF
Day, Huntington Townsend	Law	Ptnr, Wiggin & Dana, New Haven, CT
Foster, Maxwell Evarts	Law	
Hyde, Louis Kepler Jr	Investments	Chmn Bd, Dir, EW Axe & Co, Inc, Pres, Axe-Houghton Fund Tarrytown NY; Ptnr Barringer, Nelson & Hyde 41-48; Mbr 46-51, Permanent Mission to UN; Dept Trade relations Advisor 43-44, Foreign Econ Admin; Asst to Sec State 45, in charge of policy review & analysis; Dep Dir 42-43, Planning & Dev Staff, Spec Asst to Dep Administrator Lend-Lease Admin; VP 35-41, Wasserman, Nelson, Barringer & Hyde, Inc; Pres Simplex Universal Joint, Inc 29-32; VP 26-59, Riverside Coal & Timber Co; VP 26-39, Union County Investment Co; Dir 41-52, 58 - , Katzenbach & Warren, Inc; Dir 58-, Axe-Houghton Stock Fund Inc; Dir 58- , Henry WT Mali & Co, Inc; Dir Muskogee Elec Traction Co 36-55
Jones, Edwin Alfred	Industrial	Chmn-Pres Globe Iron Co, Globe Metallurgical Corp, Golden Globe Citrus Assn, Interlake Steel Corp; Chmn Naples Golf & Beach Club
Jordan, Ralph Edward	X	
Luckey, Charles Pinckney	Finance	Banker, NYC; Yale Alumni Bd; Pvt FA WWI
Matthessen, Francis Otto	Education	Bergen lecturer 48, Instr 27-29 Yale U; Cadet RAF Canada WWI
Norton, George Washington Jr.	Television	Pres, WAVE-TV (Louisville); Major, USAF WWII
Pelly, Bernard Berenger	Business	Sr VP, Balfour, Guthrie & Co, Ltd; Pres, Balfour Chemicals, Inc; Pvt 18, SATC
Tighe, Richard Lodge	Law	
Wheeler, Alfred Newton	Finance	VP, Marine Midland Grace Trust Co of NY; Pvt 17-18, WWI

1924 — PERIOD 2, DECADE 122

NAME	OCCUPATION	NOTES
Allen, Henry Elisha	Education	Prof of Religion 47-70 , U MN; Pres 41-46 Keuka Coll; 30-41 Dpt Religon, Lafayette Coll; 24-26 The Hill Schl; Dir 46-47, National Planned Parenthood, NY,
Appel, George Frederick Baer	Law	Ptnr, Townsend, Elliott & Munson (Philadelphia, PA); 44-45 Foreign Econ Admin; 42-44 Lend Lease Admin

Blair, Edwin Foster	Law	Ptnr, Hughes, Hubbard, Blair & Reed NYC; Dir, Union Bag & Paper, TD Jones & Co; Fellow 46-, Yale Corp; Chmn 42-44, Alumni Fund, Chmn 49-52, Alumni Bd, Yale U; Assoc Fellow 44-, Branford College, Yale U; many other charity and Yale football/club activities
Diller, John Cabot	Military	Assoc Dir 27-32, Bureau of Appointments; Capt 16-19, AUS Inf; Col 42-45, USAF
Ewing, Sherman	Law	Lawyer (NYC)
Haines, Thomas F. David	Industry	Pres, Ciba Pharmaceuticals Products, Inc
Heffelfinger, George Wright Peavey	Business	Exec VP, FH Peavey & Co (MN); Pres, Russell Miller Milling Co; Lt Col, USAAF WWII
Hilles, Charles Dewey Jr.	Law	Spec Legal Advisor 54-55, US High Commissioner for Germany; Dad was sec to Pres Taft
Houghton, Walter Edwards	Education, Literary	Prof of English emeritus, Editor, The Wellesley Index to Victorian Periodicals, Prof 48-68, Assoc Prof 42-48 Asst Prof 35-41, Tutor ,Wellesley College (MA); Tutor instr 31-35, Harvard Radcliffe; Master 27-29, Phillips Academy 27-29; Master 24-25, The Hill School
Lusk, William Thompson	Business	Dir 30-, Pres 55-67, Exec VP 52-55, VP 32-52 Tiffaney & Co (NY); Trustee 43-56, Pres 46-48, VP 44-46, New Canaan Country School
Mallory, William Neely	Industrial	Dir 37-45, Treas 38-45, Southwestern College; Maj, USA AF WWII
McCallum, Revell	Industrial	Chmn Propper-McCallum Hosiery; VP, Clausner Hosiery Co; Asst Dir, Rockefeller Memorial Hosp
Melton, William Davis Jr.	Law	Asst Gen Counsel, Duke Power Co (Charlotte, NC)
Spofford, Charles Merville	Law	Ptnr w/Davis, Polk & Wardwell (NYC); Instr 24-25, Yale; assoc 28-30, Isham, Lincoln & Beal (Chicago); Trustees, Carnegie Corp, NY, Mutual Life Ins Co (NY); Dir, CFR; Dirs Distillers Co, Ltd, Mutual Life Ins Co of NY, CIBA Corp, Uniroyal, Inc; Dir Metropolitan Opera Assn; Trustee, Juilliard Musical Found; Dir, Atlantic Council of US Inc; Lt Col to Brigadier Gen 42-44; Staff Officer in Mediterranean, ETO 42-45; US Deputy Rep, North Atlantic Council (perm Rep) w/rank ambassador 50-52
Thomson, Clifton Samuel	Law	Mining; Ptnr 34-, Appleto, Rice & Perrin; Gen Counsel, Dir 46-64, CIBA Corp; Mayor 40-47, (Sands Point NY)

1925 — PERIOD 2, DECADE 123

NAME	OCCUPATION	NOTES
Ardrey, Rushton Leigh	Finance	Sr VP. Republic Natl Bank (Dallas); VP, Treas, American Liberty Oil, Co; Asst Treas, Guaranty Trust; Asst VP, Bank of Manhattan
Ashburn, Frank Davis	Education	Chmn 60-62 , Coll Entrance Exam Bd; Mbr1947-54 Yale Univ Council; 53-55 Natl Council Ind Schls, Chmn; Headmaster-Brooks School; Trustee Brooks, Winsor & Miss Porter's, Brockwood Seminary
Bench, Edward Cajetan	Finance	Gen Ptnr 47-60, Clark, Dodge & Co; VP31-47, Bank of NY; Spec Asst to Asst Sec of Navy for Air, Capt 42-45, USNR
Bissell, William Truesdale	Writing	Hartford Ntl Bank & Trust; Hartford Fire Ins Co; NY Herald Tribune, Newsweek, Harper & Bros; Staff 43-45, Office of Lend-Lease Admin, DC; Chief India-SE Asia Foreign Economic Admin
Blair, James Grant	Industrial	Pres, Hopi-Grants-Pinon-Shiprock Oil Companies
Gage, Charles Stafford	Education	Treas 54-65, Yale Univ; Mbr, 25-54, ER Squibb & Son, Mathiesson Chem Co; Dir 61-74, United Illuminating Co; Dir 61-69, Union-New Haven Trust Co; 41-44, US Lend Lease Admin; Trustee 50-76, Phillips Academy; Gov 65, Mbr 50-65, Yale Athletic Bd; Mbr 52, Alumni Bd
Ives, Gerard Merrick	Finance	Sr VP, Morgan Guaranty Trust Co (NYC); Lt Col 42-45, Chief of Ordnance
Jones, Walter Clyde	Law	Gen Solicitor IL Bell Telephone Co
Lovejoy, Winslow Meston	Law	Ptnr Lovejoy, Wasson, Lundgren & Ashton (NYC); Pres 55-58, Yale Football Y Assn; Maj 42-46, AUS; Pres, RTA
Lufkin, Elgood Moulton	Finance	Deputy Dist Chief, Acting Dist Chief 41-45, NY Ordnance Dist; Mbr, Advisory Bd NY, Ordnance Dists
Luman, Richard John	Government	Deputy State Treas 59-63, WY; Mbr 53-59, Chmn 63-, WY Public Service Comm (Cheyenne); WY State Senate 45-49; Speaker 43-45, Rep 37-45, WY State Legislature
Norton, William Bunnell	Education	Prof Emeritus History, Teacher, Overseas Grad in Intrnl Relations, Boston U
Scott, Henry Clarkson	Business	Asst Proj Mgr, Dorado Beach Development, Inc, Dorado beach Puerto Rico; Gen Mgr 60-67, Pan Am Hotel Development; VP 55-60, West Indies Sugar Co; Pres 54, Caldwell & Scott, Inc; VP 38-55, Iglehart, Caldwell & Scott, Inc; Asst Supt 25-38, Thompson-Starret Const Co

Stevens, Marvin Allen	Medicine	Orthopedic Surgeon; Head Football Coach 34-41, NYU; Teaching Fellow 34-36, NYC Hosp for Special Surgery; Asst Prof 36-47, Yale Med School; Mbr Exec Comm Ntl Football and Hall of Fame; Cmdr 42-45, USN
Stevenson, Donald Day	Forestry	Chief Forester 52-68, Buckeye Cellulose Corp (Perry FL); Division Forester 45-52, Champion Papers (Canton NC); Prof 35-45, Forestry PA State; Instr, 30-33 Lingnan U (China)

1926 — PERIOD 2, DECADE 124

NAME	OCCUPATION	NOTES
Allen, Daniel	Insurance	Mayor 58-60, Larksburg; Cty Council, 56-63
Bronson, James Davis	Industrial	Dir, Pres, Boise Cascade; Pres, Prosser Orchard, Inc (Yakima); Consolodated Lumber Co; Pres 58-59, Western Pine Assoc; Pres 62-65, American Forest Ind
Coke, Henry Cornice Jr.	Law	Ptnr Coke & Coke; Major 1942-45, USAF
Crosby, Henry Stetson	Engineering	Maj, USAAF WWII
Cutler, Benjamin Crawford	Music	Owner, Ben Cutler Orchestras; Pres 63-68, Ntl Assn Orchestra Leaders
Davenport, John	Journalism	Editor 49-54, *Barron's* Magazine; Bd Editors, Asst Managing Editor, Staff 37-49, *Fortune* Magazine; 48, Hoover Plan
Ferguson, Alfred L. Jr	Finance	Investment Banker; Lt Col 42-46, Army Air Force
Hoysradt, John McArthur	Theatre	Star, NBC *Gimme A Break* John Hoyt; Actor, Writer, Director; Pres Theatre 40 Group, 75 Movies, *Spartacus, Blackboard Jungle, Cleopatra*, original doctor in *Star Trek* TV series, Mbr, Orson Welles's Mercury Theatre
Kingsbury, Howard Thayer	Education	Dean 54-69, Head 30-41, Math Dept Brooks School; Lt Col 41-46, Army
Lord, Oswald Bates	Industrial	Exec VP, Pres, Dir 1923- , Galey & Lord, Div Burlington Ind; Dir 37-, Aberfoyle Inc, Norfolk; Pres 41-51, Judson Health Ctr (NYC); Married Mary Pillsbury of the Minnesota based Pillsbury Flour Corporation.
Michel, Anthony Lee	Law	Counsel, Gardner, Carton, Douglas, Chilgren & Waud (Chicago)
Poore, Charles Graydon	Literary	Writer; formerly Book Critic New York *Times*, Chief Book Critic *Harper's* Magazine in 50's; retired to write; Mbr Yale U Council & Publications Comm; Major 42-45, GSC US Army
Root, Reginald Dean	Education	Dir Financial Aid, Dir Personnel, Dean of Men, 53-72, U WA; Coach Football 48-52, U WA; Coach 29-48, Football & Lacrosse, Yale;
Russell, Frank Ford	Industry	Chmn Bd 50-67, Pres 44, Dir 37, Sec 32, VP 29, National Aviation Corp; Gen Mgr 43-44, Ntnl Aircraft Production Council; Salesman 28, Guaranty Co of NY; Dirs, Chase Manhattan Bank, Otis Elevator, Worthington Corp, Cerro de Pasco Corp, NYC, Lockheed Aircraft Corp, South American Development Co, Union Sulphur Co
Willard, Charles Hastings	Law	Lawyer, Davis, Polk & Wardwell (NYC): Mbr, Investment Council,

1927 — PERIOD 2, DECADE 125

NAME	OCCUPATION	NOTES
Bunnell, Phil W.	Finance	Investments, Harris Upham & Co; Major 41-45 ASF
Look, Allen MacMartin	Law	Mbr 69-, Martha's Vineyard & Nantucket Steamship Authority; VP Wellington Sears Co (NYC)
McIntosh, Harris	Industrial	Pres, Toledo Scale, Co
Noble, Lawrence Mason	Education	Dir, Recruitment & Scholarships 67 -70 , United World Colleges (NYC); Lawyer 30-32, Simpson, Thacher & Bartlett (NYC); Faculty 32-66, Groton School; Varsity Hockey Coach 28-30, JV Footbal Coach 28-30, Yale U
Patterson, Thomas Cleveland	Literary	
Post, Russell Lee	Law	Lt Col, USAAF WWII
Ritchie, Wallace Parks	Medicine	Clinical Prof Neurosurgery, U MN; Major 41-45, Med Corp Army
Robbins, William Wells	Law	Lend-Lease Adminis 43, (Cairo)
Robinson, Frederick Flower	Industrial	Chmn Bd, National Aviation Corp (NYC); Asst Adminis 37-, Ntl Unemployment Census; Deputy Adminis 33-34, Ntl Recovery Adminis
Stokes, Anson Phelps Jr.	Ministry	Bishop 56-70, Episcopal Diocese MA; Asst/Rector St Mark's Church (Shreveport, LA), Rector Trinity Church (Columbus OH); Canon 45-50, St Andrews Cathedral (Honolulu); Rector St Batholomews Church (NYC)
Wadsworth, James Jeremiah	Government	Mbr 65-69, Fed Communications Comm (FCC); US Ambassador on assignment 62-65; US Rep 60-61, UN; US Rep 60-61, UN; Deputy US Rep 53-60, UN; Acting Adminis 52-53, FCDA; Deputy Adminis 50-52, Fed Civil Defense 50-52; Asst to Administrator 48-50 Econ Co-operation Adminis; Div Dir 45-46, War Asst Adminis; Mbr 31-41, NY State Assembly
Walker, George Herbert Jr.	Finance	Sr Managing Ptnr, GH Walker & Co (NYC); Gov, Assn of Stock Exchange Firms; Mbr 54-60, Yale Corp; Exec Comm of Bd, Yale Dev; Treas, RTA; Co-founder of the NY Mets; Major, USAAF WWII

Wardwell, Edward Rogers	Law	Ptnr, Davis, Polk & Wardwell (NYC); Lt Col, US Army Air Force
Warren, John Davock	Finance	Ptnr, GH Walker & Co (NYC)
Watson, Charles III	Education	Pres 37-48, Dry-Pack Corp; Ptnr 27-37, Cassatt & Co

1928 — PERIOD 2, DECADE 126

NAME	OCCUPATION	NOTES
Bartholomew, Dana Treat	Finance	CFO, Exec VP, Dir 38-70, Alcan Aluminium Ltd, Montreal; United Aircraft; Trust Bd, Citibank, 1st National Bank of NY; Asst VP 29-38, Tricontinental Corp (NY); Dir Scovil Mfg; 2nd Lt 42-44, Reserve Army of Canada
Berger, Jr., George Bart	Finance	Cmndr USNR WWII
Bingham, Charles Tiffany	Medicine	Assoc Attending Physician 49-60, Hartford Hosp, other medical pstns, many about alcholism; Clinical Instr 48-49, Medicine, Yale Medical Schl; Cmdr 43-46, (MC) USN
Fishwick, Dwight Brown	Medicine	Lt Col, Medical Corps WWII
Griggs, Herbert Stanton Jr.	Industrial	Lt Cmndr, USNR WWI
Haight, George Winthrop	Law	Lawyer, Decker, Hubbard & Welden, (NY); Lawyer of Counsel, Forsyth, Decker & Murray
Ives, Chauncey Bradley	Education	Asst Prof 60-70 Assoc Prof 70- Rutgers U; Assoc Prof 57-60, Guilford College NC; Major, Am Field Service 41-4; Civilian, OSS 45-46
Lapham, Raymond White	Business	Capt, AUS
Mallory, Barton Lee Jr	Business	Chmn Bd, Pres, Memphis Compress & Storage Co
Prentice, John Rockefeller	Business, Law	Owner 41-67, American Breeders Service, Inc Chicago; Law 31-41; Major 41-46, FA
Robertson, Arthur Clendenium	Literary	Inst 30-32, History, Yale U; Maj 42-46, Inf
Ross, Lanny Lancelot Patrick	Music	Singer, Actor; Major 43-46, Army
Scott, Stewart Patterson	Finance	Installment Credit Banking, Denver United States Ntl Bank; 1st Lt, USAAF WWII
Stewart, Peter Hellwege	Finance	
Walker, Stoughton	Business	Industrial Consultant; Dir, Fifth Ave Assn (NY); Lt Col, Ordnance Dept, Gen Staff Corps WWII

1929 — PERIOD 2, DECADE 127

NAME	OCCUPATION	NOTES
Ashforth, Albert Blackhurst	Business	Lt Cmnr USNR WWII
Costikyan, Granger Kent	Finance	Ptnr Brown Brothers Harriman, (NY); Sr VP 62-69, First Bank System, (Minneapolis, MN); VP 59-62, Chemical Bank; 29-59, NY Trust Co
Crile, George Jr	Medicine	General Surgery, Cleveland Clinc; Cmdr 42-46, USN
Decker, Edmund Lockwood Jr	Industrial	
Dodge, Washington	Finance	Broker, VP, Clark, Dodge & Co, Inc, (NYC); Mbr 41-44, NY Stock Exchange; Roberts & Co; Financial Editor, *Time*; editorial assignments, *Fortune*; Ptnr 37, Arthur Wiesenberger & Co; Public Relations 33-37, Barret & Co; Dir, AG Spaulding & Bros, Inc
Eddy, Maxon Hunter	Education Medicine	Prof of Surgery Haile Slassie U, Public Health College, Condar Ethiopia; Surgeon, Nepal; Sr Attend Surgeon, Chief General Surgery, Bridgeport Hosp; Consulting Surgeon, Milford Hosp; Lt Cmdr 43-46, MC USNR
Garvey, John Joseph	Industrial	
Gillespie, Kenrick Samson	Finance	Ptnr in Charge of Correspondent Services, Loeb, Rhoades & Co (NYC)
Grove, Manasses Jacob	Finance	Investment Analyst 57-70, U TX; VP 45-55, Mercantile-Safe Deposit & Trust Co, (Baltimore); Tech Sgt 41-42, AUS; Cmndr 42-45, USNR
Manville, Hiram Edward Jr.	Industrial	Dir, Johns-Manville Corp; Trustee, Hiram Edward Manville Foundation
Merrill, Henry Riddle	Industrial	VP, Norton Co (Troy NY)
Paine, Ralph Delahaye Jr.	Literary	VP 64-67, R&D Time, Inc; Publisher 52-64, Managing Editor 41-52, *Fortune*; War Correspondent 45, Pacific; Managing Dir 39-40, March of Time, Ltd London, in charge of all *Time* Mag European Operations, Editorial Asst to Pres, Time Inc 38-39, Business Editor 33-38, 31, w/*Time* Mag; Securities Analyst 29-31, Edward B Smith & Co (NYC); 2nd Lt 29-34, ROC;
Smith, Lloyd Hilton	Industrial	Oil Gas Production, Investments; Pres, Parafinne Oil corp; Dirs, First Ntl Bank Houston, Ntnl Review, Curtiss-Wright Corp, Information Storage Systems, Falcon Seaboard Corp, Kinetics International Corp; Adv Dir 56-70, First City National Bank Houston ; Lt Cmndr 42-45, USNR
Wack, Damon deBlois	Finance	

Wells, George	Business	Exec VP, Sexton Can Co (Everett MA); Treas, Richards, Sexton & Wells, Inc; Town Clerk (Lincoln MA); Trustees, DeCordova Museum; Concord Academy, Middlesex Institution for Savings; Phillips Exter Academy

1930 — PERIOD 2, DECADE 128

NAME	OCCUPATION	NOTES
Allison, Robert Seaman Jr.	Business	Sec, Treas Colorizer Associates; Utah art community
Ellis, Harland Montgomery	Industrial	Mbr, Yale Alumni Bd
Ellis, Raymond Walleser	Law	Ptnr, Choate, Hall & Stewart; Lt 43-46, USN
Erskine, Albert DeW. Jr	X	
Garnsey, Walter Wood	Business	Pres, Stokes Canning Co
Greene, Waldo Wittenmyer	Farming	Citrus grower; Lt Cmndr 42-46, Naval Aviation
Gwin, Samuel Lawrence	Law	Ptnr, Choate, Hall & Stewart (Boston); Major 42-45, USAAF
Hall, Robert Andrew	Law, Theatre	VP, Dir, Ntl Footbal Foundation & Hall of Fame; Staff 42-45, Office of Pres of US, Lend-Lease Admin, Australia, Spec Deputy, State Dept
Janeway, Charles Anderson	Medicine	Prof, Pediatrics Harvard U Med School; Physician-in-chief Children's Hosp Med Ctr (Boston); Pres 71, Am Pediatric Society; Pres 54-65, Iran Foundation, Inc, lots of other councils and society
Ladd, Louis Williams Jr.	Medicine	Physician, internal Medicine; Asst Prof 55-70, Medicine Western Reserve U; Capt 42-46, MC AUS
Longstreth, George Brown	Finance	Exec VP, Peoples Savings Bank (Bridgeport, CT); Trustee, Treas 60- , Fairfield Country Day School
Look, Frank Byron	Transportation	Gen Mgr, New Bedford, Woods Hole, Martha's Vineyard & Nantucket Steamship Authority (MA); Lt Cmndr 41-47, USNR
Musser, John Miller	Business	Dir, Exec Comm, Weyerhauser Co (St Paul); Dirs 1st Ntl Bank of St Paul, St Paul Insurance Cos, Aspen Inst Humanistic Studies, Weil-McLain Inc, Intrnl Time-Sharing, Inc; Chmn Bd 58-61, Trustee 47-, Carleton College; Pres 65-, VP 64-65, Yale U Council
Palmer, Arthur Edward	Law	Environmental Lawyer American reading Council, NYC; Mbr 65-68, John Lindsay's Cabinet; Ptnr 60-65, White, Weld & Co; Ptnr 47-60, Assoc 35-47, Winthrop, Stimson, Putnam & Roberts; Dir RTA
Prideaux, Tom	Writer	

1931 — PERIOD 2, DECADE 129

NAME	OCCUPATION	NOTES
Austen, David Edward	Law	
Donnelley, Gaylord	Industrial	Chmn Exec Com, RR Donnelley & Sons Company, (IL); Dir 61- Dun & Bradstreet, Inc, 46- Reuben H Donnelley Corp, 66-75 Borg Warner, 65-73 1st Natl Bank of Chicago, 1st Chicago Corp; Trustee 65-73, Chmn Bd U of Chicago; Trustee, Sarah Lawerence; Mbr 53-59, Yale U Council; Gov, Yale U Press, 64-71 Yale Dev Bd; Lt Cmmndr 42-45, USNR Air Group, IX USS Essex
Heinz, Henry John II	Business	Chmn Bd HJ Heinz Co PA Pittsburgh; Chmn Bd 59-, Pres 41-59, HJ Heinz; Dirs 41, Mellon Ntl Bank & Trust Co, 69, Overseas Development Council; Trustees 41-, Carnegie Inst, 59- Carnegie-Mellon U, Com for Econ Dev; Trustee 47, Chmn 47-51, International Chamber of Commerce; Advisor 57, Am Delegation GATT; Chmn 58-59, US Delegation, Geneva ECE
Lapham, Lewis Abbot	Finance	Dir, Pres 68-74, Chmn of Exec Comm 59-66, VChmn 66-74, Bankers Trust Co; Pres 57-59, Comm of Am Steamship Lines; VP, Dir 70- , Assn of Registered Bank Holding Companies; Pres 70, NY State Bankers Assn; Pres 53-59, Grace Line, Inc; Pres 47-53, American-Hawaiian Steamship Co; Dirs, Medusa Corp. Tri-Continental Corp, HJ Heinz Co, Macmillan Inc, Ntnl Assn Bd, Smithsonian, Celanese Corp of America, Mobil Oil Corp, Chubb Corp, Crane Co, Barber Oil Co, North American Phillips Corp, Newport News Shipbuilding & Drydock Co; Mbr Supervising Bd of NV Phillips, The Netherlands; Exec Asst to 41-45, Commanding General, SF Point of Embarkation; Sec 30-31, RTA; son served as General counsel 73-79, CIA (Anthony A '56)
Loeser, Frederic William	Industrial	Pres, Ecology, Inc (NH); NH Buick Co, Fred L Loeser & Son; Dir 38-, New Haven Boy's Club; 1st Lt 52-55 USMC
Lydgate, William Anthony	Business	Chmn, Earl Newsom & Co, Inc NY; Editor 35-, American Institute of Public Opinion (Gallop Poll); VP, Trustee, Yale-in-China Assn; Chmn 66- , Foreign Policy Assn; Public Relations; Writer 32-35, Time Mag; Author, What Our People Think
Messimer, Robert Laughlin Jr.	Business	Systems Mgr, Ward Howell Assoc, Inc, executive recruiting

Peltz, William Learned	Medicine	Prof Clinical Psychiatry, U PA Medical School; Fellow 40-42, Branford College, Yale; Med; Capt-Major, Army Med Corps, 39th Gen Hosp (Yale Unit), Pacific 42-45; Expert Civilian Consultant 51, Korean conflict 51
Rathborne, Joseph Cornelius	Industrial	Maj, USAAF WWII
Stewart, James Ross	Law	Ptnr, Arter & Hadden (Cleveland); Trustee Hathaway Brown School for Girls; Col 42-45, AUS, Gen Staff Corps
Sutherland, Richard Orlin	Education	Dept Chemical Engineering MO School of Mines & Metallurgy
Swoope, Walter Moore	Law	Ptnr, Bell, Silberblatt Swoope (Clearfield, PA); T/Sgt 43-45, Army
Tucker, Luther B.D.	Ministry	Pres, 69- Financial Management Inc, Minister, Indian Hill Church (Cincinnati); asst Christ Church (Cambridge, MA); Far East Sec 36-38, World Student Christian Fed; Trustee 36-59, Yale-in-China; Sec 38-40, Ntl Student Council, YMCA; related to Nick F Brady Y '99
Vincent, Francis Thomas	X	Southern New England Telephone Co (New Haven); CT Savings Bank (New Haven); son Fay Jr, Pres & CEO 81, Colombia Pictures Industries
Walker, John Mercer	Medicine, Finance	Lmtd Ptnr, Alex Brown & Sons (MD); Consultant, 78-82 Merrill Lynch; Consultant 74-78 White Weld; Ptnr, GH Walker & Co (NYC); Deputy Medical Dir, 51-58, Chmn Exec Comm, CEO 60-64, Memorial Sloan Kettering Hosp; Private Practice 50- Surgery; Dir Alumni Fund; Lt Col 42-46, MC US Army

1932 — PERIOD 2, DECADE 130

NAME	OCCUPATION	NOTES
Adams, Frederic Baldwin Jr.	Librarian	Dir Emeritus 48-69, Pierpoint Morgan Library (NY); Pres 59-71, Governing Brd 52-, Yale U Press; Mbr 64-71, Yale Corp; 49-58 Unvrsty Council
Barres, Herster D.	Ministry	Asst to Dir 48-51, Office of Civil Defense (DC); Chaplin 48-51, Hotchkiss Schl; 47-48 Asst Chaplin Yale; Dir 44-48, Natl Yale Alumni Placement Service; Vrsty End Football Coach 44, Yale; former headmaster; Dir 47-48, RTA
Bates, Emmert Warren	Publishing	Sr VP Litton Educational Publishing, Inc, NY; Mbr 34-37 Yale Alumni Bd
Fitch, George Hopper	Advertising	Dir, Distillers Co Ltd, Gordon's Gin Co; Bd, Yale U Art Gallery; Trustee 51, Am Federation of Arts; Dir, de Young Museum Society (SF); other Arts; Major 42-46, Army Air Force
Fulton, Robert Brank	Education	Prof Philosophy, Religion Parsons College (Fairfield IA); Teaching, Research 63-67, Western Reserve College (OH); Visiting Prof 62-63, Miles College (Brimingham, AL); Prof Chmn Dept of Philosophy, Religion 56-62, Inter-American U (Puerto Rico); 53-56 Lake Forest (IL); Chaplain, Prof Religion 51-53, Union College (Schenectady, NY); Lecturer 39-41, Yenching U (Peking); Teacher 33-35, 43-51 China, Hon Trustee 51, (Yale-in-China)
Gillespie, Samuel Hazard Jr.	Law	Of Counsel, Ptnr, Davis, Polk, Wardwell (NYC); US Attny 59-61 (So Dist of NY); Dir, Allis Chalmers Corp
Hodges, William VanDerveer Jr.	Law	Lawyer, Davis, Graham & Stubbs (CO); Lt Cmndr 42-45, USNR
Laundon, Mortimer Hamlin Jr.	Business	Pres, Bryant Equipment Corp; Mbr 67, Alumni Bd
Lindenberg, John Townsend	Literary Work	
McCrary, John Reagan Jr.	Business	Chmn, Texcomm, Inc (NYC); Tex McCary Inc (NYC)
Mills, James Paul	Finance	Dist Mgr 46-49, NYC Slick Airways; Investment Banking 33-41, Smith Barney; Dirs 41-46 Middleburg Ntl Bank, Allegheny Airlines; Trustee MC duPont Found; Dirs, Middleburg Bank; Hickory Tree Farm; Lt Col 41-46, Sr Pilot USAF
Ogden, Alfred	Law	Lawyer of Counsel 81-, Reboul, MacMurray, Hewitt, Maynard & Krostol, NYC; 79-80 w/Morgan, Lewis & Bockius; 76-78 w/Wickes, Riddell, Bloomer, Jacobi & McGuire; Ptnr 55-75, Alexander & Green (120 Bdwy, NYC) Ptnr 46-51 Blair & Ogden; Pres, Dir 52-54, C Tennant, Sons & Co (NY); 35-42 w/Dunnington, Bartholow & Miller, Shearman & Sterling & Wright, McCanliss & Early; Trustee, Finance Comm, Guggenheim Foundation; Col 42-46, US Army
O'Neill, Eugene Gladstone, Jr	Literary	
Savage, Boutelle Jr	Business	Chmn Bd Hanaford Bros Co (Portland, ME); Pres-Treas, TR Savage Co; Dir 55, Merrill Trust Co (Bangor); Trustee, Maine Central Inst
Williams, Samuel Goode	Transportation	Mgr, Pricing, Seaboard Coast Line RR Co (Jacksonville, FL)

1933 — PERIOD 2, DECADE 131

NAME	OCCUPATION	NOTES
Caldwell, Samuel Smith Jr.	Industrial	Chmn, CEO, VP, Gen Mgr, WR Willet Lumber Co; Sgt 43-45, US Army
Cooke, Francis Judd	Education	Lecturer music; 59-60 Assoc Prof Music Yale; 39-70 Teacher of Music, New England Conservatory; Music Business
Davis, Richard Marden	Law	Ptnr, Davis, Grahm & Stubbs, (Denver CO); Civilian Aide 52-54, Sec of Army; 60-62, Administrative Conference of US; Lt Col 42-45, USAF
Fletcher, Alexander Charles	Business	VP & Gen Sales Mgr, Four Roses Distillers Corp, (NYC); Lt 42-45, USN

Garnsey, William Smith	Business	Pres, Garnesy & Wheeler, Ford Dealer; Mortgage Loans & Capital Life Insurance Co; Mbr 67-75, CO State Senate; Lt Cmndr 42-45, USNR
Hall, Frederick Bagby Jr.	Industrial	Cmndr, USNR WWII
Jones, Theodore Stephen	Business	Prop, Theodore S Jones & Co (Ntl Placement Service for Designers); Consultant 68, Pathfinder Fund Latin America; Consultant, Columbia 59, Korea 59, AID; Exec Dir 48-59, Design in Industry, Boston Inst Cont Art; Dean 45-48, Hamilton College; Teacher 35-41, Pomfret school; Cmndr 42-45, USNR
Levering, Walter Barnum	Business	Ptnr 33-75, Carlisle De Coppet & Co (NYC); Dirs 58-, Oaklawn Foundation (NYC), 60- , Scott-Paine Marine Corp (Stamford), 69- , Wellington Computer Systems (NYC), 70- , Rolfite, Co (Stamford); Gov 60-62, 66-68, Assn of Stock Exchange Firms; Trustee 50-, Boys, Club (NYC); Trustee, The Hill School; Pres 67, 52-, Amsterdam House; Dir, RTA; Cmndr 42-45, USNR
Lindley, Frances Vinton	Business	
McGauley, John Michael	Insurance	Insurance Broker, New England Life (NYC); Major 42-46, Air Corps
Newton, James Quigg Jr.	Finance	Pres 63-75, The Commonwealth Fund (NYC); Pres 56-63, U CO; Dir Public Affairs, VP 55-56, Ford Found; Mayor 47-55 (Denver); Pres 46-47, Sec Bd Trustee 38-42, U Denver; Mbr 49-51, Yale U Council, Mbr 51-55, Yale Corp; Cmdr 42-46, USNR
Parker, Robert Boyd	Business	Asst to Chmn, Abex Corp (NYC)
Parsons, Henry McIlvaine	Science	Consultant Hummrro (VA); Exec Dir 74-79, Institute for Behavioral Research, Pres, Experimental College of IBR; VP Research 69-70, Riverside Research Inst; Pres 68-69, Human Factors Society; Sr Human Factors Scientist 58-64, System Development Corp; Society of Engineering Psychologists; Fellow Am Psychological Assn; Lt Cmdr 42-45, USNR
Stebbins, Hart Lyman	Ministry	Pres, Catholic United for Faith, Inc (New Rochelle, NY)
Wilbur, John Smith	Industrial	VP, Cleveland-Cliffs Iron Co (Cleveland); Capt 41-45, FA US Army

1934 — PERIOD 2, DECADE 132

NAME	OCCUPATION	NOTES
Bradford, Amory Howe	LLB	Mbr 75 -, US EPA; Mbr 73-74, Dept EPA CT; 51-52, NATO Secretariat, London; Grant Advisor 63-65, Ford Foundation; Asst to Publisher 47-54 Sec, 54-57, Dir 55-63, VP & Business Mgr 57-60, VP & General Manager 60-63, N.Y. *Times*; Attny 37-47, Davis, Polk, Wardwell, Gardiner & Reed, NYC; Married Carol Warburg Rothschild, div 1965
Cunningham, Hugh Terry	Government	Mbr 45-47, Central Intelligence Group; Director of Training 69-73, Mbr 47-73, CIA; Instructor history and literature 39-42, Harvard & Radcliffe; Rhodes Scholar; Major 42-46, AUS
Gordon, George Arthur	Literary	Editorial Dir, *Guidepost* 74-81; Staff Writer 65-74, *Reader's Digest*; Editor-in-Chief, *Cosmopolitan* 46-48; Managing Editor 39-41, *Good Housekeeping*; Lt Col 42-45, AAF
Hallett, John Folsom	Business	Pres, Concord Consultant, Inc, Boston MA; Pres Bio-Controls (SF, CA); Financial VP American Tool & Machine, Co Fitchburg, MA; Dir, Gum Products, Lion Research Corp; 69-70, International Management & Marketing Group Inc (Boston); Pres 66-69, Harbor National Bank (Boston); VP 49-62, Sr VP 62-65, First Ntl Bank (St Louis); Asst VP 47-49, Chemical Bank & Trust (NYC); Asst Treas 34-47, NY Trust Co; Representative 37-40, 46-48, 10 Dist Greenwich, CT Town Meeting; Dir 63-65, KETC (ST Louis); Lt Cmndr 42-46, Cmndr 54-, USNR,
Hambleton, Thomas Edward	Theatre	Managing Dir, Phoenix Theatre (NYC); VP, Theatre Inc; Yale U Council 55-60; Lt 42-46, Cmndr USNR
Harper, Harry Halsted Jr	Literary	Exec Editor, VP, Bd Dir, *Reader's Digest*, NY; Capt 42-46, USMC
Holmes, John Grier	Education	Pres, John Holmes Associates, Inc; Sec 52-57, Vassar College; Asst to Pres 48-52, Sarah Lawrence College
Jackson, John Herrick	Publishing	
Kilcullen, John MacHale	Transportation	Transportation Consultant; Europe Mgr 59-70, States Marine & Isthmanian Lines; Traffic Mngr 46-49, US Army Transportation Corps (Europe); Master 46-49, US Merchant Marine; Lt Cmndr 41-46, USN
Kimball, Walter Sugden	Medicine	Orthopedic Surgeon; Capt 44-47, MC
Mills, Edward Ensign	Publishing	Exec VP, David McKay Co, Inc (NYC); Gov 59-70, Yale Press
Morse, John Bolt	Art	Painter, Trustee, SF Art inst; Cmndr 41-45, USN
Nichols, Edward	Medicine	Physician; Major 42-45, MC US Army
Ranney, George Alfred	Industrial, Law	Bd Dir 54- , Sr VP 69-, Inland Steel Co (IL); Dir 67-, Harris Trust & Savings; Ptnr 51, Sidley & Austin 51; Trustee 51-, U Chicago ; Dir Chicago Urban League

Name	Occupation	Notes
Stetson, Eugene William Jr.	Business	Sr VP, Weiss, Vosin & Co, NYC; Asst Cashier 34-37, Citizens & Southern Ntl Bank; Asst Mgr 37-41, Brown Brothers Harriman & Co; VP 46-51, Adv Com 51-64, Chemical Bank; Ptnr 51-55, Stetson & Co; Chmn, Exec Comm 56-70, Winslow Cohu & Stetson, Inc; Pres, Fairhill Oil & Gas; Dirs, Scott Paine Marine corp, City Investment Co, Southeastern Compress Warehouse; Dir, Exec Comm 41-68. Canada Dry Corp; Dir 52-56, Yale & Towne Mfg, Inc; Lt Cmndr 41-46, USNR

1935 — PERIOD 2, DECADE 133

NAME	OCCUPATION	NOTES
Bowles, John Eliot	Finance	Officer, Chemical Bank; Bowery Savings Bank; Lt Comdr 42-46, USN
Collier, Samuel (Sam) Carnes	Business	Lt Cmdr USNR WWII
Curtin, Francis Clare	Education	Teacher, Needham High School; Lt 43-46, USNR
Fuller, Stanley Evert	Government	Administrator, County Juvenile Court; Chief Probation and Parole Officer (Erie County, PA)
Haas, Frederick Peter	Business, Law	VP, Gen Counsel, Dir, Ligget & Meyers, Inc (NYC); Assoc, Ptnr 38-65, Webster, Sheffield, Fleischmann, Hitchcock & Brookfield; Lt Cmndr 43-46, USN
Johnson, Joseph Hale	Business	Mgr Stamford area, Hartford Electric Light Co; Assoc Dir 58-75, State Ntnl Bank of CT; Dir 68-, Barnes Engineering Co; Trustee 68-, Citizens Savings Bank; lots civic; Lt Cmndr 42-46, USN
Kilborne, William Skinner	Business	Chmn 69-75, Harkil Corp (NYC); Spec Asst to 53-57, US Sec Commerce; 37-53 w/William Skinner & Sons; Comm 40-41, NY County
Pillsbury, John Sargent Jr.	Insurance	Chmn Bd 77-81, Chmn, CEO, Pres 56-77, Northwest Ntl Life Insurance Co (Minneapolis); 40-56 Ptnr, Faebre & Benson; 35-37, The Pillsbury Co; Chmn 67, Life Insurance Assn; Lt Cmdr 42-45, USN Air Combat Intelligence Officer
Rodd, Thomas	Finance	VChmn, Dir, VP, Morgan Guaranty Trust Co (NYC); Maj 42-45, USMCR
Seymour, Charles Jr.	Education	Prof History of Art, Curator Italian Art Yale U; Curator 39-42, 46-49, Ntl Gallery Art; 42-45 w/War Dept; Pres, RTA
Shepard, Roger Bulkley Jr.	Insurance	Sr VP, St Paul Fire & Marine Insurance Co (MN); Lt Cmdr 42-45, USN
Spitzer, Lyman B. Jr.	Education	Prof Astronomy, Chmn, Astrophysical Sciences Dept, Dir Observatory, Chmn, U Research Bd, Princeton U (NJ); Mbr, Yale U Council
Stillman, George Schley	Museum work	Sec, Museum of Modern Art (NYC); Lt Cmdr USNR WWII
Terry, Henry Porter Baldwin	Insurance	VP, Alexander & Alexander Inc (NYC); Lt Col 44-47, FA
Tufts, Bowen (Sonny) C.	Theatre	

1936 — PERIOD 2, DECADE 134

NAME	OCCUPATION	NOTES
Barr, Richard James Jr.	Art	
Bingham, Jonathan Brewster	Government	Mbr 1965-, Congress, 23rd Dist of NY; 61-64 Alt Rep to four UN General Assemblies, other UN positions; Sec 55-58, Governor, NY (Harriman); Ptnr, 39-41, 46-51, 53-54, 59-60 law practice, last, Goldwater & Flynn, NYC; Alumni Fellow 49-51, Yale Corporation; Exec comm 51-53, Yale Law Schl Assn; Head Alien Enemy Control Section 45, u/Braden, State Dept; Legal Advisor 41, Machinery Branch of the Price Division, DC; Military Intel Service 42, War Dept; Pvt to Capt 43-45, AUS
Cooke, Robert Barbour	Business	Asst to Dir Public Relations, Harry M Stevens, Inc, (NY); Dir Public Relations 61-67, F&M Brewing; Broadcaster 58-61, *CBS*; Sports Editor and Reporter 37-58, NY *Herald Tribune*; Lt 42-45, USAF
Davis, Horace Webber II	Finance	Dir, Treas 56, Farnham Neighborhood House, Inc; Bank of NY; Trust Officer, Union & New Haven Trust; Lt Cmndr USNR WWII
Gill, Brendan	Literary	Staff, *New Yorker* Magazine
Hall, Jesse Angell	Business	Sales, Lezius-Hiles, Co (OH): 45-47 Dresser Ind, (Cleveland; Teacher Math 41, Taft School; Major 42-46, FA
Hersey, John Richard	Literary	Author, writer, correspondent 40's, *Time/Life/New Yorker* (Russia, China); *A Bell for Adano, Into the Valley, Men on Bataan, Hiroshima*-author; Mbr 60-70, Yale University Council; Master 65-70, Pierson College, Yale U
Knapp, John Merrill	Education	Prof Emeritus, Dean, Woolworth Ctr, Princeton U; Intel School, DC 1942, Asst OP Officer Admiral TS Wilkinson; Lt Cmndr 42-46, USN Intelligence
Moore, Richard Anthony	Law	Ambassador 89-92, Ireland; Of Counsel 75-, Wilner & Scheiner (DC); 70-75, Government service; Pres Southwestern Cable TV Co; Pres 51-62, Times Mirror Broadcasting Co; Lawyer, Exec 46-51, *ABC*; Attny 42, Cravath, Swaine & Moore; 39-41 w/Breed, Abbot & Morgan; Founder, Ptnr TV Station, Tulsa; Dir 63-68, KCET; Spec Asst to 70, Attny Gen of US; Spec Counsel to 71-75, Pres of US; Capt 42-46, Army Air Corps, Spec Asst to Chief of Military Intelligence

Pillsbury, Edmund Pennington	Business	Pillsbury Mills (LA, CA), (Chicago), (Minneapolis); Flight Instr Army Cadets, WWII
Rankin, Bernard Courtney	Law	Consulting Ptnr, Dickinson, Wright, Moon, VanDusen & Freeman (MI); 43-47 w/Dickinson, Wright, Davis, McKean & Cudlip Detroit; 42 w/Sullivan & Cromwell (NYC); 42-43 w/Navy Dept (DC)
Shepard, Blake	Insurance	Pres, WA Lang Co (St Paul MN); 46- w/JC Griswold & Co, Inc (NYC); 38-43 w/WR Grace & Co (NYC); Lt 42-46, USNR
Train, Robert	Industrial	Pres Bibb Mfg Co (Macon GA); Lt Cmdr 41-45, USNR
Walker, Louis	Finance	VP, Tucker, Anthony, RL Day, Inc (CT); VP, White Weld, Inc; Managing Ptnr, GH Walker & Co (NYC, Hartford, CT); Sales Mgr, Dir, Western Newspaper Union Material; 43-44 w/Command AAF; Admin Officer 44-46, Psychological Warfare Div, SHEAF
Whitehead, Mather Kimbal	Business	VP, Treas, International Mining Corp (NYC); Harris Hall & Co (NY); Lt Cmdr 42-46, USN

1937 — PERIOD 2, DECADE 135

NAME	OCCUPATION	NOTES
Blake, Dexter B.	Medicine	Physician, Anesthesia, Morristown Memorial Hosp; Lt Cmdr 42-45, USN
Brooke, Frederic Hiester Jr.	Industrial	Dir of Planning, Intrnl Staff, Raytheon; Alumni Fund; Cmdr 41-4,6 USN
Burke, Charles Clinton Jr.	Finance	Sr VP, Fiduciary Trust Co of NY; 2nd Lt 43-46, US Army inf
Cross, Richard James	Medicine	1963 Dean of Faculty of Medicine U of Ghana; Prof of Medicine, Assoc Dean 1959-63, U of Pittsburgh Med Schl; Prof Medicine Rutgers Med School, New Brunswick NJ; Capt 42-46, MC AUS
Draper, Arthur Joy	Medicine	Capt, MC, USN, Commanding Officer US Naval Hosp Newport RI; many hosp and commands
Field, John Warner	Industrial	Pres, Mine Hill Consultants (CT); Pres CEO, Warnaco Inc (Bridgeport, CT); Dir, Insilco Corp, CT Ntl Bank, People Savings Bank, Speedo Holdings Ltd (Australia); Trustee 63-70, Colby College; War Correspondent, Time, Inc
Kelley, Lawrence Morgan	Education	
McLemore, John Briggs Jr.	Business	Sales Rep, TN Mirror Co; Attny 40-42, Curtis. Mallet, Prevost, Mosle (NY); Major 42-46, US Office of War Information
Miles, Richard Curtis	Business	Management Consultant, McKinsey & Co, Inc (NYC); Maj 42-46, USAF
Orrick, William Horsley Jr.	Law	US Dist Judge, Northern Dist of CA; Ptnr, Orrick, Herrington, Rowley & Sutcliffe, SF, CA; Asst Attny Gen 61-62, US, Civil Div, Anti-Trust Div 63-65; Deputy Under Sec 62-63, State for Admin; Capt 42-46, Army
Robinson, John Trumbull	Education	Teacher, Coach Watkinson School (Hartford); Lt 43-45, USN
Runnalls, John Felch B.		Theological Student; Maj, AUS Military Intelligence WWII
Stewart, Potter.	Government	Assoc Justice, 58-81 US Supreme Court; Judge 54-58, US Circuit Court of Appeals 6th Circuit, Mbr 50-54, Cincinnati City Council; Lt 42-45, USN
Stone, Louis Talcott Jr.	Law	Maj, AUS WWII, Military Intelligence, War Dept
Turner, Harold McLeod	Library Work	Lecturer, School of Library Service, Columbia U; Spec 42-46, US Coast Guard

1938 — PERIOD 2, DECADE 136

NAME	OCCUPATION	NOTES
Davenport, Bradfute Warwick	Law	Ptnr, Hunton, Williams, Gay, Powell & Gibson; Mbr 65-68, Alumni Bd; Lt Col 41-45, US Army
Dempsey, James Howard Jr.	Law	Ptnr, Squire, Sanders & Dempsey (Cleveland, OH); Mayor 52-58, (Huntington Valley, OH); Trustee, Cleveland Museum of Art; Lt Cmdr 41-45, USN
Dilworth, Joseph Richardson	Finance	Sr Financial Adviser 58-, Rockefeller Family & Assoc, (NYC); Dir, Chmn 58, Rockefeller Center; Dir 61- RH Macy, 58- Chase Manhattan Bank, 69-73, Diamond Shamrock Corp, 62- Chrysler Corp, 62- Selected Risk Investments, 59- International Basic Economy Corp, 67- Omega Fund, 66-69 Picklands Mather & Co, 50-66 Rockwell Standard Co, 56-59 Rockwell Spring & Axle Co; Buying Dept 46-51, Ptnr 52-58, Kuhn, Loeb & Co; 59- Fellow Yale Corporation; Staff 42-45, Cmdr in Chief Pacific Fleet USN
Dunham, Lawrence B. Jr.	Business	Sr Dir, Office of U Development, Yale U; Sec RTA; Lt USN WWII
Ecklund, John Edwin	Business	Treas 66-78, Yale U; Ptnr 51-66, Wiggin & Dana; Dir 66 Yale Hosp; Mbr 55-57 Alumni Bd; Pres, Dir, Sec 46-56, RTA; Lt 42-46, USNR
Fox, Joseph Carrere	Finance	VP, Kidder, Peabody & Co, Inc (NYC); Dir 61-65, Fiduciary Mutual Investment Co; Dir 67, Movie Star Inc; Mbr 68, Alumni Bd; Lt Cmdr 41-45, USN
Frank, Clinton E.	Advertising	Chmn, Bridlewood Corp; Chmn Exec Comm, Clinton E Frank, Inc (IL); Lt Col 41-45, USAF
Gordon, Edward McGuire	Finance	Lt Cmndr, USNR WWII

Hessberg, Albert II	Law	Ptnr, Poskanzer, Hessberg, Blumberg, Dolin & Muffson (Albany, NY); Trusts & Estates Sec 67, NY State Bar; Lt Cmndr 41-45, USNR
Schermerhorn, Amos E.	Finance	Stockbroker, White, Weld & Co (SF); Cmdr, USNR WWII
Stevens, Joseph Benson Jr.	Business	Chmn, CEO, Pres, Harry M Stevens, Inc (NYC); Lt Cmdr 40-45, USN
Thompson, John R.	Law	Lawyer Spec Asst Corp Counsel City NY 70-; Law Clerk Chief Justice fred Vinson US Supreme Court 47-48; Yale Law School Faculty 49-56; Asst Corp Counsel City NY 66-70,
Weed, George Haines	Business	Manufacturer's Rep, Duluth Filter Co (MN); Pres, WH Sweeney Paint Co; Pres, Lion Brand Paint Div. Valspar Corp (Minneapolis, MN); Cmdr 41-47, USNR
Whitman, Francis Slingluff Jr.	Journalism	Assoc Adv Dir, The Sunpapers (Baltimore); Pres 52-56, Baltimore Symphony; Major 41-46, Army
Wilbur, Richard Emery	Journalism	Journalist, Business Editor, Tuscon *Daily Citizen*, Tuscon; T/3 42-46, Army

1939 — PERIOD 2, DECADE 137

NAME	OCCUPATION	NOTES
Belin, Gaspard d'Andelot	Law	Ptrnr Choate, Hall & Stewart; General Counsel 62-65, US Treasury Dept; Vice-Chmn 60-, Yale Develpmnt Bd; Mbr 65-68 Yale Alumni Bd; Mbr 66- Yale Law Schl Alumni Exec Com; ; Dir 76-79, RTA; Capt 42-45, US Army
Blanchard Jerred Gurley	Law	Ptnr, Rickey, Shankman, Blanchard, Agee & Harpster; Ptnr Laskey, Dudley & Blanchard; 1968-72 Memphis City Council; 41-46, 51-53 Col Army Air Force
Bundy, William Putman	Writing	64-69, Asst Sec State for Far Eastern Affairs; 63-64, Asst Sec; 61-63, Deputy Asst Sec of Defense for International Security Affairs; Senior Research Assoc, MIT; Staff Dir 60, Pres Com on Ntl Goals; 51-61 Bd of Ntl estimates, CIA; 47-51 Covington & Burling; Mbr 61-, Yale Corp; Major 41-46, Army Signal Corps; OSS (WWII)
Chittenden, George Hastings	Finance	Bank Consultant, Arthur D Little, Inc, (NYC); SR VP 65-76, International Banking Div, Morgan Guaranty Trust; Dir, Morgan Guaranty International Finance Corp, JP Morgan of Canada, Ltd; Pres 57-59, Forex Club; Chmn 60-61, Rye United Fund; Pres 62-63, Bankers Assn for Foreign Trade; Trustee 65-73, Vassar College; Dir RTA; 48- Yale Alumni Fund; Capt 42-46, USAF
Clucas, Lowell Melcher	Finance	Principle, Harlan & Clucas; Dir Corporate Communications 58-72, Crown Zellerbach; Dir 72-, CA Life Corp, 60-72 KQED-TV; 52-54 US Public Affairs, (Bavaria); 42-45 Office of War Information
Dyess, Arthur Delma Jr.	Law	Retired Assoc Justice, Court of Appeals, Houston; Ptnr 71-78, Foreman, Dyess, Prewett, Rosenberg & Henderson; 62-71, Prewett & Henderson; Lecturer on Law 53-70, Rice U; Mbr 56-58, Alumni Bd; Lt 42-45, USN
Gile, Clement Dexter	Finance	VP, Morgan Guaranty Trust Co (NYC); Lt Cmndr 40-45, USN
Hoxton, Archibald Robinson Jr.	Education	Headmaster 67-81, Episcopal High School (Alexandria); 53-67, Green Vale Sch; Hdmstr 50-53, Fairfield County Day Sch; 45-50, w/Episcopal HS; 39-41, w/Hotchkiss Sch; Lt Cmndr 41-45, USN
Kellogg, William Welch	Science	Sr Meteorologist, Dir Lab Atmospheric Science, Assoc Dir Ntl Center for Atmospheric Research (NCAR), Boulder; Assoc Dir 64, NCAR; more science Bds, NASA, Dept Commerce; Head 51-64, Planetary Science Dept, Rand Corp; Res Assoc, Asst Prof 47-51, UCLA; Teaching Asst 40-41, U CA; Teacher 39-40, Brooks Sch; Capt 41-46, USAAF
Miller, Andrew Otterson	Law	Ptnr, White & Case; Dirs 50-56, Distillers Corp-Seagrams Ltd; 62-72, Nease Chemical Corp; 61-72, Lanvin-Charles of the Ritz, Inc; 64-74, Salant & Salant, Inc; 69-70, Argus, Inc; 60-62, Chicago Pnuematic Tool International; Major 42-46, USAF
Miller, Charles Lewis Jr.	Finance	VP, CT Bank & Trust, Co (Hartford); Mbr 66-70, Alumni Bd; 1st Lt 42-46, USAAF
Mitchell, Harry Hartwood	Business	Chmn Bd, CEO, CA Life Insurance Co & CA Life Corp (CA); Pres Vanguard intrnl (Oakland CA); Acting Chief Legal Advisor 1949, US Military Governor US Occupied Germany; Capt 43-46, US Army
Shepard, Lloyd Montgomery Jr.	Business	Pres, Berrien County Abstract & Title Co (St Joseph MI); Cmdr 41-46, USN
Wilhelmi, Frederick William Jr.	Business	Antique Dealer, The Eagle Eye
Williams, Burch	Finance	Sr VP, Blyth Eastman Dillon & Co, Inc (NY); Gen Ptnr, Eastman, Dillon, Union Securities & Co; Gen Ptnr 55-65, Reinholdt & Gardner (St Louis); VP 51-55, Murphy Oil Co; Major 41-45, USAAF

1940		PERIOD 2, DECADE 138
NAME	OCCUPATION	NOTES
Bundy, McGeorge	Finance	Scholar in Residence at the Carnegie Corporation; Chmn 90-93, Carnegie Corporation's committee on reducing nuclear danger; Pres 66-79, Ford Foundation; National Security Advisor 61-66, Kennedy and Johnson; Dean of Faculty Arts & Sciences 53-61, Prof 54, Assoc Prof 51, visiting lecturer 49, Harvard; Consultant 48, Econ Co-Op Admin; Analysis for Tom Dewey 48 campaign; Political analyst 48, CFR; Asst 46-48, Henry Stimson; Capt 42-46, US Army
Erickson, Thomas Franklin	Industrial	Ptnr, VP, Walters & Erickson Inc; Mbr 62-70, Bd Govenors, Chmn 65-68, Atlanta Mdse Mart; Bd Mbr 65-68, Natl Assn of Bedding Mfrs; Lt 42-45, Naval Air Corps
Glover, Charles Carroll III	Law	Ptnr, Wilmer, Cutler & Pickering; Dir 54, Eugene & Agnes Meyer Foundation; Trustee 57, American U, Mbr, Yale Development Corp; Dir 70, Riggs Ntl Bank; Military Intelligence 43-46, Office of Chief of staff, War Dept
Grayson, James Gordon	Finance	Sr Investment Officer, World Bank/International Finance Corp (DC); Lt Cmndr 42-46, USNR
Holden, Reuben Andrus	Education	Sec 53-71, Yale U; Assoc Sec 52-53; Asst to Pres 47-51, Asst to Dean 46-47, Yale College; Chmn Hazen Found 66- ;Trustees, Warren Wilson College (NC), Yale-in-China; Pres 65-68, Community Progress Inc; Lt Col 41-45, Inf US Army
Howe, Harold II	Education	VP 71-78, Education Ford Foundation (NYC);Harvard Graduate School Business; Program Advisor Educ Ford Found India 69-70 Dir 64-65, Learning Inst of NC; Supt Scarsdale Sch 60-64; High School Teacher, Principal 40-41, 47-50 50-60; History Teacher 47-50, Andover; Mbr 65, Pres Johnson's Task Force on Intrnl Educ; Trustee 58-66, Vassar College; Trustee 62-66, College Entrance Exams; Mbr 65-68, US Comm of Educ; Lt 42-46, USNR
Orrick, Andrew Downey	Law	Ptnr Orrick, Herrington, Rowley & Sutcliffe (SF, CA); Mbr SEC 55-60, SF Reg Admin 54-55, SEC; Dir Del Monte properties Co; United California Bank; Pres 66-, Trustee 63-69, Marin Country Day School; involved w/Monterey Inst Intrnl Studies; Capt 42-46, Army
Rodd, David Beckwith	X	
Stack, Jr., Joseph William	Business	Pres, William Stack Associates, Inc (NYC); Dir RTA; Lt Cmndr 40-45, USN
Stevens, Albert B.	Business	Sales Mgr, Lee Co (CT)
Stillman, Peter Gordon Bradley	Education	Hdmstr, Riverdale Country School (NY); Asst Headmaster, Dean of Faculty, Choate School (Wallingford CT); Capt 40-46, Army
Stucky, William McDowell	Journalism	Assoc Dir, American Press Institute, Columbia U (NYC); Lt Cmdr, USNR WWII
Swenson, Edward Francis Jr.	Finance	Owner/Mgr Investment Counselor, Edward F Swenson & Co (Miami FL); Trustee, Everglade School for Girls, U Miami ;Chmn Yale Development Bd; Capt 43-46, Army
Thorne, Peter Brinckerhoff	X	
Watson, Jr., William Berkley	Business	Chmn Bd, Pres, Chester Electronics Corp (Chester CT) subsidiary GTE Corp; Lt 42-46, USNR

1941		PERIOD 2, DECADE 139
NAME	OCCUPATION	NOTES
Cross, Walter Redmond Jr.	Finance	Pres Langeloth Foundation, (NYC); Sr VP 67-69, Morgan Guaranty Trust Co; Dir Ntnl Sugar Refining Co, 74- Amax, Inc, 70- Crompton Co, 73- NY *Times*, 75- Caramoor Inc; VP NY Trust; Mbr 52-64, Alumni Bd; Lt 43-46, USN
Devor, Donald S. Jr.	Advertising	Marketing, Citicorp Industrial Credit, Inc, (NY); VP, (Radio & TV) Wm Esty Co Inc; Lt 43-46, USN
Ellis, Franklin Henry Jr.	Medicine	Chief Cardiovascular Surgery, Lahey Clinic Foundation (Boston, MA); Harvard, Mayo Clinic; Yale Alumni Bd; Lt jg 46-48, USNR
Hall, Edward Tuck	Education	Owner, Hdmstr, 79- The Deck House, ME; Instructor 75-78, Bostwanna; Hdmstr 68-74, St Marks, School, Scouthboro MA; 52-68, The Hill School; 41-42, Phillips Andover Academy; 42-52, St Marks; 1st Lt 42-46, Infantry, Intelligence
Jackson, William Eldred	Law	Ptnr, Milbank, Tweed, Hadley & McCloy; Asst to US Chief Prosecutor, Nuremberg; Governor, St Albans School (DC); CFR; Lt, Office General Counsel, Navy Dept (DC)
Kiphuth, Delaney	Education	Dir Athletics 54-76, Yale U; Dir Athletics Hotchkiss School; Mbr 43-45, US Army

Madden, John Beckwith	Finance	Managing, Gen Ptnr Brown Brothers Harriman & Co, NYC; Pres, Bd Trustees, Packer Collegiate Inst; Trustee, Treas, Boys Club; Trustees Brooklyn Hosp, Brooklyn Savings Bank; Mngr Delaware & Hudson Co; Dirs, Delaware & Hudson Railroads Corp, Orama Securities, Merchant Sterling Corp; Treas, Dir RTA; Capt 41-46, US Army
Pickett, Lawrence Kimball	Medicine	Assoc Dean, 73-, Prof Surgery, Pediatrics, Dept Surgery, Yale U School Med; Mbr 64-68, Alumni Bd; Capt 51-53, MC US Army; Pres 70, RTA
Price, Charles Baird Jr.	Business	Chmn Bd, CEO, Booker-Price Co (KY); Pres, Wholesale Furniture Co (Louisville); Lt Col 41-46, FA
Solbert, Peter O.A.	Law	Ptnr Davis, Polk & Wardwell (NYC); Deputy Asst Sec 63-65, Defense ISA; Lt Cmndr 41-46, USN
Stevenson, Charles Porter	Industrial	Pres, Treas, Dir, Eastman Machine Co (Buffalo); Dir Ltd Eng; Dirs, Manufacturers & Traders Trust Co, Furnco Const, Millard Fillmore Hosp; Lt 42-45, USN
Thomas, Walton Dowdell	Medicine	Surgeon, Chmn Bd, Managing Ptnr, Milwaukee Medical Clinic; Assoc Clinical Prof Surgery, Med College WS, also Marquette; Lt Cmndr 44-45-53-55, USN
Tighe, Laurence Gotzian Jr.	Education	Pres 49-54 Bedford Org; English Teacher, Bedford-Rippowam School (Bedford NY); Sales 45-49, International Div, St Regis Paper Co; 1st 42-43, Lt Inf; Dir, RTA
White, Warren Benton	Industrial	Pres, Owner, Trend Petroleum, Inc OKC; Lt 41-45, USN
Zorthian, Barry	Business, Government	Sr VP, Gray & Co (DC); Pres, Washington/Baltimore Regional Assn; VP 75-79, *Time* Inc; Pres 69-74, *Time-Life* Broadcast Inc (NYC); Pres 63-64, American International Sch New Delhi; US Foreign Service Information Officer 64-68, Minister-Counselor for Information, US Mission to Vietnam, Saigon; Foreign Service Officer 61, US Information Agency; writer, editor, policy officer, program mgr 48-61, Voice of America; Senior News Writer 47-48, CBS; Reporter 46-47, New Haven Register; Col 42-46, USMCR

1942 — PERIOD 2, DECADE 140

NAME	OCCUPATION	NOTES
Aycrigg, William Anderson II	X	1st Lt, USMCR WWII
Bartholemy, Alan Edmund	Business	Pres, Bartholemy Assoc; VP, Gen Mgr, SPS, Inc; Exec Dir, 1960 Olmpic Winter Games; Major 42-46, USMC
Bell, William Tompkins	Business	VP, Administrator-Assoc Sec, National Geographic Society, DC; Bd Mbr Washington Hosp; Yale Alumni Fund; Lt Cmndr 42-46, USN
Chouteau, Rene Auguste	Student	1st Lt, USMC, Aviation, WWII
Ford, William	Law	Ptnr, Becket, Ford, Dooley & Bearns, VT; Judge 54-70, Probate Dist of Salisbury; Mbr 55, Bd of Finance (Salisbury); Incorporator 58, CT Blue Cross
Grayson, Cary Travers, Jr.	Publishing	Pres, Potomac Books (DC); Mbr 58-60, Dept of State: Mbr 61-64 Peace Corps; Capt 42-46, USMC
Halsey, Ralph Wetmore Jr.	Finance	Ptnr, Halsey Assoc (CT); Dirs, Mory's, 62-72 Security Insurance, 55-65 Kaneb Services, 76- Tropical Gas Co, 76- CT Savings Bank, 76- Middlesex Insurance, 76- IXL Mfg, 76- Essex Engineering, 52-74 Hotchkiss School; Dir, Asst Treas RTA
Harrison, Fred Harold	Education	History Teacher, Athletic Dir, Phillips Academy, Andover; Mbr 1958- , Yale Alumni Comm on Admissions and scholarships; Pres Kennedy's Council on Youth Fitness 60-63; Mbr 59-61, MA Bd of USO; Pres & Dir Andover YMCA 61- ; Lt Col 42-46 ,Active Reserve 46-70, US Army
Jessup, John Baker	Law	Ptnr 59- , Assoc 48-58, Winthrop, Stimson, Putnam & Roberts (NYC); Lt 42-46, USNR
Kemp, Frank Alexander	Business	Mbr 66-70, CO State Senate; Mbr, 52-54, 62-66 Gen Assembly (CO); Livestock Feeder Farm; VP, Wilhelm Co, Denver; Ptnr 50-62, Etcheoare & Kemp; Mbr 68-70, Yale Alumni Bd; Capt 42-47, USMC
Kirchwey, George W.	Industrial	VP, WR Grace & Co, Overseas Chem Div (NYC)
Smith, Howard Freeman Jr.	Industrial	Pres, Lasalle Building Corp (Detroit); 1st Lt 42-46, USMC
Sprole, Frank Arnoit	Law	Vchmn Bd, VP, Gen Counsel, Bristol Myers Co (NYC); Dirs, 73- Xomox Corp, 50- The Knapp Fund; Lt 42-45, USNR
Walker, John Stanley	Law	Ptnr, Reavis, Pogue, Neal & Rose (DC); Comm Counsel 51-53, Joint Comm on Atomic Energy, US Senate and House; Experiment in International Living 61-; Dir 65, COSERV; 1st Lt 41-45, Army Air Force
White, William Gardiner	X	MIA; Lt, USNR WWII

1943 — PERIOD 2, DECADE 141

NAME	OCCUPATION	NOTES
Acheson, David Campion	Law	Ptnr Drinker, Biddle & Reath, DC; Ptnr 74-78, Jones, Day, Reavis & Pogue; VP & General Consel 67-74, Communications Satelite Corp; Spcl Asst 65-67, Sec Tres; US attorney 61-65, DC; Ptnr 58-61 Covington & Burling; Mbr Bd Regents, Chmn Exec Comm Smithsonian Inst; Dir, Comm on the Present Danger, Sundstrand Corp; Pres 77-80, Natl Cathedral Assn; Lt. 42-46 USNR

Caulkins, George Peck	Business	Pres, Caulkins Management, Pres, Caulkins Oil Co; Gnrl Partner, Caulkins Citrus Partnerships; Lt USN
Daniels, John Hancok	Industrial	Dir, Mbr Exec Com, Chmn Bd, Pres, CEO, Archer-Daniels-Midland Company; Chmn National City Bankcorporation, (Minneapolis, MN); Pres 70-93, Mulberry Resources, Inc; Civilian Aide 66-69, Sec Army
Doolittle, Duncan Hunter	Industrial	Pres 79-83, RI Energy Corp; VP, Gen Mgr 46-79, Machine Tool Div, Browne & Sharpe Mfg Co (N Kingston, RI) ; Capt 43-46, FA US Army; author, A Soldier's Hero, General Sir Archibald Hunter
Drain, Richard Dale	Government	Foundation Admin 73-76, Washington Cathedral; Mbr 51-73, CIA; 1967 w/Department of Army; Reserve Officer 57-67, Foreign Service; Special Asst 57, US Sec of State; Special Asst 55, US Pres; Assoc 48-51, Drain & Weaver; Lt Cmdr 43-45, US Army
Healy, Harold Harris Jr.	Law	Ptnr, Debevoise, Plimpton, Lyons & Gates (NYC); Resident Partner 63-66 (Paris); Exec Asst US Attny General 57-58; Treas 69- , Legal Aid Society (NY); Capt 43-46, FA Army
Hoagland, Donald Wright	Law	Ptnr, Davis, Graham & Stubbs (Denver); Asst Administrator 64-66, US AID; Pres 67- , CO Urban League; Consultant 67-, Govt of Indonesia & US AID; Assoc 48-51, Winthrop, Stimson, Putnam & Roberts (NYC); Lt 42-45, USN Air Corps
Klots, Allen Trafford Jr.	Publishing	Exec Editor, Dodd, Mead & Co; Dir, City Center of Music & Drama (NYC); Lt 43-45, USNR
Liley, Frank Walder Jr.	X	1st Lt, FA AUS WWII
MacLean, John Helm	X	1st Lt, Armored Force AUS WWII
Miller, Dudley Livingston	Law	Sr Ptnr, Miller, Montgomery & Spaulding (NYC, Tokyo, Taipei); Mayor 51-59 (Laurel Hollow NY); Sec, Dir, Boys Harbor, Inc; 2nd Lt, Med Admin AUS WWII
Moseley, Spencer Dumaresq	Finance	Pres, 67-69 Mangood; Pres 69-71, REA Express; Pres 62-67, Gatax Corp; 75 w/US Olympic Com; Dirs Archer Daniels Midland, Cherry-Burrel Corp; Container Corp Am; Yale Corp 66-72; Capt 42-44, 50-53, USMC
Stewart, Zeph	Education	Prof, Greek Latin, Master of Lowell House Harvard U; Trustee, Hotchkiss school; Capt 43-47, 51-53, AUS ; Dir, Pres, RTA
Tabor, John Kaye	Law	Sec 63-67, Commerce, Sec 67-68, Internal Affairs, Sec 68-69, Labor and Industry (PA); w/Reavis & McGrath (formerly Purcell & Nelson) (DC); 50-73, w/Kirkpatrick, Lockhart, Johnson & Hutcheson (Pittsburgh); Assoc, 50-53, Winthrop Stimson Putnam & Roberts; Lt 43-46, USNR
Vogt, Tom D.	Education	Rhodes School (NY)

1944 — PERIOD 2, DECADE 142

NAME	OCCUPATION	NOTES
Brown, Samuel T. Glover	Finance	VP 67- , Smith, Barney, Harris, Upham & Co, CO; Mbr 47-60, Dean Witter & Co; Mbr 60-67, Kidder, Peabody & Co; Lt 43-46, USN
Buckley, James Lane	Government/ Business	Pres, Radio Free Europe/Radio Liberty; Undersecretary of State for Security Assistance 81-82; US Senator 71-77, R-NY; VP 53-70, The Catawba Corp; Assoc 49-53, Wiggin & Dana, (CT); Lt jg 43-46, USN
Elebash, Shehand Daniel	Theatre,	Lt 43-45, USAAF
Ellis, Alexander Jr.	Insurance	Pres, Chmn, Fairfield & Ellis, Inc Boston MA; Commissioner 65-68, Commonwealth Service Corp; Dir, Ntl Assn Casualty & Surety Agents; GHW Bush's brother-in-law; Capt 43-46 AA
Ferguson, James Lord	Law	Ptnr, Gorsuch, Kirgis, Campbell, Walker & Grover (Denver, CO); Mbr 68, Alumni Bd; Lt 43-46, AUS
Goodenough, John Bannister	Science	Prof Inorganic Chemistry, Oxford (England); Research Physicists, Leader Electronics, Materials Group, Lincoln Lab, MIT (Lexington MA); Research Engineer 51-52, Westinghouse; Capt 43-48, USAAF
Grayson, William Cabell	Communications	Consultant 64, Smithsonian Institution; Program Mgr, Sales Rep 48-62, WRC-TV, WRC Radio
Holden, John Morgan	Education, Theatre	Prof, Dir of Theatre 66-, Portville College (CA); 60-62, w/Patrian Productions (LA); 52-55, w/Stumptown Theatre; 1st Lt 43-46, Army

Hoopes, Townsend Walter	Publishing	Pres, Assoc of American Publishers, Inc, DC; VP, Dir Cresap, McCormick & Paget Inc, Intrnl Management Consultant; Under Sec 67-69, Air Force; Principal Deputy Asst Sec 66-67, Defense for Intrnl Security Affairs; Deputy Asst Sec 65-66, Defense/ISA Near east-South Asia; Ptnr 58-64, Cresao, McCormick & Paget; Sec 57-58, Military Panel, Rockefeller Bros Fund, Spec Studies project; Assoc 55-57, JH Whitney & Co; Consultant 54, White House on Organization of NSC; Consultant 54, State, Defense on overseas military bases; Asst to Pres 53-55, Spencer Chemical Co; Asst to 48-53, Sec Defense; DC Editorial Writer 47-48, Buffalo Evening News; Asst to Chmn 47-48, Comm on Armed Services, House of Rep; Mbr CFR; Lt 43-46, USMC
Kelley, William Cody II	Law	Ptnr, Brooks, Kelly & Barroni; Vice Mayor 57-59, Councilman 53-59, Cincinnati; Lt 43-46, FA
Lindsay, David Alexander	LLB	
Little, Stuart West	Literary	Writer; News Writer 54-58, NBC; former Theater news reporter NY *Herald Tribune*, monthly column *Saturday Review*; Treas, Trustee Am-Scandinavian Found; Dir Theater Dev Fund; Sgt 43-45, OSS
Walker, Jeffrey Pond	Education	Farmer; Trustee, Treas, Salisbury (CT) School, Marvelwood School (Cornwall, CT); Dir, Salisbury Bank & Trust; Lt 43-46, USNR
Whitmore, James Allen Jr.	Theatre	Actor
Witter, Dean Jr.	Finance	Ptnr, Exec VP, Dir, Mbr Exec Com, Dean Witter & Co (NYC); Lt 43-46, USNR

1945 — PERIOD 2, DECADE 143

NAME	OCCUPATION	NOTES
Allen, Archibald John Jr.	Writing	2nd Lt 43-45, AUS; Freelance writer
Blake, Gilman Dorr Jr.	Student	2nd Lt, USAAF WWII
Connick, Louis Jr.	Consulting	Coordinator 80-81, CT Senate Refugee Resettlements; Consultant to US and Foreign Governments on Third World Rural Development Proj; 79-80 International Inst of CT; 75-79, International Human Asst programs; 71-75 USAID; 62-71 Overseas Dir, Asia Foundation; 62-71 Overseas Dir, Asia Foundation; 61-62, U IL; 60-61 Fullbright Teacher, Burma; Teacher Hotchkiss School, 56-60 William Penn Charter School; Asst to Dir of Admissions 54-56, Yale U
Dale, Edwin Lyon Jr.	Journalism	Asst Dir Public Affairs, Office Management and Budget, (DC); Reporter 51-55, Worcester *Evening Gazette*; 51-55, NY *Herald Tribune*; 55-76, Washington Bureau, NY *Times*; Lt jg, USN
Davison, Endicott Peabody	Law	Ptnr, Winthrop, Stimson, Putnam & Roberts, (NYC); Yale Development Bd; Dir, RTA
Early, Hobart Evans	Law	Attny, Federal Reserve Bank of Atlanta
Elwell, Francis Bolton Jr.	Law	Asst District Attny 52-57 (NYC); Legal Adviser Defense Air Transportation Admin, US Dept Comm
Harman, Archer Jr.	Education	Hdmstr, St George's School Newport RI; Trustee St Andrew's Sch (RI); Dynamy Sch (MA);Lt 43-46, USNR
Lynch, Russell Vincent	Business	Owner, Managing Ptnr, RV Lynch & Co; Gen Ptnr, Lynch, Aberg & Co Dallas; Chmn Bds, Lane Wood Inc, Riata Oil & Gas Co, Inc, Lynch Locke Corp, RVL Operating Inc; Dir, Richardson Savings & Loan; Lt 43-45, US Naval Aviation
McElroy, Benjamin Thomas	Law	Ptnr, McElry & Boyd, White, McElroy & White (TX, Dallas); Legislative Asst 49-50, US Congressman TX; Asst Attny Gen 50-52, TX; Lt 43-46, USNR
McGaughey, Guy Ennis Jr.	Business	Proprietor, McGaughey Bldg (IL)
Moorhead, William Singer Jr.	Government	Mbr 58-80, US Congress; Ptnr 49-70, Moorehead & Knox; Asst City Solicitor 54-57 (Pittsburgh, PA); Lt 43-46, USN
Seaman, Irving Jr.	Finance	Sr Consultant 82-, Burson-Marsteller (IL); Pres, CEO, Sears Bank & Trust; Chmn Exec Com, CEO 61-76, National Boulevard Bank (Chicago); VP 47-61, Continental IL Ntl Bank & Trust Co; VP 68, Dir, Abbot Labs; Dirs, Am Chain & Cable Co, Wm Wrigley Jr Co, Pullman Co, Big Foods; Chmn, Better Business Bureau; Pres 66-69, Lake Forest Country Day School; Lt 44-46, USN
Spaulding, Josiah Augustus	Law	Attny, Ptnr Bingham, Dana & Gould (Boston); Pres, Bd Trustees, Shore Country Day School (Beverly MA); Trustee Pingree School (Hamilton MA); Dir, Boys Clubs (Boston); Capt 42-45, USMC
Sumner, William Sayre	Insurance	Managing Dir, VP Marsh & McLennan, Inc (Pittsburgh); Lt 43-46, USN

1945W — PERIOD 2, DECADE 144

NAME	OCCUPATION	NOTES
Brown, Walter Henderson	Finance	Ptnr, Brown Brothers, Harriman & Co

Carey, John	Law	Chmn 70-, Intrnl league for Rights of Man; Ptnr, Coudert Brothers, NY; Adjunct Asst Prof 66-, NYU Law Schl; Alt Mbr 66-, UN Subcomission on prevention of discrim and Protection of Minorities; Asst Dist Attny 52-54, (Philadelphia); Lt jg 43-46, USNR
Finney, J.John Warren	Journalism	News Editor, Reporter NY Times (DC Bureau); Ensign 43-46, USN
Holmes, George Burgwin	Government	Foreign Service Officer 72-80 Valletta, 68-71 London, 61-63 Yaounde, 54-57 Stockholm, 50-52 Brussells, US Embassy; Lt 43-46, USNR
Hurlbut, Gordon Buckland Jr.	Farming	Farmer, County Commissioner 68-72 (Leavenworth KS); Ensign USNR
Mallon, Thomas Ridgway	Business	Gen Mgr, Materials Div, Arundel Corp (Baltimore); Ensign 43-46, USNR
O'Brien, Phillip Jr.	Law	Attny; Army
Twichell, Charles Pratt	Education	VP Faculty, Head Classics Dept, Choate School (Wallingford, CT); Lt 43-46, USNR
Vose, Elliot Evans	Law	Sr VP, Aerospace Marketing, Grumman International, Inc (NY); Dir 67-69, VP 67-68, VP Latin American Div 61-67, Asst to Pres, Singer Co 55-61, Singer Co (NYC); Assoc 50-55, Winthrop, Stimson, Putnam & Roberts (NYC); Lt 43-46, USNR
Warren, George Upson	Education	Dean Admission, RI School of Design (Providence); Chmn 64-66, History Dept Princeton Day School; Chmn Faculty 67, Simon's Rock College; 1st Lt 44-46, 51-52, USMCR

1947 — PERIOD 2, DECADE 145

NAME	OCCUPATION	NOTES
Alling, Charles Booth Jr.	Finance	Investment Banker; Managing Dir, Eastern Region, Spencer, Stuart & Assoc, NYC; SD Fuller & Co, Inc; Mbr, 47-72 Yale Alumni Fund; Founder Independent Party; Cpt 44-45 AF, DFC
Andrews, Edward W. Jr,	Business	Pres, RD Merrill Co; Controller Skinner Corp; Cprl 43-45 USA
Boulos (Bouliaratis), William	Finance	Asst VP, Ntl Bank of Commerce (Seattle); Cprl 50-52, US Army
Bronson, David Bennet	Education/ Ministry	High School Teacher, CT; 65-66, Swartmore College; Prof 59-65, New Testament, Episcopal Theological Seminary, KY; 1950-54 Parish Ministry; 54-59 Harvard Divinity Schl; Capt 42-45, USNR, USMCR, AFB
Chafee, John Hubbard	Government	Mbr 77-, US Senate, (RI); Secretary of Navy 69-72 US; Governor 63-69, RI; Mbr 56-62, RI State Legislature; Attny 53-56, Law Practice (RI); Capt 42-45, USMC
Finley, John George Gilpin	Industrial	Gen Mgr, CIA Minera Disputada, Chile; Deputy Mgr, Corp Planning Dept, Standard Oil Co; Mbr 51-55, CIA; Economic Analyst 51-54, US Govt; Sgt 43-45, US Army
Goedecke, William Skinner	Finance	1st VP, Dir, Smith Barney, Harris Upham & Co (NYC); Sgt 41-46, US Army
Leavenworth, Donald Loyal	Education	Hdmstr, Chadwick School; Hdmstr, La Jolla Country Day School; Asst Hdmstr 54-57, Crane Country Day School (CA); Teacher 50-54, Valley School (Lignor, PA); 1st Lt 43-45, USAAAF
Moore, James I.	Law	Attny & Realtor (NYC)
O'Brien, Frank Jr.	Education	Ptnr, O'brien Associates (MA); Dir, Dev & Alumni Affairs, Mbr, English Dept, Varsity Baseball, Hockey Coach, Groton School (Groton, MA); Dir 63-, Mead Investment Co (Dayton Oh); 1st Lt 42-46, USAAF
Palmer, Charles Edgar	Business	Marketing VP, AS Harrison Co (South Norwalk, CT); 2nd Lt, USAAF WWII
Read, Richard Rollins	Insurance	Lt, USN Aviation WWII
Robinson, Howard Copeland Jr.	Business	Dir, Adv Services, Liggett & Meyers, Inc (NYC); Dir 69-73, Assn of Ntl Advertisers; 2d Lt 43-46, USAF
Tucker, Carl Jr.	Journalism	Newspaper Publisher, Patent Trader (Mt Kisco NY); Pres, Financial Management, Inc (Mt Kisco); Sec, Trustee Chatham Hall VA; Ist Lt, USAAF WWII
Whitehouse, Charles Sheldon	Government	Diplomat, Foreign Service; Ambassador 75-78, Thailand, 73-75 Laos; Deputy Ambassador 72-73, Saigon; Deputy for CORDS III CTZ, 69-70, Vietnam; Deputy Asst Sec of State for Foreign Affairs; 48-51 w/US Embassy Brussels; Consulate general, Istanbul 54-55; Pretoria 59-61; Canabry 66-68; MACU 69-71; Capt 42-46, USMC

1948 — PERIOD 2, DECADE 146

NAME	OCCUPATION	NOTES
Ashley, Thomas William Ludlow	Governemt	Business Attny NYC; Mbr 1955-81, US Congress, 9th Dist, OH; Co-Dir, Press Section, Asst Dir, Special Projects 1952-54, Radio Free Europe; Mbr 69-70, Yale Honorary Degress Com; Cprl 43-45, USA
Biglow, Lucius Horatio Jr.	Law	Attny; 43-46 AUS
Bush, George Herbert Walker	Government	Pres 89-92, VP 81-88, US; Dir 74-75, CIA; Chief US Liaison Officer 73-74, China; Chmn Republican Party; Ambassador 71-72, UN; Pres, Chmn Bd 58-66, Zapata Off-Shore Co; Mbr 66-70, US Congress; Lt jg 42-45, USNR
Caulkins, John Ervin	Finance	Treas, HJ Caulkins & Co, Detroit, MI

Clark, William Judkins	Business	Chmn 74-76, Hale & Yale Associates; Pres 66-71, Ciba Products Co, Div Ciba-Geigy Corp, Summit NJ; VP 59-63, Owens-Corning Fiberglass Corp; Bd 57-64, Deer Island Club Corp; Mbr 67-, Alumni Bd; Lt 43-46, Pilot USAF
Connelly, William James Jr.	Finance	Dir of Advertising, Mellon Ntl Bank & Trust Co, Pittsburgh, PA; 1969-74 Alumni Bd; Capt Pilot, 42-46, USAAF
Cook, George III	Industrial	Licensing Coordinator Ntl Distillers & Chemical Corp, NYC; Mgr 55-68, Owens-Corning Fiberglass, Gen Mgr 63-64, Europe; Pres 56-58, Deer Island Club Corp; 2nd Lt 43-46, Mountain Inf
Grimes, David Charles	Finance	Pres, Chmn Brentwood S&L; Pres, Dir, First Brentwood Corp; VP, 58-64 Republic Ntnl Bank, (Dallas); Ensign Pilot 43-46, USN Air Corps
Jenkins, Richard Elwood	Business	VP, Mid-Continent Sales, Fluor Engineers, Inc (TX); Pres, Ecodyne Corp, Flour Cooling Products Co, Cooling Tower Mfg; Pfc 43-45, Inf US Army
Mack, Richard Gerstle	Business	Pres, South Pacific Foods, Ltd
Moseley, Thomas Wilder	Business	General American Transportation Corp; Regional Sales Mgr 53-76, Gatax; 48-53 w/Weyerhauser Sales Co; S/Sgt 43-45, US Army
Pfau, George Harold Jr.	Finance	Sr VP, Blyth Eastman Paine Webber (CA); Gen Ptnr, White, Weld & Co (SF, CA); Dirs, Systron-Donner Corp, Sierra Pacific Industries; Trustee, Town School for Boys (SF); Cprl 42-44, US Army; Am Field Service 44-45, Italy
Walker, Samuel Sloan Jr.	Publishing	Pres, Walker Publishing Co, Inc, NY; Pres, 59- Walker & Co, NY; VP 51-59, Radio Free Europe; Dir 51-59, Free Europe Press; VP Free Europe Com, NY; Asst to Research Dir 49-51, *Time*, Inc; War Correspondent, 45-45 w/NY Post, Paris; Chmn Resources for Learning, Inc(NYC); Dir, Trustee, Am Field Service
Weaver, Howard Sayer	Education	Dean of Faculties of Art, School of Art & Architecture; Asst Dir 59-64, Yale U Press; Dir, Yale-in-China; Acting Sec 63-64 Yale U; Asst to Pres for External Relations and Assoc Sec 64-67, Yale U; Acting Dean 67-68, School of A & A; Inf Officer 51-53, US Embassy Bangkok; European Dir, Free Europe Press, Munich 54-57; 1st Lt 43-45, USAF; Sec, RTA
Wilkie, Valleau Jr.	Education	Exec VP, Sid W Richardson Foundation (TX); Headmaster, Governor, Drummer Academy (Byfield MA); Instr Hist 48-59, Phillips Academy Andover; 1st Lt 42-45, USAF

1949 **PERIOD 2, DECADE 147**

NAME	OCCUPATION	NOTES
Baribault, Richard Pfeifer	Industrial	VP Procuremnet, Alcoa; Works Mgr 70-74, International Alloys Ltd (England); Mbr Yale Schools Comm; Capt, 43-46 ETO USAAF
Bassett, Barton Bradley II	X	Circulation Dept, *Town & Country Buyers Guide* (IL); Capital Equipment Engineer 56-67, Barber Colman Co
Coffin, William S. Jr.	Ministry	Minister, The Riverside Church (NYC); Chaplain 58-75, Yale
Davison, Daniel Pomeroy	Finance	Gen Mgr, Morgan Guaranty Trust Co (London); Chmn, Pres, US Trust Corp; Sr VP, Morgan Guaranty Trust; Dir, Scovill Mfg Co; Burlington Northern; Todd Shipyards; Atlantic Companies; Discount Corp; Northwestern States Portland Cement Co; Yale Development Bd; Alumni Bd; 2nd Lt 1943-45, USAAF
Goodyear, Robert M.	Rancher	Rancher, registered Aberdeen Angus cattle
Hollister, John Baker Jr.	Business	VP Sales, Cleveland Cliffs Iron Co; VP Federal Lime & Stone, subsidiary Federal Ore & Mineral Corp, (Shaler Heights OH); Sgt 43-45, Inf Army
Lavelli, Anthony Jr.	Theatre	Director, Bella Music & Theatre Co (NYC)
Leiper, Joseph McCarrell II	Business	Deputy Asst Commissioner, NYC Dept of Transportation
Lippincott, David McCord	Literary	Author, Novelist, *E Pluribus Bang!, Voice of Armageddon, Tremor Violet* (motion picture *Armageddon*), *The Blood of October, Savage Ransom, Salt Mine, Dark Prism, Unholy Morning, The Nursery, The Home*; V Chmn 67-69, Bd Erwin Wasey, Inc; Exec Dir 65-67, McCann-Erickson Ltd (London); Sr VP 50-65, McCann Erickson Inc (NYC); Managing Dir 62-65, Ctr for Adv Practice; Intelligence Work; M/Srgt 43-45, US Army
Lord, Charles Edwin II	Finance	Chmn Bd, Dir 68- Allied Bank Intrnl; First VP, VChmnm Bank of US, DC; Sr Advisor to, First Deputy, Acting, Comptroller of the Currency 79-81, US Treasury Dept; Pres, CEO, Dir, Hartford Ntl Corp, Hartford Ntl Bank & Trust (CT); Dirs, 69-, Aetna Life & Casualty Co, 69-76 Insilco Corp, 68-76 Kamma Corp; Mbr 64-69, Alumni Bd; Mbr 67- , Yale Dev Bd
Lufkin, Sr., Peter Wende	Industry	Broker; Pres, Winner Boats, Inc (TN); S/Sgt 43-46, Army Air Force
Raymond, George Tod Perkins	Business	European Sales Dir, Cabot Corp; 53-55 w/Godfrey L Cabot Inc Boston; Acting 1st Officer 41-46, USN
Sherrill, Franklin Goldwaithe	Ministry	Rector, Grace Church (Brooklyn NY); Rector 58-67, Ascension Memorial Church (Ipswich, MA) 53-58 (St John's Dickinson ND(

Van Dine, Vance	Finance	Managing Dir, Ptnr Morgan Stanley & Co, NYC; Seaman 1/C 43-46, USN
Wickwire, Winthrop Ross	Business	VP, Operations, Wickwire Bros, Inc (Courtland, NY); 1st Lt 43-46, AAF

1950 — PERIOD 2, DECADE 148

NAME	OCCUPATION	NOTES
Breen, John Gerald	X	
Buckley, William Frank Jr.	Literary Work	Editor-in-Chief 1955- , *National Review*; Asst Instr 47-51, Spanish Yale; Assoc Editor 52, American Mercury; Syndicated Columnist 63- ; Host Firing Line 66-; USIA ADvisory Comm 69-; Chmn Bd, Starr Broadcasting Group
Draper, William Henry III	Business	Pres, Chmn Export-Import Bank of US; Chmn 86, UN Development Program; Pres, Founder Draper & Johnson Investment Co; Pres 65-70, Ptnr 70-81, Sutter Hill Capital Corp (Palo Alto, CA); Pres 67-68, Western Assn Venture Capitalists; 59-62 Assoc Draper, Gaither & Anderson; sales 54-59, Inland Steel Co; Dir 67, Measurex, Century Data System; Lt 46-47, 51-52, Inf US Army
Frank, Jr., Victor Harry	Finance	VP Info Resources, CPC International (NJ); Tax Counsel, CPC International Inc (NJ)
Galbraith, Evan Griffith	Finance	US Ambassador to France; Managing Dir 75-81, Dillon Read; Chmn 69-75, Bankers Trust International Ltd, London subsidiary Bankers Trust Co; 61-69 w/Morgan Guaranty Trust Co of NY; 61-69 w/Shearman & Sterling; Confidential Asst 60-61, Sec of Commerce; Mbr, Bar of NY, DC; Lt 53-57, USNR
Guinzburg, Thomas Henry	Publishing	Book Publisher, Doubleday & Co (NY); Pres, Viking Press (NYC); Governor 68, Yale U Press; Trustee, American Book Publishers Council, Franklin Publications; Corporal 44-46, USMCR
Henningsen, Victor William Jr.	Business	Pres, CEO Henningsen Foods (White Plains, NY); Dir, Inst of Am Poultry Ind; Mayor 69-71, (Pelham Manor, NY); Lt 43-45, USNR; Dir, Deer Island Club
Kemp, Philip Sperry	Business	Pres Playtime Equipment Co (NE); Pres Ed Myers Co (Omaha); VP Production, Data Documents, Inc (Omaha); Mbr 62-72, Yale Alumni Bd; CM 2/c 43-46, USNR
Lambert, Paul Christopher	Law	US Ambassador Ecuador, Ptnr 66, Estates & Trust Dept, Whitman, Breed, Abbott & Morgan (NYC); Lawyer 55-66, Milbank, Tweed, Hadley & McCloy (NYC); Cprl 53-55, US Army Intelligence
Lovett, Sidney	Ministry	Sr Minister, First Church of Christ, Congregational; VP 66-, Community Renewal Society (Chicago); Pastor 57-66, Rock Spring Congregational Church (VA, Arlington); Sr Minister, Union Church (IL, Hinsdale); Pastor 53-57, Congregational Church (MA, Littleton); Dir 69- , Chicago Theological Seminary
Luckey, Charles Pinckney	Ministry	Minister, Middlesbury Congregational Church, CT; Sgt 43-46, Army
MacLeish, William Hitchcock	Education	Editor, Oceanus Magazine; Spec Asst to Pres, Dir, Foundation Relations, Yale U; Exec Dir 66-68, Ctr for Inter-Am Relations; Sr Editor 58-64, Vison Magazine; Exec Com 69-, Yale Alumni Bd; 1st Lt 51-54, Army
McLean, Robert III	Business	Pres, Cushman & Wakefield of PA; VP Administration Philadelphia 1976 Bicentennial Corp; Sales 57-64, Owens-Illinois; Marketing Consultant 65-67; S/Sgt 53-56, USMC
Pionzio, Dino John	Finance/ Government	VP Dillon, Read; 1st Sec US Embassy, Bogota, Columbia; Deputy Chief of Station 70, CIA (Santiago, Chile)
Shepard, Donald Carrington Jr.	Business	CEO, Sr VP, Menasha Corp (Neenah, WS); T/Sgt 43-46, USMC

1951 — PERIOD 2, DECADE 149

NAME	OCCUPATION	NOTES
Anderson, Thomas Hill		Medical Student
Eden, John W.	Business	VP 79, Russell Reynolds Associates; Pres 78-79, TVI Corp; VP 77-78, First Municipal Leasing Corp; Asst Sec 76-77, Economic development; Deputy Undersecretary 75-76, Dept Commerce; Exec VP 68-75, Graham Engineering Corp (York, PA); Div Mgr 59-67, AMF Inc; VP 51-59, The Eden Corp; Lt 45-47, 53-5, USN
Ellis, Garrison McClintock Noel	Business	Editor, Publisher, The Country Publishers, Inc; Pres 70-73, Wilson, VanDoren-Ellis Co; Urban Affairs Consultant; Asst Dir 68-70, Baltimore Regional Planning Council; Spec Asst 65-68, Congressional and Community Relations, Office Economic Opportunity; Lt jg 51-55, USNR
Ellis, George Corson Jr.	Industrial	Chmn, CEO, Pres Kessler-Ellis Products Co
Love, Ralph Frank	Business	Stockbroker; Mgr, Plan Forecasting, IBM World Trade Corp (NY); 1st Lt 51-53, USAF
Lufkin, Chauncey Forbush Jr	Industrial	Pres Hytec, Inc (Olympia, WA)
Mathews, Craig	Law	Ptnr, Leva, Hawes, Symington, Martin & Oppenheimer (DC); Dir 65- Meriwether Home for Children; 70- w/Barker Found, 70- w/Evironmental Law Inst; 1st Lt 54-57, Inf USAR

Mayer, Charles Theodore	Industrial	Spec Asst to 82- , Undersecretary of Defense for Policy; Delegate 52-77, Societe Generale de Belgique; Chmn, Pres 68-, Foreign Policy Discussion Group (DC); 1st Lt 43-46, 51-53, Army
McNamara, Thomas Philip	Industrial	Production Mgr, Glenn Arm Plant, Koppers Co (MD)
Price, Raymond Kissam Jr.	Writing	Pres, Economic Club of NY; Consultant 83- , William S Paley & Co (NYC); Consultant 78-83, Pres Nixon; Spec Consultant 73-74, US Pres; Spec Asst 69-73, US Pres; Asst 67-68, Richard Nixon; Editor of 57-66, Editorial Page 64-66, NY *Herald Tribune*; Reporter 57, *Life*; Writer, Asst to Editor 55-56, *Colliers*; Lt 51-55, USNR; Visiting Fellow 77-, AEI; Author, *With Nixon*, wrote GHW Bush's 1992 Republican nomination speech.
Reid, Edward Snover III	Law	Ptnr 57-64, Davis, Polk & Wardwell (NYC); Dirs, Gen Mills, Inc, Metropolitan Savings Bank, The Brooklyn Museum, Metropolitan Opera Assn; Trustee & Mbr Exec Com Brooklyn Inst of Arts & Science; Capt 51-53, USMC; Lt USN Aviation WWII
Ross, Thomas Bernard	Literary	Sr VP, Corporate Affairs, RCA (NY); Asst Sec Defense, 77-81; DC Bureau Chief 70-77, DC Correspondent 58-77, Foreign Correspondent 58-68, Chicago *Sun-Times*; 58 w/*UPI*; w/55-58 *International News Service*; Lt 51-54, USN
Russell, Richard Warren	Engineering	Pres, Gen Mgr, James Russell Engineering Works (Boston); Cprl 52-55, Army
Ryan, Joseph Mather	Finance	VP Investments, Dean Witter Reynolds, Inc, MI; Institutional Salesman, Blyth & Co, MI; PFC Army 46-48
Shepard, Charles Robinson Smith	Education	Assoc fellow 70, Pierson College, Yale U; English Teacher, Hillhouse High School (New Haven); Asst Dean 55-57, Yale College; Pres 71-79, VP 70, Yale-in-China; Chmn English Dept 57-61, St John's School (Houston); Headmaster 61-62, Phoenix (AZ) Country Day School; 64-69, w/Hamden (CT) Hall; Dir, RTA; T/5 45-46, Inf Army 45-46;

1952 — PERIOD 2, DECADE 150

NAME	OCCUPATION	NOTES
Aberg, Donlan Vincent Jr.	Business	VP Sales & Marketing Abbott Labs; Pres Nutrition Products of Am (LA, CA)
Buckley, Fergus Reid	Writing	Novelist, Lecturer; Lt 1952-54, USAF
Claude, Abram Jr.	Finance	Ptnr, Ray & Berndtson; Exec VP, Security Pacific Financial Services, (NYC); Sr VP 72-80, Dillon, Read & Co; VP 69-72, Bessemer Securities Corp; VP 55-69, Morgan Guaranty Trust; 55-69 Port Authority of NY; Trustee, Lennox Hill Hosp; Pres, Treas Ntl Industries for the Blind NYC; Sgt 46-48, US Army
Connick, Andrew Jackson	Law	Ptnr, Milbank, Tweed, Hadley & McCloy; Lt 1952-54, USAF
Cruikshank, Paul Fessenden Jr.	Industrial	VP Strategic Planing 74-76, USRA; Pres 71-74, Fort Worth & Denver Ry Co; Asst VP marketing planning 67-71, Burlington Northern; Operating Dept 52-76, Great Northern; VP Operations & Maintenance, The Milwaukee Road; Alumni Fund Agent; Lt jg 52-56, USN
Eisler, Colin Tobias	Education	Prof, NYU Institute of Fine Arts (NYC)
Finney, Graham Stanley	City Government	Sr Ptnr, The Conversation Co, PA; Commissioner Addiction Services Agency NYC; Dir of Planning 57-60, (Portland ME); Many Philadelphia gov and schools positions; Spec 3 54-56, US Army
Haight, Charles Seymour Jr.	Law	US Dist Judge 76- , (Southern Dist of NY); Ptnr 57-76, Haight, Gardner, Poor & Havens (NYC); Trial Attny 55-57, US DOJ Admiralty & Shipping
Hincks, John Winslow	Law	Ptnr, Robinson, Robinson & Cole (CT); Lt 52-55, USNR; Dir 58-61, RTA
Kittredge, Frank Dutton	Business	National Foreign Trade Council; VP, Asia-Pacific Div, GE Co; Mgr, Desk Side Time Sharing Operation, GE Co; Dirs, Philippine Appliance Corp, Toshiba, Inc, Elpor Electric Co, Philippine Electric Co; Lt 54-58, USN
Roberts, George Brooke Jr.	Government	St Joseph's U, PA; Dir EA/TB 74-76, Dept of State; Spec Asst to Deputy Sec 73-74, Dept of State; Deputy Chief Mission, US Embassy, Kingston, Jamaica; 3d Sec US Embassy , Bangkok, 2d Sec US Embassy Vientiane 60-62; Intrnl relations Officer, Dept State 62-66; 1st Sec US Embassy Dar es Salaam 67-70; Lt 53-57, USN
Senay, Edward Charles	Medicine	Prof Psychiatry, Chief of Drug Studies, U Chicago
Spears, Robert Samuel	Business	Asst VP, Asst Sales Mgr, Republic Steel Corp (IL)
Steadman, John Montague	Education	Assoc Dean, Prof Law, Georgetown U (DC); Spec Asst to 65-68, Sec Defense; Deputy Under Sec 64-65, Army; Attny 63-64, US DOJ (DC); Visiting Prof Law U PA Law School, Philadelphia; Assoc 56-63, Pillsbury, Madison & Sutro (SF); Assoc Justice, D.C. Court of Appeals; Gen Counsel 68-70, Air Force
Vorys, Martin West	X	

1953 — PERIOD 2, DECADE 151

NAME	OCCUPATION	NOTES
Bulkey, Jonathan Duncan	X	

Bush, Jonathan James	Investments	Chmn Bd, J Bush & Co; Gen Ptnr 60-70, GH Walker & Co; Lt 53-55, US Army
Donaldson, William Henry	Finance	Chmn 2003- , Securities and Exchange Comm; Chmn CEO Donaldson Enterprises, Inc, NYC; Dean 75-80, Prof Management Studies, Yale; Spec Advisor 75, US Pres; Under Secretary 73-74, State US; Founder, Chmn of Bd, CEO 59-73, Donaldson, Lufkin & Jenrette, Inc (NYC); Mbr 53-70, Alumni Fund; Mbr, Yale Development; Trustee 70- Ford Foundation, Beekman Downtown Hosp, Wesleyan U; Mbr 71-7, Yale Corp; Mbr 75-, Yale Investment Comm; Dir, Deer Island Corp; 53-55 Lt USMC
Durham Edwin A. II	Mineral Exploration	Managing General Ptnr, Everest Exploration (uranium and minerals); 59-69 Southern Petroleum Exploration, Inc; Exec Asst 56-59, Frankfort Oil Co; Dir 55-59, Petroleum Exploration, Wiser Oil Co, Southern Petroleum Exploration, Inc; Dir 60-65, Thor-Jet Inc; many others; Lt 53-55, USMC
Emerson, Christy Payne	Business	Ptnr, The Bret Harte Retirement Ctr; Dir Development 65-68, Philadelphia Housing Authority; Lt jg 53-56, USNR
Lufkin, Dan Wende	Finance	Chmn, Exec Com, Donaldson, Lufkin & Jenrette, Inc (NYC); Chmn Bd, Dirs, AZ-CO Land & Cattle Co, Ontario Motor Speedway, Inc; Overseas Ntl Airways, Inc, Pan Ocean Oil Corp, Harvard Bus Sch Club NY, Opportunity Funding Corp; Gov, NY Stock Exchange; Trustees, Hotchkiss School, Pine Manor Jr Col, Dansbury Hosp, Ntl Conference Christians & Jews, Inc; 1st Lt, USMCR
Marshall, John Birnie	Industrial	
McLane, James Price	Business	Advertising Sales, Time, Inc; Venture Mgr, General Mills (Minneapolis); Chmn 69, Lee Wards subsidiary Gen Mills; Chmn 69, Bd Ed Minnetonka Schl Dist; Pfc 53-55, US Army Counter Intelligence Corps
Menton, John Dennis	X	
Mitinger, Joseph Berry	Law	Ptnr Mitinger & Mitinger (Greensburg, PA); City Solicitor (Greensburg); 1st Lt 54-56, FA US Army
Noble, Lawrence Mason Jr.	Education	Assoc Sec 71-81, Yale U; Dir 70-71, Undergraduate Financial Aid, Yale U; Asst to Dir Admissions 62, Asst Dir 63-66, Admissions, Dir 66-70, Freshman Scholarships & Assoc Dir Admissions; Trainee Hanover Bank; w/Aluminum Co Canada; w/Centre D'Etudes Industrielles; Sales Rep 57-62, Aluminum Ltd; 1st Lt 53-55, USMC
Novkov, David Arthur	Industrial	Pres, CEO, Crossville Rubber Products (TN); Factory mgr, General Tire & Rubber Co (Wabash, IN); Spec 3, 54-56 Army
Walker, George Herbert III	Finance	Chmn, Pres, CEO, Stifel, Nicolaus & Co, Inc (MO); Dirs, Mbr Exec Com, Securities Industry Assn; Bd Gov 83, Midwest Stock Exchange; Assoc Dir, A Gary Shilling & Co; Dir, VChmn, Webster College (MO); Managing Ptnr, in charge Chicago office GH Walker & Co; Dirs, GH Walker & Co, Inc, Rixson, Inc, Marine Resources, Inc, Lafayette Federal Savings & Loan Assn, Laidlaw Corp
Weber, John William	Business	Management Consultant and Principal, Pres, Putnam, Hayes & Bartlett, Inc, MA; SR VP 79-82, Boston Gas; Principal, 74-79, Temple, Barker & Sloane; Asst Administrator, 74, Federal Energy Admin; Pres 72-73, Chayes Virginia Inc; 60-71 w/ McKinsey & Co, Inc, Chicago; Prof Engineer (OH); Lt 55-58, USN
Woodsum, Harold Edward Jr.	Law	Attny, Ptnr Drummond, Woodsum, Plimpton & MacMahon (ME); Mbr 67, Cape Elizabeth Town Council; Pvt 53-55, Inf US Army

1954 **PERIOD 2, DECADE 152**

NAME	OCCUPATION	NOTES
Benninghoff, Harry Bryner	Business	Dist Sales Mgr, Proctor & Gamble Co; Lt 55-57, USAF
Evans, Tilgham Boyd	Finance	Ptnr, Shields & Co (NYC)
Fortunato, S. Joseph	Law	Ptnr, Pitney, Hardin, Kipp & Szuch (Newark NJ); Mbr 70, Alumni Bd
Giesen, Arthur Rossa, Jr	Industrial	Pres, Treas, Augusta Steel Corp (Vienna VA); Mbr 64-74, 76, VA House of Delegates
Gifford, Richard Cammann	Business	Sales, Dir Marketing, Distribution Sciences Inc (Oak Brook, IL)
Hiers, Richard Hyde	Education	Prof, Religion, U FL (Gainesville, FL); Faculty 58-61, Yale Div School; Sec 56-61, RTA
Kilrea, Walter Charles	Industrial	
Meyer, Russell William Jr.	Business	Pres, Cessna Aircraft Co (KS); Pres, American Aviation Corp (Cleveland, OH); Dir 75-, Fourth Ntnl Bank; Dir 82- KS Gas & Electric; Attny, Arter & Hadden, Cleveland; Capt 55-58, USAF
Morton, Thruston Ballard Jr.	Radio, TV	VChmn, Cosmos Broadcasting Corp (KY); Pres Orion Broadcasting, Inc (Louisville); 55-56, w/US Army
Polich, Richard Frank	Business	Pres, Tallix Inc
Price, Ross Edward	X	

Reponen, Robert Gordon	Finance	Gen Mgr, Bancode Jerez (London); Asst Mgr, First Ntl City Bank (Moorgate, London); Capt 54-58, Army
Ryan, Allan A. III	Finance	Sr VP, Smith Barney Harris Upham & Co, Inc (NYC); Dir RTA
Schnaitter, Spencer Jason	Law	City Attny (Madison, IN)
Thornton, Edmund Braxton	Business	Pres, CEO Ottawa Silica Co (Ottawa, IL); Chmn IL Nature Preserves Comm; Chmn Historic Sites Adv Council; 1st Lt 54-56, USMC

1955 — PERIOD 2, DECADE 153

NAME	OCCUPATION	NOTES
Bryan, Lloyd Thomas Jr.,	Finance	First VP, First Ntnl Bank of Boston (London); Associate 61-66, Shearman & Sterling (NY); VP 66-70, First Ntnl Bank of Chicago (Frankfur)t; Lt 59-61, US Army
DeForest, Stephen Elliott	Law	Ptnr, Riddell, Williams, Voorhees, Ivie & Bullitt, (Seattle); Lt 55-57, USN
Fehr, Gerald F.	Insurance	Dir, Sr VP Finance, Sec, Family Life Insurance Co, (WA); Lt 55-57, USNR
Gow, Richard Haigh	Industry	President, Zapata Oil; Pres, CEO, Enterprise Oil & Gas (TX); Chmn Bd, CEO, Stratford of Texas, Inc; 1st Lt 56-58 USAF
Green, Charles Grady	Finance	Exec VP, Channing Fund (NYC); Spec 3 55-57, US Army
Guidotti, Hugh George Jr.	Education	Teacher, Coach, Chmn Science Dept, Hudson High School (Hudson, MA)
Hansen, Roger Allen	Finance	Exec VP, The Chicago Corp, (IL); Gov, Midwest Stock Exchange; VP, Dean Witter & Co; Pres, Deer Island Club Corp; Lt 55-57, USN
Hudson, Franklin Donald	Business	Exec VP, Founder, Integrated Genetics, Inc, (MA); Dir of Marketing, Latin America, Sylvania Intrnl Div GTE (NYC); Advisor Domestic Peace Corp (Puerto Rico); Capt 56-58, USAF
Johanson, Stanley Morris	Education	Prof, Law U TX School of Law; Teaching Fellow 61-63, Harvard Law School; Capt 58-61, USAF
Mathias, Philip Hoffman II	Business	Dist Mgr, Bell Telephone Co (PA); E-5 56-58, Army
McCullough, David Gaub	Literary	Editor, Am Heritage Pub Co, Inc (NYC)
Searles, Paul David	Business	VP, International Group, PET Inc, MO; VP 80-82, WM Underwood Co; Philippines Dir 71-74, Asia Regional Dir 74-75, Deputy Dir 75-76, US Peace Corps; Deputy Chmn 76-80, Ntl Endowment for the Arts; High School, History Teacher (Westport, CT); Brand Mgr 58-62, Proctor & Gamble; VP Dir 62-67, Glendinning Assoc; 1st Lt, USMC
Shugart, Thorne Martin	X	
Steadman, Richard Cooke	Business	Chmn National Convenience Stores; Dir, Storage Technology, Inc; Chmn, Childrens Computer Workshop; Trustees, Children's Television Workshop, Brearly School; Author 80, Pres Mandated Study National Military Command System; Head, Defense Transition Team 76-77, Carter/Mondale; Deputy Asst Sec Defense 66-69, East Asia; Staff Office 57-59, Bd of Ntl Estimates, CIA
Walker, Ray Carter	Medicine	Psychiatrist; 59-64, w/GH Walker & Co; 1st Lt 57-59, AUS

1956 — PERIOD 2, DECADE 154

NAME	OCCUPATION	NOTES
Banks, Howard Daniel	Finance	Ist VP, VP Corp Finanace, Blyth & Co; 1st Lt 56-58, USMC
Boasberg III, James Emanuel	Law	Ptnr, Boasberg, Klores, Feldesman & Tucker (DC); Ptnr, Boasberg, Granat & Kass (DC); Spec 4, 59-60, Army
D'Avanzo, Louis A.	Medicine	Opthalmologist, (Kailua, HI)
Dempsey, Andrew Squire	Law	Attny, Squire, Sanders & Dempsey; Lt 56-59, USAF
Durfee, Charles Gibson Jr.	Industrial	Dir, International Projects, Westinghouse Electric Corp; Mgr, Quality Assurance, Westinghouse Power Systems, (PA); 65, Westinghouse commercial and Naval Nuclear programs; 60-65, General Dynamics/Electric Boat; Lt jg 56-60, USN
Esselstyn, Caldwell Blakesman Jr.	Medicine	Surgeon, Cleveland Clinic (OH); Capt 66-68, US Army
Gaines, Milton John	Business	Dir, Marketing Winfield Design Associates Inc (SF, CA); Lt 56-60, USN Aviation
Ingalls, David Sinton Jr.	Business	Mayor 80- , Local Village; Lt 56-60, USNR
Jamieson, Thomas Crawford Jr.	Law	Ptnr, Jamieson, Walsh, McCardell, Moore & Peskin, Princeton; Attny 66-68, 70-, (Lawrence Township, Mercer County); Adv Bd 67-, NJ Realty Title Insurance Co; Dir 70-, 1st Ntnl Bank Princeton; Bd Trustees 73- , RP Foundation (NJ); Sgt 59-60, Army Intelligence
Malloy, Terrence Reed	Medicine	Surgeon, Urologist; Chief Urology PA Hosp (Philadelphia); 1st Lt 56-58, Army Airborne
McGregor, Jack Edwin	Law	Pres, Hampton-Douglas Corp (NY); Chmn 81, Hampton-Windsor Corp; 81- Chmn International Water Resources, Ltd; Lawyer, Reed, Smith, Shaw & McClay (DC); Gen Counsel 72-74, Potomac Electric Power Co; 71, w/US Dept of State Trustees 65- , Point Park College (Pittsburgh), 64-70 Western PA School for the Deaf; Mbr 62-70, PA State Senate; Pres 66-70, Pitts Hockey Club; Gov 67-69, Ntl Hockey League
Menton, James Paul	Business	VP, International Marketing, Owens Corning Fiberglass Corp (OH); Stewart & Co (Baltimore); Lt 56-59, USMC

Orr, Andrew Alexander	Business	Pres, Spray Products (Oaks, PA); S/Sgt 57-58 Army
Speed, James Breckinridge	Industrial	Pres Arkansas-Best Freight System, Inc (Fort Smith, AR); Dirs, Trucking Employers, Inc, Central & Southern Motor Freight Bureau, Southern Operators, Inc, Am Trucking Assn; Dir, Transport Insurance Co (TX)
Traphagen, Peter Abraham	Business	VP, Operations, Custom Engineering Co (PA) Pres Hanley Corp; Dir, School Bd; E5 56-58, Army 56-58

1957 — PERIOD 2, DECADE 155

NAME	OCCUPATION	NOTES
Ackerman, Stephen Harry	Transportation	VP, Finance & Admin, Caesars World Inc, CA; VP, Treas, Transcon Lines; Maj Gen 57-60, USMCR
Bowman, Ralph David	Business	Acct Supervisor, Rumril Hoyt, Inc; 57-60 USMC
Carlsen, Ray Allen	Medicine	Physician, Instr Dept Medicine, Spec NIH Fellow 69-70, U of WA; Res Assoc, Seattle VA Hosp; 68-69, U of Copenhagen; Capt 63-65, USAF
Clark, Russell Inslee Jr.	Education	Headmaster 1970- , Horace Mann School, Bronx; Teacher, Admin 57-58, 60-61, Lawrenceville School; Asst Master 62-65, Trumball College, Dean 63-65, Dean of Admissions Yale U; Trustee, US Grant Foundation, Ford Foundation and many others; Capt 58-60, USAF
Cushman, Charles W.	Education	Teacher, (Punahou, HI); Camp Zama, (Tokyo)
Dunn, George J	Law	VP, Gen Counsel, Sr Attorney, Standard Oil Co, (OH); Assoc 67-68, Squire, Sanders & Dempsey; Assoc 60-67, McAfee, Hanning, Newcomer & Hazlett
Fritzche, Peter B.	Business	Chmn, Pres EAC Industries, Inc, (IL); Dir Bus Dev, Quaker Oats; Dir 65-76, Elyria Co; Dir 64-67, Neracher Investment Co; Dir 64-68, Wells Aluminum, Accurate Products, Hauske Harlen Furniture Co
Loucks, Vernon Reece Jr.,	Business	Pres, CEO 76-, Baxter Travenol Laboratories, Inc, VP for Europe & Africa, Travenol Laboratories SA, Belgium, w/company since 63; Sr Management Consultant 63-65, George Fry & Associates (IL); Dirs, John L & Helen Kellogg Foundation, Northwest U, Kemper Educ & Charitable Fund, Continental IL Corp, Continental IL Ntnl Bank & Trust, Dun & Bradstreet Corp, Emerson Electric Co Inc, Quaker Oats; 1st Lt, USMC
Loughran, Anthony Hookey	Engineer	Plant Construction Engineer, Pacific Telephone; Mbr Bohemian Club; Lt Col 50-55, USMCR
Lumpkin, Richard Anthony	Business	Pres, VP, Treas, IL Consolidated Telephone, Co; Dir, 1st National Bank (IL); 1st Lt 57-59, Army
Oberlin (Owseichik), John P.	Business	
Palmer, Lindley Guy II	Finance	Sr VP, Ayco Corp (CT); Sr VP 78-82, Fiduciary Trust Co; Managing Ptnr 66-78, Davis, Palmer & Biggs (NYC); VP 58-66, Bank of NY; Capt 58, Army
Ritchie, Wallace Parks Jr.	Medicine	Gen Surgeon, U VA School of Medicine, VA; Surgeon, Active Duty, Div Surgery Walter Reed Army Inst of Research (DC); Lt Cmndr 70
Somerville, John Wheeler	Finance	VP, Brown Management Co (HI)
Williams, William Bruce	Transportation	Chief Pilot 68-, Pan Am Business Jet Div (Teterboro, NJ); Brokerage Trainee 67-68, Merrill, Lynch, Pierce, Fenner & Smith; Major 57-67, USMC; Major 68, USMCR

1958 — PERIOD 2, DECADE 156

NAME	OCCUPATION	NOTES
Allen, Charles Edward	Law	Sr Ptrnr Hamel, Park, McCabe & Saunders, DC; Ptrnr Hogan & Hartson, DC; Chmn, 72-76 Gen Counsel, Federal Home Loan Bank Bd; 1962-68 Sullivan & Cromwell
Blue, Linden Stanley	Business	Pres, CEO, Beech Aircraft Corp; Managing Dir, CEO 80-82, Lear Fan, Ltd; Asst to the Pres 75-80, Gates Learjet Corp; Exec VP, Sec 64-74, Colorado & Western Properties Corp; 71-75 Denver City Council; Reg Chmn 67-70, Alumni Fund, Yale U; Capt 61-64, USAF
Cassel, John A.	Business	Pres, Selfin Corp
Cheney, Ronald Lawton	Law	
Cushman, Robert Edgar Jr.	Finance	Mgr, Brussels Branch First National City Bank; Managing Dir, Asia Pacific Capital Corp, Ltd, (Hong Kong); VP Citibank, NYC; E-2 58-59, Army
Embersits, John Frank	Business	Pres, CEO, Energy Resource Management Co, Operations Resource Management Co, Technical Resource Management Co, Thermtran, Ltd Exec VP, Co-Engineer Welsbach Corp, NY; Dir 69, Union Trust Co; Dir 68, NH Chamber of Commerce; Dir 65-75, University Operations, Yale U; Bus Mgr 66-69, Yale U; Officer, Mbr 70-75, Yale Corp; Asst Treas, Dir, RTA
Howe, Gary Woodson	Journalism	Bd Dir 75-, VP 74-, Exec Editor, 67- Editor, Omaha World-Herald (NE); Lt USN 58-61

Morey, Robert Willis Jr.	Finance	Pres, RW Morey, Inc (CA); William Hutchinson & Co (SF, CA); Chmn Bd Dir, Infra Red Circuits & Controls
Pendexter, John Fowler	Business	Management Consultant, Pres, Pendexter & Co (CT)
Phelan, Howard Taylor	Business	Pres, CEO, Welsbach Corp, CT; Pres, CEO, Jamaica Water & Utilities, Inc (Greenwich CT); Dir 65-70, Operations & developments, Officer 67-70 Yale Corp, asst instr 59-60, Physics Yale U;, Consultant 59-62, National Security Admin (NSA); Management Consultant 60-65, Arthur D Little, Inc; Mbr 63-, Alumni Bd; Dir 66-70, RTA
Post, Russell Lee Jr.	Law	Ptnr, Cummings & Lockwood, CT; Mbr 79-82, CT State Senate; Mbr 72-78, CT State Legislature; Deputy Commissioner 71-72 , Personnel, State of CT; Ptnr, Post & Pratt; Ptnr 65-70, Shipman & Goodwin (CT)
Preston, John Louis	Business	Pres, CEO, Action Industries, Inc (PA); Pres, Stiffler Stores, Inc (OH); Pres, Creative Service Div, Sigma Marketing Systems, Inc,(Rockville Centre, NY)
Shackelford, Robert Campbell	Education	Instr Economics Dept, U IL Urbana, IL
Van Antwerp, William Meadow Jr	Armed Services	Capt, USMC
Wheeler, Thomas Beardsley	Insurance	Exec VP, Asst Gen Mgr, MA Mutual Life Ins Co (Boston); Lt 58-60, USN

1959 — PERIOD 2, DECADE 157

NAME	OCCUPATION	NOTES
Adams, Stephen	Finance	Pres, Assoc Bankers Corp; Pres, Adams Communications Corp
Bodman, William Camp	Farming	Farmer & Business Consultant (former corporate businessman)
Connors, James Joseph III	Business	Pres Lowery Organ, IL; Consultant McKinsey and Co; Purchasing Mgr, Winchester, Div of Olin; Management Consulting Associate, NYC; Lt jg 59-62, USN
Cooke, John Patrick	Transportation	Corp Mgr Facilities, Exec offices Emery Air Freight; Dir 69- International Construction, Inc, (DC); Capt 60-65, USMC
Ercklentz, Alexander Tonio	Finance	Mgr, Foreign Investment Dept, Brown Brothers Harriman & Co, (NYC); Dir 73, Wilmar Corp, 73-75, Massassoit Management Corp; Treas, Dir 71-75, Travellers Aid; Investment Comm 69, Atlantic Funds; Treas, Dir 69, International Social Service American Branch Inc; Treas, RTA
Esselstyn, Erik Canfield	Education	Gesell Institute for Human Development, Sgt E-5 60-63
Hemphill, James Tierney	Law	Lawyer, Corcoran, Hardesty, Whyte, Hemphill & Ligon, (DC); Asst General Counsel, Consolidation Coal Co, Pittsburgh PA
Holbrook, John Jr.	Architecture	Ptnr, International Consortium of Architects Icon Arc, Pres International Construction, Icon, Inc (DC); Chmn Bd, Dir 69- , ICON Inc; Dir 70- , Decisions Analysis Corp, (DC); VP, Trustee, Foundation for Studies of Modern Science (NJ, Princeton) 68- ; Capt 59-62, USMC; Asst Sec 65-68, RTA
Kingsley, Charles Capen	Law	Ptnr 69-, Assoc 62-68, Wiggin & Dana (New Haven); Mbr 69-, Yale Alumni Bd
Lightfoot, Richard Bissett	Law	Pres, Lightfoot Broadcasting Group; Chmn, Soundings Publications, Inc (CT); Attny, Winthrop, Stimson, Putnam & Roberts, NYC; Sr Dir 67-68, Office U Development, Yale
Lord, Winston	Government	Co-Chairman of the International Rescue Committee; 93-97 Assistant Secretary of State; 85-89 Ambassador to China; 83-88 Pres, Chairman of the Council on Foreign Relations; 73-77 State Department Director of Policy Planning; 70-73 Special Assistant to the National Security Advisor to Kissinger; Mbr Planning Staff National Security Council; 1960s Defense Dept Chairman of the National Endowment for Democracy; Chairman of the Carnegie Endowment National Commission on America and the New World;
Mayor, Michael Brook	Medicine	Orthopedic Surgeon, Mary Hitchcock Clinic (Hanover NH)
Sheffield, James Rockwell	Education	Pres, US Comm UNICEF; Asst Prof, Dir, Center for Education in Africa, Teachers College Columbia U (NYC); Program Specialist 65-67, Ford Foundation (Nairobi, Kenya)
Thorson, Peter Andreas	Science	Pres, Thorson Brown (CT); Pres Optical Sciences Group, Inc (SF, CA); VP 68-70, Laird, Inc; VP 59-68, Morgan Guaranty Trust Co; Dir 82, Trade Finance Corp; Dir, RTA
Tyler, Cheever	Law	Attny, w/Wiggin & Dana (New Haven)

1960 — PERIOD 2, DECADE 158

NAME	OCCUPATION	NOTES
Ball, David George	Law	Sec, Sr VP Amax, Inc; Attny Williams, Mullen, Christian & Dobbins; Asst Sec Labor 1989-92, Bush Admin; Legal Counsel, Babcokc & Wilcox, Co; Treas 64-66, Pres 66-68, Deer island Club Corp; Pres 65-, GD Miller, Corp
Beane, Frank Eastman Jr.	Finance	Pres, Owner, JCA Limited, CT; VP United Bank of Denver; Lt 60-65, USNR
Capron, Paul III	Business	Marketing Rep IBM; Capt 61-63, US Army

Dominick, David DeWitt	Law	Ptnr, Dominick Law Offices, (CO); Asst Administrator 71-73, US EPA; Lawyer, Commissioner 69-71, Federal Water Quality Administration, Dept of Interior,(DC); Legislative Asst 66-67, Senator Milward Simpson, Senator C P Hansen 67-69, R WY; Capt 60-63, USMC
Ernst, Frederick Vincent	Industrial	VP, Marketing & International Operations, Great Southern Paper; Co-Mgr Export Sales, Great Northern Paper Co (NYC)
Garnsey, William Herrick	Business	Pres, Sec, Garnesy & Wheeler, Ford Dealer (CO); Greely Leasing Co; Dir, Weld County Credit Bureau; Bd Mbr, IntraWest Bank of Greely; Lt 60-64, USN
Giegengack, Robert F. Jr.	Education	Asst Prof Geology U PA
Holbrook, David Doubleday	Insurance	Exec VP, Marsh & McLennan, Inc (NYC)
Lindgren, Richard Hugo	Finance	VP, Private Capital, Inc; VP, White, Weld & Co (NYC); Pres, Treas, Deer Island Club Corp; Lt 62-65, USN
Lusk, Peter Anthony	Finance	Gen Ptnr, Dir Marketing, Forstmann-Leff Associates (NYC); 72-74 w/EF Hutton & Co; Co-Founder, Chmn Bd 74-76 , Federal Loan Corp; Mbr 62-72, Mgr 68-72; Lehman Bros (LA, CA)
McCarthy, Charles Edward	Education	Dean, Timothy Dwight College, Yale U
Meek, John Burgess	Engineer	VP, VA Chemicals, Inc; Mgr, Organic Chemicals, Inc (Portsmouth, VA); Lt 61-65, USN
Northrop, Robert Smitter	Medicine	Physician, Research Ntl Institutes of Health, USPHS, Laboratory Clinical Investigation, National Inst Allergy & Infectious Diseases (Bethesda); Research Physician 66-69, Pakistan-SEATO Cholera Research Lab, Dacca; House Physician 64-66, Buffalo Gen Hosp; Lt Cmndr 66-, USPHS
Scott, Eugene Lytton	Publishing	Pres, Sports Investors, Inc (NYC); Author, Feature and Free-lance Writer 65-70, NY Times, Esquire, Sports Illustrated; Dir National Leisure, Inc; Trustee Kip's Bay Boys Club; Counsel, w/Kelly, Grimes & Winston; 60-61 w/USAR
Smith, Bruce Donald III	Art, Education	Commercial Investments, Development (CO); Sculptor, Teacher

1961 — Period 2, Decade 159

Name	Occupation	Notes
Bissell, George Thomas	Finance	Treas, Low Cost Housing Corp; Lt 61-65. USN
Bockrath, Richard Charles Jr.	Education	Research, Prof, Microbiology, Indiana U Medical School
Bowles, William Carter Jr.	Law	Lawyer, Covington & Burling; Assoc 65-68, Hawkins, Delafield & Wood; Asst Campaign Mgr 68, Charles Mathais; Treas 66-68, Deer Island Fund Drive
Clark, Thomas Whitton	Industrial	Clark Paper Converting, Inc OH; Sales Mgr, Paper Mill Div, Chase Bag Co, Chagrin Falls, OH
Cogswell, John Marshall	Law	Lawyer, Ptnr Cogswell & Wehrle; Capt 1965-67, USMC
DeNeufville, John Phillip	Science	VP, Energy Conversion Devices; Research Assoc, Exxon Corp Research Lab
Hamlin, Charles B.	Medicine	Orthopedic Surgeon, Hosp for Special Surgery (NYC)
Lindsay, Dale Alton Jr.	Finance	VP Investments, White, Weld (NYC); VP Laird Inc. investments (NYC); 61-68, US Army
MacLean, Kenneth Jr.	Architecture	Ptnr, Amsler, Hagenah, MacLean Architects, Inc, McDesmond & Lord, Inc (Boston); S/Sgt E6 64-70, Army Ntnl Guard
Pyle, Michael Johnson	Finance	Mfg Rep, Mike Pyle Interests, sporting goods), Sports broadcaster, WGN; Owner/Ptnr, St Bernard Inn Restaurant; Rep White, Weld & Co (Chicago); Prof Football Player 61-69, Capt Bears 63-69, Chicago Bears; Pres 67, NFL Players Assn; Mbr 62, Ntl Guard
Seeley, George Wheeler	Education	Chmn History Dept, Belmont Hill School
Singleton, Thomas Hall	Business	Dir Marketing, Management Scope International; Business Mgr, Wilson Sporting Goods Co (IL); Abbot Labs; 62-65 w/USMC
Stewart, James Corb	Law	Asst VP, Trust Officer, Security Trust Co of Rochester (NY); Attny, Harris, Beach & Wilcox (NY); Lt 64-68, USNR
Waddel, Geoffrey Hamilton	Theater	Dir, Preforming Arts Programs, NY State Council on the Arts; Actor; Singer; Lt 62-65, USNR
Walsh, John Joseph Jr.	Education	Governing Bd, 76- Yale U Art Gallery; Assoc Curator, European Paintings, Metropolitan Museum of Art; Adjunct Assoc Prof Art History, Columbia U NYC; Lecturer, Research Asst 66-68, Frick Collection, NY; Petty Officer 3/C 57-59, USNR

1962 — Period 2, Decade 160

Name	Occupation	Notes
Back, Samuel Hutchins	Education	Assoc Dir of Development CT College; Dir of Career Plans 73-76, State U NY; Assoc Dir 1970-73 , Office of Placement and Instruction in Edu, Univ of VA; Instr 1962-68, History, The Lawerenceville School; Assoc Dir of Development Mystic Seaport Museum

Brandt, John Henry	Medicine	Resident Psychiatrist, McLean Hosp (Belmont MA); Instr, Clinical Fellow in Psychiatry, Harvard Medical School
Brewster, James Henry IV	Transportation	Owner, The Formsman, (Miami); VP Marketing Sales, Out Island Airways, (Nassau Bahamas); Spec 4, 58-61, US Army
Brooks, Tristam Anthony	Finance	Managing Dir, Salomon Brothers, Inc; Ptnr 73-77, Loeb, Rhoades & Co; Asst VP 64-73, First Boston Corp, NY; Lt 62-64, USN; Officer 70-72, Deer Island Club Corp
Burr, Charles Bentley II	Law	Sr Ptnr, Griffith & Burr; Asst US Attorney 69-71, (PA); Alumni Fund
Childs, Henry Clay	Writing	Writer (Japanologist); History Teacher 64-66, Gunnery School
Chimenti, Norman Victor	Law	Attorney, McBride, Baker & Schlosser (IL); Asst Dir Industrial Relations, Asst Corp Sec, Kroehler Mfg Co; Sgt 63-64, USMC
Hamilton, William	Cartoonist	Cartoonist, Writer, *New Yorker* Magazine; Pfc 64-65, Army
Holland, Henry Thompson	Business	Operations Mgr, Axles Europe, UK; EDP-Mgr, Management Inf Services, JL Hudson Co Detroit
LeFevre, Ronald Eaton	Medicine	Physician, Urology Res Cleveland Clinic; Lt Cmndr 68-70, USN
Ligon, Thomas B.	Theatre/TV	Actor, Producer, Director; VP Openhand Corp
Peck, Arthur John Jr.	Law	Asst Sec, Corning Glass Works (NY); Lawyer 68- 72, Shearman & Sterling, NYC; Admissions Officer 62-65, The Lawrenceville NJ School
Spitz, Robert Wayne	Business	Marketing Rep, IBM Corp (IL)
Terry, Wyllys III	Education	Asst Superintendent of Schools; Teacher, Varsity Hockey Coach Deerfield Academy (Deerfield MA); Forest Consultant, Real Estate Broker 67-70, James W Sewall, Co; 1st Lt 62-65, USMC
Zucker, Bernard Benjamin	Literary	Author, Precious Stones Co (NYC)

1963 — PERIOD 2, DECADE 161

NAME	OCCUPATION	NOTES
Ahlbrandt, Roger S. Jr.	Education	Prof & Asst Dir Ctr for Social & Urban Research U Pittsburgh; 81-82 H.U.D.; Teaching Asst U WA
Becket, Peter Logan	Finance	Real Estate, Austin, TX; Trust & Estate Administrator 72-77, US Trust Co of NY; Capt 63-66, USMCR
Boren, David Lyle	Education, Law, Government	Pres 95-, U OK; US Senator 79-94, Chmn Senate Select Comm on Intelligence; Governor 75-79, OK; Mbr 67-75, OK House of Representatives, Dist 28; Prof. Political Science, Chmn Div of Social Sciences 70-74, Baptist Univ, Shawnee OK; Amer Assn Rhodes Scholars; Lt 68, OK Army Ntl Guard, Co Commander
Clay, Jesse Loring	Social, Writing	Writer & Property Management; Bushwick Social Service (NYC)
Frank, Charles Augustus III	Finance	Sr VP, The United States Trust Co of NY; VP, Syndicate Dept, W E Hutton & Co, (NYC); Pvt 63-69, USAR
Gill, Michael Gates	Advertising	Sr VP, Creative Dir, Lansdowne Advertising; Copywriter, J Walter Thompson
Gwin, Samuel Lawrence Jr.	Student	Writer 82; Asst Sec 76-82, MA Financial Services Co; Assoc 71-76, Gaston Snow & Ely Bartlett; Capt 63-68, Army
Hewitt, Henry Hollis	Law	Attny Stoel, Rives, Boley, Fraser & Wyse; Davies, Biggs, Strayer, Stoel & Boley (OR); adjunct Prof of Law, Lewis & Clark Law School; Capt 63-65, Army
Jones, Theodore Stephen	Medicine	Medical Epidemiologist, International health program office, CDC, GA; Epidemiologist 74-77, WHO Smallpox eradication; Physician, US Public Health service Anchorage, AK; Intern, Res 67-69, Stanford U Hosp; surgeon 69, US PHS
Marsh, William Lee	Law	Gen Counsel, Health & Tennis Corp of America (CA); Administrator 73-81, IL Appellate Court, 1st Dist; Warrant Officer 63-66 , Army Intelligence
Moser, Richard Eugene	Business	Pres, CEO Lefcourt Group, Inc (CA); Exec VP, CEO, Lefcourt, Golub, Baer & Moneypenny, Inc; Pres, Lefcourt Investments, Inc: Pres, Remcourt Corp; Capt USMC 63-69; Presidential Helicopter Pilot 67-69
Nordhaus, William Dawbney	Education	Prof, Assoc, Asst Prof Economics 67-79, Yale U; Mbr 77-79, Council of Economic Advisors, US
O'Connell, Timothy James	Finance	VP, Oyster Bay Management Co, American Life of NY; Sgt 66-69, USAF
Rose, Jonathan Chapman	Government	Asst Attny Gen of US, in charge of Office of Legal Policy (DC); Ptnr 77-81, Jones, Day, Reavis & Pogue (DC); Deputy Asst Gen 75-77, Anti-trust; Assoc Deputy Attny Gen 74-75, US; General Counsel, Council on International Economic Policy, White House; Spec Asst to Pres 71-72, White House; Law Clerk, 67-68, Justice Cutter, MA Supreme Judicial Court; 1st Lt 69-71, Army
Rulon-Miller, Patrick	Finance	Investment Adviser, VP Inverness Counsel, Inc (NYC); 66-68, w/Bank of NY; 64, w/Farming in Israel at Kibutz-Galon; 64-66 w/Empire Trust; 66-68 w/Bank NY

1964		PERIOD 2, DECADE 162
NAME	OCCUPATION	NOTES
Best, Geoffry Donald Charles	Law	Assoc, Ptnr 1969-, LeBeouf, Lamb, Leiby & MacRae; English Instr 64-66, American University (Beruit, Lebanon)
Cirie, John Arthur	Marine Corps	Spec Asst to Asst Sec of Navy; Lt Col, Dir, Advertising, Marine Corps Recruiting; Capt 64-, USMC
Clay, Alexander Stephens	Law	Attny Associated Kilpatrick Cody Rogers McClatchey & Regenstein, Atlanta GA; Spec Rep of Pres 77-79, Indian Land Claims Negotiations; Dir, US-Rep of China Joint Economic Council; Counsel 69-71, Metropolitan Atlanta Council on Crime; Clerk 67-68, RC Body, US Court Eastern Dist of PA
Francis, Samuel Hopkins	Science	Research Physicist Bell Labs; Lt 64-66, USN
Gillette, Howard Frank Jr.	Education	Asst Prof, American Civilization, American Studies, George Washington U (DC); Coordinator 70, Project Pursestrings, Citizens Lobby to End the War
Kaminsky, Robert Isadore	Medicine	Urologist, TX; Physician 69-72, US Army, Beaumont Hosp (El Paso)
Lynch, Dennis Patrick	Finance	Institutional Stock Broker 76-, Lynch & Mayer, Inc, NYC; AP Sales 67-75, Smith, Barney & Co, Inc (NYC); Treas Deer Island Club; QM/2 64-65 USCG
McBride, Jonathan Evans	Finance	Pres 79-, McBride Associates, Inc (DC); VP 76-79, Simmons Associates, Inc; 72-76 Lionel D Edie & Co (NYC); 68-72 w/Merrill Lynch Pierce Fenner & Smith (DC); VP 68-70, Alumni Assn Sidwell Friends School; Lt 64-68, USNR
Prindle, Thomas Harrison	Education	Teaching Assoc 68-69, Acting Instr 69-70, German Yale U
Pulaski, Charles Alexander Jr.	Law	Prof Law, ASU (AZ); Attny, Tyler, Cooper, Grant, Bowerman & Keefe (New Haven, CT)
Rowe, Thomas D. Jr	Law	Assoc Dean, Prof Law, Duke U, School of Law; Law Clerk 70-71 , Assoc Justice Potter Stewart, Supreme Court US
Straw, Ralph Lynwood	Law	Attny, Wharton, Stewart & Davis (Somerville, NJ)
Van Loan, Eugene	Law	Capt 67-71, US Army JAGC
Wilbur, John Smith Jr.	Law Student	Attny, Ptnr, Caldwell Pacetti-Barrow & Salisbury (FL); Trial Attny, US DOJ. Asst US Attny, US Virgin Islands; Lt 64-68, USN Seal Team
Wolfe, Stephen H	Finance	Investment Planner, US Trust Co (NYC); Minister

1965		PERIOD 2, DECADE 163
NAME	OCCUPATION	NOTES
Ali, Mehdi Raza	Finance	VP 76-80, General Motors; VP Pepsico, Inc; VP 74-75, Asst VP 73, Asst Treas 70-72, Morgan Guaranty Trust
Benoit, Charles Edward Jr.	Student	Asst Program Officer, Ford Foundation; Officer in Charge 73-75, Saigon, Ford Foundation; Independent study of Chinese, Taiwan Normal U, Taipei; Research Staff 68-69, Rand Corp, Saigon; Staff 66-68, AID/Dept of State;
Clark, Gerald Holland	Theatre	Actor
Clark, Stephen Edward	Law	Lawyer, Athearn, Chandler & Hoffman; Coach 65-66, Peruvian Ntl Swim Team; Lt 69-71, USA Signal Corps
Clay, Timothy J.	Law	Lawyer, Ptnr, Phillips & Giraud, Paris; Convoy, Hewitt, O'Brien & Boardman, NYC
Coombs, Orde Musgrave	Literary & TV Work	Co-host, Conversations WPIX TV; Contributing Editor, New Yorker Magazine
Corey, Alan Lyle III	Finance	Assoc Broker NYSE, Wertheim & Co; Carlisle & DeCoppet
Desjardins, Peter Earl	Business	Managing Dir, Gulf Consulting Group, UAE; FMC International, Austria; Consultant 69-71, McKinsey & Co, (NY); Mbr 62, Certificat d'Etudes Politiques, U de Paris; Export Sales Mgr 65-67, Societe UMG, Automation, Paris; Lt 59-61, US Army
Fetner, Philip Jay	Law	Sr Ptnr, P Jay Fetner Associates, Managing Principal of African Development Group (DC); Cleary, Gottlieb, Steen & Hamilton (NYC); Teaching Fellow 69-70, Harvard
Lagercrantz, Bengt Magnus	Business	Planning Group asst, SKF Argentina 69; Trainee 67-69, Buenos Aires Branch, First Ntl City Bank of NY; LM Ericsson 70
Pinney, John Mercer	Business	Pres, John Pinnet Associates, Inc; Dir 78-81, Office on Smoking & Health, US Dept of Health & Human Services; Lt USN, Bureau Naval Personnel (DC)
Pond, Jeffrey Craig	Law	Attny, Holland & Hart, Denver
Quarles, James Perrin III	Law	Legal Staff 72-75 , Office of Enforcement, EPA (DC); Co Dir 76, Water Project, Natural Resources Defense Council; 1st Lt 65-68, Army
Shattuck, HF John III	Law	Exec Dir, ACLU (DC); Visiting Lecturer, Columbia, NYU, Princeton, Harvard, VA; Lawyer, Chambers of the Hon Edward Wienfield, US Courthouse (Foley Sq, NYC); Projects Dir 69-70, Yale Law Journal; 68 w/McCarthy Press Campaign; 69 w/Vietnam Moratorium Comm

Zallinger, Peter Franz	Art	Freelance Illustrator; Lt 66-69, USNR

1966 — PERIOD 2, DECADE 164

NAME	OCCUPATION	NOTES
Bockstoce, John R.	Education	Curator of Ethnology, New Bedford Whaling Museum; Asst to Dir 68-70, U Museum, U of PA; Intern Asst 66, Sec Smithsonian
Bradford, Timothy McFall	Education	Ptnr Hewitt Associates; 70 Dir, 71 Bd of Gov., Teacher of English, Greenwich Country Day Schools
Brown, George Clifford	Medicine	Orthopedic Surgeon; Surgical Intern, Roosevelt Hospital; Lt Army Reserve
Cross, Alan Whitmore	Medicine	Pediatrics, Strong Memorial Hosp, Rochester NY; VP, GD Miller Corp
Dalby, Michael Thomas	Education	Asst Prof, Chinese History Dept, U Chicago
Howard, James Ernest	Law	Ptnr, Kirkpatrick, Lockhart, Johnson & Hutchison, PA; Assoc Montgomery, McCracken, Walker & Rhoades; Assoc Gen Counsel, Staff Lawyer 71-80 Trustee of Penn Central Transportation Co; Mbr 69-75, PA Ntl Guard
Kerry, John Forbes	Government/ Writing	US Senator MA; Ptnr 79-83, Kerry & Sragow; 1st Asst DA 76-79 (Middlesex County, MA); Co-ordinator, MA Vietnam Veterans Against the War; Lt 66-70, USNR
Laidley, Forrest David	Law	Gen Counsel, Ptnr Wm Blair & Co
Pershing, Richard Warren	X	Lt, 101st Airborne Div
Rumsey, David McIver	Art/Finance	Pres, General Atlantic Realty Group (CA); Research Assoc 68-71, Yale Art School Faculty
Singer, Ronald Leonard	Business	VP, James River Corp, CT; VP, Gen Mgr 80-82, VP 77-80, American Can Co; SR VP, CFO Welsbach Corp; Operations Research Analyst 68-70, US DOD
Smith, Frederick Wallace	Business, Finance	Founder, CEO, Pres Federal Express; Aviation Consultants, Investments, Little Rock; Dir Business Roundtable, CATO Institute, Library of Congress James Madison Council, Mayo Foundation, VChmn U.S.-China Business Council; Capt 66-69, USMC
Stanberry, William Burks Jr.	Law	Pres, CEO Surgicare Corp (TX); Pres, CEO 74-81, VP Gen Counsel 71-73, Hycel, Inc; VP. Corporate Attny, Spec Asst to Pres 69-71, Crutcher Resources Corp
Thorne, David Hoadley	Communications	Pres, Thorne & Co (MA); Ptnr, Martilla, Payne, Kiley & Thorne; Dir 80-, Turner Corp, North American Energy Systems; Lt 66-70, USN
Vargish, Thomas	Medicine	Assoc Prof of Surgery, WV U Medical Ctr (WV); Physician, Intern Surgery Dept, NYU-Bellvue Med Ctr (NYC)

1967 — PERIOD 2, DECADE 165

NAME	OCCUPATION	NOTES
Afeoju, Bernard Ikecukwu	Engineering	Heat Transfer Engineer, The Ralph M Parsons, Co:Petroleum Engineer 68-73, Shell Oil
Ashe, Victor Henderson	Government	Mayor 75-, Knoxville, TN; TN State Senate; Mbr 68-72, TN House of Representatives; Lance Corporal, USMC
Bush, Derek George	Student	MBA Harvard
Foster, David John	Finance	Mgr, VP Results Management, Accuracy Corp, OH; Gen Mgr, VP Market Development 77-82, Accuracy Leasing, Inc; Asst to Pres 69, Rockford Aeromatic Products; Supply officer 69-72, USN
Garnsey, Walter W., Jr.	Law	Attny, Kelly, Haglund, Garnsey & Kahn (CO)
Lilley, Robert McGregor	Business	Managing Dir, Ehrmanns Wine Shippers Ltd, (UK, London); Dir, Environmental Resources, Inc (DC); Mgr 69-70, Gov Affairs Del Monte Corp; Cord Found fellowship 68-69, Public Affairs; Pfc 68-69, Army
Miller, James Whipple	Publishing	Publisher/Editor Digest of Financial Planning Ideas; Asst Prof Oriental Languages, UC Berkeley
Mitchell, H. Coleman Jr.	Television	Producer 81-, *Gimme A Break*; Sec, VP Uncle Toby Productions, CA; Writer, Story Editor, Exec Script consultant 74-77, MTM Enterprises, *The Bob Newhart Show, Rhoda,* etc, ; Independent Producer 77-81, affiliated w/Columbia Pictures TV
Neigher, Geoffrey Mark	Television	TV Writer/Producer 71-74, Writer MTM Enterprises; Producer 74-77, Columbia Pics TV; Producer 81-, NBC TV, *Gimme A Break; Law & Order: Criminal Intent, Northern Exposure, Picket Fences, Rhoda, Bob Newhart Show* and more
Preston, James Marshall	Law, Finance	Attny, Goodwin, Proctor & Hoar (MA); Assoc, Coudert Freres (Paris); Corporate Finance, First Boston Corp (NYC)
Richards, David Alan	Law	Ptnr 83- , Sidley & Austin (NY); Assoc Ptnr 77-82, Coudert Brothers; Assoc 72-77, Paul, Weiss, Rifkind, Wharton & Garrison; Spec Asst 69-71, Fgn Visitors, Yale International Office
Saxon, James M	Finance	Pres, General Syndicators of America (NYC); Bond Salesman, Salomon Brothers; Lawyer 70-72 w/Cadwalader, Wickersham & Taft
Snell, Bradford Curie	Law	Counsel, US Senate Antitrust Subcommittee; 72 w/Brookings Institution; 71-72 w/Assoc Pillsbury, Madison, (Sutro, CA)

Swil, Roy Anthony	Finance	Management Accountant; Exec Asst to Managing Dir, First National City Bank Ltd (South Africa, Johannesburg)
Thompson, Stephen Eberly Jr.	Ecology	Dir, Klah Klahnee Wildlife Sanctuary, OR; Pres 79-, Marmotological Society

1968 — PERIOD 2, DECADE 166

NAME	OCCUPATION	NOTES
Austin, Roy Leslie	Education	Asst Prof Sociology, PA State U
Birge, Robert Richards	Education	Asst Prof Chemistry, U CA (Riverside, CA); 2nd Lt, 71 USAF
Brown, Christopher Walworth	Law	Admin Asst to Hon Sam Roberts, Chief Justice Supreme Court of PA; Publishing Trainee 69-70, *Time*, Inc; Lawyer
Bush, George Walker	Armed Services	Pres 2000-, US; Governor 96-2000, TX; Investor Texas Rangers; Pres, Harken Energy; CEO Bush Exploration Co; Lt Pilot 68-74, Texas Air Ntl Guard
Cohen, Kenneth Saul	Business	Dentist, Private practice; Faculty Emory U; VP, US Dial Corp, PSA, Inc; Mbr Bd Dir 78-, Alliance Theatre Co
Cowdry, Rex William	Student	76, US Public Health Service; Assoc Clinical Dir, Intramural Research Program, NIMH, MD; Assoc Clinical Prof Georgetown U
Etra, Donald.	Student	Lawyer 95, Donald Etra; Assoc 81, Sidley & Austin; Asst US Attny 78-81, DOJ (LA); Assoc 71-73, Ralph Nader (DC); U.S. Attorney 73-77, Dept of Justice; Dir, RTA; 72-75 Pres 70-72, Dear Island Club
Gallico, G.Gregory III	Medicine	Surgeon, MA General Hosp; Asst Prof 80, Harvard Med Sch
Guthrie, Robert Karle III	Student	U of Regensberg, West Germany
Kolar, Bruton Ward (Britt)	Medicine	Family Physician; Lt, USN, attached to US Embassy, Nicosia, Cyrpus; US Naval Intelligence
McCallum, Robert Davis Jr.	Law	Asst Attny Gen 2000 US; Ptnr, Alston & Bird (GA)
Saleh, Muhammad Ahmed	Insurance	VP Timex Corporation, CT; Group Pension Dept, CT General Life Ins Co, Hartford; Adjunct Faculty, Poly Sci Dept U Hartford;
Schmidt, Thomas Carl	Consulting	Owner, Management of Montana; Spec 5 68-70, Army
Schollander, Donald Arthur	Finance	Pres North Shore Development Corp (OR); Dir, Student Employment, Financial Aids Lewis & Clark College (Portland); Institutional Sales, Eastman Dillon Securities; 67-68 w/USMC; Olympian
Thorne, Brinkley Stimson	Architecture	Ptnr, Metcalf & Thorne, Mgr Thorne Market (MA)

1969 — PERIOD 2, DECADE 167

NAME	OCCUPATION	NOTES
Arras, Robert Edward Jr.	Industrial	Gen Mgr, Far East Molasses Corp, Philippines
Bouscaren, Michael Frederic	Business	VP, Mngr, Putnam Management Co, (Boston); Dir 74-75, RTA; Lt jg, USNR (Canal Zone)
Buck, Charles Henry III	Business	Business Dir; Teaching Asst Music Dept UC Berkley;
Cosgrove, Thomas Francis Jr.	Business	Exec Search consultant, The Cosgrove Co, (CT); Asst VP for Staffing 80-82, Hartford Insurance Group; 73-78, Aetna Life & Casualty
Demaree, Frank Edward II	X	
Dowling, Brian J.	Sports	Quarterback, Boston Patriots
Fuller, Henry W.	Student	Boatyard Operator (Nova Scotia); Graduate work, London School of Economics
Livingston II, Richard H.B.	Business	VP, Treas, Admiral Shipping Services, Inc (FL); Treas 77-79, Lorentzen Shipping Agency (FL); Skaarup Shipping Corp (NYC)
Madden, Bernard Patrick	Finance	Marketing Dir, VP, First Bancorp, Inc (CT); Mbr 77-79, CT State Senate; 71-72w/ Woodbridge Bank & Trust Co; 73-75 w/First New Haven Ntnl Bank; High school teacher
Miller, Wentworth Earl	Law	Asst US Attny 80-82, Eastern Dist NY; Asst DA 77-80, Kings Co, Brooklyn; 70, Rhodes Scholar
O'Leary, John Joseph Jr.	Law	Ptnr, Pierce, Atwood, Scribner, Allen, Smith & Lancaster (ME); Mayor 80-81 (Portland, ME); Mellon Fellow literature, Clare College, Cambridge, England
Schwarzman, Stephen Allen.	Finance	Managing Director, Lehman Brothers Kuhn Loeb, Inc (NYC); Financial Analyst 69-70, Donald, Lufkin & Jenrette, Inc (NYC); National Guard
Selander, Duane Arthur	Business	The Continental Insurance Co (NJ); Supervisor Southland Corp (Denver); Cprl 62-65, USMC
Thompson, William McIlwaine Jr.	Law	Lawyer (TX); VP, Founder, Dir 74-80, Guardian Oil Co; 72-76 w/Christian, Barton, Epps, Brent & Chappell (VA)
Woodlock, Douglas Preston	Journalism	U.S. Federal District Judge 86- (MA); Asst US Attny, 79-83 (New England Organized Crime Strike Force, MA); Instr 81-82, Harvard Law School; Lawyer 76-79, Goodwin, Procter & Hoar (MA); Staff 73-75, US SEC; Newspaperman 69-73, Chicago *Sun-Times* (IL, DC)

1970 — PERIOD 2, DECADE 168

NAME	OCCUPATION	NOTES
Brown, William Scott	Writing	Publications Editor, U MT; Copy Editor 71, New Haven *Journal Courier*; Exec Dir 73-74, RTA, Resident Patriarch 77, RTA
Case, Philip Benham Jr.	Industrial	Pres, Southeast Ohio Oil & Gas Assn
Downing, Earl S. III	X	Pres, Downing & Associates (Solar Heating)
Eyre, Lawrence L.	Education	Dept of Religious Studies, U VA; Dean of Faculty, Maharishi International U School, (IA); Teacher 76, Transcendental Meditation; Yale Alumni Bd; Editor, RTA Catalogue
Friedland, Johnathan David	Law	Attny, S Freidman & Co (Israel)
Greenberg, Stephen David	Law/Sports	Attny, Manatt, Phelps, Rothenberg & Tunney, CA; Pro Baseball 70-74, Texas Rangers
Hodes, Douglas Michael	Insurance,	VP, Actuarial Asst Met Life (NYC)
Jackson, Terrence John	Education	Coal Sales Mgr, Phillips coal Co, TX; 75-81 w/Consolidation Coal Co; History Teacher, Football coach, Woodmere Academy (Woodmere, NY)
Miller, Thomas Clairborne	Banking	Exec VP, Bankers Finance Investment Management Corp (VA); Trust Dept, Riggs Ntnl Bank (DC)
Morgan, Robert McNair	Law	Lawyer, Covington & Burling (DC); 1st Lt 70-72, AUS, Vietnam
Ohene-Frempong, Kwaku	Medicine	Pediatric Hematologist, Tulane U, School of Medicine
Peters, Daniel James	Writing	Mbr, 70-72 Vietnam Resistance Brigade
Scattergood, Thomas Bevan	Education	Germantown Friends School, PA; English Teacher, Moses Brown School
Thompson, Jonathan Penfield	Engineering	Engineer, Sales Mgr, Fairchild Automated Parts, Inc, CT; Pres, 80-83, Sec 78-80 Deer Island Club Corp; Sec 80-83 GD Miller Corp
Trower, C. Christopher	Law	Ptnr, Brown, Todd & Heyburn (KY); Spec Asst to Dir 71-73, KY Crime Commission; Rhodes Scholar, Oxford

1971 — PERIOD 2, DECADE 169

NAME	OCCUPATION	NOTES
Babst, James Anthony	Student	Ptnr, Chaffe, McCall, Phillips, Toler & Sarpy, LA
Bryan, James Taylor	Law	Attny, Cooper, Williams & Bryan
Ekfelt, Richard (Dick) Henry	Law	Investment Advisor (Oil & Gas); Private Practice 76-82, (DC); Law Clerk 74-76, WV Supreme Court of Appeals
Feinerman, James Vincent	Law	Assoc, Davis, Polk & Wardwell; Fullbright Lecturer in Law 82-83, Peking U; Undergrad Admission Office 71-73, Mbr 74-75 Bd of Governors, Yale U; Staff 71-73, Yale-in-China
Fortgang, Jeffrey	Psychology	Clinical Psychologist, Bay Colony Health Services
Galvin, Michael Gerard	Advertising	Head, Galvin Advertising
Halpin, Thomas Michael	X	
Hernandez, Carols Arturo	Medicine	Physician, Columbia
Inman, Robert Davies	Medicine	Physician, Ont, Canada; Asst Prof Medicine Cornell U (NY)
Johnson, Wilbur John Jr.	Student	
Kosturko, William Theodore	Law	Sr VP, Counsel, Society for Savings, CT; Assoc 74-79, Day, Berry & Howard
Levin, Charles Herbert	Theatre	Actor
Morgan, James Wallace	Education	Superintendent (Pocantico Hills, NY); Teacher (CT, NY)
Noyes, Edward MacArthur	Medicine	Physician (Sunrise Hosp, NV)
Taft, Thomas Prindle	Education	School Teacher, Carpenter

1972 — PERIOD 2, DECADE 170

NAME	OCCUPATION	NOTES
Cangelosi, Russell Joseph	Student	
Clark, Douglas Wells	Science	Consulting Engineer 82- , Principal Engineer 80-82 , Digital Equipment Corp; Mbr 76-80, Research Staff, Xerox, Palo Alto
Csar, Michael F.	Law	Attny, Wilson & McIlvaine, (IL)
Evans, Peter Seelye	Drama	
Fisher, Scott B.	Business	Gen Mgr, Employee Relations, Petroleum Information Corp, (CO)
Lewis, Mark Sanders	Education	Ptnr, Island Technologies
Lutz, Karl Evan	Law	Ptnr, Kirkland & Ellis (IL)
MacDonald, Richard Joseph II	Student	
McLaren, Michael Glenn	Law	Ptnr, Thomason, Hendrix & Harvey (TN); Pres, Treas, Sec, Deer Island Club
Moyer, Douglas Richard	Business	Builder/woodworker; Ptnr Mendocino Recording Co (CA)
Ritterbush, Stephen Grover Jr.	Student	
Sauber, Richard Alan	Law	Attny, Chief, Defense Procurement Fraud Unit, DOJ (DC)
Walden, Robert Stewart	X	

Wilson, Zebuon Vance	Writing	Sr Dir 79-83, Independent Educational Services; Principal 77-79, Teacher 74-79, The Lovett School
Ziegler, Stan Warren	Psychology	Clinical Psychologists

1973 — PERIOD 2, DECADE 171

NAME	OCCUPATION	NOTES
Barasch, Alan Sidney	Psychiatry	80-83, w/Payne Whitney Clinic
Bellis, Tedric Lawrence	Business	Pres, Sea Hawk Transfer, Inc; Ptnr, Sierra Associates, NY
Finney, C. Roger	Architecture	
Green, Benjamin P.	Medicine	
Highfill, Philip Henry III	Music	Free-Lance Pianist; Mbr, 74 Santa Fe Opera
Huey, Mark Christopher	Education	Instructor English, Monroe Community College, (NY)
Karageorge, James Louis	Business	Freelance Commercial Photographer
Liles, Coit Redfearn	Government	Legislative Asst 75-80, Hon WG Hefner; Staff Aide 73-74, Hon Sam J Ervin; Dir, Deer Island Club Corp
Lonsdorf, David B.	X	
MacDonald, Stephen Joseph	Law	Lawyer, Assoc, Smith Lyons, Torrance, Stevenson & Mayer
Mattlin, Fred Walter	Law	Ptnr, Ross & Hardies (FL)
McPhee, Stephen Joseph	Medicine	Asst Prof, Medicine, U CA (SF, CA)
Moore, David Clement	Finance	Mgr, Schumberger Investment Service BV, Netherlands
Scott, William Ian	Law	Lawyer, w/Tilley, Carson & Findlay, Canada, Toronto; Caretaker, 75-76, Treas, RTA, Inc
Sulzer, James Sothern	Writing/ Education	Writer/Teacher, Nantucket Chamber Music Center (MA); Project Mgr 77-82, WGBH-TV (MA)

1974 — PERIOD 2, DECADE 172

NAME	OCCUPATION	NOTES
Ayeroff, Frederick Charles	Writing	
Barge, Richard Mason	Law	Attny, Fisher & Phillips; Sgt E-5 67-70, Army Intelligence
Bellis, Jon Michael	Education	79-81 Y Psychiatric Inst; Spec Educ, 75-78 Hopkins Grammar School
Bisaro, Larry R.	Accounting	Chartered Accounting
Cohen, Robert Lewis	Films	Owner, Wingstar Film Productions, Inc; writer, producer 75-76, Tele-Tactics, Inc
Connors, David Michael	Law	Attny LeBouef, Lamb, Leiby & MacRae, (UT); Missionary 74-76, LDS Italy
Diamond, Peter C.	Television	Dir, Olympic Planning, ABC; Assoc Producer 77-80, Olympics Research NBC; Olympics Researcher 74-76, ABC
Doyle, Thomas James Jr.	Finance	Asst VP, International Bond Ratings, Standard & Poor's
Eisenberg, Bruce Alan	Law	Attny, Cohen, Snyder, McCellan, Eisenberg & Katzenberg
Gonzalez, Timoteo F.	Law	Attny
Kelly, Brian Christopher	Law	Of Counsel, Ptnr 53-82, Brooks, Kelly & Barron (NV)
Lewis, George Emanuel	Music	Anthony Braxton Quartet; Count Basie Orchestra
Murchison, Brian Cameron	Law	95 w/ACUS-USIA Rule of Law in Africa Program, Ghana; Prof 90, Law, Washington and Lee U; Prof Law, Director 91-94, Frances Lewis Law Center; Assistant Prof 82-86, Assoc Prof 86-90, Prof 90-91, Law; Assoc, Hamel, Park, McCabe and Saunders (Washington, DC); Peace Corps 74-76 (Benin, West Africa)
Spear, Wesley John	Art	Painter
Thorne, Charles Hedges McKinstry	Medicine	Chief 92, Plastic Surgery Service, Bellevue Hospital; Director 89-98, Plastic Surgery Residency Program, N.Y.U. Medical Center; Program Director 98-, Aesthetic Surgery Fellowship, Manhattan Eye, Ear and Throat Hospital

1975 — PERIOD 2, DECADE 173

NAME	OCCUPATION	NOTES ONLY 14 MEMBERS
Ashenfelter, Alan Thompson	Medicine	Physician, Bascom Palmer Eye Institute, FL
Bender, Kenneth Arthur	Banking	Marketing Mgr, Mexico, Central Am, Caribbean, RBC Trade Finance, Inc, NYC
Buckley, Christopher Taylor	Writing	Managing Editor, Roving Editor, *Esquire* Magazine; Chief Speechwriter 81-83, VP of US;
Burke, James Eugene III	Law	Attorney, Keating, Muething & Klekamp, OH; 78-81, Taft, Stettinius & Hollister
English, William Deshay Jr.	Industrial	1st Lt 69-72, AUS Intelligence, Vietnam
Gaines, Edwin Frank	Entertainment	Lyricist/Playwright
Green, Rudolph	X	
Kanehl, Phillip Edwin	Farming	
MacKenzie, Kenneth M.	Accounting	Price-Waterhouse

Reigeluth, Douglas Scott	Finance	Deputy Mgr, Brown Brothers Harriman & Co (NY)
Saffen, David	X	
Struzzi, Thomas Allen	Aviation	Marketing Mgr, TWA (NY); International Marketing Mgr 81-82, TWA (London)
Wald, Stephen George	Student	Talmudist/Theologian, Doctoral Candidate, Hebrew U of Jerusalem
Zorthian, Gregory Jannig	Publishing	New Business Mgr, Circulation, *Fortune* Magazine, Time Inc (NYC); Legislative Aide, US Rep Jonathan Bingham; Dir, Deer Island Corp

1976 — PERIOD 2, DECADE 174

NAME	OCCUPATION	NOTES
Blattner, Robert William	X	
Brubaker, John Kim	Business	Mngr, Southern New England Southwestern Co
Capozzalo, Douglas Daniel	Theatre	
Casscells, Christopher Dyson	Medicine	Resident Physician, Yale-New Haven Hosp
Childs, Starling Winston	Forestry	Asst Prof 81-82, Biology, U Hartford; 81- CT Forest & Parks Assn; 76-77, New Zealand Forest Service; Dir 79-82, RTA
Davies, Philip Turner	Law	Attorney
Fort, Donald Kenneth	Student	
Gates, Edward Raymond	Student	
Gibson, Richard Channing Jr.	Literary	Screenwriter
Hart, Dennis Charles	Law	Lawyer, Testa, Hurwitz & Thibeault (MA)
Leverett, Miles Watson	X	Songwriter/Singer, On Company (NYC)
Mehta, Arjay Singh	Transportation	Indian Railway Traffic Services
Morgenstern, Marc Jaime	Journalism	Exec Producer, KNXT News (LA, CA)
Oler, Clark Kimberly Jr.	Music	Musician/Composer
Williams, Darryl L.	X	

1977 — PERIOD 2, DECADE 175

NAME	OCCUPATION	NOTES
Blakely, Marvin	Law	Law Clerk, Contra Costa Cnty, DA Office; Bd Gov, Hasting College of Law
Brubaker, James Robert	Finance	Asst VP, Citicorp; Club Agent 77-, RTA
Cooper, Carnell	Medicine	Surgery, U MN
Fredericks, Joel Richard	X	
Goldberg, Richard Julius	Consultant	Sales Consultant, Elcomp Systems (PA)
Grayson, William Cabell, Jr.	Finance	Sales Mgr, Asst VP, Coldwell Banker Real Estate Services
Kee, Christopher Andrew	X	
Lalley, Patrick William	Student	
Lawler, Quentin John	Finance	Account Exec, Paine, Webber Mitchell & Hutchins (CT)
Newman, Thomas M.	Student	
Perry, David Bulkey	Education	Writing
Rimar, Stephen III	Medicine	Pediatrics, Yale-New Haven Hosp
Schlesinger, Daniel Adam	Student	Harvard Law
Scott, Larry Glenn	Student	
Tom Chan Bruce III	Business	VP, Chinese Trading, Chinese Noodle Co, Man Chena Corp (IL)

1978 — PERIOD 2, DECADE 176

NAME	OCCUPATION	NOTES
Albritton, Paul Berem	Law	Assoc Graham & James (CA)
Baran, Mark R.	Finance	Financial Planner, Executive Planning Associates
Bassi, Keith Alan	Law	Attny, Bassi & Rega, PA
Clark, J. Bruce	X	
Gile, Lawrence Maclester	Student	Columbia, Grad School of Business; Insurance Broker, Alexander & Alexander, Inc (NY); Dir, RTA
Holmes, Peter Samuel	Student	Law Student
Hook, Noble	X	
Karp, Benjamin C	X	
Marinelli, David Leonard	Medicine	Radiology
Owens, Samuel L.	X	
Piel, Geoffrey D.	X	
Rizzo, Robert John	Medicine	Surgeon, Brigham & Women's Hosp (MA); Dir, RTA
Roy, John Marcus	Theatre	Admin Dir, The International Chamber Arts Series, Inc, PR
Sullivan, Charles S.	X	

Turner, Elvin D.	X	

1979 — PERIOD 2, DECADE 177

NAME	OCCUPATION	NOTES
Brown, Robert Nelson	Theatre	Actor, Monty Silver Agency
Edozien, Anthony O.	X	
Fore, John Arthur	Law	Dir 77-79, Yale Co-op Corp
Holmbee, Jeffrey Arthur	Student	Medical School
Lorenson, David Harold	Business/Artist	Engineer, Cumming North Atlantic, Inc (MA)
McNally, Edward E	Law, Government	Gen Counsel of the Office on Homeland Security, Senior Associate Counsel on National Security, George W Bush Admin; Spec Asst to the Asst Attny Gen, US Dept of Justice, (DC); Dir 83-, Governors Project on Organized Crime & Narcotics Trafficking; Press Aide 81-, Office of VP, US
Moses, Jack Thomas	Student	Stanford Grad School; Assoc Consultant 80-82, Data Resources, Inc
Nondorf, Kurt D.	X	
O'Brien, Donald Patrick	Law	Lawyer, Wood, Campbell, Moody & Gibbs (TX)
Peters, Eric Brooks	Writing	
Skrovan, Stephen Thomas	Theatre	Stand-up Comedian
Stevenson, Charles P.	Television	TV News, KGTV (CA)
Westerfield, Richard H.	X	
Wilson, Daniel Richard	Medicine	Psychiatry Resident, McLean Hosp (MA)
Yent, James B. Jr.	X	

1980 — PERIOD 2, DECADE 178

NAME	OCCUPATION	NOTES
Austin, Samuel Monroe	Music	Composer
Chibundu, Maxwell O.	x	
Davenport, George Leovy	Geology	Petroleum Geologist, Bolyard Oil & Gas, (CO)
DeVore, Mark Samuel	Student	MD, U of Cincinnati Med School
Dilworth, George Toby	Government	Spec Asst, US Senator Paul Tsongas
Fleming, Andrew T.	X	
Hatem, John J.	X	
Kagan, Robert William	Student	Asst editor 80-81, *The Public Interest*
Lawrence, Gary Martin	X	
Mulhern, Daniel Kevin	Social work	Pres, Coalition on Human Dignity; Dir 81-83, The Center (New Orleans)
Peters, Elliot Remsen	Student	Law
Stevens, Eric Eugene	Student	Washington U Medical School (MO)
Teig, Joseph Benjamin	Theatre	Singer, Actor; Rooms Controller 81, Marriot Corp
Tumpane, Timothy Michael	Industry	Production Planner, Quaker Oats Co (IA)
Zigerelli, Lawrence John	Industry	Asst Brand Mgr, Marketing, Procter & Gamble (OH)

1981 — PERIOD 2, DECADE 179

NAME	OCCUPATION	NOTES
Campbell, Kimberly C	Government	East Hampton Town Councilman
DeVore, Mark Samuel		
Carlsson, Mats Erik	Business	Travel Guide, Italy
Choa, Christopher James	Architecture	Architect 82-, David Paul Helpern & Associates, NYC; Designer 81-82, Leigh & Orange, Hong Kong; Designer 82-, Contractor Russell Restoration Corp
Conway, Joseph Leo Jr.	Finance	Securities Option Arbitrageur, Mabon, Nugent & Co, NYC
Grandine, Thomas Allan	Student	
Novosel, David Gerard	X	
O'Keefe, Regis James	X	
Peters, Kenneth Graham	X	
Peterson, Paul Clifford	Accounting	
Russell, Richard George	X	
Staven, Karl Eric	Psychology	Psychodrama Intern, ST Elizabeths (DC)
Stratton, Daniel James	X	
Tingey, Douglas Stuart	Business	Sales Rep, Xerox
Troy, Alexander	Student	Harvard Law School

1982 — PERIOD 2, DECADE 180

NAME	OCCUPATION	NOTES
Bass, James Edward	X	

Breslau, Jonathan	Student	
Burkus, Gregory James	X	
Campbell, Gavin Elliott	Government	Analyst, International Trade section Div, IL Dept of Agriculture
Devlin, Michael William	Education	English Lecturer, Chinese U, (Hong Kong)
Leone, Frederick Anthony	X	
McAfee, William Andrew	Publishing	City Editor, Black River Tribune (VT); Features Editor, North Country News
Meyers, Bryan Fitch	Student	Medical Student, USN
Murchison, Robert W	X	
Rachlin, David Isaiah		
Reid, Jasper	Business	VP, Transeastern, Inc; VP, Plenux International Corp; Consulting Editor, Global Digest, Inc (NY)
Salzman, Mark Joseph	Education	Teacher English, Yale-in-China, Hunan, PRC
Sanhago, Eddie	X	
Towers, Jonathan David	Television	Writer, Editor, Copy, Satellite News, Group W Satellite Communications (CT)
Wright, William Henry II	Finance	Mergers & Acquisitions, Morgan & Stanley & Co, Inc (NYC); Head Page 77-78, Republican Cloakroom, US House of Rep
Yang, James Ting-Yeh	Student	Yale Law School

1983 — PERIOD 2, DECADE 181

NAME	OCCUPATION	NOTES
Abrams, Peter Mark		
Brooks, Peter Moody	Student	
Cerveris, Michael Ernest	Student	
Franklin, Richard David	Finance	
Gale, Frederick Scott		
Kafoglis, Christian Nicholas		
Kaushal, Shalesh		
Montesano, Michael John III		
Nichols, William Allen		
Noel, Christopher		
Pinela, Carlos		
Sharp, Jonathan Douglas		
Sheffield, John Van Loon		
Wagner, Victor Edmond		

1984 — PERIOD 2, DECADE 182

NAME	OCCUPATION	NOTES
Andrie, Paul James		
Coggins, Daniel Seton		
Crawley, Brian Scott		
Davison, Henry Pomeroy		
Graves, Earl Gilbert Jr.		
Henston, Douglas Robert		
Herskovits, David Nathaniel		
Jung, Michael David		
Kahle, Jeffrey Lewis		
Lampert, Edward Scott		
Litt, David Geoffrey		
Skibell, Steven Alan		
Urquijo, Conzalo		
Weinstein, Adam		
Wiseman, David Batshaw		

1985 — PERIOD 2, DECADE 183

NAME	OCCUPATION	NOTES
Boasberg, James Emanuel		
Carlin, William John Carr Jr		
Chandrasekhar, Ashok Jai		
Frankel, Scott David		
Grossman, Jay Alan		
Kwok, Wei-Tai		
Lindy, Peter Barnes		
Misner, Timothy Charles		

Mnu Chin Steven Terner		
Petela, James Gerard		
Powers, Richard Hart		
Smock, Morgan Robert		
Taft, Horace Dutton		
Thomson, Gregory Allan		
Walsh, Kevin Sanchez		

1986 — PERIOD 2, DECADE 184

NAME	OCCUPATION	NOTES
Walton, Keith	Law	Sec 1896- Columbia U; Sr Advisor to Undersecretary of US Dept of Treas for Enforcement

1987 — PERIOD 2, DECADE 185

NAME	OCCUPATION	NOTES

1988 — PERIOD 2, DECADE 186

NAME	OCCUPATION	NOTES

1989		PERIOD 2, DECADE 187
NAME	OCCUPATION	NOTES

1990		PERIOD 2, DECADE 188
NAME	OCCUPATION	NOTES

1991		PERIOD 2, DECADE 189
NAME	OCCUPATION	NOTES

1992		PERIOD 2, DECADE 190
NAME	OCCUPATION	NOTES

1993			PERIOD 2, DECADE 191
NAME	OCCUPATION	NOTES	

1994			PERIOD 2, DECADE 192
NAME	OCCUPATION	NOTES	

1995			PERIOD 2, DECADE 193
NAME	OCCUPATION	NOTES	

* from *Rumpus*, a Yale University tabloid

1996 — Period 2, Decade 194

Name	Occupation	Notes
Oppenheimer, Mark	Writer	writer w/ Hartford Courant, NY Times BookReview, The New Yorker, Slate, Playboy Magazine

1997 — Period 2, Decade 195

Name	Occupation	Notes

1998 — Period 2, Decade 196

Name	Occupation	Notes
*Abbot, Frankie		
*Auh, Eugene		
*Benton, Scott		
*Eisenstadt, Leora		
*Falcon, Angel		
*Fromm, Julie		
*Gonzalez, Julio		
*Lee, Earl		
*McBride, Webster		
*Medard, Wilodene		
*Murphy, Maiya		
*Petit, Charlie		
*Raborar, Farrah		
*Rashid, Tauheedah		

Name	Occupation	Notes
Scott, Shannon		

1999 — PERIOD 2, DECADE 197

NAME	OCCUPATION	NOTES

2000 — PERIOD 2, DECADE 198

NAME	OCCUPATION	NOTES
*Anderson, Dargie		
*Berrelez, Manuel		
*Blake, Benjamin		
*Borghese, Luca		
*Charles, Anana		
*Denit, Kelly		
*Heikkila, Jennifer		
*Hirway, Hrishikesh		
*Hongo, Andrew		
*Johnson, Ayanna		
*Kirowski, John		
*Lester, Sara		
*Mizrahi, Celine		
*Renan, Daphna		
*Walker, Christopher		

2001 — PERIOD 2, DECADE 199

NAME	OCCUPATION	NOTES

2002 — PERIOD 2, DECADE 200

NAME	OCCUPATION	NOTES
*Banerjee, Bidisha		
*Bazzle, John Bradley		
*Gaughen, Patrick Robert		
*Goldsmith, William Dixon		

*Herlwig, Paige Lynn		
*Hudson, Jared McCabe		
*Im, Jaisohn		
*Jiminez, Carlos		
*Montgomery, Kenita Trenae		
*Montoya, Maceo		
*Penna, Timothy Rick		
*Premejee, Sharmeen Malik		
*Ruiz, Sara Elizabeth		

2003 — PERIOD 2, DECADE 201

NAME	OCCUPATION	NOTES
*Archibong, Ime		
*Cobbett, Ashley		
*Feins, Eric		
*Kelly, EB		
*Lange, Jason		
*Norris, Graham		
*Pearce, James		
*Schraufnagel, Billy		

2004 — PERIOD 2, DECADE 202

NAME	DATE	OCCUPATION	NOTES
*Almy, Chad	2004	*	
*Ashraf, Sumeyya	2004	*	
*Burke, James	2004	*	
*Melniker, Sophie	2004	*	
*So, Perry	2004	*	
*Viteli, Paul	2004	*	

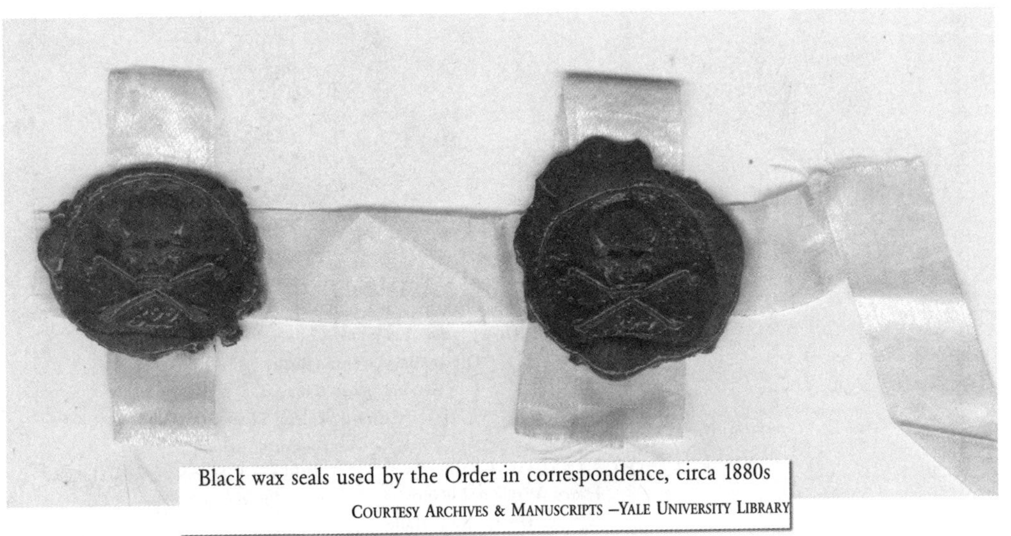

Black wax seals used by the Order in correspondence, circa 1880s

COURTESY ARCHIVES & MANUSCRIPTS –YALE UNIVERSITY LIBRARY

CLIPPINGS FROM THE YALE *BANNER*

These are the pages from the Yale *Banner* announcing some of the Bush family members initiation into the Order. The listing of new members by the *Banner* ceased in 1970 and continues halted through today, making a verified list of members for the years after difficult. The essay in the arty 1968 annual is by Lanny Davis, a presidential counselor for Bill Clinton and a member of one of Yale's seven secret societies

sential part of their program to accumulate as much information about the above-grounds—especially Bones—from year to year and thus keep adding to their file on tomb eccentricities.

But some observers see the future of societies in the flexibility of the underground system—and especially in the unique feature of Vaya or Vale. "At Yale," Professor Argyris says, "the co-ed societies undergo the same kind of experience as the all-male ones. In my view, in fact, they have a richer experience." He concludes that if Yale should go co-ed (in about five years' time) "this will not undermine the society impulse per se; but there will certainly be greater pressure to co-educate the societies."

A senior, currently in one of the co-ed societies, says: "It's fantastic, and you can forget about all that 'missed prestige'. You can get as intimate as you want with your roommates, if that's what you want to do. But talking in that way to girls, and getting to understand what a different thing the female mind is, that's another dimension altogether. Amazing, that's all."

Mr. Reisman would probably agree, He sees "a certain insulation at Yale from which some students are now breaking out." And, he adds, "I hope the place goes co-ed." And so, the argument rages on. There are those who insist that there will always be a need for an all-male society, no matter how much Yale changes. The possibility that Skull and Bones will co-educate in the near future is not strong. And others feel that the question of co-education apart, societies will have to change and adjust to the new spirit of skepticism.

[cropped from page bottom – ed.]

They probably will. Skull and Bones had to change a century of tradition in its tapping procedure merely to remain alive: pre-tapping has now become so prevalent that it is apparent that few "big men" would now turn down a sure election for the possibility of a Bones tap. And the periodic breakins to the society tombs,

Class of 1968

SKULL AND BONES

Roy Leslie Austin
Robert Richards Birge
Christopher Walworth Brown
George Walker Bush
Kenneth Saul Cohen
Rex W. F. Cowdry
Donald Etra
G. Gregory Gallico III
Robert Karl Guthrie
Britton Ward Kolar
Robert Davis Mc Callum, Jr.
Muhammad Ahmad Saleh
Thomas Carlton Schmidt
Donald Arthur Schollander
Brinkley Stimpson Thorne

Class of 1948

SKULL AND BONES

FOUNDED 1832

Edward Williamson Andrews, Jr.
Thomas William Ludlow Ashley
Lucius Horatio Biglow, Jr.
George Herbert Walker Bush
John Erwin Caulkins
William Judkins Clark
William James Connelly, Jr.
George Cook, III
Endicott Peabody Davison
David Charles Grimes
Richard Elwood Jenkins
Donald Loyal Leavenworth
Richard Gerstle Mack
Thomas Wilder Moseley
Frank O'Brien, Jr.
Philip O'Brien, Jr.
George Harold Pfau, Jr.
Samuel Sloane Walker, Jr.
Howard Sayre Weaver
Valleau Wilkie, Jr.

Class of 1917

SENIOR SOCIETY

Alfred Raymond Bellinger
Prescott Sheldon Bush
Henry Sage Fenimore Cooper
Oliver Baty Cunningham
Samuel Sloan Duryee
Edward Roland Noel Harriman
Henry Porter Isham
William Ellery Sedgwick James
Harry William LeGore
Henry Neil Mallon
Albert William Olsen
John Williams Overton
Frank Parsons Shepard, Jr.
Kenneth Farrand Simpson
Knight Woolley

ALPHABETICAL LISTING OF KNOWN MEMBERS OF THE ORDER OF SKULL & BONES

Name	Year
Abbe, Frederick Randolph	1848
Abbot, Frankie	1998
Aberg, Donlan Vincent Jr.	1952
Abrams, Peter Mark	1983
Acheson, David Campion	1943
Ackerman, Stephen Harry	1957
Acosta, John Sidney	1921
Adams, Charles Edward	1904
Adams, Charles H.	1866
Adams, Frederic Baldwin Jr.	1932
Adams, Frederick	1862
Adams, Frederick Baldwin	1900
Adams, George Webster	1904
Adams, Lewis G.	1920
Adams, Mason Tyler	1899
Adams, Stephen	1959
Afeoju, Bernard Ikecukwu	1967
Ahlbrandt, Roger S. Jr.	1963
Aiken, Edwin Edgerton	1881
Aiken, William Pope	1853
Aitchison, William	1848
Albritton, Paul Berem	1978
Aldis, Owen Franklin	1874
Aldrich, Malcolm Pratt	1922
Alexander, Eben	1873
Alexander, William DeWitt	1855
Alexander, William Felix	1851
Ali, Mehdi Raza	1965
Allen, Archibald John Jr.	1945
Allen, Arthur Dwight	1901
Allen, Arthur Huntington	1873
Allen, Calvin Durand	1913
Allen, Charles Edward	1958
Allen, Clarence Emir Jr.	1913
Allen, Daniel	1926
Allen, Frederick Winthrop	1900
Allen, Henry Elisha	1924
Allen, John DeWitt H.	1876
Allen, Parker Breese	1919
Allen, Walter	1863
Allen, William Palmer	1880
Alling, Charles Booth Jr.	1947
Allison, Robert Seaman Jr.	1930
Allison, Samuel Perkins	1847
Ames, Allen Wallace	1918
Ames, Sullivan Dobb	1899
Amundson, John Arnold	1880
Anderson, Dargie	2000
Anderson, Edwin Alexander	1835
Anderson, Thomas Hill	1951
Andrews, Edward W. Jr.	1947
Andrews, John W. Jr.	1870
Andrews, John Wolcott	1876
Andrie, Paul James	1984
Anthony, Benjamin Harris	1886
Appel, George F. Baer	1924
Ardrey, Rushton Leigh	1925
Arms, Charles Jesup	1863
Arnot, John Hulett	1885
Arnot, Matthias H.	1856
Arras, Robert Edward Jr.	1969
Ashburn, Frank Davis	1925
Ashe, Victor Henderson	1967
Ashenfelter, Alan T.	1975
Ashforth, Albert Blackhurst	1929
Ashley, Thomas W. Ludlow	1948
Auh, Eugene	1998
Austen, David Edward	1931
Austin, Roy Leslie	1968
Austin, Samuel Monroe	1980
Austin, Scott Alan	2002
Avery, Benjamin F.	1914
Avery, Charles Hammond	1875
Aycrigg, William A. II	1942
Ayeroff, Frederick Charles	1974
Babcock, Henry Harper	1853
Babst, James Anthony	1971
Back, Samuel Hutchins	1962
Backus, Joseph Willes	1846
Badger, Paul Bradford	1911
Badger, Walter Irving	1882
Bailey, Philip Horton	1897
Bair, Caitlin	2002
Baker, Richard Wheeler	1913
Baldridge, Howard M.	1918
Baldwin, George William	1853
Baldwin, Henry DeForest	1885
Baldwin, Roger Sherman	1847
Baldwin, Sherman	1919
Baldwin, Simeon Eren	1861
Ball, David George	1960
Banerjee, Bidisha	2002
Banks, Howard Daniel	1956
Bannard, Henry Clay	1869
Bannard, Otto Tremont	1876
Baran, Mark R.	1978
Barasch, Alan Sidney	1973
Baratte, Julius Adolphus	1843
Barge, Richard Mason	1974
Baribault, Richard Pfeifer	1949
Barker, George Payson	1856
Barnes, Pearce	1874
Barnes, William Deluce	1907
Barnes, William H. Lienow	1855
Barney, Danford Newton	1881
Barnum, William Milo	1877
Barr, Richard James Jr.	1936
Barres, Herster D.	1932
Barry, William Taylor S.	1841
Bartholemy, Alan Edmund	1942
Bartholomew, Dana Treat	1928
Bartlett, John Knowlton	1838
Bartlett, Philip Golden	1881
Bass, James Edward	1982
Bassett, Barton Bradley II	1949
Bassi, Keith Alan	1978
Bates, Emmert Warren	1932
Bates, Samuel Henshaw	1833
Bayard, Thomas Francis	1890
Bayne, Hugh Aiken	1892
Bayne, Thomas Levingston	1847
Bayne-Jones, Stanhope	1910
Bazzle, John Bradley	2002
Beach, John Campell	1833
Beach, John Sheldon	1839
Beane, Frank Eastman Jr.	1960
Beard, Anson McCook	1895
Beard, William Mossgrove	1896
Beaumont, George Anson O.	1834
Becket, George Campbell	1923
Becket, Peter Logan	1963
Beckley, John Werley	1860
Beebe, William	1873
Beers, Henry Augustin	1869
Begg, William Reynolds	1893
Beirne, Christopher James	1840
Belin, Gaspard d'Andelot	1939
Bell, Richard D. Spaight	1844
Bell, William Tompkins	1942
Bellinger, Alfred Rammond	1917
Bellis, Tedric Lawrence	1973
Bellis, Jon Michael	1974
Beman, Henry DeWitt	1851
Bench, Edward Cajetan	1925
Bender, Kenneth Arthur	1975
Benedict, Theodore H.	1840
Bennetto, John	1887

Name	Year
Benninghoff, Harry Bryner	1954
Benoit, Charles Edward Jr.	1965
Bent, Joseph Appleton	1865
Bentley, Edward Manross	1880
Bentley, Edward Warren	1850
Benton, Joseph Augustine	1842
Benton, Scott	1998
Berger, Jr., George Bart	1928
Berrelez, Manuel	2000
Berry, Coburn Dewees	1868
Bertron, Samuel Reading	1885
Best, Geoffry Donald C.	1964
Biddle, Thomas Bradish	1839
Bigelow, Albert	1852
Bigelow, Walter Irving	1877
Biglow, Lucius Horatio	1908
Biglow, Lucius Horatio Jr.	1948
Bingham, Charles Tiffany	1928
Bingham, Egert Byron	1863
Bingham, Jonathan B.	1936
Birge, Robert Richards	1968
Bisaro, Larry R.	1974
Bishop, Noah	1833
Bissell, Arthur Douglas	1867
Bissell, George Thomas	1961
Bissell, William Truesdale	1925
Bissell, Wilson Shannon	1869
Blackman, Charles Seymour	1857
Blackman, Samuel Curtis	1854
Blaine, Walker	1876
Blair, Edwin Foster	1924
Blair, James Grant	1925
Blair, William McCormick	1907
Blake, Benjamin	2000
Blake, Dexter B.	1937
Blake, Edward Foster	1858
Blake, Eli Whitney Jr	1857
Blake, Gilman Dorr Jr.	1945
Blake, Henry Taylor	1848
Blakely, Marvin	1977
Blakeslee, Henry Clay	1852
Blanchard Jerred Gurley	1939
Blattner, Robert William	1976
Bliss, Charles Miller	1852
Bliss, Robert	1850
Bliss, William Root	1850
Blodgett, George R.	1884
Blue, Linden Stanley	1958
Boasberg III, James E.	1956
Boasberg, James Emanuel	1985
Bockrath, Richard C.Jr.	1961
Bockstoce, John R.	1966
Bodman, William Camp	1959
Boies, Charles Alred	1860
Boltwood, Edward	1860
Boltwood, Edward	1892
Boltwood, Thomas Kast	1864
Booth, Samuel Albert	1884
Booth, Wilbur Franklin	1884
Borden, Matthew C.Durfee	1864
Boren, David Lyle	1963
Borghese, Luca	2000
Bottum, Elisha Slocum	1876
Boulos (Bouliaratis), William	1947
Bouscaren, Michael F	1969
Bowers, Lloyd Wheaton	1879
Bowles, Henry Thornton	1899
Bowles, John Eliot	1935
Bowles, William Carter Jr.	1961
Bowman, Ralph David	1957
Boyd, Francis T	1912
Boyden, Henry Paine	1864
Bradford, Amory Howe	1934
Bradford, Arthur Howe	1905
Bradford, Timothy McFall	1966
Bradley, Charles Harvey	1921
Brand, James	1866
Brandegee, Augustus	1849
Brandegee, Frank Bosworth	1885
Brandt, John Henry	1962
Breed, Edward Andrews	1844
Breen, John Gerald	1950
Bremmer, Samuel Kimball	1886
Breslau, Jonathan	1982
Brewster, Benjamin	1882
Brewster, Chauncey Bunce	1868
Brewster, James Henry IV	1962
Brewster, Walter Rice	1921
Brickell, James Noaille	1845
Bridgman, John Cloyse	1885
Brinsmade, Horatio Walsh	1851
Brisbrin, John Ball	1846
Bristol, Louis Henry	1859
Brodhead, Henry	1859
Bronson, David Bennet	1947
Bronson, James Davis	1926
Brooke, Frederic Hiester Jr.	1937
Brooke, Frederick Hiester	1899
Brooke, George Clymer	1897
Brooks, Henry Stanford	1885
Brooks, James Wilton	1875
Brooks, John Edward	1865
Brooks, Peter Moody	1983
Brooks, Tristam Anthony	1962
Brooks, Walter	1877
Brown, Alexander	1896
Brown, Alexander Lardner	1869
Brown, Christopher W.	1968
Brown, George Clifford	1966
Brown, Henry Armitt	1865
Brown, Hubert Sanford	1861
Brown, Jamot	1899
Brown, John Mason	1856
Brown, Joseph Venen	1842
Brown, Robert Nelson	1979
Brown, Samuel T. Glover	1944
Brown, Walter Henderson	
Brown, William Scott	1970
Brubaker, James Robert	1977
Brubaker, John Kim	1976
Bruce, Donald	1906
Bryan, James Taylor	1971
Bryan, Lloyd Thomas Jr.,	1955
Buchanan, Thomas Walter	1889
Buck, Charles Henry III	1969
Buckland, Joseph Payson	1857
Buckley, Christopher Taylor	1975
Buckley, Fergus Reid	1952
Buckley, James Lane	1944
Buckley, William Frank Jr.	1950
Buckner, Mortimer Norton	1895
Bulkey, Jonathan Duncan	1953
Bulkey, Jonathan Ogden	1923
Bulkey, Tuzar	1865
Bull, Cornelius Wade	1863
Bullock, Stanton B.	1981
Bumstead, Nathaniel Willis	1855
Bundy, Frederick McGeorge	1921
Bundy, Harvey Hollister	1909
Bundy, McGeorge	1940
Bundy, William Putman	1939
Bunnell, Phil W.	1927
Burch, Robert Boyd	1909
Burke, Charles Clinton r.	1937
Burke, James Eugene III	1975
Burkus, Gregory James	1982
Burnham, Curtis Field	1840
Burpee, Charles Winslow	1883
Burpee, Lucien Francis	1879
Burr, Charles Bentley II	1962
Burr, William Shedden	1834
Burrel, Joseph Dunn	1881
Burtt, Edwin Arthur	1915
Bush, Derek George	1967
Bush, George Herbert Walker	1948
Bush, George Walker	1968
Bush, James Smith	1922
Bush, Jonathan James	1953
Bush, Prescott Sheldon	1917

Name	Year
Bushnell, Samuel Clarke	1874
Bushnell, William Benedick	1865
Butler, Francis Eugene	1857
Butler, John Haskell	1863
Butterworth, Frank Seiler	1895
Buttles, Albert Barnes	1842
Cable, Benjamin Stickney	1895
Caldwell, Samuel Smith Jr.	1933
Calhoun, Governeur	1891
Callahan, Hugh Andrew	1899
Came, Charles Green	1849
Camp, Arthur Goodwin	1907
Camp, Clinton	1850
Camp, Stuart Brown	1900
Camp, Walter	1880
Campbell, Alan Barnette	1919
Campbell, Charles Soutter	1909
Campbell, Gavin Elliott	1982
Campbell, James	1849
Campbell, James Alexander	1882
Campbell, Kimberly C.	1981
Campbell, Treat	1878
Campbell, William H. W.	1856
Cangelosi, Russell Joseph	1972
Capozzalo, Douglas Daniel	1976
Capron, Paul III	1960
Capron, Samuel Mills	1853
Carey, John	
Carlin, William J Carr Jr	1985
Carlisle, James Mandeville	1901
Carlsen, Ray Allen	1957
Carlsson, Mats Erik	1981
Carpenter, George Boone	1902
Carpenter, Robert John	1859
Carter, Charles Francis	1878
Carter, Edwin Osgood	1837
Carter, Frederic Dewhurst	1919
Carter, Lyon	1915
Carter, Walter Frederick	1895
Case, George Bowen	1894
Case, Philip Benham Jr.	1970
Caskey, Taliaferro Franklin	1865
Casscells, Christopher D.	1976
Cassel, John A.	1958
Caulkins, George Peck	1943
Caulkins, John Ervin	1948
Cerveris, Michael Ernest.	1983
Chadwick, George Brewster	1903
Chafee, John Hubbard	1947
Chamberlain, Daniel Henry	1862
Chamberlain, Leander T.	1863
Chamberlain, Robert L.	1861
Chambers, William Lyon .	1843
Chandler, William Henry	1839
Chandrasekhar, Ashok Jai	1985
Chapin, Charles Frederick	1877
Charles, Anana	2000
Charnley, Charles Meigs	1865
Chase, Henry	1850
Chauvenet, William	1840
Cheney, Clifford Dudley.	1898
Cheney, Frank Dexter	1900
Cheney, Howell	1892
Cheney, Knight Dexter Jr	1892
Cheney, Philip	1901
Cheney, Ronald Lawton	1958
Cheney, Russell	1904
Cheney, Thomas Langdon	1901
Cheney, Ward	1922
Cheney, Ward	1896
Chester, Carl Thurston	1875
Chibundu, Maxwell O.	1980
Child, Linus Mason	1855
Childs, Henry Clay	1962
Childs, Starling Winston	1976
Chimenti, Norman Victor	1962
Chittenden, George H.s	1939
Choa, Christopher James	1981
Chouteau, Rene Auguste	1942
Christian, Henry Hall	1901
Cirie, John Arthur	1964
Clark, Albert Barnes	1864
Clark, Alexander Ray	1895
Clark, Avery Artison	1909
Clark, Charles Hopkins	1871
Clark, Douglas Wells	1972
Clark, Gerald Holland	1965
Clark, Harold Terry	1903
Clark, J. Bruce	1978
Clark, Russell Inslee Jr.	1957
Clark, Stephen Edward	1965
Clark, Thomas Whitton	1961
Clark, William Judkins	1948
Clarke, Thomas Slidell	1875
Clarke, William Barker	1849
Claude, Abram Jr.	1952
Clay, Alexander Stephens	1964
Clay, Cassius Marcellus	1918
Clay, Green	1859
Clay, Jesse Loring	1963
Clay, Timothy J.	1965
Clucas, Lowell Melcher	1939
Cobb, Henry Nitchie	1855
Cochran, Thomas	1894
Coe, Edward Benton	1862
Coe, Robert Elmer	1872
Coffin, Edmund	1866
Coffin, Henry Sloane	1897
Coffin, James	1868
Coffin, William S. Jr.	1949
Coffin, William Sloane	1900
Coffing, Churchill	1834
Coggins, Daniel Seton	1984
Cogswell, John Marshall	1961
Cohen, Kenneth Saul	1968
Cohen, Robert Lewis	1974
Coit, Joshua	1853
Coit, William	1837
Coke, Henry Cornice Jr.	1926
Cole, Hamilton	1866
Coleman, John Caldwell	1881
Colgate, Henry Auchincloss	1913
Collier, Samuel Carnes	1935
Collin, Frederick	1871
Collin, William Welch	1877
Colt, LeBaron Bradford	1868
Colton, Henry Martin	1848
Colton, Willis Strong	1850
Condit, Albert Pierson	1850
Condit, Charles	1848
Condit, Stephen	1856
Connelly, William James Jr.	1948
Conner, Lemuel Parker	1845
Conner, William Gustine	1845
Connick, Andrew Jackson	1952
Connick, Louis Jr.	1945
Connors, David Michael	1974
Connors, James Joseph III	1959
Converse, George Sherman	1850
Conway, Joseph Leo Jr.	1981
Cook, George III	1948
Cook, Robert Johnston	1876
Cooke, Eldridge Clinton	1877
Cooke, Francis Judd	1933
Cooke, James Barclay	1893
Cooke, John Parick	1959
Cooke, Robert Barbour	1936
Cooke, Walter Evans	1895
Cooley, Harlan Ward	1888
Coombs, Orde Musgrave	1965
Coon, John	1847
Cooper, Carnell	1977
Cooper, Henry Sage F.	1917
Cooper, Jacob	1852
Cooper, John Sherman	1923
Cooper, William Frierson	1838
Corbin, William Herbert	1889
Corey, Alan Lyle	1911
Corey, Alan Lyle III	1965

Name	Year
Cornell, Thomas Hilary	1915
Corning, Erastus	1903
Cornish, Percy Gillette Jr.	1914
Cortelyou, George Bruce	1913
Corwin, Robert Nelson	1887
Corwith, John White	1890
Cosgrove, Thomas F. Jr.	1969
Costikyan, Granger Kent	1929
Cowdry, Rex William	1968
Cowles, Alfred	1886
Cowles, Alfred	1913
Cowles, William H.	1887
Cowles, William Sheffield	1921
Cox, John Joughin	1891
Coxe, Alexander Brown	1887
Coy, Edward Harris	1910
Coy, Sherman Lockwood	1901
Crampton, Rufus Cowles	1851
Crane, Winthrop Murray	1904
Crapo, Stanford Tappan	1886
Crapo, William Wallace	1852
Crawley, Brian Scott	1984
Cressler, Alfred Miller	1902
Crile, George Jr.	1929
Crosby, Albert Hastings	1922
Crosby, Benjamin Lewis Jr.	1892
Crosby, Henry Stetson	1926
Crosby, John	1890
Cross, Alan Whitmore	1966
Cross, John Walter	1900
Cross, Richard James	1937
Cross, Walter Redmond Jr.	1941
Cross, Walter Snell	1904
Cross, William Redmond	1896
Croxton, John Thomas	1857
Cruikshank, Paul F. Jr.	1952
Crump, John	1833
Csar, Michael F.	1972
Cunningham, Hugh Terry	1934
Cunningham, Oliver Bulg	1917
Curtin, Francis Clare	1935
Curtis, George Louis	1878
Cushing, Charles Cyprian S.	1902
Cushing, William Lee	1872
Cushman, Charles W.	1957
Cushman, Isaac LaFayette	1845
Cushman, Robert Edgar Jr.	1958
Cutler, Benjamin Crawford	1926
Cutler, Carroll	1854
Dahl, George	1908
Dalby, Michael Thomas	1966
Dale, Edwin Lyon Jr.	1945
Daly, Frederick Joseph	1911
Dana, William Buck	1851
Daniels, Forest Leonard	1907
Daniels, John Hancock	1943
Daniels, Joseph Leonard	1860
Daniels, Rensselaer Wilkinson	1873
Daniels, Thomas Leonard	1914
Danielson, Richard Ely	1907
Darling, Arthur Burr	1916
Darling, Thomas	1836
D'Avanzo, Louis A.	1956
Davenport, Bradfute W.	1938
Davenport, George Leovy	1980
Davenport, John	1926
Davenport, Russell Wheeler	1923
Davenport, Stephen Rintoul	1915
Davies, Philip Turner	1976
Davies, Thomas Frederick	1853
Davies, Thomas Frederick	1894
Davis, Benjamin	1895
Davis, Benjamin Franklin	1833
Davis, Clinton Wildes	1911
Davis, Horace Webber II	1936
Davis, John	1835
Davis, Lowndes Henry	1860
Davis, Richard Marden	1933
Davis, Robert Stewart	1860
Davis, Walter Goodwin	1908
Davison, Daniel Pomeroy	1949
Davison, Endicott Peabody	1945
Davison, Fredrick Trubee	1918
Davison, Harry Pomeroy	1920
Davison, Henry Pomeroy	1984
Dawes, Chester Mitchell	1876
Day, Arthur Pomeroy	1890
Day, Clive	1892
Day, Dwight Huntington	1899
Day, Huntington Townsend	1923
Day, John Calvin	1857
Day, Melville Cox	1862
Day, Robert Webster	1875
Day, Sherwood Sunderland	1911
Day, Thomas Mills	1886
Day, Thomas Mills	1837
Day, William Edwards	1902
Deans, Robert Barr	1918
Dechert, Henry Martyn	1850
Decker, Edmund L. Jr.	1929
DeForest, Stephen Elliott	1955
Demaree, Frank Edward II	1969
Deming, Charles Clerc	1872
Deming, Clarence	1872
Deming, Henry Champion	1872
Deming, Henry Champion	1836
Deming, Lawrence Clerc	1883
Dempsey, Andrew Squire	1956
Dempsey, James Howard Jr.	1938
Dempsey, John Bourne	1911
Denegre, Thomas Bayne	1915
DeNeufville, John Phillip	1961
Denison, Lindsay	1895
Denit, Kelly	2000
Dennis, Frederic Shepard	1872
Denny, Thomas	1854
Denslow, Herbert McKenzie	1873
Dent, Henry Hatch	1836
Depew, Chauncy Mitchell	1856
Depew, Ganson Goodyear	1919
DeSa, Pompeo Ascenco	1841
DeSibour, Jules Henri	1896
DeSilver, Alber	1910
Desjardins, Peter Earl	1965
Devlin, Michael William	1982
Devor, Donald S. Jr.	1941
DeVore, Mark Samuel	1980
Dexter, Franklin Bowditch	1861
Dexter, Morton	1867
Diamond, Peter C.	1974
Dickinson, Arthur	1856
Diller, John Cabot	1924
Dilworth, George Toby	1980
Dilworth, Joseph Richardson	1938
Dimock, Henry Farnam	1863
Dines, Tyson Manzey	1908
Dixon, Theodore Polhemus	1907
Dixon, William Palmer	1868
Doane, John Wesley Jr.	1891
Dodd, Albert	1838
Dodge, Francis Talmage	1904
Dodge, Philip Lyndon	1907
Dodge, Washington	1929
Dominick, David DeWitt	1960
Dominick, Gayer Gardne	1909
Donaldson, William Henry	1953
Donnelley, Gaylord	1931
Donnelley, Thomas Elliott	1889
Doolittle, Duncan Hunter	1943
Douglas, Malcolm	1900
Douglass, Willard Robinson	1887
Dousman, Louis deVierville	1906
Dowling, Brian J.	1969
Downing, Earl S. III	1970
Doyle, Thomas James Jr.	1974
Drain, Richard Dale	1943
Draper, Arthur Joy	1937
Draper, William Henry III	1950
Dreisbach, John Martin	1903

Name	Year
DuBois, John Jay	1867
Dunham, George Elliott	1859
Dunham, Lawrence B. Jr.	1938
Dunn, George J.	1957
Dunning, Albert Elijah	1867
Dunwody, James Bulloch	1836
Durfee, Charles Gibson Jr.	1956
Durham Edwin A. II	1953
Duryee, Samuel Sloan	1917
Dwight, Timothy	1849
Dwight, Winthrop Edwards	1893
Dyess, Arthur Delma Jr.	1939
Eakin, Emmet Alexander	1856
Eakin, William Spencer	1846
Eames, Benjamin Tucker	1843
Early, Hobart Evans	1945
Eaton, Samuel Lewis	1877
Eaton, Sherburne Blake	1862
Ecklund, John Edwin	1938
Eddy, Maxon Hunter	1929
Eden, John W.	1951
Edozien, Anthony O.	1979
Edwards, Alfred Lewis	1857
Edwards, George Benjamin	1878
Edwards, Newton	1842
Edwards, Richard Henry	1901
Eels, John Shepard	1901
Eichelberger, Martin Smyser	1858
Eisenberg, Bruce Alan	1974
Eisenstadt, Leora	1998
Eisler, Colin Tobias	1952
Ekfelt, Richard Henry	1971
Elder, Samuel James	1873
Eldridge, Charles St. John	1839
Elebash, Shehand Daniel	1944
Elliot, Henry Rutherford	1871
Elliot, William Horace	1844
Ellis, Alexander Jr.	1944
Ellis, Franklin Henry Jr.	1941
Ellis, Garrison McClintock	1951
Ellis, George Corson Jr.	1951
Ellis, Harland Montgomery	1930
Ellis, Raymond Walleser	1930
Ellsworth, John Stoughton	1905
Elwell, Francis Bolton Jr.	1945
Ely, Grosvenor	1906
Embersits, John Frank	1958
Emerson, Alfred	1834
Emerson, Christy Payne	1953
Emerson, Joseph	1841
Emerson, Samuel	1848
English, William Deshay Jr.	1975
Eno, John Chester	1869
Eno, Wiliam Phelps	1882
Ercklentz, Alexander Tonio	1959
Erickson, Thomas Franklin	1940
Ernst, Frederick Vincent	1960
Erskine, Albert DeW. Jr.	1930
Esselstyn, Caldwell B. Jr	1956
Esselstyn, Erik Canfield	1959
Estill, Joe Garner	1891
Esty, Constantine Canaris	1845
Etra, Donald.	1968
Eustis, William Tappan	1841
Evans, Evan Wilhelm	1851
Evans, Peter Seelye	1972
Evans, Tilgham Boyd	1954
Evarts, Maxwell	1884
Evarts, Sherman	1881
Evarts, William Maxwell	1837
Ewell, John Lewis	1865
Ewing, Sherman	1924
Eyre, Lawrence L.	1970
Falcon, Angel	1998
Farnam, Charles Henry	1868
Farnam, Henry Walcott	1874
Farnam, William Whitman	1866
Farnham, John Dorrance	1890
Farrar, John Chipman	1918
Faulkner, Endress	1839
Fearey, Morton Lazell	1898
Fehr, Gerald F.	1955
Feinerman, James Vincent	1971
Felder, John Henry	1844
Fenn, William Henry	1854
Ferguson, Alfred L. Jr.	1926
Ferguson, Alfred Ludlow	1902
Ferguson, James Lord	1944
Ferry, Orris Sanford	1844
Fetner, Philip Jay \	1965
Fewsmith, William	1844
Field, David Irvine	1841
Field, John Warner	1937
Finch, Francis Miles	1849
Fincke, Clarence Mann	1897
Finley, John George Gilpin	1947
Finney, C. Roger	1973
Finney, Graham Stanley	1952
Finney, J.John Warren	
Fischer, Louis Christopher	1856
Fish, Stuyvesant	1905
Fisher, Irving	1888
Fisher, Samuel Herbert	1889
Fisher, Scott B.	1972
Fishwick, Dwight Brown	1928
Fisk, Franklin Woodbury	1849
Fisk, Samuel Augustus	1844
Fisk, Stuart Wilkins	1840
Fitch, George Hopper	1932
Fitch, James	1847
Flagg, Wilbur Wells	1873
Flanders, Henry Richmond	1885
Fleming, Andrew T.	1980
Fleming, William Stuart	1838
Fletcher, Alexander Charles	1933
Flinn, Alexander Rex	1906
Folsom, Henry Titus	1883
Foote, Charles Seward	1883
Foote, Harry Ward	1866
Foote, Joseph Forward	1850
Foote, Thaddeus	1844
Ford, George Tod	1865
Ford, William	1942
Fore, John Arthur	1979
Fort, Donald Kenneth	1976
Fortgang, Jeffrey	1971
Fortunato, S. Joseph	1954
Foster, David John	1967
Foster, Dwight	1848
Foster, Eleazar Kingsbury	1834
Foster, George Ferris	1879
Foster, John Pierrepont C.	1869
Foster, Joseph Taylor	1908
Foster, Maxwell Evarts	1923
Foster, Reginald	1884
Foster, Roger	1878
Fowler, Charles Newell	1876
Fowler, Horace Webster	1863
Fowler, William	1860
Fox, Joseph Carrere	1938
Franchot, Charles Pascal	1910
Francis, Samuel Hopkins	1964
Frank, Charles Augustus III	1963
Frank, Clinton E.	1938
Frank, Jr., Victor Harry	1950
Frankel, Scott David	1985
Franklin, Richard David	1983
Fredericks, Joel Richard	1977
Freeman, Henry Varnum	1869
French, Asa Palmer	1882
French, Robert Dudley	1910
Friedland, Johnathan David	1970
Fritzche, Peter B.	1957
Fromm, Julie	1998
Frost, Albert Carl, Jr.	1922
Frost, Elihu Brintnal	1883
Fuller, Henry W.	1969
Fuller, Philo Carroll	1881
Fuller, Stanley Evert	1935

Name	Year
Fuller, William Henry	1861
Fulton, Robert Brank	1932
Furbish, Edward Brown	1860
Gachet, Charles Nicholas	1843
Gage, Charles Stafford	1925
Gaillard, Edward McCrady	1919
Gaillard, Samuel G.Jr.	1916
Gaines, Edwin Frank	1975
Gaines, Milton John	1956
Galbraith, Evan Griffith	1950
Gale, Frederick Scott	1983
Gallaudet, Edson Fessenden	1893
Gallaudet, Herbert Draper	1898
Gallico, G.Gregory III	1968
Galvin, Michael Gerard	1971
Gammell, Arthur Amory	1911
Gardner, Robert Abbe	1912
Garfield, Newell	1918
Garnsey, Walter W., Jr.	1967
Garnsey, Walter Wood	1930
Garnsey, William Herrick	1960
Garnsey, William Smith	1933
Garrison, Elisha Ely	1897
Garvey, John Joseph	1929
Gates, Artemus Lamb	1918
Gates, Edward Raymond	1976
Gaughen, Patrick Robert	2002
Gerard, Sumner	1897
Gibson, Richard C. Jr.	1976
Giegengack, Robert F. Jr.	1960
Giesen, Arthur Rossa, Jr.	1954
Gifford, Richard Cammann	1954
Gile, Clement Dexter	1939
Gile, Clement Moses	1914
Gile, Lawrence Maclester	1978
Gill, Brendan	1936
Gill, Charles Otis	1889
Gill, George Metcalf	1888
Gill, Michael Gates	1963
Gillespie, Samuel H. Jr.	1932
Gillespie, Kenrick Samson	1929
Gillette, Augustus Canfield	1841
Gillette, Curtenius	1897
Gillette, Howard Frank Jr.	1964
Gilman, Daniel Coit	1852
Glaenzer, Georges Brette	1907
Gleason, William Henry	1853
Glover, Charles Carroll III	1940
Goedecke, William Skinner	1947
Goldberg, Richard Julius	1977
Goldsmith, William Dixon	2002
Gonzalez, Julio	1998
Gonzalez, Timoteo F.	1974

Name	Year
Goodenough, John Bannister	1944
Goodyear, Robert M.	1949
Gordon, Alexander Blucher	1834
Gordon, Edward McGuire	1938
Gordon, George Arthur	1934
Gould, Anthony	1877
Gould, James	1918
Gould, James Gardner	1845
Gow, Richard Haigh	1955
Grammar, Christopher	1843
Grandine, Thomas Allan	1981
Granger, Gideon	1843
Granger, John Albert	1855
Grant, Edward Dromgoole	1858
Graves, Earl Gilbert Jr.	1984
Graves, Henry Solon	1892
Graves, William Phillips	1891
Grayson, Cary Travers, Jr.	1942
Grayson, James Gordon	1940
Grayson, William Cabell	1944
Grayson, William Cabell, Jr.	1977
Gready, William Postell	1842
Green, Benjamin P.	1973
Green, Charles Grady	1955
Green, Edmund Frank	1880
Green, Henry Sherwood	1879
Green, James Payne	1857
Green, Rudolph	1975
Greenberg, Stephen David	1970
Greene, Waldo Wittenmyer	1930
Greenway, James Cowan	1900
Griggs, Herbert Stanton Jr.	1928
Griggs, John Cornelius	1889
Griggs, Maitland Fuller	1896
Grimes, David Charles	1948
Griswold, Dwight Torrey	1908
Griswold, William E. Schenck	1899
Grossman, Jay Alan	1985
Grout, Alfred	1853
Grove, Manasses Jacob	1929
Grover, Thomas Williams	1874
Grubb, Charles Ross	1873
Gruener, Gustav	1884
Guernsey, Raymond Gano	1902
Guidotti, Hugh George Jr.	1955
Guinzburg, Thomas Henry	1950
Gulliver, Henry Strong	1875
Gulliver, William Curtis	1870
Guthrie, Robert Karle III	1968
Gwin, Samuel Lawrence	1930
Gwin, Samuel Lawrence Jr.	1963
Haas, Frederick Peter	1935
Hadden, Briton	1920

Name	Year
Hadley, Arthur Twining	1876
Hadley, Hamilton	1919
Hadley, Morris	1916
Haffner, Charles C. Jr.	1919
Haight, Charles Seymour Jr.	1952
Haight, Ducald Cameron	1847
Haight, George Winthrop	1928
Haines, Thomas F.David	1924
Haldeman, Richard Jacobs	1851
Hale, Eugene Jr.	1898
Hall, Daniel Emerson	1834
Hall, Edward Tuck	1941
Hall, Frederick Bagby Jr.	1933
Hall, Jesse Angell	1936
Hall, John Loomer	1894
Hall, John Manning	1866
Hall, Robert Andrew	1930
Hall, William Kittredge	1859
Hallett, John Folsom	1934
Halpin, Thomas Michael	1971
Halsey, Jacob .	1842
Halsey, Ralph Wetmore Jr.	1942
Hambleton, Thomas E.	1934
Hamilton, William	1962
Hamlin, Charles B.	1961
Hamlin, Chauncey Jerome	1903
Hannahs, Diodate C.	1859
Hansen, Roger Allen	1955
Harding, John Wheeler	1845
Harding, Wilder Bennett	1867
Hare, Clinton Larue	1887
Hare, Meredith	1894
Harman, Archer	1913
Harman, Archer Jr.	1945
Harper, Harry Halsted Jr.	1934
Harriman, Edward Roland .	1917
Harriman, William Averell	1913
Harris, Henry Reeder	1836
Harrison, Burton Norvel	1859
Harrison, Fairfax	1890
Harrison, Francis Burton	1895
Harrison, Fred Harold	1942
Harrison, George Leslie	1910
Harrison, Henry Baldwin	1846
Hart, Dennis Charles	1976
Hart, Roswell	1843
Hart, Rufus Erastus	1833
Hartley, Cavour	1912
Hartshorn, Joseph William	1867
Haskell, Robert Chandler	1858
Haslam, Lewis Scofield	1890
Hatch, Walter Tilden	1837
Hatem, John J.	1980

Name	Year
Haven, George Griswold	1887
Havens, Daniel William	1843
Hawley, David	1846
Hay, Logan	1893
Hayden, William Hallock	1847
Healy, Harold Harris Jr.	1943
Heard, Albert Farley	1853
Heaton, Edward	1869
Hebard, Albert	1851
Hebard, Daniel	1860
Hedge, Thomas	1867
Heermance, Edgar Laing	1858
Heffelfinger, Frank Peavey	1920
Heffelfinger, George W. Peavey	1924
Heikkila, Jennifer	2000
Heinz, Henry John II	1931
Helfenstein, Charles Philip	1841
Helmer, Charles Downs	1852
Heminway, Bartow Lewis	1921
Hemphill, James Tierney	1959
Henen, William Davison	1842
Henningsen, Victor W. Jr.	1950
Henston, Douglas Robert	1984
Herlwig, Paige Lynn	2002
Hernandez, Carols Arturo	1971
Heron, John	1910
Hersey, John Richard	1936
Herskovits, David Nathaniel	1984
Hessberg, Albert II	1938
Hewitt, Brower	1903
Hewitt, Henry Hollis	1963
Hewitt, Thomas Browning	1864
Hidden, Edward	1885
Hiers, Richard Hyde	1954
Higgins, Anthony	1861
Highfill, Philip Henry III	1973
Hill, George Canning	1845
Hillard, Lord Butler	1883
Hilles, Charles Dewey Jr.	1924
Hilles, Frederick Whiley	1922
Hincks, Edward Young	1866
Hincks, John Howard	1872
Hincks, John Morris	1920
Hincks, John Winslow	1952
Hine, Charles Daniel	1871
Hinkey, Frank Augustus	1895
Hinsdale, Frank Gilbert	1898
Hirway, Hrishikesh	2000
Hitchcock, Henry	1848
Hitchcock, Henry	1879
Hixon, Robert	1901
Hoagland, Donald Wright	1943
Hobbs, Charles Buxton	1885
Hobson, Francis Thayer	1920
Hobson, Henry Wise	1914
Hodes, Douglas Michael	1970
Hodges, William VanDerveer Jr.	1932
Hogan, James Joseph	1905
Holbrook, David Doubleday	1960
Holbrook, John Jr.	1959
Holden, John Morgan	1944
Holden, Reuben Andrus	1940
Holland, Henry Thompson	1962
Hollister, Arthur Nelson	1858
Hollister, Buell	1905
Hollister, John Baker Jr.	1949
Holmbee, Jeffrey Arthur	1979
Holmes, George Burgwin	
Holmes, John Grier	1934
Holmes, John Milton	1857
Holmes, Peter Samuel	1978
Holt, George Chandler	1866
Holt, Henry Chandler	1903
Holter, Edwin Olaf	1894
Hongo, Andrew	2000
Hook, Noble	1978
Hooker, John Worthington	1854
Hooker, Thomas	1869
Hoopes, Townsend Walter	1944
Hopkins, John Morgan	1900
Hoppin, Benjamin	1872
Hoppin, James Mason	1840
Hord, Stephen Young	1921
Hothhkiss, William Henry	1875
Hough, Edward Clement	1849
Houghton, Edward	1852
Houghton, Walter Edwards	1924
Houston, John Wallace	1834
Howard, James Ernest	1966
Howard, James Merriam	1909
Howard, Oran Reed	1835
Howe, Arthur	1912
Howe, Elmer Parker	1876
Howe, Gary Woodson	1958
Howe, Harold II	1940
Howe, Henry Almy	1909
Howland, John	1894
Hoxton, Archibald R. Jr.	1939
Hoysradt, Albert	1877
Hoysradt, J Warren	1901
Hoysradt, John McArthur	1926
Hoyt, Joseph Gibson	1840
Hoyt, Lydig	1906
Hubbard, Richard Dudley	1839
Hudson, Franklin Donald	1955
Hudson, Jared McCabe	2002
Hudson, Ward Woodridge	1840
Huey, Mark Christopher	1973
Huggins, William Sidney	1842
Hughes, Berrien	1905
Hull, Louis Kossuth	1883
Hurd, John Codman	1836
Hurd, Richard Melancthon	1888
Hurlbut, Gordon B/Jr.	
Hurlbut, Joseph	1849
Husted, James William	1892
Hyatt, Robert Underwood	1837
Hyde, Alvan Pinney	1845
Hyde, Donald Robertson	1912
Hyde, Frank Eldridge	1879
Hyde, Frederick Walton	1911
Hyde, Louis Kepler Jr.	1923
Hyde, William Waldo	1876
Im, Jaisohn	2002
Ingalls, David Sinton	1920
Ingalls, David Sinton Jr	1956
Ingersoll, James W. D.	1892
Inman, Robert Davies	1971
Isbell, Orland Sidney	1888
Isham, Edward Swift	1891
Isham, Henry Porter	1917
Isham, John Beach	1869
Ives, Chauncey Bradley	1928
Ives, Gerard Merrick	1925
Ives, Henry	1881
Ives, Sherwood Bissell	1893
Jack, Thomas Mckinney	1853
Jackson, Henry Rootes	1839
Jackson, John Herrick	1934
Jackson, Joseph Cooke	1857
Jackson, Terrence John	1970
Jackson, William Eldred	1941
James, Ellery Sedgewick	1917
James, Henry Ammon	1874
James, Norman	1890
James, Robert Campbell	1894
James, Walter Belknap	1879
James, William Knowles	1878
Jamieson, Thomas C. Jr.	1956
Janeway, Charles Anderson	1930
Jay, Pierre	1892
Jefferson, Edward Francis	1909
Jenckes, Marcien	1921
Jenkins, Richard Elwood	1948
Jenks, Almet Francis	1875
Jenks, Almet Francis	1914
Jenks, Paul Emmott	1884
Jenks, Tudor Storrs	1878
Jennings, Oliver Gould	1887

Name	Year
Jennings, Percy Hall	1904
Jennings, Walter	1880
Jessup, John Baker	1942
Jesup, James Riley	1840
Jiminez, Carlos	2002
Johanson, Stanley Morris	1955
Johnes, Edward Rudolph	1873
Johnson, Ayanna	2000
Johnson, Barclay	1882
Johnson, Charles Fredrick	1855
Johnson, George Asbury	1853
Johnson, Joseph Hale	1935
Johnson, Wilbur John Jr.	1971
Johnston, Frank	1835
Johnston, Henry Phelps	1862
Johnston, Ross	1870
Johnston, William Curtis	1860
Johnston, William Preston	1852
Johnstone, Henry Webb	1916
Jones, Alfred Henry	1893
Jones, Dwight Arven	1875
Jones, Edwin Alfred	1923
Jones, Frank Hatch	1875
Jones, Frederick Scheetz	1884
Jones, George Gill	1914
Jones, Luther Maynard	1860
Jones, Seaborn Augustus	1838
Jones, Theodore Stephen	1933
Jones, Theodore Stephen	1963
Jones, Walter Clyde	1925
Jordan, Ralph Edward	1923
Judson, Frederick Newton	1866
Judson, Issac Nichols	1873
Jung, Michael David	1984
Kafoglis, Christian Nicholas	1983
Kagan, Robert William	1980
Kahle, Jeffrey Lewis	1984
Kaminsky, Robert Isadore	1964
Kanehl, Phillip Edwin	1975
Karageorge, James Louis	1973
Karp, Benjamin C	1978
Kaushal, Shalesh	1983
Kee, Christopher Andrew	1977
Kelley, Lawernce Morgan	1937
Kelley, William Cody II	1944
Kellogg, Charles Poole	1890
Kellogg, Fred William	1883
Kellogg, Stephen Wright	1846
Kellogg, William Welch	1939
Kelly, Brian Christopher	1974
Kelsey, Clarence	1878
Kemp, Frank Alexander	1942
Kemp, Philip Sperry	1950
Kendall, John Newton	1834
Kendall, William Burrage Jr.	1887
Kenerson, Vertner	1891
Kennedy, Thomas	1845
Kent, Albert Emmett	1853
Kent, William	1887
Keppelman, John Arthur	1901
Kernochan, Francis Edward	1861
Kernochan, Frederic	1898
Kernochan, Joseph F.	1863
Kerr, Albert Boardman	1897
Kerry, John Forbes	1966
Ketcham, Henry Holman	1914
Key, Thomas Marshall	1838
Kilborne, William Skinner	1935
Kilcullen, John MacHale	1934
Kilrea, Walter Charles	1954
Kimball, Arthur Reed	1877
Kimball, John Edwin	1858
Kimball, Walter Sugden	1934
King, Lyndon Marrs	1910
King, Stoddard	1914
Kingsbury, Howard Thayer	1926
Kingsley, Charles Capen	1959
Kingsley, Henry Coit	1834
Kinne, William	1848
Kinney, Herbert Evelyn	1871
Kiphuth, Delaney	1941
Kirby, Jacob Brown	1849
Kirchwey, George W.	1942
Kirowski, John	2000
Kitchel, Cornelius Ladd	1862
Kitchel, Cornelius Porter	1897
Kitchel, William Lloyd	1892
Kittle, John Caspar	1904
Kittredge, Frank Dutton	1952
Kittredge, George Alvah	1855
Klots, Allen Trafford	1909
Klots, Allen Trafford Jr.	1943
Knapp, Farwell	1916
Knapp, Howard Hoyt	1882
Knapp, John Merrill	1936
Knapp, Wallace Percy	1886
Kneeland, Yale	1890
Knight, Augustus	1910
Knight, Samuel	1887
Knott, George Tapscott	1878
Knox, Hugh Smith	1907
Kolar, Bruton Ward (Britt)	1968
Kosturko, William T.	1971
Kwok, Wei-Tai	1985
Ladd, Louis Williams Jr.	1930
Lagercrantz, Bengt Magnus	1965
Laidley, Forrest David	1966
Lalley, Patrick William	1977
Lamb, Albert Eugene	1867
Lamb, Albert Richard	1903
Lambert, Adrian VanSinderen	1893
Lambert, Alexander	1884
Lambert, Alfred	1843
Lambert, Edward W.	1854
Lambert, Paul Christopher	1950
Lampert, Edward Scott	1984
Lampman, Lewis	1866
Lampson, George	1855
Lampson, William	1862
Lane, William Griswold	1843
Lanier, Alexander Chalmers	1844
Lapham, Lewis Abbot	1931
Lapham, Raymond White	1928
Larner, Robert Johnson	1922
Lathe, Herbert William	1873
Lathrop, John Hiram	1905
Laundon, Mortimer H.Jr.	1932
Lavelli, Anthony Jr.	1949
Law, William Fabian	1837
Law, William Lyon	1838
Lawler, Quentin John	1977
Lawrance, Thomas Garner	1884
Lawrence, Gary Martin	1980
Lea, James Neilsen	1834
Lea, Robert Brinkley	1871
Leaf, Edmund	1841
Lear, Henry	1869
Learned, Dwight Whitney	1870
Learned, William Law	1841
Leavenworth, Donald Loyal	1947
Leavitt, Ashley Day	1900
Lee, Earl	1998
Lee, Samuel Henry	1858
LeFevre, Ronald Eaton	1962
LeGore, Harry William	1917
Leighton, James	1881
Leiper, Joseph McCarrell II	1949
Lent, John Abram	1843
Leone, Frederick Anthony	1982
Lester, Sara	2000
Leverett, Miles Watson	1976
Levering, Walter Barnum	1933
Levin, Charles Herbert	1971
Lewis, Asahel Hooker	1833
Lewis, Charlton Miner	1886
Lewis, George Emanuel	1974
Lewis, Henry	1842
Lewis, John	1868
Lewis, Mark Sanders	1972

Name	Year
Libbey, Frank	1867
Lightfoot, Richard Bissett	1959
Ligon, Thomas B.	1962
Liles, Coit Redfearn	1973
Liley, Frank Walder Jr.	1943
Lilley, Robert McGregor	1967
Lindenberg, John Townsend	1932
Lindgren, Richard Hugo	1960
Lindley, Frances Vinton	1933
Lindsay, Dale Alton Jr.	1961
Lindsay, David Alexander	1944
Lindy, Peter Barnes	1985
Linton, Stephen Duncan	1846
Lippincott, David McCord	1949
Lippincott, William Jackson	1914
Lippitt, Henry	1909
Litt, David Geoffrey	1984
Litt, Willard David	1921
Little, Mitchell Stuart	1907
Little, Robbins	1851
Little, Stuart West	1944
Livingston II, Richard H.B.	1969
Livingston, Herman	1879
Loeser, Frederic William	1931
Logan, Walter Seth	1910
Lohmann, Carl Albert	1910
Lombard, James Kittredge	1854
Lombardi, Cornelius Ennis	1911
Longstreth, George Brown	1930
Lonsdorf, David B.	1973
Look, Allen MacMartin	1927
Look, Frank Byron	1930
Lord, Charles Edwin II	1949
Lord, Franklin Atkins	1898
Lord, George DeForest	1854
Lord, Oswald Bates	1926
Lord, William Galey	1922
Lord, Winston	1959
Lorenson, David Harold	1979
Loucks, Vernon Reece Jr.,	1957
Loughran, Anthony H.	1957
Love, Ralph Frank	1951
Lovejoy, Winslow Meston	1925
Lovell, Joseph	1844
Lovett, August Sidney	1913
Lovett, Robert Abercrombie	1918
Lovett, Sidney	1950
Luce, Henry Robinson	1920
Luckey, Charles Pinckney	1923
Luckey, Charles Pinckney	1950
Ludden, William	1850
Lufkin, Chauncey F.	1951
Lufkin, Dan Wende	1953
Lufkin, Elgood Moulton	1925
Lufkin, Sr., Peter Wende	1949
Luman, Richard John	1925
Lumpkin, Richard Anthony	1957
Lunt, Storer Boardman	1921
Lusk, Peter Anthony	1960
Lusk, William Thompson	1924
Lutz, Karl Evan	1972
Lydgate, William Anthony	1931
Lyman, Chester Smith	1837
Lyman, Chester Wolcott	1882
Lynch, Dennis Patrick	1964
Lynch, Russell Vincent	1945
Lynde, Charles James	1838
Lyon, George Armstrong	1900
MacDonald, Ranald H. Jr	1915
MacDonald, Richard J. II	1972
MacDonald, Stephen J.	1973
Mack, Richard Gesrtle	1948
MacKenzie, Kenneth M.	1975
MacLean, Charles Fraser	1864
MacLean, John Helm	1943
MacLean, Kenneth Jr.	1961
MacLeish, Archibald	1915
MacLeish, William H.	1950
MacLellan, George B.	1858
MacVeagh, Franklin	1862
MacWhorter, Alexander	1842
Madden, Bernard Patrick	1969
Madden, John Beckwith	1941
Maffitt, Thomas Skinner	1899
Magee, James McDevitt	1899
Magee, John Gillespie	1906
Magruder, Benjamin Drake	1856
Mallon, Guy Ward	1885
Mallon, Henry Neil	1917
Mallon, John Howard	1919
Mallon, Thomas Ridgway	
Mallory, Barton Lee Jr.	1928
Mallory, William Neely	1924
Malloy, Terrence Reed	1956
Manice, William DeForest	1851
Manross, Newton Spaulding	1850
Mansfield, Howard	1871
Manville, Hiram Edward Jr.	1929
March, Daniel	1840
Marinelli, David Leonard	1978
Marmaduke, Vincent	1852
Marsh, William Lee	1963
Marshall, John Birnie	1953
Marshall, Samuel Davies	1833
Martin, George Greene	1893
Martin, John Griffith	1836
Marvin, George Lockwood	1836
Marvin, Joseph Howard	1876
Mason, Alfred Bishop	1871
Mason, Henry Burrall	1870
Mather, Frederick Ellsworth	1833
Mathews, Albert	1842
Mathews, Craig	1951
Mathias, Philip Hoffman II	1955
Matthessen, Francis Otto	1923
Mattlin, Fred Walter	1973
Mayer, Charles Theodore	1951
Mayor, Michael Brook	1959
McAfee, William Andrew	1982
McAndrew, Alexander	1913
McBride, Jonathan Evans	1964
McBride, Webster	1998
McBride, Wilber	1882
McCall, Henry	1840
McCallum, Revell	1924
McCallum, Robert Davis Jr.	1968
McCarthy, Charles Edward	1960
McClintlock, Norman	1891
McClung, Thomas Lee	1892
McClure, Archibald	1912
McClure, James Gore King	1870
McClure, James G. K.Jr.,	1906
McCormick, Alex A. Jr.	1919
McCormick, Henry	1852
McCrary, John Reagan Jr.	1932
McCullough, David Gaub	1955
McCutchen, Sam. St. John	1870
McDonnell, John Vincent	1911
McElroy, Benjamin Thomas	1945
McGaughey, Guy Ennis Jr.	1945
McGauley, John Michael	1933
McGee, Donald Ashbrook	1906
McGregor, Jack Edwin	1956
McHenry, James	1920
McHenry, John	1885
McIntosh, Harris	1927
McKee, Elmore McNeill	1919
McKee, Lanier	1895
McKee, McKee Dunn	1896
McKinney, William Allison	1868
McLallen, Philemon F.	1847
McLane, James Price	1953
McLaren, Michael Glenn	1972
McLaughlin, Edward T.	1883
McLean, Robert III	1950
McLellan, William	1835
McLemore, John Briggs Jr.	1937
McMillan, James Howard	1888
McMillan, Philip Hamilton	1894

McMillan, William Charles	1884
McNally, Edward E.	1979
McNamara, Thomas Philip	1951
McPhee, Stephen Joseph	1973
McQuaid, William Adolph	1889
Mead, Frederick	1871
Mead, Winter	1919
Medard, Wilodene	1998
Meek, John Burgess	1960
Mehta, Arjay Singh	1976
Melton, William Davis Jr.	1924
Menton, James Paul	1956
Menton, John Dennis	1953
Merriam, Alexander Ross	1872
Merriam, George Spring	1864
Merriam, James Fiske	1867
Merrill, Henry Riddle	1929
Merrill, Payson	1865
Merritt, Henry Newton	1912
Mesick, Richard Smith	1848
Messimer, Robert L. Jr.	1931
Metcalf, Harold Grant	1904
Metcalfe, Henry Laurens	1849
Metcalfe, Orrick	1845
Meyer, Russell William Jr.	1954
Meyers, Bryan Fitch	1982
Michel, Anthony Lee	1926
Middlebrook, Louis Shelton	1915
Miles, James Browning	1849
Miles, Richard Curtis	1937
Miller, Allanson Douglas	1864
Miller, Andrew Otterson	1939
Miller, Charles Lewis Jr.	1939
Miller, Dudley Livingston	1943
Miller, Francis William	1842
Miller, George Douglas	1870
Miller, James Ely	1904
Miller, James Whipple	1967
Miller, Phineas Timothy	1833
Miller, Thomas Clairborne	1970
Miller, Wentworth Earl	1969
Mills, Alfred	1847
Mills, Edward Ensign	1934
Mills, Ethelbert Smith	1835
Mills, James Paul	1932
Misner, Timothy Charles	1985
Mitchell, Donald Grant	1841
Mitchell, H. Coleman Jr.	1967
Mitchell, Harry Hartwood	1939
Mitchell, John Hanson	1861
Mitinger, Joseph Berry	1953
Mizrahi, Celine	2000
Mnu Chin Steven Terner	1985
Montesano, Michael J. III	1983
Montgomery, Grenville D.	1898
Montgomery, Kenita Trenae	2002
Montoya, Maceo	2002
Moody, Thomas Hudson	1843
Moore, David Clement	1973
Moore, Eliakim Hastings	1883
Moore, Frank Wood	1903
Moore, George Foot	1872
Moore, James I.	1947
Moore, Richard Anthony	1936
Moore, William Eves	1847
Moorhead, William Singer	1906
Moorhead, William Singer Jr.	1945
Morey, Robert Willis Jr.	1958
Morgan, James Wallace	1971
Morgan, Robert McNair	1970
Morgenstern, Marc Jaime	1976
Morison, David Whipple	1888
Morison, Samuel Benjamin	1891
Morison, Stanford Newel	1892
Morris, Edward Dafydd	1849
Morris, Luzon Burritt	1854
Morris, Ray	1901
Morse, John Bolt	1934
Morse, Samuel Finley B.	1907
Morse, Sidney Nelson	1890
Morton, Thruston B. Jr.	1954
Moseley, Spencer Dumaresq	1943
Moseley, Thomas Wilder	
Moser, Richard Eugene	1963
Moses, Jack Thomas	1979
Moyer, Douglas Richard	1972
Mulford, David Humphrey	1846
Mulford, Elisha	1855
Mulhern, Daniel Kevin	1980
Mullins, Frederic Parsons	1912
Munn, John	1847
Munroe, George Edmund	1874
Murchison, Brian Cameron	1974
Murchison, Robert W.	1982
Murphy, Frederick James	1910
Murphy, Gerald Clery	1912
Murphy, Maiya	1998
Musser, John Miller	1930
Neale, James Brown	1896
Neigher, Geoffrey Mark	1967
Nelson, Rensselaer Russell	1846
Nettleton, Edward Payson	1856
Neville, James Eugene	1921
Nevins, William Russell	1846
Newel, Stanford	1861
Newman, Thomas M.	1977
Newton, James Quigg Jr.	1933
Nichols, Alfred Bull	1880
Nichols, Edward	1934
Nichols, William Allen	1983
Nickerson, Sereno Dwight	1845
Noble, Lawerence Mason Jr.	1953
Noble, Lawrence Mason	1927
Noel, Christopher	1983
Nondorf, Kurt D.	1979
Nordhaus, William D.	1963
Norris, William Herbert	1839
Northrop, Robert Smitter	1960
Northup, Cyrus	1857
Norton, George W. Jr.	1923
Norton, William Bunnell	1925
Novkov, David Arthur	1953
Novosel, David Gerard	1981
Noyes, Edward MacArthur	1971
Oberlin (Owseichik), John P.	1957
O'Brien, Donald Patrick	1979
O'Brien, Frank	1906
O'Brien, Frank Jr.	1947
O'Brien, Phillip Jr.	
O'Connell, Timothy James	1963
Ogden, Alfred	1932
Ohene-Frempong, Kwaku	1970
O'Keefe, Regis James	1981
O'Leary, John Joseph Jr.	1969
Oler, Clark Kimberly Jr.	1976
Oler, Wesley Mardon	1916
Olmstead, John Hull	1847
Olsen, Albert William	1917
O'Neill, Eugene G., Jr	1932
Oppenheimer, Mark	1996
Ord, Joseph Pacificus	1873
Ordway, Henry Choate	1880
Orr, Andrew Alexander	1956
Orrick, Andrew Downey	1940
Orrick, William Horsley Jr.	1937
Osborn, Richard	1914
Osborne, Arthur Sherwood	1882
Osborne, Thomas Burr	1881
Otis, James Sanford	1919
Overton, John Williams	1917
Owen, Allen Ferdinand	1837
Owen, Charles Hunter	1860
Owen, Edward Thomas	1872
Owen, Henry Elijah	1864
Owens, Samuel L.	1978
Packard, Lewis Richard	1856
Paddock, Brace Whitman	1900
Page, Robert Guthrie	1922
Paine, Levi Leonard	1856

Name	Year
Paine, Ralph Delahaye	1894
Paine, Ralph Delahaye Jr.	1929
Painter, Henry McMahon	1884
Palmer, Arthur Edward	1930
Palmer, Charles Edgar	1947
Palmer, Harry Herbert	1883
Palmer, Lindley Guy II	1957
Palmer, William Henry	1864
Paris, Irving	1915
Park, William Edwards	1861
Parker, Grenville	1898
Parker, Robert Boyd	1933
Parker, Wilbur	1880
Parker, William White W.	1893
Parkin, William	1874
Parrott, Joseph Robinson	1883
Parsons, Francis	1893
Parsons, Henry McIlvaine	1933
Parsons, Langdon	1921
Partridge, Sidney Catlin	1880
Patterson, George W.	1914
Patterson, Morehead	1920
Patterson, Thomas C.	1927
Patton, John Jr	1875
Paul, Charles Henry	1912
Payson, Henry Silas	1872
Peck, Arthur John Jr.	1962
Peck, Tracy	1861
Pelly, Bernard Berenger	1923
Peltz, William Learned	1931
Pendexter, John Fowler	1958
Penna, Timothy Rick	2002
Percy, Frederick Bosworth	1877
Perkins, John	1840
Perkins, Nathaniel Shaw	1842
Perkins, Thomas Albert	1858
Perkins, William	1840
Perrin, Bernadotte	1869
Perrin, John Bates	1909
Perrin, John Orlando	1879
Perrin, Lee James	1906
Perrin, Lester William	1908
Perry, David Brainard	1863
Perry, David Bulkey	1977
Perry, John Hoyt	1870
Perry, Wilbert Warren	1871
Pershing, Richard Warren	1966
Petela, James Gerard	1985
Peters, Daniel James	1970
Peters, Elliot Remsen	1980
Peters, Eric Brooks	1979
Peters, Frank George	1886
Peters, John Andrew	1842
Peters, Kenneth Graham	1981
Peters, William Allison	1880
Peterson, Paul Clifford	1981
Petit, Charlie	1998
Pfau, George Harold Jr.	1948
Phelan, Howard Taylor	1958
Phelps, Edward Johnson	1886
Phelps, Sheffield	1886
Phelps, William Walter	1860
Phelps, Zira Bennett	1895
Philbin, Jesse Holladay	1913
Philbin, Stephen H II	1910
Phinney, Elihu	1846
Pickett, Lawrence Kimball	1941
Piel, Geoffrey D.	1978
Pierce, Frederick Erastus	1904
Pierson, Charles Wheeler	1886
Pierson, William Seward	1836
Pillsbury, Edmund P.	1936
Pillsbury, John Sargent Jr.	1935
Pinchot, Amos R. Eno	1897
Pinchot, Gifford	1889
Pinckard, Thomas Cicero	1848
Pinela, Carlos	1983
Pinney, John Mercer	1965
Pionzio, Dino John	1950
Platt, Henry Barstow	1882
Platt, Lewis Alfred	1879
Polich, Richard Frank	1954
Pollock, George Edward	1878
Pollock, William	1882
Pomeroy. John Norton	1887
Pond, Jeffrey Craig	1965
Poole, William Frederick	1891
Poore, Charles Graydon	1926
Porter, Edward Clarke	1858
Porter, Gilbert Edwin III	1916
Post, Russell LeE	1927
Post, Russell Lee Jr.	1958
Potter, Roderick	1902
Potwin. Lemuel Stoughton	1854
Powers, Richard Hart	1985
Pratt, George	1857
Pratt, Julius Howard	1842
Pratt, William Hall Brace	1864
Premejee, Sharmeen Malik	2002
Prentice, John Rockefeller	1928
Prentice, Samuel Oscar	1873
Preston, Henry Kirk	1836
Preston, James Marshall	1967
Preston, John Louis	1958
Preston, Ord	1899
Price, Charles Baird Jr.	1941
Price, Frank Julian	1892
Price, Raymond Kissam Jr.	1951
Price, Ross Edward	1954
Prideaux, Tom	1930
Prindle, Thomas Harrison	1964
Pugsley, Isaac Platt	1864
Pulaski, Charles A.Jr.	1964
Pumpelly, Harold A.	1915
Purnell, Charles Thomas	1854
Putnam, Howard Phelps	1916
Putnam, James Osborne	1839
Pyle, Michael Johnson	1961
Quarles, James Perrin III	1965
Raborar, Farrah	1998
Rachlin, David Isaiah	1982
Rafferty, John Chandler	1835
Ramsdell, Charles Benjamin	1872
Rand, Stuart Craig	1909
Randolph, Francis Fitz	1911
Rankin, Bernard Courtney	1936
Rankin, Robert	1845
Ranney, George Alfred	1934
Rashid, Tauheedah	1998
Rathborne, Joseph C.	1931
Raymond, George Tod P.s	1949
Raymond, Henry Hunter	1841
Raymond, Henry Warren	1869
Read, Richard Rollins	1947
Reed, Harry Lathrop	1889
Reed, Lansing Parmalee	1904
Reid, Edward Snover III	1951
Reid, Jasper	1982
Reigeluth, Douglas Scott	1975
Reilly, John Sylvester	1915
Renan, Daphna	2000
Reponen, Robert Gordon	1954
Ribeiro, Carlos Fernando	1838
Rich, Charles	1838
Richards, David Alan	1967
Richards, Eugene Lamb	1885
Richards, George	1840
Richardson, Allan Harvey	1901
Richardson, Gardner	1905
Richardson, Rufus Byam	1869
Richardson, Walker	1849
Riggs, Benjamin Clapp	1865
Rimar, Stephen III	1977
Ripley, George Coit	1862
Ritchie, Wallace Parks	1927
Ritchie, Wallace Parks Jr.	1957
Ritterbush, Stephen G. Jr.	1972
Rizzo, Robert John	1978
Robb, James Madison	1844

Name	Year
Robb, John Hunter	1843
Robbins, Edwards Denmore	1874
Robbins, William Wells	1927
Roberts, Charles Holmes Jr.	1916
Roberts, Ellis Henry	1850
Roberts, George Brooke Jr.	1952
Robertson, Arthur C.	1928
Robertson, Charles Franklin	1859
Robertson, Robert	1833
Robeson, Abel Bellows	1837
Robinson, Frederick Flower	1927
Robinson, George Chester	1856
Robinson, Henry Seymour	1889
Robinson, Howard C. Jr.	1947
Robinson, John Trumbull	1937
Robinson, John Trumbull	1893
Robinson, Lucius Franklin	1885
Robinson, Lucius Franklin	1843
Roby, Joseph	1893
Roby, Samuel Sidney Brese	1888
Rockefeller, Percy Avery	1900
Rockwell, Foster Haven	1906
Rockwell, John	1849
Rodd, David Beckwith	1940
Rodd, Thomas	1935
Rodman, Robert Simpson	1879
Rogers, David Francis	1898
Rogers, Derby	1893
Rogers, Edmund Pendleton	1905
Rogers, Herman Livingston	1914
Rogers, John	1887
Root, Alexander Porter	1861
Root, Reginald Dean	1926
Root, Wells	1922
Rose, Jonathan Chapman	1963
Ross, Lanny Lancelot P.	1928
Ross, Thomas Bernard	1951
Ross, William Baldwin	1852
Rowe, Thomas D. Jr.	1964
Rowland, John Tilghman	1911
Rowland, William Sherman	1836
Roy, John Marcus	1978
Ruiz, Sara Elizabeth	2002
Rulon-Miller, Patrick	1963
Rumsey, Bronson Case	1902
Rumsey, David McIver	1966
Runnalls, John Felch B.	1937
Russell, Frank Ford	1926
Russell, Philip Gray	1876
Russell, Richard George	1981
Russell, Richard Warren	1951
Russell, William Huntington	1833
Ryan, Allan A. III	1954
Ryan, Joseph Mather	1951
Ryle, Ernest	1892
Saffen, David	1975
Safford, George Blagden	1852
Safford, Theodore Lee	1920
Sage, Dean	1897
Sage, Henry Manning	1890
Saleh, Muhammad Ahmed	1968
Salzman, Mark Joseph	1982
Sanderson, Benjamin B.	1909
Sanford, Charles Frederick	1847
Sanhago, Eddie	1982
Sargent, Joseph Weir	1920
Sargent, Murray	1905
Sauber, Richard Alan	1972
Savage, Boutelle Jr.	1932
Savage, Josiah	1846
Sawyer, Homer Eugene Jr.	1913
Saxon, James M	1967
Scarborough, William S.	1837
Scattergood, Thomas Bevan	1970
Schermerhorn, Alfred C.	1920
Schermerhorn, Amos E.	1938
Schlesinger, Daniel Adam	1977
Schmidt, Thomas Carl	1968
Schnaitter, Spencer Jason	1954
Schollander, Donald Arthur	1968
Schuyler, Eugene	1859
Schwab, John Christopher.	1886
Schwab, Laurence vonPost	1913
Schwarzman, Stephen Allen.	1969
Scott, Eben Greenough	1858
Scott, Eugene Lytton	1960
Scott, Henry Clarkson	1925
Scott, Larry Glenn	1977
Scott, Shannon	1998
Scott, Stewart Patterson	1928
Scott, William Iain	1973
Scudder, Doremus	1880
Seabury, Mortimer Ashmfad	1909
Seaman, Irving Jr.	1945
Searles, Paul David	1955
Sears, Joshua Montgomery	1877
Seeley, George Wheeler	1961
Seeley, John Edward	1835
Seeley, John Frank	1860
Seely, Edward Howard Jr	1878
Seely, William Wallace	1862
Selander, Duane Arthur	1969
Selden, Edward Griffin	1870
Senay, Edward Charles	1952
Seward, William Henry	1888
Seymour, Charles	1908
Seymour, Charles Jr.	1935
Seymour, Horatio	1867
Seymour, John Forman	1835
Seymour, John Sammis	1875
Seymour, Storrs Ozias	1857
Shackelford, Robert C.	1958
Sharp, Jonathan Douglas	1983
Shattuck, HF John III	1965
Shattuck, John Waldon	1870
Shearer, Sextus	1861
Shedden, William M.	1915
Sheffey, Hugh White	1835
Sheffield, George St. John	1863
Sheffield, James Rockwell	1959
Sheffield, John Van Loon	1983
Shelden, Allan	1913
Shepard, Blake	1936
Shepard, Charles R. S.	1951
Shepard, Donald Carrington	1916
Shepard, Donald C.Jr.	1950
Shepard, Frank Parsons Jr.	1917
Shepard, Lloyd M.y Jr.	1939
Shepard, Lorrin Andrews	1914
Shepard, Roger Bulkley	1908
Shepard, Roger Bulkley Jr.	1935
Shepley, Arthur Behn	1895
Sheppard, Walter Bradley	1887
Sherman, Frederick Roger	1836
Sherrill, Franklin G.	1949
Shevlin, Edward Leonard	1921
Shipman, Arthur L.	1886
Shirley, Arthur	1869
Shugart, Thorne Martin	1955
Sill, Edward Rowland	1861
Sill, George Griswold	1852
Silliman, Benjamin Jr.	1837
Simmons, Frank Hunter	1898
Simmons, Wallace Delafield	1890
Simms, William Erskine	1891
Simpson, Kenneth Farrand	1917
Sincerbeaux, Frank Huestis	1902
Singer, Ronald Leonard	1966
Singleton, Thomas Hall	1961
Skibell, Steven Alan	1984
Skrovan, Stephen Thomas	1979
Slade, Francis Henry	1854
Slade, John Milton	1851
Sloane, Henry Thompson	1866
Sloane, John	1905
Sloane, Thomas Chalmers	1868
Sloane, William	1895
Slocum, Edwin Lyon	1915
Smith, Bruce Donald	1906

Name	Year
Smith, Bruce Donald III	1960
Smith, Charles Edgar	1865
Smith, Edward Curtis	1875
Smith, Eugene	1859
Smith, Frederick Wallace	1966
Smith, Herbert Augustine	1889
Smith, Howard Freeman Jr.	1942
Smith, James Gregory	1912
Smith, John Donnell	1847
Smith, Lloyd Hilton	1929
Smith, Rufus Biggs	1876
Smith, Traver	1919
Smith, William Thayer	1860
Smith, Winthrop D.	1896
Smock, Morgan Robert	1985
Smyth, Nathan Ayer	1897
Snell, Bradford Curie	1967
Snell, Raymond Franklin	1918
Solbert, Peter O.A.	1941
Solley, Fred Palmer	1888
Solley, Robert Folger	1922
Somerville, John Wheeler	1957
Soper, Willard Burr	1904
Soule, Leslie	1911
Southgate, Charles McC.	1866
Southmayd, Samuel Gray	1834
Southworth, Edward Wells	1875
Southworth, George C. S.	1863
Spaldin, George Atherton	1872
Spaulding, Ebenezer	1838
Spaulding, Josiah Augustus	1945
Spear, Wesley John	1974
Spears, Robert Samuel	1952
Speed, James Breckinridge	1956
Spencer, Charles Langford	1878
Spencer, Edward Curran	1880
Spencer, George Gilman	1834
Spencer, James Magoffin	1867
Sperry, Watson Robertson	1871
Spitz, Robert Wayne	1962
Spitzer, Lyman B. Jr.	1935
Spofford, Charles Merville	1924
Spring, Andrew Jackson	1855
Sprole, Frank Arnoit	1942
Stack, Jr., Joseph William	1940
Stackpole, Edward James	1915
Stagg, Amos Alonzo	1888
Stanberry, William Burks Jr.	1966
Stanley, Harold	1908
Stanley, William	1852
Stapler, Henry B. B.	1874
Staven, Karl Eric	1981
Steadman, John Montague	1952
Steadman, Richard Cooke	1955
Stearns, Edwin Russell	1870
Stebbins, Edwin Allen	1902
Stebbins, Hart Lyman	1933
Stebbins, Henry Hamlin	1862
Steele, Henry Thornton	1846
Sterling, John Williams	1864
Stetson, Eugene William Jr.	1934
Stevens, Albert B.	1940
Stevens, Eric Eugene	1980
Stevens, Frederic William	1858
Stevens, Henry	1843
Stevens, Joseph Benson Jr.	1938
Stevens, Marvin Allen	1925
Stevenson, Charles P.	1979
Stevenson, Charles Porter	1941
Stevenson, Donald Day	1925
Stevenson, Frederic A.	1888
Stewart, Charles Jacob	1918
Stewart, Donald Ogden	1916
Stewart, James Corb	1961
Stewart, James Ross	1931
Stewart, John	1921
Stewart, Percy Hamilton	1890
Stewart, Peter Hellwege	1928
Stewart, Philip Battel	1886
Stewart, Potter.	1937
Stewart, Walter Eugene Jr.	1894
Stewart, Zeph	1943
Stiles, Joseph	1846
Stiles, William Augustus	1859
Stille, Charles Janeway	1839
Stillman, George Schley	1935
Stillman, Leland Stanford	1894
Stillman, Peter Gordon B.	1940
Stimson, Henry Albert	1865
Stimson, Henry Lewis	1888
Stokes, Anson Phelps	1896
Stokes, Anson Phelps Jr.	1927
Stokes, Harold Phelps	1909
Stokes, Horace Sheldon	1889
Stone, Charles Martin	1878
Stone, Harold	1902
Stone, Louis Talcott Jr.	1937
Stone, William	1865
Storrs, Cordial	1850
Stratton, Daniel James	1981
Straw, Ralph Lynwood	1964
Street, Henry Abbott	1912
Strickler, Samuel Alexander	1848
Strong, Caleb	1835
Strong, Charles Hall	1870
Strong, George Arthur	1871
Strong, Henry Barnard	1922
Strout, Edwin Augustus Jr.	1912
Struzzi, Thomas Allen	1975
Stubbs, Alfred	1835
Stucky, William McDowell	1940
Sturges, Hezekiah	1841
Sturges, Thomas Benedict	1835
Sullivan, Charles S.	1978
Sullivan, Corlis Esmonde	1900
Sulzer, James Sothern	1973
Sumner, Graham	1897
Sumner, William Graham	1863
Sumner, William Sayre	1945
Sutherland, Richard Orlin	1931
Sutphin, Stuart Bruen	1903
Swan, Joseph Rockwell	1902
Sweet, Carroll Fuller	1899
Sweet, Edwin Forrest	1871
Swenson, Edward Francis Jr.	1940
Swift, John Morton	1836
Swift, Walker Ely	1915
Swil, Roy Anthony	1967
Swinburne, Louis Judson	1879
Swoope, Walter Moore	1931
Tabor, John Kaye	1943
Taft, Alphonso	1833
Taft, Charles Phelps	1918
Taft, Henry Waters	1880
Taft, Horace Dutton	1883
Taft, Horace Dutton	1985
Taft, Hulbert	1900
Taft, Peter Rawson	1867
Taft, Robert Alphonso	1910
Taft, Thomas Prindle	1971
Taft, William Howard	1878
Talcott, Thomas Grosvenor	1838
Tarbell, Frank Bigelow	1873
Taylor, Alan McLean	1902
Taylor, Alfred Judd	1859
Taylor, John Phelps	1862
Taylor, Richard	1845
Teig, Joseph Benjamin	1980
Tener, Alexander Campbell	1912
Tener, Kinley John	1916
Terry, Henry Porter B.	1935
Terry, Wyllys	1885
Terry, Wyllys III	1962
Thacher, James Kingsley	1868
Thacher, John Seymour	1877
Thacher, Sherman Day	1883
Thacher, Thomas	1871
Thacher, Thomas Anthony	1835
Thacher, Thomas Day	1904

Name	Year
Thacher, William Larned	1887
Thomas, Charles Henry	1873
Thomas, John Allen Miner	1922
Thomas, Walton Dowdell	1941
Thompson, Donald	1903
Thompson, John R.	1938
Thompson, Jonathan P.	1970
Thompson, Joseph Parrish	1838
Thompson, Norman F.	1881
Thompson, Oliver David	1879
Thompson, Stepehn E. Jr.	1967
Thompson, William McI. Jr.	1969
Thomson, Clifton Samuel	1924
Thomson, Gregory Allan	1985
Thomson, Samuel Clifton	1891
Thorne, Brinkley Stimson	1968
Thorne, Charles H. McK.	1974
Thorne, David Hoadley	1966
Thorne, Peter Brinckerhoff	1940
Thorne, Samuel	1896
Thorne, Samuel Brinckeroff	1896
Thornton, Edmund B.	1954
Thornton, James Carlton	1908
Thorson, Peter Andreas	1959
Tiffany, William Henry	1840
Tighe, Ambrose	1879
Tighe, Laurence Gotzian	1916
Tighe, Laurence Gotzian Jr.	1941
Tighe, Richard Lodge	1923
Tillinghast, Charles	1875
Tilney, Robert Fingland II	1905
Tilney, Thomas Joseph	1870
Tingey, Douglas Stuart	1981
Tinker, Anson Phelps	1868
Tom Chan Bruce III	1977
Tompkins, Ray	1884
Towers, Jonathan David	1982
Townsend, Frederic dePeyster Jr.	1922
Townsend, George Henry	1908
Townsend, James Mulford	1874
Townsend, James M. Jr	1908
Townsend, John Barnes	1891
Townsend, William Kneeland	1871
Tracy, Evarts	1890
Train, Robert	1936
Traphagen, Peter Abraham	1956
Trask, Charles Hooper	1846
Treadway, Ralph Bishop	1896
Trotter, Silas Flournoy	1839
Trowbridge, Mason	1902
Trower, C. Christopher	1970
Troy, Alexander	1981
Trudeau, Edward L.Jr	1896
Truesdale, Calvin	1907
Tucker, Carl Jr.	1947
Tucker, Luther B.D.	1931
Tufts, Bowen (Sonny) C.	1935
Tumpane, Timothy Michael	1980
Turner, Elvin D.	1978
Turner, Harold McLeod	1905
Turner, Harold McLeod	1937
Turner, Spencer	1906
Tuttle, George Coolidge	1907
Tuttle, George Montgomery	1877
Tweedy, Henry Hallam..	1891
Tweedy, John Hubbard	1834
Tweedy, Samuel	1868
Twichell, Charles Pratt	45W
Twombly, Alexander S.	1854
Twombly, Edward Bancroft	1912
Twombly, Henry Bancroft	1884
Tyler, Charles Mellen	1855
Tyler, Cheever	1959
Tyler, George Palmer	1836
Tyler, Moses Coit	1857
Tytus, Edward Jefferson	1868
Urquijo, Conzalo	1984
Van Antwerp, William M. Jr	58E
Van deGraaff, Adrian S.	1881
Van Dine, Vance	1949
Van Loan, Eugene	1964
Van Name, Addison	1858
Van Reypen, William K. Jr.	1905
Van Sinderen, Henry B.	1911
Van Slyck, DeForest	1920
Vanderbilt, Alfred Gwynne	1899
Vargish, Thomas	1966
Varnum, Joseph Bradley	1838
Vernon, Frederick R.	1881
Vincent, Francis Thomas	1931
Vogt, Tom D.	1943
von Holt, Herman Vademar	1916
Vorys, John Martin	1918
Vorys, Martin West	1952
Vose, Elliot Evans	45W
Vose, James Gardiner	1851
Wack, Damon deBlois	1929
Waddel, Geoffrey Hamilton	1961
Wade, Levi Clifford	1866
Wadsworth, James Jeremiah	1927
Wadsworth, James W.t Jr.	1898
Wagner, Victor Edmond	1983
Waite, Morison Remich	1888
Waite, Morris Remmick	1837
Walcott, Frederic Collin	1891
Walcott, William Stuart	1894
Wald, Stephen George	1975
Walden, Howard Talbott	1881
Walden, Robert Stewart	1972
Walden, Russell	1874
Wales, Leonard Eugene	1845
Walker, Charles Rumford	1916
Walker, Christopher	2000
Walker, George Herbert Jr.	1927
Walker, George Herbert III	1953
Walker, George Nesmith	1919
Walker, Horace Flecher	1889
Walker, Jeffrey Pond	1944
Walker, John Mercer	1931
Walker, John Stanley	1942
Walker, Joseph Burbeen	1844
Walker, Louis	1936
Walker, Ray Carter	1955
Walker, Samuel Johnson	1888
Walker, Samuel Sloan Jr.	1948
Walker, Stoughton	1928
Wallace, Henry Mitchell	1903
Wallis, Alexander Hamilton	1893
Walsh, Hugh	1835
Walsh, John Joseph Jr.	1961
Walsh, Kevin Sanchez	1985
Walton, Keith	1986
Ward, John Abbott	1862
Wardwell, Edward Rogers	1927
Waring, Antonio Johnston	1903
Warren, George Upson	45W
Warren, Henry Waterman	1865
Warren, John Davock	1927
Warren, William Candee Jr.	1914
Washburn, William Barrett	1844
Washington, George	1839
Washington, William Henry	1834
Waters, William Otis	1913
Watkins, Charles Law	1908
Watson, Charles III	1927
Watson, John Marsh	1839
Watson, Jr., William Berkley	1940
Weaver, Howard Sayer	1948
Weber, John William	1953
Weed, George Haines	1938
Weeks, Robert Kelley	1862
Weinstein, Adam	1984
Welch, George Arnold	1901
Welch, William Henry	1870
Welles, Charles Hopkins Jr.	1899
Wells, George	1929
Wells, Harold Sherman	1907
Wells, Henry Dorrance	1851
Wells, Herbert Wetmore	1889

Name	Year
Wells, John Lewis	1882
Wells, Nathan Dana	1857
Wesson, Charles Holland	1863
Westerfield, Richard H.	1979
Wetherell, John Walcott	1844
Wetmore, George Peabody	1867
Weyerhaeuser, Frederick E.	1896
Wheeler, Alfred Newton=	1923
Wheeler, Lawrence R.	1911
Wheeler, Thomas Beardsley	1958
Wheeler, William=	1855
Wheelwright, Joseph Storer	1897
White, Andrew Dickinson=	1853
White, Charles Atwood	1854
White, George	1848
White, George Edward	1866
White, Henry Charles.	1881
White, Henry Dyer	1851
White, John Richards	1903
White, Oliver Sherman.	1864
White, Percy Gardiner	1902
White, Roger Sherman	1859
White, Warren Benton	1941
White, William Gardiner	1942
Whitehead, Mather Kimbal	1936
Whitehouse, Charles S.	1947
Whitehouse, Edwin Sheldon	1905
Whitehouse, William F.	1899
Whitman, Francis S.Jr.	1938
Whitmore, James Allen Jr.	1944
Whitney, Edward Baldwin	1878
Whitney, Edward Payton	1854
Whitney, Emerson Cogswell	1851
Whitney, Harry Payne	1894
Whitney, James Lyman	1856
Whitney, Joseph Ernest	1882
Whitney, Payne	1898
Whitney, William Collins	1863
Whiton, James Morris	1853
Wickes, Forsyth	1898
Wickes, Thomas Parmelee	1874
Wickwire, Winthrop Ross	49E
Wiggin, Fredrick Holme	1904
Wilbur, John Smith	1933
Wilbur, John Smith Jr.	1964
Wilbur, Richard Emery	1938
Wilcox, Asher Henry	1859
Wilder, Amos Parker	1884
Wilhelmi, Frederick William	1903
Wilhelmi, Frederick W. Jr.	1939
Wilkie, Valleau Jr.	45/8
Willard, Andrew Jackson	1853
Willard, Charles Hastings	1926
Willcox, Giles Buckingham	1848
Williams, Burch	1939
Williams, Darryl L.	1976
Williams, Henry	1837
Williams, James Willard	1908
Williams, Norman Alton	1897
Williams, Ralph Omsted	1861
Williams, Samuel Goode	1932
Williams, Thomas Scott	1838
Williams, William Bruce	1957
Williams, William Perkins	1839
Willis, Richard Storrs	1841
Wilson, Archelaus	1844
Wilson, Daniel Richard	1979
Wilson, Hugh Robert	1906
Wilson, John	1847
Wilson, Zebuon Vance	1972
Winston, Dudley	1886
Winston, Frederick S.	1877
Winter, Daniel Robbins	1920
Winter, Edwin Wheeler II	1921
Wiseman, David Batshaw	1984
Witherbee, Frank Spencer	1874
Witherbee, Walter Crafts	1880
Witter, Dean Jr.	1944
Wodell, Ruthven AdriancE	1910
Wolcott, Elizer	1839
Wolfe, Stephen H.	1964
Wood, George Ingersoll	1833
Wood, John Seymour	1874
Wood, William Curtis	1868
Woodford, Oswald L.	1850
Woodlock, Douglas Preston	1969
Woodruff, Francis Eben	1864
Woodruff, George W.	1889
Woodruff, Timothy Lester	1879
Woodsum, Harold E. Jr.	1953
Woodward, John Butler	1883
Woodward, Richard William	1867
Woodward, Stanley	1922
Woodward, Stanley	1855
Woodward, William Herrick	1858
Woolfolk, William Grey	1841
Woolley, John Eliot	1918
Woolley, Knight	1917
Woolsey, Heathcote Muirson	1907
Woolsey, Theodore Salisbury	1872
Worcester, Edwin Dean	1876
Worcester, Franklin Eldred	1882
Worcester, Wilfred James	1885
Word, Charles Francis	1894
Wray, James McAlpin	1836
Wright, Alfred Parks	1901
Wright, Henry Burt	1898
Wright, Henry Park	1868
Wright, William Henry II	1982
Yang, James Ting-Yeh	1982
Yardley, Henry Albert	1855
Yarnall, Thomas Coffin	1841
Yent, James B. Jr.	1979
Yerkes, Stephen	1837
Young, Benham Daniel	1848
Zallinger, Peter Franz	1965
Ziegler, Stan Warren	1972
Zigerelli, Lawrence John	1980
Zorthian, Barry	1941
Zorthian, Gregory Jannig	1975
Zucker, Bernard Benjamin	1962

The Supreme Court's reputation was still suffering from its Dred Scott and Legal Tender decisions. This is the Court which nullified the 14th and 15th Amendments as guarantees of Negro rights, and commenced the historic process of construing the 14th Amendment's "due process" clause as a bulwark of property. Members: (*seated l. to r.*) Joseph P. Bradley, Samuel F. Miller, Chief Justice Morrison R. Waite, Stephen J. Field, Stanley Matthews; (*standing*) William B. Woods, Horace Gray, John M. Harlan, Samuel Blatchford.

In 1886, … in the case of *Santa Clara County v. Southern Pacific Railroad Company,* the U.S. Supreme Court decided that a private corporation is a person and entitled to the legal rights and protections the Constitutions affords to any person. Because the Constitution makes no mention of corporations, it is a fairly clear case of the Court's taking it upon itself to rewrite the Constitution.

Far more remarkable, however, is that the doctrine of corporate personhood, which subsequently became a cornerstone of corporate law, was introduced into this 1886 decision without argument. According to the official case record, Supreme Court Justice Morrison Remick Waite simply pronounced before the beginning of argument in the case of *Santa Clara County v. Southern Pacific Railroad Company* that

The court does not wish to hear argument on the question whether the provision in the Fourteenth Amendment to the Constitution, which forbids a State to deny to any person within its jurisdiction the equal protection of the laws, applies to these corporations. We are all of opinion that it does.

The court reporter duly entered into the summary record of the Court's findings that

The defendant Corporations are persons within the intent of the clause in section 1 of the Fourteen Amendment to the Constitution of the United States, which forbids a State to deny to any person within its jurisdiction the equal protection of the laws.

Thus it was that a two-sentence assertion by a single judge elevated corporations to the status of persons under the law, prepared the way for the rise of global corporate rule, and thereby changed the course of history.

The doctrine of corporate personhood creates an interesting legal contradiction. The corporation is owned by its shareholders and is therefore their property. If it is also a legal person, then it is a person owned by others and thus exists in a condition of slavery -- a status explicitly forbidden by the Thirteenth Amendment to the Constitution. So is a corporation a person illegally held in servitude by its shareholders? Or is it a person who enjoys the rights of personhood that take precedence over the presumed ownership rights of its shareholders? So far as I have been able to determine, this contradiction has not been directly addressed by the courts.

from David Korten's *The Post-Corporate World, Life After Capitalism*

RTA, Incorporated — A Shell Game

Kris Millegan
July 2003

The official name for the Order of Skull and Bones is RTA, Incorporated. Daniel Coit Gilman first incorporated the Order of Skull & Bones in 1856 as the Russell Trust Association. The name was changed in 1961 to RTA, Incorporated.

In November 1983, the members voted positively on an Amending Certificate. The proper papers filed in December increased the Board of Directors from six to eight members and the President was given more power among other changes.

Whether this was at all in reaction to the release of Antony Sutton's first Bones book, *An Introduction to the Order,* isn't known. What is interesting about the amendment is the voting record presented. There is just enough information in the documents, to satisfy the legal filing requirements, so one cannot form a definite answer about all of the group's rules for voting, but it is interesting that they list as the members required for a quorum as 35 with 71 as being "Present in Person or by Proxy and Entitled to vote." The vote required for adoption is stated as 48. Now that is the two-thirds of 71 and in RTA's Certificate of Incorporation of 1961, Section 8 (Which the amendment of 1983 negates.) it states that "any action may be taken only after a two-thirds majority vote of members." But then it goes on to state, "the vote of majority of the voting power of members shall be sufficient." This suggests that if 15 get together eight votes wins.

So who all gets to vote and what does it take to get things done in the organization? In section 5 it states, "[t]he Corporation shall have members, all of whom shall be of the same class. All persons who are at the date hereof members of the Russell Trust Association, … are members of the corporation, together with such other persons who are undergraduate students at Yale University ... who may be elected from time to time pursuant to the by-laws of the corporation." We do not have copies of RTA's bylaws so we do not know what the "voting power of the members" consists of and if every Bones member has voting rights in RTA, Incorporated or what. But we do find it interesting that an amendment change was accomplished by such small numbers. In the September 27, 1991, the New Haven Register reported "almost 700 of the club's approximately 800 surviving members narrowly voted to admit women."

Should The Order get a Tax Free Ride on it's Four Million Dollar Nest Egg?

The question of their taxes is also very interesting. RTA Incorporated tax statements are available online at www.guidestar.com and at www.fleshingoutskullandbones.com. If you can look at these documents, you will find the tax forms are quite revealing in what they say ... and do not say. There are required questions, boxes, and blanks to fill in that they just leave empty or write "not available." The most blatant and egregious action is their use of the tax code to pay no taxes on their investment earnings of sometimes over $400,000 a year and that members may take their donations to Bones as deductions off of their personal income tax liabilities.

RTA Incorporated is a non-profit 501(c) 3 corporation carrying no tax burden at all. It does all this, while spending yearly $4,000 to $10,000 *renting* their private island for "[r]ental of facility for educational programs," and $50,000 a year on "[c]onferences, conventions, and meetings," plus another $40,000 to $60,0000 thousand a year in occupancy expenses. The Order has also been spending money on renovations and improvements, spending over a quarter of a million dollars in 1998. Did they add a women's locker room to their fabled underground swimming pool or just fancy his and hers coffins?

The only charitable donations listed in their tax returns are in the years 1999 and 2000. A $5,000 donation, each of those years, to the Yale Scholarship Fund. The majority of all the expenses are declared in the tax form's Program Service Expenses column as "Educational Programs." There is no discussion of achievements, no number of clients served, nothing but "Educational Programs." The Order of Skull & Bones skirts both the spirit and letter of the law by claiming to be an educational support organization for Yale University. The 1961 Certificate of Incorporation papers give some window dressing and cover some of the 501(c)3 requirements but the activities of the group do not seem to be educational but fraternal and *secret.* How can a secret society, which does not divulge its purpose, history or even its members be considered an educational non-profit? Maybe in some of their lawyers' minds the organization is *defined* as an alumni organization. Or are they claiming to come under Yale Universities educational tax umbrella because RTA, Incorporated gives whatever assets it has left after obligations if

Bones dies to Yale? At best, what they are doing a tap-dance on the Federal Tax code for the society's *gain* and *shame.*

Historically and in reality, The Order of Skull & Bones is a fraternal organization and should be classified as a 501(c)(10) organization that should be paying taxes on the Order's investment income. A lawyer friend of mine said that the Order's tax returns, are, "skillfully prepared to look bland and innocuous." At least from the listing of the officers and board members gathered from the RTA Incorporated state corporate and federal tax records have allowed us to at least fill in some of the holes in the membership lists "dark" years.

There is no publicly held listing of members after 1972 or privately proffered list of "Bonespersons" after 1985. The only semi-confirmed list after that is 2000 when the *Rumpus,* at Yale printed a copy of the Bones printed materials. We cannot be 100% about it though, considering *Rumpus's* known irrelevancies and tabloid predilections. We have not seen the original and with today's digital methods, one could be created. Over fifteen years of members are unknown. What influence these 20 and 30-somethings are having on our current affairs is unknown.

Another item gleaned from the tax returns is that contributions have gone from $164,000 in 1997 to $45,00 in 2000. Whether the drop in contributions is part of some dissension or just a reflection of the economy is as are many things about the Order … in the dark. I have been told in several phone conversation with one researcher, who claims to have interviewed the 1967 member of Bones who tapped George W. Bush, of a *war* going on in Bones. That there are some members who are switching monetary support from Bush to Kerry. Whether this is for real or just Hegelian flim-flam of a Bonesian Wizard of Oz ploy is yet to be seen.

THE RUSSEL TRUST ASSOCIATION'S AND RTA INCORPORATED'S OFFICIAL FILINGS submitted to the Connecticut's Secretary of State's office are presented in following pages. These are all the papers registered with the Secretary of State's office for the two groups except for the yearly reports which, — as shown in the state records — begin after the name change in 1961. The earliest and latest available of these yearly reports are presented.

STATE OF CONNECTICUT

OFFICE OF THE SECRETARY OF THE STATE

I, the Connecticut Secretary of the State, and keeper of the seal thereof, and of the original record of the Acts and Resolutions of the General Assembly of said State, DO HEREBY CERTIFY, that I have compared the annexed copy of AN ACT INCORPORATING **THE RUSSELL TRUST ASSOCIATION** with the original record of the same now remaining in this office, and have found said copy to be a correct and complete transcript thereof.

And I further Certify, that said original is a public record of the State of Connecticut, now remaining in this office.

In Testimony Whereof, I have hereunto set my hand and affixed the Great Seal of the State of Connecticut, at Hartford, this 28th day of March, 2001

Susan Bysiewicz
Secretary of the State

rlb

INCORPORATING RUSSELL TRUST ASSOCIATION.

PASSED 1856.

Resolved by this Assembly, That William H. Russell, John S. Beach, Henry B. Harrison, Daniel C. Gilman, Henry T. Blake and Henry D. White, and all such other persons as may be from time to time associated with them, together with their successors, be and they are hereby constituted a body corporate and politic, by the name of "The Russell Trust Association," for the purpose of the intellectual and moral improvement of its members, and for that only, and by that name shall have perpetual succession and be capable in law to purchase and receive, hold and convey real and personal estate, to an amount not exceeding at any time fifteen thousand dollars, to sue and be sued, defend and be defended in all courts and places whatsoever, may have a common seal and may change and alter the same at pleasure; may elect such officers as they may find necessary and convenient, and make and carry into effect such by-laws as they may deem necessary, not repugnant to the laws of this state and of the United States.

SEC. 2. The first meeting of the corporation hereby established shall be holden at New Haven, on the last Wednesday in July, A. D. 1856.

SEC. 3. This act may be altered, amended or repealed at the pleasure of the general assembly.

[Vol. IV, 201.]

Amending the Charter of the Russell Trust Association.

Resolved by this Assembly, That the charter of the Russell Trust Association be, and the same is hereby, so amended that said association shall be capable in law to purchase and receive, hold and convey real and personal estate to an amount not exceeding, at any one time, three hundred and fifty thousand dollars: *provided, always*, that this resolution may be altered, amended or repealed, at the pleasure of the general assembly.

Approved, July 5th, 1870.

[House Joint Resolution No. 65.]

[121.]

CONFIRMING THE BY-LAWS OF THE RUSSELL TRUST ASSOCIATION.

Resolved by this Assembly: That the meeting of the Russell Trust Association, held on the fifth day of November, 1885, is hereby validated as a lawful and valid meeting of said corporation, and its proceedings are hereby validated and confirmed, and the by-laws then adopted by said meeting are hereby validated and confirmed as the duly established by-laws of said corporation; *provided*, that such proceedings and by-laws be not inconsistent with the laws of this state or the United States.

Approved, March 24, 1887.

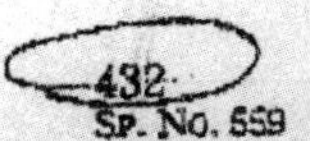

432 SPECIAL ACTS [Jan.,

Sp. No. 559

[Substitute for Senate Bill No. 214.]

[559.]

AN ACT AMENDING THE CHARTER OF THE RUSSELL TRUST ASSOCIATION.

Be it enacted by the Senate and House of Representatives in General Assembly convened:

SECTION 1. The charter of The Russell Trust Association, incorporated by a resolution approved in 1856, is amended so that said association shall be capable in law to purchase and receive, hold, convey and transfer real and personal estate to an amount not exceeding, at any time, seven hundred thousand dollars.

SEC. 2. This act shall take effect upon its acceptance by a majority of the members of said association at a meeting warned and held for that purpose within one year after its passage. An attested copy of such acceptance shall be filed with the secretary of the state.

Approved, July 9, 1943.

VOL. 16

THE RUSSELL TRUST ASSOCIATION

343 Certificate of Acceptance of Amendment to Charter

THIS IS TO CERTIFY That at a meeting of the members of The Russell Trust Association legally warned and held for the purpose at New Haven, Connecticut, on the 12th day of November, 1943, the Act amending the charter of said corporation passed at the January Session of the General Assembly, 1943, was accepted by a unanimous vote of the members present (the members present being more than a majority of the members of said corporation), of which the following is a copy:

RESOLVED: That the Act amending the charter of The Russell Trust Association passed by the General Assembly of the State of Connecticut at its January 1943 session and approved by the Governor of the State of Connecticut on July 9, 1943, be and it is hereby accepted.

Dated at New Haven, Connecticut, this 12th day of November, 1943.

ATTEST:

(CORPORATE SEAL)

Morris Hadley
President

Alfred R. Bellinger
Secretary

STATE OF CONNECTICUT)
: ss. New Haven, November 12, 1943
COUNTY OF NEW HAVEN)

Personally appeared Morris Hadley, President, and Alfred R. Bellinger, Secretary, of The Russell Trust Association, signers of the foregoing certificate and made oath to the truth of the same, before me,

(SEAL)

Huntington T. Day
Notary Public

RECEIVED AND FILED
JAN 6 1944

CERTIFICATE OF INCORPORATION

of

RTA INCORPORATED

We, the incorporators, certify that we hereby associate ourselves as a body politic and corporate, under the Nonstock Corporation Act of the State of Connecticut.

1. The name of the corporation is RTA INCORPORATED.

2. The name of the town in Connecticut in which the corporation is to be located is the Town of New Haven.

3. The nature of the activities to be conducted or the purposes to be promoted or carried out by the corporation are as follows:

The corporation is formed for exclusively educational purposes, including the intellectual and moral improvement of its members and the support of education at Yale University, New Haven, Connecticut. For these purposes the corporation shall have all the powers of a corporation formed under the Nonstock Corporation Act of the State of Connecticut except as limited by this Certificate of Incorporation.

4. No part of the corporation's income is distributable to its members, directors, officers, employees or any private shareholders or individual, and the corporation shall not have or issue shares of stock or pay dividends. The corporation is not organized and shall never be maintained or conducted for the pecuniary profit of its members, directors, officers or employees,

but is organized and shall be operated exclusively for educational purposes, and no member, director, officer or employee of the corporation shall at any time receive or be entitled to receive any pecuniary profit from the operation of the corporation except reasonable compensation for services actually rendered to the corporation in effecting one or more of its purposes. No part of the activities of the corporation shall consist of carrying on propaganda, or otherwise attempting to influence legislation, and the corporation shall not participate in, or intervene in by the publishing of or distributing of statements or otherwise, any political campaign on behalf of any candidate for public office. In the event of the dissolution of the corporation, or the termination of its corporate existence, no part of the property or assets of the corporation shall inure to the benefit of any member, director, officer or employee of the corporation or of any private shareholder or individual, but, after the payment of all lawful claims against the corporation, the same shall be paid to Yale University, New Haven, Connecticut, to be by it used for its general educational purposes. Nothing herein shall prevent the transfer of the property and assets of the corporation to another nonstock, nonprofit corporation formed for exclusively educational purposes if it has in its Certificate of Incorporation a provision for the benefit of Yale University substantially the same as that hereinbefore stated.

5. The corporation shall have members, all of whom shall be of the same class. All persons who are at the date

hereof members of The Russell Trust Association, a corporation organized and existing pursuant to special acts of the General Assembly of the State of Connecticut (Volume IV, Page 1201; Volume VI, Page 850; and Volume 24, Page 432) are members of the corporation, together with such other persons who are undergraduate students at Yale University, New Haven, Connecticut and who may be elected from time to time pursuant to the by-laws of the corporation.

6. The activities, property and affairs of the corporation shall be managed by a Board of Directors consisting of six members, two of whom shall be elected by vote of a majority of members present and voting in person or by proxy at each annual meeting of the members to serve for terms of three years and until their successors are elected and qualified. No person shall be eligible for election to two successive terms.

7. The election of directors and any other action to be voted upon by the members may be conducted and voted upon by mail if the Board of Directors so votes, and in such case a copy of the resolutions to be voted upon together with a form of written ballot and a duly addressed return envelope shall be mailed, postage prepaid to each member at least twenty days before the date fixed by the Board of Directors for the closing of the polls. Nothing in this Certificate of Incorporation shall require the Board of Directors to provide for voting by mail or to furnish proxy forms for any meeting.

8. Wherever it is provided in part VII, relating to fundamental changes, or Part VIII, relating to dissolution and winding up, of the Connecticut Nonstock Corporation Act, that any action may be taken only after a two-thirds vote of members, the vote of a majority of the voting power of members shall be sufficient.

9. The duration of the corporation shall be unlimited.

Dated at New Haven, Connecticut this 17th day of February, 1961

Henry B. Van Sinderen

John W. Hincks

Howard S. Weaver

H. P. Baldwin Terry

Sidney Lovett

[illegible signature]

STATE OF CONNECTICUT)
: ss. New Haven, February 17, 1961
COUNTY OF NEW HAVEN)

Then and there personally appeared - - - - - - - - - - - - -, Henry B. Van Sinderen, John W. Hincks, Howard S. Weaver, H. P. Baldwin Terry, and Sidney Lovett, and made oath to the truth of the foregoing certificate by them signed, before me.

John E. Ecklund

Notary Public

RTA INCORPORATED

CERTIFICATE AMENDING THE CERTIFICATE OF INCORPORATION BY ACTION OF THE BOARD OF DIRECTORS AND MEMBERS

1. The name of the corporation is RTA INCORPORATED.

2. The Certificate of Incorporation is amended only by the following resolutions of the Board of Directors and of the Members:

A. RESOLVED that Section 6 of the Certificate of Incorporation of the corporation is amended to read as follows:

"6. The activities, property and affairs of the corporation shall be managed by a Board of Directors chosen from the membership and numbering eight (or nine if the term of the president would have otherwise expired), two of whom shall be elected by vote of a majority of members present and voting in person or by proxy at each annual meeting of the members to serve for terms of four years and until their successors are elected and qualified. No person shall be eligible for election to two successive terms. Nevertheless, the president shall be entitled to continue as a director, with full authority, regardless of the expiration of the term as director for which he was originally elected and regardless of the sequence of his election by the directors as president and the election by the members of his successor on the board of directors. In such case, when he shall no longer be president, he shall cease to be a director, and no vacancy in the board shall result therefrom."

B. RESOLVED that Section 8 of the Certificate of Incorporation is deleted in its entirety.

3. The above resolutions were adopted by the Board of Directors and by the Members of the Corporation.

4. Vote of the Members:

Number of Members Required for Quorum:	35
Number of Members Present in Person or by Proxy and Entitled to Vote:	71
Total Voting Power of such Members Entitled to Vote (there being no classes of membership for purposes of voting)	
Vote Required for Adoption:	48
Vote Favoring Adoption:	71

Dated at New Haven, Connecticut, this 18th day of November, 1983.

We hereby declare, under the penalties of perjury, that the statements made in the foregoing certificate are true.

John W. Hincks
President

Coit R. Liles
Secretary

Rec + cc sent 12-21-83 fa

FILED
STATE OF CONNECTICUT
DEC - 1 1983
SECRETARY OF THE STATE
By ____ Time ____ A.M. P.M.

Rec + cc to: done 12/6/83 dp.
Robinson, Robinson + Cole
~~799 Main ST~~
Hfd, CT. 06103
ATTn: John W. Hincks

ORGANIZATION AND FIRST
BIENNIAL REPORT OF
RTA INCORPORATED

1. The name of the corporation is RTA INCORPORATED.

2. The date of the corporation's organization meeting was June 15, 1961.

3. The date of this report is June 15, 1961.

4. The principal office of the corporation is 258 Durfee Hall, Yale University, New Haven, Connecticut.

5. The names and respective residence addresses of the directors and officers of the corporation are:

DIRECTORS

Name	Residence Address
Arthur E. Palmer, Jr.	1155 Park Avenue New York 28, New York
John E. Hincks	81 Ardmore Road West Hartford, Connecticut
Sidney Lovett	31 Lincoln Street New Haven, Connecticut
Howard S. Weaver	266 Livingston Street New Haven, Connecticut
Charles S. Gage	35 Hillhouse Avenue New Haven, Connecticut
Zeph Stewart	Adams House Harvard University Cambridge, Massachusetts

OFFICERS

Name		Residence Address
Sidney Lovett	President	31 Lincoln Street New Haven, Connecticut
Howard S. Weaver	Secretary	266 Livingston Street New Haven, Connecticut
George H. Walker, Jr.	Treasurer	Dingletown Road Greenwich, Connecticut
Ralph W. Halsey, Jr.	Asst. Treasurer	Seymour Road Woodbridge, Connecticut

6. Under the penalties of perjury, I declare that the statements made in this report are true.

Signed at ~~27th~~ New Haven this 27th day of February, 1962, as of June 15, 1961.

Howard S. Weaver
Howard S. Weaver
Secretary

CONNECTICUT SECRETARY O
Document Revie
30 Trinity Stre
P.O. Box 15047o
Hartford, CT 06115-0470

FILING #0001719970 PG 01 OF 04 VOL B-00125
FILED 04/16/1997 08:30 AM PAGE 01926
SECRETARY OF THE STATE
CONNECTICUT SECRETARY OF THE STATE

Report Due: FEBRUARY, 1997.

1. Name of Corp: RTA INCORPORATED

2. Business ID: 0059060

3. Report due in the month of: FEBRUARY, 1997.

4. This corporation is DOMESTIC/NON-STOCK. Fee is $25.00.

Corporate Name: RTA INCORPORATED

Mailing: WIGGIN & DANA
Address: ONE CENTURY TOWER
NEW HAVEN,CT 06508

Changes: ______

5. Principal Office Address: (in CT only) Changes:

64 HIGH ST
NEW HAVEN,CT 06510

6. Executive Office Address: (Foreign Corps Only)

7. Principal Office in State of Formation: (Foreign Corps Only)

8. Attached hereto are the officers and directors of the corporation with their business and residence addresses.

9. Date: 3 / 25 / 97
Mo Da Yr

10. Signature: Coit R. Liles

Print Signatory Name: COIT R. LILES

Print Capacity: ASSISTANT SECRETARY

Report Officers/Di
Business ID : 005§

FILING #0001719970 PG 02 OF 04 VOL B-00125
FILED 04/16/1997 08:30 AM PAGE 01927
SECRETARY OF THE STATE
CONNECTICUT SECRETARY OF THE STATE

1. Full Legal Name: DAVID GEORGE BALL
Title(s): PRESIDENT
Residence Addr: 6760 TOWNE LANE RD
MCLEAN, VA 22101
Business Addr: WILLIAMS, MULLENS, CHRISTIAN & DOBBINS
1575 EYE ST, NW
WASHINGTON, DC 20005
Res Changes: ______
Bus Changes: ______

2. Full Legal Name: DAVID GEORGE BALL
Title(s): DIRECTOR
Residence Addr: 6760 TOWNE LANE RD
MCLEAN, VA 22101
Business Addr: WILLIAMS, MULLENS, CHRISTIAN & DOBBINS
1575 EYE ST, NW
WASHINGTON, DC 20005
Res Changes: ______
Bus Changes: ______

3. Full Legal Name: SIDNEY LOVETT
Title(s): SECRETARY
Residence Addr: COXBORO RD
HOLDERNESS, NH 03245
Business Addr: NONE
Res Changes: ______
Bus Changes: ______

4. Full Legal Name: HENRY POMEROY DAVISON II
Title(s): TREASURER
Residence Addr: 315 EAST 68TH ST, APT. 2S
NEW YORK, NY 10021
Business Addr: MORGAN GUARANTY TRUST COMPANY
9 WEST 57TH ST
NEW YORK, NY 10019
Res Changes: ______
Bus Changes: ______

Report Officers/Directors
Business ID : 005

FILING #0001719970 PG 03 OF 04 VOL B-00125
FILED 04/16/1997 08:30 AM PAGE 01928
SECRETARY OF THE STATE
CONNECTICUT SECRETARY OF THE STATE

5. Full Legal Name: COIT REDFEARN LILES
Title(s): ASSISTANT SECRETARY
Residence Addr: 40 BATTER TERRACE, APT. 24
NEW HAVEN, CT 06511
Business Addr: 64 HIGH ST
NEW HAVEN, CT 06510
Res Changes: ______
Bus Changes: ______

6. Full Legal Name: COIT REDFEARN LILES
Title(s): ASSISTANT TREASURER
Residence Addr: 40 BATTER TERRACE, APT. 24
NEW HAVEN, CT 06511
Business Addr: 64 HIGH ST
NEW HAVEN, CT 06510
Res Changes: ______
Bus Changes: ______

FILING #0001719970 PG 04 OF 04 VOL B-00125
FILED 04/16/1997 08:30 AM PAGE 01929
SECRETARY OF THE STATE
CONNECTICUT SECRETARY OF THE STATE

Annual Report - continuation

RTA Incorporated
business id: 0059060

7. Full Legal Name:	JAMES ERNEST HOWARD
Title:	DIRECTOR
Residence:	19 HARVARD STREET CHARLESTOWN, MA 02129
Business:	90 CANAL STREET BOSTON, MA 02114
8. Full Legal Name:	PAUL CHRISTOPHER LAMBERT
Title:	DIRECTOR
Residence:	1088 PARK AVENUE, APT. 3A NEW YORK, NY 10128
Business:	200 PARK AVENUE NEW YORK, NY 10166
9. Full Legal Name:	WILLIAM HENRY WRIGHT, II
Title:	DIRECTOR
Residence:	993 PARK AVENUE, APT. 9B NEW YORK, NY 10028
Business:	1585 BROADWAY NEW YORK, NY 10036
10. Full Legal Name:	CATHERINE MOIRA SHARKEY
Title:	DIRECTOR
Residence:	494 WHITNEY AVENUE, APT 1B NEW HAVEN, CT 06511
Business:	NONE
11. Full Legal Name:	JOSEPH CARRERE FOX
Title:	DIRECTOR
Residence:	5475 PALISADE AVENUE BRONX, NY 10471
Business:	237 PARK AVENUE, 21ST FLOOR NEW YORK, NY 10017
12. Full Legal Name:	JONATHAN BUSH
Title:	DIRECTOR
Residence:	2 SUTTON PLACE SOUTH, APT 18D NEW YORK, NY 10022
Business:	55 WHITNEY AVENUE NEW HAVEN, CT 06510
13. Full Legal Name:	PAUL WHYTE
Title:	DIRECTOR
Residence:	28 NASHUA STREET, APT. 5 SOMERVILLE, MA 02145
Business:	NONE
14. Full Legal Name:	DENNIS PATRICK LYNCH
Title:	DIRECTOR
Residence:	NORTH ROHALLION DRIVE RUMFORD, NJ 07760
Business:	520 MADISON AVENUE NEW YORK, NY 10022
15. Full Legal Name:	KEITH WALTON
Title:	DIRECTOR
Residence:	400 WEST 119TH STREET, APT. J NEW YORK, NY 10027
Business:	535 WEST 116TH STREET NEW YORK, NY 10027

BIBLIOGRAPHY

SKULL AND BONES - SECRET SOCIETIES:

An Introduction to the Order
By Antony Sutton
Veritas publishing 1983

America's Secret Establishment: An introduction to The Order of Skull & Bones
By Antony Sutton
Liberty House 1986
TrineDay 2002

A Brief History of the Skull & Bones Society at Yale University
By John Lawrence
Private Paper 1991

The Last Secrets of Skull and Bones
By Ron Rosenbaum
Esquire, September, 1977

Yale Society Resists Peeks Into Its Crypt
By David W. Dunlap
New York *Times*, 11/4/88

Skull and Bones -- Bush's Boy's Club
Peggy Alder-Robohm (researcher)
Covert Action Quarterly No. 33 (Winter 1990)

Skeleton in His Closet
John Schrag
Willamette Week, September 19-25, 1991

The Cyclopedia Of Fraternities
By Albert Stevens, ed.
E. B. Treat and Company 1907

Secrets of the Tomb: Skull and Bones, The Ivy League, and The Hidden Paths of Power,
Robbins, Alexandra,
Little, Brown and Co. 2002.

At Skull and Bones, Bush's Secret Club Initiates "Ream" Gore,
Rosenbaum, Ron,
New York Observer, April 23, 2001.

Rule by Secrecy: The Hidden History That Connects the Trilateral Commission, the Freemasons, and the Great Pyramids,
Marrs, Jim, New York:
Harper Collins, 2000.

The Philosophy of Right
The Philosophy of History
Georg Wilhelm Friedrich Hegel
Great Books, Encyclopedia Brittanica 1952

Life of the Party: The Biography of Pamela Digby Churchill Hayward Harriman
Christopher Ogden
Little and Brown and Company 1994

Who's Who of the Elite
Robert Gaylon Ross, Sr.
RIE 1995

Youth from Every Quarter: A Bicentennial History Of Phillips Academy, Andover"
By Frederick S. Allis, Jr.
Phillips Academy 1979

The Wise Men: Six Friends and the World They Made
Walter Issacson & Evan Thomas
Simon & Schuster, Touchstone Books 1988

Born of the Blood
John Robison
Evans and Company 1989

Secret Societies and Psychological Warfare
Michael Hoffman II
Wiswell Ruffin House 1989/1992

The Occult Conspiracy: Secret Societies -- Their Influence and Power in World History
Michael Howard
Destiny Books 1989

The Sword and the Grail: Of The Grail and the Templars and a True Discovery of America
Andrew Sinclair
Crown Publishers 1992

The Stargate Conspiracy,
Lynn Picknett & Prince, Clive,
Warner Books, 1999.

The Templar Revelation,
Picknett, Lynn & Prince, Clive,
Touchstone Book Simon & Schuster, 1997.

The Second Messiah,
Knight, Christopher & Lomas, Robert,
Century Books Limited, 1997.

The Hiram Key,
Knight, Christopher & Lomas, Robert,
Element Books, Inc. 1997.

The History of the Knights Templars,
Addison Charles G.,
Adventures Unlimited Press 1997.

The Woman With The Alabaster Jar,
Starbird, Margaret,
Bear & Co.,Inc. 1993.

The Warriors and The Bankers: A History of the Knights Templar From 1307 To The Present, Butler, Alan, Dafoe, Stephen, Templar Books, 1998.

Washington Allston, Secret Societies, and the Alchemy of Anglo-American Painting,
Bjelajac, David,
Cambridge University Press, 1997

Millennial Desire and the Apocalyptic Vision of Washington Allston,
Bjelajac, David,
Smithsonian Institution Press 1988.

Phi Beta Kappa General Catalog 1776-1922,
Editor-in-Chief Voorhees, Oscar M.,
Press of the Unionist-Gazette Association.

General Catalogue of Delta Kappa Epsilon,
Compiled by Maxwell, W.J. 1918.

A Century and a Half of DKE: The Illustrated History of Delta Kappa Epsilon,
Edited by Duncan Andrews,
Heritage Publishers, Inc. 1997

Brotherhood of Darkness
Dr. Stanley Monteith
Hearthstone Publishing 2000

The Thousand -Year Conspiracy - Secret Germany Behind the Mask
Paul Winkler
Charles Scribner's Sons 1943

The Return of the Kings
X7
Dodd, Mead & Company 1925

Pilgrims & Pioneers
Sir Harry Britain
Hutchinson & Company

Scarlet and the Beast
John Daniel
Jon Kregel, Inc 1994

Encyclopaedia of Freemasonry
Albert Mackey
Masonic History Company 1914

Secret Societies and their Power in the 20th Century
Jan van Helsing
Ewertverlag

CONSPIRACY, MIND CONTROL & THE NEW WORLD ORDER:

A Nation Of Sheep
William Lederer
W.W. Norton 1961

Who Rules America? A Century of Invisible Government
John McConaughy
Longmans, Green and Co. 1934

New World Order: The Ancient Plan of Secret Societies
William Still
Hunington House 1990

Tragedy and Hope: A History of the World in our Time
Carroll Quigley
MacMillan Company 1966

The Secret life of Ronald Reagan
Larry Flynt & Donald Freed
Prevailing Winds Research 1991

Architects Of Conspiracy: An Intriguing History
William P. Hoar
Western Islands 1984

Trance Formation Of America
Cathy O'Brien & Mark Phillips
Global Trance Formation Info Ltd. 1995

Casebook On Alternative 3: UFO's Secret Societies and World Control
Jim Keith
Illuminet Press 1994

Millennium: Peace, Promises, and the Day They Take Our Money Away
Tex Marrs
Living Truth Publishers 1990

The Franklin Cover-Up: Child Abuse, Satanism, and Murder in Nebraska
John DeCamp
AWT, Inc. 1992

Conspiracies, Cover-Ups and Crimes: From JFK to the CIA Terrorist Connection
By Jonathan Vankin
Paragon House 1992 Dell edt

Witness To A Century
George Seldes
Ballantine Books 1987

The Power Elite
C. Wright Mills
Oxford University Press 1956

Treason of the Senate, Phillips,
David Graham, Academic reprints,
Cosmopolitan Magazine Vol. XL March, 1906.

Proofs of Conspiracy
John Robison
George Forman 1798

Conspiracy in American Politics 1787-1815
J. Wendell Knoz
Arno Press 1972

Treason in America
Anton Chaitkin
Executive Intelligence Review 1998

Foundations
Rene Wormser
Covenant House 1993

Cartels in Action
George Stocking & Myron Watkins
The Twentieth Century Fund 1946

The Secret War Against the Jews
John Loftus & Mark Aarons
St. Martin's Press 1994

CIA AND INTELLIGENCE:

Cloak & Gown: Scholars of the Secret War, 1939-1961
Robin W. Winks
William Morrow, Quill Edition 1987

OSS: The Secret History of America's First Central Intelligence Agency
R. Harris Smith
University of California 1972

Defrauding America: A Pattern Of Related Scandals — Dirty Secrets Of The CIA And Other Government Operations
Rodney Stich
Diablo Western Press 1993

The Secret Team: The CIA and Its Allies in Control of the U.S. and the World
Fletcher Prouty
Prentice Hall 1973

The Crimes of Patriots: A True Tale of Dope, Dirty Money & the CIA
Jonathan Kwitney
Norton 1987

Official and Confidential: The Secret Life of J. Edgar Hoover
Anthony Summers
Pocket Star Books 1993/1994

In Banks We Trust
Penny Lernoux
Anchor Press/ Doubleday 1984

DRUG TRAFFICKING:

Kiss The Boy's Goodbye: How The United States Betrayed It's Own POWs In Vietnam
Monika Jensen Stevens & William Stevenson
Plume 1991

The Chinese Opium Wars
Jack Breeching
Harcourt Brace Jovanovich 1975

Dope, Inc.: The Book that Drove Kissinger Crazy
The Editors of Executive Intelligence Review
Executive Intelligence Review 1992

The Proper Bostonians
By Cleveland Amory
E. P. Dutton 1947

The Politics of Heroin in S.E. Asia
Alfred McCoy
Harper & Row 1991

The Great Heroin Coup: Drugs, Intelligence & International Fascism
Henrik Kruger
South End Press 1980

Double Cross: The Explosive, Inside Story of the Mobster Who Controlled America
Sam & Chuck Giancana
Warner Books 1992

The War Conspiracy: The Secret Road to the Second Indochina War
Peter Dale Scott
Bobbs-Merril 1972

The Soong Dynasty
Sterling Seagrave
Harper & Row
Perennial Library 1986

America's Secret Aristocracy
Stephen Bingham
Berkley Books 1990

The Big White Lie: The Deep Cover Operation that Exposed the CIA Sabotage of the Drug War
Michael Levine
Thunder's Mouth Press 1993

Agency of Fear
Edward Jay Epstein
Verso 1990

Out of Control: The Story of the Reagan Administration's Secret War in Nicaragua, the Illegal Bombs Pipeline, and the Contra Drug Connection
Leslie Cockburn
Little Brown 1987

The Guns 'n' Drugs Reader
Various authors
Prevailing Winds Research 1991

Contrabandista!
Evert Clark & Nicholas Hoorock
Preger 1973

Blacklisted News, Secret History: from Chicago, '68 to 1984
The New Yippie Book Collective
Bleecker Publishing 1983

Storming Heaven: LSD and The American Dream
Jay Stevens
Harper Row 1987

The Opium Monopoly,
La Motte, Ellen N.,
The Macmillan Co. 1920.

The Opium War,
Inglis, Brian,
Hodder and Stoughton, 1976.

Yankee Ships in China Seas,
Henderson, Daniel,
Hastings House, 1946.

Personal Reminiscences, Forbes, Robert B.,
MacDonald and Jane's 1974.

American Clipper Ships 1833-1858
Howe, Octavius T., Matthews, Frederick G.,
Dover Publications, Inc. 1986.

Flowers in the Blood: The Story of Opium.
Latimer, Dean and Goldberg, Jeff,
Franklin Watts, 1981.

The India-China Opium Trade in the Nineteenth Century, Janin, Hunt,
McFarland & Co., Inc 1999.

New York and The China Trade,
Howard, David Sanctuary.
Columbia Publishing Co., 1984.

Captain Prescott and The Opium Smugglers,
Stackpole, Edouard A.,
The Marine Historical Association, Inc. Reynolds Printing, Inc.1954.

Trail of the Octopus
Donal Goddard w/ Lester Coleman
Bloomsbury 1993

The I. G. in Peking
Ed. John King Fairbank
The Belknap Press of Harvard 1975

The Imperial Drug Trade
Joshua Rowntree
Methuen & Co 1906

Gold of Ophir
Sydney & Majorie Greenbie
Doubleday, Page & Co. 1925

Philadelphia and the China Trade 1682-1846
Jonathan Goldstein
The Pennsylvania State University press 1978

Americans And The China Opium Trade In The 19th Century
Charles Steele
Ayer Company Publishers, Inc 2001

Opium, Empire and the Global Political Economy
Carl A Trocki
Routledge 1999

History and Genealogy of the Cabot Family, 1475-1927
L. Vernon Briggs
Privately Printed 1927

The Boys on the Tracks
Mara Leveritt
St. Martin's Press 1999

On the Take
William J Chambliss
Indiana University Press 1978

Hot Money
RT Naylor
Simon & Schuster 1987